C OCEAN

SWEDEN
FINLAND
ESTONIA
LATVIA
LITHUANIA
MANY POLAND BELARUS
X. CZ.
SLK. UKRAINE
AUS. HUNG. MOLDOVA
N. ROMANIA
CR. SE.
ITALY B.H. BULGARIA
MO. KO. GEORGIA
MAC. ARMENIA
ALB. GREECE TURKEY
TUNISIA MALTA
CYPRUS SYRIA
ISRAEL LEBANON
West Bank IRAQ
Gaza Strip JORDAN
LIBYA EGYPT KUWAIT
SAUDI ARABIA
QATAR
UNITED ARAB
EMIRATES OMAN

RUSSIAN FEDERATION

KAZAKHSTAN
MONGOLIA
UZBEKISTAN
KYRGYZSTAN
TURKMENISTAN TAJIKISTAN
CHINA
AZERBAIJAN
AFGHANISTAN
IRAN
PAKISTAN
BHUTAN
NEPAL
BANGLADESH
INDIA MYANMAR
(BURMA)
THAILAND
CAMBODIA

N. KOREA
S. KOREA
JAPAN

PACIFIC OCEAN

Taiwan

Mariana Is.
(U.S.)

Guam
(U.S.)

MARSHALL
IS.

GER
CHAD SUDAN
ERIA
IN
CAMEROON CENTRAL
AFRICAN REP.
GABON
ME
CIPE
ANGOLA

BAHRAIN
YEMEN
DJIBOUTI
ERITREA
SOUTH
SUDAN ETHIOPIA
SOMALIA
UGANDA
RWANDA KENYA
DEM. REP. OF
THE CONGO
BURUNDI TANZANIA
COMOROS
SEYCHELLES
ZAMBIA MALAWI
ZIMBABWE
MADAGASCAR
NAMIBIA
BOTSWANA
MAURITIUS

MALDIVES
SRI
LANKA

LAOS
VIETNAM

PHILIPPINES

BRUNEI
MALAYSIA
SINGAPORE

PALAU

FEDERATED STATES
OF MICRONESIA

NAURU

KIRIBATI

TUVALU

SOLOMON
IS.

INDIAN OCEAN

INDONESIA

PAPUA
NEW
GUINEA
TIMOR
LESTE

VANUATU

FIJI

SOUTH
AFRICA MOZAMBIQUE
SWAZILAND
LESOTHO

AUSTRALIA

New Caledonia
(Fr.)

NEW
ZEALAND

Tasmania
(Aust.)

ABBREVIATIONS	
ALB.	ALBANIA
AUS.	AUSTRIA
BEL.	BELGIUM
B.H.	BOSNIA AND HERZEGOVINA
CR.	CROATIA
CZ.	CZECH REPUBLIC
DEN.	DENMARK
HUNG.	HUNGARY
KO.	KOSOVO
LUX.	LUXEMBOURG
MAC.	MACEDONIA
MO.	MONTENEGRO
NETH.	NETHERLANDS
SE.	SERBIA
SLK.	SLOVAKIA
SLN.	SLOVENIA
SWITZ.	SWITZERLAND

ANTARCTICA

20°E   40°E   60°E   80°E   100°E   120°E   140°E   160°E

◻ SEE HOW THIS BOOK CAN IMPROVE YOUR PERFORMANCE ON TESTS AND EXAMS.

Look at the Chapter Preview before you read to acquaint yourself with the topics in the chapter and the order in which they will be covered.

◻ CHAPTER PREVIEW

The Afroeurasian Trade World Before Columbus
◻ What was the Afroeurasian trade world like before the voyages of Columbus?

The European Voyages of Discovery
◻ Why and how did Europeans undertake ambitious voyages of expansion?

The Impact of Conquest
◻ How did conquest affect indigenous populations and bring about a new era of economic and cultural exchange, commercial empires, and forced migrations?

Changing Values and Beliefs
◻ How did new encounters shape cultural values and beliefs in Europe and the New World?

MAP 16.3 Seaborne Trading Empires in the Sixteenth and Seventeenth Centuries By the mid-seventeenth century, trade linked all parts of the world except for Australia. Notice that trade in slaves was not confined to the Atlantic but involved almost all parts of the world.

Get the most out of the illustrations by connecting the photos, maps, and tables to what you're reading.

value of the transatlantic trade, moved from Acapulco in New Spain to Manila (see Map 16.4). After 1640, however, the Spanish silk trade declined in the face of stiff competition from Dutch imports.

In the seventeenth century the Dutch challenged the Spanish and Portuguese Empires. Drawing on their commercial wealth and long experience in European trade, by the end of the century the Dutch emerged as the most powerful worldwide seaborne trading power. The Dutch Empire was built on spices, and the Dutch East India Company was founded in 1602 with the stated intention of capturing the spice trade from the Portuguese.

The Dutch set their sights on gaining direct access to and control of the Indonesian sources of spices. The Dutch fleet, sailing from the Cape of Good Hope in Africa and avoiding the Portuguese forts in India, steered directly for Java (modern Indonesia; see Map 16.4). In return for assisting Indonesian princes in local squabbles and disputes with the Portuguese, the Dutch won broad commercial concessions. Through agreements, seizures, and outright war, they gained control

of the western access to the Indonesian archipelago in the first half of the seventeenth century. Gradually they achieved political domination over the archipelago itself. By the 1660s the Dutch had managed to expel the Portuguese from Ceylon and other East Indian islands, thereby establishing control of the lucrative spice trade.

Changing Values and Beliefs

◻ How did new encounters shape cultural values and beliefs in Europe and the New World?

The age of overseas expansion heightened Europeans' contacts with the rest of the world. These contacts gave birth to new ideas about the inherent superiority or inferiority of different races, in part to justify European participation in the slave trade. Two great writers of the period both captured and challenged these views,

Consider the section focus questions while you read, which will give you a sense of the chapter's major themes and help to guide your reading.

Explain the significance of each key term in the Chapter Review.

◻ CHAPTER REVIEW

◻ What was the Afroeurasian trade world like before the voyages of Columbus? (p. 460)

Prior to Columbus's voyages, well-developed trade routes linked the peoples and products of Africa, Asia, and Europe. The Indian Ocean was the center of the Afroeurasian trade world, ringed by cosmopolitan commercial cities such as Mombasa in Africa, Calicut in India, and Malacca in Southeast Asia. Among the goods traded were silk, porcelain, spices, textiles, gold, and slaves. Overall, Europe played a minor role in the Afroeurasian trade world because it did not produce many products desired by Eastern elites. Nevertheless, Europeans — especially Venetian and Genoese merchants — sought to tap into the goods and wealth of Afroeurasian commerce.

KEY TERMS
bride wealth (p. 462)
conquistador (p. 465)
caravel (p. 467)
Ptolemy's *Geography* (p. 467)
Treaty of Tordesillas (p. 471)
Mexica Empire (p. 474)

Inca Empire (p. 475)
viceroyalties (p. 476)
encomienda system (p. 477)
Columbian exchange (p. 478)

◻ How did conquest affect indigenous populations and bring about a new era of economic and cultural exchange, commercial empires, and forced migrations? (p. 476)

In the aftermath of conquest, the Spanish established new forms of governance to dominate native peoples and exploit their labor. The arrival of Europeans also

Review the summary answers for the section focus questions in the Chapter Review and be sure you understand the chapter's major themes and the relationships between events.

◻ **Visit the FREE Online Study Guide at bedfordstmartins.com/ mckayworld** to check how much you've learned.

Visit the Web site for

A HISTORY OF
World Societies

bedfordstmartins.com/mckayworld

FREE Online Study Guide

GET INSTANT FEEDBACK ON YOUR PROGRESS WITH

- Chapter self-tests
- Key terms review
- Map quizzes
- Timeline activities
- Note-taking outlines

FREE History Research Writing Help

REFINE YOUR RESEARCH SKILLS AND FIND PLENTY OF GOOD SOURCES WITH

- A database of useful images, maps, documents, and more at *Make History*
- A guide to online sources for history
- Help with writing history papers
- A tool for building a bibliography
- Tips on avoiding plagiarism

A HISTORY OF
World Societies

William Hoare, Earliest Known British Portrait of a Freed Slave, 1733.

NINTH EDITION

A HISTORY OF
World Societies

JOHN P. McKAY | *University of Illinois at Urbana-Champaign*

BENNETT D. HILL | *Late of Georgetown University*

JOHN BUCKLER | *Late of University of Illinois at Urbana-Champaign*

PATRICIA BUCKLEY EBREY | *University of Washington*

ROGER B. BECK | *Eastern Illinois University*

CLARE HARU CROWSTON | *University of Illinois at Urbana-Champaign*

MERRY E. WIESNER-HANKS | *University of Wisconsin–Milwaukee*

BEDFORD/ST. MARTIN'S
Boston • New York

FOR BEDFORD/ST. MARTIN'S

Publisher for History: Mary Dougherty
Executive Editor for History: Traci M. Crowell
Director of Development for History: Jane Knetzger
Senior Developmental Editor: Laura Arcari
Senior Production Editor: Christina Horn
Senior Production Supervisor: Dennis J. Conroy
Executive Marketing Manager: Jenna Bookin Barry
Associate Editor: Lynn Sternberger
Editorial Assistant: Arrin Kaplan
Production Assistant: Laura Winstead
Copy Editor: Sybil Sosin
Map Editor: Charlotte Miller
Indexer: Leoni Z. McVey
Cartography: Mapping Specialists, Ltd.
Page Layout: Boynton Hue Studio
Photo Researcher: Carole Frohlich and Elisa Gallagher, The Visual Connection Image Research, Inc.

Permissions Manager: Kalina K. Ingham
Senior Art Director: Anna Palchik
Text and Cover Designer: Brian Salisbury
Cover Art: William Hoare, *Ayuba Suleiman Diallo (Job ben Solomon).* Property of Qatar Museums Authority (OM.762). Orientalist Museum, Doha.
Composition: NK Graphics
Printing and Binding: RR Donnelley and Sons

President: Joan E. Feinberg
Editorial Director: Denise B. Wydra
Director of Marketing: Karen R. Soeltz
Director of Production: Susan W. Brown
Associate Director, Editorial Production: Elise S. Kaiser
Managing Editor: Elizabeth M. Schaaf

Library of Congress Control Number: 2011925869

Manufactured in the United States of America.

2 3 4 5 6   15 14 13 12

For information, write: Bedford/St. Martin's, 75 Arlington Street, Boston, MA 02116   (617-399-4000)

ISBN: 978-0-312-66691-0 (Combined edition)
ISBN: 978-0-312-57013-2 (Loose leaf)
ISBN: 978-0-312-56969-3 (High School edition)
ISBN: 978-0-312-66692-7 (Volume 1)
ISBN: 978-0-312-57014-9 (Loose leaf)
ISBN: 978-0-312-66693-4 (Volume 2)
ISBN: 978-0-312-57051-4 (Loose leaf)
ISBN: 978-0-312-66694-1 (Volume A)
ISBN: 978-0-312-66695-8 (Volume B)
ISBN: 978-0-312-66696-5 (Volume C)

Distributed outside North America by:
PALGRAVE MACMILLAN
Houndmills, Basingstoke, Hampshire RG21 6XS
Companies and representatives throughout the world.
ISBN: 978-0-230-39436-0 (Combined edition)
ISBN: 978-0-230-39437-7 (Volume 1)
ISBN: 978-0-230-39438-4 (Volume 2)
ISBN: 978-0-230-39439-1 (Volume C)
A catalogue record for this book is available from the British Library.

□ IN MEMORIAM

JOHN BUCKLER 1945–2011

John Buckler, who authored many of the chapters in earlier editions of this book, was born in Louisville, Kentucky, on March 16, 1945. John received his B.A. summa cum laude from the University of Louisville in 1967 and his Ph.D. from Harvard University in 1973. From 1984 to 1986, he held an Alexander von Humboldt Fellowship at the Institut für Alte Geschichte at the University of Munich. In 1980 Harvard University Press published his *Theban Hegemony, 371–362 B.C.* In 1989 his *Philip II and the Sacred War* was published, and he also edited *BOIOTIKA: Vorträge vom 5. Internationalen Böotien-Kolloquium.* During the 1990s he contributed articles to the American Historical Association's *Guide to Historical Literature, The Oxford Classical Dictionary,* and *The Encyclopedia of Greece and the Hellenic Tradition.* In 2003 he published A*egean Greece in the Fourth Century B.C.* In the following year his editions of W. M. Leake's *Travels in the Morea* (three volumes) and *Peloponnesiaca* appeared. Cambridge University Press published his *Central Greece and the Politics of Power in the Fourth Century,* edited by Hans Beck, in 2007. At the time of his sudden and unexpected death, he was writing a book on the history of Greek warfare and also contributing to revisions of *Die Fragmente der Griechischen Historiker* by Felix Jacoby. Known internationally for his work, John was a scholar of great stature who will be missed by all who knew him.

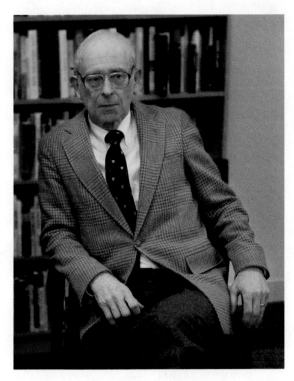

■ BRIEF CONTENTS

CONTENTS

5 The Greek Experience
3500–100 B.C.E. 114

6 The World of Rome
750 B.C.E.–400 C.E. 142

7 East Asia and the Spread of Buddhism
221 B.C.E.–800 C.E. 174

8 Continuity and Change in Europe and Western Asia
200–850 204

9 The Islamic World

600–1400 232

10 African Societies and Kingdoms

1000 B.C.E.–1500 C.E. 266

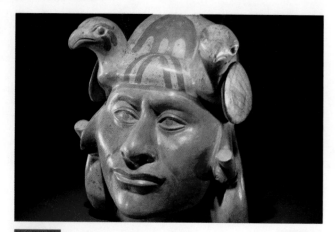

11 The Americas
2500 B.C.E.–1500 C.E. 298

12 Cultural Exchange in Central and Southern Asia
to 1400 330

13 States and Cultures in East Asia

800–1400   364

14 Europe in the Middle Ages

800–1450   392

15 Europe in the Renaissance and Reformation

1350–1600 424

16 The Acceleration of Global Contact

1450–1600 458

17 European Power and Expansion

1500–1750 490

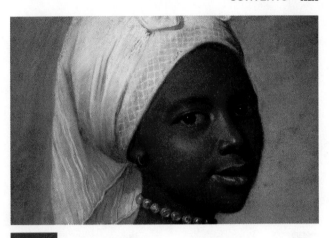

18 New Worldviews and Ways of Life

1540–1790 524

19 Africa and the World
1400–1800 556

20 The Islamic World Powers
1300–1800 586

21 Continuity and Change in East Asia

1400–1800 616

22 Revolutions in the Atlantic World

1775–1815 650

23 The Revolution in Energy and Industry

1760–1850 684

24 Ideologies of Change in Europe

1815–1914 714

25 Africa, Southwest Asia, and the New Imperialism

1800-1914 750

26 Asia in the Era of Imperialism

1800-1914 782

27 Nation Building in the Americas and Australia
1770–1914   810

28 World War and Revolution
1914–1929   842

29 Nationalism in Asia
1914–1939 876

30 The Great Depression and World War II
1929–1945 906

31 Global Recovery and Division Between Superpowers

1945 to the Present 940

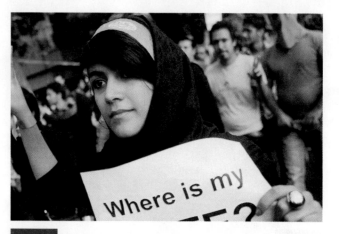

32 Independence, Progress, and Conflict in Asia and the Middle East

1945 to the Present 976

◻ MAPS, FIGURES, AND TABLES

◻ SPECIAL FEATURES

Viewpoints

Listening to the Past

Individuals In Society

Global Trade

The ninth edition of *A History of World Societies* has been particularly significant for us because it represents important changes with the author team and with our publisher. Our new publisher, Bedford/St. Martin's, gave us the opportunity to revisit our original vision and to revitalize the text and its scholarship in exciting and fulfilling ways. Sadly, founding authors John P. McKay and John Buckler retired from the book this year, but with Merry Wiesner-Hanks and Clare Haru Crowston, who joined as authors in the last edition, and Patricia Buckley Ebrey and Roger B. Beck, who joined in the fifth and seventh editions, respectively, we continue to benefit from a collaborative team of regional experts with deep experience in the world history classroom.

In this age of global connections, with its influence on the global economy, global migration patterns, popular culture, and global warming, among other things, the study of world history is more vital and urgent than ever before. An understanding of the broad sweep of the human past helps us to comprehend today's dramatic changes and enduring continuities. People now migrate enormous distances and establish new lives far from their places of birth, yet migration has been a constant in history since the first humans walked out of Africa. Satellite and cell phones now link nearly every inch of the planet, yet the expansion of communication networks is a process that is thousands of years old. Children who speak different languages at home now sit side by side in schools and learn from one another, yet intercultural encounters have long been a source of innovation, transformation, and at times, unfortunately, conflict.

This book is designed for twenty-first-century students who will spend their lives on this small interconnected planet and for whom an understanding of only local or national history will no longer be sufficient. We believe that the study of world history in a broad and comparative context is an exciting, important, and highly practical pursuit. It is our conviction, based on considerable experience in introducing large numbers of students to world history, that a book reflecting current trends in scholarship can excite readers and inspire an enduring interest in the long human experience.

Our strategy has been twofold. First, we have made social and cultural history the core elements of our narrative. We seek to re-create the lives of ordinary people in appealing human terms and also to highlight the interplay between men's and women's lived experiences and the ways they reflect on these to create meaning. Thus, in addition to foundational works of philosophy and literature, we include popular songs and stories. We present objects along with texts as important sources for studying history, and this has allowed us to incorporate the growing emphasis on material culture in the work of many historians. At the same time we have been mindful of the need to give great economic, political, and intellectual developments the attention they deserve. We want to give individual students and instructors an integrated perspective so that they can pursue — on their own or in the classroom — the themes and questions that they find particularly exciting and significant.

Second, we have made every effort to strike an effective global and regional balance. The whole world interacts today, and to understand the interactions and what they mean for today's citizens, we must study the whole world's history. Thus we have adopted a comprehensive regional organization with a global perspective that is clear and manageable for students. For example, Chapter 7 introduces students in depth to East Asia, and at the same time the chapter highlights the cultural connections that occurred via the Silk Road and the spread of Buddhism. We study all geographical areas, conscious of the separate histories of many parts of the world, particularly in the earliest millennia of human development. We also stress the links among cultures, political units, and economic systems, for these connections have made the world what it is today. We make comparisons and connections across time as well as space, for understanding the unfolding of the human story in time is the central task of history.

Textual Changes

In preparing the ninth edition of this book, we have worked hard to keep the book up-to-date and to strengthen our comprehensive, comparative, and connective approach. We carefully revisited and reconsidered every paragraph, rewriting and expanding sections for clarity and for stronger connections and comparisons and, most important, incorporating the latest scholarship, including a new first chapter on "The Earliest Human Societies, to 2500 B.C.E." informed by the most current research available. Moreover, we revised every chapter with the goal of readability and accessibility.

Several main lines of revision have guided our many changes. As in previous editions we added significantly more discussion of groups and regions that are often shortchanged in general histories of world civilizations, and we have continued to do so in this new revision, including new material on the Minoans and Mycenaeans in Chapter 5; the Celts in Chapter 8; the Pacific Islanders and Easter Island in Chapter 12; Korea during the Koryŏ dynasty in Chapter 13; the American colonies in Chapters 17 and 22; Armenian traders in Chapter 20; the Congo Free State in Chapter 25;

the Palestinians, Kurds, and Lebanese in Chapter 32; and the countries of Latin America in Chapter 33. This expanded scope reflects the awareness within the historical profession of the enormous diversity of the world's peoples.

We have also continued to increase our coverage of social and cultural history, encouraging students to consider how life in the past was both similar to and different from our lives today. This increased emphasis is supported in every chapter by the use of artifacts that make history tangible. In addition, we enhanced the discussion of religion in many chapters, including both the central ideas and lived religious practices of world religions such as Judaism and Christianity and of local religions such as those of the Celts and Egyptians. So, for example, you will find new scholarship on Amon-Ra and Isis, Zoroastrianism, and Jewish religious beliefs in Chapter 2; expanded coverage of the Jewish background of Christianity along with new material on second- and third-century Christianity in Chapter 6; and an expanded discussion of Arian Christianity along with a new discussion of the development of the Bible as a text in Chapter 8. Students are increasingly interested in the diversity of religious practices in the world around them, and we hope these additions will help them better understand the wide range of religions in the past.

Other social and cultural additions include new sections on Life in Early India in Chapter 3, Life During the Zhou Dynasty in Chapter 4, and Life in Han China in Chapter 7; a new discussion of the *Iliad* and *Odyssey* in Chapter 5; more on Roman architecture and literature in Chapter 6; new coverage of the actual workings of the law and an expanded discussion of family structure and food in Chapter 14; a new section devoted to life in the colonies of the New World in Chapter 17; and a new in-depth section devoted to the social impact of the Atlantic world in Chapter 18, including an exciting new section on Identities and Communities of the Atlantic World, where we discuss the impact of colonization and world trade on the lives of ordinary people.

As mentioned above, in this edition we have continued to strengthen the comparative coverage within the narrative to help students see and understand the cross-cultural connections of world history. In addition, we have added an exciting **NEW Connections** feature to the end of each chapter. This feature's synthesis of main developments serves to conclude the chapter, and the connections and comparisons of countries and regions explain how events relate to larger global processes, such as the influence of the Silk Road, the effects of the transatlantic slave trade, and the ramifications of colonialism. This new feature also serves to guide students in their reading, introducing related events and cultures that they will encounter in chapters to come. In this way students are introduced to history as an ongoing process of interrelated events.

The importance of cross-cultural connections to the study of world history is reflected in new scholarship and information on the impact of writing on our understanding of the past, and the relationship between the development of writing and the growth of states in Chapter 2; attention to areas of the world in which there were significant encounters between groups, such as Nubia and Kush in eastern Africa in Chapter 2 and the Indo-Bactrian kingdoms in Chapter 3; the impact of European settlement on the lives of indigenous peoples in Chapter 16; a more global perspective on European politics, culture, and economics in the early modern period, including the global impact of the Seven Years' War and treatment of the American, French, and Haitian Revolutions as interrelated events in an Atlantic world of political debates, conflicts, and aspirations in Chapter 22; an emphasis on cross-cultural encounters along the East African coast in Chapter 19; expanded coverage of Korea in Chapter 21, allowing for more in-depth analysis of the similarities of and differences between Asian countries; coverage of early efforts at modernization and industrialization outside of Europe and a discussion of how slavery impacted worldwide industrialization in Chapter 23; connections between the early European contacts in Africa and those that occurred with the empires of Southwest Asia in Chapter 25; the worldwide effects of the Great Depression in Chapter 30; and a more global treatment of both World War I and World War II, with new coverage of the ways in which these wars affected colonial peoples, in Chapters 28 and 30.

These major aspects of revision are accompanied by the incorporation of a wealth of other new scholarship and subject areas. Additions, among others, include a new section on hieroglyphics and a discussion of gender as it relates to Mesopotamian politics in Chapter 2; a more in-depth treatment of Chinese military thought and technology in Chapter 4; new scholarship on mystery religions in Chapter 5; an updated discussion of sexuality and Christianity in Chapter 8; new scholarship on race in Chapter 10; an updated discussion of mound builders and a new discussion of environmental and political changes in Chapter 11; new coverage of China under Mongol rule in Chapter 12; new scholarship on the Crusades in Chapter 14; a revised discussion of humanism to include more about women, and an updated discussion of Machiavelli to reflect new scholarship in Chapter 15; new coverage of the Atlantic world and the ways in which Enlightenment ideas and debates circulated along with many different peoples and commodities in Chapter 18; increased attention to suffrage in Chapter 24; a new discussion of politically active emigrants and the ways in which some Asians rejected Western influence, while others embraced Western ideas and practice, in Chapter 26; and updates through 2011 in Chapters 31, 32, 33, and 34, including up-to-date coverage of the economic downturn and the 2010–2011 uprisings and protests in North Africa and the Middle East. In sum, we have tried to bring new research and interpretation into our global history, believing it essential to keep our book stimulating, accurate, and current for students and instructors.

New Chapters and Organizational Changes

To meet the demands of the evolving course, we took a close and critical look at the book's organization and have made several major changes in the organization of chapters to reflect the way the course is taught today. The most dramatic change is the addition of an entirely new first chapter, "The Earliest Human Societies, to 2500 B.C.E.," which reflects a growing awareness among world historians that the human story properly begins millions, not mere thousands, of years ago. In order to provide a more global perspective on European politics, culture, and economics in the early modern period, Chapters 17, 18, and 22 have been substantially reworked and reorganized. Chapter 17 on European absolutism and constitutionalism has been broadened in scope to include European expansion, and Chapter 18 on the scientific revolution and the Enlightenment now includes coverage of the Atlantic world. As a natural extension, Chapter 22, which used to focus on the French Revolution, now examines the age of revolution in the Atlantic world. Together, the enhanced global perspectives of these chapters help connect the different regions of the globe and, in particular, help explain the crucial period when Europe began to dominate the rest of the globe.

To increase clarity and to help students see the global connections between the events surrounding World Wars I and II, we dropped the chapter on Europe in the interwar years and integrated this material into the World War chapters. Chapter 28 now focuses on the Great War, the Russian Revolution, and the interwar years, while Chapter 30 begins with the Great Depression in order to better explain the global conditions that contributed to the outbreak of World War II. The post-1945 section has also been completely reworked. In addition to updating all of the postwar chapters through 2011, we substantially reworked the last three chapters, integrating the Epilogue on the Middle East into Chapter 32 to create a more tightly focused and accessible chapter, and moving the material on Latin America and Africa to create a new Chapter 33 on the Global South. In addition to these major organizational changes, we carefully scrutinized all chapters, reorganizing material and adding clearer heads throughout as needed for clarity and to highlight important material for students.

Features

We are proud of the diverse special features that expand upon the narrative and offer opportunities for classroom discussion and assignments. For the ninth edition we have augmented our offerings to include a new feature created in response to reviewer requests for more primary source materials. This **NEW** documents feature, **Viewpoints**, offers paired primary documents on a topic that illuminates the human experience, allowing us to provide concrete examples of differences in the ways people thought. Anyone teaching world history has to emphasize larger trends and developments, but students sometimes get the wrong impression that everyone in a society thought alike. We hope that teachers can use these passages to get students thinking about diversity within and across societies. The thirty-four Viewpoints — one in each chapter — introduce students to working with sources, encourage critical analysis, and extend the narrative while giving voice to the people of the past. Each includes a brief introduction and questions for analysis. Carefully chosen for accessibility, each pair of documents presents views on a diverse range of topics, such as Chinese and Japanese Principles of Good Government, ca. 650; Roman and Byzantine Views of Barbarians; Creation in the *Popul Vuh* and in Okanogan Tradition; Lauro Quirini and Cassandra Fedele: Women and Humanist Learning; Christian Conversion in New Spain; Ottoman Travelers in Mughal and Safavid Lands; Poetry of the Great War; Gandhi and Mao on Revolutionary Means; and Ghanaian and South African Leaders on Black Nationalism.

Each chapter also continues to include a longer primary source feature titled **Listening to the Past**, chosen to extend and illuminate a major historical issue considered in each chapter. The feature presents a single original source or several voices on the subject. Each opens with an introduction and closes with questions for analysis that invite students to evaluate the evidence as historians would. Selected for their interest and significance and carefully placed within their historical context, these sources, we hope, allow students to "hear the past" and to observe how history has been shaped by individuals. **NEW** topics include Paleolithic Venus Figures; Aristotle, On the Family and On Slavery, from *The Politics*; Cicero and the Plot to Kill Caesar; Sixth-Century Biographies of Buddhist Nuns; Felipe Guaman Poma de Ayala, *The First New Chronicle and Good Government*; A German Account of Russian Life; Denis Diderot's "Supplement to Bougainville's Voyage"; Katib Chelebi on Tobacco; Abbé de Sieyès, "What Is the Third Estate?"; Mrs. Beeton's Guide for Running a Victorian Household; Mary Seacole on Her Early Life; and Aung San Suu Kyi, "Freedom from Fear."

In addition to using documents as part of our special feature program, we have quoted extensively from a wide variety of primary sources within the narrative, demonstrating in our use of these quotations that they are the "stuff" of history. Thus primary sources appear as an integral part of the narrative as well as in extended form in the Listening to the Past and new Viewpoints chapter features. We believe that this extensive program of both integrated and separate primary source excerpts will help readers learn to interpret and think critically.

In our years of teaching world history, we have often noted that students come alive when they encounter stories about real people in the past. To give students a chance to see the past through ordinary people's lives, each chapter includes one of the popular **Individuals in Society** biographical essays, each of which offers a brief study of an individual or group, informing students about the societies in which the individuals lived. This feature grew out of our long-standing focus on people's lives and the varieties of historical experience, and we believe that readers will empathize with these human beings who themselves were seeking to define their own identities. The spotlighting of individuals, both famous and obscure, perpetuates the book's continued attention to cultural and intellectual developments, highlights human agency, and reflects changing interests within the historical profession as well as the development of "micro-history." **NEW** features include essays on the Iceman, Hatshepsut and Nefertiti, Lord Mengchang, Queen Cleopatra, Josiah Wedgwood, Henry Meiggs, Liu Xiaobo, and Eva Perón.

Rounding out the book's feature program is the popular **Global Trade** feature, two-page essays that focus on a particular commodity, exploring the world trade, social and economic impact, and cultural influence of that commodity. Each essay is accompanied by a detailed map showing the trade routes of the commodity and an illustration. Retaining the eight essays of the previous edition on pottery, silk, spices, tea, slaves, indigo, oil, and arms, we have added two **NEW** features on iron and silver. We believe that careful attention to all of these essays will enable the student to appreciate the complex ways in which trade has connected and influenced the various parts of the world.

With the goal of making this the most student-centered edition yet, we paid renewed attention to the book's pedagogy. To help guide students, each chapter opens with a **Chapter Preview** with focus questions keyed to the main chapter headings. These questions are repeated within the chapter, and again in the **Chapter Reviews.** For this edition, many of the questions have been reframed, and new summary answers have been added to the chapter reviews. Each chapter review concludes with a carefully selected list of annotated **Suggestions for Further Reading**, revised and updated to stay current with the vast amount of new work being done in many fields.

To promote clarity and comprehension, bolded **key terms** in the text are defined in the margin and listed again in the chapter review. **NEW phonetic spellings** are located directly after terms that readers are likely to find hard to pronounce. The **chapter chronologies**, each of which reviews major developments discussed in the chapter, have been improved to more closely mirror the key events covered in the chapter, and the number of topic-specific **thematic chronologies** has been expanded, with new chronologies on Major Figures of the Enlightenment, and Key Events of the American Revolution, among others. Once again we also provide a **unified timeline** at the end of the text. Comprehensive and easy to locate, this useful timeline allows students to compare developments over the centuries.

The consistently high-quality art and map program has been thoroughly revised and expanded. The new edition features more than 530 **contemporaneous illustrations**. To make the past tangible, and as an extension of our attention to social and cultural history, we include over 90 **artifacts** ranging from swords and coins to a spinning wheel and a phonograph. As in earlier editions, all illustrations have been carefully selected to complement the text, and all include captions that inform students while encouraging them to read the text more deeply. Completely redesigned and reconceptualized for the new edition, **100 full-size maps** illustrate major developments in the narrative. In addition, **82 NEW spot maps** are embedded in the narrative to show specific areas under discussion. **NEW** maps in the ninth edition highlight such topics as Human Migration in the Paleolithic and Neolithic Eras; The Settling of the Americas Before 10,000 B.C.E.; Settlement of the Pacific Islands; The Slave Coast of West Africa; The Atlantic Economy in 1701; The Muslim World, ca. 1700; Emigration Out of Asia, 1820–1914; The Spanish-American War in the Philippines, 1898; Cold War Europe in the 1950s; and Authoritarian Governments in Latin America, among others.

We recognize students' difficulties with geography and visual analysis, and the new edition includes **NEW Mapping the Past map activities** and **NEW Picturing the Past visual activities.** Included in each chapter, these activities ask students to analyze the map or visual and make connections to the larger processes discussed in the narrative, giving them valuable practice in reading and interpreting maps and images.

To showcase the book's rich art program and to signal our commitment to this thorough and deep revision, the book has been completely redesigned. The dynamic new contemporary design engages and assists students with its clear, easy-to-use pedagogy.

Acknowledgments

It is a pleasure to thank the many instructors who read and critiqued the manuscript through its development:

Alemseged Abbay, Frostburg State University
Funso Afolayan, University of New Hampshire
Maria Arbelaez, University of Nebraska
Eva S. Baham, Southern University, Baton Rouge
David S. Bovee, Fort Hays State University
Nancy Cade, Pikesville College
Stephen D. Carls, Union University
Steven Cassedy, University of California
Edward J. Chess, Pulaski Technical College
Erwin F. Erhardt III, Thomas More College
Matthew D. Esposito, Drake University
Angela Feres, Grossmont Community College
Sam Giordanengo, Hawai'i Community College
Randee Goodstadt, Asheville-Buncombe Technical
    Community College
K. David Goss, Gordon College

William W. Haddad, California State Fullerton

Susan M. Hellert, University of Wisconsin, Platteville

John S. Hill, Immaculata University

Ellen Kittell, University of Idaho

Donald McGuire, SUNY Buffalo

April Najjaj, Greensboro College

Sandra L. Norman, Florida Atlantic University

Edward Paulino, John Jay College

William E. Plants, University of Rio Grande/Rio Grande Community College

Carolee Pollock, Grant MacEwan University

Charlotte Power, Black River Technical College

Salvador Rivera, SUNY Cobleskill

Mark Schneider, Suffok University and Bridgewater State

J. M. Simpson, Pierce College

Carrie Spencer, Pikes Peak Community College

Pamela Stewart, Arizona State University

Steven A. Stofferahn, Indiana State University

Jason M. Stratton, Bakersfield College

Deborah A. Symonds, Drake University

George Watters, St. Johns River Community College

Robert H. Welborn, Clayton State University

Marc Zayac, Georgia Perimeter College

It is also a pleasure to thank the many editors who have assisted us over the years, first at Houghton Mifflin and now at Bedford/St. Martin's. At Bedford/St. Martin's, these include senior development editor Laura Arcari; freelance development editors Beth Castrodale and Arthur Johnson; associate editors Lynn Sternberger and Jack Cashman; editorial assistant Arrin Kaplan; executive editor Traci Mueller Crowell; director of development Jane Knetzger; publisher for history Mary Dougherty; map editor Charlotte Miller; photo researcher Carole Frohlich; text permissions editor Heather Salus; and senior production editor Christina Horn, with the assistance of Laura Winstead, Laura Deily, and Elise Keller and the guidance of managing editor Elizabeth Schaaf and assistant managing editor John Amburg. Other key contributors were designer Brian Salisbury, page makeup artist Cia Boynton, copyeditor Sybil Sosin, proofreaders Susan Moore and Angela Morrison, indexer Leoni McVey, cover image researcher Donna Dennison, and cover designer Brian Salisbury. We would also like to thank editorial director Denise Wydra and president Joan E. Feinberg.

Many of our colleagues at the University of Illinois, the University of Washington, the University of Wisconsin–Milwaukee, and Eastern Illinois University continue to provide information and stimulation, often without even knowing it. We thank them for it. The authors also thank the many students over the years with whom we have used earlier editions of this book. Their reactions and opinions helped shape our revisions to this edition, and we hope it remains worthy of the ultimate praise that they bestowed on it, that it is "not boring like most textbooks." Merry Wiesner-Hanks would, as always, like to thank her husband Neil, without whom work on this project would not be possible. Clare Haru Crowston thanks her husband Ali and her children Lili, Reza, and Kian, who are a joyous reminder of the vitality of life that we try to showcase in this book. Roger Beck is thankful to Ann for keeping the home fires burning while he was busy writing and to the World History Association for all past, present, and future contributions to his understanding of world history.

Each of us has benefited from the criticism of his or her coauthors, although each of us assumes responsibility for what he or she has written. In addition to writing an entirely new Chapter 1, Merry Wiesner-Hanks substantially reworked and revised John Buckler's Chapters 2, 5, and 6 and has written and revised Chapters 8, 11, 14, and 15; Patricia Buckley Ebrey has written and revised Chapters 3, 4, 7, 9, 12, 13, 20, 21, 26, and 27; Roger B. Beck took responsibility for John McKay's Chapters 24 and 25 and has written and revised Chapters 10, 19, and 28–34; Clare Haru Crowston has assumed primary responsibility for Chapters 16–18 and 22 and also built upon text originally written by John McKay to revise and expand Chapter 23.

◻ VERSIONS AND SUPPLEMENTS

Adopters of *A History of World Societies* and their students have access to abundant extra resources, including documents, presentation and testing materials, the acclaimed Bedford Series in History and Culture volumes, and much more. See below for more information, visit the book's catalog site at **bedfordstmartins.com/mckayworld/catalog**, or contact your local Bedford/St. Martin's sales representative.

Get the Right Version for Your Class

To accommodate different course lengths and course budgets, *A History of World Societies* is available in several different formats, including three-hole-punched loose-leaf Budget Books versions and e-books, which are available at a substantial discount.

- Combined edition (Chapters 1–34) — available in hardcover, loose-leaf, and e-book formats
- Volume 1: To 1600 (Chapters 1–16) — available in paperback, loose-leaf, and e-book formats
- Volume 2: Since 1450 (Chapters 16–34) — available in paperback, loose-leaf, and e-book formats
- Volume A: To 1500 (Chapters 1–14) — available in paperback
- Volume B: From 800 to 1815 (Chapters 11–22) — available in paperback
- Volume C: From 1775 to the Present (Chapters 22–34) — available in paperback

The online, interactive **Bedford e-Book** can be examined or purchased at a discount at **bedfordstmartins.com/ebooks**; if packaged with the print text, it is available at no extra cost. Your students can also purchase *A History of World Societies* in other popular e-book formats for computers, tablets, and e-readers.

Online Extras for Students

The book's companion site at **bedfordstmartins.com/mckayworld** gives students a way to read, write, and study, and to find and access quizzes and activities, study aids, and history research and writing help.

FREE **Online Study Guide.** Available at the companion site, this popular resource provides students with quizzes and activities for each chapter, including multiple-choice self-tests that focus on important concepts; flashcards that test students' knowledge of key terms; timeline activities that emphasize causal relationships; and map quizzes intended to strengthen students' geography skills. Instructors can monitor students' progress through an online Quiz Gradebook or receive e-mail updates.

FREE **Research, Writing, and Anti-plagiarism Advice.** Available at the companion site, Bedford's **History Research and Writing Help** includes **History Research and Reference Sources**, with links to history-related databases, indexes, and journals; **More Sources and How to Format a History Paper**, with clear advice on how to integrate primary and secondary sources into research papers and how to cite and format sources correctly; **Build a Bibliography**, a simple Web-based tool known as The Bedford Bibliographer that generates bibliographies in four commonly used documentation styles; and **Tips on Avoiding Plagiarism**, an online tutorial that reviews the consequences of plagiarism and features exercises to help students practice integrating sources and recognize acceptable summaries.

Resources for Instructors

Bedford/St. Martin's has developed a wide range of teaching resources for this book and for this course. They range from lecture and presentation materials and assessment tools to course management options. Most can be downloaded or ordered at **bedfordstmartins.com/mckayworld/catalog**.

NEW *HistoryClass for A History of World Societies.* HistoryClass, a Bedford/St. Martin's Online Course Space, puts the online resources available with this textbook in one convenient and completely customizable course space. There you and your students can access an interactive e-book and primary sources reader; maps, images, documents, and links; chapter review quizzes; interactive multimedia exercises; and research and writing help. In HistoryClass you can get all our premium content and tools and assign, rearrange, and mix them with your own resources. For more information, visit **yourhistoryclass.com**.

Bedford Coursepack for Blackboard, WebCT, Desire2Learn, Angel, Sakai, or Moodle. We have free content to help you integrate our rich content into your course management system. Registered instructors can download coursepacks with no hassle and no strings attached. Content includes our most popular free resources and book-specific content for *A History of World Societies*. Visit bedfordstmartins.com/cms to see a demo, find your version, or download your coursepack.

Instructor's Resource Manual. The instructor's manual offers both experienced and first-time instructors tools for preparing for lecture and running discussions. It includes chapter review material, teaching strategies, and a guide to chapter-specific supplements available for the text.

Guide to Changing Editions. Designed to facilitate an instructor's transition from the previous edition of *A History of World Societies* to the current edition, this guide presents an overview of major changes as well as of changes in each chapter.

Computerized Test Bank. The test bank includes a mix of fresh, carefully crafted multiple-choice, matching, short-answer, and essay questions for each chapter. It also contains the Review, Visual Activity, Map Activity, Individuals in Society, and Listening to the Past questions from the textbook and model answers for each. The questions appear in Microsoft Word format and in easy-to-use test bank software that allows instructors to easily add, edit, re-sequence, and print questions and answers. Instructors can also export questions into a variety of formats, including WebCT and Blackboard.

PowerPoint Maps, Images, Lecture Outlines, and i>clicker Content. Look good and save time with *The Bedford Lecture Kit.* These presentation materials are downloadable individually from the Instructor Resources tab at **bedfordstmartins.com/mckayworld/catalog** and are available on *The Bedford Lecture Kit* Instructor's Resource CD-ROM. They include ready-made and fully customizable PowerPoint multimedia presentations built around lecture outlines with embedded maps, figures, and selected images from the textbook and with detailed instructor notes on key points. Also available are maps and selected images in JPEG and PowerPoint formats; content for i>clicker, a classroom response system, in Microsoft Word and PowerPoint formats; the Instructor's Resource Manual in Microsoft Word format; and outline maps in PDF format for quizzing or handing out. All files are suitable for copying onto transparency acetates.

Make History — Free Documents, Maps, Images, and Web Sites. *Make History* combines the best Web resources with hundreds of maps and images, to make it simple to find the source material you need. Browse the collection of thousands of resources by course or by topic, date, and type. Each item has been carefully chosen and helpfully annotated to make it easy to find exactly what you need. Available at **bedfordstmartins.com/makehistory**.

Videos and Multimedia. A wide assortment of videos and multimedia CD-ROMs on various topics in world history is available to qualified adopters through your Bedford/St. Martin's sales representative.

Package and Save Your Students Money

For information on free packages and discounts up to 50%, visit **bedfordstmartins.com/mckayworld/catalog**, or contact your local Bedford/St. Martin's sales representative.

Bedford e-Book. The e-book for this title, described above, can be packaged with the print text at no additional cost.

***Sources of World Societies*, Second Edition.** This two-volume primary source collection provides a revised and expanded selection of sources to accompany A *History of World Societies,* Ninth Edition. Each chapter features five or six sources by well-known figures and ordinary individuals alike. Now with visual sources and two more documents per chapter, this edition offers even more breadth and depth. Headnotes and questions supplement each document, while a new Viewpoints feature highlights two or three sources per chapter that address a single topic from different perspectives. Comparative questions ask students to make connections between sources and across time. Available free when packaged with the print text.

***Sources of World Societies* e-Book.** The reader is also available as an e-book. When packaged with the print or electronic version of the textbook, it is available for free.

The Bedford Series in History and Culture. More than one hundred titles in this highly praised series combine first-rate scholarship, historical narrative, and important primary documents for undergraduate courses. Each book is brief, inexpensive, and focused on a specific topic or period. For a complete list of titles, visit **bedfordstmartins .com/history/series**. Package discounts are available.

Rand McNally Historical Atlas of the World. This collection of almost seventy full-color maps illustrates the eras and civilizations in world history from the emergence of human societies to the present. Available for $3.00 when packaged with the print text.

The Bedford Glossary for World History. This handy supplement for the survey course gives students historically contextualized definitions for hundreds of terms — from *abolitionism* to *Zoroastrianism* — that they will encounter in lectures, reading, and exams. Available free when packaged with the print text.

World History Matters: A Student Guide to World History Online. Based on the popular "World History Matters" Web site produced by the Center for History and New Media, this unique resource, edited by Kristin Lehner (The Johns Hopkins University), Kelly Schrum (George Mason University), and T. Mills Kelly (George Mason University), combines reviews of 150 of the most useful and reliable world history Web sites with an introduction that guides students in locating, evaluating, and correctly citing online sources. Available free when packaged with the print text.

Trade Books. Titles published by sister companies Hill and Wang; Farrar, Straus and Giroux; Henry Holt and Company; St. Martin's Press; Picador; and Palgrave Macmillan are available at a 50% discount when packaged with Bedford/St. Martin's textbooks. For more information, visit **bedfordstmartins.com/tradeup**.

A Pocket Guide to Writing in History. This portable and affordable reference tool by Mary Lynn Rampolla provides reading, writing, and research advice useful to students in all history courses. Concise yet comprehensive advice on approaching typical history assignments, developing critical reading skills, writing effective history papers, conducting research, using and documenting sources, and avoiding plagiarism — enhanced with practical tips and examples throughout — have made this slim reference a best-seller. Package discounts are available.

A Student's Guide to History. This complete guide to success in any history course provides the practical help students need to be effective. In addition to introducing students to the nature of the discipline, author Jules Benjamin teaches a wide range of skills, from preparing for exams to approaching common writing assignments, and explains the research and documentation process with plentiful examples. Package discounts are available.

A HISTORY OF
World Societies

• **West African Man** Humans began to portray themselves on the surfaces of places where they lived and traveled as early as 50,000 B.C.E. Most of these paintings have vanished, but some have been redone, as in this rock painting from the region of Niger in Africa, which shows a person, perhaps a shaman, wearing a large headdress. (© David Coulson/Robert Estall Agency UK)

When does history begin? Previous generations of historians generally answered that question with "when writing begins." Thus they started their histories with the earliest known invention of writing, which happened about 3000 B.C.E. in the Tigris and Euphrates River Valleys of Mesopotamia, in what is now Iraq. Anything before that was "prehistory." That focus on only the last five thousand years leaves out most of the human story, however, and today historians no longer see writing as such a sharp dividing line. They explore all eras of the human past with many different types of sources, and some push the beginning of history back to the formation of the universe, when time itself began. This very new conceptualization of "big history" is actually similar in scope to the world's oldest histories, because for thousands and perhaps tens of thousands of years many peoples have narrated histories of their origins that also begin with the creation of the universe.

The Earliest Human Societies

to 2500 B.C.E.

Exploring the entire human past means beginning in Africa, where millions of years ago humans evolved from a primate ancestor. They migrated out of Africa in several waves, walking along coasts and over land, eventually spreading across much of the earth. Their tools were initially multipurpose sharpened stones and sticks, but gradually they invented more specialized tools that enabled them to obtain food more easily, make clothing, build shelters, and decorate their surroundings. Environmental changes, such as the advance and retreat of the glaciers, shaped life dramatically and may have led to the most significant change in all of human history, the domestication of plants and animals. •

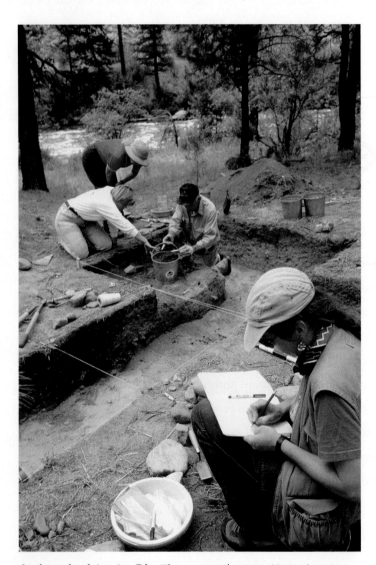

Archaeologists at a Dig These researchers at a Native American site in the Boise National Forest in Idaho follow careful procedures to remove objects from the soil and note their location. The soil itself may also yield clues, such as seeds or pollen, about what was growing in the area, allowing better understanding of the people who once lived at the site. (David R. Frazier/Photo Researcher, Inc.)

Evolution and Migration

□ How did humans evolve, and where did they migrate?

Studying the earliest era of human history involves methods that seem simple — looking carefully at an object — as well as new high-tech procedures, such as DNA analysis. Through such research, scholars have examined early human evolution, traced the expansion of the human brain, and studied migration out of Africa and across the planet. Combined with spoken language, that larger brain enabled humans to adapt to many different environments and to be flexible in their responses to new challenges.

Understanding the Early Human Past

People throughout the world have developed systems of classification that help them understand things: earth and sky; seen and unseen; animal, vegetable, and mineral; past, present, and future. Among these systems of classification was one invented in eighteenth-century Europe that divided all living things on earth into groups. Each of these divisions — such as that between plants and animals — is further subdivided into smaller and smaller groups, such as class, order, family, and genus. The final important division is the species, which is generally defined as a group of organisms that can interbreed with one another and produce fertile offspring of both sexes.

In their natural state, members of a species resemble one another, but over time they can become increasingly dissimilar. (Think of Chihuahuas and Great Danes, both members of the same species.) Ever since humans began shaping the world around them, this process has often been the result of human action. But in the long era before humans, the increasing dissimilarity resulted, in the opinion of most scientists, from the process of natural selection. Small variations within individuals in one species allowed them to acquire more food and better living conditions and made them more successful in breeding, thus passing their genetic material to the next generation. When a number of individuals within a species became distinct enough that they could no longer interbreed successfully with others, they became a new species. Species also become extinct, particularly during periods of mass extinctions such as the one that killed the dinosaurs about 65 million years ago. Natural processes of species formation and extinction continue, although today changes in the biosphere — the living matter in the world — result far more from human action than from natural selection.

The scientists who developed this system of organizing the world placed humans within it, using the same means of classification that they used for all other living things. Humans were in the animal kingdom, the order of Primates, the family Hominidae, and the genus *Homo*. Like all classifications, this was originally based on externally visible phenomena: humans were placed in the Primates order because, like other primates, they have hands that can grasp, eyes facing forward to allow better depth perception, and relatively large brains; they were placed in the **hominid** family along with chimpanzees, gorillas, and orangutans because they shared even more features with these great apes. More recently, these classifications (along with many others) have been supported by genetic evidence, particularly that provided by DNA, the basic building block of life. Over 98 percent of human DNA is the same as that of chimpanzees, which indicates to most scientists that humans and chimpanzees share a common ancestor. That common ancestor probably lived between 5 million and 7 million years ago.

Genetic analysis is one of many types of technology used by scholars who study early humans. They often use chemical and physical tests to evaluate bones and other body parts left by humans and the animals they ate, and to study the material surrounding these remains. One of the most important of these tests is the analysis of the radioactive isotope of carbon, C-14, which appears in all things that were once alive. C-14 breaks down at a rate that is known, so that measuring the amount of C-14 that remains in an object allows scientists to determine how old the object is.

Physical remains were the earliest type of evidence studied to learn about the distant human past, and scholars used them to develop another system of classification, one that distinguished between periods of time rather than types of living creatures. (Constructing models of time is called "periodization.") They gave labels to eras according to the primary materials out of which tools that survived were made. Thus the earliest human era became the Stone Age, the next era the Bronze Age, and the next

CHRONOLOGY

ca. 4.4 million years ago	*Ardipithecus* evolve in Africa
ca. 2.5–4 million years ago	*Australopithecus* evolve in Africa
ca. 500,000–2 million years ago	*Homo erectus* evolve and spread out of Africa
ca. 250,000–9000 B.C.E.	Paleolithic era
ca. 250,000 years ago	*Homo sapiens* evolve in Africa
ca. 30,000–150,000 years ago	Neanderthals flourish in Europe and western Asia
ca. 120,000 years ago	*Homo sapiens* migrate out of Africa to Eurasia
ca. 50,000 years ago	Human migration to Australia
ca. 20,000–30,000 years ago	Possible human migration from Asia to the Americas
ca. 25,000 B.C.E.	Earliest evidence of woven cloth and baskets
ca. 15,000 B.C.E.	Earliest evidence of bows and atlatls
ca. 15,000–10,000 B.C.E.	Final retreat of glaciers; humans cross the Bering Strait land bridge to the Americas; megafaunal extinctions
ca. 9000 B.C.E.	Beginning of the Neolithic; horticulture; domestication of sheep and goats
ca. 7000 B.C.E.	Domestication of cattle; plow agriculture
ca. 5500 B.C.E.	Smelting of copper
ca. 5000 B.C.E.	Invention of pottery wheel
ca. 4000 B.C.E.	Wheel adapted for use with carts
ca. 3000 B.C.E.	Earliest known invention of writing
ca. 2500 B.C.E.	Bronze technology spreads; beginning of the Bronze Age

A note on dates: This book generally uses **B.C.E.** (Before the Common Era) and **C.E.** (Common Era) when giving dates, a system of chronology based on the Christian calendar and now used widely around the world. Scholars who study the very earliest periods of hominid and human history usually use the phrase "years ago" to date their subjects, as do astrophysicists and geologists; this is often abbreviated as **B.P.** (Before the Present). Because the scale of time covered in Chapter 1 is so vast, a mere 2,000 years does not make much difference, and so **B.C.E.** and "years ago" have similar meaning.

the Iron Age. They further divided the Stone Age into the Old Stone Age, or **Paleolithic era**, during which people used stone, bone, and other natural products to

- **hominids** Members of the family Hominidae that contains humans, chimpanzees, gorillas, and orangutans.
- **Paleolithic era** Period during which humans used tools of stone, bone, and wood and obtained food by gathering and hunting. Roughly 250,000–9,000 B.C.E.

make tools and gained food largely by **foraging** — that is, by gathering plant products, trapping or catching small animals and birds, and hunting larger prey. This was followed by the New Stone Age, or **Neolithic era**, which saw the beginning of agricultural and animal domestication. People around the world adopted agriculture at various times, and some never did, but the transition between the Paleolithic and the Neolithic is usually set at about 9000 B.C.E., the point at which agriculture was first developed.

On the scale of the universe or even of the earth, human eras are short. Geologists refer to the last twelve thousand years as the Holocene epoch, a period so short given the 4.5 billion years of the solar system that it often does not show up on geologic time lines. The entire history of the human species fits well within the Holocene and the previous geologic epoch, the Pleistocene (PLIGH-stuh-seen), which began about 2.5 million years ago.

The Pleistocene was marked by repeated advances in glaciers and continental ice sheets. Glaciers tied up huge quantities of the earth's water, leading to lower sea levels, making it possible for animals and eventually humans to walk between places that were separated by oceans during interglacial times. Animals and humans were also prevented from migrating to other places by the ice sheets themselves, however, and the colder climate made large areas unfit to live in. Climate thus dramatically shaped human cultures.

Genetic analysis can indicate many things about the human family, and physical remains can provide some evidence about how people lived in the distant past, but the evidence is often difficult to interpret. By themselves, tools and other objects generally do not reveal who made or used them (though sometimes this can be determined from the location in which they were found), nor do they indicate what the objects meant to their creators or users. Thus to learn about the early human past, scholars often also study groups of people from more recent times whose technology and way of life offers parallels with those of people in the distant past. They read written reports of conquerors, government officials, and missionaries who encountered groups that lived by foraging, and they directly observe the few remaining groups that maintain a foraging lifestyle today. Such evidence is also problematic, however. Outsiders had their own perspectives, generally regarded those who lived by foraging as inferior, and often misinterpreted what they were

seeing. Contemporary foragers are not fully cut off from the modern world, nor is it correct to assume that their way of living has not changed for thousands of years, particularly because adaptability is a key feature of the foraging way of life. Thus evidence from more recent groups must be used carefully, but it can provide valuable clues.

Hominid Evolution

Using many different pieces of evidence from all over the world, archaeologists, paleontologists, and other scholars have developed a view of human evolution whose basic outline is widely shared, though there are disagreements about details. Most primates, including other hominids such as chimpanzees and gorillas, have lived primarily in trees, but at some point a group of hominids in East Africa began to spend more time on the ground, and between 5 million and 7 million years ago they began to walk upright at least some of the time. Very recently, scientists have determined that skeletal remains from the genus *Ardipithecus*, which probably date from 4.4 million years ago, indicate a combination of two-limbed movement on land and four-limbed movement in trees. *Ardipithecus* also had smaller canine teeth than do modern chimpanzees, and male and female canine teeth were equal in size, which suggests that there was less male-male combat and perhaps closer male-female relations than among earlier hominids.

Over many generations the skeletal and muscular structure of some hominids evolved to make upright walking easier, and they gradually became fully bipedal. The earliest fully bipedal hominids, whom paleontologists place in the genus *Australopithecus,* lived in southern and eastern Africa between 2.5 and 4 million years ago. Here they left bones, particularly in the Great Rift Valley that stretches from Ethiopia to Tanzania. Walking upright allowed australopithecines to carry and use tools, which allowed them to survive better and may have also spurred brain development.

Sometime around 2.5 million years ago, one group of australopithecines in East Africa began to make simple tools as well as use them, evolving into a different type of hominid that later paleontologists judged to be the first in the genus *Homo.* Called *Homo habilis* ("handy human"), they made sharpened stone pieces, which archaeologists call hand axes, and used them for various tasks. This suggests greater intelligence, and the skeletal remains sup-

The Great Rift Valley

0   200   400 mi.
0   200   400 km

White Nile R.

Omo
Lomekwi   Ileret
Koobi Fora
Nariokotome   L. Turkana
Lothagam   Kanapoi
Tabarin   Chesowanja
Baringo
Chemeron

GREAT RIFT VALLEY

Peninj
Olduvai
Gorge   Laetoli

L. Victoria

INDIAN OCEAN

Site of human fossils
● Australopithecine
● Homo habilis
● Homo erectus

port this, for *Homo habilis* had a larger brain than did the australopithecines.

About 2 million years ago another species, called *Homo erectus* ("upright human") by most paleontologists, evolved in East Africa. *Homo erectus* had still larger brains — about two-thirds the size of modern human brains — and made tools that were slightly specialized for various tasks, such as handheld axes, cleavers, and scrapers. Archaeological remains indicate that *Homo erectus* lived in larger groups than had earlier hominids and engaged in cooperative gathering, hunting, and food preparation. The location and shape of the larynx suggests that members of this species were able to make a wider range of sounds than were earlier hominids, so they may have relied more on vocal sounds than on gestures to communicate ideas to one another, through which tasks could be planned and carried out more effectively.

One of the activities that *Homo erectus* carried out most successfully was moving (Map 1.1). Gradually small groups migrated out of East Africa onto the open plains of central Africa, and from there into northern Africa. From 1 million to 2 million years ago the earth's climate was in a warming phase, and these hominids ranged still farther, moving into western Asia by as early as 1.8 million years ago. Bones and other materials from China and the island of Java in Indonesia indicate that *Homo erectus* had reached there by about 1.5 million years ago, thus migrating over large landmasses as well as along the coasts. (Sea levels were lower than they are today, and Java could be reached by walking.) *Homo erectus* also walked north, reaching what is now Spain by at least 800,000 years ago and what is now Germany by 500,000 years ago. In each of these places, *Homo erectus* adapted gathering and hunting techniques to the local environment, learning about new sources of plant food and how to best catch local animals. Although the climate was warmer than it is today, central Europe was not balmy, and these hominids may have used fire to provide light and heat, cook food, and keep away predators. Many lived in the open or in caves, but some built simple shelters, another indication of increasing flexibility and problem solving.

Homo Sapiens, "Thinking Humans"

Homo erectus was remarkably adaptable, but another hominid proved still more so: *Homo sapiens* ("thinking humans"). A few scientists think that *Homo sapiens* evolved from *Homo erectus* in a number of places in Afroeurasia, but the majority think that, like hominid evolution from earlier primates, this occurred only in East Africa. The evidence is partly archaeological, but also genetic. One type of DNA, called mitochondrial DNA, is inherited through the maternal line and can be

Fossil Footprints from Laetoli in Tanzania
About three and a half million years ago, several australopithecines walked in wet ash from a volcanic eruption. Their footprints, discovered by the archaeologist Mary Leakey, indicate that they walked fully upright and suggest that they were not solitary creatures, for they walked close together. (John Reader/Photo Researchers, Inc.)

traced far back in time. Mitochondrial DNA indicates that modern humans are so similar genetically that they cannot have been evolving for the last million or 2 million years. This evidence suggests that the evolution of *Homo sapiens* has instead taken place for only about 250,000 years. Because there is greater human

---

- **foraging** A style of life in which people gain food by gathering plant products, trapping or catching small animals and birds, and hunting larger prey.
- **Neolithic era** Period beginning in 9000 B.C.E. during which humans obtained food by raising crops and animals and continued to use tools primarily of stone, bone, and wood.

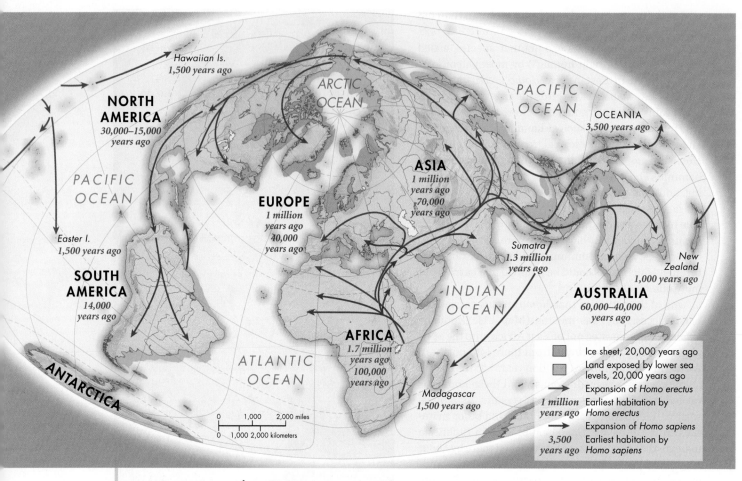

Map labels:

Hawaiian Is. 1,500 years ago

ARCTIC OCEAN

PACIFIC OCEAN

OCEANIA 3,500 years ago

NORTH AMERICA 30,000–15,000 years ago

PACIFIC OCEAN

ASIA 1 million years ago 70,000 years ago

EUROPE 1 million years ago 40,000 years ago

Easter I. 1,500 years ago

Sumatra 1.3 million years ago

New Zealand 1,000 years ago

SOUTH AMERICA 14,000 years ago

INDIAN OCEAN

AUSTRALIA 60,000–40,000 years ago

AFRICA 1.7 million years ago 100,000 years ago

ATLANTIC OCEAN

ANTARCTICA

Madagascar 1,500 years ago

0   1,000   2,000 miles
0   1,000 2,000 kilometers

Legend:
- Ice sheet, 20,000 years ago
- Land exposed by lower sea levels, 20,000 years ago
- → Expansion of *Homo erectus*
- 1 million years ago — Earliest habitation by *Homo erectus*
- → Expansion of *Homo sapiens*
- 3,500 years ago — Earliest habitation by *Homo sapiens*

◻ Mapping the Past

MAP 1.1 Human Migration in the Paleolithic and Neolithic Eras

ANALYZING THE MAP What were the major similarities with and differences between the migrations of *Homo erectus* and those of *Homo sapiens*? How did environmental factors shape human migration?

CONNECTIONS What types of technology were required for the migration patterns seen here? What do these migration patterns suggest about the social organization of early people?

genetic variety today in Africa than in other parts of the world, the evidence also suggests that *Homo sapiens* have lived there the longest, so that Africa is where they first emerged. According to this hypothesis, all modern humans are descended from a relatively small group in East Africa. (Picking up on the biblical story of the first humans, some scientists have given the name Mitochondrial Eve to the most recent common matrilineal ancestor from whom all living humans are descended.)

Although there is some debate about where and when *Homo sapiens* emerged, there is little debate about what distinguished these humans from earlier hominids: a bigger brain, in particular a bigger forebrain, the site of conscious thought. The ability to think reflectively allowed for the creation of symbolic language, that is, for language that follows certain rules

and that can refer to things or states of being that are not necessarily present. Greater intelligence allowed *Homo sapiens* to better understand and manipulate the world around them, and symbolic language allowed this understanding to be communicated within a group and passed from one generation to the next. Through spoken language *Homo sapiens* began to develop collective explanations for the world around them that we would now call religion, science, and philosophy. Spoken language also enabled *Homo sapiens* to organize socially into larger groups, thus further enhancing their ability to affect the natural world.

The advantages of a larger brain seem evident to us, so we may not think to ask why hominids evolved this way. Large brains also bring disadvantages, however. They take more energy to run than other parts of the body, so that large-brained animals have to eat more than small-brained ones. Large brains create particular problems for bipedal mammals, for the narrow pelvic structure that works best for upright walking makes giving birth to a large-headed infant difficult and painful.

The question of why hominids developed ever-larger brains might best be answered by looking at how paleontologists think it happened. As *Homo habilis, Homo erectus,* and *Homo sapiens* made and used tools, the individuals whose mental and physical abilities allowed them to do so best were able to obtain more food and were more likely to mate and have children who survived. This created what biologists term selective pressure that favored better tool users, which meant individuals with bigger brains. Thus bigger brains led to better tools, but the challenges of using and inventing better tools also created selective pressure that led to bigger brains.

The same thing may have happened with symbolic language and thought. A slightly bigger brain, or a brain that kept developing rapidly after birth and was capable of learning more, allowed for more complex thought and better language skills (aided by anatomical changes in the vocal tract and larynx that allowed for a greater range of sounds). These thinking and speaking skills enabled individuals to better attract mates and fend off rivals, which meant a greater likelihood of passing on the enhanced brain to the next generation. As we know from contemporary research on the brain, learning language promotes the development of specific areas of the brain.

The growth in brain size and complexity may also have been linked to social organization. Individuals who had better social skills were more likely to mate than those who did not—this has been observed in chimpanzees and, of course, in modern humans—and thus to pass on their genetic material. Social skills were particularly important for females, because the combination of bipedalism and growing brain size led to selective pressure for hominid infants to be born at an even earlier stage in their development than other primate infants. Thus the period when human infants are dependent on others is very long, and mothers with good social networks to assist them were more likely to have infants who survived. Humans are unique in the duration and complexity of their care for children, and cooperative child rearing, along with the development of social skills and the adaptability this encouraged, may have been an impetus to brain growth.

All these factors operated together in processes that promoted bigger and better brains. In the Paleolithic period, *Homo sapiens'* brains invented highly specialized tools made out of a variety of materials that replaced the more general-purpose stone tools made by *Homo erectus*: barbed fishhooks and har-poons, snares and traps for catching small animals, bone needles for sewing clothing, awls for punching holes in leather, nets for catching fish, sharpened flint pieces bound to wooden or bone handles for hunting or cutting, and slings for carrying infants. By 25,000 years ago, and perhaps earlier, humans in some parts of the world were weaving cloth and baskets, and by 17,000 years ago they were using bows and atlatls (AHT-lah-tuhlz)—notched throwing sticks made of bone, wood, or antler—to launch arrows and barbs with flint points bound to wooden shafts. The archaeological evidence for increasingly sophisticated language and social organization is less direct than that for tool use, but it is hard to imagine how humans could have made the tools they did—or would have chosen to decorate so many of them—without both of these.

Migration and Differentiation

Like *Homo erectus* had earlier, groups of *Homo sapiens* moved. By 200,000 years ago they had begun to spread across Africa, and by 120,000 years ago they had begun to migrate out of Africa to Eurasia (see Map 1.1). They most likely walked along the coasts of India and Southeast Asia, and then migrated inland. At the same time, further small evolutionary changes led to our own subspecies of anatomically modern humans, *Homo sapiens sapiens* (which literally translates as "thinking thinking humans"). *Homo sapiens sapiens* moved into areas where there were already *Homo erectus* populations, eventually replacing them.

The best-known example of interaction between *Homo erectus* and *Homo sapiens sapiens* is that between Neanderthals (named after the Neander Valley in Germany, where their remains were first discovered) and a group of anatomically modern humans called Cro-Magnons. **Neanderthals** lived throughout Europe and western Asia beginning about 150,000 years ago, had brains as large as those of modern humans, and used tools, including spears and scrapers for animal skins, that enabled them to survive in the cold climate of Ice Age central Europe and Russia. They built freestanding houses and decorated objects and themselves with red ochre, a form of colored clay. They sometimes buried their dead carefully with tools, animal bones, and perhaps flowers, which suggests that they understood death to have a symbolic meaning. These characteristics led them to be originally categorized as a branch of *Homo sapiens,* but DNA evidence from Neanderthal bones now indicates that they were a separate branch of highly developed *Homo erectus.*

• **Neanderthals** Group of *Homo erectus* with brains as large as those of modern humans that flourished in Europe and western Asia between 150,000 and 30,000 years ago.

Cro-Magnon peoples moved into parts of western Asia where Neanderthals lived by about 70,000 years ago, and into Europe by about 45,000 years ago. The two peoples appear to have lived side by side for millennia, hunting the same types of animals and gathering the same types of plants. In 2010 DNA evidence demonstrated that they also had sex with one another, for between 1 and 4 percent of the DNA in modern humans living outside of Africa likely came from Neanderthals. The last evidence of Neanderthals as a separate species comes from about 30,000 years ago, but it is not clear exactly how they died out. They may have been killed by Cro-Magnon peoples, or they simply may have lost the competition for food as the climate worsened around 30,000 years ago and the glaciers expanded.

Until very recently Neanderthals were thought to be the last living hominids that were not *Homo sapiens*, but in 2003 archaeologists on the Indonesian island of Flores discovered bones and tools of three-foot-tall hominids that dated from only about 18,000 years ago. A few scientists view them as very small or malformed *Homo sapiens*, but most see them as a distinct species, probably descended from *Homo erectus* just as were Neanderthals. Nicknamed "hobbits," the Flores hominids or their ancestors appear to have lived on the island for more than 800,000 years.

Homo erectus migrated great distances, but *Homo sapiens sapiens* made use of greater intelligence and better tool-making capabilities to migrate still farther. They used simple rafts to reach Australia by at least 50,000 years ago and perhaps earlier, and by 35,000 years ago had reached New Guinea. By at least 15,000 years ago humans had walked across the land bridges then linking Siberia and North America at the Bering Strait and had crossed into the Americas. Because by 14,000 years ago humans were already in southern South America, ten thousand miles from the land bridges, many scholars now think that people came to the Americas much earlier. They think humans came from Asia to the Americas, perhaps as early as 20,000 or even 30,000 years ago, walking or using rafts along the coasts. (See Chapter 11 for a longer discussion of this issue.)

With the melting of glaciers sea levels rose, and parts of the world that had been linked by land bridges, including North America and Asia as well as many parts of Southeast Asia, became separated by water. This cut off migratory paths, but also spurred innovation. Humans designed and built ever more sophisticated boats

Land Bridge Across the Bering Strait, ca. 15,000 B.C.E.

Polynesian Oceangoing Sailing Canoe This is a Hawaiian replica of the type of large double-hulled canoe in which Polynesians sailed around the Pacific as they settled many different island groups. This canoe, called the Hokule'a, has taken many voyages using traditional Pacific techniques of celestial navigation. The two hulls provided greater stability, and canoes designed like this sailed thousands of miles over the open ocean. (Photograph © Monte Costa)

and learned how to navigate by studying wind and current patterns, bird flights, and the position of the stars. They sailed to increasingly remote islands, including those in the Pacific, the last parts of the globe to be settled. The western Pacific islands were inhabited by about 2000 B.C.E., Hawaii by about 500 C.E., and New Zealand by about 1000 C.E. (For more on the settlement of the Pacific islands, see page 360.)

Once humans spread out over much of the globe, groups often became isolated from one another, and people mated only with other members of their own group or those who lived nearby, a practice anthropologists call endogamy. Thus, over thousands of generations, although humans remained one species, *Homo sapiens sapiens* came to develop differences in physical features, including skin and hair color, eye and body shape, and amount of body hair. Language also changed over generations, so that thousands of different languages were eventually spoken. Groups created widely varying cultures and passed them on to their children, further increasing diversity among humans.

Beginning in the eighteenth century, European natural scientists sought to develop a system that would explain human differences at the largest scale. They divided people into very large groups by skin color and other physical characteristics and termed these groups "races," a word that had originally meant lineage. They first differentiated these races by continent of origin — Americanus, Europaeus, Asiaticus, and Africanus — and then by somewhat different geographic areas. The word *Caucasian* was first used by the German anatomist and naturalist Johann Friedrich Blumenbach (1752–1840) to describe light-skinned people of Europe and western Asia because he thought that their original home was most likely the Caucasus Mountains on the border between Russia and Georgia. He thought that they were the first humans and the most attractive. (His judgment about Caucasian attractiveness came from studying a large collection of skulls; he measured all other skulls against one from Georgia that he judged to be the most beautiful form of the skull.) This meaning of *race* has had a long life, though biologists and anthropologists today do not use it, as it has no scientific meaning or explanatory value. All humans are one species that has less genetic variety than chimpanzees.

Paleolithic Society, 250,000–9000 B.C.E.

☐ What were the key features of Paleolithic society?

Eventually human cultures became widely diverse, but in the Paleolithic period people throughout the world lived in ways that were similar to one another. Archaeological evidence and studies of modern foragers suggest that people lived in small groups of related individuals and moved throughout the landscape in search of food. Most had few material possessions, only what they could carry, although in areas where food resources were especially rich, such as along seacoasts, they built structures and lived more permanently in one place. (See "Viewpoints: Stone Age Houses in Chile and China," page 12.) In the later Paleolithic, people in many parts of the world created art and music and developed religious ideas that linked the natural world to a world beyond.

Foraging for Food

Paleolithic peoples have often been called hunter-gatherers, but recent archaeological and anthropological research indicates that both historical and contemporary hunter-gatherers have depended much more on gathered foods than on hunted meat. Thus it would be more accurate to call them "gatherer-hunters," and

most scholars now call them foragers, a term that highlights the flexibility and adaptability in their search for food. Most of what foragers ate were plants, and much of the animal protein in their diet came from foods gathered or scavenged rather than hunted directly: insects, shellfish, small animals caught in traps, fish and other sea creatures caught in weirs and nets, and animals killed by other predators. Pointed flaked stones, which were earlier viewed as hunting implements, may have been used for a wide variety of tasks such as chopping vegetables, peeling fruits, cracking open shells, and working leather. Gathering and hunting probably varied in importance from year to year depending on environmental factors and the decisions of the group.

Paleolithic peoples did hunt large game. Groups working together forced animals over cliffs, threw spears, and, beginning about 15,000 B.C.E., used bows and atlatls to shoot projectiles so that they could stand farther away from their prey while hunting. The final retreat of the glaciers also occurred between 15,000 and 10,000 years ago, and the warming climate was less favorable to the very large mammals that had roamed the open spaces of many parts of the world. Wooly mammoths, mastodons, and wooly rhinos all died out in Eurasia in this **megafaunal extinction**, as did camels, horses, and sloths in the Americas and giant kangaroos and wombats in Australia. In many places, these extinctions occurred just about the time that modern humans appeared, and increasing numbers of scientists think that they were at least in part caused by human hunting.

Most foraging societies that exist today or did so until recently have some type of **division of labor** by sex, and also by age, with children and older people responsible for different tasks

Paleolithic Hand Axes Like most Paleolithic stone tools, these two hand axes from Libya in northern Africa were made by chipping flakes off stone to form a sharpened edge. Although they are traditionally called axes, they were used for a variety of purposes, including skinning, cutting, and chopping. (Robert Harding/ Masterfile)

- **megafaunal extinction** Die-off of large animals in many parts of the world about 15,000–10,000 B.C.E., caused by climate change and perhaps human hunting.
- **division of labor** Differentiation of tasks by gender, age, training, status, or other social distinction.

Viewpoints

Stone Age Houses in Chile and China

• *One of the central issues facing most human groups has been shelter from the elements. People's varying solutions to this issue reflect the environmental challenges and opportunities offered by their particular surroundings. Houses are not simply physical structures, however, but also reflect, communicate, and shape cultural and social values. The photographs on this page show the remains of houses built during the Paleolithic and Neolithic periods in two parts of the world very far from one another.*

QUESTIONS FOR ANALYSIS

1. From the photographs and the descriptions, what similarities and differences do you see in the two types of houses?

2. Monte Verde was a Paleolithic community of foragers, and Banpo a Neolithic community of agriculturalists. How might the differences between the two houses have been shaped by the technology of food production? What other factors might account for the differences?

3. It is easy to see the vast differences between these houses and those of today, but what similarities do you find? What social and cultural values might lie behind these similarities?

Monte Verde Monte Verde in Chile dates from about 12,000 B.C.E. The archaeologists who have studied this site have concluded that here, along a creek, a small group of perhaps twenty to thirty people built a 20-foot-long structure of wooden poles covered by animal skins. Within the structure were smaller living quarters separated by skins, each with its own small fire pit, around which archaeologists have found stone tools, rope made of reeds, and many different types of foraged food, including wild potatoes and seaweed that came from coastal areas far away. (Courtesy of Tom D. Dillehay)

Banpo The village of Banpo near Xi'an in China dates from about 4500 B.C.E. Archaeologists have concluded that a group of several hundred people built fifty or so houses there, along with kilns for making pottery and cellars for storage. They built each house by digging a shallow hole as a foundation, surrounding this with walls made of stakes interwoven with branches and twigs, and plastering this with mud, which dried to become wind- and water-resistant. They made the roof out of thatch made from millet and rice stalks, grains they raised that formed the main part of their diet. (Courtesy of China Odyssey Tours)

than adult men and women. Men are more often responsible for hunting, through which they gained prestige as well as meat, and women for gathering plant and animal products. This has led scholars to assume that in Paleolithic society men were also responsible for hunting, and women for gathering. Such a division of labor is not universal, however: in some of the world's foraging cultures, such as the Agta of the Philippines, women hunt large game, and in numerous others women are involved in certain types of hunting, such as driving herds of animals toward a cliff or compound or throwing nets over them. The stone and bone tools that remain from the Paleolithic period give no clear evidence of who used them, and the division of labor may have been somewhat flexible, particularly during periods of scarcity.

Obtaining food was a constant preoccupation, but it was not a constant job. Studies of recent foragers indicate that, other than in times of environmental disasters such as prolonged droughts, people need only about ten to twenty hours a week to gather food and carry out the other tasks needed to survive, such as

locating water and building shelters. The diet of foragers is varied and — especially compared to today's diet of highly processed foods loaded with fat, sugar, and salt — nutritious: low in fat and salt, high in fiber, and rich in vitamins and minerals. The slow pace of life and healthy diet did not mean that Paleolithic life spans approached those of the modern world, however. People avoided such contemporary killers as heart disease and diabetes, but they often died at young ages from injuries, infections, animal attacks, and interpersonal violence. Mothers and infants died in childbirth, and many children died before they reached adulthood.

Total human population thus grew very slowly during the Paleolithic. Scholars can make rough estimates only, but one of them proposes that there were perhaps 500,000 humans in the world about 30,000 years ago. By about 10,000 years ago this number had grown to 5 million — ten times as many people. This was a significant increase, but it took twenty thousand years. (By contrast, the earth's population today is approaching 7 billion; it was one-tenth this size a mere three hundred years ago.) The low population density meant

Finger Marks from Rouffignac Cave in France, 18,000–9000 B.C.E., **and Handprints from Cueva de las Manos (Cave of the Hands) in Argentina, ca. 8000** B.C.E. Paleolithic hand markings have been found in many parts of the world. The finger marks of a young girl (right) are among those made by a group of adults and children who each left such finger flutings in the wet surfaces of the cave, far from the entrance, indicating that they would have used torches to see as they decorated the walls and ceiling. The handprints below, made by blowing colored clay around the hand through a bone pipe, are from different individuals. All are slightly smaller than adult hands, which suggests that this might have been some sort of ceremony involving adolescents. Most are left hands, which indicates that even in the Paleolithic, most people were right-handed, since they would have held the pipe for blowing in the hand they normally used for tasks. (finger marks: © Leslie Van Gelder; handprints: Hubert Stadler/Corbis)

that human impact on the environment was relatively small, although still significant. In addition to contributing to the extinction of some large animals, Paleolithic people may have also shaped their environments by setting fires, which encouraged the growth of new plants and attracted animals that fed on them, making hunting or snaring game easier. This practice was a factor in the spread of plants that thrived best with occasional burning, such as the eucalyptus in Australia.

Family and Kinship Relationships

Small bands of humans — twenty or thirty people was a standard size for foragers in harsh environments — were scattered across broad areas, but this did not mean that each group lived in isolation. Their travels in search of food brought them into contact with one another, not simply for talking and celebrating, but also for providing opportunities for the exchange of sexual partners, which was essential to group survival. Today we understand that having sexual relations with close relatives is disadvantageous because it creates greater risk of genetic disorders. Earlier societies did not have knowledge of genetics, but most of them developed rules against sexual relations among immediate family members. Thus people needed to seek mates outside their own group, and the bands living in large areas became linked by bonds of kinship. Mating arrangements varied in their permanence, but many groups seem to have developed a somewhat permanent arrangement whereby a man or woman left his or her original group and joined the group of his or her mate, what would later be termed marriage.

Within each band, and within the larger kin groups, individuals had a variety of identities; they were simultaneously fathers, sons, husbands, and brothers, or mothers, daughters, wives, and sisters. Each of these identities was relational (parent to child, sibling to sibling, spouse to spouse), and some of them, especially parent to child, gave one power over others. In many areas, kin groups remained significant power structures for millennia, and in some areas they still have influence over major aspects of life, such as an individual's job or marital partner. Paleolithic people were not differentiated by wealth, for in a foraging society accumulating material goods was not advantageous. But they were differentiated by such factors as age, gender, and position in a family, and no doubt by personal qualities such as intelligence, courage, and charisma.

Stereotypical representations of Paleolithic people often portray a powerful fur-clad man holding a club and dragging off a (usually attractive) fur-clad woman by her hair, or men going off to hunt while women and children crouched around a fire, waiting for the men to bring back great slabs of meat. Studies of the relative importance of gathering to hunting, women's participation in hunting, and gender relations among contemporary foraging peoples have led some analysts to turn these stereotypes on their heads. They see Paleolithic bands as egalitarian groups in which the contributions of men and women to survival were recognized and valued, and in which both men and women had equal access to the limited amount of resources held by the group. Other scholars argue that this is also a stereotype, overly romanticizing Paleolithic society as a sort of vegetarian commune. They note that although social relations among foragers were not as hierarchical as they were in other types of societies, many foraging groups had one person who held more power than others, and that person was almost always a man. This debate about gender relations is often part of larger discussions about whether Paleolithic society — and by implication, "human nature" — was primarily peaceful and nurturing or violent and brutal, and whether these qualities are gender-related. Like much else about the Paleolithic, sources about gender and about violence are fragmentary and difficult to interpret; there may simply have been a diversity of patterns, as there is among more modern foragers.

Whether peaceful and egalitarian or violent and hierarchical, heterosexual relations produced children, who were cared for as infants by their mothers or other women who had recently given birth. Breast milk was the only food available that infants could easily digest, so mothers nursed their children for several years. Along with providing food for infants, extended nursing brings a side benefit: it suppresses ovulation and thus acts as a contraceptive. Foraging groups needed children to survive, but too many could tax scarce food resources. Many groups may have practiced selective infanticide or abandonment. They may also have exchanged children of different ages with other groups, which further deepened kinship connections between groups. Other than for feeding, children were most likely cared for by other male and female members of the group as well as by their mothers during the long period of human childhood.

Cultural Creations and Spirituality

Early human societies are often described in terms of their tools, but this misses a large part of the story. Beginning in the Paleolithic, human beings have expressed themselves through what we would now term

- **animism** Idea that animals, plants, natural occurrences, and other parts of the physical world have spirits.
- **shamans** Spiritually adept men and women who communicated with the unseen world.

the arts or culture: painting and decorating walls and objects, making music with their voices and a variety of instruments, imagining and telling stories, dancing alone or in groups. Evidence from the Paleolithic, particularly from after about 50,000 years ago, includes flutes, carvings, jewelry, and paintings done on cave walls and rock outcroppings that depict animals, people, and symbols. In many places they show the outline of a human hand — often done by blowing pigment around it — or the tracings of the fingers, a simple art form that allowed individuals to say "I was here."

Some cultural creations had a larger purpose: they were created to honor and praise ancestors or leaders, help people remember events and traditions, or promote good hunting or safe childbirth. Some were easy to do, and everyone in a culture was expected to participate in some way: to dance in order to bring rain or give thanks, to listen when stories were told, to take part in ceremonies. Others of these creations required particular talents or training and were probably undertaken only by specialists.

At the same time that people marked and depicted the world around them, they also developed ideas about supernatural forces that controlled some aspects of the natural world and the place of humans in it, what we now term spirituality or religion. The Neanderthals' careful burial of their dead suggests to some scholars that they had ideas about an afterlife or at least something beyond the visible world, and there is no doubt that this was the case for Paleolithic *Homo sapiens*. Paleolithic burials, paintings, and objects indicate that people thought of their world as extending beyond the visible. People, animals, plants, natural occurrences, and other things around them had spirits, an idea called **animism**. The only evidence of Paleolithic animism that survives is physical, of course, but more recent animist traditions carry on this understanding of the spiritual nature and interdependence of all things, as in this contemporary Chinook blessing from northwestern North America:

> ❝We call upon the Earth, our planet home, with its . . . vitality and abundance of life, and together we ask that it *Teach us, and show us the Way.*❞
>
> **CHINOOK BLESSING**

We call upon the Earth, our planet home, with its beautiful depths and soaring heights, its vitality and abundance of life, and together we ask that it *Teach us, and show us the Way.* . . .

We call upon the creatures of the fields and the forests and the seas, our brothers and sisters the wolves and the deer, the eagle and dove, the great whales and the dolphin, the beautiful orca and salmon who share our Northwest home, and ask them to *Teach Us and show us the Way.*[1]

Death took people from the realm of the living, but for Paleolithic groups people continued to inhabit an unseen world, along with spirits and deities, after death; thus kin groups included deceased as well as living members of a family. The unseen world regularly intervened in the visible world, for good and ill, and the actions of dead ancestors, spirits, and gods could be shaped by living people. Concepts of the supernatural pervaded all aspects of life; hunting, birth, death, and natural occurrences such as eclipses, comets, and rainbows all had religious meaning. Supernatural forces were understood to determine the basic rules for human existence, and upsetting these rules could lead to chaos.

Ordinary people learned about the unseen world through dreams and portents, and messages and revelations were also sent more regularly to **shamans**, spiritually adept men and women who communicated with the unseen world. Shamans created complex rituals through which they sought to ensure the health and prosperity of an individual, family, or group. Many cave paintings show herds of prey animals, and several include a masked human figure usually judged to be a shaman performing some sort of ritual. Objects understood to have special power, such as carvings or masks in the form of an animal or person, could give additional protection, as could certain plants or mixtures eaten, sniffed, or rubbed on the skin. (See "Listening to the Past: Paleolithic Venus Figures," page 16.)

Paleolithic Flute This flute, carved from the wing bone of a griffon vulture, was unearthed in a cave in Germany along with pieces of other flutes made from mammoth ivory and stone tools. Dating from at least 33,000 B.C.E., it is the oldest musical instrument ever found, and suggests that music has long been an important part of human culture. (H. Jensen/University of Tübingen)

Listening to the Past

Paleolithic Venus Figures

Written sources provide evidence about the human past only after the development of writing, allowing us to listen to the voices of people long dead. For most of human history, however, there were no written sources, so we "listen" to the past through objects. Interpreting written documents is difficult, and interpreting archaeological evidence about the earliest human belief systems is even more difficult and often contentious. For example, small stone statues of women with enlarged breasts and buttocks dating from the later Paleolithic period (roughly 33,000–9,000 B.C.E.) have been found in many parts of Europe. These were dubbed "Venus figures" by nineteenth-century archaeologists, who thought they represented Paleolithic standards of female beauty just as the goddess Venus represented classical standards. A reproduction of one of these statues is shown here. Venus figures provoke more questions than answers: Are they fertility goddesses, evidence of people's beliefs in a powerful female deity? Or are they aids to fertility, carried around by women hoping to have children — or perhaps hoping not to have more — and then discarded in the household debris where they have been most commonly found? Or are they sexualized images of women carried around by men, a sort of Paleolithic version of the centerfold in a men's magazine? Might they have represented different things to different people? Like so much Paleolithic evidence, Venus figurines provide tantalizing evidence about early human cultures, but evidence that is not easy to interpret.

QUESTIONS FOR ANALYSIS

1. Some scholars see Venus figures as evidence that Paleolithic society was egalitarian or female-dominated, but others point out that images of female deities or holy figures are often found in religions that deny women official authority. Can you think of examples of the latter? Which point of view seems most persuasive to you?

2. As you look at this statue, does it seem to link more closely with fertility or with sexuality? How might your own situation as a twenty-first-century person shape your answer to this question?

The Venus of Lespugue from France, made from tusk ivory around 25,000 years ago.
(Ronald Sheridan/Ancient Art & Architecture Ltd.)

▫ Picturing the Past

Cave Paintings of Horses and a Horned Auroch from Lascaux Cave, Southern France, ca. 15,000 B.C.E. The artist who made these amazing animals in charcoal and red ochre first smoothed the surface, just as a contemporary artist might. This cave includes paintings of hundreds of animals, including predators such as lions, as well as abstract symbols. (JM Labat/Photo Researchers, Inc.)

ANALYZING THE IMAGE The artist painted the animals so close together that they overlap. What might this arrangement have been trying to depict or convey?

CONNECTIONS Why might Paleolithic people have made cave paintings? What do these paintings suggest about Stone Age culture and society?

Shamans thus also operated as healers, with cures that included what we would term natural medicines and religious healing. Because their spiritual and the material worlds appear to have been closely intertwined, Paleolithic people most likely did not make a distinction between natural and spiritual cures.

The rituals and medicines through which shamans and healers operated were often closely guarded secrets, but they were passed orally from one spiritually adept individual to another, so that gradually a body of knowledge about the medicinal properties of local plants and other natural materials was built up. By observing natural phenomena and testing materials for their usable qualities, Paleolithic people began to invent what would later be called science.

The Development of Agriculture in the Neolithic Era, ca. 9000 B.C.E.

▫ How did plant and animal domestication develop, and what effects did it have on human society?

Foraging remained the basic way of life for most of human history, and for groups living in extreme environments, such as tundras or deserts, it was the only possible way to survive. In a few especially fertile areas, however, the natural environment provided enough

Neolithic Tools from Lakes in Switzerland These highly specialized tools include arrow points, awls, chisels, scrapers, stone ax blades in antler sockets, sickle blades, and round spindle whorls, designed to twist fibers into thread. The people who made and used them lived in wooden houses on stilts over the water, and the mud of the lake bed preserved even the bone and antler. (Courtesy of Peter A. Bostrom)

food that people could become more settled. As they remained in one place, they began to plant seeds as well as gather wild crops, to raise certain animals instead of hunting, and to selectively breed both plants and animals to make them more useful to humans. This seemingly small alteration was the most important change in human history; because of its impact it is often termed the **Agricultural Revolution**. Plant and animal domestication marked the transition from the Paleolithic to the Neolithic. It allowed the human population to grow far more quickly than did foraging, but it also required more labor, which became increasingly specialized.

The Development of Horticulture

Areas of the world differed in the food resources available to foragers. In some, acquiring enough food to sustain a group was difficult, and groups had to move constantly. In others, moderate temperatures and abundant rainfall allowed for verdant plant growth; or seas, rivers, and lakes provided substantial amounts of fish and shellfish. Groups in such areas were able to become more settled. About 15,000 years ago, the earth's cli-

mate entered a warming phase, and the glaciers began to retreat. As it became warmer, the climate became wetter, and more parts of the world were able to support sedentary or semi-sedentary groups of foragers.

In several of these places, foragers began planting seeds in the ground along with gathering wild grains, roots, and other foodstuffs. By observation, they learned the optimum times and places for planting. They removed unwanted plants through weeding and selected the seeds they planted in order to get crops that had favorable characteristics, such as larger edible parts. For grain crops, people chose plants with larger kernels clustered together that ripened all at one time and did not just fall on the ground, qualities that made harvesting more efficient. Through this human intervention, certain crops became **domesticated**, that is, modified by selective breeding so as to serve human needs, in this case to provide a more reliable source of food. Archaeologists trace the development and spread of plant-raising by noting when the seeds and other plant parts they discover show evidence of domestication.

This early crop-planting was done by individuals using hoes and digging sticks, and it is often termed **horticulture** to distinguish it from the later agriculture using plows. In some places, digging sticks were weighted with stones to make them more effective (earlier archaeologists thought these stones were the killing parts of war clubs). Intentional crop-planting developed first in the area archaeologists call the Fertile Crescent, which runs from present-day Lebanon,

- **Agricultural Revolution** Dramatic transformation in human history resulting from the change from foraging to raising crops and animals.

- **domesticated** Plants and animals modified by selective breeding so as to serve human needs; domesticated animals will behave in specific ways and breed in captivity.

- **horticulture** Crop-raising done with hand tools and human power.

Israel, and Jordan north to Turkey and then south to the Iran-Iraq border (Map 1.2). About 9000 B.C.E. people there began to plant seeds of the wild wheat and barley they had already been harvesting, along with seeds of legume crops, such as peas and lentils, and of the flax with which they made linen cloth. They then modified these crops through domestication. By about 8000 B.C.E. people were growing sorghum and millet in parts of the Nile River Valley, and perhaps yams in western Africa. By about 7000 B.C.E. they were growing domesticated rice, millet, and legumes in China, yams and taro in Papua New Guinea, and perhaps squash in Mesoamerica. In each of these places, the development of horticulture occurred independently, and it may have happened in other parts of the world as well. Archaeological evidence does not survive well in tropical areas like Southeast Asia and the Amazon Basin, which may have been additional sites of plant domestication.

Nowhere do archaeological remains alone answer the question of who within any group first began to cultivate crops, but the fact that, among foragers, women were primarily responsible for gathering plant products suggests that they may also have been the first to plant seeds in the ground. In many parts of the world, crops continued to be planted with hoes and digging sticks for millennia, and crop-raising remained primarily women's work, while men hunted or later raised animals.

Why, after living successfully as foragers for tens of thousands of years, did humans in so many parts of the world all begin raising crops at about the same time? The answer to this question is not clear, but crop-raising may have resulted from population pressures in those parts of the world where the warming climate provided more food. More food meant lower child mortality and longer life spans, which allowed communities to grow. Naturally occurring and then planted foods included cereal crops, which were soft enough for babies to eat, so that women could stop nursing their children at a younger age. They lost the contraceptive effects of breast-feeding, and children may have been born at more frequent intervals, further speeding up population growth. Thus people had a choice: they could move to a new area—the solution that foragers had relied on when faced with the same problem—or they could develop ways to increase the food supply to keep up with population growth, a solution that the warming climate was making possible. They chose the latter and began to plant more intensively, beginning cycles of expanding population

The Fertile Cresent

and intensification of land use that have continued to today.

In the Fertile Crescent, parts of China, and the Nile Valley, within several centuries of initial crop-planting, people were relying on domesticated food products alone. They built permanent houses near one another in villages with fields around them, and they invented new ways of storing foods, such as in pottery made from clay. Villages were closer together than were the camps of foragers, so population density as well as total population grew.

A field of planted and weeded crops yields ten to one hundred times as much food—measured in calories—as the same area of naturally occurring plants, a benefit that would have been evident to early crop-planters. It also requires much more labor, however, which was provided both by the greater number of people in the community and by those people working longer hours. In

Inca Farmers Planting Potatoes with a Digging Stick
Potatoes were a staple crop in the Andes for thousands of years. In this drawing from a sixteenth century C.E. book by the indigenous author Guaman Poma, the man at the left digs a hole while the woman in the middle puts in the seed potato, and the woman at the right stands ready to pound down the earth over it. (John Meek/The Art Archive)

MAP 1.2 The Spread of Agriculture and Pastoralism Local plants and animals were domesticated in many different places. Agriculturalists and pastoralists spread the knowledge of how to raise them, and spread the plants and animals themselves, through migration, trade, and conquest.

contrast to the twenty hours a week foragers spent on obtaining food, farming peoples were often in the fields from dawn to dusk, particularly during planting and harvest time, but also during the rest of the growing year because weeding was a constant task.

Foragers who lived at the edge of horticultural communities appear to have recognized the negative aspects of crop-raising, for they did not immediately adopt this new way of life. Instead farming spread when a village became too large and some residents moved to a new area, cleared land, planted seeds, and built a new village, sometimes intermarrying with the local people. Because the population of farming communities grew so much faster than that of foragers, however, horticulture quickly spread into fertile areas. By about 6500 B.C.E. farming had spread northward from the Fertile Crescent into Greece and by 4000 farther northward all the way to Britain; by 4500 it had spread southward into Ethiopia. At the same time, crop-raising spread out from others areas in which it

was first developed, and slowly larger and larger parts of China, South and Southeast Asia, and East Africa were home to horticultural villages.

People adapted crops to their local environments, choosing seeds that had qualities that were beneficial, such as drought resistance. They also domesticated new kinds of crops. In the Americas, for example, by about 3000 B.C.E. corn was domesticated in southern Mexico and potatoes and quinoa in the Andes region of South America, and by about 2500 B.C.E. squash and beans in eastern North America. These crops then spread, so that by about 1000 B.C.E. people in much of what is now the western United States were raising corn, beans, and squash. In the Indus Valley of South Asia people were growing dates, mangoes, sesame seeds, and cotton along with grains and legumes by 4000 B.C.E. Crop-raising led to dramatic human alteration of the environment.

Certain planted crops eventually came to be grown over huge areas of land, so that some scientists de-

East Asia
Millet
Rice
Soybean
Silkworm
Pig

PACIFIC
OCEAN

Southeast Asia
Banana
Yam
Chicken
Water buffalo
Zebu cattle

New Guinea
Sugar cane
Taro
Yam

AUSTRALIA

another area and began the process again, perhaps returning to the first plot many years later, after the soil had rejuvenated itself. Groups using shifting slash-and-burn cultivation remained small and continued to rely on the surrounding forest for much of their food.

Animal Domestication and the Rise of Pastoralism

At roughly the same time that they domesticated certain plants, people also domesticated animals. The earliest animal to be domesticated was the dog, which separated genetically as a subspecies from wolves at least 15,000 years ago and perhaps much earlier. The mechanism of dog domestication is hotly debated: did it result only from human action, as foragers chose and bred animals that would help them with the hunt rather than attack them, or was it also caused by selective pressure resulting from wolf action, as animals less afraid of human contact came around campsites and then bred with one another? However it happened, the relationship provided both with benefits: humans gained dogs' better senses of smell and hearing and their body warmth, and dogs gained new food sources and safer surroundings. Not surprisingly, humans and domestic dogs migrated together, including across the land bridges to the Americas and on boats to Pacific islands.

Dogs fit easily into a foraging lifestyle, but humans also domesticated animals that led them to completely alter their way of life. In about 9000 B.C.E., at the same time they began to raise crops, people in the Fertile Crescent domesticated wild goats and sheep, probably using them first for meat, and then for milk, skins, and eventually fleece (see Map 1.2). They learned from observation and experimentation that traits are passed down from generation to generation, and they began to breed the goats and sheep selectively for qualities that they wanted, including larger size, greater strength, better coats, more milk production, and more even temperaments. The book of Genesis in the Bible, written in the Fertile Crescent sometime in the first millennium B.C.E., provides an early example of selective breeding. Jacob makes a deal with his father-in-law to take only those goats and sheep that are spotted, but he secretly increases the number of spotted animals in the flock by placing a spotted stick "before the eyes . . . of the strongest of the flocks . . . whenever they were breeding" so that more and stronger spotted animals were born (Genesis 30:41). This method was based on the idea — accepted for a very long time — that what a pregnant animal or woman saw during pregnancy would influence the outcome; although this has been firmly rejected in modern science, the Bible notes that it was successful, and that Jacob "grew exceedingly rich, and had large flocks."

scribe the Agricultural Revolution as a revolution of codependent domestication: humans domesticated crops, but crops also "domesticated" humans so that they worked long hours spreading particular crops around the world. Of these, corn has probably been the most successful; more than half a million square miles around the world are now planted in corn, and one-quarter of the nearly fifty thousand items in the average American supermarket contain corn.

In some parts of the world horticulture led to a dramatic change in the way of life, but in others it did not. Horticulture can be easily combined with gathering and hunting as plots of land are usually small; many cultures, including some in Papua New Guinea and North America, remained mixed foragers and horticulturists for thousands of years. Especially in deeply wooded areas, people cleared small plots by chopping and burning the natural vegetation, and planted crops in successive years until the soil eroded or lost its fertility, a method termed "slash and burn." They then moved to

A Goat Market in Mali Pastoral economies thrive in many parts of the world today, particularly in areas that are too dry for agriculture, including central Australia, Central Asia, northern and western Africa, and much of the U.S. West. As in early pastoralism, contemporary herders choose and breed their animals for qualities that will allow them to prosper in the local environment. (Ron Giling/Lineair/Photolibrary)

After goats and sheep, pigs were domesticated somewhat later in both the Fertile Crescent and China, as were chickens in southern Asia. Like domesticated crops, domesticated animals eventually far outnumbered their wild counterparts. For example, in the United States today (excluding Alaska), there are about 77 million dogs, compared to about 6,000 wolves. (Adding Alaska would add about 150,000 dogs and 10,000 wolves.) There are more than a billion and a half cattle, with enormous consequences for the environment. Animal domestication also shaped human evolution; groups that relied on animal milk and milk products for a significant part of their diet tended to develop the ability to digest milk as adults, while those that did not remained lactose intolerant as adults, the normal condition for mammals.

Sheep and goats allow themselves to be herded, and people developed a new form of living, **pastoralism**, based on herding and raising livestock, sometimes training dogs to assist them. In areas with sufficient rainfall and fertile soil, pastoralism can be relatively sedentary, and thus easily combined with horticulture;

people built pens for animals, or in colder climates constructed special buildings or took them into their houses. They learned that animal manure increases crop yields, so they gathered the manure from enclosures and used it as fertilizer.

Increased contact with animals and their feces also increased human contact with various sorts of disease-causing pathogens, including minor illnesses such as the common cold and deadly killers such as influenza, bubonic plague, and smallpox. This was particularly the case where humans and animals lived in tight quarters, for diseases spread fastest in crowded environments. Thus pastoralists and agriculturalists developed illnesses that had not plagued foragers, and the diseases became endemic, that is, widely found within a region without being deadly. Ultimately people who lived with animals developed resistance to some of these illnesses, but foragers' lack of resistance to many illnesses meant that they died more readily after coming into contact with new endemic diseases, as was the case when Europeans brought smallpox to the Americas in the sixteenth century.

In drier areas, flocks need to travel long distances from season to season to obtain enough food, so some pastoralists became nomadic. Nomadic pastoralists

• **pastoralism** An economic system based on herding flocks of goats, sheep, cattle, or other animals.

often gather wild plant foods as well, but they tend to rely primarily on their flocks of animals for food. Pastoralism was well-suited to areas where the terrain or climate made crop-planting difficult, such as mountains, deserts, dry grasslands, and tundras. Eventually other grazing animals, including cattle, camels, horses, yak, and reindeer, also became the basis of pastoral economies in central and western Asia, many parts of Africa, and far northern Europe.

Plow Agriculture

Horticulture and pastoralism brought significant changes to human ways of life, but the domestication of certain large animals had an even bigger impact. Cattle and water buffalo were domesticated in some parts of Asia and North Africa in which they occurred naturally by at least 7000 B.C.E., and horses, donkeys, and camels by about 4000 B.C.E. All these animals consent to carry people or burdens on their backs and pull against loads dragged behind them, two qualities that are rare among the world's animal species. In many parts of the world, including North America and much of South America and sub-Saharan Africa, no naturally occurring large species could be domesticated. In the mountainous regions of South America, llamas and alpacas were domesticated to carry packs, but the steep terrain made it difficult to use them to pull loads. The domestication of large animals dramatically increased the power available to humans to carry out their tasks, which had both an immediate effect in the societies in which this happened and a long-term effect when they later encountered societies in which human labor remained the only source of power.

The pulling power of animals came to matter most, because it could be applied to food production. Sometime in the seventh millennium B.C.E., people attached wooden sticks to frames that animals dragged through the soil, thus breaking it up and allowing seeds to sprout more easily. These simple scratch plows were pulled first by cattle and water buffalo, and later by horses. (Donkeys and camels were used primarily as pack animals, but occasionally for plowing as well.) Over millennia, moldboards—angled pieces that turned the soil over, bringing fresh soil to the top—were added, which reduced the time needed to plow and allowed each person to work more land.

Using plows, Neolithic people produced a significant amount of surplus food, so that some people in the community could spend their days doing other things, increasing the division of labor. Surplus food had to be stored, and some began to specialize in making products for storage, such as pots, baskets, bags, bins, and other kinds of containers. Others specialized in making tools, houses, and other things needed in village life, or in producing specific types of food, including alcoholic beverages made from fermented fruits and grains. Families and households became increasingly interdependent, trading food for other commodities or services. In the same way that foragers had continually improved their tools and methods, people improved the processes through which they made things. Sometime in the fifth millennium B.C.E. pot-makers in Mesopotamia invented the potter's wheel, which by a millennium later had been adapted for use on carts and plows pulled by animals. Wheeled vehicles led to road-building, and wheels and roads together made it possible for people and goods to travel long distances more easily, whether for settlement, trade, or conquest.

Stored food was also valuable and could become a source of conflict, as could other issues in villages where people lived close together. Villagers needed more complex rules about how food was to be distributed and how different types of work were to be valued than did foragers. Certain individuals began to specialize in the determination and enforcement of these rules, and informal structures of power gradually became more formalized as elites developed. These elites then distributed resources to their own advantage, often using force to attain and maintain their power.

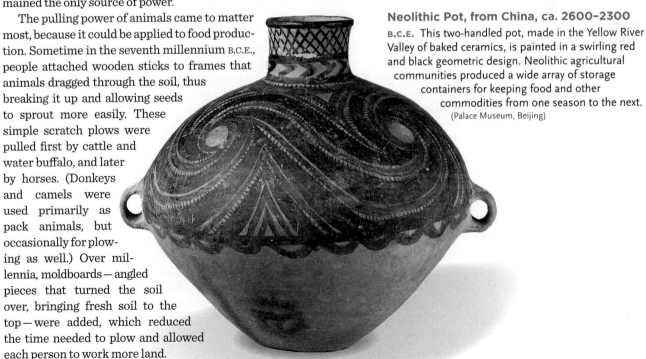

Neolithic Pot, from China, ca. 2600–2300 B.C.E. This two-handled pot, made in the Yellow River Valley of baked ceramics, is painted in a swirling red and black geometric design. Neolithic agricultural communities produced a wide array of storage containers for keeping food and other commodities from one season to the next. (Palace Museum, Beijing)

Neolithic Society

☐ How did growing social and gender hierarchies and expanding networks of trade increase the complexity of human society in the Neolithic period?

The division of labor that plow agriculture allowed led to the creation of **social hierarchies**, the divisions between rich and poor, elites and common people that have been a central feature of human society since the Neolithic era. Plow agriculture also strengthened differentiation based on gender, with men becoming more associated with the world beyond the household and women with the domestic realm. Social hierarchies were reinforced over generations as children inherited goods and status from their parents; even the gods were increasingly understood to be arranged in a hierarchy, and assuring fertility became the most important religious practice. People increasingly communicated ideas within local and regional networks of exchange, just as they traded foodstuffs, tools, and other products.

Social Hierarchies and Slavery

Archaeological finds from Neolithic villages, particularly burials, show signs of growing social differentiation. Some people were buried with significant amounts of jewelry, household goods, weapons, and other objects, while others were buried with very little. How were some people able to attain such power over their neighbors that they could even take valuable commodities with them to the grave? This is one of the key questions in all of human history. Written sources do not provide a clear answer because social hierarchies were already firmly in place by the time writing was invented, so that scholars have largely relied on archaeological sources. (See "Individuals in Society: The Iceman," page 25.)

Within foraging groups, some individuals already had more authority because of their links with the world of gods and spirits, positions as heads of kin groups, or personal characteristics. These three factors gave individuals advantages in agricultural societies, and the advantages became more significant over time as there were more resources to control. Priests and shamans developed more elaborate rituals and became full-time religious specialists, exchanging their services in interceding with the gods for food. In many communities, religious specialists were the first to work out formal rules of conduct that later became oral and written codes of law, generally explaining that these represented the will of the gods. The codes threatened divine punishment for those who broke them, and they often required people to accord deference to priests as the representatives of the gods, so that they became an elite group with special privileges.

Individuals who were the heads of large families or kin groups had control over the labor of others, which became more significant when that labor brought material goods that could be stored. Material goods—plows, sheep, cattle, sheds, pots, carts—gave one the ability to amass still more material goods, and the gap between those who had them and those who did not widened. Storage also allowed wealth to be retained over long periods of time and handed down from one family member to another, so that over generations small differences in wealth grew larger. The ability to control the labor of others could also come from physical strength, a charismatic personality, or leadership talents, and this also led to greater wealth.

Wealth itself could command labor, as individuals or families could buy the services of others to work for them or impose their wishes through force, hiring soldiers to threaten or carry out violence. Eventually some individuals bought others outright. As with social hierarchies in general, slavery predates written records, but it developed in almost all agricultural societies. Like animals, slaves were a source of physical power for their owners, providing them an opportunity to amass still more wealth and influence. In the long era before the invention of fossil fuel technology, the ability to exploit animal and human labor was the most important mark of distinction between elites and the rest of the population. As we will see in later chapters, land ownership was often what distinguished elites from others, but that land was valuable only if there were people living on it who were required to labor for the owner.

Gender Hierarchies and Inheritance

Along with hierarchies based on wealth and power, the development of agriculture was intertwined with a hierarchy based on gender. The system in which men have more power and access to resources than women and some men are dominant over other men is called **patriarchy**. Every society in the world that has left written records has been patriarchal, but patriarchy came before writing, and searching for its origins involves interpreting many different types of sources. Some scholars see the origins of gender inequality in the hominid past, noting that male chimpanzees form alliances to gain status against other males and engage in cooperative attacks on females, which might have

---

• **social hierarchies** Divisions between rich and poor, elites and common people that have been a central feature of human society since the Neolithic era.

• **patriarchy** Social system in which men have more power and access to resources than women and some men are dominant over other men.

The Iceman

ON SEPTEMBER 19, 1991, TWO GERMAN vacationers climbing in the Italian Alps came upon a corpse lying facedown and covered in ice. Scientists determined that the Iceman, as the corpse is generally known, dates to the Neolithic period, having died 5,300 years ago. He was between twenty-five and thirty-five years old at the time of his death, and he stood about five feet two inches tall. An autopsy revealed much about the man and his culture. The bluish tinge of his teeth showed a diet of milled grain, which proves that he came from an environment where crops were grown. The Iceman hunted as well as farmed: he was found with a bow and arrows and shoes of straw, and he wore a furry cap and a robe of animal skins that he had stitched together with thread that he had made from grass.

The equipment discovered with the Iceman demonstrates his mastery of several technologies. He carried a hefty copper ax, indicating a knowledge of metallurgy. He relied chiefly on archery to kill game. In his quiver were numerous wooden arrow shafts and two finished arrows. The arrows had flint heads, a sign of stoneworking, and feathers were attached to the ends of the shafts with resin-like glue. He knew the value of feathers to direct the arrows; thus he had mastered the basics of ballistics. His bow was made of yew, a relatively rare wood in central Europe that is among the best for archers.

Yet a mystery still surrounds the Iceman. When his body was first discovered, scholars assumed that he was a hapless traveler overtaken in a fierce snowstorm. But the autopsy found an arrowhead lodged under his left shoulder. The Iceman was not alone on his last day. Someone was with him, and that someone had shot him from below and behind. The Iceman is the victim in the first murder mystery of Western civilization, and the case will never be solved.

QUESTIONS FOR ANALYSIS

1. What do these images demonstrate about the Iceman's knowledge of his environment?

2. What does the Iceman reveal about the society in which he lived?

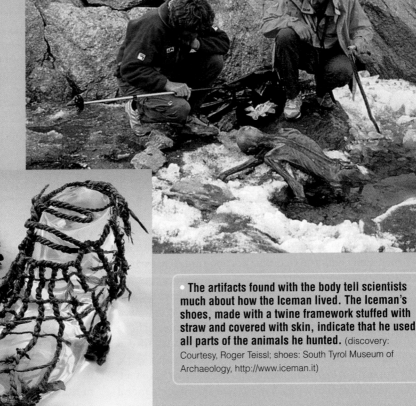

● **The artifacts found with the body tell scientists much about how the Iceman lived. The Iceman's shoes, made with a twine framework stuffed with straw and covered with skin, indicate that he used all parts of the animals he hunted.** (discovery: Courtesy, Roger Teissl; shoes: South Tyrol Museum of Archaeology, http://www.iceman.it)

Egyptian Couple Planting Grain, ca. 1500–1300 B.C.E. In this wall painting from the tomb of an official, a man guides a wooden ox-drawn plow through the soil, while the woman walking behind throws seed in the furrow. The painting was not designed to show real peasants working, but to depict the well-to-do man buried in the tomb doing work viewed as worthy of an afterlife. Nevertheless, the gender division of labor and the plow itself are probably accurate. (Erich Lessing/Art Resource, NY)

also happened among early hominids. Other scholars see the origins in the Paleolithic, with the higher status of men in lineage groups.

Plow agriculture heightened patriarchy. Although farming with a hoe was often done by women, plow agriculture came to be a male task, perhaps because of men's upper-body strength or because plow agriculture was more difficult to combine with care for infants and small children than was horticulture. The earliest depictions of plowing are on Mesopotamian cylinder seals, and they invariably show men with the cattle and plows. At the same time that cattle began to be raised for pulling plows and carts rather than for meat, sheep began to be raised primarily for wool. Spinning thread and weaving cloth became primarily women's work; the earliest Egyptian hieroglyph for weaving is, in fact, a seated woman with a shuttle, and a Confucian moral saying from ancient China asserts that "men plow and women weave." Spinning and weaving were generally done indoors and involved simpler and cheaper tools than plowing; they could also be taken up and put

down easily, and so could be done at the same time as other tasks.

Though in some ways this arrangement seems complementary, with each sex doing some of the necessary labor, plow agriculture increased gender hierarchy. Men's responsibility for plowing and other agricultural tasks took them outside the household more often than women, enlarging their opportunities for leadership. It also led to their being favored as inheritors of family land and the right to farm communally held land when inheritance systems were established to pass land and other goods on to the next generation. In some of these systems all children inherited from both parents, but more often inheritance passed from father to son (or to other male family members if there were no sons) in a patrilineal inheritance system. In some places inheritance was matrilineal, that is, traced through the female line, but in such systems women themselves did not necessarily inherit goods or property; instead a man inherited from his mother's brother rather than from his father. Thus over generations, women's independent access to resources decreased, and it became increasingly difficult for women to survive without male support.

As inherited wealth became more important, men wanted to make sure that their sons were theirs, so they restricted their wives' movements and activities. This was especially the case among elite families. Among foragers and horticulturalists, women needed to be mobile for the group to survive; their labor outdoors was essential. Among agriculturalists, the labor of animals, slaves, and hired workers could substitute for that of women in families that could afford them. Thus in some Neolithic societies, there is evidence that women spent more and more of their time within the household, either indoors or behind walls and barriers that separated the domestic realm from the wider world. Social norms and ideals gradually reinforced this pattern, so that by the time written laws and other records emerged in the second millennium B.C.E., elite women were expected to work at tasks that would not take them beyond the household or away from male supervision. Non-elite women also tended to do work that could be done within or close by the household, such as cooking, cloth production, and the care of children, the elderly, and small animals. A special program set up under the third-century B.C.E. Indian emperor Ashoka, for example, supported poor women by paying them to spin and weave in their own homes.

Social and gender hierarchies were enhanced over generations as wealth was passed down unequally, and they were also enhanced by rules and norms that shaped sexual relationships, particularly heterosexual ones. However their power originated, elites began to think of themselves as a group apart from the rest with something that made them distinctive — such as connections with a deity, military prowess, and natural superiority. They increasingly understood this distinctive quality to be hereditary and developed traditions — later codified as written laws — that stipulated which heterosexual relationships would pass this quality on, along with passing on wealth. Relationships between men and women from elite families were formalized as marriage and generally passed down both status and wealth. Relationships between elite men and non-elite women generally did not do so, or did so to a lesser degree; the women were defined as concubines or mistresses, or simply as sexual outlets for powerful men. The 1780 B.C.E. Code of Hammurabi, for example, one of the world's earliest law codes, sets out differences in inheritance for the sons a man had with his wife and those he had with a servant or slave, while not mentioning daughters at all:

> If his wife bear sons to a man, [and] his maid-servant [has] also borne sons, [but] the father while still living . . . did not say to the sons of the maid-servant:

> **"If . . . the father while still living . . . did not say to the sons of the maid-servant: "My sons," and then the father dies, then the sons of the maid-servant shall not share with the sons of the wife."**
>
> **HAMMURABI'S CODE**

"My sons," and then the father dies, then the sons of the maid-servant shall not share with the sons of the wife, but the freedom of the maid and her sons shall be granted.[2]

Relations between an elite woman and a non-elite man generally brought shame and dishonor to the woman's family and sometimes death to the man. (Early rules and laws about sex generally did not pay much attention to same-sex relations because these did not produce children that could threaten systems of inheritance.)

Thus along with the distinctions among human groups that resulted from migration and were enhanced by endogamy, distinctions developed within groups that were reinforced by social endogamy, what we might think of as the selective breeding of people. Elite men tended to marry elite women, which in some cases resulted in actual physical differences over generations, as elites had more access to food and were able to become taller and stronger. By 1800 C.E., for example, men in the highest level of the English aristocracy were five inches taller than the average height of all English people.

No elite can be completely closed to newcomers, however, because the accidents of life and death, along with the genetic problems caused by repeated close intermarriage, make it difficult for any small group to survive over generations. Thus mechanisms were developed in many cultures to adopt boys into elite families, to legitimate the children of concubines and slave women, or to allow elite girls to marry men lower on the social hierarchy. All systems of inheritance also need some flexibility. The inheritance patterns in some cultures favored male heirs exclusively, but in others close relatives were favored over those more distant, even if this meant allowing daughters to inherit. The drive to keep wealth and property within a family or kin group often resulted in women inheriting, owning, and in some cases managing significant amounts of wealth, a pattern that continues today. Hierarchies of wealth and power thus intersected with hierarchies of gender in complex ways, and in many cultures age and marital status also played roles. In many European and African cultures, for example, widows were largely able to control their own property, while unmarried sons were often under their father's control even if they were adults.

Trade and Cross-Cultural Connections

The increase in food production brought by the development of plow agriculture allowed Neolithic villages to grow ever larger. By 7000 B.C.E. or so, some villages in the Fertile Crescent may have had as many as ten thousand residents. One of the best known of these, Çatal Hüyük in what is now modern Turkey, shows evidence of trade as well as of the specialization of labor. Çatal Hüyük's residents lived in mud-brick houses whose walls were covered in white plaster and whose interiors were kept very clean, for all trash was taken outside the town. The houses were built next to one another with no lanes or paths separating them, and people seem to have entered through holes in the roofs; the rooftops may have also served as a place for people to congregate, for there is no sign of large public buildings. The men and women of the town grew wheat, barley, peas, and almonds and raised sheep and perhaps cattle, though they also seem to have hunted. They made textiles, pots, figurines, baskets, carpets, copper and lead beads, and other goods, and decorated their houses with murals showing animal and human figures. They gathered, sharpened, and polished obsidian, a volcanic rock that could be used for knives, blades, and mirrors, and then traded it with neighboring towns, obtaining seashells and flint. From here the obsidian was exchanged still farther away, for Neolithic societies slowly developed local and then regional networks of exchange and communication.

Among the goods traded in some parts of the world was copper. Pure copper occurs naturally close to the surface in some areas, and people, including those at Çatal Hüyük, hammered it into shapes for jewelry and tools. Like most metals, copper occurs more often mixed with other materials in a type of rock called ore, and by about 5500 B.C.E. people in the Balkans had learned that copper could be extracted from ore by heating it in a smelting process. Smelted copper was poured into molds and made into spear points, axes, chisels, beads, and other objects. Smelting techniques were discovered independently in many places around the world, including China, Southeast Asia, West Africa, and the Andes region. Pure copper is soft, but through experimentation artisans learned that it would become harder if they mixed it with other metals such as arsenic, zinc, or tin during heating, creating an alloy called bronze.

Because it was stronger than copper, bronze had a far wider range of uses, so much so that later historians decided that its adoption marked the beginning of a new period in human history, the Bronze Age. Like all new technologies, bronze arrived at different times in different places, but by about 2500 B.C.E. it was making a difference in many places around the world. Techniques of copper and bronze metallurgy were later applied to precious metals such as gold and silver, and then to iron, which had an even greater impact than

Stone Circle at Nabta Playa, Egypt, ca. 4800 B.C.E. This circle of stones, erected when the Egyptian desert received much more rainfall than it does today, may have been a type of calendar marking the summer solstice. Circular arrangements of stones or ditches were constructed in many places during the Neolithic era, and most no doubt had calendrical, astronomical, and/or religious purposes. (Courtesy of Raymond Betz)

bronze. (See "Global Trade: Iron," page 54). It is important to remember that all metals were expensive and hard to obtain, however, so that stone, wood, and bone remained the primary materials for tools and weapons long into the Bronze Age.

Objects were not the only things traded increasingly long distances during the Neolithic period, for people also carried ideas as they traveled on foot, boats, or camels, and in wagons or carts. Knowledge about the seasons and the weather was vitally important for those who depended on crop-raising, and agricultural peoples in many parts of the world began to calculate recurring patterns in the world around them, slowly developing calendars. Scholars have demonstrated that people built circular structures of mounded earth or huge upright stones to help them predict the movements of the sun and stars, including Nabta Playa, erected about 4500 B.C.E. in the desert west of the Nile Valley in Egypt, and Stonehenge, erected about 2500 B.C.E. in southern England.

The rhythms of the agricultural cycle and patterns of exchange also shaped religious beliefs and practices. Among foragers, human fertility is a mixed blessing, as too many children can overtax food supplies, but among crop-raisers and pastoralists, fertility of the land, animals, and people is essential. Shamans and priests developed ever more elaborate rituals designed to assure fertility, in which the gods were often given something from a community's goods in exchange for their favor, such as food offerings, animal sacrifices, or sacred objects. In many places gods came to be associated with patterns of birth, growth, death, and regeneration. They could bring death and destruction, but they also created life. Figurines, carvings, and paintings from the Neolithic include pregnant women and women giving birth, men with erect penises, and creatures that are a combination of a man and a male animal such as a bull or goat. Like humans, the gods came to have a division of labor and a social hierarchy. Thus there were rain gods and sun gods, sky goddesses and moon goddesses, gods that assured the health of cattle or the growth of corn, goddesses of the hearth and home. Powerful father and mother gods sometimes presided, but they were challenged and overthrown by virile young male gods, often in epic battles. Thus as human society was becoming more complex, so was the unseen world.

CONNECTIONS

The human story is often told as a narrative of unstoppable progress toward greater complexity. The simple stone hand axes of the Paleolithic were replaced by the specialized tools of the Neolithic and then by bronze, iron, steel, plastic, and silicon. The small kin groups of the Paleolithic gave way to Neolithic villages that grew ever larger until they became cities and eventually today's megalopolises. Egalitarian foragers became stratified by divisions of wealth and power that were formalized as aristocracies, castes, and social classes, leading to today's vast divisions between wealth and poverty. Oral rituals of worship, healing, and celebration in which everyone participated grew into a dizzying array of religions, philosophies, and branches of knowledge presided over by specialists including priests, scholars, scientists, doctors, generals, and entertainers. The rest of this book traces this story and explores the changes over time that are the central thread of history.

As you examine what — particularly in world history — can seem to be a staggering number of developments, it is also important to remember that many things were slow to change and that some aspects of human life in the Neolithic, or even the Paleolithic, continued. Foraging, horticulture, pastoralism, and agriculture have been the primary economic activities of most people throughout the entire history of the world. Though today there are only a few foraging groups in very isolated areas, there are significant numbers of horticulturalists and pastoralists, and their numbers were much greater just a century ago. At that point the vast majority of the world's people still made their living directly through agriculture. The social patterns set in early agricultural societies — with most of the population farming the land, and a small number of elite who lived off their labor — lasted for millennia. You have no doubt recognized other similarities between the early peoples discussed in this chapter and the people you see around you, and it is important to keep these continuities in mind as you embark on your examination of human history.

□ CHAPTER REVIEW

□ How did humans evolve, and where did they migrate? (p. 4)

Scholars studying the natural world and the place of humans in it have devised various ways of classifying living creatures and organizing time. Through studying the physical remains of the past, sometimes with very new high-tech procedures such as DNA analysis, they have examined human evolution from earlier hominids in eastern Africa. Evolution involved a combination of factors, including bipedalism, larger brain size, spoken symbolic language, and longer periods of infancy. All these together led humans to invent ever more complex tools that allowed them to shape the world around them. They migrated out of Africa in several waves, adapting to many different environments and developing diverse cultures.

□ What were the key features of Paleolithic society? (p. 11)

In the Paleolithic period, people lived in small groups of related individuals, moving through the landscape in the search for food. They obtained food by foraging: gathering plants, seeds, nuts, and insects; trapping fish and small animals; and sometimes hunting large game. Most had few material possessions, and social and gender hierarchies were probably much less pronounced than they would become later. Beginning around 50,000 B.C.E. people in many parts of the world began to decorate their surroundings and the objects they made, often with vivid representations of animals and people, and sometimes with symbols. These, and careful burials of the dead, suggest that people had developed ideas about supernatural or spiritual forces beyond the visible material world.

□ How did plant and animal domestication develop, and what effects did it have on human society? (p. 17)

Beginning about 9000 B.C.E. people living in the Near East, and then elsewhere, began to plant seeds as well as gather wild crops, raise certain animals instead of hunt them, and selectively breed both plants and animals to make them more useful to humans. This domestication of plants and animals, called the Agricultural Revolution, was the most important change in human history. Crop-raising began as horticulture, in which people — often women — used hand tools to plant and harvest. Animal domestication began with sheep and goats, which were often herded from place to place so that they could eat the available vegetation, an economic system called pastoralism. The domestication of large animals such as cattle and water buffalo led to plow agriculture, through which humans could raise much more food. Agriculture required more labor than did foraging, but it allowed the human population to grow far more quickly.

□ How did growing social and gender hierarchies and expanding networks of trade increase the complexity of human society in the Neolithic period? (p. 24)

The division of labor that plow agriculture required led to growing social hierarchies between those who could afford the new tools and products and those who could not. These were reinforced over generations as children inherited goods and status from their parents, and as social norms and laws were developed that led members of the elite to marry one another. Plow agriculture also strengthened differentiation based on gender, and men became more associated with the world beyond the household and women with the domestic realm. Neolithic agricultural communities developed technologies to meet their needs, including pottery, cloth-weaving, and wheeled vehicles, and they often traded with one another for products that they could not obtain locally. In some parts of the world, production and trade included copper and bronze, although most tools continued to be made of stone, bone, and wood. Religious ideas came to reflect the new agricultural society, with fertility as the most important goal and the gods, like humans, arranged in a hierarchy.

SUGGESTED READINGS

Burenhelt, Goren. *People of the Stone Age: Hunter-Gatherers and Early Farmers*. 1994. Short articles and extensive illustrations of the transition to agriculture, presented as part of the American Museum of Natural History's excellent *Illustrated History of Humankind*.

Christian, David. *Maps of Time: An Introduction to Big History*. 2002. An elegant examination of the story of the cosmos, from the Big Bang to today.

Diamond, Jared. *Guns, Germs, and Steel: The Fates of Human Societies*, 2d ed. 2005. Extremely influential and wide-ranging examination of the long-term impact of agriculture, animal domestication, and the environment on differing rates of development around the world.

Ehrlich, Paul R., and Anne H. Ehrlich. *Dominant Animal: Human Evolution and the Environment*. 2009. By two of today's leading biologists, traces the impact of humans on the planet from the Paleolithic to today.

Fagan, Brian M. *People of the Earth: An Introduction to World Prehistory*, 13th ed. 2009. A thorough survey that presents up-to-date scholarship, designed for students.

Gamble, Clive. *Timewalkers: The Prehistory of Global Colonization*. 2006. A lively examination of how and why humans came to be everywhere in the world.

Hawkes, Kristen, and Richard R. Paine. *The Evolution of Human Life History*. 2006. A series of articles that examine the ways in which what makes humans distinct from other animals came to be.

Hrdy, Sarah Bluffer. *Mothers and Others: The Evolutionary Origins of Human Understanding*. 2009. Provides the new, more egalitarian perspective on evolution.

Lewin, Roger. *Human Evolution. An Illustrated Introduction*, 5th ed. 2004. A relatively compact and very readable introduction that includes the newest archaeological and chemical evidence.

Lewis-Williams, David, and David Pearce. *Inside the Neolithic Mind: Consciousness, Cosmos, and the Realm of the Gods*. 2005. An analysis of Neolithic belief systems and the cultural products that resulted from them.

McCarter, Susan Foster. *Neolithic*. 2007. An introductory survey of the development and impact of agriculture, with many illustrations.

Pinker, Steven. *How the Mind Works*, 2d ed. 2009. An insightful examination of how the mind evolved, along with a survey of modern brain science.

Pollan, Michael. *The Omnivore's Dilemma: A Natural History of Four Meals*. 2007. A witty and thoughtful look at the way food is produced today, and how this contrasts with our foraging past.

Smith, Bruce. *The Emergence of Agriculture*. 1999. Presents both the story of the early development of agriculture around the world and the ways in which scholars study this.

NOTES

1. Chinook Blessing Litany, in Wilma Mankiller, ed., *Every Day Is a Good Day: Reflections by Contemporary Indigenous Women* (Golden, Colo.: Fulcrum Publishing, 2004), pp. 170, 171. Copyright © 2004 by Wilma P. Mankiller. Used by permission of Fulcrum Publishing.
2. Code of Hammurabi, article 171, translated by L. W. King (1910), Internet Ancient History Sourcebook, http://www.fordham.edu/halsall/ancient/hamcode.html#text.

For practice quizzes and other study tools, visit the **Online Study Guide** at bedfordstmartins.com/mckayworld.

For primary sources from this period, see *Sources of World Societies*, **Second Edition**.

For Web sites, images, and documents related to topics in this chapter, visit **Make History** at bedfordstmartins.com/mckayworld.

• **Egyptian Lyre Player** Ancient Egyptians hoped that life after death would be a pleasant continuation of life on this earth, and their tombs reflected this. This wall painting from the tomb of an official who died about 1400 B.C.E. shows a female musician — for a good afterlife would surely include music. (Werner Forman/Art Resource, NY)

Five thousand years ago, humans were living in most parts of the planet. They had designed technologies to meet the challenges presented by deep forests and jungles, steep mountains, and blistering deserts. As the climate changed, they adapted, building boats to cross channels created by melting glaciers and finding new sources of food when old sources were no longer plentiful. In some places the new sources included domesticated plants and animals, which allowed people to live in much closer proximity to one another than they had as foragers.

The Rise of the State in Southwest Asia and the Nile Valley

3200–500 B.C.E.

That proximity created opportunities, as larger groups of people pooled their knowledge to deal with life's challenges, but it also created problems. Human history from that point on can be seen as a response to these opportunities, challenges, and conflicts. As small villages grew into cities, people continued to develop technologies and systems to handle new issues.

They created structures of governance not based on the kin group to control their more complex societies, along with military forces and taxation systems to support the structures of governance. In some places they invented writing to record taxes, inventories, and payments, and they later put writing to other uses, including the preservation of stories, traditions, and history. The first places where these new technologies and systems were introduced were the Tigris and Euphrates River Valleys of southwest Asia and the Nile Valley of northeast Africa, areas whose history became linked through trade connections, military conquests, and migrations. •

Writing, Cities, and States

☐ How does writing shape what we can know about the past, and how did writing develop to meet the needs of cities and states?

Mesopotamia from Sumeria to Babylon

☐ How did the people of Mesopotamia form the world's first states, and how did their institutions spread?

The Egyptians and Their Pharaohs

☐ How did geography, leadership, and religion enable the Egyptians to build and maintain a cohesive, prosperous society, and how did migrations and invasions shape Egypt's fate?

The Hebrews

☐ How did the Hebrews create an enduring written religious tradition, and what was its significance?

The Assyrians and Persians

☐ What were the strengths of and the major differences between the Assyrian and Persian Empires?

Writing, Cities, and States

☐ How does writing shape what we can know about the past, and how did writing develop to meet the needs of cities and states?

The remains of buildings, burial sites, weapons, tools, artwork, and other handmade objects provide our only evidence of how people lived, thought, felt, and died during most of the human past. Beginning about five thousand years ago, however, people in some parts of the world developed a new technology, writing, the surviving examples of which have provided a much wider range of information. Writing was developed to meet the needs of the more complex urban societies that are often referred to as civilizations, and particularly to meet the needs of the state, a new political form that developed during the time covered in this chapter.

Written Sources and the Human Past

Writing is closely tied to the idea of history itself. The term *history* comes from the Greek word *historia*, coined by Herodotus (hi-ROD-duh-tuhs; ca. 484–ca. 425 B.C.E.) in the fifth century B.C.E. to describe his in-

Clay Letter Written in Cuneiform and Its Envelope, ca. 1850 B.C.E. In this letter (left) from a city in what is now southern Turkey, a merchant complains to his brother that life is hard and comments on the trade in silver, gold, tin, and textiles. Letters were often enclosed in envelopes (right) and sealed with a piece of soft clay that was stamped, just as you might use a stamped wax seal today. Here the sender's seal shows people approaching a king. (Courtesy of the Trustees of the British Museum)

quiry into the past. In fact, as Herodotus used them, the words *inquiry* and *history* are the same. Herodotus based his *Histories*, at their core a study of the origins of the wars between the Persians and the Greeks that had happened about the time he was born, on the oral testimony of people he had met as he traveled widely. Many of these people had been participants in the wars, and Herodotus was proud that he could rely so much on the eyewitness accounts of the people actually involved. Today we would call this methodology "oral history," and it remains a vital technique for studying the recent past. Following the standard practice of the time, Herodotus most likely read his *Histories* out loud at some sort of public gathering — one story of his life even has him doing this at the Olympic games. Herodotus also wrote down his histories, however, and consulted written documents. From his day until quite recently, this aspect of his methods has defined history and separated it from prehistory: history came to be regarded as that part of the human past for which there are written records. In this view, history began with the invention of writing — about 3200 B.C.E. in a few parts of the world and much later in others.

As we saw in Chapter 1, this line between history and prehistory has largely broken down. Historians who study human societies that developed systems of writing continue to use many of the same types of physical evidence as do those who study societies without writing. For other cultures the writing or record-keeping systems have not yet been deciphered, so our knowledge of these people also depends largely on physical evidence. Scholars can read the writing of a great many societies, however, adding greatly to what we can learn about them.

Much ancient writing survives only because it was copied and recopied, sometimes years after the writing was first produced. The oldest known copy of Herodotus's *Histories*, for example, dates from about 900 C.E., nearly a millennium and a half after he finished this book. The survival of a work means that someone from a later period — and often a long chain of someones — judged it worthy of the time, effort, and resources needed to produce copies. The copies may not be completely accurate, either, because the scribe made an error or because he (or, much less often, she)

decided to change something. Historians studying ancient works thus often try to find as many early copies as they can and compare them to arrive at the version they think is closest to the original.

Not surprisingly, the works considered worthy of copying tend to be those that, like the *Histories*, refer to political and military events involving major powers, that record religious traditions, or that come from authors who were later regarded as important. By contrast, written sources dealing with the daily life of ordinary men and women were few to begin with and were rarely saved or copied because they were not seen as significant.

Some early written texts survive in their original form because people inscribed them in stone, shells, bone, or other hard materials, intending them to be permanent. Stones with inscriptions were often erected in the open in public places for all to see, so they include things that leaders felt had enduring importance, such as laws, religious proclamations, decrees, and treaties. (This practice continues today, of course; the names etched in granite on the Vietnam Veterans Memorial in Washington, D.C., are perhaps the best-known recent example, but inscriptions can be found on nearly every major public building.) Sometimes this permanence was accidental: in ancient Mesopotamia (in the area of modern Iraq), all writing was initially made up of indentations on soft clay tablets, which then hardened. Thousands of these tablets have survived, the oldest dating to about 3200 B.C.E., and from them historians have learned about many aspects of everyday life, including taxes and wages. By contrast, writing in Egypt at the same time was often done in ink on papyrus sheets, made from a plant that grows abundantly in Egypt. Some of these papyrus sheets have survived — the oldest is an account sheet from about 2600 B.C.E. — but papyrus is a much more fragile material than hardened clay, so most have disintegrated. In China, the oldest surviving writing is on bones and turtle shells from about 1200 B.C.E., but it is clear that writing was done much earlier on less permanent materials such as silk and bamboo. (For more on the origins of Chinese writing, see page 97.)

However they have survived and however limited they are, written records often become scholars' most important original sources for investigating the past. Thus the discovery of a new piece of written evidence from the ancient past — such as the Dead Sea Scrolls, which contain sections of the Hebrew Bible, were written between 150 B.C.E. and 70 C.E., and were first seen by scholars in 1948 — is always a major event. But reconstructing and deciphering what are often crumbling documents can take decades, and disputes about how these records affect our understanding of the past can go on forever.

Cities and the Idea of Civilization

Along with writing, the growth of cities has often been a way that scholars have marked the increasing complexity of human societies. In the ancient world, residents of cities generally viewed themselves as more advanced and sophisticated than rural folk — a judgment still made today. They saw themselves as more "civilized," a word that comes from the Latin adjective *civilis*, which refers to a citizen, either a citizen of a town or of a larger political unit such as an empire. In their view, those who lived outside cities were more backward and primitive.

This depiction of people as either civilized or uncivilized was gradually extended to whole societies. Beginning in the eighteenth century European scholars described those societies in which political, economic, and social organizations operated on a large scale, not primarily through families and kin groups, as "civilizations." Civilizations had cities; laws that governed human relationships; codes of manners and

social conduct that regulated how people were to behave; and scientific, philosophical, and theological ideas that explained the larger world. Generally, only societies that used writing were judged to be civilizations, for writing allowed laws, norms, ideas, and traditions to become more complex. By comparison, societies in which people were nomadic or lived in small villages without formal laws, and in which traditions and ideas were passed down orally, were generally not regarded as civilizations. They were often seen as inferior by those who lived in large-scale societies.

The idea of a civilization came to mean not simply a system of political and social organization, but also particular ways of thinking and believing, particular styles of art, and other facets of culture. Thus the boundaries between one civilization and another were not as easy to determine as those between one political unit and another, and places were often described as being part of many different civilizations at the same time. For example, when discussing the ancient city of Athens, some historians spoke of Athenian civilization and others of Greek civilization. Others came to view Athens as part of Western civilization, a very large division of human society, often set in opposition to Eastern civilization. In the era after World War I, "Western civilization" became a standard course at colleges and universities in the United States, designed by scholars who were upset that during the war many young Americans did not seem to appreciate the importance of the links between America and Europe.

Until the middle of the twentieth century, historians often referred to the earliest places where writing and cities developed as the "cradles of civilization," proposing a model of development for all humanity patterned on that of an individual person. However, the idea that all human societies developed (or should develop) in a uniform process from a "cradle" to a "mature" civilization has now been largely discredited, and some world historians choose not to use the word *civilization* at all because its meaning is so value-laden. But they have not rejected the idea that about 5,000 years ago a new form of human society appeared, first in the valley formed by the Tigris and Euphrates Rivers — an area the Greeks later called Mesopotamia — and then in other places around the world, often in river valleys. These societies all had cities with tens of thousands of people.

The Rise of States, Laws, and Social Hierarchies

Cities concentrated people and power, and they required more elaborate mechanisms to make them work than had small agricultural villages and foraging groups. These mechanisms were part of what political scientists call "the state," an organization distinct from a tribe or kinship group in which a small share of the population is able to coerce resources out of everyone else in order to gain and then maintain power. In a state, the interest that gains power might be one particular family, a set of religious leaders, or even a charismatic or talented individual able to handle the problems of dense urban communities.

However they are established, states coerce people through violence, or the threat of violence, and develop permanent armies for this purpose. Using armed force every time they need food or other resources is not very efficient, however, so states also establish bureaucracies and systems of taxation. States also need to keep track of people and goods, so they develop systems of recording information and accounting, usually through writing, though not always. In the Inca Empire, for example, a large state established in the Andes, information about money, goods, and people was recorded on collections of colored knotted strings called *khipus* (see page 305). Systems of recording information allow the creation of more elaborate rules of behavior, often written down in the form of law codes, which facilitate further growth in state power, or in the form of religious traditions, which specify what sort of behavior is pleasing to the gods or other supernatural forces.

Written laws and traditions generally create more elaborate social hierarchies, in which divisions between elite groups and common people are established more firmly. They also generally heighten gender hierarchies. Those who gain power in states are most often men, so they tend to establish laws and norms that favor males in marriage, property rights, and other areas.

Whether we choose to call the process "the birth of civilization" or "the growth of the state," beginning about 3200 B.C.E. some human societies began to develop into a new form. Neolithic agricultural villages

expanded into cities, where most people did not raise their own food but depended on that produced by the surrounding countryside and instead carried out other tasks. The organization of this more complex division of labor was undertaken by an elite group, which enforced its will by armed force, along with laws, taxes, and bureaucracies backed up by the threat of force. Social and gender hierarchies became more complex and rigid. All this happened first in Mesopotamia, then in Egypt, and then in India and China.

Mesopotamia from Sumeria to Babylon

☐ How did the people of Mesopotamia form the world's first states, and how did their institutions spread?

States first developed in Mesopotamia, where sustained agriculture reliant on irrigation from the Euphrates and Tigris Rivers resulted in larger populations, a division of labor, and the growth of cities. Priests and rulers developed ways to control and organize these complex societies, including armies, taxation systems, and written records. Conquerors from the north unified Mesopotamian city-states into larger empires and spread Mesopotamian culture over a large area.

Environmental Challenges, Irrigation, and Religion

Mesopotamia was part of the Fertile Crescent, where settled agriculture first developed (see pages 18–19). Beginning around 7000 B.C.E., more and more villages were built in the part of southern Mesopotamia known as Sumeria (soo-MAIRE-ee-uh), where the Tigris and Euphrates Rivers brought fresh soil when they flooded each spring. The area had more rainfall than it does now, but not enough for farming the ever-expanding fields. Thus villagers began to build and maintain irrigation ditches that took water from the rivers, allowing more food to be grown and the population to expand. By about 3000 B.C.E., some villages, including Ur and Uruk, had grown into true cities with populations of 40,000 to 50,000. These cities built

Sumerian Harpist This small clay tablet, carved between 2000 B.C.E. and 1500 B.C.E., shows a seated woman playing a harp. Her fashionable dress and hat suggest that she is playing for wealthy people, perhaps at the royal court. Images of musicians are common in Sumerian art, which indicates that music was important in Sumerian culture and social life. (Erich Lessing/Art Resource, NY)

Ziggurat The ziggurat is a stepped pyramid-shaped temple that dominated the landscape of the Sumerian city. Surrounded by a walled enclosure, it stood as a monument to the gods. Religious ceremonies for the welfare of the community were often performed on the top, and grain, animals, and equipment stores were within the outer enclosure. (Charles & Josette Lemars/Corbis)

defensive walls, marketplaces, and large public buildings. Because they ruled the surrounding countryside, they were really city-states, and the irrigation system they depended on required cooperation and at least some level of social and political cohesion.

The authority to run this system was initially assumed by Sumerian priests, who created many of the institutions that are essential parts of any state. How did these priests assume power? We cannot know for certain, as this happened before the invention of writing, but it appears that the uncertainties of life in Sumerian cities, in which the rivers often flooded uncontrollably and serious droughts threatened crops, convinced people that the gods were powerful, unpredictable, and vindictive. Humans thus needed to please and obey the gods in order to bring rain, prevent floods, and ensure good harvests. They saw the cosmos as a struggle between order and disorder; to ensure order, people believed they needed to serve the gods by obeying the rules set by religious leaders. Citizens of each city worshipped a number of gods but often focused primarily on one who controlled the economic basis of the city, such as a god of the underworld who controlled the growing of grain or a god who had charge of sheep herds. Encouraged and directed by the priesthood, people erected a large temple in the center of each city, often in the form of a step-pyramid or **ziggurat** (ZIH-guh-rat), around which they built their houses. The best way to honor the gods was to make the temple as grand and as impressive as possible, for the size of the temple demonstrated the strength of the community, and gods who had a splendid ziggurat might think twice about sending floods to destroy the city.

Temples grew into elaborate complexes of buildings with storage space for grain and other products and housing for animals. To support these construction efforts, and to support themselves, temple officials developed taxation systems in which people paid a portion of their harvest to the temple or worked a certain number of days per year on land owned directly by the temple.

Sumerian Politics and Society

During times of emergencies, such as floods or invasions by other cities, a chief priest or sometimes a military leader assumed what was supposed to be temporary authority over a city. He established a regular army,

- **ziggurat** Temple in the form of a step-pyramid built in the center of a Mesopotamian city to honor the gods.
- **cuneiform** The wedge-shaped writing system that developed in Sumeria, the first writing system in the world.

trained it, and led it into battle, and he was given charge over the city's fortifications. Temporary power gradually became permanent kingship, and sometime before 2600 B.C.E. kings in some Sumerian city-states began to hand down the kingship to their sons, establishing hereditary dynasties in which power was handed down through the male line. The symbol of royal status was the palace, which came to rival the temple in its grandeur. Kings made alliances with other powerful individuals, often through marriage, and a hereditary aristocracy of nobles developed. These aristocracies were often different from those of the priests, but kings worked closely with religious authorities and relied on ideas about their connections with the gods, as well as their military might, for their power. Acting together, priests, nobles, and kings in Sumerian cities used force, persuasion, and threats of higher taxes to maintain order, keep the irrigation systems working, and keep food and other goods flowing.

The king and the nobles held extensive tracts of land that were, like the estates of the temple, worked by others — specifically, clients and slaves. Slaves were prisoners of war, convicts, and debtors. While they were subject to any treatment their owners might mete out, they could engage in trade, make profits, and even buy their freedom. Clients were free people who were dependent on the nobility. In return for their labor, they received small plots of land to work for themselves. Although this arrangement assured the clients of a livelihood, the land they worked remained the possession of the nobility or the temple. Some individuals and families owned land outright and paid their taxes in the form of agricultural products or things they had made. The city-states that developed later throughout Mesopotamia had similar social categories.

Each of these social categories included both men and women, but Sumerian society made clear distinctions based on gender. All Mesopotamian city-states were patriarchal — that is, most power was held by older adult men. Because other hierarchies such as those of hereditary aristocracy gave privilege to women connected to powerful or wealthy men, however, women saw themselves as either privileged or not, rather than as members of a single lower-ranking group. Therefore, they tended not to object to institutions and intellectual structures that subordinated them, or perhaps their objections were not recorded.

The Invention of Writing and Other Intellectual Advances

In the villages of Sumeria, people used small clay objects made into different forms to represent various types of goods that they owned, a simple system of record-keeping. By 3200 B.C.E. in the growing Sumerian cities, these objects had been replaced by tablets

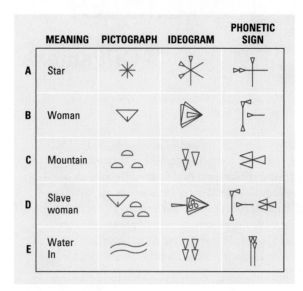

FIGURE 2.1 Sumerian Writing
(Source: Excerpted from S. N. Kramer, *The Sumerians: Their History, Culture, and Character.* Copyright © 1963 by the University of Chicago Press. Used by permission of The University of Chicago Press.)

marked with symbols standing for the goods, made either by rolling an engraved seal over soft clay or by making marks in the clay with a sharpened stylus. The stylus formed wedge-shaped marks, from which this style of writing took its name, **cuneiform** (kyoo-NEE-uh-form), the Latin term for "wedge-shaped." Initially cuneiform writing was pictographic, showing pictures of the objects, but gradually scribes simplified the system, creating stylized symbols called ideograms. These were used to represent actual objects but also came to represent ideas that were difficult to depict. Thus the sign for star (see line A in Figure 2.1) could also be used to indicate heaven, sky, or even god. Signs were also combined. For example, because many slaves in Sumeria came from mountainous regions far from cities, an inventive scribe decided to combine the sign for mountain with the sign for woman to indicate "slave woman" (see lines B, C, and D).

Certain things were still difficult to depict, and around 2700 B.C.E. scribes in some cities began to use signs to represent sounds rather than concepts. For instance, scribes drew two parallel wavy lines to indicate the word *a* or "water" (see line E in Figure 2.1). Besides water, the word *a* in Sumerian also meant "in." The word *in* expresses a relationship that is very difficult to represent pictorially. Instead of trying to invent a sign to mean "in," some clever scribe used the sign for water because the two words sounded alike. This phonetic use of signs made possible the combining of signs to convey abstract ideas.

The development of the Sumerian system of writing was piecemeal, with scribes making changes and additions as they were needed. The system became so

Listening to the Past

Gilgamesh's Quest for Immortality

The human desire to escape the grip of death appears in many cultures. The Sumerian Epic of Gilgamesh is the earliest recorded treatment of this topic. In this story, Gilgamesh, a part-real, part-mythological king of Uruk who is not fulfilling his duties as the king very well, sets out with his friend Enkidu to perform wondrous feats against fearsome agents of the gods. Together they kill several supernatural beings, and the gods decide that Enkidu must die. Here, Enkidu foresees his own death in a dream.

"Listen, my friend [Gilgamesh], this is the dream I dreamed last night. The heavens roared, and earth rumbled back an answer; between them I stood before an awful being, the somber-faced man-bird; he had directed on me his purpose. His was a vampire face, his foot was a lion's foot, his hand was an eagle's talon. He fell on me and his claws were in my hair, he held me fast and I smothered; then he transformed me so that my arms became wings covered with feathers. He turned his stare towards me, and he led me away to the palace of Irkalla, the Queen of Darkness [the goddess of the underworld; in other words, an agent of death], to the house from which none who enters ever returns, down the road from which there is no coming back."

After Enkidu sickens and dies, a distraught Gilgamesh determines to become immortal. He decides to journey to Utnapishtim and his wife, the only mortals whom the gods had granted eternal life in a beautiful paradise. Gilgamesh's journey involves the effort not only to escape from death but also to reach an understanding of the meaning of life. During his travels he meets with Siduri, the wise and good-natured goddess of wine, who gives him the following advice.

"Gilgamesh, where are you hurrying to? You will never find that life for which you are looking. When the gods created man they allotted to him death, but life they retained in their own keeping. As for you, Gilgamesh, fill your belly with good things; day and night, night and day, dance and be merry, feast and rejoice. Let your clothes be fresh, bathe yourself in water, cherish the little child that holds your hand, and make your wife happy in your embrace; for this too is the lot of man."

Ignoring Siduri's advice, Gilgamesh continues his journey until he finds Utnapishtim and puts to him the question that is the reason for his quest.

"Oh, father Utnapishtim, you who have entered the assembly of the gods, I wish to question you concerning the living and the dead, how shall I find the life for which I am searching?

Utnapishtim said, "There is no permanence. Do we build a house to stand forever, do we seal a contract to hold for all time? Do brothers divide an inheritance to keep forever, does the flood-time of rivers endure? . . . From the days of old there is no permanence. . . . What is there between the master and the servant when both have fulfilled their doom? When the Anunnaki [the gods of the underworld], the judges, and Mammetun [the goddess of fate] the mother of destinies, come together, they decree the fates of men. Life and death they allot but the day of death they do not disclose."

Then Gilgamesh said to Utnapishtim the Faraway, "I look at you now, Utnapishtim, and your appearance is no different from mine; there is nothing strange in your features. I thought I should find you like a hero prepared for battle, but you lie here taking your ease on your back. Tell me truly, how was it that you came to enter the company of the gods and to possess everlasting life?" Utnapishtim said to Gilgamesh, "I shall reveal

complicated that only professional scribes mastered it after many years of study. By 2500 B.C.E. scribal schools flourished throughout Sumeria. Most students came from wealthy families, and all were male. Each school had a master, a teacher, and monitors. Discipline was strict, and students were caned for sloppy work and misbehavior. One graduate of a scribal school had few fond memories of the joy of learning:

My headmaster read my tablet, said:
"There is something missing," caned me.
. . .
The fellow in charge of silence said:

"Why did you talk without permission," caned me.
The fellow in charge of the assembly said:
"Why did you stand at ease without permission,"
    caned me.[1]

Scribal schools were primarily intended to produce individuals who could keep records of the property and wealth of temple officials, kings, and nobles. Thus writing first developed as a way to enhance the growing power of elites, not to record speech, although it came to be used for that purpose.

Writing also came to be used to record religious traditions and stories of great heroes. These stories of-to you a mystery, I shall tell you a secret of the gods. . . . In those days the world teemed, the people multiplied, the world bellowed like wild bull, and the great god [Enlil, the warrior god] was aroused by the clamor . . . so the gods agreed to exterminate mankind."

Utnapishtim continues, telling Gilgamesh that one of the gods, Ea, had taken an oath to protect humanity, so he warned Utnapishtim to build a boat big enough to hold his family, various artisans, and all animals in order to survive the flood that was to come. The great flood killed all who were not on the boat. Although Enlil was initially infuriated by the Sumerians' survival, he ended up blessing Utnapishtim and his wife with eternal life. Gilgamesh wants this as well, but he fails two opportunities Utnapishtim provides for him to achieve it and returns to Uruk. The last part of the epic notes a different kind of immortality.

"The destiny was fulfilled which the father of the gods, Enlil of the mountain, had decreed for Gilgamesh: "In nether-earth the darkness will show him a light: of mankind, all that are known, none will leave a monument for generations to compare with his. The heroes, the wise men, like the new moon have their waxing and waning. Men will say, 'Who has ever ruled with might and power like him?' As in the dark month, the month of shadows, so without him there is no light. O Gilgamesh, this was the meaning of your dream [of immortality]. You were given the kingship, such was your destiny, everlasting life was not your destiny. Because of this do not be sad at heart, do not be grieved or oppressed; he [Enlil] has given you power to bind and to loose, to be the darkness and the light of mankind. He has given you unexampled supremacy over the people, victory in battle from which no fugitive returns, in forays and assaults from which there is no going back. But do not abuse this power, deal justly with your servants in the palace, deal justly before the face of the Sun."

Source: *The Epic of Gilgamesh*, translated with an introduction by N. K. Sanders. Penguin Classics 1960, Third edition, 1972, pp. 89–116. Copyright © N. K. Sanders, 1960, 1964, 1972. Used with permission of Penguin Group Ltd.

• **Gilgamesh, from decorative panel of a lyre unearthed at Ur.**
(Courtesy of the Penn Museum, Image #150108)

QUESTIONS FOR ANALYSIS

1. What does the *Epic of Gilgamesh* reveal about Sumerian attitudes toward the gods and human beings?
2. What does the epic tell us about Sumerian views of the nature of human life? Where do human beings fit into the cosmic world?
3. At the end of his quest, did Gilgamesh achieve immortality? If so, what was the nature of that immortality?

---

ten took the form of **epic poems**, narrations of the achievements, the labors, and sometimes the failures of heroes that embody a people's or a nation's conception of its own past. Historians can use epic poems to learn about various aspects of a society, particularly its ideals. The Sumerians produced the first epic poem, the *Epic of Gilgamesh*, which recounts the wanderings of Gilgamesh, the part real–part mythological king of the Sumerian city of Uruk. The oldest surviving cuneiform tablets that record stories of Gilgamesh date from about 2100 B.C.E., but these tales were certainly told and probably first written down much earlier. In the epic, Gilgamesh, along with his companion, Enkidu, goes off to fight monsters in a search for fame and glory. After Enkidu dies along the way, Gilgamesh is distraught and decides to search for eternal life, a quest that is unsuccessful. The *Epic of Gilgamesh* shows the Sumerians grappling with such enduring issues as life and death, people and the gods, and immortality. (See "Listening to the Past: Gilgamesh's Quest for Immortality," above.)

• **epic poems** Narrations of the achievements and sometimes the failures of heroes that embody a people's or a nation's conception of its own past. This type of writing first developed in ancient Sumeria.

Myths are the earliest known attempts to answer the question "How did it all begin?" and the story of Gilgamesh incorporates many of the myths of the Sumerians, including those about the creation of the universe. According to one myth (echoed in Genesis, the first book of the Hebrew Bible), only the primeval sea existed at first. The sea produced Heaven and earth, which were united. Heaven and earth gave birth to the god Enlil, who separated them and made possible the creation of the other gods.

The Sumerians did not spend all their time speculating about the origins of the universe. The building of cities, palaces, temples, and irrigation canals demanded practical knowledge of geometry and trigonometry. The Sumerians and later Mesopotamians made significant advances in mathematics using a numerical system based on units of sixty, ten, and six, from which we derive our division of hours into sixty minutes and minutes into sixty seconds. They also developed the concept of place value — that the value of a number depends on where it stands in relation to other numbers.

The Triumph of Babylon and the Spread of Mesopotamian Civilization

Judging by the fact that they had walls and other fortifications, the city-states of Sumeria regularly fought one another. Their battles were sometimes sparked by disputes over water, as irrigation in one area reduced or altered the flow of the rivers into other areas. During the third millennium B.C.E., the climate also became warmer and drier, which further heightened conflicts.

The wealth of Sumerian cities also attracted conquerors from the north. In 2331 B.C.E. Sargon, the chieftain of a group of loosely organized villages to the north of Sumeria, conquered a number of Sumerian cities with what was probably the world's first permanent army. He tore down their defensive walls and appointed his own sons as rulers, creating a new form of government, a state made up of several city-states, what we might think of as a small empire. The symbol of his triumph was a new capital, the city of Akkad. Sargon led his armies to the Mediterranean Sea, spreading Mesopotamian culture throughout the Fertile Crescent, and encouraged trading networks that brought in goods from as far away as the Indus River and the Nile (Map 2.1). Sargon spoke a different language than did the Sumerians, one of the many languages that scholars identify as belonging to the Semitic language family, which includes modern-day Hebrew and Arabic. However, Akkadians adapted Sumerian writing to their own language, a pattern followed by other groups that conquered the area.

Sargon's empire lasted about two hundred years and was then absorbed into the empire centered on the city of Babylon. Babylon was in an excellent position to dominate trade on both the Tigris and Euphrates Rivers, and it was fortunate in having a very able ruler in Hammurabi (hahm-moo-RAH-bee; r. 1792–1750 B.C.E.). He unified Mesopotamia using military force, strategic alliances with the rulers of smaller territories, and religious ideas. He encouraged the worship of Marduk, the all-powerful male god of Babylon, explaining that Marduk had been chosen by all the other Mesopotamian deities as their king. Thus the hierarchy among the gods reflected the hierarchy Hammurabi was establishing on earth, which gave his rule religious sanction. Under Hammurabi, Babylo-

Sargon of Akkad
This bronze head, with elaborately worked hair and beard, portrays the great conqueror Sargon of Akkad. The eyes were originally inlaid with precious jewels, which have since been gouged out. Made about 2300 B.C.E., this head was found in the Assyrian capital of Nineveh, where it had been taken as loot. (Interfoto/Alamy)

MAP 2.1 Spread of Cultures in the Ancient Near East, ca. 3000–1640 B.C.E. This map illustrates the spread of the Mesopotamian and Egyptian cultures through a semicircular stretch of land often called the Fertile Crescent. From this area, the knowledge and use of agriculture spread throughout western Asia.

nian ideas and beliefs traveled throughout Mesopotamia and beyond, with Babylonian traders spreading them farther as they reached the shores of the Mediterranean Sea and the Harappan cities of the Indus River Valley (see pages 66–69).

Hammurabi's Code and Its Social Consequences

Hammurabi's most memorable achievement was the code, introduced around 1790 B.C.E., that established the law of the land. Hammurabi claimed that divine authority stood behind the laws that promoted the welfare of the people. Laws regulating behavior and punishments set for crimes differed according to social status and gender.

Hammurabi's code provides a wealth of information about daily life in Mesopotamia. Because of farming's fundamental importance, the code dealt extensively with agriculture. It governed the duties and rights of tenant farmers, who were expected to cultivate the land carefully and to keep canals and ditches in good repair. Given that negligence in these duties could ruin or damage crops, tenants who were found negligent either bore the cost of losses or were sold into slavery.

Hammurabi gave careful attention to marriage and the family. The fathers of the prospective bride and groom legally arranged the marriage, with her father giving the bride a dowry that remained hers for the rest of her life. The groom's father gave a bridal gift to the bride's father. The wife was expected to be rigorously faithful. Adultery was defined as sex between a married woman and a man who was not her husband, and if a woman was found guilty, she could be put to death. But an accused wife could clear herself before the city council. If the investigation found her innocent, she could take her dowry and leave her husband. (Sex between a married man and a woman who was not his wife was not defined as adultery and carried no penalty.)

The husband technically had absolute power over his household. He could sell his wife and children into slavery for debt and disinherit his son, although the law made it very difficult for him to go to these extremes. Evidence other than the law code indicates that family life was not so grim. Countless wills and testaments show that husbands habitually left their estates to their wives, who in turn willed the property to their children. And though marriage was primarily an arrangement between families, a few poems speak of romantic love.

Law Code of Hammurabi Hammurabi ordered his code to be inscribed on stone pillars and set up in public throughout the Babylonian empire. At the top of the pillar Hammurabi is depicted receiving the scepter of authority from the god Shamash. (Réunion des Musées Nationaux/Art Resource, NY)

The Egyptians and Their Pharaohs

☐ How did geography, leadership, and religion enable the Egyptians to build and maintain a cohesive, prosperous society, and how did migrations and invasions shape Egypt's fate?

At about the same time that Sumerian city-states expanded and fought with one another in the Tigris and Euphrates Valleys, a more cohesive state under a single ruler grew in the valley of the Nile River in North Africa. This was Egypt, which for long stretches of history was prosperous and secure. At various times groups migrated into Egypt seeking better lives or invaded and conquered Egypt. Often these newcomers adopted aspects of Egyptian religion, art, and politics, and Egyptians also carried their traditions with them when they established an empire and engaged in trade.

The Nile and the God-King

The Greek historian and traveler Herodotus called Egypt the "gift of the Nile," and no other single geographical factor had such a fundamental and profound impact on the shaping of Egyptian life, society, and history as this river (see Map 2.2). The Nile flooded once a year, bringing fertile soil and moisture for farming. In contrast to the violent and destructive floods of the Tigris and Euphrates, Nile floods were relatively gentle, and Egyptians praised the Nile primarily as a creative and comforting force:

> Hail to thee, O Nile, that issues from the earth and comes to keep Egypt alive! . . .
> He that waters the meadows which Ra created,
> He that makes to drink the desert . . .
> He who makes barley and brings emmer [wheat] into being . . .
> He who brings grass into being for the cattle . . .
> He who makes every beloved tree to grow . . .
> O Nile, verdant art thou, who makest man and cattle to live.[2]

The regular flooding of the Nile brought life back to the fields, which may have been why the Egyptians developed strong ideas about life after death. They saw both life on this earth and life after death as pleasant, not as the bleak struggle that the Mesopotamians envisioned. The Nile also unified Egypt, serving as a highway that promoted easy communication.

The political power structures that developed in Egypt came to be linked with the Nile. Somehow the idea developed that a single individual, a living god-king whom the Egyptians called the **pharaoh**, controlled the rise and fall of the Nile. This belief came about before the development of writing in Egypt, so, as with the growth of priestly power in Sumeria, the precise details of its origins have been lost. The Egyptians themselves told of a great pharaoh, Menes, who united Upper and Lower Egypt into a single kingdom around 3100 B.C.E. Thereafter, they divided their history into dynasties, or families, of pharaohs. Modern historians have combined the many dynasties into periods with distinctive characteristics (see page 46). The political unification of Egypt ushered in the period known as the Old Kingdom (2660–2180 B.C.E.), an era remarkable for prosperity, artistic flowering, and the evolution of religious beliefs. The focal point of religious and political life in the Old Kingdom was the pharaoh, who commanded the wealth, resources, and people of Egypt.

The pharaoh was only one of the many gods honored by the Egyptians, whose **polytheistic** religious ideas

> "Hail to thee, O Nile, that issues from the earth and comes to keep Egypt alive! . . . O Nile, verdant art thou, who makest man and cattle to live."
>
> **EGYPTIAN PRAYER**

evolved over thousands of years. Egyptians often adopted new deities that they learned about through trade or conquest, or combined the powers and features of these with existing deities. Originally the mightiest of the gods were Amon (AH-muhn), the sky-god, who created the universe by his thoughts, and Ra (rah), the sun-god, who brought life to the land and its people and commanded the sky, the earth, and the underworld. The similarities between Amon and Ra eventually led the Egyptians to combine them into one god, Amon-Ra.

Other powerful deities were Osiris (oh-SIGH-ruhs) and Isis (EYE-suhs). In what became one of Egypt's important religious stories, Osiris was killed and chopped apart by his brother Seth, who was jealous of his power. But Osiris was reassembled and resurrected for a brief period by his sister Isis, who was also his wife. (Siblings who marry each other are common in polytheistic religions, for the gods have to find divine spouses somewhere.) While he was resurrected, Osiris fathered Horus, who became associated with an earlier falcon-god. In some versions of the story, Osiris dies and Isis brings him back to life each year, just as the Nile brings Egypt back to life. Osiris eventually became king of the dead, and, according to Egyptian beliefs about the afterlife, he weighed people's hearts to determine whether they had lived justly enough to deserve everlasting life. The pharaohs came to associate themselves with both Horus and Osiris, and they were regarded as avatars of Horus in life and of Osiris in death. The pharaoh's wife was associated with Isis, for both the queen and the goddess were viewed as protectors.

During the Old Kingdom, the pharaoh was widely understood to be the power who achieved the integration between gods and human beings, and this integration was seen to represent the gods' pledge to care for their people (strikingly unlike the gods of Mesopotamia). The pharaoh's surroundings had to be worthy of a god, and only a magnificent palace was suitable for his home. In fact, the word *pharaoh* means "great house." Just as the pharaoh occupied a great house in life, so he reposed in a great pyramid after death, and the massive

The Pharaoh Mykerinos and His Wife, ca. 2520 B.C.E. In this sandstone sculpture, the pharaoh and his wife look serenely toward the horizon. Stability and permanence were qualities prized by Egyptians in the Old Kingdom, and the sculptor captures them here. The figures are almost equal in size, suggesting the important role that the wives of pharaohs sometimes played. (Old Kingdom, Dynasty 4, reign of Mycerinus, 2532–2510 B.C.; Greywacke; H x W x D: 54 11/16 X 22 3/8 X 2 15/16 in. [139 x 57 x 54 cm]. Museum of Fine Arts, Boston. Harvard University–Museum of Fine Arts Expedition, 11.1738.)

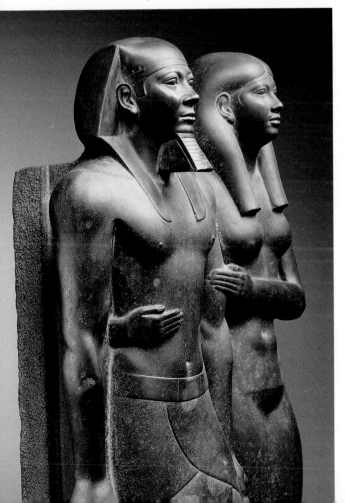

• **pharaoh** The leader of religious and political life in the Old Kingdom, he commanded the wealth, the resources, and the people of Egypt.
• **polytheism** Belief in many deities.

□ PERIODS OF EGYPTIAN HISTORY

PERIOD	DATES	SIGNIFICANT EVENTS
Archaic	3100–2660 B.C.E.	Unification of Egypt
Old Kingdom	2660–2180 B.C.E.	Construction of the pyramids
First Intermediate	2180–2080 B.C.E.	Political chaos
Middle Kingdom	2080–1640 B.C.E.	Recovery and political stability
Second Intermediate	1640–1570 B.C.E.	Political disorder resulting from Hyksos migrations
New Kingdom	1550–1070 B.C.E.	Creation of an Egyptian empire
Third Intermediate	1100–653 B.C.E.	Political fragmentation and rule by outsiders

known as the First and Second Intermediate periods, Egypt suffered invasions and internal strife. Yet the monarchy survived, and in each period a strong pharaoh arose to crush the rebels or expel the invaders and restore order.

Social Divisions and Work in Ancient Egypt

Egyptian society reflected the pyramids that it built. At the top stood the pharaoh, who relied on a circle of nobles, officials, and priests to administer his kingdom. All of them were assisted by scribes, who used a writing system perhaps adapted from Mesopotamia or perhaps developed independently. Scribes wrote with a brush on papyrus sheets or on walls in characters called **hieroglyphs** (HIGH-ruh-glifs), not with a stick on clay tablets. Therefore their writing was more elaborate than that of the Sumerians. Like cuneiform, Egyptian hieroglyphs include both ideograms and symbols used phonetically, so that learning to write was a long process, generally open only to men from relatively well-off families or whose families had high aspirations. Aside from scribes, the cities of the Nile Valley were home to artisans of all types, along with merchants and other tradespeople. The wealthier lived in spacious homes with attractive gardens, walls for privacy, and specialized rooms for eating, sleeping, and entertaining.

Most people in Egypt were farmers. The regularity of the climate meant that the agricultural year was routine and dependable, so farmers seldom suffered from foul weather and damaged crops. Farmers sowed wheat and nurtured a large variety of trees, vegetables, and vines. They also tended cattle and poultry, and when time permitted they hunted and fished in the marshlands of the Nile. Their houses were small, which suggests that they lived in small family groups, not as large extended families. Marriage was arranged by the couple's families and seems to have taken place at a young age. Once couples were married, having children, especially sons, was a high priority, as indicated by surviving charms to promote fertility and prayers for successful childbirth. In terms of property rights within marriages, women in Egypt owned and controlled property more than they did in Mesopotamia, and they were especially active in doing so when they were widows.

As in Mesopotamia, common people paid their obligations to their superiors in products and in labor, and many may not have been able to easily leave the land of their own free will. Their labor obligations may have included forced work on the pyramids and canals, although recent research suggests that most of the people who built the pyramids were paid for their work. Slavery did not become widespread until the New

tomb contained everything he needed in his afterlife. The walls of the burial chamber were inscribed with religious texts and spells relating to the pharaoh's journeys after death. To this day the great pyramids at Giza near Cairo bear silent but magnificent testimony to the god-kings of Egypt.

As the story about Osiris's duties suggests, the pharaoh was not the only one with an afterlife. For all Egyptians, life after death depended both on how one had lived one's life on earth and on the conduct of proper funeral rituals, in which mummification of the physical body was essential. Osiris's care of the dead was shared by Anubis, the jackal-headed god of mummification who annually helped Isis resuscitate Osiris. Anubis's and Osiris's roles are described in the ***Book of the Dead***, written to help guide the dead through difficulties they would encounter on the way to the underworld. This book explained that, after making the journey safely, the soul and the body became part of the divine.

To ancient Egyptians the pharaoh embodied justice and order—harmony among people, nature, and the divine. If the pharaoh was weak or allowed anyone to challenge his unique position, he opened the way to chaos. Twice in Egyptian history the pharaoh failed to maintain centralized power. During those two eras,

* ***Book of the Dead*** A book that preserved Egyptians' ideas about death and the afterlife.
* **hieroglyphs** Egyptian letters, including both ideograms and phonetic signs, written with a brush on papyrus sheets or on walls.

◻ Picturing the Past

Egyptian Home Life This grave painting depicts an intimate moment in the life of an aristocratic family, with the father and mother in the center and their children around them. Often found in Egyptian tombs are statuettes of cats (inset), family pets and the symbol of the goddess Bastet. (family: Gianni Dagli Orti/The Art Archive; cat: Courtesy of the Trustees of the British Museum)

ANALYZING THE IMAGE What evidence do you find in the painting that Egyptian artists based the size of figures on people's status in the household?

CONNECTIONS Based on your reading, how might an image of a poor family differ from this depiction?

Kingdom (1570–1075 B.C.E.; see page 48). Young men were drafted into the pharaoh's army, which served both as a fighting force and as a labor corps.

Migrations and Political Revivals

While Egypt flourished behind its bulwark of sand and sea, momentous changes were taking place around it that would leave their mark even on this rich, insular civilization. These changes involved vast movements of peoples throughout the Fertile Crescent, as various groups migrated and then accommodated themselves to local cultures.

One of these groups was made up of speakers of a Semitic language whom the Egyptians called Hyksos (HIK-sahs), which means "rulers of the uplands." Looking for good land, bands of Hyksos entered the eastern Nile Delta about 1800 B.C.E. (Map 2.2). They brought with them methods of making bronze and casting it into tools and weapons that had been developed elsewhere in the Mediterranean world. Bronze tools made farming more efficient because they were sharper and more durable than the copper, stone, or bone tools they replaced (see Chapter 1). The Hyksos also brought inventions that revolutionized Egyptian warfare, including bronze armor and weapons as well as horse-drawn chariots and the composite bow, made of multiple materials for greater strength. The migration of the Hyksos, combined with a series of famines and internal struggles for power, led Egypt to fragment politically in what later came to be known as the Second Intermediate Period. During this time the Egyptians adopted bronze technology and new forms of weaponry from the Hyksos, while the newcomers

▢ Mapping the Past

MAP 2.2 Empires and Migrations in the Eastern Mediterranean The rise and fall of empires in the eastern Mediterranean were shaped by internal developments, military conflicts, and the migration of peoples to new areas.

ANALYZING THE MAP At what point was the Egyptian Empire at its largest? The Hittite Empire? What were the other major powers in the eastern Mediterranean at this time?

CONNECTIONS What were the major effects of the migrations of the Hyksos? Of the Sea Peoples? What clues does the map provide as to why the Sea Peoples had a more powerful impact than did the Hyksos?

began to worship Egyptian deities and modeled their political structures on those of the Egyptians.

About 1570 B.C.E. a new dynasty of pharaohs seeking to unite Egypt sent armies against the Hyksos, pushing them out of the Nile Delta. These warrior-pharaohs thereby inaugurated what scholars refer to as the New Kingdom—a period characterized by enormous wealth and conscious imperialism. During this period the pharaohs expanded Egyptian power

beyond the Nile Valley and created the first Egyptian empire, which they celebrated with monuments on a scale unparalleled since the pyramids of the Old Kingdom. Also during this period, probably for the first time, widespread slavery became a feature of Egyptian life. The pharaoh's armies returned home from conquests leading hordes of slaves who constituted a new labor force for imperial building projects.

One of the most extraordinary of this unusual line of pharaohs was Akhenaten (ah-keh-NAH-tuhn; r. 1367–1350 B.C.E.), who was more concerned with religion than with conquest. Nefertiti (nef-uhr-TEE-tee), his wife and queen, encouraged his religious bent. (See "Individuals in Society: Hatshepsut and Nefertiti," page 50.) Although the precise nature of Akhenaten's religious beliefs remain debatable, most historians agree that the royal pair were monotheists: they believed in only one god, Aton, a newer version of the sun-god. Akhenaten considered all the other deities of Egypt frauds and suppressed their worship. Yet this monotheism, imposed from above, failed to find a place among the people, and Akhenaten's religion died with him.

At about the same time that the Hyksos migrated into the Nile Delta, another group, the Hittites, established an empire in the eastern Mediterranean that would eventually also confront Egyptian power. The Hittites had long been settled in Anatolia (modern Turkey), and beginning about 1600 B.C.E. they expanded their empire east and south into Mesopotamia (see Map 2.2).

The Hittites were different from other peoples in the region in two significant ways. First, they spoke a language that scholars have identified as belonging to the **Indo-European language family**, a large family of languages that includes English, most of the languages of modern Europe, Greek, Latin, Persian, Hindi, Bengali, and Sanskrit, the sacred tongue of ancient India. (For more on Sanskrit, see page 69.) This suggests that their ancestors originated in central Asia, which historians of language see as the homeland of the Indo-European languages. (Language is one of the ways that what we now call ethnic groups are differentiated from one another, although this differentiation is also based on traditions, religion, politics, and other factors, and it is shaped by history.) The Hittites began to write only after they came into contact with the literate cultures of Mesopotamia.

Second, by the end of their period of expansion the Hittites used iron weapons to some degree. Techniques for smelting iron—which must be done at a much higher temperature than bronze—appear to have been invented first in Mesopotamia or Anatolia. (They were independently invented in other places as well, including India and West Africa; see "Global Trade: Iron," page 54.) Because iron weapons were very expensive, only the highest-ranking warriors could afford them, and most soldiers continued to use bronze swords and spear tips. Iron was the technology of the future, however, and by 1000 B.C.E. the much stronger iron weapons were the deciding factors in battles in southwest Asia and the eastern Mediterranean.

Around 1300 B.C.E. the Hittites and the Egyptians confronted each other, but decided to make an alliance, which eventually included the Babylonians as

Hittite Archer in a Chariot In this stylized stone carving made about 1000 B.C.E. in Anatolia (modern-day Turkey), a Hittite archer driven in a chariot shoots toward his foes, while a victim of an earlier shot is trampled beneath the horses' hooves. The arrows would probably have been tipped with iron, an important factor in Hittite military success. (Museum of Anatolian Civilizations, Ankara/Gianni Dagli Orti/The Art Archive)

well. The alliance facilitated the exchange of ideas throughout western Asia, and the Hittite kings and Egyptian pharaohs such as Ramses II (r. ca. 1290–1224 B.C.E.) used the peace to promote prosperity and concentrate their incomes. Peace was short-lived, however. Beginning about 1200 B.C.E. waves of foreign invaders, the most famous of whom the Egyptians called the Sea Peoples, broke the Hittite Empire apart and drove the Egyptians back to the Nile Valley for a long period of political fragmentation and conquest by outsiders that scholars of Egypt refer to as the Third Intermediate Period (ca. 1100–653 B.C.E.).

Indo-European language family A large family of languages that includes English, most of the languages of modern Europe, Greek, Latin, Persian, Hindi, Bengali, and Sanskrit, the sacred tongue of ancient India.

Individuals in Society

Hatshepsut and Nefertiti

EGYPTIANS UNDERSTOOD THE PHARAOH TO BE the living embodiment of the god Horus, the source of law and morality, and the mediator between gods and humans. His connection with the divine stretched to members of his family, so that his siblings and children were also viewed as in some ways divine. Because of this, a pharaoh often took his sister or half-sister as one of his wives. This concentrated divine blood set the pharaonic family apart from other Egyptians (who did not marry close relatives) and allowed the pharaohs to imitate the gods, who in Egyptian mythology often married their siblings. A pharaoh chose one of his wives to be the "Great Royal Wife," or principal queen. Often this was a relative, though sometimes it was one of the foreign princesses who married pharaohs to establish political alliances.

The familial connection with the divine allowed a handful of women to rule in their own right in Egypt's long history. We know the names of four female pharaohs, of whom the most famous was Hatshepsut (r. 1479–1458 B.C.E.). She was the sister and wife of Thutmose II and, after he died, served as regent — as adviser and co-ruler — for her young stepson Thutmose III, who was the son of another woman. Hatshepsut sent trading expeditions and sponsored artists and architects, ushering in a period of artistic creativity and economic prosperity. She built one of the world's great buildings, an elaborate terraced temple at Deir el Bahri, which eventually served as her tomb. Hatshepsut's status as a powerful female ruler was difficult for Egyptians to conceptualize, and she is often depicted in male dress or with a false beard, thus looking more like the male rulers who were the norm. After her death, Thutmose III tried to destroy all evidence that she had ever ruled, smashing statues and scratching her name off inscriptions, perhaps because of personal animosity and perhaps because he wanted to erase the fact that a woman had once been pharaoh. Only within recent decades have historians and archaeologists begun to (literally) piece together her story.

Though female pharaohs were very rare, many royal women had power through their position as Great Royal Wives. The most famous was Nefertiti (ca. 1370–1330 B.C.E.), the wife of Akhenaten. Her name means "the perfect (or beautiful) woman has come," and inscriptions give her many other titles.

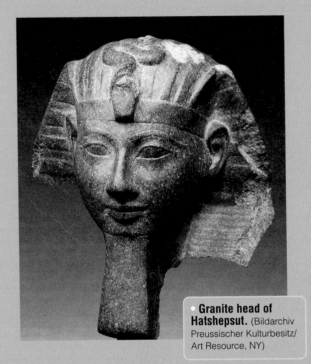

● **Granite head of Hatshepsut.** (Bildarchiv Preussischer Kulturbesitz/ Art Resource, NY)

Nefertiti used her position to spread the new religion of the sun-god Aton. Together she and Akhenaten built a new palace at Akhetaten, the present-day Amarna, away from the old centers of power. There they developed the cult of Aton to the exclusion of the traditional deities. Nearly the only literary survivor of their religious belief is the "Hymn to Aton," which declares Aton to be the only god. It describes Nefertiti as "the great royal consort whom he! Akhenaten! Loves, the mistress of the Two Lands! Upper and Lower Egypt!"

Nefertiti is often shown as being the same size as her husband, and in some inscriptions she is performing religious rituals that would normally have been carried out only by the pharaoh. The exact details of her power are hard to determine, however. An older theory held that her husband removed her from power, though there is also speculation that she may have ruled secretly in her own right after his death. Her tomb has long since disappeared, though some scholars believe that an unidentified mummy discovered in 2003 in Egypt's Valley of the Kings may be Nefertiti's.

QUESTIONS FOR ANALYSIS

1. Why might it have been difficult for Egyptians to accept a female ruler?

2. What opportunities do hereditary monarchies such as that of ancient Egypt provide for women? How does this fit with gender hierarchies in which men are understood as superior?

● **Painted limestone bust of Nefertiti.** (Bildarchiv Preussischer Kulturbesitz/Art Resource, NY)

The political and military story of waves of migrations, battles, and the rise and fall of empires can mask striking continuities and exchanges. The basic social and cultural patterns of agriculture and polytheism survived the onslaughts. Disrupted peoples and newcomers shared practical concepts of shipbuilding and of metals and textile technology, as well as of methods of trade. Cuneiform tablets and papyrus scrolls testify to commercial exchanges and cultural accommodation, adoption, and adaptation.

New Political and Economic Powers

The decline of Egypt allowed new powers to emerge. South of Egypt along the Nile was a region called Nubia (NOO-bee-uh), which as early as 2000 B.C.E. served as a conduit of trade through which ivory, gold, ebony, and other products flowed north from sub-Saharan Africa. Small kingdoms arose in this area, with large buildings and rich tombs. As Egypt expanded during the New Kingdom, it took over northern Nubia, incorporating it into the growing Egyptian empire. The Nubians adopted many features of Egyptian culture, including Egyptian gods, the use of hieroglyphs, and the building of pyramids. Many Nubians became officials in the Egyptian bureaucracy and officers in the army, and there was significant intermarriage between the two groups.

With the contraction of the Egyptian empire, an independent kingdom, Kush, rose to power in Nubia, with its capital at Napata in what is now Sudan. The Kushites conquered southern Egypt, and in 727 B.C.E. the Kushite king Piye swept through the entire Nile Valley to the delta in the north. United once again, Egypt enjoyed a brief period of peace during which the Egyptian culture continued to influence that of its conquerors. In the seventh century B.C.E. invading Assyrians (see page 57) pushed the Kushites out of Egypt, and the Kushite rulers moved their capital farther up the Nile to Meroë, where they built hundreds of pyramids. Meroë became a center of iron production, which was becoming the material of choice for weapons. Iron products from Meroë were the best in the world, smelted using wood from the vast forests in the area.

Nubian Cylinder Sheath This small silver sheath made about 520 B.C.E., perhaps for a dagger, shows a winged goddess and the Egyptian god Amon-Ra. It was found in the tombs of the king of Kush and suggests ways that Egyptian artistic styles and religious ideas influenced cultures farther up the Nile. (Nubian, Napatan Period, reign of King Amani-natakelebte, 538–519 B.C.E. Findspot: Sudan, Nubia, Nuri, Pyramid 10. Gilded silver, colored paste inclusions. Height x diameter: 12 x 3.1 cm [4¾ x 1¼ in.]. Museum of Fine Arts, Boston. Harvard University–Museum of Fine Arts Expedition, 20.275)

They were traded to much of Africa and across the Red Sea and the Indian Ocean to India. Gold and cotton textiles also provided wealth to the Kushite kingdom, which in the third century B.C.E. developed its own alphabet. It was simpler than the Egyptian alphabet, but Meroitic script has not yet been deciphered.

While Kush expanded in the southern Nile Valley, another group rose to prominence along the Mediterranean. These were the **Phoenicians** (fih-NEE-shuhnz), a Semitic-speaking people who had long inhabited several cities along the coast of modern Lebanon and who took to the sea to become outstanding explorers and merchants. Phoenician culture was urban, based on the prosperous commercial city-states of Tyre, Sidon, and Byblos, each ruled by a separate king and council of nobles. Especially from about 1100 to 700 B.C.E., the Phoenicians played a predominant role in international trade. Their most valued products were purple and blue textiles, from which originated their Greek name, Phoenicians, meaning "Purple People." They also worked metals, which they shipped processed or as ore, and made and traded glass products. Phoenician ships often carried hundreds of jars of wine, and the Phoenicians introduced grape-growing to new regions around the Mediterranean, dramatically increasing the wine available for consumption and trade. They imported rare goods and materials, including hunting dogs, gold,

---

• **Phoenicians** People of the prosperous city-states in what is now Lebanon who dominated trade throughout the Mediterranean and spread the letter alphabet.

Phoenician Settlements in the Mediterranean

and ivory, from Persia in the east and from their neighbors to the south.

The variety and quality of the Phoenicians' trade goods generally made them welcome visitors. They established colonies and trading posts throughout the Mediterranean and as far west as the Atlantic coast of modern-day Portugal. In the ninth century B.C.E. they founded the city of Carthage in modern-day Tunisia, a city that would one day struggle with Rome for domination of the western Mediterranean (see pages 150–151). The Phoenicians' voyages brought them into contact with the Greeks, to whom they introduced many as-

pects of the older and more urbanized cultures of Mesopotamia and Egypt.

The Phoenicians' overwhelming cultural legacy was the spread of a completely phonetic system of writing — that is, an alphabet (see Figure 2.2). Cuneiform and hieroglyphics had both developed signs that were used to represent sounds, but these were always used with a much larger number of ideograms. Sometime around 1800 B.C.E. Semitic workers in the Sinai peninsula, which was under Egyptian control, began to use only phonetic signs to write, with each sign designating one sound. This system vastly simplified writing and reading and spread among common people as a practical way to record things and communicate. Egyptian scribes and officials stayed with hieroglyphics, but the Phoenicians adopted the simpler system for their own Semitic language and spread it around the Mediterranean. The Greeks modified this alphabet and then used it to write their own language, and the Romans later based their alphabet — the script we use to write English today — on Greek. Alphabets based on the Phoenician alphabet were also created in the Persian Empire and formed the basis of Hebrew, Arabic, and various alphabets of south and central Asia. The system invented by ordinary people and spread by Phoenician merchants is the origin of nearly every phonetic alphabet in use today.

HIEROGLYPHIC	REPRESENTS	UGARITIC	PHOENICIAN	GREEK	ROMAN
)	Throw stick	T	∧	Γ	G
₰	Man with raised arms	⊨	≼	E	E
⊃	Basket with handle	⊳-	∨	K	K
⋎⋎⋎	Water	⊢	⋈	M	M
⌒	Snake	⋙-	⌐	N	N
⦿	Eye	◁	O	O	O
⬭	Mouth	⊨	?	Π	P
⍥	Head	⊞-	9	P	R
⛲	Pool with lotus flowers	◁⊅	W	Σ	S
⊏⊐	House	⊞	9	B	B
𓃾	Ox-head	⋙-	K	A	A

FIGURE 2.2 Origins of the Alphabet List of hieroglyphic, Ugaritic, Phoenician, Greek, and Roman sign forms. (Source: A. B. Knapp, *The History and Culture of Ancient Western Asia and Egypt.* © 1988 Wadsworth, a division of Cengage Learning, Inc. Reproduced by permission, www.cengage.com/permissions.)

The Hebrews

☐ How did the Hebrews create an enduring written religious tradition, and what was its significance?

Another people took advantage of Egypt's collapse to found an independent state, and their legacy has been even more far-reaching than that of the Phoenicians. For several centuries, a Semitic people known as the Hebrews or the Israelites controlled a small state on the western end of the Fertile Crescent. Politically unimportant when compared with the Egyptian or Babylonian empires, the Hebrews created a new form of religious belief, a monotheism based on the worship of an all-powerful god they called **Yahweh** (YAH-way, anglicized as Jehovah). They began to write down their religious ideas, traditions, laws, advice literature, prayers, hymns, history, and prophecies in a series of books. These were gathered together to form the Hebrew Bible (which Christians later adopted and termed the "Old Testament" to parallel specific Christian writings termed the "New Testament"). These writings are what came to define the Hebrews as a people, and they are the most important written record that exists from this period. The reverence for these written texts was passed down from Judaism—the religion of the Hebrews—to the other Western monotheistic religions that grew from it, Christianity and Islam.

The Hebrew State

Most of the information about the Hebrews comes from the Bible, which, like all ancient documents, must be used with care as a historical source. But archaeological evidence supports many of its details, and because it records a living religious tradition, extensive textual and physical research into everything it records continues.

The Hebrews were nomadic pastoralists who probably migrated into the Nile Delta from the east seeking good land for their herds of sheep and goats. There the Egyptians enslaved them, but, according to the Bible, a charismatic leader named Moses led them out of Egypt, and in the thirteenth century B.C.E. they settled in Palestine. There they encountered a variety of other peoples, whom they both learned from and fought. They slowly adopted agriculture and, not surprisingly, at times worshipped the agricultural gods of their neighbors, including Baal, an ancient Semitic fertility god represented as a golden calf. In this they followed the common historical pattern of newcomers by adapting themselves to the culture of an older, well-established people.

The greatest danger to the Hebrews came from a group known as the Philistines (FIH-luh-steenz), whose superior technology and military organization at first made them invincible. Sometime around 1020 B.C.E. the Hebrew leader Saul, while keeping the Philistines at bay, established a monarchy over the Hebrew tribes. After Saul died fighting the Philistines, David of Bethlehem continued Saul's work and captured the city of Jerusalem, which he enlarged and made the religious center of the realm. His work in consolidating the monarchy and enlarging the kingdom paved the way for his son Solomon. In the tenth century B.C.E. Solomon launched a building program that included cities, palaces, fortresses, and roads. The most symbolic of these projects was the Temple of Jerusalem, which became the home of the Ark of the Covenant, the chest that contained the holiest Hebrew religious articles. The Temple of Jerusalem was intended to be the religious heart of the kingdom, a symbol of Hebrew unity and of Yahweh's approval of the state built by Saul, David, and Solomon.

The Hebrew Exodus and State, ca. 1250–800 B.C.E.

➤ Possible route of the Exodus, ca. 1250 B.C.E.
☐ Solomon's kingdom, ca. 950 B.C.E.
▨ Israel, ca. 800 B.C.E.
▨ Judah, ca. 800 B.C.E.

The unified Hebrew state did not last long. Upon Solomon's death his kingdom broke into political halves. The northern part became Israel, with its capital at Samaria, and the southern half was Judah, with Jerusalem remaining its center. War broke out between the northern and southern halves, and the Assyrians wiped out the northern kingdom of Israel in 720 B.C.E. Judah survived numerous invasions until the Babylonians crushed it in 587 B.C.E. The survivors were sent into exile in Babylonia, a period commonly known as the Babylonian Captivity. In 538 B.C.E. the Persian king Cyrus the Great conquered the Babylonians and permitted some forty thousand exiles to return to Jerusalem (see page 59 and "Viewpoints: Rulers and Divine Favor: Cyrus the Great in the Cyrus Cylinder and Hebrew Scripture," page 60). They rebuilt the temple, although politically the area was simply part of the Persian Empire.

• **Yahweh** All-powerful god of the Hebrew people and the basis for the enduring religious traditions of Judaism.

Global Trade

Iron has shaped world history more than any other metal, even more than gold and silver. In its pure state iron is soft, but adding small amounts of carbon and various minerals, particularly at very high temperatures, transforms it into a material with great structural strength. Tools and weapons made of iron dramatically shaped interactions between peoples in the ancient world, and machines made of iron and steel literally created the modern world.

Human use of iron began during the Paleolithic era, when people living in what is now Egypt used small pieces of hematite, a type of iron oxide, as part of their tools, along with stone, bone, and wood. Beginning around 4000 B.C.E. people in several parts of the world began to pick up iron-nickel meteorites and pound them into shapes. Such meteorites were rare, and the objects produced from them were luxury goods, not things for everyday use. Jewelry, weapons, and occasionally tools from meteoric iron have also been found in China, Africa, and North and South America. These were traded very long distances, including thousands of miles around the Arctic, where indigenous peoples traded sharpened pieces from a gigantic iron meteorite that fell in Greenland for use as harpoon tips and knife blades.

MAP 2.3 Trade in Iron and Iron Technology, to 500 B.C.E.

This Celtic iron helmet from the first century B.C.E. fit snugly over a warrior's head, with an attached iron flap protecting the forehead and cheekbones, and a ring that would have connected a leather chin strap. Found in France, it provides evidence of the spread of iron technology, as smelting techniques as well as iron products were traded over long distances. (Courtesy, Römisch-Germanisches-Zentralmuseum, Mainz)

Iron is the most common element in the earth, but most iron on or near the earth's surface occurs in the form of ore, which must be smelted to extract the metal. This is also true of copper and tin, but these can be smelted at much lower temperatures than iron, so they were the first metals to be produced to any great extent, and were usually mixed together to form bronze. As artisans perfected bronze metalworking techniques, they also experimented with iron. They developed a long and difficult process to smelt iron, using burning charcoal and a bellows (which raised the temperature further) to extract the iron from the ore. This was done in an enclosed furnace, and the process was repeated a number of times as the ore was transformed into wrought iron, which could be formed into shapes.

Exactly where and when the first smelted iron was produced is a matter of debate—many places would like to have this honor—but it was somewhere in Mesopotamia or Anatolia (modern-day Turkey) and occurred perhaps as early as 2500 B.C.E. The Hittites became a powerful empire in the eastern Mediterranean in part through their skills in making and using iron weaponry, and by 1200 B.C.E. or so iron objects were traded throughout the Mediterranean and beyond. Knowledge of smelting traveled as well. By 1700 B.C.E. artisans in northern India were making and trading iron implements. By 1200 B.C.E. iron was being produced and sold in southern India, though scholars debate whether smelting was discovered independently there or learned through contact with iron-making cultures to the north. Iron objects were traded from Anatolia north into Greece, central Europe, and western Asia, and by 500 B.C.E. knowledge of smelting had traveled these routes as well.

Smelting was discovered independently in what is now Nigeria in western Africa about 1500 B.C.E. by a group of people who spoke Bantu languages. They carried iron hoes, axes, shovels, and weapons, and the knowledge of how to make them, as they migrated south and east over many centuries, which gave them a distinct advantage over foraging peoples. In East Africa, the Kushite people learned the advantages of iron weaponry when the iron-using Assyrians drove them out of Egypt, and they then established a major center of iron production at Meroë and traded down the African coast and across the sea to India.

Ironworkers continued to experiment and improve their products. The Chinese probably learned smelting from central Asian steppe peoples, but in about 500 B.C.E. artisans in China developed techniques of making cast iron using molds, through which implements could be made much more efficiently. Somewhere in the Near East ironworkers discovered that if the relatively brittle wrought iron objects were placed on a bed of burning charcoal and then cooled quickly, the outer layer would form into a layer of a much harder material, steel. Goods made of cast iron were usually traded locally because they were heavy, but fine sword and knife blades of steel traveled long distances, and the knowledge of how to make them followed.

The Jewish Religion

During and especially after the Babylonian Captivity, the most important Hebrew texts of history, law, and ethics were edited and brought together in the Torah, the first five books of the Hebrew Bible. The exiles redefined their beliefs and practices, thereby establishing what they believed to be the law of Yahweh. Those who lived by these precepts came to be called Jews and their religion Judaism.

Fundamental to an understanding of the Jewish religion is the concept of the Covenant, a formal agreement between Yahweh and the Hebrew people. According to the Bible, Yahweh appeared to Moses while he was leading the Hebrews out of Egypt and made the Covenant with the Hebrews: if they worshipped Yahweh as their only god, he would consider them his chosen people and protect them from their enemies. That worship was embodied in a series of rules of behavior, the Ten Commandments, which Yahweh gave to Moses; these required certain kinds of religious observances and forbade the Hebrews to steal, kill, lie, or commit adultery. From the Ten Commandments a complex system of rules of conduct was created and later written down as Hebrew law.

The monotheistic Jewish religion contrasted sharply with the polytheism of most peoples of the surrounding area. Mesopotamian and Egyptian deities — and later Greek and Roman deities — were powerful and often immortal, but they were otherwise just like humans, with good and bad personal qualities. They demanded ceremonies in their honor but were relatively unconcerned with how people behaved toward one another. The Hebrews, however, could please their god only by living up to high moral standards as well as by worshipping him. In polytheistic systems, people could easily add new gods or goddesses to the group of deities they honored, and they often did so when they moved to a new area or learned about a god with particularly appealing qualities. Yahweh, by contrast, demanded that the Hebrews worship him alone. The first of the Ten Commandments expresses this demand: "I am the Lord your God . . . you shall have no other gods besides me" (Exodus 20:23). Like Mesopotamian deities, Yahweh punished people, but the Hebrews also believed he would protect them all, not simply kings and powerful priests, and make them prosper if they obeyed his commandments. A hymn recorded in the Hebrew Bible's book of Psalms captures this idea:

> Blessed is every one who fears the Lord, who walks
>   in his ways!
> You shall eat the fruit of the labor of your hands;
>   you shall be happy, and it shall be well with you.
> Your wife will be like a fruitful vine without your
>   house;
>   your children will be like olive shoots around your
>   table.
> Lo, thus shall the man be blessed who fears the Lord.
>   (Psalms 128:1–4)

Because Yahweh is a single god, not surrounded by lesser gods and goddesses, there is no female divinity in Judaism. Occasionally, however, aspects of God are described in feminine terms, such as Sophia, the wisdom of God. Religious leaders were important in Judaism, but not as important as the written texts they interpreted; these texts came to be regarded as the word of Yahweh and thus had status that other writings did not.

The Family and Jewish Life

Although the Hebrews originally were nomadic, they adopted settled agriculture in Palestine, and some lived in cities. These shifts affected more than just how people fed themselves. Communal use of land gave way to family or private ownership, and tribal identity was replaced by loyalty to a state and then to the traditions of Judaism.

Marriage and the family were fundamentally important in Jewish life; celibacy was frowned upon, and almost all major Jewish thinkers and priests were married. As in Mesopotamia and Egypt, marriage was a family matter, too important to be left solely to the

The Golden Calf
According to the Bible, Moses descended from Mount Sinai, where he had received the Ten Commandments, to find the Hebrews worshipping a golden calf, which was against Yahweh's laws. In July 1990 an American archaeological team found this model of a gilded calf inside a pot. The figurine, which dates to about 1550 B.C.E., is strong evidence for the existence of the cult represented by the calf in Palestine. (Harvard Semitic Museum, Ashkelon Excavations)

whims of young people. Although sexual relations were seen as a source of impurity that needed to be cleansed with specific rituals, sex itself was viewed as part of Yahweh's creation and the bearing of children as in some ways a religious function. Sons were especially desired because they maintained the family bloodline while keeping ancestral property in the family. A first-born son became the head of the household upon his father's death. Mothers oversaw the early education of the children, but as boys grew older, their fathers provided more of their education.

The development of urban life among Jews created new economic opportunities, especially in crafts and trade. People specialized in certain occupations, such as milling flour, baking bread, making pottery, weaving, and carpentry, but the most important task for observant Jews was studying religious texts, especially after the return from Babylon. Until the twentieth century this activity was limited to men. For their part, women were obliged to provide for men's physical needs while they were studying. This meant that Jewish women were often more active economically than their contemporaries of other religions, trading goods the household produced.

The Assyrians and Persians

☐ What were the strengths of and the major differences between the Assyrian and Persian Empires?

Small kingdoms like those of the Phoenicians and the Jews could exist only in the absence of a major power. In the ninth century B.C.E. one major power arose in the form of the Assyrians, who starting in northern Mesopotamia created an empire through often brutal military conquest. And from a base in what is now southern Iran, the Persians established an even larger empire, developing effective institutions of government, building roads, and allowing a variety of customs, religions, and traditions to flourish.

Assyria, the Military Monarchy

Assyria rose at the beginning of the ninth century B.C.E. and came to dominate northern Mesopotamia from its chief capital at Nineveh on the Tigris River. The Assyrians were a Semitic people heavily influenced by the Babylonian culture to the south. They were also one of the most warlike people in history, carving out an empire that stretched from east and north of the Tigris River to central Egypt.

Those who stood up to Assyrian might were often systematically tortured and slaughtered, but Assyria's success was also due to sophisticated, farsighted, and effective military tactics, technical skills, and organization. For example, the Assyrians developed a wide variety of siege machinery and techniques, including excavations to undermine city walls and battering rams to knock down walls and gates. Never before in the Near East had anyone applied such technical knowledge to warfare. The Assyrians even invented the concept of a corps of engineers who bridged rivers with pontoons or provided soldiers with inflatable skins for swimming. The Assyrians also knew how to coordinate their efforts both in open battle and in siege warfare. They divided their armies into different organizational units of infantry who fought with iron swords and spears, others who fought with slings or bows and arrows, and a third group who used chariots.

Not only did the Assyrians know how to win battles, but they also knew how to take advantage of their victories. As early as the eighth century B.C.E. the Assyrian kings began to organize their conquered territories into an empire. The lands closest to Assyria became provinces governed directly by Assyrian officials. In more distant parts of the empire, including Israel, the Phoenician cities, and Egypt, Assyrian kings chose local rulers whom they favored and required them to pay tribute.

Assyrians Besiege a City In this Assyrian carving from the ninth century B.C.E., archers shoot toward a tower, foot soldiers attempt to open a chained gate, and engineers undermine the foundations of the wall. Unfortunate defenders fall toward their fate, while at the very top, a woman from the besieged city raises her arms in horror at the scene. (British Museum. Photo © Michael Holford)

In the seventh century B.C.E. Assyrian power seemed firmly established. Yet the downfall of Assyria was swift and complete. Babylon won its independence in 626 B.C.E. and joined forces with a new group, the Medes, an Indo-European-speaking people from Persia. Together the Babylonians and the Medes destroyed the Assyrian Empire in 612 B.C.E., paving the way for the rise of the Persians. The Hebrew prophet Nahum spoke for many when he asked: "Nineveh is laid waste: who will bemoan her?" (Nahum 3:7). Their cities destroyed and their power shattered, the Assyrians seemed to disappear from history.

> "Nineveh is laid waste: who will bemoan her?"
>
> **NAHUM**

Archaeology brought the Assyrians out of obscurity, however. In the nineteenth century archaeologists unearthed huge sculpted figures of winged bulls, human-headed lions, and sphinxes, along with cuneiform tablets that recounted everything from military campaigns to business relationships. Archaeologists also discovered reliefs that Assyrian artists carved for the kings' palaces. These showed scenes of war as a series of episodes that progressed from the time the army marched out until the enemy was conquered. The reliefs created a visual narrative of events, a form still favored by comic-book artists and the authors of graphic novels.

The Rise and Expansion of the Persian Empire

As we have seen, Assyria rose to power from a base in the Tigris and Euphrates River Valleys of Mesopotamia, which had been home to many earlier empires. The Assyrians were defeated by a coalition that included a Mesopotamian power — Babylon — but also a people with a base of power in a part of the world that had not been the site of earlier urbanized states: Persia (modern-day Iran), a stark land of towering mountains and flaming deserts with a broad central plateau in the heart of the country (Map 2.4).

Iran's geographical position and topography explain its traditional role as the highway between western and eastern Asia. Nomadic peoples migrating south from the broad steppes (grasslands) of Russia and Central Asia have streamed into Iran throughout much of history. (For an in-depth discussion of these groups, see Chapter 12.) Confronting the uncrossable salt deserts, most have turned either westward or eastward, moving on until they reached the advanced and wealthy urban centers of Mesopotamia and India. Cities did emerge along these routes, however, and Iran became the area where nomads met urban dwellers.

Among these nomads were various Indo-European-speaking peoples who migrated into this area about 1000 B.C.E. with their flocks and herds. They were also

MAP 2.4 The Assyrian and Persian Empires, ca. 1000–500 B.C.E. The Assyrian Empire at its height in ca. 650 B.C.E. included almost all of the old centers of power in the ancient Near East. By 513 B.C.E., however, the Persian Empire not only included more of that area but also extended as far east as western India.

horse breeders, and the horse gave them a decisive military advantage over those who already lived in the area. One of the Indo-European groups was the Medes, who settled in northern Iran and built their capital city at Ecbatana, the modern Hamadan. With the rise of the Medes, marked by their union under one king and their defeat of the Assyrian Empire with the help of the Babylonians, the balance of power in western Asia shifted east of Mesopotamia for the first time.

The Persians were another Indo-European group, and they settled in southern Iran. In 550 B.C.E. Cyrus the Great (r. 559–530 B.C.E.), king of the Persians and one of the most remarkable statesmen of antiquity, conquered the Medes. (See "Viewpoints: Rulers and Divine Favor: Cyrus the Great in the Cyrus Cylinder and Hebrew Scripture," page 60.) The conquest resulted not in slavery and slaughter but in the union of the two peoples. Having united Iran, Cyrus set out to achieve two goals. First, he wanted to win control of the west and thus of the terminal ports of the great trade routes that crossed Iran and Anatolia (modern western Turkey). Second, he strove to secure eastern Iran from the threats of nomadic invasions. In a series of major campaigns Cyrus achieved both goals. He conquered the various kingdoms of the Tigris and Euphrates Valleys and swept into Anatolia, easily overthrowing the young kingdom of Lydia. His generals subdued the Greek cities along the coast of Anatolia and the Phoenician cities south of these, thus gaining him flourishing ports on the Mediterranean. Marching to the far eastern corners of Iran from Lydia, Cyrus conquered the regions of Parthia and Bactria in central Asia, though he ultimately died on the battlefield there.

With these victories Cyrus demonstrated to the world his benevolence as well as his military might. He spared the life of the conquered king of Lydia, Croesus, who came to be Cyrus's friend and adviser. He also allowed the Greeks to live according to their customs, making possible the spread of Greek culture farther east. Cyrus's humanity likewise extended to the Jews, whom he allowed to return from Babylon to Jerusalem, where he paid for the rebuilding of their temple.

Cyrus's successors continued the Persian conquests, creating the largest empire the world had yet seen (see Map 2.4). In 525 B.C.E. his son Cambyses (r. 530–522 B.C.E.) subdued the Egyptians and the Nubians. Upon Cambyses's death (the circumstances of which are disputed), Darius (r. 521–486 B.C.E.) took over the throne and conquered Scythia in central Asia, along with much of Thrace and Macedonia, areas north of the Aegean Sea. By 510 the Persians also ruled the western coast of Anatolia and many of the islands of the Aegean. Thus, within forty years the Persians had transformed themselves from a subject people to the rulers of a vast empire that included all of the oldest kingdoms and peoples of the region, as well as many outly-

Persian Saddle-Cloth This elaborately painted piece of leather, dating from the fourth or third century B.C.E., shows running goats with huge curved horns. The fact that it survived suggests that it was not actually used, but served a ceremonial function. (© The State Hermitage Museum, St. Petersburg. Photo by Vladimir Terebenin)

ing areas (see Map 2.4) Unsurprisingly, Darius began to call himself King of Kings. Although invasions of Greece by Darius and his son Xerxes were unsuccessful, the Persian Empire lasted another two hundred years, until it became part of the empire of Alexander the Great (see page 131).

The Persians also knew how to preserve the peace they had won on the battlefield. Unlike the Assyrians, they did not resort to slaughter and torture to maintain order, preferring diplomacy instead. They created an efficient administrative system to govern the empire based in their newly built capital city of Persepolis,

Viewpoints

Rulers and Divine Favor: Cyrus the Great in the Cyrus Cylinder and Hebrew Scripture

● *In Mesopotamia — and elsewhere in the ancient world — individuals who established large empires through conquest often subsequently proclaimed that their triumph was the result of divine favor, and they honored the gods of the regions they conquered. King Cyrus the Great of Persia appears to have followed this tradition. A text written in cuneiform on a sixth-century B.C.E. Babylonian clay cylinder presents Cyrus describing the way in which the main Babylonian god Marduk selected him to conquer Babylon and restore proper government and worship. Cyrus is also portrayed as divinely chosen in the book of Isaiah in Hebrew Scripture, probably written sometime in the late sixth century B.C.E. after Cyrus allowed the Jews to return to Jerusalem. Because Cyrus was not a follower of the Jewish God, however, the issue of divine favor was more complicated.*

The Cyrus Cylinder

❝I am Cyrus, king of the universe, the great king, the powerful king, king of Babylon, king of Sumer and Akkad, king of the four quarters of the world. . . .

When I went as harbinger of peace i[nt]o Babylon I founded my sovereign residence within the palace amid celebration and rejoicing. Marduk, the great lord, bestowed on me as my destiny the great magnanimity of one who loves Babylon, and I every day sought him out in awe. My vast troops marched peaceably in Babylon, and the whole of [Sumer] and Akkad had nothing to fear. I sought the welfare of the city of Babylon and all its sanctuaries. As for the population of Babylon, . . . [w]ho as if without div[ine intention] had endured a yoke not decreed for them, I soothed their weariness, I freed them from their bond. . . . Marduk, the great lord, rejoiced at [my good] deeds, and he pronounced a sweet blessing over me, Cyrus, the king who fears him, and over Cambyses, the son [my]

issue, [and over] all my troops, that we might proceed further at his exalted command.❞

The Book of Isaiah, Chapter 45

❝Thus said the Lord to Cyrus, His anointed one — whose right hand He has grasped, Treading down nations before him, Ungirding the loins of kings, Opening doors before him, and letting no gate stay shut: I will march before you, and level the hills that loom up; I will shatter doors of bronze and cut down iron bars. I will give you treasures concealed in the dark and secret hoards — So that you may know that it is I the LORD, the God of Israel, who call you by name. For the sake of My servant Jacob, Israel My chosen one, I call you by name, I hail you by title, though you have not known Me. I am the LORD, and there is none else; beside Me, there is no God. I engird you, though you have not known Me. . . .

It was I who roused him [that is, Cyrus] for victory, and who level all roads for him. He shall rebuild My city, and let My exiled people go, without price and without payment — said the LORD of hosts.❞

Sources: Cylinder inscription translation by Irving Finkel, curator of Cuneiform Collections at the British Museum, www.britishmuseum.org. Used by permission of The British Museum; "The Book of Isaiah" in *Tanakh: A New Translation of The Holy Scriptures According to the Traditional Hebrew Text*. Copyright © 1985 by The Jewish Publication Society. Used by permission of the Jewish Publication Society.

QUESTIONS FOR ANALYSIS

1. How would you compare the portrayal of Cyrus in the two texts?

2. The Babylonians were polytheistic, and the Hebrews were monotheistic. How does this shape the way divine actions and favor are portrayed in the texts?

3. Both of these texts have been very influential in establishing the largely positive historical view of Cyrus. What limitations might there be in using these as historical sources?

near modern Schiras, Iran. Under Darius, they divided the empire into districts and appointed either Persian or local nobles as administrators called satraps to head each one. The satrap controlled local government, collected taxes, heard legal cases, and maintained order. He was assisted by a council and also by officials and army leaders sent from Persepolis who made sure that he knew the will of the king and that the king knew what was going on in the provinces. This system was in line with the Persians' usual practice of respecting their subjects and allowing them to practice their native customs and religions, giving the Near East both political unity and cultural diversity. It also lessened opposition to Persian rule by making local elites part of the system of government, although sometimes satraps used their authority to build up independent power.

● **Zoroastrianism** The religion based on the teachings of Zoroaster, who emphasized the individual's responsibility to choose between good and evil.

Throughout the Persian Empire communication and trade were eased by a sophisticated system of roads. The main highway, the famous Royal Road, spanned some 1,677 miles (see Map 2.4). Other roads branched out from this main route to link all parts of the empire from the coast of Asia Minor to the valley of the Indus River. These highways meant that the king was usually in close touch with officials and subjects, and they simplified the defense of the empire by making it easier to move Persian armies. The roads also aided the flow of trade, which Persian rulers further encouraged by building canals, including one that linked the Red Sea and the Nile.

The Persians made significant contributions to art and culture. In art they transformed the Assyrian tradition of realistic monumental sculpture from one that celebrated gory details of slaughter to one that showed both the Persians and their subjects as dignified. Because it depicted non-Persians realistically, Persian art is an excellent source of information about the weapons, tools, clothing, and even hairstyles of many peoples of the area.

The Religion of Zoroaster

Originally Persian religion was polytheistic, with many deities under a chief god Ahuramazda (ah-HOOR-uh-MAZ-duh), the creator of all living creatures. Around 600 B.C.E., however, the alternative views of one prophet, Zoroaster (zo-roh-ASS-tuhr), became more prominent. A thinker and preacher whose birth and death dates are uncertain, Zoroaster is regarded as the author of key religious texts, later collected as a collection of sacred texts called the *Avesta*. He introduced new spiritual concepts to the Persian people, stressing devotion to Ahuramazda alone and emphasizing the individual's responsibility to choose between the forces of creation, truth, and order and those of nothingness, chaos, falsehood, and disorder. He taught that people possessed the free will to decide between these and that they must rely on their own consciences to guide them through an active life in which they focused on "good thoughts, good words, and good deeds." Their decisions were crucial, Zoroaster warned, for there would come a time of reckoning. At the end of time the forces of order would win, and the victorious Ahuramazda, like the Egyptian god Osiris, would preside over a last judgment to determine each person's eternal fate.

Scholars — and contemporary Zoroastrians — debate whether Zoroaster saw the forces of disorder as a malevolent deity named Angra Mainyu who was co-eternal with and independent from Ahuramazda, or whether he was simply using this term to mean "evil thoughts" or "a destructive spirit." Forms of **Zoroastrianism** have followed each of these lines of understanding. Most Zoroastrians believed that the Ahuramazda and the Angra Mainyu were independent forces representing good and evil, respectively, who were locked together in a cosmic battle for the human race, a religious conceptualization that scholars call dualism. Others had a more monotheistic interpretation and saw Ahuramazda as the only uncreated god.

King Darius became a follower of Zoroaster's teachings and in many inscriptions proclaimed that he was divinely chosen by Ahuramazda. Continuing the common Persian pattern of toleration, Darius did not impose his religious beliefs on others, but under the protection of the Persian kings, Zoroastrianism won converts throughout Iran and the rest of the Persian Empire and spread into central China. It became the official religion of the later Persian Empire ruled by the Sassanid dynasty, and much later Zoroastrians migrated to western India, where they became known as Parsis and still live today. The religion survived the fall of the Persian Empire to influence Judaism, Christianity, Islam, and Buddhism, and its key tenets are shared by many religions: good behavior in the world, even though it might be unrecognized during one's life, will be amply rewarded in the hereafter. Evil, no matter how powerful in life, will be punished after death.

CONNECTIONS

"History is written by the victors," goes a common saying often incorrectly attributed to Winston Churchill. This is not always true; people who have been vanquished in wars or devastated by oppression have certainly made their stories known. But in other ways it is always true, for writing created records and therefore was the origin of what many people understand as history. Writing was invented to serve the needs of people who lived close to one another in cities and states, and almost everyone who could write lived in states. Because most history, including this book, concentrates on areas with states, the next two chapters examine the states that were developing in India and China during the period discussed in this chapter. In Chapter 5 we pick up on developments in the Mediterranean that link to those in Mesopotamia, Egypt, and Persia discussed in this chapter.

It is important to remember that, as was the spread of agriculture, the growth of the state was a slow process. States became the most powerful and most densely populated forms of human society, and today almost everyone on the planet is at least hypothetically a citizen of a state (or sometimes of more than one, if he or she has dual citizenship). Just three hundred years ago, however, only about a third of the world was governed by states; in the rest of the world, people lived in bands of foragers, villages led by kin leaders, family groups of pastoralists, chiefdoms, confederations of tribes, or other forms of social organization. In 500 B.C.E. perhaps only a little over 5 percent of the world's population lived in states. In his *Histories*, Herodotus pays primary attention to the Persians and the Greeks, both of whom had writing and states, but he also discusses many peoples who had neither. In their attempts to provide a balanced account of all the world's peoples, historians today are also looking beyond written sources. Those sources invariably present only part of the story, as Winston Churchill — a historian as well as a political leader — noted in something he actually *did* say: "History will bear me out, particularly as I shall write that history myself."

□ CHAPTER REVIEW

KEY TERMS

ziggurat (p. 38)	Indo-European
cuneiform (p. 39)	language family
epic poems (p. 41)	(p. 49)
pharaoh (p. 44)	Phoenicians (p. 51)
polytheism (p. 45)	Yahweh (p. 53)
Book of the Dead	Zoroastrianism
(p. 46)	(p. 61)
hieroglyphs (p. 46)	

□ **How does writing shape what we can know about the past, and how did writing develop to meet the needs of cities and states? (p. 34)**

Beginning about five thousand years ago, people in some parts of the world developed a new technology, writing. Written sources provide a wider range of information about past societies than is available from physical evidence alone, which means that we know much more about the societies that left written records than about those that did not. Writing was developed to meet the needs of the more complex urban societies that are often referred to as civilizations and particularly to meet the needs of the state, a new structure of governance distinct from tribes and kinship groups. In states, a small share of the population is able to coerce resources out of everyone else, and leaders gain and maintain power through organized violence, bureaucracies, systems of taxation, and written laws. These laws generally created more elaborate social and gender hierarchies.

□ **How did the people of Mesopotamia form the world's first states, and how did their institutions spread? (p. 37)**

States first developed in Mesopotamia, the land between the Euphrates and Tigris Rivers. Starting in the southern part of Mesopotamia known as Sumeria, sustained agriculture reliant on irrigation resulted in larger populations, a division of labor, and the growth of cities. Priests and rulers invented ways to control and organize these complex societies, including armies, taxation systems, and cuneiform writing. Conquerors from the north unified Mesopotamian city-states into larger empires and spread Mesopotamian culture over a large area. The most significant of these was the Babylonian empire, which under Hammurabi developed a written code of law and expanded trade connections.

□ **How did geography, leadership, and religion enable the Egyptians to build and maintain a cohesive, prosperous society, and how did migrations and invasions shape Egypt's fate? (p. 44)**

During the third millennium B.C.E., a period known as the Old Kingdom, Egypt grew into a cohesive state under a single ruler in the valley of the Nile, which provided rich farmland and an avenue of communication. The Egyptians developed powerful beliefs in life after death, and the focal point of religious and political life was the pharaoh, a god-king who commanded the wealth, resources, and people of Egypt. For long stretches of history Egypt was prosperous and secure in the fertile Nile Valley, although at times various groups migrated in seeking better lives or invaded and conquered. Very often these newcomers adopted aspects of Egyptian religion, art, and politics, and the Egyptians adopted aspects of the newcomers' cultures, such as the techniques for making and casting bronze of the Hyksos. During the period known as the New Kingdom, warrior-pharaohs expanded their power beyond the Nile Valley and created the first Egyptian empire, during which they first fought and then allied with the iron-using Hittites. After the collapse of the New Kingdom, the Nubian rulers of Kush conquered Egypt, and another group, the Phoenicians, came to dominate trade in the Mediterranean, spreading a letter alphabet.

☐ **How did the Hebrews create an enduring written religious tradition, and what was its significance? (p. 53)**

For several centuries after the collapse of New Kingdom Egypt, a Semitic people known as the Hebrews or the Israelites controlled a small state on the western end of the Fertile Crescent. Their most important legacy was not political, but rather a new form of religious belief, Judaism, based on the worship of a single all-powerful god, Yahweh. The Hebrews wrote down their religious ideas, traditions, laws, advice literature, prayers, hymns, history, and prophecies in a series of books, which came to define the Hebrews as a people. This group of books, the Hebrew Bible, describes the Covenant between Yahweh and the Hebrew people and sets out laws and traditions that structured Hebrew society and family life. Reverence for these written texts was passed from Judaism to the other Western monotheistic religions that grew from it, Christianity and Islam.

☐ **What were the strengths of and the major differences between the Assyrian and Persian Empires? (p. 57)**

In the ninth century the Assyrians began a rise to power from northern Mesopotamia, creating an empire by means of often brutal military conquest. Assyria's success was also due to sophisticated, far-sighted, and effective military tactics, technical skills, and organization. From a base in what is now southern Iran, the Persians established an even larger empire, developing effective institutions of government and building roads. Though conquerors, the Persians, unlike the Assyrians, usually respected their subjects and allowed them to practice their native customs, traditions, and religions. Around 600 B.C.E. a new religion based on the teachings of the prophet Zoroaster grew in Persia. This religion emphasized the individual's responsibility to choose between good and evil.

SUGGESTED READING

Brosius, Maria. *The Persians: An Introduction*. 2006. Covers all of Persian history.

Edwards, David N. *The Nubian Past*. 2004. Examines the history of Nubia and the Sudan, using archaeological and written sources.

Gates, Charles. *Ancient Cities: The Archaeology of Urban Life in the Ancient Near East and Egypt, Greece, and Rome*. 2003. Provides a survey of ancient life, including society and culture, that relies primarily on archaeological evidence.

Hawass, Zahi. *Silent Images: Women in Pharaonic Egypt*. 2000. Blends texts and pictures to depict the history of Egyptian women.

Kuhrt, Amelie. *The Ancient Near East*, 2 vols. 1995. Covers the region from the earliest times to Alexander's conquest.

Leick, Gwendolyn. *The Babylonians*. 2002. Introduces all aspects of Babylonian life and culture.

Markoe, Glenn E. *The Phoenicians*. 2000. Presents these seafarers at home and abroad in the Mediterranean.

Niditch, Susan. *Ancient Israelite Religion*. 1997. A brief but broad interpretation of Jewish religious developments.

Redford, Donald B. *Egypt, Canaan, and Israel in Ancient Times*. 1993. A study of the political, cultural, and religious relationships among the peoples of Egypt and the Near East from 3000 B.C.E. to about 500 B.C.E.

Robinson, Andrew. *The Story of Writing: Alphabets, Hieroglyphs, and Pictograms*. 2007. A brief account of the scripts used in the major civilizations of the ancient world and of the major scripts we use today, with many illustrations.

Visicato, Giuseppe. *The Power and the Writing: The Early Scribes of Mesopotamia*. 2000. Studies the practical importance of early Mesopotamian scribes.

Vivante, Bella. *Daughters of Gaia: Women of the Ancient World*. 2008. Explores the political, religious, and economic activities of actual women, and also examines ideas about gender.

NOTES

1. From *The Sumerians: Their History, Culture and Character*, p. 238. Copyright © 1963 by The University of Chicago Press. Used by permission of The University of Chicago Press.
2. J. B. Pritchard, ed., *Ancient Near Eastern Texts*, 3d ed. © 1969 Princeton University Press. Reprinted by permission of Princeton University Press.

For practice quizzes and other study tools, visit the **Online Study Guide** at bedfordstmartins.com/mckayworld.

For primary sources from this period, see *Sources of World Societies*, **Second Edition**.

For Web sites, images, and documents related to topics in this chapter, visit **Make History** at bedfordstmartins.com/mckayworld.

• **Female Spirit from an Indian Stupa** Royal patronage aided the spread of Buddhism in India, especially the patronage of King Ashoka, who sponsored the construction of numerous Buddhist monuments. This head of a female spirit (called a *yakshini*) is from the stupa that Ashoka had built at Bharhut in central India. (India Museum, Calcutta, India/Giraudon/The Bridgeman Art Library)

During the centuries when the peoples of ancient Mesopotamia and Egypt were developing urban civilizations, people in India were wrestling with the same challenges — food production, the building of cities, political administration, and questions about human life and the cosmos. Like the civilizations of the Near East, the earliest Indian civilization centered on a great river, the Indus. From about 2800 to 1800 B.C.E. the Indus Valley, or Harappan (huh-RAH-puhn), culture thrived and expanded over a huge area.

A very different Indian society emerged after the decline of this civilization. It was dominated by the Aryans, warriors who spoke an early version of Sanskrit. The Indian caste system and the Hindu religion, key features of Indian society into modern times, had their origins in early Aryan society. By the middle of the first mil-

The Foundation of Indian Society

to 300 C.E.

lennium B.C.E. the Aryans had set up numerous small kingdoms throughout north India. This was the great age of Indian religious creativity, when Buddhism and Jainism were founded and the early Brahmanic religion of the Aryans developed into Hinduism.

The first major Indian empire, the Mauryan (MAWR-ee-uhn) Dynasty, emerged in the wake of the Greek invasion of north India in 325 B.C.E. This dynasty reached its peak under King Ashoka, who actively promoted Buddhism both within his realm and beyond it. Not long after his reign, however, the empire broke up, and for several centuries India was politically divided. Although India never had a single language and only periodically had a centralized government, cultural elements dating back to the ancient period — the core ideas of Brahmanism, the caste system, and the early epics — spread through trade and other contact, even when the subcontinent was divided into hostile kingdoms. •

The Land and Its First Settlers, ca. 3000–1500 B.C.E.

□ What does archaeology tell us about the Harappan civilization in India?

The subcontinent of India, a landmass as large as western Europe, juts southward into the warm waters of the Indian Ocean. Today this region is divided into the separate countries of Pakistan, Nepal, India, Bangladesh, and Sri Lanka, but these divisions are recent, and for premodern times the entire subcontinent will be called India here.

In India, as elsewhere, the possibilities for both agriculture and communication have always been strongly shaped by geography. Some regions of the subcontinent are among the wettest on earth; others are arid deserts and scrubland. Most areas in India are warm all year, with temperatures over 100°F common. Average temperatures range from 79°F in the north to 85°F in the south. Monsoon rains sweep northward from the Indian Ocean each summer. The lower reaches of the Himalaya Mountains in the northeast are covered by dense forests that are sustained by heavy rainfall. Immediately to the south are the fertile valleys of the Indus and Ganges Rivers. These lowland plains, which stretch all the way across the subcontinent, were tamed for agriculture over time, and India's great empires were centered there. To their west are the deserts of Rajasthan and southeastern Pakistan, historically important in part because their flat terrain enabled invaders to sweep into India from the northwest. South of the great river valleys rise the jungle-clad

Vindhya Mountains and the dry, hilly Deccan Plateau. Only along the coasts of this part of India do the hills give way to narrow plains where crop agriculture flourished. India's long coastlines and predictable winds fostered maritime trade with other countries bordering the Indian Ocean.

Neolithic settlement of the Indian subcontinent occurred somewhat later than in the Near East, but agriculture followed a similar pattern of development and was well established by about 7000 B.C.E. Wheat and barley were the early crops, probably having spread in their domesticated form from the Middle East. Farmers also domesticated cattle, sheep, and goats and learned to make pottery.

The story of the first civilization in India is one of the most dramatic in the ancient world. From the Bible, people had known about ancient Egypt and Sumeria for centuries, but not until 1921 did anyone in Europe know that there was an ancient civilization in the Indus Valley. That was when archaeologists found astonishing evidence of a thriving and sophisticated Bronze Age urban culture dating to about 2500 B.C.E. at Mohenjo-daro in what is now Pakistan.

This civilization is known today as the Indus Valley or the **Harappan** civilization, from the modern names of the river and city near where the first ruins were discovered. Archaeologists have discovered some three hundred Harappan cities and many more towns and villages in both Pakistan and India, making it possible to see both the vast regional extent of the Harappan civilization and its evolution over a period of nearly a millennium (Map 3.1). It was a literate civilization, like those of Egypt and Mesopotamia, but no one has been able to decipher the more than four hundred symbols inscribed on stone seals and copper tablets. It is even possible that these symbols are not words but rather names or even nonlinguistic symbols. The civilization's most flourishing period was from 2500 to 2000 B.C.E.

• **Harappan** The first Indian civilization; also known as the Indus Valley civilization.

◻ CHRONOLOGY

2800–1800 B.C.E. Height of Harappan civilization

ca. 1500–500 B.C.E. Vedic Age; flourishing of Aryan civilization; *Rigveda*

ca. 1000 B.C.E. Introduction of iron

750–500 B.C.E. *Upanishads*

ca. 513 B.C.E. Persians conquer the Indus Valley and Kashmir

ca. 500 B.C.E. Founding of Buddhism and Jainism

ca. 400 B.C.E.–200 C.E. Gradual evolution of the Brahman religion into Hinduism

326 B.C.E. Alexander the Great enters Indus Valley

ca. 322–185 B.C.E. Mauryan Empire

ca. 300 B.C.E. Jain religion splits into two sects

ca. 269–232 B.C.E. Reign of Ashoka

ca. 200 B.C.E.–200 C.E. Classical period of Tamil culture

ca. 100 C.E. More inclusive Mahayana form of Buddhism emerges

ca. 200 C.E. Code of Manu

Harappan Artifacts Small objects like seals and jewelry found at Harappan sites provide glimpses of early Indian religious imagination and daily life. The molded tablet shown above depicts a female deity standing above an elephant battling two tigers. The jewelry found at these sites, such as the pieces shown on the right, makes much use of gold and precious stones. (both photos: J. M. Kenoyer/Harappa.com. Courtesy Department of Archaeology and Museums, Government of Pakistan)

The Harappan civilization extended over nearly five hundred thousand square miles in the Indus Valley, making it more than twice as large as ancient Egypt or Sumeria. Yet Harappan civilization was marked by a striking uniformity. Throughout the region, for instance, even in small villages, bricks were made to the same standard proportion (4:2:1). Figurines of pregnant women have been found throughout the area, suggesting common religious ideas and practices.

Like Mesopotamian cities, Harappan cities were centers for crafts and trade and were surrounded by extensive farmland. Craftsmen produced ceramics decorated with geometric designs. The Harappans were the earliest known manufacturers of cotton

MAP 3.1 Harappan Civilization, ca. 2500 B.C.E. The earliest civilization in India developed in the Indus River Valley in the west of the subcontinent.

cloth, and this cloth was so abundant that goods were wrapped in it for shipment. Trade was extensive. As early as the reign of Sargon of Akkad in the third millennium B.C.E. (see page 42), trade between India and Mesopotamia carried goods and ideas between the two cultures, probably by way of the Persian Gulf. The Harappan port of Lothal had a stone dock 700 feet long, next to which were massive granaries and bead-making factories. Hundreds of seals were found there, some of Persian Gulf origin, indicating that Lothal was a major port of exit and entry.

The cities of Mohenjo-daro in southern Pakistan, and Harappa, some 400 miles to the north, were huge for this period, more than 3 miles in circumference, with populations estimated at 35,000 to 40,000. Both were defended by great citadels that towered 40 to 50 feet above the surrounding plain. The cities had obviously been planned and built before being settled; they were not the outcomes of villages that grew and sprawled haphazardly. Large granaries stored food. Streets were straight and varied from 9 to 34 feet in width. The houses were substantial, many two stories tall, some perhaps three. The focal point of a house was a central courtyard onto which the rooms opened,

much like many houses today in both rural and urban India.

Perhaps the most surprising aspect of the elaborate planning of these cities was their complex system of drainage, which is well preserved at Mohenjo-daro. Each house had a bathroom with a drain connected to brick-lined sewers located under the major streets. Openings allowed the refuse to be collected, probably to be used as fertilizer on nearby fields. No other ancient city had such an advanced sanitation system.

Both cities also contained numerous large structures, which archaeologists think were public buildings. One of the most important was the large ventilated storehouse for the community's grain. Mohenjo-daro also had a marketplace or place of assembly, a palace, and a huge pool some 39 feet long by 23 feet wide by 8 feet deep. Like the later Roman baths, it had spacious dressing rooms for the bathers. Because the Great Bath at Mohenjo-daro resembles the ritual purification pools of later India, some scholars have speculated that power was in the hands of a priest-king and that the Great Bath played a role in the religious rituals of the city. In contrast to ancient Egypt and Mesopotamia, no great tombs have been discovered in Harappa, making it more difficult to envision the life of the elite.

The prosperity of the Indus civilization depended on constant and intensive cultivation of the rich river valley. Although rainfall seems to have been greater then than in recent times, the Indus, like the Nile, flowed through a relatively dry region made fertile by annual floods and irrigation. And as in Egypt, agriculture was aided by a long, hot growing season and near constant sunshine.

Because the written language of the Harappan people has not been deciphered, their political, intellectual, and religious life is largely unknown. There clearly was a political structure with the authority to organize city planning and facilitate trade, but we do not even know whether there were hereditary kings. There are clear connections between Harappan and Sumerian civilization, but just as clear differences. For instance, the Harappan script, like the Sumerian, was incised on clay tablets and seals, but it has no connection to Sumerian cuneiform, and the artistic style of the Harappan seals also is distinct.

Soon after 2000 B.C.E. the Harappan civilization mysteriously declined. The port of Lothal was abandoned by about 1900 B.C.E., and other major centers came to house only a fraction of their earlier populations. Scholars have offered many explanations for the mystery of the abandonment of these cities. The decline cannot be attributed to the arrival of powerful invaders, as was once thought. Rather it was internally generated. Environmental theories include an earthquake that led to a shift in the course of the river, or a

• **Aryans** The dominant people in north India after the decline of the Indus Valley civilization; they spoke an early form of Sanskrit.

Mohenjo-daro Mohenjo-daro was a planned city built of fired mud brick. Its streets were straight, and covered drainpipes were installed to carry away waste. From sites like this, we know that the early Indian political elite had the power and technical expertise to organize large, coordinated building projects. Found in Mohenjo-daro, this small ceramic figurine (left) shows a woman adorned with six necklaces. (site: J. M. Kenoyer/Harrapan.com. Courtesy, Department of Archaeology and Museums, Government of Pakistan; figurine: Angelo Hornak/Alamy)

severe drought. Perhaps the long-term practice of irrigation led to the buildup of salt and alkaline in the soil until they reached levels toxic to plants, forcing the Harappan people to move in search of arable land. Some scholars speculate that long-distance commerce collapsed, leading to an economic depression. Others theorize that the population fell prey to diseases, such as malaria, that caused people to flee the cities.

Even though the Harappan people apparently lived on after scattering to villages, the large urban centers were abandoned, and key features of their high culture were lost. For the next thousand years, India had no large cities, no kiln-fired bricks, and no written language. There are, however, many signs of continuity with later Indian civilization, ranging from the sorts of pottery ovens used to some of the images of gods. Some scholars think that the people of Harappa were the ancestors of the Tamils and other Dravidian-speaking peoples of modern south India.

The Aryans During the Vedic Age, ca. 1500–500 B.C.E.

☐ What kind of society and culture did the Indo-European Aryans create?

After the decline of the Harappan civilization, a people who called themselves **Aryans** became dominant in north India. They were speakers of an early form of Sanskrit, an Indo-European language closely related to ancient Persian and more distantly related to Latin, Greek, Celtic, and their modern descendants, such as English. For example, the Sanskrit *nava*, "ship," is related to the English word *naval*; *deva*, "god," to *divine*; and *raja*, "ruler," to *regal*. The word *Aryan* itself comes from *Arya*, "noble" or "pure" in Sanskrit, and has the same linguistic root as *Iran* and *Ireland*. The Aryans flourished during the Vedic Age (ca. 1500–500 B.C.E.).

Named for the Vedas, a large and significant body of ancient sacred works written in Sanskrit, this period witnessed the Indo-Aryan development of the caste system and Brahman religion and the writing of the great epics that represent the earliest form of Indian literature.

Aryan Dominance in North India

Until relatively recently, the dominant theory was that the Aryans came into India from outside, perhaps as part of the same movements of people that led to the Hittites occupying parts of Anatolia, the Achaeans entering Greece, and the Kassites conquering Sumer—all in the period from about 1900 to 1750 B.C.E. Some scholars, however, have proposed that the Indo-European languages spread to this area much earlier; to them it seems possible that the Harappan people were speakers of an early Indo-European language. If that was the case, the Aryans would be one of the groups descended from this early population.

Modern politics complicates analysis of the appearance of the Aryans and their role in India's history. Europeans in the eighteenth and nineteenth centuries developed the concept of Indo-European languages, and they did so in an age both highly conscious of race and in the habit of identifying races with languages. The racist potential of the concept was exploited by the Nazis, who glorified the Aryans as a superior race. Even in less politicized contexts, the notion of a group of people who entered India from outside and made themselves its rulers is troubling to many. Does it mean that the non-Aryans are the true Indians? Does it add legitimacy to those who in later times conquered India from outside? Does it justify or undermine the caste system? One of the difficulties faced by scholars who wish to take a dispassionate view of these issues is that the evidence for the earlier Harappan culture is entirely archaeological, while the evidence for the Aryans is almost entirely based on linguistic analysis of modern languages and orally transmitted texts of uncertain date.

The central source of information on the early Aryans is the ***Rigveda***, the earliest of the Vedas, an originally oral collection of hymns, ritual texts, and philosophical treatises composed in Sanskrit between 1500 and 500 B.C.E. Like Homer's epics in Greece, written in this same period, these texts were transmitted orally and are in verse. The *Rigveda* portrays the Aryans as warrior tribes who glorified military skill and heroism; loved to drink, hunt, race, and dance; and counted their wealth in cattle. The Aryans did not sweep across India in a quick campaign, nor were they a disciplined army led by one conqueror. Rather they were a collection of tribes that frequently fought with each other and only over the course of several centuries came to dominate north India.

The key to the Aryans' success probably lay in their superior military technology. Those they fought often lived in fortified towns and put up a strong defense against them, but Aryan warriors had superior technology, including two-wheeled chariots, horses, and bronze swords and spears. Their epics present the struggle for north India in religious terms, describing their chiefs as godlike heroes and their opponents as irreligious savages who did not perform the proper sacrifices. In time, however, the Aryans clearly absorbed much from those they conquered, such as agricultural techniques and foods.

At the head of each Aryan tribe was a chief, or raja (RAH-juh), who led his followers in battle and ruled them in peacetime. The warriors in the tribe elected the chief for his military skills. Next in importance to the chief was the priest. In time, priests evolved into a distinct class possessing precise knowledge of the complex rituals and of the invocations and formulas that accompanied them, rather like the priest classes in ancient Egypt, Mesopotamia, and Persia. Below them in the pecking order was a warrior nobility who rode into battle in chariots and perhaps on horseback. The warrior class met at assemblies to reach decisions and advise the raja. The common tribesmen tended herds and worked the land. To the conquered non-Aryans fell the drudgery of menial tasks. It is difficult to define precisely their social status. Though probably not slaves, they were certainly subordinate to the Aryans and worked for them in return for protection.

Possible Indo-European homeland

→ **Spread of Indo-European speakers**

☐ **Extent of Indo-European speakers**

☐ **Aryan settlement, ca. 900 B.C.E.**

Indo-European Migrations and the Vedic Age

- ***Rigveda*** The earliest collection of Indian hymns, ritual texts, and philosophical treatises, it is the central source of information on early Aryans.

- **Brahmins** Priests of the Aryans; they supported the growth of royal power in return for royal confirmation of their own religious rights, power, and status.

- **caste system** The Indian system of dividing society into hereditary groups whose members interacted primarily within the group, and especially married within the group.

Bronze Sword This bronze sword, with a rib in the middle of the blade for strength, is a striking example of the quality of Aryan arms. Superior weapons gave the Aryans military advantage. (Courtesy of the Trustees of the British Museum)

Over the course of several centuries, the Aryans pushed farther east into the valley of the Ganges River, at that time a land of thick jungle populated by aboriginal forest peoples. The tremendous challenge of clearing the jungle was made somewhat easier by the introduction of iron around 1000 B.C.E., probably by diffusion from Mesopotamia. (See "Global Trade: Iron," page 54.) Iron made it possible to produce strong axes and knives relatively cheaply.

The Aryans did not gain dominance over the entire Indian subcontinent. South of the Vindhya range, people speaking Dravidian languages maintained their control. In the great Aryan epics the *Ramayana* and *Mahabharata*, the people of the south and Sri Lanka are spoken of as dark-skinned savages and demons who resisted the Aryans' conquests. Along with the *Rigveda*, these epics would become part of the common cultural heritage of all of India.

As Aryan rulers came to dominate large settled populations, the style of political organization changed from tribal chieftainship to territorial kingship. In other words, the ruler now controlled an area with people living in permanent settlements, not a nomadic tribe that moved as a group. Moreover, kings no longer needed to be elected by the tribe; it was enough to be invested by priests and to perform the splendid royal ceremonies they designed. The priests, or **Brahmins**, supported the growth of royal power in return for royal confirmation of their own power and status. The Brahmins also served as advisers to the kings. In the face of this royal-priestly alliance, the old tribal assemblies of warriors withered away. By the time Persian armies reached the Indus around 513 B.C.E., there were sixteen major Aryan kingdoms in north India.

Life in Early India

Caste was central to the social life of these north Indian kingdoms. Early Aryan society had distinguished among the warrior elite, the priests, ordinary tribesmen, and conquered subjects. These distinctions gradually evolved into the **caste system**, which divided society into strictly defined hereditary groups. Society was conceived of as four hierarchical strata whose members did not eat with or marry each other. These strata, or varna, were Brahmin (priests), Kshatriya (warriors and officials), Vaishya (merchants), and Shudra (peasants and laborers). The Shudra stratum, which encompassed most of the conquered people, was the largest. By contrast, the three upper varnas probably accounted for no more than 30 percent of the population. The caste system thus allowed the numerically outnumbered Aryans to maintain dominance over their subjects and not be culturally absorbed by them.

Social and religious attitudes supported the caste system. Aryans considered the work of artisans impure. They left all such work to the local people, who were probably superior to them in these arts anyway. Trade, by contrast, was not viewed as demeaning. Brahmanic texts of the period refer to trade as equal in value to farming, serving the king, or being a priest.

In the *Rigveda*, the caste system is attributed to the gods:

> When they divided [the primeval man], into how
> many different portions did they arrange him?
> What became of his mouth, what of his two arms?
> What were his two thighs and his two feet called?
> His mouth became the brahman, his two arms was
> made into the [kshatriya]; his two thighs became
> the vaishyas, of his two feet the shudra was born.[1]

As priests the Brahmins were expected to memorize every syllable and tone of the Vedas so that their rituals would please the gods. Not only did they conduct the traditional ceremonies, but they also developed new ones for new circumstances. As agriculture became more important to the Aryans, for example, Brahmins acted as agents of Agni, the god of fire, to purify the land for crops. The Brahmins also knew the formulas and spells that were effective against diseases and calamities.

Those without places in the four varna—that is, newly conquered peoples and those who had lost their caste status through violations of ritual—were outcastes. That simply meant that they belonged to no caste. In time, some of them became "untouchables" because they were "impure." They were scorned because they earned their living by performing such "polluting" jobs as slaughtering animals and dressing skins.

Slavery was a feature of early social life in India, as it was in Egypt, Mesopotamia, and elsewhere in antiquity. People captured in battle often became slaves, but captives could also be ransomed by their families. Later, slavery was less connected with warfare and became

Listening to the Past

Conversations Between Rama and Sita from the *Ramayana*

The Ramayana, *an epic poem of about fifty thousand verses, is attributed to the third-century* B.C.E. *poet Valmiki. Its main character, Rama, the oldest son of a king, is an incarnation of the great god Vishnu. As a young man, he wins the princess Sita as his wife when he alone among her suitors proves strong enough to bend a huge bow. Rama and Sita love each other deeply, but court intrigue disturbs their happy life. After the king announces that he will retire and consecrate Rama as his heir, the king's beautiful junior wife, wishing to advance her own son, reminds the king that he has promised her a favor of her choice. She then asks to have him appoint her son heir and to have Rama sent into the wilderness for fourteen years. The king is forced to consent, and Rama obeys his father.*

The passage below gives the conversations between Rama and Sita after Rama learns he must leave. In subsequent parts of the very long epic, the lovers undergo many other tribulations, including Sita's abduction by the lord of the demons, the ten-headed Ravana, and her eventual recovery by Rama with the aid of monkeys.

The Ramayana *eventually appeared in numerous versions in all the major languages of India. Hearing it recited was said to bring religious merit. Sita, passionate in her devotion to her husband, has remained the favorite Indian heroine. Rama, Sita, and the monkey Hanuman are cult figures in Hinduism, with temples devoted to their worship.*

66 "For fourteen years I must live in Dandaka, while my father will appoint Bharata prince regent. I have come to see you before I leave for the desolate forest. You are never to boast of me in the presence of Bharata. Men in power cannot bear to hear others praised, and so you must never boast of my virtues in front of Bharata. . . . When I have gone to the forest where sages make their home, my precious, blameless wife, you must earnestly undertake vows and fasts. You must rise early and worship the gods according to custom and then pay homage to my father Dasaratha, lord of men. And my aged mother Kausalya, who is tormented by misery, deserves your respect as well, for she has subordinated all to righteousness. The rest of my mothers, too, must always receive your homage. . . . My beloved, I am going to the great forest, and you must stay here. You must do as I tell you, my lovely, and not give offense to anyone."

So Rama spoke, and Sita, who always spoke kindly to her husband and deserved kindness from him, grew angry just because she loved him, and said, "My lord, a man's father, his mother, brother, son, or daughter-in-law all experience the effects of their own past deeds and suffer an individual fate. But a wife, and she alone, bull among men, must share her husband's fate. Therefore I, too, have been ordered to live in the forest. It is not her father or mother, not her son or friends or herself, but her husband, and he alone, who gives a woman permanent refuge in this world and after death. If you must leave this very day for the trackless forest, Rama, I will go in front of you, softening the thorns and sharp *kusa* grass. Cast out your anger and resentment, like so much water left after drinking one's fill. Do not be reluctant to take me, my mighty husband. There is no evil in me. The shadow of a husband's feet in any circumstances surpasses the finest mansions, an aerial chariot, or even flying through the sky. . . . O Rama, bestower of honor, you have the power to protect any other person in the forest. Why then not me? . . .

"If I were to be offered a place to live in heaven itself, Rama, tiger among men, I would refuse it if you were not there. I will go to the trackless forest teeming with deer, monkeys, and elephants, and live there as in my father's house, clinging to your feet alone, in strict self-discipline. I love no one else; my heart is so attached to you that were we to be parted I am resolved to die. Take me, oh please grant my request. I shall not be a burden to you." . . .

---

more of an economic and social institution. As in ancient Mesopotamia, a free man might sell himself and his family into slavery because he could not pay his debts. And, as in Hammurabi's Mesopotamia, he could, if clever, hard-working, or fortunate, buy his and his family's way out of slavery. At birth, slave children automatically became the slaves of their parents' masters. Indian slaves could be bought, used as collateral, or given away.

Women's lives in early India varied according to their social status, much as men's did. Like most nomadic tribes, the Aryans were patrilineal and patriarchal (tracing descent through males and placing power in the senior men of the family). Thus the roles of women in Aryan society probably were more subordinate than were the roles of women in local Dravidian groups, many of which were matrilineal (tracing descent through females). But even in Aryan society women were treated somewhat more favorably than in later Indian society. They were not yet given in child-marriage, and widows had the right to remarry. In epics such as the *Ramayana*, women are often portrayed

When Sita finished speaking, the righteous prince, who knew what was right and cherished it, attempted to dissuade her. . . .

"Sita, give up this notion of living in the forest. The name 'forest' is given only to wild regions where hardships abound. . . . There are lions that live in mountain caves; their roars are redoubled by mountain torrents and are a painful thing to hear—the forest is a place of pain. At night worn with fatigue, one must sleep upon the ground on a bed of leaves, broken off of themselves—the forest is a place of utter pain. And one has to fast, Sita, to the limit of one's endurance, wear clothes of barkcloth and bear the burden of matted hair. . . . There are many creeping creatures, of every size and shape, my lovely, ranging aggressively over the ground. . . . Moths, scorpions, worms, gnats, and flies continually harass one, my frail Sita—the forest is wholly a place of pain. . . ."

Sita was overcome with sorrow when she heard what Rama said. With tears trickling down her face, she answered him in a faint voice. . . . "If from feelings of love I follow you, my pure-hearted husband, I shall have no sin to answer for, because my husband is my deity. My union with you is sacred and shall last even beyond death. . . . If you refuse to take me to the forest despite the sorrow that I feel, I shall have no recourse but to end my life by poison, fire, or water."

Though she pleaded with him in this and every other way to be allowed to go, great-armed Rama would not consent to taking her to the desolate forest. And when he told her as much, Sita fell to brooding, and drenched the ground, it seemed, with the hot tears that fell from her eyes. . . . She was nearly insensible with sorrow when Rama took her in his arms and comforted her. . . . "Without knowing your true feelings, my lovely, I could not consent to your living in the wilderness, though I am perfectly capable of protecting you. Since you are determined to live with me in the forest, Sita, I could no sooner abandon you than a self-respecting man his reputation. . . . My father keeps to the path of righteousness and truth, and I wish to act just as he instructs me. That is the eternal way of righteousness. Follow me, my timid one, be my companion in righteousness. Go now and bestow precious objects on the brahmins, give food to the mendicants and all who ask for it. Hurry, there is no time to waste."

Finding that her husband had acquiesced in her going, the lady was elated and set out at once to make the donations. "

Source: *The Ramayana of Valmiki: An Epic of India*, vol. 2: *Ayodhyakanda*, trans. Sheldon I. Pollock, ed. Robert P. Goldman (Princeton, N.J.: Princeton University Press, 1986), pp. 134–142, modified slightly. Reprinted by permission of Princeton University Press.

● **Rama and Sita in the forest, from a set of miniature paintings done in about 1600.** (National Museum, New Delhi)

QUESTIONS FOR ANALYSIS

1. What can you infer about early Indian family life and social relations from this story?
2. What do Sita's words and actions indicate about women's roles in Indian society of the time?
3. What do you think accounts for the continuing popularity of the story of Rama throughout Indian history?

---

as forceful personalities, able to achieve their goals both by using feminine ploys to cajole men and also by direct action. (See "Listening to the Past: Conversations Between Rama and Sita from the *Ramayana*," above.)

Brahmanism

The Aryans' religious beliefs recognized a multitude of gods. These gods shared some features with the gods of other early Indo-European societies such as the Per- sians and Greeks. Some of them were great brawling figures, such as Agni, the god of fire and, as in ancient Persia, a particularly important god; Indra, wielder of the thunderbolt and god of war, who each year slew a dragon to release the monsoon rains; and Rudra, the divine archer who spread disaster and disease by firing his arrows at people. Others were shadowy figures, such as Dyaus, the father of the gods, related to the Greek Zeus. Varuna, the god of order in the universe, was a hard god, quick to punish those who sinned and thus upset the balance of nature. Ushas, the goddess of dawn, was a gentle deity who welcomed the birds, gave delight to human beings, and warded off evil spirits.

Ordinary people dealt with these gods through priests who made animal sacrifices to them. By giving valued things to the gods, people strengthened both the power of the gods and their own relationships with them. Gradually, under the priestly monopoly of the Brahmins, correct sacrifice and proper ritual became so important that most Brahmins believed that a properly performed ritual would force a god to grant a worshipper's wish. Ordinary people could watch a ceremony, such as a fire ritual, which was often held outdoors, but could not perform the key steps in the ritual.

The *Upanishads* (oo-PAH-nih-shadz), composed between 750 and 500 B.C.E., record speculations about the mystical meaning of sacrificial rites and about cosmological questions of man's relationship to the universe. They document a gradual shift from the mythical worldview of the early Vedic age to a deeply philosophical one. Associated with this shift was a movement toward asceticism (uh-SEH-tuh-siz-uhm) — severe self-discipline and self-denial. In search of wisdom, some men (but not women) retreated to the forests. These ascetics concluded that disciplined meditation on the ritual sacrifice could produce the same results as the physical ritual itself. Thus they reinterpreted ritual sacrifices as symbolic gestures with mystical meanings.

Ancient Indian cosmology (theories of the universe) focused not on a creator who made the universe out of nothing, but rather on endlessly repeating cycles. Key ideas were **samsara**, the reincarnation of souls by a continual process of rebirth, and **karma**, the tally of good and bad deeds that determined the status of an individual's next life. Good deeds led to better future lives, evil deeds to worse future lives — even to reincarnation as an animal. Thus gradually arose the concept of a wheel of life that included human beings, animals, and gods. Reward and punishment worked automatically; there was no all-knowing god who judged people and could be petitioned to forgive a sin, and each individual was responsible for his or her own destiny in a just and impartial world.

To most people, especially those on the low end of the economic and social scale, these ideas were attractive. By living righteously and doing good deeds, people could improve their lot in the next life. Yet there was another side to these ideas: the wheel of life could be seen as a treadmill, giving rise to a yearning for release from the relentless cycle of birth and death. One solution offered in the *Upanishads* was moksha, or release from the wheel of life. Brahmanic mystics claimed that life in the world was actually an illusion and that the only way to escape the wheel of life was to realize that ultimate reality was unchanging.

The unchanging ultimate reality was called **brahman**. This important concept has been translated many ways. Scholars have offered both brief phrases — "the cosmic principle," "the principle of religious reality," "absolute reality," "eternal truth," and "universal soul" — and somewhat longer descriptions: "holy or sacred power that is the source and sustainer of the universe," "the ultimate unchanging reality, composed of pure being and consciousness," and "eternal, unchanging, infinite, and transcendent reality that is the divine ground of everything in this universe." Here *brahman* is defined simply as "ultimate reality."

Brahman was contrasted to the multitude of fleeting phenomena that people consider important in their daily lives. The individual soul or self was ultimately the same substance as the universal brahman, in the same way that each spark is in substance the same as a large fire.

The *Upanishads* gave the Brahmins a high status to which the poor and lowly could aspire in a future life. Consequently, the Brahmins greeted the concepts presented in these works and those who taught them with tolerance and understanding and made a place for them in traditional religious practice. The rulers of Indian society also encouraged the new trends, since the doctrines of samsara and karma encouraged the poor and oppressed to labor peacefully and dutifully. In other words, although the new doctrines were intellectually revolutionary, in social and political terms they supported the existing power structure.

India's Great Religions

☐ What ideas and practices were taught by the founders of Jainism, Buddhism, and Hinduism?

By the sixth and fifth centuries B.C.E., cities had reappeared in India, and merchants and trade were thriving. Bricks were again baked in kilns and used to build ramparts around cities. One particular kingdom, Magadha, had become much more powerful than any of the other states in the Ganges plain, defeating its enemies by using war elephants and catapults for hurling stones. Written language had reappeared.

This was a period of intellectual ferment throughout Eurasia — the period of the early Greek philosophers, the Hebrew prophets, Zoroaster in Persia, and Confucius and the early Daoists in China. In India it

---

• **samsara** The transmigration of souls by a continual process of rebirth.

• **karma** The tally of good and bad deeds that determines the status of an individual's next life.

• **brahman** The unchanging ultimate reality, according to the *Upanishads*.

led to numerous sects that rejected various elements of Brahmanic teachings. (See "Individuals in Society: Gosala," page 76.) The two most influential were Jainism and Buddhism. Their founders were contemporaries living in east India in minor states of the Ganges plain. Hinduism emerged in response to these new religions but at the same time was the most direct descendant of the old Brahmanic religion.

Jainism

The key figure of Jainism, Vardhamana Mahavira (fl. ca. 520 B.C.E.), was the son of the chief of a small state and a member of the warrior class. Like many ascetics of the period, he left home to become a wandering holy man. For twelve years, from ages thirty to forty-two, he traveled through the Ganges Valley until he found enlightenment and became a "completed soul." Mahavira taught his doctrines for about thirty years, founding a disciplined order of monks and gaining the support of many lay followers, male and female.

Mahavira accepted the Brahman doctrines of karma and rebirth but developed these ideas in new directions, founding a new religion referred to as Jainism. He argued that human beings, animals, plants, and even inanimate objects all have living souls enmeshed in matter, accumulated through the workings of karma. Even a rock has a soul locked inside it, enchained by matter but capable of suffering if someone kicks it. The souls conceived by the Jains have finite dimensions. They float or sink depending on the amount of matter with which they are enmeshed. The ascetic, who willingly undertakes suffering, can dissipate some of the accumulated karma and make progress toward liberation. If a soul at last escapes from all the matter weighing it down, it becomes lighter than ordinary objects and floats to the top of the universe, where it remains forever in inactive bliss.

Mahavira's followers pursued such liberation by living ascetic lives and avoiding evil thoughts and actions. The Jains considered all life sacred and tried to live without destroying other life. Some early Jains went to the extreme of starving themselves to death, since it is impossible to eat without destroying at least plants, but most took the less extreme step of distinguishing between different levels of life. The most sacred lifeforms were human beings, followed by animals, plants, and inanimate objects. A Jain who wished to avoid vio-

Jain Ascetic The most extreme Jain ascetics not only endured the elements without the help of clothes, but they were also generally indifferent to bodily comfort. The Jain saint depicted in this eighth-century cave temple has maintained his posture for so long that vines have grown up around him. (Courtesy, Robert Fisher)

lence to life became a vegetarian and took pains not to kill any creature, even tiny insects in the air and soil. Farming was impossible for Jains, who tended instead to take up trade. Among the most conservative Jains, priests practiced nudity, for clinging to clothes, even a loincloth, was a form of attachment. Lay Jains could pursue Jain teachings by practicing nonviolence and not eating meat. The Jains' radical nonviolence was motivated by a desire to escape the karmic consequences of causing harm to a life. In other words, violence had to be avoided above all because it harms the person who commits it.

For the first century after Mahavira's death, the Jains were a comparatively small and unimportant sect. Jainism began to flourish under the Mauryan Dynasty (ca. 322–185 B.C.E.; see pages 82–84), and Jain tradition claims the Mauryan Empire's founder, Chandragupta, as a major patron. About 300 B.C.E. the Jain scriptures were recorded, and the religion split into two sects, one maintaining the tradition of total nudity, the other choosing to wear white robes on the grounds that clothes were an insignificant external sign, unrelated to true liberation. Over the next few centuries Jain monks were particularly important in spreading northern culture into the Deccan and Tamil regions of south India.

Individuals in Society

Gosala

TEXTS THAT SURVIVE FROM EARLY INDIA ARE rich in religious and philosophical speculation and in tales of gods and heroes, but not in history of the sort written by the early Chinese and Greeks. Because Indian writers and thinkers of antiquity had little interest in recording the actions of rulers or accounting for the rise and decline of different states, few people's lives are known in any detail.

Religious literature, however, does sometimes include details of the lives of followers and adversaries. The life of Gosala, for instance, is known primarily from early Buddhist and Jain scriptures. He was a contemporary of both Mahavira, the founder of the Jains, and Gautama, the Buddha, and both of them saw him as one of their most pernicious rivals.

According to the Jain account, Gosala was born in the north Indian kingdom of Magadha, the son of a professional beggar. The name Gosala, which means "cowshed," alluded to the fact that he was born in a cowshed where his parents had taken refuge during the rainy season. The Buddhist account adds that he became a naked wandering ascetic when he fled from his enraged master after breaking an oil jar. As a mendicant he soon fell in with Mahavira, who had recently commenced his life as an ascetic. After accompanying Mahavira on his travels for at least six years, Gosala came to feel that he was spiritually more advanced than his master and left to undertake the practice of austerities on his own. According to the Jain account, after he gained magical powers, he challenged his master and gathered his own disciples.

Both Jain and Buddhist sources agree that Gosala taught a form of fatalism that they saw as dangerously wrong. A Buddhist source says that he taught that people are good or bad not because of their own efforts but because of fate. "Just as a ball of string when it is cast forth will spread out just as far and no farther than it can unwind so both fools and wise alike wandering in transmigration exactly for the allotted term shall then and only then make an end of pain."* Some people reach perfection not by their own efforts, but rather through the course of numerous rebirths over hundreds of thousands of years until they rid themselves of bad karma.

The Jains claimed that Gosala violated the celibacy expected of ascetics by living with a potter woman and, moreover, that he taught that sexual relations were not sinful. The followers of Gosala, a Buddhist source stated, wore no clothing and were particular about the food they accepted, refusing food specially prepared for them, food in a cooking pan, and food from couples or women with children. Like other ascetics, Gosala's followers owned no property, carrying the principle further than the Jains, who allowed the possession of a food bowl. They made a bowl from the palms of their hands, giving them the name "hand lickers."

Jain sources report that after sixteen years of separation, Mahavira happened to come to the town where Gosala lived. When Gosala heard that Mahavira spoke contemptuously of him, he and his followers went to Mahavira's lodgings, and the two sides came to blows. Soon thereafter, Gosala became unhinged, gave up all ascetic restraint, and, after six months of singing, dancing, drinking, and other riotous living, died, though not before telling his disciples, the Jains report, that Mahavira was right. Doubt is cast on this version of his end by the fact that for centuries to come, Gosala's followers, called the Ajivikas, were an important sect in several parts of India. The Mauryan ruler Ashoka honored them among other sects and dedicated some caves to them.

QUESTIONS FOR ANALYSIS

1. How would Gosala's own followers have described his life? What sorts of distortions are likely in a life known primarily from the writings of rivals?
2. How would the early Indian economy have been affected by the presence of ascetic beggars?

*A. F. R. Hoernle, "Ajivikas," in *Encyclopedia of Religion and Ethics*, vol. 1, ed. James Hastings (Edinburgh: T. & T. Clark, 1908), p. 262.

For several years before setting off on his own, Gosala followed Mahavira, depicted here at a Jain cave temple. (Dinodia Picture Agency)

Although Jainism never took hold as widely as Hinduism and Buddhism (discussed below), it has been an influential strand in Indian thought and has several million adherents in India today. Fasting and nonviolence as spiritual practices in India owe much to Jain teachings. In the twentieth century Mohandas Gandhi, leader of the Indian independence movement, was influenced by these ideas through his mother, and the American civil rights leader Dr. Martin Luther King, Jr., was influenced by Gandhi.

Siddhartha Gautama and Buddhism

Siddhartha Gautama (fl. ca. 500 B.C.E.), also called Shakyamuni ("sage of the Shakya tribe"), is best known as the Buddha ("enlightened one"). He was a contemporary of Mahavira and came from the same warrior social class. He was born the son of a chief of one of the tribes in the Himalayan foothills in what is now Nepal. At age twenty-nine, unsatisfied with his life of comfort and troubled by the suffering he saw around him, he left home to become a wandering ascetic. He traveled south to the kingdom of Magadha, where he studied with yoga masters, but later took up extreme asceticism. According to tradition, while meditating under a bo tree at Bodh Gaya, he reached enlightenment — that is, perfect insight into the processes of the universe. After several weeks of meditation, he preached his first sermon, urging a "middle way" between asceticism and worldly life. For the next forty-five years, the Buddha traveled through the Ganges Valley, propounding his ideas, refuting his adversaries, and attracting followers. To reach as wide an audience as possible, the Buddha preached in the local language, Magadhi, rather than in Sanskrit, which was already becoming a priestly language. Probably because he refused to recognize the divine authority of the Vedas and dismissed sacrifices, he attracted followers mostly from among merchants, artisans, and farmers, rather than Brahmins.

In his first sermon the Buddha outlined his main message, summed up in the **Four Noble Truths** and the **Eightfold Path**. The Four Noble Truths are as follows: (1) pain and suffering, frustration, and anxiety are ugly but inescapable parts of human life; (2) suffering and anxiety are caused by human desires and attachments; (3) people can understand these weaknesses and triumph over them; and (4) this triumph is made possible by following a simple code of conduct, the Eightfold Path. The basic insight of Buddhism is thus psychological. The deepest human longings can never be satisfied, and even those things that seem to give pleasure cause anxiety because we are afraid of losing them. Attachment to people and things causes sorrow at their loss.

The Buddha offered an optimistic message in that all people can set out on the Eightfold Path toward liberation. All they have to do is take a series of steps, beginning with recognizing the universality of suffering ("right knowledge"), deciding to free themselves from it ("right purpose"), and then choosing "right conduct" (including abstaining from taking life), "right speech," "right livelihood," and "right endeavor." The seventh step is "right awareness," constant contemplation of one's deeds and words, giving full thought to their importance and whether they lead to enlightenment. "Right contemplation," the last step, entails deep meditation on the impermanence of everything in the world. Those who achieve liberation are freed from the cycle of birth and death and enter the state called **nirvana**, a kind of blissful nothingness and freedom from reincarnation.

Although he accepted the Indian idea of reincarnation, the Buddha argued against belief in the integrity of the individual self or soul. He saw human beings as a collection of parts, physical and mental. As long as the parts remain combined, that combination can be called "I." When that combination changes, as at death, the various parts remain in existence, ready to become the building blocks of different combinations. According to Buddhist teaching, life is passed from person to person as a flame is passed from candle to candle.

Buddhism differed from Brahmanism and later Hinduism in that it ignored the caste system. Everyone, noble and peasant, educated and ignorant, male and female, could follow the Eightfold Path. Moreover, the Buddha was extraordinarily undogmatic. Convinced that each person must achieve enlightenment on his or her own, he emphasized that the path was important only because it led the traveler to enlightenment, not for its own sake. He compared it to a raft, essential to cross a river but useless once the traveler reaches the far shore. There was no harm in honoring local gods or observing traditional ceremonies, as long as one remembered the goal of enlightenment and did not let sacrifices become snares or attachments. The willingness of Buddhists to tolerate a wide variety of practices aided the spread of the religion.

Like Mahavira, the Buddha formed a circle of disciples, primarily men but including some women as well. He continually reminded them that each person must

- **Four Noble Truths** The Buddha's message that pain and suffering are inescapable parts of life; suffering and anxiety are caused by human desires and attachments; people can understand and triumph over these weaknesses; and the triumph is made possible by following a simple code of conduct.
- **Eightfold Path** The code of conduct set forth by the Buddha in his first sermon, beginning with "right conduct" and ending with "right contemplation."
- **nirvana** A state of blissful nothingness and freedom from reincarnation.

◻ Picturing the Past

Gandharan Frieze Depicting the Buddha This carved stone from ca. 200 C.E. is one in a series portraying scenes from the life of the Buddha. From the Gandharan kingdom (located in modern Pakistan), this frieze depicts the Buddha seated below the bo tree, where he was first enlightened.
(Freer Gallery of Art, Smithsonian Institution, Washington, D.C., Purchase. F1949.9b, F1954.20)

ANALYZING THE IMAGE What are the people around the Buddha doing? What animals are portrayed?

CONNECTIONS Does this frieze effectively convey any Buddhist principles? If so, which ones?

reach ultimate fulfillment by individual effort, but he also recognized the value of a group of people striving together for the same goal.

The Buddha's followers transmitted his teachings orally until they were written down in the second or first century B.C.E. These scriptures are called **sutras**. The form of monasticism that developed among the Buddhists was less strict than that of the Jains. Buddhist monks moved about for eight months of the year (except the rainy season), begging for their one meal a day, but they could bathe and wear clothes. Within a few centuries Buddhist monks began to overlook the rule that they should travel. They set up permanent monasteries, generally on land donated by kings or other patrons. Orders of nuns also appeared, giving

women the opportunity to seek truth in ways men had traditionally used. The main ritual that monks and nuns performed in their monastic establishments was the communal recitation of the sutras. Lay Buddhists could aid the spread of the Buddhist teachings by providing food for monks and support for their monasteries, and they could pursue their own spiritual progress by adopting practices such as abstaining from meat and alcohol.

Because Buddhism had no central ecclesiastical authority like the Christian papacy, early Buddhist communities developed several divergent traditions and came to stress different sutras. One of the most important of these, associated with the monk-philosopher Nagarjuna (fl. ca. 100 C.E.), is called **Mahayana**, or

"Great Vehicle," because it was a more inclusive form of the religion. It drew on a set of discourses allegedly given by the Buddha and kept hidden by his followers for centuries. One branch of Mahayana taught that reality is empty (that is, nothing exists independently of itself). Another branch held that ultimate reality is consciousness, that everything is produced by the mind.

Just as important as the metaphysical literature of Mahayana Buddhism was its devotional side, influenced by the religions then prevalent in Central Asia, such as Zoroastrianism (see page 61). The Buddha became deified and was placed at the head of an expanding pantheon of other Buddhas and **bodhisattvas** (boh-dih-SUHT-vuhz). Bodhisattvas were Buddhas-to-be who had stayed in the world after enlightenment to help others on the path to salvation. The Buddhas and bodhisattvas became objects of veneration, especially the Buddha of Infinite Light, Amitabha, and the bodhisattva of infinite compassion and mercy, Avalokitesvara (uh-vuh-lohk-ih-TEYSH-veh-ruh). With the growth of Mahayana, Buddhism attracted more and more laypeople.

Buddhism remained an important religion in India until about 1200 C.E. By that time it had spread widely through East, Central, and Southeast Asia. After 1200 Buddhism declined in India, losing out to both Hinduism and Islam, and the number of Buddhists in India today is small. Buddhism never lost its hold in Nepal and Sri Lanka, however, and today it is also a major religion in Southeast Asia, Tibet, China, Korea, and Japan.

Hinduism

Both Buddhism and Jainism were direct challenges to the old Brahmanic religion. Both rejected animal sacrifice, which by then was a central element in the rituals performed by Brahmin priests. Even more important, both religions tacitly rejected the caste system, accepting people of any caste into their ranks. Over the next several centuries (ca. 400 B.C.E.–200 C.E.), in response to this challenge, the Brahmanic religion evolved in a more devotional direction, developing into the religion commonly called Hinduism. In Hinduism Brahmins retained their high social status, but it became possible for individual worshippers to have more direct contact with the gods, showing their devotion without using priests as intermediaries.

The bedrock of Hinduism is the belief that the Vedas are sacred revelations and that a specific caste system is implicitly prescribed in them. Hinduism is a guide to life, the goal of which is to reach union with brahman, the unchanging ultimate reality. There are four steps in this search, progressing from study of the Vedas in youth to complete asceticism in old age. In their quest for brahman, people are to observe **dharma** (DAHR-muh), the moral law. Dharma stipulates the legitimate pursuits of Hindus: material gain, as long as it is honestly and honorably achieved; pleasure and love for the perpetuation of the family; and moksha, release from the wheel of life and unity with brahman. Because it recognizes the need for material gain and pleasure, Hinduism allows a joyful embracing of life. This certainly was part of its appeal.

Hinduism assumes that there are innumerable legitimate ways of worshipping brahman, including devotion to personal gods. After the third century B.C.E. Hinduism began to emphasize the roles and personalities of thousands of powerful gods. Brahma, the creator, Shiva, the cosmic dancer who both creates and destroys, and Vishnu, the preserver and sustainer of creation, were three of the main male deities. Important female deities included Lakshmi, goddess of wealth, and Saraswati, goddess of learning and music. These gods were usually represented by images, either small ones in homes or larger ones in temples. People could show devotion to their personal gods by reciting hymns or scriptures and by making offerings of food or flowers before these images. A worshipper's devotion to one god did not entail denial of other deities; ultimately all were manifestations of brahman, the ultimate reality. Hinduism's embrace of a large pantheon of gods enabled it to incorporate new sects, doctrines, beliefs, rites, and deities.

A central ethical text of Hinduism is the *Bhagavad Gita* (BAH-guh-vahd GEE-tuh), a part of the world's longest ancient epic, the *Mahabharata*. The *Bhagavad Gita* offers guidance on the most serious problem facing a Hindu—how to live in the world and yet honor dharma and thus achieve release from the wheel of life. The heart of the *Bhagavad Gita* is the spiritual conflict confronting Arjuna, a human hero about to ride into battle against his kinsmen. As he surveys the battlefield, struggling with the grim notion of killing his relatives, Arjuna voices his doubts to his charioteer, none other than the god Krishna. When at last Arjuna refuses to spill his family's blood, Krishna instructs him on the true meaning of Hinduism:

> You grieve for those beyond grief,
> and you speak words of insight;
> but learned men do not grieve
> for the dead or the living.

- **sutras** The written teachings of the Buddha, first transcribed in the second or first century B.C.E.
- **Mahayana** The "Great Vehicle," a tradition of Buddhism that aspires to be more inclusive.
- **bodhisattvas** Buddhas-to-be who stayed in the world after enlightenment to help others on the path to salvation.
- **dharma** The Sanskrit word for moral law, central both to Buddhist and Hindu teachings.

> 66 Never have I not existed, nor you, nor these kings; and never in the future shall we cease to exist. 99

KRISHNA, from the *Bhagavad Gita*

The God Vishnu Vishnu reclining on his protector, the serpent Shesha, is the subject of this stone relief from the Temple of Vishnu in central India at Deogarh, which dates from the Gupta period, ca. 500 C.E. (Deogarh, Uttar Pradesh, India/Giraudon/The Bridgeman Art Library)

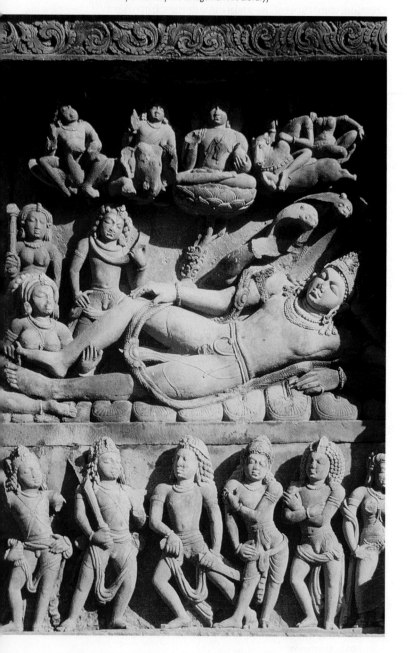

Never have I not existed,
nor you, nor these kings;
and never in the future
shall we cease to exist.

Just as the embodied self
enters childhood, youth, and old age,
so does it enter another body;
this does not confound a steadfast man.

Contacts with matter make us feel
heat and cold, pleasure and pain.
Arjuna, you must learn to endure
fleeting things — they come and go!

When these cannot torment a man,
when suffering and joy are equal
for him and he has courage,
he is fit for immortality.

Nothing of nonbeing comes to be,
nor does being cease to exist;
the boundary between these two
is seen by men who see reality.

Indestructible is the presence
that pervades all this;
no one can destroy
this unchanging reality.

Our bodies are known to end,
but the embodied self is enduring,
indestructible, and immeasurable;
therefore, Arjuna, fight the battle!

He who thinks this self a killer
and he who thinks it killed,
both fail to understand;
it does not kill, nor is it killed.

It is not born,
it does not die;
having been,
it will never not be;
unborn, enduring,
constant, and primordial,
it is not killed
when the body is killed.[2]

Krishna then clarifies the relationship between human reality and the eternal spirit. He explains compassionately to Arjuna the duty to act — to live in the world and carry out his duties as a warrior. Indeed, the *Bhagavad Gita* emphasizes the necessity of action, which is essential for the welfare of the world. For Arjuna the warrior's duty is to wage war in compliance with his dharma. Only those who live within the divine law without complaint will be released from rebirth. One person's dharma may be different from another's, but both individuals must follow their own dharmas.

Hinduism provided a complex and sophisticated philosophy of life and a religion of enormous emotional appeal that was attractive to ordinary Indians. Over time it grew to be the most common religion in India. Hinduism also inspired the preservation of literary masterpieces in Sanskrit and the major regional languages of India. Among these are the *Puranas*, which are stories of the gods and great warrior clans, and the *Mahabharata* and *Ramayana*, which are verse epics of India's early kings. Hinduism validated the caste system, adding to the stability of everyday village life, since people all knew where they stood in society.

Western Contact and the Mauryan Unification of North India, ca. 513–185 B.C.E.

◻ What was the result of Indian contact with the Persians and Greeks, and what were the consequences of unification under the Mauryan Empire?

In the late sixth century B.C.E., with the creation of the Persian empire that stretched from the west coast of Anatolia to the Indus River (see pages 58–61), west India was swept up in events that were changing the face of the ancient Near East. A couple of centuries later, by 322 B.C.E., the Greeks had supplanted the Persians in northwest India. Chandragupta saw this as an opportunity to expand his territories, and he successfully unified all of north India. The Mauryan Empire that he founded flourished under the reign of his grandson, Ashoka, but after Ashoka's death the empire declined.

Encounters with the West

India became involved in the turmoil of the sixth century B.C.E. when the Persian emperor Darius conquered the Indus Valley and Kashmir about 513 B.C.E. Persian control did not reach eastward beyond the Punjab, but even so it fostered increased contact between India and the Near East and led to the introduction of new ideas, techniques, and materials into India. From Persian administrators Indians learned more about how to rule large tracts of land and huge numbers of people. They also learned the technique of minting silver coins, and they adopted the Persian monetary standard to facilitate trade with other parts of the empire. Even states in the Ganges Valley, which were never part of the Persian Empire, adopted the use of coinage.

Another result of contact with Persia was introduction of the Aramaic script, used to write the official language of the Persian Empire. To keep records and publish proclamations just as the Persians did, Indians in northwest India adapted the Aramaic script for writing several local languages (elsewhere, Indians developed the Brahmi script, the ancestor of the script used for modern Hindi). In time the sacred texts of the Buddhists and the Jains, as well as epics and other literary works, came to be recorded using Aramaic script to write down Indian languages.

The Persian Empire in turn succumbed to Alexander the Great, and in 326 B.C.E. Alexander led his Macedonian and Greek troops through the Khyber Pass into the Indus Valley (discussed in Chapter 5 on page 131). The India

Hellenistic Influences in Gandharan Art Because Alexander the Great's army had reached this region and Hellenistic states then controlled it for more than a century, the art of Gandhara was strongly influenced by Greek artistic styles. This stucco figure was excavated from a site in eastern Afghanistan where some 23,000 Greco-Buddhist sculptures were found. Hellenistic influence, as evidenced by the drape of the clothing and the modeling of the head, is particularly easy to recognize in this piece. (Erich Lessing/Art Resource, NY) that Alexander encountered was composed of many rival states. He defeated some of these states in the northwest and heard reports of others. Porus, king of west Punjab, fought Alexander with a battalion of two thousand war elephants. After being defeated, he agreed to become a subordinate king under Alexander.

The Greeks were intrigued by the Indian culture they encountered. Alexander had heard of the sophistication of Indian philosophers and summoned some to instruct him or debate with him. The Greeks were also impressed with Indian cities, most notably Tax-

ila, a major center of trade in the Punjab. The Greeks described it as "a city great and prosperous, the biggest of those between the Indus River and the Hydaspes [the modern Jhelum River] — a region not inferior to Egypt in size, with especially good pastures and rich in fine fruits."[3] From Taxila, Alexander followed the Indus River south, hoping to find the end of the world. His men, however, mutinied and refused to continue. When Alexander turned back, he left his general Seleucus (suh-LOO-kuhs) in charge of his easternmost region.

Chandragupta and the Founding of the Mauryan Empire

The one to benefit most from Alexander's invasion was Chandragupta, the ruler of a growing state in the Ganges Valley. He took advantage of the crisis caused by Alexander's invasion to expand his territories, and by 322 B.C.E. he had made himself sole master of north India (Map 3.2). In 304 B.C.E. he defeated the forces of Seleucus.

With stunning effectiveness, Chandragupta applied the lessons learned from Persian rule. He adopted the Persian practice of dividing the area into provinces. Each province was assigned a governor, usually drawn from Chandragupta's own family. He established a complex bureaucracy to see to the operation of the state and a bureaucratic taxation system that financed public services through taxes on agriculture. He also built a regular army, complete with departments for everything from naval matters to the collection of supplies.

For the first time in Indian history, one man governed most of the subcontinent, exercising control through delegated power. From his capital at Pataliputra in the Ganges Valley (now Patna in Bihar), Chandragupta sent agents to the provinces to oversee the workings of government and to keep him informed of conditions in his realm. In designing his bureaucratic system, Chandragupta enjoyed the able assistance of his great minister Kautilya, who wrote a treatise on how a king should seize, hold, and manipulate power, rather like the Legalist treatises produced in China later that century (discussed in Chapter 4 on page 110). Kautilya urged the king to use propaganda to gain support, for instance, to disguise secret agents to look like gods so that people would be awed when they saw him in their company. He stressed the importance of seeking the enemies of his enemies, who would make good allies. When a neighboring prince was in trouble, that was the perfect time to attack him. Interstate relations were likened to the law of the fish: the large swallow the small. (See "Viewpoints: On Enemies from *The Laws of Manu* and *The Arthashastra*," page 83.)

Megasthenes, a Greek ambassador sent by Seleucus, spent fourteen years in Chandragupta's court. He left

▢ Mapping the Past

MAP 3.2 The Mauryan Empire, ca. 250 B.C.E. The Ganges River Valley was the heart of the Mauryan Empire. Although India is protected from the cold by mountains in the north, mountain passes in the northwest allowed both migration and invasion.

ANALYZING THE MAP Where are the major rivers of India? How close are they to mountains?

CONNECTIONS Can you think of any reasons that the Persian Empire and Alexander's conquests both reached into the same region of northwest India?

Viewpoints

On Enemies from *The Laws of Manu* and *The Arthashastra*

• *Advice on how to rule is found in two of the important books from early India,* The Laws of Manu, *dating perhaps to the second century* C.E., *and* The Arthashastra, *attributed to Kautilya, with material dating from the fourth century* B.C.E. *to the fourth century* C.E. *Both books cover many topics in addition to the advice on dealing with enemies excerpted below.*

"The Law for the King" from *The Laws of Manu*

❝[The King] should recognize that his immediate neighbor is his enemy, as also anyone rendering assistance to the enemy; that his enemy's immediate neighbor is an ally; and that the one beyond these two is neutral. He should prevail over them by conciliation and the other strategies, employed both separately and collectively, and by valor and policy. . . .

When he is convinced that his future dominance is certain and that any immediate disadvantage is slight, then he should resort to an alliance. When he believes that all his subjects are exceedingly content and that he himself is overwhelmingly powerful, then he should consider waging war. When he believes in his heart that his own army is in high spirit and prosperous and that the opposite is true of his adversary, then he should march into battle against his enemy. When he is weak in terms of mounted units and infantry, then he should diligently remain stationary, while gradually appeasing the enemy. When the king believes that the enemy is stronger in every respect, then he should divide his army in two and accomplish his objective. When he has become extremely vulnerable to his enemy's forces, then he should quickly seek asylum with a strong and righteous king. Should that king keep both his own subjects and the forces of his enemy in check, he should always serve him like a teacher with all his strength. Even in that case, however, if he notices a liability resulting from his asylum, he should, even in that condition, resort to the good war without hesitation. A politically astute king should employ all the strategies in such a way that his allies, neutrals, or enemies do not prevail over him.❞

"Capture of the Enemy by Means of Secret Contrivances" from *The Arthashastra*

❝Contrivances to kill the enemy may be formed in those places of worship and visit, which the enemy, under the influence of faith, frequents on occasions of worshiping gods and of pilgrimage. A wall or stone, kept by mechanical contriv-

ance, may, by loosening the fastenings, be let to fall on the head of the enemy when he has entered into a temple; stones and weapons may be showered over his head from the topmost story; or a door-panel may be let to fall; or a huge rod kept over a wall or partly attached to a wall may be made to fall over him; or weapons kept inside the body of an idol may be thrown over his head; or the floor of those places where he usually stands, sits, or walks may be besprinkled with poison mixed with cowdung or with pure water; or, under the plea of giving him flowers, scented powders, or of causing scented smoke, he may be poisoned. . . .

Or having challenged the conqueror at night, he may successfully confront the attack; if he cannot do this, he may run away by a side path; or, disguised as a heretic, he may escape with a small retinue; or he may be carried off by spies as a corpse; or disguised as a woman, he may follow a corpse [as it were, of her husband to the cremation ground]; or on the occasion of feeding the people in honor of gods or of ancestors or in some festival, he may make use of poisoned rice and water, and having conspired with his enemy's traitors, he may strike the enemy with his concealed army; or, when he is surrounded in his fort, he may lie concealed in a hole bored into the body of an idol after eating sacramental food and setting up an altar; . . . and when he is forgotten, he may get out of his concealment through a tunnel, and, entering into the palace, slay his enemy while sleeping, or loosening the fastening of a machine he may let it fall on his enemy; or when his enemy is lying in a chamber which is besmeared with poisonous and explosive substances, or which is made of lac [varnish], he may set fire to it. . . .❞

Sources: Patrick Olivelle, trans., *Manu's Code of Law* (Oxford: Oxford University Press, 2005), 162–163. © 2004 by the University of Texas Center for Asian Studies. Used by permission of Oxford University Press, Inc.; Kautilya, *Kautilya's Arthashastra*, trans. R. Shamasastry (Bangalore: Government Press, 1915).

QUESTIONS FOR ANALYSIS

1. What can you infer about interstate relations in the period these texts were written?

2. How alike are these documents in their approach toward dealing with enemies?

3. How do these texts add to your understanding of early Indian religion?

a lively description of life there. He described the city as square and surrounded by wooden walls, twenty-two miles on each side, with 570 towers and 64 gates. It had a university, a library, and magnificent palaces, temples, gardens, and parks. The king personally presided over court sessions where legal cases were heard and petitions received. The king claimed for the state all mines and forests, and there were large state farms, granaries, shipyards, and spinning and weaving factories. Even prostitution was controlled by the state. Only a portion of the empire was ruled so directly, according to Megasthenes. In outlying areas, local kings were left in place if they pledged loyalty.

Megasthenes described Chandragupta as afraid of treachery and assassination attempts:

> Attendance on the king's person is the duty of women, who indeed are bought from their fathers. Outside the gates of the palace stand the bodyguards and the rest of the soldiers. . . . Nor does the king sleep during the day, and at night he is forced at various hours to change his bed because of those plotting against him. Of his non-military departures from the palace one is to the courts, in which he passes the day hearing cases to the end, even if the hour arrives for attendance on his person. . . . When he leaves to hunt, he is thickly surrounded by a circle of women, and on the outside by spear-carrying bodyguards. The road is fenced off with ropes, and to anyone who passes within the ropes as far as the women death is the penalty.[4]

"Nor does the king sleep during the day, and at night he is forced at various hours to change his bed because of those plotting against him."

MEGASTHENES

Those measures apparently worked, as Chandragupta lived a long life. According to Jain tradition, Chandragupta became a Jain ascetic and died a peaceful death in 298 B.C.E. Although he personally adopted a nonviolent philosophy, he left behind a kingdom with the military might to maintain order and defend India from invasion.

The Reign of Ashoka, ca. 269–232 B.C.E.

The years after Chandragupta's death were an epoch of political greatness, thanks largely to his grandson Ashoka, one of India's most remarkable figures. The era of Ashoka was enormously important in the religious history of the world, because Ashoka embraced Buddhism and promoted its spread beyond India.

As a young prince, Ashoka served as governor of two prosperous provinces where Buddhism flourished. At the death of his father about 274 B.C.E., Ashoka rebelled against his older brother, who had succeeded as king, and after four years of fighting won his bid for the throne. Crowned king, Ashoka ruled intelligently and energetically. He was equally serious about his pleasures, especially those of the banquet hall and harem.

In the ninth year of his reign, 261 B.C.E., Ashoka conquered Kalinga, on the east coast of India. In a grim and savage campaign, Ashoka reduced Kalinga by wholesale slaughter. As Ashoka himself admitted, "One hundred and fifty thousand were forcibly abducted from their homes, 100,000 were killed in battle, and many more died later on."[5] Instead of exulting like a conqueror, however, Ashoka was consumed with remorse and revulsion at the horror of war. He embraced Buddhism and used the machinery of his empire to spread Buddhist teachings throughout India. He supported the doctrine of not hurting humans or animals then spreading among religious people of all sects in India. He banned animal sacrifices, and in place of hunting expeditions he took pilgrimages. Two years after his conversion, he undertook a 256-day pilgrimage to all the holy sites of Buddhism, and on his return he sent missionaries to all known countries. Buddhist tradition also credits him with erecting 84,000 stupas (structures containing Buddhist relics) throughout India, among which the ashes or other bodily remains of the Buddha were distributed, beginning the association of Buddhism with monumental art and architecture.

Ashoka's remarkable crisis of conscience, like the later conversion to Christianity of the Roman emperor Constantine, affected the way he ruled. He emphasized compassion, nonviolence, and adherence to dharma. He appointed officials to oversee the moral welfare of the realm and required local officials to govern humanely. He may have perceived dharma as a kind of civic virtue, a universal ethical model capable of uniting the diverse peoples of his extensive empire. Ashoka erected stone pillars, on the Persian model, with inscriptions to inform the people of his policies. He also had long inscriptions carved into large rock surfaces near trade routes. In his last important inscription he spoke of his efforts to encourage his people toward the path of righteousness:

> I have had banyan trees planted on the roads to give shade to man and beast; I have planted mango groves, and I have had ponds dug and shelters erected along the roads at every eight kos. Everywhere I have had wells dug for the benefit of man and beast. But his benefit is but small, for in many ways the kings of olden time have worked for the welfare of the world; but what I have done has been done that men may conform to righteousness.[6]

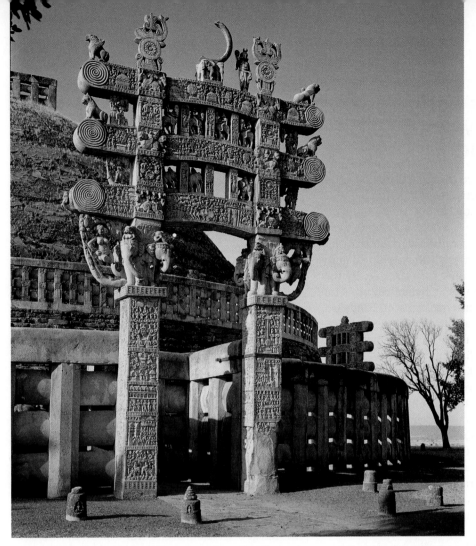

The North Gate at Sanchi
This is one of four ornately carved gates guarding the stupa at Sanchi in the state of Madhya Pradesh in India. Containing the relics of the Buddha, this Buddhist memorial shrine from the second century B.C.E. was commissioned by Ashoka. (Jean-Louis Nou/akg-images)

These inscriptions are the earliest fully dated Indian texts. (Until the script in which they were written was deciphered in 1837, nothing was known of Ashoka's achievements.) The pillars on which they are inscribed are also the first examples of Indian art to survive since the end of the Indus civilization.

Ashoka felt the need to protect his new religion and to keep it pure. He warned Buddhist monks that he would not tolerate schism — divisions based on differences of opinion about doctrine or ritual. According to Buddhist tradition, a great council of Buddhist monks was held at Pataliputra, where the earliest canon of Buddhist texts was codified. At the same time, Ashoka honored India's other religions, even building shrines for Hindu and Jain worshippers. In one edict he banned rowdy popular fairs, allowing only religious gatherings.

Despite his devotion to Buddhism, Ashoka never neglected his duties as emperor. He tightened the central government of the empire and kept a close check on local officials. He built roads and rest spots to improve communication within the realm. These measures also facilitated the march of armies and the armed enforcement of Ashoka's authority. Ashoka described his work: "Whatever good I have done has indeed been accomplished for the progress and welfare of the world. By these shall grow virtues namely: proper support of mother and father, regard for preceptors and elders,

proper treatment of Brahmans and ascetics, of the poor and the destitute, slaves and servants."[7]

Ashoka's inscriptions indirectly tell us much about the Mauryan Empire. He directly administered the central part of the empire, focusing on Magadha. Beyond it were four large provinces under princes who served as viceroys, each with its own sets of smaller districts and officials. The interior of south India was described as inhabited by undefeated forest tribes. Farther south, along the coasts, were peoples that Ashoka maintained friendly relations with but did not rule, such as the Cholas and Pandyas. Relations with Sri Lanka were especially close under Ashoka, and the king sent a branch of the tree under which the Buddha gained enlightenment to the Sri Lankan king. According to Buddhist legend, Ashoka's son Mahinda traveled to Sri Lanka to convert the people there.

Ashoka ruled for thirty-seven years. After he died in about 232 B.C.E. the Mauryan Dynasty went into decline, and India broke up into smaller units, much like those in existence before Alexander's invasion. Even though Chandragupta had instituted bureaucratic methods of centralized political control and Ashoka had vigorously pursued the political and cultural integration of the empire, the institutions they created were not entrenched enough to survive periods with weaker kings.

Small States and Trading Networks, 185 B.C.E.–300 C.E.

☐ How was India shaped by political disunity and contacts with other cultures during the five centuries from 185 B.C.E. to 300 C.E.?

After the Mauryan Dynasty collapsed in 185 B.C.E., and for much of subsequent Indian history, political unity would be the exception rather than the rule. By this time, however, key elements of Indian culture — the caste system; the religious traditions of Hinduism, Buddhism, and Jainism; and the great epics and legends — had given India a cultural unity strong enough to endure even without political unity.

In the years after the fall of the Mauryan Dynasty, a series of foreign powers dominated the Indus Valley and adjoining regions. The first were hybrid Indo-Greek states ruled by the inheritors of Alexander's defunct empire stationed in what is now Afghanistan. The city of Taxila became a major center of trade, culture, and education, fusing elements of Greek and Indian culture.

The Kushan Empire, ca. 200 B.C.E.

The great, slow movement of nomadic peoples out of East Asia that brought the Scythians to the Near East brought the Shakas to northwest India. They controlled the region from about 94 to 20 B.C.E., when they were displaced by a new nomadic invader, the Kushans, who ruled the region of today's Afghanistan, Pakistan, and west India as far south as Gujarat. Buddhist sources refer to their king Kanishka (r. ca. 78–ca. 103 C.E.) as not only a powerful ruler but also a major patron of Buddhism. Some of the coins he issued had a picture of him on one side and of the Buddha on the other. The famous silk trade from China to Rome (see "Global Trade: Silk," page 184) passed through his territory.

During the Kushan period, Greek culture had a considerable impact on Indian art. Indo-Greek artists and sculptors working in India adorned Buddhist shrines, modeling the earliest representation of the Buddha on Hellenistic statues of Apollo. Another contribution from the Indo-Greek states was coin cast with images of the king, which came to be widely adopted by Indian rulers, aiding commerce and adding evidence of rulers' names and sequence to the historical record. Places where coins are found also show patterns of trade.

Cultural exchange also went in the other direction. Old Indian animal folktales were translated into Syriac and Greek and from that source eventually made their way to Europe. South India in this period was also the center of active seaborne trade, with networks reaching all the way to Rome. Indian sailing technology was highly advanced, and much of this trade was in the hands of Indian merchants. Roman traders based in Egypt followed the routes already used by Arab traders, sailing with the monsoon from the Red Sea to the west coast of India in about two weeks, returning about six months later when the direction of the winds reversed. In the first century C.E. a Greek merchant involved in this trade reported that the traders sold coins, topaz, coral, crude glass, copper, tin, and lead and bought pearls, ivory, silk (probably originally from China), jewels of many sorts (probably many from Southeast Asia), and above all cinnamon and pepper. More Roman gold coins of the first and second centuries C.E. have been found near the southern tip of India than in any other area. The local rulers had slits made across the image of the Roman emperor to show that his sovereignty was not recognized, but they had no objection to the coins' circulating. (By contrast, the Kushan rulers in the north had Roman coins melted down to make coins with their own images on them.)

Even after the fall of Rome, many of the traders on the southwest coast of India remained. These scattered communities of Christians and Jews lived in the coastal cities into modern times. When Vasco da Gama, the Portuguese explorer, reached Calicut in 1498, he found a local Jewish merchant who was able to interpret for him.

During these centuries there were significant advances in science, mathematics, and philosophy. Indian astronomers charted the movements of stars and planets and recognized that the earth was spherical. In the realm of physics, Indian scientists, like their Greek counterparts, conceived of matter in terms of five elements: earth, air, fire, water, and ether. This was also the period when Indian law was codified. The **Code of Manu**, which lays down family, caste, and commercial law, was compiled in the second or third century C.E., drawing on older texts.

Regional cultures tend to flourish when there is no dominant unifying state, and the Tamils of south India were one of the major beneficiaries of the collapse of the Mauryan Dynasty. The third century B.C.E.

• **Code of Manu** The codification of early Indian law that lays down family, caste, and commercial law.

Kushan Gold Coin Kanishka I had coins made depicting a standing Buddha with his left hand raised in a gesture of renunciation (left). The reverse side (below) shows the king performing a sacrifice, the legend reading "Kanishka the Kushan, king of kings." (Courtesy of the Trustees of the British Museum)

to the third century C.E. is considered the classical period of Tamil culture, when many great works of literature were written under the patronage of the regional kings. Some of the poems written then take a hard look at war:

Ashokan Pillar The best preserved of the pillars that King Ashoka erected in about 240 B.C.E. is this one in the Bihar region, near Nepal. The solid shaft of polished sandstone rises 32 feet in the air. It weighs about 50 tons, making its erection a remarkable feat of engineering. Like other Ashokan pillars, it is inscribed with accounts of Ashoka's political achievements and instructions to his subjects on proper behavior. These pillars are the earliest examples of Indian writing still existing and a major historical source for the Mauryan period. (Borromeo/Art Resource, NY)

> "Harvest of War"
>
> Great king
> you shield your men from ruin,
> so your victories, your greatness
> are bywords.
>
> Loose chariot wheels
> lie about the battleground
> with the long white tusks
> of bull-elephants.
>
> Flocks of male eagles
> eat carrion
> with their mates.
>
> Headless bodies
> dance about
> before they fall
> to the ground.
>
> Blood glows,
> like the sky before nightfall,
> in the red center
> of the battlefield.
>
> Demons dance there.
> And your kingdom
> is an unfailing harvest
> of victorious wars.[8]

Other poems provide evidence of lively commerce, mentioning bulging warehouses, ships from many lands, and complex import-export procedures. From contact of this sort, the south came to absorb many cultural elements from the north, but also retained differences. Castes were present in the south before contact with the Sanskrit north, but took distinct forms, as the Kshatriya (warrior) and Vaishya (merchant) varna were hardly known in the far south.

CONNECTIONS

India was a very different place in the third century C.E. than it had been in the early phase of Harappan civilization more than two thousand years earlier. The region was still divided into many different polities, but people living there in 300 shared much more in the way of ideas and traditions. The great epics such as the *Mahabharata* and the *Ramayana* provided a cultural vocabulary for groups that spoke different languages and had rival rulers. New religions had emerged, notably Buddhism and Jainism, and Hinduism was much more a devotional religion. Contact with ancient Mesopotamia, Persia, Greece, and Rome had brought new ideas, practices, and products.

During this same time period, civilization in China underwent similar expansion and diversification. China was farther away than India from other Eurasian centers of civilization, and its developments were consequently not as closely linked. Logographic writing appeared with the Bronze-Age Shang civilization and was preserved into modern times, in striking contrast to India and lands to its west, which developed written languages that represented sounds. Still, some developments affected both India and China, such as the appearance of chariots and horseback riding. The next chapter takes up the story of these developments in early China. In Chapter 12, after considering early developments in Europe, Asia, Africa, and the Americas, we return to the story of India.

CHAPTER REVIEW

KEY TERMS

Harappan (p. 66)	Eightfold Path
Aryans (p. 69)	(p. 77)
Rigveda (p. 70)	nirvana (p. 77)
Brahmins (p. 71)	sutras (p. 78)
caste system (p. 71)	Mahayana (p. 78)
samsara (p. 74)	bodhisattvas (p. 79)
karma (p. 74)	dharma (p. 79)
brahman (p. 74)	Code of Manu
Four Noble Truths	(p. 86)
(p. 77)	

◻ **What does archaeology tell us about the Harappan civilization in India? (p. 66)**

From archaeology we know that the Harappan civilization emerged in the Indus River Valley in the third millennium B.C.E. The archaeological record suggests a striking uniformity in architecture and religious ideas and practices throughout the region dominated by the Harappan culture. The large cities that have been excavated were made of kiln-dried brick and were carefully planned, with straight streets and sewers. Seals of Mesopotamian origin indicate trade between the Harappans and the Persian Gulf. Although many intriguing artifacts have been excavated, many questions remain about this civilization, and its script has not been deciphered. Scholars can only speculate why Harappan cities were largely abandoned by 1800 B.C.E.

◻ **What kind of society and culture did the Indo-European Aryans create? (p. 69)**

From originally oral texts like the *Rigveda*, we know much about the values and social practices of the Aryans, speakers of an early form of the Indo-European language Sanskrit. During the Vedic Age Aryan warrior tribes fought using chariots and bronze swords and spears, gradually expanding into the Ganges River Valley. The first stages of the Indian caste system date to this period, when warriors and priests were ranked above merchants, artisans, and farmers. Key religious ideas were the notions of karma and rebirth and the importance of sacrifice.

◻ **What ideas and practices were taught by the founders of Jainism, Buddhism, and Hinduism? (p. 74)**

Beginning around 500 B.C.E. three of India's major religions emerged. Mahavira was the founder of the Jain religion. He taught his followers to live ascetic lives, avoid doing harm to any living thing, and renounce evil thoughts and actions. The founder of Buddhism, Siddhartha Gautama or the Buddha, similarly taught his followers a path to liberation that involved avoiding violence and freeing themselves from desires. The Buddha, however, did not think extreme asceticism was the best path and put more emphasis on mental detachment. In response to the popularity of Jainism and Buddhism, both of which rejected animal sacrifice and ignored the caste system, the traditional Brahmanic religion evolved in a devotional direction that has been called Hinduism. Hindu traditions validated sacrifice and caste but stressed the individual's relationship to the gods he or she worshipped.

◻ **What was the result of Indian contact with the Persians and Greeks, and what were the consequences of unification under the Mauryan Empire? (p. 81)**

In the sixth century B.C.E. the Persian Empire expanded into the Indus River Valley, and in the fourth century Alexander the Great's troops took the same region. From contact with the Persians and Greeks, new political techniques, ideas, art styles, and the use of money entered the Indian repertoire. Shortly after the arrival of the Greeks, much of north India was politically unified by the Mauryan Empire under Chandragupta. His grandson Ashoka was the empire's greatest ruler. Ashoka converted to Buddhism and promoted its spread inside and outside of India. The inscriptions he had carved on stones and erected in many places in his empire provide some of the best-dated sources on early Indian history and show his efforts to centralize power.

◻ **How was India shaped by political disunity and contacts with other cultures during the five centuries from 185 B.C.E. to 300 C.E.? (p. 86)**

After the decline of the Mauryan Empire, India was politically fragmented. Indian cultural identity remained strong, however, because of shared religious ideas and shared literature, including the great early epics. A series of foreign powers came to dominate the Indus Valley and surrounding regions in this period. The Indo-Greek city of Taxila became a major center of trade, culture, and education. The movement of nomadic peoples out of East Asia brought the Shakas to northeast India, where they ruled until they were displaced by the Kushans, another nomadic group. Trade and other contact with the outside world brought new elements into Indian civilization, and Greek coinage was adopted widely by Indian rulers. Just as India came to absorb Persian and Greek bureaucratic techniques and artistic styles, cultures of western Eurasia were introduced to folktales, crops, textiles, inventions, and religious ideas from India. This cultural interchange was facilitated by the silk trade in northwest India and the maritime trade of southern India.

SUGGESTED READING

Basham, A. L. *The Wonder That Was India*, 3d rev. ed. 1968. Classic appreciative account of early Indian civilization by a scholar deeply immersed in Indian literature.

Embree, Ainslee, ed. *Sources of Indian Tradition*, 2d ed. 1988. An excellent introduction to Indian religion, philosophy, and intellectual history through translations of major sources.

Keay, John. *India: A History*. 2000. Wide-ranging history of India, with a strong narrative.

Koller, John M. *The Indian Way*, 2d ed. 2004. An accessible introduction to the variety of Indian religions and philosophies.

Kulke, Hermann, and Dietmar Rothermund. *A History of India*, 3d ed. 1998. A good balanced introduction to Indian history.

Lopez, Donald S., Jr. *The Story of the Buddha: A Concise Guide to Its History and Teachings*. 2001. Emphasizes Buddhist practice, drawing examples from many different countries and time periods.

Miller, Barbara, trans. *The Bhagavad-Gita: Krishna's Counsel in Time of War*. 1986. One of several excellent translations of India's classical literature.

Possehl, Gregory L. *The Indus Civilization*. 2002. Recent overview of Harappan civilization.

Renfew, Colin. *Archaeology and Language: The Puzzle of Indo-European Origins*. 1987. In-depth analysis of the question of the origins of the Aryans.

Scharff, Harmut. *The State in Indian Tradition*. 1989. Scholarly analysis of the period from the Aryans to the Muslims.

Thapar, Romila. *Early India to 1300*. 2002. A freshly revised overview by a leading Indian historian.

Wright, Rita P. *The Ancient Indus: Urbanism, Economy, and Society*. 2010. Broad-ranging overview that brings in Mesopotamian sources.

NOTES

1. *Rigveda* 10.90, in Ainslie T. Embree, trans., *Sources of Indian Tradition*, 2d ed. Vol. 1: *From the Beginning to 1800*. Copyright © 1988 by Columbia University Press. Reprinted with permission of the publisher.
2. Excerpt from Barbara Stoler Miller, trans., *The Bhagavad-Gita: Krishna's Counsel in Time of War* (New York: Columbia University Press, 1986), pp. 31–32. Translation copyright © 1986 by Barbara Stoler Miller. Used by permission of Bantam Books, a division of Random House, Inc.
3. Arrian, *Anabasis* 5.8.2; Plutarch, *Alexander* 59.1. Translated by John Buckler.
4. *Strabo* 15.1.55. Translated by John Buckler.
5. Quoted in H. Kulke and D. Rothermund, *A History of India*, 3d ed. (London: Routledge, 1998), p. 62.
6. Embree, p. 148. Copyright © 1988 by Columbia University Press. Reprinted with permission of the publisher.
7. Quoted in B. G. Gokhale, *Asoka Maurya* (New York: Twayne Publishers, 1966), p. 169.
8. A. K. Ramanujan, ed. and trans., *Poems of Love and War: From the Eight Anthologies and the Ten Long Poems of Classical Tamil* (New York: Columbia University Press, 1985), p. 115. Copyright 1985 by Columbia University Press. Reproduced with permission of Columbia University Press in the format Textbook via Copyright Clearance Center.

For practice quizzes and other study tools, see the **Online Study Guide** at bedfordstmartins.com/mckayworld.

For primary sources from this period, see *Sources of World Societies*, **Second Edition**.

For Web sites, images, and documents related to topics in this chapter, visit **Make History** at bedfordstmartins.com/mckayworld.

• **Bronze Head from China** Archaeological discoveries continue to expand our knowledge of the cultures and civilizations of early China. This 20-inch-tall bronze head was found among a large set of sacrificial offerings in the modern province of Sichuan. These unusual objects, which were found only there, suggest a distinct culture. (Sanxingdui Museum, Guanghan, Sichuan Province, © Cultural Relics Press)

In comparison to India and the ancient Middle East, China developed in relative isolation. Communication with West and South Asia was very difficult, impeded by high mountains and vast deserts. Though there was some trade, the distances were so great that it did not allow the kind of cross-fertilization that occurred in western Eurasia. Moreover, there were no cultural breaks comparable to the rise of the Aryans in India or the Assyrians in Mesopotamia to introduce new peoples and languages. The impact of early China's relative isolation is found in many distinctive features of its culture. Perhaps the most important is its writing system; unlike the other major societies of Eurasia, China retained a logographic writing system with a symbol for each word. This writing system shaped not only Chinese literature and thought but also key social and political processes, such as the nature of the ruling class and interactions with non-Chinese.

Chinese history is commonly discussed in terms of a succession of dynasties. The Shang Dynasty (ca. 1500–1050 B.C.E.) was the first to have writing, metalworking, cities, and chariots. The Shang kings played priestly roles, serving as intermediaries with both their royal ancestors and the high god Di. The Shang were overthrown by one of their vassal states, which founded the Zhou Dynasty (ca. 1050–256 B.C.E.). The Zhou rulers set up a decentralized feudal governmental structure that evolved over centuries into a multistate system. As warfare between the states intensified in the sixth century B.C.E., social and cultural change quickened. Aristocratic privileges declined, and China entered one of its most creative periods, when the philosophies of Confucianism, Daoism, and Legalism were developed. •

China's Classical Age

to 221 B.C.E.

The Emergence of Civilization in China
□ What was the impact of China's geography on the development of Chinese societies?

The Shang Dynasty, ca. 1500–1050 B.C.E.
□ What was life like during the Shang Dynasty, and what effect did writing have on Chinese culture and government?

The Early Zhou Dynasty, ca. 1050–400 B.C.E.
□ How was China governed, and what was life like during the Zhou Dynasty?

The Warring States Period, 403–221 B.C.E.
□ How did advances in military technology contribute to the rise of independent states?

Confucius and His Followers
□ What ideas did Confucius teach, and how were they spread after his death?

Daoism, Legalism, and Other Schools of Thought
□ How did the teachings of Daoism, Legalism, and other schools of thought differ from Confucianism?

The Emergence of Civilization in China

□ What was the impact of China's geography on the development of Chinese societies?

The term *China*, like the term *India*, does not refer to the same geographical entity at all points in history. The historical China, also called China proper, was smaller than present-day China, not larger like the historical India. The contemporary People's Republic of China includes Tibet, Inner Mongolia, Turkestan, Manchuria, and other territories that in premodern times were neither inhabited by Chinese nor ruled directly by Chinese states. The geography of the region in which Chinese civilization developed has had an impact on its historical development to the present.

The Impact of Geography

China proper, about a thousand miles north to south and east to west, occupies much of the temperate zone of East Asia (Map 4.1). The northern part, drained by the Yellow River, is colder, flatter, and more arid than the south. Rainfall in many areas is less than twenty inches a year, making the land well suited to crops like wheat and millet. The dominant soil is **loess** — fine wind-driven earth that is fertile and easy to work even with simple tools. The soil gives the Yellow River its characteristic color, and because so much of the loess ends up as silt in the river, the riverbed rises and easily floods unless diked. Drought is another perennial problem for farmers in the north. The Yangzi (YANG-zuh) River is the dominant feature of the warmer, wetter, and more lush south, a region well suited to rice cultivation. Farmers in recent centuries have been able to get two rice crops a year from the land around the Yangzi River and farther south. The Yangzi and its many tributaries are navigable, so boats were traditionally the preferred means of transportation in the south.

Mountains, deserts, and grasslands separated China proper from other early civilizations. Between China and India lay Tibet, with its vast mountain ranges and high plateaus. North of Tibet are great expanses of desert where nothing grows except in rare oases, and north of the desert grasslands stretch from Ukraine to eastern Siberia. Chinese civilization did not spread into any of these Inner Asian regions, above all because they were not suited to growing crops. Inner Asia, where raising animals is a more productive use of land than planting crops, became the heartland of China's traditional enemies, such as the nomadic tribes of the Xiongnu (SHUHNG-noo) and Mongols.

Early Agricultural Societies of the Neolithic Age

From about 10,000 B.C.E. agriculture was practiced in China. It apparently originated independently of somewhat earlier developments in Egypt and Mesopotamia, but was perhaps influenced by developments in Southeast Asia, where rice was also cultivated very early. By 5000 B.C.E. there were Neolithic village settlements in several regions of China. The primary Neolithic crops were drought-resistant millet, grown in the loess soils of the north, and rice, grown in the wetlands of the lower reaches of the Yangzi River, where inhabitants supplemented their diet with fish. In both areas pigs, dogs, and cattle were domesticated, and by 3000 B.C.E. sheep had become important in the north and water buffalo in the south. Silk production can also be traced back to this period.

• **loess** Soil deposited by wind; it is fertile and easy to work.

Over the course of the fifth to third millennia B.C.E. many distinct regional Neolithic cultures emerged. One such culture emerged in the northwest during the fourth and third millennia B.C.E. These people are known for their fine red pottery vessels decorated in black pigment with bold designs, including spirals, sawtooth lines, and zoomorphic stick figures. At the same time in the east, a different culture made pottery that was rarely painted but had distinctive shapes, including three-legged, deep-bodied tripods. Jade ornaments, blades, and ritual objects, sometimes of extraordinary craftsmanship, have been found in several eastern sites but are rare in western ones.

These Neolithic societies left no written records, but we know from the material record that over time they came to share more and more social and cultural practices. Many practices related to treatment of the dead spread to other groups from their original area, including use of coffins, ramped chambers, large numbers of grave goods, and divination aimed at communicating with ancestors or gods based on interpreting cracks in cattle bones. Fortified walls made of rammed earth came to be built around settlements in many areas, suggesting not only increased contact between Neolithic societies but also increased conflict. (For more on life in Neolithic societies, see Chapter 1.)

(For more on life in Neolithic societies, see Chapter 1.)

☐ CHRONOLOGY

ca. 5000 B.C.E. Emergence of regional Neolithic settlements

ca. 1500–1050 B.C.E. Shang Dynasty

ca. 1200 B.C.E. Evidence of writing found in royal tombs; chariots come into use

ca. 1050–256 B.C.E. Zhou Dynasty

ca. 900 *Book of Songs, Book of Changes, Book of Documents*

551–479 B.C.E. Confucius

ca. 500 B.C.E. Iron technology in wide use; cities spread across the central Zhou states

500–200 B.C.E. Golden age of Chinese philosophy

453–403 B.C.E. *The Art of War*

403–221 B.C.E. Period of the Warring States; decline of the Zhou Dynasty

ca. 370–300 B.C.E. Mencius

ca. 350 B.C.E. Infantry armed with crossbows

ca. 310–215 B.C.E. Xunzi

ca. 300–200 B.C.E. Early Daoist teachings outlined in *Laozi* and the *Zhuangzi*

Neolithic Jade Plaque This small plaque (2.5 inches by 3.25 inches), dating from about 2000 B.C.E., is similar to others of the Liangzhu area near modern Shanghai. It is incised to depict a human figure who merges into a monster mask. The lower part could be interpreted as his arms and legs but at the same time resembles a monster mask with bulging eyes, prominent nostrils, and a large mouth. (Zheijiang Provincial Institute of Archaeology/© Cultural Relics Press)

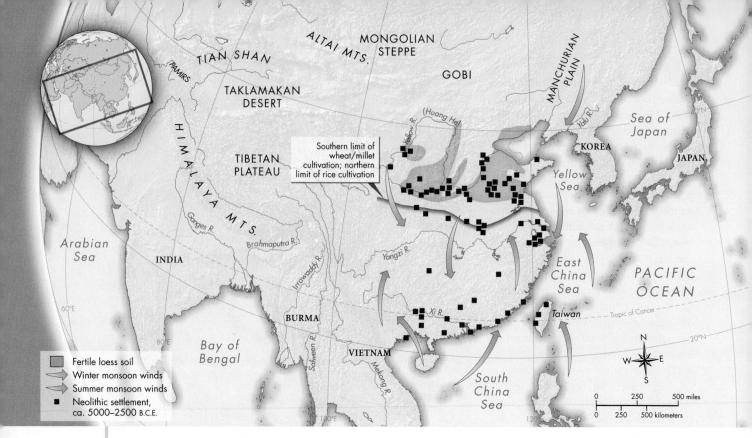

□ Mapping the Past

MAP 4.1 The Geography of Historical China Chinese civilization developed in the temperate regions drained by the Yellow and Yangzi Rivers.

ANALYZING THE MAP Trace the routes of the Yellow and Yangzi Rivers. Where are the areas of loess soil? Where are the Neolithic sites concentrated?

CONNECTIONS Does China's geography explain much about its history? (See also Map 4.2.) What geographical features had the greatest impact in the Neolithic Age? How might the fact that the Yellow and Yangzi Rivers flow west to east, rather than north to south, have influenced the development of Chinese society?

The Shang Dynasty, ca. 1500–1050 B.C.E.

□ What was life like during the Shang Dynasty, and what effect did writing have on Chinese culture and government?

After 2000 B.C.E. a Bronze Age civilization appeared in north China that shared traits with Bronze Age civilizations elsewhere in Eurasia, such as Mesopotamia, Egypt, and Greece. These traits included writing, metalworking, domestication of the horse, class stratification, and cult centers. These archaeological findings can be linked to the Shang Dynasty, long known from early texts.

• **Anyang** One of the Shang Dynasty capitals from which the Shang kings ruled for more than two centuries.

Shang Society

Shang civilization was not as densely urban as Mesopotamia, but Shang kings ruled from large settlements (Map 4.2). The best excavated is **Anyang**, from which the Shang kings ruled for more than two centuries. At the center of Anyang were large palaces, temples, and altars. These buildings were constructed on rammed-earth foundations (a feature of Chinese building practice that would last for centuries). Outside the central core were industrial areas where bronze workers, potters, stone carvers, and other artisans lived and worked. Many homes were built partly below ground level, probably as a way to conserve heat. Beyond these urban settlements were farming areas and large forests. Deer, bears, tigers, wild boars, elephants, and rhinoceros were still plentiful in north China in this era.

Texts found in the Shang royal tombs at Anyang show that Shang kings were military chieftains. The king regularly sent out armies of three thousand to five thousand men on campaigns, and when not at war they would go on hunts lasting for months. They fought rebellious vassals and foreign tribes, but the situation constantly changed as vassals became enemies and enemies accepted offers of alliance. War booty was an important source of the king's revenue, especially the war captives who could be made into slaves. Captives not needed as slaves might end up as sacrificial victims — or perhaps the demands of the gods and ancestors for sacrifices were a motive for going to war.

Bronze-tipped spears and halberds were widely used by Shang warriors, giving them an advantage over less technologically advanced groups. Bronze was also used for the fittings of the chariots that came into use around 1200 B.C.E. Chariot technology apparently spread by diffusion across Asia, passing from one society to the next. The chariot provided commanders with mobile stations from which they could supervise their troops; it also gave archers and soldiers armed with long halberds increased mobility.

Shang power did not rest solely on military supremacy. The Shang king was also the high priest, the one best qualified to offer sacrifices to the royal ancestors and the high god Di. Royal ancestors were viewed as able to intervene with Di, send curses, produce dreams,

MAP 4.2 The Shang and Early Zhou Dynasties, ca. 1500–400 B.C.E. The early Zhou government controlled larger areas than the Shang did, but the independent states of the Warring States Period were more aggressive about pushing out their frontiers, greatly extending the geographical boundaries of Chinese civilization.

Royal Tomb at Anyang Eleven large tombs and more than a thousand small graves have been excavated at the royal burial ground at Anyang. This grave, about 60 feet deep and 300 feet long, would have taken thousands of laborers many months to complete. But even more wealth was expended to fill it with bronze, stone, pottery, textiles, and jade grave goods like this 2¾-inch-tall figure, one of seven hundred jade pieces in the tomb of Lady Hao, also in Anyang. (photo: Academia Sinica, Institute of History and Philology, Taiwan; figure: Institute of Archaeology, Beijing/© Cultural Relics Press)

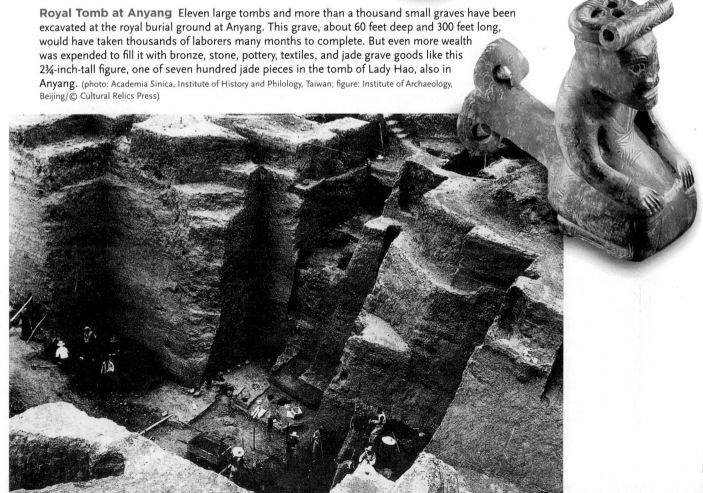

assist the king in battle, and so on. The king divined his ancestors' wishes by interpreting the cracks made in heated cattle bones or tortoise shells prepared for him by professional diviners.

The Shang royal family and aristocracy lived in large houses built on huge platforms of rammed earth similar to those used in the Neolithic period. Shang palaces were undoubtedly splendid but were constructed of perishable material like wood, and nothing of them remains today, unlike the stone buildings and monuments so characteristic of the ancient West. What has survived are the lavish underground tombs built for Shang kings and their consorts.

The one royal tomb not robbed before it was excavated was for Lady Hao, one of the many wives of the king Wu Ding (ca. 1200 B.C.E.). The tomb was filled with almost 500 bronze vessels and weapons, over 700 jade and ivory ornaments, and 16 people who would tend to Lady Hao in the afterlife. Human sacrifice did not occur only at funerals. Inscribed bones report sacrifices of war captives in the dozens and hundreds. Some of those buried with kings were not sacrificial victims but followers or servants. The bodies of people who voluntarily followed their ruler to the grave were generally buried with their own ornaments and grave goods such as weapons.

Shang society was marked by sharp status distinctions. The king and other noble families had family and clan names transmitted along patrilineal lines, from father to son. Kingship similarly passed along patrilineal lines, from elder to younger brother and father to son, but never to or through sisters or daughters. The kings and the aristocrats owned slaves, many of whom had been captured in war. In the urban centers there were substantial numbers of craftsmen who worked in stone, bone, and bronze.

Shang farmers were essentially serfs of the aristocrats. Their lives were not that different from the lives of their Neolithic ancestors, and they worked the fields with similar stone tools. They usually lived in small, compact villages surrounded by fields. Some new crops became common in Shang times, most notably wheat, which had spread from West Asia. Farmers probably also raised silkworms, from whose cocoons fine silk garments could be made for the ruling elite.

Bronze Metalworking

As in Egypt, Mesopotamia, and India, the development of more complex forms of social organization in Shang China coincided with the mastery of metalworking, specifically bronze. The bronze industry required the coordination of a large labor force and skilled artisans. Bronze was used more for ritual than for war in Shang times. Most surviving Shang bronze objects are vessels such as cups, goblets, steamers, and cauldrons that would have originally been used during sacrificial ceremonies. They were beautifully formed in a great variety of shapes and sizes. Complex designs were achieved through mold casting and prefabrication of parts. For instance, legs, handles, and other protruding members were cast first, before the body was cast onto them.

The decoration on Shang bronzes seems to say something interesting about Shang culture, but scholars do not agree about what that is. In the art of ancient Egypt, Assyria, and Babylonia, representations of agriculture (domesticated plants and animals) and of social hierarchy (kings, priests, scribes, and slaves) are very common, matching our understandings of the social, political, and economic development of those societies. In Shang China, by contrast, images of wild

Bronze Vessels The Shang Dynasty bronze vessel on the left, dating to the twelfth century B.C.E. and about 10 inches tall, is covered with symmetrical animal imagery, including stylized taotie masks. The early Zhou Dynasty inscribed bronze pan (right), dating to before 900 B.C.E., was one of 103 vessels discovered in 1975 by farmers clearing a field. The inscription tells the story of the first six Zhou kings and of the family of scribes who served them. (pan: Zhou Yuan Administrative Office of Cultural Relics, Fufeng, Shaanxi Province, © Cultural Relics Press; taotie vessel: © Image Copyright Metropolitan Museum of Art/Art Resource, NY)

WORD	ox	goat, sheep	tree	moon	earth	water	to show, declare	then (men and bowl)	heaven	to pray
SHANG SYMBOL										
MODERN CHARACTER	牛	羊	木	月	土	水	示	就	天	祝

FIGURE 4.1 The Origins of Chinese Writing The modern Chinese writing system (bottom row) evolved from the script employed by diviners in the Shang period (upper row). (Source: Adapted from Patricia Buckley Ebrey, *The Cambridge Illustrated History of China* [Cambridge: Cambridge University Press, 1996], p. 26. Reprinted by permission of Cambridge University Press.)

animals predominate. Some animal images readily suggest possible meanings. Jade cicadas were sometimes found in the mouths of the dead, and images of cicadas on bronzes are easy to interpret as images evocative of rebirth in the realm of ancestral spirits, as cicadas spend years underground before emerging. Birds, similarly, suggest to many the idea of messengers that can communicate with other realms, especially realms in the sky. More problematic is the most common image, the stylized animal face called the **taotie** (taow-tyeh). To some it is a monster—a fearsome image that would scare away evil forces. Others imagine a dragon—an animal whose vast powers had more positive associations. Some hypothesize that it reflects masks used in rituals. Others associate it with animal sacrifices, totemism, or shamanism. Still others see these images as hardly more than designs. Without new evidence, scholars can only speculate.

Bronze technology spread beyond Shang territories into areas the Shang would have considered enemy lands. In 1986, in the western province of Sichuan, discovery was made of a bronze-producing culture contemporaneous with the late Shang but very different from it. This culture did not practice human sacrifice, but two sacrificial pits contained the burned remains of elephant tusks and a wide range of gold, bronze, jade, and stone objects. Among them were a life-size statue and many life-size bronze heads, all with angular facial features and enormous eyes. No human sacrifices were found, leading some scholars to speculate that the masks were used to top wood or clay statues buried in place of humans in a sacrificial ceremony. Archaeologists are continuing to excavate in this region, and new discoveries gradually are providing fuller understanding of the religion of the people who lived there.

The Development of Writing

The survival of divination texts inscribed on bones from Shang tombs demonstrates that writing was al-

ready a major element in Chinese culture by 1200 B.C.E. Writing must have been developed earlier, but the early stages cannot be traced, probably because writing was done on wood, bamboo, silk, or other perishable materials. Once written texts survive, historians have much more material to draw on to reconstruct what life was like in a society.

The invention of writing had profound effects on China's culture and government. A written language made possible a bureaucracy capable of keeping records and corresponding with commanders and governors far from the palace. Hence literacy became the ally of royal rule, facilitating communication with and effective control over the realm. Literacy also preserved the learning, lore, and experience of early Chinese society and facilitated the development of abstract thought.

Like ancient Egyptian and Sumerian, the Chinese script was **logographic**: each word was represented by a single symbol. In the Chinese case, some of the symbols were pictures, but for the names of abstract concepts other methods were adopted. Sometimes the symbol for a different word was borrowed because the two words were pronounced alike. Sometimes two different symbols were combined; for instance, to represent different types of trees, the symbol for *tree* could be combined with another symbol borrowed for its pronunciation (Figure 4.1).

In western Eurasia logographic scripts were eventually modified or replaced by phonetic scripts, but that never happened in China (although, because of changes in the spoken language, today many words are represented by two or three characters rather than a single one). Because China retained its logographic writing system, many years were required to gain full mastery of reading and writing, which added to the prestige of education.

• **taotie** A stylized animal face commonly seen in Chinese bronzes.

• **logographic** A system of writing in which each word is represented by a single symbol, such as the Chinese script.

• **TABLE 4.1** Pronouncing Chinese Words	
LETTER	**PHONETIC EQUIVALENT IN CHINESE**
Phonetic equivalents for the vowels and especially perplexing consonants are given here.	
a	ah
e	uh
i	ee; except after *z*, *c*, and *ch*, when the sound is closer to *i* in *it*
u	oo; as in English *food*
c	ts (*ch*, however, is like English *ch*)
q	ch
z	dz
zh	j
x	sh

Why did China retain a logographic writing system even after encounters with phonetic ones? Although phonetic systems have many real advantages, especially with respect to ease of learning to read, there are some costs to dropping a logographic system. People who learned to read Chinese could communicate with a wider range of people than can people who read scripts based on speech. Since characters did not change when the pronunciation changed, educated Chinese could read texts written centuries earlier without the need for them to be translated. Moreover, as the Chinese language developed regional variants, readers of Chinese could read books and letters by contemporaries whose oral language they could not comprehend. Thus the Chinese script played a large role in holding China together and fostering a sense of connection with the past. In addition, many of China's neighbors (Japan, Korea, and Vietnam, in particular) adopted the Chinese script, allowing communication through writing between people whose languages were totally unrelated. In this regard, the Chinese language was like Arabic numerals, which have the same meaning however they are pronounced (see Table 4.1).

The Early Zhou Dynasty, ca. 1050–400 B.C.E.

☐ How was China governed, and what was life like during the Zhou Dynasty?

The Shang campaigned constantly against enemies in all directions. To the west of the Shang were the fierce Qiang (chyang), considered barbarian tribesmen by the Shang and perhaps speaking an early form of Tibetan. Between the Shang capital and the Qiang were the Zhou

(joe), who seem to have both inherited cultural traditions from the Neolithic cultures of the northwest and absorbed most of the material culture of the Shang. In about 1050 B.C.E. the Zhou rose against the Shang and defeated them in battle. The cultural and political advances that the Shang rulers had introduced were maintained by their successors.

Zhou Politics

The early Zhou period is the first one for which transmitted texts exist in some abundance. The **Book of Documents** (ca. 900 B.C.E.) describes the Zhou conquest of the Shang as the victory of just and noble warriors over decadent courtiers led by an irresponsible and sadistic king. These documents also show that the Zhou recognized the Shang as occupying the center of the known world, were eager to succeed them in that role, and saw history as a major way to legitimate power. The three early Zhou rulers who are given the most praise are King Wen (the "cultured" or "literate" king), who expanded the Zhou domain; his son King Wu (the "martial" king), who conquered the Shang; and Wu's brother, the Duke of Zhou, who consolidated the conquest and served as loyal regent for Wu's heir.

Like the Shang kings, the Zhou kings sacrificed to their ancestors, but they also sacrificed to Heaven. The *Book of Documents* assumes a close relationship between Heaven and the king, who was called the Son of Heaven. According to the documents, Heaven gives the king a mandate to rule only as long as he rules in the interests of the people. Because the last king of the Shang had been decadent and cruel, Heaven took the mandate away from him and entrusted it to the virtuous Zhou kings. Because this theory of the **Mandate of Heaven** does not seem to have had any place in Shang cosmology, it may have been elaborated by the early Zhou rulers as a kind of propaganda to win over the conquered subjects of the Shang. Whatever its origins, it remained a central feature of Chinese political ideology from the early Zhou period on.

Rather than attempt to rule all their territories directly, the early Zhou rulers set up a decentralized feudal system. They sent relatives and trusted subordinates with troops to establish walled garrisons in the conquered territories. Such a vassal was generally able to pass his position on to a son, so that in time the domains became hereditary fiefs. By 800 B.C.E. there were about two hundred lords with domains large and small. Each lord appointed officers to serve him in ritual, administrative, or military capacities. These posts and their associated titles tended to become hereditary as well.

The decentralized rule of the early Zhou period had from the beginning carried within it the danger that the regional lords would become so powerful that they

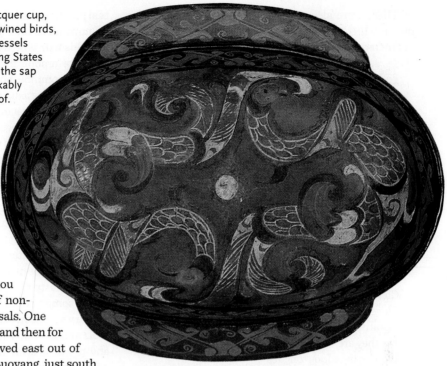

Lacquer Cup This 6-inch-long lacquer cup, decorated with images of two intertwined birds, was one of many lacquered eating vessels found in a third-century B.C.E. Warring States Period tomb. Lacquer is made from the sap of a tree native to China. It is remarkably light, strong, smooth, and waterproof. Lacquered dishes, cups, boxes, musical instruments, and sculptures became highly sought-after luxury items. (Jingzhou Prefecture Museum, © Cultural Relics Press)

would no longer obey the commands of the king. As generations passed and ties of loyalty and kinship grew more distant, this happened. In 771 B.C.E. the Zhou king was killed by an alliance of non-Chinese tribesmen and Zhou vassals. One of his sons was put on the throne, and then for safety's sake the capital was moved east out of the Wei River Valley to modern Luoyang, just south of the Yellow River in the heart of the central plains (see Map 4.2).

The revived Zhou Dynasty never fully regained control over its vassals, and China entered a prolonged period without a strong central authority. For a couple of centuries a code of chivalrous or sportsmanlike conduct still regulated warfare between the states: one state would not attack another that was in mourning for its ruler; during battles one side would not attack before the other side had time to line up; ruling houses were not wiped out, so that successors could continue to sacrifice to their ancestors; and so on. Thereafter, however, such niceties were abandoned, and China entered a period of nearly constant conflict.

Life During the Zhou Dynasty

During the early Zhou period, aristocratic attitudes and privileges were strong. Inherited ranks placed people in a hierarchy ranging downward from the king to the rulers of states with titles like duke and marquis, the hereditary great officials of the states, the lower ranks of the aristocracy — men who could serve in either military or civil capacities, known as **shi** — and finally to the ordinary people (farmers, craftsmen, and traders). Patrilineal family ties were very important in this society, and at the upper reaches, at least, sacrifices to ancestors were one of the key rituals used to forge social ties.

Glimpses of what life was like at various social levels in the early Zhou Dynasty can be found in the *Book of Songs* (ca. 900 B.C.E.), which contains the earliest Chinese poetry. Some of the songs are hymns used

in court religious ceremonies, such as offerings to ancestors. Others clearly had their origins in folk songs. The seasons set the pace for rural life, and the songs contain many references to seasonal changes, such as the appearance of insects like grasshoppers and crickets. Some of these songs depict farmers at work clearing fields, plowing and planting, gathering mulberry leaves for silkworms, and spinning and weaving. Farming life involved not merely cultivating crops like millet, hemp (for cloth), beans, and vegetables, but also hunting small animals and collecting grasses and rushes to make rope and baskets.

Many of the folk songs are love songs that depict a more informal pattern of courtship than prevailed in later China. One stanza reads:

> Please, Zhongzi,
> Do not leap over our wall,
> Do not break our mulberry trees.
> It's not that I begrudge the mulberries,
> But I fear my brothers.
> You I would embrace,
> But my brothers' words — those I dread.[1]

- ***Book of Documents*** One of the earliest Chinese books, containing documents, speeches, and historical accounts about early Zhou rule.
- **Mandate of Heaven** The theory that Heaven gives the king a mandate to rule only as long as he rules in the interests of the people.
- **shi** The lower ranks of Chinese aristocracy; these men could serve in either military or civil capacities.
- ***Book of Songs*** The earliest collection of Chinese poetry; it provides glimpses of what life was like in the early Zhou Dynasty.

There were also songs of complaint, such as this one in which the ancestors are rebuked for failing to aid their descendants:

> The drought has become so severe
> That it cannot be stopped.
> Glowing and burning, We have no place.
> The great mandate is about at an end.
> Nothing to look forward to or back upon.
> The host of dukes and past rulers
> Does not help us.
> As for father and mother and the ancestors,
> How can they bear to treat us so?[2]

Other songs in this collection are court odes that reveal attitudes of the aristocrats. One such ode expresses a deep distrust of women's involvement in politics:

> Clever men build cities,
> Clever women topple them.
> Beautiful, these clever women may be
> But they are owls and kites.
> Women have long tongues
> That lead to ruin.
> Disorder does not come down from heaven;
> It is produced by women.[3]

Part of the reason for distrust of women in politics was the practice of concubinage. Rulers regularly demonstrated their power and wealth by accumulating large numbers of concubines (legal spouses who ranked lower than the wife) and thus would have children by several women. In theory, succession went to the eldest son of the wife, then to younger sons by her, and only in their absence to sons of concubines; but in actual practice, the ruler of a state or the head of a powerful ministerial family could select a son of a concubine to be his heir if he wished. This led to much scheming for favor among the various sons and their mothers and the common perception that women were incapable of taking a disinterested view of the larger good.

Social and economic change quickened after 500 B.C.E. Cities began appearing all over north China. Thick earthen walls were built around the palaces and ancestral temples of the ruler and other aristocrats, and often an outer wall was added to protect the artisans, merchants, and farmers who lived outside the inner wall. Accounts of sieges launched against these walled citadels, with scenes of the scaling of walls and the storming of gates, are central to descriptions of military confrontations in this period.

The development of iron technology in the early Zhou Dynasty promoted economic expansion and allowed some people to become very rich. By the fifth century B.C.E. iron was being widely used for both farm tools and weapons. In the early Zhou, inherited status and political favor had been the main reasons some people had more power than others. Beginning in the fifth century wealth alone also was an important basis for social inequality. Late Zhou texts frequently mention trade across state borders in goods such as furs, copper, dyes, hemp, salt, and horses. People who grew wealthy from trade or industry began to rival rulers for influence. Rulers who wanted trade to bring prosperity to their states welcomed traders and began casting coins to facilitate trade.

Social mobility increased over the course of the Zhou period. Rulers often sent out their own officials rather than delegate authority to hereditary lesser lords. This trend toward centralized bureaucratic control created opportunities for social advancement for the shi on the lower end of the old aristocracy. Competition among such men guaranteed rulers a ready supply of able and willing subordinates, and competition among rulers for talent meant that ambitious men could be selective in deciding where to offer their services. (See "Individuals in Society: Lord Mengchang," page 101.)

Bells of the Marquis of Zeng Music played a central role in court life in ancient China, and bells are among the most impressive bronze objects of the period. The tomb of a minor ruler who died about 400 B.C.E. contained 124 musical instruments, including drums, flutes, mouth organs, pan pipes, zithers, a set of 32 chime stones, and this 64-piece bell set. The bells bear inscriptions that name the two tones each bell could make, depending on where it was struck. Five men, using poles and mallets and standing on either side of the set of bells, would have played the bells by hitting them from outside. (© Cultural Relics Press)

Lord Mengchang

DURING THE WARRING STATES PERIOD, MEN often rose to high rank on the basis of political talent. Lord Mengchang rose on the basis of his people skills: he treated his retainers so well that he attracted thousands of talented men to his service, enabling him to rise to prime minister of his native state of Qi (chee) in the early third century B.C.E.

Lord Mengchang's beginnings were not promising. His father, a member of the Qi royal family, already had more than forty sons when Mengchang was born, and he ordered the mother, one of his many concubines, to leave the baby to die. However, she secretly reared him, and while still a child he was able to win his father's approval through his cleverness.

At his father's death Mengchang succeeded him. Because Mengchang would provide room and board to men who sought to serve him, he soon attracted a few thousand retainers, many of humble background, some fleeing justice. Every night, we are told, he ate with them all in his hall, treating them equally no matter what their social origins.

Most of the stories about Mengchang revolve around retainers who solved his problems in clever ways. Once, when Mengchang had been sent as an envoy to Qin, the king of Qin was persuaded not to let so talented a minister return to help Qi. Under house arrest, Mengchang was able to ask one of the king's consorts to help him, but in exchange she wanted a fur coat kept in the king's treasury. A former thief among Mengchang's retainers stole it for him, and Mengchang was soon on his way. By the time he reached the barrier gate, Qin soldiers were pursuing him, and he knew that he had to get through quickly. One of his retainers imitated the crowing of a cock, which got the other cocks to crow, making the guards think it was dawn, so they opened the gates and let his party through.

When Mengchang served as prime minister of Qi, his retainers came up with many clever stratagems that convinced the nearby states of Wei and Han to join Qi in resisting Qin. Several times, one of his retainers of modest origins, Feng Xuan (schwan), helped Mengchang withstand the political vicissitudes of the day. When sent to collect debts owed to Mengchang in his fief of Xue, Feng Xuan instead forgave all the debts of those too poor to repay their loans. Later, when Lord Mengchang lost his post at court and returned to his fief, most of his retainers deserted him, but he found himself well loved by the local residents, all because of Feng Xuan's generosity in his name. After Mengchang reattained his court post and was traveling back to Qi, he complained to Feng Xuan about those who had deserted him. Feng Xuan, we are told, got down from the carriage and bowed to Lord Mengchang, and when pressed said that the lord should accept the retainers' departures as part of the natural order of things:

Wealth and honor attract while poverty and lowliness repel; such is the nature of things. Think of it like the market. In the morning it is crowded and in the evening it is deserted. This is not because people prefer the morning to the evening, but rather because what they want can not be found there [in the evening]. Do not let the fact that your retainers left when you lost your position lead you to bar them from returning. I hope that you will treat them just the way you did before.*

QUESTIONS FOR ANALYSIS

1. How did Mengchang attract his many retainers, and how did their service benefit him?
2. Who in this story benefited from hereditary privilege and who advanced because of ability? What does this suggest about social mobility during the Warring States Period?
3. Many of the stories about Mengchang are included in *Intrigues of the Warring States*, a book that Confucians disapproved of. What do you think they found objectionable?

*Shi ji 75.2362. Translated by Patricia Ebrey.

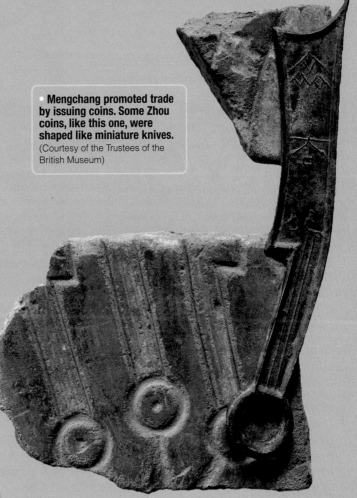

• **Mengchang promoted trade by issuing coins. Some Zhou coins, like this one, were shaped like miniature knives.** (Courtesy of the Trustees of the British Museum)

Religion in Zhou times was not simply a continuation of Shang practices. The practice of burying the living with the dead—so prominent in the royal tombs of the Shang—steadily declined in the middle Zhou period. Still, a ruler who died in 433 B.C.E. had his female musicians buried with him, evidence that some rulers still had their servants buried with them. The musicians and their instruments also testify to the role that music played in court entertainment. New deities and cults also appeared, especially in the southern state of Chu, where areas that had earlier been considered barbarian were being incorporated into the cultural sphere of the Central States, as the core region of China was called. The state of Chu expanded rapidly in the Yangzi Valley, defeating and absorbing fifty or more small states as it extended its reach north to the heartland of Zhou and east to absorb the old states of Wu and Yue. By the late Zhou period Chu was on the forefront of cultural innovation and produced the greatest literary masterpiece of the era, the *Songs of Chu*, a collection of fantastical poems full of images of elusive deities and shamans who can fly through the spirit world. Images found in Chu tombs, painted on coffins or pieces of silk, show both fearsome deities and spirit journeys.

The Warring States, 403–221 B.C.E.

The Warring States Period, 403–221 B.C.E.

☐ How did advances in military technology contribute to the rise of independent states?

By 400 B.C.E. advances in military technology were undermining the old aristocratic social structure of the Zhou. Large, well-drilled infantry armies able to withstand and defeat chariot-led forces became potent military forces in the **Warring States Period**, which lasted from 403 to 221 B.C.E. Fueled by the development of new weaponry and war tactics, the Chinese states destroyed each other one by one until only one state was left standing—the state of Qin (chin). In response to the human and economic costs of war, rulers sought ways to increase population and expand trade even while they destroyed one another.

New Technologies for War

By 300 B.C.E. states were sending out armies of a few hundred thousand drafted foot soldiers, usually accompanied by horsemen. Adding to their effectiveness was the development of the **crossbow** around 350 B.C.E. The intricate bronze trigger of the crossbow allowed a foot soldier to shoot farther than could a horseman carrying a light bow. One text of the period reports that a skilled soldier with a powerful crossbow and a sharp sword was the match of a hundred ordinary men. To defend against crossbows soldiers began wearing armor and helmets. Most of the armor was made of leader strips tied with cords. Helmets were sometimes made of iron.

The introduction of cavalry in this period further reduced the need for a chariot-riding aristocracy. Shooting bows and arrows from horseback was first perfected by non-Chinese peoples to the north of China proper who at that time were making the transition to a nomadic pastoral economy. The northern state of Jin developed its own cavalry armies to defend itself from the attacks of these horsemen. Once it started using cavalry against other Chinese states, they too had to

Mounted Swordsman This depiction of a warrior fighting a leopard decorates a bronze mirror inlaid with gold and silver dating from the Warring States Period. (From *Gugong wenwu yuekan*, 91 [1990])

> **❝**Attack where he does not expect it and go where he has not imagined. This is how military experts are victorious.**❞**
>
> **SUN WU**

master the new technology. From this time on, acquiring and pasturing horses was a key component of military preparedness.

Because these developments made commoners and craftsmen central to military success, rulers tried to find ways to increase their populations. To increase agricultural output, they brought new land into cultivation, drained marshes, and dug irrigation channels. Rulers began surveying their land and taxing farmers. They wanted to undermine the power of lords over their subjects in order to get direct access to the peasants' labor power. Serfdom thus gradually declined. Registering populations led to the extension of family names to commoners at an earlier date than anywhere else in the world.

The development of infantry armies also created the need for a new type of general, and rulers became less willing to let men lead troops merely because of aristocratic birth. Treatises on the art of war described the ideal general as a master of maneuver, illusion, and deception. In *The Art of War* (453–403 B.C.E.) Sun Wu argued that heroism is a useless virtue that leads to needless deaths. But discipline is essential, and he insisted that the entire army had to be trained to follow the orders of its commanders without questioning them. He also explicitly called for use of deceit:

> War is the Way of deceit. Thus one who is competent pretends to be incompetent; one who uses [his army] pretends not to use it; one who draws near pretends to be distant; one who is distant pretends to draw near. If [the enemy desires] some advantage, entice him [with it]. If he is in disorder, seize him. If he is substantial, be prepared for him. If he is strong, evade him. If he is enraged, irritate him [further]. If he is humble, make him haughty. If he is rested, make him toil. If he is intimate [with his ranks], separate them. Attack where he does not expect it and go where he has not imagined. This is how military experts are victorious.[4]

The Victorious States

During the Warring States Period states on the periphery of the Zhou realm had more room to expand than states in the center. With access to more resources, they were able to pick off their neighbors, one after the other. Still, for a couple of centuries the final outcome was far from clear, as alliances among states were regularly made and nearly as regularly broken.

By the third century B.C.E. there were only seven important states remaining. These states were much more centralized than their early Zhou predecessors. Their kings had eliminated indirect control through vassals and in its place dispatched royal officials to remote cities, controlling them from a distance through the transmission of documents and dismissing them at will. By the end of the third century one state, Qin, would have conquered all of the others, a development discussed in Chapter 7.

Confucius and His Followers

☐ *What ideas did Confucius teach, and how were they spread after his death?*

The Warring States Period was the golden age of Chinese philosophy, the era when the "Hundred Schools of Thought" contended. During the same period in which Indian sages and mystics were developing religious speculation about karma, souls, and eons of time (see Chapter 3), Chinese thinkers were arguing about the ideal forms of social and political organization and man's connections to nature.

Confucius

Confucius (traditional dates: 551–479 B.C.E.) was one of the first men of ideas. As a young man, he had served in the court of his home state of Lu without gaining much influence. After leaving Lu, he set out with a small band of students and wandered through neighboring states in search of a ruler who would take his advice.

Confucius's ideas are known to us primarily through the sayings recorded by his disciples in the *Analects*. The thrust of his thought was ethical rather than theoretical or metaphysical. He talked repeatedly of an ideal age in the early Zhou Dynasty when everyone was devoted to fulfilling his or her role: superiors looked after those dependent on them; inferiors devoted themselves to the service of their superiors; parents and children, husbands and wives all wholeheartedly embraced what was expected of them.

- **Warring States Period** The period of Chinese history between 403 and 221 B.C.E. when states fought each other and one state after another was destroyed.
- **crossbow** A powerful mechanical bow developed during the Warring States Period.

The Book of Mencius

The book that records the teachings of Mencius (ca. 370–300 B.C.E.) was modeled on the Analects *of Confucius. It presents, in no particular order, conversations between Mencius and several rulers, philosophers, and disciples. Unlike the* Analects, *however, the Book of Mencius includes extended discussions of particular points, suggesting that Mencius had a hand in recording the conversations.*

" Mencius had an audience with King Hui of Liang. The king said, "Sir, you did not consider a thousand *li* too far to come. You must have some ideas about how to benefit my state."

Mencius replied, "Why must Your Majesty use the word 'benefit'? All I am concerned with are the benevolent and the right. If Your Majesty says, 'How can I benefit my state?' your officials will say, 'How can I benefit my family,' and officers and common people will say, 'How can I benefit myself?' Once superiors and inferiors are competing for benefit, the state will be in danger.

"When the head of a state of ten thousand chariots is murdered, the assassin is invariably a noble with a fief of a thousand chariots. When the head of a fief of a thousand chariots is murdered, the assassin is invariably head of a subfief of a hundred chariots. Those with a thousand out of ten thousand, or a hundred out of a thousand, had quite a bit. But when benefit is put before what is right, they are not satisfied without snatching it all. By contrast, there has never been a benevolent person who neglected his parents or a righteous person who put his lord last. Your Majesty perhaps will now also say, 'All I am concerned with are the benevolent and the right.' Why mention 'benefit'?"

After seeing King Xiang (SHEE-ang) of Liang, Mencius said to someone, "When I saw him from a distance, he did not look like a ruler, and when I got closer, I saw nothing to command respect. But he asked, 'How can the realm be settled?'

"I answered, 'It can be settled through unity.'

"'Who can unify it?' he asked.

"I answered, 'Someone not fond of killing people.'

"'Who could give it to him?'

"I answered, 'Everyone in the world will give it to him. Your Majesty knows what rice plants are? If there is a drought in the seventh and eighth months, the plants wither, but if moisture collects in the sky and forms clouds and rain falls in torrents, the plants suddenly revive. This is the way it is; no one can stop the process. In the world today there are no rulers disinclined toward killing. If there were a ruler who did not like to kill people, everyone in the world would crane their necks to catch sight of him. This is really true. The people would flow toward him the way water flows down. No one would be able to repress them.'"

After an incident between Zou and Lu, Duke Mu asked, "Thirty-three of my officials died but no common people died. I could punish them, but I could not punish them all. I could refrain from punishing them, but they did angrily watch their superiors die without saving them. What would be the best course for me to follow?"

Mencius answered, "When the harvest failed, even though your granaries were full, nearly a thousand of your subjects were lost—the old and weak among them dying in the gutters, the able-bodied scattering in all directions. Your officials never reported the situation, a case of superiors callously inflicting suffering on their subordinates. Zengzi said, 'Watch out, watch out! What you do will be done to you.' This was the first chance the people had to pay them back. You should not resent them. If Your Highness practices benevolent government, the common people will love their superiors and die for those in charge of them."

King Xuan of Qi asked, "Is it true that Tang banished Jie and King Wu took up arms against Zhou?"

Mencius replied, "That is what the records say."

"Then is it permissible for a subject to assassinate his lord?"

Confucius considered the family the basic unit of society. He extolled **filial piety**, which to him meant more than just reverent obedience of children to their parents:

The Master said, "You can be of service to your father and mother by remonstrating with them tactfully. If you perceive that they do not wish to follow your advice, then continue to be reverent toward them without offending or disobeying them; work hard and do not murmur against them."[5]

The relationship between father and son was one of the five cardinal relationships stressed by Confucius. The others were between ruler and subject, husband

• **filial piety** Reverent attitude of children to their parents extolled by Confucius.

Mencius said, "Someone who does violence to the good we call a villain; someone who does violence to the right we call a criminal. A person who is both a villain and a criminal we call a scoundrel. I have heard that the scoundrel Zhou was killed, but have not heard that a lord was killed."

King Xuan of Qi asked about ministers.

Mencius said, "What sort of ministers does Your Majesty mean?"

The king said, "Are there different kinds of ministers?"

"There are. There are noble ministers related to the ruler and ministers of other surnames."

The king said, "I'd like to hear about noble ministers."

Mencius replied, "When the ruler makes a major error, they point it out. If he does not listen to their repeated remonstrations, then they put someone else on the throne."

The king blanched. Mencius continued, "Your Majesty should not be surprised at this. Since you asked me, I had to tell you truthfully."

After the king regained his composure, he asked about unrelated ministers. Mencius said, "When the king makes an error, they point it out. If he does not heed their repeated remonstrations, they quit their posts."

Bo Gui said, "I'd like a tax of one part in twenty. What do you think?"

Mencius said, "Your way is that of the northern tribes. Is one potter enough for a state with ten thousand households?"

"No, there would not be enough wares."

"The northern tribes do not grow all the five grains, only millet. They have no cities or houses, no ritual sacrifices. They do not provide gifts or banquets for feudal lords, and do not have a full array of officials. Therefore, for them, one part in twenty is enough. But we live in the central states. How could we abolish social roles and do without gentlemen? If a state cannot do without potters, how much less can it do without gentlemen.

"Those who want to make government lighter than it was under Yao and Shun are to some degree barbarians. Those who wish to make government heavier than it was under Yao and Shun are to some degree [tyrants like] Jie."

Gaozi said, "Human nature is like whirling water. When an outlet is opened to the east, it flows east; when an outlet is opened to the west, it flows west. Human nature is no more inclined to good or bad than water is inclined to east or west."

Mencius responded, "Water, it is true, is not inclined to either east or west, but does it have no preference for high or low?

• **Opening page of a 1617 edition of the Book of Mencius.** (Rare Books Collections, Harvard-Yenching Library, Harvard University)

Goodness is to human nature like flowing downward is to water. There are no people who are not good and no water that does not flow down. Still, water, if splashed, can go higher than your head; if forced, it can be brought up a hill. This isn't the nature of water; it is the specific circumstances. Although people can be made to be bad, their natures are not changed."

Source: Reprinted and edited with the permission of The Free Press, a Division of Simon & Schuster Adult Publishing Group, from *Chinese Civilization: A Sourcebook*, Second Edition, revised and expanded by Patricia Buckley Ebrey. Copyright © 1993 by Patricia Buckley Ebrey. All rights reserved.

QUESTIONS FOR ANALYSIS

1. Does Mencius give consistent advice to the kings he talks to?
2. Do you see a link between Mencius's views on human nature and his views on the true king?
3. What role does Mencius see for ministers?

and wife, elder and younger brother, and friend and friend. Mutual obligations of a hierarchical sort underlay the first four of these relationships: the senior leads and protects; the junior supports and obeys. The exception was the relationship between friends, which was conceived in terms of mutual obligations between equals.

A man of moderation, Confucius was an earnest advocate of gentlemanly conduct. He redefined the term *gentleman* (*junzi*) to mean a man of moral cultivation rather than a man of noble birth. He repeatedly urged his followers to aspire to be gentlemen rather than petty men intent on personal gain. The gentleman, he said, "feels bad when his capabilities fall short of the task. He does not feel bad when people fail to recognize him."[6] Confucius did not advocate social equality, but his teachings minimized the importance of class distinctions and opened the way for intelligent and talented people to rise in the social scale. The Confucian gentleman found his calling in service to the ruler.

> **❝**When you go out, treat everyone as if you were welcoming a great guest. . . . Do not do unto others what you would not have them do unto you.**❞**
>
> **CONFUCIUS**

Loyal advisers should encourage their rulers to govern through ritual, virtue, and concern for the welfare of their subjects, and much of the *Analects* concerns the way to govern well.

To Confucius the ultimate virtue was **ren** (humanity). A person of humanity cares about others and acts accordingly:

> [The disciple] Zhonggong asked about humanity. The Master said, "When you go out, treat everyone as if you were welcoming a great guest. Employ people as though you were conducting a great sacrifice. Do not do unto others what you would not have them do unto you. Then neither in your country nor in your family will there be complaints against you."[7]

In the Confucian tradition, studying texts came to be valued over speculation, meditation, and mystical identification with deities. Confucius encouraged the men who came to study with him to master the poetry, rituals, and historical traditions that we know today as Confucian classics. Many passages in the *Analects* reveal Confucius's confidence in the power of study:

> The Master said, "I am not someone who was born wise. I am someone who loves the ancients and tries to learn from them."
>
> The Master said, "I once spent a whole day without eating and a whole night without sleeping in order to think. It was of no use. It is better to study."[8]

The Spread of Confucian Ideas

The eventual success of Confucian ideas owes much to Confucius's followers in the three centuries following his death. The most important of them were Mencius (ca. 370–300 B.C.E.) and Xunzi (ca. 310–215 B.C.E.).

Mencius, like Confucius, traveled around offering advice to rulers of various states. (See "Listening to the Past: The Book of Mencius," page 104.) Over and over he tried to convert them to the view that the ruler able to win over the people through benevolent government would succeed in unifying "all under Heaven." Mencius proposed concrete political and financial measures to ease tax burdens and otherwise improve the people's lot. Men willing to serve an unworthy ruler earned his contempt, especially when they worked hard to fill the ruler's coffers or expand his territory. With his disciples

Serving Parents with Filial Piety This twelfth-century C.E. illustration of a passage in the *Classic of Filial Piety* shows how commoners should serve their parents: by working hard at productive jobs such as farming and tending to their parents' daily needs. The married son and daughter-in-law offer food or drink to the older couple as their own children look on, thus learning how they should treat their own parents after they become aged. (National Palace Museum, Taipei, Taiwan)

and fellow philosophers, Mencius also discussed other issues in moral philosophy, arguing strongly, for instance, that human nature is fundamentally good, as everyone is born with the capacity to recognize what is right and act on it.

Xunzi, a half century later, took the opposite view of human nature, arguing that people are born selfish and that only through education and ritual do they learn to put moral principle above their own interest. Much of what is desirable is not inborn but must be taught:

> When a son yields to his father, or a younger brother yields to his elder brother, or when a son takes on the work for his father or a younger brother for his elder brother, their actions go against their natures and run counter to their feelings. And yet these are the way of the filial son and the principles of ritual and morality.[9]

Neither Confucius nor Mencius had had much actual political or administrative experience, but Xunzi had worked for many years in the court of his home state. Not surprisingly, he showed more consideration than either Confucius or Mencius for the difficulties a ruler might face in trying to rule through ritual and virtue. Xunzi was also a more rigorous thinker than his predecessors and developed the philosophical foundations of many ideas merely outlined by Confucius and Mencius. Confucius, for instance, had declined to discuss gods, portents, and anomalies and had spoken of sacrificing as if the spirits were present. Xunzi went further and explicitly argued that Heaven does not intervene in human affairs. (See "Viewpoints: Mozi and Xunzi on Divine Response," page 108.)

Still, Xunzi did not propose abandoning traditional rituals. In contrast to Daoists (discussed below), who saw rituals as unnatural or extravagant, Xunzi saw them as an efficient way to attain order in society. Rulers and educated men should continue traditional ritual practices such as complex funeral protocols because the rites themselves have positive effects on performers and observers. Not only do they let people express feelings and satisfy desires in an orderly way, but because they specify graduated ways to perform the rites according to social rank, ritual traditions sustain the social hierarchy. Xunzi compared and contrasted ritual and music: music shapes people's emotions and creates feelings of solidarity, while ritual shapes people's sense of duty and creates social differentiation.

The Confucian vision of personal ethics and public service found a small but ardent following in the Warring States Period. In later centuries rulers came to see men educated in Confucian virtues as ideal advisers and officials. Neither revolutionaries nor flatterers, Confucian scholar-officials opposed bad government

and upheld the best ideals of statecraft. Confucian political ideals shaped Chinese society into the twentieth century.

The Confucian vision also provided the moral basis for the Chinese family into modern times. Repaying parents and ancestors came to be seen as a sacred duty. Because people owe their very existence to their parents, they should reciprocate by respecting their parents, making efforts to please them, honoring their memories, and placing the interests of the family line above personal preferences. Since the family line is a patrilineal line from father to son to grandson, placing great importance on it has had the effect of devaluing women.

Daoism, Legalism, and Other Schools of Thought

☐ How did the teachings of Daoism, Legalism, and other schools of thought differ from Confucianism?

During the Warring States Period, rulers took advantage of the destruction of states to recruit newly unemployed men to serve as their advisers and court assistants. Lively debate often resulted as these strategists proposed policies and defended their ideas against challengers. Followers took to recording their teachers' ideas, and the circulation of these "books" (rolls of silk, or strips of wood or bamboo tied together) served further to stimulate debate.

Many of these schools of thought directly opposed the ideas of Confucius and his followers. Most notable were the Daoists, who believed that the act of striving to improve something only made it worse, and the Legalists, who argued that a strong government rested not just on moral leadership but also on effective laws and procedures.

Daoism

Confucius and his followers believed in moral effort and statecraft. They thought men of virtue should devote themselves to making the government work to the benefit of the people. Those who came to be labeled Daoists disagreed. They thought striving to make things better generally made them worse. Daoists defended

---

• **ren** The ultimate Confucian virtue; it is translated as perfect goodness, benevolence, humanity, human-heartedness, and nobility.

Viewpoints

Mozi and Xunzi on Divine Response

● *Understandings of the nature of gods, ghosts, ancestors, and the deity Heaven varied a lot in early China. Confucius strongly supported the practice of ritual, especially sacrifices to ancestors, but he avoided talk about gods or ghosts, preferring to focus on the human world. Mozi, in the next century, was concerned that skepticism about the gods would lead people to act in undesirable ways because they would not fear divine punishment. Xunzi, later still, approved of rituals for their social effects and drew a distinction between what the educated and the uneducated thought.*

Mozi, from *The Mozi*

❝Long ago, in the time of Lord Zhuang of Qi [794–731 B.C.E.], there were two ministers named Wangli Guo and Zhongli Jiao. These two men had been engaged in a lawsuit for three years, but no judgment had been handed down. Lord Zhuang thought of executing them both, but he was afraid of killing an innocent man. He also thought of acquitting them both, but he was afraid of setting free one who was guilty. He therefore ordered the two men to bring a lamb and take an oath on the Qi altar of the soil. The two men agreed to take the oath of blood. The throat of the lamb was cut, its blood sprinkled on the altar, and Wangli Guo's version of the case read through to the end. Zhongli Jiao's version was read, but before it had been read half through, the lamb rose up, butted Zhongli Jiao, broke his leg, and then struck him down on the altar. At that time there were none of the attendants of Qi who did not see what happened, and no one in distant regions who did not hear about it. It was recorded in the spring and autumn annals of Qi, and the feudal lords handed down the story, saying, "All those who take oaths in insincerity will incur the punishment of the ghosts and spirits with just such rapidity!" If we examine what is written in the book, how can we doubt that ghosts and spirits exist?

Therefore Mozi said: Even in the deep valleys, the broad forests, the dark and distant places where no one lives, you must not fail to act with sincerity, for the ghosts and spirits will see you even there!❞

Xunzi, from *The Xunzi*

❝You pray for rain and it rains. Why? For no particular reason, I say. It is just as though you had not prayed for rain and it rained anyway. The sun and moon undergo an eclipse and you try to save them; a drought occurs and you pray for rain; you consult the arts of divination before making a decision on some important matter. But it is not as though you could hope to accomplish anything by such ceremonies. They are done merely for ornament. Hence the gentleman regards them as ornaments, but the common people regard them as supernatural. He who considers them ornaments is fortunate; he who considers them supernatural is unfortunate.❞

Source: Burton Watson, trans., *The Basic Writings of Mo Tzu, Hsün Tzu, and Han Fei Tzu* (Columbia University Press, 1967), 98–99, 85. Copyright © 1967 by Columbia University Press. Reprinted with permission of the publisher.

QUESTIONS FOR ANALYSIS

1. What can we infer about ordinary people's ideas about religion from these passages? How complete of a view of the religious attitudes of the time do you think these passages give us?
2. Do you find one of these thinkers more persuasive than the other, and why? How would people of the time have read these arguments?

---

private life and wanted the rulers to leave the people alone. They sought to go beyond everyday concerns and to let their minds wander freely. Rather than making human beings and human actions the center of concern, they focused on the larger scheme of things, the whole natural order identified as the Way, or **Dao**.

Early Daoist teachings are known from two surviving books, the *Laozi* and the *Zhuangzi*, both dating to the third century B.C.E. Laozi, the putative author of the *Laozi*, may not be a historical figure, but the text as-cribed to him has been of enduring importance. A recurrent theme in this brief, aphoristic text is the mystical superiority of yielding over assertion and silence over words: "The Way that can be discussed is not the constant Way."[10] The highest good is like water: "Water benefits all creatures but does not compete. It occupies the places people disdain and thus comes near to the Way."[11]

Because purposeful action is counterproductive, the ruler should let people return to a natural state of ignorance and contentment:

> Do not honor the worthy,
> And the people will not compete.

● **Dao** The Way, the whole natural order in Daoist philosophy. In Confucianism it means the moral order.

Do not value rare treasures,
And the people will not steal.
Do not display what others want,
And the people will not have their hearts confused.
A sage governs this way:
He empties people's minds and fills their bellies.
He weakens their wills and strengthens their bones.
Keep the people always without knowledge and
    without desires,
For then the clever will not dare act.
Engage in no action and order will prevail.[12]

In the philosophy of the *Laozi*, the people would be better off if they knew less, gave up tools, renounced writing, stopped envying their neighbors, and lost their desire to travel or engage in war.

Zhuangzi (369–286 B.C.E.), the author of the book of the same name, shared many of the central ideas of the *Laozi*. He was proud of his disinterest in politics. In one of his many anecdotes, he reported that the king of Chu once sent an envoy to invite him to take over the government of his realm. In response Zhuangzi asked the envoy whether a tortoise that had been held as sacred for three thousand years would prefer to be dead with its bones venerated or alive with its tail dragging in the mud. When the envoy agreed that life was preferable, Zhuangzi told the envoy to leave. He preferred to drag his tail in the mud.

The *Zhuangzi* is filled with parables, flights of fancy, and fictional encounters between historical figures, including Confucius and his disciples. A more serious strain of Zhuangzi's thought concerned death. He questioned whether we can be sure life is better than death. People fear what they do not know, the same way a captive girl will be terrified when she learns she is to become the king's concubine. Perhaps people will discover that death has as many delights as life in the palace.

When a friend expressed shock that Zhuangzi was not weeping at his wife's death but rather singing, Zhuangzi explained:

> When she first died, how could I have escaped feeling the loss? Then I looked back to the beginning before she had life. Not only before she had life, but before she had form. Not only before she had form, but before she had vital energy. In this confused amorphous realm, something changed and vital energy appeared; when the vital energy was changed, form appeared; with changes in form, life began. Now there is another change bringing death. This is like the progression of the four seasons of spring and fall, winter and summer. Here she was lying down to sleep in a huge room and I followed her, sobbing and wailing. When I realized my actions showed I hadn't understood destiny, I stopped.[13]

Zhuangzi was similarly iconoclastic in his political ideas. In one parable a wheelwright insolently tells a duke that books are useless because all they contain are the dregs of men long dead. The duke, insulted, threatens to execute the wheelwright if he cannot give an adequate explanation of his remark. The wheelwright replies:

> I see things in terms of my own work. When I chisel at a wheel, if I go slow, the chisel slides and does not stay put; if I hurry, it jams and doesn't move properly. When it is neither too slow nor too fast, I can feel it in my hand and respond to it from my heart. My mouth cannot describe it in words, but there is something there. I cannot teach it to my son, and my son cannot learn it from me. So I have gone on for seventy years, growing old chiseling wheels. The men of old died in possession of what they could not transmit. So it follows that what you are reading are their dregs.[14]

To put this another way, truly skilled craftsmen respond to situations spontaneously; they do not analyze or

□ Picturing the Past

Inscribed Bamboo Slips In 1993 Chinese archaeologists discovered a late-fourth-century B.C.E. tomb in Hubei province that contained 804 bamboo slips bearing some 12,000 Chinese characters. Scholars have been able to reconstruct more than a dozen books from them, many of them previously unknown. (Jingmen City Museum, © Cultural Relics Press)

ANALYZING THE IMAGE Can you spot any repeated characters? Can you see any very simple characters? Look in particular at the strip that is at far right. Do you see the name of the deity Taiyi (Great One) twice? Hint: *One* is a single horizontal line.

CONNECTIONS What were the consequences of recording texts on bamboo or wooden strips? How might doing so have shaped reading and writing in Zhou times? For modern archaeologists who discover these texts in tombs, would the medium used pose any challenges?

reason or even keep in mind the rules they have mastered. This strain of Daoist thought denies the validity of verbal reasoning and the sorts of knowledge conveyed through words.

Daoism can be seen as a response to Confucianism, a rejection of many of its basic premises. Nevertheless, over the course of Chinese history, many people felt the pull of both Confucian and Daoist ideas and studied the writings of both schools. Even Confucian scholars who had devoted much of their lives to public service might find that the teachings of the *Laozi* or *Zhuangzi* helped to put their frustrations in perspective. Whereas Confucianism often seems sternly masculine, Daoism is more accepting of feminine principles and even celebrates passivity and yielding. Those drawn to the arts were also often drawn to Daoism, with its validation of spontaneity and freedom. Rulers, too, were drawn to the Daoist notion of the ruler who can have great power simply by being himself without instituting anything.

Legalism

Over the course of the fourth and third centuries B.C.E. one small state after another was conquered, and the number of surviving states dwindled. Rulers fearful that their states might be next were ready to listen to political theorists who claimed expertise in the accumulation of power. These theorists, labeled **Legalists** because of their emphasis on the need for rigorous laws, argued that strong government depended not on the moral qualities of the ruler and his officials, as Confucians claimed, but on establishing effective laws and procedures. Legalism, though eventually discredited, laid the basis for China's later bureaucratic government.

In the fourth century B.C.E. the state of Qin radically reformed itself. The king of Qin, under the guidance of Lord Shang (d. 338 B.C.E.), his chief minister, adopted many Legalist policies. He abolished the aristocracy. Social distinctions were to be based on military ranks determined by the objective criterion of the number of enemy heads cut off in battle. In place of the old fiefs, the Qin king created counties and appointed officials to govern them according to the laws he decreed at court. To increase the population, Qin recruited migrants from other states with offers of land and houses. To encourage farmers to work hard and improve their land, they were allowed to buy and sell it. Ordinary farmers were thus freed from serf-like obligations to the local nobility, but direct control by the state could be even more onerous. Taxes and labor service obligations were heavy. Travel required a permit, and vagrants could be forced into penal labor service. All families were grouped into mutual responsibility groups of five and ten families; whenever anyone in the group committed a crime, all the others were equally liable unless they reported it.

In the century after Lord Shang, Legalism found its greatest exponent in Han Feizi (ca. 280?–233 B.C.E.). Han Feizi had studied with the Confucian master Xunzi but had little interest in Confucian values of goodness or ritual. In his writings he warned rulers of the political pitfalls awaiting them. They had to be careful where they placed their trust, for "when the ruler trusts someone, he falls under that person's control."[15] This is true even of wives and concubines, who think of the interests of their sons. Given subordinates' propensities to pursue their own selfish interests, the ruler should keep them ignorant of his intentions and control them by manipulating competition among them. Warmth, affection, or candor should have no place in his relationships with others.

Han Feizi saw the Confucian notion that government could be based on virtue as naive:

> Think of parents' relations to their children. They congratulate each other when a son is born, but complain to each other when a daughter is born. Why do parents have these divergent responses when both are equally their offspring? It is because they calculate their long-term advantage. Since even parents deal with their children in this calculating way, what can one expect where there is no parent-child bond? When present-day scholars counsel rulers, they all tell them to rid themselves of thoughts of profit and follow the path of mutual love. This is expecting rulers to go further than parents.[16]

If rulers would make the laws and prohibitions clear and the rewards and punishments automatic, then the officials and common people would be easy to govern. Uniform laws get people to do things they would not otherwise be inclined to do, such as work hard and fight wars, essential to the goal of establishing hegemony over all the other states.

The laws of the Legalists were designed as much to constrain officials as to regulate the common people. The third-century B.C.E. tomb of a Qin official has yielded statutes detailing the rules for keeping accounts, supervising subordinates, managing penal labor, conducting investigations, and many other responsibilities of officials. Infractions were generally punishable through the imposition of fines.

Legalism saw no value in intellectual debate or private opinion. Divergent views of right and wrong lead

---

• **Legalists** Political theorists who emphasized the need for rigorous laws and laid the basis for China's later bureaucratic government.

• **yin and yang** A concept of complementary poles, one of which represents the feminine, dark, and receptive, and the other the masculine, bright, and assertive.

to weakness and disorder. The ruler should not allow others to undermine his laws by questioning them. In Legalism, there were no laws above or independent of the wishes of the rulers, no laws that might set limits on rulers' actions in the way that natural or divine laws did in Greek thought. Indeed, a ruler's right to exercise the law as he saw fit was demonstrated by the violent deaths of the two leading Legalist thinkers: Lord Shang was drawn and quartered by chariots in 338 B.C.E., and Han Feizi was imprisoned and forced to drink poison in 233 B.C.E.

Rulers of several states adopted some Legalist ideas, but only the state of Qin systematically followed them. The extraordinary but brief success Qin had with these policies is discussed in Chapter 7.

Yin and Yang

Confucians, Daoists, and Legalists had the greatest long-term impact on Chinese civilization, but the Hundred Schools of Thought also included everyone from logicians, hedonists, and utopians to agriculturalists who argued that no one should eat who does not farm, and hermits who justified withdrawal from social life. Natural philosophy was one of the most important of these alternative schools of early Chinese thought.

One such philosophy was the cosmological concept of **yin and yang**, first described in the divination manual called the *Book of Changes* (ca. 900 B.C.E.), and developed into much more elaborate theories by late Zhou theorists. Yin is the feminine, dark, receptive, yielding, negative, and weak; yang is the masculine, bright, assertive, creative, positive, and strong. Yin and yang are complementary poles rather than distinct entities or opposing forces. The movement of yin and yang accounts for the transition from day to night and from summer to winter. These models based on observation of nature were extended to explain not only

phenomena we might classify as natural, such as illness, storms, and earthquakes, but also social phenomena, such as the rise and fall of states and conflict in families. In all these realms, unwanted things happen when the balance between yin and yang gets disturbed.

In recent decades archaeologists have further complicated our understanding of early Chinese thought by unearthing records of the popular religion of the time — astrological manuals, handbooks of lucky and unlucky days, medical prescriptions, exercises, and ghost stories. The tomb of an official who died in 316 B.C.E., for example, has records of divinations showing that illness was seen as the result of unsatisfied spirits or malevolent demons, best dealt with through exorcisms or offering sacrifices to the astral god Taiyi (Grand One).

Dagger Depicting Taiyi
Recent archaeological excavations of manuscripts from the Warring States Period have given us a much clearer understanding of religious beliefs and practices in early China. The deity Taiyi, depicted on this late-fourth-century B.C.E. drawing of a dagger, was the god of the pole star. Sacrifices were made to Taiyi to avert evil or gain his protection in battle. (Jingzhou Museum, © Cultural Relics Press)

CONNECTIONS

China's transition from Neolithic farming villages to a much more advanced civilization with writing, metalworking, iron coinage, crossbows, philosophical speculation, and competing states occurred centuries later than in Mesopotamia or India, but by the Warring States Period China was at much the same stage of development as other advanced societies in Eurasia. Although many elements of China's civilization were clearly invented in China — such as its writing system, its method of casting bronze, and its Confucian philosophy — it also adopted elements that diffused across Asia, such as the cultivation of wheat, the horse-driven chariot, and riding horseback.

Greece, the subject of the next chapter, is located very close to the ancient Near Eastern civilizations, so its trajectory was quite different from China's. It was also much smaller than China, yet in time had enormous impact on the wider world. With India and China in mind, the originality of the political forms and ideas of early Greece will stand out more clearly. We return to China's history in Chapter 7, after looking at Greece and Rome.

☐ CHAPTER REVIEW

KEY TERMS

loess (p. 92)
Anyang (p. 94)
taotie (p. 97)
logographic (p. 97)
Book of Documents
  (p. 98)
Mandate of Heaven
  (p. 98)
shi (p. 99)

Book of Songs (p. 99)
Warring States Period
  (p. 102)
crossbow (p. 102)
filial piety (p. 104)
ren (p. 106)
Dao (p. 108)
Legalists (p. 110)
yin and yang (p. 111)

☐ What was the impact of China's geography on the development of Chinese societies? (p. 92)

Chinese civilization did not spread into the Inner Asian region primarily because the mountains, deserts, and grasslands of these areas were not suited for agriculture. Instead Chinese civilizations arose in the fertile lands of the temperate zone of East Asia. The fertile loess soil of northern China was ideally suited for growing wheat and millet. Dry and cold, this region was prone to droughts and flooding from the Yellow River. Southern China was warmer and wetter, and the region around the Yangzi River was well suited for growing rice. It was in these regions of historical China that early Neolithic societies arose. By around 5000 B.C.E. many distinct regional Neolithic cultures had emerged. Over time these cultures came to share social and cultural practices, such as burial traditions, divination based on reading the cracks in bones, and fortified settlements, suggesting that there was contact and conflict between Neolithic societies.

☐ What was life like during the Shang Dynasty, and what effect did writing have on Chinese culture and government? (p. 94)

After a long Neolithic period, China entered the Bronze Age with the Shang Dynasty. Shang kings ruled over large settlements that contained palaces, temples, and altars built on rammed-earth foundations and ringed by industrial areas where artisans and craftsmen lived. War booty, including slaves who were often sacrificed to the gods, provided the king with revenue. Large armies were routinely sent out on military campaigns, and their bronze-tipped weapons and chariots gave them technological superiority over their neighbors. Shang kings served also as priests, and great wealth was invested in extraordinarily complex bronze ritual vessels. Society was sharply defined by status distinctions that were carried along patrilineal lines. From Shang times on, the Chinese language has been written in a logographic script. Written language allowed for the development of a government bureaucracy capable of ruling over a large realm. Logographic script shaped the ways people became educated and the value assigned to education.

☐ How was China governed, and what was life like during the Zhou Dynasty? (p. 98)

The Zhou Dynasty, which overthrew the Shang in about 1050 B.C.E., parceled out its territory to lords, whose titles gradually became hereditary. The *Book of Documents* described Zhou rule and the close relationship between Heaven and the king, the Son of Heaven. The Mandate of Heaven justified Zhou rule. If kings did not rule in the interests of the people, Heaven could take the Mandate away from them and confer it on a worthier person. The hereditary nature of Zhou society contributed to aristocratic attitudes and privileges. The *Book of Songs* offers glimpses into what life was like for elites and ordinary people alike. The practice of concubinage led to a distrust of women in politics. By the fifth century B.C.E. societal changes quickened as cities were built across China and iron technology promoted economic expansion. As a result, social mobility increased.

☐ How did advances in military technology contribute to the rise of independent states? (p. 102)

The ties between the Zhou king and his lords gradually weakened, and over time the domains came to act like independent states. After 500 B.C.E. China is best thought of as a multistate realm. The Warring States Period witnessed many advances in military technology. The introduction of cavalry, infantry armies, and the crossbow made warfare more deadly. The stakes rose as the independent states destroyed one another in a battle for supremacy. The warfare of this period undermined the old aristocratic social structure of Zhou society. To increase population and fund their armies, vassal lords increased agricultural output and taxed farmers. As a result, serfdom declined.

☐ What ideas did Confucius teach, and how were they spread after his death? (p. 103)

The Warring States Period was the golden age of Chinese philosophy. Confucius and his followers advocated a deeply moral view of the way to achieve order through the cultivation of virtues by everyone from the ruler on down. Key virtues were sincerity, loyalty, benevolence, and filial piety. Over the next two centuries Confucius's message was elaborated by important followers, including Mencius, who urged rulers to rule through goodness and argued that human nature is good, and Xunzi, who stressed the power of ritual and argued that human nature is selfish and must be curbed through education.

☐ **How did the teachings of Daoism, Legalism, and other schools of thought differ from Confucianism? (p. 107)**

In the contentious spirit of the age, many thinkers countered Confucian principles. Daoists like Laozi and Zhuangzi looked beyond the human realm to the entire cosmos and spoke of the relativity of concepts such as good and bad and life and death. Opposed to the Confucian emphasis on moral effort and statecraft, Daoists believed that striving to make something better could in fact make it worse. They defended the right to private life and opposed government interference. Legalists heaped ridicule on the Confucian idea that a ruler could get his people to be good by being good himself and proposed instead a strong government and rigorous laws with strict rewards and punishments. Natural philosophers explored issues that Confucius had neglected, such as the yin and yang forces that bring about the changes in the seasons, the transition from day to night, and cycles of health and illness.

SUGGESTED READING

Blunden, Caroline, and Mark Elvin. *Cultural Atlas of China.* 1983. Valuable both for its historical maps and its well-illustrated topical essays.

Chang, Kwang-chih, and Xu Pingfang. *The Formation of Chinese Civilization: An Archaeological Perspective.* 2005. Essays by leading archaeologists in China.

de Bary, William Theodore, and Irene Bloom. *Sources of Chinese Tradition.* 1999. Large collection of primary sources for Chinese intellectual history, with lengthy introductions.

Ebrey, Patricia Buckley. *Cambridge Illustrated History of China.* 2d ed. 2010. Well-illustrated brief overview of Chinese history.

Graham, A. C. *Disputers of the Tao: Philosophical Argument in Ancient China.* 1989. A philosophically rich overview of the intellectual flowering of the Warring States Period.

Ledderose, Lothar. *Ten Thousand Things: Module and Mass Production in Chinese Art.* 2000. A new interpretation of Chinese culture in terms of modules; offers fresh perspectives on the Chinese script and the production of bronzes.

Lewis, Mark. *Writing and Authority in Early China.* 1999. An examination of early Chinese thought in terms of the ways that texts create authority.

Loewe, Michael, and Edward Shaughnessy, eds. *The Cambridge History of Ancient China: From the Origins of Civilization to 221 B.C.* 1999. An authoritative collection of chapters, half by historians, half by archaeologists.

Mote, F. W. *Intellectual Foundations of China.* 1989. Brief but stimulating introduction to early Chinese thought.

Sterckx, Roel, ed. *Of Tripod and Palate: Food, Politics, and Religion in Traditional China.* 2005. Provides a fresh look at many elements in early Chinese culture.

Thorp, Robert. *China in the Early Bronze Age: Shang Civilization.* 2005. Clear synthesis based on recent research.

Thorp, Robert, and Richard Vinograd. *Chinese Art and Culture.* 2001. Broad coverage of all of China's visual arts.

Yang, Xin, ed. *The Golden Age of Chinese Archaeology.* 1999. The well-illustrated catalogue of a major show of Chinese archaeological finds.

NOTES

1. Patricia Buckley Ebrey, *Chinese Civilization: A Sourcebook,* 2d ed., revised and expanded (New York: Free Press/Macmillan, 1993), p. 11. All quotations from this work reprinted and edited with the permission of The Free Press, a Division of Simon & Schuster, Inc. Copyright © 1993 by Patricia Buckley Ebrey. Copyright © 1981 by The Free Press. All rights reserved.

2. Edward Shaughnessy, "Western Zhou History," in *The Cambridge History of Ancient China,* ed. M. Loewe and E. Shaughnessy (New York: Cambridge University Press, 1999), p. 336. Reprinted with the permission of Cambridge University Press.

3. Patricia Buckley Ebrey, *The Cambridge Illustrated History of China* (Cambridge: Cambridge University Press, 1996), p. 34.

4. Victor H. Mair, Nancy S. Steinhardt, and Paul Goldin, ed., *Hawai'i Reader in Traditional Chinese Culture* (Honolulu: University of Hawai'i Press, 2005), p. 117. Copyright © 2005 by University of Hawaii Press. Reprinted with permission of the publisher.

5. Ebrey, *Chinese Civilization,* p. 21.

6. Ibid., p. 19.

7. Ibid.

8. *Analects* 7.19, 15.30. Translated by Patricia Ebrey.

9. Ebrey, *Chinese Civilization,* p. 26.

10. Ibid., p. 27.

11. Ibid., p. 28, modified.

12. Ibid., p. 28.

13. Ibid., p. 31.

14. Ibid.

15. Ibid., p. 33.

16. Ibid., p. 35.

For practice quizzes and other study tools, see the **Online Study Guide** at bedfordstmartins.com/mckayworld.

For primary sources from this period, see *Sources of World Societies*, **Second Edition**.

For Web sites, images, and documents related to topics in this chapter, visit **Make History** at bedfordstmartins.com/mckayworld.

• **Greek Boy with Goose** In the Hellenistic culture that developed across a huge area after Alexander the Great's conquests, wealthy urban residents wanted art that showed real people rather than gods. This statue of a little boy wrestling a goose, originally carved about 200 B.C.E., no doubt found an eager buyer. (Vanni/Art Resource, NY)

The people of ancient Greece developed a culture that fundamentally shaped the civilization of the western part of Eurasia much as the Chinese culture shaped the civilization of the eastern part. The Greeks were the first in the Mediterranean and neighboring areas to explore most of the philosophical questions that still concern thinkers today. Going beyond mythmaking, the Greeks strove to understand the world in logical, rational terms. The result was the birth of philosophy and science, subjects as important to many Greeks as religion. Drawing on their day-by-day experiences, the Greeks also developed the concept of politics, and their contributions to literature still fertilize intellectual life today.

The Greek Experience 3500–100 B.C.E.

The history of the Greeks is divided into two broad periods: the Hellenic, roughly the time between the founding of the first complex societies in the area that is now the Greek islands and mainland, about 3500 B.C.E., and the rise of the kingdom of Macedonia in the north of Greece in 338 B.C.E.; and the Hellenistic, the years from the reign of Alexander the Great (336–323 B.C.E.) through the spread of Greek culture from Spain to India (ca. 100 B.C.E.; see Chapter 3). During the Hellenic period Greeks developed a distinctive form of city-state known as the polis and made lasting cultural and intellectual achievements. During the Hellenistic period Macedonian and Greek armies defeated the Persian Empire and built new cities and kingdoms. During their conquests they blended their ideas and traditions with those of the societies they encountered, creating a vibrant culture. •

Hellas: The Land and the Polis, ca. 3500–800 B.C.E.

□ How did the geography of Greece shape its earliest history and lead to the growth of the polis?

Hellas, as the Greeks call their land, encompasses the Greek peninsula with its southern peninsular extension, known as the Peloponnesus (peh-luh-puh-NEE-suhs), and the islands surrounding it, an area known as the Aegean basin (Map 5.1). In ancient times this basin included the Greek settlements in Ionia, the western coast of the area known as Anatolia in modern western Turkey. Geography acts as an enormously divisive force in Greek life; mountains divide the land, and, although there are good harbors on the sea, there are no navigable rivers. The geographical fragmentation of Greece encouraged political fragmentation. Communications were poor, with rocky tracks far more common than

MAP 5.1 Classical Greece, ca. 450 B.C.E. In antiquity the home of the Greeks included the islands of the Aegean and the western shore of Turkey as well as the Greek peninsula itself. Crete, the home of Minoan civilization, is the large island at the bottom of the map. The Peloponnesian peninsula, where Sparta is located, is connected to the rest of mainland Greece by a very narrow isthmus at Corinth.

roads. Early in Greek history several kingdoms did emerge, which later became known as the Minoan (muh-NOH-uhn) and Mycenaean (migh-suh-NEE-uhn), but the rugged terrain prohibited the growth of a great empire like those of Mesopotamia or Egypt. Instead the independent city-state, known as the polis, became the most common form of government.

The Minoans and Mycenaeans

Humans came into Greece over many thousands of years, in waves of immigration whose place of origin and cultural characteristics have been the source of much scholarly debate. The first to arrive were hunter-gatherers, but techniques of agriculture and animal domestication had spread into Greece from Turkey by about 6500 B.C.E., after which small farming communities worked much of the land. Early Greek settlers brought skills in making bronze weapons and tools, which had became more common about 3500 B.C.E.

On the large island of Crete, farmers and fishermen began to trade their surpluses with their neighbors, and cities grew, housing artisans and merchants. Beginning about 2000 B.C.E. Cretans voyaged throughout the eastern Mediterranean and the Aegean, carrying the copper and tin needed for bronze and many other goods. Social hierarchies developed, and in many cities certain individuals came to hold power, although exactly how this happened is not clear. The Cretans began to use writing about 1900 B.C.E., in a form later scholars called Linear A, but this has not been deciphered. What we can know about the culture of Crete thus depends on archaeological and artistic evidence, and of this there is a great deal. At about the same time that writing began, rulers in several cities of Crete began to build large structures with hundreds of interconnected rooms. The largest of these, at Knossos (NO-suhs), has over a thousand rooms along with pipes for bringing in drinking water and sewers to get rid of waste. The archaeologists who discovered these huge structures called them palaces, and they named the flourishing and vibrant culture of this era Minoan, after the mythical king of Crete, Minos.

Minoan society was wealthy and, to judge by the absence of fortifications on the island, relatively peaceful. Few specifics are known about Minoan political life except that a king and a group of nobles stood at its head. In terms of their religious life, Minoans appear to have worshipped goddesses far more than gods. Whether this translated into more egalitarian gender roles for real people is unclear, but surviving Minoan art, including frescoes and figurines, shows women as well as men leading religious activities, watching entertainment, and engaging in athletic competitions, such as leaping over bulls. Beginning about 1700 B.C.E. Minoan society was disrupted by a series of earthquakes and volcanic eruptions on nearby islands, some of which resulted in large tsunamis. But new settlements and palaces were often built following these disasters.

As Minoan culture was flourishing on Crete, a different type of society developed on the mainland. This society was founded by groups who had migrated in during the period after 2000 B.C.E., and its members spoke an early form of Greek. By about 1650 B.C.E. one group of these immigrants had founded a powerful kingdom at Mycenae in the Peloponnesus, from which later scholars gave the culture its name, Mycenaean. Early Mycenaean Greeks raised palaces and established cities at Thebes, Athens, and elsewhere. As in Crete, the political unit was the kingdom, and the king and his warrior aristocracy stood at the top of society. The seat and symbol of the king's power was his palace, which was also the economic center of the kingdom. Within its walls royal artisans fashioned gold jewelry and rich ornaments, made and decorated fine pottery, forged weapons, prepared hides and wool for clothing, and manufactured the other goods needed by the king and his supporters.

Mycenaean Dagger Blade This scene in gold and silver on the blade of an iron dagger depicts hunters armed with spears and protected by shields defending themselves against charging lions. The Mycenaeans were a robust, warlike people who enjoyed the thrill and the danger of hunting. (National Archaeological Museum, Athens/Ancient Art & Architecture Collection/The Bridgeman Art Library)

Palace scribes kept records with a script known as Linear B, which has been deciphered so that information on Mycenaean culture comes through inscriptions and other forms of written records as well as buildings and other objects. All of these point to a society in which war was common. Mycenaean cities were all fortified by thick stone walls, and graves contain spears, javelins, swords, helmets, and the first examples of metal armor known in the world.

Contacts between the Minoans and Mycenaeans were originally peaceful, and Minoan culture and trade goods flooded the Greek mainland. But around 1450 B.C.E., possibly in the wake of an earthquake that left Crete vulnerable, the Mycenaeans attacked Crete, destroying many towns and occupying Knossos. For about the next fifty years, the Mycenaeans ruled much of the island. The palaces at Knossos and other cities of the Aegean became grander as wealth gained through trade and tribute flowed into the treasuries of various Mycenaean kings. Prosperity, however, did not bring peace, and between 1300 and 1000 B.C.E. various kingdoms in and beyond Greece ravaged one another in a savage series of wars that destroyed both the Minoan and Mycenaean civilizations.

The fall of the Minoans and Mycenaeans was part of what some scholars see as a general collapse of Bronze Age civilizations in the eastern Mediterranean, including the end of the Egyptian New Kingdom and the fall of the Hittite Empire (see Chapter 2). This collapse appears to have had a number of causes: invasions and migrations by outsiders, including groups the Egyptians called the Sea Peoples and later Greeks called the Dorians, who destroyed cities and disrupted trade and production; changes in warfare and weaponry, which made foot soldiers the most important factor in battles and reduced the power of kings and wealthy nobles fighting from chariots; and natural disasters such as volcanic eruptions, earthquakes, and droughts, which reduced the amount of food and contributed to famines.

In Greece these factors worked together to usher in a period of poverty and disruption that historians have traditionally called the "Dark Age" of Greece (ca. 1100–800 B.C.E.). Even writing, which was not widespread in any case, was a casualty of the chaos. Traditions and stories continued to circulate orally, however. These included tales of the heroic deeds of legendary heroes similar to the epic poems of Mesopotamia. Sometime in the eighth or seventh century many of these were gathered together in two long epic poems, the *Iliad*, which tells of a war similar to those fought by Mycenaean kings, and the *Odyssey*, which records the adventures of one of the heroes of that war. These poems were recited orally, and once writing was reintroduced to Greece, they were written down and attributed to an author named Homer, about whom there are many legends but no historical sources. The two poems present human and divine characters who are larger than life but also petty, vindictive, pouting, and deceitful, flaws that drive the action forward, usually with tragic results. The first lines of the *Iliad*, which speak of the actions of the war hero Achilles against the Achaeans (uh-KEE-uhnz), capture such results well:

> Sing, O goddess, the anger of Achilles son of Peleus, that brought countless ills upon the Achaeans. Many a brave soul did it send hurrying down to Hades [hell], and many a hero did it yield as prey to dogs and vultures.[1]

The Development of the Polis

Greece's Dark Age actually saw two developments that would be central to later Greek history and to Greek influence on the world. The first of these was the migration of Greek-speaking peoples around the Aegean, spreading their culture to the islands and to the shores of Anatolia. The second, and more important, development was the **polis** (plural *poleis*), which is generally translated as "city-state." The earliest states in Sumeria were also city-states, as were many of the small Mycenaean kingdoms. What differentiated this new Greek form from the older models is the fact that the polis was more than a political institution; it was a community of citizens with their own customs and laws. The physical, religious, and political form of the polis varied from place to place, but everywhere it was relatively small, reflecting the fragmented geography of Greece. The very smallness of the polis enabled Greeks to see how they fit individually into the overall system — and in this way, how the individual parts made up the social whole. This notion of community was fundamental to the polis and was the very badge of Greekness.

The polis included a city and its surrounding countryside. The people of the polis typically lived in a compact group of houses within the city, which by the fifth century B.C.E. was generally surrounded by a wall. Another feature was a usually elevated area called the acropolis, where the people erected temples, altars, public monuments, and various dedications to the gods of the polis. The polis also contained a public square or marketplace, the agora, where there were porticoes, shops, public buildings, and courts. Originally the place where the warrior assembly met, the agora became the political center of the polis.

The *chora* (KOHR-uh), which included the surrounding countryside of the polis, was typically the community's source of wealth. Farmers left the city each morning to work their fields or tend their flocks of sheep and goats, and they returned at night. On the lands not suitable for farming or grazing, people often quarried stone or mined for precious metals. Thus the polis was the scene of both urban and agrarian life.

The average polis did not have a standing army. For protection it instead relied on its citizens, who met, when necessary, as a warrior assembly. Very rich citizens often served as cavalry, which was, however, never as important as the heavily armed infantrymen known as **hoplites**, who were the backbone of the army. Hoplites wore metal helmets and body armor, carried heavy, round shields, and armed themselves with spears and swords.

Greek poleis had several different types of government, of which the most common were democracy and oligarchy. In principle, **democracy**, which translates as "the power of the people," meant that all people, without respect to birth or wealth, had a say in how the government was run. In reality, however, Greek democracy meant the rule of citizens, not the people as a whole, and citizenship was limited to free adult men who had lived in the polis a long time. The remaining free men, resident foreigners, slaves, and all women were not citizens and had no political voice. In other words, none of the Greek democracies reflected the modern concept that all people are created equal. Still, democracy was attractive because it permitted male citizens to share equally in determining the diplomatic and military policies of the polis.

Spartan Hoplite This bronze figurine portrays an armed foot soldier about to strike an enemy. His massive helmet with its full crest gives his head nearly complete protection, while a metal corselet covers his chest and back, and greaves (similar to today's shin guards) protect his shins. In his right hand he carries a thrusting spear (now broken off), and in his left a large round shield. (Bildarchiv Preussischer Kulturbesitz/Art Resource, NY)

- **polis** Generally translated as "city-state," it was the basic political and institutional unit of ancient Greece.
- **hoplites** Heavily armed citizens who served as infantrymen and fought to defend the polis.
- **democracy** A type of Greek government in which all citizens administered the workings of government.

Oligarchy, which literally means "the rule of the few," was government by a small group of wealthy citizens. Many Greeks preferred oligarchy because it provided more political stability than did democracy. Although oligarchy was the government of the prosperous, it left the door open to political and social advancement. If members of the polis could meet property or money qualifications, they could enter the governing circle. Moreover, oligarchs generally listened to the concerns of the people, a major factor in the long success of this form of government.

Sporadic periods of violent political and social upheaval often led to a third type of government—tyranny. **Tyranny** was rule by one man who had seized power by unconstitutional means, generally by using his wealth to win a political following that toppled the existing legal government. Tyrants were not always oppressive rulers, however, and sometimes used their power to benefit average citizens.

Population and Politics in the Archaic Age, ca. 800–500 B.C.E.

☐ What were the major developments of the Archaic age, and how did Sparta and Athens create new forms of government?

The maturation of the polis coincided with an era, later termed the Archaic age, that saw two developments of lasting importance. The first was the even wider geographical reach of the Greeks, who now ventured as far east as the Black Sea and as far west as the Atlantic Ocean. The next was the rise to prominence of two particular poleis, Sparta and Athens, each with a distinctive system of government.

Greece's Overseas Expansion

With stability and prosperity, the Greek world grew in wealth and numbers, which brought new problems. The increase in population created more demand for food than the land could supply. The resulting social and political tensions drove many people to seek new homes outside of Greece (Map 5.2).

From about 750 to 550 B.C.E. Greeks poured onto the coasts of the northern Aegean and the Black Sea,

southward along the North Africa coast, and then westward to Sicily, southern Italy, and beyond to Spain and the Atlantic. In contrast to earlier military invasions and migrations of peoples, these were very often intentional colonizing ventures, organized and planned by a specific polis seeking new land for its residents. In all these places the Greeks established flourishing cities that created a much larger market for agricultural and manufactured goods. A later wave of colonization from 500 to 400 B.C.E. spread Greeks throughout the northern coast of the Black Sea as far east as southern Russia. Colonization on this scale meant that the future culture of this entire area would be Greek, a heritage that Rome would later share.

Around the time of these territorial expansions, important changes were taking place within Greece, in Sparta and Athens. These included the formation of new social and political structures.

The Growth of Sparta

During the Archaic period, one of the poleis on the Peloponnesian peninsula, Sparta, also faced problems of overpopulation and shortages of fertile land. The Spartans solved both by conquering the agriculturally rich region of Messenia to the west of Sparta in 715 B.C.E. (see Map 5.1), making the Messenians helots, state slaves. The helots soon rose in a revolt that took the Spartans thirty years to crush. Afterward, non-nobles who had shared in the fighting as foot soldiers appear to have demanded rights equal to those of the nobility and a voice in the government. (In more recent history, similar demands in the United States during the Vietnam War led to a lowering of the voting age to eighteen, to match the age at which soldiers were drafted.)

Under intense pressure the aristocrats agreed to remodel the state into a new system, called the Lycurgan regimen after Lycurgus (ligh-KUHR-guhs), a legendary lawgiver. Under this system all Spartan citizens were given equal political rights. Two kings, who were primarily military leaders, and a council of nobles shared executive power with five ephors (EH-fuhrs), overseers elected by the citizens. Economically, the helots did all the work, while Spartan citizens devoted their time to military training, and Sparta became extremely powerful.

In the Lycurgan system every citizen owed primary allegiance to Sparta, and individuals placed the defense of Sparta over their own needs. Even family life was sacrificed to the polis. After long, hard military training that began at age seven, citizens became lifelong soldiers, the best in Greece. In battle Spartans were supposed to stand and die rather than retreat. An anecdote frequently repeated about one Spartan mother sums up Spartan military values. As her son

- **oligarchy** A type of Greek government in which a small group of wealthy citizens, not necessarily of aristocratic birth, ruled.
- **tyranny** Rule by one man who took over an existing government, generally by using his wealth to gain a political following.

was setting off to battle, the mother handed him his shield and advised him to come back either victorious, carrying the shield, or dead, being carried on it. Spartan men were expected to train vigorously, do with little, and like it, qualities reflected even today in the word *spartan*.

Similar rigorous requirements applied to Spartan women, who were unique in all Greek society. Xenophon, a later Athenian admirer of the Spartans, commented that Lycurgus had:

> insisted on the training of the body as incumbent no less on the female than the male; and in pursuit of the same idea instituted rival contests in running and feats of strength for women as for men. His belief was that where both parents were strong their progeny would be found to be more vigorous.[2]

With men in military service much of their lives, women in citizen families ran the estates and owned land in their own right, and they were not physically restricted or secluded. But Spartans expected them to be good wives and strict mothers of future soldiers. Because men often did not see their wives or other women for long periods not only in times of war but also in peace, their most meaningful relations were same-sex ones. The Spartan military leaders viewed such relationships as militarily advantageous because they believed that men would fight even more fiercely for lovers and comrades. Close links among men thus contributed to Spartan civic life, which was admired throughout the Greek world.

Golden Comb This golden comb, made about 400 B.C.E. in Scythia (now part of Ukraine), shows a battle between three warriors, perhaps the three brothers who are the legendary founders of Scythia. Their dress shows a combination of Greek and Eastern details; the mounted horseman is clothed with largely Greek armor, while the warriors on foot are wearing Eastern dress. The comb may have been made by a Greek craftsman who had migrated to the Black Sea area as the Greeks established colonies there, but it was buried in a Scythian burial mound. (© Boltin Picture Library/The Bridgeman Art Library)

MAP 5.2 Greek Colonization, ca. 750–550 B.C.E. The Greeks established colonies along the shores of the Mediterranean and the Black Seas, spreading Greek culture and creating a large trading network.

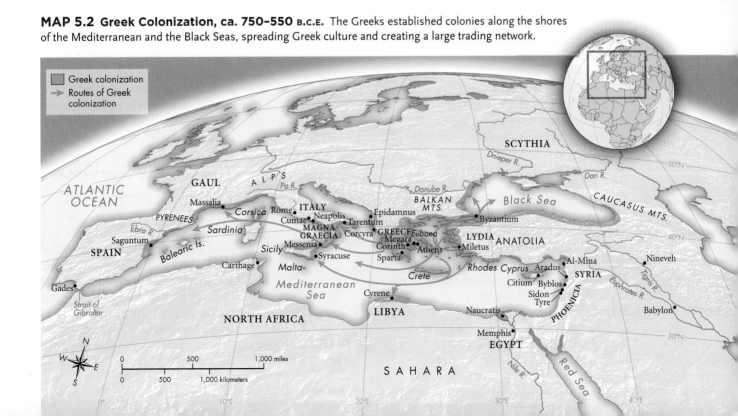

The Evolution of Athens

Like Sparta, Athens faced pressing social and economic problems during the Archaic period. The late seventh century B.C.E. was for Athens a time of turmoil because aristocrats, many of them wealthy from trade, had begun to seize the holdings of smaller landowners. In 621 B.C.E. the aristocrat Draco (DRAY-koh), under pressure from small landholders and with the consent of the nobles, published the first law code of the Athenian polis. His code was harsh—and for this reason was the origin of the word *draconian*—but it embodied the ideal that the law belonged to all citizens. Yet the aristocracy still governed Athens oppressively, and the social and economic situation remained dire. Despite Draco's code, noble landholders continued to force small farmers and artisans into economic dependence. Many families were sold into slavery as settlement for debts, while others were exiled and their land mortgaged to the rich. Solon (SOH-luhn), an aristocrat and a poet, railed against these injustices in his poems, which he recited in the agora for all to hear. Solon's sincerity and good sense convinced other aristocrats that he was no crazed revolutionary. Moreover, he gained the trust of the common people, whose problems provoked them to demand access to political life, much as commoners in Sparta had. Around 594 B.C.E. the nobles elected him *archon* (AHR-kahn), chief magistrate of the polis, and gave him extraordinary power to reform the state.

Solon allowed nobles to keep their land, but he immediately freed all people enslaved for debt, recalled all exiles, canceled all debts on land, and made enslavement for debt illegal. Also, he allowed commoners into the old aristocratic assembly, where they could vote in the election of magistrates. Later sixth-century leaders further broadened the opportunities for commoners to take part in government, transforming Athens into a democracy.

The democracy functioned on the ideal that all full citizens should play a role in government, yet not all citizens could take time from work to do this. They therefore delegated their power to other citizens by creating various offices to run the democracy. The most prestigious of these offices was the board of ten archons, whose members, elected for one year, handled legal and military affairs. After leaving office, they entered a select council of former archons who handled cases involving homicide, wounding, and arson.

Making laws was the responsibility of two bodies, the boule (BOO-lee), or council, composed of five hundred members, and the ecclesia (ee-KLEE-zhee-uh), the assembly of all citizens. The boule was perhaps the major institution of the democracy. By supervising the various committees of government and proposing bills to the assembly, it guided Athenian political life. It received foreign envoys and forwarded treaties to the assembly for ratification. However, the ecclesia, by a simple majority vote, had the final word.

Athenian democracy demonstrated that a large group of people, not just a few, could run the affairs of state. Because citizens could speak their minds, they were not forced into rebellion or conspiracy to express their views. Like all democracies in ancient Greece, however, the one in Athens was limited. Women, slaves, and outsiders could not be citizens, and their opinions were neither recorded nor legally binding.

Thought and Culture in the Classical Period, 500–338 B.C.E.

☐ What were the lasting cultural and intellectual achievements of the classical period?

Between 500 and 338 B.C.E. Greek civilization reached its highest peak in politics, thought, and art, even as it engaged in violent conflicts. First, the Greeks beat back the armies of the Persian Empire. Then, turning their spears against one another, they destroyed their own political system in a century of warfare that began with the Peloponnesian War. Some thoughtful Greek historians recorded these momentous events. This era also saw the flowering of philosophy as thinkers pondered the meaning of the universe and human nature. In other achievements of this time, the Greeks invented drama and reached their artistic zenith in architecture. Because of these various intellectual and artistic accomplishments, this age is called the classical period.

The Deadly Conflicts, 499–404 B.C.E.

Warfare marked most of the classical period. In 499 B.C.E. the Greeks who lived in Ionia unsuccessfully rebelled against the Persian Empire, which had ruled the area for fifty years (see Chapter 2). The Athenians provided feeble help to the Ionians, and in retaliation the Persians struck at Athens, only to be defeated by the Athenian hoplites at the battle of

Areas of Persian control
Greek states at war with Persia
Neutral Greek states

Thermopylae 480 B.C.E.
Artemisium 480 B.C.E.
Plataea 479 B.C.E.
Marathon 490 B.C.E.
Salamis 480 B.C.E.
Crete

The Persian Wars, 499–479 B.C.E.

Marathon. (According to legend, a Greek runner carried the news of the victory to Athens and then died from the exertion. When the modern Olympics were founded in 1896, they included a long-distance running race between Marathon and Athens, a distance of about twenty-six miles, designed to honor the ancient Greeks.) In 480 B.C.E. the Persian king Xerxes (ZUHRK-seez) personally led a massive invasion of Greece. Under the leadership of Sparta by land and Athens by sea, many Greeks united to fight the Persians, and they engaged in major battles at the pass of Thermopylae and in the waters off Artemisium. The larger Persian army was victorious and occupied Athens, but only a month or so later the Greeks defeated the Persian navy in the decisive battle of Salamis, and in 479 B.C.E. they overwhelmed the Persian army at Plataea.

The victorious Athenians and their allies then formed the **Delian League**, a grand naval alliance intended to liberate Ionia from Persian rule. While driving the Persians out of Asia Minor, the Athenians also turned the league into an Athenian empire. They often collected tribute from other cities by force and took control of their economic resources. Athenian ideas of freedom and democracy did not extend to conquered peoples, and cities that objected to or revolted over Athenian actions were put down. (See "Viewpoints:

> **"This day will be the beginning of great evils for the Greeks."**
>
> **SPARTAN AMBASSADOR**

Two Opinions About Athenian Democracy," page 124.) Under their great leader Pericles (PEHR-uh-kleez; ca. 494–429 B.C.E.) the Athenians grew so powerful and aggressive that they alarmed Sparta and its allies. In 431 B.C.E. Athenian imperialism finally drove Sparta into the conflict known as the Peloponnesian War. The Peloponnesian War lasted a generation (431–404 B.C.E.) and brought widespread civil wars, destruction, famine, and huge loss of life. With thousands of soldiers, Athens launched an attack on the island of Sicily, which ended in disaster. The Spartans encouraged revolts in cities that were subject to Athens and defeated the once-mighty Athenian fleet in naval battles. In 404 B.C.E. the Athenians finally surrendered; Sparta stripped it of its empire, but did not destroy the city itself.

The Delian League, ca. 478–431 B.C.E.

- ■ Delian League
- ▢ Allied with Delian League, 446 B.C.E.
- ● Athenian military settlement

Thasos
Corcyra
PERSIAN EMPIRE
BEOTIA
Megara *Athens*
Corinth *Delos*
Sparta

Writers at the time described and analyzed these wars, seeking to understand their causes and consequences. Herodotus (ca. 484–425 B.C.E.) traveled the Greek world to piece together the course of the Persian wars. Although he consulted documents when he could find them, he relied largely on the memories of the participants, and he presented all sides if there were conflicting views. Thucydides (ca. 460–ca. 399 B.C.E.) was an Athenian general in the Peloponnesian War but was banished early in the conflict because of a defeat; he traveled throughout Greece seeking information about the war from all sides. His account of the war saw human greed and desire for power as the root of the conflict, and he viewed the war itself as a disaster. As he told it, at the outbreak a Spartan ambassador warned the Athenians: "This day will be the beginning of great evils for the Greeks."[3] Thucydides agreed.

The Discus Thrower This marble statue shows an athlete in mid-throw, capturing the tension in the muscles and tendons. The original was made about 450 B.C.E., perhaps by the sculptor Myron of Athens. As is true of so much Greek statuary, the original is lost, and this is a Roman copy. (Scala/Art Resource, NY)

- **Delian League** A grand naval alliance created by the Athenians aimed at liberating Ionia from Persian rule.

Viewpoints

Two Opinions About Athenian Democracy

• *Modern scholars often debate the extent and character of Athenian democracy, but such debates actually started in ancient Athens itself. Pericles, the leader of Athens, portrayed Athenian democracy very positively in a public funeral speech given, according to the historian Thucydides, in 430 B.C.E. to honor those who had died in the first year of the Peloponnesian War against Sparta. By contrast, five years later an unknown author highlighted a more negative view of Athenian democracy.*

Pericles's Funeral Speech

"Our constitution does not copy the laws of neighbouring states; we are rather a pattern to others than imitators ourselves. Its administration favours the many instead of the few; this is why it is called a democracy. If we look to the laws, they afford equal justice to all in their private differences; if no social standing, advancement in public life falls to reputation for capacity, class considerations not being allowed to interfere with merit; nor again does poverty bar the way, if a man is able to serve the state, he is not hindered by the obscurity of his condition....

The magnitude of our city draws the produce of the world into our harbour, so that to the Athenian the fruits of other countries are as familiar a luxury as those of his own....

Nor are these the only points in which our city is worthy of admiration. We cultivate refinement without extravagance and knowledge without effeminacy; wealth we employ more for use than for show, and place the real disgrace of poverty not in owning to the fact but in declining the struggle against it. Our public men have, besides politics, their private affairs to attend to, and our ordinary citizens, though occupied with the pursuits of industry, are still fair judges of public matters....

In short, I say that as a city we are the school of Hellas, while I doubt if the world can produce a man who, where he has only himself to depend upon, is equal to so many emergencies, and graced by so happy a versatility, as the Athenian."

Unknown Author on the Athenian Constitution

"As for the constitution of the Athenians, their choice of this type of constitution I do not approve, for in choosing thus they choose that thieves should fare better than the elite.... I shall say that at Athens the poor and the commons seem justly to have the advantage over the well-born and the wealthy; for it is the poor which mans the fleet and has brought the state her power.... [However] in those offices which bring security to the whole people if they are in the hands of good citizens, but, if not, ruin, the poor desires to have no share.... All those offices, however, whose end is pay and family benefits the poor do seek to hold....

Secondly, some people are surprised that everywhere they give the advantage to thieves, the poor, and the radical elements rather than to the elite. This is just where they will be seen to be preserving democracy. For if the poor and the common people and the worse elements are treated well, the growth of these classes will exalt the democracy; whereas if the rich and the elite are treated well the democrats strengthen their own opponents. In every land the elite are opposed to democracy. Among the elite there is very little license and injustice, very great discrimination as to what is worthy, while among the poor there is very great ignorance, disorderliness, and thievery....

Of such mainland states as are subject to Athenian rule the large are in subjection because of fear, the small simply because of need; there is not a city which does not require both import and export trade, and it will not have that unless it is subject to Athens—the rulers of the seas.... The Athenians alone possess the wealth of the Hellenes and the foreigners."

Sources: Thucydides, *History of the Peloponnesian War*, translated by Richard Crawley (New York: Modern Library, 1951), pp. 103–106; unknown author from Fred Fling, ed., *A Source Book of Greek History*, (Boston: D. C. Heath, 1907), pp. 155–158.

QUESTIONS FOR ANALYSIS

1. What differences do you see between the views of Pericles and the unknown author about whether democracy promotes merit and good government, and about whether the poor should have a voice in government?
2. How do the two authors differ about the reasons that Athens dominated trade?

Athenian Arts in the Age of Pericles

Although Athens eventually lost to Sparta on the battlefield, in terms of cultural and intellectual legacy Athens has been long viewed as the most important polis. Some contemporary historians, noting that this Athenocentrism fails to do justice to the other Greeks who also shaped society, culture, and history, are increasingly focusing on areas other than Athens. But Athens remains the best-studied city.

In the last half of the fifth century B.C.E. Pericles turned Athens into the showplace of Greece by making the Acropolis a wonder for all time. He appropriated

Delian League money to fund a huge building program for the Acropolis, and he gained support for the program by pointing out that it would employ many Athenians and bring economic prosperity to the city. Workers erected temples and other buildings housing statues and carvings, often painted in bright colors, showing the gods in human form and celebrating the Athenian victory over the Persians. (The paint later washed away, leaving the generally white sculpture that we think of as "classical.") The Acropolis was crowned by the Parthenon, a temple that celebrated the greatness of Athens and its patron goddess, Athena, who was represented by a huge ivory and gold statue. Even though the pollution of modern Athens is destroying these ancient buildings, it cannot rob them of their nobility and charm.

Other aspects of Athenian culture, including the development of drama, were also rooted in the life of the polis. The polis sponsored plays as part of the city's religious festivals and required wealthy citizens to pay the expenses of their production. Although many plays were highly controversial, they were neither suppressed nor censored. Not surprisingly, given the incessant warfare, conflict was a constant element in Athenian drama, and playwrights used their art in attempts to portray, understand, and resolve life's basic conflicts.

Aeschylus (EHS-kuh-luhs; 525–456 B.C.E.) was the first dramatist to explore such basic questions as the rights of the individual, the conflict between the individual and society, and the nature of good and evil. In his trilogy of plays, *The Oresteia*, he treats the themes of betrayal, murder, and reconciliation, urging the use

◻ Picturing the Past

The Acropolis of Athens The natural rock formation of the Acropolis probably had a palace on top as early as the Mycenaean period, when it was also surrounded by a defensive wall. Temples were constructed beginning in the sixth century B.C.E., and after the Persian War Pericles ordered the reconstruction and expansion of many of these, as well as the building of new and more magnificent temples and an extension of the defensive walls. The largest building is the Parthenon, a temple dedicated to the goddess Athena, which originally housed a 40-foot-tall statue of Athena made of ivory and gold sheets attached to a wooden frame. Much of the Parthenon was damaged when it was shelled during a war between Venice and the Ottoman Empire in the seventeenth century, and air pollution continues to eat away at the marble. (Courtesy, Sotiris Toumbis Editions)

ANALYZING THE IMAGE Imagine yourself as an Athenian walking up the hill toward the Parthenon. What impression would the setting and the building itself convey?

CONNECTIONS What were the various functions of the Acropolis?

of reason and justice to reconcile fundamental conflicts. The final play concludes with a prayer that civil dissension never be allowed to destroy Athens.

The plays of Sophocles (SAH-fuh-kleez; 496–406 B.C.E.) also deal with matters personal, political, and divine. In *Antigone* — which tells of how a king's mistakes in judgment lead to the suicides of his son, his son's fiancée, and his wife — Sophocles emphasizes the precedence of divine law over political law and family custom. In the closing lines he writes:

> Good sense is by far the chief part of happiness; and we must not be impious towards the gods. The great words of boasters are always punished with great blows, and as they grow old teach them wisdom.[4]

In *Oedipus the King* Sophocles tells the story of a good man doomed by the gods to kill his father and marry his mother. When Oedipus fails to avoid his fate, he blinds himself in despair and flees into exile. In *Oedipus at Colonus* Sophocles treats the last days of the broken man, whose patient suffering and uncomplaining piety ultimately win the blessings and honor of the gods.

Euripides (you-RIH-puh-deez; ca. 480–406 B.C.E.) likewise explored the theme of personal conflict within the polis and sounded the depths of the individual. With Euripides drama entered a new and more personal phase. To him the gods mattered far less than people.

Aeschylus, Sophocles, and Euripides are considered writers of tragedies: the stories of flawed people who bring disaster on themselves because their passions overwhelm reason. Athens also produced writers of comic dramas, which used humor as political commentary in an effort to suggest and support the best policies for the polis. Although comedies treated the affairs of the polis bawdily and often coarsely, they too were performed at religious festivals. Best known of the comedians is Aristophanes (eh-ruh-STAH-fuh-neez; ca. 445–386 B.C.E.), a merciless critic of cranks, quacks, and fools. He used his art of sarcasm to dramatize his ideas on the right conduct of the citizen and his leaders for the good of the polis.

Daily Life and Social Conditions in Athens

The Athenians, like other Greeks, lived with comparatively few material possessions in houses that were rather simple. A typical Athenian house consisted of a series of rooms opening onto a central courtyard that contained a well, an altar, and a washbasin. Larger houses often had a front room where the men of the

> **"** Good sense is by far the chief part of happiness; and we must not be impious towards the gods. **"**
>
> **SOPHOCLES**

family ate and entertained guests, as well as women's quarters at the back. Meals consisted primarily of various grains, especially wheat and barley, as well as lentils, olives, figs, grapes, fish, and a little meat, foods that are now part of the highly touted "Mediterranean diet."

In the city a man might support himself as a craftsman, potter, bronze smith, or tanner, or he could contract with the polis to work on public buildings. Certain crafts, including spinning and weaving, were generally done by women. Men and women without skills worked as paid laborers. Slavery was commonplace in Greece, as it was throughout the ancient world. Slaves, who were paid for their work, were usually foreigners and often "barbarians," people whose native language was not Greek.

The social conditions of Athenian women have been the subject of much debate, in part because the sources are fragmentary. The available sources suggest that women rarely played notable roles in public affairs, and we know the names of no female poets, artists, or philosophers from classical Athens. The status of a free woman was strictly protected by law. Only her sons could be citizens. Only she was in charge of the household and the family's possessions, yet the law gave her these rights primarily to protect her husband's interests. Women in Athens and elsewhere in Greece, like those in Mesopotamia, brought dowries to their husbands upon marriage, which went back to their fathers in cases of divorce.

In ancient Athens the main function of women from citizen families was to bear and raise children. They ideally lived secluded lives in which the only men they usually saw were relatives and tradesmen. How far this ideal was actually a reality is impossible to say, but women in citizen families probably spent most of their time at home, leaving the house only to attend religious festivals, and perhaps occasionally plays, although this is debated. In their quarters of the house they oversaw domestic slaves and hired labor, and together with servants and friends worked wool into cloth. Women from noncitizen families lived freer lives, although they worked harder and had fewer material comforts. They performed manual labor in the fields or sold goods in the agora, going about their affairs much as men did. Prostitution was legal in Athens, and sophisticated courtesans known as hetaerae added intellectual accomplishments to physical beauty. Hetaerae accompanied men in public settings where their wives would not have been welcome, serving men as social as well as sexual partners.

Same-sex relations were generally accepted in all of ancient Greece, not simply in Sparta. In classical Athens part of a male adolescent citizen's training was supposed to entail a hierarchical sexual and tutorial relationship with an older man, who most likely was married and may have had female sexual partners as well. These relationships between adolescents and men were often celebrated in literature and art, in part because Athenians regarded perfection as possible only in the male. Women were generally seen as inferior to men, dominated by their bodies rather than their minds.

How often actual sexual relations between men or between men and women approached the ideal in Athens is very difficult to say, as most of our sources are prescriptive, idealized, or fictional. A small number of sources refer to female-female sexual desire, the most famous of which are the poems of Sappho (SA-foh), a female poet of the sixth century B.C.E. Today the English word *lesbian* is derived from Sappho's home island of Lesbos in the northern Aegean Sea.

Same-sex relations did not mean that people did not marry, for Athenians saw the continuation of the family line as essential. Sappho herself, for example, appears to have had a daughter. Sexual desire and procreation were both important aspects of life, but ancient Greeks did not necessarily link them.

Greek Religion in the Classical Period

Like most peoples of the ancient world, the Greeks were polytheists, worshipping a variety of gods and goddesses who were immortal but otherwise acted just like people. Migration, invasion, and colonization brought the Greeks into contact with other peoples and caused their religious beliefs to evolve. But by the classical era these beliefs centered on a group of gods understood to live on Mount Olympus, the highest mountain in Greece. Zeus was the king of the gods and the most powerful of them, and he was married to Hera, who was also his sister (just as, in Egypt, Isis was Osiris's wife and sister; see Chapter 2). Zeus and Hera had several children, including Ares, the god of war, and Zeus's children with other women included gods such as Apollo and Athena and heroes such as Hercules and Perseus. Apollo represented the epitome of youth, beauty, and athletic skill, and he served as the patron god of music and poetry. His half-sister Athena was a warrior-goddess who had been born from the head of Zeus. Best known for her cult at Athens, to which she gave her name, she was highly revered throughout Greece.

Besides these Olympian gods, each polis had its own minor deities, each with his or her own local group of worshippers. The polis administered the cults and religious festivals, and everyone was expected to participate in these civic rituals, which were more like today's patriotic parades or ceremonies than expressions of

belief. Individual families also honored various deities in their homes, and some people turned to what later became known as "mystery religions" (see page 136).

The Greeks had no sacred books such as the Bible, nor did religion impose an ethical code of conduct. In contrast to Mesopotamia, Egypt, and Vedic India, priests held little power in Greece; their purpose was to care for temples and sacred property and to conduct the proper rituals, but not to make religious or political rules or doctrines, much less to enforce them.

Though much of Greek religion was local and domestic, the Greeks also shared some Pan-Hellenic festivals, the chief of which were held at Olympia to honor Zeus and at Delphi to honor Apollo. The festivities at Olympia included the famous athletic contests that inspired the modern Olympic games. Held every four years after they started in 776 B.C.E., the contests attracted visitors from all over the Greek world and lasted well into Christian times. The Pythian games at Delphi were also held every four years, but these contests included musical and literary competitions. Both the Olympic and Pythian games were unifying factors in Greek life.

Hetaera and Young Man In this scene painted on the inside of a drinking cup, a hetaera holds the head of a young man who has clearly had too much to drink. Sexual and comic scenes were common on Greek pottery, particularly on objects that would have been used at a private dinner party hosted by a citizen, known as a symposium. Wives did not attend symposia, but hetaerae and entertainers were often hired to perform for the male guests. (Martin von Wagner Museum der Universität Wurzburg. Photo: Karl Oehrlein)

Listening to the Past

Aristotle, On the Family and On Slavery, from *The Politics*

The Athenian philosopher Aristotle sought to understand everything in the world around him, including human society as well as the physical world. In The Politics, *one of his most important works, he examines the development of government, which he sees as originating in the family. Thus before discussing relations of power within the city, he discusses them within the household, which requires him to confront the issue of slavery and the very unequal relations between men and women.*

66 The city belongs among the things that exist by nature, and man is by nature a political animal. . . .

He who thus considers things in their first growth and origin, whether a state or anything else, will obtain the clearest view of them. . . . Out of these two relationships between man and woman, master and slave, the first thing to arise is the family, and Hesiod is right when he says,

First house and wife and an ox for the plough,

for the ox is the poor man's slave. The family is the association established by nature for the supply of men's everyday wants.

Seeing then that the state is made up of households, before speaking of the state we must speak of the management of the household. The parts of household management correspond to the persons who compose the household, and a complete household consists of slaves and freemen. . . .

Property is a part of the household, and the art of acquiring property is a part of the art of managing the household; for no man can live well, or indeed live at all, unless he be provided with necessaries. And as in the arts which have a definite sphere the workers must have their own proper instruments for the accomplishment of their work, so it is in the management of a household. Now instruments are of various sorts; some are living, others lifeless; in the rudder, the pilot of a ship has a lifeless, in the look-out man, a living instrument; for in the arts the servant is a kind of instrument. Thus, too, a possession is an instrument for maintaining life. And so, in the arrangement of the family, a slave is a living possession. . . .

It is clear that the rule of the soul over the body, and of the mind and the rational element over the passionate, is natural and expedient; whereas the equality of the two or the rule of the inferior is always hurtful. The same holds good of animals in relation to men; for tame animals have a better nature than wild, and all tame animals are better off when they are ruled by man; for then they are preserved. Again, the male is by nature superior, and the female inferior; and the one rules, and the other is ruled; this principle, of necessity, extends to all mankind.

Where then there is such a difference as that between soul and body, or between men and animals (as in the case of those whose business is to use their body, and who can do nothing better), the lower sort are by nature slaves, and it is better for them as for all inferiors that they should be under the rule of a master. For he who can be, and therefore is, another's and he who participates in the rational principle enough to apprehend, but not to have, such a principle, is a slave by nature. Whereas the lower animals cannot even apprehend a principle; they obey their instincts. And indeed the use made of slaves and of tame animals is not very different; for both with their bodies minister to the needs of life. . . .

A question may indeed be raised, whether there is any excellence at all in a slave beyond and higher than merely instrumental and ministerial qualities—whether he can have the virtues of temperance, courage, justice, and the like; or whether slaves possess only bodily and ministerial qualities. And, whichever way we answer the question, a difficulty arises; for, if they have virtue, in what will they differ from freemen? On the other hand, since they are men and share in rational principle, it seems absurd to say that they have no virtue. A similar question may be raised about women and children, whether they too have virtues: ought a woman to be temperate

The Flowering of Philosophy

Just as the Greeks developed rituals to honor gods, they spun myths and epics to explain the origin of the universe. Over time, however, as Greeks encountered other peoples with different beliefs, some of them began to question their old gods and myths, and they sought rational rather than supernatural explanations for natural phenomena. These Greek thinkers, based in Ionia, are called the Pre-Socratics because their rational efforts preceded those of Socrates. Taking individual facts, they wove them into general theories that led them to conclude that, despite appearances, the universe is actually simple and subject to natural laws. The Pre-Socratics began an intellectual revolution that still flourishes today, creating what we now call philosophy and science.

Drawing on their observations, the Pre-Socratics speculated about the basic building blocks of the universe, and most decided that all things were made of four simple substances: fire, air, earth, and water. Democritus (dih-MAH-kruh-tuhs; ca. 460 B.C.E.) broke

• In this painting from the side of a vase made in the fifth century B.C.E., a well-to-do young woman sits on an elegant chair inside a house, spinning and weaving. The bed piled high with coverlets on the left was a symbol of marriage in Greek art. The young woman's body language and facial expression suggest that she was not particularly happy with her situation. (Erich Lessing/Art Resource, NY)

and brave and just, and is a child to be called temperate, and intemperate, or not. . . . Here the very constitution of the soul has shown us the way; in it one part naturally rules, and the other is subject, and the virtue of the ruler we maintain to be different from that of the subject; the one being the virtue of the rational, and the other of the irrational part. Now, it is obvious that the same principle applies generally, and therefore almost all things rule and are ruled according to nature. But the kind of rule differs; the freeman rules over the slave after another manner from that in which the male rules over the female, or the man over the child; although the parts of the soul are present in any of them, they are present in different degrees. For the slave has no deliberative faculty at all; the woman has, but it is without authority, and the child has, but it is immature. So it must necessarily be supposed to be with the moral virtues also; all should partake of them, but only in such manner and degree as is required by each for the fulfillment of his duty. . . . Clearly, then, moral virtue belongs to all of them; but the temperance of a man and of a woman, or the courage and justice of a man and of a woman, are not, as Socrates maintained, the same; the courage of a man is shown in commanding, of a woman in obeying. . . .

All classes must be deemed to have their special attributes; as the poet says of women,

Silence is a woman's glory,

but this is not equally the glory of man. The child is imperfect, and therefore obviously his virtue is not relative to himself alone, but to the perfect man and to his teacher, and in like manner the virtue of the slave is relative to a master. Now we determined that a slave is useful for the wants of life, and therefore he will obviously require only so much virtue as will prevent him from failing in his duty through cowardice or lack of self-control. 99

Source: Aristotle, *Politics*, Book One, translated by Benjamin Jowett, at: http://classics.mit.edu/Aristotle/politics.1.one.html.

QUESTIONS FOR ANALYSIS

1. What does Aristotle see as the purpose of the family, and why does he begin his discussion of politics with relations within the family?
2. How does Aristotle explain and justify slavery? Given what you have read about Athenian slavery, does this argument make sense to you?
3. How does Aristotle explain and justify the differences between men and women?

this down further and created the atomic theory that the universe is made up of invisible, indestructible particles. The stream of thought started by the Pre-Socratics branched into several directions. Hippocrates (hih-PAH-kruh-teez; ca. 470–400 B.C.E.), often called the father of Western medicine, sought natural explanations for diseases and natural means to treat them. Illness was not caused by evil spirits, he asserted, but by physical problems in the body, particularly by imbalances in what he saw as four basic bodily fluids: blood, phlegm, black bile, and yellow bile. In a healthy

body these fluids, called humors, were in perfect balance, and medical treatment of the ill sought to help the body bring them back into balance. Hippocrates seems to have advocated letting nature take its course and not intervening too much, though later medicine based on the humoral theory would be much more interventionist, with bloodletting emerging as the central treatment for any illness.

The Sophists (SOF-ists), a group of thinkers in fifth century B.C.E. Athens, applied philosophical speculation to politics and language, questioning the beliefs

Procession to a Temple This detail from a vase shows Greek men and women approaching a temple, where a priestess, bough in hand, greets them. In this type of Greek pottery, men are shown with dark skin and women with white, reflecting the ideal that men's lives took place largely outside in the sun-filled public squares, and women's in the shaded interiors of homes. (Image copyright © The Metropolitan Museum of Art/Art Resource, NY)

and laws of the polis to understand their origin. They believed that excellence in both politics and language could be taught, and they provided lessons for the young men of Athens who wished to learn how to persuade others in the often tumultuous Athenian democracy. Their later opponents criticized them for charging fees and also accused them of using rhetoric to deceive people instead of presenting the truth. (Today the word *sophist* is usually used in this sense, describing someone who deceives people with clever-sounding but false arguments.)

Socrates (ca. 470–399 B.C.E.), whose ideas are known only through the works of others, also applied philosophy to politics and to people. He seemed to many Athenians to be a Sophist because he also questioned Athenian traditions, although he never charged fees. His approach when exploring ethical issues and defining concepts was to start with a general topic or problem and to narrow the matter to its essentials. He did so by continuously questioning participants in a discussion or argument rather than lecturing, a process known as the Socratic dialogue. Because he posed questions rather than giving answers, it is difficult to say exactly what Socrates thought about many things, although he does seem to have felt that through knowledge people could approach the supreme good and thus find happiness. He clearly thought that Athenian leaders were motivated more by greed and opportunism than by a desire for justice in the war with Sparta, and he criticized Athenian democracy openly. His views brought him into conflict with the government. The leaders of Athens tried him for corrupting the youth of the city, and in 399 B.C.E. they executed him.

Most of what we know about Socrates comes from his student Plato (427–347 B.C.E.), who wrote dialogues in which Socrates asks questions and who also founded the Academy, a school dedicated to philosophy. Plato developed the theory that there are two worlds: the impermanent, changing world that we know through our senses, and the eternal, unchanging realm of "forms" that constitute the essence of true reality. According to Plato, true knowledge and the possibility of living a virtuous life come from contemplating ideal forms, not from observing the visible world. Thus if you want to understand justice, asserted Plato, you should think about what would make perfect justice, not study the imperfect examples of justice around you.

Plato's student Aristotle (384–322 B.C.E.) also thought that true knowledge was possible, but he believed that such knowledge came from observation of the world, analysis of natural phenomena, and logical reasoning, not contemplation. Aristotle thought that everything had a purpose, so that to know something, one also had to know its function. (See "Listening to the Past: Aristotle, On the Family and On Slavery, from *The Politics*," page 128.) The range of Aristotle's thought is staggering. His interests embraced logic, ethics, natural science, physics, politics, poetry, and art. He studied the heavens as well as earth and judged the earth to be the center of the universe, with the stars and planets revolving around it.

Plato's idealism profoundly shaped Western philosophy, but Aristotle came to have an even wider influence; for many centuries in Europe, the authority of his ideas was second only to the Bible's. His works — which are actually a combination of his lecture notes and those of his students, copied and recopied many times — were used as the ultimate proof that something was true, even if closer observation of the phenomenon indicated that it was not. Thus, ironically, Aristotle's authority was sometimes invoked in a way that contradicted his own ideas. Despite these limitations, the broader examination of the universe and the place of humans in it that Socrates, Plato, and Aristotle engaged in is widely regarded as Greece's most important intellectual legacy.

Hellenistic Society, 336–100 B.C.E.

☐ How did Alexander the Great's conquests shape society in the Hellenistic period?

The Greek city-states wore themselves out fighting one another, and Philip II, the ruler of Macedonia, a kingdom in the north of Greece, gradually conquered one after another and took over their lands. He then turned against the Persian Empire but was killed by an assassin, and his son Alexander continued the fight. A brilliant military leader, Alexander conquered the entire Persian Empire, along with many territories to the east of Persia. He also founded new cities in which Greek and local populations mixed. Although he, too, died prematurely, his successors continued to build cities and colonies, which became powerful instruments in the spread of Greek culture and in the blending of Greek traditions and ideas with those of other peoples.

Because they understood themselves to be part of "the West," Greeks generally referred to Egypt and what we now call the Near East and western Asia collectively as "the East." Many historians have continued that usage. Despite distinctions between East and West, however, they see this period as a time when Greek and "Eastern" ways of doing things blended to some degree to create a culture that is now called "Hellenistic." During the Hellenistic period, marked by the start of Alexander's reign in 336 B.C.E., Greek became the common language of learning and business, which made trade easier and contributed to the prosperity of this era.

From Polis to Monarchy, 404–200 B.C.E.

Immediately after the Peloponnesian War, Sparta began striving for empire over all of the Greeks, but could not maintain its hold. In 371 B.C.E. an army from the polis of Thebes destroyed the Spartan army, but the The-

bans were unable to bring peace to Greece. Philip II, ruler of the kingdom of Macedonia on the northern border of Greece (r. 359–336 B.C.E.), turned the situation to his advantage. By clever use of his wealth and superb army, Philip won control of the northern Aegean, and in 338 B.C.E. he defeated a combined Theban-Athenian army, conquering Greece. Because the Greek city-states could not put aside their quarrels with one another, they fell to an invader.

After his victory, Philip united the Greek states with his Macedonian kingdom and got the states to cooperate in a crusade to liberate the Ionian Greeks from Persian rule. Before he could launch his crusade, Philip fell to an assassin's dagger in 336 B.C.E. His young son Alexander, who had been tutored by Aristotle, vowed to carry on Philip's mission and led an army of Macedonians and Greeks into western Asia. He won major battles against the Persians and seized Egypt from them without a fight. He ordered the building of a new city where the Nile meets the Mediterranean, a city that would soon be called Alexandria and that within a century would be the largest city in the world. After honoring the priestly class, Alexander was proclaimed pharaoh, the legitimate ruler of Egypt. He also took the principal Persian capital of Persepolis and performed a symbolic act of retribution by burning the buildings of Xerxes, the invader of Greece during the Persian War 150 years earlier.

By 330 B.C.E. the Persian Empire had fallen, but Alexander had no intention of stopping, and he set out to conquer the rest of Asia. He plunged deeper into the East, into lands completely unknown to the Greek world. After four years of fighting his soldiers crossed the Indus River into India, but, finally, at the Hyphasis River the exhausted troops refused to go farther. Alexander reluctantly turned south to the Arabian Sea and then back west (Map 5.3). He never saw Macedonia again, however, as he died in Babylon in 323 B.C.E. from fever, wounds, and excessive drinking. He was only thirty-two, but in just thirteen years he had created an empire that stretched from his homeland of Macedonia to India, gaining the title "the Great" along the way. Alexander was instrumental in changing the face of politics in the eastern Mediterranean. His campaign swept away the Persian Empire, which had ruled the East for over two hundred years. In its place he established a Macedonian monarchy, although this fell apart with his death.

Several of the chief Macedonian generals aspired to become sole ruler, which led to a civil war lasting forty-three years that tore Alexander's empire apart. By the end of this conflict, the most successful generals had carved out their own smaller monarchies. Ptolemy (TAH-luh-mee) seized Egypt, and his descendants, the Ptolemies, assumed the powers and position of pharaohs. Antigonus (an-TIH-guh-nuhs) and his descendants, the Antigonids, maintained control of the Macedonian kingdom in Europe. Seleucus (suh-LOO-kuhs) won the bulk of Alexander's empire, his monarchy extending from western Asia to India (see page 133), but this Seleucid kingdom gradually broke into smaller states. Until the arrival of the Romans in the eastern Mediterranean in the second century B.C.E., the Hellenistic monarchies waged frequent wars that brought no lasting results. In terms of political stability and peace, these monarchies were no improvement on the Greek polis.

To encourage obedience Hellenistic kings often created ruler cults that linked the king's authority with that of the gods, or they adopted ruler cults that already existed, as Alexander did in Egypt. This created a symbol of unity within kingdoms ruling different peoples who at first had little in common; however, kingdoms never won the deep emotional loyalty that Greeks had once felt for the polis. Kings sometimes gave the cities in their territory all the external trappings of a polis, such as a council or an assembly of citizens, but these had no power. The city was not autonomous, as the polis had been, but had to follow royal orders. Hellenistic rulers generally relied on paid professionals to staff their bureaucracies and on trained, paid, full-time soldiers rather than citizen hoplites to fight their wars.

▫ Mapping the Past

MAP 5.3 Alexander's Conquests, 336–324 B.C.E. Alexander's campaign of conquest was extensive and speedy. More important than the great success of his military campaigns was his founding of Hellenistic cities.

ANALYZING THE MAP Where are most of the cities founded by Alexander located in relation to Greece? What does this suggest about his aims?

CONNECTIONS Compare this map with Map 5.2, which shows Greek colonization in the Hellenic period (page 121). What are the major differences between the two processes of expansion?

Building a Shared Society

Alexander's most important legacy was clearly not political unity. Instead it was the spread of Greek ideas and traditions across a wide area. To maintain contact with the Greek world as he moved farther eastward, he founded new cities and military colonies and settled Greek and Macedonian troops and veterans in them. This practice continued after his death, with more than 250 new cities founded in North Africa, West and Central Asia, and southeastern Europe. These cities and colonies became powerful instruments in the spread of Hellenism and in the blending of Greek and other cultures. No comparable spread and sharing of cultures had occurred in this area since the days of the Mesopotamians.

Wherever it was established, the Hellenistic city resembled a modern city. It was a cultural center with theaters, temples, and libraries — a seat of learning and a place for amusement. The Hellenistic city was also an economic center — a marketplace and a scene of trade and manufacturing.

The ruling dynasties of the Hellenistic world were Macedonian in origin, and Greeks and Macedonians initially filled all important political, military, and diplomatic positions. The prevailing institutions and laws were Greek, and Greek became the common spoken language of the entire eastern Mediterranean. Also, a new Greek dialect called the koine (kaw-NAY), which means common, became the spoken language of the royal court, bureaucracy, and army. Everyone, Greek or easterner, who wanted to find an official position or compete in business had to learn it. Those who did gained an avenue of social mobility, and as early as the third century B.C.E. local people in some Greek cities began to rise in power and prominence. Cities granted citizenship to Hellenized natives, although because real power was held by monarchs, not citizens, the political benefits of citizenship were less than they had been in the classical period. The benefits natives gave to Hellenistic society were considerable, however. Their traditions mingled with Greek traditions to create an energetic and dynamic culture.

Although cultures blended in the Hellenistic world, the kingdoms were never entirely unified in language, customs, and thought. Greek culture generally did not extend far beyond the reaches of the cities. Many urban residents adopted the aspects of Hellenism that they found useful, but people in the countryside generally did not embrace it wholly. This meant that the spread of Greek culture was wider than it was deep, a very common pattern all over the world in eras of cultural change.

The spread of Greek culture was also shaped by the actions of rulers. The Seleucid kings built a shared society through extensive colonization. Their military settlements and cities spread from western Asia Minor along the banks of the Tigris and Euphrates Rivers and father east to India. Although the Seleucids had no elaborate plan for Hellenizing the native population, they nevertheless introduced a large and vigorous Greek population to these lands. Their presence alone had an impact. Seleucid military colonies were generally founded near native villages, thus exposing one culture to the other.

In the eastern part of the large Seleucid kingdom, several Greek leaders defeated the Seleucids and established the independent kingdoms of Parthia and Bactria in today's Afghanistan and Turkmenistan (see Map 5.3). Bactria became an outpost of Hellenism, from which the Han Dynasty of China (Chapter 7) and the Mauryan Empire of India (Chapter 3) learned of sophisticated societies other than their own. The Bactrian city of Ay Khanoum on the Oxus River, on the modern border of Russia and Afghanistan not far from China, is a good example of a far-flung city where cultures met. It had Greek temples and administration

Metal Plate from Ay Khanoum This spectacular metal plate, made in the Bactrian city of Ay Khanoum in the second century B.C.E., probably depicts the goddess Cybele being pulled in a chariot by lions with the sun god above. Worship of Cybele, an earth-mother goddess, spread into Greece from Turkey and was then spread by Greek followers as they traveled and migrated. (Courtesy, National Museum, Kabul)

> " In youth, control your passions; in middle age, practice justice; in old age, be of good counsel; in death, have no regrets. "
>
> **GREEK INSCRIPTION**

buildings, and on a public square was a long inscription carved in stone in Greek verse relating Greek ideals:

> In childhood, learn good manners
> In youth, control your passions
> In middle age, practice justice
> In old age, be of good counsel
> In death, have no regrets.[5]

The city also had temples to local deities and artwork that blended Greek and local styles (for an example, see page 133). Also, some Greeks in Bactria, including several rulers, converted to Buddhism. In the second century B.C.E., after the collapse of the Mauryan Empire, Bactrian armies conquered part of northern India, establishing several small Indo-Greek states where the mixing of religious and artistic traditions was particularly pronounced (see pages 81–82).

In the booming city of Alexandria the Ptolemies generally promoted Greek culture over that of the local Egyptians. This favoritism eventually led to civil unrest, but it also led the Ptolemies to support anything that enhanced Greek learning or traditions. Ptolemaic kings established what became the largest library in the ancient world, where scholars copied works loaned from many places onto papyrus scrolls, translating them into Greek if they were in other languages. They also studied the newest discoveries in science and mathematics. Alexandria was home to the largest Jewish community in the ancient world, and here Jewish scholars translated the Hebrew Bible into Greek for the first time.

The Growth of Trade and Commerce

Alexander's conquests not only changed the political face of the ancient world but also merged it into one broad economic sphere. The period did not see a dramatic change in the way most people lived and worked; they continued to raise crops and animals, paying rents to their landlords and taxes to the state. All Hellenistic kings paid attention to agriculture, for much of their revenue came from the produce of royal lands and the rents and taxes paid by their tenants, but farming methods changed little. By contrast, trade grew significantly as the spread of Greeks eastward created new markets. The economic unity of the Hellenistic world, like its

cultural bonds, later proved valuable to the Romans, allowing them to trade products and ideas more easily over a broad area.

When Alexander conquered the Persian Empire, he found the royal treasury filled with vast sums of gold, silver, and other treasure. The victors used this wealth to finance the building of roads, the development of harbors, and, as noted earlier, especially the founding of new cities. These cities opened whole new markets to all merchants, who eagerly took advantage of the unforeseen opportunities. Whenever possible, merchants sent their goods by water, but overland trade also became more prominent in the Hellenistic era. Overland trade with India was conducted by caravans that were largely in the hands of easterners, who led camels through the harsh terrain of western Asia. Once goods reached the Hellenistic monarchies, Greek merchants took a hand in the trade. Commerce from the east arrived at Egypt and the harbors of Palestine, Phoenicia, and Syria. From these ports goods flowed to Greece, Italy, and Spain. This period also saw the development of standardized business customs, so that merchants of different nationalities, aided especially by the koine, communicated in a way understandable to them all. Trade was further facilitated by the coining of money, which provided merchants with a standard way to value goods as well as a convenient method of payment.

The increased volume of trade helped create prosperity that made luxury goods affordable to more people. As a result, overland traders brought easily transportable luxuries such as gold, silver, and precious stones to market. They extended their networks into China in order to obtain silk, which became the most valuable overland commodity and gave the major route the name the Silk Road. (See "Global Trade: Silk," page 184.) In return the peoples of the eastern Mediterranean sent east manufactured or extracted goods, especially metal weapons, cloth, wine, and olive oil. (For more on the Silk Road in East Asia, see Chapter 7.)

More economically important than trade in exotic goods were commercial dealings in essential commodities like raw materials (such as wood), grain, and industrial products. The Hellenistic monarchies usually raised enough grain for their own needs as well as a surplus for export. For the cities of the Aegean the trade in grain was essential, because many of them could not grow enough in their mountainous terrain. Fortunately for them, abundant wheat supplies were available nearby in Egypt and in the Crimea in southern Russia.

The Greek cities paid for their grain by exporting olive oil, wine, honey, dried fruit, nuts, and vegetables. Another significant commodity supplied by the Greeks was fish, which for export was salted, pickled, or dried. This trade was doubly important because fish provided poor people with an essential element of their diet.

Harbor and Marketplace at Delos During the Hellenistic period the tiny island of Delos in the Aegean became a thriving trading center, with a paved marketplace filled with shops and stands, as well as temples paid for by merchants and ship captains. From Delos cargoes were shipped to virtually every part of the Mediterranean. Liquids such as wine and oil were generally shipped in amphora (inset) made of baked clay. Amphora were easy and cheap to make and surprisingly durable. (harbor: Rolf Richardson/age footstock/superstock; amphora: Alexis Rosenfeld/Photo Researchers)

Throughout the Hellenistic world slave traders almost always found a ready market. Only the Ptolemies discouraged both the trade and slavery itself, but they did so for purely economic reasons. Their system had no room for slaves, who only would have competed with inexpensive labor provided by free people. Otherwise slave laborers could be found in cities and temples, in factories and fields, and in the homes of wealthier people.

Most trade in bulk commodities like grain and wood was seaborne, and Hellenistic merchant ships were the workhorses of the day. A merchant ship had a broad beam, which made it more stable and allowed large cargoes, and it relied on sails for propulsion. Such ships were far more seaworthy than Hellenistic warships, which were long, narrow, and built for speed. A small crew of experienced sailors easily handled the merchant vessels. Aside from providing work for sailors, maritime trade also presented opportunities for shipbuilders, dockworkers, teamsters, and pirates. Piracy was a constant factor in the Hellenistic world and remained so until Rome cleared it from the seas.

While demand for goods increased during the Hellenistic period, few new techniques of production appeared. Manual labor far more than machinery continued to turn out agricultural produce, raw materials, and the few manufactured goods the Hellenistic world used. A typical form of manual labor was mining, in which slaves, criminals, or forced laborers dug the ore under frightful conditions. The Ptolemies ran their gold mines along harsh lines, as evident from one ancient Greek historian's description of the miners' lives:

The kings of Egypt condemn [to the mines] those found guilty of wrong-doing and those taken prisoner in war, those who were victims of false accusations and were put into jail because of royal anger. . . . The condemned — and they are very many — all of them are put in chains, and they work persistently and continually, both by day and throughout the night, getting no rest and carefully cut off from escape.[6]

The Ptolemies even condemned women and children to work in the mines. Besides gold and silver, used primarily for coins and jewelry, iron was the most important metal and saw the most varied use.

Hellenistic Religion, Philosophy, and Science

❑ How did the meeting of cultures in the Hellenistic world shape religion, philosophy, and science?

The mixing of peoples in the Hellenistic era influenced religion, philosophy, and science. The Hellenistic kings built temples to the old Olympian gods and promoted rituals and ceremonies like those in earlier Greek

Hellenistic Magical Text This text, written in Greek and Egyptian on papyrus, presents a magical incantation surrounded by a lion-headed snake. Both Hellenic and Hellenistic Greeks sought to know the future through various means of divination and to control the future through rituals and formulas that called on spirits and gods. (© British Library Board, PAP. 121 fr 3)

cities. But because many people found the rituals and ceremonies spiritually unsatisfying, they turned instead to mystery religions. In these religions, which blended Greek and non-Greek elements, followers gained secret knowledge in initiation rituals and were promised eternal life. Others turned away from religion to practical philosophies that provided advice on how to live a good life. In the scholarly realm, Hellenistic thinkers made advances in mathematics, astronomy, and mechanical design. Additionally, physicians used observation and dissection to better understand the way the human body works and to develop treatments for disease.

Religion in the Hellenistic World

When Hellenistic kings founded cities, they also built temples, staffed by priests, for the old Olympian gods. In this way they spread Greek religious beliefs throughout the Near East. The transplanted religions, like those in Greece itself, sponsored literary, musical, and athletic contests, which were staged in beautiful surroundings among splendid Greek-style buildings. On the whole, however, the civic religions were primarily concerned with ritual and did not embrace such matters as morality and redemption. While lavish in pomp and display, they did not inspire deep religious feelings or satisfy spiritual yearnings.

Consequently, people increasingly sought solace from other sources. Some relied on philosophy as a guide to life, while others turned to religion, magic, or astrology. Still others shrugged and spoke of Tyche (TIE-kee), which means "fate," "chance," or "doom" — a capricious and sometimes malevolent force.

Increasingly, many people were attracted to **mystery religions**, so called because they featured a body of rituals and beliefs not divulged to anyone not initi-

ated into them. Early mystery religions in the Hellenic period were linked to specific gods in particular places, so that people who wished to become members had to travel; therefore, these religions never became very popular. But new mystery religions, like Hellenistic culture in general, were not tied to a particular place; instead they were spread throughout the Hellenistic world. People did not have to undertake long and expensive pilgrimages just to become members. In that sense the mystery religions came to the people, for temples of the new deities sprang up wherever Greeks lived.

Mystery religions, which incorporated aspects of both Greek and Eastern religions, all claimed to save their adherents from the worst that fate could do and promised life for the soul after death. Most had a single concept in common: the belief that by the rites of initiation, in which the secrets of the religion were shared, devotees became united with a deity who had also died and risen from the dead. The sacrifice of the god and his victory over death saved the devotee from eternal death. Similarly, mystery religions demanded a period of preparation in which the converts strove to become holy, that is, to live by the religion's precepts. Once aspirants had prepared themselves, they went through the initiation, usually a ritual of great emotional intensity symbolizing the entry into a new life.

Among the mystery religions the Egyptian cult of Isis took the Hellenistic world by storm. In Egyptian mythology, Isis brought her husband Osiris back to life (see page 46), and during the Hellenistic era this power

- **mystery religions** Religious systems in the Hellenistic world that incorporated aspects of both Greek and Eastern religions; they were characterized by secret doctrines, rituals of initiation, and the promise of an afterlife.
- **Epicureanism** A Greek system of philosophy founded on the teachings of Epicurus that viewed a life of contentment, free from fear and suffering, as the greatest good.
- **Stoicism** The most popular of Hellenistic philosophies, it considered nature an expression of divine will and held that people can be happy only when living in accordance with nature.

came to be understood by her followers as extending to them as well. She promised to save any mortal who came to her, and her priests asserted that she had bestowed on humanity the gift of civilization and founded law and literature. Isis was understood to be a devoted mother as well as wife, and she became the goddess of marriage, conception, and childbirth. She became the most important goddess of the Hellenistic world. Devotion to Isis, and to many other mystery religions, spread to the Romans as well as the Greeks when the two civilizations came into greater contact.

Philosophy and Its Guidance for Life

While some people turned to mystery religions to overcome Tyche and provide something permanent in a world that seemed unstable, others turned to philosophy. Several new schools of philosophical thought emerged, all of them teaching that people could be truly happy only when they had turned their backs on the world and focused full attention on one enduring thing. They differed chiefly on what that enduring thing was.

Two significant philosophies caught the minds and hearts of many Greeks and easterners, as well as many later Romans. The first was **Epicureanism**, a practical philosophy that sought serenity in an often tumultuous world. Epicurus (340–270 B.C.E.) taught that the principal good of life is pleasure, which he defined as the absence of pain. He concluded that any violent emotion is undesirable. He advocated instead mild self-discipline and even considered poverty good so long as people had enough food, clothing, and shelter. Epicurus also taught that people can most easily attain peace and serenity by ignoring the outside world and looking instead into their personal feelings. His followers ignored politics because it led to tumult, which would disturb the soul.

Isis and Horus In this small statue from Egypt, the goddess Isis is shown suckling her son Horus. Worship of Isis spread throughout the Hellenistic world; her followers believed that Isis offered them life after death, just as she had brought Horus's father Osiris back to life. (Scala/Art Resource, NY)

Opposed to the passivity of the Epicureans, Zeno (335–262 B.C.E.) formed his own school of philosophy, **Stoicism**, named after the Stoa, the building where he taught. To the Stoics the important matter was not whether they achieved anything but whether they lived virtuous lives. In that way they could triumph over Tyche, which could destroy their achievements but not the nobility of their lives. Stoicism became the most popular Hellenistic philosophy and later gained many followers among the Romans.

Zeno and his fellow Stoics considered nature an expression of divine will, and they believed that people could be happy only when living in accordance with nature. They also stressed the brotherhood of man, the concept that all people were kindred who were obliged to help one another. The Stoics' most lasting practical achievement was the creation of the concept of natural law. They concluded that as all people were brothers, partook of divine reason, and were in harmony with the universe, one natural law governed them all.

Hellenistic Science and Medicine

Hellenistic culture achieved its greatest triumphs in science and medicine. In astronomy the most notable of the Hellenistic contributors to the field was Aristarchus of Samos (ca. 310–230 B.C.E.), who was educated at Aristotle's school. Aristarchus rightly concluded that the sun is far larger than the earth and that the stars are enormously distant from the earth. He also argued against Aristotle's view that the earth is the center of the universe, instead propounding the heliocentric theory—that the earth and planets revolve around the sun. His work is all the more impressive because he lacked even a rudimentary telescope. Aristarchus's theories did not persuade the ancient world, and his heliocentric theory lay dormant until resurrected in the sixteenth century by the brilliant astronomer Nicolaus Copernicus.

In geometry Euclid (YOO-kluhd; ca. 300 B.C.E.), a mathematician living in Alexandria, compiled a valuable textbook of existing knowledge. His *The Elements of Geometry* became the standard introduction to

Individuals in Society

Archimedes, Scientist and Inventor

ARCHIMEDES (CA. 287–212 B.C.E.) WAS BORN IN the Greek city of Syracuse in Sicily, an intellectual center in which he pursued scientific interests. He was the most original thinker of his time and a practical inventor. In his book *On Plane Equilibriums* he dealt for the first time with the basic principles of mathematics, including the principle of the lever. He once said that if he were given a lever and a suitable place to stand, he could move the world. He also demonstrated how easily his compound pulley could move huge weights with little effort:

> A three-masted merchant ship of the royal fleet had been hauled on land by hard work and many hands. Archimedes put aboard her many men and the usual freight. He sat far away from her; and without haste, but gently working a compound pulley with his hand, he drew her towards him smoothly and without faltering, just as though she were running on the surface.*

He likewise invented the Archimedian screw, a pump to bring subterranean water up to irrigate fields, which quickly came into common use. In his treatise *On Floating Bodies* Archimedes founded the science of hydrostatics. He concluded that whenever a solid floats in a liquid, the weight of the solid equals the weight of the liquid displaced. This discovery and his reaction to it has become famous:

> When he was devoting his attention to this problem, he happened to go to a public bath. When he climbed down into the bathtub there, he noticed that water in the tub equal to the bulk of his body flowed out. Thus, when he observed this method of solving the problem, he did not wait. Instead, moved with joy, he sprang out of the tub, and rushing home naked he kept indicating in a loud voice that he had indeed discovered what he was seeking. For while running he was shouting repeatedly in Greek, "Eureka, eureka" ("I have found it, I have found it").†

War between Rome and Syracuse unfortunately interrupted Archimedes's scientific life. In 213 B.C.E. during the Second Punic War, the Romans besieged the city. Hiero, its king and Archimedes's friend, asked the scientist for help in repulsing Roman attacks. Archimedes began to build remarkable devices that served as artillery. One shot missiles to break up infantry attacks. Others threw huge masses of stones that fell on the enemy with incredible speed and noise. They tore gaping holes in the Roman lines and broke up attacks. Against Roman warships he built a machine consisting of huge beams that projected over the targets. Then the artillerymen dropped great weights onto the ships, like bombs. Even more complicated was an apparatus with beams from which large claws dropped onto the hulls of enemy warships, hoisted them into the air, and dropped them back into the sea. In response, the Romans brought up an exceptionally large scaling ladder carried on ships. While the ships approached, Archimedes's artillery disabled the ladders by hitting them repeatedly with stones weighing

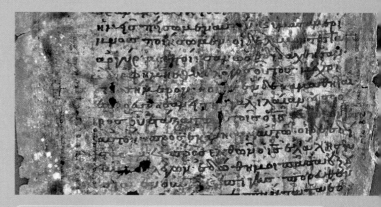

Archimedes's treatises were found on a palimpsest, a manuscript that was scraped and washed so that another text could be written over it, thus reusing the expensive parchment. In the thirteenth century Christian monks used tenth-century manuscripts of several ancient works in this way, writing over them and rebinding them into a prayer book. Scientists were able to read the original texts, which included seven works by Archimedes, using digital processing of various types of light and X-rays. (Image by the Rochester Institute of Technology. Copyright resides with the owner of the Archimedes Palimpsest, but digital images of the entire manuscript can be found at: www.archimedespalimpsest.org)

500 pounds. At last the Romans became so fearful that whenever they saw a bit of rope or a stick of timber projecting over one of the walls protecting Syracuse, they shouted, "There it is. Archimedes is trying some engine on us" and fled. When the Romans finally breached the walls of Syracuse in 212 B.C.E., a Roman soldier came upon Archimedes in his study and killed him.

Much but not all of Archimedes's work survived him. In the early twentieth century a scholar examining a thirteenth-century parchment manuscript realized that underneath the top text was another, partially scraped-off text, and that this was several works of Archimedes. He used a camera to help read the underlying text, but then the manuscript vanished. It turned up again in 1998 at a Christie's auction in New York, where it was purchased by an anonymous buyer and generously deposited at the Walters Art Museum in Baltimore. For ten years the manuscript was studied using ultraviolet and visible light and X-rays, which made the entire text visible. Contemporary science is enabling scholars of the classical world to read some of Archimedes's lost works.

QUESTIONS FOR ANALYSIS

1. What applications do you see in the world around you of the devices Archimedes improved or invented: the lever, the pulley, and artillery?
2. What effect did his weapons have on the Roman soldiers and their willingness to attack Syracuse?

*Plutarch, *Life of Marcellus*.
†Vitruvius, *On Architecture*, 9 Preface, 10.

the subject. Generations of students from antiquity to the present have learned the essentials of geometry from it.

The greatest thinker of the period was Archimedes (ah-kuh-MEE-deez; ca. 287–212 B.C.E.). A clever inventor, he devised new artillery for military purposes. In peacetime he created the Archimedian screw to draw water from a lower to a higher level. (See "Individuals in Society: Archimedes: Scientist and Inventor," page 138.) He also invented the compound pulley to lift heavy weights. His chief interest, however, lay in pure mathematics. He founded the science of hydrostatics (the study of fluids at rest) and discovered the principle that the weight of a solid floating in a liquid is equal to the weight of the liquid displaced by the solid.

Archimedes willingly shared his work with others, among them Eratosthenes (ehr-uh-TAHS-thuh-neez; 285–ca. 204 B.C.E.), who was the librarian of the vast Ptolemaic royal library in Alexandria. Eratosthenes used mathematics to further the geographical studies for which he is most famous. He calculated the circumference of the earth geometrically, estimating it at about 24,675 miles. He was not wrong by much: the earth is actually 24,860 miles in circumference. Eratosthenes further concluded that the earth is a spherical globe and that the ocean surrounds the landmass.

As the new artillery devised by Archimedes indicates, Hellenic science was used for purposes of war as well as peace. Theories of mechanics were applied to build machines that revolutionized warfare. The catapult shot large arrows and small stones against enemy targets. Engineers built wooden siege towers as artillery platforms. Generals added battering rams to bring down large portions of walls. If these new engines made warfare more efficient, they also added to the misery of the people. War came to embrace the whole population.

Physician with Young Patient This plaster cast from ca. 350 B.C.E. shows a physician examining a child, while Asclepius, the god of healing, observes. Asclepius holds a staff with a snake coiled around it, which remains the symbol of medicine today. This cast was made through a process known as intaglio in which the picture was carved onto a cylinder-shaped gemstone, then rolled across wet clay to produce the image. (Hulton Archive/Getty Images)

War and illness fed the need for medical advances, and the study of medicine flourished during the Hellenistic period, when physicians carried the work of Hippocrates into new areas. Herophilus, who lived in the first half of the third century B.C.E., approached the study of medicine in a systematic, scientific fashion. He dissected corpses and measured what he observed. He discovered the nervous system and concluded that two types of nerves, motor and sensory, existed. Herophilus also studied the brain, which he considered the center of intelligence. In the process he distinguished the cerebrum from the cerebellum. His other work dealt with the liver, lungs, and uterus. His students carried on his work, and they also discovered new means of treating disease and relieving pain, including opium.

CONNECTIONS

The ancient Greeks built on the achievements of earlier societies in the eastern Mediterranean, but they also added new elements, including history, drama, philosophy, science, and realistic art. The Greek world was largely conquered by the Romans, as you will learn in the following chapter, and the various Hellenistic monarchies became part of the Roman Empire. In cultural terms the lines of conquest were reversed: the Romans derived their alphabet from the Greek alphabet, though they changed the letters somewhat. Roman statuary was modeled on Greek and was often, in fact, made by Greek sculptors, who found ready customers among wealthy Romans. Furthermore, the major Roman gods and goddesses were largely the same as Greek ones, though they had different names. Although the Romans did not seem to have been particularly interested in the speculative philosophy of Socrates and Plato, they were drawn to the more practical philosophies of the Epicureans and Stoics. And like the Hellenistic Greeks, many Romans became dissatisfied with traditional religions, turning instead to mystery religions that offered secret knowledge and promised eternal life.

The influence of the ancient Greeks was not limited to the Romans, of course. As discussed in Chapter 3, art and thought in northern India was shaped by the blending of Greek and Buddhist traditions. And as you will see in Chapter 15, European thinkers and writers made conscious attempts to return to classical ideals in art, literature, and philosophy during the Renaissance. In America political leaders from the Revolutionary era on decided that important government buildings should be modeled on the Parthenon or other temples, complete with marble statuary of their own heroes. In some ways, capitol buildings in the United States are good symbols of the legacy of Greece — gleaming ideals of harmony, freedom, democracy, and beauty that (as with all ideals) do not always correspond with realities.

☐ CHAPTER REVIEW

KEY TERMS

polis (p. 118)
hoplites (p. 119)
democracy (p. 119)
oligarchy (p. 120)
tyranny (p. 120)
Delian League (p. 123)
mystery religions (p. 136)
Epicureanism (p. 137)
Stoicism (p. 137)

☐ **How did the geography of Greece shape its earliest history and lead to the growth of the polis? (p. 116)**

Greece's mountainous terrain and lack of navigable rivers led to the development of small, independent communities and political fragmentation. Some groups of people joined together in kingdoms, notably those of the Minoans on Crete and the Mycenaeans on the mainland, but the rugged terrain prohibited the growth of a great empire like those of Mesopotamia and Egypt. The fall of these kingdoms led to a period known as the Greek Dark Age (ca. 1100–ca. 800 B.C.E.). However, Greek culture survived, and Greeks developed the independent city-state, known as the polis, in which individuals governed themselves without elaborate political machinery. The physical, religious, and political form of the polis varied from place to place, but everywhere it was relatively small, reflecting the fragmented geography of Greece.

☐ **What were the major developments of the Archaic age, and how did Sparta and Athens create new forms of government? (p. 120)**

The maturation of the polis coincided with an era, later termed the Archaic age, that gave rise to two developments of lasting importance. The first was the spread of the Greek people, who now ventured as far east as the Black Sea and as far west as the Atlantic Ocean. The second development was the rise of Sparta and Athens, which formed new social and political structures. Sparta created a military state in which men remained in the army most of their lives and women concentrated on raising healthy soldiers. After much social conflict, Athens created a democracy in which

male citizens both voted for their leaders and had a direct voice in an assembly. As was the case in all democracies in ancient Greece, women, slaves, and outsiders could not be citizens.

☐ **What were the lasting cultural and intellectual achievements of the classical period? (p. 122)**

In the classical period, between 500 and 336 B.C.E., Greek civilization reached its highest peak in politics, thought, and art, even as it engaged in violent conflicts. The Greeks successfully defended themselves from Persian invasions but nearly destroyed themselves in the Peloponnesian War, which pitted Sparta and its allies against Athens and its allies. In the last half of the fifth century B.C.E. the brilliant Athenian leader Pericles turned Athens into the showplace of Greece by sponsoring the building of temples and other buildings. He also oversaw the creation of statues and carvings that showed the gods in human form and highlighted Athenian victories. In other artistic developments, wealthy Athenians paid for theater performances in which dramatists used their art in attempts to portray, understand, and resolve life's basic conflicts. During the classical period the Greeks honored a variety of gods and goddesses with rituals and festivals, but they did not look to religion for moral guidance. This period also saw the rise of philosophy; and Socrates, Plato, and Aristotle began a broad examination of the universe and the place of humans in it.

□ How did Alexander the Great's conquests shape society in the Hellenistic period? (p. 131)

In the middle of the fourth century B.C.E. the Greek city-states were conquered by the Macedonians under King Philip II and his son Alexander. A brilliant military leader, Alexander conquered the entire Persian Empire, along with many territories to the east of Persia. He also founded new cities in which Greek and local populations mixed. His successors continued to build cities and colonies, which became powerful instruments in the spread of Greek culture and in the blending of Greek traditions and ideas with those of other peoples. Greek became the common language of learning and business, which made trade easier and contributed to the prosperity of this era.

□ How did the meeting of cultures in the Hellenistic world shape religion, philosophy, and science? (p. 135)

The mixing of peoples in the Hellenistic era influenced religion, philosophy, and science. The Hellenistic kings built temples to the old Olympian gods and established cults like those in earlier Greek cities. But because many people found these spiritually unsatisfying, they turned instead to mystery religions. In these religions, which blended Greek and non-Greek elements, followers gained secret knowledge in initiation rituals and were promised eternal life. Others turned to practical philosophies instead of religion; these provided advice on how to live a good life. In the scholarly realm, advances were made in mathematics, astronomy, and mechanical design. The greatest thinker of the Hellenistic period was Archimedes, who devised new artillery for military purposes and created a screw to draw water from a lower to a higher level, among other inventions. Also during this period, physicians used observation and dissection to better understand the way the human body works and to develop treatments for disease.

SUGGESTED READING

Bosworth, A. B. *Conquest and Empire: The Reign of Alexander the Great.* 1988. Still the best one-volume treatment of Alexander that sets his career in a broad context.

Buckler, John. *Aegean Greece in the Fourth Century B.C.E.* 2003. Treats the history of this very influential century in detail.

Burkert, Walter. *Greek Religion.* 1987. The authoritative study of ancient religious beliefs, with much material from the sources.

Cartledge, Paul. *The Spartans: The World of the Warrior Heroes of Ancient Greece.* 2002. A readable general book on the history and legacy of Sparta.

Errington, R. Malcom. *A History of the Hellenistic World, 323–30 B.C.* 2008. Easily the best coverage of the period: full, scholarly, and readable.

Frazer, Peter M. *Cities of Alexander the Great.* 1996. Treats the impact of Greek urbanism in its eastern setting.

Hansen, Mogens Herman. *Polis: An Introduction to the Ancient Greek City-State.* 2006. The authoritative study of the polis.

Kagan, Donald. *Pericles of Athens and the Birth of Democracy.* 1991. A readable account of political changes in the era of Pericles.

Osborne, Robin. *Greece in the Making, 1200–479 B.C.* 2003. Traces the evolution of Greek communities from villages to cities and the development of their civic institutions.

Patterson, Cynthia B. *The Family in Greek History.* 2001. Treats public and private family relations.

Roochnik, David. *Retrieving the Ancients: An Introduction to Greek Philosophy.* 2004. A sophisticated and well-written narrative of ancient Greek thought designed for students.

Tsetskhladze, Gocha R., ed. *Greek Colonization: An Account of Greek Colonies and Other Settlements Overseas,* vol. 1, 2006; vol. 2, 2008. The definitive work on the entire span of Greek colonization.

NOTES

1. Homer, *Iliad,* translated by Samuel Butler, Book 1, lines 1–5.
2. In *The Works of Xenophon,* translated by Henry G. Dakyns (London: Macmillan and Co., 1892), p. 296.
3. Thucydides 2.12, translated by J. Buckler.
4. Sophocles, *Antigone,* edited and translated by Hugh Lloyd-Jones (Cambridge, Mass.: Harvard University Press, 1994), p. 127.
5. Ahmad Hasan Dani et al., *History of Civilizations of Central Asia* (Paris: UNESCO, 1992), p. 107.
6. Diodoros 3.12.2–3, translated by J. Buckler.

For practice quizzes and other study tools, visit the **Online Study Guide** at bedfordstmartins.com/mckayworld.

For primary sources from this period, see *Sources of World Societies*, **Second Edition**.

For Web sites, images, and documents related to topics in this chapter, visit **Make History** at bedfordstmartins.com/mckayworld.

• Woman from Pompeii This brightly painted fresco from a villa in Pompeii shows a young woman carrying a tray in a religious ritual. Pompeii was completely buried in ash in a volcanic explosion in 79 C.E., and excavations have revealed life in what was a vacation spot for wealthy Romans. (Villa dei Misteri, Pompeii/The Bridgeman Art Library)

6

Like the Persians under Cyrus, the Mauryans under Chandragupta, and the Macedonians
under Alexander, the Romans conquered vast territories. Their singular achievement lay in their
ability to incorporate conquered peoples into the
Roman system. Unlike the Greeks, who mostly refused to share citizenship, the Romans extended
citizenship first to other peoples in Italy and later to inhabitants of Roman provinces.
After a grim period of civil war that ended in 31 B.C.E., the emperor Augustus restored peace
and expanded Roman power and law as far east as the Euphrates River, creating the institu-

The World of Rome
750 B.C.E.–400 C.E.

tion that the modern world calls the "Roman
Empire." Later emperors extended Roman
authority farther still, so that at its largest the
Roman Empire stretched from England to
Egypt and from Portugal to Persia.

Roman history is usually divided into
two periods. The first is the republic (509–
27 B.C.E.), the age in which Rome grew through
military conquest from a small group of cities
in the middle of the Italian peninsula to a

state that ruled much of the Mediterranean. To administer their growing territory, Romans
established a republican form of government in which power was held by the senate whose
members were primarily wealthy landowners. Social conflicts and wars of conquest led to
serious political problems, and the republican constitution gave way to rule by a single individual, who took the title "emperor." Thus the second period in Roman history is the empire
(27 B.C.E.–476 C.E.), which saw further expansion, enormous building projects, and cultural
flowering but also social upheavals and economic hardship. Rome's large territory eventually was split into eastern and western halves.   •

The Romans in Italy
□ How did the Romans come to dominate Italy, and what political institutions and changes did they bring about?

Roman Expansion and Its Repercussions
□ How did Rome expand its power beyond Italy, and what were the effects of this success?

The Pax Romana
□ How did efficient Roman rule lead to a period of prosperity and relative peace?

The Coming of Christianity
□ What was Christianity, and how did it affect life in the Roman Empire?

Turmoil and Reform
□ How did the emperors Diocletian and Constantine respond to the problems created by barbarian invasions and political turmoil in the third and fourth centuries?

The Romans in Italy

□ How did the Romans come to dominate Italy, and what political institutions and changes did they bring about?

The colonies established by Greek poleis (city-states) in the Hellenic era included a number along the coast of southern Italy and Sicily, an area already populated by a variety of different groups that farmed, fished, and traded. So many Greek settlers came to this area that it later became known as Magna Graecia — Greater Greece. Although Alexander the Great created an empire that stretched from his homeland of Macedonia to India, his conquests did not reach as far as southern Italy and Sicily. Thus the Greek colonies there remained independent, and they transmitted much of their culture to people who lived farther north in the Italian peninsula. These included the Etruscans (ih-TRUHS-kuhns), who built the first cities north of Magna Graecia, and then the Romans, who eventually came to dominate the peninsula. In addition to allying with conquered peoples and granting them citizenship, the Romans established a republic ruled by a senate. However, class conflicts over the rights to power eventually erupted and had to be resolved.

The Etruscans and Rome

The culture that is now called Etruscan developed from that of peoples who either were already living in north-central Italy or who spread into this area from unknown locations about 750 B.C.E. The Etruscans

The Etruscans, ca. 500 B.C.E.

- Etruscan homeland
- Areas of expansion
- Etruscan city

spoke a language that was not in the Indo-European language family (see page 49), so it is very different from Greek and Latin; however, they adopted the Greek alphabet to write their language. Though we know they wrote letters, records, and literary works, once the Romans conquered them knowledge of how to read and write Etruscan died out. Also, the writings themselves largely disappeared, other than inscriptions on stone or engravings in metal. Modern scholars have learned to read Etruscan again to some degree, but most of what we know about their civilization comes from archaeological evidence and from the writings of other peoples who lived around them at the same time.

The Etruscans established permanent settlements that evolved into cities resembling the Greek city-states in political organization (see page 118). They spread their influence over the surrounding countryside, which they farmed and mined for its rich mineral resources. From an early period the Etruscans began to trade natural products, especially iron, with their Greek neighbors to the south and with other peoples throughout the Mediterranean in exchange for luxury goods. The Etruscans thereby built a rich cultural life, full of art and music, that became the foundation of civilization throughout Italy, and they began to take political control of a larger area.

In the process they encountered a small collection of villages subsequently called Rome. Located at an easy crossing point on the Tiber River, Rome stood astride the main avenue of communication between northern and southern Italy. Its seven hills provided safety from attackers and from the floods of the Tiber (Map 6.1).

Under Etruscan influence the Romans occupied all of Rome's seven hills and prospered. During the rule of Etruscan kings (ca. 750–509 B.C.E.) Rome enjoyed contacts with the larger Mediterranean world, while the city continued to grow. Temples and public buildings began to grace Rome, and the Forum (see Map 6.1), originally a cemetery, became a public meeting place similar to the Greek agora. In addition, trade in metalwork became common, and wealthier Romans began to import fine Greek vases. In cultural developments, the Romans adopted the Etruscan alphabet and even the Etruscan toga, the white woolen robe worn by citizens. Another custom the Romans adopted from the Etruscans was the use of a certain image, a bundle of rods tied together with an ax emerging from the center, to symbolize the Etruscan king's power. This symbol was called the fasces (FAS-eez), and it was carried by an official on ceremonial occasions. When the Romans expelled the Etruscan kings (see below), they continued using the fasces in this manner. (In the twentieth century Mussolini would use the fasces as the symbol of his political party, the Fascists, and it is also used by many other governmental groups, including some in the United States.)

The Roman Conquest of Italy

Although it is certain that the Etruscans once ruled Rome, much else about early Roman history is an uneven mixture of fact and legend. Stories about early Rome often contain an important kernel of truth, but that does not make them history. Nevertheless, legends can illustrate the ethics, morals, and ideals that Roman society considered valuable.

The Romans have several different foundation myths, which themselves were told in a number of different versions. In the most common of these, Romulus and Remus founded the city, an event later Roman authors dated precisely to 753 B.C.E. These twin brothers were descendants of a god on their father's side, and descendants on their mother's

□ CHRONOLOGY

753 B.C.E. Traditional founding of Rome

ca. 750–509 B.C.E. Etruscan rule of an evolving Rome

ca. 500–265 B.C.E. Roman conquest of Italy

509–27 B.C.E. Roman republic

494–287 B.C.E. Struggle of the Orders

264–146 B.C.E. Punic Wars

53–31 B.C.E. Civil wars among rival claimants to power

44 B.C.E. Assassination of Julius Caesar

31 B.C.E. Triumph of Augustus

27 B.C.E.–476 C.E. Roman Empire

27 B.C.E.–68 C.E. Rule of Julio-Claudian emperors

ca. 3 B.C.E.–29 C.E. Life of Jesus

284–337 C.E. Diocletian and Constantine reconstruct the empire, dividing it into western and eastern halves; construction of Constantinople

312 C.E. Constantine legalizes Christianity

380 C.E. Christianity made the official religion of the empire

Sarcophagus of Lartie Seianti The woman portrayed on this lavish sarcophagus is the noble Etruscan Lartie Seianti. Although the sarcophagus is her place of burial, she is portrayed as in life, comfortable and at rest. The influence of Greek art on Etruscan is apparent in almost every feature of the sarcophagus. (Archaeological Museum, Florence/Nimatallah/Art Resource, NY)

side of Aeneas (ih-NEE-uhs), a brave and pious Trojan who left Troy (in Anatolia, now Turkey) after it was destroyed by the Greeks. The brothers, who were left to die by a jealous uncle, were raised by a female wolf. When they were grown they decided to build a city in the hills that became part of Rome, but they quarreled over which hill should be the site of the city. Romulus chose one hill and started to build a wall around it, and Remus chose another. After Remus jumped mockingly over Romulus's wall, Romulus killed him and named the city after himself. He also established a council of advisers later called the senate, which means council of old men. He and his mostly male followers expanded their power over neighboring peoples, in part by abducting and marrying their women. The women then arranged a peace by throwing themselves between their brothers and their husbands, convincing them that killing kin would make the men cursed. The Romans, favored by the gods, continued their rise to power. Despite its tales of murder and kidnapping, this founding myth ascribes positive traits to the Romans: they are descended from gods and heroes, can thrive in wild and tough settings, will defend their boundaries at all costs, and mix with other peoples rather than simply conquering them. Also, the story portrays the mothers of Rome as virtuous and brave.

MAP 6.1 Roman Italy, ca. 265 B.C.E. As Rome expanded, it built roads linking major cities and offered various degrees of citizenship to the territories it conquered or with which it made alliances. The territories outlined in green were added by 218 B.C.E., largely as a result of the Punic Wars.

Later Roman historians continued the story by describing a series of kings after Romulus—the traditional number is seven—each elected by the senate. Because they had to fit this succession with the reality that, starting around 750 B.C.E., Rome was ruled by Etruscans, the historians described the last few of these kings as Etruscans. The kings apparently became more authoritarian, one possible reason they were overthrown. An additional reason was described in another story involving female virtue. In this story the son of the Etruscan king Tarquin raped Lucretia, a virtuous Roman wife, who committed suicide out of shame, causing the people to rise up in anger and avenge her death. Whether the rape happened can never be known, but the Romans threw out the last Etruscan king in 509 B.C.E. and established a republic, led by the senate and two **consuls** elected for one-year terms.

In the following years the Romans fought numerous wars with their Italian neighbors, including the Etruscans. They became soldiers, and the grim fighting bred tenacity, a prominent Roman trait. War also involved diplomacy, at which the Romans became masters. They very early learned the value of alliances with the towns in the province of Latium that surrounded Rome, which provided them all with security and the Romans with a large reservoir of manpower. These alliances involved the Romans in still other wars that took them farther afield in the Italian peninsula.

Around 390 B.C.E. the Romans suffered a major setback when a people new to the Italian peninsula, the Celts—or Gauls, as the Romans called them—moved down from the north, swept aside a Roman army, and sacked Rome. More intent on loot than land, they agreed to abandon Rome in return for a thousand pounds of gold. In the century that followed the Romans rebuilt their city and recouped their losses. They brought Latium and their Latin allies fully under their control and conquered the Etruscans. In a series of bitter wars the Romans also subdued southern Italy, including much of Magna Graecia, and then turned north. Their superior military institutions, organization, and manpower allowed them to conquer most of Italy by about 265 B.C.E. (see Map 6.1).

As they expanded their territory, the Romans spread their religious traditions throughout Italy, blending them with local beliefs and practices. Victorious generals made sure to honor the gods of people they had conquered, and by doing so transformed them into gods they could also call on for assistance in their future campaigns. As the Romans conquered the cities of Magna Graecia, the Greek deities were absorbed into the Roman pantheon. Their names were changed to Roman names, so that Zeus (the king of the gods), for example, became Jupiter, and Ares (the god of war) became Mars, but their personal qualities and powers were largely the same. As it was in Greece, religion was largely a matter of rites and ceremonies, not inner piety. Such rituals were an important way to express common values, however, which for Romans meant those evident in their foundation myths: bravery, morality, family, and home.

Once they had conquered an area, the Romans did what the Persians had earlier done to help cement their new territory: they built roads. Roman roads facilitated the flow of communication, trade, and armies from the capital to outlying areas. They were the tangible sinews of unity, and many were marvels of engineering, as were the stone bridges the Romans built over Italy's many rivers.

In politics the Romans shared full Roman citizenship with many of their oldest allies, particularly the inhabitants of the cities of Latium. In other instances they granted citizenship without the franchise, that is, without the right to vote or hold Roman office. These allies were subject to Roman taxes and calls for military service but ran their own local affairs.

The Distribution of Power in the Roman Republic

Along with citizenship, the republican government was another important institution of Roman political life. The Romans summed up their political existence in a single phrase: *senatus populusque Romanus*, "the Roman senate and the people," which they abbreviated "SPQR." This sentiment reflects the republican ideal of shared government rather than power concentrated in a monarchy. It stands for the beliefs, customs, and laws of the republic—its unwritten constitution that evolved over two centuries to meet the demands of the governed.

In the early republic social divisions determined the shape of politics. Political power was in the hands of the aristocracy—the **patricians**, who were wealthy landowners. Patrician men dominated the affairs of state, provided military leadership in time of war, and monopolized knowledge of law and legal procedure. The common people of Rome, the **plebeians** (plih-BEE-uhns), were free citizens with a voice in politics, but they had few of the patricians' political and social advantages. They could not hold high office or marry into patrician families. While some plebeian

---

- **consuls** Primary executives in the Roman republic, elected for one-year terms, who commanded the army in battle, administered state business, and supervised financial affairs; originally the office was limited to patricians.
- **patricians** The Roman aristocracy; wealthy landowners who held political power.
- **plebeians** The common people of Rome, who had few of the patricians' advantages.

◻ Picturing the Past

Battle Between the Romans and the Germans Rome's wars with the barbarians of western Europe come to life in this relief from a Roman sarcophagus of 225 C.E. The Romans are wearing helmets, with the soldier at the right even wearing iron or bronze chain mail, a technology they had most likely only recently picked up from the Germans. (Vanni/Art Resource, NY)

ANALYZING THE IMAGE How would you describe this depiction of war? How does the artist show Roman superiority over the barbarians through the placement, dress, and facial features of the soldiers?

CONNECTIONS How does this funeral sculpture reinforce or challenge what you have learned about Roman expansion and the Romans' treatment of the peoples they conquered?

merchants rivaled the patricians in wealth, most plebeians were poor artisans, small farmers, and landless urban dwellers.

The most important institution in the Roman government was the **senate**, which had originated under the Etruscans as a council of noble elders who advised the king. During the republic the senate advised the consuls and other officials about military and political matters and handled government finances. Because the same senators sat year after year, while the consuls changed annually, the senate also provided stability. The senate could not technically pass legislation; it could only offer its advice. Yet increasingly, because

of the senate's prestige, its advice came to have the force of law. Another responsibility of the senate was to handle relations between Rome and other powers, as Polybius, a Greek politician and historian writing in the middle of the second century B.C.E., reported:

> If it is necessary to send an embassy to reconcile warring communities, or to remind them of their duty, or sometimes to impose requisitions upon them, or to receive their submission, or finally to proclaim war against them — this too is the business of the Senate.[1]

The primary executives in the republic were the two consuls, positions initially open only to patrician men. The consuls commanded the army in battle, administered state business, and supervised financial

• **senate** The assembly that was the main institution of government in the Roman republic. It grew out of an earlier council of advisers to the king.

affairs. When the consuls were away from Rome, praetors (PREE-tuhrz) acted in their place. Otherwise, the praetors dealt primarily with the administration of justice. After the age of overseas conquest (see below), the Romans divided their lands in the Mediterranean into provinces governed by ex-consuls and ex-praetors. Because of these officials' experience in Roman politics, they were all suited to administer the affairs of the provinces and to adapt Roman law and customs to new contexts. Other officials worked with the senate to oversee the public treasury, register citizens, and supervise the city of Rome.

A lasting achievement of the Romans was their development of law. Roman civil law, the *ius civile*, consisted of statutes, customs, and forms of procedure that regulated the lives of citizens. As the Romans came into more frequent contact with foreigners, the praetors applied a broader *ius gentium*, the "law of the peoples," to such matters as peace treaties, the treatment of prisoners of war, and the exchange of diplomats. In the ius gentium, all sides were to be treated the same regardless of their nationality. By the late republic Roman jurists had widened this still further into the concept of *ius naturale*, "natural law" based in part on Stoic beliefs (see page 137). Natural law, according to these thinkers, is made up of rules that govern human behavior that come from applying reason rather than customs or traditions, and so apply to all societies.

Social Conflict in Rome

Inequality between plebeians and patricians led to a conflict known as the Struggle of the Orders. In this conflict the plebeians sought to increase their power by taking advantage of the fact that Rome's survival depended on its army, which needed plebeians to fill the ranks of the infantry. According to tradition, in 494 B.C.E. the plebeians literally walked out of Rome and refused to serve in the army. Their general strike worked, and the patricians made important concessions. For one thing they allowed patricians and plebeians to marry one another. They also recognized the right of plebeians to elect their own officials, the tribunes, who could bring plebeian grievances to the senate for resolution and could also veto the decisions of the consuls. Thus, as in Archaic age Greece (see page 120), political rights were broadened because of military needs for foot soldiers.

The law itself was the plebeians' primary target. As noted above, only the patricians knew what the law was, and only they could argue cases in court. All too often they used the law for their own benefit. The plebeians wanted the law codified and published. In response, the patricians surrendered their legal monopoly and codified and published the Laws of the Twelve Tables, so called because they were inscribed on twelve bronze plaques. The patricians also made legal procedures public so that plebeians could argue cases in court.

After a ten-year battle, the Licinian-Sextian laws passed, giving wealthy plebeians access to all the offices of Rome, including the right to hold one of the two consulships. Once plebeians could hold the consulship, they could also sit in the senate and advise on policy. Though decisive, this victory did not automatically end the Struggle of the Orders. That happened only in 287 B.C.E. with the passage of the *lex Hortensia*, which gave the resolutions of the *concilium plebis*, the plebeian assembly, the force of law for patricians and plebeians alike. This compromise established a new elite of wealthy plebeians and patricians. Yet the Struggle of the Orders had made all citizens equal before the law, resulting in a Rome stronger and more united than before.

Roman Expansion and Its Repercussions

☐ How did Rome expand its power beyond Italy, and what were the effects of this success?

With their internal affairs settled, the Romans turned their attention abroad. In a series of wars they conquered lands all around the Mediterranean, creating an overseas empire that brought them unheard of power and wealth. As a result many Romans became more cosmopolitan and comfortable, and they were especially influenced by the culture of one conquered land: Greece. Yet social unrest also came in the wake of the wars, opening unprecedented opportunities for ambitious generals who wanted to rule Rome like an empire. Civil war ensued, which was quelled briefly by the great politician and general Julius Caesar. Only his grandnephew Octavian, better known to history as Augustus, finally restored peace and order to Rome.

Overseas Conquests and the Punic Wars, 264–133 B.C.E.

In 282 B.C.E., when the Romans reached southern Italy, they embarked upon a series of wars that left them the rulers of the Mediterranean world. Although they sometimes declared war reluctantly, they nonetheless felt the need to dominate, to eliminate any state that could endanger them. Yet they did not map out grandiose strategies to conquer the world, as had Alexander the Great. Rather they responded to situations as they arose.

Two Triremes Race In this fresco painting from the temple of Isis in Pompeii, two triremes—narrow warships powered by several banks of long oars—race in what was most likely a festival celebrating the goddess. Greeks, Carthaginians, and Romans all used triremes, which had bronze front pieces designed to smash into enemy ships. The 100 to 200 oarsmen had to row in time to achieve the necessary speed, which took long practice, so this religious celebration also served a military purpose. The ruins of Pompeii provide an extremely rich source for all aspects of Roman life. (© Ministero per I Beni e le Attivita Culturali—Soprintendenza archeologia de Napoli)

Their presence in southern Italy brought the Romans to the island of Sicily, where they confronted another great power in the western Mediterranean, Carthage (CAHR-thij). The city of Carthage had been founded by Phoenicians as a trading colony in the eighth century B.C.E. (see page 51). It commanded one of the best harbors on the northern African coast and was supported by a fertile inland. By the fourth century B.C.E. the Carthaginians began to expand their holdings, and they engaged in war with the Etruscans and Greeks. At the end of a long string of wars, the Carthaginians had created and defended a mercantile empire that stretched from western Sicily to beyond Gibraltar.

The Carthaginian Empire and Roman Republic, 264 B.C.E.

The conflicting ambitions of the Romans and Carthaginians led to the First Punic (PYOO-nik) War, which lasted from 264 to 241 B.C.E. During the course of the war, Rome built a navy and defeated Carthage in a series of sea battles. Sicily became Rome's first province, but despite a peace treaty the conflict was not over.

Carthaginian armies moved into Spain, where Rome was also claiming territory. The brilliant general Hannibal (ca. 247–183 B.C.E.) marched an army of tens of thousands of troops—and, more famously, several dozen war elephants—from Spain across what is now France and over the Alps into Italy, beginning the Second Punic War (218–201 B.C.E.). Hannibal won three major victories, including a devastating blow at Cannae in southeastern Italy in 216 B.C.E. There, he inflicted some forty thousand casualties on the Romans. He then spread devastation throughout Italy, and a number of cities in central and southern Italy rebelled against Rome because it appeared to them that Hannibal would be victorious. Yet Hannibal was not able to win areas near Rome in central Italy. His allies, who included Philip V, the Antigonid king of Macedonia (see page 131), did not supply him with enough food and supplies to sustain his troops, and Rome fought back.

The Roman general Scipio Africanus (ca. 236–ca. 183 B.C.E.) copied Hannibal's methods of mobile warfare, streamlining the legions (army divisions) by making their components capable of independent action and using guerrilla tactics. He took Spain from the Carthaginians and then struck directly at Carthage itself, prompting the Carthaginians to recall Hannibal from Italy to defend the homeland. In 202 B.C.E., near the town of Zama, Scipio defeated Hannibal in one of the world's truly decisive battles. Scipio's victory meant that the world of the western Mediterranean would henceforth be Roman. Roman language, law, and culture, fertilized by Greek influences, would in time permeate this entire region.

The Second Punic War contained the seeds of still other wars. Unabated fear of Carthage led to the Third Punic War, a needless, unjust, and savage conflict that ended in 146 B.C.E. when Scipio Aemilianus, grandson of Scipio Africanus, destroyed the hated rival and burned Carthage to the ground.

After the final defeat of Carthage, the Romans turned east. They remembered the alliance between Philip of Macedonia and Hannibal, and after provocation from the current king of Macedonia, Roman legions quickly conquered Macedonia and Greece. Then they moved farther east and defeated the Seleucid monarchy. In 133 B.C.E. the king of Pergamum in Asia Minor willed his kingdom to Rome when he died. The Ptolemies of Egypt retained formal control of their kingdom, but they meekly obeyed Roman wishes in terms of trade policy. Declaring the Mediterranean *mare nostrum*, "our sea," the Romans began to create a political and administrative machinery to hold the Mediterranean together under a mutually shared cultural and political system of provinces ruled by governors sent from Rome.

Not all Romans were joyful over Rome's conquest of the Mediterranean world; some considered that victory a misfortune. The historian Sallust (86–34 B.C.E.), writing from hindsight, complained that the acquisition of an empire was the beginning of Rome's troubles:

> But when through labor and justice our Republic grew powerful . . . then fortune began to be harsh and to throw everything into confusion. The Romans had easily borne labor, danger, and hardship. To them leisure, riches — otherwise desirable — proved to be burdens and torments. So at first money, then desire for power, grew great. These things were a sort of cause of all evils.[2]

New Influences and Old Values in Roman Culture

With the conquest of the Mediterranean world, Rome became a great city. The spoils of war went to build baths, theaters, and other places of amusement, and Romans and Italian townspeople began to spend more

> **"**The Romans had easily borne labor, danger, and hardship. To them leisure, riches — otherwise desirable — proved to be burdens and torments.**"**
>
> **SALLUST**

of their time in leisure pursuits. This new urban culture reflected Hellenistic influences. Romans developed a liking for Greek literature, and it became common for an educated Roman to speak both Latin and Greek. Furthermore, the Roman conquest of the Hellenistic East resulted in wholesale confiscation of Greek paintings and sculpture to grace Roman temples, public buildings, and private homes.

The baths were built in response to another Greek influence: a passion for bathing, which Romans came to share. The large buildings containing pools supplied by intricate systems of aqueducts became essential parts of the Roman city. They were more than just places to bathe. Baths included gymnasia where men exercised, snack bars and halls where people chatted and read, and even libraries and lecture halls. Women had opportunities to bathe, generally in separate facilities or at separate times, and both women and men went to the baths to see and be seen. Conservative commentators objected to these new pastimes as a corruption of traditional Roman values, but they were widely adopted in the cities, and they do not seem to have interfered with Romans' abilities to rule their huge territory.

New customs did not change the core Roman social structures. The head of the family remained the **paterfamilias**, the oldest dominant male of the family. He held nearly absolute power over his wife and children as long as he lived. Until he died, his sons could not legally own property. To deal with important matters, he usually called a council of the family's adult males. The women of the family had no formal part in these councils, but they could inherit and own property. The Romans praised women, like Lucretia of old, who were virtuous and loyal to their husbands. (See "Viewpoints: On Roman Wives from a Tombstone Inscription and Juvenal's Sixth Satire," page 152.) They also accorded respect to women as mothers and thought that children should be raised by their mothers. Though women handled the early education of their children, after the age of seven, sons and occasionally daughters in wealthy families began a formal

---

• **paterfamilias** The oldest dominant male of the family, who held nearly absolute power over the lives of family members as long as he lived.

Viewpoints

On Roman Wives from a Tombstone Inscription and Juvenal's Sixth Satire

• *Most Romans married, and a great variety of sources portray husbands and wives visually and in words. These include idealizations, such as those found on tombstones, and biting critiques, including those by satirists such as the poet Juvenal.*

Epitaph on a Roman Tombstone from Around 130 B.C.E.

Stranger, my message is short. Stand by and read it through. Here is the unlovely tomb of a lovely woman. Her parents called her Claudia by name. She loved her husband with all her heart. She bore two sons; of these she leaves one on earth; under the earth she has placed the other. She was charming in converse, yet gentle in bearing. She kept house, she made wool. That's my last word. Go your way.

Juvenal's Sixth Satire, Written Sometime in the Early Second Century C.E.

[Y]ou are preparing for a covenant, a marriage-contract and a betrothal; you are by now getting your hair combed by a master barber; you have also perhaps given a pledge to her finger. What! Postumus, are you, you who once had your wits, taking to yourself a wife? Tell me . . . what snakes are driving you mad? Can you submit to a she-tyrant when there is so much rope to be had, so many dizzy heights of windows standing open? . . . If you are honestly uxorious, and devoted to one woman, then bow your head and submit your neck ready to bear the yoke. Never will you find a woman who spares the man who loves her; for though she be herself aflame, she delights to torment and plunder him. So the better the man, the more desirable he be as a husband, the less good by far will he get out of his wife. No present will you ever make if your wife forbids; nothing will you ever sell if she objects; nothing will you buy without her consent. She will arrange your friendships for you; she will turn your now-aged friend from the door which saw the beginnings of his beard. . . . Give up all hope of peace so long as your mother-in-law is alive. It is she that teaches her daughter to revel in stripping and despoiling her husband; it is she that teaches her to reply to a seducer's love-letters in no unskilled and innocent fashion; she eludes or bribes your guards. . . . The bed that holds a wife is never free from wrangling and mutual bickerings; no sleep is to be got there! It is there that she sets upon her husband, more savage than a tigress that has lost her cubs; conscious of her own secret slips, she affects a grievance, abusing his boys, or weeping over some imagined mistress. She has an abundant supply of tears always ready in their place, awaiting her command in which fashion they should flow. . . . But whence come these monstrosities? you ask; from what fountain do they flow? In days of old, the wives of Latium were kept chaste by their humble fortunes. It was toil and brief slumbers that kept vice from polluting their modest homes; hands chafed and hardened by Tuscan fleeces, Hannibal nearing the city, and husbands standing to arms. . . . We are now suffering the calamities of long peace. Luxury, more deadly than any foe, has laid her hand upon us, and avenges a conquered world.

QUESTIONS FOR ANALYSIS

1. How does the wife in Juvenal's satire compare to the wife in the epitaph?

2. How does the type of sources that these are—one a tombstone inscription and one a satire—shape their portrayals of Roman wives?

3. Juvenal wrote more than two centuries after the tombstone was erected. In his opinion, how had Roman history in the intervening centuries shaped the behavior of Roman wives?

Sources: Tombstone: Naphtali Lewis and Meyer Reinhold, *Roman Civilization*, vol. 1 (New York: Columbia University Press, 1990), p. 524; Juvenal: *Juvenal*, translated by G. G. Ramsay, Loeb Classical Library (Cambridge, Mass.: Harvard University Press, 1918), pp. 85, 99, 101, 103, 105, 107.

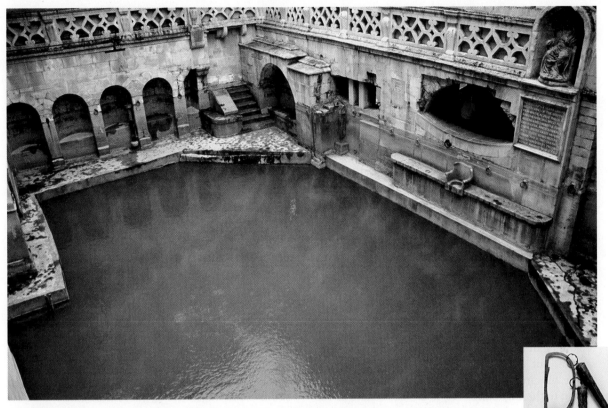

Roman Bath This Roman bath in Bath, England (a city to which it gave its name), was built around a natural hot spring beginning in the first century C.E. The Romans spread the custom of bathing, which they had adopted from the Greeks, to the outer reaches of their empire. In addition to hot water, bathers used oil for massage and metal scrapers (inset) to clean and exfoliate their skin. Many Roman artifacts have been unearthed at Bath, including a number of curse tablets, small tablets made of lead calling on the gods to harm someone, which were common in the Greco-Roman world. Not surprisingly, many of the curse tablets found at Bath relate to the theft of clothing while people were bathing. (baths: Horst Schafer/Photolibrary/Peter Arnold Inc.; artifact: Courtesy of the Trustees of the British Museum)

education under Greek tutors. Most children learned what they needed from their parents or through apprenticeships with artisans.

Most Romans continued to work long days, but an influx of slaves from Rome's conquests provided labor for the fields and cities. To the Romans slavery was a misfortune that befell some people, but it was not based on racial theories. For loyal slaves the Romans always held out the possibility of freedom, and **manumission**, the freeing of individual slaves by their masters, became common. Nonetheless, slaves rebelled from time to time.

Religion played an important role in the lives of most Romans before and after the conquests. They honored Jupiter (Zeus's counterpart) and his wife Juno, as well as Mars, the god of war who also guaranteed the welfare of the farm. The Romans honored the cults of their gods, hoping for divine favor. For example, in the city of Rome the shrine of Vesta, the goddess of hearth and home, was tended by six "vestal virgins" chosen from patrician families. Roman military losses were sometimes blamed on inattention by the vestal virgins, another link between female honor and the Roman state. In addition to the great gods, the Romans believed in spirits who haunted fields and even homes. Some of the deities were hostile, and only magic could ward them off. Some spirits were ghosts who haunted places where they had lived.

The Late Republic and the Rise of Augustus, 133–27 B.C.E.

The wars of conquest eventually created serious political problems for the Romans. When the legionaries (soldiers) returned home, they found their farms practically in ruins. Many were forced to sell their land to ready buyers who had grown rich from the wars. These wealthy men created huge estates called latifundia. Now landless, veterans moved to the cities, especially

• **manumission** The freeing of individual slaves by their masters.

Rome, but could not find work. These developments not only created unrest in the city but also threatened Rome's army by reducing its ranks. The Romans had always believed that only landowners should serve in the army, for only they had something to fight for. Landless men, even if they were Romans and lived in Rome, were forbidden to serve. The landless veterans were willing to follow any leader who promised help. The leader who answered their call was Tiberius Gracchus (163–133 B.C.E.), an aristocrat who was appalled by the situation. Elected tribune in 133 B.C.E., he proposed dividing public land among the poor. But a group of wealthy senators murdered him, launching a long era of political violence that would destroy the republic. Still, Tiberius's brother Gaius Gracchus (153–121 B.C.E.) passed a law providing the urban poor with cheap grain and urged practical reforms. Once again senators tried to stem the tide of reform by murdering him.

The next reformer, Gaius Marius (ca. 157–86 B.C.E.), recruited landless men into the army to put down a rebel king in Africa. He promised them land for their service. But after his victory, the senate refused to honor his promise. From then on, Roman soldiers looked to their commanders, not to the senate or the state, to protect their interests. The turmoil continued until 88 B.C.E., when the Roman general Sulla made himself dictator, an official office in the Roman republic given to a man who was granted absolute power temporarily to handle an emergency such as a war. Dictators were supposed to step down after six months — and more than eighty dictators had done so in Roman history — but Sulla held this position for nine years, and after that it was too late to restore the republican constitution. The senate and other institutions of the Roman state had failed to meet the needs of the people, and they had lost control of their generals and army. The soldiers put their faith in generals rather than the state, and that doomed the republic.

The history of the late republic is the story of power struggles among many famous Roman figures, which led to a series of civil wars. Pompey (PAHM-pee), who had been one of Sulla's officers, used military success in Spain to force the senate to allow him to run for consul. In 59 B.C.E. he was joined in a political alliance called the First Triumvirate by Crassus, another ambitious politician, and by Julius Caesar (100–44 B.C.E.). Born of a noble family, Caesar, an able general, was also a brilliant politician with unbridled ambition and a superb orator with immense literary ability. Recognizing that military success led to power, he led his troops to victory in Spain and Gaul, modern France. The First Triumvirate fell apart after Crassus was killed in battle in 53 B.C.E., leaving Caesar and Pompey in competition with each other for power. The result was civil war. The Ptolemaic rulers of Egypt became mixed up in this war, particularly Cleopatra VII, who allied herself with Caesar and had a son by him. (See "Individuals in Society: Queen Cleopatra," page 155.) Although the senate backed Pompey, Caesar was victorious. The senate then began appointing Caesar to various offices, including that of consul, dictator, and imperator (ihm-puh-RAH-tuhr), a title given to victorious commanders.

Using his victory wisely, Caesar enacted basic reforms. He extended citizenship to many provincials outside Italy who had supported him. To relieve the pressure of Rome's huge population, he sent eighty thousand poor people to establish colonies in Gaul, Spain, and North Africa. These new communities — formed of Roman citizens, not subjects — helped spread Roman culture.

In 44 B.C.E. a group of conspirators assassinated Caesar and set off another round of civil war. (See "Listening to the Past: Cicero and the Plot to Kill Caesar," page 156.) His grandnephew and heir, the eighteen-year-old Octavian (63 B.C.E.–14 B.C.E.), joined with two of Caesar's followers, Marc Antony and Lepidus, in the Second Triumvirate. After defeating Caesar's murderers, they had a falling-out. Octavian forced Lepidus out of office and waged war against Antony, who had now also become allied with Cleopatra. In 31 B.C.E., with the might of Rome at his back, Octavian defeated the combined forces of Antony and Cleopatra at the Battle of Actium in Greece. His victory ended the age of civil war. For his success, the senate in 27 B.C.E. gave Octavian the name Augustus, meaning "revered one." Tradition recognizes this date and Augustus's leadership as the start of the Roman Empire.

The Successes of Augustus

After Augustus ended the civil wars, he faced the monumental problems of reconstruction, and from 29–23 B.C.E. he toiled to heal Rome's wounds. He first had to rebuild the constitution and the organs of government. Next he had to demobilize much of the army and care for the welfare of the provinces. Then he had to address the danger of various groups on Rome's European frontiers. Augustus was highly successful in meeting these challenges.

Augustus claimed that in restoring the constitutional government he was also restoring the republic. Yet he had to modify republican forms and offices to meet the new circumstances. While expecting the senate to shoulder heavy administrative burdens, he failed to give it enough actual power to do the job. Many of the senate's prerogatives thus shifted to Augustus and his successors.

Augustus also had to fit his own position into the republican constitution. He did this not by creating a new

Individuals in Society

Queen Cleopatra

CLEOPATRA VII (69–30 B.C.E.) WAS A MEMBER OF the Ptolemy Dynasty, the Hellenistic rulers of Egypt who had established power in the third century B.C.E. Although she was a Greek, she was passionately devoted to her Egyptian subjects and was the first in her dynasty who could speak Egyptian in addition to Greek. Just as ancient pharaohs had linked themselves with the gods, she had herself portrayed as the goddess Isis and may have seen herself as a reincarnation of Isis (see page 45).

At the time civil war was raging in the late Roman republic, Cleopatra and her brother Ptolemy XIII were in a dispute over who would be supreme ruler in Egypt. Julius Caesar captured the Egyptian capital of Alexandria, Cleopatra arranged to meet him, and the two became lovers, although Cleopatra was much younger and Caesar was married. The two apparently had a son, Caesarion, and Caesar's army defeated Ptolemy's army, ending the power struggle. Cleopatra came to Rome in 46 B.C.E., where Caesar put up a statue of her as Isis in one of the city's temples. The Romans hated her because they saw her as a decadent Eastern queen and a threat to what were considered traditional Roman values.

After Caesar's assassination, Cleopatra returned to Alexandria. There she witnessed the outbreak of another Roman civil war that pitted Octavian, Caesar's heir, against Marc Antony, who commanded the Roman army in the East. When Antony visited Alexandria in 41 B.C.E. he met Cleopatra, and though he was already married to Octavian's sister, he became her lover. He abandoned (and later divorced) his Roman wife, married Cleopatra in 37 B.C.E., and changed his will to favor his children by Cleopatra. Antony's wedding present to Cleopatra was a huge grant of territory, much of it Roman, that greatly increased her power and that of all her children, including Caesarion. Antony also declared Caesarion to be Julius Caesar's rightful heir.

Octavian used the wedding gift as the reason to declare Antony a traitor. He and other Roman leaders described Antony as a romantic fool captivated by the seductive Cleopatra. Roman troops turned against Antony and joined with Octavian, and at the battle of Actium in 31 B.C.E. Octavian defeated the army and navy of Antony and Cleopatra. Antony committed suicide, as did Cleopatra shortly afterward. Octavian ordered the teenage Caesarion killed, but the young children of Antony and Cleopatra were allowed to go back to Rome, where they were raised by Antony's widow. In another consequence of Octavian's victory, Egypt became a Roman province.

Roman sources are viciously hostile to Cleopatra, and she became the model of the femme fatale whose sexual attraction led men to their doom. Stories about her beauty, sophistication, allure, lavish spending, desire for power, and ruthlessness abounded and were retold for centuries. The most dramatic story was that she committed suicide through the bite of a poisonous snake, which may have been true and which has been the subject of countless paintings. Her tumultuous relationships with Caesar and Antony have been portrayed in plays, novels, movies, and television programs.

● **Bust of Cleopatra, probably from Alexandria.**
(Bildarchiv Preussischer Kulturbesitz/Art Resource, NY)

QUESTIONS FOR ANALYSIS

1. How did Cleopatra benefit from her relationships with Caesar and Antony? How did they benefit from their relationships with her?

2. How did ideas about gender and Roman suspicion of the more sophisticated Greek culture combine to shape Cleopatra's fate and the way she is remembered?

3. The "Individuals in Society" in Chapter 2 also focuses on leading female figures in Egypt, but they lived more than a thousand years before Cleopatra. How would you compare their situation with hers?

Listening to the Past

Cicero and the Plot to Kill Caesar

Marcus Tullius Cicero was born in January 106 B.C.E. After an excellent education, he settled in Rome to practice law. His meteoric career took him to the consulship in 63 B.C.E. By the time of Caesar's death in 44 B.C.E., Cicero was sixty-two years old and a senior statesman. Like many others, he was fully caught up in the events leading to Caesar's assassination and the resulting revolution. Shortly before the plot was carried out on March 15, 44 B.C.E. — the Ides of March — Caesar wrote Cicero a flattering letter telling him that "your approval of my actions elates me beyond words. . . . As for yourself, I hope I shall see you at Rome so that I can avail myself as usual of your advice and resources in all things."[1] By then, however, Cicero knew of and supported the plot to assassinate Caesar and prudently decided not to meet him. The following letters and speeches offer a personal account of Cicero's involvement in the plot and its aftermath.

Trebonius, one of the assassins, wrote to Cicero describing the murder, and on February 2, 43 B.C.E., Cicero gave this frank opinion of the events:

Would to heaven you had invited me to that noble feast that you made on the Ides of March: no remnants, most assuredly, should have been left behind. Whereas the part you unluckily spared gives us so much perplexity that we find something to regret, even in the godlike service that you and your illustrious associates have lately rendered to the republic. To say the truth, when I reflect that it was owing to the favor of so worthy a man as yourself that Antony now lives to be our general bane, I am sometimes inclined to be a little angry with you for taking him aside when Caesar fell as by this means you have occasioned more trouble to myself in particular than to all the rest of the whole community.[2]

By the "part [of the feast] you unluckily spared" he meant Marc Antony, Caesar's firm supporter and a fierce enemy of the assassins. Another reason that Cicero was not entirely pleased with the results of the assassination was that it led to civil war. Two men led the cause for restoring the republic: Brutus, an aristocrat who favored traditional Roman values,

and Cassius, an unpopular but influential senator. Still undecided about what to do after the assassination, Cassius wrote to Cicero asking for advice. Cicero responded:

Where to advise you to begin to restore order I must acknowledge myself at a loss. To say the truth, it is the tyrant alone, and not the tyranny, from which we seem to be delivered: for although the man [Caesar] is destroyed, we still servilely maintain all his despotic ordinances. We do more: and under the pretence of carrying his designs into execution, we approve of measures which even he himself would never have pursued. . . . This outrageous man [Antony] represents me as the principal advisor and promoter of your glorious efforts. Would to heaven the charge were true! For had I been a party in your councils, I should have put it out of his power thus to bother and embarrass our plans. But this was a point that depended on yourselves to decide; and since the opportunity is now over, I can only wish that I were capable of giving you any effective advice. But the truth is that I am utterly at a loss in how to act myself. For what is the purpose of resisting where one cannot oppose force by force?[3]

At this stage the young Octavian, the future Augustus and Caesar's heir, appeared to claim his inheritance. He too sought Cicero's advice, and in a series of letters to his close friend Atticus, Cicero discussed the situation:

On the second or third of November 44 B.C.E. a letter arrived from Octavian. He has great schemes afoot. He has won the veterans at Casilinum and Calatia over to his views, and no wonder since he gives them 500 denarii apiece. He plans to make a round of the other colonies. His object is plain: war with Antony and himself as commander-in-chief. So it looks to me as though in a few days' time we shall be in arms. But whom are we to follow? Consider his name; consider his age. . . . In short, he proffers himself as our leader and expects me to back him up. For my part I have recommended him to go to Rome. I imagine he will have the city rabble behind him, and the honest men too if he convinces them of his sincerity. Ah Brutus, where are you? What a golden opportunity you are losing! I could not foretell *this*, but I thought something of the kind would happen.[4]

office for himself but by gradually taking over many of the offices that traditionally had been held by separate people. The senate named him as a consul every year and also as a tribune, though the former office was normally held by a patrician and the latter by a plebeian. He was also named imperator and held control of the

army, which he made a permanent standing organization. Furthermore, recognizing the importance of religion, he had himself named pontifex maximus, or chief priest. The senate also gave him the honorary title princeps civitatis, "first citizen of the state." That title had no official powers attached to it, but the fact that it

Four days later Cicero records news of the following developments:

"Two letters for me from Octavian in one day! Now he wants me to return to Rome at once, says he wants to work through the senate.... In short, he presses and I play for time. I don't trust his age and I don't know what he's after.... I'm nervous of Antony's power and don't want to leave the coast. But I'm afraid of some star performance during my absence. Varro [an enemy of Antony] doesn't think much of the boy's [Octavian's, who was only eighteen] plan; I take a different view. He has a strong force at his back and *can* have Brutus. And he's going to work quite openly, forming companies at Capua and paying out bounties. War is evidently coming any minute now."[5]

At last Cicero openly sided with Octavian. On April 21, 43 B.C.E., he denounced Antony in a speech to the senate. He reminded his fellow senators how they had earlier opposed Antony:

"Do you not remember, in the name of the immortal gods, what resolutions you have made against these men [Antony and his supporters]? You have repealed the acts of Antony. You have taken down his law. You have voted that they were carried by violence and with a disregard of the auspices. You have called out the troops throughout all Italy. You have pronounced that colleague and ally of all wickedness a public enemy. What peace can there be with this man? Even if he were a foreign enemy, still, after such actions as have taken place, it would be scarcely possible by any means whatever to have peace. Though seas and mountains and vast regions lay between you, still you would hate such a man without seeing him. But these men will stick to your eyes, and when they can to your very throats; for what fences will be strong enough for us to restrain savage beasts? Oh, but the result of war is uncertain. It is at all events in the power of brave men such as you ought to be to display your valor, for certainly brave men can do that, and not to fear the caprice of fortune."[6]

When war broke out Cicero continued to speak out in the senate against Antony. Yet Cicero commanded no legions, and only legions commanded respect. At last Antony got his revenge when he had Cicero prosecuted as a public enemy. An ill and aging Cicero fled to the sea in a litter but was intercepted by Antony's men. With dignity Cicero stretched his head out of the window of the litter, and a centurion cut it off together, along with the hand that had written the speeches against Antony. Cicero's hands and head were displayed in the Roman Forum, showing the revenge taken on an enemy of the state. But years later Octavian, then the Roman emperor Augustus, said of Cicero: "A learned man, learned and a lover of his country."[7]

• **Bust of Cicero.**
(Alinari/Art Resource, NY)

QUESTIONS FOR ANALYSIS

1. What can you infer from these letters about how well prepared Brutus and Cassius were to take control of the government after Caesar's death?
2. What do these sources suggest about Cicero's importance?
3. What was Cicero's view of Octavian? Of Antony?

1. *To Atticus* 9.16.2 in D. R. Shackleton-Bailey, *Cicero's Letters to Atticus*, vol. IV (Cambridge, U.K.: Cambridge University Press, 1968), pp. 203–205.
2. *To Trebonius* in T. de Quincy, *Cicero: Offices, Essays, and Letters* (New York: E. P. Dutton, 1942), pp. 328–329.
3. *To Cassius*, ibid., pp. 324–325.
4. *To Atticus* 16.8.1–2 in D. R. Shackleton-Bailey, *Cicero's Letters to Atticus*, vol. VI (Cambridge, U.K.: Cambridge University Press, 1967), pp. 185–187.
5. *To Atticus* 16.9, ibid., p. 189.
6. *The Fourteenth Phillipic* in C. D. Yonge, *Cicero, Select Orations* (New York: Harper and Brothers, 1889), p. 499.
7. Plutarch, *Cicero* 49.15.

is the origin of the word *prince*, meaning sovereign ruler, is an indication of what Augustus actually did.

Considering what had happened to Julius Caesar, Augustus wisely kept all this power in the background, and his period of rule is officially called the "principate." Although principate leaders were said to be "first among equals," Augustus's tenure clearly marked the end of the republic, and without specifically saying so, Augustus created the office of emperor. That word is derived from *imperator*, commander of the army, a link that reflects the fact that the main source of Augustus's power was his position as commander of the Roman army. The changes that Augustus made created a stable government, although the fact that the army was loyal to him as a person, not as the head of the Roman state, would lead to trouble later.

In other political reforms, Augustus made provincial administration more orderly and improved its functioning. He encouraged local self-government and the development of cities. As a spiritual bond between the provinces and Rome, Augustus encouraged the cult of *Roma et Augustus* (Rome and Augustus) as the guardian of the state. The cult spread rapidly and became a symbol of Roman unity. Augustus had himself portrayed on coins standing alongside the goddess Victory and on celebratory stone arches built to commemorate military victories. In addition, he had temples, stadiums, marketplaces, and public buildings constructed in Rome and other cities.

In the social realm, Augustus promoted marriage and childbearing through legal changes that released free women and freedwomen (female slaves who had been freed) from male guardianship if they had given birth to a certain number of children. Men and women who were unmarried or had no children were restricted in the inheritance of property. Same-sex relationships were denounced as immoral for not producing children, although no laws were passed against them.

Aside from addressing legal issues and matters of state, Augustus actively encouraged poets and writers. For this reason the period of his rule is known as the golden age of Latin literature. Roman poets and prose writers celebrated human accomplishments in works that were highly polished, elegant in style, and intellectual in conception.

Rome's greatest poet was Virgil (70–19 B.C.E.), whose masterpiece is the *Aeneid* (uh-NEE-id), an epic poem that is the Latin equivalent of the Greek *Iliad* and *Odyssey* (see page 118). Virgil's account of the founding of Rome and the early years of the city gave final form to the legend of Aeneas, the Trojan hero (and ancestor of Romulus and Remus; see page 145) who escaped to Italy at the fall of Troy:

> Arms and the man I sing, who first made way,
> predestined exile, from the Trojan shore
> to Italy, the blest Lavinian strand.
> Smitten of storms he was on land and sea
> by violence of Heaven, to satisfy
> stern Juno's sleepless wrath; and much in war
> he suffered, seeking at the last to found
> the city, and bring o'er his fathers' gods
> to safe abode in Latium; whence arose
> the Latin race, old Alba's reverend lords,
> and from her hills wide-walled, imperial Rome.[3]

As Virgil told it, Aeneas became the lover of Dido (DIE-doh), the widowed queen of Carthage, but left her because his destiny called him to found Rome. Dido committed suicide, and, according to Virgil, distress over the end of their relationship helped cause the Punic Wars. In leaving Dido, an "Eastern" queen, Aeneas put the good of the state ahead of marriage or

Augustus as Imperator In this marble statue, found in the villa of Augustus's widow, Augustus is dressed in a military uniform and in a pose usually used to show leaders addressing their troops. This emphasizes his role as imperator, the head of the army. The figures on his breastplate show various peoples the Romans had defeated or with whom they had made treaties, along with assorted deities. Although Augustus did not declare himself a god—as later Roman emperors would—this statue shows him barefoot, just as gods and heroes were in classical Greek statuary, and accompanied by Cupid riding a dolphin, both symbols of the goddess Venus, whom he claimed as an ancestor. (Scala /Art Resource, NY)

Roman territory

- At outset of Punic Wars, 264 B.C.E.
- Added by death of Tiberius Gracchus, 133 B.C.E.
- Added by death of Julius Caesar, 44 B.C.E.
- Added by death of Augustus, 14 B.C.E.
- Added by death of Hadrian, 138 B.C.E.
- Territory gained and lost, with dates held
- Parthian Empire, ca. 200 C.E.
- Principal land trade route

□ Mapping the Past

MAP 6.2 Roman Expansion, 282 B.C.E.–138 B.C.E. Rome expanded in all directions, eventually controlling every shore of the Mediterranean and vast amounts of land.

ANALYZING THE MAP How would you summarize the pattern of Roman expansion—that is, which areas were conquered first and which later? How long was Rome able to hold on to territories at the outermost boundaries of its empire?

CONNECTIONS Many of today's major cities in these areas were founded as Roman colonies. Why do you think so many of these cities were founded along the northern border of Roman territory?

pleasure. The parallels between this story and the real events involving Antony and Cleopatra were not lost on Virgil's audience. Making the public aware of these parallels, and of Virgil's description of Aeneas as an ancestor of Julius Caesar, fit well with Augustus's aims. Therefore, he encouraged Virgil to write the *Aeneid* and made sure it was circulated widely immediately after Virgil died.

One of the most momentous aspects of Augustus's reign was Roman expansion into northern and west-ern Europe (Map 6.2). Augustus completed the conquest of Spain, founded twelve new towns in Gaul, and saw that the Roman road system linked new settlements with one another and with Italy. After hard fighting, he made the Rhine River the Roman frontier in Germania (Germany). Meanwhile, generals conquered areas as far as the Danube River, and Roman legions penetrated the areas of modern Austria, southern Bavaria, and western Hungary. The regions of modern Serbia, Bulgaria, and Romania also fell. Within this

Ara Pacis In the middle years of Augustus's reign, the Roman senate ordered a huge altar, the Ara Pacis, built to honor him and the peace he had brought to the empire. This was decorated with life-size reliefs of Augustus and members of his family, prominent Romans, and other people and deities. One side shows a goddess figure, most likely the goddess Peace herself, with twin babies on her lap, surrounded by symbols of fertility and dominance, thus linking the imperial family with continued prosperity. (Scala/Art Resource, NY)

area the legionaries built fortified camps. Roads linked these camps with one another, and settlements grew up around the camps, eventually becoming towns. Traders began to frequent the frontier and to do business with the native people who lived there; as a result, for the first time, central and northern Europe came into direct and continuous contact with Mediterranean culture. Romans generally referred to these native people as barbarians, a word derived from a Greek word for people who did not speak Greek. The Romans maintained peaceful relations with the barbarians whenever possible, but Roman legions remained on the frontier to repel hostile barbarians.

Romans did not force their culture on native people in Roman territories. However, just as earlier ambitious people in the Hellenistic world knew that the surest path to political and social advancement lay in embracing Greek culture and learning to speak Greek (see page 133), those determined to get ahead now learned Latin and adopted aspects of Roman culture.

The Pax Romana

☐ How did efficient Roman rule lead to a period of prosperity and relative peace?

Augustus's success in creating solid political institutions was tested by the ineptness of some leaders who followed him, but later in the first century C.E. Rome entered a period of political stability, prosperity, and relative peace that lasted until the end of the second century. In the eighteenth century historians dubbed this period the **pax Romana**, the Roman peace. During this time the growing city of Rome saw great improvements, and trade and production flourished in the provinces. Rome also expanded eastward and came into indirect contact with China.

Political and Military Changes in the Empire

For fifty years after Augustus's death in 14 C.E. the dynasty that he established—known as the Julio-Claudians because all were members of the Julian and

Claudian clans — provided the emperors of Rome. Some of the Julio-Claudians, such as Tiberius and Claudius, were sound rulers and created a bureaucracy of able administrators to help them govern. Others, including Caligula and Nero, were weak and frivolous.

In 68 C.E. Nero's inept rule led to military rebellion and widespread disruption. Yet only two years later Vespasian (r. 69–79 C.E.), who established the Flavian dynasty, restored order. He also turned Augustus's principate into a hereditary monarchy and expanded the emperor's powers. The Flavians (69–96 C.E.) repaired the damage of civil war to give the Roman world peace and paved the way for the Antonines (96–192 C.E.), a dynasty of emperors under whose leadership the Roman Empire experienced a long period of prosperity. Wars generally ended victoriously and were confined to the frontiers. In addition to the full-blown monarchy of the Flavians, other significant changes had occurred in Roman government since Augustus's day. Hadrian (HAY-dree-uhn), who became emperor in 117 C.E., made the imperial bureaucracy created by Claudius more organized. He established imperial administrative departments and separated civil from military service. In addition, he demanded professionalism from members of the bureaucracy. These innovations helped the empire run more efficiently while increasing the authority of the emperor, who was now the ruling power of the bureaucracy.

The Roman army also saw changes, transforming from a mobile unit to a defensive force. The frontiers became firmly fixed and defended by a system of forts and walls, some of which, such as sections of Hadrian's Wall in England, are still standing today. Behind them the network of roads was expanded and improved both to supply the forts and to reinforce them in times of trouble. The Roman road system eventually grew to over fifty thousand miles, longer than the current interstate highway system in the United States; some of those roads are still usable today.

The personnel of the legions were changing, too. Because Italy could no longer supply all the recruits needed for the army, increasingly only the officers came from Italy, while the soldiers were mostly drawn from the provinces. Among the provincial soldiers were barbarians who joined the army to gain Roman citizenship.

Life in Rome

The era of peace created great wealth, much of which flowed into Rome. The city, with a population of somewhere between 500,000 and 750,000, became the largest in the world at that time. Although Rome could boast of stately palaces, noble buildings, and beautiful residential areas, most people lived in shoddily constructed houses. They took whatever work was available, making food, clothing, construction materials, and the many other things needed by the city's residents, or selling these products from small shops or at the city's many marketplaces.

Fire and crime were perennial problems even in Augustus's day, and sanitation was poor. In the second century urban planning and new construction greatly improved the situation. For example, engineers built an elaborate system that collected sewage from public baths, the ground floors of buildings, and public latrines. They also built hundreds of miles of aqueducts, most of them underground, to bring fresh water into the city from the surrounding hills. The aqueducts, powered entirely by gravity, were a sophisticated system that required regular maintenance. But they were a great improvement and helped make Rome a very attractive place to live. Building aqueducts required thousands and sometimes tens of thousands of workers, who were generally paid out of the imperial treasury.

Rome grew so large that it became ever more difficult to feed. Emperors solved the problem by providing citizens with free bread, oil, and wine. By doing so, they also stayed in favor. They likewise entertained the people with gladiatorial contests in which participants fought to the death using swords and other weapons. Many gladiators were criminals, some the slaves of gladiatorial schools, and others prisoners of war. A few free people, men and very occasionally women, volunteered for the arena. The Romans actually preferred chariot racing to gladiatorial contests. In these races two-horse and four-horse chariots ran a course of seven laps, about five miles. Four permanent teams, each with its own color, competed against one other. Winning charioteers were idolized just as sports stars are today.

Prosperity in the Roman Provinces

Like Rome, the Roman provinces and frontiers saw extensive prosperity in the second century C.E. through the growth of agriculture, trade, and industry, among other factors. Peace and security opened Britain, Gaul, Germany, and the lands of the Danube to settlers from other parts of the Roman Empire. Many of these settlers became tenant farmers on small parcels of land, and eventually these farmers became the backbone of Roman agriculture.

In continental Europe the army was largely responsible for the new burst of expansion. The areas where legions were stationed became Romanized because legionaries, upon retirement, often settled where they had served, frequently marrying local women. Having learned a trade, such as carpentry or metalworking, in

pax Romana A period of Roman security, order, harmony, flourishing culture, and expanding economy during the first and second centuries C.E.

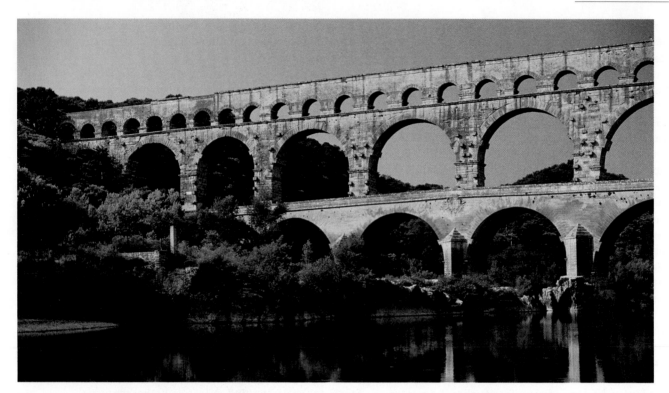

Roman Architecture These three structures demonstrate the beauty and utility of Roman architecture. The Coliseum in Rome (below),a sports arena that could seat 50,000 spectators built between 70 and 80 C.E., was the site of gladiatorial games, animal spectacles, executions, and mock naval battles. The Pantheon in Rome (right) is a temple dedicated to all the gods, built in its present form about 130 C.E. after earlier temples on this site burned down. Its dome, 140 feet in diameter, remains the largest unreinforced concrete dome in the world. Romans also used concrete for more everyday purposes. The Pont du Gard at Nîmes in France (above), is a bridge over a river carrying an aqueduct that supplied millions of gallons of water per day to the Roman city of Nîmes in Gaul; the water flowed in a channel at the very top. Although this bridge was built largely without mortar or concrete, many Roman aqueducts and bridges relied on concrete for their strength. (Pont du Gard: Vanni/Art Resource, NY; Pantheon: Gianni Dagli Orti/The Art Archive; Coliseum: Scala/Art Resource, NY)

the army, they brought essential skills to areas that badly needed trained men. These veterans also used their retirement pay to set themselves up in business.

The eastern part of the empire, including Greece, Anatolia, and Syria, shared in the boom in part by trading with other areas and in part because of local industries. The cities of the East built extensively, beautifying themselves with new amphitheaters, temples, and other public buildings.

The expansion of trade during the pax Romana made the Roman Empire an economic as well as a political force. Britain and Belgium became prime grain producers, with much of their harvests going to the armies of the Rhine, and Britain's wool industry probably got its start under the Romans. Italy and southern Gaul produced huge quantities of wine, which was shipped in large pottery jugs wherever merchant vessels could carry it. Roman colonists introduced the olive to southern Spain and northern Africa, which soon produced most of the oil consumed in the western part of the empire. In the East the olive oil production of Syrian farmers reached an all-time high, and Egypt produced tons of wheat that fed the Roman populace. Additionally, the Roman army in Mesopotamia consumed a high percentage of the raw materials and manufactured products from Syria and Asia Minor.

The growth of industry in the provinces was another striking development of this period. Cities in Gaul and Germany eclipsed the old Mediterranean manufacturing centers, and in the second century C.E. Gaul and Germany took over the pottery market. Lyons in Gaul and later Cologne in Germany became the new centers of the glassmaking industry, and the cities of Gaul were nearly unrivaled in the manufacture of bronze and brass. Aided by all this growth in trade and industry, Europe and western Asia were linked in ways they had not been before.

Eastward Expansion and Contacts Between Rome and China

The expansion of their empire took the Romans into West and Central Asia, which had two immediate effects. The first was a long military confrontation between the Romans and several western Asian empires. The second was a period of contact (often indirect) between the major ancient civilizations of the world, as Roman movement eastward coincided with Chinese expansion into the West (see page 183).

As the Romans drove farther eastward, they encountered the Parthians, who had established a kingdom in what is now Afghanistan and Iran in the Helle-

nistic period (see page 133). In the second century the Romans tried unsuccessfully to drive the Parthians out of Armenia and the Tigris and Euphrates Valleys. In 226 C.E. the Parthians were defeated by the Sassanids, a new dynasty in the area (see page 208). When the Romans continued their attacks against this new enemy, the Sassanid king Shapur conquered the Roman legions of the emperor Valerian, whom he took prisoner.

Although warfare disrupted parts of Asia, it did not stop trade that had prospered from Hellenistic times (see pages 134–135). Rarely did a merchant travel the entire distance from China to Mesopotamia. The Chinese and Romans were prevented from making direct contact because Parthians acted as middlemen between them. Chinese merchants sold their wares to the Parthians at the Stone Tower, located in modern Tashkurghan in Afghanistan. The Parthians then carried the goods overland to Mesopotamia or Egypt, from where they were shipped throughout the Roman Empire. Silk was still a major commodity from east to west, along with other luxury goods. In return the Romans traded glassware, precious gems, and slaves. The Parthians added exotic fruits, rare birds, and other products desired by the Chinese. (See "Global Trade: Pottery," page 164.)

The pax Romana was also an era of maritime trade, and Roman ships sailed from Egyptian ports to the mouth of the Indus River, where they traded local merchandise and wares imported by the Parthians. Merchants who made the voyage contended with wind, shoal waters, and pirates. Despite the dangers and discomforts, hardy mariners pushed into the Indian Ocean and beyond, reaching Malaya, Sumatra, and Java in Southeast Asia, where they traded with equally hardy local sailors.

Maritime trade between Chinese and Roman ports began in the second century C.E., though no merchant traveled the entire distance. The period of this contact coincided with the era of Han greatness in China (see pages 178–183). The Han emperor Wu encouraged trade by sea as well as by land, and during the reign of the Roman emperor Nerva (r. 96–98 C.E.), a later Han emperor sent an ambassador, Gan Ying, to make contact with the Roman Empire. Gan Ying made it as far as the Persian Gulf ports, where he heard about the Romans from Parthian sailors and reported back to his emperor that the Romans were wealthy, tall, and strikingly similar to the Chinese. His report became part of a group of accounts about the Romans and other "western" peoples that circulated widely among scholars and officials in Han China. Educated Romans did not have a corresponding interest in China. For them, China remained more of a mythical than a real place, and they never bothered to learn more about it.

Global Trade

Pottery

is used primarily for dishes today, but it served a surprisingly large number of purposes in the ancient world. Families used earthen pottery for cooking and tableware, for storing grains and liquids, and for lamps. On a larger scale pottery was used for the transportation and protection of goods traded overseas, much as today's metal storage containers are used.

The creation of pottery dates back to the Neolithic period. Few resources were required to make it, only abundant sources of good clay and wheels upon which potters could throw their vessels. Once made, the pots were baked in specially constructed kilns. Although the whole process was relatively simple, skilled potters formed groups that made utensils for entire communities. Later innovations occurred when the artisans learned to glaze their pots by applying a varnish before baking them in a kiln.

The earliest potters focused on coarse ware: plain plates, cups, and cooking pots that remained virtually unchanged throughout antiquity. Increasingly, however, potters began to decorate these pieces with simple designs. In this way pottery became both functional and decorative. One of the most popular pieces was the amphora, a large two-handled jar with a wide mouth, a round belly, and a base. It became the workhorse of maritime shipping because it protected contents from water and rodents, was easy and cheap to produce, and could be

MAP 6.3 The Roman Pottery Trade, ca. 200 C.E.

reused. Amphorae contained goods as varied as wine and oil, spices and unguents, dried fish and pitch. The amphora's dependability and versatility kept it in use from the fourth century B.C.E. to the beginning of the Middle Ages.

In the Hellenistic and Roman periods amphorae became common throughout the Mediterranean and carried goods eastward to the Black Sea, Persian Gulf, and Red Sea. The Ptolemies of Egypt sent amphorae and their contents even farther, to Arabia, eastern Africa, and India. Thus merchants and mariners who had never seen the Mediterranean depended on these containers.

Other pots proved as useful as the amphora, and all became a medium of decorative art. By the eighth century B.C.E. Greek potters and artists began to decorate their wares by painting them with patterns and scenes from mythology, legend, and daily life. They portrayed episodes such as famous chariot races or battles from the *Iliad*. Some portrayed the gods, such as

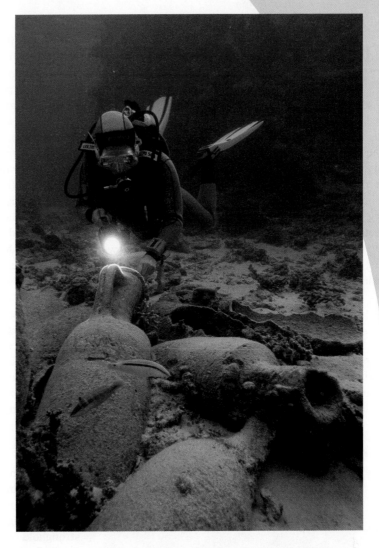

Wrecks of Roman ships in the Mediterranean often contain amphorae. This merchant ship from the first century C.E., discovered off the island of Sicily, contained 500 amphorae originally filled with oil, fruits, and vegetables. (Corrado Giavara/ StockphotoPro)

Dionysus at sea. These images widely spread knowledge of Greek religion and culture. In the West, especially, the Etruscans in Italy and the Carthaginians in North Africa eagerly welcomed the pots, their decoration, and their ideas. The Hellenistic kings shipped these pots as far east as China. Pottery thus served as a means of cultural exchange among people scattered across huge portions of the globe.

The Romans took the manufacture of pottery to an advanced stage by introducing a wider range of vessels and by making some in industrial-scale kilns that were large enough to fire tens of thousands of pots at once. The most prized pottery was *terra sigillata*, reddish decorated tableware with a glossy surface. Methods for making *terra sigillata* spread from Italy northward into Europe, often brought by soldiers in the Roman army who had been trained in pottery making in Italy. They set up facilities to make roof tiles, amphorae, and dishes for their units, and local potters began to copy their styles and methods of manufacturing. *Terra sigillata* often portrayed Greco-Roman gods and heroes, and so the pottery spread Mediterranean myths and stories. Local artisans added their own distinctive flourishes and sometimes stamped their names on the pots; these individual touches have allowed archaeologists to trace the pottery trade throughout the Roman Empire in great detail.

The Coming of Christianity

☐ What was Christianity, and how did it affect life in the Roman Empire?

During the reign of the emperor Tiberius (r. 14–37 C.E.), in the Roman province of Judaea, which had been created out of the Jewish kingdom of Judah, a Jewish man named Jesus of Nazareth preached, attracted a following, and was executed on the order of the Roman prefect Pontius Pilate. At the time this was a minor event, but Christianity, the religion created by Jesus's followers, came to have an enormous impact first in the Roman Empire and later throughout the world.

Factors Behind the Rise of Christianity

The civil wars that destroyed the Roman republic left their mark on Judaea, where Jewish leaders had taken sides in the conflict. The turmoil created a climate of violence throughout the area, and among the Jews two movements in opposition to the Romans spread. First were the Zealots (ZEH-luhts), who fought to rid Judaea of the Romans. The second movement was the growth of militant apocalypticism — the belief that the end of the world was near and that it would happen with the coming of a savior, or Messiah, who would destroy the Roman legions and inaugurate a period of happiness and plenty for Jews. This belief was an old one among Jews, but by the first century C.E. it had become more widespread than ever.

The pagan world also played its part in the story of early Christianity. The term **pagan** refers to all those who believed in the Greco-Roman gods. Paganism at the time of Jesus's birth can be broadly divided into three spheres: the official state religion of Rome; the traditional Roman veneration of hearth, home, and countryside; and the new mystery religions that arose in the Hellenistic world (see pages 136–137). The mystery religions gave their adherents what neither the official religion nor traditional practices could — spiritual satisfaction and the promise of eternal life — but they were exclusive. Therefore, many people's spiritual needs were unmet by these religious traditions, further paving the way for the rise of Christianity.

The Life and Teachings of Jesus

Into this climate of Messianic hope and Roman religious yearning came Jesus of Nazareth (ca. 3 B.C.E.–29 C.E.). According to Christian scripture, he was born to deeply religious Jewish parents and raised in Galilee, stronghold of the Zealots and a trading center where Greeks and Romans interacted with Jews. His ministry began when he was about thirty, and he taught by preaching and telling stories.

Like Socrates and the Buddha, Jesus left no writings. Accounts of his sayings and teachings first circulated orally among his followers and were later written down. The principal evidence for his life and deeds are the four Gospels of the Bible, books that are part of what Christians later termed the New Testament. These Gospels — the name means "good news" — are records of Jesus's teachings, written to build a community of faith sometime in the late first century. The Gospels include certain details of Jesus's life, but they were not meant to be biographies. Their authors had probably heard many different people talk about what

Depiction of Jesus This mural, from a Roman camp at Dura-Europos on the Euphrates River, may be the earliest known depiction of Jesus. Dating to 235 C.E., it depicts Jesus healing a paralytic man, an incident described in the New Testament. Early Christians used art to spread their message. (Yale University Art Gallery, Dura-Europos Collection)

Catacombs of Rome Christians favored burial of the dead rather than the more common Roman practice of cremation, and in the second century they began to dig tunnels in the soft rock around Rome for burials. The bodies were placed in niches along the walls of these passageways and then sealed up. Memorial services for martyrs were sometimes held in or near catacombs, but they were not regular places of worship. Many catacombs contain some of the earliest examples of Christian art, and others, dug by Jews for their own dead, contain examples of Jewish art from this period. (Catacombe di Priscilla, Rome/Scala/Art Resource, NY)

Jesus said and did, and there are discrepancies among the four accounts. These differences indicate that early followers had a diversity of beliefs about Jesus's nature and purpose. This diversity of beliefs about Jesus continues today. Some see him as a moral teacher, some as a prophet, and many as the son of God who rose from the dead and is himself divine.

However, almost all the early sources agree on certain aspects of Jesus's teachings: he preached of a heavenly kingdom of eternal happiness in a life after death and of the importance of devotion to God and love of others. His teachings were essentially Jewish, based on a group of Jewish books and with a conception of God and morality that came from Jewish tradition. Jesus's orthodoxy enabled him to preach in the synagogue and the temple, but he deviated from orthodoxy in insisting that he taught in his own name, not in the name of Yahweh (the Hebrew name for God). Was he the Messiah — in the Greek translation of the Hebrew word *Messiah*, the Christ? A small band of followers thought so, and Jesus claimed that he was. Yet Jesus had his own conception of the Messiah. He would establish a spiritual kingdom, not an earthly one. As recounted in one of the Gospels, he commented:

Do not lay up for yourselves treasures on earth, where moth and rust consume and where thieves break in and steal, but lay up for yourselves treasures in heaven, where neither moth nor rust consumes and where thieves do not break in and steal. For where your treasure is, there will your heart be also.[4]

The prefect Pontius Pilate knew little about Jesus's teachings. He was concerned with maintaining peace and order. Crowds followed Jesus at the time of Passover, a highly emotional time in the Jewish year that marked the Jewish people's departure from Egypt under the leadership of Moses (see page 53). The prospect that these crowds would spark violence alarmed Pilate. Some Jews believed that Jesus was the long-awaited Messiah. Others hated and feared him because they thought him religiously dangerous. To avert riot and bloodshed, Pilate condemned Jesus to death, and his soldiers carried out the sentence. On the third day after Jesus's crucifixion, some of his followers claimed that he had risen from the dead. For his earliest followers and for generations to come, the resurrection of Jesus became a central element of faith.

The Spread of Christianity

The memory of Jesus and his teachings survived and flourished. Believers in his divinity met in small assemblies or congregations, often in one another's homes, to discuss the meaning of Jesus's message and to celebrate a ritual (later called the Eucharist or Lord's Supper) commemorating his last meal with his disciples before his arrest. Because they expected Jesus to return to the world very soon, they regarded

pagan From a Latin term meaning "of the country," used to describe non-Christian followers of Greco-Roman gods.

earthly life and institutions as unimportant. Only later did these congregations evolve into what came to be called the religion of Christianity, with a formal organization and set of beliefs.

The catalyst in the spread of Jesus's teachings and the formation of the Christian Church was Paul of Tarsus, a well-educated Hellenized Jew who was comfortable in both the Roman and the Jewish worlds. At first he persecuted members of the new sect, but on the road to the city of Damascus in Syria he was converted to belief in Jesus and became a vigorous promoter of Jesus's ideas. Paul traveled all over the Roman Empire and wrote letters of advice to many groups. These letters were copied and widely circulated, transforming Jesus's ideas into more specific moral teachings. As a result of his efforts Paul became the most important figure in changing Christianity from a Jewish sect into a separate religion, and many of his letters became part of Christian scripture.

The breadth of the Roman Empire was another factor behind the spread of Christianity. If all roads led to Rome, they also led outward to the provinces. This enabled early Christians to spread their faith easily throughout the known world, as Jesus had told his followers to do, thus making his teachings universal. The pagan Romans also considered their secular empire universal, and the early Christians combined the two concepts of universalism.

Though most of the earliest converts seem to have been Jews, or Greeks and Romans who were already interested in Jewish moral teachings, Paul urged that Gentiles, or non-Jews, be accepted on an equal basis. The earliest Christian converts included people from all social classes. These people were reached by missionaries and others who spread the Christian message through family contacts, friendships, and business networks. Many women were active in spreading Christianity. Paul greeted male and female converts by name in his letters and noted that women often provided financial support for his activities. The growing Christian communities differed about the extent to which women should participate in the workings of the religion; some favored giving women a larger role in church affairs, while others were more restrictive.

People were attracted to Christian teachings for a variety of reasons. It was in many ways a mystery religion, offering its adherents special teachings that would give them immortality. But in contrast to traditional mystery religions, Christianity promised this immortality widely, not only to a select few. Christianity also offered the possibility of forgiveness, for believers accepted that human nature is weak and that even the best Christians could fall into sin. But Jesus loved sinners and forgave those who repented. Christianity was also attractive to many because it gave the Roman world a cause. Instead of passivity, Christians stressed the ideal of striving for a goal. By spreading the word of Christ, Christians played their part in God's plan for the triumph of Christianity on earth. They were not discouraged by temporary setbacks, believing Christianity to be invincible. Christianity likewise gave its devotees a sense of community, which was very welcome in the often highly mobile world of the Roman Empire. To stress the spiritual kinship of this new type of community, Christians often called one another brother and sister. Also, many Christians took Jesus's commandment to love one another as a guide and provided support for widows, orphans, and the poor, just as they would for family members.

The Growing Acceptance and Evolution of Christianity

At first many pagans in the Roman Empire misunderstood Christian practices and beliefs. Pagans thought that Christianity was one of the worst of the mystery cults, with immoral and indecent rituals. For instance, they thought that the ritual of the Lord's Supper, at which Christians said that they ate and drank the body and blood of Jesus, was an act of cannibalism. Pagans also feared that the Greco-Roman gods would withdraw their favor from the Roman Empire because of the Christian insistence that the pagan gods either did not exist or were evil spirits. And many worried that Christians were trying to destroy the Roman family with their insistence on a new type of kinship.

Christians themselves were partly responsible for the religious misunderstandings. They exaggerated the degree of pagan hostility to them, and most of the gory stories about the martyrs (Christians who were tortured and executed because of their beliefs) are fictitious. Although there were some cases of pagan persecution of the Christians, with few exceptions they were local and sporadic in nature. Even Emperor Nero's notorious persecution of Christians was temporary and limited to Rome. As time went on, pagan hostility and suspicion decreased. Pagans realized that Christians were not working to overthrow the state and that Jesus was no rival of Caesar. The emperor Trajan (r. 98–117 C.E.) forbade his governors to hunt down Christians. Though admitting that he considered Christianity an abomination, he preferred to leave Christians in peace.

By the second century C.E. Christianity was also changing. The belief that Jesus was soon coming again gradually waned, and as the number of converts in-

• **bishop** A Christian Church official with jurisdiction over a certain area and the power to determine the correct interpretation of Christian teachings.

• **heresy** A religious practice or belief judged unacceptable by church officials.

creased, permanent institutions were established instead of simple house churches. These included buildings and a hierarchy of officials often modeled on those of the Roman Empire. **Bishops**, officials with jurisdiction over a certain area, became especially important. They began to assert that they had the right to determine the correct interpretation of Christian teachings and to choose their successors. As the rise of the bishops shows, lines began to be drawn between what was considered correct teaching and what was considered incorrect, or **heresy**.

Christianity also began to attract more highly educated individuals who developed complex theological interpretations of issues that were not clear in scripture. Often drawing on Greek philosophy and Roman legal traditions, they worked out understandings of such issues as how Jesus could be both divine and human and how God could be both a father and a son (and later a spirit as well, a Christian doctrine known as the Trinity). Bishops and theologians often modified teachings that seemed upsetting to Romans, such as Jesus's harsh words about wealth. Given all these changes, Christianity became more formal in the second century, with power more centralized.

Turmoil and Reform

☐ How did the emperors Diocletian and Constantine respond to the problems created by barbarian invasions and political turmoil in the third and fourth centuries?

The prosperity of the second century gave way to a period of chaos and stress in the Roman Empire. Trying to repair the damage was the major work of the emperors Diocletian and Constantine (r. 306–337 C.E.), both of whom rose to leadership through the ranks of the military. They enacted political and religious reforms that dramatically changed the empire.

Diocletian's Reforms

During the third century C.E. the Roman Empire was stunned by civil war, as different individuals claimed rights to leadership of the empire. Emperors often ruled for only a few years or even months. Army leaders in the provinces declared their loyalty to one faction or another, or they broke from the empire entirely, thus ceasing to supply troops or taxes. Barbarian groups invaded Roman-held territory along the Rhine and Danube, occasionally even crossing the Alps to maraud in Italy. In the East, Sassanid armies advanced all the way to the Mediterranean. By the time peace was restored, the empire's economy was shattered, cities had shrunk in size, and many farmers had left their lands.

At the close of the third century C.E. the emperor Diocletian ended the period of chaos. Under Diocletian the princeps became *dominus*, "lord," reflecting the emperor's claim that he was "the elect of god," ruling because of divine favor. To underscore the emperor's exalted position, Diocletian and his successor, Constantine, adopted the court ceremonies and trappings of the Persian Empire.

The Division of the Roman World, 293

Diocletian recognized that the empire had become too great for one man to handle and so divided it into a western and an eastern half. He assumed direct control of the eastern part, giving a colleague the rule of the western part along with the title *augustus*, which had become synonymous with *emperor*. Diocletian and his fellow augustus further delegated power by appointing two men to assist them. Each man was given the title *caesar* to indicate his exalted rank. Although this system is known as the Tetrarchy (TEH-trahr-kee) because four men ruled the empire, Diocletian was clearly the senior partner and final source of authority.

Although the Tetrarchy soon failed, Diocletian's division of the empire into two parts became permanent. Throughout the fourth century C.E. the eastern and western sections drifted apart. In later centuries the western part witnessed the decline of Roman government and the rise of barbarian kingdoms, while the eastern half evolved into the Byzantine Empire.

Economic Hardship and Its Consequences

Major economic problems also confronted Diocletian and Constantine at a time when the empire was less capable of recovery than in previous eras. The emperors needed additional revenues to support the army and the imperial court, but the wars and invasions had harmed Roman agriculture, the primary source of tax revenues. The wars and invasions had also disrupted normal commerce and the means of production. Mines were exhausted by the attempt to supply much-needed ores, especially gold and silver. In the cities, markets, trade, and industry were disrupted, and travel between cities became dangerous, with pirates attacking ships at sea and robber bands capturing merchant caravans. The devastation of the countryside increased the difficulty of feeding and supplying the cities, and merchant and artisan families rapidly left devastated regions.

Economic hardship had been met by cutting the silver content of coins until money was virtually worthless. The immediate result was crippling inflation throughout the empire.

In an attempt to curb inflation, Diocletian took a step unprecedented in Roman history: he issued an edict that fixed maximum prices and wages throughout the empire. He and his successors dealt with the tax system just as strictly and inflexibly. Taxes became payable in kind, that is, in goods and services instead of money. All those involved in the growing, preparation, and transportation of food and other essentials were locked into their professions, as the emperors tried desperately to assure a steady supply of these goods. A baker, for example, could not go into any other business, and his son was required to take up the trade at his death. In this period of severe depression, many localities could not pay their taxes. In such cases local tax collectors, who were themselves locked into service, had to make up the difference from their own funds. This system soon wiped out a whole class of moderately wealthy people.

During the third century C.E. many free tenant farmers and their families were killed in barbarian invasions. Others fled in advance of the invasions or after devastation from the fighting. Large tracts of land consequently lay deserted. Great landlords with ample resources began at once to claim as much of this land as they could. The huge estates that resulted, called villas, were self-sufficient. Because they often produced more than they consumed, they successfully competed with the declining cities by selling their surpluses in the countryside. They became islands of stability in an

> "Every man, when dying, shall have the right to bequeath as much of his property as he desires to the holy and venerable Catholic Church. And such wills are not to be broken."
>
> **MEGASTHENES**

unsettled world, and in return for the protection and security landlords could offer, many small landholders who remained in the countryside gave over their lands and their freedom. They continued to work the land, but it was no longer their own, and they could no longer decide to move elsewhere. In this way, free people become what would later be called serfs.

Constantine, Christianity, and the Rise of Constantinople

The stress of the third century C.E. seemed to some emperors the punishment of the gods. Diocletian increased persecution of Christians, hoping that the gods would restore their blessing on Rome. Yet his persecutions were never very widespread or long-lived, and by the late third century most pagans accepted Christianity, even if they did not practice it. Constantine made this toleration official, legalizing the practice of Christianity throughout the empire in 312 and later being baptized as a Christian. He supported the church throughout his reign, expecting in return the support of church officials in maintaining order. Constantine also freed the clergy from imperial taxation and endowed the building of Christian churches. He allowed others to make gifts to the church as well, decreeing in 321 that "Every man, when dying, shall have the right to bequeath as much of his property as he desires to the holy and venerable Catholic Church. And such wills are not to be broken."[5] Constantine also declared Sunday a public holiday, choosing it over the Jewish holy

Gold Solidi of Constantine and Helena
These gold coins, issued in the fourth century by the emperor Constantine and his mother Helena, show the imperial figures in profile, surrounded by their names and shortened versions of their titles. Every Roman emperor issued coins, which served as means of exchange and also as transmitters of political propaganda. The front showed a carefully chosen portrait, and the reverse often depicted a recent victory or an abstract quality such as health or peace. Helena's ability to issue her own coins indicates her status in the imperial household. (Constantine: Yale University Art Gallery/Art Resource, NY; Helena: Morelli Collection, Lugano, Switzerland/Visual Connection Archive)

day of Saturday because it fit with his own worship of the sun god, a practice shared by many Romans. Christians altered their practices to follow the emperor's decrees, and because of its favored position in the empire, Christianity slowly became the leading religion.

In time the Christian triumph would be complete. In 380 C.E. the emperor Theodosius (r. 379–395 C.E.) made Christianity the official religion of the Roman Empire. He allowed the church to establish its own courts and to use its own body of law, called "canon law." At that point Christians began to persecute the pagans for their religion. History had come full circle.

The acceptance of Christianity was not the only event that made Constantine's reign a turning point in Roman history. Constantine took the bold step of building a new capital for the empire. Constantinople, the New Rome, was constructed on the site of Byzantium, an old Greek city on the Bosporus, a strait on the boundary between Europe and Asia. Byzantium was chosen as the site of Constantinople for several reasons. First, it was in the eastern part of the empire, which was easier to defend than the western part and thus had escaped the worst of the barbarian devastation. Also, it was wealthy and its urban life still vibrant. Moreover, Christianity was more widespread in the East than in the West, and the city of Constantinople was intended to be a Christian center.

In his new capital Constantine built palaces, warehouses, public buildings, and even a hippodrome for horse racing, modeling them on Roman buildings. In addition, he built defensive works along the borders of the empire, trying hard to keep it together, as did his successors. Despite their efforts, the eastern and the western halves drifted apart throughout the fourth century.

CONNECTIONS

The Roman Empire, with its powerful — and sometimes bizarre — leaders, magnificent buildings, luxurious clothing, and bloody amusements, has long fascinated people. Politicians and historians have closely studied the reasons for its successes and have even more closely analyzed the weaknesses that led to its eventual collapse. Despite the efforts of emperors and other leaders, the Western Roman Empire slowly broke apart and by the fifth century no longer existed. By the fourteenth century European scholars were beginning to see the fall of the Roman Empire as one of the great turning points in Western history, the end of the classical era. That began the practice of dividing Western history into different periods — eventually, the ancient, medieval, and modern eras. Those categories still shape the way that Western history is taught and learned.

This three-part conceptualization also shapes the periodization of world history. As you saw in Chapter 4 and will see in Chapter 7, China is also understood to have had a classical age, and, as you will read in Chapter 11, the Maya of Mesoamerica did as well. The dates of these ages are different from those of the classical period in the Mediterranean, but there are striking similarities among all three places: successful large-scale administrative bureaucracies were established, trade flourished, cities grew, roads were built, and new cultural forms developed. In all three places — and in other countries described as having a classical era — this period was followed by an era of less prosperity and more warfare and destruction.

No large-scale story of rise and fall captures the experience of everyone, of course. For many people in the Roman world, neither the change from republic to empire nor the end of the empire altered their lives very much. They farmed or worked in cities, and hoped for the best for their families. They took in new ideas but blended them with old traditions. And for some, the judgment of later scholars that there was a pax Romana would have seemed a cruel joke. In a speech the Roman historian Tacitus put in the mouth of Calgacus, a leader of the Britons, right before a battle with Roman invaders of his homeland, "They make a desert and call it 'peace.'"[6]

▢ CHAPTER REVIEW

▢ How did the Romans come to dominate Italy, and what political institutions and changes did they bring about? (p. 144)

The Etruscans and Romans both settled in Italy, with the Etruscans establishing permanent settlements that evolved into cities resembling the Greek city-states. The Etruscans introduced Romans to urbanism, industry, trade, and the alphabet. Under Etruscan rule, the Romans prospered, making contact with the larger Mediterranean world, while the city of Rome continued to grow. In 509 B.C.E. the Romans won independence from Etruscan rule and continued to expand their territories. They also established a republic, which functioned through a shared government of the people directed by the senate, summarized by the expression SPQR — *senatus populusque Romanus*, meaning "the Roman senate and people." In the resolution to a social conflict known as the Struggle of the Orders, nobles and ordinary people created a state administered by magistrates elected from the entire population and established a uniform legal code.

▢ How did Rome expand its power beyond Italy, and what were the effects of this success? (p. 149)

In a series of wars (most significantly, the Punic Wars) the Romans conquered the Mediterranean, creating an overseas empire that brought them unheard of power and wealth. Yet social unrest came in the wake of the war, opening unprecedented opportunities for ambitious generals who wanted to rule Rome like an empire. Civil war ensued, and it appeared as if the great politician and general Julius Caesar would emerge victorious, but he was assassinated by a group of senators. After his assassination and another period of civil war, his grandnephew Augustus finally restored peace and order to Rome. Augustus did not create a new office for himself but instead assumed control over many of the offices that traditionally had been held by separate people. His tenure clearly marked the end of the republic, and without specifically saying so, Augustus created the office of emperor. One of the most momentous aspects of his reign was the further expansion of Roman territories.

▢ How did efficient Roman rule lead to a period of prosperity and relative peace? (p. 160)

Augustus's success in creating solid political institutions was tested by the ineptness of some leaders who followed him, but later in the first century C.E. Rome entered a period of political stability, prosperity, and relative peace that lasted until the end of the second century C.E. During this period, later dubbed the pax Romana, the city of Rome became the magnificent capital of the empire, increasingly adorned with beautiful buildings and improved urban housing, and harboring a well-fed populace. To entertain the public, Roman rulers presented gladiatorial games and chariot racing. The Roman provinces and frontiers also saw extensive prosperity in the second century through the growth of agriculture, trade, and industry, among other factors. As the Roman Empire expanded eastward from Europe, it met opposition; yet even during the fighting, commerce among the Romans, the Parthians, and the Chinese empire thrived along a series of trade routes.

▢ What was Christianity, and how did it affect life in the Roman Empire? (p. 166)

Christianity was a religion created by the followers of Jesus of Nazareth, a Jewish man who taught that belief in his divinity led to eternal life. His followers spread their belief across the empire, transforming Christianity from a Jewish sect into a new religion. Christian groups were informal at first, but by the second century they began to develop hierarchical institutions modeled on those of the Roman Empire. At first many pagans in the Roman Empire misunderstood Christian practices and rites, and they feared that the gods would withdraw their favor from the Roman Empire because of the Christian insistence that the pagan gods either did not exist or were evil spirits. As a result, Christians suffered sporadic persecution under certain Roman emperors. Gradually, however, tensions between pagans and Christians lessened, particularly as Christianity modified its teachings to make them more acceptable to wealthy and educated Romans.

☐ How did the emperors Diocletian and Constantine respond to the problems created by barbarian invasions and political turmoil in the third and fourth centuries? (p. 169)

The prosperity of the second century C.E. gave way in the third century to a period of civil war, barbarian invasions, and conflict with foreign armies. These disrupted agriculture, trade, and production and damaged the flow of taxes and troops. At the close of the third century the emperor Diocletian ended the period of chaos, in part because he recognized that the empire had become too great for one man to handle. He therefore divided it into a western and an eastern half, assuming direct control of the eastern part and giving a colleague the rule of the western part. Diocletian and his successor, Constantine, also took rigid control of the struggling economy, but their efforts were not successful. Free tenant farmers lost control of their lands, exchanging them for security that landlords offered against barbarians and other threats. Meanwhile, tolerance of Christianity grew, and Constantine legalized the practice of this religion throughout the empire. The symbol of all the changes in the empire became the establishment of its new capital, Constantinople, the new Rome.

SUGGESTED READING

Aldrete, Gregory S. *Daily Life in the Roman City*. 2004. Reveals the significance of ordinary Roman life in the city of Rome, its port Ostia, and Pompeii.

Canfora, Luciano. *Julius Caesar: The Life and Times of the People's Dictator*. 2007. Provides a new interpretation of Caesar that puts him fully in the context of his times.

Clark, Gillian. *Christianity and Roman Society*. 2004. Surveys the evolution of Christian life among Christians and with their pagan neighbors.

Evans, J. K. *War, Women, and Children in Ancient Rome*. 2000. Provides a concise survey of how war affected the home front in wartime.

Forsythe, Gary A. *A Critical History of Early Rome from Prehistory to the First Punic War*. 2005. Uses archaeological findings as well as written sources to examine the political, social, and religious developments of early Rome.

Goldsworthy, Adrian. *Roman Warfare*. 2000. A concise treatment of warfare from republican to imperial times.

Haynes, Sybille. *Etruscan Civilization: A Cultural History*. 2000. Deals with cultural history, with special emphasis on Etruscan women.

Holland, Tom. *Rubicon, the Triumph and Tragedy of the Roman Republic*. 2003. Gives a lively account of the disintegration of the republic from the Gracchi to Caesar's death.

Kyle, Donald G. *Sport and Spectacle in the Ancient World*. 2007. Deals in grim detail with the ritualized violence of the gladiatorial games.

MacMullen, R. *Roman Social Relations, 50 B.C.–A.D. 284*. 1981. Still an excellent discussion of the topic by a leading scholar.

Matz, David. *Daily Life of the Ancient Romans*. 2008. A brief but valuable account of the ordinary things in Roman life.

Scullard, H. H. *A History of the Roman World*. 4th ed. 1993. Still the best single account of Roman history.

Turcam, R. *The Gods of Ancient Rome*. 2000. Provides a concise survey of the Roman pantheon.

NOTES

1. Polybius, *Histories*, vol. 1, translated by Evelyn Shuckburgh (New York: Macmillan and Co., 1889), p. 469.
2. Sallust, *War with Cataline* 10.1–3, translated by John Buckler.
3. Virgil, *Aeneid*, translated by Theodore C. Williams (Boston: Houghton Mifflin, 1910).
4. Matthew 6: 19-21.
5. Maude Aline Huttman, ed. and trans., *The Establishment of Christianity and the Proscription of Paganism* (New York: AMS Press, 1967), p. 164.
6. Tacitus, *Agricola*, translated by A.R. Birley (Oxford: Oxford University Press, 1999), p. 22.

For practice quizzes and other study tools, visit the **Online Study Guide** at bedfordstmartins.com/mckayworld.

For primary sources from this period, see *Sources of World Societies*, **Second Edition**.

For Web sites, images, and documents related to topics in this chapter, visit **Make History** at bedfordstmartins.com/mckayworld.

• **Buddhist Monk** Buddhism became the religion of much of Asia in the period from 200 to 800 C.E. Art styles spread as well, with Buddhas, bodhisattvas, and monks depicted in both sculpture and painting. This statue of a monk is among the many that have survived in the cave temples of Dunhuang in northwest China. (Wang Lu/ChinaStock)

East Asia was transformed over the millennium from 221 B.C.E. to 800 C.E. At the beginning of this era, China had just been unified into a single state upon the Qin defeat of all the rival states of the Warring States Period, but it still faced major military challenges with the confederation of the nomadic Xiongnu to its north. At the time China was the only place in East Asia with writing, iron technology, large cities, and complex state organizations. Over the next several centuries East Asia changed dramatically as new states emerged. To protect an emerging trade in silk and other valuables, Han China sent armies far into Central Asia. War, trade, diplomacy, missionary activity, and the pursuit of learning led the Chinese to travel to distant lands and people from distant lands to go to China. Among the results were the spread of Buddhism from India and Central Asia to China and the adaptation of many elements of Chinese culture by near neighbors, especially Korea and Japan. Buddhism came to provide a common set of ideas and visual images to all of the cultures of East Asia, much the way Christianity linked societies in Europe.

Increased communication stimulated state formation among China's neighbors: Tibet, Korea, Manchuria, Vietnam, and Japan. Written Chinese was increasingly used as an international language by the ruling elites of these countries, and the new states usually adopted political models from China as well. By 800 C.E. each of these regions was well on its way to developing a distinct political and cultural identity. •

East Asia and the Spread of Buddhism

221 B.C.E.–800 C.E.

The Age of Empire in China: The Qin and Han Dynasties

□ What were the social, cultural, and political consequences of the unification of China under the strong centralized governments of the Qin and Han empires?

In much the same period in which Rome created a huge empire, the Qin and Han rulers in China created an empire on a similar scale. Like the Roman Empire (see Chapter 6), the Chinese empire was put together through force of arms and held in place by sophisticated centralized administrative machinery. The bureaucracies created by the Qin and Han empires affected many facets of Chinese social, cultural, and intellectual life.

The Qin Unification, 221–206 B.C.E.

In 221 B.C.E., after decades of constant warfare, Qin (chin), the state that had adopted Legalist policies during the Warring States Period (see page 110), succeeded in defeating the last of its rivals, and China was unified for the first time in many centuries. Deciding that the title *king* was not grand enough, the king of Qin invented the title emperor (*huangdi*). He called himself the First Emperor (*Shihuangdi*) in anticipation of a long line of successors. His state, however, did not long outlast him.

Once Qin ruled all of China, the First Emperor and his shrewd Legalist minister Li Si embarked on a sweeping program of centralization that touched the lives of nearly everyone in China. To cripple the nobility of the defunct states, who could have posed serious threats, the First Emperor ordered the nobles to leave their lands and move to the capital. The private possession of arms was outlawed to make it more difficult for subjects to rebel. The First Emperor dispatched officials to administer the territory that had been conquered and controlled the officials through a long list of regulations, reporting requirements, and penalties for inadequate performance. These officials owed their power and positions entirely to the favor of the em-

Army of the First Emperor The thousands of life-size ceramic soldiers buried in pits about a half mile from the First Emperor's tomb help us imagine the Qin military machine. It was the Qin emperor's concern with the afterlife that led him to construct such a lifelike guard. The soldiers were originally painted in bright colors, and they held real bronze weapons. (Robert Harding World Imagery)

peror and had no hereditary rights to their offices.

To harness the enormous human resources of his people, the First Emperor ordered a census of the population. Census information helped the imperial bureaucracy to plan its activities: to estimate the cost of public works, the tax revenues needed to pay for them, and the labor force available for military service and building projects. To make it easier to administer all regions uniformly, Chinese script was standardized, outlawing regional variations in the ways words were written. This standardization would prove to be one of the most significant contributions of the Qin Dynasty. The First Emperor also standardized weights, measures, coinage, and even the axle lengths of carts (important because roads became deeply rutted from carts' wheels). To make it easier for Qin armies to move rapidly, thousands of miles of roads were built. These achievements indirectly facilitated trade. Most of the labor on the projects came from drafted farmers or convicts working out their sentences.

Some twentieth-century Chinese historians have glorified the First Emperor as a bold conqueror who let no obstacle stop him, but the traditional evaluation was almost entirely negative. For centuries Chinese historians castigated him as a cruel, arbitrary, impetuous, suspicious, and superstitious megalomaniac. Hundreds of thousands of subjects were drafted to build the **Great Wall** (ca. 230–208 B.C.E.), a rammed-earth fortification along the northern border between the Qin realm and the land controlled by the nomadic Xiongnu. After Li Si complained that scholars (especially Confucians) used records of the past to denigrate the emperor's achievements and undermine popular support, the emperor had all writings other than useful manuals on topics such as agriculture, medicine, and divination collected and burned. As a result of this massive book burning, many ancient texts were lost.

Assassins tried to kill the First Emperor three times, and perhaps as a consequence he became obsessed with discovering the secrets of immortality. He spent lavishly on a tomb designed to protect him in the

▢ CHRONOLOGY

ca. 230–208 B.C.E. Construction of Great Wall

221 B.C.E. China unified under Qin Dynasty

206 B.C.E.–220 C.E. Han Dynasty

145–ca. 85 B.C.E. Sima Qian, Chinese historian

114 B.C.E. Han government gains control over Silk Road trade routes across Central Asia

111 B.C.E. Emperor Wu conquers Nam Viet

108 B.C.E. Han government establishes colonies in Korea

105 C.E. Chinese invention of paper

ca. 200 C.E. Buddhism begins rapid growth in China

220–589 C.E. Age of Division in China

313–668 C.E. Three Kingdoms Period in Korea

372 C.E. Buddhism introduced in Korea

538 C.E. Buddhism introduced in Japan

581–618 C.E. Sui Dynasty

604 C.E. Prince Shōtoku introduces Chinese-style government in Japan

605 C.E. Introduction of merit-based examination system for the selection of officials in China

618–907 C.E. Tang Dynasty; great age of Chinese poetry

668 C.E. First political unification of Korea under Silla

690 C.E. Empress Wu declares herself emperor, becoming the only Chinese woman emperor

710 C.E. Nara made the capital of Japan

735–737 C.E. Smallpox epidemic in Japan

845 C.E. Tang emperor begins persecution of Buddhism

afterlife. Although the central chambers have not yet been excavated, in nearby pits archaeologists have unearthed thousands of life-size terra-cotta figures of armed soldiers and horses lined up to protect him.

Like Ashoka in India a few decades earlier (see page 84), the First Emperor erected many stone inscriptions to inform his subjects of his goals and accomplishments. He had none of Ashoka's modesty,

• **Great Wall** A rammed-earth fortification built along the northern border of China during the reign of the First Emperor.

however. On one stone he described the conquest of the other states this way:

> The six states, insatiable and perverse, would not make an end of slaughter, until, pitying the people, the emperor sent troops to punish the wicked and display his might. His penalties were just, his actions true, his power spread far, all submitted to his rule. He wiped out tyrants, rescued the common people, brought peace to the four corners of the earth. His enlightened laws spread far and wide as examples to All Under Heaven until the end of time. Great is he indeed! The whole universe obeys his sagacious will; his subjects praise his achievements and have asked to inscribe them on stone for posterity.[1]

After the First Emperor died in 210 B.C.E., the Qin state unraveled. The Legalist institutions designed to concentrate power in the hands of the ruler made the stability of the government dependent on his strength and character, and his heir proved ineffective. The heir was murdered by his younger brother, and uprisings soon followed.

The Han Dynasty, 206 B.C.E.–220 C.E.

The eventual victor in the struggle for power that ensued in the wake of the collapse of the Qin Dynasty was Liu Bang, known in history as Emperor Gaozu (r. 202–195 B.C.E.). The First Emperor of Qin was from the Zhou aristocracy. Gaozu was, by contrast, from a modest family of commoners, so his elevation to emperor is evidence of how thoroughly the Qin Dynasty had destroyed the old order.

Gaozu did not disband the centralized government created by the Qin, but he did remove its most unpopular features. Harsh laws were canceled, taxes were sharply reduced, and a policy of noninterference was adopted in an effort to promote economic recovery. With policies of this sort, relative peace, and the extension of China's frontiers, the Chinese population grew rapidly in the first two centuries of the Han Dynasty (Map 7.1). The census of 2 C.E. recorded a population of 58 million, the earliest indication of the large size of China's population. Few other societies kept as good records, making comparisons difficult, but high-end estimates for the Roman Empire are in a similar range (50–70 million).

The Han government was largely supported by the taxes and forced labor demanded of farmers, but this revenue regularly fell short of the government's needs. To pay for his military campaigns, Emperor Wu, the "Martial Emperor" (r. 141–87 B.C.E.), took over the minting of coins, confiscated the land of nobles, sold offices and titles, and increased taxes on private businesses. A widespread suspicion of commerce as an unproductive exploitation of the true producers made it easy to levy especially heavy assessments on merchants. The worst blow to businessmen, however, was the government's decision to enter into market competition with them by selling the commodities that had been collected as taxes. In 119 B.C.E. government monopolies were established in the production of iron, salt, and liquor. These enterprises had previously been sources of great profit for private entrepreneurs. Large-scale grain dealing also had been a profitable business, and the government now took that over as well. Grain was to be bought where it was plentiful and its price low and to be either stored in granaries or transported to areas of scarcity. This procedure was supposed to eliminate speculation in grain, provide more constant prices, and bring profit to the government.

Han Intellectual and Cultural Life

In contrast to the Qin Dynasty, which favored Legalism, the Han came to promote Confucianism and recruit officials on the basis of their Confucian learning or Confucian moral qualities. The Han government's efforts to recruit men trained in the Confucian classics marked the beginning of the Confucian scholar-official system, one of the most distinctive features of imperial China.

Under the most activist of the Han emperors, Emperor Wu, Confucian scholars were given a privileged position. Confucian officials did not always please Emperor Wu and other emperors. Seeing criticism of the government as one of their duties, the officials tried to check abuse of power. Their willingness to stand up to the ruler also reflected the fact that most of the Confucian scholars selected to serve as officials came from landholding families, much like those who staffed the Roman government, which gave them some economic independence.

The Confucianism that made a comeback during the Han Dynasty was a changed Confucianism. Although Confucian texts had fed the First Emperor's bonfires, some dedicated scholars had hidden their books, and others had memorized whole works: one ninety-year-old man was able to recite two long books almost in their entirety. The ancient books recovered in this way—called the **Confucian classics**—were revered as repositories of the wisdom of the past. Confucian scholars treated these classics with piety and attempted to make them more useful as sources of moral guidance by writing commentaries on them. Many Confucian scholars specialized in a single classic, and teachers passed on to their disciples their understanding of

• **Confucian classics** The ancient texts recovered during the Han Dynasty that Confucian scholars treated as sacred scriptures.

each sentence in the work. Other Han Confucians went to the opposite extreme, developing comprehensive cosmological theories that explained the world in terms of cyclical flows of yin and yang (see page 111) and the five phases (fire, water, earth, metal, and wood). Some used these theories to elevate the role of the emperor, who alone had the capacity to link the realms of Heaven, earth, and man. Natural disasters such as floods or earthquakes were viewed as portents that the emperor had failed in his role of maintaining the proper balance among the forces of Heaven and earth.

Han art and literature reveal a fascination with omens, portents, spirits, immortals, and occult forces. Emperor Wu tried to make contact with the world of

gods and immortals through elaborate sacrificial offerings of food and wine, and he welcomed astrologers, alchemists, seers, and shamans to his court. He marveled at stories of deities such as the Queen Mother of the West and the Yellow Emperor, who had taken his entire court with him when he ascended to the realm of the immortals. Much of this interest in immortality and communicating with the spirit world was absorbed into the emerging religion of Daoism, which also drew on the philosophical ideas of Laozi and Zhuangzi (see pages 107–110).

A major intellectual accomplishment of the Han Dynasty was history writing. Sima Qian (145–ca. 85 B.C.E.) wrote a comprehensive history of China from the time

MAP 7.1 The Han Empire, 206 B.C.E.–270 C.E. The Han Dynasty asserted sovereignty over vast regions from Korea in the east to Central Asia in the west and Vietnam in the south. Once garrisons were established, traders were quick to follow, leading to considerable spread of Chinese material culture in East Asia. Chinese goods, especially silk, were in demand far beyond East Asia, promoting long-distance trade across Eurasia.

Bronze Mirror The back side of a bronze mirror was frequently decorated with images of deities and animals and with auspicious words. As the viewer turned the mirror, he saw different scenes. This Han mirror features an outer border with semicircles decorated with cloud patterns and squares with words written on them. In the center are deities. (Mirror Featuring Deities and Kings in Three Sections Surrounded by Rings of Squares and Semicircles. China, Eastern Han dynasty [25–220], late 2nd–early 3rd century. Bronze; diameter 13.9 cm. The Cleveland Museum of Art. Gift of Drs. Thomas and Martha Carter in Honor of Sherman E. Lee 1995.328)

of the mythical sage-kings of high antiquity to his own day, dividing his account into a chronology recounting political events, biographies of key individuals, and treatises on subjects such as geography, taxation, and court rituals. As an official of the emperor, he had access to important people and documents and to the imperial library. Like the Greek historians Herodotus and Thucydides (see page 123), Sima Qian believed fervently in visiting the sites where history was made, examining artifacts, and questioning people about events. He was also interested in China's geography and local history. The result of his research, ten years or more in the making, was ***Records of the Grand Historian***, a massive work of literary and historical genius. In the chapter devoted to moneymakers, he described how the Ping family made its fortune:

> Lu people are customarily cautious and miserly, but the Ping family of Cao were particularly so. They started out by smelting iron and in time accumulated a fortune of a hundred million cash. All the members of the family from the father and elder brothers down to the sons and grandsons, however, made a promise that they would "Never look down without picking up something useful; never look up without grabbing something of value." They traveled about to all the provinces and kingdoms, selling goods on credit, lending money and trading. It was because of their influence that so many people in Zou and Lu abandoned scholarship and turned to the pursuit of profit.[2]

From examples like these Sima Qian concluded that wealth has no permanent master: "It finds its way to the man of ability like the spokes of a wheel converging upon the hub, and from the hands of the worthless it falls like shattered tiles."[3] For centuries to come, Sima Qian's work set the standard for Chinese historical writing, although most of the histories modeled after it covered only a single dynasty. The first of these was the work of three members of the Ban family in the first century C.E. (See "Individuals in Society: The Ban Family," page 186.)

The circulation of books like Sima Qian's was made easier by the invention of paper, which the Chinese traditionally date to 105 C.E. Scribes had previously written on strips of bamboo and wood or rolls of silk. Cai Lun, to whom the Chinese attribute the invention of paper, worked the fibers of rags, hemp, bark, and other scraps into sheets of paper. Paper, thus, was somewhat similar to the papyrus made from pounded reeds in ancient Egypt. Though much less durable than wood, paper was far cheaper than silk and became a convenient means of conveying the written word. Compared to papyrus, it depended less on a specific source of plant fiber and so could be produced many places.

Inner Asia and the Silk Road

The difficulty of defending against the nomadic pastoral peoples to the north in the region known as Inner Asia is a major reason China came to favor a centralized bureaucratic form of government. Resources from the entire subcontinent were needed to maintain control of the northern border.

Beginning long before the Han Dynasty, China's contacts with its northern neighbors had involved both trade and military conflict. China's neighbors sought Chinese products such as silk and lacquer ware. When they did not have goods to trade or when trading relations were disrupted, raiding was considered an acceptable alternative in the tribal cultures of the region. Chinese sources speak of defending against raids of "barbarians" from Shang times (ca. 1500–ca. 1050 B.C.E.) on, but not until the rise of nomadism in the mid-Zhou period (fifth to fourth centuries B.C.E.) did the horsemen of the north become China's main threat.

The economy of these nomads was based on raising sheep, goats, camels, and horses. Families lived in tents that could be taken down and moved north in summer and south in winter when groups of families moved in search of pasture. Herds were tended on horseback, and everyone learned to ride from a young age. Especially awesome from the Chinese perspective was the ability of nomad horsemen to shoot arrows while riding horseback. The typical social structure of the steppe nomads was fluid, with family and clan units linked through loyalty to tribal chiefs selected for their military prowess. Charismatic tribal leaders could form large coalitions and mobilize the entire society for war.

Chinese farmers and Inner Asian herders had such different modes of life that it is not surprising that they had little respect for each other. For most of the imperial period, Chinese farmers looked on the northern non-Chinese horsemen as gangs of bullies who thought

robbing was easier than working for a living. The nomads identified glory with military might and viewed farmers as contemptible weaklings.

In the late third century B.C.E. the Xiongnu (known in the West as the Huns) formed the first great confederation of nomadic tribes (see Map 7.1). The Qin's Great Wall was built to defend against them, and the Qin sent out huge armies in pursuit of them. The early Han emperors tried to make peace with them, offering generous gifts of silk, rice, cash, and even imperial princesses as brides. But these policies were controversial, since critics thought they merely strengthened the enemy. Xiongnu power did not decline, and in 166 B.C.E. 140,000 Xiongnu raided to within a hundred miles of the Chinese capital.

Emperor Wu decided that China had to push the Xiongnu back. He sent several armies of 100,000 to 300,000 troops deep into Xiongnu territory. These costly campaigns were of limited value because the Xiongnu were a moving target: fighting nomads was not like attacking walled cities. If the Xiongnu did not want to fight the Chinese troops, they simply moved their camps. To try to find allies and horses, Emperor Wu turned his attention west, toward Central Asia. From the envoy he sent into Bactria, Parthia, and Ferghana in 139 B.C.E., the Chinese learned for the first time of other civilized states comparable to China (see Map 7.1). The envoy described Ferghana as an urban society 10,000 *li* (about 3,000 miles) west of China, where grapes were grown for wine and the horses were particularly fine. In Parthia he was impressed by the use of silver coins stamped with the image of the king's face. These regions, he reported, were familiar with Chinese products, especially silk, and did a brisk trade in them.

In 114 B.C.E. Emperor Wu sent an army into Ferghana and gained recognition of Chinese overlordship in the area, thus obtaining control over the trade routes across Central Asia commonly called the **Silk Road** (see Map 7.1). The city-states along this route did not resist the Chinese presence. They could carry out the trade on which they depended more conveniently with Chinese garrisons to protect them than with rival tribes raiding them.

Xiongnu Metalwork The metal ornaments of the Xiongnu provide convincing evidence that they were in contact with nomadic pastoralists farther west in Asia, such as the Scythians, who also fashioned metal plaques and buckles in animal designs. This buckle or ornament is made of gold and is about 3 inches tall. (Image copyright © The Metropolitan Museum of Art/Art Resource, NY)

- **Records of the Grand Historian** A comprehensive history of China written by Sima Qian.
- **Silk Road** The trade routes across Central Asia through which Chinese silk and other items were traded.

> **"If a country possesses a wealth of fertile land and yet its people are underfed, the reason is that merchants and workers have prospered while agriculture has been neglected."**

CONFUCIAN SCHOLAR, 81 B.C.E.

At the same time, Emperor Wu sent troops into northern Korea to establish military districts that would flank the Xiongnu on their eastern border. By 111 B.C.E. the Han government also had extended its rule south into Nam Viet, which extended from south China into what is now northern Vietnam. Thus during Emperor Wu's reign, the territorial reach of the Han state was vastly extended.

During the Han Dynasty China developed a **tributary system** to regulate contact with foreign powers. States and tribes beyond its borders sent envoys bearing gifts and received gifts in return. Over the course of the dynasty the Han government's outlay on these gifts was huge, perhaps as much as 10 percent of state revenue. In 25 B.C.E., for instance, the government gave tributary states twenty thousand rolls of silk cloth and about twenty thousand pounds of silk floss. Although the tributary system was a financial burden to the Chinese, it reduced the cost of defense and offered China confirmation that it was the center of the civilized world.

The silk given to the Xiongnu and other northern tributaries often entered the trading networks of Sogdian, Parthian, and Indian merchants, who carried it by caravans across Asia. There was a market both for skeins of silk thread and for silk cloth woven in Chinese or Syrian workshops. Caravans returning to China carried gold, horses, and occasionally handicrafts of West Asian origin, such as glass beads and cups. Through the trade along the Silk Road, the Chinese learned of new foodstuffs, including walnuts, pomegranates, sesame, and coriander, all of which came

to be grown in China. This trade was largely carried by the two-humped Bactrian camel, which had been bred in Central Asia since the first century B.C.E. With a heavy coat of hair to withstand the bitter cold of winter, each camel could carry about five hundred pounds of cargo. (See "Global Trade: Silk," page 184.)

Maintaining a military presence so far from the center of China was expensive. To cut costs, the government set up self-supporting military colonies, recruited Xiongnu tribes to serve as auxiliary forces, and established vast government horse farms. Still, military expenses threatened to bankrupt the Han government.

Life in Han China

How were ordinary people's lives affected by the creation of a huge Han bureaucratic empire? The lucky ones who lived in Chang'an or Luoyang, the great cities of the empire, got to enjoy the material benefits of increased long-distance trade and a boom in the production of luxury goods.

The government did not promote trade per se. The Confucian elite, like ancient Hebrew wise men, considered trade necessary but lowly. Agriculture and crafts were more honorable because they produced something, but merchants merely took advantage of others' shortages to make profits as middlemen. In a debate conducted in 81 B.C.E., the Confucian scholars argued that "If a country possesses a wealth of fertile land and yet its people are underfed, the reason is that merchants and workers have prospered while agriculture has been neglected."[4] This attitude justified the government's takeover of the grain,

Ceramic Model of a Pigsty Chinese farmers regularly raised pigs, keeping them in walled-off pens and feeding them scraps. This Han Dynasty model of such a pigsty was placed in a tomb to represent the material goods one hoped the deceased would enjoy in the afterlife. (The Minneapolis Institute of Arts, Gift of Alan and Dena Naylor in memory of Thomas E. Leary)

iron, and salt businesses. Still, the government indirectly promoted commerce by building cities and roads.

Markets were the liveliest places in the cities. Besides stalls selling goods of all kinds, markets offered fortune-tellers and entertainers. People flocked to puppet shows and performances of jugglers and acrobats. The markets also were used for the execution of criminals, to serve as a warning to onlookers.

Government patronage helped maintain the quality of craftsmanship in the cities. By the beginning of the first century C.E. China also had about fifty state-run ironworking factories. Chinese metalworking was the most advanced in the world at the time. In contrast to Roman blacksmiths, who hammered heated iron to make wrought iron tools, the Chinese knew how to liquefy iron and pour it into molds, producing tools with a higher carbon content that were harder and more durable. Han workmen turned out iron plowshares, agricultural tools with wooden handles, and weapons and armor.

Iron was replacing bronze in tools, but bronzeworkers still turned out a host of goods. Bronze was prized for jewelry, mirrors, and dishes. Bronze was also used for minting coins and for precision tools such as carpenters' rules and adjustable wrenches. Surviving bronze gear-and-cog wheels bear eloquent testimony to the sophistication of Han machinery. Han metalsmiths were mass-producing superb crossbows long before the crossbow was dreamed of in Europe.

The bulk of the population in Han times and even into the twentieth century consisted of peasants living in villages of a few hundred households. Because the Han empire, much like the contemporaneous Roman Empire, drew its strength from a large population of free peasants who contributed both taxes and labor services to the state, the government had to try to keep peasants independent and productive. The economic insecurity of smallholders was described by one official in 178 B.C.E. in terms that could well have been repeated in most later dynasties:

> They labour at plowing in the spring and hoeing in the summer, harvesting in the autumn and storing foodstuff in winter, cutting wood, performing labour service for the local government, all the while exposed to the dust of spring, the heat of summer, the storms of autumn, and the chill of winter. Through all four seasons they never get a day off. They need funds to cover such obligations as entertaining guests, burying the dead, visiting the sick, caring for orphans, and bringing up the young. No matter how hard they work they can be ruined by floods or droughts, or cruel and arbitrary officials who impose taxes at the wrong times or keep changing their

orders. When taxes fall due, those with produce have to sell it at half price [to raise the needed cash], and those without [anything to sell] have to borrow [at such high rates] they will have to pay back twice what they borrowed. Some as a consequence sell their lands and houses, even their children and grandchildren.[5]

To fight peasant poverty, the government kept land taxes low (one-thirtieth of the harvest), provided relief in time of famine, and promoted up-to-date agricultural methods. Still, many hard-pressed peasants were left to choose between migration to areas where new lands could be opened and quasi-servile status as the dependents of a magnate. Throughout the Han period Chinese farmers in search of land to till pushed into frontier areas, expanding Chinese domination at the expense of other ethnic groups, especially in central and south China.

The Chinese family in Han times was much like the Roman (see page 151) and the Indian (see page 72) families. In all three societies senior males had great authority, marriages were arranged by parents, and brides normally joined their husbands' families. Other practices were more distinctive to China, such as the universality of patrilineal family names, the practice of dividing land equally among the sons in a family, and the great emphasis placed on the virtue of filial piety. The brief *Classic of Filial Piety*, which claimed that filial piety was the root of all virtue, gained wide circulation in Han times. The virtues of loyal wives and devoted mothers were extolled in the *Biographies of Exemplary Women*, which told the stories of women from China's past who were notable for giving their husbands good advice, knowing how to educate their sons, and sacrificing themselves when forced to choose between their fathers and husbands. The book also contained a few cautionary tales of scheming, jealous, manipulative women who brought destruction to all around them. One of the most commonly used texts for the education of women is Ban Zhao's *Admonitions for Women*, in which she extols the feminine virtues, such as humility. (See "Individuals in Society: The Ban Family," page 186.)

China and Rome

The empires of China and Rome (discussed in Chapter 6) were large, complex states governed by monarchs, bureaucracies, and standing armies. Both reached

---

• **tributary system** A system first established during the Han Dynasty to regulate contact with foreign powers. States and tribes beyond its borders sent envoys bearing gifts and received gifts in return.

Global Trade

Silk was one of the earliest commodities to stimulate international trade. By 2500 B.C.E. Chinese farmers had domesticated *Bombyx mori*, the Chinese silkworm, and by 1000 B.C.E. they were making fine fabrics with complex designs. Sericulture (silk making) is labor-intensive. In order for silkworms to spin their cocoons, they have to be fed chopped leaves from mulberry trees every few hours, day and night, during the month between hatching and spinning. The cocoons consist of a single filament several thousand feet long but a minuscule 0.025 millimeter thick. More than two thousand cocoons are needed to make a pound of silk. After the cocoons are boiled to loosen the natural gum that binds the filament, several strands of filament are twisted together to make yarns.

What made silk the most valued of all textiles was its beauty and versatility. It could be made into sheer gauzes, shiny satins, multicolored brocades, and plush velvets. Fine Han silks have been found in Xiongnu tombs in northern Mongolia. Korea and Japan not only imported silk but also began silk production themselves, and silk came to be used in both places in much the way it was used in China—for the clothes of the elite, for temple banners, and as a surface for writing and painting. Central Asia, Persia, India, and Southeast Asia also became producers of silk in distinctive local styles. Lacking suitable climates to produce silk, Mongolia and Tibet remained major importers of Chinese silks into modern times.

MAP 7.2 The Silk Trade in the Seventh Century C.E.

Designed to be worn by a priest in the Eastern Orthodox Church, this fourteenth-century silk garment is embellished with silver- and silver-gilt-covered threads. It was probably made in Constantinople, though the silk floss may well have been imported, perhaps from Syria or Persia. (Courtesy, Library of the Chapter of St. Peter and the Museum of the Treasury, Vatican City)

What makes the silk trade famous, however, is not the trade within Asia but the trade across Asia to Europe. In Roman times silk carried by caravans across Asia or by ships across the Indian Ocean became a high-status luxury item, said to cost its weight in gold. To satisfy Roman taste, imported silk fabrics were unraveled and rewoven in Syrian workshops. Although the techniques of sericulture gradually spread through Asia, they remained a mystery in the West until the Byzantine emperor Justinian in the sixth century had two monks bring back silkworms from China along with knowledge of how to care for them and process their cocoons.

In medieval times most of the silk imported into Europe came from Persia, the Byzantine Empire, or the Arab world. Venetian merchants handled much of the trade. Some of this fabric still survives in ancient churches, where it was used for vestments and altar clothes and to wrap relics. In the eleventh century Roger I, king of Sicily, captured groups of silk-workers from Athens and Corinth and moved them to Sicily, initiating the production of silk in western Europe. Over the next couple of centuries, Italy became a major silk producer, joined by France in the fifteenth century.

When the Venetian merchant Marco Polo traveled across Asia in the late thirteenth century, he found local silk for sale in Baghdad, Georgia, Persia, and elsewhere, but China remained the largest producer. He claimed that more than a thousand cartloads of silk were brought into the capital of China every day.

With the development of the sea route between western Europe and China from the sixteenth century on, Europe began importing large quantities of Chinese silk, much of it as silk floss—raw silk—to supply Italian, French, and English silk weavers. In 1750 almost 77.2 tons of raw silk and nearly 20,000 bolts of silk cloth were carried from China to Europe. By this period the aristocracy of Europe regularly wore silk clothes, including silk stockings.

Mechanization of silkmaking began in Europe in the seventeenth century. The Italians developed machines to "throw" the silk—doubling and twisting raw silk into threads suitable for weaving. In the early nineteenth century the introduction of Jacquard looms using punched cards made complex patterns easier to weave.

In the 1920s the silk industry was hit hard by the introduction of synthetic fibers, especially rayon and nylon. In the 1940s women in the United States and Europe switched from silk stockings to the much less expensive nylon stockings. European production of silk almost entirely collapsed. After China reentered world trade in the early 1980s China rapidly expanded its silk production for export. By 2003 there were more than two thousand silk enterprises in China, employing a million workers and supplying 80 percent of the total world trade in silk.

Individuals in Society

The Ban Family

BAN BIAO (3–54 C.E.), A SUCCESSFUL OFFICIAL from a family with an envied library, had three highly accomplished children: his twin sons, the general Ban Chao (32–102) and the historian Ban Gu (32–92), and his daughter, Ban Zhao (ca. 45–120). After distinguishing himself as a junior officer in campaigns against the Xiongnu, Ban Chao was sent in 73 C.E. to the Western Regions to see about the possibility of restoring Chinese overlordship there, lost several decades earlier. Ban Chao spent most of the next three decades in Central Asia. Through patient diplomacy and a show of force, he re-established Chinese control over the oasis cities of Central Asia, and in 92 he was appointed protector general of the area.

His twin brother Ban Gu was one of the most accomplished writers of his age, excelling in a distinctive literary form known as the rhapsody *(fu)*. His "Rhapsody on the Two Capitals" is in the form of a dialogue between a guest from Chang'an and his host in Luoyang. It describes the palaces, spectacles, scenic spots, local products, and customs of the two great cities. Emperor Zhang (r. 76–88) was fond of literature and often had Ban Gu accompany him on hunts or travels. He also had him edit a record of the court debates he held on issues concerning the Confucian classics.

Ban Biao was working on the *History of the Western Former Han Dynasty*, when he died in 54. Ban Gu took over this project, modeling it on Sima Qian's *Records of the Grand Historian*. He added treatises on law, geography, and bibliography, the last a classified list of books in the imperial library.

Because of his connection to a general out of favor, Ban Gu was sent to prison in 92, where he soon died. At that time the *History of the Former Han Dynasty* was still incomplete. The emperor called on Ban Gu's widowed sister, Ban Zhao, to finish it. She came to the palace, where she not only worked on the history but also became a teacher of the women of the palace. According to the *History of the Later Han*, she taught them the classics, history, astronomy, and mathematics. In 106 an infant succeeded to the throne, and the widow of an earlier emperor became regent. This empress frequently turned to Ban Zhao for advice on government policies.

Ban Zhao credited her own education to her learned father and cultured mother and became an advocate of the education of girls. In her *Admonitions for Women* Ban Zhao objected that many families taught their sons to read but not their daughters. She did not claim girls should have the same education as boys; after all, "just as yin and yang differ, men and women have different characteristics." Women, she wrote, will do well if they cultivate the womanly virtues such as humility. "Humility means yielding and acting respectful, putting others first and oneself last, never mentioning one's own good deeds or denying one's own faults, enduring insults and bearing with mistreatment, all with due trepidation."* In subsequent centuries Ban Zhao's *Admonitions* became one of the most commonly used texts for the education of Chinese girls.

QUESTIONS FOR ANALYSIS

1. What inferences can you draw from the fact that a leading general had a brother who was a literary man?
2. What does Ban Zhao's life tell us about women in her society? How do you reconcile her personal accomplishments with the advice she gave for women's education?

*Patricia Buckley Ebrey, ed., *Chinese Civilization: A Sourcebook*, rev. ed. (New York: Free Press, 1993), p. 75.

● **Ban Zhao continued to be considered the ideal woman teacher into the eighteenth century, when this imaginary portrait depicted her taking up her brush among women and children.** (National Palace Museum, Taipei, Taiwan)

directly to the people through taxation and conscription policies, and both invested in infrastructure such as roads and waterworks. The empires faced the similar challenge of having to work hard to keep land from becoming too concentrated in the hands of hard-to-tax wealthy magnates. In both empires people in neighboring areas that came under political domination were attracted to the conquerors' material goods, productive techniques, and other cultural products, resulting in gradual cultural assimilation. China and Rome also had similar frontier problems and tried similar solutions, such as recruiting "barbarian" soldiers and settling soldier-colonists.

Nevertheless, the differences between Rome and Han China are worth as much notice as the similarities. The Roman Empire was linguistically and culturally more diverse than China. In China there was only one written language; people in the Roman Empire still wrote in Greek and several other languages, and people in the eastern Mediterrean could claim more ancient civilizations. China did not have comparable cultural rivals. Politically the dynastic principle was stronger in China than in Rome. Han emperors were never chosen by the army or by any institution comparable to the Roman senate, nor were there republican ideals in China. In contrast to the graduated forms of citizenship in Rome, Han China drew no distinctions between original and added territories. The social and economic structures also differed in the two empires. Slavery was much more important in Rome than in China, and merchants were more favored. Over time these differences put Chinese and Roman social and political development on different trajectories.

The Fall of the Han and the Age of Division

In the second century c.e. the Han government suffered a series of blows. A succession of child emperors required regents to rule in their place until they reached maturity, allowing the families of empresses to dominate the court. Emperors, once grown, turned to **eunuchs** (castrated palace servants) for help in ousting the empresses' families, only to find that the eunuchs were just as difficult to control. In 166 and 169 scholars who had denounced the eunuchs were arrested, killed, or banished from the capital and official life. Then in 184 a millenarian religious sect rose in massive revolt. The armies raised to suppress the rebels soon took to fighting among themselves. In 189 one general slaughtered two thousand eunuchs in the palace and took the Han emperor captive. After years of fighting, a stalemate was reached, with three warlords each controlling distinct territories in the north, the southeast, and the southwest. In 220 one of them

forced the last of the Han emperors to abdicate, formally ending the Han Dynasty.

The period after the fall of the Han Dynasty is often referred to as the **Age of Division** (220–589). A brief reunification from 280 to 316 came to an end when non-Chinese who had been settling in north China since Han times seized the opportunity afforded by the political turmoil to take power. For the next two and a half centuries north China was ruled by one or more non-Chinese dynasties (the Northern Dynasties), and the south was ruled by a sequence of four short-lived Chinese dynasties (the Southern Dynasties) centered in the area of the present-day city of Nanjing.

In the south a hereditary aristocracy entrenched itself in the higher reaches of officialdom. These families intermarried only with families of equivalent pedigree and compiled lists and genealogies of the most eminent families. They saw themselves as maintaining the high culture of the Han and looked on the emperors of the successive dynasties as upstarts — as military men rather than men of culture. In this aristocratic culture, the arts of poetry and calligraphy flourished, and people began collecting writings by famous calligraphers.

Establishing the capital at Nanjing, south of the Yangzi River, had a beneficial effect on the economic development of the south. To pay for an army and to support the imperial court and aristocracy in a style that matched their pretensions, the government had to expand the area of taxable agricultural land, whether by settling migrants or converting the local inhabitants into taxpayers. The south, with its temperate climate and ample supply of water, offered nearly unlimited possibilities for such development.

The Northern Dynasties are interesting as the first case of alien rule in China. Ethnic tensions flared from time to time. In the late fifth century the Northern Wei (way) Dynasty (386–534) moved the capital from near the Great Wall to the ancient city of Luoyang, adopted Chinese-style clothing, and made Chinese the official language. But the armies remained in the hands of the Xianbei tribesmen. Soldiers who saw themselves as marginalized by the pro-Chinese reforms rebelled in 524. For the next fifty years north China was torn apart by struggles for power. It had long been the custom of the northern pastoral tribes to enslave those they captured; sometimes the residents of entire cities were enslaved. In 554, when the city of Jiangling was taken, a hundred thousand civilians were enslaved and distributed to generals and officials.

- **eunuchs** Castrated males who played an important role as palace servants.
- **Age of Division** The period after the fall of the Han Dynasty, when China was politically divided.

The Spread of Buddhism Out of India

☐ How did Buddhism find its way into East Asia, and what was its appeal and impact?

In much the same period that Christianity was spreading out of its original home in ancient Israel, Buddhism was spreading beyond India. Buddhism came to Central, East, and Southeast Asia with merchants and missionaries along the overland Silk Road, by sea from India and Sri Lanka, and also through Tibet. Like Christianity, Buddhism was shaped by its contact with cultures in the different areas into which it spread, leading to several distinct forms.

Meditating Monk This monk, wearing the traditional patchwork robe, sits in the crossed-legged meditation position. His small niche is to the left of the main image of the Buddha in cave 285 at Dunhuang, a cave completed in 539 under the patronage of a prince of the Northern Wei imperial house who was then the local governor. (Photo: Lois Conner. Courtesy, Dunhuang Academy)

Buddhism's Path Through Central Asia

Central Asia is a loose term used to refer to the vast area between the ancient civilizations of Persia, India, and China. Modern political borders are a product of competition for empire among the British, Russians, and Chinese in the mid-nineteenth century and have relatively little to do with the earlier history of the region. Through most of recorded history, the region was ethnically and culturally diverse; it was home to urban centers, especially at the oases along the Silk Road, and to animal herders in the mountains and grasslands.

Under Ashoka in India (see pages 84–85) Buddhism began to spread to Central Asia. This continued under the Kushan empire (ca. 50–250 C.E.), especially under the greatest Kushan king Kanishka I (ca. 100 C.E.). In this region, where the influence of Greek art was strong, artists began to depict the Buddha in human form. Over the next several centuries most of the city-states of Central Asia became centers of Buddhism, from Bamiyan northwest of Kabul, to Kucha, Khotan, Loulan, Turfan, and Dunhuang (Map 7.3). Because the remarkable Buddhist civilization of Central Asia was later supplanted by Islam, it was not until early in the twentieth century that European archaeologists discovered its traces. The main sites yielded not only numerous Buddhist paintings but also thousands of texts in a variety of languages. In Khotan, for instance, an Indian language was used for administrative purposes long after the fall of the Kushan empire. Other texts were in various Persian languages, showing the cultural mix of the region.

The form of Buddhism that spread from Central Asia to China, Japan, and Korea was called Mahayana, which means "Great Vehicle" (see page 78), reflecting the claims of its adherents to a more inclusive form of the religion. Influenced by the Iranian religions then prevalent in Central Asia, Buddhism became more devotional. The Buddha came to be treated as a god, the head of an expanding pantheon of other Buddhas and bodhisattvas (Buddhas-to-be). With the growth of this pantheon, Buddhism became as much a religion for laypeople as for monks and nuns.

The first translators of Buddhist texts into Chinese were not Indians but Parthians, Sogdians, and Kushans from Central Asia. One of the most important interpreters of Buddhism in China was the eminent Central

□ Mapping the Past

MAP 7.3 The Spread of Buddhism, ca. 500 B.C.E.–800 C.E. Buddhism spread throughout India in Ashoka's time and beyond India in later centuries. The different forms of Buddhism found in Asia today reflect this history. The Mahayana Buddhism of Japan came via Central Asia, China, and Korea, with a secondary later route through Tibet. The Theravada Buddhism of Southeast Asia came directly from India and indirectly through Sri Lanka.

ANALYZING THE MAP Trace the routes of the spread of Buddhism by time period. How fast did Buddhism spread?

CONNECTIONS Why do you think Buddhism spread more to the east of India than to the west?

Asian monk Kumarajiva (350–413) from Kucha, who settled in Chang'an and directed several thousand monks in the translation of Buddhist texts.

The Appeal and Impact of Buddhism in China

Why did Buddhism find so many adherents in China during the three centuries after the fall of the Han Dynasty in 220? There were no forced conversions, but still the religion spread rapidly. In the unstable political environment, many people were open to new ideas. To Chinese scholars the Buddhist concepts of the rein-carnation of souls, karma, and nirvana posed a stimulating intellectual challenge. To rulers the Buddhist religion offered a source of magical power and a political tool to unite Chinese and non-Chinese. In a rough and tumultuous age Buddhism's emphasis on kindness, charity, and eternal bliss was deeply comforting. As in India, Buddhism posed no threat to the social order, and the elite who were drawn to Buddhism encouraged its spread to people of all classes.

The monastic establishment grew rapidly in China. Like their Christian counterparts in medieval Europe, Buddhist monasteries played an active role in social, economic, and political life. By 477 there were said to

Listening to the Past

Sixth-Century Biographies of Buddhist Nuns

Women drawn to Buddhism could leave secular life to become nuns. Most nuns lived with other nuns in convents, but they could also work to spread Buddhist teachings outside the cloister. The first collection of biographies of eminent nuns in China was written in 516. Among the sixty-five nuns whose lives it recounted are these three.

Kang Minggan

"Minggan's secular surname was Zhu, and her family was from Kaoping. For generations the family had venerated the [Buddhist] teachings known as the Great Vehicle.

A bandit who wanted to make her his wife abducted her, but, even though she suffered increasing torment, she vowed not to give in to him. She was forced to serve as a shepherdess far from her native home. Ten years went by and her longing for her home and family grew more and more intense, but there seemed to be no way back. During all this she kept her mind fixed on the Three Treasures, and she herself wished to become a nun.

One day she happened to meet a Buddhist monk, and she asked him to bestow on her the five fundamental precepts [of a Buddhist householder]. He granted her request and also presented her with a copy of the Bodhisattva Guanshiyin Scripture, which she then practiced chanting day and night without pause.

Deciding to return home to build a five-story pagoda, she fled to the east in great anxiety and distress. At first she did not know the road but kept traveling both day and night. When crossing over a mountain she saw a tiger lying only a few steps away from her. After momentary terror she composed her mind, and her hopes were more than met, for the tiger led the way for her, and, after the days had grown into weeks, she finally arrived in her home territory of Qing Province. As she was about to enter the village, the tiger disappeared, but at that moment, having arrived in the province, Minggan was again abducted, this time by Ming Bolian. When word reached her family, her husband and son ransomed her, but the family did not let her carry out her wishes [to enter the life of a Buddhist nun]. Only after three years of cultivating stringent religious practices was she able to follow her intention. As a nun, she especially concentrated on the cultivation of meditation, and she kept all the regulations of a monastic life without any transgressions. If she happened to commit a minor fault, she would confess it several mornings in a row, ceasing only after she received a sign or a good omen. Sometimes as a good omen she saw flowers rain down from the sky or she heard a voice in the sky or she saw a Buddha image or she had auspicious dreams.

As Minggan approached old age, her moral cultivation was even more strict and lofty. All the men and women north of the Yangtze River honored her as their spiritual teacher in whom they could take refuge.

In the spring of 348 of the Jin dynasty, she, together with Huichan and others—ten in all—traveled south, crossed the Yangtze River, and went to see the minister of public works, He Chong, in the capital of the Eastern Jin dynasty. As soon as he met them, he showed them great respect. Because at that time there were no convents in the capital region He Chong converted one of his private residences into a convent for them.

He asked Minggan, "What should the convent be named?"

She replied, "In the great realm of the Jin dynasty all the four Buddhist assemblies of monks, nuns, and male and female householders are now established for the first time. Furthermore, that which you as donor have established will bestow blessings and merit. Therefore, let us call the convent 'Establishing Blessings Convent.'" He Chong agreed to her suggestion. Not long afterward Minggan took sick and died."

Daoqiong

"Daoqiong's secular surname was Jiang. Her family was from Danyang. When she was a little more than ten years old, she was already well educated in the classics and history, and after her full admission to the monastic assembly she became learned in the Buddhist writings as well and also diligently cultivated a life of asceticism. In the Taiyuan reign period [376–396] of the Eastern Jin dynasty, the empress admired her exalted

be 6,478 Buddhist temples and 77,258 monks and nuns in the north. Some decades later south China had 2,846 temples and 82,700 clerics. Given the importance of family lines in China, becoming a monk was a major decision, since a man had to give up his surname and take a vow of celibacy, thus cutting himself off from the ancestral cult. Those not ready to become monks or nuns could pursue Buddhist goals as pious laypeople by performing devotional acts and making contributions to monasteries. Among the most generous patrons were rulers in both the north and south.

In China women turned to Buddhism as readily as men. Although birth as a female was considered lower than birth as a male, it was also viewed as temporary, and women were encouraged to pursue salvation on terms nearly equal to men. Joining a nunnery became conduct, and, whenever she wished to gain merit by giving gifts or by listening to religious exhortations, she most often depended on the convent where Daoqiong lived for such opportunities. Ladies of noble family vied with one another to associate with Daoqiong.

In 431 she had many Buddhist images made and placed them everywhere: in Pengcheng Monastery, two gold Buddha images with a curtained dais and all accessories; in Pottery Office Monastery, a processional image of Maitreya, the future Buddha, with a jeweled umbrella and pendants; in Southern Establishing Joy Monastery, two gold images with various articles, banners, and canopies. In Establishing Blessings Convent, she had an image of the reclining Buddha made, as well as a hall to house it. She also had a processional image of the bodhisattva, Puxian [or Samantabhadra], made. Of all these items, there was none that was not extremely beautiful. Again, in 438, Daoqiong commissioned a gold Amitayus [or Infinite Life] Buddha, and in the fourth month and tenth day of that same year a golden light shone forth from the mark between the eyebrows of the image and filled the entire convent. The news of this event spread among religious and worldly alike, and all came to pay honor, and, gazing at the unearthly brilliance, there was none who was not filled with great happiness. Further, using the materials bequeathed to her by the Yuan empress consort, she extended the convent to the south to build another meditation hall.

On the full-moon night of the fifteenth day of the third month, in 463 . . . , Daozong, as an offering to the Buddha, purified herself in a fire fed by oil. Even though she was engulfed by flames up to her forehead, and her eyes and ears were nearly consumed, her chanting of the scriptures did not falter. Monastics and householders sighed in wonder; the demonic and upright were alike startled. When the country heard this news, everyone aspired to attain enlightenment. The appointed court scholar . . . , Liu Qiu, especially revered her and composed a Buddhist-style poetic verse to praise her. **"**

Source: Kathryn Ann Tsai, trans., *Lives of the Nuns: Biographies of Chinese Buddhist Nuns from the Fourth to Sixth Centuries*. Copyright © 1994 University of Hawai'i Press. Reprinted with permission.

Daozong

" Daozong, whose family origins are unknown, lived in Three-Story Convent in Jiangling. As a child she had no intention of setting herself apart; as an adult she did not consider associating with others a defilement. She merely followed a course along the boundary between the wise and the foolish, and, although outwardly she seemed muddled, yet within she traversed hidden profundities.

QUESTIONS FOR ANALYSIS

1. Why were the lives of these three particular nuns considered worth recording? What was admirable or inspiring about their examples?

2. What do the nuns' spiritual journeys reveal about the virtues associated with Buddhist monastic life?

3. Do you see a gender element in these accounts? Were the traits that made a nun admirable also appropriate for monks?

an alternative for a woman who did not want to marry or did not want to stay with her husband's family in widowhood. (See "Listening to the Past: Sixth-Century Biographies of Buddhist Nuns," above.) Later, the only woman ruler of China, Empress Wu, invoked Buddhist principles to justify her role (see page 194), which reveals how significant a break with Confucianism Buddhism was for women.

Buddhism had an enormous impact on the visual arts in China, especially sculpture and painting. Before Buddhism, Chinese had not set up statues of gods in temples, but now they decorated temples with a profusion of images. Inspired by the cave-temples of India and Central Asia, in China, too, caves were carved into rock faces to make temples.

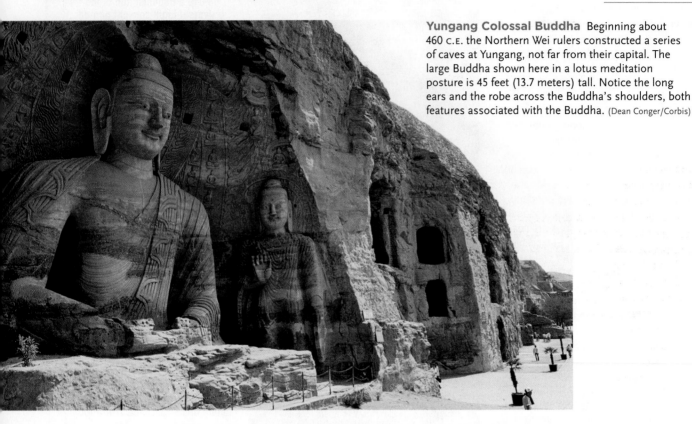

Yungang Colossal Buddha Beginning about 460 C.E. the Northern Wei rulers constructed a series of caves at Yungang, not far from their capital. The large Buddha shown here in a lotus meditation posture is 45 feet (13.7 meters) tall. Notice the long ears and the robe across the Buddha's shoulders, both features associated with the Buddha. (Dean Conger/Corbis)

Urban temples could be just as splendid. One author described the ceremony held each year on the seventh day of the fourth month at the largest monastery in the northern capital, Luoyang. All the Buddhist statues in the city, more than a thousand altogether, would be brought to the monastery, and the emperor would come in person to scatter flowers as part of the Great Blessing ceremony:

> The gold and the flowers dazzled in the sun, and the jewelled canopies floated like clouds; there were forests of banners and a fog of incense, and the Buddhist music of India shook heaven and earth. All kinds of entertainers and trick riders performed shoulder to shoulder. Virtuous hosts of famous monks came, carrying their staves; there were crowds of the Buddhist faithful, holding flowers; horsemen and carriages were packed beside each other in an endless mass.[6]

Not everyone was won over by Buddhist teachings. Critics of Buddhism labeled it immoral, unsuited to China, and a threat to the state since monastery land was not taxed and monks did not perform labor service. Twice in the north orders were issued to close monasteries and force monks and nuns to return to lay life, but these suppressions did not last long. No attempt was made to suppress belief in Buddhism, and the religion continued to thrive in the subsequent Sui and Tang periods.

The Chinese Empire Re-created: Sui (581–618) and Tang (618–907)

☐ What were the lasting accomplishments of the Sui and Tang Dynasties?

Political division was finally overcome when the Sui Dynasty conquered its rivals to reunify China in 581. Although the dynasty lasted only thirty-seven years, it left a lasting legacy in the form of political reform, the construction of roads and canals, and the institution of merit-based exams for the appointment of officials. The Tang Dynasty that followed would last for centuries and would build upon the Sui's accomplishments to create an era of impressive cultural creativity and political power.

The Sui Dynasty, 581–618

In the 570s and 580s, the long period of division in China was brought to an end under the leadership of the Sui (sway) Dynasty. Yang Jian, who both founded

• **Grand Canal** A canal, built during the Sui Dynasty, that connected the Yellow and Yangzi Rivers, notable for strengthening China's internal cohesion and economic development.

the Sui Dynasty and oversaw the reunification of China, was from a Chinese family that had intermarried with the non-Chinese elite of the north. His conquest of the south involved naval as well as land battles, with thousands of ships on both sides contending for control of the Yangzi River. The Sui reasserted Chinese control over northern Vietnam and campaigned into Korea and against the new force on the steppe, the Turks. The Sui strengthened central control of the government by curtailing the power of local officials to appoint their own subordinates and by instituting in 605 C.E. competitive written examinations for the selection of officials, a practice that would come to dominate the lives of educated men in later centuries.

The crowning achievement of the Sui Dynasty was the construction of the **Grand Canal**, which connected the Yellow and Yangzi River regions. The canal facilitated the shipping of tax grain from the prosperous Yangzi Valley to the centers of political and military power in north China. Henceforth the rice-growing Yangzi Valley and south China played an ever more influential role in the country's economic and political life, strengthening China's internal cohesion and facilitating maritime trade with Southeast Asia, India, and areas farther west.

Despite these accomplishments, the Sui Dynasty lasted for only two reigns. The ambitious projects of the two Sui emperors led to exhaustion and unrest, and in the ensuing warfare Li Yuan, a Chinese from the same northwest aristocratic circles as the founder of the Sui, seized the throne.

The Tang Dynasty, 618–907

The dynasty founded by Li Yuan, the Tang, was one of the high points of traditional Chinese civilization. Especially during this dynasty's first century, its capital, Chang'an, was the cultural center of East Asia, drawing in merchants, pilgrims, missionaries, and students to a degree never matched before or after. This position of strength gave the Chinese the confidence to be open to learning from the outside world, leading to a more cosmopolitan culture than in any other period before the twentieth century.

The first two Tang rulers, Gaozu (r. 618–626) and Taizong (r. 626–649), were able monarchs. Adding auxiliary troops composed of Turks, Tanguts, Khitans, and other non-Chinese led by their own chieftains to their

Tang China, ca. 750 C.E.

Chang'an

Urban Planning Chang'an in Tang times attracted merchants, pilgrims, and students from all over East Asia. The city was laid out on a square grid (left) and divided into walled wards, the gates to which were closed at night. Temples were found throughout the city, but trade was limited to two government-supervised markets. In the eighth and ninth centuries the Japanese copied the general plan of Chang'an in designing their capitals—first at Nara, then at Heian, shown on the right. (Cradles of Civilization/Visual Connection Archive)

Heian (Kyoto)

armies, they campaigned into Korea, Vietnam, and Central Asia. In 630 the Chinese turned against their former allies, the Turks, gaining territory from them and winning for Taizong the title of Great Khan, so that for a short period he was simultaneously head of both the Chinese and the Turkish empires.

In the civil sphere Tang accomplishments far outstripped anything known in Europe until the growth of national states in the seventeenth century. Tang emperors subdivided the administration of the empire into departments, much like the numerous agencies of modern governments. They built on the Sui precedent of using written examinations to select officials. Although only about thirty men were recruited this way each year, the prestige of passing the examinations became so great that more and more men attempted them. Candidates had to master the Confucian classics and the rules of poetry, and they had to be able to analyze practical administrative and political matters. Government schools were founded to prepare the sons of officials and other young men for service as officials.

The mid-Tang Dynasty saw two women—Empress Wu and Consort Yang Guifei—rise to positions of great political power. Empress Wu was the consort of the weak and sickly Emperor Gaozong. After Gaozong suffered a stroke in 660, she took full charge. She continued to rule after Gaozong's death, summarily deposing her own two sons and dealing harshly with all opponents. In 690 she proclaimed herself emperor, the only woman who took that title in Chinese history. To gain support, she circulated a Buddhist sutra that predicted the imminent reincarnation of the Buddha Maitreya as a female monarch, during whose reign the world would be free of illness, worry, and disaster. Although despised by later Chinese historians as an evil usurper, Empress Wu was an effective leader. It was not until she was over eighty that members of the court were able to force her out in favor of her son.

Her grandson, the emperor Xuanzong (r. 713–756), presided over a brilliant court and patronized leading poets, painters, and calligraphers in his early years. In his later years, however, after he became enamored of his consort Yang Guifei, he did not want to be bothered by the details of government. In this period ample and rounded proportions were much admired in women,

and Yang was said to be such a full-figured beauty. The emperor allowed her to place friends and relatives in important positions in the government. One of her favorites was the general An Lushan, who, after getting into a quarrel with Yang's brother over control of the government, rebelled in 755. Xuanzong had to flee the capital, and the troops that accompanied him forced him to have Yang Guifei executed.

The rebellion of An Lushan was devastating to the Tang Dynasty. Peace was restored only by calling on the Uighurs (WEE-grz), a Turkish people allied with the Tang, who looted the capital after taking it from the rebels. After the rebellion was finally suppressed in

Figurine of a Woman Notions of what makes women attractive have changed over the course of Chinese history. Figurines found in Tang tombs like this one show that full-figured women with plump faces were admired in the mid- and late Tang. Emperor Xuanzong's favorite, Yang Guifei, was said to be a plump woman, and the fashion is thought to have spread from the court. (Werner Forman/Art Resource, NY)

• **Pure Land** A school of Buddhism that taught that by calling on the Buddha Amitabha and his chief helper, one could achieve rebirth in Amitabha's Pure Land paradise.

763, the central government had to keep meeting the extortionate demands of the Uighurs. Many military governors came to treat their provinces as hereditary kingdoms and withheld tax returns from the central government. In addition, eunuchs gained increasing power at court and were able to prevent both the emperors and the Confucian officials from doing much about them.

Tang Culture

The reunification of north and south led to cultural flowering. The Tang capital cities of Chang'an and Luoyang became great metropolises; Chang'an and its suburbs grew to more than 2 million inhabitants (probably making it the largest city in the world at the time). The cities were laid out in rectangular grids and contained a hundred-odd walled "blocks" inside their walls. Like the gates of the city, the gates of each block were locked at night.

In these cosmopolitan cities, knowledge of the outside world was stimulated by the presence of envoys, merchants, and pilgrims who came from neighboring states in Central Asia, Japan, Korea, Tibet, and Southeast Asia. Because of the presence of foreign merchants, many religions were practiced, including Nestorian Christianity, Manichaeism, Zoroastrianism, Judaism, and Islam, although none of them spread into the Chinese population the way Buddhism had a few centuries earlier. Foreign fashions in hair and clothing were often copied, and foreign amusements such as the Persian game of polo found followings among the well-to-do. The introduction of new musical instruments and tunes from India, Iran, and Central Asia brought about a major transformation in Chinese music.

The Tang Dynasty was the great age of Chinese poetry. Skill in composing poetry was tested in the civil service examinations, and educated men had to be able to compose poems at social gatherings. The pain of parting, the joys of nature, and the pleasures of wine and friendship were all common poetic topics. One of Li Bo's (701–762) most famous poems describes an evening of drinking with only the moon and his shadow for company:

> A cup of wine, under the flowering trees;
> I drink alone, for no friend is near.
> Raising my cup I beckon the bright moon,
> For he, with my shadow, will make three men.
> The moon, alas, is no drinker of wine;
> Listless, my shadow creeps about at
>   my side.
> . . .
> Now we are drunk, each goes his way.
> May we long share our odd, inanimate feast,
> And we meet at last on the cloudy River of the sky.[7]

> **"**How can I govern these people and lead them aright? I cannot even understand what they say. But at least I am glad, now that the taxes are in, To learn that in my province there is no discontent.**"**
>
> **BO JUYI**

The poet Bo Juyi (772–846) often wrote of more serious subjects. At times he worried about whether he was doing his job justly and well:

> From these high walls I look at the town below
> Where the natives of Pa cluster like a swarm of flies.
> How can I govern these people and lead them aright?
> I cannot even understand what they say.
> But at least I am glad, now that the taxes
>   are in,
> To learn that in my province there is no
>   discontent.[8]

In Tang times Buddhism fully penetrated Chinese daily life. Stories of Buddhist origin became widely known, and Buddhist festivals, such as the festival for feeding hungry ghosts in the summer, became among the most popular holidays. Buddhist monasteries became an important part of everyday life. They ran schools for children. In remote areas they provided lodging for travelers. Merchants entrusted their money and wares to monasteries for safekeeping, in effect transforming the monasteries into banks and warehouses. The wealthy often donated money or land to support temples and monasteries, making monasteries among the largest landlords.

At the intellectual and religious level, Buddhism was developing in distinctly Chinese directions. Two schools that thrived were Pure Land and Chan. **Pure Land** appealed to laypeople because its simple act of calling on the Buddha Amitabha

Five-Stringed Pipa/Biwa
This musical instrument, decorated with fine wood marquetry, was probably presented by the Tang court to a Japanese envoy. It was among the objects placed in a Japanese royal storage house (Shōsōin) in 756.
(Kyodo)

and his chief helper, the compassionate bodhisattva Guanyin, could lead to rebirth in Amitabha's paradise, the Pure Land. Among the educated elite the **Chan** school (known in Japan as Zen) also gained popularity. Chan teachings rejected the authority of the scriptures and claimed the superiority of mind-to-mind transmission of Buddhist truths. The "northern" Chan tradition emphasized meditation and monastic discipline. The "southern" tradition was even more iconoclastic, holding that enlightenment could be achieved suddenly through insight into one's own true nature, even without prolonged meditation.

Opposition to Buddhism re-emerged in the late Tang period. In addition to concerns about the fiscal impact of removing so much land from the tax rolls and so many men from the labor service force, there were concerns about Buddhism's foreign origins. As China's international position weakened, xenophobia surfaced. During the persecution of 845, more than 4,600 monasteries and 40,000 temples and shrines were destroyed, and more than 260,000 Buddhist monks and nuns were forced to return to secular life. Although this ban was lifted after a few years, the monastic establishment never fully recovered. Buddhism retained a strong hold among laypeople, and basic Buddhist ideas like karma and reincarnation had become fully incorporated into everyday Chinese thinking. But Buddhism was never again as central to Chinese life.

The East Asian Cultural Sphere

☐ What elements of Chinese culture were adopted by Koreans, Vietnamese, and Japanese, and how did they adapt them to their own circumstances?

During the millennium from 200 B.C.E. to 800 C.E. China exerted a powerful influence on its immediate neighbors, who began forming states of their own. By Tang times China was surrounded by independent states in Korea, Manchuria, Tibet, the area that is now Yunnan province, Vietnam, and Japan. All of these states were much smaller than China in area and population, making China by far the dominant force politically and culturally until the nineteenth century. Nevertheless, each of these separate states developed a strong sense of uniqueness and independent identity. In the case of Tibet, cultural borrowing was more often from neighboring India than from China.

The earliest information about each of these countries is found in Chinese sources. Han armies brought Chinese culture to Korea and Vietnam, but even in those cases much cultural borrowing was entirely voluntary as the elite, merchants, and craftsmen adopted the techniques, ideas, and practices they found appealing. In Japan much of the process of absorbing elements of Chinese culture was mediated via Korea. In Korea, Japan, and Vietnam the fine arts — painting, architecture, and ceramics in particular — were all strongly influenced by Chinese models. Tibet, though a thorn in the side of Tang China, was as much in the Indian sphere of influence as in the Chinese and thus followed a somewhat different trajectory. Most significantly, it never adopted Chinese characters as its written language, nor was it as influenced by Chinese artistic styles as other areas. Moreover the form of Buddhism that became dominant in Tibet came directly from India, not through Central Asia and China.

In each area, Chinese-style culture was at first adopted by elites, but in time many Chinese products and ideas, ranging from written language to chopsticks and soy sauce, became incorporated into everyday life. By the eighth century the written Chinese language was used by educated people throughout East Asia. Educated Vietnamese, Koreans, and Japanese could communicate in writing when they could not understand each other's spoken languages, and envoys to Chang'an could in this way carry out "brush conversations" with each other. The books that educated people read included the Chinese classics, histories, and poetry, as well as Buddhist sutras translated into Chinese. The great appeal of Buddhism known primarily through Chinese translation was a powerful force promoting cultural borrowing.

Vietnam

Vietnam is today classed with the countries to its west as part of Southeast Asia, but its ties are at least as strong to China, and its climate is much like that of southernmost China — subtropical, with abundant rain and rivers. The Vietnamese first appear in Chinese sources as a people of south China called the Yue, who gradually migrated farther south as the Chinese state expanded. The people of the Red River Valley in northern Vietnam had achieved a relatively advanced level of Bronze Age civilization by the first century B.C.E. The bronze heads of their arrows often were dipped in poison to facilitate killing large animals such as elephants, whose tusks were traded to China for iron. Power was held by hereditary tribal chiefs who served as civil, religious, and military leaders, with the king as the most powerful chief.

The collapse of the Qin Dynasty in 206 B.C.E. had an impact on this area because a former Qin general, Zhao Tuo (Trieu Da in Vietnamese), finding himself in the

• **Chan** A school of Buddhism (known in Japan as Zen) that rejected the authority of the sutras and claimed the superiority of mind-to-mind transmission of Buddhist truths.

far south, set up his own kingdom of Nam Viet (Nan Yue in Chinese). This kingdom covered much of south China and was ruled by Trieu Da from his capital near the present site of Guangzhou. Its population consisted chiefly of the Viet people. After killing all officials loyal to the Chinese emperor, Trieu Da adopted the customs of the Viet and made himself the ruler of a vast state that extended as far south as modern-day Da Nang.

After almost a hundred years of diplomatic and military duels between the Han Dynasty and Trieu Da and his successors, Nam Viet was conquered in 111 B.C.E. by Chinese armies. Chinese administrators were assigned to replace the local nobility. Chinese political institutions were imposed, and Confucianism was treated as the official ideology. The Chinese language was introduced as the medium of official and literary expression, and Chinese characters were adopted as the written form for the Vietnamese spoken language. The Chinese built roads, waterways, and harbors to facilitate communication within the region and to ensure that they maintained administrative and military control over it. Chinese art, architecture, and music had a powerful impact on their Vietnamese counterparts.

Chinese innovations that were beneficial to the Vietnamese were readily integrated into the indigenous culture, but the local elite were not reconciled

The Kingdom of Nam Viet, ca. 200 B.C.E.

to Chinese political domination. The most famous early revolt took place in 39 C.E., when two widows of local aristocrats, the Trung sisters, led an uprising against foreign rule. After overwhelming Chinese strongholds, they declared themselves queens of an independent Vietnamese kingdom. Three years later a powerful army sent by the Han emperor re-established Chinese rule.

China retained at least nominal control over northern Vietnam through the Tang Dynasty, and there were no real borders between China proper and Vietnam during this time. The local elite became culturally dual, serving as brokers between the Chinese governors and the native people.

Korea

Korea is a mountainous peninsula some 600 miles long extending south from Manchuria and Siberia. At its tip it is about 120 miles from Japan (Map 7.4). Archaeological, linguistic, and anthropological evidence indicates that the Korean people share a common ethnic origin with other peoples of North Asia, including those of Manchuria, Siberia, and Japan. Linguistically, Korean is not related to Chinese.

Korea began adopting elements of technology from China in the first millennium B.C.E., including bronze and iron technology. Chinese-Korean contact expanded

Bronze Drum By 300 B.C.E. large bronze drums were being cast in what is now northern Vietnam. They were regularly decorated with scenes of daily life, war, and rituals. This drum, called the Ngoc Lu drum, has depictions of boats carrying warriors on its sides. The three concentric rings on top show birds, deer, houses, and pairs of people pounding rice (see below). (From A. J. Bernet Kempers, *The Kettledrums of South Asia: A Bronze Age World and Its Aftermath* [Leiden, The Netherlands: A. A. Balkema, 1988]. Courtesy, CRC Press, Balkema)

during the Warring States Period when the state of Yan extended into part of Korea. In about 194 B.C.E. Wiman, an unsuccessful rebel against the Han Dynasty, fled to Korea and set up a state called Choson in what is now northwest Korea and southern Manchuria. In 108 B.C.E. this state was overthrown by the armies of the Han emperor Wu. Four prefectures were established there, and Chinese officials were dispatched to govern them.

The impact of the Chinese prefectures in Korea was similar to that of the contemporaneous Roman colonies in Britain in encouraging the spread of culture and political forms. The prefectures survived not only through the Han Dynasty, but also for nearly a century after the fall of the dynasty, to 313 C.E. The Chinese never controlled the entire Korean peninsula, however. The Han commanderies coexisted with the native Korean kingdom of Koguryŏ, founded in the first century B.C.E. Chinese sources describe this kingdom as a society of aristocratic tribal warriors who had under them a mass of serfs and slaves, mostly from conquered tribes. After the Chinese colonies were finally overthrown, the kingdoms of Paekche and Silla emerged farther south on the peninsula in the third and fourth centuries C.E., leading to what is called the Three Kingdoms Period (313–668 C.E.). In all three Korean kingdoms Chinese was used as the language of government and learning. Each of the three kingdoms had hereditary kings, but their power was curbed by the existence of very strong hereditary elites.

Buddhism was officially introduced in Koguryŏ from China in 372 and in the other states not long after. Buddhism connected Korea to societies across Asia. Buddhist monks went back and forth between China and Korea. One even made the journey to India and back, and others traveled on to Japan to aid in the spread of Buddhism there.

When the Sui Dynasty finally reunified China in 589, it tried to establish control of at least a part of Korea. But the Korean kingdoms were much stronger than their predecessors in Han times, and they repeat-

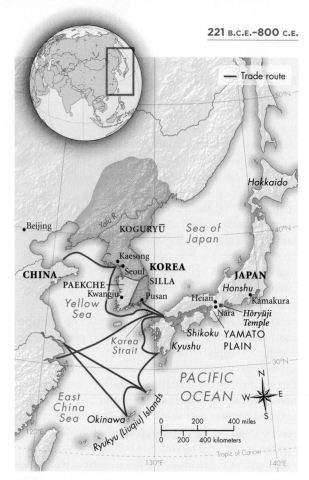

MAP 7.4 Korea and Japan, ca. 600 Korea and Japan are of similar latitude, but Korea's climate is more continental, with harsher winters. Of Japan's four islands, Kyushu is closest to Korea and mainland Asia.

edly repulsed Chinese attacks. The Tang government then tried allying itself with one state, Silla, to fight the others. Silla and Tang jointly destroyed Paekche in 660 and Koguryŏ in 668. With its new resources Silla was able to repel Tang efforts to make Korea a colony but agreed to vassal status. The unification under Silla marked the first political unification of Korea.

For the next century Silla embarked on a policy of wholesale borrowing of Chinese culture and institutions. Annual embassies were sent to Chang'an, and large numbers of students studied in China. The Silla government was modeled on the Tang, although modifications were made to accommodate Korea's more aristocratic social structure.

Japan

Japan does not touch China as do Korea, Tibet, and Vietnam. The heart of Japan is four mountainous islands off the coast of Korea (see Map 7.4). Since the land is rugged and lacking in navigable waterways, the Inland Sea, like the Aegean in Greece, was the easiest avenue of communication in early times. Hence the land bordering the Inland Sea — Kyushu, Shikoku, and

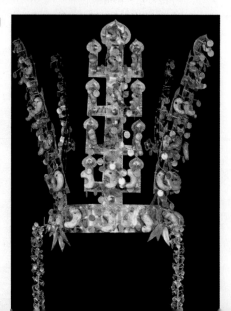

Gold Crown Excavated from a fifth- to sixth-century royal Silla tomb, this magnificent crown reflects metalwork traditions found in scattered places across the Eurasian steppe. The crown is decorated with dangling gold disks and comma-shaped beads of jadeite. The upright bars at the top are thought to represent deer antlers. (Courtesy, Gyeonju National Museum)

Honshu—developed as the political and cultural center of early Japan. Geography also blessed Japan with a moat—the Korea Strait and the Sea of Japan. Consequently, the Japanese for long periods were free to develop their way of life without external interference.

Japan's early development was closely tied to that of the mainland, especially to Korea. Physical anthropologists have discerned several major waves of immigrants into Japan. People of the Jōmon culture, established by about 10,000 B.C.E. after an influx of people from Southeast Asia, practiced hunting and fishing and fashioned clay pots. New arrivals from northeast Asia brought agriculture and a distinct culture called Yayoi (ca. 300 B.C.E.–300 C.E.). Later Yayoi communities were marked by complex social organization with rulers, soldiers, artisans, and priests. During the Han Dynasty objects of Chinese and Korean manufacture found their way into Japan, an indication that people were traveling back and forth as well. In the third century C.E. Chinese histories begin to report on the land called Wa made up of mountainous islands. It had numerous communities, markets, granaries, tax collection, and class distinctions. The people ate with their fingers, used body paint, purified themselves by bathing after a funeral, and liked liquor.

One of the most distinctive features of early Japan was its women rulers. A Chinese historian wrote:

> The country formerly had a man as ruler. For some seventy or eighty years after that there were disturbances and warfare. Thereupon the people agreed upon a woman for their ruler. Her name was Himiko. She occupied herself with magic and sorcery, bewitching the people. Though mature in age, she remained unmarried. She had a younger brother who assisted her in ruling the country. After she became the ruler, there were few who saw her. She had one thousand women as attendants, but only one man. He served her food and drink and acted as a medium of communication. . . .
>
> When Himiko passed away, a great mound was raised, more than a hundred paces in diameter. Over a hundred male and female attendants followed her to the grave. Then a king was placed on the throne, but the people would not obey him. Assassination and murder followed; more than one thousand were thus slain.
>
> A relative of Himiko named Iyo, a girl of thirteen, was then made queen and order was restored.[9]

During the fourth through sixth centuries, new waves of migrants from Korea brought the language that evolved into Japanese. They also brought sericulture (silkmaking), bronze swords, crossbows, iron plows, and the Chinese written language. In this period a social order similar to Korea's emerged, dominated by a warrior aristocracy organized into clans. Clad in helmet and armor, these warriors wielded swords, battle-axes, and often bows, and some rode into battle on horseback. Those vanquished in battle were made slaves. Each clan had its own chieftain, who marshaled clansmen for battle and served as chief priest. Over time the clans fought with each other, and their numbers were gradually reduced through conquest and alliance. By the fifth century the chief of the clan that claimed descent from the sun-goddess, located in the Yamato plain around modern Osaka, had come to occupy the position of Great King—or Queen, for as the quotation above shows, female rulers were not uncommon in this period.

The Yamato rulers used their religion to subordinate the gods of their rivals, much as Hammurabi had used Marduk in Babylonia (see page 42). They established the chief shrine of the sun-goddess near the seacoast, where she could catch the first rays of the rising sun. Cults to other gods also were supported as long as they were viewed as subordinate to the sun-goddess. This native religion was later termed **Shinto**, the Way of the Gods. Buddhism was formally introduced in 538 C.E. and coexisted with the Shinto reverence for the spirits of ancestors and all living things.

In the sixth century Prince Shōtoku (574–622) undertook a sweeping reform of the state designed to strengthen Yamato rule by adopting Chinese-style bureaucratic practices (though not the recruitment of officials by examination). His "Seventeen Principles" of 604 drew from both Confucian and Buddhist teachings. In it he likened the ruler to Heaven and instructed officials to put their duty to the ruler above the interest of their families. He instituted a ladder of official ranks similar to China's, admonished the nobility to avoid strife and opposition, and urged adherence to Buddhist precepts. Near his seat of government, Prince Shōtoku built the magnificent Hōryūji Temple and staffed it with monks from Korea. He also opened direct relations with China, sending four missions during the brief Sui Dynasty. (See "Viewpoints: Chinese and Japanese Principles of Good Government, ca. 650," page 200.)

State-building efforts continued through the seventh century and culminated in the establishment in 710 of Japan's first long-term true city, the capital at **Nara**, north of modern Osaka. Nara, which was modeled on the Tang capital of Chang'an, gave its name to an era that lasted until 794 and that was characterized by the avid importation of Chinese ideas and methods. Seven times missions with five hundred to six hundred men were sent on the dangerous sea crossing and long overland journey to Chang'an. As Buddhism developed a stronghold in Japan, it inspired many trips to China

- **Shinto** The Way of the Gods, it was the native religion espoused by the Yamato rulers in Japan.
- **Nara** Japan's capital and first true city; it was established in 710 and modeled on the Tang capital of Chang'an.

Viewpoints

Chinese and Japanese Principles of Good Government, ca. 650

• *Confucian principles of government, first developed in the Han dynasty, in time had considerable influence beyond China's borders, especially in Korea and Japan. The two seventh-century texts below look at good government from different sides. The first comes from an essay written in 648 in China by the Tang emperor Taizong, addressed to the heir apparent to encourage him to aspire to the Confucian understanding of the ideal ruler. The second text, issued by Prince Shōtoku in Japan in about the same period, is addressed to his officials. In both cases only the first item is included in full, but the titles of the other items are listed.*

Taizong's Plan for an Emperor

1. The Body of the Sovereign: The people are the origin of the state. The state is the foundation of the sovereign. The body of the lord of men should be like the great holy peaks, lofty and towering and unmovable. It should be like sun and moon, constant in their brilliance, and illuminating all alike. He is the one to whom the myriad people look up, to whom the entire empire turns. His will should be broad and magnanimous, sufficient to bind them together. His heart should be impartial and just, sufficient for him to make forceful decisions. Without awesome power, he will have no means to affect the most distant regions: without benign liberality he will have no means to cherish his people. He must comfort the nine grades of his kinsfolk by humanity. He must bind his great ministers to him by the rites. In serving his ancestors, he must bear in mind his filial obligations: in occupying his position [as ruler] he must remember to be reverent. He must repress his own [personal interests] and toil diligently, so as to put into practice virtue and righteousness. Such then is the body of the sovereign.
2. Establishing One's Kinsmen. . . .
3. Seeking Sage-Worthies. . . .
4. Carefully Examine Candidates for Offices. . . .
5. Accepting Remonstrance. . . .
6. Ridding Yourself of Flatterers. . . .
7. Guarding Against Excess. . . .
8. Esteem Frugality. . . .
9. Rewards and Punishments. . . .
10. Giving Due Attention to Agriculture. . . .
11. Reviewing Preparations for War. . . .
12. Honoring Learning. . . .

Prince Shōtoku's Seventeen-Article Edict

1. Harmony is to be valued, and contentiousness avoided. All men are inclined to partisanship and few are truly discerning. Hence there are some who disobey their lords and fathers or who maintain feuds with the neighboring villages. But when those above are harmonious and those below are conciliatory and there is concord in the discussion of all matters, the disposition of affairs comes about naturally. Then what is there that cannot be accomplished?
2. Sincerely reverence the Three Treasures [The Buddha, the Law, and the Sangha]. . . .
3. When you receive the imperial commands, fail not scrupulously to obey them. . . .
4. The ministers and functionaries should make ritual decorum their leading principle, for the leading principle in governing the people consists in ritual decorum. . . .
5. Ceasing from gluttony and abandoning covetous desires, deal impartially with the suits which are submitted to you. . . .
6. Chastise that which is evil and encourage that which is good. . . .
7. Let every man have his own charge, and let not the spheres of duty be confused. . . .
8. Let the ministers and functionaries attend the court early in the morning, and retire late. . . .
9. Trustworthiness is the foundation of right. . . .
10. Let us cease from wrath and refrain from angry looks. . . .
11. Give clear appreciation to merit and demerit, and deal out to each its sure reward or punishment. . . .
12. Let not the provincial authorities or the local nobles levy exaction on the people. . . .
13. Let all persons entrusted with office attend equally to their functions. . . .
14. Ye ministers and functionaries! Be not envious. . . .
15. To turn away from that which is private and to set our faces toward that which is public—this is the path of a minister. . . .
16. Let the people be called up for labor service only at seasonable times. . . .
17. Matters should not be decided by one person alone. . . .

Sources: Denis Twitchett, "*How to Be an Emperor*: T'ang T'ai-tsung's Vision of His Role," *Asia Major* 3d ser. 9.1–2 (1996), 57–58. Reprinted by permission of the Institute of History and Philology of Academic Sinica, Taipei, Taiwan; Prince Shōtoku adapted from W. G. Aston, *Nihongi: Chronicles of Japan from the Earliest Times to A.D. 697* (London: Kegan Paul, Trench and Trübner, 1896), II, 128–133.

QUESTIONS FOR ANALYSIS

1. What similarities do you see in these two documents? In what sense can both be considered Confucian?
2. What differences in these documents can you attribute to the differences between China and Japan in the seventh century?

to acquire sources and to study at Chinese monasteries. Chinese and Korean craftsmen were often brought back to Japan, especially to help with the decoration of the many Buddhist temples then under construction. Musical instruments and tunes were imported as well, many originally from Central Asia. Chinese practices were instituted, such as the compilation of histories and law codes, the creation of provinces, and the appointment of governors to collect taxes from them. By 750 some seven thousand men staffed the central government.

Increased contact with the mainland had unwanted effects as well. In contrast to China and Korea, both part of the Eurasian landmass, Japan had been relatively isolated from many deadly diseases, so when diseases arrived with travelers, people did not have immunity. The great smallpox epidemic of 735–737 is thought to have reduced the population of about 5 million by 30 percent. (Smallpox did not become an endemic childhood disease in Japan until the tenth or eleventh century, measles until even later.)

The Buddhist monasteries that ringed Nara were both religious centers and wealthy landlords, and the monks were active in the political life of the capital. Copying the policy of the Tang Dynasty in China, the government ordered every province to establish a Buddhist temple with twenty monks and ten nuns to chant sutras and perform other ceremonies on behalf of the emperor and the state. When an emperor abdicated in 749 in favor of his daughter, he became a Buddhist priest-monk, a practice many of his successors would later follow.

Many of the temples built during the Nara period still stand, the wood, clay, and bronze statues in them exceptionally well preserved. The largest of these temples was the Tōdaiji, with its huge bronze statue of

□ Picturing the Past

Hōryūji Temple Japanese Buddhist temples, like those in China and Korea, consisted of several buildings within a walled compound. The buildings of the Hōryūji Temple (built between 670 and 711, after Prince Shōtoku's original temple burned down) include the oldest wooden structures in the world and house some of the best early Buddhist sculpture in Japan. The three main buildings depicted here are the pagoda, housing relics; the main hall, with the temple's principal images; and the lecture hall, for sermons. The five-story pagoda could be seen from far away, much like the steeples of cathedrals in medieval Europe. (Michael Hitoshi/The Image Bank/Getty Images)

ANALYZING THE IMAGE How are the buildings arranged? How large is the compound? Do you see anything interesting about the roofs?

CONNECTIONS Was this temple laid out primarily for the convenience of monks who resided there or more for lay believers coming to worship? How would their needs differ?

the Buddha, which stood fifty-three feet tall and was made from more than a million pounds of metal. When the temple and statue were completed in 752, an Indian monk painted the eyes, and the ten thousand monks present for the celebration had a magnificent vegetarian feast. Objects from the dedication ceremony were placed in a special storehouse, the Shōsōin, and about ten thousand of them are still there, including books, weapons, mirrors, screens, and objects of gold, lacquer, and glass, most made in China but some coming from Central Asia and Persia via the Silk Road.

CONNECTIONS

East Asia was transformed in the years between the Qin unification in 221 B.C.E. and the end of the eighth century. The Han Dynasty and four centuries later the Tang Dynasty had proved that a centralized, bureaucratic monarchy could bring peace and prosperity to populations of 50 million or more spread across China proper. By 800 C.E. neighboring societies along China's borders, from Korea and Japan on the east to the Uighurs and Tibetans to the west, had followed China's lead, forming states and building cities. Buddhism had transformed the lives of all of these societies, bringing new ways of thinking about life and death and new ways of pursuing spiritual goals.

In the same centuries that Buddhism was adapting to and simultaneously transforming the culture of much of eastern Eurasia, comparable processes were at work in western Eurasia, where Christianity continued to spread, and in India where Brahmanism evolved into Hinduism. The spread of these religions was aided by increased contact between different cultures, facilitated in Eurasia by the merchants traveling the Silk Road or sailing the Indian Ocean. Where contact between cultures wasn't as extensive, as in Africa (discussed in Chapter 10), religious beliefs were more localized. The collapse of the Roman Empire in the west during this period was not unlike the collapse of the Han Dynasty, but in Europe the empire was never put back together at the level that it was in China, where the Tang Dynasty by many measures was more splendid than the Han. The story of these centuries in western Eurasia are taken up in the next two chapters, which trace the rise of Christianity and Islam and the movement of peoples throughout Europe and Asia. Before returning to the story of East Asia after 800 in Chapter 13, we will also examine the empires in Africa (Chapter 10) and the Americas (Chapter 11).

☐ CHAPTER REVIEW

> ### KEY TERMS
>
> | | |
> |---|---|
> | Great Wall (p. 177) | eunuchs (p. 187) |
> | Confucian classics | Age of Division |
> | (p. 178) | (p. 187) |
> | *Records of the Grand* | Grand Canal (p. 193) |
> | *Historian* (p. 180) | Pure Land (p. 195) |
> | Silk Road (p. 181) | Chan (p. 196) |
> | tributary system | Shinto (p. 199) |
> | (p. 182) | Nara (p. 199) |

☐ **What were the social, cultural and political consequences of the unification of China under the strong centralized governments of the Qin and Han empires? (p. 176)**

After unifying China in 221 B.C.E., the Qin Dynasty created a strongly centralized government that abolished noble privilege and kept ordinary people in place through strictly enforced laws. The First Emperor of Qin standardized script, coinage, weights, and measures. Building roads for the army facilitated trade and helped establish China as a world power. During the four centuries of the subsequent Han Dynasty, the harsher laws and taxes of the Qin were lifted, though a strong centralized government was retained. The government sent huge armies against the nomadic Xiongnu, who regularly raided settlements in the north, but the Xiongnu remained a potent foe. The Han government promoted internal peace by providing relief in cases of floods, droughts, and famines and by keeping land taxes low for the peasantry. As a result, the population grew, reaching 58 million. Han armies expanded Chinese territory both to the south and into Central Asia, which helped trade along the Silk Road. Confucian teachers attracted many students, and popular religion flourished as people spread stories of gods and immortals and their paradises. The invention of paper reduced the cost of keeping records and aided the circulation of books.

☐ **How did Buddhism find its way into East Asia, and what was its appeal and impact? (p. 188)**

In the final years of the Han Dynasty, Buddhism reached China from Central Asia. Conquest had little to do with the spread of Buddhism in East Asia (in contrast to the spread of Christianity and Islam, which often followed a change of rulers). Rather it was merchants and missionaries who brought Buddhism, especially Mahayana Buddhism, across the Silk Road. Buddhism brought much that was new to China: a huge body of scriptures, celibate monks and nuns, traditions of depicting Buddhas and bodhisattvas in statues and paintings, and a strong proselytizing tradition. Buddhism was intellectually appealing to the educated, and rulers welcomed it as a tool to unite Chinese and non-Chinese citizens. It posed no threat to the social order, and people from all classes were drawn to its emphasis on kindness and charity. Buddhism offered new opportunities to women as nuns and let them pursue enlightenment on terms almost equal to men.

☐ **What were the lasting accomplishments of the Sui and Tang Dynasties? (p. 192)**

After centuries of division, China was reunified in 589 C.E. by the Sui Dynasty. The Sui strengthened the central control of government by limiting the power of local officials to appoint their own subordinates. The competitive written exams that the Sui instituted for the selection of officials would dominate China and other parts of East Asia in the centuries to come. The building of the Grand Canal strengthened China internally and connected the north to the maritime trade with Southeast Asia and India. The Tang built upon Sui accomplishments, establishing government schools to prepare men for service as officials. China regained overlordship along the Silk Road into Central

Asia and once again had to deal with powerful northern neighbors, this time the Turks and Uighurs. In the wake of a huge internal rebellion, eunuchs gained power at court, and military governors treated their provinces as hereditary kingdoms. The Tang period was one of cultural flowering, especially in music and poetry. The introduction of new instruments and music from India, Iran, and Central Asia transformed Chinese music.

□ **What elements of Chinese culture were adopted by Koreans, Vietnamese, and Japanese, and how did they adapt them to their own circumstances?** (p. 196)

From 200 B.C.E. to 800 C.E., China's neighbors, especially Korea, Japan, and Vietnam, began to adopt elements of China's material, political, and religious culture, including the Chinese writing system. Force of arms helped bring Chinese culture to both Korea and Vietnam, but military might was not the primary means by which culture spread in this period. Particularly in Korea and Japan, ambitious rulers sought Chinese expertise and Chinese products — such as, sericulture, bronze swords, crossbows, iron plows, and Chinese-style centralized governments — believing the adoption of the most advanced ideas and technologies to be to their advantage. In more isolated Japan, Koreans played a large role in the spread of Chinese culture. Korea, Vietnam, and Japan all retained many features of their earlier cultures even as they adopted Chinese practices, in the process developing distinctive national styles. For example, in Korea the government was modeled on the Tang, but was modified to accommodate Korea's aristocratic social structure.

SUGGESTED READING

Barfield, Thomas. *Perilous Frontier: Nomadic Empires and China, 221 B.C.–A.D. 1757.* 1989. A bold interpretation of the relationship between the rise and fall of dynasties in China and the rise and fall of nomadic confederations that derived resources from them.

Elvin, Mark. *The Pattern of the Chinese Past.* 1973. Analyzes the military dimensions of China's unification.

Farris, Wayne. *Population, Disease, and Land in Early Japan, 645–900.* 1985. Shows the impact of the eighth-century introduction of smallpox to Japan on the government and rural power structure.

Hardy, Grant. *Worlds of Bronze and Bamboo: Sima Qian's Conquest of History.* 1999. An excellent introduction to the methods of China's earliest historian. Although Sima Qian seems to present just the facts, Hardy shows how he brings out different perspectives and interpretations in different chapters.

Holcomb, Charles. *The Genesis of East Asia, 221 B.C.–A.D. 907.* 2001. A thought-provoking analysis of the connections between China and Korea, Japan, and Vietnam that emphasizes the use of the Chinese script.

Lee, Peter H. *Sourcebook of Korean Civilization.* 1993. Excellent collection of primary sources.

Lewis, Mark Edward. *China's Cosmopolitan Empire: The Tang Dynasty.* 2009. This accessible and lively survey complements the author's works on the Han Dynasty (*The Early Chinese Empires*) and the period of division (*China Between Empires*).

Schafer, Edward. *The Golden Peaches of Samarkand.* 1963. Draws on Tang literature to show the place of the western regions in Tang life and imagination.

Seth, Michael J. *A Concise History of Korea: From the Neolithic Period Through the Nineteenth Century.* 2006. An up-to-date and well-balanced introduction to Korean history.

Totman, Conrad. *A History of Japan.* 1999. A broad and up-to-date history of Japan.

Varley, H. Paul. *Japanese Culture.* 2000. An accessible introduction to Japanese history and culture.

Waley, Arthur. *The Life and Times of Po Chu-i, 772–846 A.D.* 1949. A lively biography of a Tang official, that draws heavily on his poetry.

Watt, James C. Y. *China: Dawn of a Golden Age 200–750 A.D.* 2004. A well-illustrated catalogue of a major art and archaeological exhibition.

Wright, Arthur. *Buddhism in Chinese History.* 1959. This short book remains a good introduction to China's encounter with Buddhism and the ways Buddhism was adapted to China.

NOTES

1. Li Yuning, ed., *The First Emperor of China* (White Plains, N.Y.: International Arts and Sciences Press, 1975), pp. 275–276, slightly modified.
2. Burton Watson, trans., *Records of the Grand Historian of China,* vol. 2 (New York: Columbia University Press, 1961), p. 496.
3. Ibid., p. 499.
4. From Patricia Buckley Ebrey, ed., *Chinese Civilization: A Sourcebook,* 2d ed. (New York: The Free Press, 1993), p. 62.
5. Patricia Buckley Ebrey, *The Cambridge Illustrated History of China* (Cambridge: Cambridge University Press, 1996), p. 74.
6. W. F. Jenner, *Memories of Loyang: Yang Hsüan-chih and the Lost Capital (493–534)* (Oxford: Clarendon Press, 1981), p. 208.
7. Arthur Waley, trans., *More Translations from the Chinese* (New York: Knopf, 1919), p. 27. Reprinted by permission of the Arthur Waley Estate.
8. Ibid., p. 71.
9. *Sources of Japanese Tradition,* by William Theodore de Bary, Donald Keene, George Tanabe, and Paul Varley, eds. Copyright © 2001 by Columbia University Press. Reproduced with permission of the publisher.

For practice quizzes and other study tools, visit the **Online Study Guide** at bedfordstmartins.com/mckayworld.

For primary sources from this period, see *Sources of World Societies*, **Second Edition**.

For Web sites, images, and documents related to topics in this chapter, visit **Make History** at bedfordstmartins.com/mckayworld.

• French Reliquary of Sainte Foy Preachers who spread Christianity often told stories of spiritually heroic saints and martyrs, and placed their remains in reliquaries for people to venerate. This jeweled ninth-century French reliquary contains the bones of Sainte Foy, a young woman thought to have been martyred centuries earlier. (Erich Lessing/Art Resource, NY)

From the third century onward the Western Roman Empire slowly disintegrated. The last Roman emperor in the West, Romulus Augustus, was deposed by the Ostrogothic chieftain Odoacer (OH-duh-way-suhr) in 476, but much of the empire had already come under the rule of various barbarian tribes well before this. Scholars have long seen this era as one of the great turning points in Western history, but during the last several decades focus has shifted to continuities as well as changes. What is now usually termed "late antiquity" has been recognized as a period of creativity and adaptation in Europe and western Asia, not simply of decline and fall.

Continuity and Change in Europe and Western Asia

200–850

The two main agents of continuity were the Eastern Roman (or Byzantine) Empire and the Christian Church. The Byzantine Empire lasted until 1453, a thousand years longer than the Western Roman Empire, and preserved and transmitted much of Greco-Roman law, philosophy, and institutions. Missionaries and church officials spread Christianity within and far beyond the borders of what had been the Roman Empire, transforming a small sect into the most important and wealthiest institution in Europe. The main agent of change in late antiquity was the migration of barbarian groups throughout much of Europe and western Asia. They brought different social, political, and economic structures with them, but as they encountered Roman and Byzantine culture and became Christian, their own ways of doing things were also transformed. •

The Byzantine Empire

□ How was the Byzantine Empire able to survive for so long, and what were its most important achievements?

The Growth of the Christian Church

□ What factors enabled the Christian Church to expand and thrive?

Christian Ideas and Practices

□ How did Christian thinkers and missionaries adapt Greco-Roman ideas to Christian theology and develop effective techniques for converting barbarian peoples?

Migrating Peoples

□ How did the barbarians shape social, economic, and political structures in Europe and western Asia?

The Byzantine Empire

□ How was the Byzantine Empire able to survive for so long, and what were its most important achievements?

The emperor Constantine (see page 169) had tried to maintain the unity of the Roman Empire, but during the fifth and sixth centuries the western and eastern halves drifted apart. From Constantinople, Eastern Roman emperors worked to hold the empire together and to reconquer at least some of the West from barbarian tribes. Justinian (r. 527–565) waged long wars against the Ostrogoths (members of a Germanic barbarian tribe) and temporarily regained Italy and North Africa, but the costs were high. Justinian's wars exhausted the resources of the state, destroyed Italy's economy, and killed a large part of Italy's population.

By the late sixth century, after Justinian's death, a weakened Italy had fallen easily to another Germanic tribe, the Lombards. With this defeat, the lands that had been the Western Roman Empire were again under Germanic sway.

However, the Roman Empire continued in the East. The Eastern Roman or Byzantine Empire (Map 8.1) preserved the institutions and traditions of the old Roman Empire. Byzantium passed the intellectual heritage of Greco-Roman civilization on to later cultures as it also developed its own distinctive characteristics.

Sources of Byzantine Strength

Byzantine emperors traced their lines back past Constantine to Augustus (see page 154). While evolving into a Christian and Greek-speaking state with a mul-

MAP 8.1 The Byzantine and Sassanid Empires, ca. 600 Both the Byzantine and Sassanid Empires included territory that had earlier been part of the Roman Empire. The Sassanid Persians fought Roman armies before the founding of the Byzantine Empire. Later Byzantium and the Sassanids engaged in a series of wars that weakened both and brought neither lasting territorial acquisitions.

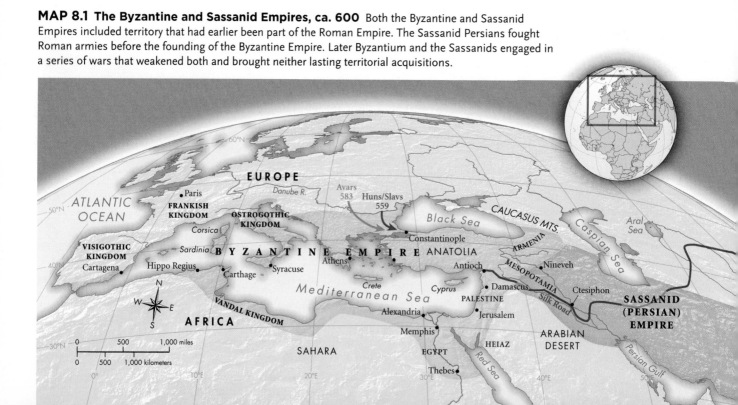

tiethnic population centered in the eastern Mediterranean and the Balkans, the Byzantines retained the legal and administrative system of the empire centered at Rome. (In fact, the Byzantines called themselves "Romans" and their state the "Roman Empire"; only in the sixteenth century did people begin to use the term "Byzantine Empire.") Thus, the senate that sat in Constantinople carried on the traditions and preserved the glory of the old Roman senate. The army that defended the empire was the direct descendant of the old Roman legions.

That army was kept very busy, for the Byzantine Empire survived waves of attacks. In 559 a force of Xiongnu (whom the Greeks and Romans called Huns) and Slavs reached the gates of Constantinople. In 583 the Avars, a mounted Mongol people who had swept across Russia and the Balkans, seized Byzantine forts along the Danube and also reached the walls of Constantinople. Between 572 and 630 the Greeks were repeatedly at war with the Sassanid Persians (see page 208). In 632 the Arabs began pressuring the Greek empire. Why didn't one or a combination of these enemies capture Constantinople, as the Germanic tribes had taken Rome? The answer lies, first, in the strong military leadership the Greeks possessed. General Priskos (d. 612) skillfully led Byzantine armies to a decisive victory over the Avars in 601. Then, after a long war, the well-organized emperor Heraclius I (r. 610–641) crushed the Persians at Nineveh in Mesopotamia (now Iraq).

Second, the city's location and excellent fortifications proved crucial. Constantinople had the most powerful defenses in the ancient world. One defense was natural: the sea that surrounded Constantinople on three sides. The other defense was the walls that surrounded the city, protecting it from invasions by both land and sea. Massive triple walls protected the city from sea invasion. Within the walls huge cisterns provided water, and vast gardens and grazing areas supplied vegetables and meat. Such strong fortifications and provisions meant that if attacked by land or sea, Constantinople's defenders could hold out far longer than a besieging army. In essence, the site chosen for the imperial capital in the fourth century enabled Con-

▫ CHRONOLOGY

226–651	Sassanid dynasty
325	Nicene Creed produced
340–419	Life of Saint Jerome
354–430	Life of Saint Augustine
380	Theodosius makes Christianity official religion of Roman Empire
ca. 385–461	Life of Saint Patrick
ca. 481–511	Reign of Clovis
527–565	Reign of Justinian
529	Writing of *The Rule of Saint Benedict*
541–543	"Justinian plague"
730–843	Iconoclastic controversy
768–814	Reign of Charlemagne
843	Treaty of Verdun ratified

Sassanid Cameo In this cameo—a type of jewelry made by carving into a multicolored piece of rock—the Sassanid king Shapur and the Byzantine emperor Valerian fight on horseback, each identifiable by his distinctive clothing and headgear. This does not record an actual hand-to-hand battle, but uses the well-muscled rulers as symbols of their empires. (Erich Lessing/Art Resource, NY)

stantinople to survive longer than it might have otherwise. Because the city survived, the empire, though reduced in territory, endured.

The Sassanid Empire and Conflicts with Byzantium

For several centuries the Sassanid empire of Persia was Byzantium's most regular foe. In 226 Ardashir I (r. 226–243) founded the Sassanid dynasty, which lasted until 651, when it was overthrown by the Muslims. Ardashir expanded his territory and absorbed the Roman province of Mesopotamia.

Centered in the fertile Tigris-Euphrates Valley, but with access to the Persian Gulf and extending south to Meshan (modern Kuwait), the Sassanid empire depended on agriculture for its economic prosperity; its location also proved well suited for commerce (see Map 8.1). A lucrative caravan trade from Ctesiphon (TE-suh-fahn) north to Merv and then east to Samarkand linked the Sassanid empire to the Silk Road and China (see page 184). Persian metalwork, textiles, and glass were exchanged for Chinese silks, and this trade brought about considerable cultural contact between the Sassanids and the Chinese.

> "Slaves become our property by the Law of Nations when they are either taken from the enemy, or are born of our female slaves."
>
> **JUSTINIAN'S** *Digest*

Whereas the Parthians (who fell to the Sassanids in 226) had tolerated many religions, the Sassanid Persians made Zoroastrianism the official state religion. Religion and the state were inextricably tied together. The king's power rested on the support of nobles and Zoroastrian priests, who monopolized positions in the court and in the imperial bureaucracy. A highly elaborate court ceremonial and ritual exalted the status of the king and emphasized his semidivine pre-eminence over his subjects. (The Byzantine monarchy, the Roman papacy, and the Muslim caliphate subsequently copied aspects of this Persian ceremonial.)

Adherents to religions other than Zoroastrianism, such as Jews and Christians, faced discrimination. The Jewish population in the Sassanid empire was sizable because the Romans had forced many Jews out of Israel and Judaea after a series of revolts against Roman rule, a dispersal later termed the diaspora. Jews suffered intermittent persecution under the Sassanids, as did Christians, whom followers of Zoroastrianism saw as being connected to Rome and Constantinople.

An expansionist foreign policy brought Persia into frequent conflict with Byzantium, and neither side was able to achieve a clear-cut victory. The long wars financed by higher taxation, on top of the arrival of the plague (see page 209), compounded discontent in both Byzantine and Persian societies. Moreover, internal political instability weakened the Sassanid dynasty,

and in the seventh century Persian territories were absorbed into the Islamic caliphate (see page 237).

The Law Code of Justinian

Byzantine emperors organized and preserved Roman law, making a lasting contribution to the medieval and modern worlds. Roman law had developed from many sources — decisions by judges, edicts of emperors, legislation passed by the senate, and opinions of jurists expert in the theory and practice of law. By the fourth century Roman law had become a huge, bewildering mass. Its sheer bulk made it almost unusable.

To address this problem, the emperor Justinian appointed a committee of eminent jurists to sort through and organize the laws. The result was the *Code*, which distilled the legal genius of the Romans into a coherent whole, eliminated outmoded laws and contradictions, and clarified the law itself.

Justinian next set about bringing order to the equally huge body of Roman jurisprudence, the science or philosophy of law. To harmonize the often differing opinions of Roman jurists, Justinian directed his jurists to clear up disputed points and to issue definitive rulings. Accordingly, in 533 his lawyers published the *Digest*, which codified Roman legal thought and contained provisions such as these on slavery:

> Slaves are brought under our ownership either by the Civil Law or by that of Nations. This is done by the Civil Law where anyone who is over twenty years of age permits himself to be sold for the sake of sharing in his own price [that is, for debt]. Slaves become our property by the Law of Nations when they are either taken from the enemy, or are born of our female slaves. . . .
>
> He who conceals a fugitive slave is a thief. . . . And the magistrates are very properly notified to detain fugitive slaves carefully in custody to prevent their escape. . . . Careful custody permits the use of leg irons.[1]

Finally, Justinian's lawyers compiled a handbook of civil law, the *Institutes*. These three works — the *Code*, the *Digest*, and the *Institutes* — are the backbone of the **corpus juris civilis**, the "body of civil law," which is the foundation of law for nearly every modern European nation.

Byzantine Intellectual Life

Just as they valued the law, the Byzantines prized education, and because of them many masterpieces of an-

corpus juris civilis The "body of civil law," it is composed of the *Code*, the *Digest*, and the *Institutes*.

Πῶρρ κῶρ · Ἠραιοδὲ καιτααοκλαςιω πυρωωολώ ωπυρι

τό λεερ ωμας πυρπολ · ΤΟΝΤΩΝΪΕΝΑΗ ΠΤΦΟΛΟΝ ·

Greek Fire In this illustration from a twelfth-century manuscript, sailors shoot Greek fire toward an attacking ship from a pressurized tube that looks strikingly similar to a modern flamethrower. The exact formula for Greek fire has been lost, but it was probably made from a petroleum product because it continued burning on water. Greek fire was particularly important in Byzantine defenses of Constantinople from Muslim forces in the late seventh century. (Prado, Madrid/The Bridgeman Art Library)

cient Greek literature survived to influence the intellectual life of the modern world. The literature of the Byzantine Empire was predominately Greek, although Latin was long spoken by top politicians, scholars, and lawyers. Among members of the large reading public, history was a favorite subject.

The most remarkable Byzantine historian was Procopius (ca. 500–ca. 562), who left a rousing account of Justinian's reconquest of North Africa and Italy. Procopius's *Secret History*, on the other hand, is a vicious and uproarious attack on Justinian and his wife, the empress Theodora, which continued the wit and venom of earlier Greek and Roman writers. (See "Individuals in Society: Theodora of Constantinople," page 210.)

In mathematics and science the Byzantines discovered little that was new, though they passed Greco-Roman learning on to the Arabs. The best-known Byzantine scientific discovery was an explosive compound known as "Greek fire" made of crude oil mixed with resin and sulfur, which were heated and propelled by a pump through a bronze tube. As the liquid jet left the tube, it was ignited, somewhat like a modern flamethrower. Greek fire saved Constantinople from Arab assault in 678.

The Byzantines devoted a great deal of attention to medicine, and their general level of medical compe-tence was far higher than that of western Europeans, for they could read about and use Hellenistic methods of treating illness and relieving pain. Yet Byzantine physicians could not cope with the terrible disease, often called "the Justinian plague," that swept through the Byzantine Empire and parts of western Europe between 541 and 543. Probably originating in northwestern India and carried to the Mediterranean region by ships, the disease was similar to the bubonic plague. Characterized by high fevers, chills, delirium, and enlarged lymph nodes, or by inflammation of the lungs that caused hemorrhages of black blood, the plague carried off tens of thousands of people. The epidemic had profound political as well as social consequences. It weakened Justinian's military resources, thus hampering his efforts to restore unity to the Mediterranean world. Losses from the plague also further weakened Byzantine and Persian forces that had long been fighting each other, contributing to their inability to offer more than token opposition to Muslim armies (see page 237).

Life in Constantinople

By the tenth century Constantinople was the greatest city in the Christian world: the seat of the imperial court and administration, a large population center,

Individuals in Society

Theodora of Constantinople

THE MOST POWERFUL WOMAN IN BYZANTINE history was the daughter of a bear trainer for the circus. Theodora (ca. 497–548) grew up in what her contemporaries regarded as an undignified and morally suspect atmosphere, and she worked as a dancer and actress, both dishonorable occupations in the Roman world. Despite her background, she caught the eye of Justinian, who was then a military leader and whose uncle (and adoptive father) Justin had himself risen from obscurity to become the ruler of the Byzantine Empire. Under Justinian's influence, Justin changed the law to allow an actress who had left her disreputable life to marry whom she liked, and Justinian and Theodora married in 525. When Justinian was proclaimed co-emperor with his uncle Justin on April 1, 527, Theodora received the rare title of *augusta*, empress. Thereafter her name was linked with Justinian's in the exercise of imperial power.

Most of our knowledge of Theodora's early life comes from the *Secret History*, a tell-all description of the vices of Justinian and his court written by Procopius around 550. Procopius was the official court historian and thus spent his days praising those same people. In the *Secret History*, however, he portrays Theodora and Justinian as demonic, greedy, and vicious, killing courtiers to steal their property. In scene after detailed scene, Procopius portrays Theodora as particularly evil, sexually insatiable, and cruel, a temptress who used sorcery to attract men, including the hapless Justinian.

In one of his official histories, *The History of the Wars of Justinian*, Procopius presents a very different Theodora. Riots between the supporters of two teams in chariot races had turned deadly, and Justinian wavered in his handling of the perpetrators. Both sides turned against the emperor, besieging the palace while Justinian was inside it. Shouting "*Nika!*" (Victory), the rioters swept through the city, burning and looting. Justinian's counselors urged flight, but, according to Procopius, Theodora rose and declared:

> For one who has reigned, it is intolerable to be an exile. . . . If you wish, O Emperor, to save yourself, there is no difficulty: we have ample funds and there are the ships. Yet reflect whether, when you have once escaped to a place of security, you will not prefer death to safety. I agree with an old saying

● **A sixth-century mosaic of the empress Theodora, made of thousands of tiny cubes of glass, shows her with a halo—a symbol of power—and surrounded by officials, priests, and court ladies.** (Scala/Art Resource, NY)

that the purple [that is, the color worn only by emperors] is a fair winding sheet [to be buried in].

Justinian rallied, ordered more than thirty thousand men and women executed, and crushed the revolt.

Other sources describe or suggest Theodora's influence on imperial policy. Justinian passed a number of laws that improved the legal status of women, such as allowing women to own property and to be guardians over their own children. He forbade the exposure of unwanted infants, which happened more often to girls than to boys, since boys were valued more highly. Theodora presided at imperial receptions for Arab sheiks, Persian ambassadors, Germanic princesses from the West, and barbarian chieftains from southern Russia. When Justinian fell ill from the bubonic plague in 542, Theodora took over his duties. Justinian is reputed to have consulted her every day about all aspects of state policy, including religious policy regarding the doctrinal disputes that continued throughout his reign.

Theodora's influence over her husband and her power in the Byzantine state continued until she died, perhaps of cancer, twenty years before Justinian. Her influence may have even continued after death, for Justinian continued to pass reforms favoring women and, at the end of his life, accepted an interpretation of Christian doctrine she had favored. Institutions that she established, including hospitals and churches, continued to be reminders of her charity and piety.

Theodora has been viewed as a symbol of the use of beauty and cleverness to attain position and power, and also as a strong and capable co-ruler who held the empire together during riots, revolts, and deadly epidemics. Just as she fascinated Procopius, she continues to intrigue writers today, who make her a character not only in historical works, but also in science fiction and fantasy

QUESTIONS FOR ANALYSIS

1. How would you assess the complex legacy of Theodora?
2. Since Procopius's public and private views of the empress are so different, should he be trusted at all as a historical source? Why?

and the pivot of a large volume of international trade. Given that the city was a natural geographical connecting point between East and West, its markets offered goods from many parts of the world. Furs and timber flowed across the Black Sea from the Rus (Russia) to the capital, as did slaves across the Mediterranean from northern Europe and the Balkans via Venice. Spices, silks, jewelry, and other luxury goods came to Constantinople from India and China by way of Arabia, the Red Sea, and the Indian Ocean. In return, the city exported glassware, mosaics, gold coins, silk cloth, carpets, and a host of other products, with much foreign trade in the hands of Italian merchants. At the end of the eleventh century Constantinople may have been the world's third largest city, with only Córdoba in Spain and Kaifeng in China larger.

Although merchants could become fabulously wealthy, as in western Europe and China, the landed aristocracy always held the dominant social position. By contrast, merchants and craftsmen, even when they acquired considerable wealth, never won social prominence. Aristocrats and monasteries usually invested their wealth in real estate, which involved little risk but brought little gain.

Constantinople did not enjoy constant political stability. Between the accession of Emperor Heraclius in 610 and the fall of the city to western Crusaders in 1204 (see page 407), four separate dynasties ruled at Constantinople. Imperial government involved such intricate court intrigue, assassination plots, and military revolts that the word *byzantine* is sometimes used in English to mean extremely entangled and complicated politics.

What do we know about private life in Constantinople? Research has revealed a fair amount about the Byzantine *oikos* (OY-kohs), or household. The typical household in the city included family members and servants, some of whom were slaves. Artisans lived and worked in their shops, while clerks, civil servants, minor officials, and businesspeople—those who today would be called middle class—commonly dwelled in multistory buildings perhaps comparable to the apartment complexes of modern American cities. Wealthy aristocrats resided in freestanding mansions that frequently included interior courts, galleries, large reception halls, small sleeping rooms, reading and writing rooms, baths, and chapels.

In the homes of the upper classes, the segregation of women seems to have been the first principle of interior design. As in ancient Athens, private houses contained a *gynaeceum* (jihn-uh-SEE-um), or women's apartment, where women were kept strictly separated from the outside world. The fundamental reason for this segregation was the family's honor: "An unchaste daughter is guilty of harming not only herself but also her parents and relatives. That is why you should keep your daughters under lock and key, as if proven guilty or imprudent, in order to avoid venomous bites," as an eleventh-century Byzantine writer put it.[2]

Marriage was part of a family's strategy for social advancement. Both the immediate family and the larger kinship group participated in the selection of a bride or a groom, choosing a spouse who might enhance the family's wealth or prestige.

The Growth of the Christian Church

☐ What factors enabled the Christian Church to expand and thrive?

As the Western Roman Empire disintegrated, the Christian Church survived and grew, becoming the most important institution in Europe. The church gained strength by taking more authority over religious issues away from the state. Also, the church's western realm, increasingly left to its own devices after the imperial capital moved from Rome to Constantinople, gained more power. Even so, the state continued to intervene in theological disputes. Meanwhile, new Christian orders emphasizing asceticism arose and made important contributions to religious and secular society.

The Evolution of Church Leadership and Orthodoxy

Believers in early Christian communities elected their leaders, but as the centuries passed appointment by existing church leaders or secular rulers became the common practice. During the reign of Diocletian (r. 284–305), the Roman Empire had been divided for administrative purposes into geographical units called **dioceses**, and Christianity adopted this pattern. Each diocese was headed by a bishop, who was responsible for delegating responsibilities for preaching and teaching, organizing preaching, overseeing the community's goods, and maintaining orthodox (established or correct) doctrine. The center of a bishop's authority was his cathedral, a word deriving from the Latin *cathedra*, meaning "chair."

Some bishops brought significant administrative skills to the early Christian Church. Bishop Ambrose of Milan (339–397), for example, had a solid education, was a trained lawyer, and had once been the governor

---

• **dioceses** Geographic administrative districts of the church, each under the authority of a bishop and centered around a cathedral.

> "It is written, God's to God and Caesar's to Caesar. The palace is the Emperor's, the churches are the Bishop's."

BISHOP AMBROSE OF MILAN

of a province. He was typical of the Roman aristocrats who held high public office, were converted to Christianity, and subsequently became bishops. He had a strong sense of his authority and even stood up to Emperor Theodosius (r. 379–395), who had ordered Ambrose to hand over his major church—called a basilica—to the emperor:

> At length came the command, "Deliver up the Basilica"; I reply, "It is not lawful for us to deliver it up, nor for your Majesty to receive it. By no law can you violate the house of a private man, and do you think that the house of God may be taken away? . . . But do not burden your conscience with the thought that you have any right as Emperor over sacred things. . . . It is written, God's to God and Caesar's to Caesar. The palace is the Emperor's, the churches are the Bishop's. To you is committed jurisdiction over public, not over sacred buildings."[3]

The emperor relented, and Ambrose's assertion that the church was supreme in spiritual matters and the state in secular issues remained the Christian leadership's position on church-state relations for centuries. Because of his strong influence Ambrose came to be regarded as one of the fathers of the church, and his authority was regarded as second only to the Bible's in later centuries. Although conflicts like these between religious and secular leaders were frequent, the church also received support from the emperors. In return the emperors expected the Christian Church's support in maintaining order and unity.

In the fourth century, disputes also arose within the Christian community, though these concerned theological issues. Some disagreements had to do with the nature of Christ. For example, **Arianism**, which originated with Arius (ca. 250–336), a priest of Alexandria, held that Jesus was created by the will of God the Father and thus was not co-eternal with him. Arius also reasoned that Jesus the Son must be inferior to God the Father, because the Father was incapable of suffering and did not die. Arian Christianity attracted many followers, including Greeks, Romans, and especially barbarian migrants to Europe who were converted by Arian Christian missionaries.

Emperor Constantine, who legalized Christianity in 312, rejected the Arian interpretation and decided that religious disagreement meant civil disorder. In 325 he summoned a council of church leaders to Nicaea in Asia Minor and presided over it personally. The council produced the Nicene Creed, which defined the orthodox position that Christ is "eternally begotten of the Father" and of the same substance as the Father. Arius and those who refused to accept the creed were banished, the first case of civil punishment for heresy. This participation of the emperor in a theological dispute within the church paved the way for later emperors to claim that they could do the same. The Nicene interpretation was modified slightly by councils later in the fourth century, but it eventually became the most widely held understanding of the nature of Christ. (It is accepted today by the Roman Catholic Church, the Eastern Orthodox churches, and most Protestant churches.) Although Arian Christianity slowly died out among Greeks and Romans, it remained the most

Sarcophagus of Helena This marble sarcophagus was made for Helena, the mother of Emperor Constantine, at her death. Its detailed carvings show victorious Roman horsemen and barbarian prisoners. Like her son, Helena became a Christian, and she was sent by Constantine on a journey to bring sacred relics from Jerusalem to Constantinople as part of his efforts to promote Christianity in the empire. (Vanni/Art Resource, NY)

common form of Christianity among barbarian groups for centuries.

In 380 Theodosius went even further than Constantine and made Christianity the official religion of the empire. He stripped Roman pagan temples of statues, made the practice of the old Roman state religion a treasonable offense, and persecuted Christians who dissented from orthodox doctrine. Most significantly, he allowed the church to establish its own courts and develop its own body of law, called canon law. These courts, not the Roman government, had jurisdiction over the clergy and ecclesiastical disputes. The foundation for later growth in church power had thus been laid.

The Western Church and the Eastern Church

The leader of the church in the West, the bishop of Rome, became more powerful than his counterpart in the Byzantine East for a variety of reasons. The change began in the fourth century with the move of the imperial capital and the emperor from Rome to Constantinople. Because the bishop of Rome no longer had any real competition for leadership in the West, he began to exercise more influence there.

The power of successive bishops of Rome increased as they repeatedly called on the emperors at Constantinople for military support against barbarian invaders. Because the emperors had no troops to spare, they rarely could send such support. The Western Church thus became less dependent on the emperors' power and gradually took over political authority in central Italy, charging taxes, sending troops, and enforcing laws.

The bishops of Rome also stressed their special role within the church. They pointed to words spoken by Jesus to one of his disciples, Peter, and the fact that, according to tradition, Peter had lived in Rome and been its first bishop, to assert a privileged position in the church hierarchy, an idea called the Petrine Doctrine. As successors of Peter, they stated, the bishops of Rome—known as **popes**, from the Latin word *papa*, meaning "father"—should be supreme over other Christian communities. They urged other churches to appeal to Rome for the resolution of disputed issues. (The Christian Church headed by the pope in Rome was generally called the Roman Church in this era, and later the Roman Catholic Church. The word *catholic* derives from a Greek word meaning "general," "universal," or "worldwide.")

By contrast, in the East the emperor's jurisdiction over the church was fully acknowledged, even though the bishops of Antioch, Alexandria, Jerusalem, and Constantinople had more power than other bishops. As in Rome, there was a head of the church in Constantinople, called the patriarch, but he did not develop the same powers that the pope did in the West because there was never a similar power vacuum into which he needed to step. He and other high church officials were appointed by the emperor. The Eastern emperors looked on religion as a branch of the state, and they considered it their duty to protect the faith not only against heathen outsiders but also against heretics within the empire. Following the pattern set by Constantine, the emperors summoned councils of bishops and theologians to settle doctrinal disputes. They and the Eastern bishops did not accept Rome's claim to primacy, and gradually the Eastern Christian Church, generally called the **Orthodox Church**, and the Roman Church began to diverge. (*Orthodoxy* with a capital *O* refers to the Eastern Church, and *orthodoxy* with a small *o* means correct doctrine as defined by church leaders.)

The Iconoclastic Controversy

In the centuries after Constantine the most serious dispute within the Orthodox Church concerned icons—images or representations of God the Father, Jesus, and the saints in a painting, bas-relief, or mosaic. Since the third century the church had allowed people to venerate icons. Although all prayer had to be directed to God the Father, Christian teaching held that icons representing the saints fostered reverence and that Jesus and the saints could most effectively plead a cause to God the Father. (For more about the role of saints, see page 219.) Iconoclasts, those who favored the destruction of icons, argued that people were worshipping the image itself rather than what it signified. This, they claimed, constituted idolatry, a violation of one of the Ten Commandments, a religious and moral code sacred to Christians.

The result of this dispute was a terrible theological conflict, the **iconoclastic controversy**, that split the Byzantine world for a century. In 730 the emperor Leo III (r. 717–741) ordered the destruction of icons. The removal of these images from Byzantine churches provoked a violent reaction: entire provinces revolted, and the empire and Roman papacy severed relations. Since Eastern monasteries were the fiercest defenders of icons, Leo's son Constantine V (r. 741–775),

---

- **Arianism** A theological belief, originating with Arius, a priest of Alexandria, that denied that Christ was co-eternal with God the Father.
- **popes** Heads of the Roman Catholic Church, who became political as well as religious authorities. The period of a pope's term in office is called a "pontificate."
- **Orthodox Church** Another name for the Eastern Christian Church, over which emperors continued to have power.
- **iconoclastic controversy** The conflict over the veneration of religious images in the Byzantine Empire.

nicknamed "Copronymous" ("Dung-name") by his enemies, took the war to the monasteries. He seized their property, executed some of the monks, and forced other monks into the army. Theological disputes and civil disorder over the icons continued intermittently until 843, when the icons were restored.

The implications of the iconoclastic controversy extended far beyond strictly theological issues. Iconoclasm raised the question of the right of the emperor to intervene in religious disputes — a central problem in the relations between church and state. Iconoclasm antagonized the pope and served to encourage him in his quest for an alliance with the Frankish monarchy (see page 225). This further divided the two parts of Christendom, and in 1054 a theological disagreement led the pope in Rome and the patriarch of Constantinople to excommunicate each other. The outcome was a continuing schism, or split, between the Roman Catholic and the Orthodox Churches.

From a cultural perspective, the acceptance of icons profoundly influenced subsequent religious art within Christianity. That art rejected the Judaic and Islamic prohibition against images of religious figures and continued the Greco-Roman tradition of giving these figures human forms.

Christian Monasticism

Like the great East Asian religions of Jainism and Buddhism (see pages 74–79), Christianity began and spread as a city religion. With time, however, some especially pious Christians started to feel that a life of asceticism (extreme material sacrifice, including fasting and the renunciation of sex) was a better way to show their devotion to Christ's teachings. Asceticism was — and is — a common part of many religious traditions, either as a temporary practice during especially holy times or as a permanent way of life.

Ascetics often separate themselves from their families and normal social life, and this is what Christian ascetics did. Individuals and small groups withdrew from cities and moved to the Egyptian desert, where they sought God through prayer in caves and shelters in the desert or mountains. These individuals were called "hermits," from the Greek word *eremos*, meaning "desert," or "monks," from the Greek word *monos*, meaning "alone." Gradually, large groups of monks emerged in the deserts of Upper Egypt, creating a style of life known as "monasticism." Many devout women also were attracted to this eremitical type of monasticism, becoming nuns. Although monks and nuns led isolated lives, ordinary people soon recognized them as holy people and sought them as spiritual guides.

Church leaders did not really approve of eremitical life. Hermits sometimes claimed to have mystical experiences — direct communications with God. If hermits could communicate directly with the Lord, what need had they for priests, bishops, and the institutional church? The church hierarchy instead encouraged those who wanted to live ascetic lives of devotion to do so in communities. Communal living in a monastery, they argued, provided an environment for training the aspirant in the virtues of charity, poverty, and freedom from self-deception. Consequently, in the fourth, fifth, and sixth centuries many different kinds of communal monasticism developed in Gaul, Italy, Spain, Anglo-Saxon England, and Ireland.

In 529 Benedict of Nursia (ca. 480–547), who had experimented with both the eremitical and the communal forms of monastic life, wrote a brief set of regulations for the

Saint Benedict Holding his *Rule* in his left hand, the seated and hooded patriarch of Western monasticism blesses a monk with his right hand. His monastery, Monte Cassino, is in the background. (Biblioteca Apostolica Vaticana)

monks who had gathered around him at Monte Cassino, between Rome and Naples. Benedict's guide for monastic life, known as *The Rule of Saint Benedict*, slowly replaced all others, and it has influenced all forms of organized religious life in the Roman Church. The guide outlined a monastic life of regularity, discipline, and moderation in an atmosphere of silence. Under Benedict's regulations, monks spent part of each day in formal prayer, chanting psalms and other prayers from the Bible. The rest of the day was passed in manual labor, study, and private prayer.

Why did the Benedictine form of monasticism eventually replace other forms of western monasticism? The monastic life as conceived by Saint Benedict struck a balance between asceticism and activity. It thus provided opportunities for men of entirely different abilities and talents—from mechanics and gardeners to literary scholars. The Benedictine form of religious life also proved congenial to women. Five miles from Monte Cassino at Plombariola, Benedict's twin sister Scholastica (ca. 480–543) adapted *The Rule of Saint Benedict* for her community of nuns.

Another reason for Benedictine monasticism's dominance was its material success. In the seventh and eighth centuries Benedictine monasteries pushed back forests and wastelands, drained swamps, and experimented with crop rotation, making a significant contribution to the agricultural development of Europe. In the process they earned immense wealth. The communal nature of their organization, whereby property was held in common and profits were pooled and reinvested, made their contributions to agriculture possible.

Monasteries also conducted schools for local young people. Some learned about prescriptions and herbal remedies and went on to provide medical treatment for their localities. Others copied manuscripts and wrote books. Local and royal governments drew on the services of the literate men and able administrators the monasteries produced.

Because all monasteries followed rules, men who lived a communal monastic life came to be called regular clergy, from the Latin word *regulus* (rule). In contrast, priests and bishops who staffed churches in which people worshipped and who were not cut off from the world were called secular clergy. According to official church doctrine, women were not members of the clergy, but this distinction was not clear to most people.

Monasticism in the Greek Orthodox world differed in fundamental ways from the monasticism that evolved in western Europe. First, while *The Rule of Saint Benedict* gradually became the universal guide for all western European monasteries, each monastic house in the Byzantine world developed its own set of rules for organization and behavior. Second, education never became a central feature of the Greek houses. Monks and nuns had to be literate to perform the services of the choir, and children destined for the monastic life were taught to read and write, but no monastery assumed responsibility for the general training of the local young. Since bishops and patriarchs of the Greek Church were recruited only from the monasteries, Greek houses did, however, exercise a cultural influence.

Christian Ideas and Practices

❑ How did Christian thinkers and missionaries adapt Greco-Roman ideas to Christian theology and develop effective techniques for converting barbarian peoples?

The growth of Christianity was tied not just to institutions such as the papacy and monasteries, but also to ideas. Initially, Christians rejected Greco-Roman culture. Gradually, however, Christian leaders and thinkers developed ideas that drew on classical influences. At the same time missionaries sponsored by bishops and monasteries spread Christian ideas and institutions far beyond the borders of the Roman and Byzantine Empires, often adapting them to local spiritual beliefs and practices as they assimilated pagan peoples to Christianity.

Christian Beliefs and the Greco-Roman Tradition

In the first century Christians believed that Christ would soon fulfill his promise to return and that the end of the world was near; therefore, they saw no point in devoting time to learning. By the second century, however, these apocalyptic expectations were diminishing, and church leaders began to incorporate elements of Greek and Roman philosophy and learning into Christian teachings (see page 168). They found support for this incorporation in the written texts that circulated among Christians. In the third and fourth centuries these texts were brought together as the New Testament of the Bible, with general agreement about most of what should be included but sharp disputes about some books. Although some of Jesus's sermons as recorded in the Gospels (see page 166) urged followers to avoid worldly attachments, other parts of the Bible advocated acceptance of existing social, economic, and political structures. Christian thinkers built on these, adapting Christian teachings to fit with Roman realities and Roman ideas to fit with Christian aims.

Procession to a New Church In this sixth-century ivory carving, two men in a wagon, accompanied by a procession of people holding candles, carry relics of a saint to a Christian church under construction. New churches often received holy items when they were dedicated, and processions were common ways in which people expressed community devotion. (Cathedral Treasury, Trier. Photo: Ann Muenchow)

Saint Jerome (340–419), a distinguished theologian and linguist regarded as a father of the church, translated the Bible's Old Testament and New Testament from Hebrew and Greek, respectively, into vernacular Latin (a form of Latin common among Christians of the time). Called the "Vulgate," his edition of the Bible served as the official translation until the sixteenth century, and scholars rely on it even today. Familiar with the writings of classical authors such as Cicero and Virgil, Saint Jerome believed that Christians should study the best of ancient thought because it would direct their minds to God. He maintained that the best ancient literature should be interpreted in light of the Christian faith.

Christian attitudes toward gender and sexuality provide a good example of the ways early Christians challenged and then adopted the views of their contemporary world, modifying these as they did. In his plan of salvation Jesus considered women the equal of men. He attributed no disreputable qualities to women and did not refer to them as inferior creatures. On the contrary, women were among his earliest and most faithful converts.

Accordingly, women took an active role in the spread of Christianity, preaching, acting as missionaries, being martyred alongside men, and perhaps even baptizing believers. Because early Christians believed that the second coming of Christ was imminent, they devoted their energies to their new spiritual family of co-believers. Also, they often met in people's homes and called one another brother and sister, a metaphorical use of family terms that was new to the Roman Em-

pire. Some women embraced the ideal of virginity and either singly or in monastic communities declared themselves "virgins in the service of Christ." All this made Christianity seem dangerous to many Romans, especially when becoming Christian led some young people to avoid marriage, which was viewed by Romans as the foundation of society and a necessity for maintaining the power of the paterfamilias (see page 151).

Not all Christian teachings represented a radical break from Roman tradition, however. In the first century male church leaders began to place restrictions on female believers. Paul (see page 168) and later writers forbade women to preach, and women were gradually excluded from holding official positions in Christianity other than in women's monasteries. In so limiting the activities of female believers Christianity was following well-established social patterns, just as it modeled its official hierarchy after that of the Roman Empire.

Christian teachings about sexuality also built on and challenged classical models. The church's unfavorable view of sexual activity involved an affirmation of the importance of a spiritual life, but it also incorporated hostility toward the body found in some Hellenistic philosophies. Just as spirit was superior to matter, the thinking went, the mind was superior to the body. Though Christian teachings affirmed that God had created the material world and sanctioned marriage, most Christian thinkers also taught that celibacy was the better life and that anything that distracted one's attention from the spiritual world performed an evil function. Most church fathers saw women as just such a distraction and temptation, and in some of their writings women are portrayed as evil. Thus these writings contain a strong streak of misogyny (hatred of women), which was passed down to later Christian thinkers. Same-sex relations — which were generally acceptable in the Greco-Roman world, especially if they were between socially unequal individuals — were also evil in the eyes of church fathers. Their misogyny and hostility toward sexuality had a greater influence on the formation of later attitudes than did the relatively egalitarian actions and words of Jesus.

Saint Augustine

One thinker had an especially strong role in shaping Christian views about sexual activity and many other issues: Saint Augustine of Hippo (354–430), the most influential church father in the West. Augustine was born into an urban family in what is now Algeria in North Africa. His father, a minor civil servant, was a pagan; his mother, Monica, a devout Christian. It was not until adulthood that he converted to his mother's religion, eventually becoming bishop of the city of Hippo Regius. Augustine gained renown as a preacher, a vigorous defender of orthodox Christianity, and the author of more than ninety-three books and treatises.

Augustine's autobiography, *The Confessions*, is a literary masterpiece and one of the most influential books in history. Written in the rhetorical style and language of late Roman antiquity, it nonetheless challenges Greco-Roman views of human behavior and morality. *The Confessions* describes Augustine's moral struggle, the conflict between his spiritual aspirations and his sensual self. Many Greek and Roman philosophers had taught that knowledge and virtue are the same: a person who knows what is right will do what is right. Augustine rejected this idea, arguing that people do not always act on the basis of rational knowledge. Instead, the basic or dynamic force in any individual is the will. When Adam ate the fruit forbidden by God in the Garden of Eden (Genesis 3:6), he committed the "original sin" and corrupted the will, wrote Augustine. Adam's sin was not simply his own but was passed on to all later humans through sexual intercourse; even infants were tainted. Augustine viewed sexual desire as the result of the disobedience of Adam and Eve (who also ate the forbidden fruit), linking sexuality even more clearly with sin than had earlier church fathers. According to Augustine, because Adam disobeyed God, all human beings have an innate tendency to sin: their will is weak. But Augustine held that God restores the strength of the will through grace, which is transmitted in certain rituals that the church defined as **sacraments**. Augustine's ideas on sin, grace, and redemption became the foundation of all subsequent Western Christian theology, Protestant as well as Catholic.

Missionary Activity

Christ had said that his teaching was for all peoples, and Christians sought to make their faith catholic — that is, worldwide or believed everywhere. The Mediterranean served as the highway over which Christianity spread to the cities of the Byzantine Empire (Map 8.2). From there missionaries took Christian teachings to the countryside, and then to areas beyond the borders of the empire.

Because the religion of a region's chieftain or king determined the religion of the people, missionaries concentrated their initial efforts on these leaders and members of their families, and the leaders then ordered their people to convert. Queens and other female members of the royal family were often the first converts in an area, and they influenced their husbands and brothers. Barbarian kings accepted Christianity because they believed that the Christian God was more powerful than pagan gods and that the Christian God — either the Arian or the Nicene version — would deliver victory in battle, because Christianity taught obedience to (kingly) authority, or because Christian priests possessed knowledge and a charisma that could be associated with kingly power.

Many barbarian groups were converted by Arian missionaries, who also founded dioceses. Even before Saint Jerome translated the Bible into Latin, one of these Arian missionaries, Bishop Ulfilas (ca. 310–383), an Ostrogoth himself, translated the Bible from Greek into the Gothic language, creating a new Gothic script in order to write it down. Over the next several centuries this text was recopied many times and carried with the Gothic tribes as they migrated throughout southern Europe. In the sixth and seventh centuries most Goths and other Germanic tribes converted to Roman Christianity, sometimes peacefully and sometimes as a result of conquest. Ulfilas's Bible — and the Gothic script he invented — were forgotten and rediscovered only a thousand years later.

Tradition identifies the conversion of Ireland with Saint Patrick (ca. 385–461). After a vision urged him to Christianize Ireland, Patrick studied in Gaul and in 432 was consecrated a bishop. He then returned to Ireland, where he converted the Irish tribe by tribe, first baptizing the king.

The Christianization of the English really began in 597, when Pope Gregory I (pontificate 590–604) sent a delegation of monks to England. The conversion of the English had far-reaching consequences because Britain later served as a base for the Christianization of Germany and other parts of northern Europe (see

• **sacraments** Certain rituals of the church believed to act as a conduit of God's grace, such as the Eucharist and baptism.

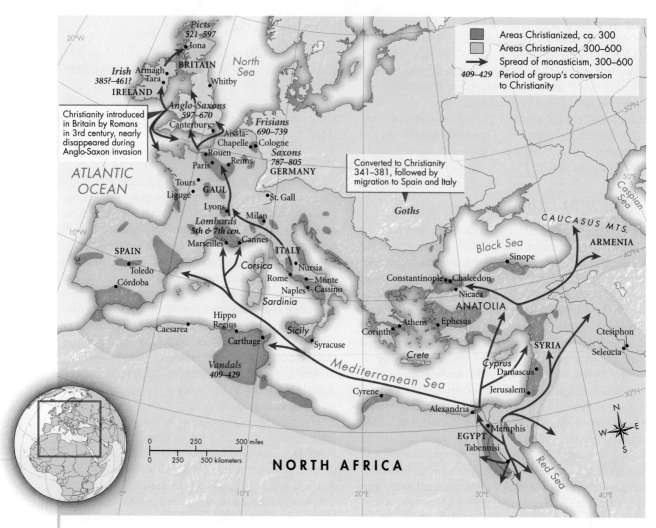

Legend:
- Areas Christianized, ca. 300
- Areas Christianized, 300–600
- → Spread of monasticism, 300–600
- 409–429 Period of group's conversion to Christianity

Christianity introduced in Britain by Romans in 3rd century, nearly disappeared during Anglo-Saxon invasion

Converted to Christianity 341–381, followed by migration to Spain and Italy

▢ Mapping the Past

MAP 8.2 The Spread of Christianity, ca. 300–800 Originating in the area near Jerusalem, Christianity spread throughout the Roman world.

ANALYZING THE MAP Based on the map, how did the roads and sea-lanes of the Roman Empire influence the spread of Christianity?

CONNECTIONS How does the map support the conclusion that Christianity began as an urban religion and then spread into more rural areas?

Map 8.2). Between the fifth and tenth centuries the majority of people living on the European continent and the nearby islands accepted the Christian religion — that is, they received baptism, though baptism in itself did not automatically transform people into Christians.

In eastern Europe missionaries traveled far beyond the boundaries of the Byzantine Empire. In 863 the emperor Michael III (r. 842–867) sent the brothers Cyril (826–869) and Methodius (815–885) to preach Christianity in Moravia (an eastern region of the modern Czech Republic). Other missionaries succeeded in converting the Russians in the tenth century. Another

Byzantine influence on Russia was the Slavic alphabet invented by Cyril (called the "Cyrillic alphabet"). This made possible the birth of Russian literature, and it is still in use today. Similarly, Byzantine art and architecture became the basis of and inspiration for Russian forms, particularly in the creation of religious icons.

Conversion and Assimilation

When a ruler marched his people to the waters of baptism, the work of Christianization had only begun. Christian kings could order their subjects to be bap-

Staffordshire Hoard Artifact with Biblical Inscription This strip of gold bears a biblical inscription in somewhat misspelled Latin asking God for help against enemies. Made in the seventh century, it was buried sometime later along with hundreds of garnet-inlaid gold and silver weapons parts, and it was discovered in 2009 in Staffordshire, England, as part of the largest hoard of Anglo-Saxon gold ever found. Who made it, who owned it, and who buried it will no doubt be a source of debate for decades, as the hoard modifies scholarly opinion about Anglo-Saxon England. (Courtesy, www.staffordshirehoard.org.uk)

tized, married, and buried in Christian ceremonies, which they did increasingly across Europe. Churches could be built, and people could be required to attend services and belong to parishes, but the church could not compel people to accept Christian beliefs, many of which, such as "love your enemies," seemed strange or radical.

How, then, did missionaries and priests get masses of pagan and illiterate peoples to understand and become more accepting of Christian ideals and teachings? They did it through preaching, assimilation, the ritual of penance, and veneration of the saints.

Preaching aimed at presenting the basic teachings of Christianity and strengthening the newly baptized in their faith through stories about the lives of Christ and the saints. Deeply ingrained pagan customs and practices, however, could not be stamped out by words alone or even by imperial edicts. Thus Christian missionaries often pursued a policy of assimilation, easing the conversion of pagan men and women by stressing similarities between their customs and beliefs and those of Christianity. In the same way that classically trained scholars such as Jerome and Augustine blended Greco-Roman and Christian ideas, missionaries and converts mixed barbarian pagan ideas and practices with Christian ones. For example, bogs and lakes sacred to Germanic gods became associated with saints (discussed in more detail below), as did various aspects of ordinary life, such as traveling, planting crops, and worrying about a sick child. Aspects of existing midwinter celebrations, which often centered on the return of the sun as the days became longer, were incorporated into celebrations of Christmas. Spring rituals involving eggs and rabbits (both symbols of fertility) were added to celebrations of Easter.

The ritual of **penance** was also instrumental in teaching Christian beliefs, in this case concerning sins, actions and thoughts that went against God's commands. Christianity taught that only by confessing sins and asking forgiveness could a sinning believer be reconciled with God. Confession was initially a public ritual, but by the fifth century individual confession to a parish priest was more common. During this ritual the individual knelt before the priest, who questioned him or her about sins he or she might have committed. The priest then set a penance, such as fasting or saying specific prayers, to allow the person to atone for the sin. Penance gave new converts a sense of the behavior expected of Christians, encouraged the private examination of conscience, and offered relief from the burden of sinful deeds.

Although confession became mostly a private affair, most religious observances continued to be community matters, as they had been in the ancient world. People joined with family members, friends, and neighbors to celebrate baptisms and funerals, presided over by a priest.

Veneration of **saints**, people who had lived (or died) in a way that was spiritually heroic or noteworthy, was another way that Christians formed stronger connections with their religion. Saints were understood to provide protection and assistance to worshippers, and parish churches often housed saints' relics, that is, bones, articles of clothing, or other objects associated with them. The relics served as links between the material world and the spiritual, and miracle stories about saints and their relics were an important part of Christian preaching and writing. For example, Gregory of Tours (ca. 538–594), a bishop in the Frankish kingdom, described his father's faith in relics:

> Because my father wished himself to be protected by relics of saints, he asked a cleric to grant him something from these relics, so that with their protection he might be kept safe as he set out on this long journey. He put the sacred ashes in a gold medallion and

- **penance** Ritual in which Christians asked a priest for forgiveness for sins, and the priest set certain actions to atone for the sins.
- **saints** People who were venerated for having lived or died in a way that was spiritually heroic or noteworthy.

> **"**He claimed that often, because of the powers of these relics, he had avoided the violence of bandits, the dangers of floods, the threats of turbulent men, and attacks from swords.**"**
>
> **GREGORY OF TOURS**

carried it with him. Although he did not even know the names of the blessed men, he was accustomed to recount that he had been rescued from many dangers. He claimed that often, because of the powers of these relics, he had avoided the violence of bandits, the dangers of floods, the threats of turbulent men, and attacks from swords.[4]

Christians came to venerate the saints as powerful and holy. They prayed to saints or to the Virgin Mary to intercede with God, or they simply asked the saints to assist and bless them. The entire village participated in processions marking saints' days or important points in the agricultural year, often carrying images of saints or their relics around the houses and fields. Although the decision to adopt Christianity was often made first by an emperor or king, actual conversion was a local matter, as people came to feel that the parish priest and the saints provided them with benefits in this world and the world to come. Christianity became an important means through which barbarian groups migrating into Europe gained access to at least some of Greco-Roman culture.

Migrating Peoples

☐ How did the barbarians shape social, economic, and political structures in Europe and western Asia?

The migration of peoples from one area to another has been a continuing feature of world history. One of the most enduring patterns of migration was the movement of peoples west and south from Central Asia and northern Europe beginning in the second century C.E. (Map 8.3). The Greeks who encountered these peoples called them *barbaros* because they seemed to the Greeks to be speaking nonsense syllables — bar, bar, bar. ("Barbar" is the Greek equivalent of "blah-blah" or "yada-yada.") Although *barbaros* originally meant someone who did not speak Greek, gradually people labeled as such were also seen as unruly, savage, and more primitive than members of the advanced civilization of

Greece. (See "Viewpoints: Roman and Byzantine Views of Barbarians," page 222.) The word brought this broader meaning with it when it came into Latin and other European languages.

Barbarians included many different ethnic groups with social and political structures, languages, laws, and beliefs developed in central and northern Europe and western Asia over many centuries. Among the largest barbarian groups were the Celts (whom the Romans called Gauls) and Germans; Germans were further subdivided into various tribes, such as Ostrogoths, Visigoths, Burgundians, and Franks. *Celt* and *German* are often used as ethnic terms, but they are better understood as linguistic terms, a Celt being a person who spoke a Celtic language, an ancestor of the modern Gaelic or Breton languages, and a German one who spoke a Germanic language, an ancestor of modern German, Dutch, Danish, Swedish, and Norwegian. Celts, Germans, and other barbarians brought their customs and traditions with them when they moved south and west, and these gradually combined with classical and Christian customs and beliefs to form a new type of society. From this cultural mix the Franks emerged as an especially strong and influential force, and they built a lasting empire (see page 225).

Social and Economic Structures

Barbarians generally had no notion of the state as we use the term today; they thought in social, not political, terms. The basic social unit was the tribe, made up of kin groups, and tribe members believed that they were all descended from a common ancestor. Blood united them; kinship protected them. Kin groups were made up of families, which were responsible for the debts and actions of their members and for keeping the peace in general.

Barbarian groups usually resided in small villages, and climate and geography determined the basic patterns of agricultural and pastoral life. Many groups settled on the edges of clearings where they raised barley, wheat, oats, peas, and beans. Men and women tilled their fields with simple scratch plows, which broke the soil with wooden spikes, and harvested their grain with small iron sickles. The kernels of grain were eaten as porridge, ground up for flour, or fermented into strong, thick beer. Most of people's caloric intake came from grain in some form.

Within the small villages, there were great differences in wealth and status. Free men and their families constituted the largest class, and the number of cattle these men possessed indicated their wealth and determined their social status. Free men also took part in tribal warfare. Slaves (prisoners of war) worked as farm laborers, herdsmen, and household servants.

MAP 8.3 The Barbarian Migrations, ca. 340–500 Various barbarian groups migrated throughout Europe and western Asia in late antiquity, pushed and pulled by a number of factors. Many of them formed loosely structured states, of which the Frankish kingdom would become the most significant.

Barbarian society was patriarchal: within each household the father had authority over his wife, children, and slaves. Some wealthy and powerful men had more than one wife, a pattern that continued even after they became Christian, but polygamy was not widespread among ordinary people. A woman was considered to be under the legal guardianship of a man, and she had fewer rights to own property than did Roman women in the late empire. However, once they were widowed (and there must have been many widows in such a violent, warring society), women sometimes assumed their husbands' rights over family property and took guardianship of their children.

Chiefs, Warriors, and Laws

Barbarian tribes were led by chieftains, the tribe members recognized as the strongest and bravest in battle. Each chief was elected from among the male members of the strongest family. He led the tribe in war, settled disputes among its members, conducted negotiations

with outside powers, and offered sacrifices to the gods. As barbarian groups migrated into and conquered parts of the Western Roman Empire, their chiefs became even more powerful. Often chiefs adopted the title of king, though this title implies broader power than they actually had.

Closely associated with the chief in some tribes was the comitatus (kuhm-ee-TAH-tuhs), or "war band." The warriors swore loyalty to the chief and fought alongside him in battle. Warriors may originally have been relatively equal to one another, but during the migrations and warfare of the second through the fourth centuries, the war band was transformed into a system of stratified ranks. When tribes settled down, warriors also began to acquire land as both a mark of prestige and a means to power. Social inequalities emerged and gradually grew stronger. These inequalities help explain the origins of the European noble class.

Early barbarian tribes had no written laws. Instead, law was custom—preserved in the minds of tribal elders and handed down by word of mouth from

Viewpoints

Roman and Byzantine Views of Barbarians

• *The earliest written records about the barbarian groups that migrated, attacked, and sometimes conquered the more urbanized and densely populated areas of Europe and western Asia all come from the pens of educated Greeks, Romans, and Byzantines. They provide us with important information about barbarians, but always from the perspective of outsiders with a particular point of view. The selections below are typical of such commentary. The first is from the fourth-century Roman general and historian Ammianus Marcellinus, who fought in Roman armies against Germanic tribes, the Huns, and the Persians, and later wrote a history of the Roman Empire. The second is from the sixth-century Byzantine historian Agathias, describing recent encounters between the forces of the Byzantine emperor Justinian and various Germanic tribes.*

Ammianus Marcellinus on the Huns, ca. 380

The people of the Huns, but little known from ancient records, dwelling beyond the Maeotic Sea near the ice-bound ocean, exceed every degree of savagery. . . . They all have compact, strong limbs and thick necks, and are so monstrously ugly and misshapen, that one might take them for two legged-beasts or for the stumps, rough-hewn into images, that are used in putting sides to bridges. But although they have the form of men, however ugly, they are so hardy in their mode of life that they have no need of fire nor of savory food, but eat the roots of wild plants and the half-raw flesh of any kind of animal whatever, which they put between their thighs and the backs of their horses, and thus warm a little. They are never protected by any buildings, but they avoid these like tombs. . . . They are not at all adapted to battles on foot, but they are almost glued to their horses, which are hardy, it is true, but ugly. . . . They fight from a distance with missiles having sharp bone [points], instead of the usual (metal) parts, joined to the shafts with wonderful skill; then they gallop over the intervening spaces and fight hand to hand with swords, regardless of their own lives. . . . No one in their country ever plows a field or touches a plow-handle. They are all without fixed abode, without hearth, or law, or settled mode of life, and keep roaming from place to place, like fugitives, accompanied by wagons in which they live; in wagons their wives weave for them their hideous garments, in wagons they cohabit with their husbands, bear children, and rear them to the age of puberty.

Agathias on the Franks

The Franks are not nomads, as indeed some barbarian peoples are, but their system of government, administration and laws are modelled more or less on the Roman pattern, apart from which they uphold similar standards with regard to contracts, marriage, and religious observance. They are in fact all Christians and adhere to the strictest orthodoxy. They also have magistrates in their cities and priests and celebrate the feasts in the same way we do, and, for a barbarian people, strike me as extremely well-bred and civilized and as practically the same as ourselves except for their uncouth style of dress and peculiar language. I admire them for their other attributes and especially for the spirit of justice and harmony which prevails amongst them.

Sources: Reprinted by permission of the publishers and the Trustees of the Loeb Classical Library from *Ammianus Marcellinus: Volume I*, Loeb Classical Library Volume 300, translated by J. C. Rolfe, pp. 383, 385, Cambridge, Mass.: Harvard University Press, Copyright © 1935, 1950 by the President and Fellows of Harvard College. Loeb Classical Library ® is a registered trademark of the President and Fellows of Harvard College; Agathias, *The Histories*, translated by Joseph D. Frendo (Berlin: Walter de Gruyter, 1975), p. 10.

QUESTIONS FOR ANALYSIS

1. What qualities of the Huns does Ammianus Marcellinus find admirable? What does he criticize?

2. What qualities of the Franks does Agathias praise? Why does he find these qualities admirable?

3. How does the fact that both Ammianus Marcellinus and Agathias come from agricultural societies with large cities shape their views of barbarians?

---

generation to generation. Beginning in the late sixth century, however, some tribal chieftains began to collect, write, and publish lists of their customs at the urging of Christian missionaries. The churchmen wanted to understand barbarian ways in order to assimilate the tribes to Christianity. Moreover, by the sixth century many barbarian chieftains needed regulations for the Romans under their jurisdiction as well as for their own people.

Barbarian law codes often included clauses designed to reduce interpersonal violence. Any crime that involved a personal injury, such as assault, rape, and murder, was given a particular monetary value, called the **wergeld** (WUHR-gehld) (literally "man-money" or "money to buy off the spear"), that was to be paid by a person accused of a crime to the victim or the victim's family. If the accused agreed to pay the wergeld and if the victim or his or her family accepted the payment, there was peace. If the accused refused to pay the wergeld or if the victim or family refused to accept it, a blood feud ensued.

The wergeld varied according to the severity of the crime and also the social status and gender of the victim, as shown in these clauses from the law code of the Salian Franks, one of the barbarian tribes.

> If any person strike another on the head so that the brain appears, and the three bones which lie above the brain shall project, he shall be sentenced to 1200 denars, which make 300 shillings. . . .
>
> If any one have killed a free woman after she has begun bearing children, he shall be sentenced to 2400 denars, which make 600 shillings.[5]

In other codes as well, a crime against a woman of childbearing years often carried a wergeld as substantial as that for a man of higher stature, suggesting that barbarians were concerned about maintaining their population levels.

Like Greeks, Romans, and Hindus, barbarians worshipped hundreds of gods and goddesses with specialized functions. They regarded certain mountains, lakes, rivers, or groves of trees as sacred because these were linked to deities. Rituals to honor the gods were held outdoors rather than in temples or churches, often at certain points in the yearly agricultural cycle. Among the Celts, religious leaders called druids had legal and educational as well as religious functions, orally passing down laws and traditions from generation to generation. Bards singing poems and ballads also passed down myths and stories of heroes and gods, which were written down much later.

• **wergeld** Compensatory payment for death or injury set in many barbarian law codes.

Migrations and Political Change

Migrating groups that the Romans labeled barbarians had pressed along the Rhine-Danube frontier of the Roman Empire since about 150 C.E. (see page 169). In the third and fourth centuries increasing pressures on the frontiers from the east and north placed greater demands on Roman military manpower, which plague and a declining birthrate had reduced. Roman generals therefore recruited refugees and barbarian tribes allied with the Romans to serve in the Roman army, and some rose to the highest ranks.

Anglo-Saxon Helmet This ceremonial bronze helmet from seventh-century England was found inside a ship buried at Sutton Hoo. The nearly 100-foot-long ship was dragged overland before being buried completely. It held one body and many grave goods, including swords, gold buckles, and silver bowls made in Byzantium. The unidentified person who was buried here was clearly wealthy and powerful, and so was very likely a chief. (Courtesy of the Trustees of the British Museum)

Why did the barbarians migrate? In part, they were searching for more regular supplies of food, better farmland, and a warmer climate. Conflicts within and among barbarian groups also led to war and disruption, which motivated groups to move. Franks fought Alemanni (another Germanic tribe) in Gaul, while Visigoths fought Vandals in the Iberian peninsula and across North Africa. Roman expansion led to further movement of barbarian groups but also to the blending of cultures.

The spread of the Celts presents a good example of both conflict and assimilation. Celtic-speaking peoples had lived in central Europe since at least the fifth century B.C.E. and had spread out from there to the Iberian peninsula in the west, Hungary in the east, and the British Isles in the north. As Julius Caesar advanced northward into what he termed Gaul (present-day France), he defeated many Celtic tribes (see page 154). Celtic peoples conquered by the Romans often assimilated to Roman ways, adopting the Latin language and many aspects of Roman culture. Also, Celts and Romans intermarried, and many Celtic men became Roman citizens and joined the Roman army. By the fourth century C.E., however, Gaul and Britain were under pressure from Germanic groups moving westward. Roman troops withdrew from Britain, and Celtic-speaking peoples clashed with Germanic-speaking invaders, of whom the largest tribes were the Angles and the Saxons. Some Celtic-speakers moved farther west, to Brittany (modern northwestern France), Wales, Scotland, and Ireland. Others remained and intermarried with Germanic peoples, their descendants forming a number of small Anglo-Saxon kingdoms.

In eastern Europe, a significant factor in barbarian migration and the merging of various Germanic groups was pressure from nomadic steppe peoples from central Asia. These included the Alans, Avars, Bulghars, Khazars, and most prominently the Huns, who attacked the Black Sea area and the Eastern Roman Empire beginning in the fourth century. Under the leadership of their warrior-king Attila, the Huns swept into central Europe in 451, attacking Roman settlements in the Balkans and Germanic settlements along the Danube and Rhine Rivers. After Attila turned his army southward and crossed the Alps into Italy, a papal delegation, including Pope Leo I himself, asked him not to attack Rome. Though papal diplomacy was later credited with stopping the advance of the Huns, dwindling food supplies for Hunnic troops, as well as a plague that had spread among them, were probably much more important factors. The Huns retreated from Italy, and within a year Attila was dead. Later leaders were not as effective, and the Huns never again played a significant role in European history. Their conquests had pushed many Germanic groups together, however, which transformed smaller bands of people into larger, more unified groups that could more easily pick the Western Roman Empire apart.

After they conquered an area, barbarians generally established rulership under kings (chieftains). The kingdoms did not have definite geographical borders, and their locations shifted as tribes moved. Eventually, barbarian kingdoms came to include Italy itself. The Western Roman emperors increasingly relied on barbarian commanders and their troops to maintain order. In 476 the barbarian chieftain Odoacer deposed Romulus Augustus, the last person to have the title of Roman emperor in the West. Odoacer did not take the title of emperor, calling himself instead the king of Italy, so that this date marks the official end of the Roman Empire in the West. From Constantinople, Eastern Roman emperors such as Justinian (see page 208) worked to reconquer at least some of the West from barbarian tribes. They were occasionally successful but could not hold the empire together for long.

The Frankish Kingdom

Most barbarian kingdoms did not last very long, but one that did, and that came to have a decisive role in history, was that of the Franks. The Franks were a confederation of Germanic peoples who came from the marshy lowlands north and east of the northernmost part of the Roman Empire. In the fourth and fifth centuries they settled within the empire and allied with the Romans, some attaining high military and civil positions. The Franks believed that Merovech, a semi-legendary figure, founded their ruling dynasty, which was thus called **Merovingian** (mehr-uh-VIHN-jee-uhn).

The reign of Clovis (ca. 481–511) was decisive in the development of the Franks as a unified people. Through military campaigns, Clovis acquired the central provinces of Roman Gaul and began to conquer southern Gaul from other Germanic tribes. His wife Clotild, a Roman Christian, converted her husband and supported the founding of churches and monasteries. Her actions typify the role women played in the Christianization of barbarian kingdoms. (See "Listening to the Past: Gregory of Tours, The Conversion of Clovis," page 226.) Clotild, and other Frankish queens, frequently influenced events, for they had a say in how royal funds were spent and often spent long periods as regents for their sons until they came of age.

Clovis's conversion to Roman Christianity brought him the crucial support of the bishops of Gaul in his campaigns against tribes that were still pagan or had accepted the Arian version of Christianity. As the defender of Roman Christianity against heretical tribes,

Clovis went on to conquer the Visigoths, extending his domain to include much of what is now France and southwestern Germany.

When Clovis died his kingdom was divided among his four sons, following Frankish custom. For the next two centuries rulers of the various kingdoms fought one another in civil wars, and other military leaders challenged their authority. So brutal were these wars that historians used to use the term *Dark Ages* to apply to the entire Merovingian period, although more recently they have noted that the Merovingians also developed new political institutions, so the era was not uniformly bleak.

Merovingian kings based some aspects of their government on Roman principles. For example, they adopted the Roman concept of the *civitas* — Latin for a city and its surrounding territory. A count presided over the civitas, raising troops, collecting royal revenues, and providing justice on the basis of local, not royal, law. At the king's court — that is, wherever the king was present — an official called the mayor of the palace supervised legal, financial, and household officials; the mayor of the palace also governed in the king's absence. In the seventh century that position was held by members of an increasingly powerful family, the **Carolingians** (ka-ruh-LIHN-jee-uhns), who advanced themselves through advantageous marriages, a well-earned reputation for military strength, and the help of the church.

Eventually the Carolingians replaced the Merovingians as rulers of the Frankish kingdom, cementing their authority when the Carolingian Charles Martel defeated Muslim invaders in 732 at the Battle of Poitiers (pwah-ty-AY) in central France. Muslims and Christians have interpreted the battle differently. Muslims considered it a minor skirmish and attributed the Frankish victory to Muslim difficulties in maintaining supply lines over long distances and to ethnic conflicts and unrest in Islamic Spain. Charles Martel and later Carolingians used the victory to portray themselves as defenders of Christendom against the Muslims.

The Battle of Poitiers helped the Carolingians acquire more support from the church, perhaps their most important asset. They further strengthened their ties to the church by supporting the work of missionaries who preached Christian principles — including the duty to obey secular authorities — to pagan peoples, and

- **Merovingian** A dynasty founded in 481 by the Frankish chieftain Clovis in what is now France. *Merovingian* derives from *Merovech*, the name of the semi-legendary leader from whom Clovis claimed descent.
- **Carolingian** A dynasty of rulers that took over the Frankish kingdom from the Merovingians in the seventh century; *Carolingian* derives from the Latin word for "Charles," the name of several members of this dynasty.

Listening to the Past

Gregory of Tours, The Conversion of Clovis

Modern Christian doctrine holds that conversion is a process, the gradual turning toward Jesus and the teachings of the Christian Gospels. But in the early medieval world, conversion was perceived more as a one-time event determined by the tribal chieftain. If he accepted baptism, the mass conversion of his people followed. The selection here about the Frankish king Clovis is from The History of the Franks *by Gregory, bishop of Tours (ca. 504–594), written about a century after the events it describes.*

❝The first child which Clotild bore for Clovis was a son. She wanted to have her baby baptized, and she kept urging her husband to agree to this. "The gods whom you worship are no good," she would say.

"They haven't even been able to help themselves, let alone others. . . . Take your Saturn, for example, who ran away from his own son to avoid being exiled from his kingdom, or so they say; and Jupiter, that obscene perpetrator of all sorts of mucky deeds, who couldn't keep his hands off other men, who had his fun with all his female relatives and couldn't even refrain from intercourse with his own sister. . . .

"You ought instead to worship Him who created at a word and out of nothing heaven, and earth, the sea and all that therein is, who made the sun to shine, who lit the sky with stars, who peopled the water with fish, the earth with beasts, the sky with flying creatures, by whose hand the race of man was made, by whose gift all creation is constrained to serve in deference and devotion the man He made." However often the Queen said this, the King came no nearer to belief. . . .

The Queen, who was true to her faith, brought her son to be baptized. . . . The child was baptized; he was given the name Ingomer; but no sooner had he received baptism than he died in his white robes. Clovis was extremely angry. He began immediately to reproach his Queen. "If he had been dedicated in the name of my gods," he said, "he would have lived without

question; but now that he has been baptized in the name of your God he has not been able to live a single day!"

"I give thanks to Almighty God," replied Clotild, "the Creator of all things who has not found me completely unworthy, for He has deigned to welcome into his Kingdom a child conceived in my womb. . . ."

Some time later Clotild bore a second son. He was baptized Chlodomer. He began to ail and Clovis said, "What else do you expect? It will happen to him as it happened to his brother: no sooner is he baptized in the name of your Christ than he will die!" Clotild prayed to the Lord and at His commands the baby recovered.

Queen Clotild continued to pray that her husband might recognize the true God and give up his idol-worship. Nothing could persuade him to accept Christianity. Finally war broke out against the Alemanni and in this conflict he was forced by necessity to accept what he had refused of his own free will. It so turned out that when the two armies met on the battlefield there was a great slaughter and the troops of Clovis were rapidly being annihilated. He raised his eyes to heaven when he saw this, felt compunction in his heart and was moved to tears. "Jesus Christ," he said, "you who Clotild maintains to be the Son of the living God, you who deign to give help to those in travail and victory to those who trust in you, in faith I beg the glory of your help. If you will give me victory over my enemies, and if I may have evidence to that miraculous power which the people dedicated to your name say that they have experienced, then I will believe in you and I will be baptized in your name. I have called upon my own gods, but, as I see only too clearly, they have no intention of helping me. I therefore cannot believe that they possess any power for they do not come to the assistance of those who trust them. I now call upon you. I want to believe in you, but I must first be saved from my enemies." Even as he said this the Alemanni turned their backs and began to run away. As soon as they saw that their King was killed, they submitted to Clovis. "We beg you," they said, "to put an end to

by allying themselves with the papacy against other Germanic tribes.

Charlemagne

The most powerful of the Carolingians was Charles the Great (r. 768–814), generally known as Charlemagne (SHAHR-luh-mayn). In the autumn of the year 800, Charlemagne visited Rome, where on Christmas Day

Pope Leo III crowned him emperor. The event had momentous consequences. In taking as his motto *Renovatio romani imperi* (Revival of the Roman Empire), Charlemagne was deliberately perpetuating old Roman imperial ideas while identifying with the new Rome of the Christian Church. From Baghdad, the Abbasid Empire's caliph, Harun al-Rashid (r. 786–809), congratulated Charlemagne on his coronation with the gift of an elephant. The elephant survived for nearly a this slaughter. We are prepared to obey you." Clovis stopped the war. He made a speech in which he called for peace. Then he went home. He told the Queen how he had won a victory by calling on the name of Christ. This happened in the fifteenth year of his reign (496).

The Queen then ordered Saint Remigius, Bishop of the town of Rheims, to be summoned in secret. She begged him to impart the word of salvation to the King. The Bishop asked Clovis to meet him in private and began to urge him to believe in the true God, Maker of heaven and earth, and to forsake his idols, which were powerless to help him or anyone else. The King replied: "I have listened to you willingly, holy father. There remains one obstacle. The people under my command will not agree to forsake their gods. I will go and put to them what you have just said to me." He arranged a meeting with his people, but God in his power had preceded him, and before he could say a word all those present shouted in unison: "We will give up worshipping our mortal gods, pious King, and we are prepared to follow the immortal God about whom Remigius preaches." This news was reported to the Bishop. He was greatly pleased and he ordered the baptismal pool to be made ready. . . . The baptistry was prepared, sticks of incense gave off clouds of perfume, sweet-smelling candles gleamed bright and the holy place of baptism was filled with divine fragrance. God filled the hearts of all present with such grace that they imagined themselves to have been transported to some perfumed paradise. King Clovis asked that he might be baptized first by the Bishop.

Like some new Constantine he stepped forward to the baptismal pool, ready to wash away the sores of his old leprosy and to be cleansed in flowing water from the sordid stains which he had borne so long.

King Clovis confessed his belief in God Almighty, three in one. He was baptized in the name of the Father, the Son, and the Holy Ghost, and marked in holy chrism [an anointing oil] with the sign of the Cross of Christ. More than three thousand of his army were baptized at the same time.

Source: Gregory of Tours, from *The History of the Franks*, translated with an introduction by Lewis Thorpe, pp. 141–144. Copyright © Lewis Thorpe, 1974, London. Reproduced by permission of Penguin Books Ltd.

QUESTIONS FOR ANALYSIS

1. Who took the initiative in urging Clovis's conversion? What can we deduce from that?

2. According to this account, why did Clovis ultimately accept Christianity?

3. How does Gregory of Tours portray the workings of divine power in Clovis's conversion?

4. On the basis of this selection, do you consider *The History of the Franks* reliable? Why?

decade, though like everyone else at Charlemagne's capital of Aachen (on the western border of modern Germany), it lived in a city that was far less sophisticated, healthy, and beautiful than Abbasid Baghdad. Although the Muslim caliph recognized Charlemagne as a fellow sovereign, the Byzantines regarded his papal coronation as rebellious and Charlemagne as a usurper. His crowning as emperor thus marks a decisive break between Rome and Constantinople.

Charlemagne's most striking characteristic was his phenomenal energy, which helps explain his great military achievements. Continuing the expansionist policies of his ancestors, he fought more than fifty campaigns, and by around 805 the Frankish kingdom included all of continental Europe except Spain, Scandinavia, southern Italy, and the Slavic fringes of the East.

▫ Picturing the Past

Charlemagne and His Wife This illumination from a ninth-century manuscript portrays Charlemagne with one of his wives. Marriage was an important tool of diplomacy for Charlemagne, and he had a number of wives and concubines. (Erich Lessing/Art Resource, NY)

ANALYZING THE IMAGE What does Charlemagne appear to be doing? How would you characterize his wife's reaction?

CONNECTIONS Does this depiction of a Frankish queen match what you've read about female rulers in this era, such as Theodora and Clotild?

For administrative purposes, Charlemagne divided his entire kingdom into counties. Each of the approximately six hundred counties was governed by a count, who had full military and judicial power and held his office for life but could be removed by the emperor for misconduct. As a link between local authorities and the central government, Charlemagne appointed officials called *missi dominici*, "agents of the lord king." Each year beginning in 802 two missi, usually a count and a bishop or abbot, visited assigned districts. They checked up on the counts and their districts' judicial, financial, and clerical activities.

It is ironic that Charlemagne's most enduring legacy was the stimulus he gave to scholarship and learning. Barely literate, preoccupied with the control of vast territories, and much more a warrior than a thinker, Charlemagne nevertheless set in motion a cultural revival that later historians called the "Carolingian Renaissance." The Carolingian Renaissance was a rebirth of interest in, study of, and preservation of the language, ideas, and achievements of classical Greece and Rome. Scholars at Aachen copied Greco-Roman and Christian books and manuscripts and built up libraries. Furthermore, Charlemagne urged monasteries to promote Christian learning, and both men's and

• **Treaty of Verdun** A treaty ratified in 843 that divided Charlemagne's territories among his three surviving grandsons; their kingdoms set the pattern for the modern states of Germany, France, and Italy.

Charlemagne's Conquests, ca. 768–814

Frankish Kingdom, 768
Areas conquered by Charlemagne
Tributary peoples
Byzantine Empire

women's houses produced beautiful illustrated texts, preserving Christian and classical works for subsequent generations.

Charlemagne left his vast empire to his sole surviving son, Louis the Pious (r. 814–840), who attempted to keep the empire intact. This proved to be impossible.

Members of the nobility engaged in plots and open warfare against the emperor, often allying themselves with one of Louis's three sons. In 843, shortly after Louis's death, those sons agreed to the **Treaty of Verdun**, which divided the empire into three parts: Charles the Bald received the western part, Lothair the middle and the title of emperor, and Louis the eastern part, from which he acquired the title "the German." Though of course no one knew it at the time, this treaty set the pattern for political boundaries in Europe that has been maintained to today. Other than brief periods under Napoleon and Hitler, Europe would never again see as large a unified state as it had under Charlemagne, which is one reason he has become a symbol of European unity in the twenty-first century.

The Treaty of Verdun, 483

The weakening of central power was hastened by invasions and migrations from the north, south, and east. Thus Charlemagne's empire ended in much the same way that the Roman Empire had earlier, from a combination of internal weakness and external pressure.

CONNECTIONS

For centuries the end of the Roman Empire in the West was seen as a major turning point in history, the fall of the sophisticated and educated classical world to uncouth and illiterate tribes. Over the last several decades, however, many historians have put a greater emphasis on continuities. Barbarian kings relied on officials trained in Roman law, and Latin remained the language of scholarly communication and the Christian Church. Greco-Roman art and architecture still adorned the land, and people continued to use Roman roads, aqueducts, and buildings. In eastern Europe and western Asia, the Byzantine Empire preserved the traditions of the Roman Empire and protected the intellectual heritage of Greco-Roman culture for another millennium.

Very recently, however, some historians and archaeologists have returned to an emphasis on change. They note that people may have traveled on Roman roads after the end of the Roman Empire, but the roads were rarely maintained, and travel itself was much less secure than during the empire. Merchants no longer traded over long distances, so people's access to goods produced outside their local area plummeted. Knowledge about technological processes such as the making of glass and roof tiles declined or disappeared. Although there was intermarriage and cultural assimilation among Romans and barbarians, there was also violence and great physical destruction, even in Byzantium.

In the middle of the era covered in this chapter, a new force emerged that had a dramatic impact on much of Europe and western Asia — Islam. In the seventh and eighth centuries Sassanid Persia, much of the Byzantine Empire, and the barbarian kingdoms in the Iberian peninsula fell to Arab forces carrying this new religion. As we have seen in this chapter, a reputation as victors over Islam helped the Franks establish the most powerful state in Europe. As we will see in Chapter 14, Islam continued to shape European culture and politics in subsequent centuries. In terms of world history, the expansion of Islam may have been an even more dramatic turning point than the fall of the Roman Empire. Here, too, however, there were continuities, as the Muslims adopted and adapted Greek, Byzantine, and Persian political and cultural institutions.

◻ CHAPTER REVIEW

◻ How was the Byzantine Empire able to survive for so long, and what were its most important achievements? (p. 206)

During the sixth and seventh centuries the Byzantine Empire survived waves of attacks, owing to effective military leadership and to fortifications around Constantinople. From this strong position Byzantine emperors organized and preserved Roman institutions, and the Byzantine Empire survived until 1453, nearly a millennium longer than the Roman Empire in the West. In particular, the emperor Justinian oversaw creation of the *Code*, which distilled the legal genius of the Romans into a coherent whole, eliminated outmoded laws and contradictions, and clarified the law itself. Just as they valued the law, the Byzantines prized education, and because of them many masterpieces of ancient Greek literature survived to influence the intellectual life of the modern world. In mathematics and science, the Byzantines passed Greco-Roman learning on to the Arabs, and they discovered an explosive compound, "Greek fire," that saved Constantinople from Arab assault. The Byzantines also devoted a great deal of attention to medicine, and their general level of medical competence was far higher than that of western Europeans.

◻ What factors enabled the Christian Church to expand and thrive? (p. 211)

Christianity gained the support of the fourth-century emperors and gradually adopted the Roman system of hierarchical organization. The church possessed able administrators and leaders whose skills were tested in the chaotic environment of the end of the Roman Empire in the West. Bishops expanded their activities, and in the fifth century the bishops of Rome, taking the title "pope," began to stress their supremacy over other Christian communities. Monasteries offered opportunities for individuals to develop deeper spiri-

KEY TERMS

corpus juris civilis (p. 208)	sacraments (p. 217)
dioceses (p. 211)	penance (p. 219)
Arianism (p. 212)	saints (p. 219)
popes (p. 213)	wergeld (p. 222)
Orthodox Church (p. 213)	Merovingian (p. 225)
	Carolingian (p. 225)
iconoclastic controversy (p. 213)	Treaty of Verdun (p. 229)

tual devotion and also provided a model of Christian living, methods that advanced agricultural development, and places for education and learning.

◻ How did Christian thinkers and missionaries adapt Greco-Roman ideas to Christian theology and develop effective techniques for converting barbarian peoples? (p. 215)

Christian thinkers reinterpreted the classics in a Christian sense, incorporating elements of Greek and Roman philosophy and of various pagan religious groups into Christian teachings. Of these early thinkers, Augustine of Hippo was the most influential. His ideas about sin, free will, and sexuality shaped western European thought from the fifth century on. Missionaries and priests got pagan and illiterate peoples to understand and become more accepting of Christianity by preaching the basic teachings of the religion, stressing similarities between pagan customs and beliefs and those of Christianity, and introducing the ritual of penance and the veneration of saints.

◻ How did the barbarians shape social, economic, and political structures in Europe and western Asia? (p. 220)

The barbarian groups that, beginning in the second century, migrated throughout Europe and Central Asia brought with them customs and traditions that combined with classical and Christian customs and beliefs. Barbarians generally had no notion of the state as we use the term today; they thought in social, not political, terms. The basic social unit was the tribe, made up of kin groups formed by families. Family groups lived in small agriculture-based villages, where there were great differences in wealth and status. Most barbarian kingdoms were weak and short-lived, though the kingdom of the Franks was relatively more unified and powerful. Rulers first in the Merovingian Dynasty, and then in the Carolingian, used military victories, strategic marriage alliances, and the help of the church to enhance their authority. Carolingian government reached the peak of its power under Charlemagne, who continued the expansionist policies of his ancestors, extending the Frankish kingdom to include all of continental Europe except Spain, Scandinavia, southern Italy, and the Slavic areas of the East.

SUGGESTED READING

Barbero, Allesandro. *Charlemagne: Father of a Continent.* 2004. A wonderful biography of Charlemagne and a study of the times in which he lived that argues for the complexity of his legacy.

Brown, Peter. *Augustine of Hippo,* rev. ed. 2000. The best biography of Saint Augustine, which treats him as a symbol of change.

Brown, Peter. *The World of Late Antiquity,* A.D. *150–750,* rev. ed. 1989. A lavishly illustrated survey that stresses social and cultural change and has clearly written introductions to the entire period.

Burns, Thomas S. *Rome and the Barbarians, 100* B.C.–*400 A.D.* 2003. Argues that Germanic and Roman cultures assimilated more than they conflicted.

Cameron, Averil. *The Mediterranean World in Late Antiquity,* A.D. *395–600.* 1993. Focuses especially on political and economic changes.

Clark, Gilian. *Women in Late Antiquity: Pagan and Christian Lifestyles.* 1994. Explores law, marriage, and religious life.

Dunn, Marilyn. *The Emergence of Monasticism: From the Desert Fathers to the Early Middle Ages.* 2003. Focuses on the beginnings of monasticism.

Fletcher, Richard. *The Barbarian Conversion: From Paganism to Christianity.* 1998. A superbly written analysis of conversion to Christianity.

Herrin, Judith. *Byzantium: The Surprising Life of a Medieval Empire.* 2009. An examination of many aspects of Byzantine culture that focuses on people and demonstrates Byzantium's continuing significance for world history.

Herrin, Judith. *The Formation of Christendom.* 1987. The best synthesis of the development of the Christian Church from the third to the ninth centuries.

Pelikan, Jaroslav. *The Excellent Empire: The Fall of Rome and the Triumph of the Church.* 1987. Describes how interpretations of the fall of Rome have influenced our understanding of Western culture.

Riche, Pierre. *Daily Life in the World of Charlemagne,* trans. JoAnn McNamara. 1978. A detailed study of many facets of Carolingian society.

Todd, Malcolm. *The Early Germans,* 2d ed. 2004. Uses archaeological and literary sources to analyze Germanic social structure, customs, and religion and to suggest implications for an understanding of migration and ethnicity.

Ward-Perkins, Bryan. *The Fall of Rome and the End of Civilization.* 2006. Uses material evidence to trace the physical destruction and economic dislocation that accompanied the barbarian migrations.

Wells, Peter S. *The Barbarians Speak: How the Conquered Peoples Shaped Roman Europe.* 1999. Presents extensive evidence of Celtic and Germanic social and technical development.

Wickham, Chris. *Framing the Early Middle Ages: Europe and the Mediterranean, 400–800.* 2007. A massive, yet accessible survey of economic and social changes in many regions, with great attention to ordinary people.

NOTES

1. S. P. Scott, trans., *Corpus Juris Civilis: The Civil Law* (Cincinnati: The Central Trust, 1932), sections 1.5.5, 11.4.1.
2. Quoted in E. Patlagean, "Byzantium in the Tenth and Eleventh Centuries," in *A History of Private Life.* Vol. 1: *From Pagan Rome to Byzantium,* ed. P. Ariès and G. Duby (Cambridge, Mass.: Harvard University Press, 1987), p. 573.
3. R. C. Petry, ed., *A History of Christianity: Readings in the History of Early and Medieval Christianity* (Englewood Cliffs, N.J.: Prentice Hall, 1962), p. 70.
4. Gregory of Tours, *The Glory of the Martyrs,* trans. Raymond Van Dam (Liverpool: Liverpool University, 1988), p. 108. Used by permission of Liverpool University Press.
5. E. F. Henderson, ed., *Select Historical Documents of the Middle Ages* (London: G. Bell and Sons, 1912), pp. 176, 189.

For practice quizzes and other study tools, visit the **Online Study Guide** at bedfordstmartins.com/mckayworld.

For primary sources from this period, see *Sources of World Societies*, **Second Edition**.

For Web sites, images, and documents related to topics in this chapter, visit **Make History** at bedfordstmartins.com/mckayworld.

• **Egyptian Man** Life remained gracious in the great cities of North Africa and the Middle East even as Islam brought new traditions. This image of a man wearing a turban and holding a cup is from a wall painting. Found in Egypt, it dates to the eleventh century, during the Fatimid caliphate. (Museum of Islamic Art, Cairo/Gianni Dagli Orti/The Art Archive)

Around 610 in the city of Mecca in what is now Saudi Arabia, a merchant called Muhammad had a religious vision that inspired him to preach God's revelations to the people of Mecca. By the time he died in 632, he had many followers in Arabia, and a century later his followers controlled what is now Syria, Palestine, Egypt, Iraq, Iran, northern India, northern Africa, Spain, and southern France. Within another century Muhammad's beliefs had been carried across Central Asia to the borders of China and India. The speed with which Islam spread is one of the most amazing stories in world history, and scholars have pointed to many factors that must have contributed to its success. Military victories were rooted in strong military organization and the practice of establishing garrison cities in newly conquered territories. The religious zeal of new converts certainly played an important role. So too did the political weakness of many of the governments then holding power in the lands where Islam extended, such as the Byzantine government centered in Constantinople. Commerce and trade also spread the faith of Muhammad.

The Islamic World

600–1400

Although its first adherents were nomads, Islam developed and flourished in a mercantile milieu. By land and sea, Muslim merchants transported a rich variety of goods across Eurasia. On the basis of the wealth that trade generated, a gracious, sophisticated, and cosmopolitan culture developed with centers at Baghdad and Córdoba. During the ninth, tenth, and eleventh centuries, the Islamic world witnessed enormous intellectual vitality and creativity. Muslim scholars produced important work in many disciplines, especially mathematics, medicine, and philosophy. This brilliant civilization profoundly influenced the development of both Eastern and Western civilizations.   •

The Origins of Islam

☐ From what kind of social and economic environment did Muhammad arise, and what did he teach?

The Arabian peninsula, about a third of the size of Europe or the United States, covers about a million square miles, much but not all of the land desert. By the seventh century C.E. farming prevailed in the southwestern mountain valleys with their ample rainfall. In other areas scattered throughout the peninsula, oasis towns sustained sizable populations including artisans, merchants, and religious leaders. Outside the towns were Bedouin (BEH-duh-uhn) nomadic tribes who moved from place to place, grazing their sheep, goats, and camels. Though always small in number, Bedouins were the most important political and military force in the region because of their toughness, solidarity, fighting traditions, possession of horses and camels, and ability to control trade and lines of communication. Mecca became the economic and cultural center of western Arabia, in part because pilgrims came to visit the Ka'ba, a temple containing a black stone thought to be a god's dwelling place as well as other holy objects connected to other gods. Muhammad's roots were in this region.

Arabian Social and Economic Structure

The basic social unit of the Bedouins and other Arabs was the tribe. Consisting of people connected through kinship, tribes provided protection and support and in turn expected members' total loyalty. Like the Germanic peoples in the age of their migrations (see pages 220–229), Arab tribes were not static entities but rather continually evolving groups. A particular tribe might include both nomadic and sedentary members.

As in other nomadic societies, nomads in Arabia depended on agriculturally productive communities for food they could not produce, cloth, metal products, and weapons. Nomads paid for these goods with livestock, milk and milk products, hides, and hair, items in demand in oasis towns. Nomads acquired additional income by serving as desert guides and as guards for caravans, or by creating the need for guards by plundering caravans and extorting protection money.

Page from the Qur'an The aesthetic appeal of Arabic calligraphy is easy to recognize in this thirteenth-century Qur'an. (Museum of Islamic Art, Cairo/Gianni Dagli Orti/The Art Archive)

In northern and central Arabia in the early seventh century, tribal confederations with their warrior elite were dominant. In the southern parts of the peninsula, however, religious aristocracies tended to hold political power. Many oasis or market towns contained members of one holy family who served the deity of the town and acted as guardians of the deity's shrine. At the shrine, a cultic leader tried to settle disputes among warring tribes. All Arabs respected the shrines because they served as neutral places for such arbitration.

The power of the northern warrior class rested on its fighting skills. The southern religious aristocracy, by contrast, depended on its religious and economic power. Located in agricultural areas that were also commercial centers, the religious aristocracy had a stronger economic base than did the warrior-aristocrats. The political genius of Muhammad was to bind together these different tribal groups into a strong, unified state.

□ CHRONOLOGY

622 Muhammad and his followers emigrate from Mecca to Medina

632 Muhammad dies; Abu Bakr becomes the first caliph

642 Muslim defeat of the Persians marks end of the Sassanid empire

651 Publication of the Qur'an

661 Ali assassinated; split between Shi'a and Sunnis

711 Muslims defeat Visigothic kingdom in Spain

722–1492 Progressive loss of most of Spain to the Christian reconquest (*reconquista*)

750–1258 Abbasid caliphate

762 Baghdad founded by Abbasids

800–1300 Height of Muslim learning and creativity

869–883 Zanj (slave) revolts

950–1100 Entry on a large scale of Turks into the Middle East

1055 Baghdad falls to Seljuk Turks

1099–1187 Christian Crusaders hold Jerusalem

1258 Mongols capture Baghdad and kill the last Abbasid caliph

Muhammad's Rise as a Religious Leader

Much like the earliest sources for Jesus, the earliest account of the life of Muhammad (ca. 570–632) comes from oral traditions passed down among followers and not written down for several decades or generations. According to these traditions, Muhammad was orphaned at the age of six and brought up by his paternal uncle. As a young man, he became a merchant in the caravan trade that crisscrossed the Arabian desert. Later he entered the service of a wealthy widow, Khadija, and their subsequent marriage brought him financial security. Muhammad was extremely pious and devoted to contemplation. At about age forty, in a cave in the hills near Mecca where he was accustomed to praying, Muhammad had a vision of an angelic being who commanded him to preach the revelations that God would be sending him. Muhammad began to preach to the people of Mecca, urging them to give up their idols and to submit to the one indivisible God. During his lifetime, Muhammad's followers jotted down his revelations haphazardly on animal bones and skins (paper was very scarce) and committed them to memory. After his death, scribes organized the revelations into chapters. In 651 they published the version of them that Muslims consider authoritative, the **Qur'an** (kuh-RAHN). Muslims revere the Qur'an for its sacred message and for the beauty of its Arabic language.

For the first two or three centuries after the death of Muhammad, there was considerable debate about theological issues, such as the oneness of God, the role of angels, the prophets, the Scriptures, and Judgment Day, as well as about political issues, such as the authority of Muhammad and that of the caliph (KAY-lif; political ruler, successor to Muhammad). Likewise, religious scholars had to sort out and assess the **hadith** (huh-DEETH), collections of the sayings of or anecdotes about Muhammad. Controversies over the authenticity of particular sayings continued for centuries. Muhammad's example as revealed in the hadith became the legal basis for the conduct of every Muslim. The life of Muhammad, who is also known as the Prophet, provides the "normative example," or **Sunna**, for the Muslim believer. Once Islamic theology and law had developed into a religious system, Muhammad was revealed as the perfect man, the embodiment of

- **Qur'an** The sacred book of Islam.
- **hadith** Collections of the sayings of and anecdotes about Muhammad.
- **Sunna** An Arabic term meaning "trodden path." The term refers to the deeds and sayings of Muhammad, which constitute the obligatory example for Muslim life.

the will of God. Muhammad's example became central to the Muslim way of life.

The Tenets of Islam

Islam, the strict monotheistic faith that is based on the teachings of Muhammad, rests on the principle of the oneness and omnipotence of God (Allah). The word *Islam* means "surrender to God," and *Muslim* means "a person who submits." Muslims believe that Muhammad was the last of the prophets, completing the work begun by Abraham, Moses, and Jesus. According to the Qur'an, the coming of the final prophet was acknowledged by both Jewish and Christian authorities. The Qur'an asserts that the Prophet Muhammad descended from Adam, the first man, and that the Prophet Abraham built the Ka'ba. The Qur'an holds that the holy writings of both Jews and Christians represent divine revelation, but it claims that both Jews and Christians tampered with the books of God.

Muslims believe that they worship the same God as Jews and Christians. Monotheism had flourished in Middle Eastern Semitic and Persian cultures for centuries before Muhammad. Islam appropriates much of the Old and New Testaments of the Bible but often retells the narratives with significant shifts in meaning. Islam recognizes Moses's laws about circumcision, ritual bathing, and restrictions on eating pork and shellfish, and the Qur'an calls Christians "nearest in love" to Muslims. Muhammad insisted that he was not preaching a new message; rather, he was calling people back to the one true God, urging his contemporaries to reform their lives, to return to the faith of Abraham, the first monotheist.

Unlike the Old Testament, much of which is a historical narrative, or the New Testament, which is a collection of essays on the example and teachings of Jesus, the Qur'an is a collection of directives issued in God's name. Its organization is not strictly topical or chronological. To deal with seeming contradictions, later commentators explained the historical circumstances behind each revelation.

The Qur'an prescribes a strict code of moral behavior. A Muslim must recite the profession of faith in God and in Muhammad as his prophet: "There is no God but God, and Muhammad is his Prophet." A believer must also pray five times a day, fast and pray during the sacred month of Ramadan, make a pilgrimage (hajj) to the holy city of Mecca once during his or her lifetime, and give alms to the Muslim poor. These fundamental obligations are known as the **Five Pillars of Islam**.

Dome of the Rock, Jerusalem Completed in 691 and revered by Muslims as the site where Muhammad ascended to Heaven, the Dome of the Rock is the oldest surviving Islamic sanctuary and, after Mecca and Medina, the holiest place in Islam. Although influenced by Byzantine and Persian architecture, it also has distinctly Arabic features, such as the 700 feet of carefully selected Qur'anic inscriptions and vegetal motifs that grace the top of the outer walls. (imagebroker.net/SuperStock)

Islam forbids alcoholic beverages and gambling. It condemns usury in business — that is, lending money and charging the borrower interest — and taking advantage of market demand for products by charging high prices. Most scholars hold that compared with earlier Arab standards, the Qur'an set forth a strict sexual code. Muslim jurisprudence condemned licentious behavior by both men and women and specified the same punishments for both. (By contrast, contemporary Frankish law punished prostitutes, but not their clients.)

Islam warns about Judgment Day and the importance of the life to come. Like the Christian Judgment Day, on that day God will separate the saved and the damned. The Qur'an describes in detail the frightful tortures with which God will punish the damned and the heavenly rewards of the saved and the blessed.

Islamic States and Their Expansion

☐ What made possible the spread of Islam, and what forms of government were established to rule Muslim lands?

According to Muslim tradition, Muhammad's preaching at first did not appeal to many people. Legend has it that for the first three years he attracted only fourteen believers. In preaching a transformation of the social order and calling for the destruction of the idols in the Ka'ba, Muhammad challenged the power of the local elite and the pilgrimage-based local economy. As a result, the townspeople of Mecca turned against him, and he and his followers were forced to flee to Medina. This *hijra* (hih-JIGH-ruh), or emigration, occurred in 622, and Muslims later dated the beginning of their era from that event.

At Medina, Muhammad attracted increasing numbers of believers, and his teachings began to have an impact. His followers supported themselves by raiding caravans en route to Mecca, setting off a violent conflict between Mecca and Medina. After eight years of strife, Mecca capitulated. Thus, by the time he died in 632, Muhammad had welded together all the Bedouin tribes.

Muhammad displayed genius as both a political strategist and a religious teacher. He gave Arabs the idea of a unique and unified **umma** (UH-muh), or community, that consisted of all those whose primary identity and bond was a common religious faith and commitment, not a tribal tie. The umma was to be a religious and political community led by Muhammad for the achievement of God's will on earth. In the early

seventh century the southern Arab tribal confederations lacked cohesiveness and were constantly warring. The Islamic notion of an absolute higher authority transcended the boundaries of individual tribal units and fostered the political consolidation of the tribal confederations. All authority came from God through Muhammad. Within the umma, the law of God was discerned and applied through Muhammad.

Islam's Spread Beyond Arabia

After the Prophet's death, Islam spread far beyond Arabia (Map 9.1). In the sixth century two powerful empires divided the Middle East: the Greek-Byzantine empire centered at Constantinople and the Persian-Sassanid empire concentrated at Ctesiphon (near Baghdad in present-day Iraq). The Byzantine Empire stood for Hellenistic culture and championed Christianity (see Chapter 8). The Sassanid empire espoused Persian cultural traditions and favored the religious faith known as Zoroastrianism (see pages 61, 208). Although each empire maintained an official state religion, neither possessed religious unity. Both had sizable Jewish populations, and within Byzantium sects that Orthodox Greeks considered heretical — Monophysites and Nestorians — were politically divisive forces. During the fourth through sixth centuries these two empires fought each other fiercely, each trying to expand its territories at the expense of the other and to control and tax the rich trade coming from Arabia and the Indian Ocean region. Many peripheral societies were drawn into the conflict. The resulting disorder facilitated the growth of Muslim states.

The second and third successors of Muhammad, Umar (r. 634–644) and Uthman (r. 644–656), launched a two-pronged attack against the Byzantine and Sassanid empires. One force moved north from Arabia against the Byzantine provinces of Syria and Palestine, and the Greek armies there could not halt them (see page 207). From Syria, the Muslims conquered the rich province of Egypt, taking the commercial and intellectual hub of Alexandria in 642. Simultaneously, Arab armies swept into the Sassanid empire. The Muslim defeat of the Persians at Nihawand in 642 signaled the collapse of this empire (see Map 9.1).

The Muslims continued their drive eastward. In the mid-seventh century they occupied the province of Khurasan, where the city of Merv became the center

---

• **Five Pillars of Islam** The basic tenets of the Islamic faith; they include reciting a profession of faith in God and in Muhammad as God's prophet, praying five times daily, fasting and praying during the month of Ramadan, making a pilgrimage to Mecca once in one's lifetime, and contributing alms to the poor.

• **umma** A community of people who share a religious faith and commitment rather than a tribal tie.

Expansion of Islam
- Under Muhammad, 622–632
- 632–656
- 656–750
- 750–900
- Byzantine Empire, ca. 600
- Major battle or siege

▢ Mapping the Past

MAP 9.1 The Expansion of Islam, 622–900 The rapid expansion of Islam in a relatively short span of time testifies to the Arabs' superior fighting skills, religious zeal, and economic ambition as well as to their enemies' weakness. Plague, famine, and political troubles in Sassanid Persia contributed to Muslim victory there.

ANALYZING THE MAP Trace the routes of the spread of Islam by time period. How fast did it spread? How similar were the climates of the regions that became Muslim?

CONNECTIONS Which were the most powerful and populous of the societies that were absorbed into the Muslim world? What regions or societies were more resistant?

of Muslim control over eastern Persia and the base for campaigns farther east. By 700 the Muslims had crossed the Oxus River and swept toward Kabul, today the capital of Afghanistan. They then penetrated Kazakhstan and then seized Tashkent, one of the oldest cities in Central Asia. The clash of Muslim horsemen with a Chinese army at the Talas River in 751 marked the farthest Islamic penetration into Central Asia (see Map 9.1). From southern Persia, a Muslim force marched into the Indus Valley in northern India and in 713 founded an Islamic community there. Beginning in the eleventh century Muslim dynasties from Ghazni in Afghanistan carried Islam deeper into the Indian subcontinent (see page 349).

Likewise, to the west Arab forces moved across North Africa and crossed the Strait of Gibraltar. In 711

at the Guadalete River they easily defeated the Visigothic kingdom of Spain. A few Christian princes supported by Merovingian rulers held out in the Cantabrian Mountains, but the Muslims controlled most of Spain until the thirteenth century. Advances into France were stopped in 732 when the Franks defeated Arab armies in a battle near the city of Tours, and Muslim occupation of parts of southern France did not last long.

Reasons for the Spread of Islam

By the beginning of the eleventh century the crescent of Islam flew from the Iberian heartlands to northern India. How can this rapid and remarkable expansion be explained? The internal view of Muslim historians was that God supported the Islamic faith and aided its spread. The external, especially European, view used to be that religious fervor was the main driving force; the Muslim concept of jihad (JEE-hahd), or struggle, seemed the key element. The Qur'an does not precisely explain jihad. Some Muslim scholars hold that it signifies the individual struggle against sin and toward perfection on "the straight path" of Islam. Others claim that jihad has a social and communal implication — a militancy as part of a holy war against unbelievers living in territories outside the control of the Muslim community. The Qur'an states, "Fight those in the way of God who fight you" (Qur'an 4:74).[1] Just as Christians have a missionary duty to spread their faith, so Muslims have the obligation, as individuals and as a community, to extend the power of Islam.

Today, few historians emphasize religious zeal alone but rather point to a combination of Arab military advantages and the political weaknesses of their opponents. The Byzantine and Sassanid empires had just fought a grueling century-long war and had also been weakened by the plague, which hit urban, stationary populations harder than nomadic populations. Equally important are the military strength and tactics of the Arabs. For example, rather than scattering as landlords of peasant farmers over conquered lands, Arab soldiers remained together in garrison cities, where their Arab ethnicity, tribal organization, religion, and military success set them apart. All soldiers were registered in the **diwān** (dih-WAHN), an administrative organ adopted from the Persians or Byzantines. Soldiers received a monthly ration of food for themselves and their families and an annual cash stipend. In return, they had to be available for military service. Fixed salaries, regular pay, and the lure of battlefield booty attracted rugged tribesmen from Arabia. Except for the Berbers of North Africa, whom the Arabs could not pacify, Muslim armies initially did not seek to convert or recruit warriors from conquered peoples. In later campaigns to the east, many recruits were recent converts to Islam from Christian, Persian, and Berber backgrounds. The assurance of army wages secured the loyalty of these very diverse men.

The Arab commanders recognized the economic benefits of capturing the major cities of the region. Arab caravans frequented the market towns of southern Syria and the rich commercial centers of the north, such as Edessa, Aleppo, and Damascus. Syria's economic prosperity probably attracted the Muslims, and perhaps Muhammad saw the land as a potential means of support for the poor who flooded into Medina. Syria also contained sites important to the faith: Jerusalem, where Jesus and other prophets mentioned in the Qur'an had lived and preached, and Hebron, the traditional burial place of Abraham, the father of monotheism.

How did the conquered peoples make sense of their new subordinate situations? Jews and Christians tried to minimize the damage done to their former status and played down the gains of their new masters. Whereas Christians regarded the conquering Arabs as God's punishment for their sins, Jews saw the Arabs as instruments for their deliverance from Greek and Sassanid persecution.

While the conquered peoples figured out their situations as subordinates, Muslims had to figure out how to rule their new territories after Muhammad's death. The government they established is called the caliphate.

The Caliphate and the Split Between Shi'a and Sunni Alliances

When Muhammad died in 632, he left a large Muslim umma, but this community stood in danger of disintegrating into separate tribal groups. How was the vast empire that came into existence within one hundred years of his death to be governed? Neither the Qur'an nor the Sunna offered guidance for the succession.

In this crisis, according to tradition, a group of Muhammad's ablest followers elected Abu Bakr (573–634), a close supporter of the Prophet and his father-in-law, and hailed him as caliph, a term combining the ideas of leader, successor, and deputy (of the Prophet). This election marked the victory of the concept of a universal community of Muslim believers.

Because the law of the Qur'an was to guide the community, there had to be an authority to enforce the law, and the caliph assumed this responsibility. Muslim teaching holds that the law is paramount. God is the sole source of the law, and the ruler is bound to obey the law. Government exists not to make law but to enforce it. Islam draws no distinction between the temporal and spiritual domains: social law is a basic strand in the fabric of comprehensive religious law. Religious leaders and institutions nevertheless act as a check on political leaders who drift too far from religious standards. The creation of Islamic law in an institutional sense took three or four centuries and is one of the great achievements of medieval Islam.

In the two years of his rule (632–634), Abu Bakr governed on the basis of his personal prestige within the Muslim umma. He sent out military expeditions, collected taxes, dealt with tribes on behalf of the entire community, and led the community in prayer. Gradually, under Abu Bakr's first three successors, Umar, Uthman, and Ali (r. 656–661), the caliphate emerged as an institution. Umar succeeded in exerting his

---

• **diwān** A unit of government.

authority over the Bedouin tribes involved in ongoing conquests. Uthman asserted the right of the caliph to protect the economic interests of the entire umma. Also, Uthman's publication of the definitive text of the Qur'an showed his concern for the unity of the umma. However, Uthman was from a Mecca family that had resisted the Prophet until the capitulation of Mecca in 630, and he aroused resentment when he gave favors to members of his family. Opposition to Uthman coalesced around Ali, and when Uthman was assassinated in 656, Ali was chosen to succeed him.

The issue of responsibility for Uthman's murder raised the question of whether Ali's accession was legitimate. Uthman's cousin Mu'awiya, a member of the Umayyad family who had built a power base as governor of Syria, refused to recognize Ali as caliph. In the ensuing civil war, Ali was assassinated, and Mu'awiya (r. 661–680) assumed the caliphate. Mu'awiya founded the Umayyad Dynasty and shifted the capital of the Islamic state from Medina in Arabia to Damascus in Syria. Although electing caliphs remained the Islamic ideal, beginning with Mu'awiya, the office of caliph increasingly became hereditary. Two successive dynasties, the Umayyad (661–750) and the Abbasid (750–1258), held the caliphate.

From its inception the caliphate rested on the theoretical principle that Muslim political and religious unity transcended tribalism. Mu'awiya sought to enhance the power of the caliphate by making tribal leaders dependent on him for concessions and special benefits. At the same time, his control of a loyal and well-disciplined army enabled him to take the caliphate in an authoritarian direction. Through intimidation he forced the tribal leaders to accept his son Yazid as his heir, thereby establishing the dynastic principle of succession. By distancing himself from a simple life within the umma and withdrawing into the palace that he built at Damascus, and by surrounding himself with symbols and ceremony, Mu'awiya laid the foundations for an elaborate caliphal court. Many of Mu'awiya's innovations were designed to protect him from assassination. A new official, the *hajib*, or chamberlain, restricted access to the caliph, who received visitors while he was seated on a throne surrounded by bodyguards.

The assassination of Ali and the assumption of the caliphate by Mu'awiya had another profound consequence. It gave rise to a fundamental division in the umma and in Muslim theology. Ali had claimed the caliphate on the basis of family ties — he was Muhammad's cousin and son-in-law. When Ali was murdered, his followers argued that Ali had been the Prophet's designated successor — partly because of the blood tie, partly because Muhammad had designated Ali **imam** (ih-MAHM), or leader in community prayer. These supporters of Ali were called **Shi'a** (SHEE-uh), meaning "supporters" or "partisans" of Ali (Shi'a are also known as Shi'ites). In succeeding generations, opponents of the Umayyad Dynasty emphasized their blood descent from Ali and claimed to possess divine knowledge that Muhammad had given them as his heirs.

Those who accepted Mu'awiya as caliph insisted that the central issue was adhering to the practices and beliefs of the umma based on the precedents of the Prophet. They came to be called **Sunnis** (SOO-neez), which derived from *Sunna* (examples from Muhammad's life). When a situation arose for which the Qur'an offered no solution, Sunni scholars searched for a precedent in the Sunna, which gained an authority comparable to the Qur'an itself.

Both Sunnis and Shi'a maintain that authority within Islam lies first in the Qur'an and then in the Sunna. Who interprets these sources? Shi'a claim that the imam does, for he is invested with divine grace and insight. Sunnis insist that interpretation comes from the consensus of the **ulama**, the group of religious scholars.

Throughout the Umayyad period the Shi'a constituted a major source of discontent. They condemned the Umayyads as worldly and sensual rulers, in contrast to the pious true successors of Muhammad. The Abbasid (uh-BA-suhd) clan, which based its claim to the caliphate on the descent of Abbas, Muhammad's uncle, exploited the situation. The Abbasids agitated the Shi'a, encouraged dissension among tribal factions, and contrasted Abbasid piety with the pleasure-loving style of the Umayyads.

The Abbasid Caliphate

In 747 Abu' al-Abbas led a rebellion against the Umayyads, and in 750 he won general recognition as caliph. Damascus had served as the headquarters of Umayyad rule. Abu' al-Abbas's successor, al-Mansur (r. 754–775), founded the city of Baghdad in 762 and made it his capital. Thus the geographical center of the caliphate shifted eastward to former Sassanid territories. The first three Abbasid caliphs crushed their opponents, turned against many of their supporters, and created a new ruling elite drawn from newly converted Persian families that had traditionally served the ruler. The Abbasid revolution established a basis for rule and

• **imam** The leader in community prayer.
• **Shi'a** Arabic term meaning "supporters of Ali"; they make up one of the two main divisions of Islam.
• **Sunnis** Members of the larger of the two main divisions of Islam; the division between Sunnis and Shi'a began in a dispute about succession to Muhammad, but over time many differences in theology developed.
• **ulama** A group of religious scholars whom Sunnis trust to interpret the Qur'an and the Sunna.

citizenship more cosmopolitan and Islamic than the narrow, elitist, and Arab basis that had characterized Umayyad government.

The Abbasids worked to identify their rule with Islam. They patronized the ulama, built mosques, and supported the development of Islamic scholarship. Moreover, during the Abbasid caliphate, provincial governors gradually won semi-independent power, whereas under the Umayyads the Muslim state had been a federation of regional and tribal armies. Although at first Muslims represented only a small minority of the conquered peoples, Abbasid rule provided the religious-political milieu in which Islam gained, over time, the allegiance of the vast majority of the populations from Spain to Afghanistan.

The Abbasids also borrowed heavily from Persian culture. Following Persian tradition, the Abbasid caliphs claimed to rule by divine right, as reflected in the change of their title from "successor of the Prophet" to "deputy of God." A majestic palace with hundreds of attendants and elaborate court ceremonies deliberately isolated the caliph from the people he ruled. Subjects had to bow before the caliph, kissing the ground, a symbol of his absolute power.

Under the third caliph, Harun al-Rashid (r. 786–809), Baghdad emerged as a flourishing commercial, artistic, and scientific center—the greatest city in Islam and one of the most cosmopolitan cities in the world. Its population of about a million people—an astoundingly large size for preindustrial times—created a huge demand for goods and services, and Baghdad became an entrepôt (trading center) for textiles, slaves, and foodstuffs coming from Oman, East Africa, and India. The city also became intellectually influential. Harun al-Rashid organized the translation of Greek medical and philosophical texts. As part of this effort the Christian scholar Hunayn ibn Ishaq (808–873) translated Galen's medical works into Arabic and made Baghdad a center for the study and practice of medicine. Likewise, impetus was given to the study of astronomy, and through a program of astronomical observations, Muslim astronomers sought to correct and complement Ptolemaic astronomy, which held that the earth is a stationary object at the center of the universe. Above all, studies in Qur'anic textual analysis, history, poetry, law, and philosophy—all in Arabic—reflected the development of a distinctly Islamic literary and scientific culture.

An important innovation of the Abbasids was the use of slaves as soldiers. The caliph al-Mu'tasim (r. 833–842) acquired several thousand Turkish slaves who were converted to Islam and employed in military service. Scholars have offered varied explanations for this practice: that the use of slave soldiers was a response to a manpower shortage; that as highly skilled horsemen, the Turks had military skills superior to those

Abbasid Wooden Doors These ninth-century wooden doors are thought to come from Samarra, a city about 125 miles upstream from Baghdad, which briefly served as the capital in the ninth century. (Image copyright © The Metropolitan Museum of Art/Art Resource, NY)

of the Arabs and other peoples; and that al-Mu'tasim felt he could trust the Turks more than the Arabs, Persians, Khurasans, and other recruits. In any case, slave soldiers—later including Slavs, Indians, and sub-Saharan blacks—became a standard feature of Muslim armies in the Middle East down to the twentieth century.

Administration of the Islamic Territories

The Islamic conquests brought into being a new imperial system. The Muslims adopted the patterns of administration used by the Byzantines in Egypt and Syria and by the Sassanids in Persia. Specifically, Arab **emirs**, or governors, were appointed and given overall responsibility for public order, maintenance of the armed forces, and tax collection. Below them, experienced native officials — Greeks, Syrians, and Copts (Egyptian Christians) — remained in office. Thus there was continuity with previous administrations.

The Umayyad caliphate witnessed the further development of the imperial administration. At the head stood the caliph, who led military campaigns against unbelievers. Theoretically, he had the ultimate responsibility for the interpretation of the sacred law. In practice, however, the ulama interpreted the law as revealed in the Qur'an and the Sunna. In the course of time, the ulama's interpretations constituted a rich body of law, the **shari'a** (shuh-REE-uh), which covered social, criminal, political, commercial, and religious matters. The ulama enjoyed great prestige in the Muslim community and were consulted by the caliph on difficult legal and spiritual matters. The *qadis* (KAH-dees), or judges, who were well versed in the sacred law, carried out the judicial functions of the state. Nevertheless, Muslim law prescribed that all people have access to the caliph, and he set aside special times for hearing petitions and for directly redressing grievances.

The central administrative organ was the diwān, which collected the taxes that paid soldiers' salaries (see page 239) and financed charitable and public works, such as aid to the poor and the construction of mosques, irrigation works, and public baths. Another important undertaking was a relay network established to convey letters and intelligence reports rapidly between the capital and distant outposts. The relay system made it possible for the caliph to respond quickly when news reached him of revolts by emirs and other officials far from the capital.

The early Abbasid period witnessed considerable economic expansion and population growth, complicating the work of government. New and specialized departments emerged, each with a hierarchy of officials. The most important new official was the **vizier** (vuh-ZEER), a position that the Abbasids adopted from the Persians. The vizier was the caliph's chief assistant, advising the caliph on matters of general policy, supervising the bureaucratic administration, and, under the caliph, overseeing the army, the provincial governors, and relations with foreign governments. Depending on the caliph's personality, viziers could acquire extensive power, and some used their offices for personal gain. Although some viziers' careers ended with their execution, there were always candidates seeking the job.

Ivory Chest of Pamplona, Spain The court of the Spanish Umayyads prized small, intricately carved ivory chests, often made in a royal workshop and used to store precious perfumes. This exquisite side panel depicts an eleventh-century caliph flanked by two attendants. An inscription on the front translates as "In the Name of God. Blessings from God, goodwill, and happiness." (Museo Navarra, Pamplona/Institut Amatller d'Art Hispanic)

Fragmentation and Military Challenges, 900–1400

☐ How were the Muslim lands governed from 900 to 1400, and what new challenges did rulers face?

In theory, the caliph and his central administration governed the whole empire, but in practice, the many parts of the empire enjoyed considerable local independence. As long as public order was maintained and taxes were forwarded, the central government rarely interfered. At the same time, the enormous distance between many provinces and the imperial capital, and the long time it took to travel this distance by horse or camel, made it difficult for the caliph to prevent provinces from breaking away. Local, ethnic, or tribal loyalties, combined with fierce ambition, led to the creation of regional dynasties in much of the Islamic world, including Spain, Persia, Central Asia, northern India, and Egypt. None of these states repudiated Islam, but they did stop sending tax revenues to Baghdad. Moreover, most states became involved with costly wars against their neighbors in their attempts to expand. Sometimes these conflicts were worsened by Sunni-Shi'a antagonisms. All these developments, as well as invasions by Turks and Mongols, posed challenges to central Muslim authority.

Breakaway Territories and Shi'a Gains

One of the first territories to break away from the Baghdad-centered caliphate was Spain. In 755 an Umayyad prince who had escaped death at the hands of the triumphant Abbasids and fled to Spain set up an independent regime at Córdoba (see Map 9.1). Other territories soon followed. In 800 the emir in Tunisia in North Africa set himself up as an independent ruler and refused to place the caliph's name on the local coinage. And in 820 Tahir, the son of a slave, was rewarded with the governorship of Khurasan because he had supported the caliphate. Once he took office, Tahir ruled independently of Baghdad, not even mentioning the caliph's name in the traditional Friday prayers in recognition of caliphal authority.

In 946 a Shi'a Iranian clan overran Iraq and occupied Baghdad. The caliph was forced to recognize the clan's leader as commander-in-chief and to allow the celebration of Shi'a festivals — though the caliph and most of the people were Sunnis. A year later the caliph was accused of plotting against his new masters, snatched from his throne, dragged through the streets,

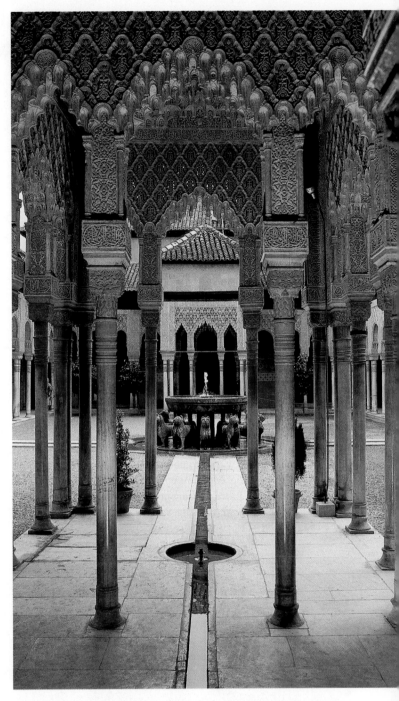

The Patio of the Lions at Alhambra, Fourteenth Century
The fortress that the Moorish rulers of Spain built at Granada is considered one of the masterpieces of Andalusian art, notable for the fine carving of geometrical designs and Arabic calligraphy. (George Holton/Photo Researchers, Inc.)

- **emirs** Arab governors who were given overall responsibility for public order, maintenance of the armed forces, and tax collection.
- **shari'a** Muslim law, which covers social, criminal, political, commercial, and religious matters.
- **vizier** The caliph's chief assistant.

and blinded. Blinding was a practice adopted from the Byzantines as a way of rendering a ruler incapable of carrying out his duties. This incident marked the practical collapse of the Abbasid caliphate. Abbasid caliphs, however, remained as puppets of a series of military commanders and symbols of Muslim unity until the Mongols killed the last Abbasid caliph in 1258 (see page 245).

In another Shi'a advance, the Fatimids, a Shi'a dynasty that claimed descent from Muhammad's daughter Fatima, conquered North Africa then expanded into the Abbasid province of Egypt, founding the city of Cairo as their capital in 969. For the next century or so, Shi'a were in ascendancy in much of the western Islamic world.

The Ascendancy of the Turks

In the mid-tenth century the Turks began to enter the Islamic world in large numbers. First appearing in Mongolia in the sixth century, groups of Turks gradually appeared across the grasslands of Eurasia. Skilled horsemen, they became prime targets for Muslim slave raids, as they made good slave soldiers. Once they understood that Muslims could not be captured for slaves, more and more of them converted to Islam (and often became *ghazi*, frontier raiders, who attacked unconverted Turks to capture slaves). The first to convert accepted Sunni Islam near Bukhara, then a great Persian commercial and intellectual center.

In the 1020s and 1030s Seljuk Turks overran Persia then pushed into Iraq and Syria. Baghdad fell to them on December 18, 1055, and the caliph became a puppet of the Turkish sultan—literally, "he with authority." The Turkic elite rapidly gave up pastoralism and took up the sedentary lifestyle of the people they governed.

The Fatimid Caliphate, 909–1171

The Turks brought badly needed military strength to the Islamic world. They played a major part in recovering Jerusalem after it was held for nearly a century, from 1099 to 1187, by the European Crusaders (who had fought to take Christian holy lands back from the Muslims; see pages 405–408). They also were important in preventing the later Crusades from accomplishing much. Moreover, the Turks became staunch Sunnis and led a campaign against Shi'a.

The influx of Turks from 950 to 1100 also helped provide a new expansive dynamic. At the battle of Manzikert in 1071, Seljuk Turks broke through Byzantine border defenses, opening Anatolia to Turkish migration. Over the next couple of centuries, perhaps a million Turks entered the area—including bands of ghazis and dervishes (Sufi brotherhoods). Seljuk Turks set up the Sultanate of Rum in Anatolia, which lasted until the Mongols invaded in 1243. With the Turks came many learned men from the Persian-speaking East. Over time, many of the Christians in Anatolia converted to Islam and became fluent in Turkish.

The Mongol Invasions

In the early thirteenth century the Mongols arrived in the Middle East. Originally from the grasslands of Mongolia, in 1206 they proclaimed Chinggis Khan (1162–1227) as their leader, and he welded Mongol, Tatar, and Turkish tribes into a strong confederation that rapidly subdued neighboring settled societies (see pages 336–345). After conquering much of north China, the Mongols swept westward, leaving a trail of blood and destruction. They used terror as a weapon, and out of fear many cities surrendered without a fight.

In 1219–1221, when the Mongols first reached the Islamic lands, the areas from Persia through the Central Asian cities of Herat and Samarkand were part of the kingdom of Khwarizm. The ruler—the son of a Turkish slave who had risen to governor of a province—was a conqueror himself, having conquered much of Persia. He had the audacity to execute Chinggis's envoy, and Chinggis retaliated with a force of a hundred thousand soldiers that sacked city after city, often slaughtering the residents or enslaving them and sending them to Mongolia. Millions are said to have died. The irrigation systems that were needed for agriculture in this dry region had been neglected for some time, and with the Mongol invasions suffered a fatal blow.

The Seljuk Empire in 1000

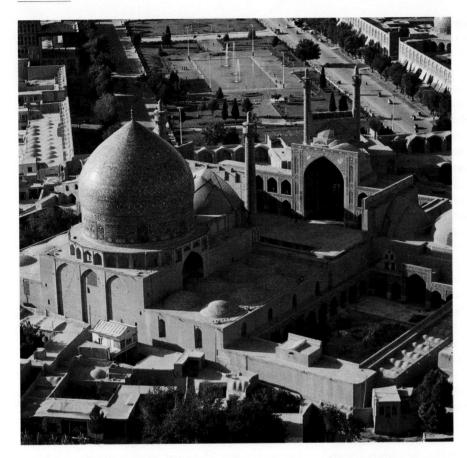

Great Mosque at Isfahan in Persia
Begun in the late eighth century and added to over the centuries, the Great Mosque in Isfahan is one of the masterpieces of Islamic architecture. The huge dome and the vaulted niches around the courtyard are covered with blue, turquoise, white, and yellow tile. (© Roger Wood/Corbis)

Not many Mongol forces were left in Persia after the campaign of 1219–1221, and another army, sent in 1237, captured the Persian city of Isfahan. In 1251 the decision was taken to push farther west. Chinggis Khan's grandson, Hülegü (1217–1265) led an attack on the Abbasids in Baghdad, sacking and burning the city and killing the last Abbasid caliph in 1258. The fall of Damascus followed in 1260. Mamluk soldiers from Egypt, however, were able to withstand the Mongols and win a major victory at Ayn Jalut in Syria, which has been credited with saving Egypt and the Muslim lands in North Africa and perhaps Spain. At any rate, the desert ecology of the region did not provide suitable support for the Mongol armies, which required five horses for each soldier. Moreover, in 1260 the Great Khan (ruler of Mongolia and China) died, and the top Mongol generals withdrew to Mongolia for the selection of the next Great Khan.

Hülegü and his descendants ruled the central Muslim lands (referred to as the Il-Khanate) for eighty years. In 1295 his descendant Ghazan embraced Islam and worked for the revival of Muslim culture. As the Turks had done earlier, the Mongols, once converted, injected new vigor into the faith and spirit of Islam. In the Il-Khanate, the Mongols governed through Persian viziers and native financial officials.

Muslim Society: The Life of the People

☐ What social distinctions were important in Muslim society?

When the Prophet appeared, Arab society consisted of independent Bedouin tribal groups loosely held together by loyalty to a strong leader and by the belief that all members of a tribe were descended from a common ancestor. Heads of families elected the *sheik,* or tribal chief. He was usually chosen from among elite warrior families who believed their bloodlines made them superior. According to the Qur'an, however, birth counted for nothing; piety was the only criterion for honor: "O ye folk, verily we have created you male and female. . . . Verily the most honourable of you in the sight of God is the most pious of you."[2] The idea of social equality was a basic Muslim doctrine.

When Muhammad defined social equality, he was thinking about equality among Muslims alone. But even among Muslims, a sense of pride in ancestry could not be destroyed by a stroke of the pen. Claims based on birth remained strong among the first Muslims, and after Islam spread outside of Arabia, full-blooded Arab tribesmen regarded themselves as superior to foreign converts.

The Social Hierarchy

In the Umayyad period, Muslim society was distinctly hierarchical. At the top of the hierarchy were the caliph's household and the ruling Arab Muslims. Descended from Bedouin tribespeople and composed of warriors, veterans, governing officials, and town settlers, this class constituted the ruling elite. Because birth continued to determine membership, it was more a caste than a class. It was also a relatively small group, greatly outnumbered by Muslim villagers and country people.

Converts constituted the second class in Islamic society, one that grew slowly over time. Converts to Islam had to attach themselves to one of the Arab tribes in a subordinate capacity. Many resented having to do this, since they believed they represented a culture superior to that of Arab tribespeople. From the Muslim converts eventually came the members of the commercial and learned professions — merchants, traders, teachers, doctors, artists, and interpreters of the shari'a. Second-class citizenship led some Muslim converts to adopt Shi'ism (see page 240). Even so, over the centuries, Berber, Copt, Persian, Aramaean, and other converts to Islam intermarried with their Muslim conquerors. Gradually, assimilation united peoples of various ethnic backgrounds.

Dhimmis (zih-MEEZ) — including Jews, Christians, and Zoroastrians — formed the third stratum. Considered "protected peoples" because they worshipped only one God, they were allowed to practice their religions, maintain their houses of worship, and conduct their business affairs as long as they gave unequivocal recognition to Muslim political supremacy and paid a small tax. Because many Jews and Christians were well educated, they were often appointed to high positions in provincial capitals as well as in Damascus and Baghdad. Restrictions placed on Christians and Jews were not severe, and outbursts of violence against them were rare. However, their social position deteriorated during the Crusades and the Mongol invasions, when there was a general rise of religious loyalties. At those times, Muslims suspected the dhimmis, often rightly, of collaborating with the enemies of Islam.

How did the experience of Jews under Islam compare with that of Jews living in Christian Europe? Recent scholarship shows that in Europe Jews were first marginalized in the Christian social order then completely expelled from it. In Islam Jews, though marginalized, participated fully in commercial and professional activities, some attaining economic equality with their Muslim counterparts. (See "Viewpoints: Jews in Muslim Lands," page 247.) The seventeenth Sura (chapter) of the Qur'an, titled Bani Isra'il, "The Children of Israel," accords to the Jews a special respect because they were "the people of the Book." Also, Islamic culture was urban and commercial and gave the merchant considerable respect; medieval Christian culture was basically rural and agricultural and did not revere the businessperson.

Slavery

Slavery had long existed in the ancient Middle East, and the Qur'an accepted slavery much the way the Old and New Testaments did. But the Qur'an prescribes just and humane treatment of slaves, saying that a master should feed and clothe his slaves adequately; give them moderate, not excessive, work; and not punish them severely. The Qur'an also explicitly encourages the freeing of slaves and urges owners whose slaves ask for their freedom to give them the opportunity to buy it. In fact, the freeing of slaves was thought to pave the way to paradise.

Muslim expansion ensured a steady flow of slaves captured in war. The great Muslim commander Musa ibn Nusayr (640–716), himself the son of a Christian enslaved in Iraq, is reputed to have taken 300,000 prisoners of war in his North African campaigns and 30,000 virgins from the Visigothic nobility of Spain. (These numbers are surely inflated, as most medieval numbers are.) Every soldier, from general to private, had a share of slaves from captured prisoners.

Women slaves worked as cooks, cleaners, laundresses, and nursemaids. A few performed as singers, musicians, dancers, and reciters of poetry. Many female slaves also served as concubines. Not only rulers but also high officials and rich merchants owned many concubines. Down the economic ladder, artisans and tradesmen often had a few concubines who assumed domestic as well as sexual duties.

According to tradition, the seclusion of women in a harem protected their virtue (see page 252), and when men had the means the harem was secured by eunuch (castrated) guards. The use of eunuch guards seems to have been a practice Muslims adopted from the Byzantines and Persians. Early Muslim law forbade castration, so in the early Islamic period Muslims secured eunuchs from European, African, and Central Asian slave markets. In contrast to China, where only the emperor could have eunuch servants, the well-to-do in the Muslim world could purchase them to guard their harems.

• **dhimmis** A term meaning "protected peoples"; they included Jews, Christians, and Zoroastrians.

Viewpoints

Jews in Muslim Lands

- *Under Islam, Jews were considered protected people whose religion was tolerated as long as they abided by rules such as refraining from proselytizing. Often Jews rose to high positions in government service. The two documents below, both written by Jews, show some of the possibilities open to Jews as well as some of the difficulties. The first document is one of the thousands of medieval Jewish documents found in the nineteenth century at a synagogue in Cairo. It is addressed to Abu Sad al-Tustari (d. 1047), a Jew then powerful at court through his connection to the caliph's mother. The second document was written by the eminent Jewish philosopher Maimonides (1137 or 1138–1204). In it he explains how busy he was kept as a physician by both the court and the populace at large after he moved from Spain to Egypt.*

Letter from the Congregation of a Synagogue in Tripoli to Abu Sad al-Tustari

We the entire congregation of Tripoli send our greetings to our Lord, the honorable Elder, and ask the Lord our God, Who hears the cry of the downtrodden, to grant you eternal life. We wish to inform your Excellency that we are in great distress because we have no place to pray. Everywhere else, the synagogues have been returned to the House of Israel—except in our town. The reason for this is that our synagogue was converted into a mosque. We are, therefore, petitioning our Master to show us kindness with an edict from the Government permitting us to build for ourselves a synagogue—as has been done everywhere else—on one of our ruined properties on which servants of the ruler dwell without paying any rent. We may point out to our Lord that this very year the congregation in [the port city of] Jubayl rebuilt their synagogue, and no Muslim said anything. We also wish to inform our Lord that we will pay an annual rent for the place to the Gentiles.

There is no need to mention that this is a matter which would be pleasing to God. Your welfare and blessings will increase forever. Selah.

May salvation come swiftly.

Maimonides, On His Life as a Jewish Physician in Cairo

I live in Fustat, and the king lives in Cairo, and between the two places there is a distance of [about 1½ miles]. With the king I have a very heavy program. It is impossible for me not to see him first thing every day. If he suffers any indisposition, or if any of his sons or concubines falls sick, I cannot leave Cairo, and I spend most of my day in the palace. It may also happen that one or two of his officers fall sick, and I must attend to them. In short, I go to Cairo early every morning, and if there is no mishap and nothing new, I return to Fustat in the afternoon, and certainly not before then. By then I am hungry, and I find the anterooms all filled with people: Gentiles and Jews, great and small, judges and bailiffs, friends and enemies, a mixed multitude, who await the moment of my return. I dismount from my beast and wash my hands and go to them to soothe them and placate them and beg them to excuse me and wait while I eat a quick meal, my only one in the whole day. Then I go out to treat them and write prescriptions and instructions for their illnesses. They come and go without a break until night, and sometimes, I swear by my faith in the Torah, until two hours of the night or more. I talk to them and instruct them and converse with them, lying on my back from exhaustion. By nightfall I am so worn out that I cannot speak. In fine, no Jew can speak to me or keep company with me or have private conversation with me except on the Sabbath.

Sources: Norman A. Stillman, *The Jews of Arab Lands: A History and Source Book* (Philadelphia: The Jewish Publication Society of America, 1979), p. 204: Reprinted with permission from the Jewish Publication Society. © 1979, Norman Stillman; Bernard Lewis, ed. and trans., *Islam from the Prophet Muhammad to the Capture of Constantinople* (Oxford University Press, 1987), pp. 228–229. Used by permission of Oxford University Press, Inc.

QUESTIONS FOR ANALYSIS

1. Why would a Jewish community member appeal to a Jew with connections at court rather than to the ruler himself?

2. How does Maimonides talk about himself? Does he see his court appointment as an honor or a burden?

3. Taking these two documents together, what would you infer about Jewish communities under Islam?

Slaves Dancing A few women slaves performed as dancers, singers, and musicians, usually before an elite audience of rulers, officials, and wealthy merchants. This reconstructed wall-painting from the ninth century adorned a harem in a royal palace in Samarra. (Bildarchiv Preussischer Kulturbesitz/Art Resource, NY)

Muslims also employed eunuchs as secretaries, tutors, and commercial agents, possibly because eunuchs were said to be more manageable and dependable than men with ordinary desires. Male slaves, eunuchs or not, were also set to work as longshoremen on the docks, as oarsmen on ships, in construction crews, in workshops, and in gold and silver mines.

As already noted, male slaves also fought as soldiers. Any free person could buy a slave, but only a ruler could own military slaves. In the ninth century the rulers of Tunisia formed a special corps of black military slaves, and at the end of that century the Tulunid rulers of Egypt built an army of 24,000 white and 45,000 black slaves. The Fatimid rulers of Egypt (969–1171) raised large black battalions, and a Persian visitor to Cairo between 1046 and 1049 estimated an army of 100,000 slaves, of whom 30,000 were black soldiers.

Slavery in the Islamic world differed in at least two fundamental ways from the slavery later practiced in the Americas. First, race had no particular connection to slavery among Muslims, who were as ready to take slaves from Europe as from Africa. Second, slavery in the Islamic world was not the basis for plantation agriculture, as it was in the southern United States, the Caribbean, and Brazil in the eighteenth and nineteenth centuries. True, in the tenth century large numbers of black slaves worked on date plantations in northeastern Arabia. But massive revolts of black slaves called

Zanj from East Africa (see pages 288–289), provoked by mercilessly harsh labor conditions in the salt flats and on the sugar and cotton plantations of southwestern Persia, erupted in 869. Gathering momentum, the Zanj captured the rich cities of Ahwaz, Basra, and Wasit and threatened Baghdad. Only the strenuous efforts of the commander of the caliph's armies, which were composed of Turkish slaves and included naval as well as land forces, halted and gradually crushed the Zanj in 883. The long and destructive Zanj revolt ended the Muslim experiment with plantation agriculture.

Slavery was rarely hereditary in the Muslim world. Most slaves who were taken from non-Muslim peoples later converted, which often led to emancipation. The children of female slaves by Muslim masters were by definition Muslim and thus free. To give Muslim slavery the most positive possible interpretation, one could say that it provided a means to fill certain socioeconomic and military needs and that it assimilated rather than segregated outsiders.

Women in Classical Islamic Society

Before Islam, Arab tribal law gave women virtually no legal status. Girls were sold into marriage by their guardians, and their husbands could terminate the union at will. Also, women had virtually no property or succession rights. Seen from this perspective, the Qur'an sought to improve the social position of women.

The hadith — records of what Muhammad said and did, and what believers in the first two centuries after his death believed he said and did (see page 235) — provide information about the Prophet's wives. Some hadith portray them as subject to common human frailties, such as jealousy; others report miraculous events in their lives. Most hadith describe the wives as "mothers of the believers" — models of piety and righteousness whose every act illustrates their commitment to promoting God's order on earth by personal example.

Although the hadith usually depict women in terms of moral virtue, domesticity, and saintly ideals, they also show some prominent women in political roles. For example, Aisha, daughter of the first caliph and probably Muhammad's favorite wife, played a leading role in rallying support for the movement opposing Ali, who succeeded Uthman in 656 (see page 240). Likewise, Umm Salama, a member of a wealthy and prominent clan in Mecca, first supported Ali, then switched sides and supported the Umayyads.[3] (See "Listening to the Past: Abu Hamid Al-Ghazali, The Etiquette of Marriage," page 250.)

The Qur'an, like the religious writings of other traditions, represents moral precept rather than social practice, and the texts are open to different interpretations. Modern scholars tend to agree that the Islamic sacred book intended women to be the spiritual and sexual equals of men and gave them considerable economic rights. In the early Umayyad period, moreover, women played active roles in the religious, economic, and political life of the community. They owned property. They had freedom of movement and traveled widely. They participated with men in public religious rituals and observances. But this Islamic ideal of women and men having equal value to the community did not last, and, as Islamic society changed, the precepts of the Qur'an were interpreted in more patriarchal ways.

By the Abbasid period, the status of women had declined. The practices of the Byzantine and Persian lands that had been conquered, including seclusion of women, were absorbed. The supply of slave women increased substantially. Some scholars speculate that as wealth replaced ancestry as the criterion of social status, men more and more viewed women as possessions, as a form of wealth.

Men were also seen as dominant in their marriages. The Qur'an states that "men are in charge of women because Allah hath made the one to excel the other, and because they (men) spend of their property (for the support of women). So good women are obedient, guarding in secret that which Allah hath guarded."[4] A tenth-century interpreter, Abu Ja'far Muhammad ibn-Jarir al-Tabari, commented on that passage this way:

> Men are in charge of their women with respect to disciplining (or chastising) them, and to providing them with restrictive guidance concerning their duties toward God and themselves (i.e., the men), by virtue of that by which God has given excellence (or preference) to the men over their wives: i.e., the payment of their dowers to them, spending of their wealth on them, and providing for them in full.[5]

A thirteenth-century commentator on the same Qur'anic passage goes into more detail and argues that women are incapable of and unfit for any public duties, such as participating in religious rites, giving evidence in the law courts, or being involved in any public political decisions. This view came to be accepted, and later interpreters further categorized the ways in which men were superior to women.

Separating Men and Women in a Mosque In this mid-sixteenth-century illustration of the interior of a mosque, a screen separates the women, who are wearing veils and tending children, from the men. The women can hear what is being said, but the men cannot see them. (Bodleian Library, University of Oxford, Ms. Ouseley Add 24, fol. 55v)

Listening to the Past

Abu Hamid Al-Ghazali, The Etiquette of Marriage

Abu Hamid Al-Ghazali (1058–1111) was a Persian philosopher, theologian, jurist, and Sufi, and a prolific author of more than seventy books. His magnum opus, the Revival of the Religious Sciences, *is divided into four parts:* Acts of Worship, Norms of Daily Life, The Ways to Perdition, *and* The Ways of Salvation. *The passages on marriage presented here are only a small part of* Norms of Daily Life, *a lengthy treatise full of quotations from the Qur'an and traditions about the words and actions of Muhammad. His writings reflect the trend toward more patriarchal readings of Muslim teachings.*

❝There are five advantages to marriage: procreation, satisfying sexual desire, ordering the household, providing companionship, and disciplining the self in striving to sustain them. The first advantage—that is, procreation—is the prime cause, and on its account marriage was instituted. The aim is to sustain lineage so that the world would not want for humankind. . . .

It was for the purpose of freeing the heart that marriage with the bondmaid was permitted when there was fear of hardship, even though it results in enslaving the son, which is a kind of attrition; such marriage is forbidden to anyone who can obtain a free woman. However, the enslaving of a son is preferable to destroying the faith, for enslavement affects temporarily the life of the child, while committing an abomination results in losing the hereafter; in comparison to one of its days the longest life is insignificant. . . .

It is preferable for a person with a temperament so overcome by desire that one woman cannot curb it to have more than one woman, up to four. For God will grant him love and mercy, and will appease his heart by them; if not, replacing them is recommended. Seven nights after the death of Fatimah, Ali got married. It is said that al-Hasan, the son of Ali, was a great lover having married more than two hundred women. Perhaps he would marry four at a time, and perhaps he would divorce four at a time replacing them with others. . . .

The fourth advantage [of marriage]: being free from the concerns of household duties, as well as of preoccupation with cooking, sweeping, making beds, cleaning utensils, and means for obtaining support. . . .

Ali used to say, "The worst characteristics of men constitute the best characteristics of women; namely, stinginess, pride, and cowardice. For if the woman is stingy, she will preserve her own and her husband's possessions; if she is proud, she will refrain from addressing loose and improper words to everyone; and if she is cowardly, she will dread everything and will therefore not go out of her house and will avoid compromising situations for fear of her husband. . . ."

Some God-fearing men as a precaution against delusion would not marry off their daughters until they are seen. Al-Amash said, "Every marriage occurring without looking ends in worry and sadness." It is obvious that looking does not reveal character, religion, or wealth; rather, it distinguishes beauty from ugliness. . . .

The Messenger of God declared that "The best women are those whose faces are the most beautiful and whose dowries are the smallest." He enjoined against excessiveness in dowries. The Messenger of God married one of his wives for a dowry of ten dirhams and household furnishings that consisted of a hand mill, a jug, a pillow made of skin stuffed with palm fibers, and a stone; in the case of another, he feasted with two measures of barley; and for another, with two measures of dates and two of mush. . . .

It is incumbent upon the guardian also to examine the qualities of the husband and to look after his daughter so as not to give her in marriage to one who is ugly, ill-mannered, weak in faith, negligent in upholding her rights, or unequal to

---

The Sunni aphorism "There shall be no monkery in Islam" captures the importance of marriage in Muslim culture and the Muslim belief that a sexually frustrated person is dangerous to the community. Islam had no roles for the celibate. In the Muslim world, as in China, every man and woman is expected to marry unless physically incapable or financially unable. Marriage is seen as a safeguard of virtue, essential to the stability both of the family and of society.

As in medieval Europe and traditional India and China, marriage in Muslim society was considered too important an undertaking to be left to the romantic emotions of the young. Families or guardians, not the prospective bride and groom, identified suitable partners and finalized the contract. The official wedding ceremony consisted of an offer and its acceptance by representatives of the bride's and groom's parents at a meeting before witnesses. A wedding banquet at which men and women feasted separately followed; the quality of the celebration, of the gifts, and of the food depended on the relative wealth of the two families. Because it was absolutely essential that the bride be a virgin, marriages were arranged shortly after the onset of the girl's menstrual period at age twelve or

● 1308 Persian edition of the *Alchemy of Happiness*, titled in the original Arabic version the *Revival of Religious Sciences*. (Bibliothèque nationale de France)

her in descent. The Prophet has said, "Marriage is enslavement; let one, therefore, be careful in whose hands he places his daughter." . . .

The Prophet asked his daughter Fatimah, "What is best for a woman?" She replied, "That she should see no man, and that no man should see her." So he hugged her and said they were "descendants one of another" [Qur'an 3:33]. Thus he was pleased with her answer. . . .

The Prophet permitted women to go to the mosques; the appropriate thing now, however, is to prevent them [from doing so], except for the old [ones]. Indeed such [prevention] was deemed proper during the days of the companions; A'ishah declared, "If the Prophet only knew of the misdeeds that women would bring about after his time, he would have prevented them from going out." . . .

If [a man] has several wives, then he should deal equitably with them and not favor one over the other; should he go on a journey and desire to have one [of his wives] accompany him, he should cast lots among them, for such was the practice of the Messenger. If he cheats a woman of her night, he should make up for it, for making up for it is a duty upon him. . . .

Let [a man] proceed with gentle words and kisses. The Prophet said, "Let none of you come upon his wife like an animal, and let there be an emissary between them." He was asked, "What is this emissary, O Messenger of God?" He said, "The kiss and [sweet] words."

One should not be overjoyed with the birth of a male child, nor should he be excessively dejected over the birth of a female child, for he does not know in which of the two his blessings lie. Many a man who has a son wishes he did not have him, or wishes that he were a girl. The girls give more tranquility and [divine] remuneration, which are greater.

Concerning divorce, let it be known that it is permissible; but of all permissible things, it is the most detestable to Almighty God. 🙶

Source: Madelain Farah, *Marriage and Sexuality in Islam: A Translation of Al-Ghazāli's Book on the Etiquette of Marriage from the Ihyā'* (Salt Lake City: University of Utah Press, 1984), pp. 53, 63, 64, 66, 85–86, 88–89, 91, 95–96, 100, 103, 106, 113, 116, slightly modified.

QUESTIONS FOR ANALYSIS

1. In what ways are the views toward marriage and gender expressed by Al-Ghazali similar to those seen in other traditions?

2. Were there situations in which the author did not think it was appropriate to do what Muhammad and his early followers did? What was his reasoning?

thirteen. Husbands were perhaps ten to fifteen years older. Youthful marriages ensured a long period of fertility.

A wife's responsibilities depended on the wealth and occupation of her husband. A farmer's wife helped in the fields, ground the corn, carried water, prepared food, and did the myriad of tasks necessary in rural life. Shopkeepers' wives in the cities sometimes helped in business. In an upper-class household, the lady supervised servants, looked after all domestic arrangements, and did whatever was needed for her husband's comfort.

In every case, children were the wife's special domain. A mother exercised authority over her children and enjoyed their respect. A Muslim tradition asserts that "Paradise is at the mother's feet." Thus, as in Chinese culture, the prestige of the young wife depended on the production of children — especially sons — as rapidly as possible. A wife's failure to have children was one of the main reasons for a man to take a second wife or to divorce his wife entirely.

Like the Jewish tradition, Muslim law permits divorce. The law prescribes that if a man intends to divorce his wife, he should avoid hasty action and not have intercourse with her for three months; it is hoped that during that time they will reconcile. If the woman turns out to be pregnant, her husband knows that he is the father. Although divorce is allowed, it is not encouraged. One commentator cited the Prophet as saying, "The lawful thing which God hates most is divorce."[6]

In contrast to the traditional Christian view of sexual activity as something inherently shameful and only a cure for lust even within marriage, Islam maintains a healthy acceptance of sexual pleasure for both males and females. The Qur'an permits a man to have four wives, provided that all are treated justly. Some modern Muslim commentators link this provision to a surplus of women that resulted from the wars during the Prophet's lifetime. As in other societies that allowed men to take several wives, only wealthy men could afford to do so. The vast majority of Muslim males were monogamous because they had difficulty enough supporting one wife.

In many present-day Muslim cultures, few issues are more sensitive than the veiling and seclusion of women. These practices have their roots in pre-Islamic times, and they took firm hold in classical Islamic society. As Arab conquerors subjugated various peoples, they adopted some of the vanquished peoples' customs. Veiling was probably of Byzantine or Persian origin. The head veil seems to have been the mark of freeborn urban women; wearing it distinguished them from slave women. Country and desert women did not wear veils because they interfered with work. The veil also indicated respectability and modesty. The Qur'an contains no specific rule about the veil, but its few vague references have been interpreted as sanctioning the practice. Gradually, the custom of covering women extended beyond the veil. Eventually, all parts of a woman's body were considered best covered in public.

An even greater restriction on women than veiling was the practice of purdah, literally, seclusion behind a screen or curtain—the harem system. The English word *harem* comes from the Arabic *haram*, meaning "forbidden" or "sacrosanct," which the women's quarters of a house or palace were considered to be. The practice of secluding women in a harem also derives from Arabic contacts with Persia and other Eastern cultures. Scholars do not know precisely when the harem system began, but by 800 women in more prosperous households stayed out of sight. The harem became another symbol of male prestige and prosperity, as well as a way to distinguish upper-class women from peasants.

Trade and Commerce

☐ Why did trade thrive in Muslim lands?

Islam looked favorably on profit-making enterprises. From 1000 to 1500 there was less ideological resistance to striving for profit in trade and commerce in the Muslim world than in the Christian West or the Confucian East. Also in contrast to the social values of the medieval West and the Confucian East, Muslims tended to look with disdain on agricultural labor. Muhammad had earned his living in business as a representative of the city of Mecca, which carried on a brisk trade from southern Palestine to southwestern Arabia. According to the sayings of the Prophet: "The honest, truthful Muslim merchant will stand with the martyrs on the Day of Judgment. I commend the merchants to you, for they are the couriers of the horizons and God's trusted servants on earth."[7]

> "The honest, truthful Muslim merchant will stand with the martyrs on the Day of Judgment."
>
> **THE PROPHET MUHAMMAD**

The Qur'an, moreover, has no prohibition against trade with Christians or other unbelievers. In fact, non-Muslims, including the Jews of Cairo and the Armenians in the central Islamic lands, were prominent in mercantile networks.

Waterways served as the main commercial routes of the Islamic world (Map 9.2). They included the Mediterranean and Black Seas; the Caspian Sea and the Volga River, which gave access deep into Russia; the Aral Sea, from which caravans departed for China; the Gulf of Aden; and the Arabian Sea and the Indian Ocean, which linked the Persian Gulf region with eastern Africa, the Indian subcontinent, and eventually Indonesia and the Philippines.

Cairo was a major Mediterranean entrepôt for intercontinental trade. Foreign merchants from Central Asia, Persia, Iraq, northern Europe (especially Venice), the Byzantine Empire, and Spain sailed up the Nile to the Aswan region, traveled east from Aswan by caravan to the Red Sea, and then sailed down the Red Sea to Aden, where they entered the Indian Ocean on their way to India. They exchanged textiles, glass, gold, silver, and copper for Asian spices, dyes, and drugs and for Chinese silks and porcelains. Muslim and Jewish merchants dominated the trade with India, and all spoke and wrote Arabic. Their commercial practices included the *sakk*, an Arabic word that is the root of the English *check*, an order to a banker to pay money held on account to a third party; the practice can be traced to Roman Palestine. Muslims also developed other business innovations, such as the bill of exchange, a writ-

MAP 9.2 The Expansion of Islam and Its Trading Networks in the Thirteenth and Fourteenth Centuries By 1500 Islam had spread extensively in North and East Africa, and into the Balkans, the Caucasus, Central Asia, India, and island Southeast Asia. Muslim merchants played a major role in bringing their religion as they extended their trade networks. They were active in the Indian Ocean long before the arrival of Europeans.

ten order from one person to another to pay a specified sum of money to a designated person or party, and the idea of the joint stock company, an arrangement that lets a group of people invest in a venture and share its profits (and losses) in proportion to the amount each has invested.

Trade also benefited from improvements in technology. The adoption from the Chinese of the magnetic compass, an instrument for determining directions at sea by means of a magnetic needle turning on a pivot, greatly helped navigation of the Arabian Sea and the Indian Ocean. The construction of larger ships led to a shift in long-distance cargoes from luxury goods such as pepper, spices, and drugs to bulk goods such as sugar, rice, and timber. Venetian galleys sailing the Mediterranean came to carry up to 250 tons of cargo, but the

Arab and Persian ships plying the Indian Ocean were built to carry up to 400 tons. The teak forests of western India supplied the wood for Arab ships.

In this period Egypt became the center of Muslim trade, benefiting from the decline of Iraq caused by the Mongol capture of Baghdad and the fall of the Abbasid caliphate (see page 245). Beginning in the late twelfth century Persian and Arab seamen sailed down the east coast of Africa and established trading towns between Somalia and Sofala (see pages 286–291). These thirty to fifty urban centers — each merchant-controlled, fortified, and independent — linked Zimbabwe in southern Africa with the Indian Ocean trade and the Middle Eastern trade.

A private ninth-century list mentions a great variety of commodities transported into and through the

Individuals in Society

Ibn Battuta

IN 1354 THE SULTAN OF MOROCCO APPOINTED a scribe to write an account of the travels of Abu ʾAbdallah Ibn Battuta (1304–1368), who between 1325 and 1354 had traveled through most of the Islamic world. The two men collaborated. The result was a travel book written in Arabic and later hailed as the richest eyewitness account of fourteenth-century Islamic culture. It has often been compared to the slightly earlier *Travels* of the Venetian Marco Polo (see page 346).

Ibn Battuta was born in Tangiers to a family of legal scholars. As a youth, he studied Muslim law, gained fluency in Arabic, and acquired the qualities considered essential for a civilized Muslim gentleman: courtesy, manners, and the social polish that eases relations among people.

At age twenty-one he left Tangiers to make the *hajj* (pilgrimage) to Mecca. He crossed North Africa and visited Alexandria, Cairo, Damascus, and Medina. Reaching Mecca in October 1326, he immediately praised God for his safe journey, kissed the Holy Stone at the Ka'ba, and recited the ritual prayers. There he decided to see more of the world.

In the next four years Ibn Battuta traveled to Iraq and to Basra and Baghdad in Persia, then returned to Mecca before sailing down the coast of Africa as far as modern Tanzania. On the return voyage he visited Oman and the Persian Gulf region, then traveled by land across central Arabia to Mecca. Strengthened by his stay in the holy city, he decided to go to India by way of Egypt, Syria, and Anatolia; across the Black Sea to the plains of western Central Asia, detouring to see Constantinople; back to the Asian steppe; east to Khurasan and Afghanistan; and down to Delhi in northern India.

For eight years Ibn Battuta served as a judge in the service of the sultan of Delhi. In 1341 the sultan chose him to lead a diplomatic mission to China. After the expedition was shipwrecked off the southeastern coast of India, Ibn Battuta traveled through southern India, Sri Lanka, and the Maldive Islands. Then he went to China, stopping in Bengal and Sumatra before reaching the southern coast of China, then under Mongol rule. Returning to Mecca in 1346, he set off for home, getting to Morocco in 1349. After a brief trip across the Strait of Gibraltar to Granada, he undertook his last journey, by camel caravan across the Sahara to Mali in the west African Sudan (see page 280), returning home in 1354. Scholars estimate that he had traveled about seventy-five thousand miles.

Ibn Battuta had a driving intellectual curiosity to see and understand the world. At every stop, he sought the learned jurists and pious men at the mosques and madrasas. He marveled at the Lighthouse of Alexandria, then in ruins; at the

• **A traveler, perhaps Ibn Battuta, as depicted on a 1375 European map.** (The Granger Collection, New York)

vast harbor at Kaffa (in southern Ukraine on the Black Sea), whose two hundred Genoese ships were loaded with silks and slaves for the markets at Venice, Cairo, and Damascus; and at the elephants in the sultan's procession in Delhi, which carried machines that tossed gold and silver coins to the crowds.

Ibn Battuta must have had an iron constitution. Besides walking long distances on his land trips, he endured fevers, dysentery, malaria, the scorching heat of the Sahara, and the freezing cold of the steppe. His thirst for adventure was stronger than his fear of nomadic warriors and bandits on land and the dangers of storms and pirates at sea.

Source: R. E. Dunn, *The Adventures of Ibn Battuta: A Muslim Traveler of the Fourteenth Century* (Berkeley: University of California Press, 1986).

QUESTIONS FOR ANALYSIS

1. Trace the routes of Ibn Battuta's travels on Map 9.2 (page 253).
2. How did a common Muslim culture facilitate Ibn Battuta's travels?

Arab Trade and Commerce A mariner's compass determines direction at sea. Arab traders brought this Chinese south-pointing compass (right) to the West, probably in the twelfth century. In 1984 archaeologists unearthed these coins (left) on the island of Pemba, off the coast of modern Kenya. Deriving from Tunisian, Egyptian, and Syrian mints and bearing Arabic scripts, the coins testify to Muslim trade with the Swahili city-states. (compass: Ontario Science Center, Toronto; coins: Courtesy, Dr. Mark Horton, Department of Archaeology and Anthropology, University of Bristol, Bristol, UK)

Islamic world by land and by sea:

> Imported from India: tigers, leopards, elephants, leopard skins, red rubies, white sandal-wood, ebony, and coconuts
> From China: aromatics, silk, porcelain, paper, ink, peacocks, fiery horses, saddles, felts, cinnamon
> From the Byzantines: silver and gold vessels, embroidered cloths, fiery horses, slave girls, rare articles in red copper, strong locks, lyres, water engineers, specialists in plowing and cultivation, marble workers, and eunuchs
> From Egypt: ambling donkeys, fine cloths, papyrus, balsam oil, and, from its mines, high-quality topaz
> From the Khazars [a people living on the northern shore of the Black Sea]: slaves, slave women, armor, helmets, and hoods of mail
> From Ahwaz [a city in southwestern Persia]: sugar, silk brocades, castanet players and dancing girls, kinds of dates, grape molasses, and candy.[8]

Did Muslim economic activity amount to a kind of capitalism? If capitalism is defined as private (not state) ownership of the means of production, the production of goods for sale, profit as the main motive for economic activity, competition, and a money economy, then, unquestionably, the medieval Muslim economy had capitalistic features. Until the sixteenth century much more world trade went through Muslim than European hands.

One by-product of the extensive trade through Muslim lands was the spread of useful plants. Cotton, sugar cane, and rice spread from India to other places with suitable climates. Citrus fruits made their way to Muslim Spain from Southeast Asia and India. The value of this trade contributed to the prosperity of the Abbasid era.

Cultural Developments

☐ What new ideas and practices emerged in the arts, sciences, education, and religion?

Long-distance trade provided the wealth that made possible a gracious and sophisticated culture in the cities of the Muslim world. (See "Individuals in Society: Ibn Battuta," page 254.) Education helped foster achievements in the arts and sciences, and Sufism brought a new spiritual and intellectual tradition.

The Cultural Centers of Baghdad and Córdoba

Although cities and mercantile centers dotted the entire Islamic world, the cities of Baghdad and Córdoba, at their peak in the tenth century, stand out as the finest examples of cosmopolitan Muslim civilization. On Baghdad's streets thronged a kaleidoscope of races, creeds, costumes, and cultures, an almost infinite variety of peoples: returning travelers, administrative officials, slaves, visitors, and merchants from Asia, Africa, and Europe. Shops and marketplaces offered a dazzling and exotic array of goods from all over the world.

The caliph Harun al-Rashid presided over a glamorous court. He invited writers, dancers, musicians, poets, and artists to live in Baghdad, and he is reputed to have rewarded one singer with 100,000 silver pieces for a single song. This brilliant era provided the background for the tales that appear in *The Thousand and One Nights*.

The central story of this fictional collection concerns the attempt of a new bride, Scheherazade, to keep her husband, Shahyar, legendary king of Samarkand, from killing her out of certainty that she will be unfaithful like his first wife. In efforts to delay her execution, she entertains him with one tale a night for 1,001 nights. In the end, Scheherazade's efforts succeed, and her husband pardons her. Among the tales she tells him are such famous ones as "Aladdin and His Lamp," "Sinbad the Sailor," and "Ali Baba and the Forty Thieves." Though filled with folklore, the *Arabian Nights* (as it is also called) has provided many of the images through which Europeans have understood the Islamic world.

Córdoba in southern Spain competed with Baghdad for the cultural leadership of the Islamic world. In the tenth century no city in Asia or Europe could equal dazzling Córdoba. Its streets were well paved and lighted, and the city had an abundant supply of fresh water. With a population of about 1 million, Córdoba contained 1,600 mosques, 900 public baths, 213,177 houses for ordinary people, and 60,000 mansions for generals, officials, and the wealthy. In its 80,455 shops, 13,000 weavers produced silks, woolens, and brocades that were internationally famous. Córdoba was also a great educational center with 27 free schools and a library containing 400,000 volumes. (By contrast, the great Benedictine abbey of Saint-Gall in Switzerland had about 600 books.) Moreover, Córdoba's scholars made contributions in chemistry, medicine and surgery, music, philosophy, and mathematics. It was through Córdoba and Persia that the Indian game of chess entered western Europe. The contemporary Saxon nun Hrosthwita of Gandersheim (d. 1000) described Córdoba as the "ornament of the world."[9]

Education and Intellectual Life

Muslim culture valued learning, especially religious learning, because knowledge provided the guidelines by which men and women should live. Parents, thus, established elementary schools for the training of their children. After the caliph Uthman (see page 240) ordered the preparation of an approved text of the Qur'an and had copies of it made, the Qur'an became the basic text. From the eighth century onward formal education for young men involved reading, writing, and the study of the Qur'an, believed essential for its religious message and for its training in proper grammar and syntax.

Teachers Disputing in a Madrasa Although Islamic education relied heavily on memorization of the Qur'an, religious scholars frequently debated the correct interpretation of a particular text. Listening to this lively disputation, the students illustrated in this 1222 book are learning to think critically and creatively. (Bibliothèque nationale de France, Ms. Arabe 6094, fol. 16)

Islam is a religion of the law, and the institution for instruction in Muslim jurisprudence was the **madrasa** (muh-DRA-suh), the school for the study of Muslim law and religion. Many madrasas were founded between 1000 and 1350. By 1193 thirty madrasas existed in Damascus, with sixty more established there between 1200 and 1250. Aleppo, Jerusalem, Alexandria, and above all Cairo also witnessed the foundation of madrasas.

Schools were urban phenomena. Wealthy merchants endowed them, providing salaries for teachers, stipends for students, and living accommodations for both. The teacher served as a guide to the correct path of living. All Islamic higher education rested on a close relationship between teacher and students, so in selecting a teacher, the student (or his father) considered the character and intellectual reputation of the teacher, not that of the institution. Students built their subsequent careers on the reputation of their teachers.

Learning depended heavily on memorization. In primary school, which was often attached to an institution of higher learning, a boy began his education by memorizing the entire Qur'an. Normally, he achieved this feat by the time he was seven or eight! In adolescence a student learned by heart an introductory work in one of the branches of knowledge, such as jurisprudence or grammar. Later he analyzed the texts in detail. Memorizing four hundred to five hundred lines a day was considered outstanding. Every class day, the teacher examined the student on the previous day's learning and determined whether the student fully understood what he had memorized. Students, of course, learned to write, for they had to record the teacher's commentary on a particular text. But the overwhelming emphasis was on the oral transmission of knowledge.

Because Islamic education focused on particular books, when the student had mastered a text to his teacher's satisfaction, the teacher issued the student a certificate stating that he had studied the book or collection of traditions with his teacher. The certificate allowed the student to transmit a text to the next generation on the authority of his teacher.

As the importance of books suggests, the Muslim transmission and improvement of papermaking techniques had special significance to education. For centuries the Chinese had been making paper from rags and from the fibers of hemp, jute, bamboo, and other plants. After these techniques spread westward, Muslim papermakers improved on them by adding starch to fill the pores in the surfaces of the sheets. Muslims carried this new method to Baghdad in Iraq, Damascus in Syria, Cairo in Egypt, and the Maghrib (North Africa), from which it entered Spain. Even before the invention of printing, papermaking had a revolutionary impact on the collection and diffusion of knowledge and thus on the transformation of society.

Mechanical Hand Washer Building on the work of the Greek engineer and inventor Archimedes (see page 138), the Arab scientist Ibn al-Razzaz al-Raziri (ca. 1200) designed practical devices to serve general social needs and illustrated them in a mechanical engineering handbook. In this diagram, a device in the form of a servant pours water with its right hand and offers a towel with its left. The device resembles a modern faucet that releases water when hands are held under it. (Freer Gallery of Art, Smithsonian Institution, Washington, D.C./The Bridgeman Art Library)

Muslim higher education, apart from its fundamental goal of preparing men to live wisely and in accordance with God's law, aimed at preparing them to perform religious and legal functions as Qur'an — or hadith — readers; as preachers in the mosques; as professors, educators, or copyists; and especially as judges. Judges issued fatwas, or legal opinions, in the public courts; their training was in the Qur'an, hadith, or some text forming part of the shari'a.

What educational opportunities were available to women? Although tradition holds that Muhammad

---

• **madrasa** A school for the study of Muslim law and religious science.

said, "The seeking of knowledge is a duty of every Muslim," Islamic culture was ambivalent on the issue of female education. Because of the basic Islamic principle that "Men are the guardians of women, because God has set the one over the other," the law excluded women from participating in the legal, religious, or civic occupations for which the madrasa prepared young men. Moreover, educational theorists insisted that men should study in a sexually isolated environment because feminine allure would distract them. Nevertheless, many young women received substantial educations from their parents or family members; the initiative invariably rested with their fathers or older brothers. The daughter of Ali ibn Muhammad al-Diruti al Mahalli, for example, memorized the Qur'an, learned to write, and received instruction in several sacred works. According to one biographical dictionary covering the lives of 1,075 women, 411 of them had memorized the Qur'an, studied with a particular teacher, and received a certificate. After marriage, responsibility for a woman's education belonged to her husband.

How does Islamic higher education during the twelfth through fourteenth centuries compare with that available in Europe or China at the same time (see pages 412–413, 373–378)? There are some striking similarities and some major differences. In both Europe and the Islamic countries, religious authorities ran most schools, while in China the government, local villages, and lineages ran schools, and private tutoring was very common. In the Islamic world, as in China, the personal relationship of teacher and student was seen as key to education. In Europe the reward for satisfactorily completing a course of study was a degree granted by the university. In China, at the very highest levels, the state ran a civil service examination system that rewarded achievement with appointments in the state bureaucracy. In Muslim culture, by contrast, it was not the school or the state but the individual teacher whose evaluation mattered and who granted certificates.

Still, there were also some striking similarities in the practice of education. Students in all three cultures had to master a sacred language (Latin, Arabic, or classical Chinese). In all three cultures education rested heavily on the study of basic religious, legal, or philosophical texts: the Old and New Testaments or the Justinian *Code* in Europe; the Confucian classics and commentaries in China; the Qur'an, hadith, and legal texts deriving from them in the Muslim world. Also in all three cultures memorization played a large role in

Pharmacist Preparing Drugs The translation of Greek scientific treatises into Arabic, combined with considerable botanical experimentation, gave Muslims virtually unrivaled medical knowledge. Many ailments were treated with prescription drugs. In this thirteenth-century illustration a pharmacist prepares a drug in a cauldron over a brazier. It has been said that the pharmacy as an institution is an Islamic invention. (Image copyright © The Metropolitan Museum of Art/Art Resource, NY)

the acquisition and transmission of learning. Furthermore, teachers in all three societies lectured on particular passages, and leading teachers might disagree fiercely about the correct interpretations of a particular text, forcing students to question, to think critically, and to choose among divergent opinions. All these similarities in educational practice contributed to cultural cohesion and ties among the educated living in scattered localities.

In the Muslim world the spread of the Arabic language, not only among the educated classes but also among all the people, was the decisive element in the creation of a common culture. Recent scholarship demonstrates that after the establishment of the Islamic empire, the major influence in the cultural transformation of the Byzantine–Sassanid–North African and the Central Asian worlds was language. The Arabic language proved more important than religion in this regard. Whereas conversion to Islam was gradual, linguistic conversion went much faster. Arabic became the official language of the state and its bureaucracies in former Byzantine and Sassanid territories, and Muslim conquerors forbade Persian-speaking people to use their native language. Islamic rulers required tribute from monotheistic peoples — the Persians and Greeks — but they did not force them to change their religions. Conquered peoples were, however, compelled to submit to a linguistic conversion — to adopt the Arabic language. In time Arabic produced a cohesive and "international" culture over a large part of the Eurasian world.

As a result of Muslim creativity and vitality, modern scholars consider the years from 800 to 1300 to be one of the most brilliant periods in the world's history. Near the beginning of this period the Persian scholar al-Khwarizmi (d. ca. 850) harmonized Greek and Indian findings to produce astronomical tables that formed the basis for later Eastern and Western research. Al-Khwarizmi also studied mathematics, and his textbook on algebra (from the Arabic *al-Jabr*) was the first work in which the word *algebra* is used to mean the "transposing of negative terms in an equation to the opposite side."

Muslim medical knowledge far surpassed that of the West. The Baghdad physician al-Razi (865–925), the first physician to make the clinical distinction between measles and smallpox, produced an encyclopedic treatise on medicine that was translated into Latin and circulated widely in the West. In Córdoba the great surgeon al-Zahrawi (d. 1013) produced an important work in which he discussed the cauterization of wounds (searing them with a branding iron) and the crushing of stones in the bladder. Muslim science reached its peak in the work of Ibn Sina of Bukhara (980–1037), known in the West as Avicenna. His *al-Qanun* codified all Greco-Arabic medical thought, described the con-

> " O my lord, if I worship thee from fear of hell, and if I worship thee in hope of paradise, exclude me thence, but if I worship thee for thine own sake, then withhold not from me thine eternal beauty. "
>
> **RABI'A**

tagious nature of tuberculosis and the spreading of diseases, and listed 760 drugs.

Muslim scholars also wrote works on geography, jurisprudence, and philosophy. Al-Kindi (d. ca. 870) was the first Muslim thinker to try to harmonize Greek philosophy and the religious precepts of the Qur'an. He sought to integrate Islamic concepts of human beings and their relations to God and the universe with the principles of ethical and social conduct discussed by Plato and Aristotle. Inspired by Plato's *Republic* and Aristotle's *Politics*, the distinguished philosopher al-Farabi (d. 950) wrote a political treatise describing an ideal city whose ruler is morally and intellectually perfect and who has as his goal the citizens' complete happiness. Avicenna maintained that the truths found by human reason cannot conflict with the truths revealed in the Qur'an. Ibn Rushid, or Averroës (1126–1198), of Córdoba, a judge in Seville and later the royal court physician, paraphrased and commented on the works of Aristotle. He insisted on the right to subject all knowledge, except the dogmas of faith, to the test of reason and on the essential harmony of religion and philosophy.

The Mystical Tradition of Sufism

Like the world's other major religions — Buddhism, Hinduism, Judaism, and Christianity — Islam also developed a mystical tradition: Sufism (SOO-fizm). It arose in the ninth and tenth centuries as a popular reaction to the materialism and worldliness of the later Umayyad regime. Sufis sought a personal union with God — divine love and knowledge through intuition rather than through rational deduction and study of the shari'a. The earliest of the Sufis followed an ascetic routine (denial of physical desires to achieve a spiritual goal), dedicating themselves to fasting, prayer, meditation on the Qur'an, and the avoidance of sin.

The woman mystic Rabi'a (717–801) epitomized this combination of renunciation and devotion. An attractive woman who refused marriage so that nothing would distract her from a total commitment to God, Rabi'a attracted followers, whom she served as a spiritual guide. One of her poems captures her deep devotion: "O my lord, if I worship thee from fear of hell, and if I worship thee in hope of paradise, exclude me thence, but if I worship thee for thine own sake, then withhold not from me thine eternal beauty."[10]

Between the tenth and the thirteenth centuries groups of Sufis gathered around prominent leaders called *shaykhs*; members of these groups were called *dervishes*. Dervishes entered hypnotic or ecstatic trances, either through the constant repetition of certain prayers or through physical exertions such as whirling or dancing (hence the English phrase "whirling dervish" for one who dances with abandonment).

Some Sufis acquired reputations as charismatic holy men to whom ordinary Muslims came seeking spiritual consolation, healing, charity, or political mediation between tribal and factional rivals. Other Sufis became known for their writings. Probably the most famous medieval Sufi was the Spanish mystic-philosopher Ibn al'Arabi (1165–1240). He traveled widely in Spain, North Africa, and Arabia seeking masters of Sufism. In Mecca he received a "divine commandment" to begin his major work, *The Meccan Revelation*, which

□ Picturing the Past

Sufi Collective Ritual Collective or group rituals, in which Sufis tried through ecstatic experiences to come closer to God, have always fascinated outsiders, including non-Sufi Muslims. Here the sixteenth-century Persian painter Sultan Muhammad illustrates the writing of the fourteenth-century lyric poet Hafiz. Notice the various musical instruments and the delicate floral patterns so characteristic of Persian art. (Edinburgh University Library, Scotland/With kind permission of the University of Edinburgh/The Bridgeman Art Library)

ANALYZING THE IMAGE What sort of architectural space is depicted here? What distinctions do you see among the people in terms of how they dress and what they are doing?

CONNECTIONS How common are music and dance in religion? What do they provide?

evolved into a personal encyclopedia of 560 chapters. Also at Mecca the wisdom of a beautiful young girl inspired him to write a collection of love poems, *The Interpreter of Desires*, for which he composed a mystical commentary. In 1223, after visits to Egypt, Anatolia, Baghdad, and Aleppo, Ibn al'Arabi concluded his pilgrimage through the Islamic world at Damascus, where he produced *The Bezels [Edges] of Wisdom*, considered one of the greatest works of Sufism.

Muslim-Christian Encounters

☐ How did Muslims and Christians come into contact with each other, and how did they view each other?

During the early centuries of its development, Islam came into contact with the other major religions of Eurasia—Hinduism in India, Buddhism in Central Asia, Zoroastrianism in Persia, and Judaism and Christianity in western Asia and Europe. However, the relationship that did the most to define Muslim identity was the one with Christianity. To put this another way, the most significant "other" to Muslims in the heartland of Islam was Christendom. The close physical proximity and the long history of military encounters undoubtedly contributed to making the Christian-Muslim encounter so important to both sides.

European Christians and Middle Eastern Muslims shared a common cultural heritage from the Judeo-Christian past. In the classical period of Islam, Muslims learned about Christianity from the Christians they met in conquered territories; from the Old and New Testaments; from Jews; and from Jews and Christians who converted to Islam. Before 1400 a wide spectrum of Muslim opinion about Jesus and Christians existed. At the time of the Crusades and of the Christian reconquest of Muslim Spain (the *reconquista*, 722–1492), polemical anti-Christian writings appeared. In other periods, Muslim views were more positive.

In the medieval period Christians and Muslims met frequently in business and trade. Commercial contacts, especially when European merchants resided for a long time in the Muslim East, gave Europeans, notably the Venetians, familiarity with Muslim art and architecture. Likewise, when in the fifteenth century Muslim artists in the Ottoman Empire and in Persia became acquainted with Western artists, such as Gentile Bellini, they admired and imitated them. Also, Christians very likely borrowed aspects of their higher education practices from Islam.

In the Christian West, Islam had the greatest cultural impact in Andalusia in southern Spain. Between roughly the eighth and twelfth centuries, Muslims, Christians, and Jews lived in close proximity in Andalusia, and some scholars believe the period represents a remarkable era of interfaith harmony. Many Christians adopted Arabic patterns of speech and dress, gave up the practice of eating pork, and developed a special appreciation for Arabic music and poetry. Some Christian women of elite status chose the Muslim practice of going out in public with their faces veiled. Records describe Muslim and Christian youths joining in celebrations and merrymaking. These assimilated Christians, called **Mozarabs** (moh-ZAR-uhbz), did not attach much importance to the doctrinal differences between the two religions.

However, Mozarabs soon faced the strong criticism of both Muslim scholars and Christian clerics. Muslim teachers feared that close contact between people of the two religions would lead to Muslim contamination and become a threat to the Islamic faith. Christian bishops worried that a knowledge of Islam would lead to confusion about essential Christian doctrines. Both Muslim scholars and Christian theologians argued that assimilation led to moral decline.

Thus, beginning in the late tenth century, Muslim regulations closely defined what Christians and Muslims could do. A Christian, however much assimilated, remained an unbeliever, a word that carried a pejorative connotation. Because of their status as unbelievers, Mozarabs had to live in special sections of cities; could not learn the Qur'an, employ Muslim workers or servants, or build new churches; and had to be buried in their own cemeteries. A Muslim who converted to Christianity immediately incurred a sentence of death. By about 1250 the Christian reconquest of Muslim Spain had brought most of the Iberian peninsula under Christian control. With their new authority Christian kings set up schools that taught both Arabic and Latin to train missionaries.

Beyond Andalusian Spain, mutual animosity limited contact between people of the two religions. The Muslim assault on Christian Europe in the eighth and ninth centuries—with villages burned, monasteries sacked, and Christians sold into slavery—left a legacy of bitter hostility. Christians felt threatened by a faith that acknowledged God as creator of the universe but denied the Trinity (the doctrine of God as the union of a holy father, his son, and the holy spirit); that accepted Jesus as a prophet but denied his divinity; and that believed in the Last Judgment but seemed to make

---

• **Mozarabs** Christians who adopted some Arabic customs but did not convert.

sensuality Heaven's greatest reward. Europeans' perception of Islam as a menace helped inspire the Crusades of the eleventh through thirteenth centuries (see pages 404–408).

Despite the conflicts between the two religions, Muslim scholars often wrote sympathetically about Jesus. For example, the great historian al Tabari (d. 923), relying on Arabic sources, wrote positively of Jesus's life, focusing on his birth and crucifixion. Also, Ikhwan al-Safa, an eleventh-century Islamic brotherhood, held that in his preaching Jesus deliberately rejected the harsh punishments reflected in the Jewish Torah and tried to be the healing physician teaching by parables and trying to touch people's hearts by peace and love. In terms of more critical views of Christianity, al Tabari used Old Testament books to prove Muhammad's prophethood. The prominent theologian and qadi (judge) of Teheran, Abd al-Jabbar (d. 1024), though not critical of Jesus, argued that Christians had rejected Jesus's teachings: they failed to observe the ritual purity of prayer, substituting poems by Christian scholars for scriptural prayers; they gave up circumcision, the sign of their covenant with God and Abraham; they moved the Sabbath from Saturday to Sunday; they allowed the eating of pork and shellfish; and they adopted a Greek idea, the Trinity, defending it by quoting Aristotle. Thus, al-Jabbar maintained — and he was followed later by many other Muslim theologians and scholars — that Christians failed to observe the laws of Moses and Jesus and distorted Jesus's message.

In the Christian West, both positive and negative views of Islam appeared in literature. The Bavarian knight Wolfram von Eschenbach's *Parzival* and the En-

Mozarabic Bible In this page from a tenth-century Mozarabic Bible, Moses is depicted closing the passage through the Red Sea, thus drowning the Egyptians. (Real Collegiata San Isidoro de León/Gianni Dagli Orti/The Art Archive)

glishman William Langland's *Piers the Plowman* — two medieval poems that survive in scores of manuscripts, suggesting that they circulated widely — reveal broad-mindedness and tolerance toward Muslims. Some travelers in the Middle East were impressed by the kindness and generosity of Muslims and with the strictness and devotion with which Muslims observed their faith. Frequently, however, Christian literature portrayed Muslims as the most dreadful of Europe's enemies, guilty of every kind of crime. In his *Inferno*, for example, the great Florentine poet Dante (1265–1321) placed the Muslim philosophers Avicenna and Averroës with other virtuous "heathens," among them Socrates and Aristotle, in the first circle of Hell, where they endured only moderate punishment. Muhammad, however, Dante consigned to the ninth circle, near Satan himself, where he was condemned as a spreader of discord and scandal and suffered perpetual torture.

Even when they rejected each other most forcefully, the Christian and Muslim worlds had a significant impact on each other. Art styles, technology, and even institutional practices spread in both directions. During the Crusades Muslims adopted Frankish weapons and methods of fortification. Christians in contact with Muslim scholars recovered ancient Greek philosophical texts that survived only in Arabic translation.

CONNECTIONS

During the five centuries that followed Muhammad's death, his teachings came to be revered in large parts of the world from Spain to Afghanistan. Although in some ways similar to the earlier spread of Buddhism out of India and Christianity out of Palestine, in the case of Islam, military conquests played a large part in the extension of Muslim lands. Still, conversion was never complete; both Christians and Jews maintained substantial communities within Muslim lands. Moreover, cultural contact among Christians, Jews, and Muslims was an important element in the development of each culture.

Muslim civilization in these centuries drew from many sources, including Persia and Byzantium, and in turn had broad impact beyond its borders. Muslim scholars preserved much of early Greek philosophy and science through translation into Arabic. Trade connected the Muslim lands both to Europe and to India and China.

During the first and second centuries after Muhammad, Islam spread along the Mediterranean coast of North Africa, which had been part of the Roman world. The next chapter explores other developments in the enormous and diverse continent of Africa during this time. Many of the written sources that tell us about the African societies of these centuries were written in Arabic by visitors from elsewhere in the Muslim world. Muslim traders traveled through many of the societies in Africa north of the Congo, aiding the spread of Islam to the elites of many of these societies. Ethiopia was an exception, as Christianity spread there from Egypt before the time of Muhammad and retained its hold in subsequent centuries. Africa's history is introduced in the next chapter.

◻ CHAPTER REVIEW

◻ **From what kind of social and economic environment did Muhammad arise, and what did he teach? (p. 234)**

Muhammad was born in the Arabian peninsula among farmers, traders, merchants, and herders, where tribes were the basic social unit. After experiencing a religious vision, Muhammad began to preach to the people, urging them to give up their idols and submit to the one indivisible God. He taught strict monotheism — that there is one and only one God and that believers must submit to God's will. This God is the same God of the Christians and Jews, and Islam, the religion based on Muhammad's teachings, appropriates much of the Old and New Testaments of the Bible. Through his religious teaching, Muhammad helped to bind different tribal groups into a strong, unified state by emphasizing commitment to a common religious faith over tribal ties. After Muhammad's death, religious leaders organized his revelations into chapters, eventually producing the Qur'an, which prescribes a strict code of moral behavior.

◻ **What made possible the spread of Islam, and what forms of government were established to rule Muslim lands? (p. 237)**

A mixture of religious zeal, desire for plunder, and the weakness of their neighbors pushed Muslims to carry their faith from the Arabian peninsula through the Middle East, to North Africa and Spain, and to the borders of China and northern India — all within the relatively short span of a century. Successors to Muhammad established the caliphate, which through two successive dynasties — the Umayyad, centered at Damascus in Syria, and the Abbasid, with its capital at Baghdad in Iraq — coordinated rule over Muslim lands through emirs (governors), qadi (judges), and viziers (chief assistants to caliphs). A key challenge faced by the caliphate was a fundamental division in Muslim theology between the Sunnis and the Shi'a.

◻ **How were the Muslim lands governed from 900 to 1400, and what new challenges did rulers face? (p. 243)**

In theory, the caliph and his central administration governed the whole Muslim empire, but in practice, the many parts of the empire enjoyed considerable local independence. Local, ethnic, or tribal loyalties, combined with fierce ambition, led to the creation of regional dynasties in much of the Islamic world. As a result, various territories, including Spain, began to break away from the Baghdad-centered caliphate. In

KEY TERMS

Qur'an (p. 235)
hadith (p. 235)
Sunna (p. 235)
Five Pillars of Islam (p. 236)
umma (p. 237)
diwān (p. 239)
imam (p. 240)
Shi'a (p. 240)
Sunnis (p. 240)
ulama (p. 240)
emirs (p. 242)
shari'a (p. 242)
vizier (p. 242)
dhimmis (p. 246)
madrasa (p. 257)
Mozarabs (p. 261)

this situation, Turks played more and more important roles in the armies and came to be the effective rulers in many places. They were succeeded by the Mongols who invaded the Middle East in the thirteenth century and ruled the central Muslim lands for eighty years.

◻ **What social distinctions were important in Muslim society? (p. 245)**

In the Umayyad period Muslim society was distinctly hierarchical. At the top of the hierarchy were the caliph's household and the ruling Arab Muslims. Next were converts to Islam, including the Copts, Berbers, Persians, and Aramaeans. Below the converts were Jews, Christians, and Zoroastrians, recognized as protected people because they recognized only one God, who were allowed to continue practicing their religions. In addition there were a substantial number of slaves, many of whom were war captives. Slaves normally were converted to Islam and might come to hold important positions, especially in the army. Distinctions between men and women in Islamic society were strict. In the Qur'an men were said to be in charge of women because God "made the one to excel the other," and women were enjoined to be obedient. In time, the seclusion and veiling of women became common practices, especially among the well-to-do.

◻ **Why did trade thrive in Muslim lands? (p. 252)**

Muhammad was said to see merchants as "God's trusted servants on earth," and Islam did not discourage profit-making. Merchants were respected and treated well. By land and sea Muslim merchants transported a rich variety of goods across Asia, the Middle East, Africa, and western Europe. As trade thrived, innovations such as money orders to bankers, bills of exchange, and joint stock companies aided the conduct of business.

◻ **What new ideas and practices emerged in the arts, sciences, education, and religion? (p. 255)**

Trade provided the wealth that made possible a gracious and sophisticated culture in the cities of the Muslim world. Urban culture, with centers at Baghdad and Córdoba, also thrived because of the strong foundation provided by education (at madrasas and other institutions). Education fostered achievements in the arts and sciences and in other intellectual pursuits, and as a result of Muslim creativity and vitality, modern scholars consider the years from 800 to 1300 one of the most brilliant periods in world history. During this period Muslim scholars produced important work in many disciplines, especially mathematics, medicine, and philosophy. As the larger culture blossomed, a new spiritual and intellectual tradition arose in the mystical practices of Sufism. Sufis sought a personal union with God — divine love and knowledge through intuition rather than through rational deduction and study of the shari'a.

□ How did Muslims and Christians come into contact with each other, and how did they view each other? (p. 261)

European Christians and Middle Eastern Muslims shared a common cultural heritage from the Judeo-Christian past. In the classical period of Islam, Muslims learned about Christianity from the Christians they met in conquered territories, from the Old and New Testaments, from Jews, and from Jews and Christians who converted to Islam. Before 1500 a wide spectrum of Muslim opinion about Jesus and Christians existed. At the time of the Crusades and of the Christian reconquest of Muslim Spain, polemical anti-Christian writings appeared. In other periods Muslim views were more positive. For their part some Christians, such as the Mozarabs, assimilated into Muslim culture, while others, including writers of certain literary works, saw Muslims as enemies and criminals.

SUGGESTED READING

Ahmed, Leila. *Women and Gender in Islam*. 1993. Links modern issues to their historical roots.

Berkey, Jonathan. *The Transmission of Knowledge in Medieval Cairo*. 1992. A study of religious education and its social context.

Bulliet, Richard W. *Cotton, Climate, and Camels in Early Islamic Iran*. 2009. Links a cooling of the climate to a decline in the Iranian cotton industry and cross-breeding of one- and two-hump camels.

Cohen, Mark R. *Under Crescent and Cross: The Jews in the Medieval Ages*. 1994. Argues that Jews were less marginalized and persecuted under Islamic states than under Christian states.

Constable, Olivia Remie. *Trade and Traders in Muslim Spain: The Commercial Realignment of the Iberian Peninsula, 900–1500*. 1994. An excellent study of Muslim trade and commerce drawing on a wide range of both Western and Arabic sources.

Ettinghausen, Richard, Oleg Grabar, and Marilyn Jenkins-Madina. *The Art and Architecture of Islam, 650–1250*. 2001. A stunningly illustrated overview of Islamic art.

Fletcher, Richard. *The Cross and the Crescent*. 2003. A balanced, fascinating, and lucidly written short account of the earliest contacts between Christians and Muslims.

Hourani, Albert, and Malise Ruthven. *A History of the Arab Peoples*, 2d ed. 2003. An important synthesis.

Lewis, Bernard, ed. and trans. *Islam from the Prophet Muhammad to the Capture of Constantinople: Religion and Society*. 1987. A collection of original sources on many topics.

Lewis, Bernard. *Race and Slavery in the Middle East*. 1990. Explores the culture of slavery beginning from before Islam, with particular attention to slaves from Africa.

Long, Pamela O. *Technology and Society in the Medieval Centuries: Byzantium, Islam, and the West, 500–1300*. 2003. A useful survey of Arab scientific and military developments.

Peters, F. E. *The Hajj: The Muslim Pilgrimage to Mecca and the Holy Places*. 1994. Covers the social, commercial, and political significance of the obligatory Muslim pilgrimage to Mecca.

Sells, Michael. *Approaching the Qur'an*. 2007. Includes selected translations set in historical and cultural context.

Stowasser, Barbara Freyer. *Women in the Qur'an: Traditions and Interpretation*. 1994. A fine analysis of the Qur'an's statement on women.

Turner, Howard R. *Science in Medieval Islam: An Illustrated Introduction*. 1995. A fascinating exploration of Islamic science with chapters on astronomy, medicine, geography, alchemy, mathematics, and other topics.

NOTES

1. F. E. Peters, *A Reader on Classical Islam* (Princeton: Princeton University Press, 1994), pp. 154–155.

2. Quoted in R. Levy, *The Social Structure of Islam*, 2d ed. (Cambridge: Cambridge University Press, 1957), p. 56.

3. See B. F. Stowasser, *Women in the Qur'an, Traditions, and Interpretation* (New York: Oxford University Press, 1994), pp. 94–118.

4. Quoted in B. F. Stowasser, "The Status of Women in Early Islam," in *Muslim Women*, ed. F. Hussain (New York: St. Martin's Press, 1984), p. 25.

5. Quoted ibid., pp. 25–26.

6. Peters, *A Reader on Classical Islam*, p. 250.

7. Quoted in B. Lewis, ed. and trans., *Islam from the Prophet Muhammad to the Capture of Constantinople*, vol. 2: *Religion and Society* (New York: Harper & Row, 1975), p. 126.

8. Ibid, pp. 154–157. Used by permission of Oxford University Press, Inc.

9. R. Hillenbrand, "Cordoba," in *Dictionary of the Middle Ages*, vol. 3, ed. J. R. Strayer (New York: Scribner's, 1983), pp. 597–601.

10. Margaret Smith, *Readings from the Mystics of Islam* (London: Luzac and Co., 1950), p. 11.

For practice quizzes and other study tools, visit the **Online Study Guide** at bedfordstmartins.com/mckayworld.

For primary sources from this period, see *Sources of World Societies*, **Second Edition**.

For Web sites, images, and documents related to topics in this chapter, visit **Make History** at bedfordstmartins.com/mckayworld.

● **Ife Ruler** West African rulers, such as the one shown in this bronze head of a Yoruban king, or *Oni*, from the thirteenth or fourteenth century, were usually male. (© Jerry Thompson)

Until fairly recently, most of the outside world knew little about the African continent, its history, or its people. The sheer size of the continent, along with tropical diseases and the difficulty of navigating Africa's rivers inland, limited travel there to a few intrepid Muslim adventurers such as Ibn Battuta. Ethnocentrism and racism became critical factors with the beginning of the Atlantic slave trade in the ... the nineteenth century by European colonialism, which distorted and ... ... e and information about Africa. But recent scholarship has allowed us ... ... more about early African civilizations, and we are able to appreciate the richness, diversity, and dynamism of those cultures. We know now that between about 400 and 1500 some highly centralized, bureaucratized, and socially stratified civilizations developed in Africa alongside communities with a looser form of social organization that were often held together simply through common bonds of kinship.

African Societies and Kingdoms

1000 B.C.E.–1500 C.E.

In West Africa there arose during this period several large empires that were closely linked to the trans-Saharan trade in salt, gold, cloth, ironware, ivory, and other goods. After 700 this trade connected West Africa with the Muslim societies of North Africa and the Middle East. Vast stores of new information, contained in books and carried by visiting scholars, now arrived from an Islamic world that was experiencing a Golden Age.

Meanwhile, Bantu-speaking peoples carried ironworking and the domestication of crops and animals from modern Cameroon to Africa's southern tip. They established kingdoms, such as Great Zimbabwe, in the interior, while one group, the Swahili, established large and prosperous city-states along the Indian Ocean coast.   •

The Land and Peoples of Africa

□ How did Africa's geography shape its history and contribute to its diverse population, and how has this fueled the debate over who is African?

Early African Societies

□ How did settled agriculture affect life among the early societies in the western Sudan and among the Bantu-speaking societies of central and southern Africa?

The Trans-Saharan Trade

□ What characterized trans-Saharan trade, and how did it affect West African society?

African Kingdoms and Empires, ca. 800–1500

□ How were the East African city-states, Aksum, and Great Zimbabwe different from and similar to the kingdoms of the western Sudan?

The Land and Peoples of Africa

□ How did Africa's geography shape its history and contribute to its diverse population, and how has this fueled the debate over who is African?

The world's second largest continent (after Asia), Africa covers 20 percent of the earth's land surface. The student beginning the study of African history should bear in mind the enormous diversity of African peoples and cultures both within and across regions. It is difficult and often wrong to make broad generalizations about African life. Statements that begin "African culture is . . ." or "African people are . . ." are virtually meaningless. African peoples are not now and never have been homogeneous. This rich diversity helps explain why the study of African history is so exciting and challenging.

Africa's Geographical and Human Diversity

Five main climatic zones roughly divide the continent (Map 10.1). Fertile land with unpredictable rainfall borders parts of the Mediterranean coast in the north and the southwestern coast of the Cape of Good Hope in the south. Inland from these areas lies dry steppe country with little plant life. The steppe gradually gives way to Africa's great deserts: the Sahara in the north and the Namib (NAH-mihb) and Kalahari in the south. The vast Sahara—3.5 million square miles—takes its name from the Arabic word for "tan," the color of the desert. (Folk etymology ascribes the word *Sahara* to an ancient Arabic word that sounds like a parched man's gasp for water.) The Sahara's southern sub-desert fringe is called the Sahel (SA-hihl), from the Arabic word for "shore." The savanna—flat grassland—extends in a swath across the widest part of the continent, across parts of south-central Africa, and along

the eastern coast. It is one of the richest habitats in the world and accounts for perhaps 55 percent of the African continent. Dense, humid tropical rain forests stretch along coastal West Africa and on both sides of the equator in central Africa. Africa's climate is mostly tropical, with subtropical climates limited to the northern and southern coasts and to regions of high elevation. Rainfall is seasonal on most of the continent and is very sparse in desert and semidesert areas.

Geography and climate have significantly shaped African economic development. In the eastern African plains the earliest humans hunted wild animals. The drier steppe regions favored herding. Wetter savanna regions, like the Nile Valley, encouraged grain-based agriculture. Tropical forests favored hunting and gathering and, later, root-based agriculture. Root crops, such as yams, potatoes, and cassava, are high in carbohydrates and are usually grown in areas that are not suitable for grains. Rivers and lakes supported economies based on fishing.

Africa's peoples are as diverse as the continent's topography. In North Africa contacts with Asian and European civilizations date back to the ancient Phoenicians, Greeks, and Romans (see Chapters 5 and 6). Groups living on the coast or along trade routes had the greatest degree of contact with outside groups. The native Berbers of North Africa, living along the Mediterranean, intermingled with many different peoples—with Muslim Arabs, who first conquered North Africa in the seventh and eighth centuries C.E. (see page 238); with Spanish Muslims and Jews, many of whom settled in North Africa after their expulsion from Spain in 1492 (see page 440); and with sub-Saharan blacks with whom they traded across the Sahara Desert. The peoples living along the Swahili coast in East Africa developed a maritime civilization and had rich commercial contacts with southern Arabia, the Persian Gulf, India, China, and the Malay Archipelago.

Black Africans inhabited the region south of the Sahara, an area of savanna and rain forest. The ancient Greeks called them *Ethiopians*, which means "people with burnt faces." The Berbers also described this region based on its inhabitants, coining the term *Akal-n-Iquinawen*, which survives today as *Guinea*. Similarly, the Arabs used the term *Bilad al-Sudan*, which survives as *Sudan*. The Berber and Arab terms both mean "land of the blacks." Short-statured peoples, sometimes inaccurately referred to as Pygmies, inhabited the equatorial rain forests. South of those forests, in the continent's southern third, lived the Khoisan (KOY-sahn), a small people with yellow-brown skin color who primarily were hunters but also had domesticated livestock.

Egypt, Race, and Being African

When Europeans first started exploring sub-Saharan Africa's interior in the nineteenth century they were amazed at the quality of the art and architecture they came across, which included the ruins at Great Zimbabwe and the Nok heads, both of which are discussed in this chapter. In response they developed the **Hamitic thesis**, which argued that Africans were not capable of such work, so a "Hamitic race" related to the Caucasian race must have settled in Africa in the distant past, practiced their advanced technologies, including ironworking, and then blended into nearby African populations or departed. Although completely discredited today, the Hamitic thesis survived throughout much of the twentieth century.

As is evident from the nineteenth century's artificial construction of a Hamitic race, popular usage of the term *race* has often been imprecise and inaccurate. The application of general characteristics and patterns of behavior to peoples based on perceptions of physical differences is one of the legacies of imperialism and colonialism. Anthropologists have long insisted that when applied to geographical, national, religious, linguistic, or cultural groups, the concept of race is inappropriate and has been refuted by the scientific data. But race remains an essential category in the popular psyche, and the issue of race continues to engender fierce debate. Nowhere in African studies has this debate been more strident than over questions relating to Egyptian identity and civilization, and Africa's contribution to European civilization.

Geographically, Egypt, located in North Africa, is part of the African continent. But from the days of the ancient Greek historian Herodotus, who visited Egypt in the fifth century B.C.E. (see page 123), down to the present, scholars have vigorously, even violently,

□ CHRONOLOGY

ca. 1000 B.C.E.–1500 C.E. Bantu-speakers expand across central and southern Africa

ca. 600 C.E. Christian missionaries convert Nubian rulers

642 C.E. Muslim conquest of Egypt; Islam introduced to Africa

650–1500 C.E. Slave trade from sub-Saharan Africa to the Mediterranean

700–900 C.E. Berbers develop caravan routes

ca. 900–1100 C.E. Kingdom of Ghana; bananas and plantains arrive in Africa from Asia

ca. 1100–1400 C.E. Great Zimbabwe is built, flourishes

ca. 1200–1450 C.E. Kingdom of Mali

ca. 1312–1337 C.E. Reign of Mansa Musa in Mali

1314–1344 C.E. Reign of Amda Siyon in Ethiopia

1324–1325 C.E. Mansa Musa's pilgrimage to Mecca

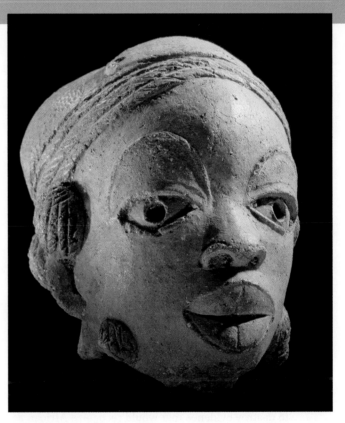

Nok Woman Hundreds of terra-cotta sculptures such as the head of this woman survive from the Nok culture, which originated in the central plateau of northern Nigeria in the first millennium B.C.E. (Werner Forman/Art Resource, NY)

• **Hamitic thesis** A nineteenth-century concept, tied to scientific racism, that a subgroup of the Caucasian race, the Hamites, brought superior technology and knowledge to Africa in the ancient past; now completely discredited.

MAP 10.1 The Geography of Africa Africa's climate zones have always played a critical role in the history of the continent and its peoples. These zones mirror each other north and south of the equator: tropical forest, savanna, sub-desert, desert, and Mediterranean climate.

debated whether racially and culturally Egypt is part of the Mediterranean world or part of the African world. More recently, the debate has also included the question of whether Egyptians of the first century B.C.E. made such contributions to the Western world as architecture (the pyramids), mathematics, philosophy, science, and religion (the idea of divine kingship), and, if so, whether they were black people.

Some African and African American scholars have argued that much Western historical writing since the eighteenth century has been a "European racist plot" to destroy evidence that would recognize African accomplishments. They have amassed architectural and linguistic evidence, as well as a small mountain of quotations from Greek and Roman writers and from the Bible, to insist that the ancient Egyptians belonged to the black race. The late Senegalese scholar Cheikh Anta Diop claimed to have examined the skin of ancient Egyptian mummies and said that it "was pigmented in the same way as that of all other (sub-Saharan) Afri-

can negroes."[1] Similarly, in 1987 the English historian Martin Bernal argued that Egypt and therefore Africa had never received enough credit for their contributions to Greek civilization.[2]

Against this view, another group of scholars holds that the ancient Egyptians were Caucasians. They believe that Phoenician, Berber, Libyan, Hebrew, and Greek peoples populated Egypt and created its civilization. Whereas Diop relied on the book of Genesis to support his thesis, his detractors argue that the Hebrew Scriptures are not an anthropological treatise but a collection of Hebrew, Mesopotamian, and Egyptian legends concerned with the origins of all human peoples, not racial groups in the twentieth-century sense. They point out that the pharaohs of the first century B.C.E. descended from the (white) Macedonian generals whom Alexander the Great had placed over Egypt.

A third proposition, perhaps the most plausible, holds that ancient Egypt, at the crossroads of three continents, was a melting pot of different cultures and peoples. To attribute Egyptian civilization to any one group is blatant racism and ultimately extremist. Many diverse peoples contributed to the great achievements of Egyptian culture. Moderate scholars believe that black Africans resided in ancient Egypt, primarily in Upper Egypt (south of what is now Cairo), but that other racial groups constituted the majority of the population. The argument put forward by Bernal and others that Egypt significantly contributed to Greek civilization has been critically challenged by a number of these scholars, including Mary Lefkowitz and Guy MacLean Rogers, for the selective gathering of evidence and poor historical and linguistic scholarship.[3] On these complex issues, the jury remains out.[4]

Early African Societies

☐ How did settled agriculture affect life among the early societies in the western Sudan and among the Bantu-speaking societies of central and southern Africa?

The introduction of new crops from Asia and methods of settled agriculture profoundly changed many African societies, although the range of possibilities was greatly dependent on local variations in climate and geography. Bantu-speakers took the knowledge of domesticated livestock and agriculture and the iron-working skills that developed in northern and western Africa and spread them south across central and southern Africa. The most prominent feature of early West African society was a strong sense of community based on blood relationships and on religion. Extended families made up the villages that collectively formed small kingdoms.

Settled Agriculture and Its Impact

Agriculture began very early in Africa. Knowledge of plant cultivation moved west from ancient Judaea (southern Palestine), arriving in the Nile Delta in Egypt about the fifth millennium B.C.E. Settled agriculture then traveled down the Nile Valley and moved west across the Sahel to the central and western Sudan. By the first century B.C.E. settled agriculture existed in West Africa. From there it spread to the equatorial forests. African farmers learned to domesticate plants, including millet, sorghum, and yams. Cereal-growing people probably taught forest people to plant grains on plots of land cleared by a method known as "slash and burn." Gradually most Africans evolved a sedentary way of life: living in villages, clearing fields, relying on root crops such as yams and cassava, and fishing. Hunting-and-gathering societies survived only in scattered parts of Africa, particularly in the central rain forest region and in southern Africa.

Between 1500 and 1000 B.C.E. settled agriculture also spread southward from Ethiopia along the Great Rift Valley of present-day Kenya and Tanzania. Archaeological evidence reveals that the peoples of this region grew cereals, raised cattle, and used wooden and stone tools. Cattle raising spread more quickly than did planting, prospering on the open savannas that are free of tsetse flies, which are devastating to cattle. The early African peoples of this region prized cattle highly. Many trading agreements, marriage alliances, political compacts, and treaties were negotiated in terms of cattle.

Cereals such as millet and sorghum are indigenous to Africa. Scholars speculate that traders brought bananas, taros (a type of yam), sugarcane, and coconut palms to Africa from Southeast Asia. Because tropical forest conditions were ideal for banana plants, their cultivation spread rapidly. Throughout sub-Saharan Africa native peoples also domesticated donkeys, pigs, chickens, geese, and ducks.

The evolution from a hunter-gatherer life to a settled life had profound effects. In contrast to nomadic conditions, settled societies made shared or common needs more apparent, and those needs strengthened ties among extended families. Agricultural and pastoral populations also increased, though scholars speculate that this increase was not steady, but rather fluctuated over time. Nor is it clear that the growth in numbers of people was accompanied by a commensurate increase in agricultural output.

Early African societies were similarly influenced by the spread of ironworking, though scholars dispute the route by which this technology spread to sub-Saharan Africa. Some believe the Phoenicians brought the iron-smelting technique to northwestern Africa, from where it spread southward. Others insist it spread westward from the Meroë (MEHR-oh-ee) region on the Nile. Most of West Africa had acquired knowledge of ironworking by 250 B.C.E., however, and archaeologists believe Meroë achieved pre-eminence as an iron-smelting center only in the first century B.C.E. Thus a stronger case can probably be made for the Phoenicians. The great trans-Saharan trade routes (see page 274) may have carried ironworking south from the Mediterranean coast. In any case, ancient iron tools found at the village of Nok on the Jos Plateau in present-day Nigeria seem to prove a knowledge of ironworking in West Africa by at least 700 B.C.E. The Nok culture, which enjoys enduring fame for its fine terra-cotta (baked clay) sculptures, flourished from about 800 B.C.E. to 200 C.E.

Tassili Rock Painting
This scene of cattle grazing near a group of huts (represented on the left by ovals) reflects the domestication of animals and the development of settled pastoral agriculture in Africa. Women and children seem to perform most of the domestic chores. Tassili is a mountainous region in the Sahara where over 15,000 of these paintings have been catalogued, with the oldest dating back 9,000–10,000 years. (Photo: Henri Lhote. Courtesy, Irene Lhote)

Bantu Migrations

The spread of ironworking is linked to the migrations of Bantu-speaking peoples. Today the overwhelming majority of the 70 million people living south of the Congo River speak a **Bantu** language. Because very few Muslims or Europeans penetrated into the interior, and few Bantu-speakers, except the Swahili, for example, wrote down their languages, very few written sources for the early history of central and southern Africa survive. Lacking written sources, modern scholars have tried to reconstruct the history of the Bantu-speakers on the basis of linguistics, oral traditions (rarely reliable beyond three hundred years back), archaeology, and anthropology. Botanists and zoologists have played particularly critical roles in providing information about early diets and environments.

The word *Bantu* is a linguistic classification, and linguistics (the study of the nature, structure, and modification of human speech) has helped scholars explain the migratory patterns of African peoples east and south of the equatorial forest. There are hundreds of Bantu languages, including Zulu, Sotho, and Tswana, which are part of the southern African linguistic and cultural nexus, and Swahili, which is spoken in eastern, and to a limited extent central, Africa.

Bantu-speaking peoples originated in the Benue region, the borderlands of modern Cameroon and Nigeria. In the second millennium B.C.E. they began to spread south and east into the forest zone of equatorial Africa.

Why they began this movement is still a matter of dispute among historians. Some hold that rapid population growth sent people in search of land. Others believe that the evolution of centralized kingdoms allowed rulers to expand their authority, while causing newly subjugated peoples to flee in the hope of regaining their independence.

Since the early Bantu-speakers had words for fishing, fishhooks, fish traps, dugout canoes, paddles, yams, and goats, linguists assume that they were fishermen and that they cultivated roots. Because initially they lacked words for grains and cattle herding, they probably were not involved in grain cultivation or the domestication of cattle. During the next fifteen hundred years, however, Bantu-speakers migrated throughout the savanna, adopted mixed agriculture, and learned ironworking. Mixed agriculture (cultivating cereals and raising livestock) and ironworking were practiced in western East Africa (the region of modern Burundi) in the first century B.C.E. In the first millennium C.E. Bantu-speakers migrated into eastern and southern Africa. Here the Bantu-speakers, with their iron weapons, either killed, drove off, or assimilated the hunting-gathering peoples they met. Some of the earlier assimilated inhabitants gradually adopted a Bantu language, contributing to the spread of Bantu culture.

The settled cultivation of cereals, the keeping of livestock, and the introduction of new crops such as the banana — together with Bantu-speakers' intermarriage with indigenous peoples — led over a long time to considerable population increases and the need to migrate farther. The so-called Bantu migrations should not be seen as a single movement sweeping across Africa from west to east to south and displacing all peoples in their path. Rather, those migrations were a series of group interactions between Bantu-speakers and pre-existing peoples in which bits of culture, languages, economies, and technologies were shared and exchanged to produce a wide range of cultural variation across central and southern Africa.[5]

The Bantu-speakers' expansion and subsequent land settlement that dominated eastern and southern African history in the first fifteen hundred years of the Common Era was uneven. Enormous differences in the quality of the environment determined settlement patterns. Some regions were well watered; others were very arid. This situation resulted in very uneven population distribution. The largest concentration of people seems to have been in the region bounded on the west by the Congo River and on the north, south, and east by Lakes Edward and Victoria and Mount Kilimanjaro, comprising parts of modern Uganda, Rwanda, and Tanzania. There the agricultural system rested on sorghum and yam cultivation. Between 900 and 1100 bananas and plantains (a starchy form of the banana) arrived from Asia. Because little effort was needed for their cultivation and the yield was much higher than for yams, bananas soon became the Bantu people's staple crop. The rapid growth of the Bantu-speaking population led to further migration southward and eastward. By the eighth century the Bantu-speaking people had crossed the Zambezi River and had begun settling in the region of present-day Zimbabwe, and by the fifteenth century they had reached Africa's southeastern coast.

Life in the Kingdoms of the Western Sudan, ca. 1000 B.C.E.–800 C.E.

The **Sudan** is the region bounded by the Sahara to the north, the Gulf of Guinea to the south, the Atlantic Ocean to the west, and the mountains of Ethiopia to the east (see Map 10.1). In the savanna of the western Sudan — where the Bantu migrations originated — a series of dynamic kingdoms emerged in the millennium before European intrusion began in the 1400s and 1500s.

Between 1000 B.C.E. and 200 C.E. the peoples of the western Sudan made the momentous shift from nomadic hunting to settled agriculture. The rich savanna proved ideally suited to the production of cereals, es-

Bantu Migrations, ca. 1000 B.C.E.–1500 C.E.

pecially rice, millet, and sorghum. People situated near the Senegal River and Lake Chad supplemented their diet with fish. Food supply affects population, and the peoples of the region — known as the Mande-speakers and the Chadic-speakers, or Sao (sowl) — increased dramatically in number. By 400 C.E. the entire savanna, particularly the areas around Lake Chad, the Niger River bend, and present-day central Nigeria (see Map 10.1), had a large population.

Families and clans affiliated by blood kinship lived together in villages or small city-states. The basic social unit was the extended family. A chief, in consultation with a council of elders, governed a village. Some villages seem to have formed kingdoms. Village chiefs were responsible to regional heads, who answered to provincial governors, who in turn were responsible to a king. The chiefs and their families formed an aristocracy.

Kingship in the Sudan may have emerged from the priesthood, whose members were believed to make rain and to have contact with spirit powers. African kings always had religious sanction or support for their authority and were often considered divine. In this respect, early African kingship bears a strong resemblance to Germanic kingship of the same period (discussed in Chapter 14): the king's authority rested in part on the ruler's ability to negotiate with outside powers, such as the gods.

Among the Asante in modern-day Ghana, one of the most prominent West African peoples, the king was considered divine but shared some royal power with the Queen Mother. She was a full member of the governing council and enjoyed full voting power in various matters of state. The future king was initially chosen by the Queen Mother from eligible royal candidates, and then had to be approved by both his elders and by the commoners. Among the Yoruba in modern Nigeria the Queen Mother held the royal insignia and could refuse it if the future king did not please her. It was she who also placed the royal beaded crown on the king's head. Although the Mende in modern Sierra Leone was one of the few African societies to be led by female rulers, women exercised significant power and autonomy in many African societies. The institutions of female chiefs, known as *iyalode* among the Yoruba and *omu* among the Igbo in modern Nigeria, were established to

---

- **Bantu** Speakers of a Bantu language living south and east of the Congo River.
- **Sudan** The African region surrounded by the Sahara, the Gulf of Guinea, the Atlantic Ocean, and the mountains of Ethiopia.

represent women in the political process. The *omu* was even considered a female co-ruler with the male chief.

Religious practices in the western Sudan, like African religions elsewhere, were animistic and polytheistic. Most people believed that a supreme being had created the universe and was the source of all life. Most African religions also recognized ancestral spirits, which people believed might seek God's blessings for the prosperity and security of their families and communities as long as these groups behaved appropriately. If not, the ancestral spirits might not protect them from harm, and illness and misfortune could result. Some African religions believed as well that nature spirits lived in such things as the sky, forests, rocks, and rivers. These spirits controlled the forces of nature and had to be appeased. During the annual agricultural cycle, for example, all the spirits had to be propitiated from the time of clearing the land through sowing the seed to the final harvest. Because special ceremonies were necessary to satisfy the spirits, special priests with the knowledge and power to communicate with them through sacred rituals were needed. The heads of families and villages were often priests. Each family head was responsible for ceremonies honoring the dead and living members of the family.[6]

In some societies of West Africa oracles who spoke for the gods were particularly important. Some of the most famous oracles were those among the Ibo in modern Nigeria. These were female priestesses who were connected with a particular local deity that resided in a sacred cave or other site, as is vividly described in the Nigerian author Chinua Achebe's 1958 novel *Things Fall Apart*. All the members of the surrounding villages

would come to the priestess to seek advice about such matters as crops and harvests, war, marriage, legal issues, and religion. Clearly, these priestesses held much power and authority, even over the local male rulers.

Kinship patterns and shared religious practices helped to bind together the early African kingdoms of the western Sudan. The spread of Islam across the Sahara by at least the ninth century C.E., however, created a north-south religious and cultural divide in the western Sudan. Islam advanced across the Sahel into modern Mauritania, Mali, Burkina Faso, Niger, northern Nigeria, and Chad, but halted when it reached the savanna and forest zones of West Africa. The societies in the south maintained their traditional animistic religious practices. Muslim empires lying along the great northern bend of the Niger River evolved into formidable powers ruling over sizable territory as they seized control of the southern termini of the trans-Saharan trade. What made this long-distance trade possible was the "ship of the desert," the camel.

The Trans-Saharan Trade

☐ What characterized trans-Saharan trade, and how did it affect West African society?

The expression "trans-Saharan trade" refers to the north-south trade across the Sahara (see Map 10.2). The camel had an impact on this trade comparable to the very important impact of horses and oxen on European agriculture. Although scholars dispute exactly when the camel was introduced from Central Asia — first into North Africa, then into the Sahara and the Sudan — they agree that it was before 200 C.E. Camels can carry about five hundred pounds as far as twenty-five miles a day and can go for days without drinking, living on the water stored in their stomachs. Temperamental and difficult to work with, camels had to be loaded on a daily, sometimes twice-daily, basis, and much of the cargo for a long trip was made up of provisions for the journey itself. Nevertheless, camels proved more efficient for desert transportation than horses or oxen. The trans-Saharan trade brought lasting economic and social change to Africa, facilitating the spread of Islam via Muslim Arab traders, and affected the development of world commerce.

The Berbers of North Africa

Sometime in the fifth century C.E. the North African **Berbers** fashioned a saddle for use on the camel. This saddle had no direct effect on commercial operations, for a merchant usually walked and guided the camel on foot. But the saddle gave the Berbers and later the region's Arabian inhabitants maneuverability on the

Trans-Saharan Trade A Berber caravan driver adjusts the salt block on his camel in a timeless ritual of the trans-Saharan trade. (© James Michael Dorsey)

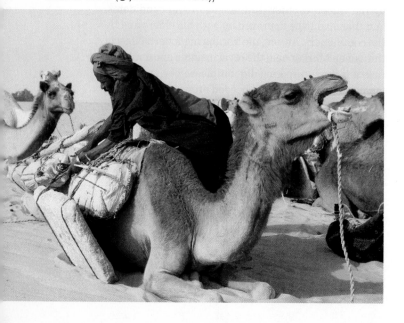

animal and thus a powerful political and military advantage: they came to dominate the desert and to create lucrative routes across it. The Berbers determined who could enter the desert, and they extracted large sums of protection money from merchant caravans in exchange for a safe trip.

Between 700 and 900 C.E. the Berbers developed a network of caravan routes between the Mediterranean coast and the Sudan (see Map 10.2). The long expedition across the Sahara testifies to the spirit of the traders and to their passion for wealth. Because of the blistering sun and daytime temperatures reaching 110 degrees, caravan drivers preferred night travel, when temperatures might drop to the low 20s. Ibn Battuta, an Arab traveler in the fourteenth century when the trade was at its height, left one of the best descriptions of the trans-Saharan traffic. (See "Individuals in Society: Ibn Battuta," page 254.) It took Ibn Battuta twenty-five days to travel from Sijilmasa to the oasis of Taghaza and another sixty-five days to travel from Taghaza to the important market town of Walata.

Nomadic raiders, the Tuareg (TWAH-reg), posed a serious threat to trans-Saharan traders. The Tuareg were Berbers who lived in the desert uplands and preyed on the caravans as a way of life. To avoid being victimized, merchants made safe-conduct agreements with them and selected guides from among them. Large numbers of merchants crossed the desert together to discourage attack; caravans of twelve thousand camels were reported in the fourteenth century. Blinding sandstorms often separated part of a line of camels and on at least one recorded occasion buried alive some camels and drivers. Water was the biggest problem. To satisfy normal thirst and to compensate for constant sweating, each person required a gallon of water per day. Desperate thirst sometimes forced the traders to kill camels and drink the foul, brackish water in their stomachs. The Tuareg used this problem to their advantage, sometimes poisoning wells to wipe out caravans and steal their goods.

The Arab Berber merchants from North Africa who controlled the caravan trade carried dates, salt (essential in tropical climates to replace the loss from perspiration) from the Saharan salt mines, and some manufactured goods — silk and cotton cloth, beads, mirrors — to the Sudan. These products were exchanged for the much-coveted commodities of the West African savanna — gold, ivory, gum, kola nuts (eaten as a stimulant), and enslaved West African men and women who were sold to Muslim slave markets in Morocco, Algiers, Tripoli, and Cairo.

Effects of Trade on West African Society

The steady growth of trans-Saharan trade had three important effects on West African society. First, trade

• TABLE 10.1 Estimated Magnitude of Trans-Saharan Slave Trade, 650–1500

YEARS	ANNUAL AVERAGE OF SLAVES TRADED	TOTAL
650–800	1,000	150,000
800–900	3,000	300,000
900–1100	8,700	1,740,000
1100–1400	5,500	1,650,000
1400–1500	4,300	430,000

Source: R. A. Austen, "The Trans-Saharan Slave Trade: A Tentative Census," in *The Uncommon Market: Essays in the Economic History of the Atlantic Slave Trade*, ed. H. A. Gemery and J. S. Hogendorn (New York: Academic Press, 1979). Used with permission.

stimulated gold mining. Parts of modern-day Senegal, Nigeria, and Ghana contained rich veins of gold. Both sexes shared in mining it. Men hacked out gold-bearing rocks and crushed them, separating the gold from the soil. Women washed the gold in gourds. Alluvial gold (mixed with soil, sand, or gravel) was separated from the soil by panning. Scholars estimate that by the eleventh century nine tons of gold were exported to the Mediterranean coast and Europe annually — a prodigious amount for the time, since even with modern machinery and sophisticated techniques, the total gold exports from the same region in 1937 amounted to only twenty-one tons. Some of this metal went to Egypt. From there it was transported down the Red Sea and eventually to India (see Map 9.2 on page 253) to pay for the spices and silks demanded by Mediterranean commerce. In this way, African gold linked the entire world, exclusive of the Western Hemisphere.

Second, trade in gold and other goods created a desire for slaves. Slaves were West Africa's second most valuable export (after gold). Slaves worked the gold and salt mines, and in Muslim North Africa, southern Europe, and southwestern Asia there was a high demand for household slaves among the elite. African slaves, like their early European and Asian counterparts, seem to have been peoples captured in war. Recent research suggests, moreover, that large numbers of black slaves were also recruited for Muslim military service through the trans-Saharan trade. High death rates from disease, manumission, and the assimilation of some blacks into Muslim society meant that the demand for slaves remained high for centuries. Table 10.1 shows the scope of the trans-Saharan slave trade. The total number of blacks enslaved over an 850-year period may be tentatively estimated at more than 4 million.[7]

Slavery in Muslim societies, as in European and Asian countries before the fifteenth century, was not

---

Berbers North African peoples who controlled the caravan trade between the Mediterranean and the Sudan.

based on skin color. Muslims also enslaved Caucasians who had been purchased, seized in war, or kidnapped from Europe. Wealthy Muslim households in Córdoba, Alexandria, and Tunis often included slaves of a number of races, all of whom had been completely cut off from their cultural roots. Likewise, West African kings who sold blacks to northern traders also bought a few white slaves — Slavic, British, and Turkish — for their own domestic needs. Race had little to do with the phenomenon of slavery.

The third important effect on West African society was the role of trans-Saharan trade in stimulating the development of urban centers. Scholars date the growth of African cities from around the early ninth century. Families that had profited from trade tended to congregate in the border zones between the savanna and the Sahara. They acted as middlemen between the miners to the south and Muslim merchants from the north. By the early thirteenth century these families had become powerful black merchant dynasties. Muslim traders from the Mediterranean settled permanently in the trading depots, from which they organized the trans-Saharan caravans. The concentration of people stimulated agriculture and the craft industries. Gradually cities of sizable population emerged. Jenne, Gao, and Timbuktu, which enjoyed commanding positions on the Niger River bend, became centers of the export-import trade. Sijilmasa grew into a thriving market center. Koumbi Saleh, with between fifteen thousand and twenty thousand inhabitants, was probably the largest city in the western Sudan in the twelfth century. (By European standards, Koumbi Saleh was a metropolis; London and Paris achieved this size only in the late thirteenth century.) Between 1100 and 1400 these cities played a dynamic role in the commercial life of West Africa and Europe and became centers of intellectual creativity.

The Spread of Islam in Africa

Perhaps the most influential consequence of the trans-Saharan trade was the introduction of Islam to West African society. In the eighth century Arab invaders overran all of coastal North Africa. They introduced the Berbers living there to the religion of Islam (see page 238), and gradually the Berbers became Muslims. As traders, these Berbers carried Islam to sub-Saharan West Africa. From the eleventh century onward militant Almoravids, a coalition of fundamentalist western Saharan Berbers, preached Islam to the rulers of Ghana, Mali, Songhai, and Kanem-Bornu, who, admiring

The Spread of Islam in Africa

Muslim administrative techniques and wanting to protect their kingdoms from Muslim Berber attacks, accepted Islamic conversion. Some merchants also sought to preserve their elite mercantile status with the Berbers by adopting Islam. By the tenth century Muslim Berbers controlled the north-south trade routes to the savanna. By the eleventh century African rulers of Gao and Timbuktu had accepted Islam. The king of Ghana was also influenced by Islam. Muslims quickly became integral to West African government and society. Hence in the period from roughly 1000 to 1400, Islam in West Africa was a class-based religion with conversion inspired by political or economic motives. Rural people in the Sahel region and the peoples of the savanna and forest regions farther south, however, largely retained their traditional animism.

Conversion to Islam introduced West Africans to a rich and sophisticated culture. By the late eleventh century Muslims were guiding the ruler of Ghana in the operation of his administrative machinery. The king of Ghana adopted the Muslim dīwān, the agency for keeping financial records (see page 239). Because efficient government depends on the preservation of records, the arrival of Islam in West Africa marked the advent of written documents there. Arab Muslims also taught the rulers of Ghana how to manufacture bricks, and royal palaces and mosques began to be built of brick. African rulers corresponded with Arab and North African Muslim architects, theologians, and other intellectuals, who advised them on statecraft and religion. Islam accelerated the development of the West African empires of the ninth through fifteenth centuries.

After the Muslim conquest of Egypt in 642 (see page 237), Islam spread southward from Egypt up the Nile Valley and west to Darfur and Wadai. This Muslim penetration came not by military force but, as in the trans-Saharan trade routes in West Africa, by gradual commercial passage.

Muslim expansion from the Arabian peninsula across the Red Sea to the Horn of Africa, then southward along the coast of East Africa, represents a third direction of Islam's growth in Africa. From ports on the Red Sea and the Gulf of Aden, maritime trade carried the Prophet's teachings to East Africa and the Indian Ocean. Muslims founded the port city of **Mogadishu**, today Somalia's capital. In the twelfth century Mogadishu developed into a Muslim sultanate, a monarchy that employed a slave military corps against foreign and domestic enemies. Archaeological evidence, confirmed by Arabic sources, reveals a rapid Islamic expansion along Africa's east coast in the thirteenth century as far south as Kilwa, where Ibn Battuta came across a center for Islamic law during a visit in 1331.

African Kingdoms and Empires, ca. 800–1500

☐ How were the East African city-states, Aksum, and Great Zimbabwe different from and similar to the kingdoms of the western Sudan?

All African societies shared one basic feature: a close relationship between political and social organization. Ethnic or blood ties bound clan members together. What scholars call **stateless societies** were culturally homogeneous ethnic societies, generally organized around kinship groups. The smallest ones numbered fewer than a hundred people and were nomadic hunting groups. Larger stateless societies of perhaps several thousand people, such as the Tiv in modern central Nigeria, lived a settled and often agricultural or herding life. These societies lacked a central authority figure, such as a king, capital city, or military; hence their designation by some historians as decentralized societies. A village or group of villages might recognize a chief who held very limited powers and whose position was not hereditary, but more commonly they were governed by local councils, whose members were either elders or persons of merit. Although stateless societies functioned successfully, their weakness lay in their inability to organize and defend themselves against attack by the powerful armies of neighboring kingdoms or by the European powers of the colonial era.

While stateless societies were relatively common in Africa, the period from about 800 to 1500 is best known as the age of Africa's great empires (Map 10.2). It witnessed the flowering of several powerful African states. In the western Sudan the large empires of Ghana, Mali, and Songhai developed, complete with sizable royal bureaucracies. On the east coast emerged powerful city-states based on sophisticated mercantile activities and, like Sudan, very much influenced by Islam. In Ethiopia, in central East Africa, kings relied on the Christian faith of their people to strengthen political authority. In southern Africa the empire of Great Zimbabwe, built on the gold trade with the east coast, flourished.

The Kingdom of Ghana, ca. 900–1100

So remarkable was the kingdom of **Ghana** during the age of Africa's great empires that Arab and North African visitors praised it as a model for other rulers. Even in modern times, ancient Ghana holds a central place in Africa's historical consciousness. When the Gold Coast colony gained its independence from British colonial rule in 1957, its new political leaders paid tribute to this glorious heritage by naming their new country Ghana. Although modern Ghana lies far from the site of the old kingdom, the name was selected to signify the rebirth of ancient Ghana's illustrious past in black Africa.

The nucleus of the territory that became the kingdom of Ghana was inhabited by Soninke people who called their ruler *ghana*, or war chief. By the late eighth century Muslim traders and other foreigners applied the king's title to the region where the Soninke lived, the black kingdom south of the Sahara. The Soninke themselves called their land Wagadou (WAH-guh-doo). Only the southern part of Wagadou received enough rainfall to be agriculturally productive, and it was in this area that the civilization of Ghana developed (see Map 10.2). Skillful farming and an efficient system of irrigation led to the production of abundant crops, which eventually supported a population of as many as two hundred thousand.

The Soninke name for their king — war chief — aptly describes the king's major preoccupation in the tenth century. In 992 Ghana captured the Berber town of Awdaghost, strategically situated on the trans-Saharan trade route. Thereafter Ghana controlled the southern portion of a major caravan route. Before the year 1000 the rulers of Ghana had extended their influence almost to the Atlantic coast and had captured a number of small kingdoms in the south and east. By the early eleventh century the Ghanaian king exercised sway over a territory approximately the size of Texas. No other power in the West African region could successfully challenge him.

Throughout this vast West African area, all authority sprang from the king. Religious ceremonies and court rituals emphasized the king's sacredness and were intended to strengthen his authority. The king's position was hereditary in the matrilineal line — that is, the ruling king's heir was one of the king's sister's sons (presumably the eldest or fittest for battle). According to the eleventh-century Spanish Muslim geographer al-Bakri (1040?–1094), "This is their custom . . . the kingdom is inherited only by the son of the king's sister. He the king has no doubt that his successor is a son of his sister, while he is not certain that his son is in fact his own."[8]

- **Mogadishu** A Muslim port city in East Africa founded between the eighth and tenth centuries; today it is the capital of Somalia.
- **stateless societies** African societies bound together by ethnic or blood ties rather than being political states.
- **Ghana** From the word for ruler, the name of a large and influential African kingdom inhabited by the Soninke people.

▢ Mapping the Past

MAP 10.2 African Kingdoms and Trade, ca. 800–1500 Throughout world history powerful kingdoms have generally been closely connected to far-flung trade networks.

ANALYZING THE MAP Which kingdoms, empires, and city-states were linked to the trans-Saharan trade network? Which were connected to the Indian Ocean trade network? To the Portuguese route?

CONNECTIONS How were the kingdoms, empires, and city-states shown on this map shaped by their proximity to trade routes?

A council of ministers assisted the king in the work of government, and from the ninth century on most of these ministers were Muslims. Detailed evidence about the early Ghanaian bureaucracy has not survived, but scholars suspect that separate agencies were responsible for taxation, royal property, foreigners, forests, and the army. The royal administration was well served by ideas, skills, and especially literacy brought from the North African and Arab Muslim worlds. The king and his people, however, clung to their ancestral religion and basic cultural institutions.

The king of Ghana held his court in the large and vibrant city of **Koumbi Saleh**, which al-Bakri actually describes as two towns — one in which the king and the royal court lived, and the other Muslim. Al-Bakri provides a valuable picture of the Muslim part of the town in the eleventh century:

> The city of Ghana consists of two towns lying on a plain, one of which is inhabited by Muslims and is large, possessing twelve mosques — one of which is a congregational mosque for Friday prayer; each has its imam, its muezzin and paid reciters of the Quran. The town possesses a large number of jurisconsults and learned men.[9]

Either for their own protection or to preserve their special identity, the Muslims of Koumbi Saleh lived separate from the African artisans and tradespeople. The Muslim community in Ghana must have been large and prosperous to have supported twelve mosques. Muslim religious leaders exercised civil authority over their fellow Muslims. The imam was the religious leader who conducted the ritual worship, especially the main prayer service on Fridays (see page 240). The muezzin led the prayer responses after the imam; he needed a strong voice so that those at a distance and the women in the harems, or enclosures, could hear (see page 252). The presence of the religious leaders and of other learned Muslims suggests that Koumbi Saleh was a city of vigorous intellectual activity.

Al-Bakri also described the royal court:

> The town inhabited by the king is six miles from the Muslim one and is called Al Ghana. . . . The residence of the king consists of a palace and a number of dome-shaped dwellings, all of them surrounded by a strong enclosure, like a city wall. In the town . . . is a mosque, where Muslims who come on diplomatic missions to the king pray.[10]
>
> The king adorns himself, as do the women here, with necklaces and bracelets; on their heads they wear caps decorated with gold, sewn on material of fine cotton stuffing. When he holds court in order to hear the people's complaints and to do justice, he sits in a pavilion around which stand ten horses wearing golden trappings; behind him ten

> **" When [the king] holds court . . . he sits in a pavilion around which stand ten horses wearing golden trappings . . . ; at his right are the sons of the chiefs of the country, splendidly dressed and with their hair sprinkled with gold. "**
>
> **AL-BAKRI**

> pages stand, holding shields and swords decorated with gold; at his right are the sons of the chiefs of the country, splendidly dressed and with their hair sprinkled with gold. . . . When the king's coreligionists appear before him, they fall on their knees and toss dust on their heads — this is their way of greeting their sovereign. Muslims show respect by clapping their hands.[11]

Justice derived from the king, who heard cases at court or on his travels throughout his kingdom. As al-Bakri recounts:

> When a man is accused of denying a debt or of having shed blood or some other crime, a headman (village chief) takes a thin piece of wood, which is sour and bitter to taste, and pours upon it some water which he then gives to the defendant to drink. If the man vomits, his innocence is recognized and he is congratulated. If he does not vomit and the drink remains in his stomach, the accusation is accepted as justified.[12]

This appeal to the supernatural for judgment was similar to the justice by ordeal that prevailed among the Germanic peoples of western Europe at the same time (discussed in Chapter 14). Complicated cases were appealed to the king, who often relied on the advice of Muslim legal experts.

The king's elaborate court, the administrative machinery he built, and the extensive territories he governed were all expensive. To support the kingdom, the royal estates — some hereditary, others conquered in war — produced annual revenue, mostly in the form of foodstuffs for the royal household. The king also received tribute annually from subordinate chieftains. Customs duties on goods entering and leaving the country generated revenues. Salt was the largest import. Berber merchants paid a tax to the king on the cloth, metalwork, weapons, and other goods that they brought into the country from North Africa; in return these traders received royal protection from bandits. African traders bringing gold into Ghana from the south also paid the customs duty.

• **Koumbi Saleh**   The city in which the king of Ghana held his court.

Finally, the royal treasury held a monopoly on the export of gold. The gold industry was undoubtedly the king's largest source of income. It was on gold that the fame of medieval Ghana rested. The ninth-century Persian geographer al-Ya-qubi wrote, "Its king is mighty, and in his lands are gold mines. Under his authority are various other kingdoms — and in all this region there is gold."[13]

The governing aristocracy — the king, his court, and Muslim administrators — occupied the highest rung on the Ghanaian social ladder. On the next rung stood the merchant class. Considerably below the merchants stood the farmers, cattle breeders, gold mine supervisors, and skilled craftsmen and weavers — what today might be called the middle class. Some merchants and miners must have enjoyed great wealth, but, as in all aristocratic societies, money alone did not suffice. High status was based on blood and royal service. On the social ladder's lowest rung were slaves, who worked in households, on farms, and in the mines. As in Asian and European societies of the time, slaves accounted for only a small percentage of the population.

Apart from these social classes stood the army. According to al-Bakri, "the king of Ghana can put 200,000 warriors in the field, more than 40,000 being armed with bow and arrow." Like most medieval estimates, this is probably a gross exaggeration. The king of Ghana, however, was not called "war chief" for nothing. He maintained at his palace a standing force of a thousand men, comparable to the bodyguards of the emperors of the Roman republic. These thoroughly disciplined, well-armed, totally loyal troops protected the king and the royal court. They lived in special compounds, enjoyed the king's favor, and sometimes acted as his personal ambassadors to subordinate rulers. In wartime this regular army was augmented by levies of soldiers from conquered peoples and by the use of slaves and free re-

> **"Its king is mighty, and in his lands are gold mines. Under his authority are various other kingdoms — and in all this region there is gold."**
>
> **AL-YA-QUBI**

serves. The force that the king could field was sizable, if not as huge as al-Bakri estimated.

The reasons for ancient Ghana's decline are still a matter of much debate. By al-Bakri's time there were other increasingly powerful neighbors, such as the Mandinke, to challenge Ghana's influence in the region. The most commonly accepted theory for Ghana's rapid decline held, however, that the Berber Almoravid dynasty of North Africa invaded and conquered Ghana around 1100 and forced its rulers and people to convert to Islam. A close study of this question has recently concluded that while Almoravid and Islamic pressures certainly disrupted the empire, weakening it enough for its incorporation into the rising Mali empire, there was no Almoravid military invasion and subsequent forced conversion to Islam.[14]

The Kingdom of Mali, ca. 1200–1450

There can be no doubt that Ghana and its capital of Koumbi Saleh were in decline between 1100 and 1200, and a cloud of obscurity hung over the western Sudan. The kingdom of Ghana split into several small kingdoms that feuded among themselves. One people, the Mandinka, from the kingdom of Kangaba on the upper Niger River, gradually asserted their dominance over these kingdoms. The Mandinka had long been part of the Ghanaian empire, and the Mandinka and Soninke belonged to the same language group. Kangaba formed the core of the new empire of Mali. Building on Ghanaian foundations, Mali developed into a better-organized and more powerful state than Ghana.

The kingdom of Mali owed its greatness to two fundamental assets. First, its strong agricultural and commercial base provided for a large population and enormous wealth. Second, Mali had two rulers, Sundiata (soon-JAH-tuh) and Mansa Musa, who combined military success with exceptionally creative personalities.

The earliest surviving evidence about the Mandinka, dating from the early eleventh century, indicates that they were extremely successful at agriculture. Consistently large harvests throughout the twelfth and thirteenth centuries meant a plentiful supply of food, which encouraged steady population growth. The geographical location of Kangaba also placed the Mandinka in an ideal position in West African trade. Earlier, during the period of Ghanaian hegemony, the Mandinka had acted as middlemen in the gold and salt traffic flowing north and south. In the thirteenth century Mandinka traders

The Expansion of Mali, ca. 1200–1450

Territory of Mali
- ca. 1100
- ca. 1350
- ca. 1500

formed companies, traveled widely, and gradually became a major force in the entire West African trade.

The founder of Mali, Sundiata (r. ca. 1230–1255) set up his capital at Niani, transforming the city into an important financial and trading center. He then embarked on a policy of imperial expansion. Through a series of military victories, Sundiata and his successors absorbed into Mali other territories of the former kingdom of Ghana and established hegemony over the trading cities of Gao, Jenne, and Walata.

These expansionist policies were continued in the fourteenth century by Sundiata's descendant Mansa Musa (r. ca. 1312–1337), early Africa's most famous ruler. In the language of the Mandinke, *mansa* means "emperor." Mansa Musa fought many campaigns and checked every attempt at rebellion. Ultimately his influence extended northward to several Berber cities in the Sahara, eastward to the trading cities of Timbuktu and Gao, and westward as far as the Atlantic Ocean. Throughout his territories, he maintained strict royal control over the rich trans-Saharan trade. Thus this empire, roughly twice the size of the Ghanaian kingdom and containing perhaps 8 million people, brought Mansa Musa fabulous wealth.

Mansa Musa built on the foundations of his predecessors. The stratified aristocratic structure of Malian society perpetuated the pattern set in Ghana, as did the system of provincial administration and annual tribute. The emperor took responsibility for the territories that formed the heart of the empire and appointed governors to rule the outlying provinces or dependent kingdoms. But Mansa Musa made a significant innovation: in a practice strikingly similar to a system used in both China and France at the time, he appointed members of the royal family as provincial governors. He could count on their loyalty, and they received valuable experience in the work of government.

In another aspect of administration, Mansa Musa also differed from his predecessors. He became a devout Muslim. Although most of the Mandinke clung to their ancestral animism, Islamic practices and influences in Mali multiplied.

The most celebrated event of Mansa Musa's reign was his pilgrimage to Mecca in 1324–1325, during which he paid a state visit to the sultan of Egypt. Mansa Musa's entrance into Cairo was magnificent. Preceded by five hundred slaves, each carrying a six-pound staff of gold, he followed with a huge host of retainers, including one hundred elephants each bearing one hundred pounds of gold. The emperor lavished his wealth on the citizens of the Egyptian capital. Writing twelve years later, al-Omari, one of the sultan's officials, recounts:

> This man Mansa Musa spread upon Cairo the flood of his generosity: there was no person, officer of the court, or holder of any office of the Sultanate who did not receive a sum of gold from him. The people of Cairo earned incalculable sums from him, whether by buying and selling or by gifts. So much gold was current in Cairo that it ruined the value of money.[15]

The Great Friday Mosque, Jenne The mosque at Jenne was built in the form of a parallelogram. Inside, nine long rows of adobe columns run along a north-south axis and support a flat roof of palm logs. A pointed arch links each column to the next in its row, forming nine east-west archways facing the *mihrab*, the niche in the wall of the mosque indicating the direction of Mecca and from which the imam speaks. This mosque (rebuilt in 1907 on a thirteenth-century model) testifies to the considerable wealth, geometrical knowledge, and manpower of Mali. (© Gavin Hellier/Alamy)

For the first time, the Mediterranean world gained concrete knowledge of Mali's wealth and power, and the black kingdom began to be known as one of the world's great empires. Mali retained this international reputation into the fifteenth century. Musa's pilgrimage also had significant consequences within Mali. He gained some understanding of the Mediterranean countries and opened diplomatic relations with the Muslim rulers of Morocco and Egypt. His zeal for the Muslim faith and Islamic culture increased. Musa brought back from Arabia the distinguished architect al-Saheli, whom he commissioned to build new mosques at Timbuktu and other cities. These mosques served as centers for the conversion of Africans to Islam. Musa employed Muslim engineers to build in brick. He also encouraged Malian merchants and traders to wear the distinctive flowing robes and turbans of Muslim males.

Timbuktu began as a campsite for desert nomads, but under Mansa Musa, it grew into a thriving trading post, or entrepôt (AHN-truh-poh), attracting merchants and traders from North Africa and all parts of the Mediterranean world. They brought with them cosmopolitan attitudes and ideas. In the fifteenth century Timbuktu developed into a great center for scholarship and learning. Architects, astronomers, poets, lawyers, mathematicians, and theologians flocked there. One hundred fifty schools, for men only, were devoted to Qur'anic studies. The school of Islamic law enjoyed a distinction in Africa comparable to the prestige of the school at Cairo (see page 257). The vigorous traffic in books that flourished in Timbuktu made them the most common items of trade. Timbuktu's tradition and reputation for African scholarship lasted until the eighteenth century.

Moreover, in the fourteenth and fifteenth centuries many Arab and North African Muslim intellectuals and traders married native African women. These unions brought into being a group of racially mixed people. The necessity of living together harmoniously, the traditional awareness of diverse cultures, and the cosmopolitan atmosphere of Timbuktu all contributed to a rare degree of racial toleration and understanding. After visiting the court of Mansa Musa's successor in 1352–1353, Ibn Battuta observed:

> [T]he Negroes possess some admirable qualities. They are seldom unjust, and have a greater abhorrence of injustice than any other people. Their sultan shows no mercy to anyone who is guilty of the least act of it. There is complete security in their country. Neither traveler nor inhabitant in it has anything to fear from robbers. . . . They do not confiscate the property of any white man who dies in their country, even if it be uncounted wealth. On the contrary, they give it into the charge of some trustworthy person among the whites.[16]

The third great West African empire, Songhai, succeeded Mali in the fourteenth century. It encompassed the old empires of Ghana and Mali and extended its territory farther north and east to become one of the largest African empires in history (see Map 10.2).

Ethiopia: The Christian Kingdom of Aksum

Just as the ancient West African empires were significantly affected by Islam and the Arab culture that accompanied it, the African kingdoms that arose in modern Sudan and Ethiopia in northeast Africa were heavily influenced by Egyptian culture, and they influenced it in return. This was particularly the case in ancient Nubia. Nubia's capital was at Meroë (see Map 10.2); thus the country is often referred to as the Nubian kingdom of Meroë.

As part of the Roman Empire, Egypt was subject to Hellenistic and Roman cultural forces, and it became an early center of Christianity. Nubia, however, was never part of the Roman Empire; its people clung to ancient Egyptian religious ideas. Christian missionaries went to the Upper Nile region and succeeded in converting the Nubian rulers around 600 C.E. By that time, there were three separate Nubian states, of which the kingdom of Nobatia, centered at Dongola, was the strongest. The Christian rulers of Nobatia had close ties with the kingdom of **Aksum** in Ethiopia, and through this relationship Egyptian culture spread to Ethiopia.

Two-thirds of the country consists of the Ethiopian highlands, the rugged plateau region of East Africa. The Great Rift Valley divides this territory into two massifs (mountain masses), of which the Ethiopian Plateau is the larger. Sloping away from each side of the Great Rift Valley are a series of mountains and valleys. Together with this mountainous environment, the three Middle Eastern religions—Judaism, Christianity, and Islam—have influenced Ethiopian society, bringing symbols of its cultural identity via trade and contact with it neighbors in the Upper Nile,

The Kingdom of Aksum, ca. 600

SASSANID EMPIRE

ROMAN EMPIRE

EGYPT

ARABIAN PENINSULA

Nile R.

Red Sea

NOBATIA

NUBIA

Dongola   Meroë

Adulis

Blue Nile R.

White Nile R.

Aksum

KINGDOM OF AKSUM

Christianity and Islam in Ethiopia The prolonged contest between the two religions in Ethiopia was periodically taken to the battlefield. This drawing from the eighteenth century by an Ethiopian artist shows his countrymen (left) advancing victoriously and celebrates national military success. (© British Library Board. OR 533 f50v)

including Nobatia, and via its proximity to the Middle East.

By the first century C.E. the kingdom of Aksum in northwestern Ethiopia was a sizable trading state. Merchants at Adulis, its main port on the Red Sea, sold ivory, gold, emeralds, rhinoceros horns, shells, and slaves to the Sudan, Arabia, Yemen, and various cities across the Indian Ocean in exchange for glass, ceramics, fabrics, sugar, oil, spices, and precious gems. Adulis contained temples, stone-built houses, and irrigated agriculture. Between the first and eighth centuries Aksum served as the capital of an empire extending over much of what is now northern Ethiopia. The empire's prosperity rested on trade. Aksum even independently minted specie (coins) modeled on the Roman *solidus;* at that time, only the Roman Empire, Persia, and some Indian states issued coins that circulated in Middle Eastern trade. It was the first and only sub-Saharan African state to have its own currency, and the last after its decline until the Swahili city-state of Kilwa minted gold coins beginning perhaps as early as the eleventh century.

The expansion of Islam into northern Ethiopia in the eighth century (see page 276) weakened Aksum's commercial prosperity. The Arabs first ousted the Greek Byzantine merchants who traded on the Dahlak Archipelago (in the southern Red Sea) and converted the islands' inhabitants. Then, Muslims attacked and destroyed Adulis. Some Aksumites converted to Islam; many others found refuge in the rugged mountains north of the kingdom, where they were isolated from outside contacts. Thus began the insularity that characterized later Ethiopian society.

Tradition ascribes to Frumentius (ca. 300–380 C.E.), a Syrian Christian trader, the introduction of Coptic Christianity, an Orthodox form of Christianity that originated in Egypt, into Ethiopia. Kidnapped as a young boy en route from India to Tyre (in southern Lebanon), Frumentius was taken to Aksum, given his freedom, and appointed tutor to the future king, Ezana. Upon Ezana's accession to the throne, Frumentius went to Alexandria, Egypt, where he was consecrated the first bishop of Aksum around 340 C.E. He then returned to Ethiopia with some priests to spread Christianity. Shortly after members of the royal court accepted Christianity, it became the Ethiopian state religion. Ethiopia's future was to be inextricably tied up with Christianity, a unique situation in black Africa.

- **Timbuktu** Originally a campsite for desert nomads, it grew into a thriving city under Mansa Musa, king of Mali and Africa's most famous ruler.

- **Aksum** A kingdom in northwestern Ethiopia that was a sizable trading state and the center of Christian culture.

Ethiopia's acceptance of Christianity led to the production of ecclesiastical documents and royal chronicles, making Ethiopia the first black African society that can be studied from written records. The Scriptures were translated into Ge'ez (gee-EHZ), an ancient language and script used in Ethiopia and Aksum. Pagan temples were dedicated to Christian saints; and, as in early medieval Ireland and in the Orthodox Church of the Byzantine world, the monasteries were the main cultural institutions of the Christian faith in Ethiopia. Monks went out from the monasteries to preach and convert the people, who resorted to the monasteries in times of need. As the Ethiopian state expanded, vibrant monasteries provided inspiration for the establishment of convents for nuns, as in medieval Europe (see page 400).

Monastic records provide fascinating information about early Ethiopian society. Settlements were made on the warm and moist plateau lands, not in the arid lowlands or the river valleys. Farmers used a scratch plow (unique in sub-Saharan Africa) to cultivate wheat and barley, and they regularly rotated those cereals. Plentiful rainfall seems to have helped produce abundant crops, which in turn led to population growth. In contrast to people in most of sub-Saharan Africa, both sexes probably married young. Because of ecclesiastical opposition to polygyny, monogamy was the norm, other than for kings and the very rich. The abundance of land meant that young couples could establish independent households. Widely scattered farms, with the parish church as the central social unit, seem to have been the usual pattern of existence.

Above the broad class of peasant farmers stood warrior-nobles. Their wealth and status derived from their fighting skills, which kings rewarded with grants of estates and with the right to collect tribute from the peasants. To acquire lands and to hold warriors' loyalty, Ethiopian kings had to pursue a policy of constant territorial expansion. (See "Individuals in Society: Amda Siyon," page 285.) Nobles maintained order in their regions, supplied kings with fighting men, and displayed their superior status by the size of their households and their generosity to the poor.

Sometime in the fourteenth century six scribes in the Tigrayan highlands of Ethiopia combined oral tradition, Jewish and Islamic commentaries, apocryphal (noncanonical) Christian texts, and the writings of the early Christian Church fathers to produce the *Kebra Negast* (The Glory of Kings). This history served the authors' goals: it became an Ethiopian national epic, glorifying a line of rulers descended from the Hebrew king Solomon (see page 53), arousing patriotic feelings, and linking Ethiopia's identity to the Judeo-Christian tradition. The book mostly deals with the origins of Emperor Menilek I of Ethiopia in the tenth century B.C.E.

The *Kebra Negast* asserts that Queen Makeda of Ethiopia (called Sheba in the Jewish tradition) had little governmental experience when she came to the throne. So she sought the advice and wise counsel of King Solomon (r. 961–922 B.C.E.) in Jerusalem. Makeda learned Jewish statecraft, converted to Judaism, and expressed her gratitude to Solomon with rich gifts of spices, gems, and gold. Desiring something more precious, Solomon prepared a lavish banquet for his attractive pupil. Satiated with spicy food and rich wines, Makeda fell asleep. In the middle of the night Solomon tricked Makeda into allowing him into her bed. Their son, Menilek, was born some months later. When Menilek reached maturity, he visited Solomon in Jerusalem. There Solomon anointed him crown prince of Ethiopia and sent a retinue of young Jewish nobles to accompany him home as courtiers. Unable to face life without the Hebrews' Ark of the Covenant, the courtiers stole the cherished wooden chest, which the Hebrews believed contained the Ten Commandments. God apparently approved the theft, for he lifted the youths, pursued by Solomon's army, across the Red Sea and into Ethiopia. Thus, according to the *Kebra Negast*, Menilek avenged his mother's shame, and God gave his legal covenant to Ethiopia, Israel's successor.[17] Although written around twenty-three hundred years after the events, the myths and legends contained in the *Kebra Negast* effectively served the purpose of building nationalistic fervor.

Consuming a spiked drink may not be the most dignified or auspicious way to found an imperial dynasty, but from the tenth to the sixteenth centuries, and even in the Ethiopian constitution of 1955, rulers of Ethiopia claimed that they belonged to the Solomonic line of succession. Thus the church and state in Ethiopia were inextricably linked.

Ethiopia's high mountains isolated the kingdom and hindered access from the outside, but through trade word gradually spread about the Christian devotion of this African kingdom. Twelfth-century Crusaders returning from the Middle East told of a powerful Christian ruler, Prester John, whose lands lay behind Muslim lines and who was eager to help restore the Holy Land to Christian control. The story of Prester John sparked European imagination and led to exploration aimed at finding his legendary kingdom, which was eventually identified with Ethiopia. In the later thirteenth century the dynasty of the Solomonic kings witnessed a literary and artistic renaissance particularly notable for works of hagiography (biographies of saints), biblical exegesis (critical explanation or interpretation of the bible), and manuscript illumination. The most striking feature of Ethiopian society in the period from 500 to 1500 was the close relationship between the church and the state. Christianity inspired

Amda Siyon

SCHOLARS CONSIDER AMDA SIYON (r. 1314–1344) the greatest ruler of Ethiopia's Solomonic dynasty. Yet we have no image or representation of him. We know nothing of his personal life, though if he followed the practice of most Ethiopian kings, he had many wives and children. Nor do we know anything about his youth and education. The evidence of what he did, however, suggests a tough military man who personified the heroic endurance and physical pain expected of warriors. According to a chronicle of Siyon's campaign against the Muslim leader of Ifat, he

> clove the ranks of the rebels and struck so hard that he transfixed two men as one with the blow of his spear, through the strength of God. Thereupon the rebels scattered and took to flight, being unable to hold their ground in his presence.

Amda Siyon reinforced control over his kingdom's Christian areas. He then expanded into neighboring regions of Shewa, Gojam, and Damot. Victorious there, he gradually absorbed the Muslim states of Ifat and Hedya to the east and southeast. These successes gave him effective control of the central highlands and also the Indian Ocean trade routes to the Red Sea (see Map 10.2). He governed in a quasi-feudal fashion. Theoretically the owner of all land, he assigned *gults*, or fiefs, to his ablest warriors. In return for nearly complete authority in their regions, these warrior-nobles conscripted soldiers for the king's army, required agricultural services from the farmers working on their land, and collected taxes in kind.

Ethiopian rulers received imperial coronation at Aksum, but their kingdom had no permanent capital. Rather, the ruler and court were peripatetic. They constantly traveled around the country to check the warrior-nobles' management of the gults, to crush revolts, and to impress ordinary people with royal dignity.

Territorial expansion had important economic and religious consequences. Amda Siyon concluded trade agreements with Muslims by which they were allowed to trade with his country in return for Muslim recognition of his authority, and their promise to accept his administration and pay taxes. Economic growth followed. As a result of these agreements, the flow of Ethiopian gold, ivory, and slaves to Red Sea ports for export to the Islamic heartlands and to South Asia accelerated. Profits from commercial exchange improved people's lives, or at least the lives of the upper classes.

Monk-missionaries from traditional Christian areas flooded newly conquered regions, stressing that Ethiopia was a new Zion, or second Israel; a Judeo-Christian nation defined by religion. Ethiopian Christianity focused on the divinity of the Old Testament Jehovah, rather than on the humanity of the New Testament Jesus. Jewish dietary restrictions, such as the avoidance of pork and shellfish, shaped behavior, and the holy Ark of the Covenant had a prominent place in the liturgy. But the monks also taught New Testament values, especially the importance of charity and spiritual reform. Following

the Byzantine pattern, the Ethiopian priest-king claimed the right to summon church councils and to issue doctrinal degrees. Christianity's stress on monogamous marriage, however, proved hard to enforce. As in other parts of Africa (and in Islamic lands, China, and South Asia), polygyny remained common, at least among the upper classes.

QUESTIONS FOR ANALYSIS

1. What features mark Ethiopian culture as unique and distinctive among early African societies?
2. Referring to Solomonic Ethiopia, assess the role of legend in history.

Sources: G. W. B. Huntingford, ed., *The Glorious Victories of Amda Seyon* (Oxford: Oxford University Press, 1965), pp. 89–90; H. G. Marcus, *A History of Ethiopia*, updated ed. (Berkeley: University of California Press, 2002); J. Iliffe, *Africans: The History of a Continent*, 2d ed. (New York: Cambridge University Press, 2007).

• **Colorful biblical scenes adorn the interior of the Urai Kidane Miharet Church, one of the many monasteries established by Amda Siyon.**
(Ariadne Van Zandberger/The Africa Image Library, photographersdirect.com)

▫ Picturing the Past

The Queen of Sheba and King Solomon Sheba, Queen Makeda, figured prominently in European as well as Ethiopian art. Created in about 1180 by a French artist as part of a series of biblical scenes for an abbey in Austria, this image shows Solomon receiving gifts from Sheba's servants. The inscription surrounding the scene reads "Solomon joins himself to the Queen of Sheba and introduces her to his faith." (Erich Lessing/Art Resource, NY)

ANALYZING THE IMAGE What are King Solomon and Queen Sheba wearing and holding? How are the other figures depicted, and what are they doing?

CONNECTIONS What does the style of this image suggest about the background of the artist and about the audience for whom the image was intended?

fierce devotion and tended to equate doctrinal heresy with political rebellion, thus reinforcing central monarchical power.

The East African City-States

Like Ethiopia, the city-states of East Africa were shaped by their proximity to the trade routes of the Red Sea and Indian Ocean. In the first century C.E. a merchant seaman from Alexandria in Egypt sailed down the Red Sea and out into the Indian Ocean, where he stopped at seaports along the coasts of East Africa, Arabia, and India. He took careful notes on all he observed, and the result, *Periplus of the Erythraean Sea* ("Red Sea" in Greek, but the word can designate the Indian Ocean as well), is the earliest surviving literary evidence of the city-states of the East African coast. (See "Viewpoints: Early Descriptions of Africa," page 287.) Although primarily preoccupied with geography and navigation, the *Periplus* includes accounts of the local East African peoples and their commercial activities. Since the days of the Roman emperors, the *Periplus* testifies, the East African coast had strong commercial links with India and the Mediterranean.

Greco-Roman ships traveled from Adulis on the Red Sea around the tip of the Gulf of Aden and down the portion of the East African coast that the Greeks called Azania in modern-day Kenya and Tanzania (see Map 10.2). These ships carried manufactured goods — cotton cloth, copper and brass, iron tools, and gold and silver plate. At the African coastal emporiums, Mediterranean merchants exchanged these goods for

Viewpoints

Early Descriptions of Africa

• *One of the earliest surviving documents describing any part of Africa is the* Periplus of the Erythraean Sea. *Written in Greek around 70 C.E., probably by an Egyptian merchant from Alexandria, the* Periplus *provides a detailed account of the author's sea voyage for use by future travelers. The excerpt below describes the East African coast.*

Over fourteen hundred years after the Periplus, *a Portuguese mariner named Gomes Eannes de Azarar left the first account of the people and places along the West African coast. The selection here recounts the capture of the first slaves of the Atlantic slave trade along the West African coast in 1441 by two Portuguese ship captains, Antam Gonçalvez and Nuno Tristam.*

Periplus of the Erythraean Sea

15. . . . [A]fter two courses of a day and night along the Ausanitic coast,* is the island Menuthias, about three hundred stadia from the mainland, low and wooded, in which there are rivers and many kinds of birds and the mountain-tortoise. There are no wild beasts except the crocodiles; but there they do not attack men. In this place there are sewed boats, and canoes hollowed from single logs, which they use for fishing and catching tortoise. In this island they also catch them in a peculiar way, in wicker baskets, which they fasten across the channel-opening between the breakers.

16. Two days' sail beyond, there lies the very last market-town of the continent of Azania, which is called Rhapta. . . . Along this coast live men of piratical habits, very great in stature, and under separate chiefs for each place. The . . . chief governs it under some ancient right that subjects it to the sovereignty of the state that is become first in Arabia. And the people of Muza now hold it under his authority and send thither many large ships; using Arab captains and agents, who are familiar with the natives and intermarry with them, and who know the whole coast and understand the language.

17. There are imported into these markets the lances made at Muza especially for this trade, and hatchets and daggers and awls, and various kinds of glass; and at some places a little wine, and wheat, not for trade, but to serve for getting the good-will of the savages. There are exported from these places a great quantity of ivory, but inferior to that of Adulis, and rhinoceros-horn and tortoise-shell (which is in best demand after that from India), and a little palm-oil.

Gomes Eannes de Azarar

Thereupon [Nuno Tristam] caused Antam Gonçalvez to be called . . . "You", said he, "my friend Antam Gonçalvez, are not ignorant of the will of the Infant† our Lord, and you know that . . . he hath toiled in vain in this part of the world, never being able to arrive at any certainty as to the people of this land, under what law or lordship they do live. And although you are carrying off these two captives, and by their means the Infant may come to know something about this folk, yet that doth not prevent what is still better, namely, for us to carry off many more; for, besides the knowledge which the Lord Infant will gain by their means, profit will also accrue to him by their service or ransom. Wherefore, it seemeth to me that we should do well to act after this manner. That is to say, in this night now following, you should choose ten of your men and I another ten of mine . . . and let us then go together and seek those whom you have found. . . ."

And so it chanced that in the night they came to where the natives lay scattered in two encampments. . . . And when our men had come nigh to them, they attacked them very lustily, shouting at the top of their voices, "Portugal" . . . the fright of which so abashed the enemy, that it threw them all into disorder. And so, all in confusion, they began to fly without any order or carefulness. Except indeed that the men made some show of defending themselves . . . , especially one of them who fought face to face with Nuno Tristam, defending himself till he received his death. And besides this one, . . . the others killed three and took ten prisoners, what of men, women and boys.

Sources: W. H. Schoff, trans. and ed., *The Periplus of the Erythraean Sea: Travel and Trade in the Indian Ocean by a Merchant of the First Century* (London, Bombay, and Calcutta, 1912), pp. 27–29; Gomes Eannes de Azurara, *The Chronicle of the Discovery and Conquest of Guinea*, vol. 1, trans. C. R. Beazley and E. Prestage (New York: Burt Franklin, 1963), pp. 46–48.

QUESTIONS FOR ANALYSIS

1. What aspects of the East African coast did the author of the *Periplus* write about, and how might these details benefit future travelers to the region?

2. What reasons are given in the second document for enslaving the ten Africans?

3. What are the main concerns of the authors of these documents?

*Coast of modern Zanzibar.

†Portuguese term for any prince other than the eldest; here it refers to Prince Henry the Navigator (see page 466).

Listening to the Past

A Tenth-Century Muslim Traveler Describes Parts of the East African Coast

Other than Ethiopia, early African societies left no written accounts of their institutions and cultures, so modern scholars rely for information on the chronicles of travelers and merchants. Outsiders, however, come with their own preconceptions, attitudes, and biases. They tend to measure what they visit and see by the conditions and experiences with which they are familiar.

Sometime in the early tenth century the Muslim merchant-traveler Al Mas'udi (d. 945 C.E.), in search of African ivory, visited Oman, the southeast coast of Africa, and Zanzibar. He referred to all the peoples he encountered as Zanj, a term that was also applied to the maritime Swahili culture of the area's towns. Al Mas'udi's report, excerpted here, offers historians a wealth of information about these peoples.

"Omani seamen cross the strait [of Berbera, off northern Somalia] to reach Kanbalu island [perhaps modern Pemba], located in the sea of Zanj. The island's inhabitants are a mixed population of Muslims and idolatrous Zanj. . . . I have sailed many seas, the Chinese sea, the Rum sea [Mediterranean], the Khazar [Caspian Sea], the Kolzom [Red Sea], and the sea of Yemen. I have encountered dangers without number, but I know no sea more perilous than the sea of Zanj. Here one encounters a fish called el-Owal [whale]. . . . The sailors fear its approach, and both day and night they strike pieces of wood together or beat drums to drive it away. . . . The Zanj sea also contains many other fish species possessing the most varied shapes and forms. . . . Ambergris* is found in great quantities along the Zanj coast and also along the coastline of Shihr in Arabia. . . . The best ambergris is found in the islands and on the shores of the Zanj sea: it is round, of a pale blue tint, sometimes the size of an ostrich egg, sometimes a little less. Lumps of it are swallowed by the whale. . . . When the sea becomes very rough the whale vomits up large rock size balls of ambergris. When it tries to gulp them down again it chokes to death and its body floats to the surface. Quickly the men of Zanj, or from other lands, who have been waiting for a favorable moment, draw the fish near with harpoons and tackle, cut open its stomach, and extract the ambergris. The pieces found in its intestines emit a nauseating odor, and Iraqi and Persian chemists call these *nedd:* but the fragments found near the back are much purer as these have been longer inside the body. . . .

The lands of the Zanj provide the people with wild leopard skins that they wear and that they export to Muslim countries. These are the largest leopard skins and make the most beautiful saddles. The Zanj also export tortoise-shell for making combs, and ivory is likewise employed for this purpose. The giraffe is the most common animal found in these lands. . . . They [the Zanj] settled in this country and spread south to Sofala, which marks the most distant frontier of this land and the terminus of the ship voyages made from Oman and Siraf on the Zanj sea. Just as the China sea ends with the land of Japan, the limits of the sea of Zanj are the lands of Sofala and the Waqwaq, a region with a warm climate and fertile soil that produces gold in abundance and many other marvelous things. This is where the Zanj built their capital and chose their king, whom they call *Mfalme*, the traditional title for their sovereigns. The *Mfalme* rules over all other Zanj kings and commands 300,000 cavalrymen. The Zanj employ the ox as a beast of burden, for their country contains no horses, mules, or camels, and they do not even know of these animals. Nor do they know of snow or hail. . . . The territory of the Zanj commences where a branch diverts from the upper Nile and continues to the land of Sofala and the Waqwaq. Their villages extend for about 700 parasangs in length and breadth along the coast. The country is divided into valleys, mountains, and sandy deserts. It abounds in wild elephants but you will not see a single tame one. The Zanj employ them neither for war nor for anything else. . . . When they want to catch them, they throw into the water the leaves, bark, and branches of a particular tree that grows in their country: then they hide in ambush until the elephants come to drink. The tainted water burns them and makes them drunk, causing them to fall down and be unable to get up. The Zanj then rush upon them, armed with very long spears, and kill them for their tusks. Indeed, the lands of the Zanj produce tusks each weighing fifty pounds

cinnamon, myrrh and frankincense, captive slaves, and animal byproducts such as ivory, rhinoceros horns, and tortoise shells. The ships then headed back north and, somewhere around Cape Guardafui on the Horn of Africa, caught the monsoon winds eastward to India, where ivory was in great demand.

In the early centuries of the Common Era many merchants and seamen from the Mediterranean settled in East African coastal towns. Succeeding centuries saw the arrival of more traders. The great emigration from Arabia after the death of Muhammad accelerated Muslim penetration of the area, which the Arabs called the Zanj, "land of the blacks," a land inhabited by a Bantu-speaking peoples also called the Zanj. Along the coast, Arabic Muslims established small trading colonies whose local peoples were ruled and more. They generally go to Oman, and are then sent on to China and India. These are the two primary destinations, and if they were not, ivory would be abundant in Muslim lands.

In China the kings and military and civil officers ride in ivory palanquins:† no official or dignitary would dare to enter the royal presence in an iron palanquin. Only ivory can serve on this occasion. Thus they prefer straight tusks to curved. . . . They also burn ivory before their idols and incense their altars with its perfume, just as Christians use the Mary incense and other scents in their churches. The Chinese derive no other benefit from the elephant and believe it brings bad fortune when used for domestic purposes or war. In India ivory is much in demand. There dagger handles, as well as curved sword-scabbards, are fashioned from ivory. But ivory is chiefly used in the manufacture of chessmen and backgammon pieces. . . .

Although the Zanj are always hunting the elephant and collecting its ivory, they still make no use of ivory for their own domestic needs. For their finery they use iron rather than gold and silver, and oxen, as we mentioned above, as beasts of burden or for war, as we use camels or horses. The oxen are harnessed like horses and run at the same speed.

To return to the Zanj and their kings, these are known as *Wfalme*, meaning son of the Great Lord. They refer thus to their king because he has been selected to govern them fairly. As soon as he exerts tyrannical power or strays from the rule of law they put him to death and exclude his descendants from accession to the throne. They claim that through his wrongful actions he ceases to be the son of the Master, that is, the King of Heaven and Earth. They give God the name *Maliknajlu*, meaning the Sovereign Master.

The Zanj express themselves eloquently and have preachers in their own language. Often a devout man will stand in the center of a large crowd and exhort his listeners to render themselves agreeable to God and to submit to his commands. He depicts for them the punishments their disobedience exposes them to, and recalls the example of their ancestors and former kings. These people possess no religious code: their kings follow custom and govern according to traditional political practices.

The Zanj eat bananas, which are as abundant as they are in India; but the staples in their diets are millet and a plant called *kalari* that is pulled from the earth like truffles. It is similar to the cucumber of Egypt and Syria. They also eat honey and meat. Every man worships what he pleases, be it a plant, an animal or a mineral.‡ The coconut grows on many of the islands: its fruit is eaten by all the Zanj peoples. One of these islands, situated one or two days' sail off the coast, contains a Muslim population and a hereditary royal family. This is the island of Kanbalu, which we have already mentioned. 🙶

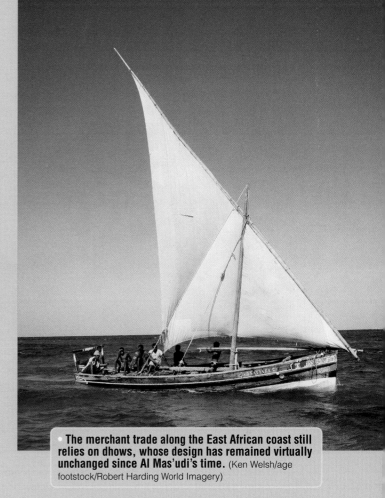

● **The merchant trade along the East African coast still relies on dhows, whose design has remained virtually unchanged since Al Mas'udi's time.** (Ken Welsh/age footstock/Robert Harding World Imagery)

Source: Al Mas'udi, *Les Prairies d'Or*, trans. Arab to French by C. Barbier de Meynard and Pavet de Courteille (Paris: Imperial Printers, 1861, 1864), vol. I: pp. 231, 234, 333–335; vol. III: pp. 2, 3, 5–9, 26–27, 29, 30–31. Trans. French to English by Roger B. Beck.

QUESTIONS FOR ANALYSIS

1. What does Al Mas'udi's report tell us about the Zanj peoples and their customs? How would you describe his attitude toward them?

2. What commodities were most sought after by Muslim traders? Why? Where were they sold?

*A solid, waxy, flammable substance, produced in the digestive system of sperm whales, not swallowed as Mas'udi purports. Principally used in perfumery, and not to be confused with amber, the fossil resin used in the manufacture of ornamental objects such as beads and women's combs.

†An enclosed litter attached to poles that servants supported on their shoulders.

‡These are forms of animism.

by kings and practiced various animistic religions. Eventually—whether through Muslim political hegemony or gradual assimilation—the coastal peoples slowly converted to Islam. Indigenous African religions, however, remained strong in the continent's interior. (See "Listening to the Past: A Tenth-Century Muslim Traveler Describes Parts of the East African Coast," above.)

Migrants from the Arabian peninsula and the Malay Archipelago had a profound influence on the lives of the coastal people of East Africa. Beginning in the late twelfth century fresh waves of Arabs and of Persians from Shiraz poured down the coast, first settling at Mogadishu, then pressing southward to Kilwa. Everywhere they landed, they introduced Islamic culture to the indigenous population. Similarly, from the first to

Great Mosque at Kilwa Built between the thirteenth and fifteenth centuries to serve the Muslim commercial aristocracy of Kilwa on the Indian Ocean, the mosque attests to the wealth and power of the East African city-states. (Karen Samson Photography)

the fifteenth centuries Indonesians crossed the Indian Ocean and settled on the African coast and on the large island of Madagascar, or Malagasy, an Indonesian name. All these immigrants intermarried with Africans, and the resulting society combined Asian, African, and especially Islamic traits. The East African coastal culture was called **Swahili**, after a Bantu language whose vocabulary and poetic forms exhibit a strong Arabic influence. The thirteenth-century Muslim mosque at Mogadishu and the fiercely Muslim populations of Mombasa and Kilwa in the fourteenth century attest to strong Muslim influence.

By the late thirteenth century **Kilwa** had become the most powerful city on the coast, exercising political hegemony as far north as Pemba and as far south as Sofala (see Map 10.2). In the fourteenth and fifteenth centuries the coastal cities were great commercial empires comparable to the Italian city-state of Venice (discussed in Chapter 14). Like Venice, Swahili cities such as Kilwa, Mombasa, and Pemba were situated on offshore islands. The tidal currents that isolated them from the mainland also protected them from landside attack.

Much current knowledge about life in the East African trading societies rests on the account of Ibn Battuta. When he arrived at Kilwa, he found "a large

city on the seacoast, most of whose inhabitants are Zinj, jet-black in colour. They have tattoo marks on their faces. . . . The city of Kilwa is one of the finest and most substantially built towns; all the buildings are of wood, and the houses are roofed with al-dis [reeds]."[18] On the mainland were fields and orchards of rice, millet, oranges, mangoes, and bananas and pastures and yards for cattle, sheep, and poultry. Yields were apparently high; Ibn Battuta noted that the rich enjoyed three enormous meals a day and were very fat.

From among the rich mercantile families that controlled the coastal cities arose a ruler who by the fourteenth century had taken the Arabic title *sheik*. The sheik governed both the island city of Kilwa and the nearby mainland. Farther inland, tribal chiefs ruled with the advice of councils of elders.

Approaching the East African coastal cities in the late fifteenth century, Portuguese traders were astounded at their enormous wealth and prosperity. This wealth rested on the sheik's monopolistic control of all trade in the area. Some coastal cities manufactured goods for export: Mogadishu produced cloth for the Egyptian market; Mombasa and Malindi processed iron tools; and Sofala made cottons for the interior trade. The bulk of the cities' exports, however, consisted of animal products — leopard skins, tortoise shell, ambergris, ivory — and gold. The gold originated in the Mutapa region south of the Zambezi River, where the Bantu mined it. As in tenth-century Ghana, gold was a royal monopoly in the fourteenth-century coastal city-states. The Mutapa kings received it as annual tribute, prohibited outsiders from entering the mines or participating in the trade, and controlled shipments down the Zambezi to the coastal markets. Kilwa's prosperity rested on its traffic in gold.

African goods satisfied the global aristocratic demand for luxury goods. In Arabia leopard skins were made into saddles, shells were made into combs, and ambergris was used in the manufacture of perfumes. Because African elephants' tusks were larger and more durable than the tusks of Indian elephants, African ivory was in great demand in India for sword and dagger handles, carved decorative objects, and the ceremonial bangles used in Hindu marriage rituals. Wealthy Chinese valued African ivory for use in the construction of sedan chairs.

In exchange for these natural products, the Swahili cities bought in, among many other items, incense, glassware, glass beads, and carpets from Arabia; textiles, spices, rice, and cotton from India; and grains, fine porcelain, silk, and jade from China. Swahili kings imposed enormous duties on imports, perhaps more than 80 percent of the value of the goods themselves. Even so, traders who came to Africa made fabulous profits.

Slaves were another export from the East African coast. Reports of slave trading in East Africa began with the publication of the *Periplus*. The trade accelerated with the establishment of Muslim settlements in the eighth century and continued down to the arrival of the Portuguese in the late fifteenth century, who provided a market for African slaves in the New World (discussed in Chapter 15). In fact, the global market for slaves would fuel the East African coastal slave trade until at least the beginning of the twentieth century.

As in West Africa, traders obtained slaves primarily through raids and kidnapping. As early as the tenth century Arabs from Oman enticed hungry children with dates. When the children accepted the sweet fruits, they were abducted and enslaved. Profit was the traders' motive.

The Arabs called the northern Somalia coast *Ras Assir* (Cape of Slaves). From there, Arab traders transported slaves northward up the Red Sea to the markets of Arabia and Persia. Muslim dealers also shipped blacks from the region of Zanzibar across the Indian Ocean to markets in India. Rulers of the Deccan Plateau in central India used large numbers of black slave soldiers in their military campaigns. Slaves also worked on the docks and dhows (typical Arab lateen-rigged

Copper Coin from Mogadishu, Twelfth Century Islamic proscriptions against representation of the human form prevented the use of rulers' portraits on coinage, unlike the practice of the Romans, Byzantines, and Sassanids. Instead, Islamic coins since the Umayyad period were decorated exclusively with writing. Sultan Haran ibn Sulayman of Kilwa on the East African coast minted this coin, a symbol of the region's Muslim culture and of its rich maritime trade. (Courtesy of the Trustees of the British Museum)

ships) in the Muslim-controlled Indian Ocean and as domestic servants and concubines throughout South and East Asia.

As early as the tenth century sources mention persons with "lacquer-black bodies" in the possession of wealthy families in Song China.[19] In 1178 a Chinese official noted in a memorial to the emperor that Arab traders were shipping thousands of blacks from East Africa to the Chinese port of Guangzhou (Canton) by way of the Malay Archipelago. The Chinese employed these slaves as household servants, as musicians, and, because East Africans were often expert swimmers, as divers to caulk the leaky seams of ships below the water line.

By the thirteenth century Africans living in many parts of South and East Asia had made significant economic and cultural contributions to their societies. It appears, however, that in Indian, Chinese, and East African markets, slaves were never as valuable a commodity as ivory. Thus the volume of the Eastern slave trade did not approach that of the trans-Saharan slave trade.[20]

Southern Africa and Great Zimbabwe

Southern Africa, bordered on the northwest by the Kalahari Desert and on the northeast by the Zambezi River (see Map 10.2), enjoys a mild and temperate climate. Desert conditions prevail along the Atlantic coast, which gets less than five inches of annual rainfall. Eastward toward the Indian Ocean, rainfall increases, amounting to between fifty to ninety inches a year in some places. Temperate grasslands characterize the highlands in the interior. Considerable variations in climate occur throughout much of southern Africa from year to year.

- **Swahili** The East African coastal culture, named after a Bantu language whose vocabulary and poetic forms exhibit strong Arabic influences.
- **Kilwa** The most powerful city on the east coast of Africa by the late thirteenth century.

Ruins of Great Zimbabwe Considered the most impressive monument in the African interior south of the Ethiopian highlands, these ruins of Great Zimbabwe consist of two complexes of dry-stone buildings, some surrounded by a massive serpentine wall 32 feet high and 17 feet thick at its maximum. Among the archaeological finds are monoliths crowned by soapstone birds (left). This 14½-inch-high monolith also appears to have an alligator-like creature on its side. Scholars debate the significance of these birds: Were they symbols of royal power? Messengers from the spiritual world to the terrestrial? What does the alligator mean? (photo: Robert Harding World Imagery/SuperStock; bird: Courtesy of the National Archives of Zimbabwe)

Southern Africa has enormous mineral resources: gold, copper, diamonds, platinum, and uranium. Preindustrial peoples mined some of these deposits in open excavations down several feet, but fuller exploitation required modern technology. (Today, gold mining operations can penetrate two miles below the surface.)

Located at the southern extremity of the Afroeurasian landmass, southern Africa has a history that is very different from the histories of West Africa, the Nile Valley, and the East African coast. Unlike the rest of coastal Africa, southern Africa remained far removed from the outside world until the Portuguese arrived in the late fifteenth century — with one important exception. Bantu-speaking people reached southern Africa in the eighth century. They brought skills in ironworking and mixed farming (settled crop production plus cattle and sheep raising) and immunity to the kinds of diseases that later decimated the Amerindians of South America (discussed in Chapter 16).

The earliest residents of southern Africa were hunters and gatherers. In the first millennium C.E. new farming techniques from the north arrived. Lack of water and timber (both needed to produce the charcoal used in iron smelting) slowed the spread of iron technology and tools and thus of crop production in southwestern Africa. These advances reached the western coastal region by 1500. By that date, Khoisan-speakers were farming in the arid western regions. The area teemed with wild game — elephants, buffalo, lions, hippopotamuses, leopards, zebras, and many varieties of antelope. To the east, descendants of Bantu-speaking immigrants grew sorghum, raised cattle and sheep, and fought with iron-headed spears. However, disease-bearing insects such as the tsetse (SET-see) fly, which causes sleeping sickness, attacked the cattle and sheep and retarded their domestication.

The nuclear family was the basic social unit among early southern African peoples, who practiced polygyny and traced descent in the male line. Several families formed bands numbering between twenty and eighty people. Such bands were not closed entities; people in neighboring territories identified with bands speaking the same language. As in most preindustrial societies, a division of labor existed whereby men hunted and women cared for children and raised edible plants. People lived in caves or in camps made of portable material, and they moved from one watering or hunting region to another as seasonal or environmental needs required.

In 1871 a German explorer came upon the ruined city of **Great Zimbabwe** southeast of what is now Masvingo in Zimbabwe. Archaeologists consider Great Zimbabwe the most impressive monument in Africa south of the Nile Valley and the Ethiopian highlands.

The ruins consist of two vast complexes of dry-stone buildings, a fortress, and an elliptically shaped enclosure commonly called the Temple. Stone carvings, gold and copper ornaments, and Asian ceramics once decorated the buildings. The ruins extend over sixty acres and are encircled by a massive wall. The entire city was built from local granite between the eleventh and fifteenth centuries without any outside influence.

These ruins tell a remarkable story. Great Zimbabwe was the political and religious capital of a vast empire. During the first millennium C.E. settled crop cultivation, cattle raising, and work in metal led to a steady buildup in population in the Zambezi-Limpopo region. The area also contained a rich gold-bearing belt. Gold ore lay near the surface; alluvial gold lay in the Zambezi River tributaries. In the tenth century the inhabitants collected the alluvial gold by panning and washing; after the year 1000, the gold was worked in open mines with iron picks. Traders shipped the gold eastward to Sofala (see Map 10.2). Great Zimbabwe's wealth and power rested on this gold trade.

Great Zimbabwe declined in the fifteenth century, perhaps because the area had become agriculturally exhausted and could no longer support the large population. Some people migrated northward and settled in the Mazoe River Valley, a tributary of the Zambezi. This region also contained gold, and the settlers built a new empire in the tradition of Great Zimbabwe. This empire's rulers were called "Mwene Mutapa," and their power was also based on the gold trade down the Zambezi River to Indian Ocean ports. It was this gold that the Portuguese sought when they arrived on the East African coast in the late fifteenth century.

• **Great Zimbabwe** A ruined South African city discovered by a German explorer in 1871; it is considered the most powerful monument south of the Nile Valley and Ethiopian highlands.

CONNECTIONS

Because our ancestors first evolved in Africa, Africa's archaeological record is rich with material artifacts, such as weapons, tools, ornaments, and eating utensils. But its written record is much less complete, and thus the nonmaterial dimensions of human society — human interaction in all its facets — is much more difficult to reconstruct. The only exception is in Egypt, where hieroglyphic writings give us a more complete picture of Egyptian society than of nearly any other ancient culture.

Not until the Phoenicians, Greeks, and Romans were there written accounts of the peoples of North and East Africa. These accounts document Africa's early connections and contributions to the vast trans-Saharan and Indian Ocean trading networks that stretched from Europe to China. This trade brought wealth to the kingdoms, empires, and city-states that developed alongside the routes. But the trade in ideas most profoundly connected the growing African states to the wider world, most notably through Islam, which arrived by the eighth century, and Christianity, which developed a foothold in Ethiopia.

Prior to the late fifteenth century Europeans had little knowledge about African societies. All this would change during the European Age of Discovery. Chapter 16 traces the expansion of Portugal from a small and poor European nation to an overseas empire, as it established trading posts and gained control of the African gold trade. Portuguese expansion led to competition, spurring Spain and then England to strike out for gold of their own in the Americas. The acceleration of this conquest would forever shape the history of Africa and the Americas (discussed in Chapters 11 and 15) and intertwine them via the African slave trade that fueled the labor needs of the colonies in the Americas.

☐ CHAPTER REVIEW

KEY TERMS

Hamitic thesis (p. 269)	Ghana (p. 277)
Bantu (p. 272)	Koumbi Saleh (p. 279)
Sudan (p. 273)	Timbuktu (p. 282)
Berbers (p. 274)	Aksum (p. 282)
Mogadishu (p. 276)	Swahili (p. 290)
stateless societies (p. 277)	Kilwa (p. 290)
	Great Zimbabwe (p. 293)

☐ **How did Africa's geography shape its history and contribute to its diverse population, and how has this fueled the debate over who is African? (p. 268)**

Africa is a huge continent with many different climatic zones and diverse geography. The peoples of Africa are as diverse as the topography. Groups relying on herd animals developed in the drier, disease-free steppe regions well-suited to domesticated animals, while agricultural settlements developed in the wetter savanna regions. In the tropical forests of central Africa and arid zones of southern Africa, hunter-gatherers dominated. Along the coasts and by lakes and rivers, maritime communities grew whose inhabitants relied on fishing and trade for their livelihood.

The peoples of North Africa were closely connected with the Middle Eastern and European civilizations of the Mediterranean basin. Similarly, the peoples of the Swahili coast participated in trade with Arabia, the Persian Gulf, India, China, and the Malay Archipelago. Black Africans living in the Sahel zone of West Africa traded across the Sahara and became part of the larger world of Islam. Because the peoples south of the Sahara are generally described as black Africans, the inappropriate concept of race has engendered fierce debate over just who is African. Since the days of ancient Greece, historians have debated whether Egypt, because of its proximity to the Mediterranean, should be identified as part of Africa or part of the Mediterranean world. Race as a concept for determining one's "Africanness" has been discredited as extremist.

☐ **How did settled agriculture affect life among the early societies in the western Sudan and among the Bantu-speaking societies of central and southern Africa? (p. 271)**

With the introduction of new crops from Asia and settled agriculture, early societies across the western Sudan were profoundly affected as they switched from hunting and gathering in small bands to form settled farming communities. Populations increased significantly in this rich savanna zone that was ideally suited for grain production. Blood kinship brought together families in communities governed by chiefs or local councils. Animistic religions that recognized ancestral and nature spirits developed. The nature spirits were thought to dwell in nearby streams, forests, mountains, or caves.

The migrations of the Bantu-speakers over a two-thousand-year period began in modern Cameroon and Nigeria, and spread across all of central and southern Africa. Possessing iron tools and weapons, domesticated livestock, and a knowledge of settled agriculture, these Bantu-speakers assimilated, killed, or drove away all the previous inhabitants of these regions.

☐ **What characterized trans-Saharan trade, and how did it affect West African society? (p. 274)**

The most essential component in the trans-Saharan trade was the camel. The camel made it possible for great loads to be hauled across vast stretches of hot, dry desert. The Berbers of North Africa endured these long treks south and then north again across the Sahara. To control this trade they fashioned camel saddles that gave them great political and military advantage. The primary items of trade were salt from the north and gold from the south, although textiles, fruit, ivory, kola nuts, gum, beads, and other goods were also prized by one side or the other. Enslaved West Africans, males and females, were also traded north to slave markets in Morocco, Algiers, Tripoli, and Cairo.

The trans-Saharan trade had three important effects on West African society. First, it stimulated gold mining. Second, it increased the demand for West Africa's second most important commodity, slaves. Third, the trans-Saharan trade stimulated the development of large urban centers in West Africa, such as Gao, Timbuktu, Koumbi Saleh, Sijilmasa, and Jenne.

◻ How were the East African city-states, Aksum, and Great Zimbabwe different from and similar to the kingdoms of the western Sudan? (p. 277)

East African city-states were centered on individual cities, such as Kilwa and Mogadishu. Their existence was based on Indian Ocean commercial networks, in which they traded African products for luxury items from Arabia, Southeast Asia, and East Asia. Like East Africa, South Africa was made up of city-states, chief among them Great Zimbabwe. Located at the southernmost reach of the Indian Ocean trade network, these city-states exchanged their gold for the riches of Arabia and Asia. Somewhat more isolated, the kingdom of Aksum in Ethiopia utilized its access to the Red Sea to trade north to the Mediterranean and south to the Indian Ocean. While Ghana and Mali in the western Sudan also owed their prosperity to trade — primarily the trade of gold — they were great empires whose kings ruled over millions of people.

The East African city-states and the kingdoms of the western Sudan were both part of the world of Islam. Arabian merchants brought Islam with them as they settled along the East African coast, and Berber traders brought Islam to West Africa. Differing from its neighbors, Ethiopia formed a unique enclave of Christianity in the midst of Islamic societies. The Bantu-speaking peoples of Great Zimbabwe were neither Islamic nor Christian, and they practiced indigenous forms of worship such as animism.

SUGGESTED READING

Allen, J. de Vere. *Swahili Origins*. 1993. A study of the problem of Swahili identity.

Austen, Ralph. *African Economic History*. 1987. Classic study of Africa's economic history.

Austen, Ralph. *Trans-Saharan Africa in World History*. 2010. Excellent new introduction to the Sahara region and the trans-Saharan trade that gave it life.

Beck, Roger B. *The History of South Africa*. 2000. Introduction to this large and important country.

Bouvill, E. W., and Robin Hallett. *The Golden Trade of the Moors: West African Kingdoms in the Fourteenth Century*. 1995. Classic description of the trans-Saharan trade.

Bulliet, R. W. *The Camel and the Wheel*. 1995. The importance of the camel to African trade.

Ehret, Christopher. *An African Classical Age: Eastern and Southern Africa in World History, 1000 B.C. to A.D. 400*. 2001. Solid introduction by a renowned African scholar.

Ehret, Christopher. *The Civilizations of Africa: A History to 1800*. 2002. The best study of pre-1800 African history.

Gilbert, Erik, and Jonathan Reynolds. *Africa in World History*. 2007. Groundbreaking study of Africa's place in world history.

Iliffe, John. *Africans: The History of a Continent*, 2d ed. 2007. Thoughtful introduction to African history.

Levtzion, Nehemia, and Randall L. Pouwels. *History of Islam in Africa*. 2000. Comprehensive survey of Islam's presence in Africa.

Marcus, H. G. *A History of Ethiopia*. 2002. Standard introduction to Ethiopian history.

Mitchell, Peter. *African Connections: Archaeological Perspectives on Africa and the Wider World*. 2005. Places ancient Africa and its history in a global context.

Newman, J. L. *The Peopling of Africa: A Geographic Interpretation*. 1995. Explores population distribution and technological change down to the late nineteenth century.

Schmidt, Peter R. *Historical Archaeology in Africa: Representation, Social Memory, and Oral Traditions*. 2006. An excellent introduction to archaeology and the reconstruction of Africa's history.

NOTES

1. C. A. Diop, "The African Origins of Western Civilization," and R. Mauny, "A Review of Diop," in *Problems in African History: The Precolonial Centuries*, ed. R. O. Collins et al. (New York: Markus Weiner Publishing, 1994), pp. 32–40, 41–49; the quotations are from p. 42.

2. Martin Bernal, *Black Athena: Afroasiatic Roots of Classical Civilization*, Volume I: *The Fabrication of Ancient Greece, 1785–1965* (New Brunswick, N.J.: Rutgers University Press, 1987).

3. Mary R. Lefkowitz and Guy MacLean Rogers, *Black Athena Revisited* (Chapel Hill: University of North Carolina Press, 1996).

4. Mauny, "A Review of Diop." For contrasting views of Afrocentrism in American higher education, see T. Martin, *The Jewish Onslaught: Dispatches from the Wellesley Battlefront* (Dover, Mass.: The Majority Press, 1993), and M. Lefkowitz, *Not Out of Africa: How Afrocentrism Became an Excuse to Teach Myth as History* (New York: Basic Books, 1996).

5. T. Spear, "Bantu Migrations," in *Problems in African History: The Precolonial Centuries*, p. 98.

6. J. S. Trimingham, *Islam in West Africa* (Oxford: Oxford University Press, 1959), pp. 6–9.

7. R. A. Austen, "The Trans-Saharan Slave Trade: A Tentative Census," in *The Uncommon Market: Essays in the Economic History of the Atlantic Slave Trade*, ed. H. A. Gemery and J. S. Hogendorn (New York: Academic Press, 1979), pp. 1–71, esp. p. 66.

8. Quoted in J. O. Hunwick, "Islam in West Africa, A.D. 1000–1800," in *A Thousand Years of West African History*, ed. J. F. Ade Ajayi and I. Espie (New York: Humanities Press, 1972), pp. 244–245.

9. Quoted in A. A. Boahen, "Kingdoms of West Africa, c. A.D. 500–1600," in *The Horizon History of Africa* (New York: American Heritage, 1971), p. 183.

10. Al-Bakri, *Kitab al-mughrib fdhikr bilad Ifriqiya wa'l-Maghrib (Description de l'Afrique Septentrionale)*, trans. De Shane (Paris: Adrien-Maisonneuve, 1965), pp. 328–329.

11. Quoted in R. Oliver and C. Oliver, eds., *Africa in the Days of Exploration* (Englewood Cliffs, N.J.: Prentice-Hall, 1965), p. 10.

12. Quoted in Boahen, "Kingdoms of West Africa," p. 184.

13. This quotation and the next appear in E. J. Murphy, *History of African Civilization* (New York: Delta, 1972), pp. 109, 111.

14. Pekka Masonen and Humphrey J. Fisher, "Not Quite Venus from the Waves: The Almoravid Conquest of Ghana in the Modern Historiography of Western Africa," *History in Africa* 23 (1996): 197–232.

15. Quoted in Murphy, *History of African Civilization*, p. 120.

16. Quoted in Oliver and Oliver, *Africa in the Days of Exploration*, p. 18.

17. See H. G. Marcus, *A History of Ethiopia*, updated ed. (Berkeley: University of California Press, 2002), pp. 17–20.

18. Ibn Battuta, *The Travels of Ibn Battuta*, A.D. 1325–1354, vol. 1, ed. H.A.R. Gibb (London: University Press, 1972), pp. 379–380.

19. Austen, "The Trans-Saharan Slave Trade," p. 65; J. H. Harris, *The African Presence in Asia* (Evanston, Ill.: Northwestern University Press, 1971), pp. 3–6, 27–30; P. Wheatley, "Analecta Sino-Africana Recensa," in Neville Chittick and Robert Rotberg, *East Africa and the Orient* (New York: Africana Publishing, 1975), p. 109.

20. I. Hrbek, ed., *General History of Africa*, vol. 3, *Africa from the Seventh to the Eleventh Century* (Berkeley: University of California Press; New York: UNESCO, 1991), pp. 294–295, 346–347.

For practice quizzes and other study tools, visit the **Online Study Guide** at bedfordstmartins.com/mckayworld.

For primary sources from this period, see *Sources of World Societies*, **Second Edition**.

For Web sites, images, and documents related to topics in this chapter, visit **Make History** at bedfordstmartins.com/mckayworld.

● **Moche Portrait Vessel** A Moche artist captured the commanding expression of a ruler in this ceramic vessel. The Moche were one of many cultures in Peru that developed technologies that were simultaneously useful and beautiful, including brightly colored cloth, hanging bridges made of fiber, and intricately fit stone walls. (Private Collection/Photo © Boltin Picture Library/The Bridgeman Art Library)

The first humans settled in the Americas between 40,000 and 15,000 B.C.E. after emigrating from Asia. The melting of glaciers 13,000 to 11,000 years ago separated the Americas and Afroeurasia, and the Eastern and Western Hemispheres developed in isolation from one another. There were many parallels, however. In both areas people initially gathered and hunted their food, and then some groups began to plant crops, adapting plants that were native to the areas they settled. Techniques of plant domestication spread, allowing for population growth because harvested crops provided a more regular food supply than did gathered food. In certain parts of both hemispheres, efficient production and transportation of food supplies led to the growth of cities, with monumental buildings honoring divine and human power, specialized production of a wide array of products, and marketplaces where those products were exchanged. New products included improved military equipment, which leaders used to enhance their authority and build up the large political entities we call kingdoms and empires. The power of those leaders also often rested on religious ideas, so that providing service to a king or obeying the laws he set forth was viewed as a way to honor the gods. In the Western Hemisphere strong and prosperous empires developed first in Mesoamerica — consisting of present-day Mexico and Central America — and then in the Andes. •

The Americas
2500 B.C.E.–1500 C.E.

The First Peoples of the Americas

☐ How did early peoples in the Americas adapt to their environment as they created technologies of food production and economic systems?

Early Societies

☐ What physical, social, and intellectual features characterized early societies in the Americas?

Classical Era Mesoamerica and North America, 300–900 C.E.

☐ How did Mesoamerican and North American peoples develop prosperous and stable societies in the classical era?

The Aztecs

☐ How did the Aztecs both build on the achievements of earlier Mesoamerican cultures and develop new traditions to create their large empire?

The Incas

☐ What were the sources of strength and prosperity, and of problems, for the Incas as they created their enormous empire?

MAP 11.1 The Settling of the Americas Before 10,000 B.C.E. Genetic evidence is currently providing new information about the ways that people migrated across the Bering Strait through the region known as Beringia. It suggests that this occurred in waves, that people settled in Beringia for a while before going on, and that people also migrated back to Asia.

The First Peoples of the Americas

☐ How did early peoples in the Americas adapt to their environment as they created technologies of food production and economic systems?

As in the development of early human cultures worldwide, the environment shaped the formation of settlements in the Americas. North America includes arctic tundra, dry plains, coastal wetlands, woodlands, deserts, and temperate rain forests. **Mesoamerica** is dominated by high plateaus with a temperate climate and good agricultural land bounded by coastal plains. The Caribbean coast of Central America—modern Belize, Guatemala, Honduras, Nicaragua, El Salvador, Costa Rica, and Panama—is characterized by thick jungle lowlands, heavy rainfall, and torrid heat. South America has extremely varied terrain. The entire western coast is edged by the Andes, the highest mountain range in the Western Hemisphere, while three-fourths of the continent—almost the whole interior—is lowland plains. South America's Amazon River, at four thousand miles the second-longest river in the world, is bordered by tropical lowland rain forests with dense growth and annual rainfall in excess of eighty inches. Not surprisingly, the varied environments of the Americas contributed to the great diversity of peoples, cultures, and linguistic groups. While all these environments have supported extensive human settlement at various times, it is easier to learn about those people who lived in drier areas, such as the high mountains of the Andes or the deserts of southwestern North America, because artifacts survive longer there.

Describing the Americas and Their Peoples

The environment shaped the history of the Americas, but history shaped the words we use to describe the lands and peoples of these areas. Perhaps more than anywhere else in the world, these words resulted from errors and misunderstandings, and they are often controversial.

About a decade after Christopher Columbus's first voyage in 1492, another Italian explorer and adventurer, Amerigo Vespucci, wrote a letter to his old employers, the Medici rulers in Italy, trumpeting the wonders of the "new world" he had seen. He claimed to have been the first explorer to travel to what is now Venezuela in 1497, a year before Columbus got to the South American mainland. This letter was published many times in many different languages, and the name "New World" began to show up on world maps around 1505. Shortly after that, the word *America*, meaning "the land of Amerigo," also appeared, because mapmakers read and believed Vespucci's letter. But by just a few years later, mapmakers and others knew that Columbus had been the first to this new world. They wanted to omit the label "America" from future maps, but the name had already stuck.

Our use of the word *Indian* for the indigenous peoples of the Americas stems from another mistake. Columbus was trying to reach Asia by sailing west and thought he was somewhere in the East Indies when he landed, which is why he called the people he met "Indians." They apparently called themselves "Tainos," and people who lived on nearby islands called themselves other things. In many cases native people died so fast from the germs brought by Europeans that we have no idea what they called themselves, so the words we use for various indigenous groups come from other indigenous groups or from European languages, and some were originally derogatory nicknames. Many indigenous groups are returning to designations from their own languages, and scholars are attempting to use terminology that is historically accurate, so certain groups are known by multiple names. The use of the word *Indian* is itself highly controversial, and various other terms are often used, including Native Americans, Amerindians, and (in Canada) First Peoples. Each of these substitutes has supporters and opponents, including people who are themselves of indigenous background. No single term for all the indigenous inhabitants of the Western Hemisphere is universally accepted, though in the United States "American Indians" is now becoming more common. The many peoples of the Americas did not think of themselves as belonging to a single group, any more than the peoples living in Europe at Columbus's time thought of themselves as Europeans.

Settling the Americas

The traditions of many American Indian peoples teach that their group originated independently, often through the actions of a divine figure. Many creation accounts, including that of the book of Genesis in the Bible, begin with people who are created out of earth and receive assistance from supernatural beings who set out certain ways the people are supposed to behave. Both Native American and biblical creation accounts continue to have deep spiritual importance for many people.

□ CHRONOLOGY

ca. 40,000–13,000 B.C.E. Initial human migration to the Americas (date disputed)

ca. 8000 B.C.E. Beginnings of agriculture

ca. 2500 B.C.E. First cities in Norte Chico region of Peru; earliest mound building in North America

ca. 1500–300 B.C.E. Olmec culture

ca. 1200 B.C.E. Emergence of Chavin culture

ca. 200 B.C.E.–600 C.E. Hopewell culture

ca. 100–800 C.E. Moche culture

ca. 450 C.E. Peak of Teotihuacán's influence

ca. 600–900 C.E. Peak of Maya culture

ca. 1050–1250 C.E. Construction of mounds at Cahokia

ca. 1325 C.E. Construction of Aztec city of Tenochtitlán begins

ca. 1450 C.E. Height of Aztec culture

ca. 1500 C.E. Inca Empire reaches its largest extent

Archaeological and DNA evidence indicates that the earliest humans came to the Americas from Siberia and East Asia, but exactly when and how this happened is hotly debated. The traditional account is that people crossed the Bering Strait from what is now Russian Siberia to what is now Alaska sometime between 15,000 and 13,000 B.C.E., mostly by walking (Map 11.1). This was the end of the last Ice Age, so more of the world's water was frozen and ocean levels were much lower than they are today. (This situation is the opposite of what is occurring today; global warming is melting polar ice, which is raising water levels around the world.) The migrants traveled southward through North America between two large ice sheets that were slowly melting and retreating. They lived by gathering and hunting, using spears with distinctive fluted stone tips that archaeologists term "Clovis points" after the town in New Mexico where they were first discovered.

Clovis points have been found widely throughout the Americas, and archaeologists used to see the Clovis people who first created these spear points about 11,000 B.C.E as the ancestors of most indigenous people in the Western Hemisphere. Within the last several decades, however, sites in many places have yielded stone tools that appear to predate Clovis.

• **Mesoamerica** The term used by scholars to designate the area of present-day Mexico and Central America.

301

Archaeologists working at Monte Verde along the coast of Chile have excavated a site that they date to at least 12,000 B.C.E., which would have required a very fast walk from the Bering land bridge. Other sites have been excavated in Brazil, Colombia, Chile, Venezuela, and in many parts of the United States. The pre-Clovis dating of many of these sites has been controversial, in part because the number of objects found at any one site has been small. But in 2011 more than fifteen thousand artifacts were found at one site in Texas, dating to between 11,200 B.C.E. and 13,500 B.C.E. A large group of prominent archaeologists affirmed that this site provides compelling evidence there were humans in the Americas before the Clovis people.

These new archaeological discoveries are leading increasing numbers of archaeologists to conclude that migrants over the land bridge were preceded by people coming originally from Asia who traveled along the coast in skin boats, perhaps as early as 40,000 years ago. They lived by gathering and fishing in the rich coastal estuaries and kelp beds, and they slowly worked their way southward. The coasts that they traveled along are today far under water, and so archaeological evidence is difficult to obtain, but DNA and other genetic evidence have lent support to the theory of coastal migration.

However and whenever people got to the Western Hemisphere — and a consensus about this may emerge in the next decade — they lived by gathering, fishing, and hunting, as did everyone throughout the world at that point. Some groups were nomadic and followed migrating game, while others did not have to travel to be assured of a regular food supply. Coastal settlements from the Pacific Northwest to the southern end of South America relied on fish and shellfish, and some also hunted seals and other large marine mammals.

The Development of Agriculture

About 8000 B.C.E. people in some parts of the Americas began raising crops as well as gathering wild produce. As in the development of agriculture in Afroeurasia, people initially planted the seeds of native plants. Pumpkins and other members of the gourd family were among the earliest crops, as were chilies, beans, and avocados. At some point people living in what is now southern Mexico also began raising what would become the most important crop in the Americas — maize, which we generally call corn. Exactly how this happened is not clear. In contrast to other grains such as wheat and rice, the kernels of maize — which are the seeds as well as the part that is eaten for food — are wrapped in a husk, so the plant cannot propagate itself easily. In addition, no wild ancestor of maize has been found. What many biologists now think happened is that a related grass called "teosinte" developed mutant forms with large kernels enclosed in husks, and people living in the area quickly realized the benefits of these new forms. They began to intentionally plant kernels from them and crossbred the results to get better crops each year.

People bred various types of maize for different purposes and for different climates, making it the staple food throughout the highlands of Mesoamerica. They often planted maize along with squash, beans, and other crops in a field called a milpa (MIHL-puh); the beans use the maize stalks for support as they grow and also fix nitrogen in the soil, acting as a natural fertilizer. Crops can be grown in milpas year after year, in contrast to single-crop planting in which rotation is needed so as not to exhaust the soil.

Inca Terraces In order to create more land for farming and limit soil erosion, Andean peoples built terraces up steep slopes. Later the Incas built systems of aqueducts and canals to bring water to terraced fields. (Wolfgang Kaehler/Corbis)

Maize was viewed as the source of human life and therefore came to have a symbolic and religious meaning. It featured prominently in sculptures of gods and kings, and it was often associated with a specific deity, the corn god. Ceremonies honoring this god were held regularly. In them, people asked for good harvests, as in this Mexica (meh-SHEE-kah) hymn, recorded in the sixteenth century:

> The god of corn, born in Paradise,
> where flowers bloom,
> on the day One Flower . . .
> The god of corn,
> born in the region of rain and mist,
> where the children of men are conceived.[1]

In central Mexico, along with milpas, people also built *chinampas* (chee-NAHM-pahs), floating gardens. They dredged soil from the bottom of a lake or pond, placed the soil on mats of woven twigs, and then planted maize and other crops in the soil. Chinampas were enormously productive, yielding up to three harvests a year.

Knowledge of maize cultivation and maize seeds themselves spread from Mesoamerica into both North and South America. By 3000 B.C.E. farmers in what is now Peru and Uruguay were planting maize, and by 2000 B.C.E. farmers in southwest North America were as well. The crop then spread into the Mississippi Valley and to northeastern North America, where farmers bred slightly different variants for the different growing conditions. After 1500 C.E. maize cultivation spread to Europe, Africa, and Asia as well, becoming an essential food crop there. (In the twentieth century maize became even more successful; about one-quarter of the nearly fifty thousand items in the average American supermarket now contains corn.)

The expansion of maize was the result of contacts between different groups that can be traced through trade goods as well. Copper from the Great Lakes, used for jewelry and ornaments, was a particularly valuable item and was traded throughout North America, reaching Mexico by 3000 B.C.E. Obsidian from the Rocky Mountains, used for blades, was traded widely, as were shells and later pottery.

Various cultivars of maize were developed for many different climates, but maize was difficult to grow in high altitudes. Thus in the high Andes, people relied on potatoes, with the ear-

"The god of corn, born in Paradise, where flowers bloom."

MEXICA HYMN

liest evidence of people eating potatoes dating from about 11,000 B.C.E. in Monte Verde. Potatoes first grew wild and then were cultivated, and selective breeding produced many different varieties. The slopes on which potatoes were grown were terraced with stone retaining walls, keeping the hillsides from sliding. High-altitude valleys were connected to mountain life and vegetation to form a single interdependent agricultural system, called "vertical archipelagos," capable of supporting large communities. Such vertical archipelagos often extended more than thirty-seven miles from top to bottom. The terraces were shored up with earthen walls to retain moisture, enabling the production of bumper crops of potatoes. Potatoes ordinarily cannot be stored for long periods, but Andean peoples developed a product called *chuñu*, freeze-dried potatoes made by subjecting potatoes alternately to nightly frosts and daily sun. Chuñu will keep unspoiled for several years. Coca (the dried leaves of a plant native to the Andes from which cocaine is derived), chewed in moderation as a dietary supplement, enhanced people's stamina and their ability to withstand the cold that was part of living at high altitudes.

Maize will also not grow well in hot, wet climates. In the Amazon rain forest manioc, a tuber that can be cooked in many ways, became the staple food instead. It was planted along with other crops, including fruits, nuts, and various types of palm trees such as domesticated peach palms, which produce fruit, pulp that is made into flour, heart of palm that is eaten raw, and juice that can be fermented into beer. Just how many people Amazonian agriculture supported before the introduction of European diseases (see "Connections" on page

Lime Container from the Andes This 9-inch gold bottle for holding lime, made between 500 C.E. and 1000 C.E., shows a seated female figure with rings in her ears and beads across her forehead and at her neck, wrists, knees, and ankles. Lime helped release the active ingredients in coca, which was used by many peoples of South America in rituals and to withstand bodily discomfort. Pieces of coca leaves were placed in the mouth with small amounts of powdered lime made from seashells and then chewed. (Image © The Metropolitan Museum of Art/Art Resource, NY)

327) is hotly debated by anthropologists, but increasing numbers see the original tropical rain forest not as a pristine wilderness, but as an ecosystem managed effectively by humans for thousands of years.

Farming in the Americas was not limited to foodstuffs. Beginning about 2500 B.C.E. people living along the coast of Peru used irrigation to raise cotton, and textiles became an important part of Peruvian culture. Agriculture in the Americas was extensive, though it was limited by the lack of an animal that could be harnessed to pull a plow. People throughout the Americas domesticated dogs for hunting, and in the Andes they domesticated llamas and alpacas to carry loads through the mountains. But no native species allowed itself to be harnessed as horses, oxen, and water buffalo did in Asia and Europe, which meant that all agricultural labor was human-powered.

Early Societies

□ What physical, social, and intellectual features characterized early societies in the Americas?

Agricultural advancement had definitive social and political consequences. Careful cultivation of the land brought a reliable and steady food supply, which contributed to a relatively high fertility rate. As a result, population in the Americas grew steadily and may have reached about 15 million by the first century B.C.E. This growth in population allowed for the creation of the first urban societies.

Mounds, Towns, and Trade in North and South America

By 2500 B.C.E. some groups in North America began to build massive earthworks, mounds of earth and stone serving a variety of purposes (see page 311). Some mounds were conical, others elongated or wall-like, others pyramidical, and still others, called effigy mounds, in serpentine, bird, or animal form. The Ohio and Mississippi River Valleys contain the richest concentration of mounds, but these earthworks have been found from the Great Lakes down to the Gulf of Mexico (see Map 11.1). One early large mound at Poverty Point, Louisiana, on the banks of the Mississippi dates from about 1300 B.C.E. It consists of six octagonal ramparts, one within the other, that measure six feet high and more than four hundred yards across. The area was

home to perhaps five thousand people and was inhabited for hundreds of years, with trade goods brought in by canoe and carved stone beads exported.

Large structures for political and religious purposes began to be built earlier in South America than in North America. By about 2500 B.C.E. cities grew along river valleys on the coast of Peru in the region called Norte Chico (NAWR-tay CHEE-koh). Stepped pyramids, some more than ten stories high, dominated these settlements, and they were built at about the same time as the pyramids in Egypt. Cities in Norte Chico often used irrigation to produce squash, beans, cotton, and other crops. People who lived along the coast relied extensively on fish and shellfish, which they traded with residents of inland cities for the cotton needed to make nets. The largest city, Caral, had many plazas, houses, and temples built with large pieces of quarried stone, supported by woven cotton and grass bags filled with smaller stones. Cotton was used in Norte Chico for many other things, including the earliest example yet discovered of a **khipu** (also spelled *quipu*), a collection of knotted strings that was used to record information. Later Peruvian cultures, including the Incas, developed ever more complex khipu, using the colors of the string and the style and position of the knots to represent tax obligations, census records, and other numeric data.

Along with khipu, Norte Chico culture also developed religious ideas and representations of deities. Dating to about 2250 B.C.E. the oldest religious image yet found in the Americas, a piece of gourd with a drawing of a fanged god holding a staff, comes from Norte Chico. This staff god became a major deity in many Andean cultures, one of a complex pantheon of deities. Religious ceremonies, as well as other festivities, in Norte Chico likely involved music, as a large number of bone flutes have been discovered.

The earliest cities in the Andes were built by the Chavin people beginning about 1200 B.C.E. These people built pyramids and other types of monumental architecture, quarrying and trimming huge blocks of stone and assembling them without mortar. They worked gold and silver into human and animal figurines, trading these and other goods to coastal peoples.

Olmec Agriculture, Technology, and Religion

The **Olmecs** created the first society with cities in Mesoamerica. The word *Olmec* comes from an Aztec term for the peoples living in southern Veracruz and western Tabasco, Mexico, between about 1500 and 300 B.C.E. Until 1993 knowledge of the Olmecs rested on archaeological evidence — pyramids, jade objects, axes, figurines, and stone monuments — but that year two linguists deciphered Olmec writing. Since then, un-

---

• **khipu** An intricate system of knotted and colored strings used by early Peruvian cultures to store information such as census and tax records.

• **Olmecs** The oldest of the early advanced Mesoamerican civilizations.

This khipu, a collection of colored, knotted strings, recorded numeric information and allowed Inca administrators to keep track of the flow of money, goods, and people in their large empire. Every aspect of the khipu—the form and position of the knots, the colors and spin of the string—may have provided information. Administrators read them visually and by running their hands through them, as Braille text is read today. (Museo Arqueologico Rafael Larco Herrera, Lima, Peru)

derstanding of Olmec and other contemporary Mesoamerican cultures such as the Zapotecs also has come from the written records they left.

The Olmecs cultivated maize, squash, beans, and other plants and supplemented that diet with wild game and fish. They engaged in long-distance trade, exchanging rubber, cacao (from which chocolate is made), pottery, figurines, jaguar pelts, and the services of painters and sculptors for obsidian (a hard, black volcanic glass from which paddle-shaped weapons were made), basalt, iron ore, shells, and various perishable goods. Trading networks extended as far away as central and western Mexico and the Pacific coast.

Originally the Olmecs lived in egalitarian societies that had few distinctions based on status or wealth. After 1500 B.C.E., however, more complex, hierarchical societies evolved. Most Olmecs continued to live in small villages along the rivers of the region, while their leaders resided in large cities, including those today known as San Lorenzo and La Venta. These cities contained palaces (large private houses) for the elite, large plazas, temples (ritual centers), water reservoirs, and carved stone drains for the disposal of wastes. They also contained special courts on which men played a game with a hard rubber ball that was both religious ritual and sport.

Later Mesoamerican groups played a similar ball game, and they also adopted other aspects of Olmec culture: large pyramid-shaped buildings, huge stone heads of rulers or gods, sacrifice at sacred ceremonial sites, and a calendar that traced celestial phenomena, which they believed influenced human life. The need to record time led the Olmecs to develop a symbolic writing system, which they also passed down.

Around 900 B.C.E. San Lorenzo, the center of early Olmec culture, was destroyed, probably by migrating peoples from the north, and power passed to La Venta in Tabasco. Archaeological excavation at La Venta has uncovered a huge volcano-shaped pyramid. Standing 110 feet high at an inaccessible site on an island in the Tonala River, the so-called Great Pyramid was the center of the Olmec religion. The upward thrust of this monument, like ziggurats in Mesopotamia or cathedrals

The Olmecs, ca. 1500–300 B.C.E.

in medieval Europe, may have represented the human effort to get closer to the gods. Built of huge stone slabs, the Great Pyramid required, scholars estimate, some eight hundred thousand hours of human labor. It testifies to the region's good harvests, which were able to support a labor force large enough to build such a monument.

Classical Era Mesoamerica and North America, 300–900 C.E.

☐ How did Mesoamerican and North American peoples develop prosperous and stable societies in the classical era?

The urban culture of the Olmecs and other Mesoamerican peoples influenced subsequent Mesoamerican societies. Especially in what became known as the classical era (300–900 C.E.), various groups developed large states centered on cities, with high levels of technological and intellectual achievement. The city-states established by the **Maya** were the longest lasting, but others were significant as well. Peoples living in North America built communities that, although smaller than those in Mesoamerica, featured significant achieve-

Palace Doorway Lintel at Yaxchilan, Mexico Lady Xoc, principal wife of King Shield-Jaguar, who holds a torch over her, pulls a thorn-lined rope through her tongue to sanctify with her blood the birth of a younger wife's child—reflecting the importance of blood sacrifice in Maya culture. The elaborate headdresses and clothes of the couple show their royal status. (Photograph K2887 © Justin Kerr)

ments, such as the use of irrigation to enhance agricultural production.

Maya Agriculture and Trade

The word *Maya* seems to derive from *Zamna*, the name of a Maya god. Linguistic evidence suggests that the first Maya were a small North American Indian group that emigrated from the area that is now southern Oregon and northern California to the western highlands of Guatemala. Between the third and second millennia B.C.E. various groups, including the Cholans and Tzeltalans, broke away from the parent group and moved north and east into the Yucatán peninsula. The Cholan-speaking Maya, who occupied the area during the time of great cultural achievement, apparently created the culture.

Maya communities relied on agriculture. The staple crop in Mesoamerica was maize, often raised in multiple-crop milpas with other foodstuffs, including beans, squash, chili peppers, some root crops, and fruit trees. The Maya also practiced intensive agriculture in raised, narrow, rectangular plots that they built above the low-lying, seasonally flooded land bordering rivers.

The raised-field and milpa systems yielded food sufficient to support large population centers. The entire Maya region could have had as many as 14 million inhabitants. At Uxmal, Uaxactún, Copán, Piedras Negras, Tikal, Palenque, and Chichén Itzá (Map 11.2), archaeologists have uncovered the palaces of nobles, elaborate pyramids where nobles were buried, engraved pillars, masonry temples, altars, sophisticated polychrome pottery, and courts for games played with a rubber ball. The largest site, Tikal, may have had forty thousand people and served as a religious and ceremonial center.

At these population centers, public fairs for trading merchandise accompanied important religious festivals. Jade, obsidian, beads of red spiny oyster shell, lengths of cloth, and cacao beans—all in high demand in the Mesoamerican world—served as media of exchange. The extensive trade among Maya communities, plus a common language, promoted unity among the peoples of the region and gave them a common sense of identity. Merchants trading beyond Maya regions, such as with the Zapotecs of the Valley of Oaxaca and with the Teotihuacános of the central valley of Mexico, were considered state ambassadors bearing "gifts" to royal neighbors, who reciprocated with their own "gifts." Since this long-distance trade played an important part in international relations, the merchants conducting it were high nobles or even members of the royal family.

The extensive networks of rivers and swamps in the area ruled by the Maya were the main arteries of transportation; over them large canoes carved out of hardwood trees carried cargoes of cloth and maize. Wide roads also linked Maya centers; on the roads merchants and lords were borne in litters, goods and produce on human backs. Trade produced considerable wealth that seems to have been concentrated in a noble class, for the Maya had no distinctly mercantile class. They did have a sharply defined hierarchical society. A hereditary elite owned private land, defended society, carried on commercial activities, exercised political power, and directed religious rituals. Artisans and scribes made up the next social level. The rest of the people were farmers, unskilled laborers, and slaves, the latter including prisoners of war.

Wars were fought in Maya society for a variety of reasons. Long periods without rain caused crop failure, which led to famine and then war with other centers for food. Certain cities, such as Tikal, extended their authority over larger areas through warfare with neighboring cities. Within the same communities, domestic strife between factions over the succession to the kingship or property led to violence.

Maya Science and Religion

The Maya developed the most complex writing system in the Americas, a script with nearly a thousand characters that represent concepts and sounds. With this script important events and observations were re-

MAP 11.2 The Maya World, 300–900 C.E.

The Maya built dozens of cities linked together in trading networks of roads and rivers. Only the largest of them are shown here.

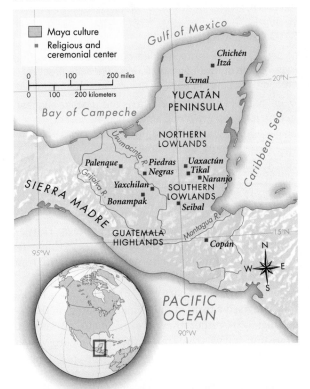

> " In the year 3114 B.C. my forefathers were present, during the Creation of the World. "
>
> **MAYA STELE FROM TIKAL**

corded in books made of bark paper and deerskin, on stone pillars archaeologists term "steles," on pottery, and on the walls of temples and other buildings. The deciphering of this writing over the last fifty years has demonstrated that the inscriptions are historical documents recording the births, accessions, marriages, wars, and deaths of Maya kings and nobles, in contrast to the earliest writings from Mesopotamia, which are tax records for payments to the temple (see page 39). As was common for elites everywhere, Maya leaders often stressed the ancient ancestry of their families. "In the year 3114 B.C. my forefathers were present, during the Creation of the World," reads one stele in the city of Tikal, recording the lineage of the Maya Lord Kan Boar.[2] The writing and pictorial imagery often represent the same events, allowing for a fuller understanding of Maya dynastic history.

Learning about Maya religion through written records is more difficult. In the sixteenth century Spanish religious authorities ordered all books of Maya writing to be destroyed, viewing them as demonic. Only three (and part of a fourth) survived, because they were already in Europe. These texts provide information about religious rituals and practices, as well as astronomical calculations. Further information comes from the **Popul Vuh** (poh-POHL VOO), or *Book of Council*, a book of mythological narratives and dynastic history written in the middle of the sixteenth century in the Maya language but in European script, which Spanish friars had taught to Maya students. Like the Bible in Judeo-Christian tradition, the *Popul Vuh* gives the Maya view of the creation of the world, concepts of good and evil, and the entire nature and purpose of the living experience. (See "Viewpoints: Creation in the *Popul Vuh* and in Okanogan Tradition," page 308.) Because almost all religious texts from Mesoamerica—not just Maya texts but also those from other cultures—were destroyed by Spanish Christian authorities, this book's significance is enormous.

Maya religious practice emphasized performing rituals at specific times, which served as an impetus for further refinements of the calendar. From careful

- **Maya** A highly developed Mesoamerican culture centered in the Yucatán peninsula of Mexico. The Maya created the most intricate writing system in the Western Hemisphere.
- **Popul Vuh** The *Book of Council*, a collection of mythological narratives and dynastic histories that constitutes the primary record of the Maya civilization.

Viewpoints

Creation in the *Popul Vuh* and in Okanogan Tradition

> • *Every people of the world appears to have had a creation account that describes the way the world and the people within it came to be. These are excerpts from the accounts of the Maya people, as recorded in the sixteenth century in the* Popul Vuh, *and of the Okanogan people of the Pacific Northwest, as recorded in the twentieth century from oral traditions.*

Popul Vuh

"Heart of Sky arrived here with Sovereign and Quetzal Serpent [three creator gods] in the darkness, in the night. . . . They thought and they pondered. They reached an accord, bringing together their words and their thoughts. . . . Then the earth was created by them. Merely their word brought about the creation of it. In order to create the earth, they said, "Earth," and immediately it was created. . . . Then were conceived the animals of the mountains, the guardians of the forest, and all that populate the mountains—the deer and the birds, the puma and the jaguar, the serpent and the rattlesnake. . . . This, then, is the beginning of the conception of humanity, when that which would become the flesh of mankind was sought. Then spoke they who are called She Who Has Borne Children and He Who Has Begotten Sons, the Framer and the Shaper [four other gods associated with creation], Sovereign and Quetzal Serpent: "The dawn approaches, and our work is not completed. A provider and a sustainer have yet to appear—a child of light, a son of light. Humanity has yet to appear to populate the face of the earth," they said. Thus they gathered together and joined their thoughts in the darkness, in the night. They searched and they sifted. Here they thought and they pondered. Their thoughts came forth bright and clear. They discovered and established that which would become the flesh of humanity. . . . Thus their frame and shape were given expression by our first Mother and our first Father. Their flesh was merely yellow ears of maize and white ears of maize. . . . And so there were four who were made, and mere food was their flesh. . . . Then their companions, their wives, also came to be. It was the gods who conceived them as well."

Okanogan Tradition

"The earth was once a human being: Old One made her out of a woman. "You will be the mother of all people," he said.

Earth is alive yet, but she has been changed. The soil is her flesh, the rocks are her bones, the wind is her breath, trees and grass are her hair. She lives spread out, and we live on her. When she moves, we have an earthquake.

After taking the woman and changing her to earth, Old One gathered some of her flesh and rolled it into balls, as people do with mud or clay. He made the first group of these balls into the ancients, the beings of the early world. . . .

Besides the ancients, real people and real animals lived on the earth at that time. Old One made the people out of the last balls of mud he took from the earth. He rolled them over and over, shaped them like Indians, and blew on them to bring them alive. They were so ignorant that they were the most helpless of all the creatures Old One had made.

Old One made people and animals into males and females so that they might breed and multiply. Thus all living things came from the earth. When we look around, we see part of our mother everywhere."

Sources: Allen Christensen, trans., *Popul Vuh: The Sacred Book of the Maya* (Winchester, U.K.: O Books, 2003), pp. 70, 71, 74, 192, 195, 201. Used by permission of O Books; "Creation of the Animal People" from Ella C. Clark, *Indian Legends of the Pacific Northwest*. Copyright © 1981 by Ella C. Clark. Reprinted by permission of the University of California Press.

QUESTIONS FOR ANALYSIS

1. Who carries out the creation of the world and human beings in each of these accounts? How does the process of creation combine the spiritual and the material world?

2. How are humans created? What does this process suggest about the relations between humans and the rest of creation?

observation of the earth's movements around the sun, the Maya devised a calendar of eighteen 20-day months and one 5-day month, for a total of 365 days. They also used a second calendar with a cycle of 260 days, perhaps inherited from the Olmecs. When these two cyclical calendars coincided, which happened once every fifty-two years, the Maya celebrated with a period of feasting, ball-game competitions, and religious observance. These observances—and those at other times as well—included human sacrifice to honor the gods and demonstrate the power of earthly kings. The actions of those kings were recorded using yet a third calendar, which counted in a linear fashion forward from a specific date.

Using a system of bars (— = 5) and dots (○ = 1), the Maya devised a form of mathematics based on the vigesimal (20) rather than the decimal (10) system. More unusual was their use of the number zero, which

Maya Ballplayers and Writing This model of a ball court, made in Mesoamerica sometime before 250 C.E., shows the widely played game in which players used their hips, protected by padding, to hit a rubber ball through a vertical ring high on the wall. Spectators watched and bet on the games, which were also religious rituals and could result in death for the loser. The stone disk showing a player with an elaborate feather headdress comes from a Maya ball court built in 591 C.E. Maya glyphs rim the edge of the disk. (ball court: Yale University Art Gallery/Art Resource, NY; stone disk: National Anthropological Museum Mexico/The Art Archive)

allows for more complex calculations than are possible in number systems without it. The zero may have actually been discovered by the Olmecs, who used it in figuring their calendar, but the Maya used it mathematically as well. (At about the same time, mathematicians in India also began using zero.) The Maya's proficiency with numbers made them masters of abstract knowledge — notably in astronomy, mathematics, calendric development, and the recording of history.

Maya civilization lasted about a thousand years, reaching its peak between approximately 600 and 900 C.E., the period when the Tang Dynasty was flourishing in China, Islam was spreading in the Middle East, and Carolingian rulers were extending their sway in Europe. Between the eighth and tenth centuries the Maya abandoned their cultural and ceremonial centers, and Maya civilization collapsed. Archaeologists and historians attribute the decline to a combination of agricultural failures due to land exhaustion and drought; overpopulation; disease; and constant wars fought to achieve economic and political goals. These wars brought widespread destruction, which aggravated agrarian problems. Royalty also suffered from the decline in Maya civilization: just as in good times

kings attributed moral authority and prosperity to themselves, so in bad times, when military, economic, and social conditions deteriorated, they were blamed.

Growth and Assimilation of the Teotihuacán and Toltec Cultures

The Maya were not alone in creating a complex culture in Mesoamerica during the classic period. In the isolated valley of Oaxaca at modern-day Monte Albán in southern Mexico, Zapotecan-speaking peoples established a great religious center whose temples and elaborately decorated tombs testify to the wealth of the nobility. To the north of Monte Albán, Teotihuacán (tay-oh-tee-wah-KAHN) in central Mexico witnessed the flowering of a remarkable civilization built by a new people from regions east and south of the Valley of Mexico. In about 450 C.E. the city of Teotihuacán had a population of over two hundred thousand — more than any European city at the time. The inhabitants were stratified into distinct social classes. The rich and powerful resided in houses of palatial splendor in a special precinct. Ordinary working people, tradespeople, artisans, and obsidian craftsmen lived in apartment compounds, or barrios, on the edge of the city. Agricultural laborers lived outside the city. Teotihuacán became the center of trade and culture for all of Mesoamerica.

In the center of the city stood several great pyramids, which the Aztecs later referred to as the Pyramids of the Sun and the Moon. The Pyramid of the Sun, built of sun-dried bricks and faced with stone, is the world's third-largest pyramid, only a bit smaller than the largest ancient Egyptian pyramid. (The world's largest pyramid is also in Mesoamerica: the great pyramid of Cholula in Puebla, Mexico, built at about the same time as the pyramids of Teotihuacán.) Exactly what deities were worshipped there is unknown, although they appear to have included the feathered serpent god worshipped by many Mesoamerican peoples, called Quetzalcoatl (kwet-suhl-kuh-WAH-tuhl) or "quetzal serpent" by the Aztecs, named for the brilliant plumage of the quetzal bird.

Around 750 C.E. less-developed peoples from the southwest burned Teotihuacán, and the city-state fell

The Toltecs, ca. 900–1200 C.E.

- Toltec site
- Other site

apart. This collapse, plus that of the Maya in about 900 B.C.E., marks the end of the classical period in Mesoamerica for most scholars, just as the end of the Roman Empire in the West marks the end of the classical era in Europe (see Chapter 6). As in Europe, a period of disorder, militarism, and domination by smaller states followed.

Whereas nature gods and their priests seem to have governed the great cities of the earlier period, militant gods and warriors dominated the petty states that now arose. Among these states, the most powerful heir to Teotihuacán was the Toltec confederation, a weak union of strong states. The Toltecs admired the culture of their predecessors and sought to absorb and preserve it. Through intermarriage, they assimilated with the Teotihuacán people. In fact, every new Mesoamerican confederation became the cultural successor of earlier confederations.

Under Topiltzin (r. ca. 980–1000), the Toltecs extended their hegemony over most of central Mexico. Topiltzin established his capital at Tula, and its splen-

The Pyramid of the Sun at Teotihuacán Built in several stages beginning in about 100 C.E., the Pyramid of the Sun has sides measuring 700 feet long and 200 feet high. Originally it was covered with lime plaster decorated with brightly colored murals. Smaller pyramids surround it in what was the heart of the bustling city of Teotihuacán. (© age footstock/SuperStock)

Great Serpent Mound, Adams County, Ohio Made by people in the Hopewell culture, this 1,254-foot-long mound in the form of a writhing snake has its "head" at the highest point, suggesting an open mouth ready to swallow a huge egg formed by a heap of stones. (Georg Gerster/ Photo Researchers, Inc.)

dor and power became legendary during his reign. After the reign of Topiltzin, troubles beset the Toltec state. Drought led to crop failure. Northern peoples, the Chichimecas, attacked the borders in waves. Weak, incompetent rulers could not quell domestic uprisings. When the last Toltec king committed suicide in 1174, the Toltec state collapsed.

Hohokam, Hopewell, and Mississippian Societies

Mesoamerican trading networks extended into southwestern North America, where by 300 B.C.E. the Hohokam people and other groups were using irrigation canals, dams, and terraces to enhance their farming of the arid land (Map 11.3). The Hohokam built platforms for ceremonial purposes and, like the Olmecs and other Mesoamerican peoples, played games with rubber balls. The balls themselves were imported, for rubber trees do not grow in the desert, and turquoise and other precious stones were exported in return. Religious ideas came along with trade goods. Along with local divinities who created, preserved, and destroyed, the feathered serpent god became important to desert peoples. They planted desert crops such as agave, as well as cotton and maize that came from Mexico. Other groups, including the Anasazi (ah-nuh-SAH-zee), the Yuma, and later the Pueblo and Hopi also built settlements in this area, using large sandstone blocks and masonry to construct thick-walled houses that offered protection from the heat. Mesa Verde, the largest Anasazi town, had a population of about twenty-five hundred living in houses built into and on cliff walls. Roads connected Mesa Verde to other Anasazi towns, allow-

ing timber and other construction materials to be brought in more easily. Drought, deforestation, and soil erosion led to decline in both the Hohokam and Anasazi cultures, increasing warfare between towns.

To the east, the mound building introduced at settlements along the Mississippi River around 2000 B.C.E. spread more widely in the valleys of other rivers. One of the most important mound-building cultures was that of the Hopewell (200 B.C.E.–600 C.E.), named for a town in Ohio near where the most extensive mounds were built. Some mounds were burial chambers for priests, leaders, and other high-status individuals, or for thousands of more average people. Others were platforms for the larger houses of important people. Still others were simply huge mounds of earth shaped like animals or geometric figures, which may have served some sort of ceremonial purpose. Mound building thus had many purposes: to honor the gods, to remember the dead, and to make distinctions between leaders and common folk.

Hopewell earthworks also included canals that enabled trading networks to expand, bringing products from the Caribbean far into the interior. Those trading networks also carried maize, allowing more intensive agriculture to spread throughout the eastern woodlands of North America.

At Cahokia (kuh-HOE-kee-uh), near the confluence of the Mississippi and Missouri Rivers in Illinois, archaeologists have uncovered the largest mound of all, part of a ceremonial center and city that housed perhaps thirty-eight thousand people. Work on this complex of mounds, plazas, and houses — which covered five and a half square miles — began about 1050 C.E. and was completed about 1250 C.E. A fence of wooden posts

□ Mapping the Past

MAP 11.3 Major North American Agricultural Societies, ca. 600–1500 C.E.

Many North American groups used agriculture to increase the available food supply and allow greater population density and the development of urban centers. Shown here are three of these cultures: the Mississippian, Anasazi, and Hohokam.

ANALYZING THE MAP How did the location of the Mississippian and other mound-building cultures facilitate trade?

CONNECTIONS The climate and natural vegetation of North America in this period did not differ significantly from those of today. What different types of challenges might these have posed for crop-raising in the three societies shown here?

Approximate extent of mound-building cultures

Approximate extent of the Mississippian culture

Approximate extent of the Anasazi culture

Approximate extent of the Hohokam culture

0   500   1,000 miles
0   500   1,000 kilometers

---

surrounded the center of the complex. Several hundred rectangular mounds inside and outside the fence served as tombs and as the bases for temples and palaces. Within the fence, the largest mound rose in four stages to a height of one hundred feet and was nearly one thousand feet long. On its top stood a large building, used perhaps as a temple.

The mounds at Cahokia are the most impressive physical achievement of the **Mississippian** mound builders, who built cities and mounds throughout much of the eastern United States. What do the mounds tell us about Mississippian societies? The largest mounds served as burial chambers for leaders and, in many cases, for the leaders' male and female servants, who were sacrificed in order to assist the leader in the after-

life. Mounds also contain valuable artifacts, such as jewelry made from copper from Michigan, mica (a mineral used in building) from the Appalachians, obsidian from the Rocky Mountains, conch shells from the Caribbean, and pipestone from Minnesota.

From these burial items, archaeologists have deduced that mound culture was hierarchical and that power was increasingly centralized. The leader had religious responsibilities and also managed long-distance trade and gift-giving. The exchange of goods was not perceived as a form of commerce but as a means of showing respect and of establishing bonds among diverse groups. Large towns housed several thousand inhabitants and served as political and ceremonial centers. They controlled surrounding villages of a few hundred people but did not grow into large, politically unified city-states the way Tikal and Teotihuacán did.

Mississippian mound builders relied on agriculture to support their complex cultures, and by the time Cahokia was built, maize agriculture had spread to the Atlantic coast. Particularly along riverbanks and the

---

• **Mississippian** An important mound-building culture that thrived between 800 and 1500 C.E. in a territory that extended from the Mississippi River to the Appalachian Mountains. The largest mound produced by this culture is found at Cahokia, Illinois.

• **Nahuatl** The language of both the Toltecs and the Aztecs.

Engraved Mississippian Copper Plate This ornamental copper plate was excavated in Etowah Mound, Georgia, a Mississippian site first settled in about 1000 C.E. The copper may have been mined along the shore of Lake Superior in what is now northern Michigan, the largest source of copper in North America. Falcons were associated with success in warfare and long life among Mississippians, and warriors with falcon wings were frequently shown in the handiworks of this culture. (Catalogue No. A91117, Department of Anthropology, Smithsonian Institution; photo by D. E. Hurlbert)

coastline, fields of maize, beans, and squash surrounded large, permanent villages containing many houses, all surrounded by walls made of earth and timber. Hunting and fishing provided animal protein, but the bulk of people's food came from farming. For recreation, people played various ball games and chunkey, a game in which spears were thrown at a disk rolled across the ground. As in Mesoamerica, these games were sometimes played in large arenas with many spectators, who frequently gambled on the outcome.

Mississippian people's religious ideas are revealed in pottery in the form of bowls, jars, and bottles; in effigy pipes in various shapes; and in engraved shells, decorated copper plates, and carved stone statues. Along with the visible world, the Mississippian cosmos included an Overworld and an Underworld filled with supernatural beings; the three worlds were linked together by an axis usually portrayed as a tree or a striped pole. The forces and beings of both spiritual worlds, which often took the form of falcons, serpents, panthers, or creatures that combined parts from various animals, were honored through ceremonies and rituals, and they offered supernatural power to humans who performed these rites correctly.

At its peak in about 1150 Cahokia was the largest city north of Mesoamerica. However, construction of the interior wooden fence denuded much of the surrounding countryside of trees, which made spring floods worse and eventually destroyed much of the city. An earthquake at the beginning of the thirteenth century furthered the destruction, and the city never recovered. The worsening climate of the fourteenth century that brought famine to Europe probably also contributed to Cahokia's decline, and the site's population dispersed. Throughout Mississippian areas the fifteenth century brought increased warfare, as evidenced by the building of walls and defensive works around towns, and more migration. Iroquois-speaking peoples in particular migrated south from what is now New York into the valleys of the Ohio River and its

tributaries, sometimes displacing groups that had been living in these areas through warfare. In the fifteenth or early sixteenth century a group of Iroquois nations formed an association known as the Iroquois League to lessen intergroup violence. This league was a powerful force when European colonists first entered these areas.

The Aztecs

☐ How did the Aztecs both build on the achievements of earlier Mesoamerican cultures and develop new traditions to create their large empire?

The Aztecs provide a spectacular example of a culture that adopted many things from earlier peoples and also adapted them to create an even more powerful state. Around 1300 a group of **Nahuatl**-speaking people are believed to have migrated southward from what is now northern Mexico, settling on the shores and islands of Lake Texcoco in the central valley of Mexico (Map 11.4). Here they built the twin cities of Tenochtitlán (tay-nawch-teet-LAHN) and Tlatelolco, which by 1500 were probably larger than any city in Europe except

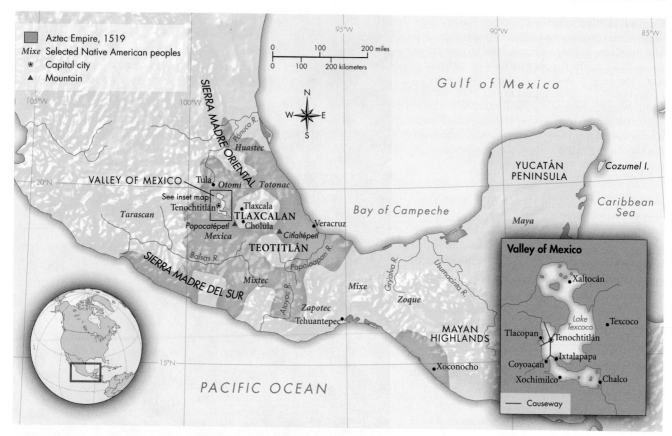

MAP 11.4 The Aztec (Mexica) Empire in 1519 The Mexica migrated into the central valley of what is now Mexico from the north, conquering other groups and establishing an empire, later called the Aztec Empire. The capital of the Aztec Empire was Tenochtitlán, built on islands in Lake Texcoco.

Istanbul. As they migrated, these people, who were later called the Aztecs, conquered many neighboring city-states and established an empire later termed the Aztec Empire. The word *Aztec* was not used at the time, however, and most scholars now prefer the term **Mexica** to refer to the empire and its people; we use both terms here.

Religion and War in Aztec Society

In Mexica society, religion was the dynamic factor that transformed other aspects of the culture: economic security, social mobility, education, and especially war. War was an article of religious faith. The state religion of the Aztecs initially gave them powerful advantages over other groups in central Mexico; it inspired them to conquer vast territories in a remarkably short time. War came to be seen as a religious duty; through it

nobles, and occasionally commoners, honored the gods, gained prestige, and often acquired wealth.

The Mexicas worshipped a number of gods and goddesses as well as some deities that had dual natures as both male and female. The basic conflict in the world was understood as being between order and disorder, though the proper life was seen as balancing these two, because disorder could never be completely avoided. Disorder was linked to dirt and uncleanness, so temples, shrines, and altars were kept very clean; rituals of purification often involved sweeping or bathing. Like many polytheists, Mexicas took the deities of people they encountered into their own pantheon or mixed their attributes with those of existing gods. Quetzalcoatl, for example, the feathered serpent god found among many Mesoamerican groups, was generally revered by the Mexicas as a creator deity and a source of knowledge.

Among the deities venerated by Mexica and other Mesoamerican groups was Huitzilopochtli (weet-zeel-oh-POHCH-tlee), a young warrior-god whose name translates fully as "Blue Hummingbird of the South" (or "Blue Hummingbird on the Left") and who symbolized the sun blazing at high noon. The sun, the source

• **Mexica** The dominant ethnic group of what is now Mexico, which created an empire based on war and religion that reached its height in the mid-1400s; in the nineteenth century the people became known as Aztecs.

of all life, had to be kept moving in its orbit if darkness was not to overtake the world. To keep it moving, Aztecs believed, the sun had to be frequently fed precious fluids — that is, human blood. Therefore, human sacrifice was seen as a sacred duty, essential for the preservation and prosperity of humankind. (See "Individuals in Society: Tlacaélel," page 316.)

Most victims were war captives, for the Aztecs controlled their growing empire by sacrificing prisoners seized in battle, by taking hostages from among defeated peoples as ransom against future revolt, and by demanding that subject states provide an annual tribute of people to be sacrificed to Huitzilopochtli. In some years it was difficult to provide enough war captives, so other types of people, including criminals and slaves, were sacrificed as well. Additionally, unsuccessful generals, corrupt judges, and careless public officials — even people who accidentally entered forbidden precincts of the royal palaces — were routinely sacrificed. Non-captive victims had a lower status than did captives, however, and Mexicas engaged in special wars simply to provide victims for sacrifices, termed "flower (or flowery) wars." Flowers were frequently associated metaphorically with warfare in Mexica culture, with blood described as a flower of warfare, swords and banners as blooming like flowers, and a warrior's life as being as fleeting as a flower's blooming. The objective of flower wars was to capture warriors from the other side, not to kill them.

The Mexica state religion required constant warfare for two basic reasons. One was to meet the gods' needs for human sacrifice; the other was to acquire warriors for the next phase of imperial expansion. Moreover, defeated peoples had to pay tribute in foodstuffs to support rulers, nobles, warriors, and the imperial bureaucracy. The vanquished supplied laborers for agriculture, the economic basis of Mexica society. Likewise, conquered peoples had to produce workers for the construction and maintenance of the entire Aztec infrastructure — roads, dike systems, aqueducts, causeways, and royal palaces. Finally, merchants also benefited from warfare, for it opened new markets for traders' goods in subject territories.

Social Distinctions Among Aztecs

A wealth of information has survived about fifteenth- and sixteenth-century Mexico. The Aztecs wrote many books recounting their history, geography, and religious practices, and they loved making speeches, which scribes wrote down. The Aztecs also preserved records of their legal disputes, which alone amounted to vast files. The Spanish conquerors subsequently destroyed much of this material, but enough documents remain to construct a picture of the Mexica people at the time of the Spanish intrusion.

Few sharp social distinctions existed among the Aztecs during their early migrations, but by the early sixteenth century Aztec society had changed. A stratified social structure had come into being, and the warrior aristocracy exercised great authority. Men who had

Huitzilopochtli This painting of the hummingbird god of war carrying a shield in one hand and serpent-headed knife in the other was made by Aztec priests in a book written on bark paper about the time of the Spanish conquest. He is shown descending from a step-pyramid, perhaps a reference to the great pyramid in the center of Tenochtitlán, where he was worshipped.
(© Foundation for the Advancement of Mesoamerican Studies, Inc., www.famsi.org)

Individuals in Society

Tlacaélel

THE HUMMINGBIRD GOD HUITZILOPOCHTLI was originally a somewhat ordinary god of war and of young men, but in the fifteenth century he was elevated in status among the Mexica. He became increasingly associated with the sun and gradually became the Mexicas' most important deity. This change appears to have been primarily the work of Tlacaélel, the very long-lived chief adviser to the emperors Itzcóatl (r. 1427–1440), Montezuma I (r. 1440–1469), and Axayacatl (r. 1469–1481). Tlacaélel first gained influence during wars in the 1420s in which the Mexicas defeated the rival Tepanecs, after which he established new systems of dividing military spoils and enemy lands. At the same time, he advised the emperor that new histories were needed in which the destiny of the Mexica people was made clearer. Tlacaélel ordered the destruction of older historical texts, and under his direction the new chronicles connected Mexicas' fate directly to Huitzilopochtli. Mexica writing was primarily pictographic, drawn and then read by specially trained scribes who used written records as an aid to oral presentation, especially for legal issues, historical chronicles, religious and devotional poetry, and astronomical calculations.

According to these new texts, the Mexicas had been guided to Lake Texcoco by Huitzilopochtli; there they saw an eagle perched on a cactus, which a prophecy foretold would mark the site of their new city. Huitzilopochtli kept the world alive by bringing the sun's warmth, but to do this he required the Mexicas, who increasingly saw themselves as the "people of the sun," to provide a steady offering of human blood.

The worship of Huitzilopochtli became linked to cosmic forces as well as daily survival. In Nahua tradition, the universe was understood to exist in a series of five suns, or five cosmic ages. Four ages had already passed, and their suns had been destroyed; the fifth sun, the age in which the Mexicas were now living, would also be destroyed unless the Mexicas fortified the sun with the energy found in blood. Warfare thus not only brought new territory under Mexica control but also provided sacrificial victims to nourish the sun god. With these ideas, Tlacaélel created what Miguel León-Portilla, a leading contemporary scholar of Nahuatl religion and philosophy, has termed a "mystico-militaristic" conception of Aztec destiny.

Human sacrifice was practiced in many cultures of Mesoamerica, including the Olmec and the Maya as well as the Mexica, before the changes introduced by Tlacaélel, but the number of victims is believed to have increased dramatically during the last period of Mexica rule. A huge pyramid-shaped temple in the center of Tenochtitlán, dedicated to Huitzilopochtli and the water god Tlaloc, was renovated and expanded many times, the last in 1487. Each expansion was dedicated by priests sacrificing war captives. Similar ceremonies were held regularly throughout the year on days dedicated to Huitzilopochtli and were attended by many observers, including representatives from neighboring states as well as masses of Mexicas. According to many accounts, victims were placed on a stone slab, and their hearts were cut out with an obsidian knife; the officiating priest then held the heart up as an offering to the sun. Sacrifices were also made to other gods at temples elsewhere in Tenochtitlán, and perhaps in other cities controlled by the Mexicas.

Estimates of the number of people sacrificed to Huitzilopochtli and other Mexica gods vary enormously and are impossible to verify. Both Mexica and later Spanish accounts clearly exaggerated the numbers, but most historians today assume that between several hundred and several thousand people were killed each year.

Sources: Miguel León-Portilla, *Pre-Columbian Literatures of Mexico* (Norman: University of Oklahoma Press, 1969); Inga Clendinnen, *Mexicas: An Interpretation* (Cambridge: Cambridge University Press, 1991).

QUESTIONS FOR ANALYSIS

1. How did the worship of Huitzilopochtli contribute to Aztec expansion? To hostility toward the Aztecs?

2. Why might Tlacaélel have seen it as important to destroy older texts as he created this new Aztec mythology?

Tlacaélel emphasized human sacrifice as one of the Aztecs' religious duties. (Scala/Art Resource, NY)

▢ Picturing the Past

Aztec Adolescents This scene of adults supervising the tasks that young people at each age (indicated by dots) were expected to learn appeared in a painted book made by Mexica artists in the middle of the sixteenth century. It includes Nahuatl and Spanish words, including "dos [two] tortillas," the basic amount of food the artists thought was appropriate for these adolescents. (The Bodleian Library, University of Oxford, MS Arch. Selden. A.1, fol. 60r)

ANALYZING THE IMAGE What tasks are boys expected to learn? What tasks are girls expected to learn? What do these differences suggest about Aztec society?

CONNECTIONS This painting was made about a generation after the Spanish conquest so that in some ways it represents an idealized past rather than current reality. How might this have shaped the artists' views of adolescence?

distinguished themselves in war occupied the highest military and social positions in the state. Generals, judges, and governors of provinces were appointed by the emperor from among his servants who had earned reputations as war heroes. These great lords, or tecuhtli (teh-COOT-lee), dressed luxuriously and lived in palaces. Acting as provincial governors, they exercised full political, judicial, and military authority on the emperor's behalf. In their territories they maintained order, settled disputes, and judged legal cases; oversaw the cultivation of land; and made sure that tribute — in food or gold — was paid. The governors also led troops in wartime. These functions resembled those of feudal lords in western Europe during the Middle Ages. Just as only nobles in France and England could wear fur and carry swords, just as gold jewelry and

elaborate hairstyles for women distinguished royal and noble classes in African kingdoms, so in Mexica societies only the tecuhtli could wear jewelry and embroidered cloaks. As the empire expanded, the growth of a strong mercantile class led to an influx of tropical wares and luxury goods: cotton, feathers, cocoa, skins, turquoise jewelry, and gold. These goods contributed to the elegant and extravagant lifestyle that the upper classes enjoyed.

Beneath the great nobility of military leaders and imperial officials was the class of warriors. Theoretically, every free man could be a warrior, and parents dedicated their male children to war, burying a male child's umbilical cord with some arrows and a shield on the day of his birth. In actuality the sons of nobles were more likely to become warriors because of their fathers' positions and influence in the state. At the age of six boys entered a school that trained them for war. They were taught to fight with a *ma-cana*, a paddle-shaped wooden club edged with bits of obsidian. Youths were also trained in the use of spears, bows and arrows, lances fitted with obsidian points, and atlatls, notched throwing sticks made of bone, wood, or antler. They learned to live on little food and sleep and to accept pain without complaint. At about age eighteen a warrior fought his first campaign. If he captured a prisoner for ritual sacrifice, he acquired the title *iyac*, or warrior. If in later campaigns he succeeded in killing or capturing four of the enemy, he became a *tequiua*—one who shared in the booty and thus was a member of the nobility. If a young man failed in several campaigns to capture the required four prisoners, he became a *macehualli* (plural *macehualtin*), a commoner.

> "O great Lord of All Things, remember your servant who has gone to exalt your honor and the greatness of your name. He will offer blood in that sacrifice that is war."
>
> **PRAYER TO HUITZILOPOCHTLI**

The macehualtin were the ordinary citizens—the backbone of Aztec society and the vast majority of the population. The word *macehualli* means "worker" and implies boorish speech and vulgar behavior. Members of this class performed all sorts of agricultural, military, and domestic services and carried heavy public burdens not required of noble warriors. Government officials assigned them work on the temples, roads, and bridges. Army officers called them up for military duty, but Mexica considered this an honor and a religious rite, not a burden. Unlike nobles, priests, orphans, and slaves, macehualtin paid taxes. Macehualtin in the capital, however, possessed certain rights: they held their plots of land for life, and they received a small share of the tribute paid by the provinces to the emperor.

Beneath the macehualtin were the *tlalmaitl*, the landless workers or serfs. Some social historians speculate that this class originated during the period of migrations and upheavals following the end of the classical period (see page 306), when weak and defenseless people placed themselves under the protection of strong warriors, just as European peasants had become serfs after the end of the Roman Empire (see Chapter 6). The tlalmaitl provided agricultural labor, paid rents in kind, and were bound to the soil—they could not move off the land. In many ways the tlalmaitl resembled the serfs of western Europe, but unlike serfs they performed military service when called on

to do so. They enjoyed some rights as citizens and generally were accorded more respect than slaves.

Slaves were the lowest social class. Like Asian, European, and African slaves, most were prisoners captured in war or kidnapped from enemy tribes. But Aztecs who stole from a temple or private house or plotted against the emperor could also be enslaved, and people in serious debt sometimes voluntarily sold themselves into slavery. Female slaves often became their masters' concubines. Mexica slaves differed fundamentally from European ones, for they could possess goods; save money; buy land, houses, and even slaves for their own service; and purchase their freedom. If a male slave married a free woman, their offspring were free, and a slave who escaped and managed to enter the emperor's palace was automatically free. Most slaves eventually gained their freedom. Mexica slavery, therefore, had some humane qualities and resembled slavery in Islamic societies (see pages 246–248).

Women of all social classes played important roles in Mexica society, but those roles were restricted largely to the domestic sphere. As the little hands of the newborn male were closed around a tiny bow and arrow indicating his warrior destiny, so the infant female's hands were wrapped around miniature weaving instruments and a small broom: weaving was a sacred and exclusively female art; the broom signaled a female's responsibility for the household shrines and for keeping the home swept and free of contamination. Almost all Mexica people married, men at about twenty and women several years earlier. As in premodern Asian and European societies, parents selected their children's spouses, using neighborhood women as go-betweens. Save for the few women vowed to the service of the temple, marriage and the household were a woman's fate, and marriage represented social maturity for both sexes. Pregnancy became the occasion for family and neighborhood feasts, and a successful birth launched celebrations lasting from ten to twenty days.

Women were expected to pray for their husbands' success in battle while they were gone. One prayer to Huitzilopochtli went:

O great Lord of All Things, remember your servant
Who has gone to exalt your honor and the greatness
  of your name.
He will offer blood in that sacrifice that is war.
Behold, Lord, that he did not go out to work for me
Or for his children. . . . He went for your sake,
In your name, to obtain glory for you. . . .
Give him victory in this war so that he may return
To rest in his home and so that my children and I
  may see
His countenance again and feel his presence.[3]

Alongside the secular social classes stood the temple priests. Huitzilopochtli and each of the numerous

• **Tenochtitlán** A large and prosperous Aztec city that was built starting in 1325. It was admired by the Spanish when they entered in 1519.

lesser gods were attended to by many priests who oversaw the upkeep of the temple, assisted at religious ceremonies, and performed ritual sacrifices. The priests also did a brisk business in foretelling the future from signs and omens. Aztecs consulted priests on the selection of wives and husbands, on the future careers of newborn babies, and before leaving on journeys or for war. Temples possessed enormous wealth in gold and silver ceremonial vessels, statues, buildings, and land. From the temple revenues and resources, the priests supported schools, aided the poor, and maintained hospitals. The chief priests had the ear of the emperor and often exercised great power and influence.

The emperor stood at the peak of the social pyramid. Aztec historians contradict one another about the origin of the imperial dynasty, but modern scholars tend to accept the verdict of one sixteenth-century authority that the "custom has always been preserved among the Mexicans (that) the sons of kings have not ruled by right of inheritance but by election."[4] A small oligarchy of the chief priests, warriors, and state offi-

cials made the selection. If none of the sons of the previous emperor proved satisfactory, a brother or nephew of the emperor was chosen, but election was always restricted to the royal family.

The Aztec emperor was expected to be a great warrior who had led Mexica and allied armies into battle. All his other duties pertained to the welfare of his people. It was up to the emperor to see that justice was done; he was the final court of appeal. He also held ultimate responsibility for ensuring an adequate food supply. The emperor Montezuma I (r. 1440–1469) distributed twenty thousand loads of stockpiled grain when a flood hit Tenochtitlán. This deed and other recorded actions show that the Aztec emperors took their public duties seriously.

The City of Tenochtitlán

When the Spanish entered **Tenochtitlán** (which they called Mexico City) in November 1519, they could not believe their eyes. According to Bernal Díaz, one of

The Aztec Capital of Tenochtitlán This 1524 map of Tenochtitlán, made by a European mapmaker, was included with a Latin edition of one of the letters of Cortés, printed in Germany. It was based on Cortés's written description of the city and shows the city laid out in concentric circles, with causeways and people paddling canoes. The administrative and religious buildings were at the heart of the city, surrounded by residential quarters. The smaller map at the left shows the Gulf of Mexico as Cortés understood it, with Yucatan as an island instead of a peninsula. This map has north at the bottom, and if you rotate it 180 degrees, you will see some familiar landmarks, including the mouth of the Mississippi River (which the Spanish called Río del Espíritu Santo) and Florida. This was the first printed map on which the name "Florida" appeared. (The Newberry Library)

Cortés's companions:

> When we saw all those cities and villages built in the water, and other great towns on dry land, and that straight and level causeway leading to Mexico, we were astounded. These great towns and cues (temples) and buildings rising from the water, all made of stone, seemed like an enchanted vision. . . . Indeed, some of our soldiers asked whether it was not all a dream.[5]

As of 1500 Tenochtitlán had about 60,000 households and a total population of around 250,000, making it one of the largest cities in the world. At the time, no European city and few Asian cities could boast a population even half that size. The total Aztec Empire has been estimated at around 5 million inhabitants, with the total population of Mesoamerica at between 20 and 30 million.

Originally built on salt marshes, Tenochtitlán was approached by four great causeways that connected it with the mainland. Openings in the causeways, covered by bridges, provided places for boats to pass through. Stone and adobe walls surrounded the city itself, making it (somewhat like medieval Constantinople; see page 207) highly defensible and capable of resisting a prolonged siege. Wide, straight streets as well as canals plied by boats and canoes crisscrossed the city. Lining the roads and canals stood thousands of rectangular one-story houses of mortar faced with stucco. Although space was limited, many small gardens and parks were alive with the colors and scents of flowers.

A large aqueduct whose sophisticated engineering astounded Cortés carried pure water from distant springs and supplied fountains in the parks. Streets and canals opened onto public squares and marketplaces, where tradespeople offered every kind of merchandise. Butchers hawked turkeys, ducks, chickens, rabbits, and deer; grocers sold kidney beans, squash, avocados, maize, and all kinds of peppers. Artisans sold intricately designed gold, silver, and feathered jewelry, while seamstresses offered various items of clothing customarily worn by ordinary people: sandals, loincloths and cloaks for men, and blouses and long skirts for women. The seamstresses also provided embroidered robes and cloaks for the rich. Slaves for domestic service, wood for building, herbs for seasoning and medicine, honey and sweets, knives, jars, smoking tobacco, even human excrement used to cure animal skins — all these wares added to the dazzling spectacle.

At one side of the central square of Tenochtitlán stood the great temple of Huitzilopochtli. Built as a pyramid and approached by three flights of 120 steps each, the temple was about one hundred feet high and dominated the city's skyline. According to Cortés, it was "so large that within the precincts, which are surrounded by a very high wall, a town of some five hundred inhabitants could easily be built. All round inside this wall there are very elegant quarters with very large rooms and corridors where their priests live."[6]

Travelers, perhaps inevitably, compare what they see abroad with what is familiar to them at home. Tenochtitlán thoroughly astounded Cortés, and in his letter to the emperor Charles V he describes the city in comparison to his homeland: "the market square," where sixty thousand people a day came to buy and sell, "was twice as big as Salamanca"; the beautifully constructed "towers," as the Spaniards called the pyramids, rose higher "than the cathedral at Seville"; Montezuma's palace was "so marvelous that it seems to me to be impossible to describe its excellence and grandeur[;] . . . in Spain there is nothing to compare with it." Accustomed to the squalor and filth of their own cities, the Spaniards were dumbfounded by the cleanliness of Tenochtitlán and by all the evidence of its ordered and elegant planning.[7] Unfortunately their amazement was not matched by an ability to maintain the city's splendor. Very shortly after the Spanish conquered the city in 1521 (see page 474), disease killed off most of its residents, much of its treasure was shipped back to Spain, and its temples and palaces were demolished.

The Incas

☐ What were the sources of strength and prosperity, and of problems, for the Incas as they created their enormous empire?

In the center of Peru rise the cold highlands of the Andes. Six valleys of fertile and wooded land at altitudes ranging from eight thousand to eleven thousand feet punctuate highland Peru. The largest of these valleys are the Huaylas, Cuzco, and Titicaca. It was there that Inca civilization developed and flourished. Like the Aztecs, the Incas started as a small militaristic group. But they grew in numbers and power as they conquered surrounding groups, eventually establishing one of the most extraordinary empires in the world. Gradually, Inca culture spread throughout Peru.

• **Moche** A Native American culture that thrived along Peru's northern coast between 100 and 800 C.E. The culture existed as a series of city-states and is distinguished by an extraordinarily rich and diverse pottery industry.

• **Incas** The Andean people who created a large empire that was at its peak around 1500 and was held together by an extensive system of roads.

Earlier Peruvian Cultures

Inca achievements built on those of cultures that preceded them in the Andes and on the Peruvian coast. These included the Chavin civilization (see page 304) and the **Moche** (MO-cheh) civilization, which flourished along a 250-mile stretch of Peru's northern coast between 100 and 800 C.E. Rivers that flowed out of the Andes into the valleys allowed the Moche people to develop complex irrigation systems, with which they raised food crops and cotton. Each Moche valley contained a large ceremonial center with palaces and pyramids surrounded by settlements of up to ten thousand people. Their dazzling gold and silver artifacts, elaborate headdresses, and ceramic vessels display a remarkable skill in metalwork and pottery.

Politically, Moche civilization was made up of a series of small city-states rather than one unified state, and warfare was common among them. As in Aztec culture, war provided victims for human sacrifice, frequently portrayed on Moche pottery. Beginning about 500, the Moche suffered several severe El Niños, the changes in ocean current patterns in the Pacific that bring both searing drought and flooding. Their leaders were not able to respond effectively to the devastation, and the cities lost population.

The Moche civilization was one of several that were able to carve out slightly larger empires than their predecessors, the Chavin. These newer civilizations built cities around large public plazas, with temples, palaces, and elaborate stonework. Using terraces and other means to increase the amount of arable soil, they grew potatoes and other crops, even at very high altitudes. Enough food was harvested to feed not only the farmers themselves but also massive armies, administrative bureaucracies, and thousands of industrial workers. These cultures were skilled at using fibers for a variety of purposes, including building boats to use on Lake Titicaca and hanging bridges to take humans and pack llamas across steep valleys.

Inca Imperialism and Its Religious Basis

Who were the **Incas**? *Inca* was originally the name of the governing family of a group that settled in the basin

The Inca Empire, 1532

of Cuzco. From that family, the name was gradually extended to all peoples living in the Andes valleys. The Incas themselves used the word to identify their ruler or emperor. Here the term is used for both the ruler and the people. As with the Aztecs, so with the Incas: religious ideology was the force that transformed the culture, and it also created pressure for imperialist expansion.

The Incas believed their ruler descended from the sun-god and that the health and prosperity of the state depended on him. Dead rulers were thought to link the people to the sun-god. When the ruler died, his corpse was preserved as a mummy in elaborate clothing and housed in a sacred and magnificent chamber. A sixteenth-century account of the death of the emperor Pachacuti Inca (r. 1438–1471) in 1471 described the practices for burying him and honoring him after his death:

He was buried by putting his body in the earth in a large new clay urn, with him very well dressed. Pachacuti Inca [had] ordered that a golden image made to resemble him be placed on top of his tomb. And it was to be worshiped in place of him by the people who went there. . . . [He had] ordered those of his own lineage to bring this statue out for the feasts that were held in Cuzco. When they brought it out like this, they sang about the things that the Inca did in his life, both in the wars and in his city. Thus they served and revered him, changing its garments as he used to do, and serving it as he was served when he was alive.[8]

As a group, the descendants of a dead ruler managed his lands and sources of income and used the revenues to care for his mummy, maintain his cult, and support themselves. The costs of maintaining the cult were high; therefore, the next ruler had to find new sources of income through higher taxes or imperial expansion, as the account about Pachacuti Inca points out:

Word should be sent to all the land, and from all the provinces and towns they should bring again all that is necessary for the service of the new lord [the successor to Pachacuti Inca], including gold, silver, livestock, clothing, and the rest of the things needed to replenish all the storehouses that, because of his death, had been emptied for the sacrifices and things he ordered to be done.[9]

Around 1000 C.E. the Incas were one of many small groups fighting among themselves for land and water. The cult of royal mummies provided the impetus for expanding Inca power. The desire for conquest provided incentives for courageous (or ambitious) nobles: those who were victorious in battle and gained new territories for the state could expect lands, additional wives, servants, herds of llamas, gold, silver, fine clothes, and other symbols of high status. Even common soldiers who distinguished themselves in battle could be rewarded with booty and raised to noble status. The imperial interests of the emperor paralleled those of other social groups. Under Pachacuti Inca and his successors, Inca domination was gradually extended by warfare to the frontier of present-day Ecuador and Colombia in the north and to the Maule River in present-day Chile in the south, an area of about 350,000 square miles. Eighty provinces, scores of ethnic groups, and 16 million people came under Inca control. A remarkable system of roads held the empire together. Conquered peoples were forced to adopt the Inca language, which the Spanish called **Quechua** (KEH-chuh-wuh), and this was another way in which the Inca way of life was spread throughout the Andes. Before Inca civilization, each group that entered the Andes valleys had its own distinct language. These languages were not written and have become extinct. Scholars will probably never understand the linguistic condition of Peru before the fifteenth century, when Pachacuti made Quechua the official language of his people and administration. Though not written until the Spanish in Peru adopted it as a second official language, Quechua had replaced local languages by the seventeenth and eighteenth centuries and is still spoken by most Peruvians today.

Both the Aztecs and the Incas ruled very ethnically diverse peoples. Whereas the Aztecs tended to control their subject peoples through terror, the Incas governed by means of imperial unification. They imposed not only their language but also their entire panoply of gods. Magnificent temples scattered throughout the expanding empire housed images of these gods. Priests led prayers and elaborate rituals, and on such occasions as a terrible natural disaster or a great military victory, they sacrificed human beings to the gods.

Imperial unification was also achieved through the forced participation of local chieftains in the central bureaucracy and through a policy of colonization. To prevent rebellion in newly conquered territories, Pachacuti Inca and subsequent rulers transferred all the inhabitants of these territories to other parts of the

empire, replacing them with workers who had lived longer under Inca rule. The rulers also drafted men from conquered territories for distant wars, breaking up kin groups that had existed in Andean society for centuries.

An excellent system of roads — averaging three feet in width, some paved and others not — facilitated the transportation of armies and the rapid communication of royal orders by runners. The roads followed straight lines wherever possible but also crossed pontoon bridges and tunneled through hills. Like Persian and Roman roads, these great feats of Inca engineering linked an empire.

On these roads, Inca officials, tax collectors, and accountants traveled throughout the empire, using increasingly elaborate khipus (see page 304) to record financial and labor obligations, the output of fields, population levels, land transfers, and other numerical records. Scholars have deciphered the way numbers were recorded on khipus, finding a base-ten system. Khipus may also have been used to record narrative history, but this theory is more speculative, as knowledge of how to read them died out after the Spanish conquest. Just as the Spanish destroyed books in Mesoamerica, they also destroyed khipus in the Andes because they thought they might contain religious messages and encourage people to resist Spanish authority. About 750 Inca khipus survive today, more than half in museums in Europe.

Although the pressure for growth of the Inca empire continued unabated, it produced stresses. For example, open lands began to be scarce, so the Incas attempted to penetrate the tropical Amazon forest east of the Andes, an effort that led to repeated military disasters. Traditionally, the Incas waged wars with highly trained armies drawn up in massed formation and fought pitched battles on level ground, often engaging in hand-to-hand combat. But in dense jungles the troops could not maneuver or maintain order against enemies using guerrilla tactics and sniping at them with deadly blowguns. Another source of stress was revolts among subject peoples in conquered territories. Even the system of roads and message-carrying runners couldn't keep up with the administrative needs of the empire. The average runner could cover about 50 leagues, or 175 miles, per day — a remarkable feat of physical endurance, especially at a high altitude — but the larger the empire became, the greater the distances to be covered. The roundtrip from the capital at Cuzco to Quito in Ecuador, for example, took from ten to twelve days, so that an emperor might have to base urgent decisions on incomplete or out-of-date information. The empire was overextended.

When the Inca Huayna Capac died in 1525, his throne was bitterly contested by two of his sons,

• **Quechua** First deemed the official language of the Incas under Pachacuti, it is still spoken by most Peruvians today.

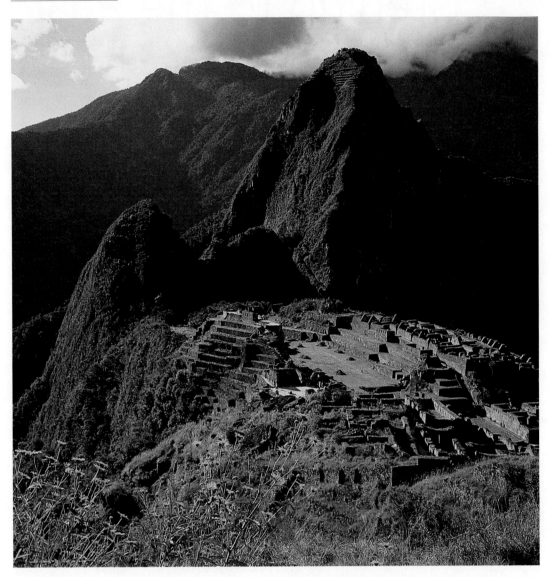

Machu Picchu The Inca city of Machu Picchu, surrounded by mountains in the clouds, clings to a spectacular crag in upland Peru. It was built around 1450, when the Inca Empire was at its height, and abandoned about a century later. (Will McIntyre/Photo Researchers, Inc.)

Huascar and Atahualpa. Huascar's threat to do away with the cult of royal mummies led the nobles — who often benefited from managing land and wealth for a deceased ruler — to throw their support behind Atahualpa. In the civil war that began in 1532, Atahualpa's veteran warriors easily defeated Huascar's green recruits, but the conflict weakened the Incas. On his way to his coronation at Cuzco, Atahualpa encountered Pizarro and 168 Spaniards who had recently entered the kingdom. The Spaniards quickly became the real victors in the Inca kingdom (see pages 475–476).

The Clan-Based Structure of Inca Society

The *ayllu* (EYE-yoo), or clan, served as the fundamental social unit of Inca society. All members of the ayllu owed allegiance to the *curacas*, or clan leaders, who conducted relations with outsiders. The ayllu held specific lands granted by village or provincial authorities on a long-term basis, and individual families tended to work the same plots for generations. Cooperation in the cultivation of the land and intermarriage among members of the ayllu wove people into a tight web of connections. (See "Listening to the Past: Felipe Guaman Poma de Ayala, *The First New Chronicle and Good Government*," page 324.)

Listening to the Past

Felipe Guaman Poma de Ayala, *The First New Chronicle and Good Government*

According to his own self-description, Felipe Guaman Poma de Ayala (1550?–1620?) was a member of an indigenous noble family in Peru. His native language was Quechua, but he was baptized as a Christian, learned to read and write Spanish, and served as an assistant to a Spanish friar and a Spanish judge. He saw and experienced firsthand the abuses of the Spanish authorities in what had been the Inca Empire. In the early seventeenth century he began writing and illustrating what became his masterpiece, a handwritten book of almost eight hundred pages of text and nearly four hundred line drawings addressed to the king of Spain that related the history of the Inca Empire and the realities of Spanish rule. Finishing in about 1615, he hoped to send the book to Spain, where it would convince the king to make reforms that would bring about the "good government" of the book's title. (The book apparently never reached the king, though it did make it to Europe. It was discovered in the Danish Royal Library in Copenhagen in 1908; how it got there is unknown.) Guaman Poma's descriptions of Inca life before the conquest are shaped by his purpose, but they also portray some important aspects of Andean culture that appear from other sources to have been quite accurate. In the following section, Guaman Poma sets out certain traditional age-group categories of Inca society, which he terms "paths," ten for men and ten for women. Through these, he gives us a glimpse of Inca values and everyday activities, and suggests that this orderly structure underlay Inca power.

❝The first path was that of the brave men, the soldiers of war. They were thirty-three years of age (they entered this path as young as twenty-five, and left it at fifty). These brave men were held very much apart and distinguished in every manner possible. The Inca [the Inca ruler] selected some of these Indians to serve in his battles and wars. He selected some from among these brave Indians to settle as *mitmacs* (foreigners) in other provinces, giving them more than enough land, both pasture and cropland, to multiply, and giving each of them a woman from the same land. He did this to keep his kingdom secure; they served as overseers. He selected some of these brave Indians to serve as plowmen and as skilled workers in every task that was necessary for the Inca and the other lords, princes, noblemen, and ladies of this kingdom; those selected in this way were called *mitmac* (foreigners). Others of these

brave men were selected to work in the mines and for other labor, toil, and obligations. . . .

The Fifth Path was that of the *sayapayac* [those who stand upright]. These were the Indians of the watch, aged from eighteen to twenty years. They served as messenger boys between one pueblo and another, and to other nearby places in the valley. They also herded flocks, and accompanied the Indians of war and the great lords and captains. They also carried food. . . .

The Eighth Path was that of boys aged from five to nine years. These were the "boys who play" (*puellacoc wamracuna*). They served their mothers and fathers in whatever ways they could, and bore many whippings and thumpings; they also served by playing with the toddlers and by rocking and watching over the babies in cradles. . . .

The Tenth Path was that of those called *wawa quirawpi cac* (newborn babies at the breast, in cradles), from the age of one month. It is right for others to serve them; their mothers must necessarily serve them for no other person can give milk to these children. . . .

The First Path was that of the married women and widows called *auca camayocpa warmin* [the warriors' women], whose occupation is weaving fine cloth for the Inca, the other lords, the captains, and the soldiers. They were thirty-three years of age when they married; up until then, they remained virgins and maidens. . . . These wives of brave men were not free [from tribute obligations]. These women had the occupation of weaving fine *awasca* cloth and spinning yarn; they assisted the commons in their pueblos and provinces, and they assisted with everything their titled noble lords decreed. . . .

The Sixth Path was that of those called *coro tasquicunas*, *rotusca tasqui*, which means "young girls with short-cropped hair." They were from twelve to eighteen years of age and served their fathers, mothers, and grandmothers. They also began to serve the great ladies so that they could learn to spin yarn and weave delicate materials. They served as animal herders and workers in the fields, and in making *chica* [corn beer] for their fathers and mothers, and they assisted in other occupations insofar as they could, helping out . . . they were filled with obedience and respect, and were taught to cook, spin, and weave. Their hair was kept cropped until they reached the age of thirty, when they were married and given the dowry of their destitution and poverty.

The Seventh Path was that of the girls called flower pickers. . . . They picked flowers to dye wool for *cumpis*, cloth, and other things, and they picked the edible herbs mentioned above, which they dried out and stored in the warehouse to be

• Guaman Poma's line drawings show a man and woman on the "first path," the man a warrior holding an obsidian blade in one hand and the severed head of an enemy in the other, and the woman weaving fine cloth on a back-strap loom. (Nick Saunders/Barbara Heller Photo Library, London/Art Resource, NY)

eaten the following year. These girls were from nine to twelve years of age. . . .

The Ninth Path was that of the girls aged one and two, who were called *llucac warmi wawa* ("young girls who crawl"). They do nothing; instead, others serve them. Better said, they ought to be served by their mothers, who should be exempt [from tribute] because of the work of raising their children. Their mothers have to walk around carrying them, and never let go of their hands. **"**

Source: Felipe Guaman Poma de Ayala, *The First New Chronicle and Good Government*, selected, translated and annotated by David Frye, pp. 70, 72, 74, 75, 77, 80, 81, 82. Copyright © 2006 by Hackett Publishing Company, Inc. Reprinted by permission of Hackett Publishing Company, Inc. All rights reserved.

QUESTIONS FOR ANALYSIS

1. The "first path" among both men and women is the one with the highest status. Judging by the way Guaman Poma describes these, what do the Incas especially value? How do his descriptions of other paths support your conclusions about this?

2. In what ways are the paths set out for boys and men different from those for girls and women? In what ways are they similar? What does this suggest about Inca society?

3. Guaman Poma wrote this about eighty years after the Spanish conquest of Peru. How does the date and the colonial setting affect our evaluation of this work as a source?

In return for the land, every family had to provide crops for the Inca nobles, bureaucracy, and religious personnel, and also send a person to work a certain number of days per year at other tasks. These included providing military service; building and maintaining palaces, temples, roads, and irrigation systems; terracing and irrigating new arable land; acting as runners on the post roads; weaving and dying cotton cloth; and excavating imperial gold, silver, and copper mines. This labor tax, called the *mit'a* (MEE-tuh), was rotated among households in an ayllu throughout the year, and it was similar to the labor obligations required of peasant families in Europe. The government also made an ayllu responsible for maintaining state-owned granaries, which distributed grain in times of shortage and famine, and supplied assistance in natural disasters.

As the Inca Empire expanded, it imposed this pattern of social and labor organization on newly conquered indigenous peoples. After the conquest, the Spaniards adopted the Incas' ways of organizing their economy and administration, just as the Incas (and, in Mesoamerica, the Aztecs) had built on earlier cultures.

The state required everyone to marry and even decided when and sometimes whom a person should marry. Women married in their late teens, men when they were a little older. The marriage ceremony consisted of the joining of hands and the exchange of a pair of sandals. This ritual was followed by a large wedding feast at which the state presented the bride and groom with two sets of clothing, one for everyday wear and the other for festive occasions. Sometimes, marriage was used as a symbol of conquest; Inca rulers and nobles married the daughters of elite families among the peoples they conquered. Very high-ranking Inca men sometimes had many wives, but marriage among common people was generally monogamous.

An Inca Cape Inca artisans could produce gorgeous textiles, and on ceremonial occasions nobles proudly paraded in brightly colored feathers or in garments made of luxurious alpaca wool. This exquisite cape is fashioned from the feathers of a blue and yellow macaw; the pattern, befitting aristocratic tastes, features lordly pelicans carried on litters by less exalted birds. (The Textile Museum, Washington, D.C., 91.395. Acquired by George Hewitt Myers in 1941)

The backbreaking labor of ordinary people in the fields and mines made possible the luxurious lifestyle of the great Inca nobility. The nobles — called *orejones*, or "big ears," by the Spanish because they pierced their ears and distended the lobes with heavy jewelry — were the ruling Inca's kinsmen. Lesser nobles included the curacas, royal household servants, public officials, and religious leaders.

In the fifteenth century Inca rulers ordered that allegiance be paid to the ruler at Cuzco rather than to the curacas, and they relocated the entire populations of certain regions and disrupted clan groups, which led to resentment. As the empire expanded, there arose a noble class of warriors, governors, and local officials whose support the ruling Inca secured with gifts of land, precious metals, and llamas and alpacas (llamas were used as beasts of burden; alpacas were raised for their long, fine wool). The nobility was exempt from agricultural work and from other kinds of public service.

CONNECTIONS

Research on all the cultures discussed in this chapter is providing new information every year, provoking vigorous debates among scholars. Archaeologists are discovering new objects and reinterpreting the sites where they were found; historians are learning to better read indigenous writing systems; biologists are using more complex procedures to study genetic linkages; anthropologists are integrating information from oral histories and preserved traditions, and scholars in other disciplines are using both traditional and new methods to expand their understanding. In no other chapter of this book are the basic outlines of what most people agree happened changing as fast as they are for the Americas. Together the various fields of study have produced a history of the Western Hemisphere in the centuries before 1500 that looks more like the history of the Eastern Hemisphere than it did twenty years ago. We now know that there were large, settled agricultural communities in many parts of North and South America that traded ideas and goods with one another, and that the empires of Mesoamerica and the Andes were as rich and powerful as any in Asia, Africa, or Europe.

The parallel paths of the two hemispheres were radically changed by Columbus's arrival and the events that followed, however. The greater availability of metals, especially iron, in the Eastern Hemisphere meant that the military technology of the Europeans who came to the Western Hemisphere was more deadly than anything indigenous peoples had developed. Even more deadly, however, were the germs Europeans brought with them, from which the people of the Western Hemisphere died in astounding numbers. In some cases one or two indigenous people who had made contact with Europeans would spread disease throughout the native population. As a result, when Europeans arrived in the home areas of these people they would find deserted villages with only a few residents. Often, they could not imagine how so few people could have built huge earth mounds or massive stone works. Therefore, they speculated that that these structures must have been built by wandering Egyptians or Israelites, a tribe of giants, or (in the early twentieth century) space aliens, giving rise to myths that have been slow to die.

☐ CHAPTER REVIEW

☐ **How did early peoples in the Americas adapt to their environment as they created technologies of food production and economic systems? (p. 300)**

The environment shaped the history of human settlements in the Americas, but later history shaped the way the lands and peoples of these areas have been described. Early peoples crossed into the Western Hemisphere from Asia, although exactly when this happened is hotly debated. All the highly varied environments, from polar tundra to tropical rain forests, came to support human settlement. About 8000 B.C.E., people in some parts of the Americas began raising crops as well as gathering wild produce. Maize became the most important crop, with knowledge about its cultivation spreading from Mesoamerica into North and South America.

☐ **What physical, social, and intellectual features characterized early societies in the Americas? (p. 304)**

Agricultural advancement led to an increase in population, which allowed greater concentrations of people and the creation of the first urban societies. In certain parts of North and South America, towns dependent on agriculture flourished. Some groups in North America began to build large earthwork mounds, while others in Mesoamerica and South America practiced irrigation. The Olmecs created the first society with cities in Mesoamerica, with large ceremonial buildings, an elaborate calendar, and a symbolic writing.

☐ **How did Mesoamerican and North American peoples develop prosperous and stable societies in the classical era? (p. 306)**

The urban culture of the Olmecs and other Mesoamerican peoples influenced subsequent societies. Especially in what became known as the classical era (300–900 C.E.), various groups developed large states centered on cities, with high levels of technological and intellectual achievement. Of these, the Maya were the longest-lasting, creating a complex written language, multiple-crop milpas and raised beds for agriculture, roads connecting population centers, trading practices that built unity among Maya communities as well as wealth, and striking art. Peoples living in North America built communities that were smaller than those in Mesoamerica, but many also used irrigation techniques to enhance agricultural production and continued to build earthwork mounds for religious purposes.

☐ **How did the Aztecs both build on the achievements of earlier Mesoamerican cultures and develop new traditions to create their large empire? (p. 313)**

The Aztecs, also known as the Mexica, built a unified culture based heavily on the heritage of earlier Mesoamerican societies and distinguished by achievements in engineering, sculpture, and architecture, including the streets, canals, public squares, and aqueduct of Tenochtitlán, the most spectacular and one of the largest cities in the world in 1500. In Mexica society, religion was the dynamic factor that transformed other aspects of the culture: economic security, social mobility, education, and especially war. War was an article of religious faith, providing riches and land, sacrificial victims for ceremonies honoring the Aztec gods, warriors for imperial expansion, and laborers. Aztec society was hierarchical, with nobles and priests having special privileges.

☐ **What were the sources of strength and prosperity, and of problems, for the Incas as they created their enormous empire? (p. 320)**

Inca achievements built on those of cultures that preceded theirs in the Andes, including the Moche and Chavin civilizations. Moche, Chavin, and Inca cultures made their home in the valleys along the Peruvian coast and in the Andean highlands, cultivating food crops and cotton. The Incas, who began as a small militaristic group, eventually created the largest empire in South America and conquered surrounding groups. The Incas' far-flung empire stretched along the Andes, kept together through a system of roads, along which moved armies and administrators. The Incas achieved imperial unification by imposing their gods on conquered peoples, forcing local chieftains to participate in the central bureaucracy, and pursuing a policy of colonization. The imperial expansion that increased the Incas' strength also caused stress. Andean society was dominated by clan groups, and Inca measures to disrupt these groups and move people great distances created resentment.

SUGGESTED READING

Carassco, David, and Scott Sessions. *Daily Life of the Aztecs: People of the Sun and Earth.* 2008. An overview of Aztec culture designed for general readers.

Clendinnen, Inga. *Aztecs: An Interpretation.* 1992. Pays particular attention to the role that rituals and human sacrifice played in Aztec culture.

Coe, Michael D. *The Maya.* 2005. A new edition of a classic survey that incorporates the most recent scholarship.

Conrad, G. W., and A. A. Demarest. *Religion and Empire: The Dynamics of Aztec and Inca Expansionism.* 1993. Compares the two largest American empires.

D'Altroy, Terence. *The Incas.* 2003. Examines the ways in which the Incas drew on earlier traditions to create their empire; by a leading scholar.

Freidel, David. *A Forest of Kings: The Untold Story of the Ancient Maya.* 1990. A splendidly illustrated work providing expert treatment of the Maya world.

Kehoe, Alice Beck. *America Before the European Invasion.* 2002. An excellent survey of North America before the coming of the Europeans, by an eminent anthropologist.

Knight, Alan. *Mexico: From the Beginnings to the Spanish Conquest.* 2002. Provides information on many Mesoamerican societies.

León-Portilla, Miguel. *The Aztec Image of Self and Society: An Introduction to Nahua Culture.* 1992. The best appreciation of Aztec religious ritual and symbolism.

Mann, Charles C. *1491: New Revelations of the Americas Before Columbus.* 2005. A thoroughly researched overview of all the newest scholarship, written for a general audience.

Milner, George R. *The Moundbuilders: Ancient Peoples of Eastern North America.* 2005. Beautifully illustrated book that discusses the mounds and the societies that built them; could also be used as a tourist guide.

Wright, Ronald. *Time Among the Maya: Travels in Belize, Guatemala, and Mexico.* 1989. A highly readable account of Maya agricultural and religious calendars and their influence on modern Maya culture.

NOTES

1. Florentine Codex, Book 2, trans. John M. Curl, author of *Ancient American Poets.* Reprinted by permission.
2. "Maya Writing," Authentic Maya, http://www.authenticmaya.com/maya_writing.htm.
3. Fray Diego Durán, *Mexicas: The History of the Indies of New Spain,* trans. with notes, by Doris Heyden and Fernand Horcasitas (New York: Orion Press, 1964), p. 203. Copyright © 1994 by the University of Oklahoma Press. Reprinted with permission of the publisher.
4. Quoted in J. Soustelle, *Daily Life of the Aztecs on the Eve of the Spanish Conquest,* trans. P. O'Brian (Stanford, Calif.: Stanford University Press, 1970), p. 89.
5. Bernal Díaz, *The Conquest of New Spain,* trans. J. M. Cohen (New York: Penguin Books, 1978), p. 214.
6. Quoted in J. H. Perry, *The Discovery of South America* (New York: Taplinger, 1979), pp. 161–163.
7. Quoted in Inga Clendinnen, *Aztecs: An Interpretation* (New York: Cambridge University Press, 1992), pp. 16–17.
8. *Narrative of the Incas by Juan de Betanzos,* trans. and ed. Roland Hamilton and Dana Buchanan from the Palma de Mallorca manuscript, p. 138. Copyright © 1996. By permission of the University of Texas Press.
9. Ibid.

For practice quizzes and other study tools, visit the **Online Study Guide** at bedfordstmartins.com/mckayworld.

For primary sources from this period, see *Sources of World Societies*, **Second Edition**.

For Web sites, images, and documents related to topics in this chapter, visit **Make History** at bedfordstmartins.com/mckayworld.

• **Mongol Woman** Women played influential roles among the Mongols. The Mongol woman portrayed in this painting is Chabi, wife of Khubilai Khan. Like other Mongols, she maintained Mongol dress even though she spent much of her time in China. (National Palace Museum, Taipei, Taiwan)

12

The large expanse of Asia treated in this chapter underwent profound changes during the centuries examined here. The north saw the rise of nomadic pastoral societies, first the Turks, then more spectacularly the Mongols. The nomads' mastery of the horse and mounted warfare gave them a military advantage that agricultural societies could rarely match. From the fifth century on, groups of Turks appeared along the fringes of the settled societies of Eurasia, from China and Korea to India and Persia. Often Turks were recruited as auxiliary soldiers; sometimes they gained the upper hand. By the tenth century many were converting to Islam.

Cultural Exchange in Central and Southern Asia

to 1400

Much more dramatic was the rise of the Mongols under the charismatic leadership of Chinggis Khan in the late twelfth and early thirteenth centuries. A military genius, with a relatively small army Chinggis subdued one society after another from Byzantium to the Pacific. For a century Mongol hegemony fostered unprecedented East-West trade and contact. More Europeans made their way east than ever before, and Chinese inventions such as printing and the compass made their way west.

Over the course of several centuries Arab and Turkish armies brought Islam to India, but the Mongols never gained power there. In the Indian subcontinent during these centuries, regional cultures flourished. Although Buddhism declined, Hinduism continued to flourish. India continued to be the center of a very active seaborne trade, and this trade helped carry Indian ideas and practices to Southeast Asia. Buddhism was adopted in much of Southeast Asia, along with other ideas and techniques from India. The maritime trade in spices and other goods brought increased contact with the outside world to all but the most isolated of islands in the Pacific. •

Central Asian Nomads
□ What aspects of nomadic life gave the nomads of Central Asia military advantages over nearby settled civilizations?

Chinggis Khan and the Mongol Empire
□ How did Chinggis Khan and his successors conquer much of Eurasia, and how did the Mongol conquests change the regions affected?

East-West Communication During the Mongol Era
□ How did the Mongol conquests facilitate the spread of ideas, religions, inventions, and diseases?

India, Islam, and the Development of Regional Cultures, 300–1400
□ What was the result of India's encounters with Turks, Mongols, and Islam?

Southeast Asia, the Pacific Islands, and the Growth of Maritime Trade
□ How did states develop along the maritime trade routes of Southeast Asia and beyond?

Manichean Priests Many religions spread through Central Asia before it became predominantly Muslim after 1300. This fragment of a tenth- to twelfth-century illustrated document, found at the Silk Road city of Turfan, is written in the Uighur language and depicts Manichean priests. (Archives Charmet/The Bridgeman Art Library)

Central Asian Nomads

□ What aspects of nomadic life gave the nomads of Central Asia military advantages over nearby settled civilizations?

One experience Rome, Persia, India, and China all shared was conflict with **nomads** who came from the very broad region referred to as Central Asia. This region was dominated by the **steppe**, arid grasslands that stretched from modern Hungary, through southern Russia and across Central Asia (today's Tajikistan, Turkmenistan, Kazakhstan, Kyrgyzstan, and Uzbekistan) and adjacent parts of China, to Mongolia and parts of today's northeast China. Initially small in number, the nomadic peoples of this region would use their military superiority to conquer first other nomads, then the settled societies they encountered. In the process, they created settled empires of their own that drew on the cultures they absorbed.

Nomadic Society

Easily crossed by horses but too dry for crop agriculture, the grasslands could support only a thin population of nomadic herders who lived off their flocks of sheep, goats, camels, horses, or other animals. Following the seasons, they would break camp at least twice a year and move their animals to new pastures, going north in the spring and south in the fall.

In their search for water and good pastures, nomadic groups often came into conflict with other nomadic groups pursuing the same resources, which the two would then fight over, as there was normally no higher political authority able to settle disputes. Groups on the losing end, especially if they were small, faced the threat of extermination or slavery, which prompted them to make alliances with other groups or move far away. Groups on the winning end of intertribal conflicts could exact tribute from those they defeated, sometimes so much that they could devote themselves entirely to war, leaving the work of tending herds to their slaves and vassals.

To get the products of nearby agricultural societies, especially grain, woven textiles, iron, tea, and wood, nomadic herders would trade their own products, such as horses and furs. When trade was difficult, they would turn to raiding to seize what they needed. Much of the time nomadic herders raided other nomads, but nearby agricultural settlements were common targets as well. The nomads' skill as horsemen and archers made it difficult for farmers and townsmen to defend against them. It was largely to defend against the raids of the Xiongnu nomads, for example, that the Chinese built the Great Wall.

Political organization among nomadic herders was generally very simple. Clans—members of an extended family—had chiefs, as did tribes (coalitions of clans). Leadership within a group was based on military prowess and was often settled by fighting. Occasionally a charismatic leader would emerge who was able to extend alliances to form confederations of tribes. From the point of view of the settled societies, which have left most of the records about these nomadic groups, large confederations were much more of a threat, since they could plan coordinated attacks on cities and towns. Large confederations rarely lasted more than a century or so, however, and when they broke up, tribes again spent much of their time fighting with each other, relieving some of the pressure on their settled neighbors.

The three most wide-ranging and successful confederations were those of the Xiongnu—Huns, as they were known in the West—who emerged in the third century B.C.E. in the area near China; the Turks, who had their origins in the same area in the fourth and fifth centuries C.E.; and the Mongols, who did not become important until the late twelfth century. In all three cases, the entire steppe region was eventually swept up in the movement of peoples and armies.

The Turks

The Turks were the first of the Inner Asian peoples to have left a written record in their own language; the earliest Turkish documents date from the eighth century. Turkic languages may have already been spoken

in dispersed areas of the Eurasian steppe when the Turks first appeared; today these languages are spoken by the Uighurs in western China; the Uzbeks, Kazakhs, Kyrghiz, and Turkmens of Central Asia; and the Turks of modern Turkey. The original religion of the Turks was shamanistic and involved worship of Heaven, making it similar to the religions of many other groups in the steppe region.

In 552 a group called Turks who specialized in metalworking rebelled against their overlords, the Rouruan, whose empire dominated the region from the eastern Silk Road cities of Central Asia through Mongolia. The Turks quickly supplanted the Rouruan as overlords of the Silk Road in the east. When the first Turkish khagan (ruler) died a few years later, the Turkish empire was divided between his younger brother, who took the western part (modern Central Asia), and

- **nomads** Groups of people who move from place to place in search of food, water, and pasture for their animals, usually following the seasons.
- **steppe** Grasslands that are too dry for crops but support pasturing animals; they are common across much of the center of Eurasia.

his son, who took the eastern part (modern Mongolia). Sogdians—who were influential merchants along the Silk Road—convinced them to send a delegation to both the Persian (see Chapter 9) and the Byzantine courts (see Chapter 8). Repeated diplomatic overtures in both directions did not prevent hostilities, however, and in 576 the Western Turks captured the Byzantine city of Bosporus in the Crimea.

The Eastern Turks frequently raided China and just as often fought among themselves. The Chinese history of the Sui Dynasty records that "The Turks prefer to destroy each other rather than to live side-by-side. They have a thousand, nay ten thousand clans who are hostile to and kill one another. They mourn their dead with much grief and swear vengeance."[1] In the early seventh century the empire of the Eastern Turks ran up against the growing military might of the Tang Dynasty in China and soon broke apart.

In the eighth century a Turkic people called the Uighurs formed a new empire based in Mongolia that survived about a century. It had close ties to Tang China, providing military aid but also extracting large payments in silk. During this period many Uighurs adopted religions then current along the Silk Road, notably Buddhism, Nestorian Christianity, and Manichaeism. In the ninth century this Uighur empire was destroyed by another Turkic people from north of Mongolia called the Kyrghiz (KIHR-guhz). Some fled to what is now western China. Setting up their capital city in Kucha, these Uighurs created a remarkably stable and prosperous kingdom that lasted four centuries (ca. 850–1250). Because of the dry climate of the region, many buildings, wall paintings, and manuscripts written in a variety of languages have been preserved from this era. They reveal a complex urban civilization in which Buddhism, Manichaeism, and Christianity existed side by side, practiced by Turks as well as by Tokharians, Sogdians, and other Iranian peoples.

Farther west in Central Asia other groups of Turks, such as the Karakhanids, Ghaznavids, and Seljuks, rose to prominence. Often local Muslim forces would try to capture them, employ them as slave soldiers, and convert them. By the mid- to late tenth century many were serving in the Islamic Abbasid armies. Also in the tenth century Central Asian Turks began converting to Islam (which protected them from being abducted as slaves). Then they took to raiding unconverted Turks.

In the mid-eleventh century the Turks had gained the upper hand in the caliphate, and the caliphs became little more than figureheads. From there Turkish power was extended into Syria, Palestine, and Asia Minor. (Asia Minor is now called Turkey because Turks mi-grated there by the thousands over several centuries.) In 1071 Seljuk Turks inflicted a devastating defeat on the Byzantine army in eastern Anatolia (see page 244). Other Turkish confederations established themselves in Afghanistan and extended their control into north India (see page 352).

In India, Persia, and Anatolia, the formidable military skills of nomadic Turkish warriors made it possible for them to become overlords of settled societies. By the end of the thirteenth century nomad power prevailed through much of Eurasia. Just as the Uighurs developed a hybrid urban culture along the eastern end of the Silk Road, adopting many elements from the mercantile Sogdians, the Turks of Central and West Asia created an Islamic culture that drew from both Turkish and Iranian sources. Often Persian was used as the administrative language of the states they formed. Nevertheless, despite the presence of Turkish overlords all along the southern fringe of the steppe, no one group of Turks was able to unite them all into a single political unit. That feat had to wait for the next major power on the steppe, the Mongols.

The Mongols

In the twelfth century ambitious Mongols did not aspire to match the Turks or other groups that had migrated west, but rather wanted to be successors to the Khitans and Jurchens, nomadic groups that had stayed in the east and mastered ways to extract resources from China, the largest and richest country in the region. In the tenth and eleventh centuries the Khitans had accomplished this; in the twelfth century the Jurchens had overthrown the Khitans and extended their reach even deeper into China. The Khitans and Jurchens formed hybrid nomadic-urban states, with northern sections where tribesmen continued to live in the traditional way and southern sections politically controlled by the non-Chinese rulers but settled largely by taxpaying Chinese. The Khitans and Jurchens had scripts created to record their languages and adopted many Chinese governing practices. They built cities in pastoral areas that served as trading centers and places to enjoy their newly acquired wealth. In both cases, their elite became culturally dual, adept in Chinese ways as well as in their own traditions.

The Mongols lived north of these hybrid nomadic-settled societies and maintained their traditional ways. Chinese, Persian, and European observers have all left descriptions of the daily life of the Mongols, which they found strikingly different from their own. The daily life of the peasants of China, India, Vietnam, and Japan, all tied to the soil, had much more in common with each other than with the Mongol pastoralists. Before considering the military conquests of the Mongols, it is useful to look more closely at their way of life.

• **yurts** Tents in which the pastoral nomads lived; they could be quickly dismantled and loaded onto animals or carts.

Mongol Daily Life

Before their great conquests the Mongols, like other steppe nomads, did not have cities, towns, or villages. Rather, they moved with their animals between winter and summer pastures. To make their settlements portable, the Mongols lived in tents called **yurts** rather than in houses. The yurts, about twelve to fifteen feet in diameter, were constructed of light wooden frames covered by layers of wool felt, greased to make them waterproof. Yurts were round, since this shape held up better against the strong winds that blew across the treeless grasslands. They could be dismantled and loaded onto pack animals or carts in a short time. The floor of a yurt was covered first with dried grass or straw, then with felt, skins, or rugs. In the center, directly under the smoke hole, was the hearth. The master's bed was on the north. Goat horns attached to the frame of the yurt were used as hooks to hang joints of meat, cooking utensils, bows, quivers of arrows, and the like. A group of families traveling together would set up their yurts in a circle open to the south and draw up their wagons in a circle around the yurts for protection.

Because the steppe was too cold and dry for agriculture, the Mongol diet consisted mostly of animal products. Without granaries to store food, the Mongols' survival was endangered when weather or diseases of their animals threatened their food supply. The most common meat was mutton, supplemented with wild game. When grain or vegetables could be obtained through trade, they were added to the diet. Wood was scarce, so dried animal dung or grasses fueled the cook fires.

The Mongols milked sheep, goats, cows, and horses and made cheese and fermented alcoholic drinks from the milk. A European visitor to Mongolia in the 1250s described how they milked mares, a practice unfamiliar to Europeans:

> They fasten a long line to two posts standing firmly in the ground, and to the line they tie the young colts of the mares which they mean to milk. Then come the mothers who stand by their foals, and allow themselves to be milked. And if any of them be too unruly, then one takes her colt and puts it under her, letting it suck a while, and presently taking it away again, and the milker takes its place.[2]

He also described how they made the alcoholic drink koumiss from the milk, a drink that "goes down very pleasantly, intoxicating weak brains."[3]

Because of the intense cold of the winter, the Mongols made much use of furs and skins for clothing. Both men and women usually wore silk trousers and tunics (the silk obtained from China). Over these they wore robes of fur, for the very coldest times in two layers — an inner layer with the hair on the inside and an outer layer with the hair on the outside. Hats were of felt or fur, boots of felt or leather. Men wore leather belts to which their bows and quivers could be attached. Women of high rank wore elaborate headdresses decorated with feathers.

Mongol Yurt A Chinese artist in the thirteenth or fourteenth century captured the essential features of a Mongol yurt to illustrate the story of a Chinese woman who married a nomad. (Image © The Metropolitan Museum of Art/Art Resource, NY)

Mongol women had to work very hard and had to be able to care for the animals when the men were away hunting or fighting. They normally drove the carts and set up and dismantled the yurts. They also milked the sheep, goats, and cows and made the butter and cheese. In addition, they made the felt, prepared the skins, and sewed the clothes. Because water was scarce, clothes were not washed with water, nor were dishes. Women, like men, had to be expert riders, and many also learned to shoot. They participated actively in family decisions, especially as wives and mothers. In *The Secret History of the Mongols*, a work written in Mongolian in about 1240, the mother and wife of the Mongol leader Chinggis Khan frequently make impassioned speeches on the importance of family loyalty. (See "Listening to the Past: The Abduction of Women in *The Secret History of the Mongols*," page 338.)

Mongol men kept as busy as the women. They made carts and wagons and the frames for the yurts. They also made harnesses for the horses and oxen, leather saddles, and the equipment needed for hunting and war, such as bows and arrows. Men also had charge of the horses, and they milked the mares. Young horses were allowed to run wild until it was time to break them in. Catching them took great skill in the use of a long springy pole with a noose at the end. One specialist among the nomads was the blacksmith, who made stirrups, knives, and other metal tools.

Kinship underlay most social relationships among the Mongols. Normally each family occupied a yurt, and groups of families camping together were usually related along the male line (brothers, uncles, nephews, and so on). More distant patrilineal relatives were recognized as members of the same clan and could call on each other for aid. People from the same clan could not marry each other, so men had to get wives from other clans. When a woman's husband died, she would be inherited by another male in the family, such as her husband's brother or his son by another woman. Tribes were groups of clans, often distantly related. Both clans and tribes had chiefs who would make decisions on where to graze and when to retaliate against another tribe that had stolen animals or people. Women were sometimes abducted for brides. When tribes stole men from each other, they normally made them into slaves, and slaves were forced to do much of the heavy work. They would not necessarily remain slaves their entire lives, however, as their original tribes might be able to recapture them or make exchanges for them, or their masters might free them.

Even though population was sparse in the regions where the Mongols lived, conflict over resources was endemic, and each camp had to be on the alert for attacks. Defending against attacks and retaliating against raids was as much a part of the Mongols' daily life as caring for their herds and trading with nearby settlements.

Mongol children learned to ride at a young age, first on goats. The horses they later rode were short and stocky, almost like ponies, but nimble and able to endure long journeys and bitter cold. Even in the winter the horses survived by grazing, foraging beneath the snow. The prime weapon boys had to learn to use was the compound bow, which had a pull of about 160 pounds and a range of more than 200 yards, well suited for using on horseback, giving Mongol soldiers an advantage in battle. Other commonly used weapons were small battle-axes and lances fitted with hooks to pull enemies off their saddles.

From their teenage years Mongol men participated in battles, and among the Mongols courage in battle was essential to male self-esteem. Hunting was a common form of military training. Each year tribes would organize one big hunt; mounted hunters would form a vast ring perhaps ten or more miles in circumference, then gradually shrink it down, trapping all the animals before killing them. On military campaigns a Mongol soldier had to be able to ride for days without stopping to cook food; he ate from a supply of dried milk curd and cured meat, which could be supplemented by blood let from the neck of his horse. When time permitted, the soldiers would pause to hunt, adding dogs, wolves, foxes, mice, and rats to their food.

As with the Turks and other steppe nomads, religious practices centered around the shaman, a religious expert believed to be able to communicate with the gods. The high god of the Mongols was Heaven/Sky, but they recognized many other gods as well. Some groups of Mongols, especially those closer to settled communities, converted to Buddhism, Nestorian Christianity, or Manichaeism.

Chinggis Khan and the Mongol Empire

☐ How did Chinggis Khan and his successors conquer much of Eurasia, and how did the Mongol conquests change the regions affected?

In the mid-twelfth century the Mongols were just one of many peoples in the eastern grasslands, neither particularly numerous nor especially advanced. Why then did the Mongols suddenly emerge as an overpowering force on the historical stage? One explanation is ecological. A drop in the mean annual temperature created a subsistence crisis. As pastures shrank, the Mon-

• **Chinggis Khan** The title given to the Mongol ruler Temujin in 1206 and later to his successors; it means Great Ruler.

gols and other nomads had to look beyond the steppe to get more of their food from the agricultural world. A second reason for their sudden rise was the appearance of a single individual, the brilliant but utterly ruthless Temujin (ca. 1162–1227), later and more commonly called Chinggis Khan (sometimes spelled Genghis or Ghengis).

Chinggis Khan

What we know of Temujin's early career was recorded in *The Secret History of the Mongols*, written within a few decades of his death. In Temujin's youth his father had built a modest tribal following. When Temujin's father was poisoned by a rival, his followers, not ready to follow a boy of twelve, drifted away, leaving Temujin and his mother and brothers in a vulnerable position. Temujin slowly collected followers. In 1182 Temujin was captured and carried in a cage to a rival's camp. After a daring midnight escape, he led his followers to join a stronger chieftain whom his father had once aided. With the chieftain's help, Temujin began avenging the insults he had received.

Temujin proved to be a natural leader, and as he subdued the Tartars, Kereyids, Naimans, Merkids, and other Mongol and Turkish tribes, he built up an army of loyal followers. He mastered the art of winning allies through displays of personal courage in battle and generosity to his followers. To those who opposed him, he could be merciless. He once asserted that nothing gave more pleasure than massacring one's enemies, seizing their horses and cattle, and ravishing their women. Sometimes Temujin would kill all the men in a defeated tribe to prevent later vendettas. At other times he would take them on as soldiers in his own armies. Courage impressed him. One of his leading generals, Jebe, first attracted his attention when he held his ground against overwhelming opposition and shot Temujin's horse out from under him. Another prominent general, Mukhali, became Temujin's personal slave at age twenty-seven after his tribe was defeated by Temujin in 1197. Within a few years he was leading a corps of a thousand men from his own former tribe.

In 1206, at a great gathering of tribal leaders, Temujin was proclaimed **Chinggis Khan**, or Great Ruler. Chinggis decreed that Mongol, until then an

The Tent of Chinggis Khan In this fourteenth-century Persian illustration from Rashid al-Din's *History of the World*, two guards stand outside while Chinggis is in his tent. (The Granger Collection, New York)

Listening to the Past

The Abduction of Women in *The Secret History of the Mongols*

Within a few decades of Chinggis Khan's death, oral traditions concerning his rise were written down in the Mongolian language. They begin with the cycles of revenge among the tribes in Mongolia, many of which began when women were abducted for wives. These passages relate how Temujin's (Chinggis Khan's) father Yesugei seized Hogelun, Temujin's future mother, from a passing Merkid tribesman; how twenty years later three Merkids in return seized women from Temujin; and Temujin's revenge.

That year Yesugei the Brave was out hunting with his falcon on the Onan. Yeke Chiledu, a nobleman of the Merkid tribe, had gone to the Olkhunugud people to find himself a wife, and he was returning to the Merkid with the girl he'd found when he passed Yesugei hunting by the river. When he saw them riding along Yesugei leaned forward on his horse. He saw it was a beautiful girl. Quickly he rode back to his tent and just as quick returned with his two brothers, Nekun Taisi and Daritai Odchigin. When Chiledu saw the three Mongols coming he whipped his dun-colored horse and rode off around a nearby hill with the three men behind him. He cut back around the far side of the hill and rode to Lady Hogelun, the girl he'd just married, who stood waiting for him at the front of their cart. "Did you see the look on the faces of those three men?" she asked him. "From their faces it looks like they mean to kill you. As long as you've got your life there'll always be girls for you to choose from. There'll always be women to ride in your cart. As long as you've got your life you'll be able to find some girl to marry. When you find her, just name her Hogelun for me, but go now and save your own life!" Then she pulled off her shirt and held it out to him, saying: "And take this to remember me, to remember my scent." Chiledu reached out from his saddle and took the shirt in his hands. With the three Mongols close behind him he struck his dun-colored horse with his whip and took off down the Onan River at full speed.

The three Mongols chased him across seven hills before turning around and returning to Hogelun's cart. Then Yesugei the Brave grasped the reins of the cart, his elder brother Nekun Taisi rode in front to guide them, and the younger brother Daritai Odchigin rode along by the wheels. As they rode her back toward their camp, Hogelun began to cry, . . . and she cried till she stirred up the waters of the Onan River, till she shook the trees in the forest and the grass in the valleys. But as the party approached their camp Daritai, riding beside her, warned her to stop: "This fellow who held you in his arms, he's already ridden over the mountains. This man who's lost you, he's crossed many rivers by now. You can call out his name, but he can't see you now even if he looks back. If you tried to find him now you won't even find his tracks. So be still now," he told her. Then Yesugei took Lady Hogelun to his tent as his wife. . . .

[Some twenty years later] one morning just before dawn Old Woman Khogaghchin, Mother Hogelun's servant, woke with a start, crying: "Mother! Mother! Get up! The ground is shaking, I hear it rumble. The Tayichigud must be riding back to attack us. Get up!"

Mother Hogelun jumped from her bed, saying: "Quick, wake my sons!" They woke Temujin and the others and all ran for the horses. Temujin, Mother Hogelun, and Khasar each took a horse. Khachigun, Temuge Odchigin, and Belgutei each took a horse. Bogorchu took one horse and Jelme another. Mother Hogelun lifted the baby Temulun onto her saddle. They saddled the last horse as a lead and there was no horse left for [Temujin's wife] Lady Borte. . . .

Old Woman Khogaghchin, who'd been left in the camp, said: "I'll hide Lady Borte." She made her get into a black covered cart. Then she harnessed the cart to a speckled ox. Whipping the ox, she drove the cart away from the camp down the Tungelig. As the first light of day hit them, soldiers rode up and told them to stop. "Who are you?" they asked her, and Old Woman Khogaghchin answered: "I'm a servant of Temujin's. I've just come from shearing his sheep. I'm on my way back to my own tent to make felt from the wool." Then they asked her: "Is Temujin at his tent? How far is it from here?" Old Woman Khogaghchin said: "As for the tent, it's not far. As for Temujin, I couldn't see whether he was there or not. I was just shearing his sheep out back." The soldiers rode off toward the camp, and Old Woman Khogaghchin whipped the ox. But as the cart moved faster its axletree snapped. "Now we'll have to run for the woods on foot," she thought, but before she could start the soldiers returned. They'd made [Temujin's half brother] Belgutei's mother their captive, and had her slung over one of their horses with her feet swinging down. They rode up to the old woman shouting: "What have you got in that cart!" "I'm just carrying wool," Khogaghchin replied, but an old soldier turned to the younger ones and said, "Get off your horses and see what's in there." When they opened the door of the cart they found Borte inside. Pulling her out, they forced Borte and Khogaghchin to ride on their horses, then they all set out after Temujin. . . .

The men who pursued Temujin were the chiefs of the three Merkid clans, Toghtoga, Dayin Usun, and Khagatai Darmala. These three had come to get their revenge, saying: "Long ago Mother Hogelun was stolen from our brother, Chiledu." When they couldn't catch Temujin they said to each other: "We've got our revenge. We've taken their wives from them," and they rode down from Mount Burkhan Khaldun back to their homes. . . .

Having finished his prayer Temujin rose and rode off with Khasar and Belgutei. They rode to [his father's sworn brother] Toghoril Ong Khan of the Kereyid camped in the Black Forest on the Tula River. Temujin spoke to Ong Khan, saying: "I was attacked by surprise by the three Merkid chiefs. They've stolen my wife from me. We've come to you now to say, 'Let my father the Khan save my wife and return her.'" . . .

[Temujin and his allies] moved their forces from Botoghan Bogorjin to the Kilgho River where they built rafts to cross over to the Bugura Steppe, into [the Merkid] Chief Toghtoga's land. They came down on him as if through the smoke-hole of his tent, beating down the frame of his tent and leaving it flat, capturing and killing his wives and his sons. They struck at his door-frame where his guardian spirit lived and broke it to pieces. They completely destroyed all his people until in their place there was nothing but emptiness. . . .

As the Merkid people tried to flee from our army running down the Selenge with what they could gather in the darkness, as our soldiers rode out of the night capturing and killing the Merkid, Temujin rode through the retreating camp shouting out: "Borte! Borte!"

Lady Borte was among the Merkid who ran in the darkness and when she heard his voice, when she recognized Temujin's voice, Borte leaped from her cart. Lady Borte and Old Woman Khogaghchin saw Temujin charge through the crowd and they ran to him, finally seizing the reins of his horse. All about them was moonlight. As Temujin looked down to see who had stopped him he recognized Lady Borte. In a moment he was down from his horse and they were in each other's arms, embracing. "

Source: Paul Kahn, trans., *The Secret History of the Mongols: The Origin of Chinghis Khan*. Copyright © 1984. Reprinted with permission of Paul Kahn.

QUESTIONS FOR ANALYSIS

1. What do you learn from these stories about the Mongol way of life?

2. "Marriage by capture" has been practiced in many parts of the world. Can you infer from these stories why such a system would persist? What was the impact of such practices on kinship relations?

3. Can you recognize traces of the oral origins of these stories?

• **Chinggis and his wife Borte are seated together at a feast in this fourteenth-century Persian illustration.**
(Bibliothèque nationale de France/The Bridgeman Art Library)

unwritten language, be written down in the script used by the Uighur Turks. With this script a record was made of the Mongol laws and customs, ranging from the rules for the annual hunt to punishments of death for robbery and adultery. Another measure adopted at this assembly was a postal relay system to send messages rapidly by mounted courier, suggesting that Chinggis already had ambitions to rule a vast empire.

With the tribes of Mongolia united, the energies previously devoted to infighting and vendettas were redirected to exacting tribute from the settled populations nearby, starting with the Jurchen (Jin) state that extended into north China (see Map 13.2, page 372). Because of his early experiences with intertribal feuding, Chinggis mistrusted traditional tribal loyalties, and as he fashioned a new army, he gave it a new, non-tribal structure. He conscripted soldiers from all the tribes and assigned them to units that were composed of members from different tribes. He selected commanders for each unit whom he could remove at will, although he allowed commanders to pass their posts to their sons. Marco Polo, the famous European traveler who later attended the Mongol court of Chinggis's grandson, explained the decimal hierarchy of his armies this way:

> When one of the great Tartar chiefs proceeds on an expedition, he puts himself at the head of an army of a hundred thousand horses, and organizes them in the following manner. He appoints an officer to the command of every ten men, and others to command a hundred, a thousand, and ten thousand men, respectively. Thus ten of the officers commanding ten men take their orders from him who commands a hundred; of these, each ten, from him who commands a thousand; and each ten of these latter, from him who commands ten thousand. By this arrangement each officer has only to attend to the management of ten men or ten bodies of men.[4]

After Chinggis subjugated a city, he would send envoys to cities farther out to demand submission and threaten destruction. Those who opened their city gates and submitted without fighting could become allies and retain local power, but those who resisted faced the prospect of mass slaughter. He despised city dwellers and would sometimes use them as living shields in the next battle. After the Mongol armies swept across north China in 1212–1213, ninety-odd cities lay in rubble. Beijing, captured in 1215, burned for more than a month. Not surprisingly many governors of cities and rulers of small states hastened to offer submission.

Chinggis preferred conquest to administration and did not stay in north China to set up an administrative structure. He left that to subordinates and turned his attention westward, to Central Asia and Persia, then dominated by different groups of Turks. In 1218 Chinggis proposed to the Khwarizm shah of Persia that he accept Mongol overlordship and establish trade relations. The shah, to show his determination to resist, ordered the envoy and the merchants who had accompanied him killed. The next year Chinggis led an army of one hundred thousand soldiers west to retaliate. Mongol forces destroyed the shah's army and sacked one Persian city after another, demolishing buildings and massacring hundreds of thousands of people.

After returning from Central Asia, Chinggis died in 1227 during the siege of a city in northwest China. Before he died, he instructed his sons not to fall out among themselves but instead to divide the spoils.

Chinggis's Successors

Although Mongol leaders traditionally had had to win their positions, after Chinggis died the empire was divided into four states called **khanates**, with one of the lines of his descendants taking charge of each one (Map 12.1). Chinggis's third son, Ögödei, assumed the title of khan, and he directed the next round of invasions.

In 1237 representatives of all four lines led 150,000 Mongol, Turkish, and Persian troops into Europe. During the next five years they gained control of Moscow and Kievan Russia and looted cities in Poland and Hungary. They were poised to attack deeper into Europe when they learned of the death of Ögödei in 1241. To participate in the election of a new khan, the army returned to the Mongols' new capital city, Karakorum.

Once Ögödei's son was certified as his successor, the Mongols turned their attention to Persia and the Middle East. In 1256 a Mongol army took northwest Iran, then pushed on to the Abbasid capital of Baghdad. When it fell in 1258, the last Abbasid caliph was murdered, and the population was put to the sword. The Mongol onslaught was successfully resisted, however, by both the Delhi sultanate (see page 353) and the Mamluk rulers in Egypt (see page 245).

Under Chinggis's grandson Khubilai Khan (r. 1260–1294) the Mongols completed their conquest of China. South China had never been captured by non-Chinese, in large part because horses were of no strategic advantage in a land of rivers and canals. Perhaps because they were entering a very different type of terrain, the Mongols proceeded deliberately. First they surrounded the Song empire in central and south China (discussed in Chapter 13) by taking its westernmost province in 1252, as well as Korea to its east in 1258, destroying the Nanzhao kingdom in modern Yunnan in 1254, and then

khanates The states ruled by a khan; the four units into which Chinggis divided the Mongol Empire.

→ Mongol campaign before 1240
→ Mongol campaign after 1240
→ Route of Marco Polo, 1271–1295

EUROPE

• Moscow

• Kiev

• Bulgar

Venice •

KHANATE OF THE GOLDEN HORDE

ASIA

MONGOLIA

EMPIRE OF THE GREAT KHAN

• Karakorum

MANCHURIA

KAMAKURA JAPAN

Sea of Japan

BYZANTINE EMPIRE

Black Sea

Volga R.

Aral Sea

Syr Darya

KHANATE OF CENTRAL ASIA

GOBI

• Shangdu

• Beijing

KORYŎ KOREA

Danube R.

Caspian Sea

Bukhara •

• Samarkand

Amu Darya

Yellow R. (Huang He)

• Kaifeng

East China Sea

Mediterranean Sea

Tigris R.

Euphrates R.

IL-KHAN EMPIRE

• Khotan

• Hangzhou

Yangzi R.

• Jerusalem

• Baghdad

EGYPT

HIMALAYA MTS.

Brahmaputra R.

SOUTHERN SONG CHINA (Fell 1279)

• Guangzhou

ARABIA

Red Sea

Nile R.

Indus R.

Delhi •

Ganges R.

Irrawaddy R.

Salween R.

DELHI SULTANATE

NANZHAO

Xi R.

ANNAM

BURMA

Mekong R.

South China Sea

Arabian Sea

Bay of Bengal

• Pagan

KHMER EMPIRE

AFRICA

N W E S

INDIAN OCEAN

Equator

60°E

90°E

120°E

150°E

30°N

SRIVIJAYA EMPIRE

0   500   1,000 miles
0   500   1,000 kilometers

◻ Mapping the Past

MAP 12.1 The Mongol Empire The creation of the vast Mongol Empire facilitated communication across Eurasia and led to both the spread of deadly plagues and the transfer of technical and scientific knowledge. After the death of Chinggis Khan in 1227, the empire was divided into four khanates ruled by different lines of his successors. In the 1270s the Mongols conquered southern China, but most of their subsequent campaigns did not lead to further territorial gains.

ANALYZING THE MAP Trace the campaigns of the Mongols. Which ones led to acquisition of territory, and which ones did not?

CONNECTIONS Would the division of the Mongol Empire into separate khanates have made these areas easier for the Mongols to rule? What drawbacks might it have had from the Mongols' point of view?

continuing south and taking Annam (northern Vietnam) in 1257. A surrendered Song commander advised them to build a navy to attack the great Song cities located on rivers. During the five-year siege of a central Chinese river port, both sides used thousands of boats and tens of thousands of troops. The Mongols employed experts in naval and siege warfare from all over their empire — Chinese, Korean, Jurchen, Uighur, and Persian. Catapults designed by Muslim engineers launched a barrage of rocks weighing up to a hundred pounds

Viewpoints

Chinese and European Accounts About the Mongol Army

• *The Mongols received little attention from historians until they were united under Chinggis and began their military conquests. The following documents offer different perspectives on the Mongol army. The first, one of the earliest surviving accounts, was written about 1220 by a Chinese historian, Li Xinchuan, living in south China under the Song Dynasty. He would have learned of the Mongols secondhand, as the Song had diplomatic relations with Jin, then under attack by the Mongols. He reported how the Tartars — referring to the Mongols — gained control of north China in 1213–1214. The second excerpt refers to the time that the state of Song in South China sustained its first major attack by the Mongols in 1236, when Mongol armies entered the western province of Sichuan and destroyed major cities like Chengdu. A man who survived the slaughter, Zhu Sisun, later reported what he went through. Marco Polo, encountering the Mongols a half century later after most of their conquests through Eurasia were complete, had a different view of the warriors.*

Li Xinchuan

"In the spring of 1213 [the Tartars] attacked Yanjing [modern Beijing] and that fall Yunji [the Jin emperor] was killed. Chinggis left Samohe in charge of Yanjing and incorporated the 46 divisions of the surrendered [Jin] armies of Yang Boyu and Liu Bolin into the great Tartar armies, which were divided into three divisions to conquer the prefectural cities of [the circuits of] River North, River East, and Mountains East. . . . At this time the troops of the various circuits of north China pulled back to defend the region west of the mountains, but there were not enough troops, so commoners were drafted as soldiers and put on the tops of the city walls to defend them. The Tartars drove their family members to attack them, and fathers and sons or brothers often got close enough to recognize and call out to each other. Because of this, [the drafted soldiers] were not firmly resolved, and all of the cities surrendered as soon as the fighting began. From the twelfth month of 1213 to the first month of 1214, more than ninety prefectures fell. Every place the armies passed through was devastated. For several thousand *li*, throughout River East, River North, and Mountains East, the people were slaughtered. Gold and silk, boys and girls, oxen and sheep, horses and other animals were all "rolled up" and taken away. Houses were burnt down and defensive walls smashed."

Zhu Sisun

"Here is how the people of Sichuan went to their deaths: groups of fifty people were clustered together, and the Mongols impaled them all with swords and piled up the corpses. At sunset, those who did not appear dead were again stabbed. Sisun lay at the bottom of a pile of corpses, and by chance the evening stabbing did not reach him. The blood of the corpses above him dripped steadily into his mouth. Halfway through the night Sisun began to revive, and crawling into the woods he made his escape."

Marco Polo

"They are brave in battle, almost to desperation, setting little value upon their lives, and exposing themselves without hesitation to all manner of danger. Their disposition is cruel. They are capable of supporting every kind of privation, and when there is a necessity for it, can live for a month on the milk of their mares, and upon such wild animals as they may chance to catch. The men are habituated to remain on horseback during two days and two nights, without dismounting, sleeping in that situation whilst their horses graze. No people on earth can surpass them in fortitude under difficulties, nor show greater patience under wants of every kind."

Sources: Li Xinchuan, *Jianyan yilai chaoye zaji* (Beijing: Zhonghua shuju, 2000), pp. 847–851, translated by Patricia Ebrey; Paul J. Smith, "Family, *Landsmann*, and Status-Group Affinity in Refugee Mobility Strategies: The Mongol Invasions and the Diaspora of Sichuanese Elites, 1230–1330," *Harvard Journal of Asiatic Studies* 52.2 (1992), 671–672, slightly modified; *The Travels of Marco Polo, the Venetian*, ed. Manuel Komroff (New York: Boni and Liveright, 1926), p. 93.

QUESTIONS FOR ANALYSIS

1. How would you explain the differences in what these writers chose to mention?

2. If you were writing a history of the Mongols, would you consider these sources as equally valid evidence, or do you find some more reliable than others? Does anything in the accounts seem exaggerated? How can you judge?

each. During their advance toward the Chinese capital of Hangzhou, the Mongols ordered the total slaughter of the people of the major city of Changzhou, and in 1276 the Chinese empress dowager surrendered in hopes of sparing the people of the capital a similar fate.

Having overrun China and Korea, Khubilai turned his eyes toward Japan. In 1274 a force of 30,000 soldiers and support personnel sailed from Korea to Japan. In 1281 a combined Mongol and Chinese fleet of about 150,000 made a second attempt to conquer Japan. On both occasions the Mongols managed to land but were beaten back by Japanese samurai armies. Each time fierce storms destroyed the Mongol fleets. The Japanese claimed that they had been saved by the *kamikaze*, the "divine wind" (which later lent its name to the thousands of Japanese aviators who crashed their airplanes into American warships during World War II). A decade later, in 1293, Khubilai tried sending a fleet to the islands of Southeast Asia, including Java, but it met with no more success than the fleets sent to Japan.

Why were the Mongols so successful against so many different types of enemies? Even though their population was tiny compared to the populations of the large agricultural societies they conquered, their tactics, their weapons, and their organization all gave them advantages. Like other nomads before them, they were superb horsemen and excellent archers. Their horses were extremely nimble, able to change direction quickly, thus allowing the Mongols to maneuver easily and ride through infantry forces armed with swords, lances, and javelins. Usually only other nomadic armies, like the Turks, could stand up well against the Mongols. (See "Viewpoints: Chinese and European Accounts About the Mongol Army," page 342.)

The Mongols were also open to trying new military technologies. To attack walled cities, they learned how to use catapults and other engines of war. At first they employed Chinese catapults, but when they learned that those used by the Turks in Afghanistan were more powerful, they adopted the better model. The Mongols also used exploding arrows and gunpowder projectiles developed by the Chinese.

☐ MONGOL CONQUESTS

1206	Temujin made Chinggis Khan
1215	Fall of Beijing (Jurchens)
1219–1220	Fall of Bukhara and Samarkand in Central Asia
1227	Death of Chinggis
1237–1241	Raids into eastern Europe
1257	Conquest of Annam (northern Vietnam)
1258	Conquest of Abbasid capital of Baghdad; conquest of Korea
1260	Khubilai succeeds to khanship
1274	First attempt at invading Japan
1276	Surrender of Song Dynasty (China)
1281	Second attempt at invading Japan
1293	Mongol fleet unsuccessful in invasion of Java
mid-14th century	Decline of Mongol power

The 1258 Fall of Baghdad This illustration from a fourteenth-century Persian manuscript shows the Mongol army attacking the walled city of Baghdad. Note the use of catapults on both sides. (Bildarchiv Preussischer Kulturbesitz/Art Resource, NY)

The Mongols made good use of intelligence and tried to exploit internal divisions in the countries they attacked. Thus, in north China they appealed to the Khitans, who had been defeated by the Jurchens a century earlier, to join them in attacking the Jurchens. In Syria they exploited the resentment of Christians against their Muslim rulers.

The Mongols as Rulers

The success of the Mongols in ruling vast territories was due in large part to their willingness to incorporate other ethnic groups into their armies and governments. Whatever their original country or religion, those who served the Mongols loyally were rewarded. Uighurs, Tibetans, Persians, Chinese, and Russians came to hold powerful positions in the Mongol government. Chinese helped breach the walls of Baghdad in the 1250s, and Muslims operated the catapults that helped reduce Chinese cities in the 1270s. Mongol armies incorporated the armies they vanquished and in time had large numbers of Turkish troops.

Since, in Mongol eyes, the purpose of fighting was to gain riches, they regularly would loot the settlements they conquered, taking whatever they wanted, including the residents. Land would be granted to military commanders, nobles, and army units to be governed and exploited as the recipients wished. Those working the land would be given to them as serfs. The Mongols built a capital city called Karakorum in modern Mongolia, and to bring it up to the level of the cities they conquered, they transported skilled workers from those cities. For instance, after Bukhara and Samarkand were captured in 1219–1220, some thirty thousand artisans

were seized and transported to Mongolia. Sometimes these slaves gradually improved their status. A French goldsmith from Budapest named Guillaume Boucher was captured by the Mongols in 1242 and taken to Karakorum, where he gradually won favor and was put in charge of fifty workers to make gold and silver vessels for the Mongol court.

The traditional nomad disdain for farmers led some commanders to suggest turning north China into a gigantic pasture after it was conquered. In time, though, the Mongols came to realize that simply appropriating the wealth and human resources of the settled lands was not as good as extracting regular revenue from them. A Chinese-educated Khitan who had been working for the Jurchens in China explained to the Mongols that collecting taxes from farmers would be highly profitable: they could extract a revenue of 500,000 ounces of silver, 80,000 bolts of silk, and more than 20,000 tons of grain from the region by taxing it. The Mongols gave this a try, but soon political rivals convinced the khan that he would gain even more by letting Central Asian Muslim merchants bid against each other for licenses to collect taxes any way they could, a system called **tax-farming**. Ordinary Chinese found this method of tax collecting much more oppressive than traditional Chinese methods, since there was little to keep the tax collectors from seizing everything they could.

By the second half of the thirteenth century there was no longer a genuine pan-Asian Mongol Empire. Much of Asia was in the hands of Mongol successor states, but these were generally hostile to each other. Khubilai was often at war with the khanate of Central Asia, then held by his cousin Khaidu, and he had little contact with the khanate of the Golden Horde in south Russia. The Mongols adapted their methods of government to the existing traditions of each place they ruled, and the regions now went their separate ways.

In China the Mongols resisted assimilation and purposely avoided many Chinese practices. The rulers conducted their business in the Mongol language and spent their summers in Mongolia. Khubilai discouraged Mongols from marrying Chinese and took only Mongol women into the palace. Some Mongol princes preferred to live in yurts erected on the palace grounds rather than in the grand palaces constructed at Beijing. Chinese were treated as legally inferior not only to the Mongols but also to all other non-Chinese. In cases of assault the discrepancy was huge, as a Mongol

Gold Belt Plaques Like earlier nomads, the Mongols favored art with animal designs, such as these two gold belt plaques, which depict deer under trees or flowers. Belts and horses were often exchanged to seal or commemorate an alliance. (Nasser D. Khalili Collection of Islamic Art, © Nour Foundation, Courtesy of the Khalili Family Trust)

who murdered a Chinese could get off with a fine, but a Chinese who hit a Mongol to defend himself would face severe penalties.

In Central Asia, Persia, and Russia the Mongols tended to merge with the Turkish groups already there and, like them, converted to Islam. Russia in the thirteenth century was not a strongly centralized state, and the Mongols allowed Russian princes and lords to continue to rule their territories as long as they turned over adequate tribute (thus adding to the burden on peasants). The city of Moscow became the center of Mongol tribute collection and grew in importance. In the Middle East the Mongol Il-khans (as they were known in Persia) were more active as rulers, again continuing the traditions of the caliphate. In Mongolia itself, however, Mongol traditions were maintained.

Mongol control in each of the khanates lasted about a century. In the mid-fourteenth century the Mongol dynasty in China deteriorated into civil war, and in the 1360s the Mongols withdrew back to Mongolia. There was a similar loss of Mongol power in Persia and Central Asia. Only on the south Russian steppe did the Golden Horde maintain its hold for another century.

As Mongol rule in Central Asia declined, a new conqueror emerged, Timur, also known as Tamerlane (Timur the Lame). Not a nomad but a highly civilized Turkish noble, Timur in the 1360s struck out from his base in Samarkand into Persia, north India (see page 353), southern Russia, and beyond. His armies used the terror tactics that the Mongols had perfected, massacring the citizens of cities that resisted. In the decades after his death in 1405, however, Timur's empire went into decline.

East-West Communication During the Mongol Era

☐ How did the Mongol conquests facilitate the spread of ideas, religions, inventions, and diseases?

The Mongol governments did more than any earlier political entities to encourage the movement of people and goods across Eurasia. With these vast movements came cultural accommodation as the Mongols, their conquered subjects, and their trading partners learned from one another. This cultural exchange included both physical goods and the sharing of ideas, including the introduction of new religious beliefs and the adoption of new ways to organize and rule the Mongol empire. It also facilitated the spread of the plague and the unwilling movement of enslaved captives.

The Movement of Peoples

The Mongols had never looked down on merchants the way the elites of many traditional states did, and they welcomed the arrival of merchants from distant lands. Even when different groups of Mongols were fighting among themselves, they usually allowed caravans to pass without harassing them.

The Mongol practice of transporting skilled people from the lands they conquered also brought people into contact with each other in new ways. Besides those forced to move, the Mongols recruited administrators from all over. Chinese, Persians, and Arabs served the Mongols, and the Mongols often sent them far from home. Especially prominent were the Uighur Turks of Chinese Central Asia, whose familiarity with Chinese civilization and fluency in Turkish were extremely valuable in facilitating communication. Literate Uighurs staffed much of the Mongol administration.

One of those who served the Mongols was Rashid al-Din (ca. 1247–1318). A Jew from Persia and the son of an apothecary, Rashid al-Din converted to Islam at the age of thirty and entered the service of the Mongol Il-khan of Persia as a physician. He rose in government service, traveled widely, and eventually became prime minister. Rashid al-Din became friends with the ambassador from China, and together they arranged for translations of Chinese works on medicine, agronomy, and statecraft. He had ideas on economic management that he communicated to Mongol officials in Central Asia and China. Aware of the great differences between cultures, he believed that the Mongols should try to rule in accord with the moral principles of the majority in each land. On that basis he convinced the Mongol khan of Persia to convert to Islam. Rashid al-Din undertook to explain the great variety of cultures by writing a world history more comprehensive than any previously written.

The Mongols were remarkably open to religious experts from all the lands they encountered. More Europeans made their way as far as Mongolia and China in the Mongol period than ever before. Popes and kings sent envoys to the Mongol court in the hope of enlisting the Mongols on their side in their long-standing conflict with Muslim forces over the Holy Land. European visitors were also interested in finding Christians who had been cut off from the West by the spread of Islam, and in fact there were considerable numbers of Nestorian Christians in Central Asia. In 1245 Pope Innocent IV wrote two letters to the "King and people of the Tartars" asking him to become a Christian and cease attacks against Europe. They were delivered to a Mongol general in Armenia. The next year another

• **tax-farming** Assigning the collection of taxes to whoever bids the most for the privilege.

Depictions of Europeans The Mongol Empire, by facilitating travel across Asia, increased knowledge of faraway lands. Rashid al-Din's *History of the World* included a history of the Franks, illustrated here with images of Western popes (left) conferring with Byzantine emperors (right). (Topkapi Saray Museum, Ms. H.1654, fol. 303a)

our own eyes, to which they reduce all peoples who have submitted to them."5

A few years later, in 1253, Flemish friar William of Rubruck set out with the permission of King Louis IX of France as a missionary to convert the Mongols. He too made his way to Karakorum, where he found many Europeans. At Easter, Hungarians, Russians, Georgians, Armenians, and Alans all took communion in a Nestorian church. Rubruck also recorded information he heard about China while in Mongolia, such as the Chinese practice of writing with a brush.

The most famous European visitor to the Mongol lands was the Venetian Marco Polo (ca. 1254–1324). In his famous *Travels*, Marco Polo described all the places he visited or learned about during his seventeen years away from home. He reported being warmly received by Khubilai, who impressed him enormously. He was also awed by the wealth and splendor of Chinese cities and spread the notion of Asia as a land of riches. In Marco Polo's lifetime, some skeptics did not believe his tale, and even today some scholars speculate that he may have learned about China from Persian merchants he met in the Middle East without actually going to China. But Mongol scholars staunchly defend Marco Polo, even though they admit that he stretched the truth to make himself look good in several places. Regardless of the final verdict on Marco Polo's veracity, there is no doubt that the great popularity of his book contributed to European interest in finding new routes to Asia.

The Spread of Disease, Goods, and Ideas

The rapid transfer of people and goods across Central Asia spread more than ideas and inventions. It also spread diseases, the most deadly of which was the plague known in Europe as the Black Death, which most scholars identify today as the bubonic plague. In the early fourteenth century, transmitted by rats and fleas, the plague began to spread from Central Asia into West Asia, the Mediterranean, and western Europe. When the Mongols were assaulting the city of Kaffa in the Crimea in 1346, they were infected by the plague and had to withdraw. In retaliation, they purposely spread the disease to their enemy by catapulting the bodies of victims into the city of Kaffa. Soon the disease was carried from port to port throughout the Mediterranean by ship. The confusion of the mid-fourteenth century that led to the loss of Mongol power in China, Iran, and Central Asia undoubtedly owes something to the effect of the spread of the plague and other diseases. (For more on the Black Death, see Chapter 14.)

Traditionally, the historians of each of the countries conquered by the Mongols portrayed them as a scourge.

envoy, Giovanni di Pian de Carpine, reached the Volga River and the camp of Batu, the khan of the Golden Horde. Batu sent him on to the new Great Khan in Karakorum with two Mongol guides, riding so fast that they had to change horses five to seven times a day. Their full journey of more than three thousand miles took a remarkably short five and a half months. Carpine spent four months at the Great Khan's court but never succeeded in convincing the khan to embrace Christianity or drop his demand that the pope appear in person to tender his submission to the khan. When Carpine returned home, he wrote a report that urged preparation for a renewed Mongol attack on Europe. The Mongols had to be resisted "because of the harsh, indeed intolerable, and hitherto unheard-of slavery seen with

Russian historians, for instance, saw this as a period of bondage that set Russia back and cut it off from western Europe. Among contemporary Western historians, it is now more common to celebrate the genius of the Mongol military machine and treat the spread of ideas and inventions as an obvious good, probably because we see global communication as a good in our own world. There is no reason to assume, however, that people benefited equally from the improved communications and the new political institutions of the Mongol era. Merchants involved in long-distance trade prospered, but those enslaved and transported hundreds or thousands of miles from home would have seen themselves not as the beneficiaries of opportunities to encounter cultures different from their own, but rather as the most pitiable of victims.

The places that were ruled by Mongol governments for a century or more — China, Central Asia, Persia, and Russia — do not seem to have advanced at a more rapid rate during that century than they did in earlier centuries, either economically or culturally. By Chinese standards Mongol imposition of hereditary status distinctions was a step backward from a much more mobile and open society, and placing Persians, Arabs, or Tibetans over Chinese did not arouse interest in foreign cultures. Much more foreign music and foreign styles in clothing, art, and furnishings were integrated into Chinese civilization in Tang times than in Mongol times.

In terms of the spread of technological and scientific ideas, Europe seems to have been by far the main beneficiary of increased communication, largely because in 1200 it lagged farther behind than the other areas. Chinese inventions such as printing, gunpowder, and the compass spread westward. Persian and Indian expertise in astronomy and mathematics also spread. In terms of the spread of religions, Islam probably gained the most. It came to dominate in Chinese Central Asia, which had previously been Buddhist.

Another element promoting Eurasian connection was maritime trade, which linked all the societies of the Indian Ocean and East Asia. The products of China and other areas of the East introduced to Europe by merchants like Marco Polo whetted the appetites of Europeans for goods from the East, and the demand for Asian goods eventually culminated in the great age of European exploration and expansion (discussed in Chapter 16). By comparison, in areas the Mongols had directly attacked, protecting their own civilization became a higher priority than drawing from the outside to enrich or enlarge it.

India, Islam, and the Development of Regional Cultures, 300–1400

☐ What was the result of India's encounters with Turks, Mongols, and Islam?

South Asia, although far from the heartland of the steppe, still felt the impact of the arrival of the Turks in Central Asia. Over the course of many centuries, horsemen from both the east and the west (Scythians, Huns, Turks, and Mongols) all sent armies south to raid or invade north India. After the Mauryan Empire broke apart in 185 B.C.E. (see page 85), India was politically divided into small kingdoms for several centuries. Only the Guptas in the fourth century would emerge to unite much of north India, though their rule was cut short by the invasion of the Huns in about 450. In the centuries that followed, India witnessed the development of regional cultures and was profoundly shaped by Turkish nomads from Central Asia who brought their culture and, most importantly, Islam to India. Despite these

Horse and Groom Zhao Mengfu (1254–1322), the artist of this painting and a member of the Song imperial family, took up service under the Mongol emperor Khubilai. The Mongol rulers, great horsemen themselves, would likely have appreciated this depiction of a horse buffeted by the wind. (National Palace Museum, Taipei, Taiwan)

> **❝**I see your body in the sinuous creeper, your gaze in the startled eyes of deer, your cheek in the moon.**❞**
>
> **KALIDASA**

events, the lives of most Indians remained unchanged, with the majority of the people living in villages in a society defined by caste.

The Gupta Empire, ca. 320–480

In the early fourth century a state emerged in the Ganges plain that was able to bring large parts of north India under its control. The rulers of this Indian empire, the Guptas, consciously modeled their rule after that of the Mauryan Empire, and the founder took the name of the founder of that dynasty, Chandragupta. Although the Guptas never controlled as much territory as the Mauryans had, they united north India and received tribute from states in Nepal and the Indus Valley, thus giving large parts of India a period of peace and political unity.

The Gupta Empire, ca. 320–480

The Guptas' administrative system was not as centralized as that of the Mauryans. In the central regions they drew their revenue from a tax on agriculture of one-quarter of the harvest and maintained monopolies on key products such as metals and salt (reminiscent of Chinese practice). They also exacted labor service for the construction and upkeep of roads, wells, and irrigation systems. More distant areas were assigned to governors who were allowed considerable leeway, and governorships often became hereditary. Areas still farther away were encouraged to become vassal states, able to participate in the splendor of the capital and royal court in subordinate roles and to engage in profitable trade, but not required to turn over much in the way of revenue.

The Gupta kings were patrons of the arts. Poets composed epics for the courts of the Gupta kings, and other writers experimented with prose romances and popular tales. India's greatest poet, Kalidasa (ca. 380–450), like Shakespeare, wrote poems as well as plays in verse. His most highly esteemed play, *Shakuntala*, con-

cerns a daughter of a hermit who enthralls a king who is out hunting. The king sets up house with her, then returns to his court and, owing to a curse, forgets her. Only much later does he acknowledge their child as his true heir. Equally loved is Kalidasa's one-hundred-verse poem "The Cloud Messenger" about a demigod who asks a passing cloud to carry a message to his wife, from whom he has long been separated. At one point he instructs the cloud to tell her: "I see your body in the sinuous creeper, your gaze in the startled eyes of deer, your cheek in the moon, your hair in the plumage of peacocks, and in the tiny ripples of the river I see your sidelong glances, but alas, my dearest, nowhere do I see your whole likeness."[6]

In mathematics, too, the Gupta period could boast of impressive intellectual achievements. The so-called Arabic numerals are actually of Indian origin. Indian mathematicians developed the place-value notation system, with separate columns for ones, tens, and hundreds, as well as a zero sign to indicate the absence of units in a given column. This system greatly facilitated calculation and spread as far as Europe by the seventh century.

The Gupta rulers were Hindus, but they tolerated all faiths. Buddhist pilgrims from other areas of Asia reported that Buddhist monasteries with hundreds or even thousands of monks and nuns flourished in the cities. The success of Buddhism did not hinder Hinduism with its many gods, which remained popular among ordinary people.

The great crisis of the Gupta Empire was the invasion of the Huns (Xiongnu). The migration of these nomads from Central Asia shook much of Eurasia. Around 450 a group of them known as the White Huns thundered into India. Mustering his full might, the Gupta ruler Skandagupta (r. ca. 455–467) threw back the invaders. Although the Huns failed to uproot the Gupta Empire, they dealt the dynasty a fatal blow.

India's Medieval Age and the First Encounter with Islam

After the decline of the Gupta Empire, India once again broke into separate kingdoms that were frequently at war with each other. Most of the dynasties of India's medieval age (ca. 500–1400) were short-lived, but a balance of power was maintained between the major regions of India, with none gaining enough of an advantage to conquer the others. Particularly notable are the Cholas, who dominated the southern tip of the peninsula, Sri Lanka, and much of the eastern Indian Ocean to the twelfth century (Map 12.2).

Political division fostered the development of regional cultures. Literature came to be written in India's regional languages, among them Marathi, Bengali, and Assamese. Commerce continued as before, and the

Wall Painting at Ajanta Many of the best surviving examples of Gupta period painting are found at the twenty-nine Buddhist cave temples at Ajanta in central India. The walls of these caves were decorated in the fifth and sixth centuries with scenes from the former lives of the Buddha. These two scenes, showing a royal couple on the right and a princess and her attendants on the left, offer glimpses of what the royal courts of the period must have looked like. (Benoy K. Behl)

coasts of India remained important in the sea trade of the Indian Ocean.

The first encounters with Islam occurred in this period. In 711, after pirates had plundered a richly laden Arab ship near the mouth of the Indus, the Umayyad governor of Iraq sent a force with six thousand horses and six thousand camels to seize the Sind area in western India (modern day Pakistan). The western part of India remained part of the caliphate for centuries, but Islam did not spread much beyond this foothold. During the ninth and tenth centuries Turks from Central Asia moved into the region of today's northeastern Iran and western Afghanistan, then known as Khurasan. Converts to Islam, they first served as military forces for the caliphate in Baghdad, but as its authority weakened (see pages 243–244), they made themselves rulers of an effectively independent Khurasan and frequently sent raiding parties into north India. Beginning in 997, Mahmud of Ghazni (r. 997–1030) led seventeen annual forays into India from his base in modern Afghanistan. His goal was plunder to finance his wars against other Turkish rulers in Central Asia. Toward this end, he systematically looted Indian palaces and temples, viewing religious statues

as infidels' idols. Eventually even the Arab conquerors of the Sind fell to the Turks. By 1030 the Indus Valley, the Punjab, and the rest of northwest India were in the grip of the Turks.

The new rulers encouraged the spread of Islam, but the Indian caste system (see page 71) made it difficult to convert higher-caste Indians. Al-Biruni (d. 1048), a Persian scholar who spent much of his later life at the court of Mahmud and learned Sanskrit, wrote of the obstacles to Hindu-Muslim communication. The most basic barrier was language, but the religious gulf was also fundamental:

They totally differ from us in religion, as we believe in nothing in which they believe, and vice versa. On the whole, there is very little disputing about theological topics among them; at the utmost they fight with words, but they will never stake their soul or body or property on religious controversy. . . . They call foreigners impure and forbid having any connection with them, be it by intermarriage or any kind of relationship, or by sitting, eating, and drinking with them, because thereby, they think, they would be polluted.[7]

MAP 12.2 South and Southeast Asia in the Thirteenth Century The extensive coastlines of South and Southeast Asia and the predictable monsoon winds aided seafaring in this region. Note the Strait of Malacca, through which most east-west sea trade passed.

After the initial period of raids and destruction of temples, the Muslim Turks came to an accommodation with the Hindus, who were classed as a **protected people**, like the Christians and Jews, and allowed to follow their religion. They had to pay a special tax but did not have to perform military service. Local chiefs and rajas were often allowed to remain in control of their domains as long as they paid tribute. Most Indians looked on the Muslim conquerors as a new ruling caste, capable of governing and taxing them but otherwise peripheral to their lives. The myriad castes largely governed themselves, isolating the newcomers.

Nevertheless, over the course of several centuries Islam gained a strong hold on north India, especially in the Indus Valley (modern Pakistan) and in Bengal at the mouth of the Ganges River (modern Bangladesh). Moreover, the sultanate seems to have had a positive effect on the economy. Much of the wealth confiscated

from temples was put to more productive use, and India's first truly large cities emerged. The Turks also were eager to employ skilled workers, giving new opportunities to low-caste manual and artisan labor.

The Muslim rulers were much more hostile to Buddhism than to Hinduism, seeing Buddhism as a competitive proselytizing religion. In 1193 a Turkish raiding party destroyed the great Buddhist university at Nalanda in Bihar. Buddhist monks were killed or forced to flee to Buddhist centers in Southeast Asia, Nepal, and Tibet. Buddhism, which had thrived for so long in peaceful and friendly competition with Hinduism, went into decline in its native land.

Hinduism, however, remained as strong as ever. South India was largely unaffected by these invasions, and traditional Hindu culture flourished there under native kings ruling small kingdoms. (See "Individuals in Society: Bhaskara the Teacher," page 351.) Temple-centered Hinduism flourished, as did devotional cults and mystical movements. This was a great age of religious art and architecture in India. Extraordinary temples covered with elaborate bas-relief were built in many areas. Sexual passion and the union of men and

• **protected people** The Muslim classification used for Hindus, Christians, and Jews; they were allowed to follow their religions but had to pay a special tax.

Individuals in Society

Bhaskara the Teacher

IN INDIA, AS IN MANY OTHER SOCIETIES, astronomy and mathematics were closely linked, and many of the most important mathematicians served their rulers as astronomers. Bhaskara (1114–ca. 1185) was such an astronomer-mathematician. For generations his Brahmin family had been astronomers at the Ujjain astronomical observatory in north-central India, and his father had written a popular book on astrology.

Bhaskara was a highly erudite man. A disciple wrote that he had thoroughly mastered eight books on grammar, six on medicine, six on philosophy, five on mathematics, and the four Vedas. Bhaskara eventually wrote six books on mathematics and mathematical astronomy. They deal with solutions to simple and quadratic equations and show his knowledge of trigonometry, including the sine table and relationships between different trigonometric functions, and even some of the basic elements of calculus. Earlier Indian mathematicians had explored the use of zero and negative numbers. Bhaskara developed these ideas further, in particular improving on the understanding of division by zero.

A court poet who centuries later translated Bhaskara's book titled *The Beautiful* explained its title by saying Bhaskara wrote it for his daughter named Beautiful (Lilavati) as consolation when his divination of the best time for her to marry went awry.

> **The observatory where Bhaskara worked in Ujjain today stands in ruins.** (Dinodia Photo Library)

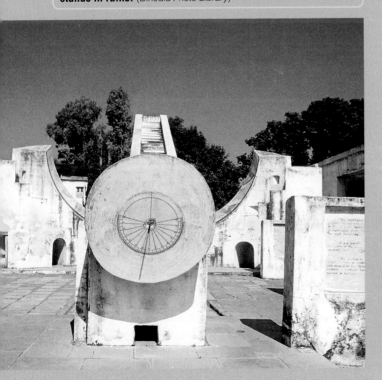

Whether Bhaskara did or did not write this book for his daughter, many of the problems he provides in it have a certain charm:

> On an expedition to seize his enemy's elephants, a king marched two yojanas the first day. Say, intelligent calculator, with what increasing rate of daily march did he proceed, since he reached his foe's city, a distance of eighty yojanas, in a week?*
>
> Out of a heap of pure lotus flower, a third part, a fifth, and a sixth were offered respectively to the gods Siva, Vishnu, and the Sun; and a quarter was presented to Bhavani. The remaining six lotuses were given to the venerable preceptor. Tell quickly the whole number of lotus.†
>
> If eight best variegated silk scarfs, measuring three cubits in breadth and eight in length, cost a hundred nishkas, say quickly, merchant, if thou understand trade, what a like scarf, three and a half cubits long and half a cubit wide will cost.‡

In the conclusion to *The Beautiful*, Bhaskara wrote:

> Joy and happiness is indeed ever increasing in this world for those who have *The Beautiful* clasped to their throats, decorated as the members are with neat reduction of fractions, multiplication, and involution, pure and perfect as are the solutions, and tasteful as is the speech which is exemplified.

Bhaskara had a long career. His first book on mathematical astronomy, written in 1150 when he was thirty-six, used mathematics to calculate solar and lunar eclipses or planetary conjunctions. Thirty-three years later he was still writing on the subject, this time providing simpler ways to solve problems encountered before. Bhaskara wrote his books in Sanskrit, already a literary language rather than a vernacular language, but even in his own day some of them were translated into other Indian languages.

Within a couple of decades of his death, a local ruler endowed an educational institution to study Bhaskara's works, beginning with his work on mathematical astronomy. In the text he had inscribed at the site, the ruler gave the names of Bhaskara's ancestors for six generations, as well as of his son and grandson, who had continued in his profession.

QUESTIONS FOR ANALYSIS

1. What might have been the advantages of making occupations like astronomer hereditary in India?
2. How does Bhaskara link joy and happiness to mathematical concepts?

*Quotations from Haran Chandra Banerji, *Colebrooke's Translation of the Lilanvanti*, 2d ed. (Calcutta: The Book Co., 1927), pp. 80–81, 30, 51, 200. The answer is that each day he must travel 22/7 yojanas farther than the day before.

†The answer is 120.

‡The answer, from the formula $x = (1 \times 7 \times 1 \times 100) / (8 \times 3 \times 8 \times 2 \times 2)$, is given in currencies smaller than the nishka: 14 drammas, 9 panas, 1 kakini, and 6⅔ cowry shells. (20 cowry shells = 1 kakini, 4 kakini = 1 pana, 16 panas = 1 dramma, and 16 drammas = 1 nishka.)

Kandariyâ Mahâdeva Hindu Temple Built around 1050 by a local king in central India, this is one of the best preserved Hindu temples from the medieval period. The main spire rises 100 feet, and the sides are decorated with more than 600 stone statues. (Yvan Travert/akg images)

women were frequently depicted, symbolically representing passion for and union with the temple god.

The Delhi Sultanate

In the twelfth century a new line of Turkish rulers arose in Afghanistan, led by Muhammad of Ghur (d. 1206). Muhammad captured Delhi and extended his control nearly throughout north India. When he fell to an assassin in 1206, one of his generals, the former slave Qutb-ud-din, seized the reins of power and established a government at Delhi, separate from the government in Afghanistan. This sultanate of Delhi lasted for three centuries, even though dynasties changed several times.

The North African Muslim world traveler Ibn Battuta (1304–1368; see page 254), served for several years as a judge at the court of one of the Delhi sultans. He praised the sultan for his insistence on the observance of ritual prayers and many acts of generosity to those in need, but he also considered the sultan overly violent. Here is just one of many examples he offered of how quick the sultan was to execute:

During the years of the famine, the Sultan had given orders to dig wells outside the capital, and have grain crops sown in those parts. He provided the cultivators with the seed, as well as with all that was necessary for cultivation in the way of money and supplies, and required them to cultivate these crops for the [royal] grain-store. When the jurist 'Afif al-Din heard of this, he said, "This crop will not produce what is hoped for." Some informer told the Sultan what he had said, so the Sultan jailed him, and said to him, "What reason have you to meddle with the government's business?" Some time later he released him, and as 'Afif al-Din went to his house he was met on the way by two friends of his, also jurists, who said to him, "Praise be to God for your release," to which our jurist replied, "Praise be to God who has delivered us from the evildoers." They then separated, but they had not reached their houses before this was reported to the Sultan, and he commanded all three to be fetched and brought before him. "Take out this fellow," he said, referring to 'Afif al-Din, "and cut off his head baldrickwise," that is, the head is cut off along with an arm and part of the chest, "and behead the other two." They said to him, "He deserves punishment, to be sure, for what he said, but in our case for what crime are you killing us?" He replied, "You heard what he said and did not disavow it, so you as good as agreed with it." So they were all put to death, God Most High have mercy on them.[8]

A major accomplishment of the Delhi sultanate was holding off the Mongols. Chinggis Khan and his troops entered the Indus Valley in 1221 in pursuit of the shah of Khurasan. The sultan wisely kept out of the way, and when Chinggis Khan left some troops in the area, the sultan made no attempt to challenge them. Two generations later, in 1299, a Mongol khan launched a campaign into India with two hundred thousand men, but the sultan of the time was able to defeat them. Two years later the Mongols returned and camped at Delhi for two months, but they eventually left without taking the sultan's fort. Another Mongol raid in 1306–1307 also was successfully repulsed.

Although the Turks by this time were highly cosmopolitan and no longer nomadic, they had retained their martial skills and understanding of steppe warfare. They were expert horsemen, and horses thrived in northwest India. The south and east of India, however, like the south of China, were less hospitable to raising horses, and generally people had to import them. In India's case, though, the climate of the south and east was well suited to elephants, which had been used as weapons of war in India since early times. Rulers in the northwest imported elephants from more tropical regions. The Delhi sultanate is said to have had as many as one thousand war elephants at its height.

During the fourteenth century, however, the Delhi sultanate was in decline and proved unable to ward off the armies of Timur (see page 345), who took Delhi in 1398. Timur's chronicler reported that when the troops drew up for battle outside Delhi, the sultanate had 10,000 horsemen, 20,000 foot soldiers, and 120 war elephants. Though alarmed at the sight of the elephants, Timur's men dug trenches to trap them and shot at their drivers. The sultan fled, leaving the city to surrender. Timur took as booty all the elephants, loading them with treasures seized from the city. Ruy Gonzalez de Clavijo, an ambassador from the king of Castile (now part of Spain), who arrived in Samarkand in 1403, was greatly impressed by these well-trained elephants. "When all the elephants together charged abreast, it seemed as though the solid earth itself shook at their onrush," he observed, noting that he thought each elephant was worth a thousand foot soldiers in battle.[9]

Timur's invasion left a weakened sultanate. The Delhi sultanate endured under different rulers until 1526, when it was conquered by the Mughals, a Muslim dynasty that would rule over most of northern Indian from the sixteenth into the nineteenth century.

Life in Medieval India

Local institutions played a much larger role in the lives of the overwhelming majority of people in medieval India than did the state. Craft guilds oversaw conditions of work and trade; local councils handled law and

> **"**When all the elephants together charged abreast, it seemed as though the solid earth itself shook at their onrush.**"**
>
> **RUY GONZALEZ DE CLAVIJO**

order at the town or village level; and local castes gave members a sense of belonging and identity.

Like peasant societies elsewhere, including in China, Japan, and Southeast Asia, agricultural life in India ordinarily meant village life. The average farmer worked a small plot of land outside the village. All the family members pooled their resources — human, animal, and material — under the direction of the head of the family. These joint efforts strengthened family solidarity.

The agricultural year began with spring plowing. The traditional plow, drawn by two oxen wearing yokes and collars, had an iron-tipped share and a handle with which the farmer guided it. Rice, the most important and popular grain, was sown at the beginning of the long rainy season. Beans, lentils, and peas were the farmer's friends, for they grew during the cold season and were harvested in the spring, when fresh food was scarce. Cereal crops such as wheat, barley, and millet provided carbohydrates and other nutrients. Sugar cane was another important crop. Some families cultivated vegetables, spices, fruit trees, and flowers in their gardens.

Farmers also raised livestock. Most highly valued were cattle, which were raised for plowing and milk, hides, and horns, but Hindus did not slaughter them for meat. Like the Islamic and Jewish prohibition on the consumption of pork, the eating of beef was forbidden among Hindus.

Local craftsmen and tradesmen lived and worked in specific parts of a town or village. They were frequently organized into guilds, with guild heads and guild rules. The textile industries were particularly well developed. Silk (which had entered India from China), linen, wool, and cotton fabrics were produced in large quantities and traded throughout India and beyond. The cutting and polishing of precious stones was another industry associated closely with foreign trade.

In the cities shops were open to the street; families lived on the floors above. The busiest tradesmen dealt in milk and cheese, oil, spices, and perfumes. Equally prominent but disreputable were tavern keepers. Indian taverns were haunts of criminals and con artists, and in the worst of them fighting was as common as drinking. In addition to these tradesmen and merchants, a host of peddlers shuffled through towns and villages selling everything from needles to freshly cut flowers.

The Chinese Buddhist pilgrim Faxian (FAH-shen), during his six years in Gupta India, described it as a

Men at Work This stone frieze from the Buddhist stupa in Sanchi depicts Indian men doing a variety of everyday jobs. Although the stone was carved to convey religious ideas, we can use it as a source for such details of daily life as the sort of clothing men wore while working and how they carried loads. (Dinodia Photo Library)

peaceful land where people could move about freely without needing passports and where the upper castes were vegetarians. He was the first to make explicit reference to "untouchables," remarking that they hovered around the margins of Indian society, carrying gongs to warn upper-caste people of their polluting presence.

In this period the caste system reached its mature form. Within the broad division into the four *varna* (strata) of Brahmin, Kshatriya, Vaishya, and Shudra (see page 71), the population was subdivided into numerous castes, or **jati**. Each caste had a proper occupation. In addition, its members married only within the caste and ate only with other members. Members of high-status castes feared pollution from contact with lower-caste individuals and had to undertake rituals of purification to remove the taint.

Eventually Indian society comprised perhaps as many as three thousand castes. Each caste had its own governing body, which enforced the rules of the caste. Those incapable of living up to the rules were expelled,

becoming outcastes. These unfortunates lived hard lives, performing tasks that others considered unclean or lowly.

Villages were often walled, as in north China and the Middle East. The streets were unpaved, and the rainy season turned them into a muddy soup. Cattle and sheep roamed as freely as people. Some families kept pets, such as cats or parrots. Half-wild mongooses served as effective protection against snakes. The pond outside the village was its main source of water and also a spawning ground for fish, birds, and mosquitoes. Women drawing water frequently encountered water buffalo wallowing in the shallows. After the farmers returned from the fields in the evening, the village gates were closed until morning.

The life of the well-to-do is described in the *Kamasutra* (Book on the Art of Love). Comfortable surroundings provided a place for men to enjoy poetry, painting, and music in the company of like-minded friends. Courtesans well-trained in entertaining men added to the pleasures of wealthy men. A man who had more than one wife was advised not to let one wife speak ill of the other and to try to keep each of them happy by taking them to gardens, giving them presents, telling them secrets, and loving them well.

- **jati** The thousands of Indian castes.
- **sati** A practice whereby a high-caste Hindu woman would throw herself on her husband's funeral pyre.

For all members of Indian society regardless of caste, marriage and family were the focus of life. As in China, the family was under the authority of the eldest male, who might take several wives, and ideally sons stayed home with their parents after they married. The family affirmed its solidarity by the religious ritual of honoring its dead ancestors — a ritual that linked the living and the dead, much like ancestor worship in China (see pages 95–96). People commonly lived in extended families: grandparents, uncles and aunts, cousins, and nieces and nephews all lived together in the same house or compound.

Children were viewed as a great source of happiness. The poet Kalidasa described children as the greatest joy of their father's life:

> With their teeth half-shown in causeless laughter,
> and their efforts at talking so sweetly uncertain,
> when children ask to sit on his lap
> a man is blessed, even by the dirt on their bodies.[10]

Children in poor households worked as soon as they were able. Children in wealthier households faced the age-old irritations of learning reading, writing, and arithmetic. Less attention was paid to daughters than to sons, though in more prosperous families they were often literate. Because girls who had lost their virginity could seldom hope to find good husbands and thus would become financial burdens and social disgraces to their families, daughters were customarily married as children, with consummation delayed until they reached puberty.

A wife was expected to have no life apart from her husband. A widow was expected to lead the hard life of the ascetic, sleeping on the ground; eating only one simple meal a day, without meat, wine, salt, or honey; wearing plain undyed clothes without jewelry; and shaving her head. She was viewed as inauspicious to everyone but her children, and she did not attend family festivals. Among high-caste Hindus, a widow would be praised for throwing herself on her husband's funeral pyre. Buddhist sects objected to this practice, called **sati**, but some Hindu religious authorities declared that by self-immolation a widow could expunge both her own and her husband's sins, so that both would enjoy eternal bliss in Heaven.

Within the home the position of a wife often depended on her own intelligence and strength of character. Wives were supposed to be humble, cheerful, and diligent even toward worthless husbands. As in other patriarchal societies, however, occasionally a woman ruled the household. For women who did not want to accept the strictures of married life, the main way out was to join a Buddhist or Jain religious community (see pages 190–191).

Southeast Asia, the Pacific Islands, and the Growth of Maritime Trade

☐ How did states develop along the maritime trade routes of Southeast Asia and beyond?

Much as Roman culture spread to northern Europe and Chinese culture spread to Korea, Japan, and Vietnam, in the first millennium C.E. Indian learning, technology, and material culture spread to Southeast Asia, both mainland and insular. The spread of Indian culture was facilitated by the growth of maritime trade, but this interchange did not occur uniformly, and by 1400 there were still isolated societies in this region, most notably in the Pacific islands east of Indonesia.

Southeast Asia is a tropical region that is more like India than China, with temperatures hovering around 80°F and rain falling dependably throughout the year. The topography of mainland Southeast Asia is marked by north-south mountain ranges separated by river valleys. It was easy for people to migrate south along these rivers but harder for them to cross the heavily forested mountains that divided the region into areas that had limited contact with each other. The indigenous population was originally mostly Malay, but migrations over the centuries brought many other peoples, including speakers of Austro-Asiatic (such as Vietnamese and Cambodian), Austronesian (such as Malay and Polynesian), and Sino-Tibetan-Burmese (such as Burmese and possibly Thai) languages, some of whom moved to the islands offshore and farther into the Pacific Ocean.

State Formation and Indian Influences

Southeast Asia was long a crossroads. Traders from China, India, Africa, and Europe either passed through the region when traveling from the Indian to the Pacific Ocean, or came for its resources, notably spices. (See "Global Trade: Spices," page 356.)

The northern part of modern Vietnam was under Chinese political control off and on from the second century B.C.E. to the tenth century C.E. (see pages 196–197), but Indian influence was of much greater significance for the rest of Southeast Asia. The first state to appear in historical records, called Funan by Chinese visitors, had its capital in southern Vietnam. In the first to sixth centuries C.E. Funan extended its control over much of Indochina and the Malay Peninsula. Merchants from northwest India would offload their goods and carry them across the narrowest part of the Malay Peninsula. The ports of Funan offered food and

Global Trade

Spices

were a major reason from ancient times on for both Europeans and Chinese to trade with South and Southeast Asia. Pepper, nutmeg, cloves, cinnamon, and other spices were in high demand not only because they could be used to flavor food but also because they were thought to have positive pharmacological properties. Unlike other highly desired products of India and farther east—such as sugar, cotton, rice, and silk—no way was found to produce the spices close to where they were in demand. Because of the location where these spices were produced, this trade was from earliest times largely a maritime trade conducted through a series of middlemen. The spices were transported from where they were grown to nearby ports, and from there to major entrepôts (trading centers), where merchants would take them in many different directions.

Two types of pepper grew in India and Southeast Asia. Black pepper is identical to our familiar peppercorns. "Long pepper," from a related plant, was hotter. The Mediterranean world imported its pepper from India; China imported it from Southeast Asia. After the discovery of the New World, the importation of long pepper declined, as the chili pepper found in Mexico was at least as spicy and grew well in Europe and China.

By Greek and Roman times trade in pepper was substantial. According to the Greek geographer Strabo (64 B.C.E.–24 C.E.), 120 ships a year made the trip to India to acquire pepper, the round

MAP 12.3 The Spice Trade, ca. 100 B.C.E.–1500 C.E.

trip taking a year because sailors had to wait for the monsoon winds to shift direction. Pliny in about 77 C.E. complained that the Roman Empire wasted fifty million sesterces per year on long pepper and white and black pepper combined.

Cloves and nutmeg entered the repertoire of spices somewhat later than pepper. They are interesting because they could be grown in only a handful of small islands in the eastern part of the Indonesian archipelago. Merchants in China, India, Arab lands, and Europe got them through intermediaries and did not know where they were grown. An Arab source from about 1000 C.E. reported that cloves came from an island near India that had a Valley of Cloves, and that they were acquired by a silent barter. The sailors would lay the items they were willing to trade out on the beach, and the next morning they would find cloves in their place.

The demand for these spices in time encouraged Chinese, Indian, and Arab seamen to make the trip to the Strait of Malacca or east Java. Malay seamen in small craft such as outrigger canoes would bring the spices the thousand or more

A fifteenth-century Italian painter depicted a bag of cinnamon bark nearly as large as the merchant holding it. (Biblioteca Estense, Modena, Italy/The Bridgeman Art Library)

miles to the major ports where foreign merchants would purchase them. This trade was important to the prosperity of the Srivijaya kingdom. The trade was so profitable, however, that it also attracted pirates.

In the Mongol era travelers like Marco Polo, Ibn Battuta, and Odoric of Pordenone (in modern Italy) reported on the cultivation and marketing of spices in the various places they visited. Ibn Battuta described pepper plants as vines planted to grow up coconut palms. He also reported seeing the trunks of cinnamon trees floated down rivers in India. Odoric reported that pepper was picked like grapes from groves so huge it would take eighteen days to walk around them. Marco Polo referred to the 7,459 islands in the China Sea that local mariners could navigate and that produced a great variety of spices as well as aromatic wood. He also reported that spices, including pepper, nutmeg, and cloves, could be acquired at the great island of Java, perhaps not understanding that they had often been shipped from the innumerable small islands to Java.

Gaining direct access to the spices of the East was one of the motivations behind Christopher Columbus's voyages. Not long after, Portuguese sailors did reach India by sailing around Africa, and soon the Dutch were competing with them for control of the spice trade and setting up rival trading posts. Pepper was soon successfully planted in other tropical places, including Brazil. India, however, has remained the largest exporter of spices to this day.

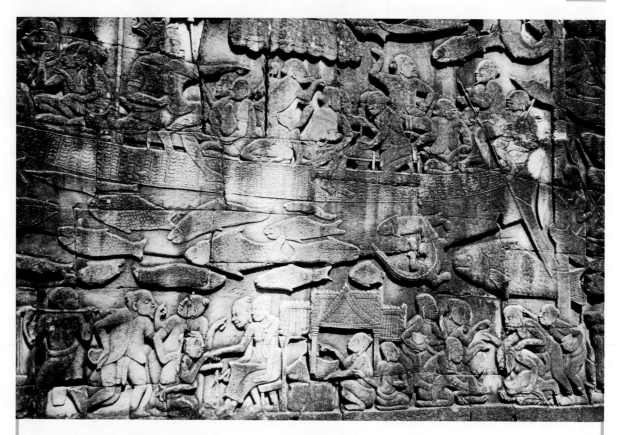

◻ Picturing the Past

Bayan Relief, Angkor Among the many relief sculptures at the temples of Angkor are depictions of royal processions, armies at war, trade, cooking, cockfighting, and other scenes of everyday life. In the relief shown here, the boats and fish convey something of the significance of the sea to life in Southeast Asia.
(Robert Wilson, photographer)

READING THE IMAGE Find the boat. What do the people on it seem to be doing? What fish and animals do you see in the picture? Can you find the alligator eating a fish?

CONNECTIONS Why would a ruler devote so many resources to decorating the walls of a temple? Why include scenes like this one?

lodging to the merchants as they waited for the winds to shift to continue their voyages. Brahmin priests and Buddhist monks from India settled along with the traders, serving the Indian population and attracting local converts. Rulers often invited Indian priests and monks to serve under them, using them as foreign experts knowledgeable about law, government, architecture, and other fields.

Sixth-century Chinese sources report that the Funan king lived in a multistory palace and the common people lived in houses built on piles with roofs of bamboo leaves. The king rode around on an elephant, but narrow boats measuring up to ninety feet long

were a more important means of transportation. The people enjoyed both cockfighting and pig fighting. Instead of drawing water from wells, as the Chinese did, they made pools, from which dozens of nearby families would draw water.

After the decline of Funan, maritime trade continued to grow, and petty kingdoms appeared in many places. Indian traders frequently established small settlements, generally located on the coast. Contact with the local populations led to intermarriage and the creation of hybrid cultures. Local rulers often adopted Indian customs and values, embraced Hinduism and Buddhism, and learned **Sanskrit**, India's classical literary language. Sanskrit gave different peoples a common mode of written expression, much as Chinese did in East Asia and Latin did in Europe.

When Indian traders, migrants, and adventurers entered mainland Southeast Asia, they encountered both

• **Sanskrit** India's classical literary language.
• **Srivijaya** A maritime empire that held the Strait of Malacca and the waters around Sumatra, Borneo, and Java.

long-settled peoples and migrants moving southward from the frontiers of China. As in other such extensive migrations, the newcomers fought one another as often as they fought the native populations. In 939 the north Vietnamese became independent of China and extended their power southward along the coast of present-day Vietnam. The Thais had long lived in what is today southwest China and north Burma. In the eighth century the Thai tribes united in a confederacy and expanded northward against Tang China. Like China, however, the Thai confederacy fell to the Mongols in 1253. Still farther west another tribal people, the Burmese, migrated to the area of modern Burma in the eighth century. They also established a state, which they ruled from their capital, Pagan, and came into contact with India and Sri Lanka.

The most important mainland state was the Khmer (kuh-MAIR) Empire of Cambodia (802–1432), which controlled the heart of the region. The Khmers were indigenous to the area. Their empire eventually extended south to the sea and the northeast Malay Peninsula. Indian influence was pervasive; the impressive temple complex at Angkor Wat built in the early twelfth century was dedicated to the Hindu god Vishnu. Social organization, however, was modeled not on the Indian caste system but on indigenous traditions of social hierarchy. A large part of the population was of slave status, many descended from non-Khmer mountain tribes defeated by the Khmers. Generally successful in a long series of wars with the Vietnamese, the Khmers reached the peak of their power in 1219 and then gradually declined.

The Srivijaya Maritime Trade Empire

Far different from these land-based states was the maritime empire of **Srivijaya**, based on the island of Sumatra in modern Indonesia. From the sixth century on, it held the important Strait of Malacca, through which most of the sea traffic between China and India passed. This state, held together as much by alliances as by direct rule, was in many ways like the Gupta state of the same period in India, securing its prominence and binding its vassals and allies through its splendor and the promise of riches through trade.

Much as the Korean and Japanese rulers adapted Chinese models (see pages 199–201), the Srivijayan rulers drew on Indian traditions to justify their rule and organize their state. The Sanskrit writing system was used for government documents, and Indians were often employed as priests, scribes, and administrators.

Angkor Wat Temple The Khmers built several stone temple complexes at Angkor. This aerial view catches something of the scale of the largest of these complexes, Angkor Wat. (Roy Garner/Alamy)

Using Sanskrit overcame the barriers raised by the many different native languages of the region. Indian mythology took hold, as did Indian architecture and sculpture. Kings and their courts, the first to embrace Indian culture, consciously spread it to their subjects. The Chinese Buddhist monk Yixing (d. 727) stopped at Srivijaya for six months in 671 on his way to India and for four years on his return journey. He found a thousand monks there, some of whom helped him translate Sanskrit texts.

After several centuries of prosperity, Srivijaya suffered a stunning blow in 1025. The Chola state in south India launched a large naval raid and captured the Srivijayan king and capital. Unable to hold their gains, the Indians retreated, but the Srivijaya Empire never regained its vigor.

During the era of the Srivijayan kingdom, other kingdoms flourished as well in island Southeast Asia. Borobudur, the magnificent Buddhist temple complex, was begun under patronage of Javan rulers in around 780. This stone monument depicts the ten tiers of Buddhist cosmology. When pilgrims made the three-mile-long winding ascent, they passed numerous sculpted reliefs depicting the journey from ignorance to enlightenment.

Buddhism became progressively more dominant in Southeast Asia after 800. Mahayana Buddhism became important in Srivijaya and Vietnam, but Theravada Buddhism, closer to the original Buddhism of early India, became the dominant form in the rest of mainland Southeast Asia. Buddhist missionaries from India and Sri Lanka played a prominent role in these developments. Local converts continued the process by making pilgrimages to India and Sri Lanka to worship and to observe Indian life for themselves.

The Spread of Indian Culture in Comparative Perspective

The social, cultural, and political systems developed in India, China, and Rome all had enormous impact on neighboring peoples whose cultures were originally not as technologically advanced. Some of the mechanisms for cultural spread were similar in all three cases, but differences were important as well.

In the case of Rome and both Han and Tang China, strong states directly ruled outlying regions, bringing their civilizations with them. India's states, even its largest empires, such as the Mauryan and Gupta, did not have comparable bureaucratic reach. Outlying areas tended to be in the hands of local lords who had consented to recognize the overlordship of the stronger state. Moreover, most of the time India was politically divided.

The expansion of Indian culture into Southeast Asia thus came not from conquest and extending direct political control, but from the extension of trading networks, with missionaries following along. This made it closer to the way Japan adopted features of Chinese culture, often through the intermediary of Korea. In both cases, the cultural exchange was largely voluntary, as the Japanese or Southeast Asians sought to adopt more up-to-date technologies (such as writing) or were persuaded of the truth of religious ideas they learned from foreigners.

The Settlement of the Pacific Islands

Through most of Eurasia, societies became progressively less isolated over time. But in 1400 there still remained many isolated societies, especially in the islands east of modern Indonesia. As discussed in Chapter 1, *Homo sapiens* began settling the western Pacific islands very early, reaching Australia by 50,000 years ago and New Guinea by 35,000 years ago. The process did not stop there, however. The ancient Austronesians (speakers of Austronesian languages) were skilled mariners who used double-canoes and brought pottery, the root vegetable taro, pigs, and chickens to numerous islands of the Pacific in subsequent centuries, generally following the coasts. Their descendants, the Polynesians, learned how to sail into the open ocean with only the stars, currents, wind patterns, paths of birds, and perhaps paths of whales and dolphins to help them navigate. They reached Tahiti and the Marquesas Islands in the central Pacific by about 200 C.E. Undoubtedly, seafarers were sometimes blown off their intended course, but communities would not have developed unless the original groups had included women as well as men, so probably in many cases they were looking for new places to live.

After reaching the central Pacific, Polynesians continued to fan out, in some cases traveling a thousand or more miles away. They reached the Hawaiian Islands in about 300 C.E., Easter Island in perhaps 1000, and New Zealand not until about 1000–1300. There even were groups who sailed west, eventually settling in Madagascar between 200 and 500.

In the more remote islands, such as Hawai'i, Easter Island, and New Zealand, the societies that developed were limited by the small range of domesticated plants and animals that the settlers brought with them and those that were indigenous to the place. Easter Island is perhaps the most extreme case. Only 15 miles wide at its widest point (only 63 square miles in total area), it is 1,300 miles from the nearest inhabited island (Pitcairn) and 2,240 miles from the coast of South America. At some point there was communication with South America, as sweet potatoes originally from there made their way to Easter Island. The community that developed on the island raised chickens and cultivated sweet potatoes, taro, and sugarcane. The inhabitants also engaged in deep-sea fishing, catching dolphins and tuna. Their tools were made of stone, wood, or bone.

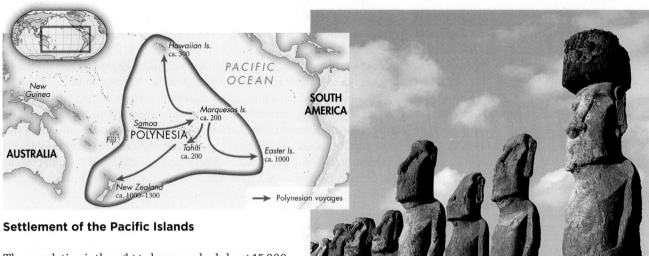

Settlement of the Pacific Islands

The population is thought to have reached about 15,000 at Easter Island's most prosperous period, which began about 1200 C.E. It was then that its people devoted remarkable efforts to fashioning and erecting the large stone statues that still dot the island.

What led the residents of such a small island to erect more than eight hundred statues, most weighing around ten tons and standing twenty to seventy feet tall? When the first Europeans arrived in 1722, no statues had been erected for several generations, and the local residents explained them as representing ancestors. One common theory is that they were central to the islanders' religion and that rival clans competed with each other to erect the most impressive statues. The effort they had to expend to carve them with stone tools, move them to the chosen site, and erect them would have been formidable.

After its heyday, Easter Island suffered severe environmental stress with the decline of its forests. Whether the rats that came with the original settlers ate too many of the trees' seeds or the islanders cut down too many of the trees to transport the stone statues, the impact of deforestation was severe. The islanders could not make boats to fish in the ocean, and bird colonies shrank, as nesting areas decreased, also reducing the food supply. Scholars still disagree on how much weight to give the many different elements that contributed to a decline in the prosperity of Easter Island from the age when the statues were erected.

Easter Island Statues Archaeologists have excavated and restored many of Easter Island's huge statues, which display remarkable stylistic consistency, with the head disproportionately large and the legs not visible. (JP De Mann/Robert Harding World Imagery)

Certainly, early settlers of an island could have drastic impact on its ecology. When Polynesians first reached New Zealand, they found large birds up to ten feet tall. They hunted them so eagerly that within a century the birds had all but disappeared. Hunting seals and sea lions also led to their rapid depletion. But the islands of New Zealand were much larger than Easter Island, and in time the Maori (the indigenous people of New Zealand) found more sustainable ways to feed themselves, depending more and more on agriculture.

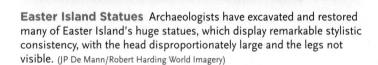

CONNECTIONS

The societies of Eurasia became progressively more connected to each other during the centuries discussed in this chapter. One element promoting connection was the military superiority of the nomadic warriors of the steppe, first the Turks, then the Mongols, who conquered many of the settled civilizations near them. Through conquest they introduced their culture and, in the case of the Turks, the religion of Islam to India.

Another element was maritime trade, which connected all the societies of the Indian Ocean and East Asia. As the Mongol Empire declined, maritime trading routes became an even more important part of the African, European, and Asian economic integration, with long-lasting consequences for the Afro-Eurasian trading world (see Chapter 16). Maritime trade was also one of the key elements in the spread of Indian culture to both mainland and insular Southeast Asia. Other elements connecting these societies included Sanskrit as a language of administration and missionaries who brought both Hinduism and Buddhism far beyond their homelands. Some societies did remain isolated, probably none more than the remote islands of the Pacific, such as Hawai'i, Easter Island, and New Zealand.

East Asia was a key element in both the empires created by nomadic horsemen and the South Asian maritime trading networks. As discussed in Chapter 13, before East Asia had to cope with the rise of the Mongols, it experienced one of its most prosperous periods, during which China, Korea, and Japan became more distinct culturally. China's economy boomed during the Song Dynasty, and the scholar-official class, defined through the civil service examination, came more and more to dominate culture. In Korea and Japan, by contrast, aristocrats and military men gained ascendancy. Although China, Korea, and Japan all drew on both Confucian and Buddhist teachings, they ended up with elites as distinct as the Chinese scholar-official, the Korean aristocrat, and the Japanese samurai.

CHAPTER REVIEW

KEY TERMS

nomads (p. 332)
steppe (p. 332)
yurts (p. 335)
Chinggis Khan (p. 337)
khanates (p. 340)
tax-farming (p. 344)

protected people (p. 350)
jati (p. 354)
sati (p. 355)
Sanskrit (p. 358)
Srivijaya (p. 359)

□ **What aspects of nomadic life gave the nomads of Central Asia military advantages over nearby settled civilizations? (p. 332)**

The nomadic pastoral societies that stretched across Eurasia had the great military advantage of being able to raise horses in large numbers and support themselves from their flocks. Their mastery of the horse and mounted archery allowed them repeatedly to overawe or conquer their neighbors. On military campaigns, Mongol horsemen were able to travel without stopping for days. Nomadic pastoralists generally were organized on the basis of clans and tribes that selected chiefs for their military talent. Much of the time these tribes fought with each other, but several times in history leaders formed larger confederations capable of coordinated attacks on cities and towns. From the fifth to the twelfth centuries the most successful nomadic groups on the Eurasian steppes were Turks of one sort or another.

□ **How did Chinggis Khan and his successors conquer much of Eurasia, and how did the Mongol conquests change the regions affected? (p. 336)**

In the early thirteenth century, through his charismatic leadership and military genius, Chinggis Khan was able to lead victorious armies from one side of Eurasia to another. To avoid tribal feuding, he gave his army a non-tribal structure. He rewarded loyalty and displays of courage, but he could be merciless to those who opposed him. His initial conquests were quite destructive, with the inhabitants of many cities enslaved or killed. Those who opened their city gates and submitted without fighting could become allies and retain local power, but those who resisted faced

the prospect of mass slaughter. After the empire was divided into four khanates ruled by different lines of Chinggis's descendants, more stable forms of government were developed. The Mongols gave important positions to people willing to serve them faithfully, and they did not try to change the cultures or religions of the countries they conquered. In Mongolia and China the Mongol rulers welcomed those learned in all religions. In Central Asia and Persia the Mongol khans converted to Islam and gave it the support earlier rulers there had done.

□ **How did the Mongol conquests facilitate the spread of ideas, religions, inventions, and diseases? (p. 345)**

For a century the Mongol Empire fostered unprecedented East-West contact. The Mongols encouraged trade and often moved craftsmen and other specialists from one place to another. Missionaries were tolerated, as were all religions. As more Europeans made their way east than ever before, Chinese inventions such as printing and the compass made their way west. Because Europe was further behind in 1200, it benefited most from the spread of technical and scientific ideas. Diseases also spread, including the Black Death, carried by fleas and rats that found their way into the goods of merchants and other travelers.

☐ What was the result of India's encounters with Turks, Mongols, and Islam? (p. 347)

India was invaded by the Mongols, but not conquered. After the fall of the Gupta Empire in about 480, India was for the next millennium ruled by small kingdoms, which allowed regional cultures to flourish. The north and northwest were frequently raided by Turks from Afghanistan or Central Asia, and for several centuries Muslim Turks ruled a state in north India called the Delhi sultanate. Over time Islam gained adherents throughout South Asia. Hinduism continued to flourish, but Buddhism went into decline.

☐ How did states develop along the maritime trade routes of Southeast Asia and beyond? (p. 355)

Throughout the medieval period India continued to be the center of a very active seaborne trade, and this trade helped carry Indian ideas and practices to Southeast Asia. Local rulers used experts from India to establish strong states, such as the Khmer kingdom in modern Cambodia and the Srivijaya kingdom in modern Malaysia and Indonesia. Buddhism became the dominant religion throughout the region, though Hinduism also played an important role. Indian influences did not spread uniformly, and the Pacific islands east of Indonesia remained isolated culturally for centuries.

SUGGESTED READING

Abu-Lughod, Janet L. *Before European Hegemony: The World System A.D. 1250–1350*. 1989. Examines the period of Mongol domination from a global perspective.

Ali, Daud. *Courtly Culture and Political Life in Early Medieval India*. 2004. Explores the growth of royal households and the development of a courtly worldview in India from 350 to 1200.

Beckwith, Christopher I. *Empires of the Silk Road: A History of Central Eurasia from the Bronze Age to the Present*. 2009. Makes Central Asia the center of Eurasian history.

Chaudhuri, K. N. *Asia Before Europe*. 1990. Discusses the economy and civilization of cultures within the basin of the Indian Ocean.

Di Cosmo, Nicola, Allen J. Frank, and Peter B. Golden. *The Cambridge History of Inner Asia: The Chinggisid Age*. 2009. Authoritative account of the Mongols and their successors in Central Asia.

Findley, Carter Vaughn. *The Turks in World History*. 2005. Covers both the early Turks and the connections between the Turks and the Mongols.

Fischer, Steven Roger. *A History of the Pacific Islands*. 2002. A broad-ranging history, from early settlement to modern times.

Franke, Herbert, and Denis Twitchett, eds. *The Cambridge History of China*, vol. 6, *Alien Regimes and Border States*. 1994. Clear and thoughtful accounts of the Mongols and their predecessors in East Asia.

Jackson, Peter. *The Delhi Sultanate*. 2003. Provides a close examination of north India in the thirteenth and fourteenth centuries.

Jackson, Peter. *The Mongols and the West, 1221–1410*. 2005. A close examination of many different types of connections between the Mongols and both Europe and the Islamic lands.

Lane, George. *Daily Life in the Mongol Empire*. 2006. Treats many topics, including food, health, dwellings, women, and folktales.

Liberman, Victor. *Strange Parallels: Southeast Asia in Global Context, c. 800–1830*, 2 vols. 2003, 2009. Ambitious and challenging effort to see Southeast Asia as a part of Eurasia.

Ratchnevsky, Paul. *Genghis Khan: His Life and Legacy*. 1992. A reliable account by a leading Mongolist.

Rossabi, Morris. *Khubilai Khan: His Life and Times*. 1988. Provides a lively account of the life of one of the most important Mongol rulers.

Shaffer, Lynda. *Maritime Southeast Asia to 1500*. 1996. A short account of early Southeast Asia from a world history perspective.

NOTES

1. Trans. in Denis Sinor, "The Establishment and Dissolution of the Türk Empire," in *The Cambridge History of Early Inner Asia*, ed. Denis Sinor (Cambridge: Cambridge University Press, 1990), p. 307.
2. Manuel Komroff, ed., *Contemporaries of Marco Polo* (New York: Dorset Press, 1989), p. 65.
3. Ibid.
4. *The Travels of Marco Polo, the Venetian*, ed. Manuel Komroff (New York: Boni and Liveright, 1926), pp. 93–94.
5. Cited in John Larner, *Marco Polo and the Discovery of the World* (New Haven, Conn.: Yale University Press, 1999), p. 22.
6. Quoted in A. L. Basham, *The Wonder That Was India*, 2d ed. (New York: Grove Press, 1959), p. 420. Copyright © A. L. Basham. All quotations from this work are reprinted by permission of Pan Macmillan, London, and Namita Catherine Basham.
7. Edward C. Sachau, *Alberuni's India*, vol. 1 (London: Kegan Paul, 1910), pp. 19–20, slightly modified.
8. H. A. R. Gibb, *The Travels of Ibn Battuta* (Cambridge: Cambridge University Press for the Hakluyt Society, 1971), pp. 700–701. Reprinted by permission of David Higham Associates on behalf of the Hakluyt Society.
9. Guy le Strang, trans., *Clavijo, Embassy to Tamerlane, 1403–1406* (London: Routledge, 1928), pp. 265–266.
10. Quoted in Basham, *The Wonder That Was India*, p. 161.

For practice quizzes and other study tools, visit the **Online Study Guide** at bedfordstmartins.com/mckayworld.

For primary sources from this period, see *Sources of World Societies*, **Second Edition**.

For Web sites, images, and documents related to topics in this chapter, visit **Make History** at bedfordstmartins.com/mckayworld.

• First Song Emperor China enjoyed a period of great cultural and economic development under the Song Dynasty, whose founder, Taizu, is depicted in this painting. (The Granger Collection, New York)

During the six centuries between 800 and 1400, East Asia was the most advanced region of the world. For several centuries the Chinese economy had grown spectacularly, and China's methods of production were highly advanced in fields as diverse as rice cultivation, the production of iron and steel, and the printing of books. Philosophy and the arts all flourished. China's system of government was also advanced for its time. In the Song period the principle that the government should be in the hands of highly educated scholar-officials, selected through competitive written civil service examinations, became well established. Song China's great wealth and sophisticated government did not give it military advantage, however, and in this period China had to pay tribute to militarily more powerful northern neighbors, the Khitans, the Jurchens, and finally the Mongols, who conquered all of China in 1279.

During the previous millennium basic elements of Chinese culture had spread beyond China's borders, creating the East Asian cultural sphere based on the use of Chinese as the language of civilization. Beginning around 800, however, the pendulum shifted toward cultural differentiation as Japan, Korea, and China developed in distinctive ways. In both Korea and Japan, for several centuries court aristocrats were dominant both politically and culturally, and then aristocrats lost out to generals with power in the countryside. By 1200 Japan was dominated by warriors — known as samurai — whose ethos was quite unlike China's literati elite. In both Korea and Japan, Buddhism retained a very strong hold, one of the ties that continued to link the countries of East Asia. In addition, China and Korea both had to deal with the same menacing neighbors to the north. Even Japan had to mobilize its resources to fend off two seaborne Mongol attacks. •

States and Cultures in East Asia

800-1400

The Medieval Chinese Economic Revolution, 800–1100
□ What made possible the expansion of the Chinese economy, and what were the outcomes of this economic growth?

China During the Song and Yuan Dynasties, 960–1368
□ How did the civil service examinations and the scholar-official class shape Chinese society and culture, and what impact did the Mongol conquest have on them?

Korea Under the Koryŏ Dynasty, 935–1392
□ How did Korean society and culture develop in an age when its northern neighbors were Khitans, Jurchens, and Mongols?

Japan's Heian Period, 794–1185
□ How did the Heian form of government contribute to the cultural flowering of Japan in the period?

The Samurai and the Kamakura Shogunate, 1185–1333
□ What were the causes and consequences of military rule in Japan?

The Medieval Chinese Economic Revolution, 800–1100

□ What made possible the expansion of the Chinese economy, and what were the outcomes of this economic growth?

Chinese historians traditionally viewed dynasties as following a standard cyclical pattern. Founders were vigorous men able to recruit capable followers to serve as officials and generals. Externally they would extend China's borders; internally they would bring peace. They would collect low but fairly assessed taxes. Over time, however, emperors born in the palace would get used to luxury and lack the founders' strength and wisdom. Families with wealth or political power would find ways to avoid taxes, forcing the government to impose heavier taxes on the poor. As a result, impoverished peasants would flee; the morale of those in the government and armies would decline; and the dynasty would find itself able neither to maintain internal peace nor to defend its borders.

Viewed in terms of this theory of the **dynastic cycle**, by 800 the Tang Dynasty (see pages 193–196) was in decline. It had ruled China for nearly two centuries, and its high point was in the past. A massive rebellion had wracked it in the mid-eighth century, and the Uighur Turks and Tibetans were menacing its borders. Many of the centralizing features of the government had been abandoned, with power falling more and more to regional military governors.

Historically, Chinese political theorists always assumed that a strong, centralized government was better than a weak one or than political division, but if anything the Tang toward the end of its dynastic cycle seems to have been both intellectually and economically more vibrant than the early Tang had been. Less control from the central government seems to have stimulated trade and economic growth.

A government census conducted in 742 shows that China's population was still approximately 50 million, very close to what it had been in 2 C.E. Over the next three centuries, with the expansion of wet-field rice cultivation in central and south China, the country's food supply steadily increased, and so did its popula-

Chinese Paper Money Chinese paper currency indicated the unit of currency and the date and place of issue. The Mongols continued the use of paper money, as this note from the Mongol period attests. (© Cultural Relics Press)

tion, which reached 100 million by 1100. China was certainly the largest country in the world at the time; its population probably already exceeded that of all the Islamic countries of the time or that of all the countries of Europe put together.

Agricultural prosperity and denser settlement patterns aided commercialization of the economy. Peasants in Song China no longer merely aimed at self-sufficiency. They had found that producing for the market made possible a better life. Peasants sold their surpluses and used their profits to buy charcoal, tea, oil, and wine. In many places farmers specialized in commercial crops, such as sugar, oranges, cotton, silk, and tea. (See "Global Trade: Tea," page 368.) The need to transport the products of interregional trade stimulated the inland and coastal shipping industries, providing employment for shipbuilders and sailors and business opportunities for enterprising families with enough capital to purchase a boat. Marco Polo, the Venetian merchant who wrote of his visit to China from about 1275 to 1292, was astounded at the boat traffic on the Yangzi River. He claimed to have seen no fewer than fifteen thousand vessels at one city on the river, "and yet there are other towns where the number is still greater."[1]

As marketing increased, demand for money grew enormously, leading eventually to the creation of the world's first paper money. The decision by the late Tang government to abandon the use of bolts of silk as supplementary currency had increased the demand for copper coins. By 1085 the output of coins had increased tenfold to more than 6 billion coins a year. To avoid the weight and bulk of coins for large transactions, local merchants in late Tang times started trading receipts from deposit shops where they had left money or goods. The early Song authorities awarded a small set of these shops a monopoly on the issuing of these certificates of deposit, and in the 1120s the government took over the system, producing the world's first government-issued paper money. Marco Polo was amazed:

> The coinage of this paper money is authenticated with as much form and ceremony as if it were actually of pure gold or silver; for to each note a number of officers, specially appointed, not only subscribe their names, but affix their signets also; and when this has been regularly done by the whole of them,

> "The coinage of this paper money is authenticated with as much form and ceremony as if it were actually of pure gold or silver."
>
> **MARCO POLO**

the principal officer . . . having dipped into vermilion the royal seal committed to his custody, stamps with it the piece of paper, so that the form of the seal tinged with the vermilion remains impressed upon it.[2]

With the intensification of trade, merchants became progressively more specialized and organized. They set up partnerships and joint stock companies, with a separation of owners (shareholders) and managers. In the large cities merchants were organized into guilds according to the type of product sold, and they arranged sales from wholesalers to shop owners and periodically set prices. When government officials wanted to

• **dynastic cycle** The theory that Chinese dynasties go through a predictable cycle from early vigor and growth to subsequent decline as administrators become lax and the well-off find ways to avoid paying taxes, cutting state revenues.

Global Trade

Tea is made from the young leaves and leaf buds of *Camellia sinensis*, a plant native to the hills of southwest China. As an item of trade, tea has a very long history. Already by Han times (206 B.C.E.–220 C.E.) tea was being grown and drunk in southwest China, and for several centuries thereafter it was looked on as a local product of the region with useful pharmacologic properties, such as countering the effects of wine. By Tang times (608–907) it was being widely cultivated in the Yangzi River Valley and was a major item of interregional trade. Tea was common enough in Tang life that poets often mentioned it in their poems. In the eighth century the Chinese poet Lu Yu wrote an entire treatise on the wonders of tea.

The most intensive time for tea production was the harvest season, since young leaves were of much more value than mature ones. Mobilized for about a month each year, women would come out to help pick the tea. Not only were Chinese tea merchants among the wealthiest merchants, but from the late eighth century on, taxes on tea became a major source of government revenue.

Tea circulated in several forms, loose and compressed (brick), powder and leaf. The cost of tea varied both by form and by region of origin. In Song times (960–1279), the cheapest tea could cost as little as 18 cash per catty, the most expensive 275. In Kaifeng in the 1070s the most popular type was loose tea powdered at water mills. The tea exported from Sichuan to Tibet, however, was formed into solid bricks for ease of transport.

MAP 13.1 The Tea Trade

The Song Dynasty established a government monopoly on tea. Only those who purchased government licenses could legally trade in tea. The dynasty also used its control of tea to ensure a supply of horses, needed for military purposes. The government could do this because the countries on its borders that produced the best horses—Tibet, Central Asia, Mongolia, and so on—were not suitable for growing tea. Thus the Song government insisted on horses for tea.

Tea reached Korea and Japan as a part of Buddhist culture. Buddhist monks drank it to help them stay awake during long hours of recitation or meditation. The priest Saichō, patriarch of

Tea drinkers were fastidious about the utensils they used, the temperature of the water, and how the tea was prepared. In this detail from a Song period painting, a gentleman is supervising three servants who are preparing tea outdoors for his guests. The fourteenth-century Chinese tea-leaf jar (right) was imported to Japan, where it was treasured as an art object and used by tea masters. (ceremony: National Palace Museum, Taipei, Taiwan; jar: Tokugawa Art Museum, Nagoya)

Tendai Buddhism, visited China in 804 and reportedly brought back tea seeds. Tea drinking did not become widespread in Japan, however, until the twelfth century, when Zen monasteries popularized its use. By the fourteenth century tea imported from China was still prized, but the Japanese had already begun to appreciate the distinctive flavors of teas from different regions of Japan. With the development of the tea ceremony, tea drinking became an art in Japan, with much attention to the selection and handling of tea utensils. In both Japan and Korea, offerings of tea became a regular part of offerings to ancestors, as they were in China.

Tea did not become important in Europe until the seventeenth century. Tea first reached Russia in 1618, when a Chinese embassy presented some to the tsar. Under agreements between the Chinese and Russian governments, camel trains would arrive in China laden with furs and would return carrying tea, taking about a year for the round trip. By 1700 Russia was receiving more than 600 camel loads of tea annually. By 1800 it was receiving more than 6,000 loads, amounting to more than 3.5 million pounds. Tea reached western Europe in the sixteenth century, both via Arabs and via Jesuit priests traveling on Portuguese ships.

In Britain, where tea drinking would become a national institution, tea was first drunk in coffeehouses. In his famous diary Samuel Pepys recorded having his first cup of tea in 1660. By the end of the seventeenth century tea made up more than 90 percent of China's exports to England. In the eighteenth century tea drinking spread to homes and tea gardens. Queen Anne (r. 1702–1714) was credited with starting the custom of drinking tea instead of ale for breakfast. Afternoon tea became a central feature of British social life in the nineteenth century.

Already by the end of the eighteenth century Britain imported so much tea from China that it worried about the outflow of silver to pay for it. Efforts to balance trade with China involved promoting the sale of Indian opium to China and efforts to grow tea in British colonies. Using tea seeds collected in China and a tea plant indigenous to India's Assam province, both India and Sri Lanka eventually grew tea successfully. By the end of the nineteenth century huge tea plantations had been established in India, and India surpassed China as an exporter of tea.

The spread of the popularity of drinking tea also stimulated the desire for fine cups to drink it from. Importation of Chinese ceramics, therefore, often accompanied adoption of China's tea customs.

requisition supplies or assess taxes, they dealt with the guild heads.

Foreign trade also flourished in the Song period. In 1225 the superintendent of customs at the coastal city of Quanzhou wrote an account of the foreign places Chinese merchants visited. It includes sketches of major trading cities from Srivijaya and Malabar in Southeast Asia to Cairo and Baghdad in the Middle East. Pearls were said to come from the Persian Gulf, ivory from the Red Sea port of Aden, pepper from the Indonesian islands of Java and Sumatra, and cotton from the various kingdoms of India. In this period Chinese ships began to displace Indian and Arab merchants in the South Seas. Ship design was improved in several ways. Watertight bulkheads improved buoyancy and protected cargo. Stern-mounted rudders improved steering. Some of the ships were powered by both oars and sails and were large enough to hold several hundred men.

Also important to oceangoing travel was the perfection of the **compass**. The way a magnetic needle would point north had been known for some time, but in Song times the needle was reduced in size and attached to a fixed stem (rather than floated in water). In some cases it was put in a small protective case with a glass top, making it suitable for sea travel. The first reports of a compass used in this way date to 1119.

The Song also witnessed many advances in industrial techniques. Heavy industry, especially iron, grew astoundingly. With advances in metallurgy, iron production reached around 125,000 tons per year in 1078, a sixfold increase over the output in 800. At first charcoal was used in the production process, leading to deforestation of parts of north China. By the end of the eleventh century, however, bituminous coke had largely taken the place of charcoal. Much of the iron was put to military purposes. Mass-production methods were used to make iron armor in small, medium, and large sizes. High-quality steel for swords was made through high-temperature metallurgy. Huge bellows, often driven by water wheels, were used to superheat the molten ore. The needs of the army also brought Chinese engineers to experiment with the use of gunpowder. In the twelfth-century wars against the Jurchens (see page 334), those defending a besieged city used gunpowder to propel projectiles at the enemy.

The quickening of the economy fueled the growth of cities. Dozens of cities had fifty thousand or more residents, and quite a few had more than a hundred thousand — very large populations compared to other places in the world at the time. Both the capitals, Kaifeng (kigh-fuhng) and Hangzhou (hahng-joh), are estimated to have had in the vicinity of a million residents. Marco Polo described Hangzhou as the finest and most splendid city in the world. He reported that it had ten marketplaces, each half a mile long, where forty thousand to fifty thousand people would shop on any given day. There were also bathhouses; permanent shops selling things such as spices, drugs, and pearls; and innumerable courtesans — "adorned in much finery, highly

City Life A well-developed system of river and canal transport kept the Song capital well supplied with goods from across China, as shown in this detail from a 17-foot-long hand scroll painted in the twelfth century. (Palace Museum, Beijing)

Transplanting Rice To get the maximum yield per plot and to make it possible to grow two crops in the same field, Chinese farmers grew rice seedlings in a seed bed and then, when a field was free, transplanted the seedlings into the flooded field. Because the Song government wanted to promote up-to-date agricultural technology, in the twelfth century it commissioned a set of twelve illustrations of the steps to be followed. This painting comes from a later version of those illustrations. (Freer Gallery of Art, Smithsonian Institution, Washington, D.C., Purchase F1949.9b, F1954.20)

perfumed, occupying well-furnished houses, and attended by many female domestics."³

The medieval economic revolution shifted the economic center of China south to the Yangzi River drainage area. This area had many advantages over the north China plain. Rice, which grew in the south, provides more calories per unit of land and therefore allows denser settlement. The milder temperatures often allowed two crops to be grown on the same plot of land, first a summer and then a winter crop. The abundance of rivers and streams facilitated shipping, which reduced the cost of transportation and thus made regional specialization economically more feasible. In the first half of the Song Dynasty, the capital was still at Kaifeng in the north, close to the Grand Canal (see page 193), which linked the capital to the rich south.

The economic revolution of Song times cannot be attributed to intellectual change, as Confucian scholars did not reinterpret the classics to defend the morality of commerce. But neither did scholar-officials take a unified stand against economic development. As officials they had to work to produce revenue to cover government expenses such as defense, and this was much easier to do when commerce was thriving.

Ordinary people benefited from the Song economic revolution in many ways. There were more opportunities for the sons of farmers to leave agriculture and find work in cities. Those who stayed in agriculture had a better chance to improve their situations by taking up sideline production of wine, charcoal, paper, or textiles. Energetic farmers who grew cash crops such as sugar, tea, mulberry leaves (for silk), and cotton (recently introduced from India) could grow rich. Greater interregional trade led to the availability of more goods at the rural markets held every five or ten days.

Of course, not everyone grew rich. Poor farmers who fell into debt had to sell their land, and if they still owed money they could be forced to sell their daughters as maids, concubines, or prostitutes. The prosperity of the cities created a huge demand for women to serve the rich in these ways, and Song sources mention that criminals would kidnap girls and women to sell in distant cities at huge profits.

China During the Song and Yuan Dynasties, 960–1368

☐ How did the civil service examinations and the scholar-official class shape Chinese society and culture, and what impact did the Mongol conquest have on them?

In the tenth century Tang China broke up into separate contending states, some of which had non-Chinese rulers. The two states that proved to be long-lasting were the Song, which came to control almost all of China proper south of the Great Wall, and the Liao, whose ruling house was Khitan and which held the territory of modern Beijing and areas north (Map 13.2). Although the Song Dynasty had a much larger population, the Liao was militarily the stronger of the two. In

• **compass** A tool developed in Song times to aid in navigation at sea; it consisted of a magnetic needle that would point north that was placed in a small protective case.

◻ Mapping the Past

MAP 13.2 East Asia in 1000 and 1200 The Song Empire did not extend as far as its predecessor, the Tang, and faced powerful rivals to the north—the Liao Dynasty of the Khitans and the Xia Dynasty of the Tanguts. Koryŏ Korea maintained regular contact with Song China, but Japan, by the late Heian period, was no longer deeply involved with the mainland. By 1200 military families dominated both Korea and Japan, but the borders were little changed. On the mainland, the Liao Dynasty had been overthrown by the Jurchens' Jin Dynasty, which also seized the northern third of the Song Empire. Because the Song relocated its capital to Hangzhou in the south, this period is called the Southern Song period.

ANALYZING THE MAP What are the countries of East Asia in 1000? What are the major differences in 1200?

CONNECTIONS What connections do you see between the length of their northern borders and the histories of China, Korea, and Japan?

the early twelfth century the Liao state was defeated by the Jurchens, another non-Chinese people, who founded the Jin Dynasty and went on to conquer most of north China, leaving Song to control only the south. After a century the Jurchens' Jin Dynasty was defeated by the Mongols who extended their Yuan Dynasty to control all of China by 1276.

The Song Dynasty

The founder of the Song Dynasty, Taizu (r. 960–976), was a general whose troops elevated him to emperor (somewhat reminiscent of Roman practice). Taizu worked to make sure that such an act could not happen

in the future by placing the armies under central government control. To curb the power of his generals, he retired or rotated them and assigned civil officials to supervise them. In time these civil bureaucrats came to dominate every aspect of Song government and society. The civil service examination system established during the Sui Dynasty (see page 192) was greatly expanded to provide the dynasty with a constant flow of men trained in the Confucian classics.

Curbing the generals' power ended warlordism but did not solve the military problem of defending against the nomadic Khitans's Liao Dynasty to the north. After several attempts to push the Liao back beyond the Great Wall, the Song concluded a peace treaty with them. The Song agreed to make huge annual payments of gold and silk to the Khitans, in a sense paying them not to invade. Even so, the Song rulers had to maintain a standing army of more than a million men. By the middle of the eleventh century military expenses consumed half the government's revenues. Song had the industrial base to produce swords, armor, and arrowheads in huge quantities, but had difficulty maintaining enough horses and well-trained horsemen. Even though China was the economic powerhouse of the region, with by far the largest population, the horse was a major weapon of war in this period, and it was not easy to convert wealth to military advantage.

In the early twelfth century the military situation rapidly worsened when the Khitan state was destroyed by another tribal confederation led by the Jurchens. Although the Song allied with the Jurchens, the Jurchens quickly realized how easy it would be to defeat the Song. When they marched into the Song capital in 1126, they captured the emperor and took him and his entire court hostage, and he died eight years later in captivity. Song forces rallied around one of his sons who escaped capture, and this prince reestablished a Song court in the south at Hangzhou (see Map 13.2). This Southern Song Dynasty controlled only about two-thirds of the former Song territories, but the social, cultural, and intellectual life there remained vibrant until the Song fell to the Mongols in 1279.

The Scholar-Officials and Neo-Confucianism

The Song period saw the full flowering of one of the most distinctive features of Chinese civilization, the **scholar-official class** certified through highly competitive civil service examinations. This elite was both broader and better educated than the elites of earlier periods in Chinese history. Once the **examination system** was fully developed, aristocratic habits and prejudices largely disappeared. Ancestry did not matter as much when office depended more on study habits than on connections.

The examination system came to carry such prestige that the number of scholars entering each competition escalated rapidly, from fewer than 30,000 early in the eleventh century, to nearly 80,000 by the end of that century, to about 400,000 by the dynasty's end. To prepare for the examinations, men had to memorize the classics in order to be able to recognize even the most obscure passages. They also had to master specific forms of composition, including poetry, and be ready to discuss policy issues, citing appropriate historical examples. Those who became officials this way had usually tried the exams several times and were on average a little over thirty years of age when they succeeded. Because the competition was so fierce, the

great majority of those who devoted years to preparing for the exams never became officials.

The invention of printing should be given some credit for the trend toward a better-educated elite. Tang craftsmen developed the art of carving words and pictures into wooden blocks, inking the blocks, and pressing paper onto them. Each block held an entire page of text and illustrations. Such whole-page blocks were used for printing as early as the middle of the ninth century, and in the eleventh century **movable type** (one piece of type for each character) was invented, but it was rarely used because whole-block printing was cheaper. In China as in Europe a couple of centuries later, the introduction of printing dramatically lowered the price of books, thus aiding the spread of literacy.

Among the upper class the availability of cheaper books enabled scholars to amass their own libraries. Song publishers printed the classics of Chinese literature in huge editions to satisfy scholarly appetites. Works on philosophy, science, and medicine also were avidly consumed, as were Buddhist texts. Han and Tang poetry and historical works became the models for Song writers. One popular literary innovation was the encyclopedia, which first appeared in the Song period, at least five centuries before the publication of the first European encyclopedia.

The life of the educated man involved more than study for the civil service examinations and service in office. Many took to refined pursuits such as collecting antiques or old books and practicing the arts — especially poetry writing, calligraphy, and painting. For many individuals these cultural interests overshadowed any philosophical, political, or economic concerns; others found in them occasional outlets for creative activity and aesthetic pleasure. In the Song period the engagement of the elite with the arts led to extraordinary achievement in calligraphy and painting, especially landscape painting. A large share of the social life of upper-class men was centered on these refined pastimes, as they gathered to compose or criticize poetry, to view each other's art treasures, and to patronize young talents.

The new scholar-official elite produced some extraordinary men able to hold high court offices while pursuing diverse intellectual interests. (See "Individuals in Society: Shen Gua," page 375.) Ouyang Xiu spared

- **scholar-official class** Chinese educated elite that included both scholars and officials. The officials had usually gained office by passing the highly competitive civil service examination. Scholars without office had often studied for the examinations but failed repeatedly.

- **examination system** A system of selecting officials based on competitive written examinations.

- **movable type** A system of printing in which one piece of type is used for each unique character.

◻ Picturing the Past

On a Mountain Path in Spring With spare, sketchy strokes, the court painter Ma Yuan (ca. 1190–1225) depicts a scholar on an outing accompanied by his boy servant carrying a lute. The scholar gazes into the mist, his eyes attracted by a bird in flight. The poetic couplet was inscribed by Emperor Ningzong (r. 1194–1124), at whose court Ma Yuan served. It reads: "Brushed by his sleeves, wild flowers dance in the wind. / Fleeing from him, hidden birds cut short their songs." (National Palace Museum, Taipei, Taiwan)

ANALYZING THE IMAGE Find the key elements in this picture: the scholar, the servant boy, the bird, the willow tree. Are these elements skillfully conveyed? Are there other elements in the painting that you find hard to read?

CONNECTIONS What do you think is the reason for writing a poetic couplet on this painting? Does it enhance the experience of viewing the painting or detract from it?

time in his busy official career to write love songs, histories, and the first analytical catalogue of rubbings of ancient stone and bronze inscriptions. Sima Guang, besides serving as prime minister, wrote a narrative history of China from the Warring States Period (403–221 B.C.E.) to the founding of the Song Dynasty. Su Shi wrote more than twenty-seven hundred poems and eight hundred letters while active in opposition politics. He was also an esteemed painter, calligrapher, and theorist of the arts. Su Song, another high official, constructed an eighty-foot-tall mechanical clock. He adapted the water-powered clock invented in the Tang period by adding a chain-driven mechanism. The clock told not only the time of day but also the day of the month, the phase of the moon, and the position of certain stars and planets in the sky. As in Renaissance

Europe a couple of centuries later (discussed in Chapter 15), gifted men made advances in a wide range of fields.

These highly educated men accepted the Confucian responsibility to aid the ruler in the governing of the country. In this period, however, this commitment tended to embroil them in unpleasant factional politics. In 1069 the chancellor Wang Anshi proposed a series of sweeping reforms designed to raise revenues and help small farmers. Many well-respected scholars and officials thought that Wang's policies would do more harm than good and resisted enforcing them. Animosities grew as critics were assigned offices far from the capital. Later, when they returned to power, they retaliated against those who had pushed them out, escalating the conflict.

Individuals in Society

Shen Gua

IN THE ELEVENTH CENTURY IT WAS NOT RARE for Chinese men of letters to have broad interests, but few could compare to Shen Gua (1031–1095), a man who tried his hand at everything from mathematics, geography, economics, engineering, medicine, divination, and archaeology to military strategy and diplomacy.

In his youth Shen Gua traveled widely with his father, who served as a provincial official, which added to his knowledge of geography. In 1063 he passed the civil service examinations, and in 1066 he received a post in the capital, just before Wang Anshi's rise to power. He generally sided with Wang in the political disputes of the day. He eventually held high astronomical, ritual, and financial posts and became involved in waterworks and the construction of defense walls. He was sent as an envoy to the Khitans in 1075 to try to settle a boundary dispute. When a military campaign that he advised failed in 1082, he was demoted and later retired to write.

It is from his book of notes that we know the breadth of his interests. In one note Shen describes how, on assignment to inspect the frontier, he made a relief map of wood and glue-soaked sawdust to show the mountains, roads, rivers, and passes. The emperor was so impressed when he saw it that he ordered all the border prefectures to make relief maps. Elsewhere Shen describes the use of petroleum and explains how to make movable type from clay. Shen Gua often applied a mathematical approach to issues that his contemporaries did not think of in those terms. He once computed the total number of possible situations on a Go board, and another time he calculated the longest possible military campaign given the limits of human carriers, who had to carry their own food as well as food for the soldiers.

Shen Gua is especially known for his scientific explanations. He explained the deflection of the compass from due south. He identified petrified bamboo and from its existence argued that the region where it was found must have been much warmer and more humid in ancient times. He argued against the theory that tides are caused by the rising and setting of the sun, demonstrating that they correlate with the cycles of the moon. He proposed switching from a lunar calendar to a solar one of 365 days, saying that even though his contemporaries would reject his idea, "surely in the future some will adopt my idea." To convince his readers that the

sun and the moon were spherical, not flat, he suggested that they cover a ball with fine powder on one side and then look at it obliquely. The powder was the part of the moon illuminated by the sun, and as the viewer looked at it obliquely, the white part would be crescent shaped, like a waxing moon. Shen Gua, however, did not realize that the sun and moon had entirely different orbits, and he explained why they did not collide by positing that both were composed of qi (vital energy) and had form but not substance.

Shen Gua also wrote on medicine and criticized his contemporaries for paying more attention to old treatises than to clinical experience. Yet he, too, was sometimes stronger on theory than on observation. In one note he argued that longevity pills could be made from cinnabar. He reasoned that if cinnabar could be transformed in one direction, it ought to be susceptible to transformation in the opposite direction as well. Therefore, since melted cinnabar causes death, solid cinnabar should prevent death.

QUESTIONS FOR ANALYSIS

1. How did Shen Gua's travels add to his curiosity about the material world?

2. In what ways could Shen Gua have used his scientific interests in his work as a government official?

3. How does Shen Gua's understanding of the natural world compare to that of the early Greeks? (See Chapter 5, pages 128–131.)

• **Shen Gua played Go with white and black markers on a grid-like board like this one.**
(Library of Congress, LC-USZC4-8471/8472)

Besides politics, scholars also debated issues in ethics and metaphysics. For several centuries Buddhism had been more vital than Confucianism. Beginning in the late Tang period Confucian teachers began claiming that the teachings of the Confucian sages contained all the wisdom one needed and that a true Confucian would reject Buddhist teachings. During the eleventh century many Confucian teachers urged students to set their sights not on exam success but on the higher goals of attaining the wisdom of the sages. Metaphysical theories about the workings of the cosmos in terms of *li* (principle) and *qi* (vital energy) were developed in response to the challenge of the sophisticated metaphysics of Buddhism.

Neo-Confucianism, as this movement is generally termed, was more fully developed in the twelfth century by the immensely learned Zhu Xi (joo shee) (1130–1200). Besides serving in office, he wrote, compiled, or edited almost a hundred books; corresponded with dozens of other scholars; and still regularly taught groups of disciples, many of whom stayed with him for years at a time. Although he was treated as a political threat during his lifetime, within decades of his death his writings came to be considered orthodox, and in subsequent centuries candidates for the examinations had to be familiar with his commentaries on the classics. (See "Viewpoints: Zhu Xi and Yuan Cai on Family Management," page 377.)

Women's Lives in Song Times

Thanks to the spread of printing, more books survive from the Song period than from earlier periods, giving us more glimpses of women's lives. Song stories, documents, and legal cases show us widows who ran inns, maids sent out by their mistresses to do errands, midwives who delivered babies, pious women who spent their days chanting Buddhist sutras, nuns who called on such women to explain Buddhist doctrine, girls who learned to read with their brothers, farmers' daughters who made money by weaving mats, child-

less widows who accused their nephews of stealing their property, wives who were jealous of the concubines their husbands brought home, and women who used part of their own large dowries to help their husbands' sisters marry well.

Families who could afford it usually tried to keep their wives and daughters within the walls of the house, rather than let them work in the fields or in shops or inns. At home there was plenty for them to do. Not only was there the work of tending children and preparing meals, but spinning, weaving, and sewing were considered women's work and took a great deal of time. Families that raised silkworms also needed women to do much of the work of coddling the worms and getting them to spin their cocoons. Within the home women generally had considerable say and took active interest in issues such as the selection of marriage partners for their children.

Women tended to marry between the ages of sixteen and twenty. Their husbands were, on average, a couple of years older than they were. Marriages were arranged by their parents, who would have either called on a professional matchmaker (most often an older woman) or turned to a friend or relative for suggestions. Before a wedding took place, written agreements were exchanged, listing the prospective bride's and groom's birth dates, parents, and grandparents; the gifts that would be exchanged; and the dowry the bride would bring. The goal was to match families of approximately equal status, but a young man who had just passed the civil service exams would be considered a good prospect even if his family had little wealth.

A few days before the wedding the bride's family sent her dowry to the groom's family, which at a minimum contained boxes full of clothes and bedding. In better-off families, the dowry also included items of substantial value, such as gold jewelry or deeds to land. On the day of the wedding the groom and some of his friends and relatives went

Woman Attendant The Song emperors were patrons of a still-extant temple in northern China that enshrined a statue of the "holy mother," the mother of the founder of the ancient Zhou Dynasty. The forty-two maids who attend her, one of whom is shown here, seem to have been modeled on the palace ladies who attended Song emperors. (© Cultural Relics Press)

• **Neo-Confucianism** The revival of Confucian thinking that began in the eleventh century, characterized by the goal of attaining the wisdom of the sages, not exam success.

Viewpoints

Zhu Xi and Yuan Cai on Family Management

• *The Confucian tradition put considerable emphasis on the correct way for family members to treat each other and on the rituals that should govern family life. Filial piety was considered a central virtue in Confucius's* Analects, *and the early Confucian text, the* Greater Learning, *argued that a man who wanted to serve the ruler or bring peace to the realm had to first manage his own family.*

What could one do to attain harmony in his family? Zhu Xi (1130–1200), one of the leading Neo-Confucian philosophers of his day, placed emphasis on ritual. His discussion of the importance of setting up an ancestral shrine is the first item in his influential Family Rituals. *Other parts of this book detail the steps to be taken in funerals, weddings, coming-of-age ceremonies, and ancestral rites. His contemporary Yuan Cai (ca. 1140–ca. 1190) was a local government official whose views about how to attain family harmony seem to have come from his personal experience rather than the study of Confucian texts. His book also gives advice on arranging marriages, managing servants, and avoiding bankruptcy These two books, while written in Chinese, circulated in Korea and Japan as well as China, with Zhu Xi's* Family Rituals *becoming especially important in Korea.*

Zhu Xi on the Offering Hall

❝When a man of virtue builds a house his first task is always to set up an offering hall to the east of the main room of his house. For this hall four altars to hold the spirit tablets of the ancestors are made; collateral relatives who died without descendants may have associated offerings made to them there according to their generational seniority. Sacrificial fields should be established and sacrificial utensils prepared. Once the hall is completed, early each morning the master enters the outer gate to pay a visit. All comings and goings are reported there. On New Year's Day, the solstices, and each new and full moon, visits are made. On the customary festivals, seasonal foods are offered, and when an event occurs, reports are made. Should there be flood, fire, robbers, or bandits, the offering hall is the first thing to be saved. The spirit tablets, inherited manuscripts, and then the sacrificial utensils should be moved; only afterward may the family's valuables be taken. As one generation succeeds another, the spirit tablets are reinscribed and moved to their new places.❞

Yuan Cai on Forbearance

❝People say that lasting harmony in families begins with the ability to forbear. But knowing how to forbear without knowing how to live with forbearing can lead to a great many errors. Some seem to think that forbearance means to repress anger; that is, when someone offends you, you repress your feelings and do not reveal them. If this happens only once or twice it would be all right. But if it happens repeatedly the anger will come bursting forth like an irrepressible flood.

A better method is to dissipate anger as the occasion arises instead of hiding it in your chest. Do this by saying to yourself, "He wasn't thinking," "He doesn't know any better," "He made a mistake," "He is narrow in his outlook," "How much harm can this really do?" If you keep the anger from entering your heart, then even if someone offends you ten times a day, neither your speech nor your behavior will be affected. You will then see the magnitude of the benefits of forbearance.❞

Yuan Cai on Dislike Among Relatives

❝Dislike among blood relatives may start from a very minor incident but end up ingrained. It is just that once two people take a dislike to each other they become irascible, and neither is willing to be the first to cool off. When they are in each other's company day in and day out, they cannot help but irritate each other. If, having reached this state, one of them would be willing to take the initiative in cooling off and would talk to the other, then the other would reciprocate, and the situation would return to normal. This point is worth deep consideration.❞

Sources: Patricia Buckley Ebrey, trans., *Family and Property in Sung China: Yuan Ts'ai's* Precepts for Social Life (Princeton, N.J.: Princeton University Press, 1984), pp. 186–187. Reprinted by permission of Princeton University Press; Patricia Buckley Ebrey, trans., *Chu Hsi's Family Rituals: A Twelfth-Century Chinese Manual for the Performance of Cappings, Weddings, Funerals, and Ancestral Rites* (Princeton, N.J.: Princeton University Press, 1991), p. 5. Reprinted by permission of Princeton University Press.

QUESTIONS FOR ANALYSIS

1. Would attention to the details of ancestral rites of the sort Zhu Xi outlines help avoid the sorts of problems among relatives that Yuan Cai discusses, or could it make them worse?

2. The ideal Chinese family was one that did not divide during the parents' lifetimes, so that adult brothers and their families all lived together with their elderly parents. What can you infer about problems connected to such large, complex families from these two authors?

to the bride's home to get her. She would be elaborately dressed and would tearfully bid farewell to everyone in her family. She was carried to her new home in a fancy sedan chair to the sound of music, alerting everyone on the street that a wedding was taking place. Meanwhile the groom's family's friends and relatives had gathered at his home, ready to greet the bridal party. The bride would kneel and bow to her new parents-in-law and later also to the tablets representing her husband's ancestors. A classical ritual still practiced was for the new couple to drink wine from the same cup. A ritual that had become popular in Song times was to attach a string to the bride and groom, literally tying them together. Later they were shown to their new bedroom, where the bride's dowry had already been placed, and people tossed beans or rice on the bed, symbolizing the desired fertility. After teasing them, the guests left them alone and went out to the courtyard for a wedding feast.

The young bride's first priority was to try to win over her mother-in-law, since everyone knew that mothers-in-law were hard to please. One way to do this was to quickly bear a son for the family. Within the patrilineal system, a woman fully secured her position in the family by becoming the mother of one of the men. Every community had older women skilled in midwifery who were called to help when a woman went into labor. If the family was well-to-do, arrangements might be made for a wet nurse to help her take care of the newborn.

Women frequently had four, five, or six children, but likely one or more would die in infancy. If a son reached adulthood and married before the woman herself was widowed, she would be considered fortunate, for she would have always had an adult man who could take care of business for her—first her husband, then her grown son. But in the days when infectious diseases took many people in their twenties and thirties, it was not uncommon for a woman to be widowed while in her twenties, when her children were still very young.

A woman with a healthy and prosperous husband faced another challenge in middle age: her husband could bring home a **concubine** (and more than one if he could afford it). Moralists insisted that it was wrong for a wife to be jealous of her husband's concubines, but contemporary documents suggest that jealousy was very common. Wives outranked concubines and could give them orders in the house, but a concubine had her own ways of getting back through her hold on the husband. The children born to a concubine were considered just as much children of the family as the wife's children, and if the wife had had only daughters and the concubine had a son, the wife would find herself dependent on the concubine's son in her old age.

As a woman's children grew up, she would start thinking of suitable marriage partners. Many women liked the idea of bringing other women from their families of birth—perhaps a brother's daughter—to be their daughters-in-law. No matter who was selected, a woman's life became easier once she had a daughter-in-law to do the cooking and cleaning. Many found more time for religious devotions at this stage of their lives. Their sons, still living with them, could be expected to look after them and do their best to make their late years comfortable.

Neo-Confucianism is sometimes blamed for a decline in the status of women in Song times, largely because one of the best known of the Neo-Confucian teachers, Cheng Yi, once told a follower that it would be better for a widow to die of starvation than to lose her virtue by remarrying. In later centuries this saying was often quoted to justify pressuring widows, even very young ones, to stay with their husbands' families and not remarry. In Song times, however, widows frequently remarried.

It is true that **foot binding** began during the Song Dynasty, but it was not recommended by Neo-Confucian teachers; rather it was associated with the pleasure quarters and with women's efforts to beautify themselves. Mothers bound the feet of girls aged five to eight with long strips of cloth to keep them from growing and to bend the four smaller toes under to make the foot narrow and arched. The hope was that the girl would be judged more beautiful. Foot binding spread gradually during Song times but was probably still largely an elite practice. In later centuries it became extremely common in north and central China, eventually spreading to all classes. Women with bound feet were less mobile than women with natural feet, but only those who could afford servants bound their feet so tightly that walking was difficult.

China Under Mongol Rule

As discussed in Chapter 12, the Mongols conquered China in stages, gaining much of north China by 1215 and all of it by 1234, but not taking the south till the 1270s. The north suffered the most devastation. The non-Chinese rulers in the north, the Jin Dynasty of the Jurchen—with 150,000 cavalry, mostly Jurchen, and more than 300,000 Chinese infantrymen—thought they had the strongest army known to history, and they certainly had one of the largest. Yet Mongol tactics frustrated them. The Mongols would take a city, plunder it, and then withdraw, letting the Jin take it back and deal with the resulting food shortages and destruction.

• **concubine** A woman contracted to a man as a secondary spouse; although subordinate to the wife, her sons were considered legitimate heirs.

• **foot binding** The practice of binding the feet of girls with long strips of cloth to keep them from growing large.

Under these circumstances, Jurchen power rapidly collapsed.

Not until Khubilai was Great Khan was the Song Dynasty defeated and south China brought under the control of the Mongol's Yuan Dynasty. Non-Chinese rulers had gained control of north China several times in Chinese history, but none of them had been able to secure control of the region south of the Yangzi River, which required a navy. By the 1260s Khubilai had put Chinese shipbuilders to work building a fleet, crucial to his victory over Song (see page 341).

Life in China under the Mongols was much like life in China under earlier alien rulers. Once order was restored, people did their best to get on with their lives. Some were deprived of their land, business, or freedom and suffered real hardship. Yet people still spoke Chinese, followed Chinese customary practices in arranging their children's marriages or dividing their family property, made offerings at local temples, celebrated the new year and other customary festivals, and turned to local landowners when in need. Teachers still taught students the classics; scholars continued to write books; and books continued to be printed.

The Mongols, like other foreign rulers before them, did not see anything particularly desirable in the social mobility of Chinese society. Preferring stability, they assigned people hereditary occupations such as farmer, Confucian scholar, physician, astrologer, soldier, artisan, salt producer, miner, and Buddhist monk; the occupations came with obligations to the state. Besides these occupational categories, the Mongols classified the population into four grades, with the Mongols occupying the top grade. Next came various non-Chinese, such as the Uighurs and Persians. Below them were Chinese former subjects of the Jurchen, called the Han. At the bottom were the former subjects of the Song, called southerners.

The reason for codifying ethnic differences this way was to preserve the Mongols' privileges as conquerors. Chinese were not allowed to take Mongol names, and great efforts were made to keep them from passing as Mongols or marrying Mongols. To keep Chinese from rebelling, they were forbidden to own weap-

ons or congregate in public. Khubilai even prohibited Chinese from dealing in bamboo because it could be used to make bows and arrows.

As the Mongols captured Chinese territory, they recruited Chinese into their armies and government. Although some refused to serve the Mongols, others argued that the Chinese would fare better if Chinese were the administrators and could shield Chinese society from the most brutal effects of Mongol rule. A few Confucian scholars devoted themselves to the task of patiently teaching Mongol rulers the principles of Confucian government.

Nevertheless, government service, which had long been central to the identity and income of the educated elite in China, was not as widely available under the Mongols. The Mongols reinstituted the civil service examinations in 1315, but filled only about 2 percent of the positions in the bureaucracy through it and reserved half of those places for Mongols.

The scholar-official elite without government employment turned to alternative ways to support themselves. Those who did not have land to live off of found work as physicians, fortune-tellers, children's teachers, Daoist priests, publishers, booksellers, or playwrights. Many took leadership roles at the local level, such as founding academies for Confucian learning or promoting local charitable ventures. Through such

Blue-and-White Jars of the Yuan Period
Chinese ceramics had long been in demand outside of China, and an innovation of the Mongol period— decorating white porcelain with underglaze designs in blue—proved especially popular. Persia imported large quantities of Chinese blue-and-white ceramics, and Korean, Japanese, and Vietnamese potters took up versions of the style themselves. (© The Trustees of the British Museum/Art Resource, NY)

activities, scholars out of office could assert the importance of civil over military values and see themselves as trustees of the Confucian tradition.

Since the Mongols wanted to extract wealth from China, they had every incentive to develop the economy. They encouraged trade both within China and beyond its borders and tried to keep paper money in circulation. They repaired the Grand Canal, which had been ruined during their initial conquest of north China. Chinese industries with strong foreign markets, such as porcelain, thrived. Nevertheless, the economic expansion of late Tang and Song times did not continue under the alien rule of the Jurchen and Mongols. The economy of north China, with its strong iron industry, contracted under the Jurchen, and the destruction of cities was extensive during the first five decades of Mongol rule of the north. Although the Mongols did not discourage commerce, they were not as experienced in controlling currency, leading to serious inflation. The combination of war, disease, and a shrinking economy led to a population decline, probably of tens of millions.

The Mongols' Yuan Dynasty began a rapid decline in the 1330s as disease, rebellions, and poor leadership led to disorder throughout the country. When a Chinese strongman succeeded in consolidating the south, the Mongol rulers retreated to Mongolia before he could take Beijing. By 1368 the Yuan Dynasty had given way to a new Chinese-led dynasty: the Ming.

The Koryŏ Dynasty, 935–1392

YUAN DYNASTY

Yalu R.

1253–1254

1231

Kaegyong

1236–1239

Sea of Japan

KORYŎ KOREA

Yellow Sea

Tonggyang

1281

1274—

Korea Strait

JAPAN

➤ Mongol invasion
ⵊⵊ Wall

Korea Under the Koryŏ Dynasty, 935–1392

☐ How did Korean society and culture develop in an age when its northern neighbors were Khitans, Jurchens, and Mongols?

During the Silla period Korea was strongly tied to Tang China and avidly copied China's model (see page 198). This changed along with much else in North Asia between 800 and 1400. In this period Korea lived more in the shadows of the powerful nomad states of the Khitans, Jurchens, and Mongols than of the Chinese.

The Silla Dynasty began to decline after the king was killed in a revolt in 780. For the next 155 years the

kings were selected from several collateral lines, and the majority of them met violent deaths. Rebellions and coups d'état followed one after the other, as different groups of nobles placed their candidates on the throne and killed as many of their opponents as they could. As conditions deteriorated, serfs absconded in large numbers, and independent merchants and seamen of humble origins came to dominate the three-way trade between China, Korea, and Japan.

The dynasty that emerged from this confusion was called Koryŏ (KAW-ree-oh) (935–1392). (The English word *Korea* derives from the name of this dynasty.) During this time Korea developed more independently of the China model than it had in Silla times, just as contemporary Japan was doing (see the next section). This was not because the Chinese model was rejected; the Koryŏ capital was laid out on the Chinese model, and the government was closely patterned on the Tang system. But despite Chinese influence, Korean society remained deeply aristocratic.

The founder of the dynasty, Wang Kon (877–943), was a man of relatively obscure maritime background, and he needed the support of the old aristocracy to maintain control. His successors introduced civil service examinations on the Chinese model, as well as examinations for Buddhist clergy, but because the aristocrats were the best educated and the government schools admitted only the sons of aristocrats, this system served primarily to solidify their control. Politics was largely the competition among aristocratic clans for influence at court and marriage of their daughters to the royal princes. Like the Heian aristocrats in Japan (see pages 382–386), the Koryŏ aristocrats wanted to stay in the capital and only reluctantly accepted posts in the provinces.

At the other end of the social scale, the number of people in the serf-slave stratum seems to have increased. This lowborn stratum included not only privately held slaves but also large numbers of government slaves as well as government workers in mines, porcelain factories, and other government industries. Sometimes entire villages or groups of villages were considered lowborn. There were occasional slave revolts, and some manumitted (freed) slaves did rise in status, but prejudice against anyone with slave ancestors was so strong that the law provided that "only if there is no evidence of lowborn status for eight generations in one's official household registration may one receive a position in the government."[4] In China and

Wooden Blocks for Printing
The Heainsa Buddhist Temple in Korea has preserved the 80,000 woodblocks used to print the huge Buddhist canon in the thirteenth century. The monk shown here is replacing a block. All the blocks are carved on both sides and stabilized by wooden frames that have kept them from warping. (© OUR PLACE THE WORLD HERITAGE COLLECTION, www. ourplaceworldheritage.com)

Japan, by contrast, slavery was a much more minor element in the social landscape.

The commercial economy declined in Korea during this period, showing that it was not closely linked to China's then booming economy. Except for the capital, there were no cities of commercial importance, and in the countryside the use of money declined. One industry that did flourish was ceramics. Connoisseurs have long appreciated the elegance of the pale green Koryŏ celadon pottery, decorated with designs executed in inlaid white or gray clay.

Buddhism remained strong throughout Korea, and monasteries became major centers of art and learning. As in Song China and Kamakura Japan, Chan (Zen) and Tiantai (Tendai) were the leading Buddhist teachings (see pages 196, 385). The founder of the Koryŏ Dynasty attributed the dynasty's success to the Buddha's protection, and he and his successors were ardent patrons of the church. The entire Buddhist canon was printed in the eleventh century and again in the thirteenth. (The 81,258 individual woodblocks used to print it still survive in a monastery in southern Korea.) As in medieval Europe, aristocrats who entered the church occupied the major abbacies. Monasteries played the same roles as they did in China and Japan, such as engaging in money lending and charitable works. As in Japan (but not China), some monasteries accumulated military power.

Not all cultural advances were connected to monasteries or Buddhism. The most important literary work of the Koryŏ period is *The History of the Three Kingdoms*, compiled in 1145 in Chinese. Modeled on Chinese histories, it is the best source of information on early Korean history.

The Koryŏ Dynasty was preserved in name long after the ruling family had lost most of its power. In 1170 the palace guards massacred the civil officials at court and placed a new king on the throne. The coup leaders scrapped the privileges that had kept the aristocrats in power and appointed themselves to the top posts. After incessant infighting among the generals and a series of coups, in 1196 the general Ch'oe Ch'ung-hon took control. Ch'oe had a private army of about three thousand warrior-retainers and an even larger number of slaves. The domination of Korea by the Ch'oe family was much like the contemporaneous situation in Japan, where warrior bands were seizing power. Moreover, because the Ch'oe were content to dominate the government while leaving the Koryŏ king on the throne, they had much in common with the Japanese shoguns, who followed a similar strategy.

Although Korea adopted many ideas from China, it could not so easily adopt the Chinese assumption that it was the largest, most powerful, and most advanced society in the world. Korea, from early times, recognized China as being in many ways senior to it, but when strong non-Chinese states emerged to its north in Manchuria, Korea was ready to accommodate them as well. Koryŏ's first neighbor to the north was the Khitan state of Liao, which in 1010 invaded and sacked the capital. To avoid destruction, Koryŏ acceded to vassal status, but Liao invaded again in 1018. This time Koryŏ was able to repel the nomadic Khitans. Afterward a defensive wall was built across the Korean peninsula south of the Yalu River. When the Jurchens and their Jin Dynasty supplanted the Khitans's Liao Dynasty, Koryŏ agreed to send them tribute as well.

As mentioned in Chapter 12, Korea was conquered by the Mongols, and the figurehead Koryŏ kings were moved to Beijing, where they married Mongol princesses, their descendants becoming more Mongol than Korean. This was a time of hardship for the Korean people. In the year 1254 alone, the Mongols enslaved two hundred thousand Koreans and took them away. Ordinary people in Korea suffered grievously when their land was used as a launching pad for the huge Mongol invasions of Japan: nine hundred ships and the provisions for the soldiers on them had to be procured from the Korean countryside. In this period Korea also suffered from frequent attacks by Japanese pirates, somewhat like the depredations of the Vikings in Europe a little earlier (see page 394). The Mongol overlords did little to provide protection, and the harried coastal people had little choice but to retreat inland.

When Mongol rule in China fell apart in the mid-fourteenth century, it declined in Korea as well. Chinese rebels opposing the Mongols entered Korea and even briefly captured the capital in 1361. When the Ming Dynasty was established in China in 1368, the Koryŏ court was unsure how to respond. In 1388 a general, Yi Song-gye, was sent to oppose a Ming army at the northwest frontier. When he saw the strength of the Ming, he concluded that making an alliance was more sensible than fighting, and he led his troops back to the capital, where in 1392 he usurped the throne, founding the Choson Dynasty.

Japan's Heian Period, 794–1185

☐ How did the Heian form of government contribute to the cultural flowering of Japan in the period?

As described in Chapter 7, during the seventh and eighth centuries the Japanese ruling house pursued a vigorous policy of adopting useful ideas, techniques, and policies from the more advanced civilization of China. The rulers built a splendid capital along Chinese lines in Nara and fostered the growth of Buddhism. Monasteries grew so powerful in Nara, however, that in less than a century the court decided to move away from them and encourage other sects of Buddhism.

The new capital was built about twenty-five miles away at Heian (HAY-ahn; modern Kyoto). Like Nara, Heian was modeled on the Tang capital of Chang'an

(although neither of the Japanese capitals had walls, a major feature of Chinese cities). For the first century at Heian the government continued to follow Chinese models, but it turned away from them with the decline of the Tang Dynasty in the late ninth century. The last official embassy to China made the trip in 894. During the Heian period (794–1185) Japan witnessed a literary and cultural flowering under the rule of the Fujiwara family.

Fujiwara Rule

Only the first two Heian emperors were much involved in governing. By 860 political management was taken over by a series of regents from the Fujiwara family, who supplied most of the empresses in this period. The emperors continued to be honored, even venerated, because of their presumed divine descent, but the Fujiwaras ruled. Fujiwara dominance represented the privatization of political power and a return to clan politics. Political history thus took a very different course in Japan than in China, where, when a dynasty weakened, military strongmen would compete to depose the emperor and found their own dynasties. In Japan for the next thousand years, political contenders sought to manipulate the emperors rather than supplant them.

The Fujiwaras reached the apogee of their glory under Fujiwara Michinaga (r. 995–1027). Like many aristocrats of the period, he was learned in Buddhism, music, poetry, and Chinese literature and history. He dominated the court for more than thirty years as the father of four empresses, the uncle of two emperors, and the grandfather of three emperors. He acquired great landholdings and built fine palaces for himself and his family. After ensuring that his sons could continue to rule, he retired to a Buddhist monastery, all the while continuing to maintain control.

By the end of the eleventh century several emperors who did not have Fujiwara mothers found a device to counter Fujiwara control: they abdicated but continued to exercise power by controlling their young sons on the throne. This system of rule has been called **cloistered government** because the retired emperors took Buddhist orders, while maintaining control of the government from behind the scenes. Thus for a time the imperial house was a contender for political power along with other aristocratic groups.

Aristocratic Culture

A brilliant aristocratic culture developed in the Heian period. It was strongly focused on the capital at Heian, where nobles, palace ladies, and imperial family members lived a highly refined and leisured life. In their society niceties of birth, rank, and breeding counted for everything. From their diaries we know of the pains

The Tale of Genji
In this scene from a twelfth-century painting illustrating *The Tale of Genji*, Genji has his inkstone and brushes ready to respond to the letter he is reading. (Tokugawa Reimeikai Foundation, Tokyo, Japan/Photo AISA/The Bridgeman Art Library)

aristocratic women took in their dress, selecting the color combinations of the kimonos they wore, layer upon layer. Even among men, presentation and knowing how to dress tastefully were more important than skill with a horse or sword. The elegance of one's calligraphy and the allusions in one's poems were matters of intense concern to both men and women at court. Courtiers did not like to leave the capital, and some like the court lady Sei Shonagon shuddered at the sight of ordinary working people. In her *Pillow Book*, she wrote of encountering a group of commoners on a pilgrimage: "They looked like so many basket-worms as they crowded together in their hideous clothes, leaving hardly an inch of space between themselves and me. I really felt like pushing them all over sideways."[5] (See "Listening to the Past: *The Pillow Book* of Sei Shonagon," page 384.)

In this period a new script was developed for writing Japanese phonetically. Each symbol was based on a simplified Chinese character and represented one of the syllables used in Japanese (such as *ka, ki, ku, ke, ko*). Although "serious" essays, histories, and government documents continued to be written in Chinese, less formal works such as poetry and memoirs were written in Japanese. Mastering the new writing system took much less time than mastering writing in Chinese and aided the spread of literacy, especially among women in court society.

> "They looked like so many basket-worms as they crowded together in their hideous clothes, leaving hardly an inch of space between themselves and me. I really felt like pushing them all over sideways."
>
> **SEI SHONAGON**

In the Heian period women played important roles at all levels of society. Women educated in the arts and letters could advance at court as attendants to the ruler's empress and other consorts. Women could inherit property from their parents, and they would compete with their brothers for shares of the family property. In political life, marrying a daughter to an emperor or shogun (see page 386) was one of the best ways to gain power, and women often became major players in power struggles.

The literary masterpiece of this period is **The Tale of Genji**, written in Japanese by Lady Murasaki over several years (ca. 1000–1010). This long narrative

- **cloistered government** A system in which an emperor retired to a Buddhist monastery but continued to exercise power by controlling his young son on the throne.
- **The Tale of Genji** A Japanese literary masterpiece about court life written by Lady Murasaki.

Listening to the Past

The Pillow Book of Sei Shonagon

Beginning in the late tenth century Japan produced a series of great women writers. At the time women were much freer than men to write in vernacular Japanese, giving them a large advantage. Lady Murasaki, author of the novel The Tale of Genji, *is the most famous of the women writers of the period, but her contemporary Sei Shonagon is equally noteworthy. Sei Shonagon served as a lady in waiting to Empress Sadako during the last decade of the tenth century (990–1000). Her only known work is* The Pillow Book, *a collection of notes, character sketches, anecdotes, descriptions of nature, and eccentric lists such as boring things, awkward things, hateful things, and things that have lost their power.*

The Pillow Book portrays the lovemaking/marriage system among the aristocracy more or less as it is depicted in The Tale of Genji. *Marriages were arranged for family interests, and a man could have more than one wife. Wives and their children commonly stayed in their own homes, where their husbands and fathers would visit them. But once a man had an heir by his wife, there was nothing to prevent him from establishing relations with other women. Some relationships were long-term, but many were brief, and men often had several lovers at the same time. Some women became known for their amorous conquests, others as abandoned women whose husbands ignored them. The following passage from* The Pillow Book *looks on this lovemaking system with amused detachment.*

"It is so stiflingly hot in the Seventh Month that even at night one keeps all the doors and lattices open. At such times it is delightful to wake up when the moon is shining and to look outside. I enjoy it even when there is no moon. But to wake up at dawn and see a pale sliver of a moon in the sky—well, I need hardly say how perfect that is.

I like to see a bright new straw mat that has just been spread out on a well-polished floor. The best place for one's three-foot curtain of state is in the front of the room near the veranda. It is pointless to put it in the rear of the room, as it is most unlikely that anyone will peer in from that direction.

It is dawn and a woman is lying in bed after her lover has taken his leave. She is covered up to her head with a light mauve robe that has a lining of dark violet; the colour of both the outside and the lining is fresh and glossy. The woman, who appears to be asleep, wears an unlined orange robe and a dark crimson skirt of stiff silk whose cords hang loosely by her side, as if they have been left untied. Her thick tresses tumble over each other in cascades, and one can imagine how long her hair must be when it falls freely down her back.

Nearby another woman's lover is making his way home in the misty dawn. He is wearing loose violet trousers, an orange hunting costume, so lightly coloured that one can hardly tell whether it has been dyed or not, a white robe of still silk, and a scarlet robe of glossy, beaten silk. His clothes, which are damp from the mist, hang loosely about him. From the dishevelment of his side locks one can tell how negligently he must have tucked his hair into the black lacquered headdress when he got up. He wants to return and write his next-morning letter before the dew on the morning glories has had time to vanish; but the path seems endless, and to divert himself he hums "the sprouts in the flax fields."

As he walks along, he passes a house with an open lattice. He is on his way to report for official duty, but cannot help stopping to lift up the blind and peep into the room. It amuses him to think that a man has probably been spending the night here and has only recently got up to leave, just as happened to himself. Perhaps that man too had felt the charm of the dew.

Looking around the room, he notices near the woman's pillow an open fan with a magnolia frame and purple paper; and at the foot of her curtain of state he sees some narrow

depicts a cast of characters enmeshed in court life, with close attention to dialogue and personality. Murasaki also wrote a diary that is similarly revealing of aristocratic culture. In one passage she tells of an occasion when word got out that she had read the Chinese classics:

Worried what people would think if they heard such rumors, I pretended to be unable to read even the inscriptions on the screens. Then Her Majesty asked me to read to her here and there from the collected works of [the Tang Chinese poet] Bo Juyi, and, because she evinced a desire to know much more about such things, we carefully chose a time when other women would not be present and, amateur that I was, I read with her the two books of Bo Juyi's New Ballads in secret; we started the summer before last.[6]

Despite the reluctance of Murasaki and the lady she served to let others know of their learning, there were, in fact, quite a few women writers in this period. The wife of a high-ranking court official wrote a poetic memstrips of Michinoku paper and also some other paper of a faded colour, either orange-red or maple.

The woman senses that someone is watching her and, looking up from under her bedclothes, sees a gentleman leaning against the wall by the threshold, a smile on his face. She can tell at once that he is the sort of man with whom she need feel no reserve. All the same, she does not want to enter into any familiar relations with him, and she is annoyed that he should have seen her asleep.

"Well, well, Madam," says the man, leaning forward so that the upper part of his body comes behind her curtains, "what a long nap you're having after your morning adieu! You really are a lie-abed!"

"You call me that, Sir," she replied, "only because you're annoyed at having had to get up before the dew had time to settle."

Their conversation may be commonplace, yet I find there is something delightful about the scene.

Now the gentleman leans further forward and, using his own fan, tries to get hold of the fan by the woman's pillow. Fearing his closeness, she moves further back into her curtain enclosure, her heart pounding. The gentleman picks up the magnolia fan and, while examining it, says in a slightly bitter tone, "How standoffish you are!"

But now it is growing light; there is a sound of people's voices, and it looks as if the sun will soon be up. Only a short while ago this same man was hurrying home to write his next-morning letter before the mists had time to clear. Alas, how easily his intentions have been forgotten!

While all this is afoot, the woman's original lover has been busy with his own next-morning letter, and now, quite unexpectedly, the messenger arrives at her house. The letter is attached to a spray of bush-clover, still damp with dew, and the paper gives off a delicious aroma of incense. Because of the new visitor, however, the woman's servants cannot deliver it to her.

Finally it becomes unseemly for the gentleman to stay any longer. As he goes, he is amused to think that a similar scene may be taking place in the house he left earlier that morning. 🙶

Source: Ivan Morris, trans., *The Pillow Book of Sei Shonagon* (New York: Penguin Books, 1970), pp. 60–62. © Ivan Morris 1967. Reprinted by permission of Oxford University Press and Columbia University Press.

QUESTIONS FOR ANALYSIS

1. What sorts of images does Sei Shonagon evoke to convey an impression of a scene?

2. What can you learn from this passage about the material culture of Japan in this period?

3. Why do you think Sei Shonagon was highly esteemed as a writer?

oir of her unhappy twenty-year marriage to him and his rare visits. A woman wrote both an autobiography that related her father's efforts to find favor at court and a love story of a hero who travels to China. Another woman even wrote a history that concludes with a triumphal biography of Fujiwara Michinaga.

Buddhism remained very strong throughout the Heian period. A mission sent to China in 804 included two monks in search of new texts. One of the monks, Saichō, spent time at the monasteries on Mount Tiantai and brought back the Buddhist teachings associated with that mountain (called Tendai in Japanese). Tendai's basic message is that all living beings share the Buddha nature and can be brought to salvation. Tendai practices include strict monastic discipline, prayer, textual study, and meditation. Once back in Japan, Saichō established a monastery on Mount Hiei outside Kyoto, which grew to be one of the most important monasteries in Japan. By the twelfth century this monastery and its many branch temples had vast lands and a powerful army of monk-soldiers to protect its interests. Whenever the monastery felt that its interests were at risk, it sent the monk-soldiers into the capital to parade its sacred symbols in an attempt to intimidate the civil authorities.

Kūkai, the other monk on the 804 mission to China, came back with texts from another school of Buddhism — Shingon, "True Word," a form of **Esoteric Buddhism**. Esoteric Buddhism is based on the idea that teachings containing the secrets of enlightenment had been secretly transmitted from the Buddha. An adept (expert) can gain access to these mysteries through initiation into the mandalas (cosmic diagrams), mudras (gestures), and mantras (verbal formulas). On his return to Japan, Kūkai attracted many followers and was allowed to establish a monastery at Mount Kōya, south of Osaka. The popularity of Esoteric Buddhism was a great stimulus to Buddhist art.

The Samurai and the Kamakura Shogunate, 1185–1333

☐ What were the causes and consequences of military rule in Japan?

The gradual rise of a warrior elite over the course of the Heian period finally brought an end to the domination of the Fujiwaras and other Heian aristocratic families. In 1156 civil war broke out between the Taira and Minamoto warrior clans based in western and eastern Japan, respectively. Both clans relied on skilled warriors, later called samurai, who were rapidly becoming a new social class. A samurai and his lord had a double bond: in return for the samurai's loyalty and service, the lord granted him land or income. From 1159 to 1181 a Taira named Kiyomori dominated the court, taking the position of prime minister and marrying his daughter to the emperor. His relatives became governors of more than thirty provinces, managed some five hundred tax-exempt estates, and amassed a fortune in the trade with Song China and Koryŏ Korea. Still, the Minamoto clan managed to defeat the Taira, and the Minamoto leader, Yoritomo, became **shogun**, or general-in-chief. With him began the Kamakura Shogunate (1185–1333). This period is often referred to as Japan's feudal period

because it was dominated by a military class whose members were tied to their superiors by bonds of loyalty and supported by landed estates rather than salaries.

Military Rule

The similarities between military rule in Japan and feudalism in medieval Europe during roughly the same period have fascinated scholars, as have the very significant differences. In Europe feudalism emerged out of the fusion of Germanic and Roman social institutions and flowered under the impact of Muslim and Viking invasions. In Japan military rule evolved from a combination of the native warrior tradition and Confucian ethical principles of duty to superiors.

The emergence of the samurai was made possible by the development of private landholding. The government land allotment system, copied from Tang China, began breaking down in the eighth century (much as it did in China). By the ninth century local lords began escaping imperial taxes and control by commending (formally giving) their land to tax-exempt entities such as monasteries, the imperial family, and certain high-ranking officials. The local lord then received his land back as a tenant and paid his protector a small rent. The monastery or privileged individual received a steady income from the land, and the local lord escaped imperial taxes and control. By the end of the thirteenth century most land seems to have been taken off the tax rolls this way. Each plot of land could thus have several people with rights to shares of its produce, ranging from the cultivator, to a local lord, to an estate manager working for him, to a regional strongman, to a noble or temple in the capital. Unlike peasants in medieval Europe, where similar practices of commendation occurred, those working the land in Japan never became serfs. Moreover, Japanese lords rarely lived on the lands they had rights in, unlike English or French lords who lived on their manors.

Samurai resembled European knights in several ways. Both were armed with expensive weapons, and both fought on horseback. Just as the knight was supposed to live according to the chivalric code, so Japanese samurai were expected to live according to **Bushido** (or "way of the warrior"), a code that stressed military honor, courage, stoic acceptance of hardship, and, above all, loyalty. Physical hardship was accepted as routine, and soft living was despised as weak and unworthy. Disloyalty brought social disgrace, which the samurai could avoid only through *seppuku*, ritual suicide by slashing his belly.

The Kamakura Shogunate derives its name from Kamakura, a city near modern Tokyo that was the seat of the Minamoto clan. The founder, Yoritomo, ruled the country much the way he ran his own estates, appoint-

• **Esoteric Buddhism** A sect of Buddhism that maintains that the secrets of enlightenment have been secretly transmitted from the Buddha and can be accessed through initiation into the mandalas, mudras, and mantras.

• **shogun** The Japanese general-in-chief, whose headquarters was the shogunate.

• **Bushido** Literally, the "way of the warrior"; the code of conduct by which samurai were expected to live.

ing his retainers to newly created offices. To cope with the emergence of hard-to-tax estates, he put military land stewards in charge of seeing to the estates' proper operation. To bring order to the lawless countryside, he appointed military governors to oversee the military and enforce the law in the provinces. They supervised the conduct of the land stewards in peacetime and commanded the provincial samurai in war.

Yoritomo's wife Masako protected the interests of her own family, the Hōjōs, especially after Yoritomo died. She went so far as to force her first son to abdicate when he showed

**Kamakura Shogunate,
1185–1333**

signs of preferring the family of his wife to the family of his mother. She later helped her brother take power away from her father. Thus the process of reducing power holders to figureheads went one step further in 1219 when the Hōjō family reduced the shogun to a figurehead. The Hōjō family held the reins of power until 1333.

The Mongols' two massive seaborne invasions in 1274 and 1281 (see page 343) were a huge shock to the shogunate. The Kamakura government was hard-pressed to gather adequate resources for its defense. Temples were squeezed, farmers were taken away from their fields to build walls, and warriors were promised generous rewards in return for their service. Although the Hōjō regents, with the help of a "divine wind" (*kamikaze*), repelled the Mongols, they were unable to reward their vassals in the traditional way because little booty was found among the wreckage of the Mongol fleets. Discontent grew among the samurai, and by the fourteenth century the entire political system was breaking down. Both the imperial and the

shogunate families were fighting among themselves. As land grants were divided, samurai became impoverished and took to plunder and piracy, or shifted their loyalty to local officials who could offer them a better living.

The factional disputes among Japan's leading families remained explosive until 1331, when the emperor Go-Daigo tried to recapture real power. His attempt sparked an uprising by the great families, local lords, samurai, and even Buddhist monasteries, which had thousands of samurai retainers. Go-Daigo destroyed the Kamakura Shogunate in 1333 but soon lost the loyalty of his followers. By 1338 one of his most important military supporters, Ashikaga Takauji, had turned on him and established the Ashikaga Shogunate, which lasted until 1573. Takauji's victory was also a victory for the samurai, who took over civil authority throughout Japan.

Cultural Trends

The cultural distance between the elites and the commoners narrowed a little during the Kamakura period. Buddhism was vigorously spread to ordinary Japanese by energetic preachers. Honen (1133–1212) propagated the Pure Land teaching, preaching that

The Shogun Minamoto Yoritomo in Court Dress
This wooden sculpture, 27.8 inches tall (70.6 cm), was made about a half century after Yoritomo's death for use in a shrine dedicated to his memory. The bold shapes convey Yoritomo's dignity and power. (Tokyo National Museum/ image: TNM Image Archives)

The Itinerant Preacher Ippen
The monk Ippen spread Pure Land teaching as he traveled through Japan urging people to call on the Amitabha Buddha through song and dance. This detail from a set of twelve paintings done in 1299, a decade after his death, shows him with his belongings on his back as he approaches a village. (Tokyo National Museum/image: TNM Image Archives)

paradise could be reached through simple faith in the Buddha and repeating the name of the Buddha Amitabha. Neither philosophical understanding of Buddhist scriptures nor devotion to rituals was essential. His follower Shinran (1173–1263) taught that monks should not shut themselves off in monasteries but should marry and have children. A different path was promoted by Nichiren (1222–1282), a fiery and intolerant preacher who proclaimed that to be saved people had only to invoke sincerely the Lotus Sutra, one of the most important of the Buddhist sutras. These lay ver-sions of Buddhism found a receptive audience among ordinary people in the countryside.

It was also during the Kamakura period that **Zen** came to flourish in Japan. Zen teachings originated in Tang China, where they were known as Chan (see page 196). Rejecting the authority of the sutras, Zen teachers claimed the superiority of mind-to-mind transmission of Buddhist truth. When Japanese monks went to China in the twelfth century looking for ways to revitalize Japanese Buddhism, they were impressed by the rigorous monastic life of the Chan/Zen monasteries. One school of Zen held that enlightenment could be achieved suddenly through insight into one's own true nature. This school taught rigorous meditation and the use of kōan riddles to unseat logic and free

• **Zen** A school of Buddhism that emphasized meditation and truths that could not be conveyed in words.

the mind for enlightenment. This teaching found eager patrons among the samurai, who were attracted to its discipline and strong master-disciple bonds.

Buddhism remained central to the visual arts. Many temples in Japan still house fine sculptures done in this period. In painting, narrative hand scrolls brought to life the miracles that faith could bring and the torments of Hell awaiting unbelievers. All forms of literature were depicted in these scrolls, including *The Tale of Genji*, war stories, and humorous anecdotes.

During the Kamakura period war tales continued the tradition of long narrative prose works. *The Tale of the Heike* tells the story of the fall of the Taira family and the rise of the Minamoto clan. The tale reached a large and mostly illiterate audience because blind minstrels would chant sections to the accompaniment of a lute. The story is suffused with the Buddhist idea of the transience of life and the illusory nature of glory. Yet it also celebrates strength, courage, loyalty, and pride. The Minamoto warriors from the east are portrayed as the toughest. In one scene one of them dismisses his own prowess with the bow, claiming that other warriors from his region could pierce three sets of armor with their arrows. He then brags about the martial spirit of warriors from the east: "They are bold horsemen who never fall, nor do they let their horses stumble on the roughest road. When they fight they do not care if even their parents or children are killed; they ride over their bodies and continue the battle."[7] In this they stood in contrast to the warriors of the west, who in good Confucian fashion would retire from battle to mourn their parents.

> "They are bold horsemen who never fall, nor do they let their horses stumble on the roughest road. When they fight they do not care if even their parents or children are killed; they ride over their bodies and continue the battle."
>
> **THE TALE OF THE HEIKE**

After stagnating in the Heian period, agricultural productivity began to improve in the Kamakura period, and the population grew, reaching perhaps 8.2 million by 1333. Much like farmers in contemporary Song China, Japanese farmers in this period adopted new strains of rice, often double-cropped in warmer regions, made increased use of fertilizers, and improved irrigation for paddy rice. Besides farming, ordinary people made their livings as artisans, traders, fishermen, and entertainers. Although trade in human beings was banned, those who fell into debt might sell themselves or their children, and professional slave traders kidnapped women and children. A vague category of outcastes occupied the fringes of society, in a manner reminiscent of India. Buddhist strictures against killing and Shinto ideas of pollution probably account for the exclusion of butchers, leatherworkers, morticians, and lepers, but other groups, such as bamboo whisk makers, were also traditionally excluded for no obvious reason.

CONNECTIONS

East Asia faced many internal and external challenges between 800 and 1400, and the ways the societies responded to them shaped their subsequent histories. In China the first four centuries of this period were a time of economic growth, urbanization, the spread of printing, and the expansion of the educated class. In Korea and Japan aristocracy and military rule were more typical of the era. All three areas, but especially China and Korea, faced an unprecedented challenge from the Mongols, with Japan less vulnerable because it did not share a land border. The challenges of the period did not hinder creativity in the literary and visual arts; among the greatest achievements of this era are the women's writings of Heian Japan, such as *The Tale of Genji*, and landscape painting of both Song and Yuan China.

Europe during these six centuries, the subject of the next chapter, also faced invasions from outside; in its case, the pagan Vikings were especially dreaded. Europe had a social structure more like that of Korea and Japan than of China, with less centralization and a more dominant place in society for military men. The centralized church in Europe, however, was unlike anything known in East Asian history. These centuries in Europe saw a major expansion of Christendom, especially to Scandinavia and eastern Europe, both through conversion and migration. Although there were scares that the Mongols would penetrate deeper into Europe, the greatest challenge in Europe was the Black Death and the huge loss of life that it caused.

□ CHAPTER REVIEW

□ What made possible the expansion of the Chinese economy, and what were the outcomes of this economic growth? (p. 366)

The loosening of the central government's control of the economy in the late Tang period seems to have stimulated trade and economic growth. In the period from 800 to 1100, China's population doubled to 100 million, reflecting in part the spread of wet-field rice cultivation, especially in the south. At the same time, the economy became increasingly commercialized. There was a huge increase in the use of money and the introduction of paper money to meet demand. Cities grew, and the economic center of China shifted from the north China plain to the south, the region drained by the Yangzi River. Merchants became more specialized, and foreign trade grew.

□ How did the civil service examinations and the scholar-official class shape Chinese society and culture, and what impact did the Mongol conquest have on them? (p. 371)

In the Song period the booming economy and the invention of printing allowed a great expansion in the size of the scholar-official class, which came to dominate the government. The life of the educated class was strongly shaped by the civil service examinations, which most educated men spent a decade or more studying for, often unsuccessfully. Their high levels of education fostered interest in literature, antiquities, philosophy, and art. Because there were more educated men, more books were written, and because of the spread of printing, a much greater share of them have survived to the present, making it possible to see dimensions of life poorly documented for earlier periods, such as the lives of women. China's great wealth and its elite's high levels of education could not be easily converted to military supremacy, and the Song had to pay tribute to its northern neighbors, eventually falling to the Mongols. During the Mongols' Yuan Dynasty, China's economic expansion came to an end. The Mongols instituted hereditary occupations, ending much of the social mobility that characterized the Song Dynasty. The status of scholars was made hereditary, but there were many fewer opportunities for them to serve in the government.

KEY TERMS

dynastic cycle (p. 366)
compass (p. 370)
scholar-official class (p. 373)
examination system (p. 373)
movable type (p. 373)
Neo-Confucianism (p. 376)
concubine (p. 378)
foot binding (p. 378)
cloistered government (p. 382)
The Tale of Genji (p. 383)
Esoteric Buddhism (p. 386)
shogun (p. 386)
Bushido (p. 386)
Zen (p. 388)

□ How did Korean society and culture develop in an age when its northern neighbors were Khitans, Jurchens, and Mongols? (p. 380)

During the Koryŏ dynasty Korea evolved more independently of China than it had for the past several centuries, in part because it had to placate powerful non-Chinese neighbors. The commercial economy declined, and an increasing portion of the population was unfree; slaves worked much of the agricultural land in the hands of aristocrats and local magnates, and the government compelled others to work for it in mines or factories. Buddhism continued to flourish. Military strongmen dominated the government, but the armies were no match for the much larger empires to their north and had to accede to often onerous demands, especially during the period of Mongol domination.

□ How did the Heian form of government contribute to the cultural flowering of Japan in the period? (p. 382)

In marked contrast to Song China, in Heian Japan a tiny aristocracy dominated government and society. More important than the emperors were a series of regents, most of them from the Fujiwara family and fathers-in-law of the emperors. The aristocratic court society put great emphasis on taste and refinement. Women were influential at the court and wrote much of the best literature of the period. Buddhism remained popular, and the teachings of Esoteric Buddhism were introduced from China, stimulating art. The Heian aristocrats had little interest in life in the provinces, which gradually came under the control of military clans.

□ What were the causes and consequences of military rule in Japan? (p. 386)

After a civil war between the two leading military clans, a military government, called the shogunate, was established in the east. The Kamakura Shogunate was dominated by a military class of samurais who were bound to their lord by loyalty and service in return for land and income. A change in landownership practices made possible the emergence of this warrior class. Emperors were still placed on the throne, but they had little power. A major crisis in military control was caused by the two invasions of the Mongols. Although both times the invaders were repelled, the costs of defense were high. During this period of military rule, culture was no longer so capital-centered, and Buddhism was vigorously spread to ordinary people. Arts that appealed to the samurai, such as war stories and Zen Buddhism, all flourished.

SUGGESTED READING

Bowring, Richard. *The Religious Traditions of Japan 500–1600*. 2005. A wide-ranging study that puts Buddhism in the context of local cults.

Chaffee, John W. *The Thorny Gates of Learning in Sung China: A Social History of Examinations*. 1985. Documents the wide-ranging impact of the examination system and the ways men could improve their chances.

Ebrey, Patricia Buckley. *The Inner Quarters: Marriage and the Lives of Chinese Women in the Sung Period*. 1993. Overview of the many facets of women's lives, from engagements to dowries, childrearing, and widowhood.

Ebrey, Patricia Buckley, Anne Walthall, and James B. Palais. 2009. *East Asia: A Cultural, Social, and Political History*, 2d ed. Textbook with strong coverage of this period.

Egan, Ronald. *Word, Image, and Deed in the Life of Su Shi*. 1994. A sympathetic portrait of one of the most talented men of the age.

Farris, Wayne W. *Heavenly Warriors*. 1992. Argues against Western analogies in explaining the dominance of the samurai.

Friday, Karl F. *Hired Swords*. 1992. Treats the evolution of state military development in connection with the emergence of the samurai.

Hansen, Valerie. *Changing the Gods in Medieval China, 1127–1276*. 1990. A portrait of the religious beliefs and practices of ordinary people in Song times.

Kuhn, Dieter. *The Age of Confucian Rule: The Song Transformation of China*. 2009. Accessible overview, especially strong on economic history and material culture.

Lorge, Peter. 2009. *War, Politics and Society in Early Modern China, 900–1795*. Examines dynasties as military powers.

Morris, Ivan. *The World of the Shining Prince: Court Life in Ancient Japan*. 1964. An engaging portrait of Heian culture based on both fiction and nonfiction sources.

Rossabi, Maurice. *China Among Equals*. 1983. Essays on Song, Liao, Jin, and Yuan, as well as Korea.

Souyri, Pierre François. *The World Turned Upside Down: Medieval Japanese Society*. 2001. A thought-provoking analysis of both the social system and the mentalities of Japan's Middle Ages.

NOTES

1. *The Travels of Marco Polo, the Venetian*, ed. Manuel Komroff (New York: Boni and Liveright, 1926), p. 227.
2. Ibid., p. 159.
3. Ibid., p. 235.
4. Peter H. Lee, ed., *Sourcebook of Korean Civilization* (New York: Columbia University Press, 1993), p. 327.
5. Ivan Morris, trans., *The Pillow Book of Sei Shonagon* (New York: Penguin Books, 1970), p. 258.
6. Quoted in M. Collcott, M. Jansen, and I. Kumakura, *Cultural Atlas of Japan* (New York: Facts on File, 1988), p. 82, slightly modified.
7. Ibid., p. 101.

For practice quizzes and other study tools, visit the **Online Study Guide** at bedfordstmartins.com/mckayworld.

For primary sources from this period, see *Sources of World Societies*, **Second Edition**.

For Web sites, images, and documents related to topics in this chapter, visit **Make History** at bedfordstmartins.com/mckayworld.

• Hedwig of Bavaria Noble women in medieval Europe played a wide variety of roles. Hedwig of Bavaria conducted diplomatic negotiations, ruled her husband's territory when he was away, founded monasteries, and worked to expand Christianity in eastern Europe. (The John Paul Getty Museum, Los Angeles, Ms Ludwig XI, fol.12v [detail], Court Atelier of Duke Ludwig I of Liegnitz and Brieg [illuminator], *Vita beatae Hedwigis*, 1353. Tempera colors, colored washes and ink bound between wood boards covered with red-stained pigskin, 34.1 x 24.8 cm)

By the fifteenth century scholars in the growing cities of northern Italy began to think that they were living in a new era, one in which the glories of ancient Greece and Rome were being reborn. What separated their time from classical antiquity, in their opinion, was a long period of darkness and barbarism, to which a seventeenth-century professor gave the name "Middle Ages." In this conceptualization, the history of Europe was divided into three periods — ancient, medieval, and modern — an organization that is still in use today. Later, the history of other parts of the world was sometimes fit into this three-period schema as well, with discussions of the "classical" period in Maya history, of "medieval" India and China, and of "modern" everywhere.

Europe in the Middle Ages
800–1450

Today historians often question whether labels of past time periods for one culture work on a global scale, and some scholars are uncertain about whether "Middle Ages" is a just term even for European history. They assert that the Middle Ages was not simply a period of stagnation between two high points but rather a time of enormous intellectual energy and creative vitality. While agrarian life continued to dominate Europe, political structures that would influence later European history began to form, and Christianity continued to spread. People at the time did not know that they were living in an era that would later be labeled "middle" or sometimes even "dark," and we can wonder whether they would have shared this negative view of their own times.   •

Political Developments

□ How did medieval rulers overcome internal divisions and external threats, and work to create larger and more stable territories?

The Christian Church

□ How did the Christian Church enhance its power and create new institutions and religious practices?

The Crusades

□ What were the motives, course, and consequences of the Crusades?

The Life of the People

□ How did the lives of common people, nobles, and townspeople differ, and what new commercial developments increased wealth?

Learning and Culture

□ What were the primary educational and cultural developments in medieval Europe?

Crises of the Later Middle Ages

□ Why have the later Middle Ages been seen as a time of calamity and crisis?

Political Developments

□ How did medieval rulers overcome internal divisions and external threats, and work to create larger and more stable territories?

Later scholars dated the beginning of the Middle Ages to the fifth century, the time of the fall of the Roman Empire in the West. However, the growth of Germanic kingdoms such as those of the Merovingians and the Carolingians (see Chapter 8) is generally viewed as the beginning of "medieval" politics in Europe, and that is why we begin this chapter with the ninth century. In 800 Charlemagne, the most powerful of the Carolingians, was crowned the Holy Roman emperor. After his death his empire was divided among his grandsons, and their kingdoms were weakened by nobles vying for power. In addition, beginning around 800 western Europe was invaded by several different groups. Local nobles were the strongest power, and common people turned to them for protection. By the eleventh century, however, rulers in some parts of Europe reasserted authority and slowly built centralized states.

Invasions and Migrations

From the moors of Scotland to the mountains of Sicily, there arose in the ninth century the prayer, "Save us, O God, from the violence of the Northmen." The Northmen were pagan Germanic peoples from Norway, Sweden, and Denmark who came to be known as Vikings. Some scholars believe that the name *Viking* derives from the Old Norse word *vik*, meaning "creek." A Viking was someone who waited in a creek or bay to attack passing vessels.

Viking assaults began around 800, and by the mid-tenth century the Vikings had brought large sections of continental Europe and Britain under their sway. In the east they sailed the rivers of Russia as far as the Black Sea. In the west they established permanent settlements in Iceland and short-lived ones in Greenland and Newfoundland in Canada (Map 14.1).

The Vikings were superb seamen with advanced methods of boatbuilding. Propelled either by oars or by sails, lacking decks, and about sixty-five-feet long, a Viking ship could carry between forty and sixty men—enough to harass an isolated monastery or village. Against these ships navigated by experienced and fearless sailors, the Carolingian Empire, with no navy, was helpless. At first the Vikings attacked and sailed off laden with booty. Later, on returning, they settled down and colonized the areas they had conquered, often marrying local women and adopting the languages and some of the customs of their new homes.

Along with the Vikings, groups of central European steppe peoples known as Magyars (MAG-yahrz) also raided villages in the late ninth century, taking plunder and captives and forcing leaders to pay tribute in an effort to prevent further looting and destruction. Moving westward, small bands of Magyars on horseback reached far into Europe. They subdued northern Italy, compelled Bavaria and Saxony to pay tribute, and penetrated into the Rhineland and Burgundy. Western Europeans thought of them as returning Huns, so the Magyars came to be known as Hungarians. They settled in the area that is now Hungary, became Christian, and in the eleventh century allied with the papacy.

From North Africa, the Muslims also began new encroachments in the ninth century. They already ruled most of Spain and now conquered Sicily, driving northward into central Italy and the south coast of France.

What was the impact of these invasions? From the perspective of those living in what had been

• **vassal** A knight who has sworn loyalty to a particular lord.

" Save us, O God, from the violence of the Northmen. "

NINTH-CENTURY PRAYER

Charlemagne's empire, Viking, Magyar, and Muslim attacks contributed to increasing disorder and violence. Italian, French, and English sources often describe this period as one of terror and chaos. People in other parts of Europe might have had a different opinion. In Muslim Spain and Sicily scholars worked in thriving cities, and new crops such as cotton and sugar enhanced ordinary people's lives. In eastern Europe states such as Moravia and Hungary became strong kingdoms. A Viking point of view might be the most positive, for by 1100 descendants of the Vikings not only ruled their homelands in Norway, Sweden, and Denmark but also ruled northern France (a province known as Normandy, or land of the Northmen), England, Sicily, Iceland, and Russia, with an outpost in Greenland and occasional voyages to North America.

Feudalism and Manorialism

The large-scale division of Charlemagne's empire led to a decentralization of power at the local level. Civil wars weakened the power and prestige of kings, who could do little about regional violence. Likewise, the invasions of the ninth century, especially those of the Vikings, weakened royal authority. The Frankish kings were unable to halt the invaders, and the local aristocracy had to assume responsibility for defense. Thus, in the ninth and tenth centuries great aristocratic families increased their authority in their local territories, and distant and weak kings could not interfere. Common people turned for protection to the strongest power, the local nobles.

The most powerful nobles were those who gained warriors' allegiance, often symbolized in an oath-swearing ceremony of "homage and fealty" that grew out of earlier Germanic oaths of loyalty. In this ceremony a warrior (knight) swore his loyalty as a **vassal**—from a Celtic term meaning "servant"—to the more powerful individual, who became his lord. In return for the vassal's loyalty, aid,

Animal Headpost from a Viking Ship Skilled woodcarvers produced ornamental headposts for ships, sledges, wagons, and bedsteads. The fearsome quality of many carvings suggests that they were intended to ward off evil spirits and to terrify. (© University Museum of Cultural Heritage, Oslo. Photographer: Eirik Irgens Johnsen)

◻ Mapping the Past

MAP 14.1 Invasions and Migrations of the Ninth Century This map shows the Viking, Magyar, and Arab invasions and migrations in the ninth century. Compare it with Map 8.3 (page 221) on the barbarian migrations of late antiquity to answer the following questions.

ANALYZING THE MAP What similarities do you see in the patterns of migration in these two periods? What significant differences?

CONNECTIONS How did Viking expertise in shipbuilding and sailing make their migrations different from those of earlier Germanic tribes? How did this set them apart from the Magyar and Muslim invaders of the ninth century?

and military assistance, the lord promised him protection and material support. This support might be a place in the lord's household but was more likely land of the vassal's own, called a **fief** (*feudum* in Latin). The fief, which might contain forests, churches, and towns, technically still belonged to the lord, and the vassal had only the use of it. Peasants living on a fief produced the food and other goods necessary to maintain the knight.

Though historians debate this, fiefs appear to have been granted extensively first by Charles Martel (688–741) and then by his successors, including Charlemagne

and his grandsons. These fiefs went to the most powerful nobles, who often took the title of count. As the Carolingians' control of their territories weakened, the practice of granting fiefs moved to the local level, with lay lords, bishops, and abbots as well as kings granting fiefs. This system, later named **feudalism**, was based on personal ties of loyalty cemented by grants of land rather than on allegiance to an abstract state or governmental system.

The economic power of the warrior class rested on landed estates, which were worked by peasants under

Homage and Fealty Although the rite of entering a feudal relationship varied widely across Europe and sometimes was entirely verbal, a few illustrations exist. Here the vassal kneels before the lord, places his clasped hands between those of the lord, and declares, "I become your man." Sometimes the lord handed over a clump of earth, representing the fief, and the ceremony concluded with a kiss, symbolizing peace between them. (Osterreichische Nationalbibliothek, Vienna #E 8.037-C/D [Cod. 2262, fol 174r])

a system of **manorialism**. Free farmers surrendered themselves and their land to the lord's jurisdiction in exchange for protection. The land was given back to them to farm, but they were tied to the land by various payments and services. Most significantly, a peasant lost his or her freedom and became a **serf**, part of the lord's permanent labor force. Unlike slaves, serfs were personally free, but they were bound to the land and unable to leave it without the lord's permission.

The transition from freedom to serfdom was slow, but by the year 800 perhaps 60 percent of the population of western Europe had been reduced to serfdom. Over the next several centuries unstable conditions and insecurity further increased the need for protection, so that by around 1000 the majority of western Europeans were serfs. While serfs ranged from the highly prosperous to the desperately poor, all had lost their freedom. In eastern Europe the transition was slower but longer lasting. Western European peasants began to escape from serfdom in the later Middle Ages, at the very point that serfs were more firmly tied to the land in eastern Europe, especially in eastern Germany, Poland, and Russia.

The Restoration of Order

The eleventh century witnessed the beginnings of political stability in western Europe. Foreign invasions gradually declined, and in some parts of Europe lords in control of large territories built up their power even further, becoming kings over growing and slowly centralizing states. As rulers expanded their territories and extended their authority, they developed larger bureaucracies, armies, judicial systems, and other institutions to maintain control, as well as taxation systems to pay for them. These new institutions and practices laid the foundations for modern national states. Political developments in England, France, and Germany provide good examples of the beginnings of the national state in the central Middle Ages.

Under the pressure of Viking invasions in the ninth and tenth centuries, the seven kingdoms of Anglo-Saxon England united under one king. At the same time, England was divided into local shires, or counties, each under the jurisdiction of a sheriff appointed by the king. When Edward the Confessor (r. 1042–1066) died, his cousin, Duke William of Normandy, a French-speaking descendant of the Vikings, crossed the channel and won the English throne by defeating his Anglo-

- **fief** A portion of land, the use of which was given by a lord to a vassal in exchange for the latter's oath of loyalty.
- **feudalism** A medieval European political system that defines the military obligations and relations between a lord and his vassals and involves the granting of fiefs.
- **manorialism** The economic system that governed rural life in medieval Europe, in which the landed estates of a lord were worked by the peasants under the lord's jurisdiction in exchange for his protection.
- **serf** A peasant who lost his or her freedom and became permanently bound to the landed estate of a lord.

Saxon rival at the Battle of Hastings. Later dubbed "the Conqueror," William (r. 1066–1087) subdued the rest of the country, distributed land to his Norman followers, and required all feudal lords to swear an oath of allegiance to him as king. He retained the Anglo-Saxon institution of sheriff.

In 1085 William decided to conduct a systematic survey of the entire country to determine how much wealth there was and who had it. This process was described by a contemporary chronicler:

> He sent his men over all England into every shire and had them find out . . . what or how much everybody had who was occupying land in England, in land or cattle, and how much money it was worth. So very narrowly did he have it investigated, that there was no single . . . yard of land, nor indeed . . . one ox nor one cow nor one pig was there left out, and not put down in his record: and all these records were brought to him afterwards.[1]

The resulting record, called the *Domesday Book* (DOOMZ-day) from the Anglo-Saxon word *doom*, meaning "judgment," provided William and his descendants with vital information for governing the country. Completed in 1086, the book still survives, and it is an invaluable source of social and economic information about medieval England.

In 1128 William's granddaughter Matilda married a powerful French noble, Geoffrey of Anjou. Their son, who became Henry II of England, inherited provinces in northwestern France from his father. When Henry married the great heiress Eleanor of Aquitaine in 1152, he claimed lordship over Aquitaine and other provinces in southwestern France as well. The histories of England and France were thus closely intertwined in the Middle Ages.

In the early twelfth century France consisted of a number of nearly independent provinces, each governed by its local ruler. The work of unifying France began under Philip II (r. 1180–1223), called "Augustus" because he vastly enlarged the territory of the kingdom. By the end of his reign Philip was effectively master of northern France, and by 1300 most of the provinces of modern France had been added to the royal domain through diplomacy, marriage, war, and inheritance.

In central Europe the German king Otto I (r. 936–973) defeated many other lords to build up his power, based on an alliance with and control of the church.

The Norman Conquest, 1066

Norman territory, ca. 1066
Major battle

Otto asserted the right to control church appointments, and bishops and abbots had to perform feudal homage for the lands that accompanied their church positions. German rulers were not able to build up centralized power, however. Under Otto I and his successors, a loose confederation stretching from the North Sea to the Mediterranean developed. In this confederation, later called the Holy Roman Empire, the emperor shared power with princes, dukes, counts, city officials, archbishops, and bishops.

Frederick Barbarossa (r. 1152–1190) of the house of Hohenstaufen tried valiantly to make the Holy Roman Empire a united state. He made alliances with the high nobles and even compelled the great churchmen to become his vassals. When he tried to enforce his authority over the cities of northern Italy, however, they formed a league against him in alliance with the pope, and infantrymen from the cities defeated Frederick's mounted knights. Frederick's absence from the German part of his empire allowed the princes and other rulers of independent provinces to consolidate their power there as well.

Law and Justice

Throughout Europe in the twelfth and thirteenth centuries, the law was a hodgepodge of customs, feudal rights, and provincial practices. Rulers wanted to blend these elements into a uniform system of rules acceptable and applicable to all their peoples, though their success in doing so varied.

The French king Louis IX (r. 1226–1270) was famous in his time for his concern for justice. Each French province, even after being made part of the kingdom of France, retained its unique laws and procedures. But Louis IX created a royal judicial system, establishing the Parlement of Paris, a kind of supreme court that heard appeals from lower courts.

Under Henry II (r. 1154–1189), England developed and extended a common law—a law common to and accepted by the entire country. No other country in medieval Europe did so. Each year Henry sent out circuit judges (royal officials who traveled in a given circuit or district) to hear civil and criminal cases. Wherever the king's judges sat, there sat the king's court. Slowly, the king's court gained jurisdiction over all property disputes and criminal actions.

Henry's son John (r. 1199–1216) met with serious disappointment after taking the throne. He lost the

French province of Normandy to Philip Augustus in 1204 and spent the rest of his reign trying to win it back. Saddled with heavy debt from his father and brother Richard (r. 1189–1199), John tried to squeeze more money from nobles and town dwellers, creating an atmosphere of resentment. When John's military campaign failed in 1214, it was clear that the French lands that had once belonged to the English king were lost for good. His ineptitude as a soldier in a culture that idealized military glory turned the people against him. The barons revolted and in 1215 forced him to attach his seal to the Magna Carta — the "Great Charter," which became the cornerstone of English justice and law.

To contemporaries the Magna Carta was intended to redress the grievances that particular groups had against King John. It came to have much broader significance, however, and every English king in the Middle Ages reissued the Magna Carta as evidence of his promise to observe the law. It came to signify the principle that everyone, including the king and the government, must obey the law, and it gradually came to be seen as almost sacred. Some clauses of the Magna Carta contain the germ of the idea of due process of law: a person may not be arbitrarily arrested and held indefinitely in prison without being accused of crime and brought to trial.

Statements of legal principles such as the Magna Carta were not how most people experienced the law in medieval Europe. Instead they were involved in actual cases. Judges determined guilt or innocence in a number of ways. In some cases, particularly those in which there was little clear evidence, they ordered a trial by ordeal, in which the accused might be tied hand and foot and dropped in a lake or river. People believed that water was a pure substance and would reject anything foul or unclean, although God could always affect the outcome. Thus a person who sank was considered innocent, while a person who floated was found guilty. Trials by ordeal are fascinating to modern audiences, but they were relatively rare, and their use declined as courts increasingly favored more rational procedures, in which judges heard testimony, sought witnesses, and read written evidence if it was available. Violent crimes were often punished by public execution. Hanging was the most common method of execution, although nobles might be beheaded because hanging was seen as demeaning. Executioners were feared figures, but they were also well-paid public officials and were a necessary part of the legal structure.

The Christian Church

☐ How did the Christian Church enhance its power and create new institutions and religious practices?

Kings and emperors were not the only rulers consolidating their power in the eleventh and twelfth centuries; the papacy did as well, although the popes' efforts were sometimes challenged by medieval kings and emperors. Despite such challenges, monasteries continued to be important places for learning and devotion, and new religious orders were founded. Also, Christianity expanded into Europe's northern and eastern regions, and Christian rulers expanded their holdings in Muslim Spain.

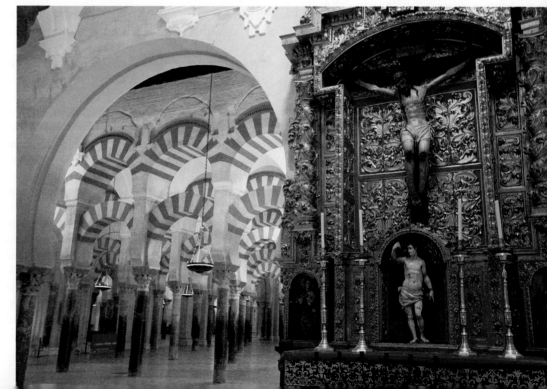

Córdoba Mosque and Cathedral The huge arches of the Great Mosque at Córdoba dwarf the cathedral built in its center after the city was conquered by Christian armies in 1236. During the reconquista (see page 404), Christian kings often transformed mosques into churches, often by simply adding Christian elements such as crosses and altars to existing structures. (dbimages/ Alamy)

Papal Reforms

During the ninth and tenth centuries the church came under the control of kings and feudal lords, who chose priests, bishops, abbots, and other church officials in their territories, granting them fiefs that provided an income and expecting loyalty and service in return. Church offices were sometimes sold outright — a practice called *simony*. Although the Roman Church encouraged clerical celibacy, many priests were married or living with women. Popes were chosen by wealthy Roman families from among their members, and after gaining the papal office they paid more attention to their families' political fortunes or their own pleasures than to the institutional or spiritual health of the church. Not surprisingly, clergy at all levels who had bought their positions or had been granted them for political reasons provided little spiritual guidance, and their personal lives were rarely models of high moral standards.

Serious efforts to change all this began in the eleventh century. A series of popes believed that secular or lay control over the church was largely responsible for the lack of moral leadership, so they proclaimed the church independent from secular rulers. The Lateran Council of 1059 decreed that the authority and power to elect the pope rested solely in the college of cardinals, a special group of priests from the major churches in and around Rome. The college retains that power today.

Pope Gregory VII (pontificate 1073–1085) vigorously championed reform and the expansion of papal power. He ordered all priests to give up their wives and children or face dismissal, invalidated the ordination of church officials who had purchased their offices, and placed nuns under firmer control of male authorities. He believed that the pope, as the successor of Saint Peter, was the vicar of God on earth and that papal orders were the orders of God. Thus he was the first pope to emphasize the political authority of the papacy. He ordered that any church official selected or appointed by a layperson should be deposed, and any layperson, including rulers, who appointed a church official should be excommunicated — cut off from the sacraments and the Christian community.

European rulers immediately protested this restriction of their power, and the strongest reaction came from Henry IV, the ruler of Germany who would later become the Holy Roman emperor. Henry continued to appoint officials, and Gregory responded by excommunicating bishops who supported Henry and threatening to depose him. In January 1077 Henry arrived at the pope's residence in Canossa in northern Italy and, according to legend, stood outside in the snow for three days seeking forgiveness. As a priest, Gregory was obliged to grant absolution and readmit the emperor into the Christian community. Although Henry bowed before the pope, he actually won a victory, maintaining authority over his subjects and in 1084 being crowned emperor. This victory was temporary, however, for high nobles within the empire took advantage of further conflicts with the pope to enhance their position, siding with the church to gain power. They subordinated lesser nobles, expanded restrictions on peasants, and prevented later emperors such as Frederick Barbarossa from unifying the empire.

Monastic Life

Although they were in theory cut off from the world (see page 214), monasteries and convents were deeply affected by issues of money, rank, and power. By the eighth century monasteries and convents dotted the European landscape, and during the ninth and tenth centuries they were often the target of Viking attacks or raids by local looters seeking valuable objects. Some religious communities fled and dispersed, while others fell under the control and domination of local feudal lords. Powerful laymen appointed themselves or their relatives as abbots, took the lands and goods of monasteries, and spent monastic revenues.

Medieval monasteries fulfilled the needs of the feudal system in other ways as well. They provided noble boys with education and opportunities for ecclesiastical careers. Although a few men who rose in the ranks of church officials were of humble origins, most were from high-status families. Social class also defined the kinds of religious life open to women. Kings and nobles usually established convents for their female relatives and other elite women, and the position of abbess, or head of a convent, became the most powerful position a woman could hold in medieval society. (See "Individuals in Society: Hildegard of Bingen," page 401.) People of lower social standing did live and work in monasteries, but as lay brothers and sisters who performed manual labor, not religious duties.

Routines within individual monasteries varied widely from house to house and from region to region. In every monastery, however, daily life centered on the liturgy or Divine Office, psalms, and other prayers, which monks and nuns said seven times a day and once during the night. Praying was looked on as a vital service, as crucial as the labor of peasants and the military might of nobles. Prayers were said for peace, rain, good harvests, the civil authorities, the monks' and nuns' families, and their benefactors. Monastic patrons in turn lavished gifts on the monasteries, which often became very wealthy, controlling large tracts of land and the peasants who farmed them.

The combination of lay control and wealth created problems for monasteries as monks and nuns concentrated on worldly issues and levels of spiritual observance and intellectual activity declined. Several waves

Hildegard of Bingen

THE TENTH CHILD OF A LESSER NOBLE FAMILY, Hildegard (1098–1179) was turned over to the care of an abbey in the Rhineland when she was eight years old. There she learned Latin and received a good education. She spent most of her life in various women's religious communities, two of which she founded herself. When she was a child, she began having mystical visions, often of light in the sky, but told few people about them. In middle age, however, her visions became more dramatic: "And it came to pass . . . when I was 42 years and 7 months old, that the heavens were opened and a blinding light of exceptional brilliance flowed through my entire brain. And so it kindled my whole heart and breast like a flame, not burning but warming . . . and suddenly I understood of the meaning of expositions of the books."* She wanted the church to approve of her visions and wrote first to St. Bernard of Clairvaux, who answered her briefly and dismissively, and then to Pope Eugenius, who encouraged her to write them down. Her first work was *Scivias* (Know the Ways of the Lord), a record of her mystical visions that incorporates extensive theological learning (see the illustration).

Obviously possessed of leadership and administrative talents, Hildegard left her abbey in 1147 to found the convent of Rupertsberg near Bingen. There she produced *Physica* (On the Physical Elements) and *Causa et Curae* (Causes and Cures), scientific works on the curative properties of natural elements; poems; a mystery play; and several more works of mysticism. She carried on a huge correspondence with scholars, prelates, and ordinary people. When she was over fifty, she left her community to preach to audiences of clergy and laity, and she was the only woman of her time whose opinions on religious matters were considered authoritative by the church.

Hildegard's visions have been explored by theologians and also by neurologists, who judge that they may have originated in migraine headaches, as she reports many of the same phenomena that migraine sufferers do: auras of light around objects, areas of blindness, feelings of intense doubt and intense euphoria. The interpretations that she develops come from her theological insight and learning, however, not from her illness. That same insight also emerges in her music, which is what she is best known for today. Eighty of her compositions survive—a huge number for a medieval composer—most of them written to be sung by the nuns in her convent, so they have strong lines for female voices. Many of her songs and chants have been recorded recently by various artists and are available on compact disk, as downloads, and on several Web sites.

QUESTIONS FOR ANALYSIS

1. Why do you think Hildegard might have kept her visions secret at first? Why do you think she eventually sought church approval for them?
2. In what ways were Hildegard's accomplishments extraordinary given women's general status in the Middle Ages?

*From *Scivias*, trans. Mother Columba Hart and Jane Bishop, *The Classics of Western Spirituality* (New York/Mahwah: Paulist Press, 1990).

Inspired by heavenly fire, Hildegard begins to dictate her visions to her scribe. The original of this elaborately illustrated copy of *Scivias* disappeared from Hildegard's convent during World War II, but fortunately a facsimile had already been made. (Private Collection/The Bridgeman Art Library)

Agricultural Work In this scene from a German manuscript written about 1190, men and women of different ages are sowing seeds and harvesting grain. All residents of a village, including children, engaged in agricultural tasks. (Rheinisches Landesmuseum, Bonn/The Bridgeman Art Library)

of reform improved the situation in some monasteries, but when deeply impressed laypeople showered gifts on monasteries with good reputations, monastic observance and spiritual fervor again declined. New religious orders, such as the Cistercians (sihs-TUHR-shuhnz), founded in 1098, attempted to solve the problem by establishing their houses in isolated areas, rejecting the traditional feudal sources of income (such as the possession of mills and serfs), and living very simply. Their innovative methods of farming, sheep-raising, and cloth production brought financial success, however, and by the late twelfth century economic prosperity and political power had begun to compromise the original Cistercian ideals.

In the thirteenth century the growth of cities provided a new challenge for the church. Many urban people thought that the church did not meet their spiritual needs. They turned instead to heresies — that is, to versions of Christianity outside of those approved by the papacy. Ironically, many of these belief systems denied the value of material wealth. Combating **heresy** became a principal task of new religious orders, most prominently the Dominicans and Franciscans, who preached and ministered to city dwellers; the Dominicans also staffed the papal Inquisition, a special court designed to root out heresy.

Popular Religion

Apart from the land, the weather, and local legal and social conditions, religion had the greatest impact on the daily lives of ordinary people in medieval Europe. Religious practices varied widely from country to country and even from province to province. But nowhere was religion a one-hour-a-week affair.

For Christians, the village church was the center of community life — social, political, and economic as well as religious — with the parish priest in charge of a host of activities. Every Sunday and on holy days the villagers stood at Mass or squatted on the floor (there were no chairs), breaking the painful routine of work. The feasts that accompanied baptisms, weddings, funerals, and other celebrations were commonly held in the churchyard. Popular religion consisted largely of rituals heavy with symbolism. For example, before slicing a loaf of bread, the pious woman tapped the sign of the cross on it with her knife. Before planting began on local lands, the village priest customarily went out and sprinkled the fields with water, symbolizing refreshment and life. Everyone participated in village processions. The entire calendar was designed with reference to Christmas, Easter, and Pentecost, events in the life of Jesus and his disciples.

The Christian calendar was also filled with saints' days. Saints were individuals who had lived particularly holy lives and were honored locally or more widely for their connection with the divine. The cult of the saints, which developed in a rural and uneducated en-

• **heresy** An opinion, belief, or action counter to doctrines that church leaders defined as correct; heretics could be punished by the church.

vironment, represents a central feature of popular culture in the Middle Ages. People believed that the saints possessed supernatural powers that enabled them to perform miracles, and each saint became the special property of the locality in which his or her relics—remains or possessions—rested. Relics such as the saint's bones, articles of clothing, tears, and saliva, and even the dust from his or her tomb, were enclosed in the church altar. In return for the saint's healing powers and support, peasants would offer prayers, loyalty, and gifts.

Just as they felt connections to saints, people had a strong sense of the presence of God. They believed that God rewarded the virtuous with peace, health, and material prosperity and punished sinners with disease, poor harvests, and war. Sin was caused by the Devil, who lurked everywhere and constantly incited people to evil deeds.

Most people in medieval Europe were Christian, but there were small Jewish communities scattered through many parts of Europe, as well as Muslims in the Iberian Peninsula, Sicily, other Mediterranean islands, and southeastern Europe. Increasing suspicion and hostility marked relations among believers in different religions throughout the Middle Ages, but there were also important similarities in the ways that European Christians, Jews, and Muslims understood and experienced their faiths. In all three traditions, every major life transition, such as marriage or the birth of a child, was marked by a ceremony that involved religious officials or spiritual elements. In all three faiths, death was marked by religious rituals, and the living had obligations to the dead, including prayers and special mourning periods.

The Expansion of Christianity

The eleventh and twelfth centuries saw not only reforms in monasticism and the papacy but also an expansion of Christianity into Scandinavia, the Baltic lands, eastern Europe, and Spain that had profound cultural consequences. The expansion was accomplished through wars, the establishment of new bishoprics, and the vast migration of Christian colonists into non-Christian territories. As it occurred, more and more Europeans began to think of themselves as belonging to a realm of Christianity that was political as well as religious, a realm they called Christendom.

Christian influences entered Scandinavia and the Baltic lands primarily through the creation of dioceses (church districts headed by bishops). This took place in Denmark in the tenth and eleventh centuries, and the institutional church spread rather quickly due to the support offered by the strong throne. Dioceses were established in Norway and Sweden in the eleventh century, and in 1164 Uppsala, Sweden, long the center of the pagan cults of Odin and Thor, became a Catholic archdiocese.

Otto I (see page 398) planted a string of dioceses along his northern and eastern frontiers, hoping to pacify the newly conquered Slavs in eastern Europe. However, frequent Slavic revolts illustrate the people's resentment of German lords and clerics and indicate that the church did not easily penetrate the region.

The church also moved into central Europe, first into Bohemia in the tenth century and from there into Poland and Hungary in the eleventh century. In the twelfth and thirteenth centuries thousands of settlers poured into eastern Europe from the west. These new

Baking Bread Bread and beer or ale were the main manorial products for local consumption. While women dominated the making of ale and beer, men and women cooperated in the making and baking of bread—the staple of the diet. Most people did not have ovens in their own homes because of the danger of fire; they used the communal manorial oven, which, like a modern pizza oven, could bake several loaves at once. (Bibliothèque nationale de France)

immigrants, German in descent, name, language, and law, settled in Silesia, Mecklenburg, Bohemia, Poland, Hungary, and Transylvania, where they established towns.

The Iberian Peninsula was another area of Christian expansion. About 950 Caliph Abd al-Rahman III (912–961) of the Umayyad Dynasty of Córdoba ruled most of the peninsula. Christian Spain consisted of the small kingdoms of Castile, León, Catalonia, Aragon, Navarre, and Portugal. When civil wars erupted among Rahman's descendants, Muslim lands were split among several small kingdoms, making it easier for Christians to take over these lands. By 1248 Christians held all of the peninsula save for the small state of Granada in the south. As the Christians advanced, they changed the face of Spanish cities, transforming mosques into cathedrals.

Fourteenth-century clerical propagandists would call the movement to expel the Muslims the **reconquista** (reconquest) — a sacred and patriotic crusade to wrest the country from "alien" Muslim hands from about 722 to 1492. This religious idea became part of Spanish political culture and of the national psychology. Rulers of the Christian kingdoms of Spain increasingly passed legislation discriminating against Muslims and Jews living under Christian rule, and they attempted to exclude anyone from the nobility who could not prove "purity of blood" — that is, that they had no Muslim or Jewish ancestors. As a consequence of the reconquista (ray-kon-KEES-tah), the Spanish and Portuguese also learned how to administer vast tracts of newly acquired territory. In the sixteenth century they used their claims about the rightful dominance of Christianity to justify their colonization of new territories in Mexico, Brazil, Peru, Angola, and the Philippines, and relied on their experiences at home to provide models of how to govern.

Spain was not the only place in Europe where "blood" became a way of understanding differences among people and a basis for discriminatory laws. When Germans moved into eastern Europe and English forces took over much of Ireland, they increasingly barred local people from access to legal courts and denied them positions in monasteries or craft guilds. They banned intermarriage between ethnic groups in an attempt to maintain ethnic purity, even though everyone was Christian. As Europeans later came into contact with people from Africa and Asia, and particularly as they developed co-

Date of Christian reconquest
By 814 ■ By 1097 ■ By 1275
By 910 ■ By 1150 ■ By 1492
By 1037 ■ By 1190

The Reconquista, 722–1492

lonial empires there, these notions of blood also became a way of conceptualizing racial categories.

The Crusades

☐ What were the motives, course, and consequences of the Crusades?

The expansion of Christianity in the Middle Ages was not limited to Europe but extended to the eastern Mediterranean in what were later termed the **Crusades**. Occurring in the late eleventh and early twelfth centuries, the Crusades were wars sponsored by the papacy to recover the holy city of Jerusalem from the Muslims. The word *crusade* was not actually used at the time and did not appear in English until the late sixteenth century. It means literally "taking the cross," a vow to spread Christianity symbolized by the cross that soldiers sewed on their garments. Although people of all ages and classes participated in the Crusades, so many knights did that crusading became a distinctive feature of the upper-class lifestyle. In an aristocratic military society, men coveted reputations as Crusaders; the Christian knight who had been to Jerusalem enjoyed great prestige.

Background and Motives

In the eleventh century the papacy had strong reasons for wanting to launch an expedition against Muslims in the East. If the pope could muster a large army against the enemies of Christianity, his claim to be the leader of Christian society in the West would be strengthened. Moreover, in 1054 a serious theological disagreement had split the Greek Church of Byzantium and the Roman Church of the West. The pope believed that a crusade would lead to strong Roman influence in Greek territories and eventually the reunion of the two churches.

Popes and other church officials gained support for war in defense of Christianity by promising spiritual benefits to those who joined a campaign or died fighting. Church leaders said that these people would be forgiven for their sins without having to do penance, that is, without having to confess to a priest and carry out some action to make up for the sins. Preachers communicated these ideas widely and told stories about warrior-saints who slew hundreds of enemies.

Religious zeal led increasing numbers of people to go on pilgrimages to holy places, including Jerusalem. The Arabic Muslims who had ruled Jerusalem and the surrounding territory for centuries allowed Christian pilgrims to travel freely, but in the late eleventh century the Seljuk Turks took over Palestine, defeating

MAP 14.2 The Crusades, 1096–1270 The Crusaders took many different sea and land routes on their way to Jerusalem, often crossing the lands of the Byzantine Empire, which led to conflict with Eastern Christians. The Crusader kingdoms in the East lasted only briefly.

Legend:
- First Crusade, 1096–1099
- Second Crusade, 1147–1149
- Third Crusade, 1189–1192
- Fourth Crusade, 1202–1204
- Crusade of Frederick II, 1228–1229
- Crusades of Louis IX, 1248–1254 and 1270
- Crusader kingdoms in the East
- Major battle

both Arabic and Byzantine armies, and pilgrimage became more difficult. The Byzantine emperor at Constantinople appealed to western European Christians for support. The emperor's appeal fit well with papal aims, and in 1095 Pope Urban II called for a great Christian holy war against the infidels. He urged Christian knights who had been fighting one another to direct their energies against those he claimed were the true enemies of God, the Muslims.

The Course of the Crusades

Thousands of people of all classes responded to Urban's call, streaming southward and then toward Jerusalem in what became known as the First Crusade. The First Crusade was successful, mostly because of the dynamic enthusiasm of the participants, who had little more than religious zeal. They knew little of the geography or climate of the Middle East, and although there were several counts with military experience, the Crusaders could never agree on a leader. Adding to these disadvantages, supply lines were never set up, starvation and disease wracked the army, and the Turks slaughtered hundreds of noncombatants. Nevertheless, the army pressed on, defeating the Turks in several battles,

and after a monthlong siege it took Jerusalem in July 1099 (Map 14.2). Fulcher of Chartres, a chaplain on the First Crusade, described the scene:

> Amid the sound of trumpets and with everything in an uproar they attacked boldly, shouting "God help us!" . . . They ran with the greatest exultation as fast as they could into the city and joined their companions in pursuing and slaying their wicked enemies without cessation. . . . If you had been there your feet would have been stained to the ankles in the blood of the slain. What shall I say? None of them were left alive. Neither women nor children were spared.[2]

With Jerusalem taken, some Crusaders regarded their mission as accomplished and set off for home, but the appearance of more Muslim troops convinced the Crusaders that they needed to stay. Slowly institutions were set up to rule local territories and the Muslim

- **reconquista** A fourteenth-century term used to describe the Christian crusade to wrest Spain back from the Muslims from 722 to 1492; clerics believed it was a sacred and patriotic mission.
- **Crusades** Holy wars sponsored by the papacy for the recovery of the Holy Land from the Muslims.

Listening to the Past

An Arab View of the Crusades

The Crusades helped shape the understanding that Arabs and Europeans had of each other and all subsequent relations between the Christian West and the Arab world. To medieval Christians, the Crusades were papally approved military expeditions to recover holy places in Palestine; to the Arabs, these campaigns were "Frankish wars" or "Frankish invasions" for the acquisition of territory.

Early in the thirteenth century, Ibn Al-Athir (1160–1223), a native of Mosul, an important economic and cultural center in northern Mesopotamia (modern Iraq), wrote a history of the First Crusade. He relied on Arab sources for the events he described. Here is his account of the Crusaders' capture of Antioch.

❝The power of the Franks first became apparent when in the year 478/1085–86* they invaded the territories of Islam and took Toledo and other parts of Andalusia [in Spain]. Then in 484/1091 they attacked and conquered the island of Sicily and turned their attention to the African coast. Certain of their conquests there were won back again, but they had other successes, as you will see.

In 490/1097 the Franks attacked Syria. This is how it all began: Baldwin, their King, a kinsman of Roger the Frank who had conquered Sicily, assembled a great army and sent word to Roger saying: "I have assembled a great army and now I am on my way to you, to use your bases for my conquest of the African coast. Thus you and I shall become neighbors."

Roger called together his companions and consulted them about these proposals. "This will be a fine thing for them and for us!" they declared, "for by this means these lands will be converted to the Faith!" At this Roger raised one leg and farted loudly, and swore that it was of more use than their advice. "Why?" "Because if this army comes here it will need quantities of provisions and fleets of ships to transport it to Africa, as well as reinforcements from my own troops. Then, if the Franks succeed in conquering this territory they will take it over and will need provisioning from Sicily. This will cost me my annual profit from the harvest. If they fail they will return here and be an embarrassment to me here in my own domain." . . .

He summoned Baldwin's messenger and said to him: "If you have decided to make war on the Muslims your best course will be to free Jerusalem from their rule and thereby win great honor. I am bound by certain promises and treaties of allegiance with the ruler of Africa." So the Franks made ready to set out to attack Syria.

Another story is that the Fatimids of Egypt were afraid when they saw the Seljuqids extending their empire through Syria as far as Gaza, until they reached the Egyptian border and Atsiz invaded Egypt itself. They therefore sent to invite the Franks to invade Syria and so protect Egypt from the Muslims.† But God knows best.

When the Franks decided to attack Syria they marched east to Constantinople, so that they could cross the straits and advance into Muslim territory by the easier, land route. When they reached Constantinople, the Emperor of the East refused them permission to pass through his domains. He said: "Unless you first promise me Antioch, I shall not allow you to cross into the Muslim empire." His real intention was to incite them to attack the Muslims, for he was convinced that the Turks, whose invincible control over Asia Minor he had observed, would exterminate every one of them. They accepted his conditions and in 490/1097 they crossed the Bosphorus at Constantinople. . . . They . . . reached Antioch, which they besieged.

When Yaghi Siyan, the ruler of Antioch, heard of their approach, he was not sure how the Christian people of the city would react, so he made the Muslims go outside the city on their own to dig trenches, and the next day sent the Christians out alone to continue the task. When they were ready to return home at the end of the day he refused to allow them. "Antioch is yours," he said, "but you will have to leave it to me until I see what happens between us and the Franks." "Who will protect our children and our wives?" they said. "I shall look after them for you." So they resigned themselves to their fate, and lived in the Frankish camp for nine months, while the city was under siege.

*Muslims traditionally date events from Muhammad's hegira, or emigration, to Medina, which occurred in 622 according to the Christian calendar.

†Although Muslims, Fatimids were related doctrinally to the Shi'ites, but the dominant Sunni Muslims considered the Fatimids heretics.

population. Four small "Crusader states" — Jerusalem, Edessa, Tripoli, and Antioch — were established, and castles and fortified towns were built in these states to defend against Muslim reconquest. Reinforcements arrived in the form of pilgrims and fighters from Europe, so that there was constant coming and going by land and more often by sea after the Crusaders conquered port cities.

Between 1096 and 1270 the crusading ideal was expressed in eight papally approved expeditions, though none after the First Crusade accomplished very much. The Muslim states in the Middle East were politically fragmented when the Crusaders first came, and it took them about a century to reorganize. They did so dramatically under Saladin (Salah al-Din), who unified Egypt and Syria. In 1187 the Muslims retook Jerusa-

Yaghi Siyan showed unparalleled courage and wisdom, strength and judgment. If all the Franks who died had survived they would have overrun all the lands of Islam. He protected the families of the Christians in Antioch and would not allow a hair of their heads to be touched.

After the siege had been going on for a long time the Franks made a deal with . . . a cuirass [breastplate]-maker called Ruzbih whom they bribed with a fortune in money and lands. He worked in the tower that stood over the riverbed, where the river flowed out of the city into the valley. The Franks sealed their pact with the cuirass-maker, God damn him! and made their way to the water-gate. They opened it and entered the city. Another gang of them climbed the tower with their ropes. At dawn, when more than 500 of them were in the city and the defenders were worn out after the night watch, they sounded their trumpets. . . . Panic seized Yaghi Siyan and he opened the city gates and fled in terror, with an escort of thirty pages. His army commander arrived, but when he discovered on enquiry that Yaghi Siyan had fled, he made his escape by another gate. This was of great help to the Franks, for if he had stood firm for an hour, they would have been wiped out. They entered the city by the gates and sacked it, slaughtering all the Muslims they found there. This happened in Jumada I (491/April/May 1098). . . .

It was the discord between the Muslim princes . . . that enabled the Franks to overrun the country. 99

Source: *Arab Historians of the Crusades*, selected and translated from the Arabic sources by Francesco Gabrieli. Translated from the Italian by E. J. Costello. © 1969 by Routledge & Kegan Paul Ltd. Reproduced by permission of Taylor & Francis Books UK and The University of California Press.

QUESTIONS FOR ANALYSIS

1. Most Christian histories of the Crusades begin with Pope Urban II's call in 1095. What does Ibn Al-Athir see as the beginning? How would this make his view of the Crusades different from that of Christian chroniclers?

2. How does Ibn Al-Athir characterize the Christian leaders Roger and Baldwin? How does this compare with his characterization of Yaghi Siyan, the Muslim ruler of Antioch?

3. To what does Ibn Al-Athir attribute the fall of Antioch? To what does he attribute Christian defeats of the Muslims more generally? What does this suggest about his view of Christian military capabilities?

lem, but the Christians kept their hold on port towns, and Saladin allowed pilgrims safe passage to Jerusalem. From that point on, the Crusader states were more important economically than politically or religiously, giving Italian and French merchants direct access to Eastern products such as perfumes and silk.

After the Muslims retook Jerusalem the crusading movement faced other setbacks. During the Fourth Crusade (1202–1204), Crusaders stopped in Constantinople, and when they were not welcomed they sacked the city and grabbed thousands of relics, which were later sold in Europe. The Byzantine Empire splintered into three parts and soon consisted of little more than the city of Constantinople. Moreover, the assault of one Christian people on another — when one of the goals of the Crusades was reunion of the Greek and Latin

Churches — made the split between the churches permanent and discredited the entire crusading movement in the eyes of many Christians.

The battles of the Crusades were typical of much medieval warfare, which consisted of the besieging of towns and castles. Help could not enter nor could anyone leave; the larger the number of besiegers, the greater was the chance the fortification would fall. Women swelled the numbers of besiegers. In the Crusades, women assisted in filling the moats surrounding fortified places with earth so that ladders and war engines could be brought close, provided water to fighting men, worked as washerwomen, foraged for food, and provided sexual services.

In the late thirteenth century Turkish armies, after gradually conquering all other Muslim rulers, turned against the Crusader states. In 1291 the Christians' last stronghold, the port of Acre, fell in a battle that was just as bloody as the first battle for Jerusalem two centuries earlier. Knights then needed a new battlefield for military actions, which some found in Spain, where the rulers of Aragon and Castile continued fighting Muslims until 1492.

Consequences of the Crusades

The Crusades testified to the religious enthusiasm of the High Middle Ages and the influence of the papacy, gave kings and the pope opportunities to expand their bureaucracies, and provided an outlet for nobles' dreams of glory. The Crusades also introduced some Europeans to Eastern luxury goods, but their immediate cultural impact on the West remains debatable. By the late eleventh century strong economic and intellectual ties with the East had already been made. However, the Crusades were a boon to Italian merchants, who profited from outfitting military expeditions as well as from the opening of new trade routes and the establishment of trading communities in the Crusader states.

Despite these advantages, the Crusades had some seriously negative sociopolitical consequences. For one thing, they proved to be a disaster for Jewish-Christian relations. Inspired by the ideology of holy war, Christian armies on their way to Jerusalem on the First Crusade joined with local mobs to attack Jewish families and communities, sometimes burning people alive in the synagogue or Jewish section of town. Later Crusades brought similar violence, enhanced by accusations that Jews engaged in the ritual murder of Christians to use their blood in religious rites.

Legal restrictions on Jews gradually increased throughout Europe. Jews were forbidden to have Christian servants or employees, to hold public office, to appear in public on Christian holy days, or to enter Christian parts of town without a badge marking them as Jews. They were prohibited from engaging in any trade with Christians except money-lending — which only fueled popular resentment — and were banished from England and France.

The Crusades also left an inheritance of deep bitterness in Christian-Muslim relations. Each side dehumanized the other, viewing those who followed the other religion as unbelievers. (See "Listening to the Past: An Arab View of the Crusades," page 406.) Whereas Europeans perceived the Crusades as sacred religious movements, Muslims saw them as expansionist and imperialistic. The ideal of a sacred mission to conquer or convert Muslim peoples entered Europeans' consciousness and became a continuing goal. When in 1492 Christopher Columbus sailed west, he used the language of the Crusades in his diaries, and he hoped to establish a Christian base in India from which a new crusade against Islam could be launched (see page 470).

The Life of the People

☐ How did the lives of common people, nobles, and townspeople differ, and what new commercial developments increased wealth?

In the late ninth century medieval intellectuals described Christian society as composed of those who pray (the monks), those who fight (the nobles), and those who work (the peasants). This image of society became popular in the Middle Ages, especially among people who were worried about the changes they saw around them. They asserted that the three categories of citizens had been established by God and that every person had been assigned a fixed place in the social order.

This three-category model does not fully describe medieval society; there were degrees of wealth and status within each group. Also, the model does not take townspeople and the emerging commercial classes into consideration, and it completely excludes those who were not Christian, such as Jews, Muslims, and pagans. Furthermore, those who used the model, generally bishops and other church officials, ignored the fact that each of these groups was made up of both women and men; they spoke only of warriors, monks, and farmers. Despite — or perhaps because of — these limitations, the model of the three categories was a powerful mental construct. Therefore, we can use it to organize our investigation of life in the Middle Ages, broadening it to include groups and issues that medieval authors did not. (See page 400 for a discussion of the life of monks and nuns — "those who pray.")

The Life and Work of Peasants

The men and women who worked the land in the Middle Ages made up probably more than 90 percent of the population. The evolution of localized feudal systems into more centralized states had relatively little impact on the daily lives of these peasants except when it involved warfare. While only nobles fought, their battles often destroyed the houses, barns, and fields of ordinary people, who might also be killed either directly or as a result of the famine and disease that often accompanied war. Villagers might seek protection in the local castle during times of war, but typically they worked and lived without paying much attention to political developments within castle walls.

This lack of attention went in the other direction as well. Since villagers did not perform what were considered "noble" deeds, the aristocratic monks and clerics who wrote the records that serve as historical sources did not spend time or precious writing materials on them. So it is more difficult to find information on the majority of Europeans who were peasants than on the small group at the top of society.

Medieval theologians lumped everyone who worked the land into the category of "those who work," but in fact there were many levels of peasants, ranging from slaves to free and very rich farmers. Most peasants were serfs, required to stay in the village and perform labor on the lord's land. The number of workdays varied, but serfs usually worked three days a week except in the planting or harvest seasons, when the number of days increased. Serfs frequently had to pay arbitrary levies, as for marriage or inheritance of property. A free person had to do none of these things. For his or her landholding, rent had to be paid to the lord, but a free person could move and live as he or she wished.

Serfdom was a hereditary condition. A person born a serf was likely to die a serf, though many serfs did secure their freedom, and the economic revival that began in the eleventh century (see pages 410–412) allowed many to buy their freedom. Further opportunities for increased personal freedom came when lords organized groups of villagers to migrate to sparsely settled frontier areas or to cut down forests or fill in swamps so that there was more land available for farming. Those who took on this extra work often gained a reduction in traditional manorial obligations and an improvement of their social and legal conditions.

In the Middle Ages most European peasants, free and unfree, lived in family groups in small villages that were part of a manor, the estate of a lord (see page 397). The manor was the basic unit of medieval rural organization and the center of rural life. Within the manors of western and central Europe, villages were made up of small houses for individual families, a church, and perhaps the large house of the lord. Peasant households consisted of one married couple, their children (including stepchildren), and perhaps one or two other relatives, such as a grandparent or unmarried aunt. In southern and eastern Europe, extended families were more likely to live in the same household or very near one another. Between one-third and one-half of children died before age five, though many people lived into their sixties.

The arable land of the manor was divided between the lord and the peasantry, with the lord's portion known as the demesne (dih-MAYN) or home farm. A peasant family's land was not usually one particular field but a scattering of strips across many fields, some of which would be planted in grain, some in other crops, and some left unworked to allow the soil to rejuvenate. That way if one field yielded little, strips in a different field might be more bountiful.

The peasants' work was typically divided according to gender. Men and boys were responsible for clearing new land, plowing, and caring for large animals; women and girls were responsible for the care of small animals, spinning, and food preparation. Both sexes harvested and planted, though often there were gender-specific tasks within each of these major undertakings. Women and men worked in the vineyards and in the harvest and preparation of crops needed by the textile industry — flax and plants used for dyeing cloth. Beginning in the eleventh century water mills and windmills aided in some tasks, especially grinding grain, and an increasing use of horses rather than oxen speeded up plowing.

The mainstay of the diet for peasants everywhere — and for all other classes — was bread. Peasants also ate vegetables, not because they appreciated their importance for good health but because there was usually little else available. Animals were too valuable to be used for food on a regular basis, but weaker animals were often slaughtered in the fall so that they did not need to be fed through the winter, and their meat was preserved with salt and eaten on great feast days such as Christmas and Easter. Ale was the universal drink of common people, and it provided needed calories and some relief from the difficult and monotonous labor that filled people's lives. In many places, severe laws forbidding hunting and trapping in the forests restricted deer and other game to the king and nobility.

The Life and Work of Nobles

The nobility, though a small fraction of the total population, strongly influenced all aspects of medieval culture. Despite political, scientific, and industrial revolutions, nobles continued to hold real political and social power in Europe into the nineteenth century.

In the early Middle Ages noble status was limited to a very few families, but in the eleventh century knights in service to kings began to claim such status because it gave them special legal privileges. Nobles generally paid few taxes, and they had power over the people living on their lands. They maintained order, resolved disputes, and protected their dependents from attacks. They appointed officials who oversaw agricultural production. The liberty and privileges of the noble were inheritable, perpetuated by blood and not by wealth alone.

Nobles did have military obligations to their lords, but by the mid-twelfth century their duty to fight was limited in most parts of western Europe to forty days a year. The noble was obliged to attend his lord's court on important occasions when the lord wanted to put on great displays, such as on religious holidays or the wedding of a son or daughter.

Originally, most knights focused solely on military skills, but gradually a different ideal of knighthood emerged, usually termed **chivalry**. Chivalry was a code of conduct originally devised by the clergy to transform the typically crude and brutal behavior of the knightly class. It may have originated in oaths administered to Crusaders in which fighting was declared to have a sacred purpose and knights vowed loyalty to the church as well as to their lords. Qualities other than loyalty gradually

became part of chivalry: bravery, generosity, honor, graciousness, mercy, and eventually gallantry toward women. The chivalric ideal — and it was an ideal, not a standard pattern of behavior — created a new standard of masculinity for nobles, in which loyalty and honor remained the most important qualities, but graceful dancing and intelligent conversation were not considered unmanly.

Noblewomen played a large and important role in the functioning of the estate. They were responsible for managing the household's "inner economy" — cooking, brewing, spinning, weaving, and caring for yard animals. When the lord was away for long periods, his wife became the sole manager of the family properties. Often the responsibilities of the estate fell permanently to her if she became a widow.

Towns, Cities, and the Growth of Commercial Interests

The rise of towns and the growth of a new business and commercial class were a central part of Europe's recovery after the disorders of the tenth century. The growth of towns was made possible by several factors: a rise in population; increased agricultural output, which provided an adequate food supply for new town dwellers; and a minimum of peace and political stability, which allowed merchants to transport and sell goods. The development of towns was to lay the foundations for Europe's transformation, centuries later, from a rural agricultural society into an urban industrial society — a change with global implications.

Medieval towns had a few characteristics in common, one being that walls enclosed them. (The terms *burgher* and *bourgeois* derive from the Old English and Old German words *burg, burgh, borg,* and *borough* for "a walled or fortified place.") Most towns were first established as trading centers, with a marketplace in the middle, and they were likely to have a mint for coining money and a court for settling disputes. In each town, many people inhabited a small, cramped area. As population increased, towns rebuilt their walls, expanding the living space to accommodate growing numbers. Residents bargained with lords to make the town

Saint Maurice Some of the individuals who were held up to young men as models of ideal chivalry were probably real, but their lives were embellished with many stories. One such individual was Saint Maurice (d. 287), a soldier apparently executed by the Romans for refusing to renounce his Christian faith. He first emerges in the Carolingian period, and later he was held up as a model knight and declared a patron of the Holy Roman Empire and protector of the imperial army in wars against the pagan Slavs. His image was used on coins, and his cult was promoted by the archbishops of Magdeburg, who moved his relics to their cathedral. Until 1240 he was portrayed as a white man, but after that he was usually represented as a black man, as in this sandstone statue from Magdeburg Cathedral (ca. 1250). We have no idea why this change happened. (The Menil Collection)

politically independent, which gave them the right to hold legal courts, select leaders, and set taxes.

Townspeople also tried to acquire liberties, above all personal freedom, for themselves. It gradually developed that an individual who lived in a town for a year and a day, and was accepted by the townspeople, was free of servile obligations and status. Thus serfs who fled their manors for towns and were able to find work and avoid recapture became free of personal labor obligations. In this way the growth of towns contributed to a slow decline of serfdom in western Europe, although the complete elimination of serfdom would take centuries.

Merchants constituted the most powerful group in most towns, and they were often organized into merchant guilds, which prohibited nonmembers from trading, pooled members' risks, monopolized city offices, and controlled the economy of the town. Towns became centers of production as well, and artisans in particular trades formed their own **craft guilds**, including guilds of butchers, weavers, blacksmiths, bakers, silversmiths, and so on. Members of the craft guilds determined the quality, quantity, and price of the goods produced and the number of apprentices and journeymen affiliated with the guild. Formal membership in guilds was generally limited to men, but women often worked in guild shops without official membership.

Artisans generally made and sold products in their own homes, with production taking place on the ground floor. A window or door opened from the main workroom directly onto the street, and passersby could look in and see the goods being produced. The family lived above the business on the second or third floor. As the business and the family expanded, additional stories were added.

Most medieval towns and cities developed with little planning or attention to sanitation. Horses and oxen, the chief means of transportation and power, dropped tons of dung on the streets every year. It was universal practice in the early towns to dump household waste, both animal and human, into the road in front of one's house. The stench must have been abominable, as officials of the king noted in their order to the citizens of one English town in 1298:

> The air is so corrupted and infected by the pigsties situated in the king's highways and in the lanes of that town and by the swine feeding and frequently wandering about . . . and by dung and dunghills and many other foul things placed in the streets and lanes, that great repugnance overtakes the king's ministers staying in that town and . . . the advantage of more wholesome air is impeded. . . . [So] the king, being unwilling longer to tolerate such great and unbearable defects there, orders . . . the pigsties, aforesaid streets and lanes to be cleansed from all dung.[3]

> 66 The air is so corrupted . . . by dung and dunghills and many other foul things placed in the streets and lanes, that great repugnance overtakes the king's ministers staying in that town. 99

ROYAL ORDER TO THE CITIZENS OF BOUTHAM, ENGLAND

Despite such unpleasant aspects of urban life, people wanted to get into medieval towns because they represented opportunities for economic advancement, social mobility, and improvement in legal status.

The Expansion of Trade and the Commercial Revolution

The growth of towns went hand in hand with a remarkable expansion of trade as artisans and craftsmen manufactured goods for local and foreign consumption. Most trade centered in towns and was controlled by merchants. They began to pool their money to finance trading expeditions, sharing the profits and also sharing the risks. If disaster struck the ship or caravan, an investor's loss was limited to the amount of that individual's investment, a legal concept termed "limited liability" that is essential to the modern capitalist economy.

Italian cities, especially Venice, led the West in trade in general and completely dominated trade with Asia and North Africa. Venetian ships carried salt from the Venetian lagoon; pepper and other spices from North Africa; and slaves, silk, and purple textiles from the East to northern and western Europe. Wealthy European consumers had greater access to foreign luxuries than they had earlier, and their tastes became more sophisticated. Merchants from other cities in northern Italy such as Florence and Milan were also important traders, and they developed new methods of accounting and record keeping that facilitated the movement of goods and money. The towns of Bruges, Ghent, and Ypres in Flanders were also leaders in long-distance trade and built up a vast industry in the manufacture of cloth, aided by ready access to wool from England, which was just across the channel. The availability of raw wool also encouraged the development of cloth manufacture within England itself, and commercial families in manufacturing towns grew fabulously rich.

In much of northern Europe, the Hanseatic League (known as the Hansa for short), a mercantile associa-

- **chivalry** A code of conduct that was supposed to govern the behavior of a knight.
- **craft guilds** Associations of artisans organized to regulate the quality, quantity, and price of the goods produced as well as the number of affiliated apprentices and journeymen.

tion of towns formed to achieve mutual security and exclusive trading rights, controlled trade. During the thirteenth century perhaps two hundred cities from Holland to Poland joined the league, but Lübeck always remained the dominant member. The ships of the Hansa cities carried furs, wax, copper, fish, grain, timber, and wine. These goods were exchanged for other products, mainly cloth and salt, from western cities. At cities such as Bruges and London, Hanseatic merchants secured special concessions exempting them from all tolls and allowing them to trade at local fairs. Hanseatic merchants also established foreign trading centers, which they called "factories," because the commercial agents within them were called "factors." (Later the word *factory* would be applied to centers of production as well.)

The Hanseatic League, ca. 1300–1400

These developments added up to what is often called the **commercial revolution**. In giving the transformation this name, historians point not only to an increase in the sheer volume of trade and in the complexity and sophistication of business procedures, but also to the new attitude toward business and making money. Some even detect a "capitalist spirit" in which making a profit was regarded as a good thing in itself, regardless of the uses to which that profit was put.

The commercial revolution created a great deal of new wealth, which did not escape the attention of kings and other rulers. Wealth could be taxed, and through taxation kings could create strong and centralized states. In the years to come, alliances with the middle classes were to enable kings to defeat feudal powers and aristocratic interests and to build the states that came to be called "modern." The commercial revolution also provided the opportunity for thousands of serfs in western Europe to improve their social position; however, many people continued to live hand to mouth on low wages. Also, it is important to remember that most towns remained small throughout the Middle Ages.

- **commercial revolution** The transformation of the economic structure of Europe, beginning in the eleventh century, from a rural, manorial society to a more complex mercantile society.
- **Scholastics** Medieval professors who developed a method of thinking, reasoning, and writing in which questions were raised and authorities cited on both sides of a question.
- **Gothic** The term for the architectural and artistic style that prevailed in Europe from the mid-twelfth to the sixteenth century.

Feudal nobility and churchmen continued to determine the preponderant social attitudes, values, and patterns of thought and behavior.

Learning and Culture

☐ What were the primary educational and cultural developments in medieval Europe?

The towns that became centers of trade and production in the High Middle Ages also developed into cultural and intellectual centers. Trade brought in new ideas as well as merchandise, and in many cities a new type of educational institution—the university—emerged, meeting the needs of the new bureaucratic states and the church for educated administrators. As universities emerged, so did other cultural advancements, such as new forms of architecture and literature.

Universities and Scholasticism

Since the time of the Carolingian Empire, monasteries and cathedral schools had offered the only formal instruction available. Monasteries, geared to religious concerns, were located in rural environments. In contrast, schools attached to cathedrals and run by the bishop and his clergy were frequently situated in bustling cities, where people of many backgrounds stimulated the growth and exchange of ideas. In the eleventh century in Bologna and other Italian cities wealthy businessmen established municipal schools, and in the twelfth century municipal schools in Italy and cathedral schools in France developed into much larger universities, a transformation parallel to the opening of madrasas in Muslim cities (see page 257).

The growth of the University of Bologna coincided with a revival of interest in Roman law. The study of Roman law as embodied in Justinian's *Code* (see page 208) had never completely died out in the West, but this sudden burst of interest seems to have been inspired by Irnerius (ca. 1055–ca. 1130), a great teacher at Bologna. Irnerius not only explained the Roman law of Justinian's *Code* but also applied it to practical situations, such as cases of inheritance and landownership.

At the Italian city of Salerno, interest in medicine had persisted for centuries. Greek and Muslim physicians there had studied the use of herbs as cures and had experimented with surgery. The twelfth century ushered in a new interest in Greek medical texts and in the work of Arab and Greek doctors. Ideas from this medical literature spread throughout Europe from Salerno and became the basis of training for physicians at other medieval universities. University training gave physicians high social status and allowed them to charge high fees, although their diagnoses and treatments were based on classical theories, not on interactions with patients.

Although medicine and law were important academic disciplines in the Middle Ages, theology was "the queen of sciences," so termed because it involved the study of God, who was said to make all knowledge possible. Paris became the place to study theology, and in the first decades of the twelfth century students from all over Europe crowded into the cathedral school of Notre Dame in that city.

University professors (a term first used in the fourteenth century) were known as "schoolmen" or **Scholastics**. They developed a method of thinking, reasoning, and writing in which questions were raised and authorities cited on both sides of a question. The goal of the Scholastic method was to arrive at definitive answers and to provide a rational explanation for what was believed on faith.

One of the most famous Scholastics was Peter Abélard (1079–1142). Fascinated by logic, which he believed could be used to solve most problems, Abélard used a method of systematic doubting in his writing and teaching. As he put it, "By doubting we come to questioning, and by questioning we perceive the truth." Other scholars merely asserted theological principles; Abélard discussed and analyzed them.

Thirteenth-century Scholastics devoted an enormous amount of time to collecting and organizing knowledge on all topics. These collections were published as summa (SOO-muh), or reference books. There were summa on law, philosophy, vegetation, animal life, and theology. Thomas Aquinas (1225–1274), a professor at the University of Paris, produced the most famous collection, the *Summa Theologica*, which deals with a vast number of theological questions.

In northern Europe — at Paris and later at Oxford and Cambridge in England — university faculties grouped themselves according to academic disciplines, or schools: law, medicine, arts, and theology. Students lived in privately endowed residential colleges and were considered to be lower-level members of the clergy, so that any student accused of a crime was tried in church, rather than in city, courts. This clerical status, along with widely held ideas about women's lesser intellectual capabilities, meant that university education was restricted to men.

At all universities, the standard method of teaching was the lecture — that is, a reading. With this method the professor read a passage from the Bible, Justinian's *Code*, or one of Aristotle's treatises. He then explained

> " By doubting we come to questioning, and by questioning we perceive the truth. "
>
> **PETER ABÉLARD**

and interpreted the passage. Students wrote down everything. Because books had to be copied by hand, they were extremely expensive, and few students could afford them. Examinations were given after three, four, or five years of study, when the student applied for a degree. Examinations were oral and very difficult. If the candidate passed, he was awarded the first, or bachelor's, degree. Further study, about as long, arduous, and expensive as it is today, enabled the graduate to try for the master's and doctor's degrees. Degrees were technically licenses to teach. Most students, however, did not become teachers. They staffed the expanding royal and papal administrations.

Cathedrals and a New Architectural Style

As we have seen, religious devotion was expressed through daily rituals, holiday ceremonies, and the creation of new institutions such as universities and religious orders. People also wanted permanent visible representations of their piety, and both church and city leaders wanted physical symbols of their wealth and power. These aims found their outlet in the building of tens of thousands of churches, chapels, abbeys, and, most spectacularly, cathedrals. A cathedral is the church of a bishop and the administrative headquarters of a diocese. The word comes from the Greek word *kathedra*, meaning "seat," because the bishop's throne, a symbol of the office, is located in the cathedral.

In the tenth and eleventh centuries cathedrals were built in a style that resembled ancient Roman architecture, with massive walls, rounded stone arches, and small windows — features later labeled Romanesque. In the twelfth century a new style spread out from central France. It was dubbed **Gothic** by later Renaissance architects who thought that only the uncouth Goths could have invented such a disunified style. The basic features of Gothic architecture — pointed arches, high ceilings, and exterior supports called flying buttresses that carried much of the weight of the roof — allowed unprecedented interior lightness. Stained-glass windows were cut into the stone, so that the interior, one French abbot exclaimed, "would shine with the wonderful and uninterrupted light of most sacred windows, pervading the interior beauty."[4] Between 1180 and 1270 in France alone, eighty cathedrals, about five hundred abbey churches, and tens of thousands of parish churches were constructed in this new style. They are testimony to the deep religious faith and piety of medieval people and also to the civic pride of urban residents, for towns competed with one another to build the largest and most splendid cathedral. In addition to marriages,

Notre Dame Cathedral, Paris, begun 1163 This view offers a fine example of the twin towers (left), the spire, the great rose window over the south portal (center), and the flying buttresses that support the walls and the vaults. Like hundreds of other churches in medieval Europe, it was dedicated to the Virgin Mary. With a spire rising more than 300 feet, Notre Dame was the tallest building in Europe at the time of its construction. (David R. Frazier/Photo Researchers, Inc.)

baptisms, and funerals, there were scores of feast days on which the entire town gathered in the cathedral.

Cathedrals served secular as well as religious purposes. Local guilds met in the cathedrals to arrange business deals, and municipal officials held political meetings there. Pilgrims slept there, lovers courted there, and traveling actors staged plays there. First and foremost, however, the cathedral was intended to teach the people the doctrines of Christian faith through visual images such as those found in stained-glass windows and religious statuary. In this way architecture became the servant of theology.

Troubadour Poetry

Educational and religious texts were typically written in Latin, but poems, songs, and stories were written down in local dialects and celebrated things of concern to ordinary people. In southern Europe, especially in the area of southern France known as Provence, poets who called themselves **troubadours** wrote lyric verses celebrating love, desire, beauty, and gallantry and sang them at the courts of nobles and rulers.

Troubadour poets celebrated *fin'amor*, a Provençal word for the pure or perfect love a knight was supposed to feel for his lady, which has in English come to be called "courtly love." In courtly love poetry, the writer praises his or her love object, idealizing the beloved and promising loyalty and great deeds. Poetry in praise of love originated in the Muslim culture of the Iberian Peninsula, where heterosexual romantic love had long been the subject of poems and songs. Southern France was a border area where Christian and Muslim cultures mixed; Spanish Muslim poets sang at the courts of Christian nobles, and Provençal poets picked up their romantic themes.

Troubadours included a few women, with their poetry often chiding knights who did not live up to the ideal, as in this twelfth-century verse:

> I've suffered great distress
> From a knight whom I once owned.
> Now, for all time, be it known:
> I loved him — yes, to excess. His jilting I've regretted,
> Yet his love I never really returned.[5]

- **troubadours** Medieval poets in southern Europe who wrote and sang lyrical verses. The word *troubadour* comes from the Provençal word *trobar*, which in turn derives from the Arabic *taraba*, meaning "to sing" or "to sing poetry."
- **Black Death** The plague that first struck Europe in 1347, killing perhaps one-third of the population.

Crises of the Later Middle Ages

☐ Why have the later Middle Ages been seen as a time of calamity and crisis?

During the later Middle Ages, the last book of the New Testament, the book of Revelation, inspired thousands of sermons and hundreds of religious tracts. Revelation deals with visions of the end of the world, with disease, war, famine, and death—often called the "Four Horsemen of the Apocalypse"—triumphing everywhere. It is no wonder that this part of the Bible was so popular. Between 1300 and 1450 Europeans experienced a frightful series of shocks: climate change, economic decline, plague, war, social upheaval, and increased crime and violence. Death and preoccupation with death made the fourteenth century one of the most wrenching periods of history in Europe.

The Great Famine and the Black Death

In the first half of the fourteenth century Europe experienced a series of climate changes, especially the beginning of a period of colder and wetter weather that historical geographers label the "little ice age." Its effects were dramatic and disastrous. Population had steadily increased in the twelfth and thirteenth centuries, but with colder weather, poor harvests led to scarcity and starvation. The costs of grain, livestock, and dairy products rose sharply. Almost all of northern Europe suffered a terrible famine between 1315 and 1322, with dire social consequences: peasants were forced to sell or mortgage their lands for money to buy food, and the number of vagabonds, or homeless people, greatly increased, as did petty crime. An undernourished population was ripe for the Grim Reaper, who appeared in 1347 in the form of a virulent new disease, later called the **Black Death** (Map 14.3). The symptoms of this disease were first described in 1331 in southwestern China, part of the Mongol Empire (see page 334). From there it spread across Central Asia by way of Mongol armies and merchant caravans, arriving in the ports of the Black Sea by the 1340s. In October 1347 Genoese ships traveling from the Crimea in southern Russia brought the plague to Messina, from which it spread across Sicily and into Italy. From Italy it traveled in all directions.

Most historians and almost all microbiologists identify the disease that spread in the fourteenth century as the bubonic plague, caused by the bacillus *Yersinia pestis*. The disease normally afflicts rats. Fleas living

Procession of Flagellants In this manuscript illumination from 1349, shirtless flagellants, men and women who whipped and scourged themselves as penance for their and society's sins, walk through the Flemish city of Tournai, which had just been struck by the plague. Many people believed that the Black Death was God's punishment for humanity's wickedness. (Ann Ronan Picture Library/HIP/Art Resource, NY)

MAP 14.3 The Course of the Black Death in Fourteenth-Century Europe The plague followed trade routes as it spread into and across Europe. A few cities that took strict quarantine measures were spared.

on the infected rats drink their blood and pass the bacteria that cause the plague on to the next rat they bite. Usually the disease is limited to rats and other rodents, but at certain points in history the fleas have jumped from their rodent hosts to humans and other animals. The fourteenth-century disease showed some differences from later outbreaks of bubonic plague; there are no reports of massive rat die-offs, and the disease was often transmitted directly from one person to another through coughing and sneezing. These differences have led a few historians to ask whether the fourteenth-century outbreak was some disease other than the bubonic plague — perhaps something like the Ebola virus. Debates about the nature of the disease fuel continued study of medical aspects of the plague, with scientists using innovative techniques such as studying the tooth pulp of bodies in medieval cemeteries to see if it contains DNA from plague-causing agents.

Whatever it was, the disease had dreadful effects on the body. The classic symptom was a growth the size of a nut or an apple in the armpit, in the groin, or on the neck. This was the boil, or *bubo,* that gave the disease

its name and caused agonizing pain. If the bubo was lanced and the pus thoroughly drained, the victim had a chance of recovery. The secondary stage was the appearance of black spots or blotches caused by bleeding under the skin. Finally, the victim began to cough violently and spit blood. This stage, indicating the presence of millions of bacilli in the bloodstream, signaled the end, and death followed in two or three days. Physicians could sometimes ease the pain but had no cure.

Most people — lay, scholarly, and medical — believed that the Black Death was caused by poisons or by "corrupted air" that carried the disease from place to place. They sought to keep poisons from entering the body by smelling or ingesting strong-smelling herbs, and they tried to remove the poisons through bloodletting. They also prayed and did penance. Anxiety and fears about the plague caused people to look for scapegoats, and they found them in the Jews, who they believed had poisoned the wells of Christian communities and thereby infected the drinking water. This charge led to the murder of thousands of Jews across Europe.

Viewpoints

Italian and English Views of the Plague

> • *Eyewitness commentary on the plague includes the Italian writer Giovanni Boccaccio (1313–1375), who portrayed the course of the disease in Florence in the preface to his book of tales,* The Decameron, *and the English monastic chronicler Henry Knighton (d. 1396), who described the effects of the plague on English towns and villages in his four-volume chronicle of English history.*

Giovanni Boccaccio

"Against this pestilence no human wisdom or foresight was of any avail.... Men and women in great numbers abandoned their city, their houses, their farms, their relatives, and their possessions and sought other places, going at least as far away as the Florentine countryside—as if the wrath of God could not pursue them with this pestilence wherever they went but would only strike those it found within the walls of the city! ... [A]lmost no one cared for his neighbor, and relatives hardly ever visited one another—they stayed far apart. This disaster had struck such fear into the hearts of men and women that brother abandoned brother, uncle abandoned nephew, sister left brother, and very often wife abandoned husband, and—even worse, almost unbelievable—fathers and mothers neglected to tend and care for their children as if they were not their own.... So many corpses would arrive in front of a church every day and at every hour that the amount of holy ground for burials was certainly insufficient for the ancient custom of giving each body its individual place; when all the graves were full, huge trenches were dug in all the cemeteries of the churches and into them the new arrivals were dumped by the hundreds; and they were packed in there with dirt, one on top of another, like a ship's cargo, until the trench was filled.... Oh how many great palaces, beautiful homes and noble dwellings, once filled with families, gentlemen, and ladies, were now emptied, down to the last servant!"

Henry Knighton

"Then that most grievous pestilence penetrated the coastal regions [of England] by way of Southhampton, and came to Bristol, and people died as if the whole strength of the city were seized by sudden death. For there were few who lay in their beds more than three days or two and half days; then that savage death snatched them about the second day. In Leicester, in the little parish of St. Leonard, more than three hundred and eighty died; in the parish of Holy Cross, more than four hundred.... And so in each parish, they died in great numbers.... At the same time, there was so great a lack of priests everywhere that many churches had no divine services.... One could hardly hire a chaplain to minister to the church for less than ten marks, whereas before the pestilence, when there were plenty of priests, one could hire a chaplain for five or four marks.... Meanwhile, the king ordered that in every county of the kingdom, reapers and other labourers should not receive more than they were accustomed to receive, under the penalty provided in the statute, and he renewed the statute at this time. The labourers, however, were so arrogant and hostile that they did not heed the king's command, but if anyone wished to hire them, he had to pay them what they wanted, and either lose his fruits and crops or satisfy the arrogant and greedy desire of the labourers as they wished.... Similarly, those who received day-work from their tenants throughout the year, as is usual from serfs, had to release them and to remit such service. They either had to excuse them entirely or had to fix them in a laxer manner at a small rent, lest very great and irreparable damage be done to the buildings and the land everywhere remain uncultivated."

Sources: Giovanni Boccaccio, *The Decameron*, trans. Mark Musa and Peter Bondanella (New York: W.W. Norton, 1982), pp. 7, 9, 12. Copyright © 1982 by Mark Musa and Peter Bondanella. Used by permission of W. W. Norton & Company, Inc.; Henry Knighton, *Chronicon Henrici Knighton*, in James Bruce Ross and Mary Martin McLaughlin, eds., *The Portable Medieval Reader* (New York: Viking, 1949), pp. 218, 220, 222.

QUESTIONS FOR ANALYSIS

1. How did the residents of Florence respond to the plague, as described by Boccaccio?
2. What were some of the effects of the plague in England, as described by Knighton?
3. How might the fact that Boccaccio was writing in an urban setting and Knighton was writing from a rural monastery that owned a large amount of land have shaped their perspectives?

Because population figures for the period before the arrival of the plague do not exist for most countries and cities, only educated guesses can be made about mortality rates. Of a total English population of perhaps 4.2 million, probably 1.4 million died of the Black Death in its several visits. In Italy densely populated cities endured incredible losses. Florence lost between one-half and two-thirds of its population when the plague visited in 1348. The disease recurred intermittently in the 1360s and 1370s and reappeared many times, as late as the early 1700s in Europe. (It still continues to infect rodent and human populations sporadically today.)

In the short term the economic effects of the plague were severe because the death of many peasants disrupted food production. But in the long term the dramatic decline in population eased pressure on the land, and wages and per capita wealth rose for those who survived. The psychological consequences of the plague were profound. (See "Viewpoints: Italian and English Views of the Plague," page 417.) Some people sought release in wild living, while others turned to the severest forms of asceticism and frenzied religious fervor.

The Hundred Years' War

While the plague ravaged populations in Asia, North Africa, and Europe, a long international war in western Europe added further death and destruction. England and France had engaged in sporadic military hostilities from the time of the Norman Conquest in 1066 (see page 398), and in the middle of the fourteenth century these became more intense. From 1337 to 1453 the two countries intermittently fought one another in what was the longest war in European history, ultimately dubbed the Hundred Years' War, though it actually lasted 116 years.

The Hundred Years' War had a number of causes. Both England and France claimed the duchy of Aquitaine in southwestern France, and the English king Edward III argued that, as the grandson of an earlier French king, he should have rightfully inherited the French throne. Nobles in provinces on the borders of France who were worried about the growing power of the French king supported Edward, as did wealthy wool merchants and cloth makers in Flanders who depended on English wool. The governments of both England and France promised wealth and glory to those who fought and manipulated public opinion to support their side in the war, with each country portraying the other as evil.

The war, fought almost entirely in France, consisted mainly of a series of random sieges and raids. During the war's early stages, England was highly successful, primarily through the use of longbows fired by well-trained foot soldiers against mounted knights and, after 1375, by early cannons. By 1419 the English had advanced to the walls of Paris. But the French cause was not lost. Though England scored the initial victories, France won the war.

The ultimate French success rests heavily on the actions of an obscure French peasant girl, Joan of Arc, whose vision and military leadership revived French

Suit of Armor This fifteenth-century suit of Italian armor protected its wearer, but its weight made movement difficult. Both English and French mounted knights wore full armor at the beginning of the Hundred Years' War, but by the end they wore only breastplates and helmets, which protected their vital organs but allowed greater mobility. This suit has been so well preserved that it was most likely never used in battle; it may have been made for ceremonial purposes. (Image copyright © The Metropolitan Museum of Art/Art Resource, NY)

□ Picturing the Past

Siege of the Castle of Mortagne near Bordeaux This miniature of a battle in the Hundred Years' War shows the French besieging an English-held castle. Medieval warfare usually consisted of small skirmishes and attacks on castles. (© British Library Board, MS Royal 14 e. IV f. 23)

ANALYZING THE IMAGE What types of weapons are the attackers and defenders using? How have the attackers on the left enhanced their position?

CONNECTIONS This painting shows a battle that occurred in 1377, but it was painted about a hundred years later and shows the military technology available at the time it was painted, not at the time of the actual siege. Which of the weapons represent newer forms of military technology? What impact would you expect them to have on warfare?

fortunes and led to victory. Born in 1412 to well-to-do peasants, Joan grew up in a pious household. During adolescence she began to hear voices, which she later said belonged to Saint Michael, Saint Catherine, and Saint Margaret. In 1428 these voices told her that the dauphin of France — Charles VII, who was uncrowned as king because of the English occupation — had to be crowned and the English expelled from France. Joan went to the French court disguised as a male for safety and secured the support of the dauphin to travel, dressed as a knight, with the French army to the besieged city of Orléans.

At Orléans, Joan inspired and led French attacks, and the English retreated. As a result of her successes, Charles made Joan co-commander of the entire army, and she led it to a string of military victories in the summer of 1429; many cities surrendered without a fight. Two months after the victory at Orléans, Charles VII was crowned king at Reims.

Joan and the French army continued their fight against the English. In 1430 England's allies, the Burgundians, captured Joan and sold her to the English, and the French did not intervene. The English wanted Joan eliminated for obvious political reasons, but the primary charge against her was heresy, and the trial was conducted by church authorities. She was interrogated about the angelic voices and about why she wore men's clothing. She apparently answered skillfully, but in 1431 the court condemned her as a heretic, and she was burned at the stake in the marketplace at Rouen. (A new trial in 1456 cleared her of all charges, and in 1920 she was canonized as a saint.) Joan continues to be a symbol of deep religious piety to some, of conservative nationalism to others, and of gender-bending cross-dressing to others. Beneath the pious and popular legends is a teenage girl who saved the French monarchy, which was the embodiment of France. The French army continued its victories without her, and demands for an end to the war increased among the English, who were growing tired of the mounting loss of life and the flow of money into a seemingly bottomless pit. Slowly the French reconquered Normandy and finally ejected the English from Aquitaine. At the war's end in 1453, only the town of Calais remained in English hands.

The Great Schism, 1378–1417

Allegiance to Rome
Allegiance to Avignon
Official allegiance to Rome but with shifting local allegiances

The long war had a profound impact on the two countries. In England and France the war promoted nationalism — the feeling of unity and identity that binds together a people. It led to technological experimentation, especially with gunpowder weaponry, whose firepower made the protective walls of stone castles obsolete. However, such weaponry also made warfare increasingly expensive. The war also stimulated the development of the English Parliament. Between 1250 and 1450 representative assemblies from several classes of society flourished in many European countries, but only the English Parliament became a powerful national body. Edward III's constant need for money to pay for the war compelled him to summon it many times, and its representatives slowly built up their powers.

Challenges to the Church

In times of crisis or disaster people of all faiths have sought the consolation of religion, but in the fourteenth century the official Christian Church offered little solace. While local clergy eased the suffering of many, a dispute over who was the legitimate pope weakened the church as an institution. In 1309 pressure by the French monarchy led the pope to move his permanent residence to Avignon in southern France, the location of the papal summer palace. This marked the start of seven successive papacies in Avignon. Not surprising, all these popes were French — a matter of controversy among church followers outside France. Also, the popes largely concentrated on bureaucratic and financial matters to the exclusion of spiritual objectives.

In 1376 one of the French popes returned to Rome, and when he died there several years later Roman citizens demanded an Italian pope who would remain in Rome. The cardinals elected Urban VI, but his tactless, arrogant, and bullheaded manner caused them to regret their decision. The cardinals slipped away from Rome and declared Urban's election invalid because it had come about under threats from the Roman mob. They elected a French cardinal who took the name Clement VII (pontificate 1378–1394) and set himself up at Avignon in opposition to Urban. There were thus two popes, a situation that was later termed the Great Schism.

The powers of Europe aligned themselves with Urban or Clement along strictly political lines. France recognized the Frenchman, Clement; England, France's historic enemy, recognized Urban. The rest of Europe lined up behind one or the other. In all European countries the common people — hard-pressed by inflation, wars, and plague — were thoroughly confused about which pope was legitimate. In the end the schism weakened the religious faith of many Christians and brought church leadership into serious disrepute.

A first attempt to heal the schism led to the installation of a third pope and a threefold split, but finally a church council meeting at Constance (1414–1418) successfully deposed the three schismatic popes and elected a new leader, who took the name Martin V (pontificate 1417–1431). The schism was over, but those who had hoped that the council would also reform problems in the church were disappointed. In the later fifteenth century the papacy concentrated on building up its wealth and political power in Italy rather than on the concerns of the whole church. As a result, many people decided that they would need to rely on their own prayers and pious actions rather than on the institutional church for their salvation.

Peasant and Urban Revolts

The difficult conditions of the fourteenth and fifteenth centuries spurred a wave of peasant and urban revolts across Europe. In 1358, when French taxation for the Hundred Years' War fell heavily on the poor, the frustrations of the French peasantry exploded in a massive uprising called the Jacquerie (zhah-kuh-REE), after a supposedly happy agricultural laborer, Jacques Bonhomme (Good Fellow). Adding to the anger over taxes was the toll taken by the plague and by the famine that had struck some areas. Crowds swept through the countryside, slashing the throats of nobles, burning their castles, raping their wives and daughters, and killing or maiming their horses and cattle. Artisans, small merchants, and parish priests joined the peasants, and residents of both urban and rural areas committed terrible destruction. For several weeks the nobles were on the defensive, until the upper class united to repress the revolt with merciless ferocity. Thousands of the "Jacques," innocent as well as guilty, were cut down.

Taxes and other grievances also led to the 1381 English Peasants' Revolt, involving tens of thousands of people. The Black Death had dramatically reduced the supply of labor, and peasants had demanded higher wages and fewer manorial obligations. Parliament countered with a law freezing wages and binding workers to their manors. Although the law was difficult to enforce, it contributed to an atmosphere of discontent, which was further enhanced by popular preachers who proclaimed that great disparities between rich and poor went against Christ's teachings. Moreover, decades of aristocratic violence, much of it perpetrated against the weak peasantry, had bred hostility and bitterness.

In 1380 Parliament imposed a poll tax on all citizens to fund the Hundred Years' War, requiring rich and poor to pay the same amount and ordering sheriffs to collect it. This tax imposed a greater burden on the poor than on wealthier citizens, and it sparked revolt. Beginning with assaults on the tax collectors, the uprising in England followed much the same course as had the Jacquerie in France. Castles and manors were sacked; manorial records were destroyed; nobles were murdered. Urban discontent merged with rural violence. Apprentices and journeymen, frustrated because the highest positions in the guilds were closed to them, rioted.

The boy-king Richard II (r. 1377–1399) met the leaders of the revolt, agreed to charters ensuring the peasants' freedom from manorial obligations, tricked them with false promises, and then proceeded to crush the uprising with terrible ferocity. The nobility tried to use this defeat to restore the ancient obligations of serfdom, but the increasingly commercialized economy made that difficult, and serfdom slowly disappeared in England, though peasants remained poor.

Conditions in England and France were not unique. In Florence in 1378 the *ciompi*, or poor propertyless workers, revolted, and serious social unrest occurred in Lübeck, Brunswick, and other German cities. In Spain in 1391 massive uprisings in Seville and Barcelona took the form of vicious attacks on Jewish communities. Rebellions and uprisings everywhere revealed deep peasant and worker frustration with the socioeconomic conditions of the time.

CONNECTIONS

Medieval Europe continues to fascinate us today. We go to medieval banquets, fairs, and even weddings; visit castle-themed hotels and amusement parks; watch movies about knights and their conquests; play video games in which we become warriors, trolls, or sorcerers; and read stories with themes of great quests, some set in the Middle Ages and some set in places that just seem medieval, with humble but brave villagers, beautiful ladies, powerful wizards, and gorgeous warriors on horseback. From all these amusements the Middle Ages emerges as a strange and wonderful time, when people's emotions were more powerful, challenges more dangerous, and friendships more lasting than in the safe, shallow, fast-paced modern world. Characters from other parts of the world often heighten the exoticism: a Muslim soldier joins the fight against a common enemy, a Persian princess rescues the hero and his sidekick, a Buddhist monk teaches martial arts techniques. These characters from outside Europe are fictional, but they also represent aspects of reality, because medieval Europe was not isolated, and political and social structures similar to those in Europe developed elsewhere.

In reality few of us would probably want to live in the real Middle Ages, when most people worked in the fields all day, a banquet meant a piece of tough old rooster instead of the usual meal of pea soup and black bread, and even wealthy lords lived in damp and drafty castles. We do not really want to return to a time when one-third to one-half of all children died before age five and alcohol was the only real pain reliever. But the contemporary appeal of the Middle Ages is an interesting phenomenon, particularly because it stands in such sharp contrast to the attitude of educated Europeans who lived in the centuries immediately afterward. They were the ones who dubbed the period "middle" and viewed the soaring cathedrals as dreadful "Gothic." They saw their own era as the one to be celebrated, and the Middle Ages as best forgotten.

□ CHAPTER REVIEW

KEY TERMS

vassal (p. 395)   chivalry (p. 410)
fief (p. 396)   craft guilds (p. 411)
feudalism (p. 396)   commercial
manorialism (p. 397)   revolution (p. 412)
serf (p. 397)   Scholastics (p. 413)
heresy (p. 402)   Gothic (p. 413)
reconquista (p. 404)   troubadours (p. 414)
Crusades (p. 404)   Black Death (p. 415)

□ How did medieval rulers overcome internal divisions and external threats, and work to create larger and more stable territories? (p. 394)

As Charlemagne's empire broke down, no European political power was strong enough to put up effective resistance to external attack, which came from many directions. Vikings from Scandinavia carried out raids for plunder along the coasts and rivers of Europe and traveled as far as Iceland, Greenland, North America, and Russia. In many places they set up permanent states, as did the Magyars, who came into central Europe from the east. From the south came Muslims, who conquered Sicily and drove northward into Italy. All these invasions as well as civil wars weakened the power of kings, and local nobles became the strongest powers against external threats. They established a new form of decentralized government, later known as feudalism. Common people turned to nobles for protection, paying with their land, labor, and freedom. By the twelfth century, however, rulers in some parts of Europe reasserted authority and began to develop new institutions of government and legal codes that enabled them to assert power over lesser lords and the general population.

□ How did the Christian Church enhance its power and create new institutions and religious practices? (p. 399)

The papacy also consolidated its power in the eleventh and twelfth centuries, though these moves were sometimes challenged by kings and emperors. Monasteries continued to be important places for learning and devotion, and new religious orders were founded. Meanwhile, Christianity expanded into Europe's northern and eastern regions, and Christian rulers expanded their holdings in Muslim Spain. On a more personal scale, religion structured people's daily lives and the yearly calendar.

□ What were the motives, course, and consequences of the Crusades? (p. 404)

A papal call to retake the holy city of Jerusalem led to the Crusades, nearly two centuries of warfare between Christians and Muslims. The enormous popular response to this call reveals the influence of the papacy and a new sense that war against the church's enemies was a duty of nobles. The Crusades were initially successful, and small Christian states were established in the Middle East. They did not last

very long, however, and other effects of the Crusades were disastrous: Jewish communities in Europe were regularly attacked; relations between the Western and Eastern Christian Churches were poisoned by the Crusaders' attack on Constantinople; and Christian-Muslim relations became more uniformly hostile than they had been earlier.

□ How did the lives of common people, nobles, and townspeople differ, and what new commercial developments increased wealth? (p. 408)

The vast majority of medieval Europeans were rural peasants who lived in small villages and worked their own and their lords' land. Peasants led hard lives, and most were bound to the land, although there were some opportunities for social mobility. Nobles were a tiny fraction of the total population, but they exerted great power over all aspects of life. Aristocratic values and attitudes, often called chivalry, shaded all aspects of medieval culture. Medieval towns and cities grew initially as trading centers and recruited people from the countryside with the promise of greater freedom and new possibilities. They also became centers of production, and merchants and artisans formed guilds to protect their livelihoods. Not everyone in medieval towns and cities shared in the prosperity; many residents lived hand to mouth on low wages.

□ What were the primary educational and cultural developments in medieval Europe? (p. 412)

The towns that became centers of trade and production in the High Middle Ages also developed into cultural and intellectual centers. Trade brought in new ideas as well as merchandise, and in many cities a new type of educational institution — the university — emerged from cathedral and municipal schools. Universities developed theological, legal, and medical courses of study based on classical models and provided trained officials for the new government and church bureaucracies. People also wanted permanent visible representations of their piety, and church and city leaders supported the building of churches and cathedrals as symbols of their Christian faith and their civic pride. Cathedrals grew larger and more sumptuous, with high towers and exquisite stained-glass windows. New types of vernacular literature arose in which poems, songs, and stories were written down in local dialects. The troubadours of southern France led the way with this new art form, using Arabic models to create romantic stories of heterosexual love.

□ **Why have the later Middle Ages been seen as a time of calamity and crisis? (p. 415)**

In the fourteenth century bad weather brought poor harvests, which contributed to an international economic depression and fostered disease. The Black Death caused enormous population losses and had social, psychological, and economic consequences. Additional difficulties included the Hundred Years' War, which devastated much of the French countryside and bankrupted England; a schism among rival popes that weakened the Western Christian Church; and peasant and worker frustrations that exploded in uprisings. These revolts were usually crushed, though noble landlords were not always successful in reasserting their rights to labor services instead of cash rents.

SUGGESTED READING

Allmand, Christopher. *The Hundred Years War: England and France at War, ca. 1300–1450*, rev. ed. 2005. Designed for students; examines the war from political, military, social, and economic perspectives and compares the way England and France reacted to the conflict.

Bartlett, Robert. *The Making of Europe: Conquest, Colonization and Cultural Change, 950–1350*. 1993. A broad survey of many of the developments traced in this chapter.

Bennett, Judith M. *A Medieval Life: Cecelia Penifader of Brigstock, c. 1297–1344*. 1998. An excellent brief introduction to all aspects of medieval village life from the perspective of one woman; designed for students.

Brooke, Rosalind, and Christopher Brooke. *Popular Religion in the Middle Ages*. 1984. A readable synthesis of material on the beliefs and practices of ordinary Christians.

Epstein, Steven A. *An Economic and Social History of Later Medieval Europe, 1000–1500*. 2009. Examines the most important themes in European social and economic history, with a wide geographic sweep.

Glick, Leonard B. *Abraham's Heirs: Jews and Christians in Medieval Europe*. 1999. Provides information on many aspects of Jewish life and Jewish-Christian relations.

Herlihy, David. *The Black Death and the Transformation of the West*, 2d ed. 1997. A fine treatment of the causes and cultural consequences of the disease that remains the best starting point for study of the great epidemic.

Janin, Hunt. *The University in Medieval Life, 1179–1499*. 2008. An overview of medieval universities designed for general readers.

Kaeuper, Richard W. *Chivalry and Violence in Medieval Europe*. 2006. Examines the role chivalry played in promoting violent disorder.

Madden, Thomas. *The New Concise History of the Crusades*. 2005. A highly readable brief survey by the preeminent American scholar of the Crusades.

Sawyer, Peter, ed. *The Oxford Illustrated History of the Vikings*. 1997. A sound account of the Vikings by an international team of scholars.

Shahar, Shulamit. *The Fourth Estate: A History of Women in the Middle Ages*, 2d ed. 2003. Analyzes attitudes toward women and provides information on the lives of a variety of women, including nuns, peasants, noblewomen, and townswomen.

Shinners, John. *Medieval Popular Religion, 1000–1500*, 2d ed. 2006. An excellent collection of a wide variety of sources that provide evidence about the beliefs and practices of ordinary Christians.

Tuchman, Barbara. *A Distant Mirror: The Calamitous Fourteenth Century*. 1978. A vivid description of this tumultuous time written for a general audience.

Wickham, Chris. *Framing the Early Middle Ages: Europe and the Mediterranean, 400–800*. 2007. A massive yet accessible survey of economic and social changes in many regions, with great attention to ordinary people.

NOTES

1. D. C. Douglas and G. E. Greenaway, eds., *English Historical Documents*, vol. 2 (London: Eyre & Spottiswoode, 1961), p. 853.
2. Fulcher of Chartres, *A History of the Expedition to Jerusalem, 1095–1127*, trans. Frances Rita Ryan, ed. Harold S. Fink (Knoxville: University of Tennessee Press, 1969), pp. 121–123.
3. H. Rothwell, ed., *English Historical Documents*, vol. 3 (London: Eyre & Spottiswoode, 1975), p. 854.
4. Erwin Panofsky, trans. and ed., *Abbot Suger on the Abbey Church of St.-Denis and Its Art Treasures* (Princeton, N.J.: Princeton University Press, 1946), p. 101.
5. Quoted in J. J. Wilhelm, ed., *Lyrics of the Middle Ages: An Anthology*. Copyright 1990. Reproduced with permission of TAYLOR & FRANCIS GROUP LLC in the format Textbook and Other Book via Copyright Clearance Center.

For practice quizzes and other study tools, visit the **Online Study Guide** at bedfordstmartins.com/mckayworld.

For primary sources from this period, see *Sources of World Societies*, **Second Edition**.

For Web sites, images, and documents related to topics in this chapter, visit **Make History** at bedfordstmartins.com/mckayworld.

• **Portrait of Baldassare Castiglione** The author and courtier Baldassare Castiglione directs his calm gaze toward the viewer in this portrait by the renowned Italian Renaissance artist Raphael. Individual portraits like this one expressed the ideals of the Renaissance: elegance, balance, proportion, and self-awareness. (© Samuel Courtauld Trust, The Courtauld Gallery, London/The Bridgeman Art Library)

15

While disease, famine, and war marked the fourteenth century in much of Europe, the era also witnessed the beginnings of remarkable changes in many aspects of intellectual and cultural life. First in Italy and then elsewhere, artists and writers thought that they were living in a new golden age, later termed the Renaissance, French for *rebirth*. The word *renaissance* was used initially to describe art that seemed to recapture, or perhaps even surpass, the glories of the classical past, and then came to be used for many aspects of life of the period. The new attitude diffused slowly out of Italy, with the result that the Renaissance "happened" at different times in different parts of Europe. It shaped the lives of Europe's educated elites, although families, kin networks, religious beliefs, and the rhythms of the agricultural year still remained important.

Religious reformers carried out even more dramatic changes. Calls for reform of the Christian Church began very early in its history and continued throughout the Middle Ages. In the sixteenth century these calls gained wide acceptance, due not only to religious issues and problems within the church but also to political and social factors. In a movement termed the Protestant Reformation, Western Christianity broke into many divisions, a situation that continues today. The Renaissance and the Reformation were very different types of movements, but both looked back to a time they regarded as purer and better than their own, and both offered opportunities for strong individuals to shape their world in unexpected ways. Both have also been seen as key elements in the creation of the "modern" world. •

Europe in the Renaissance and Reformation

1350–1600

Renaissance Culture

□ What were the major cultural developments of the Renaissance?

The **Renaissance** was characterized by self-conscious awareness among fourteenth- and fifteenth-century Italians, particularly scholars and writers known as humanists, that they were living in a new era. Their ideas influenced education and were spread through the new technology of the printing press. Interest in the classical past and in the individual also shaped Renaissance art in terms of style and subject matter. Also important to Renaissance art were the wealthy patrons who helped fund it.

Wealth and Power in Renaissance Italy

Economic growth laid the material basis for the Italian Renaissance and its cultural achievements. Ambitious merchants gained political power to match their economic power and then used their money and power to buy luxuries and hire talent in a **patronage** system. Through this system cities, groups, and individuals commissioned writers and artists to produce specific works. Thus, economics, politics, and culture were interconnected.

The Renaissance began in the northern Italian city of Florence, which possessed enormous wealth. From their position as tax collectors for the papacy, Florentine mercantile families began to dominate Euro-

Italian States, 1494

pean banking on both sides of the Alps, setting up offices in major European and North African cities. The profits from loans, investments, and money exchanges allowed banking families to control the city's politics and culture. Although Florence was officially a republic, starting in 1434 the great Medici (MEH-duh-chee) banking family held power almost continually for centuries. They supported an academy for scholars and a host of painters, sculptors, poets, and architects.

In other Italian cities as well, wealthy merchants and bankers built magnificent palaces and required that all political business be done there. They became patrons of the arts, hiring not only architects to design and build these palaces but also artists to fill them with paintings and sculptures, and musicians and composers to fill them with music. Attractions like these appealed to the rich, social-climbing residents of Venice, Florence, Genoa, and Rome, who came to see life more as an opportunity for enjoyment than as a painful pilgrimage to Heaven.

This cultural flowering took place amid political turmoil. In the fifteenth century five powers dominated the Italian peninsula: Venice, Milan, Florence, the Papal States, and the kingdom of Naples. These powers competed furiously for territory and ruthlessly tried to extend their authority over smaller city-states. While the states of northern Europe were moving toward centralization and consolidation, Italian politics resembled a jungle where the powerful dominated the weak.

In one significant respect, however, the Italian city-states anticipated future relations among competing European states after 1500.

Whenever one Italian state appeared to gain a predominant position within the peninsula, other states combined to establish a balance of power against the major threat. In the formation of these alliances, Renaissance Italians invented the machinery of modern diplomacy: permanent embassies with resident ambassadors in capitals where political relations and commercial ties needed continual monitoring.

Although the resident ambassador was one of the great political achievements of the Italian Renaissance, diplomacy did not prevent invasions of Italy. These began in 1494 as Italy became the focus of international ambitions and the battleground of foreign armies, and Italian cities suffered severely from continual warfare for decades. Thus the failure of the city-states to form some type of federal system, to consolidate, or at least to establish a common foreign policy led to centuries of subjugation by outside invaders. Italy was not to achieve unification until 1870.

The Rise of Humanism

The Renaissance was a self-conscious intellectual movement. The realization that something new and unique was happening first came to writers in the fourteenth century, especially to the Italian poet and humanist Francesco Petrarch (frahn-CHEH-skoh PEH-trahrk; 1304–1374). For Petrarch, the barbarian migrations (see pages 220–225) had caused a sharp cultural break with the glories of Rome and inaugurated what he called the "dark ages." Along with many of his contemporaries, Petrarch sought to reconnect with the classical past, and he believed that such efforts were bringing on a new golden age of intellectual achievement.

Petrarch and other poets, writers, and artists showed a deep interest both in the physical remains of the Roman Empire and in classical Latin texts. The study of Latin classics became known as the *studia humanitates*, usually translated as "liberal studies" or the "liberal arts." People who advocated it were known as *humanists*, and their program as **humanism**. Like all programs of study, humanism contained an implicit philosophy: that human nature and achievements, evident in the classics, were worthy of contemplation. Humanists did not reject religion, however. Instead they sought to synthesize Christian and classical teachings, pointing out the harmony between them.

Families, religious brotherhoods, workers' organizations, and other groups continued to have meaning in peoples' lives, but humanists and other Renaissance thinkers increasingly viewed these groups as springboards to far greater individual achievement. They were especially interested in individuals who had risen above their background to become brilliant, powerful,

- **Renaissance** A French word meaning rebirth, used to describe a cultural movement that began in fourteenth-century Italy and looked back to the classical past.
- **patronage** Financial support of writers and artists by cities, groups, and individuals, often to produce specific works or works in specific styles.
- **humanism** A program of study designed by Italians that emphasized the critical study of Latin and Greek literature with the goal of understanding human nature.

Viewpoints

Lauro Quirini and Cassandra Fedele: Women and Humanist Learning

• *Italian humanists promoted the value of their new style of education, and several women from the bustling cities of northern Italy obtained humanist education, writing letters, dialogues, and orations. Some male humanists criticized women who publicly shared their ideas, but others celebrated them. The Venetian humanist nobleman Lauro Quirini (ca. 1420–ca. 1475) wrote to one of these, the learned Isotta Nogarola (1418–1466), praising her accomplishments and advising her on a plan of study. The second document is an excerpt from an oration that the Venetian Cassandra Fedele (1465–1558) gave in Latin at the University of Padua in honor of her (male) cousin's graduation. Fedele applied advice such as Quirini's to her own studies and became the best known female scholar in her time.*

Letter from Lauro Quirini to Isotta Nogarola, ca. 1450

❝This letter asks of you nothing else than that you pursue in the most splendid way, until death, that same course of right living that you have followed since childhood. . . . Rightful therefore, should you also, famous Isotta, receive the highest praises, since you have, if I may so speak, overcome your own nature. For that true virtue that is proper to men you have pursued with remarkable zeal—not the mediocre virtue that many men seek, but that which would befit a man of the most flawless and perfect wisdom. . . . Therefore dissatisfied with the lesser studies, you have applied your noble mind to those highest disciplines, in which there is need for keenness of intelligence and mind. For you are engaged in the art of dialectic, which shows the way to learning the truth. After you have also digested this part of philosophy, which is concerned with human matters, equipped with your nobility of the soul you should also set out for that ample and vast other part [divine matters]. . . . Here you should begin especially with those disciplines that we call by the Greek term mathematics. . . . You should also make use of those studies, moreover, that you have splendidly embraced from your youth, and especially history, for history is as it were the teacher of life.❞

Cassandra Fedele, In Praise of Letters, ca. 1485

❝I shall speak very briefly on the study of the liberal arts, which for humans is useful and honorable, pleasurable and enlightening since everyone, not only philosophers but also the most ignorant man, knows and admits that it is by reason that man is separated from beasts. For what is it that so greatly helps both the learned and the ignorant? What so enlarges and enlightens men's minds the way that an education in and knowledge of literature and the liberal arts do? . . . But erudite men who are filled with the knowledge of divine and human things turn all their thoughts and considerations toward reason as though toward a target, and free their minds from all pain, though plagued by many anxieties. . . .

But enough on the utility of literature since it produces not only an outcome that is rich, precious, and sublime, but also provides one with advantages that are extremely pleasurable, fruitful, and lasting—benefits that I myself have enjoyed. And when I meditate on the idea of marching forth in life with the lowly and execrable weapons of the little woman—the needle and the distaff [the rod onto which yarn is wound after spinning]—even if the study of literature offers women no rewards or honors, I believe women must nonetheless pursue and embrace such studies alone for the pleasure and enjoyment they contain.❞

Sources: Isotta Nogarola, *Complete Writings, Letterbook, Dialogue on Adam and Eve, Orations*, ed. and trans. Margaret L. King and Diana Robin, pp. 108–113. Copyright © 2004 by University of Chicago Press. Used by permission of University of Chicago Press; Cassandra Fedele, *Letters and Orations*, ed. and trans. Diana Robin, pp. 159–162. Copyright © 2000 by University of Chicago Press. Used by permission of University of Chicago Press.

QUESTIONS FOR ANALYSIS

1. What do Quirini and Fedele view as the best course and purposes of study? How are these different, or similar, for men and women?

2. Quirini is male and Fedele female. Does the gender of the authors shape their ideas about the appropriateness of humanist learning for women? If so, how?

or unique. (See "Individuals in Society: Leonardo da Vinci," page 434.) Such individuals had the admirable quality of *virtù* (ver-TOO), which is not virtue in the sense of moral goodness, but the ability to shape the world around them according to their will.

Humanists thought that their recommended course of study in the classics would provide essential skills for future diplomats, lawyers, military leaders, businessmen, and politicians, as well as for writers and artists. They also taught that taking an active role in the world should be the aim of all educated individuals and that education was not simply for private or religious purposes, but to benefit the public good.

Humanists put their educational ideas into practice. They opened schools and academies in Italian cities and courts in which pupils began with Latin grammar and rhetoric, went on to study Roman history and political philosophy, and then learned Greek in order to study Greek literature and philosophy. These classics, humanists taught, would provide models of how to write clearly, argue effectively, and speak persuasively. Gradually humanist education became the basis for intermediate and advanced education for well-to-do urban boys and men.

Humanists disagreed about education for women. Many saw the value of exposing women to classical models of moral behavior and reasoning, but they also wondered whether a program of study that emphasized eloquence and action was proper for women, whose sphere was generally understood to be private and domestic. Humanists never established schools for girls, though through tutors or programs of self-study a few women did become educated in the classics. (See "Viewpoints: Lauro Quirini and Cassandra Fedele: Women and Humanist Learning," page 428.)

Humanists looked to the classical past for political as well as literary models. The best-known political theorist of this era was Niccolò Machiavelli (1469–1527), who worked as an official for the city of Florence until he was ousted in a power struggle. He spent the rest of his life writing, and his most famous work is the short political treatise *The Prince* (1513). Using the examples of classical and contemporary rulers, *The Prince* argues that the function of a ruler (or a government) is to preserve order and security. The inability to do so would lead to disorder, which might end in civil war or conquest by an outsider, situations clearly not conducive to any people's well-being. To preserve the state a ruler should use whatever means necessary—brutality, lying, manipulation—but he should not do anything that would make the populace turn against him. Stealing or cruel actions done for a ruler's own pleasure

> ❝It is much safer for the prince to be feared than loved, but he ought to avoid making himself hated.❞
>
> **NICCOLÒ MACHIAVELLI**

would lead to resentment and destroy the popular support needed for a strong, stable realm. "It is much safer for the prince to be feared than loved," Machiavelli advised, "but he ought to avoid making himself hated."[1]

The Prince is often seen as the first modern guide to politics, though Machiavelli was denounced for writing it, and people later came to use the word *Machiavellian* to mean cunning and ruthless. Machiavelli put a new spin on the Renaissance search for perfection, arguing that ideals needed to be measured in the cold light of the real world.

Christian Humanism

In the last quarter of the fifteenth century, students from the Low Countries, France, Germany, and England flocked to Italy, absorbed the "new learning" of humanism, and carried it back to their own countries. Northern humanists shared the Italians' ideas about the wisdom of ancient texts and felt even more strongly that the best elements of classical and Christian cultures should be combined. These **Christian humanists**, as they were later called, saw humanist learning as a way to bring about reform of the church and to deepen people's spiritual lives.

The Englishman Thomas More (1478–1535) began life as a lawyer, studied the classics, and entered government service. He became best known for his controversial dialogue *Utopia* (1516), a word More invented from the Greek words for "nowhere." *Utopia* describes a community on an island somewhere beyond Europe where all children receive a good humanist education, and adults divide their days between manual labor or business pursuits and intellectual activities. The problems that plagued More's fellow citizens, such as poverty and hunger, are solved by a beneficent government. Inequality and greed are prevented because profits from business and property are held in common, not privately. Furthermore, there is religious toleration, and order and reason prevail. Because Utopian institutions are perfect, however, dissent and disagreement are not acceptable.

More's purposes in writing *Utopia* have been hotly debated. Some view it as a revolutionary critique of More's own hierarchical and violent society, some as a call for an even firmer hierarchy, and others as part of the humanist tradition of satire. It was widely read by

---

• **Christian humanists** Humanists from northern Europe who thought that the best elements of classical and Christian cultures should be combined and saw humanist learning as a way to bring about reform of the church and deepen people's spiritual lives.

Procession of the Magi, 1461 This segment of a huge fresco by the Italian artist Bennozzo Gozzoli covering three walls of a chapel in the Medici palace in Florence shows members of the Medici family and other contemporary individuals in a procession accompanying the biblical three wise men (*magi* in Italian) as they brought gifts to the infant Jesus. Reflecting the self-confidence of his patrons, Gozzoli places several members of the Medici family at the head of the procession, accompanied by their grooms. (Erich Lessing/Art Resource, NY)

cal, and especially religious institutions; and, most important, a critical edition of the Greek New Testament (1516). For Erasmus, education was the key to moral and intellectual improvement, and true Christianity was an inner attitude of the spirit, not a set of outward actions.

Printing and Its Social Impact

Although the fourteenth-century humanist Petrarch and the sixteenth-century humanist Erasmus had many similar ideas, the immediate impact of their ideas was very different because of one thing: the printing press with movable metal type. While Petrarch's works spread slowly from person to person by hand copying, Erasmus's works spread quickly through printing, in which hundreds or thousands of identical copies could be made in a short time.

While printing with movable type was invented in China (see page 373), movable metal type was actually developed in the thirteenth-century in Korea, though it was tightly controlled by the monarchy and did not have the broad impact there that printing did in Europe. Printing with movable metal type developed in Germany in the middle of the fifteenth century as a combination of existing technologies. Several metal-smiths, most prominently Johann Gutenberg (ca. 1400–1468), transformed the metal stamps used to mark signs on jewelry into type that could be covered with ink and used to mark symbols onto a page. This type could be rearranged for every page and so used over and over. Historians have speculated whether German printers somehow learned of the Korean invention, but there is no evidence that they did. The printing revolution was also

learned Europeans in the Latin in which More wrote it, and later in vernacular translations, and its title quickly became the standard word for any idealized imaginary society.

Better known by contemporaries than Thomas More was the Dutch humanist Desiderius Erasmus (1466?–1536) of Rotterdam. His fame rested largely on his exceptional knowledge of Greek and the Bible. Erasmus's long list of publications includes *The Education of a Christian Prince* (1504), a book combining idealistic and practical suggestions for the formation of a ruler's character through the careful study of Plutarch, Aristotle, Cicero, and Plato; *The Praise of Folly* (1509), a witty satire poking fun at social, politienabled by the ready availability of paper, which was made using techniques that had originated in China and spread from Muslim Spain to the rest of Europe.

The effects of the invention of movable-type printing were not felt overnight. Nevertheless, within a half century of the publication of Gutenberg's Bible of 1456, movable type had brought about radical changes. Historians estimate that somewhere between 8 million and 20 million books were printed in Europe between 1456 and 1500, many more than the total number of books that had been produced in the West during the many millennia between the invention of writing and 1456.

Printing transformed both the private and the public lives of Europeans. In the public realm, government and church leaders both used and worried about printing. They printed laws, declarations of war, battle accounts, and propaganda, but they also attempted to censor or ban books and authors whose ideas they thought were wrong. These efforts were rarely effective.

In the private realm, printing enabled people to read identical books so that they could more easily discuss the ideas that the books contained. Although most of the earliest books and pamphlets dealt with religious subjects, printers produced anything that would sell: professional reference sets, historical romances, biographies, poetry, prose fiction, and how-to manuals for the general public. Illustrations increased a book's sales, so they published both history and pornography full of woodcuts and engravings. Additionally, single-page broadsides and flysheets allowed public events and "wonders" such as comets and two-headed calves to be experienced vicariously by the stay-at-home. Since books and other printed materials were read aloud to illiterate listeners, print bridged the gap between the written and oral cultures.

Because many laypeople could not read Latin, printers put out works in Italian, French, Spanish, and English, fostering standardization in these languages. Works in these languages were also performed on stage, for plays of all types were popular everywhere. Traveling companies of actors performed before royal courts and in town squares, and in larger cities public theaters offered bawdy comedies and bloody tragedies. In London the works of William Shakespeare (1564–1616) were especially popular (see page 485).

Art and the Artist

No feature of the Renaissance evokes greater admiration than its artistic masterpieces. In Renaissance Italy wealthy merchants, bankers, popes, and princes spent vast sums to commission art as a means of glorifying themselves and their families. Patrons varied in their level of involvement as a work progressed; some simply ordered a specific subject or scene, while others oversaw the work of the artist or architect very closely, suggesting themes and styles and demanding changes while the work was in progress.

As a result of patronage certain artists gained great public acclaim and adulation, leading many historians to view the Renaissance as the beginning of the concept of the artist as genius. In the Middle Ages people believed that only God created, albeit through individuals, and artistic originality was not particularly valued. By contrast, Renaissance artists and humanists came to think that a work of art was the deliberate creation of a unique personality, of an individual who transcended traditions, rules, and theories.

In terms of artistic themes, religious topics, such as the Annunciation of the Virgin Mary and the Nativity, remained popular among both patrons and artists, but frequently the patron had himself and his family portrayed in the scene. As the fifteenth century advanced and humanist ideas spread more widely, classical

Printing Press In this reproduction of Gutenberg's printing press, metal type sits in a frame ready to be placed in the bottom part of the press, with a leather-covered ink ball nearby for spreading ink on the type. Paper was then placed over the type, and a heavy metal plate was brought down onto the paper with a firm pull of a large wooden handle, a technology adapted from wine presses. (Erich Lessing/Art Resource, NY)

themes and motifs, such as the lives and loves of pagan gods and goddesses, figured increasingly in painting and sculpture, with the facial features of the gods sometimes modeled on those of living people. Classical styles also influenced architecture, as architects designed buildings that featured carefully proportioned arches and domes modeled on the structures of ancient Rome.

The individual portrait emerged as a distinct genre in Renaissance art. Rather than reflecting a spiritual ideal, as medieval painting and sculpture tended to do,

Renaissance portraits showed human ideals, often portrayed in a more realistic style. The Florentine sculptor Donatello (1386–1466) revived the classical figure, with its balance and self-awareness. Leonardo da Vinci (1452–1519) was particularly adept at portraying female grace and beauty in his paintings of upper-class urban women and biblical figures such as the Virgin Mary. (See "Individuals in Society: Leonardo da Vinci," page 434.) Another Florentine artist, Raphael Sanzio (1483–1520), painted hundreds of portraits and devo-

Michelangelo's *David* (1501–1504) and the *Last Judgment* (detail, 1537–1541) Like all Renaissance artists, Michelangelo worked largely on commissions from patrons. Officials of the city of Florence contracted the young sculptor to produce a statue of the Old Testament hero David (left) to be displayed in the city's main square. Michelangelo portrayed David anticipating his fight against the giant Goliath, and the statue came to symbolize the republic of Florence standing up to its larger and more powerful enemies. More than thirty years later, Michelangelo was commissioned by the pope to paint a scene of the Last Judgment on the altar wall of the Sistine Chapel, where he had earlier spent four years covering the ceiling with magnificent frescoes. The massive work shows a powerful Christ standing in judgment, with souls ascending into Heaven while others are dragged by demons into Hell (above). The *David* captures ideals of human perfection and has come to be an iconic symbol of Renaissance artistic brilliance, while the dramatic and violent *Last Judgment* conveys both terror and divine power. (sculpture: Scala/Minertero per I Beni e le Attività Culturali/Art Resource, NY; painting: Alinari/The Bridgeman Art Library)

tional images in his relatively short life, becoming the most sought after artist in Europe (see page 424).

In the late fifteenth century the center of Renaissance art shifted from Florence to Rome, where wealthy cardinals and popes wanted visual expression of the church's and their own families' power and piety. To meet this demand Michelangelo Buonarroti (1475–1564) went to Rome from Florence about 1500 and began the series of statues, paintings, and architectural projects from which he gained an international reputation. For example, he produced sculptures of Moses and of the Virgin Mary holding Jesus after his crucifixion (the Pietà), he redesigned the Capitoline Hill in central Rome, and most famously, between 1508 and 1512, he painted religiously themed frescoes on the ceiling and altar wall of the Sistine Chapel. Pope Julius II, who commissioned Michelangelo for the Sistine Chapel project, demanded that the artist work as fast as he could and frequently visited him to offer suggestions and criticism. Michelangelo complained in person and by letter about the pope's meddling, but his fame did not match the power of the pope, and he kept working.

Though they might show individual genius, Renaissance artists were still expected to be schooled in proper artistic techniques and stylistic conventions, for the notion that artistic genius could show up in the work of the untrained did not emerge until the twentieth century. Therefore, in both Italy and northern Europe most aspiring artists were educated in the workshops of older artists. By the later sixteenth century formal academies were also established to train artists. Like universities, artistic workshops and academies were male-only settings in which students of different ages came together to learn and to create bonds of friendship, influence, patronage, and sometimes intimacy. Several women did become well-known as painters during the Renaissance, but they were trained by their artist fathers and often quit painting when they married.

Women were not alone in being excluded from the institutions of Renaissance culture. Though a few talented artists such as Leonardo and Michelangelo emerged from artisanal backgrounds, most scholars and artists came from families with at least some money. The audience for artists' work was also exclusive, limited mostly to educated and prosperous citizens. Although common people in large cities might have occasionally seen plays such as those of Shakespeare, most people lived in villages with no access to formal schooling or to the work of prominent artists. In general a small, highly educated minority of literary humanists and artists created the culture of and for a social elite. In this way the Renaissance maintained, and even enhanced, a gulf between the learned minority and the uneducated multitude that has survived for many centuries.

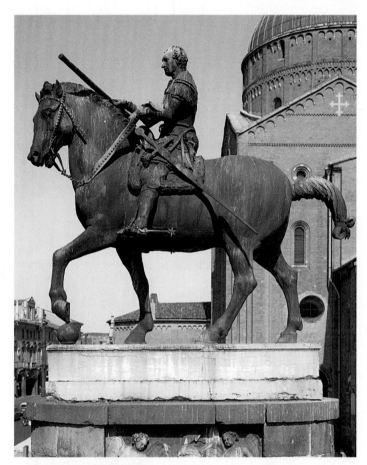

Donatello, *Gattamelata*, 1450 The Florentine sculptor Donatello's bronze statue of the powerful military captain nicknamed Gattamelata ("Honey-Cat") mounted on his horse was erected in the public square of Padua. The first bronze equestrian statue made since Roman times, the larger-than-life-size work seems to capture in metal the shrewd and determined type of ruler Machiavelli described in *The Prince*. (Scala/Art Resource, NY)

Social Hierarchies

❑ What were the key social hierarchies in Renaissance Europe, and how did these hierarchies shape people's lives?

The division between the educated and uneducated was one of many social hierarchies evident in the Renaissance. Other hierarchies built on those of the Middle Ages, but also developed new features that contributed to modern social hierarchies, such as those of race, class, and gender.

Race and Slavery

Renaissance people did not use the word *race* the way we do, but often used *race*, *people*, and *nation* interchangeably for ethnic, national, and religious groups — for example, the French race, the Irish people, the

Leonardo da Vinci

WHAT MAKES A GENIUS? AN INFINITE CAPACITY for taking pains? A deep curiosity about an extensive variety of subjects? A divine spark as manifested by talents that far exceed the norm? Or is it just "one percent inspiration and ninety-nine percent perspiration," as Thomas Edison said? To most observers, Leonardo da Vinci was one of the greatest geniuses in the history of the Western world. In fact, Leonardo was one of the individuals that the Renaissance label "genius" was designed to describe: a special kind of human being with exceptional creative powers.

Leonardo (who, despite the title of a recent bestseller, is always called by his first name) was born in Vinci, near Florence, the illegitimate son of Caterina, a local peasant girl, and Ser Piero da Vinci, a notary public. Caterina later married another native of Vinci. When Ser Piero's marriage to Donna Albrussia produced no children, he and his wife took in Leonardo. Ser Piero secured Leonardo's apprenticeship with the painter and sculptor Andrea del Verrocchio in Florence. In 1472, when Leonardo was just twenty years old, he was listed as a master in Florence's "Company of Artists."

Leonardo's most famous portrait, *Mona Lisa*, shows a woman with an enigmatic smile that the sixteenth-century artist and writer Giorgio Vasari described as "so pleasing that it seemed divine rather than human." The portrait, probably of the young wife of a rich Florentine merchant (her exact identity is hotly debated), may be the best-known painting in the history of art. One of its competitors for that designation is another work of Leonardo's, *The Last Supper*, which has been called "the most revered painting in the world."

Leonardo's reputation as a genius does not rest simply on his paintings, however, which are few in number, but rather on the breadth of his abilities and interests. In these, he is often understood to be the first "Renaissance man," a phrase we still use for a multitalented individual. He wanted to reproduce what the eye can see, and he drew everything he saw around him, including executed criminals hanging on gallows as well as the beauties of nature. Trying to understand how the human body worked, Leonardo studied live and dead bodies, doing autopsies and dissections to investigate muscles and circulation. He carefully analyzed the effects of light, using his analysis to paint strong contrasts of light and shadow, and he experimented with perspective, which gave his drawings and paintings a realistic, three-dimensional look.

Leonardo used his drawings as the basis for his paintings and also as a tool of scientific investigation. He drew plans for hundreds of inventions, many of which would become reality centuries later, such as the helicopter, tank, machine gun, and parachute. He was hired by one of the powerful new rulers in Italy, Duke Ludovico Sforza of Milan, to design practical things that the duke needed, including weapons, fortresses, and water systems, as well as to produce works of art. Leonardo left Milan when Sforza was overthrown in war and spent the last years of his life painting, drawing, and designing for the pope and the French king.

Leonardo experimented with new materials for painting and sculpture, some of which worked and some of which did not. The experimental method he used to paint *The Last Supper* caused the picture to deteriorate rapidly, and it began to flake off the wall as soon as it was finished. Leonardo regarded it as never quite completed, for he could not find a model for the face of Christ that would evoke the spiritual depth he felt it deserved. His gigantic equestrian statue in honor of Ludovico's father, Duke Francesco Sforza, was never made. The clay model collapsed, and only notes survived. He planned to write books on many subjects but never finished any of them, leaving only notebooks. Leonardo once said that "a painter is not admirable unless he is universal." The patrons who supported him— and he was supported very well—perhaps wished that his inspirations would have been a bit less universal in scope, or at least accompanied by more perspiration.

• **The enigmatic smile and smoky quality of Leonardo da Vinci's *Lady with an Ermine* can be found in many of Leonardo's works.** (Czartoryski Museum, Krakow/The Bridgeman Art Library)

Sources: Giorgio Vasari, *Lives of the Artists*, vol. 1, trans. G. Bull (London: Penguin Books, 1965); S. B. Nuland, *Leonardo da Vinci* (New York: Lipper/ Viking, 2000).

QUESTIONS FOR ANALYSIS

1. In what ways do the notion of a genius and the notion of a Renaissance man support one another? In what ways do they contradict one another? Which seems a better description of Leonardo?
2. Has the idea of artistic genius changed since the Renaissance? If so, how?

Artemisia Gentileschi, *Esther Before Ahaseurus*, ca. 1630 In this oil painting, Gentileschi shows an Old Testament scene of the Jewish woman Esther who saved her people from being killed by her husband, King Ahaseurus. This deliverance is celebrated in the Jewish holiday of Purim. The elaborate clothes shown here are the type worn in Renaissance courts. Typical of a female painter, Artemisia Gentileschi was trained by her father. She mastered the dramatic style favored in the early seventeenth century and became known especially for her portraits of strong biblical and mythological heroines. (Image copyright © The Metropolitan Museum of Art/Art Resource, NY)

Jewish nation. They did make distinctions based on skin color that were in keeping with later conceptualizations of race, but these distinctions were interwoven with other characteristics when people thought about human differences.

Ever since the time of the Roman republic, a few black Africans had lived in western Europe. They had come, along with white slaves, as the spoils of war. After the collapse of the Roman Empire and throughout the Middle Ages, Muslim and Christian merchants continued to import black slaves, and long tradition sanctioned the practice of slavery. The black population was especially concentrated in the cities of the Iberian Peninsula, where African slaves sometimes gained their freedom and intermingled with the local population. By the mid-sixteenth century blacks, slave and free, constituted roughly 3 percent of the Portuguese population, and because of intermarriage cities such as Lisbon had significant numbers of people of mixed African and European descent.

In Renaissance Portugal, Spain, and Italy, African slaves supplemented the labor force in virtually all occupations — as servants, agricultural laborers, crafts-men, and seamen on ships. Slaves also formed the primary workforce on the sugar plantations set up by Europeans on the Atlantic islands in the late fifteenth century (see page 479). European aristocrats sometimes had themselves painted with their black servants to indicate their wealth or, in the case of noblewomen, to highlight their fair skin.

Until their voyages down the African coast in the late fifteenth century, Europeans had little concrete knowledge of Africans and their cultures. They perceived Africa as a remote place, the home of strange people isolated by heresy and Islam from superior European civilization. Africans' contact, even as slaves, with Christian Europeans would improve the blacks, they believed. The expanding slave trade reinforced negative preconceptions about the inferiority of black Africans.

Wealth and the Nobility

The word *class* — as in working class, middle class, upper class — was not used in the Renaissance to describe social division, but by the thirteenth century, and even

▫ Picturing the Past

Laura de Dianti, **1523** The Venetian artist Titian shows a young Italian woman with a gorgeous blue dress and an elaborate pearl and feather headdress accompanied by a young black page with a gold earring. Slaves from Africa and the Ottoman Empire were common in wealthy Venetian households. (Courtesy, Friedrich Kisters, Heinz Kisters Collection)

ANALYZING THE IMAGE How does the artist convey the message that this woman comes from a wealthy family? How does he use the skin color of the slave to highlight the woman's fair skin, which was part of Renaissance ideals of female beauty?

CONNECTIONS Household slaves worked at various tasks, but they were also symbols of the exotic. What other elements does Titian include in the painting to represent foreign places and the wealth brought to Venice by overseas trade? What does this painting suggest about Venetian attitudes toward slaves, who were part of that trade?

more so by the fifteenth, the idea of a changeable hierarchy based on wealth was emerging alongside the medieval concept of orders (see page 408). This was particularly true in towns. Most residents of towns were technically members of the third order — "those who work" rather than "those who fight" and "those who pray." With the rise of trade and commerce, however, townspeople could now gain status through wealth. Wealthy merchants oversaw vast trading empires, held positions of political power, and lived in splendor rivaling that enjoyed by the richest nobles.

The development of a hierarchy of wealth did not mean an end to the hierarchy of orders, however, and even poorer nobles still had higher status than merchants. If this had not been the case, wealthy Italian merchants would not have bothered to buy noble titles

and country villas, nor would wealthy English and Spanish merchants have been eager to marry their daughters and sons into often impoverished noble families. The nobility maintained its status in most parts of Europe not by maintaining rigid boundaries, but by taking in and integrating the new social elite of wealth.

Gender Roles

Renaissance people would not have understood the word *gender* to refer to categories of people, but they would have easily grasped the concept. Toward the end of the fourteenth century learned men (and a few women) began what was termed the **debate about women** (*querelle des femmes*), an argument about women's character and nature that would last for centuries. Misogynist critiques of women from both clerical and secular authors denounced females as devious, domineering, and demanding. In response, several authors compiled long lists of famous and praisewor-

• **debate about women** A discussion, which began in the later years of the fourteenth century, that attempted to answer fundamental questions about gender and to define the role of women in society.

thy women exemplary for their loyalty, bravery, and morality. Some writers, including a few women who had gained a humanist education, were interested not only in defending women but also in exploring the reasons behind women's secondary status — that is, why the great philosophers, statesmen, and poets had generally been men. In this they were anticipating more recent discussions about the "social construction of gender" by six hundred years.

Beginning in the sixteenth century the debate about women also became one about female rulers, because in Spain, England, France, and Scotland women served as advisers to child kings or ruled in their own right. There were no successful rebellions against female rulers simply because they were women, but in part this was because female rulers, especially Queen Elizabeth I of England, emphasized qualities regarded as masculine — physical bravery, stamina, wisdom, duty — whenever they appeared in public.

The dominant notion of the "true" man was that of the married head of household, so men whose class and age would have normally conferred political power but who remained unmarried were sometimes excluded from ruling positions. Actual marriage patterns in Europe left many women unmarried until late in life, but this did not lead to greater equality. Women who worked for wages, as was typical, earned about half to two-thirds of what men did even for the same work. Regulations for German vineyard workers in the early sixteenth century, for example, specified that

> Men who work in the vineyards, doing work that is skilled, are to be paid 16 pence per day; in addition, they are to receive soup and wine in the morning, at midday beer, vegetables and meat, and in the evening soup, vegetables and wine. Young boys are to be paid 10 pence per day. Women who work as haymakers are to be given 6 pence a day. If the employer wants to have them doing other work, he may make an agreement with them to pay them 7 or 8 pence. He may also give them soup and vegetables to eat in the morning — but no wine — milk and bread at midday, but nothing in the evening.[2]

Of all the ways in which Renaissance society was hierarchically arranged — by class, age, level of education, rank, race, occupation — gender was regarded as the most "natural" distinction and therefore the most important one to defend.

Italian City Scene In this detail from a fresco, the Italian painter Lorenzo Lotto captures the mixing of social groups in a Renaissance Italian city. The crowd of men in the left foreground includes wealthy merchants in elaborate hats and colorful coats. Two mercenary soldiers (carrying a sword and a pike) wear short doublets and tight hose stylishly slit to reveal colored undergarments, while boys play with toy weapons at their feet. Clothing like that of the soldiers, which emphasized the masculine form, was frequently criticized for its expense and its "indecency." At the right, women sell vegetables and bread, which would have been a common sight at any city marketplace. (Scala/Art Resource, NY)

Politics and the State in the Renaissance, ca. 1450–1521

☐ How did the nation-states of western Europe evolve in this period?

The High Middle Ages had witnessed the origins of many of the basic institutions of the modern state. Sheriffs, inquests, juries, circuit judges, professional bureaucracies, and representative assemblies all trace their origins to the twelfth and thirteenth centuries. The linchpin for the development of states, however, was strong monarchy. Beginning in the fifteenth century rulers used aggressive methods to build up their governments. They began the work of reducing violence, curbing unruly nobles, and establishing domestic order. They emphasized royal majesty and royal sovereignty and insisted on the respect and loyalty of all subjects. Here, we examine how monarchies throughout western Europe built and maintained power.

France

The Hundred Years' War left France drastically depopulated, commercially ruined, and agriculturally weak (see page 420). Nonetheless, the ruler whom Joan of Arc had seen crowned at Reims, Charles VII (r. 1422–1461), revived the monarchy and France. He reorganized the royal council, giving increased influence to middle-class men, and strengthened royal finances through such taxes as the *gabelle* (on salt) and the *taille* (on land). These taxes remained the Crown's chief sources of income until the Revolution of 1789. By establishing regular companies of cavalry and archers—recruited, paid, and inspected by the state—Charles created the first permanent royal army.

Two further developments strengthened the French monarchy. The marriage of Louis XII (r. 1498–1515) and Anne of Brittany added the large western duchy of Brittany to the state. Louis XII's successor, Francis I (r. 1515–1547), and Pope Leo X reached a mutually satisfactory agreement about church and state powers in 1516 that gave French kings the power to control the appointment and thus the policies of church officials in the kingdom.

England

English society suffered severely in the fourteenth and fifteenth centuries. Population, decimated by the Black Death, continued to decline. Between 1455 and 1471 adherents of the ducal houses of York and Lancaster waged civil wars over control of the English throne.

These conflicts were commonly called the Wars of the Roses because the symbol of the Yorkists was a white rose and that of the Lancastrians a red one. The chronic disorder hurt trade, agriculture, and domestic industry, and the authority of the monarchy sank lower than it had been in centuries.

The Yorkist Edward IV (r. 1461–1483) succeeded in defeating the Lancastrian forces and after 1471 began to reconstruct the monarchy and consolidate royal power. Henry VII (r. 1485–1509) of the Welsh house of Tudor worked to restore royal prestige, to crush the power of the nobility, and to establish order and law at the local level. Because the government halted the long period of anarchy, it won the key support of the merchant and agricultural upper middle class. Early in his reign Henry VII summoned several meetings of Parliament, primarily to confirm laws, but the center of royal authority was the royal council, which governed at the national level. There Henry VII revealed his distrust of the nobility: very few great lords were among the king's closest advisers, who instead were lesser landowners and lawyers. They were, in a sense, middle class. The royal council handled any business the king put before it—executive, legislative, and judicial.

Secretive, cautious, and thrifty, Henry VII rebuilt the monarchy. He encouraged the cloth industry and built up the English merchant marine. He crushed an invasion from Ireland, secured peace with Scotland through the marriage of his daughter Margaret to the Scottish king, and enhanced English prestige through the marriage of his eldest son, Arthur, to Catherine of Aragon, the daughter of Ferdinand and Isabella of Spain. (After Arthur's death, Catherine would become the wife of his younger brother and the future king of England, Henry VIII; see page 448.) When Henry VII died in 1509, he left a country at peace both domestically and internationally, a substantially augmented treasury, and the dignity and role of the royal majesty much enhanced.

Spain

While England and France laid the foundations of unified nation-states during the Renaissance, Spain remained a conglomerate of independent kingdoms. Even the wedding in 1469 of the dynamic and aggressive Isabella of Castile and the crafty and persistent Ferdinand of Aragon did not bring about administrative unity. Isabella and Ferdinand were, however, able to exert their authority in ways similar to the rulers of France and England. They curbed aristocratic power by excluding aristocrats and great territorial magnates from the royal council, and instead appointed only men of middle-class background. The council and various government boards recruited men trained in Roman law, which exalted the power of the Crown. They also

Felipe Bigarny: Ferdinand and Isabella In these wooden sculptures, the Burgundian artist Felipe Bigarny portrays Ferdinand and Isabella as paragons of Christian piety, kneeling at prayer. Ferdinand is shown in armor, a symbol of his military accomplishments and masculinity. Isabella wears a simple white head covering rather than something more elaborate to indicate her modesty, a key virtue for women, though her actions and writings indicate that she was more determined and forceful than Ferdinand. (Laurie Platt Winfrey/The Granger Collection, NY)

secured from the Spanish pope Alexander VI the right to appoint bishops in Spain and in the Hispanic territories in America, enabling them to establish the equivalent of a national church. In 1492 their armies conquered Granada, the last territory held by Arabs in southern Spain.

Ferdinand and Isabella's rule also marked the start of a dark chapter in Spanish history, greater persecution of the Jews. In the Middle Ages the kings of France and England had expelled the Jews from their kingdoms, and many had sought refuge in Spain. During the long centuries of the reconquista (see page 404), Christian kings in Spain had renewed Jewish rights and privileges; in fact, Jewish industry, intelligence, and money had supported royal power. But while Christians of all classes borrowed from Jewish moneylenders and while all who could afford them sought Jewish physicians, a strong undercurrent of resentment of Jewish influence and wealth festered.

In the fourteenth century anti-Semitism in Spain was aggravated by fiery anti-Jewish preaching, by economic dislocation, and by the search for a scapegoat during the Black Death. Anti-Semitic pogroms swept the towns of Spain, and perhaps 40 percent of the Jewish population was killed or forced to convert. Those who converted were called *conversos* (kuhn-VEHR-sohz) or New Christians. Conversos were often well-educated and held prominent positions in government, the church, medicine, law, and business.

Such successes bred resentment. Aristocrats resented their financial dependence on conversos; the poor hated the converso tax collectors; and churchmen doubted the sincerity of their conversions. Queen Isabella shared these suspicions, and she and Ferdinand received permission from Pope Sixtus IV to establish an Inquisition to "search out and punish converts from Judaism who had transgressed against Christianity by secretly adhering to Jewish beliefs and performing rites of the Jews."[3] Investigations and trials began immediately, with officials of the Inquisition looking for conversos who showed any sign of incomplete conversion, such as not eating pork.

Recent scholarship has carefully analyzed documents of the Inquisition. Most conversos identified themselves as sincere Christians; many came from families that had received baptism generations before.

In response, officials of the Inquisition developed a new type of anti-Semitism. A person's status as a Jew, they argued, could not be changed by religious conversion, but was in the person's blood and was heritable, so Jews could never be true Christians. Under what were known as "purity of blood" laws, having "pure Christian blood" became a requirement for noble status. Ideas about Jews developed in Spain became important components in European concepts of race, and discussions of "Jewish blood" later expanded into discriminatory definitions of the "Jewish race."

In 1492, shortly after the conquest of Granada, Isabella and Ferdinand issued an edict expelling all practicing Jews from Spain. Of the community of perhaps 200,000 Jews, 150,000 fled. Absolute religious orthodoxy and "purity of blood" served as the theoretical foundation of the Spanish national state.

The Habsburgs

War and diplomacy were important ways that states increased their power in sixteenth-century Europe, but so was marriage. Because almost all of Europe was ruled by hereditary dynasties—the Papal States and a few cities being the exceptions—claiming and holding resources involved shrewd marital strategies, for it was far cheaper to gain land by inheritance than by war.

The benefits of an advantageous marriage stretched across generations, as can be seen most dramatically with the Habsburgs. The Holy Roman emperor Frederick III, a Habsburg who was the ruler of most of Austria, acquired only a small amount of territory—but a great deal of money—with his marriage to Princess Eleanore of Portugal in 1452. He arranged for his son Maximilian to marry Europe's most prominent heiress, Mary of Burgundy, in 1477; she inherited the

MAP 15.1 The Global Empire of Charles V, ca. 1556 Charles V exercised theoretical jurisdiction over more European territory than anyone since Charlemagne. He also claimed authority over large parts of North and South America, although actual Spanish control was weak in much of this area.

Netherlands, Luxembourg, and the county of Burgundy in what is now eastern France. Through this union with the rich and powerful duchy of Burgundy, the Austrian house of Habsburg, already the strongest ruling family in the empire, became an international power. The marriage of Maximilian and Mary angered the French, who considered Burgundy French territory, and it inaugurated centuries of conflict between the Habsburgs and the kings of France. Within the empire, German principalities that resented Austria's pre-eminence began to see that they shared interests with France.

Maximilian learned the lesson of marital politics well, marrying his son and daughter to the children of Ferdinand and Isabella, the rulers of Spain, much of southern Italy, and eventually the Spanish New World empire. His grandson Charles V (1500–1558) fell heir to a vast and incredibly diverse collection of states and peoples, each governed in a different manner and held together only by the person of the emperor (Map 15.1). Charles was convinced that it was his duty to maintain the political and religious unity of Western Christendom. This conviction would be challenged far more than Charles ever anticipated.

The Protestant Reformation

☐ What were the central ideas of Protestant reformers, and why were they appealing to various groups across Europe?

Calls for reform in the church came from many quarters in early-sixteenth-century Europe — from educated laypeople such as Christian humanists and urban residents, from villagers and artisans, and from church officials themselves. This dissatisfaction helps explain why the ideas of Martin Luther, an obscure professor from a new and not very prestigious German university, found a ready audience. Within a decade of his first publishing his ideas (using the new technology of the printing press), much of central Europe and Scandinavia had broken with the Catholic Church in a movement that came to be known as the **Protestant Reformation**. In addition, even more radical concepts of the Christian message were being developed and linked to calls for social change.

Criticism of the Church

Sixteenth-century Europeans were deeply pious. Despite — or perhaps because of — the depth of their piety, many people were also highly critical of the Roman Catholic Church and its clergy. Papal conflicts with rulers and the Great Schism (see page 420) badly damaged the prestige of church leaders. Papal tax collec-

tion methods were also attacked, and some criticized the papacy itself as an institution. Court records, written descriptions of bishops' visitations of parishes, and even popular songs and printed images show widespread anticlericalism, or opposition to the clergy.

In the early sixteenth century critics of the church concentrated their attacks on clerical immorality, clerical ignorance, and clerical absenteeism. Charges of clerical immorality were aimed at a number of priests who were drunkards, neglected the rule of celibacy, gambled, or indulged in fancy dress. Charges of clerical ignorance applied to barely literate priests who delivered poor quality sermons and who were obviously ignorant of the Latin words of the Mass.

In regard to absenteeism, many clerics, especially higher ecclesiastics, held several benefices (or offices) simultaneously — a practice termed pluralism. However, they seldom visited the communities served by the benefices, let alone performed the spiritual responsibilities those offices entailed. Instead, they collected revenues from all of the benefices assigned to them and hired a poor priest to fulfill their spiritual duties, paying him just a fraction of the income.

There was also local resentment of clerical privileges and immunities. Priests, monks, and nuns were exempt from civic responsibilities, such as defending the city and paying taxes. Yet religious orders frequently held large amounts of urban property, in some cities as much as one-third. City governments were increasingly determined to integrate the clergy into civic life. This brought city leaders into opposition with bishops and the papacy, which for centuries had stressed the independence of the church from lay control and the distinction between members of the clergy and laypeople.

Martin Luther

By itself, widespread criticism of the church did not lead to the dramatic changes of the sixteenth century. Those resulted from the personal religious struggle of a German university professor, Martin Luther (1483–1546). Luther's middle-class father wanted him to be a lawyer, but a sense of religious calling led him to join the Augustinian friars, an order whose members often preached to, taught, and assisted the poor. Luther was ordained a priest in 1507 and after additional study earned a doctorate of theology. From 1512 until his death in 1546 he served as professor of the Scriptures at the new University of Wittenberg.

Martin Luther was a very conscientious friar, but his scrupulous observance of the religious routine, frequent confessions, and fasting gave him only temporary relief from anxieties about sin and his ability to

• **Protestant Reformation** A religious reform movement that began in the early sixteenth century that split the Western Christian Church.

Selling Indulgences
A German single-page pamphlet shows a monk offering an indulgence, with the official seals of the pope attached, as people run to put their money in the box in exchange for his promise of heavenly bliss, symbolized by the dove above his head. Indulgences were sold widely in Germany, and they were the first Catholic practice that Luther criticized openly. This pamphlet also attacks the sale of indulgences, calling it devilish and deceitful, a point of view expressed in the woodcut by the peddler's riding on a donkey, an animal that had long been used as a symbol of ignorance. Indulgences were often printed as fill-in-the-blank forms. This one, purchased in 1521, has space for the indulgence seller's name at the top, the buyer's name in the middle, and the date at the bottom. (woodcut: akg-images; indulgence: Visual Connection Archive)

meet God's demands. Through his study of Saint Paul's letters in the New Testament, he gradually arrived at a new understanding of Christian doctrine. His understanding is often summarized as "faith alone, grace alone, scripture alone." He believed that salvation and justification (righteousness in God's eyes) come through faith, and that faith is a free gift of God, not the result of human effort. God's word is revealed only in biblical scripture, not in the traditions of the church.

At the same time Luther was engaged in scholarly reflections and professorial lecturing, Pope Leo X authorized a special Saint Peter's indulgence to finance his building plans in Rome. An **indulgence** was a document, signed by the pope or another church official, that substituted for penance. The archbishop who controlled the area in which Wittenberg was located, Albert of Mainz, also promoted the sale of indulgences, in his case to pay off a debt he had incurred to be named bishop of several additional territories. Albert's sales campaign, run by a Dominican friar who mounted an advertising blitz, promised that the purchase of indulgences would bring full forgiveness for one's own sins or buy release from purgatory for a loved one. One of the slogans — "As soon as coin in coffer rings, the soul from purgatory springs" — brought phenomenal success.

Luther was severely troubled that many people believed that they had no further need for repentance once they had purchased indulgences. He wrote a letter to Archbishop Albert on the subject and enclosed in Latin "Ninety-five Theses on the Power of Indulgences." His argument was that indulgences undermined the seriousness of the sacrament of penance and competed with the preaching of the Gospel. After Luther's death, biographies reported that the theses were also posted on the door of the church at Wittenberg Castle on October 31, 1517. Such an act would have been very strange — they were in Latin and written for those learned in theology, not for normal churchgoers — but it has become a standard part of Luther lore. In any case, Luther intended the theses for academic debate, but by December 1517 they had been translated into German and were read throughout the Holy Roman Empire.

Luther was ordered to go to Rome, but he was able to avoid this because the ruler of the territory in which he lived protected him. The pope nonetheless ordered him to recant many of his ideas, and Luther publicly burned the letter containing the papal order. In this highly charged atmosphere, the twenty-one-year-old emperor Charles V summoned Luther to appear before the **Diet of Worms**. When ordered to recant at this assembly, Luther replied in language that rang all over Europe:

> Unless I am convinced by the evidence of Scripture or by plain reason — for I do not accept the authority of the Pope or the councils alone, since it is established that they have often erred and contradicted themselves — I am bound by the Scriptures I have cited and my conscience is captive to the Word of God. I cannot and will not recant anything, for it is neither safe nor right to go against conscience. God help me. Amen.[4]

Protestant Thought and Its Appeal

As he developed his ideas, Luther gathered followers, who came to be called Protestants. The word **Protestant** derives from a "protest" drawn up by a small group of reforming German princes in 1529. At first *Protestant* meant "a follower of Luther," but with the appearance of many protesting sects, it became a general term applied to all non-Catholic western European Christians.

Catholic teaching held that salvation is achieved by both faith and good works. Protestants held that salvation comes by faith alone, irrespective of good works or the sacraments. God, not people, initiates salvation. (See "Listening to the Past: Martin Luther, *On Christian Liberty*," page 444.) Second, where does religious authority reside? Christian doctrine had long maintained that authority rests both in the Bible and in the traditional teachings of the church. For Protestants, however, authority rests in the Bible alone, and for a doctrine or issue to be valid, it has to have a scriptural basis. Third, what is the church? Protestants held that the church is a spiritual priesthood of all believers, an invisible fellowship not fixed in any place or person, which differed markedly from the Roman Catholic practice of looking to a clerical, hierarchical institution headed by the pope in Rome. Fourth, what is the highest form of Christian life? The medieval church had stressed the superiority of the monastic and religious life over the secular. Luther disagreed and argued that every person should serve God in his or her individual calling.

Pulpits and printing presses spread Luther's message all over Germany. By the time of his death, Lutherans could be found in all social classes in Germany and many other parts of Europe as well. What was the immense appeal of Luther's religious ideas and those of other Protestants?

Educated people and humanists were attracted by Luther's ideas. He advocated a simpler personal religion based on faith, a return to the spirit of the early church, the centrality of the Scriptures in the liturgy and in Christian life, and the abolition of elaborate ceremonies — precisely the reforms the Christian humanists had been calling for. His insistence that everyone should read and reflect on the Scriptures attracted the literate middle classes, including many priests and monks who became clergy in the new Protestant churches. Luther's ideas also appealed to townspeople who envied the church's wealth and resented paying for it. After cities became Protestant, the city council taxed the clergy and placed them under the jurisdiction of civil courts.

Scholars in many disciplines have attributed Luther's fame and success to the invention of the printing press, which rapidly reproduced and made known his ideas. Many printed works included woodcuts and other illustrations, so that even those who could not read could grasp the main ideas. Hymns were also important means of conveying central points of doctrine, as was Luther's translation of the New Testament into German in 1523.

Luther worked closely with political authorities, viewing them as fully justified in reforming the church in their territories. He instructed all Christians to obey their secular rulers, whom he saw as divinely ordained to maintain order. Individuals may have been convinced of the truth of Protestant teachings by hearing sermons, listening to hymns, or reading pamphlets, but a territory became Protestant when its ruler, whether a noble or a city council, brought in a reformer or two to reeducate the territory's clergy, sponsored public sermons, and confiscated church property. This happened in many of the states of the empire during the 1520s and then moved beyond the empire to Denmark-Norway and Sweden.

The Radical Reformation and the German Peasants' War

In the sixteenth century the practice of religion remained a public matter. The ruler determined the official form of religious practice in his (or occasionally her) jurisdiction. Almost everyone believed that the presence of a faith different from that of the majority represented a political threat to the security of the state. Few believed in religious liberty; people with different ideas had to convert or leave.

Some individuals and groups rejected the idea that church and state needed to be united, however, and

---

- **indulgence** A papal statement granting remission of a priest-imposed penalty for sin. (No one knew what penalty God would impose after death.)
- **Diet of Worms** An assembly of the Estates of the Holy Roman Empire convened by Charles V in the German city of Worms. It was here, in 1521, that Martin Luther refused to recant his writings.
- **Protestant** Originally meaning "a follower of Luther," this term came to be generally applied to all non-Catholic western European Christians.

Listening to the Past

Martin Luther, *On Christian Liberty*

The idea of liberty or freedom has played a powerful role in the history of human society and culture, but the meaning and understanding of liberty have undergone continual change and interpretation. In the Roman world, where slavery was a basic institution, liberty meant the condition of being a free man, independent of obligations to a master. In the Middle Ages, possessing liberty meant having special privileges or rights that other persons or institutions did not have. A lord or a monastery, for example, might speak of his or its liberties, and citizens in London were said to possess the "freedom of the city," which allowed them to practice trades and own property without interference. Likewise, the first chapter of Magna Carta (1215), often called the "Charter of Liberties," states: "Holy Church shall be free and have its rights entire and its liberties inviolate," meaning that the English Church was independent of the authority of the king.

The idea of liberty also has a religious dimension, and the reformer Martin Luther formulated a classic interpretation of liberty in his treatise On Christian Liberty *(sometimes translated as* On the Freedom of a Christian*), arguably his finest piece. Written in Latin for the pope but translated immediately into German and published widely, it contains the main themes of Luther's theology: the importance of faith, the relationship of Christian faith and good works, the dual nature of human beings, and the fundamental importance of scripture. Luther writes that Christians were freed through Christ, not by their own actions, from sin and death.*

❝Christian faith has appeared to many an easy thing; nay, not a few even reckon it among the social virtues, as it were; and this they do because they have not made proof of it experimentally, and have never tasted of what efficacy it is. For it is not possible for any man to write well about it, or to understand well what is rightly written, who has not at some time tasted of its spirit, under the pressure of tribulation; while he who has tasted of it, even to a very small extent, can never write, speak, think, or hear about it sufficiently. . . .

I hope that . . . I have attained some little drop of faith, and that I can speak of this matter, if not with more elegance, certainly with more solidity. . . .

A Christian man is the most free lord of all, and subject to none; a Christian man is the most dutiful servant of all, and subject to everyone.

Although these statements appear contradictory, yet, when they are found to agree together, they will do excellently for my purpose. They are both the statements of Paul himself, who says, "Though I be free from all men, yet have I made myself a servant unto all" (I Corinthians 9:19), and "Owe no man anything but to love one another" (Romans 13:8). Now love is by its own nature dutiful and obedient to the beloved object. Thus even Christ, though Lord of all things, was yet made of a woman; made under the law; at once free and a servant; at once in the form of God and in the form of a servant.

Let us examine the subject on a deeper and less simple principle. Man is composed of a twofold nature, a spiritual and a bodily. As regards the spiritual nature, which they name the soul, he is called the spiritual, inward, new man; as regards the bodily nature, which they name the flesh, he is called the fleshly, outward, old man. The Apostle speaks of this: "Though our outward man perish, yet the inward man is renewed day by day" (II Corinthians 4:16). The result of this diversity is that in the Scriptures opposing statements are made concerning the same man, the fact being that in the same man these two men are opposed to one another; the flesh lusting against the spirit, and the spirit against the flesh (Galatians 5:17).

We first approach the subject of the inward man, that we may see by what means a man becomes justified, free, and a true Christian; that is, a spiritual, new, and inward man. It is certain that absolutely none among outward things, under whatever name they may be reckoned, has any influence in producing Christian righteousness or liberty, nor, on the other hand, unrighteousness or slavery. This can be shown by an easy argument.

What can it profit to the soul that the body should be in good condition, free, and full of life, that it should eat, drink, and act according to its pleasure, when even the most impious slaves of every kind of vice are prosperous in these matters? Again, what harm can ill health, bondage, hunger, thirst, or any other outward evil, do to the soul, when even the most pious of men, and the freest in the purity of their conscience, are harassed by these things? Neither of these states of things has to do with the liberty or the slavery of the soul.

they sought to create a voluntary community of believers as they understood it to have existed in New Testament times. In terms of theology and spiritual practices, these individuals and groups varied widely, though they are generally termed "radicals" for their insistence on a more extensive break with prevailing ideas. Some adopted the custom of baptizing adult believers — for which they were given the title of "Anabaptists" or re-baptizers by their enemies — while others saw all outward sacraments or rituals as misguided. Some groups attempted communal ownership of property, living very simply and rejecting anything they thought unbiblical. Some reacted harshly to members who deviated from the group's accepted practices,

And so it will profit nothing that the body should be adorned with sacred vestment, or dwell in holy places, or be occupied in sacred offices, or pray, fast, and abstain from certain meats, or do whatever works can be done through the body and in the body. Something widely different will be necessary for the justification and liberty of the soul, since the things I have spoken of can be done by an impious person, and only hypocrites are produced by devotion to these things. On the other hand, it will not at all injure the soul that the body should be clothed in profane raiment, should dwell in profane places, should eat and drink in the ordinary fashion, should not pray aloud, and should leave undone all the things above mentioned, which may be done by hypocrites.

. . . One thing, and one alone, is necessary for life, justification, and Christian liberty; and that is the most Holy Word of God, the Gospel of Christ, as He says, "I am the resurrection and the life; he that believeth in me shall not die eternally" (John 9:25), and also, "If the Son shall make you free, ye shall be free indeed" (John 8:36), and "Man shall not live by bread alone, but by every word that proceedeth out of the mouth of God" (Matthew 4:4).

Let us therefore hold it for certain and firmly established that the soul can do without everything except the Word of God, without which none at all of its wants is provided for. But, having the Word, it is rich and wants for nothing, since that is the Word of life, of truth, of light, of peace, of justification, of salvation, of joy, of liberty, of wisdom, of virtue, of grace, of glory, and of every good thing. . . .

But you will ask, "What is this Word, and by what means is it to be used, since there are so many words of God?" I answer, "The Apostle Paul (Romans 1) explains what it is, namely the Gospel of God, concerning His Son, incarnate, suffering, risen, and glorified through the Spirit, the Sanctifier." To preach Christ is to feed the soul, to justify it, to set it free, and to save it, if it believes the preaching. For faith alone, and the efficacious use of the Word of God, bring salvation. "If thou shalt confess with thy mouth the Lord Jesus, and shalt believe in thine heart that God hath raised Him from the dead, thou shalt be saved" (Romans 9:9); . . . and "The just shall live by faith" (Romans 1:17). . . .

But this faith cannot consist of all with works; that is, if you imagine that you can be justified by those works, whatever they are, along with it. . . . Therefore, when you begin to believe, you learn at the same time that all that is in you is utterly guilty, sinful, and damnable, according to that saying, "All have sinned, and come short of the glory of God" (Romans 3:23). . . . When you have learned this, you will know that Christ is necessary for you, since He has suffered and risen again for you, that, believing on Him, you might by this faith become another man, all your sins being remitted, and you being justified by the merits of another, namely Christ alone.

. . . [A]nd since it [faith] alone justifies, it is evident that by no outward work or labour can the inward man be at all justified, made free, and saved; and that no works whatever have any relation to him. . . . Therefore the first care of every Christian ought to be to lay aside all reliance on works, and strengthen his faith alone more and more, and by it grow in knowledge, not of works, but of Christ Jesus, who has suffered and risen again for him, as Peter teaches (I Peter 5). 99

Source: *Luther's Primary Works*, ed. H. Wace and C. A. Buchheim (London: Holder and Stoughton, 1896). Reprinted in *The Portable Renaissance Reader*, ed. James Bruce Ross and Mary Martin McLaughlin (New York: Penguin Books, 1981), pp. 721–726.

QUESTIONS FOR ANALYSIS

1. What did Luther mean by liberty?
2. Why, for Luther, was scripture basic to Christian life?

but others argued for complete religious toleration and individualism.

Religious radicals were met with fanatical hatred and bitter persecution, including banishment and execution. Both Protestant and Catholic authorities felt threatened by the social, political, and economic implications of radicals' religious ideas and by their rejection of a state church, which the authorities saw as key to maintaining order. Their community spirit and heroism in the face of martyrdom, however, contributed to the survival of radical ideas. Later, the Quakers, with their pacifism; the Baptists, with their emphasis on inner spiritual light; the Congregationalists, with their democratic church organization; and in 1787 the

> "Let everyone who can smite, slay, and stab [the peasants], secretly and openly, remembering that nothing can be more poisonous, hurtful or devilish than a rebel."
>
> **MARTIN LUTHER**

authors of the U.S. Constitution, with their opposition to the "establishment of religion" (state churches), would all trace the origins of their beliefs, in part, to the radicals of the sixteenth century.

Another group to challenge state authorities was the peasantry. In the early sixteenth century the economic condition of peasants varied from place to place but was generally worse than it had been in the fifteenth century and was deteriorating. Peasants demanded limitations on the new taxes and services their noble landlords were imposing. They believed that their demands conformed to the Scriptures and cited Luther as a theologian who could prove that they did.

Wanting to prevent rebellion, Luther initially sided with the peasants, blasting the lords for robbing their subjects. But when rebellion broke out, the peasants who expected Luther's support were soon disillusioned. Freedom for Luther meant independence from the authority of the Roman Church, not opposition to legally established secular powers. Firmly convinced that rebellion would hasten the end of civilized society, he wrote the tract *Against the Murderous, Thieving Hordes of the Peasants*, which said, in part, "Let everyone who can smite, slay, and stab [the peasants], secretly and openly, remembering that nothing can be more poisonous, hurtful or devilish than a rebel."[5] The nobility ferociously crushed the revolt, which became known as the German Peasants' War of 1525. That year, historians estimate, more than seventy-five thousand peasants were killed.

The peasants' war greatly strengthened the authority of lay rulers. Because Luther turned against the peasants who revolted, the Reformation lost much of its popular appeal after 1525, though peasants and urban rebels sometimes found a place for their social and religious ideas in radical groups. Peasants' economic conditions did moderately improve, however. For example, in many parts of Germany, enclosed fields, meadows, and forests were returned to common use instead of being controlled by noble landlords.

Marriage and Women's Roles

Luther and other Protestants believed that a priest's or nun's vows of celibacy went against human nature and God's commandments. Luther married a former nun,

Katharina von Bora (1499–1532), who quickly had several children. Most other Protestant reformers also married, and their wives had to create a new and respectable role for themselves — pastor's wife — to overcome being viewed as simply a new type of priest's concubine. They were living demonstrations of their husband's convictions about the superiority of marriage to celibacy, and they were expected to be models of wifely obedience and Christian charity.

Catholics viewed marriage as a sacramental union that, if validly entered into, could not be dissolved. Protestants saw marriage as a contract in which each partner promised the other support, companionship, and the sharing of mutual goods. They believed that spouses who did not comfort or support one another endangered their own souls and the surrounding community; therefore, most Protestants came to allow divorce. Divorce remained rare, however, because marriage was such an important social and economic institution.

Protestants did not break with medieval scholastic theologians in their view that, within marriage, women were to be subject to men. Women were advised to be cheerful rather than grudging in their obedience, for in doing so they demonstrated their willingness to follow God's plan. Men were urged to treat their wives kindly and considerately, but also to enforce their authority, through physical coercion if necessary. Both continental and English marriage manuals use the metaphor of breaking a horse for teaching a wife obedience, though laws did set limits on the husband's power to control his wife. A few women took the Protestant idea about the priesthood of all believers to heart and wrote religious pamphlets and hymns, but no sixteenth-century Protestants officially allowed women to hold positions of religious authority. Monarchs such as Elizabeth I of England and female territorial rulers of the states of the Holy Roman Empire did determine religious policies, however.

Because the Reformation generally brought the closing of monasteries and convents, marriage became virtually the only occupation for upper-class Protestant women. Recognizing this, women in some convents fought the Reformation or argued that they could still be pious Protestants within convent walls. Most nuns left, however, and we do not know what happened to them. The Protestant emphasis on marriage made unmarried women (and men) suspect, for they did not belong to the type of household regarded as the cornerstone of a proper, godly society.

The Reformation and German Politics

Criticism of the church was widespread in Europe in the early sixteenth century, and calls for reform came from many areas. Yet such movements could be more

Martin Luther and Katharina von Bora Lucas Cranach the Elder painted this double marriage portrait to celebrate Luther's wedding in 1525 to Katharina von Bora, a former nun. The artist was one of the witnesses at the wedding and, in fact, had presented Luther's marriage proposal to Katharina. The couple quickly became a model of the ideal marriage, and many churches wanted their portraits. More than sixty similar paintings, with slight variations, were produced by Cranach's workshop and hung in churches and wealthy homes. (Uffizi, Florence/ Scala/Art Resource, NY)

easily squelched by the strong central governments of Spain, France, and England. The Holy Roman Empire, in contrast, included hundreds of largely independent states in which the emperor had far less authority than did the monarchs of western Europe. Thus local rulers in the empire continued to exercise great power.

Germany was one place where local leadership remained strong, and Luther's ideas appealed to its rulers for a variety of reasons. Though Germany was not a nation, people did have an understanding of being German because of their language and traditions. Luther frequently used the phrase "we Germans" in his attacks on the papacy, and his appeal to national feeling influenced many rulers. Also, while some German rulers were sincerely attracted to Lutheran ideas, material considerations swayed many others to embrace the new faith. The rejection of Roman Catholicism and the adoption of Protestantism would mean the legal confiscation of lush farmlands, rich monasteries, and wealthy shrines owned by monasteries, bishops, and other officials. Thus many political authorities in the empire used the religious issue to extend their financial and political power and to enhance their independence from the emperor.

The Habsburg Charles V, elected as emperor in 1521, was a vigorous defender of Catholicism, so it is not surprising that the Reformation led to religious wars. Protestant territories in the empire formed military alliances, and the emperor could not oppose them effectively given other military engagements. In southeastern Europe Habsburg troops were already fighting the Ottoman Turks, who were expanding their holdings at just the point that the Reformation began. Habsburg soldiers were also engaged in a series of wars with the Valois (VAL-wah) kings of France. The cornerstone of French foreign policy in the sixteenth and seventeenth centuries was the desire to keep the German states divided. Thus Europe witnessed the paradox of the Catholic king of France supporting Lutheran princes in their challenge to his fellow Catholic, Charles V. The Habsburg-Valois wars advanced the cause of Protestantism and promoted the political fragmentation of the German Empire.

Finally, in 1555, Charles agreed to the Peace of Augsburg, which officially recognized Lutheranism and ended religious war in Germany for many decades. Under this treaty, the political authority in each territory of the Holy Roman Empire was permitted to decide whether the territory would be Catholic or Lutheran. Most of northern and central Germany became Lutheran, while southern Germany was divided between Lutheran and Catholic. His hope of uniting his empire under a single church dashed, Charles V abdicated in 1556, transferring power over his Spanish and Netherlandish holdings to his son Philip II and his imperial power to his brother Ferdinand.

England's Shift Toward Protestantism

States within the Holy Roman Empire and the kingdom of Denmark-Norway were the earliest territories to accept the Protestant Reformation, but by the later 1520s religious change also came to England, France, and eastern Europe. In all these areas, a second generation of reformers, most prominently John Calvin (see below), built on earlier ideas to develop their own theology and plans for institutional change.

As on the continent, the Reformation in England had economic and political as well as religious causes. The impetus for England's break with Rome was the desire of King Henry VIII (r. 1509–1547) for a new wife. When the personal matter of his need to divorce his first wife became enmeshed with political issues, a complete break with Rome resulted.

In 1527, after eighteen years of marriage, Henry's wife Catherine of Aragon had failed to produce a male child, and Henry had also fallen in love with a court lady-in-waiting, Anne Boleyn. So Henry petitioned Pope Clement VII for an annulment of his marriage to Catherine. When the pope procrastinated in granting the annulment, Henry decided to remove the English Church from papal authority. In this way, he was able to get the annulment and marry Anne.

Henry used Parliament to legalize the Reformation in England and to make himself the supreme head of the Church of England. Some opposed the king and were beheaded, among them Thomas More, the king's chancellor and author of *Utopia* (see page 429). Anne had a daughter, Elizabeth, but failed to produce a son, so Henry VIII charged her with adulterous incest and in 1536 had her beheaded. His third wife, Jane Seymour, gave Henry the desired son, Edward, but she died in childbirth. Henry went on to three more wives.

Between 1535 and 1539, influenced by his chief minister, Thomas Cromwell, Henry decided to dissolve the English monasteries because he wanted their wealth. Hundreds of former church properties were sold to the middle and upper classes, strengthening the upper classes and tying them to the Tudor dynasty, to which Henry belonged. How did everyday people react to Henry's break from the Catholic Church? Recent scholarship points out that people rarely "converted" from Catholicism to Protestantism overnight. Instead, they responded to the local consequences of the shift from Catholicism—for example, the closing of a monastery, the ending of masses for the dead—with a combination of resistance, acceptance, and collaboration.

Loyalty to the Catholic Church remained particularly strong in Ireland. Ireland had been claimed by English kings since the twelfth century, but in reality the English had firm control of only the area around Dublin known as the Pale. In 1536, on orders from Lon-don, the Irish Parliament, which represented only the English landlords and the people of the Pale, approved the English laws severing the church from Rome. The (English) ruling class adopted the new reformed faith, but most of the Irish people remained Roman Catholic. Irish armed opposition to the Reformation led to harsh repression by the English, thus adding religious antagonism to the ethnic hostility that had been a feature of English policy toward Ireland for centuries (see page 404).

In the short reign of Henry's sickly son Edward VI (r. 1547–1553), strongly Protestant ideas exerted a significant influence on the religious life of the country. The equally brief reign of Mary Tudor (r. 1553–1558), the devoutly Catholic daughter of Catherine of Aragon, witnessed a sharp move back to Catholicism, and many Protestants fled to the continent. Mary's death raised to the throne her half-sister Elizabeth (r. 1558–1603) and inaugurated the beginning of religious stability.

Elizabeth had been raised a Protestant, but at the start of her reign sharp differences existed in England. On the one hand, Catholics wanted a Roman Catholic ruler. On the other hand, a vocal number of returning exiles wanted all Catholic elements in the Church of England eliminated. Members of the latter group, because they wanted to "purify" the church, were called "Puritans." Shrewdly, Elizabeth chose a middle course between Catholic and Puritan extremes. She referred to herself as the "supreme governor of the Church of England," which allowed Catholics to remain loyal to her without denying the pope. She required her subjects to attend church or risk a fine but did not interfere with their privately held beliefs. The Anglican Church, as the Church of England was called, moved in a moderately Protestant direction.

Calvinism and Its Moral Standards

In 1509, while Luther was preparing for a doctorate at Wittenberg, John Calvin (1509–1564) was born in Noyon in northwestern France. As a young man he studied law, but in 1533 he experienced a religious crisis, as a result of which he converted from Catholicism to Protestantism. Calvin believed that God had specifically selected him to reform the church. Accordingly, he accepted an invitation to assist in the reformation of the city of Geneva. There, beginning in 1541, Calvin worked assiduously to establish a Christian society ruled by God through civil magistrates and reformed ministers. Geneva thereby became the model of a Christian community for sixteenth-century Protestant reformers.

To understand Calvin's Geneva, it is necessary to understand Calvin's ideas. These he embodied in *The Institutes of the Christian Religion*, first published in

Allegory of the Tudor Dynasty The unknown creator of this work intended to glorify the virtues of the Protestant succession; the painting has no historical reality. Henry VIII (seated) hands the sword of justice to his Protestant son Edward VI. At left the Catholic Queen Mary and her husband Philip of Spain are followed by Mars, god of war, signifying violence and civil disorder. At right the figures of Peace and Plenty accompany the Protestant Elizabeth I, symbolizing England's happy fate under her rule. (Yale Center for British Art, Paul Mellon Collection/The Bridgeman Art Library)

1536 and modified several times afterward. The cornerstone of Calvin's theology was his belief in the absolute sovereignty and omnipotence of God and the total weakness of humanity. Before the infinite power of God, he asserted, men and women are as insignificant as grains of sand.

Calvin did not ascribe free will to human beings because that would detract from the sovereignty of God. According to his beliefs, men and women could not actively work to achieve salvation; rather, God decided at the beginning of time who would be saved and who damned. This viewpoint constitutes the theological principle called **predestination**. Many people consider the doctrine of predestination, which dates back to Saint Augustine and Saint Paul, to be a pessimistic view of the nature of God. But "this terrible decree," as even Calvin called it, did not lead to pessimism or fatalism. Rather, predestination served as an energizing dynamic, convincing people that hardships were part of the constant struggle against evil.

Calvin aroused Genevans to a high standard of morality. In the reformation of the city, the Genevan Consistory also exercised a powerful role. This body of laymen and pastors was assembled "to keep watch over every man's life [and] to admonish amiably those whom they see leading a disorderly life."[6] Although all municipal governments in early modern Europe regulated citizens' conduct, none did so with the severity of Geneva's Consistory under Calvin's leadership. Absence from sermons, criticism of ministers, dancing, card playing, family quarrels, and heavy drinking were all investigated and punished by the Consistory.

Religious refugees from France, England, Spain, Scotland, and Italy visited Calvin's Geneva. Subsequently, the Reformed Church of Calvin served as the model for the Presbyterian Church in Scotland, the Huguenot (HYOO-guh-naht) Church in France, and the Puritan churches in England and New England.

For Calvinists, one's own actions could do nothing to change one's fate, but many people came to believe that hard work, thrift, and proper moral conduct could be signs that an individual was among the "elect" chosen for salvation. Any occupation or profession could be a God-given calling, and work should be done with diligence and dedication. These factors helped to make Calvinism the most dynamic force in sixteenth- and seventeenth-century Protestantism.

> • **predestination** Calvin's teaching that, by God's decree, some persons are guided to salvation and others to damnation; that God has called us not according to our works but according to his purpose and grace.

The Catholic Reformation

☐ How did the Catholic Church respond to the new religious situation?

Between 1517 and 1547 Protestantism made remarkable advances. Nevertheless, the Roman Catholic Church made a significant comeback. After about 1540 no new large areas of Europe, other than the Netherlands, accepted Protestant beliefs (Map 15.2). Many historians see the developments within the Catholic Church after the Protestant Reformation as two interrelated movements, one a drive for internal reform linked to earlier reform efforts, and the other a Counter-Reformation that opposed Protestants intellectually, politically, militarily, and institutionally. In both movements, papal reforms and new religious orders were important agents.

Papal Reforms and the Council of Trent

Renaissance popes and advisers were not blind to the need for church reforms, but they resisted calls for a general council representing the entire church, fearing loss of power, revenue, and prestige. This changed beginning with Pope Paul III (pontificate 1534–1549), under whom the papal court became the center of the reform movement rather than its chief opponent.

In 1542 Pope Paul III established the Supreme Sacred Congregation of the Roman and Universal Inquisition, often called the Holy Office, with jurisdiction over the Roman Inquisition, a powerful instrument of the Catholic Reformation. The Inquisition was a committee of six cardinals with judicial authority over all Catholics and the power to arrest, imprison, and execute. Within the Papal States, the Inquisition effectively destroyed heresy (and some heretics).

Pope Paul III also called a general council, which met intermittently from 1545 to 1563 at Trent, an imperial city close to Italy. It was called not only to reform the church but also to secure reconciliation with the Protestants. Lutherans and Calvinists were invited to participate, but their insistence that the Scriptures be the sole basis for discussion made reconciliation impossible.

Nonetheless, the decrees of the Council of Trent laid a solid basis for the spiritual renewal of the Catholic Church. It gave equal validity to the Scriptures and to tradition as sources of religious truth and authority. It reaffirmed the seven sacraments and the traditional

Catholic teaching on transubstantiation (the transformation of bread and wine into the body and blood of Christ in the Eucharist). It tackled the disciplinary matters that had disillusioned the faithful, requiring bishops to reside in their own dioceses, suppressing pluralism and the selling of church offices, and forbidding the sale of indulgences. Clerics who kept concubines were to give them up. In a highly original decree, the council also required every diocese to establish a seminary for educating and training clergy. Seminary professors were to determine whether candidates for ordination had vocations, genuine callings to the priesthood. This was a novel idea, since from the time of the early church, parents had determined their sons' (and daughters') religious careers. Finally, great emphasis was placed on preaching to and instructing the laity, especially the uneducated. One decision had especially important social consequences for laypeople. The Council of Trent stipulated that for a marriage to be valid, consent (the essence of marriage) as given in the vows had to be made publicly before witnesses, one of whom had to be the parish priest. Trent thereby ended the widespread practice of secret marriages in Catholic countries. For four centuries the doctrinal and disciplinary legislation of Trent served as the basis for Roman Catholic faith, organization, and practice.

New Religious Orders

Just as seminaries provided education, so did new religious orders, which aimed to raise the moral and intellectual level of the clergy and people. The Ursuline (UHR-suh-luhn) order of nuns, founded by Angela Merici (1474–1540), attained enormous prestige for the education of women. The daughter of a country gentleman, Merici worked for many years among the poor, sick, and uneducated around her native Brescia in northern Italy. In 1535 she established the first women's religious order concentrating exclusively on teaching young girls, with the goal of re-Christianizing society by training future wives and mothers. After receiving papal approval in 1565, the Ursulines rapidly spread to France and the New World.

Another important new order was the Society of Jesus, or **Jesuits**. Founded by Ignatius Loyola (1491–1556) in 1540, this order played a powerful international role in strengthening Catholicism in Europe and spreading the faith around the world. While recuperating from a severe battle wound in his legs, Loyola studied the life of Christ and other religious books and decided to give up his military career and become a soldier of Christ. The first Jesuits, whom Loyola recruited primarily from wealthy merchant and professional families, saw the causes and cures of church problems as related not to doctrinal issues but to people's spiritual condition. Reform of the church, as Luther and Calvin understood that term, played no role in the

---

• **Jesuits** Members of the Society of Jesus, founded by Ignatius Loyola and approved by the papacy in 1540, whose goal was the spread of the Roman Catholic faith through humanistic schools and missionary activity.

Predominant religion in 1555

- Lutheran
- Calvinist (Reformed)
- Church of England
- Roman Catholic
- Eastern Orthodox
- Muslim
- → Spread of Calvinism, from 1541
- ▲ Huguenot center
- — Ottoman Empire, 1566

0   150   300 miles
0   150   300 kilometers

Penetration of Calvinism to England after 1558

Wittenburg
Martin Luther writes Ninety-five Theses 1517

Worms
Edict of Worms 1521

Nantes
Edict of Nantes 1598

Trent
Council of Trent 1545–1563

Augsburg
Peace of Augsburg 1555

Geneva
Calvin assists in Reformation beginning in 1541

◻ Mapping the Past

MAP 15.2 Religious Divisions in Europe, ca. 1555 The Reformation shattered the religious unity of Western Christendom. The situation was even more complicated than a map of this scale can show. Many cities within the Holy Roman Empire, for example, accepted a different faith than did the surrounding countryside; Augsburg, Basel, and Strasbourg were all Protestant, though surrounded by territory ruled by Catholic nobles.

ANALYZING THE MAP Which countries were most religiously diverse in Europe? Which were least diverse?

CONNECTIONS Where was the first arena of religious conflict in Europe, and why did it develop there and not elsewhere? To what degree can nonreligious factors be used as an explanation of the religious divisions that developed in sixteenth-century Europe?

Teresa of Ávila Teresa of Ávila (1515–1582) was a Spanish nun who experienced mystical visions that led her to reform convents, making them stricter and less hierarchical. This seventeenth-century enamelwork shows one of her visions, of an angel piercing her heart. Teresa founded new religious houses, seeing them as answers to the Protestant takeover of Catholic churches. She became a saint and in 1970 was the first woman declared a Doctor of the Church, a title given to a theologian of outstanding merit. (By gracious permission of Catherine Hamilton Kappauf)

future the Jesuits planned for themselves. Instead, their goal was "to help souls." The Society of Jesus developed into a highly centralized, tightly knit organization whose professed members vowed to go anywhere the pope said they were needed. They established schools that adopted the modern humanist curricula and methods and that educated the sons of the nobility as well as the poor. The Jesuits attracted many recruits and achieved phenomenal success for the papacy and the reformed Catholic Church, carrying Christianity to India and Japan before 1550 and to Brazil, North America, and the Congo in the seventeenth century. Within Europe the Jesuits brought almost all of southern Germany and much of eastern Europe back to Catholicism. Also, as confessors and spiritual directors to kings, Jesuits exerted great political influence.

Religious Violence

☐ What were the causes and consequences of religious violence, including riots, wars, and witch-hunts?

In 1559 France and Spain signed the Treaty of Cateau-Cambrésis, which ended the long conflict known as the Habsburg-Valois wars. However, over the next century religious differences led to riots, civil wars, and international conflicts. Especially in France and the Netherlands, Protestants and Catholics opposed one another through preaching, teaching, and violence, for each side regarded the other as a poison in the community that would provoke the wrath of God. Catholics and Protestants alike feared people of other faiths, whom they often saw as agents of Satan. Even more, they feared those explicitly identified with Satan: people believed to be witches. This era saw the most virulent witch per-

secutions in European history, as both Protestants and Catholics tried to make their cities and states more godly.

French Religious Wars

The costs of the Habsburg-Valois wars, waged intermittently through the first half of the sixteenth century, forced the French to increase taxes and borrow heavily. King Francis I's treaty with the pope (see page 438) gave the French crown a rich supplement of money and offices, and also a vested financial interest in Catholicism. Significant numbers of French people, however, were attracted to the "reformed religion," as Calvinism was called. Calvinism drew converts from among reform-minded members of the Catholic clergy, the industrious middle classes, and artisan groups. Additionally, some French nobles became Calvinist, either because of religious conviction or because this allowed them to oppose the monarchy. By the middle of the sixteenth century perhaps one-tenth of the French population had become **Huguenots**, the name given to French Calvinists.

Both Calvinists and Catholics believed that the others' books, services, and ministers polluted the community. Preachers communicated these ideas in sermons, triggering violence at the baptisms, marriages, and funerals of the other faith. Armed clashes between Catholic royalist nobles and Calvinist antimonarchical nobles occurred in many parts of France.

Calvinist teachings called the power of sacred images into question, and mobs in many cities destroyed statues, stained-glass windows, and paintings. Though it was often inspired by fiery Protestant sermons, this iconoclasm is an example of men and women carrying out the Reformation themselves, rethinking the church's system of meaning. Catholic mobs responded by defending the sacred images, and crowds on both sides killed their opponents, often in gruesome ways.

A savage Catholic attack on Calvinists in Paris on August 24, 1572 — Saint Bartholomew's Day — followed the usual pattern. The occasion was the marriage of the king's sister Margaret of Valois to the Protestant Henry of Navarre, which was intended to help reconcile Catholics and Huguenots. Instead, Huguenot wedding guests in Paris were massacred, and other Protestants were slaughtered by mobs. Violence spread to the provinces, where thousands were killed. The Saint Bartholomew's Day massacre led to a civil war that dragged on for fifteen years. As a result, agriculture in many areas was destroyed, commercial life declined severely, and starvation and death haunted the land.

What ultimately saved France was a small group of moderates of both faiths called **politiques** (POH-lee-teeks) who believed that only the restoration of a strong

Massacre of the Huguenots, 1573 The Italian artist Giorgio Vasari depicts the Saint Bartholomew's Day massacre in Paris, one of many bloody events in the religious wars that accompanied the Reformation. Here Admiral Coligny, a leader of the French Protestants (called Huguenots) is hurled from a window while his followers are slaughtered. This fresco was commissioned by Pope Gregory XIII to decorate a hall in the Vatican Palace in Rome. Both sides used visual images to win followers and celebrate their victories. (Vatican Palace/Scala/Art Resource, NY)

in France, the reign of Henry IV and the Edict of Nantes paved the way for French kings to claim absolute power in the seventeenth century.

Civil Wars in the Netherlands

In the Netherlands a movement for church reform developed into a struggle for Dutch independence. The Catholic emperor Charles V had inherited the seventeen provinces that compose present-day Belgium and the Netherlands (see page 441). In the Netherlands, as elsewhere, corruption in the Roman Catholic Church and the critical spirit of the Renaissance provoked pressure for reform, and Lutheran ideas took root. Charles V had grown up in the Netherlands, however, and he was able to limit the impact of the new ideas. Charles V abdicated in 1556 and transferred power over the Netherlands to his son Philip II, who had grown up in Spain. Although Philip, like his father, opposed Protestantism, Protestant ideas spread in the Netherlands.

By the 1560s Protestants in the Netherlands were primarily Calvinists. Calvinism's intellectual seriousness, moral gravity, and emphasis on any form of labor well done appealed to middle-class merchants and financiers and to working-class people. Whereas Lutherans taught respect for the powers that be, Calvinism tended to encourage opposition to authorities who were judged to be ungodly.

In the 1560s Spanish authorities attempted to suppress Calvinist worship and raised taxes, which sparked riots and a wave of iconoclasm. In response, Philip II sent twenty thousand Spanish troops, and from 1568 to 1578 civil war raged in the Netherlands between Catholics and Protestants and between the seventeen provinces and Spain. Eventually the ten southern provinces—the Spanish Netherlands (the future Belgium)—came under the control of the Spanish Habsburg forces. The seven northern provinces, led by Holland, formed the **Union of Utrecht** (the United

monarchy could reverse the trend toward collapse. The politiques also favored officially recognizing the Huguenots. The death of the French queen Catherine de' Medici, followed by the assassination of her son King Henry III, paved the way for the accession of Henry of Navarre (the unfortunate bridegroom of the Saint Bartholomew's Day massacre), a politique who became Henry IV (r. 1589–1610).

Henry's willingness to sacrifice religious principles to political necessity saved France. He converted to Catholicism but also, in 1598, issued the Edict of Nantes (nahnt), which granted liberty of conscience (freedom of thought) and liberty of public worship to Huguenots in 150 fortified towns. By helping restore internal peace

- **Huguenots** French Calvinists.
- **politiques** Catholic and Protestant moderates who sought to end the religious violence in France by restoring a strong monarchy and granting official recognition to the Huguenots.
- **Union of Utrecht** The alliance of seven northern provinces of the Netherlands, all of which were Protestant, that declared independence from Spain and formed the United Provinces of the Netherlands.

Provinces), and in 1581 they declared their independence from Spain. The north was Protestant, and the south remained Catholic. Philip did not accept the independence of the north, and war continued. England was even drawn into the conflict, supplying money and troops to the United Provinces. (Spain launched the Spanish Armada, an unsuccessful invasion of England, in response.) Hostilities ended in 1609 when Spain agreed to a truce that recognized the independence of the United Provinces.

The Great European Witch-Hunt

Insecurity created by the religious wars contributed to persecution for witchcraft, which actually began before the Reformation in the 1480s but became especially common about 1560. Both Protestants and Catholics tried and executed those accused of being witches, with church officials and secular authorities acting together.

The heightened sense of God's power and divine wrath in the Reformation era was an important factor in the witch-hunts, but other factors were also significant. In the later Middle Ages, many educated Christian theologians, canon lawyers, and officials added a demonological component to existing ideas about witches. For them, the essence of witchcraft was making a pact with the Devil that required the witch to do the Devil's bidding. Witches were no longer simply people who used magical power to do harm and get what they wanted, but rather people used by the Devil to do what he wanted. Some demonological theorists also claimed that witches were organized in an international conspiracy to overthrow Christianity.

Trials involving this new notion of witchcraft as diabolical heresy began in Switzerland and southern Germany in the late fifteenth century; became less numerous in the early decades of the Reformation, when Protestants and Catholics were busy fighting each other; and then picked up again about 1560, spreading to much of western Europe and to European colonies in the Americas. Scholars estimate that during the sixteenth and seventeenth centuries somewhere between 100,000 and 200,000 people were officially tried for witchcraft, and between 40,000 and 60,000 were executed. While the trials were secret, executions were not, and the list of charges was read out for all to hear.

Though the gender balance of the accused varied widely in different parts of Europe, between 75 and 85 percent of those tried and executed were women, whom some demonologists viewed as weaker and so more likely to give in to the Devil. Tensions within families, households, and neighborhoods also played a role in witchcraft accusations, as grievances and jealousies led to accusations. Suspects were questioned and tortured by legal authorities, and they often implicated others. The circle of the accused grew, sometimes into a much larger hunt that historians have called a "witch panic." Panics were most common in the part of Europe that saw the most witch accusations in general — the Holy Roman Empire, Switzerland, and parts of France. Most of this area consisted of very small governmental units that were jealous of each other and, after the Reformation, were divided by religion. The rulers of these small territories often felt more threatened than did the monarchs of western Europe, and they saw persecuting witches as a way to demonstrate their piety and concern for order.

Even in the sixteenth century a few individuals questioned whether witches could ever do harm, make a pact with the Devil, or engage in the wild activities attributed to them. Furthermore, doubts about whether secret denunciations were valid or torture would ever yield a truthful confession gradually spread among the same type of religious and legal authorities who had so vigorously persecuted witches. By about 1660, prosecutions for witchcraft became less common. The last official execution for witchcraft in England was in 1682, though the last one in the Holy Roman Empire was not until 1775.

CONNECTIONS

The Renaissance and the Reformation are often seen as key to the creation of the modern world. The radical changes of these times contained many elements of continuity, however. Artists, humanists, and religious reformers looked back to the classical era and early Christianity for inspiration, viewing those times as better and purer than their own. Political leaders played important roles in cultural and religious developments, just as they had for centuries in Europe and other parts of the world.

The events of the Renaissance and Reformation thus were linked with earlier developments, and they were also closely connected with another important element in the modern world: European exploration and colonization (discussed in Chapter 16). Renaissance monarchs paid for expeditions' ships, crews, and supplies, expecting a large share of any profits gained and increasingly viewing overseas territory as essential to a strong state. Only a week after Martin Luther stood in front of Charles V at the Diet of Worms declaring his independence in matters of religion, Ferdinand Magellan, a Portuguese sea captain using Spanish ships, was killed by indigenous people in a group of islands off the coast of southeast Asia. Charles V had provided the backing for Magellan's voyage, the first to circumnavigate the globe. Magellan viewed one of the purposes of his trip as the spread of Christianity, and later in the sixteenth century institutions created as part of the Catholic Reformation, including the Jesuit order and the Inquisition, would operate in European colonies overseas as well as in Europe itself. The islands where Magellan was killed were later named the Philippines, in honor of Charles's son Philip, who sent the ill-fated Spanish Armada against England. The desire for fame, wealth, and power that was central to the Renaissance, and the religious zeal central to the Reformation, were thus key to the European voyages and to colonial ventures as well.

CHAPTER REVIEW

KEY TERMS

Renaissance (p. 426)
patronage (p. 426)
humanism (p. 427)
Christian humanists (p. 429)
debate about women (p. 436)
Protestant Reformation (p. 441)
indulgence (p. 442)

Diet of Worms (p. 443)
Protestant (p. 443)
predestination (p. 449)
Jesuits (p. 450)
Huguenots (p. 452)
politiques (p. 452)
Union of Utrecht (p. 453)

□ **What were the major cultural developments of the Renaissance? (p. 426)**

The Renaissance was characterized by self-conscious awareness among fourteenth- and fifteenth-century Italians, particularly scholars and writers known as humanists, that they were living in a new era. Key to this attitude was a serious interest in the Latin classics, a belief in individual potential, and a more secular attitude toward life. Humanists opened schools for boys and young men to train them for active lives of public service, but they had doubts about whether humanist education was appropriate for women. As humanism spread to northern Europe, religious concerns became more pronounced, and Christian humanists set out plans for the reform of church and society. Their ideas were spread to a much wider audience than those of early humanists as a result of the development of the printing press with movable metal type, which revolutionized communication. Interest in the classical past and in the individual shaped Renaissance art in terms of style and subject matter. Also important to Renaissance art were the wealthy patrons who helped fund it.

□ **What were the key social hierarchies in Renaissance Europe, and how did these hierarchies shape people's lives? (p. 433)**

Social hierarchies in the Renaissance developed new features that contributed to the modern social hierarchies of race, class, and gender. The distinction between free people and slaves was one such hierarchy. Although in the Renaissance slavery in Europe was not limited to Africans, increasing numbers of black Africans entered Europe as slaves to supplement the labor force, and black skin color was increasingly viewed as a mark of inferiority. In terms of class, the medieval hierarchy of orders based on function in society intermingled with a new hierarchy that created a new social elite whose status was based on wealth. In regard to gender, the Renaissance debate about women led many to discuss women's nature and proper role in society, a discussion sharpened by the presence of a number of ruling queens in this era. Nevertheless, women continued to lag behind men in social status and earnings.

□ **How did the nation-states of western Europe evolve in this period? (p. 438)**

Feudal monarchies gradually evolved into nation-states, and beginning in the fifteenth century rulers in western Europe used aggressive methods to build up their governments, reducing violence, curbing unruly nobles, and establishing domestic order. They emphasized royal majesty and royal sovereignty and insisted on the respect and loyalty of all subjects. War and diplomacy were important ways that states increased their power, but so was marriage. Because almost all of Europe was ruled by hereditary dynasties, claiming and holding resources involved shrewd marital alliances.

□ **What were the central ideas of Protestant reformers, and why were they appealing to various groups across Europe? (p. 441)**

The Catholic Church in the early sixteenth century had serious problems, and many individuals and groups had long called for reform. This discontent helps explain why the ideas of one reformer, Martin Luther, found such a ready audience. Luther and other Protestants developed a new understanding of Christian doctrine that emphasized faith, the power of God's grace, and the centrality of the Bible. Protestant ideas were attractive to the literate middle classes, and they spread rapidly through preaching, hymns, and the printing press. Some reformers developed more radical ideas about baptism, the ownership of property, and the separation between church and state. Both Protestants and Catholics regarded these ideas as dangerous, and radicals were banished or executed. The progress of the Reformation was shaped by the political situation in the Holy Roman Empire, the decentralization of which allowed the Reformation to spread. In England the king's need for a church-approved divorce triggered the break with Rome, and a Protestant church was established. Protestant ideas also spread into France and eastern Europe. In all these areas, a second generation of reformers, most prominently John Calvin, developed their own theology and plans for institutional change.

◻ How did the Catholic Church respond to the new religious situation? (p. 450)

The Roman Catholic Church responded slowly to the Protestant challenge, but by the middle of the sixteenth century the papacy was leading a movement for reform within the church. Decrees of the Council of Trent (1545–1563) banned the holding of multiple church offices and the selling of such offices. The council also required every diocese to establish a seminary for educating and training clergy. Additionally, new religious orders such as the Jesuits and the Ursulines spread Catholic ideas through teaching, and in the case of the Jesuits through missionary work.

◻ What were the causes and consequences of religious violence, including riots, wars, and witch-hunts? (p. 452)

Religious differences led to riots, civil wars, and international conflicts in the later sixteenth century. In France and the Netherlands Calvinist Protestants and Catholics attacked each other, and religious differences mixed with political and economic grievances. Long civil wars resulted, with the civil war in the Netherlands becoming an international conflict. War ended in France with the Edict of Nantes, in which Protestants were given some civil rights, and in the Netherlands with the division of the country into a Protestant north and a Catholic south. The era of religious wars was also marked by the most extensive witch persecutions in European history, as both Protestants and Catholics tried to rid their cities and states of people they regarded as linked to the Devil.

For practice quizzes and other study tools, visit the **Online Study Guide** at bedfordstmartins.com/mckayworld.

For primary sources from this period, see *Sources of World Societies*, **Second Edition**.

For Web sites, images, and documents related to topics in this chapter, visit **Make History** at bedfordstmartins.com/mckayworld.

SUGGESTED READING

Bossy, John. *Christianity in the West, 1500–1700*. 1985. A lively brief overview.

Earle, T. F., and K. J. P. Lowe, eds. *Black Africans in Renaissance Europe*. 2005. Includes essays discussing many aspects of ideas about race and the experience of Africans in Europe.

Ertman, Thomas. *The Birth of Leviathan: Building States and Regimes in Medieval and Early Modern Europe*. 1997. A good introduction to the creation of nation-states.

Grafton, Anthony, and Lisa Jardine. *From Humanism to the Humanities: Education and the Liberal Arts in Fifteenth and Sixteenth Century Europe*. 1986. Discusses humanist education and other developments in Renaissance learning.

Hale, J. R. *The Civilization of Europe in the Renaissance*. 1994. A comprehensive treatment of the period, arranged thematically.

Hendrix, Scott. *Luther*. 2009. A brief introduction to his thought; part of the Abingdon Pillars of Theology series.

Holmes, George, ed. *Art and Politics in Renaissance Italy*. 1993. Treats the art of Florence and Rome against a political background.

Hsia, R. Po-Chia. *The World of Catholic Renewal, 1540–1770*. 1998. Situates the Catholic Reformation in a global context and examines colonial Catholicism.

Johnson, Geraldine. *Renaissance Art: A Very Short Introduction*. 2005. Excellent brief survey that includes male and female artists, and sets the art in its cultural and historical context.

Levack, Brian. *The Witchhunt in Early Modern Europe*, 3d ed. 2007. A good introduction to the vast literature on witchcraft, with helpful bibliographies.

Lindbergh, Carter. *The European Reformations*. 1996. Provides a thorough discussion of the Protestant Reformation and some discussion of Catholic issues.

Man, John. *Gutenberg Revolution: The Story of a Genius and an Invention That Changed the World*. 2002. Presents a rather idealized view of Gutenberg but has good discussions of his milieu and excellent illustrations.

Nauert, Charles. *Humanism and the Culture of Renaissance Europe*, 2d ed. 2006. A thorough introduction to humanism throughout Europe.

Wiesner-Hanks, Merry E. *Women and Gender in Early Modern Europe*, 3d ed. 2008. Discusses all aspects of women's lives and ideas about gender.

NOTES

1. Niccolò Machivelli, *The Prince*, trans. Leo Paul S. de Alvarez (Prospect Heights, Ill.: Waveland Press, 1980), p. 101.
2. Stuttgart, Württembergische Hauptstaatsarchiv, Generalreskripta, A38, Bü. 2, 1550; trans. Merry Wiesner-Hanks.
3. Quoted in Benzion Netanyahu, *The Origins of the Inquisition in Fifteenth Century Spain* (New York: Random House, 1995), p. 921.
4. Quoted in E. H. Harbison, *The Age of Reformation* (Ithaca, N.Y.: Cornell University Press, 1963), p. 52.
5. Quoted ibid., p. 284.
6. Ibid., p. 137.

16

The Acceleration of Global Contact
1450–1600

Before 1500 Europeans were relatively marginal players in a centuries-old trading system that linked Africa, Asia, and Europe. Elite classes everywhere prized Chinese porcelains and silks, while wealthy Chinese wanted ivory and black slaves from East Africa and exotic goods and peacocks from India. African people wanted textiles from India and cowrie shells from the Maldives. Europeans craved spices and silks, but they had few desirable goods to offer their trading partners.

The Indian Ocean was the locus of these desires and commercial exchanges, which sparked competition among Arab, Persian, Turkish, Indian, African, Chinese, and European merchants and adventurers. They fought each other for the trade that brought great wealth. They also jostled with Muslim scholars, Buddhist teachers, and Christian missionaries, who competed for the religious adherence of the peoples of Sumatra, Java, Borneo, and the Philippine Islands.

The European search for better access to Asian trade goods led to a new overseas empire in the Indian Ocean and the accidental discovery of the Western Hemisphere. With this discovery South and North America soon joined an international network of trade centers and political empires, which Europeans came to dominate. The era of globalization had begun, creating new forms of cultural exchange, assimilation, conversion, and resistance. Europeans sought to impose their cultural values on the peoples they encountered while struggling to comprehend them and their societies. The Age of Discovery from 1450 to 1650, as the time of these encounters is known, laid the foundations for the modern world as we know it today.   •

The Afroeurasian Trade World Before Columbus
☐ What was the Afroeurasian trade world like before the voyages of Columbus?

The European Voyages of Discovery
☐ Why and how did Europeans undertake ambitious voyages of expansion?

The Impact of Conquest
☐ How did conquest affect indigenous populations and bring about a new era of economic and cultural exchange, commercial empires, and forced migrations?

Changing Values and Beliefs
☐ How did new encounters shape cultural values and beliefs in Europe and the New World?

The Afroeurasian Trade World Before Columbus

☐ What was the Afroeurasian trade world like before the voyages of Columbus?

Historians now recognize that a type of world economy, known as the Afroeurasian trade world, linked the products and people of Europe, Asia, and Africa in the fifteenth century. Before Christopher Columbus began his voyages to the New World in 1492, the West was not the dominant player in world trade. Nevertheless, wealthy Europeans were eager consumers of luxury goods from the East, which they received through Venetian and Genoese middlemen.

The Trade World of the Indian Ocean

The Indian Ocean was the center of the Afroeurasian trade world, serving as a crossroads for commercial and cultural exchanges between China, India, the Middle East, Africa, and Europe (Map 16.1). From the seventh through the fourteenth centuries, the volume of this trade steadily increased, declining only during the years of the Black Death.

Merchants congregated in a series of multicultural, cosmopolitan port cities strung around the Indian Ocean. Most of these cities had some form of autonomous self-government, and mutual self-interest had largely limited violence and attempts to monopolize trade. The most developed area of this commercial web was made up of the ports surrounding the South China Sea. In the fifteenth century the port of Malacca became a great commercial entrepôt (AHN-truh-poh), a trading post to which goods were shipped for storage while awaiting redistribution to other places. To Malacca came Chinese porcelains, silks, and camphor (used in the manufacture of many medications); pepper, cloves, nutmeg, and raw materials such as sandalwood from the Moluccas; sugar from the Philippines;

and Indian textiles, copper weapons, incense, dyes, and opium.

The Mongol emperors opened the doors of China to the West, encouraging Europeans like the Venetian trader and explorer Marco Polo to do business there. Marco Polo's tales of his travels from 1271 to 1295 and his encounter with the Great Khan (one of the successors of the famous Mongol ruler Chinggis Khan) fueled Western fantasies about the Orient. After the Mongols fell to the Ming Dynasty in 1368, China entered a period of agricultural and commercial expansion, population growth, and urbanization. Historians agree that China had the most advanced economy in the world until at least the beginning of the eighteenth century.

China also took the lead in exploration, sending Admiral Zheng He's fleet as far west as Egypt. (See "Individuals in Society: Zheng He," page 463.) From 1405 to 1433, each of his seven expeditions involved hundreds of ships and tens of thousands of men. In one voyage alone, Zheng sailed more than 12,000 miles, compared to Columbus's 2,400 miles on his first voyage some sixty years later.[1] Although the ships brought back many wonders, such as giraffes and zebras, the purpose of the voyages was primarily diplomatic, to enhance China's prestige and seek tribute-paying alliances. The voyages came to a sudden halt after the deaths of Zheng and the emperor who initiated his voyages, probably due to court opposition to their high cost and contact with foreign peoples.

By ending large-scale exploration on China's part, this decision marked a turning point in history. Nonetheless, Zheng He's voyages left a legacy of increased Chinese trading in the South China Sea and Indian Ocean. Following Zheng He's voyages, tens of thousands of Chinese emigrated to the Philippines, where they acquired commercial dominance of the island of Luzon by 1600.

Another center of Indian Ocean trade was India, the crucial link between the Persian Gulf and the Southeast Asian and East Asian trade networks. The subcontinent had ancient links with its neighbors to the northwest: trade between South Asia and Mesopotamia dates back to the origins of human civilization. Trade among ports bordering the Indian Ocean was revived in the Middle Ages by Arab merchants who circumnavigated India on their way to trade in the South China Sea. The need for stopovers led to the establishment of trading posts at Gujarat and on the Malabar coast, where the cities of Calicut and Quilon became thriving commercial centers.

The inhabitants of India's Coromandel coast traditionally looked to Southeast Asia, where they had ancient trading and cultural ties. Hinduism and Buddhism arrived in Southeast Asia from India during the Middle Ages, and a brisk trade between Southeast Asian and Coromandel port cities persisted from that time until the arrival of the Portuguese in the sixteenth century. India itself was an important contributor of goods to the world trading system. Most of the world's pepper was grown in India, and Indian cotton and silk textiles, mainly from the Gujarat region, were also highly prized.

Peoples and Cultures of the Indian Ocean

Indian Ocean trade connected peoples from the Malay Peninsula (the southern extremity of the Asian continent), India, China, and East Africa, among whom there was an enormous variety of languages, cultures,

and religions. In spite of this diversity, certain sociocultural similarities linked these peoples, especially in Southeast Asia.

For example, by the fifteenth century, inhabitants of what we call Indonesia, Malaysia, the Philippines, and the many islands in between all spoke languages of the Austronesian family, reflecting continuing interactions among them. A common environment led to a diet based on rice, fish, palms, and palm wine. Rice, harvested by women, is probably indigenous to the region, and it formed the staple of the diet. The seas provided many varieties of fish, crabs, and shrimp, and fishing served as the chief male occupation, well ahead of agriculture. Also, sugar cane

The Port of Calicut in India The port of Calicut, located on the west coast of India, was a center of the Indian Ocean spice trade during the Middle Ages. Vasco da Gama arrived in Calicut in 1498 and obtained permission to trade there, leading to hostilities between the Portuguese and the Arab traders who had previously dominated the port. (Private Collection/The Stapleton Collection/The Bridgeman Art Library)

CALECHVT CELEBERRI: MVM INDIÆ EMPORIVM.

MAP 16.1 The Fifteenth-Century Afroeurasian Trading World After a period of decline following the Black Death and the Mongol invasions, trade revived in the fifteenth century. Muslim merchants dominated trade, linking ports in East Africa and the Red Sea with those in India and the Malay archipelago. The Chinese admiral Zheng He's voyages (1405–1433) followed the most important Indian Ocean trade routes, hoping to impose Ming dominance of trade and tribute.

grew in profusion, and it was chewed as a confectionery and used as a sweetener.[2]

In comparison to India, China, or even Europe after the Black Death, Southeast Asia was sparsely populated. People were concentrated in port cities and in areas of intense rice cultivation.

Another difference between Southeast Asia and India, China, and Europe was the higher status of women in the region. Their primary role in planting and harvesting rice gave them authority and economic power. At marriage, which typically occurred around age twenty, the groom paid the bride (or sometimes her family) a sum of money called **bride wealth**, which remained under her control. This practice was in sharp contrast to the Chinese, Indian, and European dowry,

which came under the husband's control. Property was administered jointly, in contrast to the Chinese principle and Indian practice that wives had no say in the disposal of family property. All children, regardless of gender, inherited equally, and when Islam arrived in the region, the rule requiring sons to receive double the inheritance of daughters was never implemented.

Respect for women carried over to the commercial sphere. Women participated in business as partners and independent entrepreneurs, even undertaking long sea voyages to accompany their wares. When Portuguese and Dutch men settled in the region and married local women, their wives continued to play important roles in trade and commerce.

In contrast to most parts of the world other than Africa, Southeast Asian peoples had an accepting attitude toward premarital sexual activity, and no premium was placed on virginity at marriage. Divorce carried no social stigma, and it was easy if a pair proved

• **bride wealth** In early modern Southeast Asia, a sum of money the groom paid the bride or her family at the time of marriage, in contrast to the husband's control of dowry in China, India, and Europe.

Individuals in Society

Zheng He

IN 1403 THE CHINESE EMPEROR YONGLE ordered his coastal provinces to build a vast fleet of ships, with construction centered at Longjiang near Nanjing. The inland provinces were to provide wood for the ships and float it down the Yangzi River. Thirty thousand shipwrights, carpenters, sailmakers, ropers, and caulkers worked in a frenzy. As work progressed, Yongle selected a commander for the fleet. The emperor chose Zheng He (1371–1433), despite fearing that the thirty-five-year-old was too old for so politically important an expedition. The decision rested on Zheng's unquestioned loyalty, strength of character, energy, ability, and eloquence. These qualities apparently were expected to compensate for Zheng's lack of seamanship.

The southwestern province of Yunnan, where Zheng was born, had a large Muslim population, and he was raised in that faith. When the then prince Zhi Di defeated the Mongols in Yunnan, Zheng's father was killed in the related disorder. The young boy was taken prisoner and, as was the custom, castrated. Raised in Zhi Di's household, he learned to read and write, studied Confucian writings, and accompanied the prince on all military expeditions. By age twenty Zheng was not the soft, effeminate stereotype of the eunuch; rather he was "seven feet tall and had a waist five feet in circumference. His cheeks and forehead were high . . . [and] he had glaring eyes . . . [and] a voice loud as a bell. . . . He was accustomed to battle." Zheng must have looked imposing. A devout Muslim, he persuaded the emperor to place mosques under imperial protection after a period of persecution. On his travels, he prayed at mosques at Malacca and Hormuz. Unable to sire sons, he adopted a nephew. When Zheng became a naval commander under Yongle, he was the first eunuch in Chinese history to hold such an important position.

The fleet for Zheng's first expedition was composed of 317 ships, including junks, supply ships, water tankers, warships, transports for horses, and patrol boats, and carried twenty-eight thousand sailors and soldiers; it was the largest naval force in world history before World War I. Because it bore tons of beautiful porcelains, elegant silks, lacquer ware, and exquisite artifacts to be exchanged for goods abroad, it was called the "treasure fleet."

Between 1405 and 1433, Zheng led seven voyages, which combined the emperor's diplomatic, political, geographical, and commercial goals (see Map 16.1). During the voyages he worked toward Yongle's goal of securing China's hegemony over tributary states and collecting pledges of loyalty from them. Zheng also sought information on winds, tides, distant lands, and rare plants and animals, and he sailed as far west as Egypt to gather it. Because smallpox epidemics had recently hit China, another purpose of his voyages was to gather pharmacological products. An Arab text on drugs and therapies was secured and translated into Chinese. He also brought back a giraffe and mahogany, a wood ideal for ships' rudders because of its hardness.

Just before his death, Zheng recorded his accomplishments on stone tablets. The expeditions had unified "seas and continents . . . the countries beyond the horizon from the ends of the earth have all become subjects . . . and the distances and routes between distant lands may be calculated," implying that China had accumulated considerable geographical information. From around the Indian Ocean, official tribute flowed to the Ming court as a result of Zheng's efforts. A vast immigration of Chinese people into Southeast Asia, sometimes called the Chinese diaspora, came into being after the expeditions. Immigrants carried with them Chinese culture, including social customs, diet, and practical objects of Chinese technology — calendars, books, scales for weights and measures, and musical instruments. With legends collected about him and monuments erected to him, Zheng became a great cult hero.

Source: Louise Levathes, *When China Ruled the Seas: The Treasure Fleet of the Dragon Throne, 1405–1433* (New York: Oxford University Press, 1996).

QUESTIONS FOR ANALYSIS

1. What do the voyages of the treasure fleet tell us about China in the fifteenth century?
2. What was Zheng He's legacy?

Zheng He (right), voyager to India, Persia, Arabia, and Africa. (From Lo Monteng, *The Western Sea Cruises of Eunuch San Pao*, 1597)

incompatible. Either the woman or the man could initiate a divorce, and common property and children were divided.

Trade with Africa and the Middle East

On the east coast of Africa, Swahili-speaking city-states engaged in the Indian Ocean trade, exchanging ivory, rhinoceros horn, tortoise shells, copra (dried coconut), and slaves for textiles, spices, cowrie shells, porcelain, and other goods. The most important cities were Mogadishu, Mombasa, and Kilwa, which had converted to Islam by the eleventh century. Peopled by confident and urbane merchants, the cities were known for their prosperity and culture.

West Africa also played an important role in world trade. In the fifteenth century most of the gold that reached Europe came from Sudan in West Africa and, in particular, from the kingdom of Mali near present-

day Ghana. Transported across the Sahara by Arab and African traders on camels, the gold was sold in the ports of North Africa. Other trading routes led to the Egyptian cities of Alexandria and Cairo, where the Venetians held commercial privileges.

Inland nations that sat astride the north-south caravan routes grew wealthy from this trade. In the mid-thirteenth century the kingdom of Mali emerged as an important player on the overland trade route. In later centuries, however, the diversion of gold away from the trans-Sahara routes would weaken the inland states of Africa politically and economically.

Gold was one important object of trade; slaves were another. Slavery was practiced in Africa, as virtually everywhere else in the world, even before the arrival of Europeans. Arabic and African merchants took West African slaves to the Mediterranean to be sold in European, Egyptian, and Middle Eastern markets and also brought eastern Europeans to West Africa as slaves. In addition, Indian and Arabic merchants traded slaves in the coastal regions of East Africa.

The Middle East served as an intermediary for trade between Europe, Africa, and Asia and was also an important supplier of goods for foreign exchange, especially silk and cotton. Two great rival empires, the Persian Safavids and the Turkish Ottomans, dominated the region, competing for control over western trade routes to the East. By the mid-sixteenth century the Ottomans had established control over eastern Mediterranean sea routes to trading centers in Syria, Palestine, Egypt, and the rest of North Africa. Their power also extended into Europe as far west as Vienna.

Genoese and Venetian Middlemen

Compared to the East, Europe constituted a minor outpost in the world trading system, for European craftsmen produced few products to rival those of Asia. However, Europeans desired luxury goods from the East, and in the late Middle Ages such trade was controlled by the Italian city-states of Venice and Genoa. Venice had opened the gateway to Asian trade in 1304, when it established formal relations with the sultan of Mamluk Egypt and started operations in Cairo. In exchange for European products like Spanish and English wool, German metal goods, Flemish textiles, and silk cloth made with imported raw materials, the Venetians obtained luxury items like spices, silks, and carpets. They accessed these from middlemen in the eastern Mediterranean and Asia Minor. Because Eastern demand for these European goods was low, Venetians made up the difference by earning currency in the shipping industry and through trade in firearms and slaves.

Venice's ancient trading rival was Genoa. By the time the Crusades ended around 1270, Genoa domi-

Mansa Musa This detail from the Catalan Atlas of 1375 depicts a king of Mali, Mansa Musa, who was legendary for his wealth in gold. European desires for direct access to the trade in sub-Saharan gold helped inspire Portuguese exploration of the west coast of Africa in the fifteenth century. (Bridgeman-Giraudon/Art Resource, NY)

nated the northern route to Asia through the Black Sea. From then until the fourteenth century, the Genoese expanded their trade routes as far as Persia and the Far East. In 1291 they sponsored a failed expedition into the Atlantic in search of India. This voyage reveals the long roots of Genoese interest in Atlantic exploration.

In the fifteenth century, with Venice claiming victory in the spice trade, the Genoese shifted focus from trade to finance and from the Black Sea to the western Mediterranean. Located on the northwestern coast of Italy, Genoa had always been active in the western Mediterranean, trading with North African ports, southern France, Spain, and even England and Flanders through the Strait of Gibraltar. When Spanish and Portuguese voyages began to explore the western Atlantic (see page 467), Genoese merchants, navigators, and financiers provided their skills to the Iberian monarchs.

A major element of both Venetian and Genoese trade was slavery. Merchants purchased slaves, many of whom were fellow Christians, in the Balkans of southeastern Europe. After the loss of the Black Sea trade routes — and thus the source of slaves — to the Ottomans, the Genoese sought new supplies of slaves in the West, eventually seizing or buying and selling the Guanches (indigenous peoples from the Canary Islands), Muslim prisoners and Jewish refugees from Spain, and by the early 1500s both black and Berber Africans. With the growth of Spanish colonies in the New World, Genoese and Venetian merchants became important players in the Atlantic slave trade.

Italian experience in colonial administration, the slave trade, and international trade and finance served as a model for the Iberian states as they pushed European expansion to new heights. Mariners, merchants, and financiers from Venice and Genoa — most notably Christopher Columbus — played crucial roles in bringing the fruits of this experience to the Iberian Peninsula and to the New World.

The European Voyages of Discovery

☐ Why and how did Europeans undertake ambitious voyages of expansion?

As we have seen, Europe was by no means isolated before its discovery of the New World. But because Europeans did not produce many products desired by Eastern elites, they were modest players in the Indian Ocean trading world. In the fifteenth and early sixteenth centuries, however, they launched new voyages of exploration, commerce, and conquest out of a desire to spread Christianity, to undo Italian and Ottoman domination of trade with the East, and to tap entirely new sources of wealth. Ultimately, their efforts landed them in the New World.

Causes of European Expansion

Europeans sought to expand their international reach for many reasons. By the middle of the fifteenth century, Europe was experiencing a revival of population and economic activity after the lows of the Black Death. This revival created demands for luxury goods, especially spices, from the East. However, the conquest of Constantinople by the Ottomans gave the Muslim empire control of trade routes to the east and blocked the fulfillment of European demands. Europeans thus needed to find new sources of precious metal to trade with the Ottomans or to find trade routes that bypassed the Ottomans.

Religious fervor was another important catalyst for expansion. The passion and energy ignited by the Christian reconquista of the Iberian Peninsula encouraged the Portuguese and Spanish to continue the Christian crusade. In 1492 Spain conquered Granada, the last remaining Muslim state on the Iberian Peninsula. Since the remaining Muslim states, such as the mighty Ottoman Empire, were too strong to defeat, Iberians turned their attention elsewhere. Just seven months after the Spanish conquest of Granada, Columbus departed across the Atlantic.

Combined with eagerness to gain wealth and to spread Christianity were the desire for glory and the urge to chart new waters. Scholars have frequently described the European discoveries as a manifestation of Renaissance curiosity about the physical universe. The detailed journals kept by European voyagers attest to their fascination with the new peoples and places they visited.

Individual explorers combined these motivations in unique ways. Columbus, a devout Christian, aimed to discover new territories where Christianity could be spread while seeking a direct trade route to Asia. The motives of Portuguese explorer Bartholomew Diaz were, in his own words, "to serve God and His Majesty, to give light to those who were in darkness and to grow rich as all men desire to do." When the Portuguese explorer Vasco da Gama reached the port of Calicut, India, in 1498 and a native asked what he wanted, he replied, "Christians and spices."[3] The bluntest of the Spanish **conquistadors** (kahn-KEES-tuh-dorz),

---

• **conquistador** Spanish for "conqueror"; Spanish soldier-explorer, such as Hernando Cortés and Francisco Pizarro, who sought to conquer the New World for the Spanish crown.

> " I have come to win gold, not to plow the fields like a peasant. "

HERNANDO CORTÉS

Hernando Cortés, announced as he prepared to conquer Mexico, "I have come to win gold, not to plow the fields like a peasant."[4]

Eagerness for exploration was heightened by a lack of opportunity at home. After the reconquista, young men of the Spanish upper classes found their economic and political opportunities greatly limited. The ambitious turned to the sea to seek their fortunes.

Whatever the reasons, the voyages were made possible by the growth of government power. The Spanish monarchy was stronger than before and in a position to support foreign ventures. In Portugal explorers also looked to the monarchy, to Prince Henry the Navigator in particular (page 467), for financial support and encouragement. Like voyagers, monarchs shared a mix of motivations, from the desire to please God to the desire to win glory and profit from trade. Competition among European monarchs was an important factor in encouraging the steady stream of expeditions that began in the late fifteenth century.

Ordinary men chose to join these voyages to escape poverty at home, to continue a family trade, to win a few crumbs of the great riches of empire, or to find better lives as illegal immigrants in the colonies. However, common sailors were ill-paid, and life at sea meant danger, unbearable stench, hunger, and overcrowding. For months at a time, 100 to 120 people lived and worked in a space of 1,600 to 2,000 square feet.

The people who stayed at home had a powerful impact on the process and a strong interest in it. Royal ministers and factions at court influenced monarchs to provide or deny support for exploration. The small number of people who could read served as an audience for tales of fantastic places and unknown peoples. Cosmography, natural history, and geography aroused enormous interest among educated people in the fifteenth and sixteenth centuries. One of the most popular books of the time was the fourteenth-century text *The Travels of Sir John Mandeville*, which purported to be a firsthand account of the author's travels in the

The Travels of Sir John Mandeville The author of this tale claimed to be an English knight who traveled extensively in the Middle East and Asia from the 1320s to the 1350s. Although historians now consider the work a skillful fiction, it had a great influence on how Europeans understood the world at the time. This illustration, from an edition published around 1410, depicts Mandeville approaching a walled city on the first stage of his voyage to Constantinople. (© British Library Board, Add 24289, f 14v)

Middle East, India, and China. Although we now know they were fictional, these fantastic tales of cannibals, one-eyed giants, men with the heads of dogs, and other marvels were believed for centuries. Columbus took a copy of Mandeville and the equally popular and more reliable *The Travels of Marco Polo* on his voyage in 1492.

Technology and the Rise of Exploration

Technological developments in shipbuilding, navigation, and weaponry provided another impetus for European expansion. Since ancient times, most seagoing vessels had been narrow, open boats called galleys, propelled largely by slaves or convicts manning the oars. Though well suited to the placid waters of the Mediterranean, galleys could not withstand the rougher conditions in the Atlantic. The need for sturdier craft,

---

- **caravel** A small, maneuverable, three-mast sailing ship developed by the Portuguese in the fifteenth century that gave the Portuguese a distinct advantage in exploration and trade.
- **Ptolemy's *Geography*** A second century C.E. work that synthesized the classical knowledge of geography and introduced the concepts of longitude and latitude. Reintroduced to Europeans in 1410 by Arab scholars, its ideas allowed cartographers to create more accurate maps.

as well as population losses caused by the Black Death, forced the development of a new style of ship that would not require much manpower to sail. In the course of the fifteenth century, the Portuguese developed the **caravel**, a small, light, three-mast sailing ship. The caravel was much more maneuverable than the galley. When fitted with cannon, it could dominate larger vessels.

Great strides in cartography and navigational aids were also made during this period. Around 1410 Arab scholars reintroduced Europeans to **Ptolemy's *Geography***. Written in the second century, the work synthesized the geographical knowledge of the classical world. It represented a major improvement over medieval cartography, showing the world as round and introducing the idea of latitude and longitude to plot position accurately. It also contained significant errors. Unaware of the Americas, Ptolemy showed the world as much smaller than it is, so that Asia appeared not very distant from Europe. Both the assets and the flaws of Ptolemy's work, combined with the latest information from mariners, became part of the new maps that European explorers would use on their voyages.

The magnetic compass enabled sailors to determine their direction and position at sea. The astrolabe, an instrument invented by the ancient Greeks and perfected by Muslim navigators, was used to determine the altitude of the sun and other celestial bodies. It permitted mariners to plot their latitude, that is, their precise position north or south of the equator.

Like the astrolabe, much of the new technology that Europeans used on their voyages was borrowed from the East. Gunpowder, the compass, and the sternpost rudder were Chinese inventions. The lateen sail, which allowed European ships to tack against the wind, was a product of the Indian Ocean trade world and was brought to the Mediterranean on Arab ships. Advances in cartography also drew on the rich tradition of Judeo-Arabic mathematical and astronomical learning in Iberia. In exploring new territories, European sailors thus called on techniques and knowledge developed over centuries in China, the Muslim world, and trading centers along the Indian Ocean.

The Expanding Portuguese Empire

For centuries Portugal was a small and poor nation on the margins of European life whose principal activities were fishing and subsistence farming. It would have been hard for a medieval European to predict Portugal's phenomenal success overseas after 1450. Yet Portugal had a long history of seafaring and navigation. Blocked from access to western Europe by Spain, the Portuguese turned to the Atlantic, whose waters they knew better than did other Europeans. Nature favored the Portuguese: winds blowing along their coast offered passage to Africa, its Atlantic islands, and, ultimately, Brazil.

In the early phases of Portuguese exploration, Prince Henry (1394–1460), a younger son of the king, played a leading role. A nineteenth-century scholar dubbed Henry "the Navigator" because of his support for the study of geography and navigation and for the annual expeditions he sponsored down the western coast of Africa.

The Portuguese Fleet Embarked for the Indies This image shows a Portuguese trading fleet in the late fifteenth century bound for the riches of the Indies. Between 1500 and 1635 over nine hundred ships sailed from Portugal to ports on the Indian Ocean in annual fleets composed of five to ten ships. Portuguese sailors used astrolabes, such as the one pictured here, to accurately plot their position. (fleet: British Museum/HarperCollins Publishers/The Art Archive; astrolabe: Courtesy of the Trustees of the British Museum)

Pepper Harvest To break the monotony of their bland diet, Europeans had a passion for pepper, which—along with cinnamon, cloves, nutmeg, and ginger—was the main object of the Asian trade. We can appreciate the fifteenth-century expression "as dear as pepper": one kilo of pepper cost 2 grams of silver at the place of production in the East Indies and from 1 to 10 grams of silver in Alexandria, Egypt; 14 to 18 grams in Venice; and 20 to 30 grams at the markets of northern Europe. Here natives fill vats, and the dealer tastes a peppercorn for pungency. (Bibliothèque nationale de France/ Archives Charmet/The Bridgeman Art Library)

Through their exploration voyages the Portuguese had several goals: to achieve military glory; to Christianize Muslims and locate a mythical Christian king of Africa, Prester John; and to find gold, slaves, and an overseas route to the spice markets of India. Portugal's conquest of Ceuta, an Arab city in northern Morocco, in 1415 marked the beginning of European overseas expansion. In the 1420s, under Henry's direction, the Portuguese began to settle the Atlantic islands of Madeira (ca. 1420) and the Azores (1427). In 1443 they founded their first African commercial settlement at Arguin in North Africa. By the time of Henry's death in 1460, his support for exploration was vindicated by thriving sugar plantations on the Atlantic islands, the first arrival of enslaved Africans in Portugal (see page 479), and new access to African gold.

Portuguese Expansion into Africa

The Portuguese next established trading posts and forts on the gold-rich Guinea coast and penetrated into the African continent all the way to Timbuktu (Map 16.2). By 1500 Portugal controlled the flow of African gold to Europe.

The Portuguese then pushed farther south down the west coast of Africa. In 1487 Bartholomew Diaz (ca. 1451–1500) rounded the Cape of Good Hope at the southern tip, but storms and a threatened mutiny forced him to turn back. A decade later Vasco da Gama (ca. 1469–1524) succeeded in rounding the Cape while commanding a fleet in search of a sea route to India. With the help of an Indian guide, da Gama reached the port of Calicut in India. He returned to Lisbon with spices and samples of Indian cloth, having proved the possibility of lucrative trade with the East via the Cape route. Thereafter, a Portuguese convoy set out for passage around the Cape every March.

Lisbon became the entrance port for Asian goods into Europe, but this was not accomplished without a fight. Muslim-controlled port city-states had long controlled the rich spice trade of the Indian Ocean, and they did not surrender it willingly. Portuguese cannon blasted open the port of Malacca in 1511, followed by Calicut, Hormuz, and Goa. The bombardment of these cities laid the foundation for Portuguese imperialism

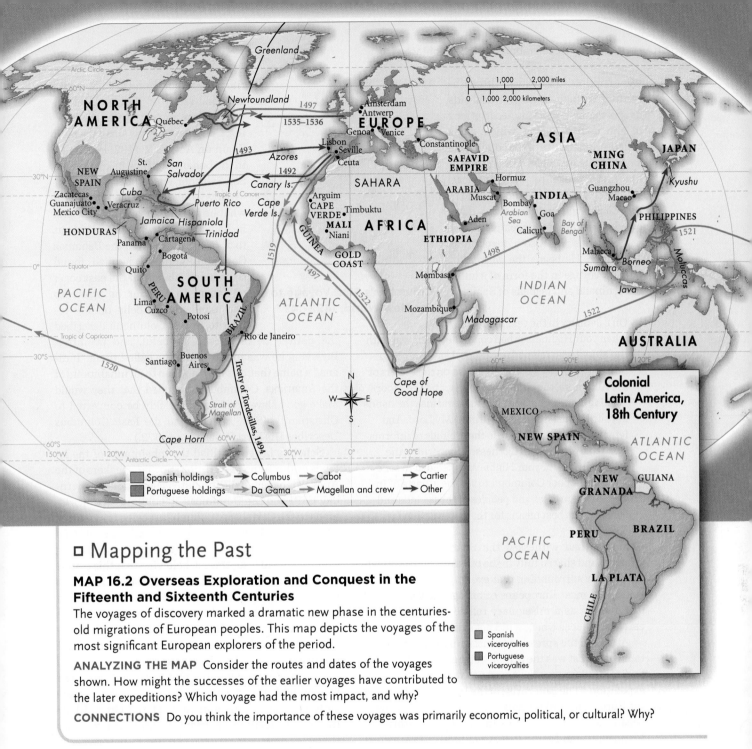

□ Mapping the Past

MAP 16.2 Overseas Exploration and Conquest in the Fifteenth and Sixteenth Centuries

The voyages of discovery marked a dramatic new phase in the centuries-old migrations of European peoples. This map depicts the voyages of the most significant European explorers of the period.

ANALYZING THE MAP Consider the routes and dates of the voyages shown. How might the successes of the earlier voyages have contributed to the later expeditions? Which voyage had the most impact, and why?

CONNECTIONS Do you think the importance of these voyages was primarily economic, political, or cultural? Why?

---

in the sixteenth and seventeenth centuries. The acquisition of port cities and their trade routes brought riches to Portugal but had limited impact on the lives and religious faith of Asian peoples beyond Portuguese coastal holdings. In the meantime, Spain also had begun the quest for an empire.

Christopher Columbus's Voyages to the Americas

Christopher Columbus (1451–1506) is a controversial figure in history — glorified by some as the brave discoverer of America, vilified by others as a cruel exploiter of

Native Americans. Rather than judging Columbus by the debates and standards of our time, it is more important to understand him in the context of his own time. First, what kind of man was Columbus, and what forces or influences shaped him? Second, in sailing westward from Europe, what were his goals? Third, did he achieve his goals, and what did he make of his discoveries?

The westward voyages of Columbus, a native of Genoa, embodied a long-standing Genoese ambition to circumvent Venetian, and then Portuguese, domination of eastward trade. Columbus was knowledgeable about the sea. He had worked as a mapmaker, and he was familiar with such fifteenth-century Portuguese navigational aids as *portolans* — written descriptions of the courses along which ships sailed — and the use of the compass as a nautical instrument. The success of his first voyage to the Americas, which took him across the Atlantic to the Caribbean in thirty-three days, owed a great deal to his seamanship.

Columbus was also a deeply religious man. He began the *Journal* of his first voyage in the form of a letter to Ferdinand and Isabella of Spain:

Columbus's First Voyage to the New World, 1492–1493

> On 2 January in the year 1492, when your Highnesses had concluded their war with the Moors who reigned in Europe, I saw your Highnesses' banners victoriously raised on the towers of the Alhambra, the citadel of the city, and the Moorish king come out of the city gates and kiss the hands of your Highnesses and the prince, My Lord. And later in that same month, on the grounds of information I had given your Highnesses concerning the lands of India . . . your Highnesses decided to send me, Christopher Columbus, to see these parts of India and the princes and peoples of those lands and consider the best means for their conversion.[5]

Columbus had witnessed the Spanish conquest of Granada and shared fully in the religious and nationalistic fervor surrounding that event. Like the Spanish rulers and most Europeans of his age, he understood Christianity as a missionary religion that should be carried to places where it did not exist.

Although the spread of Christianity was an important goal, what was the primary object of this first voyage? Columbus gave the answer in the very title of the expedition, "The Enterprise of the Indies," *Indies* being the European word for Asia. He wanted to find a direct ocean trading route to Asia. Inspired by the stories of Mandeville and Marco Polo, Columbus also dreamed of reaching the court of the Mongol emperor, the Great Khan (not realizing that the Ming Dynasty had overthrown the Mongols in 1368). Based on Ptolemy's *Geography* and other texts, he expected to pass the islands of Japan and then land on the east coast of China.

Before Columbus could begin his voyage he needed financing. Rejected for funding by the Portuguese in 1483 and by Ferdinand and Isabella in 1486, he finally won the support of the Spanish monarchy in 1492. The Spanish crown agreed to make him viceroy over any territory he might discover and to give him one-tenth of the material rewards of the journey. With this backing, Columbus and his small fleet left Spain on August 3, 1492. He landed in the Bahamas, which he christened San Salvador, on October 12, 1492.

How did Columbus interpret what he had found, and did he think he had achieved what he had set out to do? On his arrival in the Bahamas Columbus believed he had found some small islands off the east coast of Japan. In a letter he wrote to Ferdinand and Isabella on his return to Spain, Columbus described the natives as handsome, peaceful, and primitive. Believing he was in the Indies, he called them "Indians," a name that was later applied to all inhabitants of the Americas. Columbus concluded that they would make good slaves and could quickly be converted to Christianity. (See "Listening to the Past: Columbus Describes His First Voyage," page 472.)

Scholars have identified the inhabitants of the islands as the Taino (TIGH-noh) people, speakers of the Arawak language, who inhabited Hispaniola (modern-day Haiti and the Dominican Republic) and other islands in the Caribbean. Columbus received reassuring reports from Taino villagers of the presence of gold and of a great king in the vicinity. From San Salvador, Columbus sailed southwest, believing that this course would take him to Japan or the coast of China. He landed instead on Cuba on October 28. Deciding that he must be on the mainland of China near the coastal city of Quinsay (now Hangzhou), he sent a small embassy inland with letters from Ferdinand and Isabella and instructions to locate the grand city.

The landing party found only small villages. Confronted with this disappointment, Columbus apparently gave up on his aim to meet the Great Khan. Instead, he focused on trying to find gold or other valuables among the peoples he had discovered. The sight of Taino people wearing gold ornaments on Hispaniola seemed to prove that gold was available in the region. In January, confident that its source would soon be found, he headed back to Spain to report on his discovery.

Over the next decades, the Spanish would follow a policy of conquest and colonization in the New World (see pages 474–476). On his second voyage, Columbus forcibly subjugated the island of Hispaniola and enslaved its indigenous peoples. On this and subsequent voyages, he brought with him settlers for the new Spanish territories, along with agricultural seed and livestock. Columbus himself, however, had little interest in or capacity for governing. Arriving in Hispaniola

• **Treaty of Tordesillas** The 1494 agreement giving Spain everything west of an imaginary line drawn down the Atlantic and giving Portugal everything to the east.

on this third voyage, he found revolt had broken out against his brother. A royal expedition sent to investigate returned the brothers to Spain in chains. Although Columbus was quickly cleared of wrongdoing, he did not recover his authority over the territories.

> " Those new regions which we found and explored with the fleet . . . we may rightly call a New World. "
>
> **AMERIGO VESPUCCI**

Columbus was very much a man of his times. To the end of his life in 1506, he believed that he had found small islands off the coast of Asia. He never realized the scope of his achievement: that he had found a vast continent unknown to Europeans, except for a fleeting Viking presence centuries earlier. He could not know that the lands he discovered would become a crucial new arena for international trade and colonization, with grave consequences for native peoples.

Later Explorers

The Florentine navigator Amerigo Vespucci (veh-SPOO-chee; 1454–1512) realized what Columbus had not. Writing about his discoveries on the coast of modern-day Venezuela, Vespucci stated: "Those new regions which we found and explored with the fleet . . . we may rightly call a New World." This letter, titled *Mundus Novus* (The New World), was the first document to describe America as a continent separate from

Asia. In recognition of Amerigo's bold claim, the continent was named for him.

To settle competing claims to the Atlantic discoveries, Spain and Portugal turned to Pope Alexander VI. The resulting **Treaty of Tordesillas** (tor-duh-SEE-yuhs) in 1494 gave Spain everything to the west of an imaginary line drawn down the Atlantic and Portugal everything to the east. This arbitrary division worked in Portugal's favor when in 1500 an expedition led by Pedro Alvares Cabral, en route to India, landed on the coast of Brazil, which Cabral claimed as Portuguese territory.

The search for profits determined the direction of Spanish exploration and expansion in South America. Because its profits from the Caribbean were insignificant compared to Portugal's enormous riches from the Asian spice trade, Spain renewed the search for a western passage to Asia. In 1519 Charles V of Spain commissioned Ferdinand Magellan (1480–1521) to find a direct sea route to the spices of the Moluccas, islands off the southeast coast of Asia. Magellan sailed southwest across the Atlantic to Brazil, and after a long search along the coast he located the treacherous strait off the southern tip of South America that now bears his name (see Map 16.2). After passing through the

World Map of Diogo Ribeiro, 1529 This map integrates the wealth of new information provided by European explorers in the decades after Columbus's 1492 voyage. Working on commission for the Spanish king Charles V, mapmaker Diogo Ribeiro incorporated new details on Africa, South America, India, the Malay Archipelago, and China. Note the inaccuracy in his placement of the Moluccas, or Spice Islands, which are much too far east. This "mistake" was intended to serve Spain's interests in trade negotiations with the Portuguese. (Biblioteca Apostolica Vaticana)

Listening to the Past

Columbus Describes His First Voyage

On his return voyage to Spain in February 1493, Christopher Columbus composed a letter intended for wide circulation and had copies of it sent ahead to Isabella, Ferdinand, and others when the ship docked at Lisbon. Because the letter sums up Columbus's understanding of his achievements, it is considered the most important document of his first voyage.

"Since I know that you will be pleased at the great success with which the Lord has crowned my voyage, I write to inform you how in thirty-three days I crossed from the Canary Islands to the Indies, with the fleet which our most illustrious sovereigns gave me. I found very many islands with large populations and took possession of them all for their Highnesses; this I did by proclamation and unfurled the royal standard. No opposition was offered.

I named the first island that I found "San Salvador," in honour of our Lord and Saviour who has granted me this miracle.... When I reached Cuba, I followed its north coast westwards, and found it so extensive that I thought this must be the mainland, the province of Cathay.* ... From there I saw another island eighteen leagues eastwards which I then named "Hispaniola."† ...

Hispaniola is a wonder. The mountains and hills, the plains and meadow lands are both fertile and beautiful. They are most suitable for planting crops and for raising cattle of all kinds, and there are good sites for building towns and villages. The harbours are incredibly fine and there are many great rivers with broad channels and the majority contain gold.‡ The trees, fruits and plants are very different from those of Cuba. In Hispaniola there are many spices and large mines of gold and other metals.§ ...

*Cathay is the old name for China. In the logbook and later in this letter Columbus accepts the native story that Cuba is an island that they can circumnavigate in something more than twenty-one days, yet he insists here and during the second voyage that it is in fact part of the Asiatic mainland.

†Hispaniola is the second largest island of the West Indies; Haiti occupies the western third of the island, the Dominican Republic the rest.

‡This did not prove to be true.

§These statements are also inaccurate.

The inhabitants of this island, and all the rest that I discovered or heard of, go naked, as their mothers bore them, men and women alike. A few of the women, however, cover a single place with a leaf of a plant or piece of cotton which they weave for the purpose. They have no iron or steel or arms and are not capable of using them, not because they are not strong and well built but because they are amazingly timid. All the weapons they have are canes cut at seeding time, at the end of which they fix a sharpened stick, but they have not the courage to make use of these, for very often when I have sent two or three men to a village to have conversation with them a great number of them have come out. But as soon as they saw my men all fled immediately, a father not even waiting for his son. And this is not because we have harmed any of them; on the contrary, wherever I have gone and been able to have conversation with them, I have given them some of the various things I had, a cloth and other articles, and received nothing in exchange. But they have still remained incurably timid. True, when they have been reassured and lost their fear, they are so ingenuous and so liberal with all their possessions that no one who has not seen them would believe it. If one asks for anything they have they never say no. On the contrary, they offer a share to anyone with demonstrations of heartfelt affection, and they are immediately content with any small thing, valuable or valueless, that is given them. I forbade the men to give them bits of broken crockery, fragments of glass or tags of laces, though if they could get them they fancied them the finest jewels in the world.

I hoped to win them to the love and service of their Highnesses and of the whole Spanish nation and to persuade them to collect and give us of the things which they possessed in abundance and which we needed. They have no religion and are not idolaters; but all believe that power and goodness dwell in the sky and they are firmly convinced that I have come from the sky with these ships and people. In this belief they gave me a good reception everywhere, once they had overcome their fear; and this is not because they are stupid—far from it, they are men of great intelligence, for they navigate all those seas, and give a marvellously good account of everything—but because they have never before seen men clothed or ships like these....

strait, his fleet sailed north up the west coast of South America and then headed west into the Pacific toward the Malay Archipelago. Some of these islands were conquered in the 1560s and named the Philippines for Philip II of Spain.

Terrible storms, disease, starvation, and violence haunted the expedition. Sailors on two of Magellan's five ships attempted mutiny on the South American coast; one ship was lost, and another ship deserted and returned to Spain before even traversing the strait. Magellan himself was killed in a skirmish in the Philippines. At this point, the expedition had enough survivors to man only two ships, and one of them was captured by the Portuguese. Finally, in 1522 one ship with only eighteen men returned to Spain, having traveled from the east by way of the Indian Ocean, the Cape of

In all these islands the men are seemingly content with one woman, but their chief or king is allowed more than twenty. The women appear to work more than the men and I have not been able to find out if they have private property. As far as I could see whatever a man had was shared among all the rest and this particularly applies to food. . . . In another island, which I am told is larger than Hispaniola, the people have no hair. Here there is a vast quantity of gold, and from here and the other islands I bring Indians as evidence.

In conclusion, to speak only of the results of this very hasty voyage, their Highnesses can see that I will give them as much gold as they require, if they will render me some very slight assistance; also I will give them all the spices and cotton they want. . . . I will also bring them as much aloes as they ask and as many slaves, who will be taken from the idolaters. I believe also that I have found rhubarb and cinnamon and there will be countless other things in addition. . . .

So all Christendom will be delighted that our Redeemer has given victory to our most illustrious King and Queen and their renowned kingdoms, in this great matter. They should hold great celebrations and render solemn thanks to the Holy Trinity with many solemn prayers, for the great triumph which they will have, by the conversion of so many peoples to our holy faith and for the temporal benefits which will follow, for not only Spain, but all Christendom will receive encouragement and profit.

This is a brief account of the facts.

Written in the caravel off the Canary Islands.**

15 February 1493

At your orders
THE ADMIRAL ""

**Actually, Columbus was off Santa Maria in the Azores.

Source: J. M. Cohen, ed. and trans., *The Four Voyages of Christopher Columbus* (Penguin Classics, 1958), pp. 115–123. Copyright © J. M. Cohen, 1969, London. Reproduced by permission of Penguin Books Ltd.

QUESTIONS FOR ANALYSIS

1. How did Columbus explain the success of his voyage?

2. What was Columbus's view of the Native Americans he met?

3. Evaluate his statements that the Caribbean islands possessed gold, cotton, and spices.

4. Why did Columbus cling to the idea that he had reached Asia?

Good Hope, and the Atlantic. The voyage — the first to circumnavigate the globe — had taken close to three years.

Despite the losses, this voyage revolutionized Europeans' understanding of the world by demonstrating the vastness of the Pacific. The earth was clearly much larger than Columbus had believed. Magellan's expedition also made Spain rethink its plans for overseas commerce and territorial expansion. Although the voyage made a small profit in spices, the westward passage to the Indies was too long and dangerous for commercial purposes. Thus Spain soon abandoned the attempt to oust Portugal from the Eastern spice trade and concentrated on exploiting its New World territories.

The English and French also set sail across the Atlantic during the early days of exploration, in their case to search for a northwest passage to the Indies. In 1497 John Cabot (ca. 1450–1499), a Genoese merchant living in London, discovered Newfoundland. The next year he returned and explored the New England coast. These forays proved futile, and at that time the English established no permanent colonies in the territories they explored. Later English efforts to find a passage to Asia focused on the extreme north. Between 1576 and 1578, Martin Frobisher (ca. 1535–1594) made three voyages in and around the Canadian bay that now bears his name. Frobisher hopefully brought a quantity of ore back to England with him, but it proved to be worthless.

Early French exploration of the Atlantic was equally frustrating. Between 1534 and 1541 Frenchman Jacques Cartier (1491–1557) made several voyages and explored the St. Lawrence region of Canada, searching for a passage to the wealth of Asia. When this hope proved vain, the French turned to a new source of profit within Canada itself: trade in beavers and other furs. French fisherman also competed with the Spanish and English for the teeming schools of cod they found in the Atlantic waters around Newfoundland.

Spanish Conquest in the New World

After Columbus's voyages Spanish explorers penetrated farther into the New World. This territorial expansion began in 1519, when the Spanish governor in Cuba sent an expedition, under the command of the conquistador Hernando Cortés (1485–1547), to what is now Mexico. Accompanied by six hundred men, sixteen horses, and ten cannon, Cortés was to launch the conquest of the **Mexica Empire**. Its people were later called the Aztecs, but now most scholars prefer to use the term *Mexica* to refer to them and their empire.

The Mexica Empire was ruled by Montezuma II (r. 1502–1520) from his capital at Tenochtitlán (taynawch-teet-LAHN), now Mexico City. Larger than any European city of the time, it was the heart of a sophisticated civilization with an advanced understanding of mathematics, astronomy, and engineering; with a complex social system; and with oral poetry and historical traditions.

Invasion of Tenochtitlán, 1519–1521

Gulf of Mexico

Texcoco
Otumba
Zautla
Jalapa
Tlaxcala
Cholula
Veracruz
Tenochtitlán

→ Cortés's original route, 1519
→ Cortés's retreat, 1520
→ Cortés's return route, 1520–1521

Soon after Cortés landed on the Mexican coast on April 21, 1519, his camp was visited by delegations of unarmed Mexica leaders bearing gifts and news of their great emperor. Impressed by the wealth of the local people, Cortés decided to defy his orders from the governor in Cuba, which restricted him to trading and exploration, and set up a settlement under his own authority. He thus founded the settlement of Veracruz and burned his ships to prevent any disloyal or frightened followers from returning to Cuba.

The Mexica state religion necessitated constant warfare against neighboring peoples to secure captives for religious sacrifices and laborers for agricultural and building projects. Conquered peoples were required to pay tribute to the Mexica state through their local chiefs. Realizing that he could exploit dissension over this practice to his own advantage, Cortés forged an alliance with the Tlaxcala (tlah-SKAH-lah) and other subject kingdoms, which chafed under the tribute demanded by the Mexicas. In October a combined Spanish-Tlaxcalan force occupied the city of Cholula and massacred many thousand inhabitants. Strengthened by this display of power, Cortés made alliances with other native kingdoms. In November 1519, with a few hundred Spanish men and some six thousand indigenous warriors, he marched on Tenochtitlán.

Montezuma refrained from attacking the Spaniards as they advanced toward his capital and welcomed Cortés and his men into Tenochtitlán. Other native leaders attacked the Spanish, but Montezuma relied on the advice of his state council, itself divided, and on the dubious loyalty of tribute-paying communities subjugated by the Mexica. Historians have largely discredited one long-standing explanation, that he feared the Spaniards as living gods. This idea seems to have been a myth spread by Spanish missionaries and their converts after the fact, as a way of justifying and explaining the conquest. Montezuma's long hesitation proved disastrous. When Cortés — with incredible boldness — took Montezuma hostage, the emperor's influence over his people crumbled.

During the ensuing attacks and counterattacks, Montezuma was killed. The Spaniards and their allies escaped from the city and began gathering forces and making new alliances against the Mexica. In May 1521 Cortés led a second assault on Tenochtitlán, leading an army of approximately 1,000 Spanish and 75,000 native warriors.[6] The Spanish victory in late summer 1521 was hard-won and greatly aided by the effects of smallpox, which had weakened and reduced the Mexica population. After the defeat of Tenochtitlán, Cortés and

• **Mexica Empire** Also known as the Aztec Empire, a large and complex Native American civilization in modern Mexico and Central America that possessed advanced mathematical, astronomical, and engineering technology.

• **Inca Empire** The vast and sophisticated Peruvian empire centered at the capital city of Cuzco that was at its peak from 1438 until 1532.

□ Picturing the Past

Doña Marina Translating for Hernando Cortés During His Meeting with Montezuma

In April 1519 Doña Marina (or La Malinche as she is known in Mexico) was among twenty women given to the Spanish as slaves. Fluent in Nahuatl (NAH-wha-tuhl) and Yucatec Mayan (spoken by a Spanish priest accompanying Cortés), she acted as an interpreter and diplomatic guide for the Spanish. She had a close relationship with Cortés and bore his son, Don Martín Cortés, in 1522. This image was created by Tlaxcalan artists shortly after the conquest of Mexico and represents one indigenous perspective on the events. (The Granger Collection, New York)

ANALYZING THE IMAGE What role does Doña Marina (far right) appear to be playing in this image? Does she appear to be subservient or equal to Cortés (right, seated)? How did the painter indicate her identity as non-Spanish?

CONNECTIONS How do you think the native rulers negotiating with Cortés might have viewed Doña Marina? What about a Spanish viewer of this image? What does the absence of other women suggest about the role of women in these societies?

other conquistadors began the systematic conquest of Mexico. Over time a series of indigenous kingdoms fell under Spanish domination, although not without decades of resistance.

More surprising than the defeat of the Mexicas was the fall of the remote **Inca Empire** in Peru. Living in a settlement perched more than 9,800 feet above sea level, the Incas were isolated from other indigenous cultures. Like the Mexicas, they had created a vast empire that rivaled that of the Europeans in population and complexity. However, by the time of the Spanish invasion the Inca Empire had been weakened by a civil war over succession and an epidemic of disease, possibly smallpox.

The Spanish conquistador Francisco Pizarro (ca. 1475–1541) landed on the northern coast of Peru on May 13, 1532, the very day Atahualpa (ah-tuh-WAHL-puh) won control of the empire after five years of fighting his brother for the throne. As Pizarro advanced across the Andes toward Cuzco, the capital of the Inca Empire, Atahualpa was also heading there for his coronation.

Like Montezuma in Mexico, Atahualpa was aware of the Spaniards' movements. He sent envoys to greet the Spanish and invite them to meet him in the provincial town of Cajamarca. His plan was to lure the Spaniards into a trap, seize their horses and ablest men for his army, and execute the rest. Instead, the Spaniards ambushed and captured him, collected an enormous ransom in gold, and then executed him in 1533. The Spanish then marched on to Cuzco, profiting once again from internal conflicts to form alliances with local peoples. When Cuzco fell in 1533, the Spanish plundered immense riches in gold and silver.

As with the Mexica, decades of violence and resistance followed the defeat of the Incan capital. Nevertheless, the Spanish conquest opened a new chapter in European relations with the New World. It was not long before rival European nations attempted to forge their own overseas empires.

The Impact of Conquest

☐ How did conquest affect indigenous populations and bring about a new era of economic and cultural exchange, commercial empires, and forced migrations?

The growing European presence in the New World transformed its land and its peoples forever. Violence and disease wrought devastating losses, while surviving peoples encountered new political, social, and economic organizations imposed by Europeans. Although the exchange of goods and people between Europe and the New World brought diseases to the Americas, it also gave both the New and Old Worlds new crops that eventually altered consumption patterns across the globe.

Also, the centuries-old Afroeurasian trade world was forever changed by the European voyages of discovery and their aftermath. For the first time, a truly global economy emerged in the sixteenth and seventeenth centuries, and it forged new links among far-flung peoples, cultures, and societies. The ancient civilizations of Europe, Africa, the Americas, and Asia confronted each other in new and rapidly evolving ways. Those confrontations often led to conquest, forced migration, and brutal exploitation, but they also contributed to cultural exchange and renewal.

- **viceroyalties** The name for the four administrative units of Spanish possessions in the Americas: New Spain, Peru, New Granada, and La Plata.
- **encomienda system** A system whereby the Spanish crown granted the conquerors the right to forcibly employ groups of Indians; it was a disguised form of slavery.

Colonial Administration

Columbus, Cortés, and Pizarro had claimed the lands they had discovered for the Spanish crown. How were these lands governed? Already in 1503, the Spanish had granted the port of Seville a monopoly over all traffic to the New World and established the House of Trade or *Casa de la Contratación* to oversee economic matters. In 1524 Spain added to this body the Royal and Supreme Council of the Indies, with authority over all colonial affairs subject to approval by the king. Spanish territories themselves were divided initially into two **viceroyalties** or administrative divisions: New Spain, created in 1535, with its capital at Mexico City, and Peru, created in 1542, with its capital at Lima. In the eighteenth century two additional viceroyalties were added: New Granada, with Bogotá as its administrative center; and La Plata, with Buenos Aires as its capital (see Map 16.2).

Within each territory, the viceroy, or imperial governor, exercised broad military and civil authority as the direct representative of Spain. The viceroy presided over the *audiencia* (ow-dee-EHN-see-ah), a board of twelve to fifteen judges that served as his advisory council and the highest judicial body. Later, King Charles III (r. 1759–1788) introduced the system of intendants to Spain's New World territories. These royal officials possessed broad military, administrative, and financial authority within their intendancies, smaller divisions within each viceroyalty, and were responsible not to the viceroy but to the monarchy in Madrid. The intendant system was pioneered by the Bourbon kings of France and was also used by the French in their overseas colonies.

The Portuguese governed their colony of Brazil in a similar manner. After the union of the crowns of Portugal and Spain in 1580, Spanish administrative forms were introduced. Local officials called *corregidores* (kuh-REH-gih-dawr-eez) held judicial and military powers. Royal policies placed severe restrictions on Brazilian industries that might compete with those of Portugal and Spain. These restrictions were just one of the many challenges native peoples faced under colonial rule.

The Impact of European Settlement on the Lives of Indigenous Peoples

Before Columbus's arrival, the Americas were inhabited by thousands of groups of indigenous peoples with different languages and cultures. These groups ranged from hunter-gatherer tribes organized into tribal confederations to large-scale agriculture-based empires connecting bustling cities and towns. The best estimate is that the peoples of the Americas numbered around 50 million in 1492.

Mixed Races The unprecedented mixing of peoples in the Spanish New World colonies inspired great fascination. An elaborate terminology emerged to describe the many possible combinations of indigenous, African, and European blood, which were known collectively as *castas*. This painting belongs to a popular genre of the eighteenth century depicting couples composed of individuals of different ethnic origin and the children produced of their unions. (Schalkwijk/Art Resource, NY)

Español con India, Mestizo.

Mestizo con Española Castizo.

Mulato con Española, Morisco.

Morisco con Española Chino.

Lobo con China Gibaro.

Gibaro con Mulata Albarazado

Sanbaigo con Loba

Calpamulato con Canbula

Their lives were radically transformed by the arrival of Europeans. In the sixteenth century perhaps two hundred thousand Spaniards immigrated to the New World. Conquistadors carved out vast estates called *haciendas* (ah-see-EHN-duhz) in temperate grazing areas and imported Spanish livestock for the kinds of ranching with which they were familiar. In coastal tropical areas, the Spanish erected huge plantations to supply sugar to the European market. Around 1550 silver was discovered in present-day Bolivia and Mexico. To work the cattle ranches, sugar plantations, and silver mines, the conquistadors first turned to the indigenous peoples.

The Spanish quickly established the **encomienda system**, in which the Crown granted the conquerors the right to employ groups of Native Americans as laborers or to demand tribute from them in exchange for providing food and shelter. In practice, the encomiendas (ehn-koh-mee-EHN-duhz) were a legalized form of slavery.

The new conditions and hardships imposed by conquest and colonization resulted in enormous native population losses. The major cause of death was disease. Having little or no resistance to diseases brought from the Old World, the inhabitants of the New World fell victim to smallpox, typhus, influenza, and other illnesses. Another factor behind the decline in population was overwork. Unaccustomed to forced labor, native workers died in staggering numbers. Moreover, forced labor diverted local people from tending to their own crops, leading to malnutrition, reduced fertility rates, and starvation. Women forced to work were separated from their infants, leading to high infant mortality rates in a population with no livestock to supply alternatives to breast milk. Malnutrition and hunger in turn lowered resistance to disease. Finally, many indigenous peoples also died through outright violence in warfare.[7]

The Franciscan Bartolomé de Las Casas (1474–1566) documented the brutal treatment of indigenous peoples at the hands of the Spanish:

> To these quiet Lambs . . . came the Spaniards like
> most c(r)uel Tygres, Wolves and Lions, enrag'd with
> a sharp and tedious hunger; for these forty years
> past, minding nothing else but the slaughter of these
> unfortunate wretches, whom with divers kinds of

torments neither seen nor heard of before, they have so cruelly and inhumanely butchered, that of three millions of people which Hispaniola itself did contain, there are left remaining alive scarce three hundred persons.[8]

Las Casas and other missionaries asserted that the Indians had human rights, and through their persistent pressure the Spanish emperor Charles V abolished the worst abuses of the encomienda system in 1531.

The pattern of devastating disease and population loss established in the Spanish colonies was repeated everywhere Europeans settled. The best estimate is that the native population declined from roughly 50 million in 1492 to around 9 million by 1700. It is important to note, however, that native populations and cultures did survive the conquest period, sometimes by blending with European incomers and sometimes by maintaining cultural autonomy. Mixed-race populations sometimes rose to the colonial elite. The Spanish conquistadors often consolidated their power through marriage to the daughters of local rulers, and their descendants were among the most powerful inhabitants of Spanish America.

For colonial administrators the main problem posed by the astronomically high death rate was the loss of a subjugated labor force to work the mines and sugar plantations. The search for fresh sources of labor gave birth to the new tragedy of the Atlantic slave trade (see page 479).

The Columbian Exchange

The travel of people and goods between the Old and New Worlds led to an exchange of animals, plants, and diseases, a complex process known as the **Columbian exchange**. As we have seen, the introduction of new diseases to the Americas had devastating consequences. But other results of the exchange brought benefits not only to the Europeans but also to native peoples.

European immigrants wanted to eat foods familiar to them, so they searched the Americas for climatic zones favorable to crops grown in their homelands. Everywhere they settled, the Spanish and Portuguese brought and raised wheat with labor provided by the encomienda system. Grapes and olives brought over from Spain did well in parts of Peru and Chile. Perhaps the most significant introduction to the diet of Native Americans came via the meat and milk of the livestock that the early conquistadors brought with them, including cattle, sheep, and goats. The horse enabled both the Spanish conquerors and native populations to travel faster and farther and to transport heavy loads.

In turn, Europeans returned home with many food crops that became central elements of their diet. Crops originating in the Americas included tomatoes as well as many varieties of beans, squash, pumpkins, and peppers. One of the most important of such crops was maize (corn), first introduced to Europe by Columbus in 1493. Because maize gives a high yield per unit of land, has a short growing season, and thrives in climates too dry for rice and too wet for wheat, it proved an especially important crop for Europeans. By the late seventeenth century maize had become a staple in Spain, Portugal, southern France, and Italy, and in the eighteenth century it became one of the chief foods of southeastern Europe.

Even more valuable was the nutritious white potato, which slowly spread from west to east—to Ireland, England, and France in the seventeenth century, and to Germany, Poland, Hungary, and Russia in the eighteenth, contributing everywhere to a rise in popu-

Incan Women Milking Cows This illustration of Incan women milking cows is from a collection of illustrations by a Spanish bishop that offers a valuable view of life in Peru in the 1780s. (Archivo Fotografos Oronoz)

lation. Ironically, the white potato reached New England from old England in the early eighteenth century. The Portuguese quickly began exporting chili peppers from Brazil to Africa, India, and Southeast Asia along the trade routes they dominated. The chili pepper arrived in continental North America when plantation owners began to plant them as a food source for enslaved Africans, for whom they were a dietary staple.

Europeans' initial reaction to these crops was often fear or hostility. Adoption of the tomato and the potato, for example, was long hampered by belief that they were unfit for human consumption and potentially poisonous. Both plants belong to the deadly nightshade family, and both contain poison in their leaves and stems. Consequently, it took time and persuasion for these plants to win over tradition-minded European peasants, who used potatoes mostly as livestock feed. During the eighteenth-century Enlightenment, scientists and doctors played an important role in popularizing the nutritive benefits of the potato.

While the exchange of foods was a great benefit to both cultures, the introduction of European pathogens to the New World had a disastrous impact on the native population. The wave of catastrophic epidemic disease that swept the Western Hemisphere after 1492 can be seen as an extension of the swath of devastation wreaked by the Black Death in the 1300s, first on Asia and then on Europe. The world after Columbus was thus unified by disease as well as by trade and colonization.

Sugar and Early Transatlantic Slavery

Two crucial and interrelated elements of the Columbian exchange were the transatlantic trade in sugar and slaves. Throughout the Middle Ages slavery was deeply entrenched in the Mediterranean, but it was not based on race; many slaves were white. How, then, did black African slavery enter the European picture and take root in South and then North America? In 1453 the Ottoman capture of Constantinople halted the flow of white slaves from the eastern Mediterranean. Additionally, the successes of the Christian reconquest of the Iberian Peninsula drastically diminished the supply of Muslim captives. Cut off from its traditional sources of slaves, Mediterranean Europe turned to sub-Saharan Africa, which had a long history of slave trading.

As Portuguese explorers began their voyages along the western coast of Africa, one of the first commodities they sought was slaves. In 1444 the first ship returned to Lisbon with a cargo of enslaved Africans. While the first slaves were simply seized by small raiding parties, Portuguese merchants soon found that it was easier to trade with African leaders, who were accustomed to dealing in slaves captured through warfare with neighboring powers. From 1490 to 1530 Portuguese traders brought between three hundred and two thousand black slaves to Lisbon each year. There, they performed most of the manual labor and constituted 10 percent of the city's population.

In this stage of European expansion, the history of slavery became intertwined with the history of sugar. Originally sugar was an expensive luxury that only the very affluent could afford, but population increases and greater prosperity in the fifteenth century led to increasing demand. The establishment of sugar plantations on the Canary and Madeira Islands in the fifteenth century testifies to this demand.

Sugar was a particularly difficult crop to produce for profit. Seed-stems were planted by hand, thousands to the acre. When mature, the cane had to be harvested and processed rapidly to avoid spoiling, forcing days and nights of work with little rest. Moreover, sugar cane has a virtually constant growing season, meaning that there was no fallow period when workers could recuperate. The demands of sugar production were increased with the invention of roller mills to crush the cane more efficiently. Yields could be augmented, but only if a sufficient labor force was found to supply the mills. Europeans solved the labor problem by forcing first native islanders and then enslaved Africans to perform the backbreaking work.

The transatlantic slave trade began in 1518 when Spanish king Charles I authorized traders to bring African slaves to New World colonies. The Portuguese brought the first slaves to Brazil around 1550; by 1600 four thousand were being imported annually. After its founding in 1621, the Dutch West India Company transported thousands of Africans to Brazil and the Caribbean, mostly to work on sugar plantations. In the late seventeenth century, with the chartering of the Royal African Company, the English got involved in bringing slaves to Barbados and other English colonies in the Caribbean and mainland North America.

The Transatlantic Slave Trade

Before 1700, when slavers decided it was better business to improve conditions, some 20 percent of slaves died on the voyage from Africa to the Americas.[9] The most common cause of death was dysentery induced

• **Columbian exchange** The exchange of animals, plants, and diseases between the Old and the New Worlds.

A New World Sugar Refinery in Brazil Sugar was the most important and most profitable plantation crop in the New World. This image shows the processing and refinement of sugar on a Brazilian plantation. Sugar cane was grown, harvested, and processed by African slaves who labored under brutal and ruthless conditions to generate enormous profits for plantation owners. (The Bridgeman Art Library/Getty Images)

by poor-quality food and water, lack of sanitation, and intense crowding. (To increase profits, slave traders packed several hundred captives on each ship.) Men were often kept in irons during the passage, while women and girls were considered fair game for sailors. On sugar plantations, death rates among slaves from illness and exhaustion were extremely high, leading to a constant stream of new shipments of slaves from Africa. Driven by rising demands for sugar, cotton, tobacco, and other plantation crops, the tragic transatlantic slave trade reached its height in the eighteenth century.

The Birth of the Global Economy

With Europeans' discovery of the Americas and their exploration of the Pacific, the entire world was linked for the first time in history by seaborne trade. The opening of that trade brought into being three successive commercial empires: the Portuguese, the Spanish, and the Dutch.

The Portuguese were the first worldwide traders. In the sixteenth century they controlled the sea route to India (Map 16.3). From their fortified bases at Goa on the Arabian Sea and at Malacca on the Malay Peninsula, ships carried goods to the Portuguese settlement at Macao in the South China Sea. From Macao Portuguese ships loaded with Chinese silks and porcelains sailed to the Japanese port of Nagasaki and to the Phil-

ippine port of Manila, where Chinese goods were exchanged for Spanish silver from New Spain. Throughout Asia the Portuguese traded in slaves. They also exported horses from Mesopotamia and copper from Arabia to India; from India they exported hawks and peacocks for the Chinese and Japanese markets. Back to Portugal they brought Asian spices that had been purchased with textiles produced in India and with gold and ivory from East Africa. They also shipped back sugar from their colony in Brazil, produced by African slaves whom they had transported across the Atlantic.

Becoming an imperial power a few decades later than the Portuguese, the Spanish were determined to claim their place in world trade. This was greatly facilitated by the discovery of immense riches in silver, first at Potosí in modern-day Bolivia and later in Mexico. Silver poured into Europe through the Spanish port of Seville, contributing to steep inflation across Europe. Demand for silver also created a need for slaves to work in the mines. (See "Global Trade: Silver," page 482.)

The Spanish Empire in the New World was basically land-based, but across the Pacific the Spaniards built a seaborne empire centered at Manila in the Philippines. The city of Manila served as the transpacific bridge between Spanish America and China. In Manila, Spanish traders used silver from American mines to purchase Chinese silk for European markets. The European demand for silk was so huge that in 1597, for example, 12 million pesos of silver, almost the total

MAP 16.3 Seaborne Trading Empires in the Sixteenth and Seventeenth Centuries By the mid-seventeenth century, trade linked all parts of the world except for Australia. Notice that trade in slaves was not confined to the Atlantic but involved almost all parts of the world.

value of the transatlantic trade, moved from Acapulco in New Spain to Manila (see Map 16.4). After 1640, however, the Spanish silk trade declined in the face of stiff competition from Dutch imports.

In the seventeenth century the Dutch challenged the Spanish and Portuguese Empires. Drawing on their commercial wealth and long experience in European trade, by the end of the century the Dutch emerged as the most powerful worldwide seaborne trading power. The Dutch Empire was built on spices, and the Dutch East India Company was founded in 1602 with the stated intention of capturing the spice trade from the Portuguese.

The Dutch set their sights on gaining direct access to and control of the Indonesian sources of spices. The Dutch fleet, sailing from the Cape of Good Hope in Africa and avoiding the Portuguese forts in India, steered directly for Java (modern Indonesia; see Map 16.4). In return for assisting Indonesian princes in local squabbles and disputes with the Portuguese, the Dutch won broad commercial concessions. Through agreements, seizures, and outright war, they gained control

of the western access to the Indonesian archipelago in the first half of the seventeenth century. Gradually they achieved political domination over the archipelago itself. By the 1660s the Dutch had managed to expel the Portuguese from Ceylon and other East Indian islands, thereby establishing control of the lucrative spice trade.

Changing Values and Beliefs

☐ How did new encounters shape cultural values and beliefs in Europe and the New World?

The age of overseas expansion heightened Europeans' contacts with the rest of the world. These contacts gave birth to new ideas about the inherent superiority or inferiority of different races, in part to justify European participation in the slave trade. Two great writers of the period both captured and challenged these views,

Global Trade

Silver in vast quantities was discovered in 1545 by the Spanish, at an altitude of fifteen thousand feet, at Potosí in unsettled territory conquered from the Inca Empire. A half-century later, 160,000 people lived in Potosí, making it about the size of the city of London. In the second half of the sixteenth century the mine (in present-day Bolivia) yielded perhaps 60 percent of all the silver mined in the world. From Potosí and the mines at Zacatecas and Guanajuato in Mexico, huge quantities of precious metals poured forth.

Mining became the most important industry in the colonies. The Spanish crown claimed the quinto, one-fifth of all precious metals mined in South America, and gold and silver yielded the Spanish monarchy 25 percent of its total income. One scholar has estimated that 260 tons of silver arrived in Europe each year by 1600.* Seville was the official port of entry for all Spanish silver, although a lively smuggling trade existed.

The real mover of world trade was not Europe, however, but China, which in this period had a population approaching 100 million. By 1450 the collapse of its paper currency led the Ming government to shift to a silver-based currency. Instead of rice, the traditional form of payment, all Chinese now had to pay their taxes in silver. The result was an insatiable demand for the world's production of silver.

*Artur Attman, *American Bullion in the European World Trade, 1600–1800* (Goteborg, 1986).

MAP 16.4 The Global Silver Trade

The incredibly rich silver mines at Potosí (in modern-day Bolivia) were the source of this eight-reale coin (lower right) struck at the mine during the reign of Charles II. Such coins were the original "pieces of eight" prized by pirates and adventurers. (silver mine: Courtesy of The Hispanic Society of America; coin: Hoberman Collection/SuperStock)

Japan was China's original source, and the Japanese continued to ship large quantities of silver ore until the depletion of its mines near the end of the seventeenth century. The discovery of silver in the New World provided a vast and welcome new supply for the Chinese market. In 1571 the Spanish founded a port city at Manila in the Philippines to serve as a bridge point for bringing silver to Asia. Throughout the seventeenth century Spanish galleons annually carried 2 million pesos (or more than fifty tons) of silver from Acapulco to Manila, where Chinese merchants carried it on to China. Even more silver reached China through exchange with European merchants who purchased Chinese goods using silver shipped across the Atlantic. European trade routes to China passed through the Baltic, the Mediterranean, and the Ottoman Empire, as well as around the Cape of Good Hope in Africa. Historians estimate that ultimately the majority of the world's silver in this period ended up in China.

In exchange for silver, the Chinese traded high-quality finished goods much desired by elites across the world, including fine silks, porcelain, and spices. To ensure continued demand for their products, enterprising Chinese merchants adapted them to Western tastes.

Silver had a mixed impact on the regions involved. Spain's immense profits from silver paid for the tremendous expansion of its empire and for the large armies that defended it. However, the easy flow of money also dampened economic innovation. It exacerbated the rising inflation Spain was already experiencing in the mid-sixteenth century. When the profitability of the silver mines diminished in the 1640s, Spain's power was fundamentally undercut

China experienced similarly mixed effects. On the one hand, the need for finished goods to trade for silver led to the rise of a merchant class and a new specialization of regional production. On the other hand, the inflation resulting from the influx of silver weakened the finances of the Ming Dynasty. As the purchasing power of silver declined in China, so did the value of silver taxes. The ensuing fiscal crisis helped bring down the Ming and led to the rise of the Qing in 1644. Ironically, the two states that benefited the most from silver also experienced political decline as a direct result of their reliance on it.

The consequences were most tragic elsewhere. In New Spain millions of indigenous laborers suffered brutal conditions and death in the silver mines. Demand for new sources of labor for the mines contributed to the intensification of the African slave trade.

Silver ore mined at Potosí thus built the first global trade system in history. Previously, a long-standing Afroeurasian trading world had involved merchants and consumers from the three Old World continents. Once Spain opened a trade route across the Pacific through Manila, all continents except Australia and Antarctica were linked.

Silver remained a crucial element in world trade through the nineteenth century. When Mexico won independence from Spain in 1821, it began to mint its own silver dollar, which became the most prized coin in trade in East Asia. By the beginning of the twentieth century, when the rest of the world had adopted gold as the standard of currency, only China and Mexico remained on the silver standard, testimony to the central role this metal had played in their histories.

providing insights still valued today. The essays of Michel de Montaigne epitomized a new spirit of skepticism and cultural relativism, while the plays of William Shakespeare reflected his efforts to come to terms with the cultural complexities of his day. Religion became another means of cultural contact, as European missionaries aimed to spread Christianity in both the New World and East Asia, with mixed results. While Christianity was embraced in parts of the New World, it was met largely with suspicion in China and Japan. However, the East-West contacts led to exchanges of influential cultural and scientific ideas.

New Ideas About Race

At the beginning of the transatlantic slave trade, most Europeans would have thought of Africans, if they thought of them at all, as savages because of their eating habits, religious practices, morals, clothing, and social customs, and as barbarians because of their language and methods of war. They grouped Africans into the despised categories of pagan heathens or Muslim infidels. Africans were certainly not the only peoples subject to such dehumanizing attitudes. To Christian Europeans, Jews were also an alien group and were, like Africans, naturally given to sin and depravity. More generally, elite people across Europe were accustomed to viewing the peasant masses as a lower form of humanity.

As Europeans turned to Africa for new sources of slaves, they drew on beliefs about Africans' primitiveness and barbarity to defend slavery and even argue that enslavement benefited Africans by bringing the light of Christianity to heathen peoples. In 1444 an observer defended the enslavement of the first Africans by Portuguese explorers as necessary for their salvation "because they lived like beasts, without any of the customs of rational creatures, since they did not even know what were bread and wine, nor garments of cloth, nor life in the shelter of a house; and worse still was their ignorance, which deprived them of knowledge of good, and permitted them only a life of brutish idleness."[10] Compare this with an early seventeenth-century Englishman's complaint that the Irish "be so beastly that they are better like beasts than Christians."[11]

Over time the institution of slavery fostered a new level of racial inequality. Africans gradually became seen as utterly distinct from and wholly inferior to Europeans. In a transition from rather vague assumptions about African's non-Christian religious beliefs and general lack of civilization, Europeans developed increasingly rigid ideas of racial superiority and inferiority to safeguard the growing profits gained from plantation slavery. Black skin became equated with slavery itself as Europeans at home and in the colonies convinced themselves that blacks were destined by God to serve them as slaves in perpetuity.

Support for this belief went back to the Greek philosopher Aristotle's argument that some people are naturally destined for slavery and to biblical associations between darkness and sin. A more explicit justification was found in the story of Noah's curse upon the descendants of his disobedient son Ham to be the "servant[s] of servants." Biblical genealogies listing Ham's sons as those who peopled North Africa and Kush (which includes parts of modern Egypt and Sudan) were interpreted to mean that all inhabitants of those regions bore Noah's curse. From the sixteenth century onward, many defenders of slavery cited this story as justification for the enslavement of an entire race.

After 1700 the emergence of new methods of observing and describing nature led to the use of science to define race. From referring to a nation or an ethnic group, henceforth "race" would be used to describe supposedly biologically distinct groups of people whose physical differences produced differences in culture, character, and intelligence. Biblical justifications for inequality thereby gave way to allegedly scientific ones.

Michel de Montaigne and Cultural Curiosity

Racism was not the only possible reaction to the new worlds emerging in the sixteenth century. Decades of religious fanaticism, bringing civil anarchy and war, led both Catholics and Protestants to doubt that any one faith contained absolute truth. Added to these doubts was the discovery of peoples in the New World who had radically different ways of life. These shocks helped produce ideas of skepticism and cultural relativism in the sixteenth and seventeenth centuries. Skepticism is a school of thought founded on doubt that total certainty or definitive knowledge is ever attainable. Cultural relativism suggests that one culture is not necessarily superior to another, just different. Both notions found expression in the work of Frenchman Michel de Montaigne (MEE-shel duh mahn-TAYN; 1533–1592).

Montaigne developed a new literary genre, the essay — from the French *essayer*, meaning "to test or try" — to express his thoughts and ideas. Published in 1580, Montaigne's *Essays* consisted of short personal reflections. Intending to be accessible to ordinary people, Montaigne wrote in French rather than in Latin and used an engaging conversational style.

Montaigne's essay "On Cannibals" reveals the impact of overseas discoveries on his consciousness. In contrast to the prevailing views of the time, he rejected the notion that one culture is superior to another. Speaking of native Brazilians, he wrote:

I find that there is nothing barbarous and savage in this nation [Brazil], . . . except, that everyone gives the title of barbarism to everything that is not according to his usage; as, indeed, we have no other criterion of truth and reason, than the example and pattern of the opinions and customs of the place wherein we live. . . . They are savages in the same way that we say fruits are wild, which nature produces of herself and by her ordinary course; whereas, in truth, we ought rather to call those wild whose natures we have changed by our artifice and diverted from the common order.[12]

In his own time and throughout the seventeenth century, few would have agreed with Montaigne's challenging of European superiority. The publication of his ideas, however, contributed to a basic shift in attitudes. Montaigne inaugurated an era of doubt. "Wonder," he said, "is the foundation of all philosophy, research is the means of all learning, and ignorance is the end."[13]

William Shakespeare and His Influence

In addition to marking the introduction of the essay as a literary genre, the period fostered remarkable creativity in other branches of literature. England — especially in the latter part of Queen Elizabeth I's reign

and in the first years of her successor, James I (r. 1603–1625) — witnessed remarkable literary expression.

The undisputed master of the period was the dramatist William Shakespeare, whose genius lay in the originality of his characterizations, the diversity of his plots, his understanding of human psychology, and his unsurpassed gift for language. Born in 1564, Shakespeare was a Renaissance man with a deep appreciation of classical culture, individualism, and humanism.

Like Montaigne's, Shakespeare's work reveals the impact of new connections between Europeans and peoples of other cultures. The title character of *Othello* is described as a "Moor of Venice." In Shakespeare's day, the word *moor* referred to Muslims of Moroccan or North African origin, including those who had migrated to the Iberian Peninsula. It could also be applied, though, to natives of the Iberian Peninsula who converted to Islam or to non-Muslim Berbers in North Africa. To complicate things even more, references in the play to Othello as "black" in skin color have led many to believe that Shakespeare intended him to be a sub-Saharan African, and he is usually depicted as such in modern performances. This confusion in the play reflects the uncertainty in Shakespeare's own day about racial and religious classifications.

The character of Othello is both vilified in racist terms by his enemies and depicted as a brave warrior, a key member of the city's military leadership, and a

Titus Andronicus With classical allusions, fifteen murders and executions, a Gothic queen who takes a black lover, and incredible violence, this early Shakespearean tragedy (1594) was a melodramatic thriller that enjoyed enormous popularity with the London audience. The shock value of a dark-skinned character on the English stage is clearly shown in this illustration. (Reproduced by permission of the Marquess of Bath, Longleat House, Warminster, Wilts)

Viewpoints

Christian Conversion in New Spain

• *In justifying their violent conquest of the Mexica and Inca civilizations, Spanish conquistadors emphasized the need to bring Christianity to heathen peoples. For the conquered, the imposition of Christianity and repression of their pre-existing religions were often experienced as yet another form of loss. The first document describes the response of the recently vanquished Mexica leaders of Tenochtitlán to Franciscan missionaries. Despite resistance, missionaries eventually succeeded in converting much of the indigenous population to Catholicism. In his firsthand account of the Spanish conquest, written a few decades after the fall of Tenochtitlán, Bernal Díaz del Castillo expressed great satisfaction at the Catholic piety of some indigenous communities.*

Mexica Response to the Franciscans' Explanation of Their Mission in 1524

❝You have told us that we do not know the One who gives us life and being, who is Lord of the heavens and of the earth. You also say that those we worship are not gods. This way of speaking is entirely new to us, and very scandalous. We are frightened by this way of speaking because our forebears who engendered and governed us never said anything like this. On the contrary, they left us this our custom of worshiping our gods, in which they believed and which they worshiped all the time that they lived here on earth. They taught us how to honor them. And they taught us all the ceremonies and sacrifices that we make. They told us that through them [our gods] we live and are, and that we were beholden to them, to be theirs and to serve countless centuries before the sun began to shine and before there was daytime. They said that these gods that we worship give us everything we need for our physical existence: maize, beans, chia seeds, etc.

. . .All of us together feel that it is enough to have lost, enough that the power and royal jurisdiction have been taken from us. As for our gods, we will die before giving up serving and worshiping them.❞

Bernal Díaz del Castillo, from *The True History of the Conquest of New Spain*

❝It is a thing to be grateful for to God, and for profound consideration, to see how the natives assist in celebrating a holy Mass. . . . There is another good thing they do [namely]

that both men, women and children, who are of the age to learn them, know all the holy prayers in their own languages and are obliged to know them. They have other good customs about their holy Christianity, that when they pass near a sacred altar or Cross they bow their heads with humility, bend their knees, and say the prayer "Our Father," which we Conquistadores have taught them, and they place lighted wax candles before the holy altars and crosses, for formerly they did not know how to use wax in making candles. In addition, to what I have said, we taught them to show great reverence and obedience to all the monks and priests, and, when these went to their pueblos, to sally forth to receive them with lighted wax candles and to ring the bells, and to feed them very well. . . . Beside the good customs reported by me they have others both holy and good, for when the day of Corpus Christ comes, or that of Our Lady, or other solemn festivals when among us we form processions, most of the pueblos in the neighbourhood of this city of Guatemala come out in procession with their crosses and lighted wax tapers, and carry on their shoulders, on a litter, the image of the saint who is the patron of the pueblo.❞

Sources: Mexica Response: "The Lords and Holy Men of Tenochtitlan Reply to the Franciscans Bernardino de Sahagún, Coloquios y doctrina Cristiana," ed. Miguel León-Portilla, in *Spanish Colonial America: A Documentary History*, ed. Kenneth Mills and William B. Taylor. Copyright 1998. Reproduced with permission of SR BOOKS in the format Textbook and Other Book via Copyright Clearance Center; Bernal Díaz del Castillo: Bernal Diaz, *The True History of the Conquest of New Spain*, in Stuart B. Schwarz, *Victors and Vanquished: Spanish and Nahua Views of the Conquest of Mexico*, pp. 218–219.

QUESTIONS FOR ANALYSIS

1. What reasons do the leaders of Tenochtitlán offer for rejecting the teachings of Franciscan missionaries? What importance do they accord their own religious traditions?

2. What evidence does Bernal Diaz provide for the conversion of the indigenous people in the city of Guatemala?

3. How and why do you think indigenous peoples might have evolved from the attitudes expressed in the first document to those described in the second? Do you think the second document tells the whole story of religious attitudes under Spanish rule?

man capable of winning the heart of an aristocratic white woman. In contrast to the prevailing view of Moors as inferior, Shakespeare presents Othello as a complex human figure. Shakespeare's play thus demonstrates both the intolerance of contemporary society and the possibility for some individuals to look beyond racial stereotypes.

Shakespeare's last play, *The Tempest*, displays a similar interest in race and race relations. The plot involves the stranding on an island of sorcerer Prospero and his daughter, Miranda. There Prospero finds and raises Caliban, a native of the island, whom he instructs in his own language and religion. After Caliban's attempted rape of Miranda, Prospero enslaves him, earning the rage and resentment of his erstwhile pupil. Modern scholars often note the echoes between this play and the realities of imperial conquest and settlement in Shakespeare's day. It is no accident, they argue, that the playwright portrayed Caliban as a monstrous dark-skinned island native who was best-suited for slavery. However, Shakespeare himself borrows words from Montaigne's essay "On Cannibals," suggesting that he may have intended to criticize, rather than endorse, racial intolerance. Shakespeare's work shows us one of the finest minds of the age struggling to come to terms with the racial and religious complexities around him.

Religious Conversion in the New World

Converting indigenous people to Christianity was a key ambition for all European powers in the New World. Galvanized by the desire to spread their religion and prevent any gains by Protestants, Catholic powers actively sponsored missionary efforts. Franciscans, Dominicans, Jesuits, and members of other religious orders who accompanied the conquistadors and sub-

sequent settlers established Catholic missions throughout Spanish and Portuguese colonies. Later French explorers were also accompanied by missionaries who preached to the Native American tribes with whom they traded.

Rather than a straightforward imposition of Christianity, conversion entailed a complex process of cultural exchange. Catholic friars were among the first Europeans to seek understanding of native cultures and languages as part of their effort to render Christianity comprehensible to indigenous people. In addition to spreading Christianity, missionaries taught indigenous peoples European methods of agriculture and instilled loyalty to colonial masters. In turn, Christian ideas and practices in the New World took on a distinctive character. For example, a sixteenth-century apparition of the Virgin Mary in Mexico City, known as the Virgin of Guadalupe, became a central icon of Spanish-American Catholicism.

Missionaries' success in the New World varied over time and space. In Central and South America large-scale conversion forged enduring Catholic cultures in Portuguese and Spanish colonies. (See "Viewpoints: Christian Conversion in New Spain," page 486.) For example, it is estimated that missionaries had baptized between four and nine million indigenous people in New Spain by the mid-1530s.[14] Conversion efforts in seventeenth-century North America were less effective due to the scattered nature of settlement and the lesser integration of native people into the colonial community. On the whole, Protestants were less active than Catholics as missionaries, although some dissenters like Quakers and Methodists did seek converts among native people. Efforts to Christianize indigenous peoples in the New World were paralleled by missionary work by the Jesuits and other orders in the Far East.

CONNECTIONS

Just three years separated Martin Luther's attack on the Catholic Church in 1517 and Ferdinand Magellan's discovery of the Pacific Ocean in 1520. Within a few short years western Europeans' religious unity and notions of terrestrial geography were shattered. Old medieval certainties about Heaven and earth collapsed. In the ensuing decades Europeans struggled to come to terms with religious differences among Protestants and Catholics at home and with the multitudes of new peoples and places they encountered abroad. While some Europeans were fascinated and inspired by this new diversity, too often the result was violence. Europeans endured decades of religious civil war, and indigenous peoples overseas suffered massive population losses as a result of European warfare, disease, and exploitation. Tragically, both Catholic and Protestant religious leaders condoned the trade in slaves that was to bring suffering and death to millions of Africans.

Even as the voyages of discovery contributed to the fragmentation of European culture, they also factored into state centralization and consolidation in the longer term.

Henceforth, competition to gain overseas colonies became an integral part of European politics. Spain's investment in conquest proved spectacularly profitable, and yet, the ultimate result was a weakening of its power. Over time the Netherlands, England, and France also reaped tremendous profits from colonial trade, which helped them build modernized, centralized states.

The most important consequence of the European voyages of discovery was the creation of enduring contacts among five of the seven continents of the globe — Europe, Asia, Africa, North America, and South America. From the sixteenth century onward, the peoples of the world were increasingly entwined in divergent forms of economic, social, and cultural exchange. Our modern era of globalization had begun.

◻ CHAPTER REVIEW

◻ What was the Afroeurasian trade world like before the voyages of Columbus? (p. 460)

Prior to Columbus's voyages, well-developed trade routes linked the peoples and products of Africa, Asia, and Europe. The Indian Ocean was the center of the Afroeurasian trade world, ringed by cosmopolitan commercial cities such as Mombasa in Africa, Calicut in India, and Malacca in Southeast Asia. Among the goods traded were silk, porcelain, spices, textiles, gold, and slaves. Overall, Europe played a minor role in the Afroeurasian trade world because it did not produce many products desired by Eastern elites. Nevertheless, Europeans — especially Venetian and Genoese merchants — sought to tap into the goods and wealth of Afroeurasian commerce.

◻ Why and how did Europeans undertake ambitious voyages of expansion? (p. 465)

A revival of populations and economies after the time of the Black Death created markets for spices and other goods from the East. In addition to searching for routes that would undo the Italian and Ottoman dominance of trade in the East, Europeans were motivated by intellectual curiosity, driving ambition, religious zeal, and a lack of opportunities at home. Strengthened monarchies possessed sufficient resources to back ambitious seafarers like Christopher Columbus, Vasco da Gama, and Ferdinand Magellan. Technological developments such as the invention of the caravel and magnetic compass enabled Europeans to undertake ever more ambitious voyages. Driven by desires for conquest and wealth, Europeans — first Hernando Cortés and then Francisco Pizarro — eventually penetrated farther into the New World than Columbus had.

KEY TERMS

bride wealth (p. 462)
conquistador (p. 465)
caravel (p. 467)
Ptolemy's *Geography* (p. 467)
Treaty of Tordesillas (p. 471)
Mexica Empire (p. 474)
Inca Empire (p. 475)
viceroyalties (p. 476)
encomienda system (p. 477)
Columbian exchange (p. 478)

◻ How did conquest affect indigenous populations and bring about a new era of economic and cultural exchange, commercial empires, and forced migrations? (p. 476)

In the aftermath of conquest, the Spanish established new forms of governance to dominate native peoples and exploit their labor. The arrival of Europeans also brought enormous population losses to native communities, primarily through the spread of infectious diseases. Disease was one element of the Columbian exchange, a complex transfer of germs, plants, and animals between the Old and New Worlds. Although this exchange brought diseases to the Americas, it also gave both the New and Old Worlds new crops that eventually altered consumption patterns internationally. These new cultural linkages were part of the creation of the first truly global economy. Tragically, a major component of global trade was the transatlantic slave trade, in which Europeans transported, under horrific conditions, many thousands of Africans to labor in the sugar plantations and silver mines of the New World. European nations vied for supremacy in global trade, with early Portuguese success in India and Asia being challenged first by the Spanish and then by the Dutch, who took control of trade with the East in the mid-seventeenth century.

◻ How did new encounters shape cultural values and beliefs in Europe and the New World? (p. 481)

Increased contact with the outside world led Europeans to develop new ideas about cultural and racial differences. Europeans had long held negative attitudes about Africans; as the slave trade grew, they began to express more rigid notions of racial inequality and to claim that Africans were inherently suited for slavery. Most Europeans, with some important exceptions, shared such views. In his essays, Michel de Montaigne challenged the idea that natives of the Americas were inferior barbarians, while William Shakespeare's plays contain ambivalent attitudes toward complex non-European characters. Religion became another means of cultural contact, as European missionaries aimed to spread Christianity in the New World, with mixed results. Christianity was especially embraced in Central and South America, where large-scale conversion led to the development of distinct and enduring Catholic cultures. Missionaries were less successful in North America because of the distance between settlements and the lesser integration of native populations into colonial society.

SUGGESTED READING

Crosby, Alfred W. *The Columbian Exchange: Biological and Cultural Consequences of 1492*. 30th anniversary ed. 2003. An innovative and highly influential account of the environmental impact of Columbus's voyages.

Elliot, J. H. *Empires of the Atlantic World: Britain and Spain in America, 1492–1830*. 2006. A masterful account of the differences and similarities between the British and Spanish Empires in the Americas.

Fernández-Armesto, Felip. *Columbus*. 1992. An excellent biography of Christopher Columbus.

Greenblatt, Stephen. *Marvelous Possessions: The Wonder of the New World*. 1991. Describes the cultural impact of New World discoveries on Europeans.

Menard, Russell. *Sweet Negotiations: Sugar, Slavery, and Plantation Agriculture in Early Barbados*. 2006. Explores the intertwined history of sugar plantations and slavery in seventeenth-century Barbados.

Northrup, David, ed. *The Atlantic Slave Trade*. 1994. Collected essays by leading scholars on many different aspects of the slave trade.

Pérez-Mallaína, Pablo E. *Spain's Men of the Sea: Daily Life on the Indies Fleet in the Sixteenth Century*. 1998. A description of recruitment, daily life, and career paths of ordinary sailors and officers in the Spanish fleet.

Pomeranz, Kenneth, and Steven Topik. *The World That Trade Created: Society, Culture, and the World Economy, 1400 to the Present*. 1999. Explores the creation of a world market through the rich and vivid stories of merchants, miners, slaves, and farmers.

Restall, Matthew. *Seven Myths of Spanish Conquest*. 2003. A re-examination of common ideas about why and how the Spanish conquered native civilizations in the New World.

Scammell, Geoffrey V. *The World Encompassed: The First European Maritime Empires, c. 800–1650*. 1981. A detailed overview of the first European empires, including the Italian city-states, Portugal, and Spain.

Schmidt, Benjamin. *Innocence Abroad: The Dutch Imagination and the New World, 1570–1670*. 2001. Examines changing Dutch attitudes toward the New World, from criticism of the cruelty of the Spanish conquest to eagerness for their own overseas empire.

Subrahamanyam, Sanjay. *The Career and Legend of Vasco da Gama*. 1998. A probing biography that places Vasco da Gama in the context of Portuguese politics and society.

NOTES

1. Thomas Benjamin, *The Atlantic World: Europeans, Africans, Indians and Their Shared History, 1400–1900* (Cambridge, U.K.: Cambridge University Press, 2009), p. 56.
2. A. Reid, *Southeast Asia in the Age of Commerce, 1450–1680*. Vol. 1: *The Land Under the Winds* (New Haven, Conn.: Yale University Press, 1988), pp. 3–20.
3. Quoted in C. M. Cipolla, *Guns, Sails, and Empires: Technological Innovation and the Early Phases of European Expansion, 1400–1700* (New York: Minerva Press, 1965), p. 132.
4. Quoted in F. H. Littell, *The Macmillan Atlas: History of Christianity* (New York: Macmillan, 1976), p. 75.
5. Quoted in R. L. Kagan, "The Spain of Ferdinand and Isabella," in *Circa 1492: Art in the Age of Exploration*, ed. J. A. Levenson (Washington, D.C.: National Gallery of Art, 1991), p. 60.
6. Benjamin, *The Atlantic World*, p. 141.
7. Ibid., pp. 35–59.
8. Quoted in C. Gibson, ed., *The Black Legend: Anti-Spanish Attitudes in the Old World and the New* (New York: Knopf, 1971), pp. 74–75.
9. Herbert S. Klein, "Profits and the Causes of Mortality," in *The Atlantic Slave Trade*, ed. David Northrup (Lexington, Mass.: D. C. Heath and Co., 1994), p. 116.
10. Quoted in James H. Sweet, "The Iberian Roots of American Racist Thought," *The William and Mary Quarterly*, Third Series, 54 (Jan. 1997): 155.
11. Quoted in Sean J. Connolly, *Contested Island: Ireland, 1460–1630* (Oxford, U.K.: Oxford University Press, 2007), p. 397.
12. C. Cotton, trans., *The Essays of Michel de Montaigne* (New York: A. L. Burt, 1893), pp. 207, 210.
13. Ibid., p. 523.
14. David Carrasco, *The Oxford Encyclopedia of Mesoamerican Cultures* (Oxford: Oxford University Press, 2001), p. 208.

For practice quizzes and other study tools, visit the **Online Study Guide** at bedfordstmartins.com/mckayworld.

For primary sources from this period, see *Sources of World Societies*, **Second Edition**.

For Web sites, images, and documents related to topics in this chapter, visit **Make History** at bedfordstmartins.com/mckayworld.

• **Louis XIV** Representations of royal power emphasized the aristocratic bearing, elegance, and innate authority of absolutist kings. This was one of Louis XIV's favorite portraits of himself. He liked it so much that he had many copies of the portrait made, in full and half-size format. (Louvre/Giraudon/The Bridgeman Art Library)

17

The seventeenth century was a period of crisis and transformation in Europe. What one historian described as the long European "struggle for stability" that originated with conflicts sparked by the Reformation in the early sixteenth century and continued with economic and social breakdown was largely resolved by 1680.[1] To meet the demands of war, armies grew larger, taxes increased, and new bureaucracies came into being. Thus at the same time that powerful governments were emerging and evolving in Asia — such as the Qing Dynasty in China, the Tokugawa Shogunate in Japan (see Chapter 21), and the Mughal Empire in India (see Chapter 20) — European rulers also increased the power of the central state.

Important differences existed, however, in terms of which authority within the state possessed sovereignty — the Crown or privileged groups. Between roughly 1589 and 1715 two basic patterns of government emerged in Europe: absolute monarchy and the constitutional state. Almost all subsequent European governments have been modeled on one of these patterns, which have also influenced greatly the rest of the world in the past three centuries.

European Power and Expansion

1500-1750

Constitutional or absolutist, European states sought to further increase their power through colonial expansion. Jealous of the silver that had flowed into Spain from the New World, England, France, and the Netherlands vied for new acquisitions on the mainland and in the Caribbean. •

Estonian Serfs in the 1660s The Estonians were conquered by German military nobility in the Middle Ages and reduced to serfdom. The German-speaking nobles ruled the Estonian peasants with an iron hand, and Peter the Great reaffirmed their domination when Russia annexed Estonia. (Mansell Collection/Time Life Pictures/Getty Images)

Seventeenth-Century Crisis and Rebuilding

☐ What were the common crises and achievements of seventeenth-century European states?

Historians often refer to the seventeenth century as an "age of crisis." After the economic and demographic growth of the sixteenth century, Europe was challenged by population losses, economic decline, and social and political unrest. These difficulties were partially due to climate changes that reduced agricultural productivity. But they also resulted from religious divides, increased taxation, and war. Peasants and the urban poor were hit especially hard by the economic problems, and peasants took action against rising food prices, sometimes rioting for food to obtain relief. In the long run, however, governments proved increasingly able to impose their will on the populace. This period witnessed a spectacular growth in army size as well as increased taxation, expansion of government bureaucracies, and strides toward state sovereignty.

Crises Among Peasants and the Urban Poor

In the seventeenth century a period of colder and wetter climate throughout Europe, dubbed the "little ice age" by historians, meant a shorter growing season with lower yields. The result was recurrent famines that significantly reduced the population of early modern Europe. Most people did not die of outright starvation, but rather of diseases brought on by malnutrition and exhaustion. Facilitated by the weakened population, outbreaks of the Black Death (bubonic plague) continued in Europe until the 1720s.

In 1651 the estates of Normandy, a provincial assembly, reported on the dire conditions in northern France during an outbreak of plague in which disease was compounded by the disruption of agriculture and a lack of food:

> Of the 450 sick persons whom the inhabitants were unable to relieve, 200 were turned out, and these we saw die one by one as they lay on the roadside. A large number still remain, and to each of them it is only possible to dole out the least scrap of bread. We only give bread to those who would otherwise die. The staple dish here consists of mice, which the inhabitants hunt, so desperate are they from hunger. They devour roots which the animals cannot eat; one can, in fact, not put into words the things one sees.[2]

When food prices were high, industry also suffered because consumers had little money to purchase goods.

The result was low wages and widespread unemployment, which further exacerbated economic problems. The output of woolen textiles, one of the most important manufactured products from Europe, declined sharply in many parts of Europe in the first half of the seventeenth century. This economic crisis was not universal: it struck various regions at different times and to different degrees. In the middle decades of the century, Spain, France, Germany, and England all experienced great economic difficulties. In the Netherlands, however, an influx of foreign capital, among other factors, made these years a golden age (see page 515).

The urban poor and peasants were the hardest hit. When the price of bread rose beyond their capacity to pay, they frequently expressed their anger by rioting. In towns they invaded bakers' shops to seize bread and resell it at a "just price." In rural areas they attacked convoys taking grain to the cities. Women often led these actions, since their role as mothers gave them some protection against punishment by authorities. Historians have labeled this vision of a world in which community needs predominate over competition and profit a moral economy.

The Return of Serfdom in Eastern Europe

While economic and social hardship was common across Europe, important differences existed between east and west. In the west the demographic losses of the Black Death allowed peasants to escape the bonds of working the landed estate of a lord (serfdom) as they acquired enough land to feed themselves and the livestock and ploughs necessary to work their land. In eastern Europe, however, the Black Death had the opposite effect, and peasants largely lost their ability to own land independently. Before the arrival of the plague, starting in about 1050, rulers and nobles in eastern Europe had attracted new settlers to their sparsely populated estates by offering them land on excellent terms and granting them much personal freedom. But in the fourteenth century eastern lords addressed labor shortages caused by the Black Death by restricting the right of their peasants to move to take advantage of better opportunities elsewhere. Moreover, lords steadily took

more and more of their peasants' land and arbitrarily imposed heavier and heavier labor obligations. By the early 1500s lords in many eastern territories could command their peasants to work for them without pay for as many as six days a week.

The power of the lord reached far into serfs' everyday lives. Not only was their freedom of movement restricted, but they required permission to marry or could be forced to marry. Lords could reallocate the lands worked by their serfs at will or break up serf families by selling individual members. The local lord also monopolized the legal system, acting as prosecutor, judge, and jailer. There were no independent royal officials to provide justice or uphold the common law.

Between 1500 and 1650 the consolidation of serfdom in eastern Europe was accompanied by the growth of commercial agriculture, particularly in Poland and

□ CHRONOLOGY

ca. 1500–1650 Consolidation of serfdom in eastern Europe

1533–1584 Reign of Ivan the Terrible in Russia

1589–1610 Reign of Henry IV in France

1598–1613 Time of Troubles in Russia

1612–1697 Caribbean islands colonized by France, England, and the Netherlands

1620–1740 Growth of absolutism in Austria and Prussia

1642–1649 English civil war, ending with the execution of Charles I

1643–1715 Reign of Louis XIV in France

1651 First of the Navigation Acts

1653–1658 Oliver Cromwell's military rule in England (the Protectorate)

1660 Restoration of English monarchy under Charles II

1665–1683 Jean-Baptiste Colbert applies mercantilism to France

1670 Charles II agrees to re-Catholicize England in secret agreement with Louis XIV

1670–1671 Cossack revolt led by Stenka Razin

1682 Louis XIV moves court to Versailles

1682–1725 Reign of Peter the Great in Russia

1683–1718 Habsburgs push the Ottoman Turks from Hungary

1685 Edict of Nantes revoked

1688–1689 Glorious Revolution in England

1701–1713 War of the Spanish Succession

eastern Germany. As economic expansion and population growth resumed after 1500, eastern lords increased the production of their estates by squeezing sizable surpluses out of the impoverished peasants. They then sold these surpluses to foreign merchants, who exported them to the growing cities of wealthier western Europe.

The worsened conditions for serfs in eastern Europe reflected the fact that eastern lords enjoyed much greater political power than their western counterparts. In the late Middle Ages, when much of eastern Europe was experiencing innumerable wars and general public chaos, the noble landlord class had greatly increased its political power at the expense of the ruling monarchs. Moreover, the western concept of a king as one who protects the interests of all his people was not well developed in eastern Europe before 1650.

With the approval of weak kings, landlords in eastern Europe systematically undermined the medieval privileges of the towns and the power of the urban classes. For example, eastern towns lost their medieval right to provide refuge to runaways and were compelled to return escaped peasants to their lords. The populations of the towns and the urban middle classes declined greatly. This development both reflected and promoted the supremacy of noble landlords in most of eastern Europe in the sixteenth century. Although noble landlords held onto their powers in the seventeenth century, kings increased their authority during this period (see pages 501–509).

The Thirty Years' War

In the first half of the seventeenth century, the fragile balance of life was violently upturned by the ravages of the Thirty Years' War (1618–1648). Leading up to the war were conflicts between Catholics and Protestants in the Holy Roman Empire, a confederation of hundreds of principalities, independent cities, duchies, and other polities loosely united under an elected emperor. Although the emperor was Catholic, Protestantism had started to take hold in parts of the empire, including Germany, and clashes resulted. In 1555 the two religious groups came to an uneasy truce under the Peace of Augsburg, which officially recognized Lutheranism and allowed political authorities in each German territory to decide whether the territory would be Catholic or Lutheran. But the truce deteriorated as the faiths of various areas shifted. Lutheran princes felt compelled to form the Protestant Union (1608), and Catholics retaliated with the Catholic League (1609). Each alliance was determined that the other should make no religious

or territorial advance. Dynastic interests were also involved; the Spanish Habsburgs strongly supported the goals of their Austrian relatives: the unity of the empire and the preservation of Catholicism within it.

The war is traditionally divided into four phases. The first, or Bohemian, phase (1618–1625) was characterized by civil war in Bohemia (part of the present-day Czech Republic) between the Catholic League and the Protestant Union. In 1620 Catholic forces defeated Protestants at the Battle of the White Mountain. The second, or Danish, phase of the war (1625–1629) — so called because of the leadership of the Protestant king Christian IV of Denmark (r. 1588–1648) — witnessed additional Catholic victories.

The third, or Swedish, phase of the war (1630–1635) began with the arrival in Germany of the Swedish king Gustavus Adolphus (r. 1594–1632) and his army. The ablest administrator of his day and a devout Lutheran, he intervened to support the empire's Protestants. The French chief minister, Cardinal Richelieu, subsidized the Swedes, hoping to weaken Habsburg power in Europe. Gustavus Adolphus won two important battles but was fatally wounded in combat. The final, or French, phase of the war (1635–1648) was prompted by Richelieu's concern that the Habsburgs, France's greatest rival for power, would rebound after the death of Gustavus Adolphus. Richelieu declared war on Spain and sent military as well as financial assistance. Finally, in October 1648 peace was achieved.

The 1648 **Peace of Westphalia** that ended the Thirty Years' War marked a turning point in European history. The treaties that established the peace not only ended conflicts fought over religious faith but also recognized the independent authority of more than three hundred German princes (Map 17.1), reconfirming the emperor's severely limited authority. The Augsburg agreement of 1555 became permanent, adding Calvinism to Catholicism and Lutheranism as legally permissible creeds. The north German states remained Protestant; the south German states, Catholic.

The Thirty Years' War was probably the most destructive event for the central European economy and society prior to the world wars of the twentieth century. Perhaps one-third of urban residents and two-fifths of the rural population died, leaving entire areas depopulated. Trade in southern German cities was virtually destroyed. Agricultural areas also suffered catastrophically. Many small farmers lost their land, allowing nobles to enlarge their estates and consolidate their control.[3]

Achievements in State Building

In this context of economic and demographic depression, monarchs began to make new demands on their people. Traditionally, historians have distinguished be-

---

• **Peace of Westphalia** The name of a series of treaties that concluded the Thirty Years' War in 1648 and marked the end of large-scale religious violence in Europe.

MAP 17.1 Europe After the Thirty Years' War Which country emerged from the Thirty Years' War as the strongest European power? What dynastic house was that country's major rival in the early modern period?

tween the absolutist governments of France, Spain, eastern and central Europe, and Russia and the constitutionalist governments of England and the Dutch Republic. Whereas absolutist monarchs gathered all power under their personal control, English and Dutch rulers were obliged to respect laws passed by representative institutions. More recently, historians have emphasized commonalities among these powers. Despite their political differences, all these states sought to protect and expand their frontiers, raise new taxes, consolidate central control, and compete for the colonies opening up in the New and Old Worlds.

Rulers who wished to increase their authority encountered formidable obstacles. Without paved roads, telephones, or other modern technology, it took weeks to convey orders from the central government to the provinces. Rulers also suffered from lack of information about their realms, making it impossible to police and tax the population effectively. Local power structures presented another serious obstacle. Nobles, the church, provincial and national assemblies, town councils, guilds, and other bodies held legal privileges that could not easily be rescinded. In some kingdoms many people spoke a language different from the Crown's, further diminishing their willingness to obey the Crown's commands.

Nonetheless, over the course of the seventeenth century both absolutist and constitutional governments achieved new levels of central control. This increased authority focused on four areas in particular: greater taxation, growth in armed forces, larger and more efficient bureaucracies, and the increased ability to compel obedience from subjects. Over time, centralized power added up to something close to sovereignty. A state may be termed sovereign when it possesses a monopoly over the instruments of justice and the use of force within clearly defined boundaries. In a sovereign state, no nongovernmental system of courts, such as ecclesiastical tribunals, competes with state courts in the dispensation of justice. Also, private armies, such as those of feudal lords, present no threat to central authority. While seventeenth-century states did not acquire total sovereignty, they made important strides toward that goal.

Absolutism in France and Spain

◻ Why and how did the French absolutist state arise under Louis XIV, and why did absolutist Spain experience decline in the same period?

Kings in absolutist states asserted that, because they were chosen by God, they were responsible to God alone. They claimed exclusive power to make and enforce laws, denying any other institution or group the authority to check their power. Louis XIV of France is often seen as the epitome of an absolute monarch. In truth, his success relied on collaboration with nobles, and thus his example illustrates both the achievements and the compromises of absolutist rule.

As French power rose in the seventeenth century, the glory of Spain faded. Once the fabulous revenue from American silver declined, Spain's economic stagnation could no longer be disguised, and the country faltered under weak leadership.

The Foundations of Absolutism

Louis XIV's absolutism had long roots. In 1589 his grandfather Henry IV (r. 1589–1610), the founder of the Bourbon dynasty, acquired a devastated country. Civil wars between Protestants and Catholics had wracked France since 1561. Poor harvests had reduced peasants to starvation, and commercial activity had declined drastically.

Henry IV inaugurated a remarkable recovery by keeping France at peace during most of his reign. Although he had converted to Catholicism, he issued the Edict of Nantes, allowing Huguenots (French Protestants) the right to worship in 150 traditionally Protes-

tant towns throughout France. He sharply lowered taxes and instead charged royal officials an annual fee to guarantee the right to pass their positions down to their heirs. He also improved the country's infrastructure, building new roads and canals and repairing the ravages of years of civil war. Despite his efforts at peace, Henry was murdered in 1610 by a Catholic zealot.

After the death of Henry IV his wife, the queen-regent Marie de' Medici, headed the government for their eldest son, nine-year-old Louis XIII (r. 1610–1643). In 1628 Armand Jean du Plessis — Cardinal Richelieu (1585–1642) — became first minister of the French crown. Richelieu's maneuvers allowed the monarchy to maintain power within Europe and within its own borders despite the turmoil of the Thirty Years' War.

Cardinal Richelieu's domestic policies were designed to strengthen royal control. He extended the use of intendants, commissioners for each of France's thirty-two districts who were appointed directly by the monarch, to whom they were solely responsible. They recruited men for the army, supervised the collection of taxes, presided over the administration of local law, checked up on the local nobility, and regulated economic activities in their districts. As the intendants' power increased under Richelieu, so did the power of the centralized French state.

Under Richelieu, the French monarchy also acted to repress Protestantism. Louis XIII personally supervised the siege of La Rochelle, an important port city and a major commercial center with strong ties to Protestant Holland and England. The fall of La Rochelle in October 1628 was one step in the removal of Protestantism as a strong force in French life.

Richelieu did not aim to wipe out Protestantism in the rest of Europe, however. His main foreign policy goal was to destroy the Catholic Habsburgs' grip on territories that surrounded France. Consequently, Richelieu supported Habsburg enemies, including Protestants (see page 494). For the French cardinal, interests of state outweighed religious considerations.

In 1642 Cardinal Jules Mazarin (1602–1661) succeeded Richelieu as chief minister for the next child-king, the four-year-old Louis XIV. Along with the regent, Queen Mother Anne of Austria, Mazarin continued Richelieu's centralizing policies. His struggle to increase royal revenues to meet the costs of the Thirty Years' War led to the uprisings of 1648–1653 known as the **Fronde**. In Paris, magistrates of the Parlement of Paris, the nation's most important law court, were outraged by the Crown's autocratic measures. These so-called robe nobles (named for the robes they wore in court) encouraged violent protest by the common people. As rebellion spread outside Paris and to the sword nobles (the traditional warrior nobility), civil order broke down completely, and young Louis XIV had to flee Paris for his safety. In 1651 Anne's regency

Louis XIV Receiving Ambassadors from Siam
The kings of France and Siam (today's Thailand) sent ambassadors to each other's courts in the 1680s. This engraving commemorates Louis XIV's reception of the second Siamese diplomatic mission at Versailles, a visit that aroused great excitement and enthusiasm throughout western Europe. (Private Collection/Photo © Luca Tettoni/The Bridgeman Art Library)

ended with the declaration of Louis as king in his own right. Much of the rebellion died away, and its leaders came to terms with the government.

The twin evils of noble rebellion and popular riots left the French wishing for peace and for a strong monarch to reimpose order. This was the legacy that Louis XIV inherited when he assumed personal rule of the largest and most populous country in western Europe. Humiliated by his flight from Paris during the Fronde, he was determined to avoid any recurrence of rebellion when he assumed personal rule at Mazarin's death in 1661.

Louis XIV and Absolutism

In the long reign of Louis XIV (r. 1643–1715) the French monarchy reached the peak of absolutist development. Louis believed in the doctrine of the divine right of kings: God had established kings as his rulers on earth, and they were answerable ultimately to him alone. However, though kings were divinely anointed and shared in the sacred nature of divinity, they could not simply do as they pleased. They had to obey God's laws and rule for the good of the people. To symbolize his central role in the divine order, when he was fifteen years old Louis danced at a court ballet dressed as the sun, thereby acquiring the title "Sun King."

Louis worked very hard at the business of governing. He ruled his realm through several councils of state and insisted on taking a personal role in many of the councils' decisions. He selected councilors from the recently ennobled or the upper middle class because he believed "that the public should know, from the rank of those whom I chose to serve me, that I had no intention of sharing power with them."[4] Despite increasing financial problems, Louis never called a meeting of the Estates General, the traditional French representative assembly composed of the three estates of clergy, nobility, and commoners. The French people, and its noble leaders, therefore, had no means to form united views or exert joint pressure on the monarch.

• **Fronde** A series of violent uprisings early in the reign of Louis XIV triggered by growing royal control and oppressive taxation.

Also, Louis freed himself from the inordinate power of a Richelieu by not appointing a first minister.

Although personally tolerant, Louis hated division within the realm and insisted that religious unity was essential to his royal dignity and to the security of the state. He thus pursued the policy of Protestant repression launched by Richelieu. In 1685 Louis revoked the Edict of Nantes and took steps to suppress the Huguenots.

Despite his claims to absolute authority, there were multiple constraints on Louis's power. As a representative of divine power, he was obliged to rule in a way that seemed consistent with virtue and benevolent authority. He had to uphold the laws issued by his royal predecessors. Moreover, he also relied on the collaboration of nobles, who maintained authority in their ancestral lands. Without their cooperation, it would have been impossible for Louis to extend his power throughout France or wage his many foreign wars (see page 499). His need to elicit noble cooperation led him to revolutionize court life at his palace at Versailles.

Life at Versailles

Through most of the seventeenth century, the French court had no fixed home, following the monarch to his numerous palaces and country residences. In 1682 Louis moved his court and government to the newly renovated palace at Versailles, in the countryside southwest of Paris. The palace quickly became the center of political, social, and cultural life. The king required all great nobles to spend at least part of the year in attendance on him there. Since he controlled the distribution of state power and wealth, nobles had no choice but to obey and compete with each other for his favor at Versailles.

Louis further revolutionized court life by establishing an elaborate set of etiquette rituals to mark every moment of his day, from waking up and dressing in the morning to removing his clothing and retiring at night. He required nobles to serve him in these rituals, and they vied for the honor of doing so. Endless squabbles broke out over what type of chair one could sit on at court and the order in which great nobles entered and were seated in the chapel for Mass.

These rituals may seem absurd, but they were far from meaningless or trivial. The king controlled immense resources and privileges; access to him meant favored treatment for government offices, military and religious posts, state pensions, honorary titles, and a host of other benefits. The Duke of Saint-Simon wrote

of the king's power at court in his memoirs:

> No one understood better than Louis XIV the art of enhancing the value of a favour by his manner of bestowing it; he knew how to make the most of a word, a smile, even of a glance. If he addressed any one, were it but to ask a trifling question or make some commonplace remark, all eyes were turned on the person so honored; it was a mark of favour which always gave rise to comment.[5]

Courtiers sought these rewards for themselves and their family members and followers. A system of patronage — in which a higher-ranked individual protected a lower-ranked one in return for loyalty and services — flowed from the court to the provinces. Through this mechanism Louis gained cooperation from powerful nobles.

Although they were denied public offices and posts, women played a central role in the patronage system. At court the king's wife, mistresses, and other female relatives recommended individuals for honors, advocated policy decisions, and brokered alliances between noble factions. Noblewomen played a similar role among courtiers, bringing their family connections into their marriages to form powerful social networks.

Louis XIV was also an enthusiastic patron of the arts. He commissioned many sculptures and paintings for Versailles as well as performances of dance and music. Louis loved the stage, and in the plays of Molière and Racine his court witnessed the finest achievements in the history of the French theater.

With Versailles as the center of European politics, French culture grew in international prestige. French became the language of polite society and international diplomacy, gradually replacing Latin as the language of scholarship and learning. The royal courts of Sweden, Russia, Poland, and Germany all spoke French. France inspired a cosmopolitan European culture in the late seventeenth century that looked to Versailles as its center.

French Finances

France's ability to build armies and fight wars depended on a strong economy. Fortunately for Louis, his controller general, Jean-Baptiste Colbert (1619–1683), proved to be a financial genius. Colbert's central principle was that the wealth and the economy of France should serve the state. To this end, from 1665 to his death in 1683, Colbert rigorously applied mercantilist policies to France.

Mercantilism is a collection of governmental policies for the regulation of economic activities by and for the state. It derives from the idea that a nation's international power is based on its wealth, specifically its

• mercantilism A system of economic regulations aimed at increasing the power of the state based on the belief that a nation's international power was based on its wealth, specifically its supply of gold and silver.

supply of gold and silver. To accumulate wealth, a country always had to sell more goods abroad than it bought. Thus, to reduce imports Colbert insisted that French industry should produce everything needed by the French people.

To increase exports, Colbert supported old industries and created new ones. He enacted new production regulations, created guilds to boost quality standards, and encouraged foreign craftsmen to immigrate to France. To encourage the purchase of French goods, he abolished many domestic tariffs and raised tariffs on foreign products. In 1664 Colbert founded the Company of the East Indies with (unfulfilled) hopes of competing with the Dutch for Asian trade. Colbert also sought to increase France's control over and presence in New France (Canada)—rich in untapped minerals and some of the best agricultural land in the world (see page 516).

During Colbert's tenure as controller general, Louis was able to pursue his goals without massive tax increases and without creating a stream of new offices.

The constant pressure of warfare after Colbert's death, however, undid many of his economic achievements.

Louis XIV's Wars

Louis XIV kept France at war for thirty-three of the fifty-four years of his personal rule. François le Tellier, Marquis de Louvois, Louis's secretary of state for war, equaled Colbert's achievements in the economic realm. Louvois created a professional army in the employ of the French state. The French army grew in size from roughly 125,000 men in the Thirty Years' War (1630–1648) to 250,000 during the Dutch War (1672–1678) and 340,000 during the War of the League of Augsburg (1688–1697).[6] Uniforms and weapons were standardized, and a rational system of training and promotion was devised. As in so many other matters, Louis's model was followed across Europe.

During this long period of warfare Louis's goal was to expand France to what he considered its natural borders. His armies managed to extend French borders

Spanish Troops The long wars that Spain fought over Dutch independence, in support of Habsburg interests in Germany, and against France left the country militarily exhausted and financially drained by the mid-1600s. In this detail from a painting by Peeter Snayers, Spanish troops—thin, emaciated, and probably unpaid—straggle away from battle. (Prado, Madrid/Index/The Bridgeman Art Library)

Mapping the Past

MAP 17.2 Europe After the Peace of Utrecht, 1715 The series of treaties commonly called the Peace of Utrecht ended the War of the Spanish Succession and redrew the map of Europe. A French Bourbon king succeeded to the Spanish throne. France surrendered the Spanish Netherlands (later Belgium), then in French hands, to Austria and recognized the Hohenzollern rulers of Prussia. Spain ceded Gibraltar to Great Britain, for which it has been a strategic naval station ever since. Spain also granted Britain the *asiento*, the contract for supplying African slaves to America.

ANALYZING THE MAP Identify the areas on the map that changed hands as a result of the Peace of Utrecht. How did these changes affect the balance of power in Europe?

CONNECTIONS How and why did so many European countries possess scattered or discontiguous territories? What does this suggest about European politics in this period? Does this map suggest potential for future conflict?

to include important commercial centers in the Spanish Netherlands and Flanders as well as the entire province of Franche-Comté between 1667 and 1678. In 1681 Louis seized the city of Strasbourg, and three years later he sent his armies into the province of Lorraine. At that moment the king seemed invincible. In fact, Louis had reached the limit of his expansion. The wars of the 1680s and 1690s brought no additional territories but placed unbearable strains on French resources. Colbert's successors resorted to desperate

measures to finance these wars, including devaluation of the currency and new taxes.

Louis's last war was endured by a French people suffering high taxes, crop failure, and widespread malnutrition and death. This war resulted from a dispute over the rightful successor to the Spanish throne. In 1700 the childless Spanish king Charles II (r. 1665–1700) died. His will bequeathed the Spanish crown and its empire to Philip of Anjou, Louis XIV's grandson (Louis's wife, Maria-Theresa, had been Charles's sister). The will violated a prior treaty by which the European powers had agreed to divide the Spanish possessions between the king of France and the Holy Roman emperor, both brothers-in-law of Charles II. Claiming that he was following both Spanish and French interests, Louis broke with the treaty and accepted the will, thereby triggering the War of the Spanish Succession (1701–1713).

In 1701 the English, Dutch, Austrians, and Prussians formed the Grand Alliance against Louis XIV. War dragged on until 1713, when it was ended by the **Peace of Utrecht**. This series of treaties allowed Louis's grandson Philip to remain king of Spain on the understanding that the French and Spanish crowns would never be united. France surrendered large territories overseas to England (Map 17.2; see also page 519).

The Peace of Utrecht marked the end of French expansion. Thirty-three years of war had given France the rights to all of Alsace (on France's present-day border with Germany and Switzerland) and some commercial centers in the north. But at what price? In 1714 an exhausted France hovered on the brink of bankruptcy. It is no wonder that when Louis XIV died on September 1, 1715, many subjects felt as much relief as they did sorrow.

The Decline of Absolutist Spain

At the beginning of the seventeenth century, France's position appeared extremely weak. Struggling to recover from decades of religious civil war, France could not compete with Spain's European and overseas empire or its mighty military. Yet by the end of the century the countries' positions were reversed.

By the early seventeenth century the seeds of Spanish disaster were sprouting. Between 1610 and 1650 Spanish trade with the colonies in the New World fell 60 percent due to competition from local industries in the colonies and from Dutch and English traders. At the same time, frightful epidemics of disease reduced the number of native Indian and African slaves who toiled in the South American silver mines. Ultimately, the mines that filled the Spanish Empire's treasury started to run dry, and the quantity of metal produced steadily declined after 1620.

In Madrid, royal expenditures constantly exceeded income. To meet mountainous state debt, the Spanish crown repeatedly devalued the coinage and declared bankruptcy, which resulted in the collapse of national credit. Meanwhile, commerce and manufacturing shrank. In the textile industry manufacturers were forced out of business by steep inflation that pushed their production costs to the point where they could not compete in colonial and international markets.[7] To make matters worse, the Crown expelled some three hundred thousand Moriscos, or former Muslims,

in 1609, significantly reducing the pool of skilled workers and merchants.

Spanish aristocrats, attempting to maintain an extravagant lifestyle they could no longer afford, increased the rents on their estates. High rents and heavy taxes drove the peasants from the land, leading to a decline in agricultural productivity. In cities wages and production stagnated.

The Spanish crown had no solutions to these dire problems. Philip III (r. 1598–1621) handed the running of the government over to the duke of Lerma, who used the position to increase his personal and familial wealth. Philip IV (r. 1621–1665) left the management of his several kingdoms to Gaspar de Guzmán, Count-Duke of Olivares. Olivares was an able administrator who has often been compared to Richelieu. He did not lack energy and ideas, and he succeeded in devising new sources of revenue. But he clung to the belief that the solution to Spain's difficulties rested in a return to the imperial tradition of the sixteenth century. Unfortunately, the imperial tradition demanded the revival of war with the Dutch at the expiration of a twelve-year truce in 1622 and a long war with France over Mantua (1628–1659). These conflicts, on top of an empty treasury, brought disaster.

Spain's situation worsened with internal conflicts and fresh military defeats through the remainder of the seventeenth century. In 1640 Spain faced serious revolts in Catalonia and Portugal. In 1643 the French inflicted a crushing defeat on the Spanish army at Rocroi in what is now Belgium. By the Treaty of the Pyrenees of 1659, which ended the French-Spanish conflict, Spain was compelled to surrender extensive territories to France. And in 1688 the Spanish crown reluctantly recognized the independence of Portugal. With these losses the era of Spanish dominance in Europe ended.

Absolutism in Austria, Prussia, and Russia

☐ How did Austrian, Prussian, and Russian rulers transform their nations into powerful absolutist monarchies?

Rulers in eastern and central Europe and in Russia also labored to build strong absolutist states in the seventeenth century. But they built on social and economic foundations far different from those in western Europe, namely serfdom and the strong nobility who

> • **Peace of Utrecht** A series of treaties, from 1713 to 1715, that ended the War of the Spanish Succession, ended French expansion in Europe, and marked the rise of the British Empire.

MAP 17.3 The Growth of Austria and Brandenburg-Prussia to 1748 Austria expanded to the southwest into Hungary and Transylvania at the expense of the Ottoman Empire. It was unable to hold the rich German province of Silesia, however, which was conquered by Brandenburg-Prussia.

benefited from it. The endless wars of the seventeenth century allowed monarchs to increase their power by building large armies, increasing taxation, and suppressing representative institutions. In exchange for their growing political authority, monarchs allowed nobles to remain unchallenged masters of their peasants, a deal that appeased both king and nobility but left serfs at the mercy of the lords.

There were important variations on the absolutist theme in eastern Europe, central Europe, and Russia. The royal absolutism created in Prussia was stronger and more effective than that established in Austria. As for Russia, it developed its own form of absolutism, which was quite different from that of France or even Prussia.

The Austrian Habsburgs

In 1521 Habsburg emperor Charles V ceded power over his Austrian territories to his brother Ferdinand I, thus permanently separating the dynasty into Austrian and Spanish branches. Like all of central Europe, the Austrian Habsburgs emerged from the Thirty Years' War impoverished and exhausted. Their efforts to destroy Protestantism in the German lands and to turn the weak Holy Roman Empire into a real state had failed. Defeat in central Europe encouraged the Austrian Habsburgs to turn away from a quest for imperial dominance and to focus inward and eastward in an attempt to unify their diverse holdings.

Habsburg victory over Bohemia during the Thirty Years' War was an important step in this direction. Ferdinand II (r. 1619–1637) drastically reduced the power of the Bohemian Estates, the largely Protestant representative assembly. He also confiscated the landholdings of Protestant nobles and gave them to loyal Catholic nobles and to the foreign aristocratic mercenaries who led his armies. After 1650 a large portion of the Bohemian nobility was of recent origin and owed its success to the Habsburgs.

With the support of this new nobility, the Habsburgs established direct rule over Bohemia. Under their rule the condition of the enserfed peasantry worsened substantially, and Protestantism was stamped out. These changes were important steps in creating absolutist rule in Bohemia.

Ferdinand III (r. 1637–1657) continued to build state power. He centralized the government in the empire's German-speaking provinces, which formed the core Habsburg holdings. For the first time, a permanent standing army was ready to put down any internal opposition.

The Habsburg monarchy then turned east toward Hungary, which had been divided between the Ottomans and the Habsburgs in the early sixteenth century. Between 1683 and 1699 the Habsburgs pushed the Ottomans from most of Hungary and Transylvania. The recovery of all the former kingdom of Hungary was completed in 1718 (Map 17.3).

The Hungarian nobility, despite its reduced strength, effectively thwarted the full development of Habsburg absolutism. Throughout the seventeenth century Hungarian nobles rose in revolt against the Habsburgs. They never triumphed decisively, but neither were they crushed. In 1703, with the Habsburgs bogged down in the War of the Spanish Succession, the Hungarians rose in one last patriotic rebellion under Prince Francis Rákóczy (RAH-cohtsee).

Rákóczy and his forces were eventually defeated, but the Habsburgs agreed to restore many of the traditional privileges of the Hungarian aristocracy in return for the country's acceptance of hereditary Habsburg rule. Thus Hungary was never fully integrated into a centralized, absolute Habsburg state. Despite checks on their ambitions in Hungary, the Habsburgs made significant achievements in state-building elsewhere by forging consensus with the church and the nobility.

Prussia in the Seventeenth Century

In the fifteenth and sixteenth centuries the Hohenzollern family ruled parts of eastern Germany as the

A Prussian Giant Grenadier Frederick William I wanted tall, handsome soldiers. He dressed them in tight bright uniforms to distinguish them from the peasant population from which most soldiers came. He also ordered several portraits of his favorites, such as this one, from his court painter, J. C. Merk. Grenadiers wore the miter cap instead of an ordinary hat so that they could hurl their heavy grenades unimpeded by a broad brim. (The Royal Collection © 2011, Her Majesty Queen Elizabeth II)

imperial electors of Brandenburg and the dukes of Prussia, but they had little real power. Although the elector of Brandenburg enjoyed the right to help choose the Holy Roman emperor, nothing would suggest that the Hohenzollern territories would come to play an important role in European affairs.

When he came to power, twenty-year-old Frederick William (r. 1640–1688), later known as the Great Elector, was determined to unify his three provinces and enlarge them by diplomacy and war. These provinces were Brandenburg; Prussia, inherited in 1618; and scattered holdings along the Rhine inherited in 1614 (see Map 17.3). Each had its own representative assembly, or estates, and taxes could not be levied without their consent. The estates of Brandenburg and Prussia were dominated by the nobility and the landowning classes, known as the **Junkers**.

In 1660 Frederick William persuaded Junkers in the estates to accept taxation without consent in order to fund a permanent army. They agreed to do so in exchange for reconfirmation of their own privileges, including authority over the serfs. Opposition from the towns was crushed ruthlessly.

Thereafter, the estates' power declined rapidly, for the Great Elector had both financial independence and superior force. State revenue tripled during his reign, and the army expanded dramatically. In 1688 a population of one million supported a peacetime standing army of thirty thousand. In 1701 the elector's son, Frederick I, received the elevated title of king of

Junkers The nobility of Brandenburg and Prussia; they were reluctant allies of Frederick William in his consolidation of the Prussian state.

> ❝A formidable army and a war chest large enough to make this army mobile in times of need can create great respect for you in the world, so that you can speak a word like the other powers.❞

KING FREDERICK WILLIAM I

Prussia (instead of elector) as a reward for aiding the Holy Roman emperor in the War of the Spanish Succession.

The Consolidation of Prussian Absolutism

The son of the first king of Prussia, Frederick William I (r. 1713–1740), completed his grandfather's work, eliminating the last traces of parliamentary estates and local self-government. Known as "the Soldiers' King," Frederick William firmly established Prussian absolutism and transformed Prussia into a military state. He summed up his life's philosophy in his instructions to his son: "A formidable army and a war chest large enough to make this army mobile in times of need can create great respect for you in the world, so that you can speak a word like the other powers."[8]

Twelfth in Europe in population, Prussia had the fourth largest army by 1740. The Prussian army was the best-trained in Europe, astonishing foreign observers with its precision, skill, and discipline. As one western traveler put it:

> There is no theatre in Berlin whatsoever, diversion is understood to be the handsome troops who parade daily. A special attraction is the great Potsdam Grenadier Regiment . . . when they practice drill, when they fire and when they parade up and down, it is as if they form a single body.[9]

In spite of his restrictive rule, Frederick William and his ministers built an exceptionally honest and conscientious bureaucracy to administer the country and foster economic development. Nevertheless, Prussians paid a heavy and lasting price for bureaucratic and military achievements. Civil society became rigid and highly disciplined. As a Prussian minister later summed up, "To keep quiet is the first civic duty."[10] Thus the policies of Frederick

William I, combined with harsh peasant bondage and Junker tyranny, laid the foundations for a highly militaristic country.

Frederick II (r. 1740–1786), commonly known as Frederick the Great, built masterfully on the work of his father. When the young Maria Theresa of Austria inherited the Habsburg dominions upon the death of her father Charles VI, Frederick was quick to make use of the splendid army his own father had left him. He invaded Austria's rich, mainly German province of Silesia, defying solemn Prussian promises to respect the Pragmatic Sanction, a diplomatic agreement that had guaranteed Maria Theresa's succession. In 1742, as other powers vied for her lands in the European War of the Austrian Succession (1740–1748), Maria Theresa was forced to cede almost all of Silesia to Prussia. In one stroke Prussia had doubled its population to 6 million people. Now Prussia unquestionably towered above all the other German states and stood as a European Great Power.

Mongol Rule in Russia and the Rise of Moscow

Absolutism in Russia had its roots in two hundred years of rule under the king (khan) of the Mongols, a group of nomadic tribes from present-day Mongolia. These tribes had come together under Chinggis Khan (ca. 1162–1227). In the thirteenth century the Mongols conquered Kievan Rus, the medieval Slavic state centered first at Novgorod and then at Kiev, a city on the

Dnieper River, which included most of present-day Ukraine, Belarus, and part of northwest Russia. The Mongols forced the Slavic princes to submit to their rule and to give them tribute and slaves. The princes of the Grand Duchy of Moscow, a principality within Kievan Rus, became particularly adept at serving the Mongols. They loyally put down uprisings and collected the khan's taxes. Eventually the Muscovite princes were able to destroy the other princes who were their rivals for power. Ivan III (r. 1462–1505), known as Ivan the Great, successfully expanded the principality of Moscow eastward toward the Baltic Sea and westward to the Ural Mountains and the Siberian frontier.

By 1480 Ivan III felt strong enough to stop acknowledging the khan as his supreme ruler. To legitimize their new autonomy, he and his successors

The Expansion of Russia, to 1725

Russian Peasant An eighteenth-century French artist visiting Russia recorded his impressions of the daily life of the Russian people in this etching of a fish merchant pulling his wares through a snowy village on a sleigh. Two caviar vendors behind him make a sale to a young mother standing at her doorstep with her baby in her arms. (From Jean-Baptiste Le Prince's second set of Russian etchings, 1765. Private Collection/www.amis-paris-petersbourg.org)

declared themselves to be autocrats, meaning that they were the sole source of power. The Muscovite state also borrowed Mongol institutions such as the tax system, postal routes, and the census. Loyalty from the highest-ranking nobles, or **boyars**, helped the Muscovite princes consolidate their power.

Another source of legitimacy lay in Moscow's claim to the political and religious inheritance of the Byzantine Empire. After the empire's capital, Constantinople, fell to the Turks in 1453, the princes of Moscow saw themselves as the heirs of both the caesars (or emperors) and of Orthodox Christianity. Ivan III's marriage to the daughter of the last Byzantine emperor enhanced Moscow's claim to have inherited imperial authority. The title *tsar*, first taken by Ivan IV in 1547, is a contraction of *caesar*.

The Tsar and His People

Developments in Russia took a chaotic turn with the reign of Ivan IV (r. 1533–1584), the famous Ivan the Terrible, who ascended to the throne at age three. His mother died, possibly poisoned, when he was eight,

leaving Ivan to suffer insults and neglect from the boyars at court. At age sixteen he suddenly pushed aside his hated advisers and crowned himself tsar.

Ivan's reign was successful in defeating the remnants of Mongol power, adding vast new territories to the realm, and laying the foundations for the huge multiethnic Russian empire. After the sudden death of his beloved first wife, Anastasia Romanov, however, Ivan began a campaign of persecution against those he suspected of opposing him. Many were intimates of the court from leading boyar families, whom he killed along with their families, friends, servants, and peasants. To further crush the power of the boyars, Ivan created a new service nobility, who received noble titles and estates in return for serving in the tsar's army.

Ivan also moved toward making all commoners servants of the tsar. (See "Listening to the Past: A German Account of Russian Life," page 506.) As landlords demanded more from the peasants who survived the wars and persecutions, growing numbers of them fled

• **boyars** The highest-ranking members of the Russian nobility.

Listening to the Past

A German Account of Russian Life

Seventeenth-century Russia remained a remote and mysterious land for western and even central Europeans, who had few direct contacts with the tsar's dominion. Westerners portrayed eastern Europe as more "barbaric" and less "civilized" than their homelands. Thus they expanded eastern Europe's undeniably harsher social and economic conditions to encompass a very debatable cultural and moral inferiority.

Knowledge of Russia came mainly from occasional travelers who had visited Muscovy and sometimes wrote accounts of what they saw. The most famous of these accounts was by the German Adam Olearius (ca. 1599–1671), who was sent to Moscow on three diplomatic missions in the 1630s. These missions ultimately proved unsuccessful, but they provided Olearius with a rich store of information for his Travels in Muscovy, *from which the following excerpts are taken. Published in German in 1647 and soon translated into several languages (but not Russian), Olearius's unflattering but well-informed study played a major role in shaping European ideas about Russia.*

❝The government of the Russians is what political theorists call a "dominating and despotic monarchy," where the sovereign, that is, the tsar or the grand prince who has obtained the crown by right of succession, rules the entire land alone, and all the people are his subjects, and where the nobles and princes no less than the common folk—townspeople and peasants—are his serfs and slaves, whom he rules and treats as a master treats his servants. . . .

If the Russians be considered in respect to their character, customs, and way of life, they are justly to be counted among the barbarians. . . . The vice of drunkenness is so common in this nation, among people of every station, clergy and laity, high and low, men and women, old and young, that when they are seen now and then lying about in the streets, wallowing in the mud, no attention is paid to it, as something habitual. If a cart driver comes upon such a drunken pig whom he happens to know, he shoves him onto his cart and drives him home, where he is paid his fare. No one ever refuses an opportunity to drink and to get drunk, at any time and in any place, and usually it is done with vodka. . . .

The Russians being naturally tough and born, as it were, for slavery, they must be kept under a harsh and strict yoke and must be driven to do their work with clubs and whips, which they suffer without impatience, because such is their station,

and they are accustomed to it. Young and half-grown fellows sometimes come together on certain days and train themselves in fisticuffs, to accustom themselves to receiving blows, and, since habit is second nature, this makes blows given as punishment easier to bear. Each and all, they are slaves and serfs. . . .

Because of slavery and their rough and hard life, the Russians accept war readily and are well suited to it. On certain occasions, if need be, they reveal themselves as courageous and daring soldiers. . . .

Although the Russians, especially the common populace, living as slaves under a harsh yoke, can bear and endure a great deal out of love for their masters, yet if the pressure is beyond measure, then it can be said of them: "Patience, often wounded, finally turned into fury." A dangerous indignation results, turned not so much against their sovereign as against the lower authorities, especially if the people have been much oppressed by them and by their supporters and have not been protected by the higher authorities. And once they are aroused and enraged, it is not easy to appease them. Then, disregarding all dangers that may ensue, they resort to every kind of violence and behave like madmen. . . . They own little; most of them have no feather beds; they lie on cushions, straw, mats, or their clothes; they sleep on benches and, in winter, like the non-Germans [natives] in Livonia, upon the oven, which serves them for cooking and is flat on the top; here husband, wife, children, servants, and maids huddle together. In some houses in the countryside we saw chickens and pigs under the benches and the ovens. . . . Russians are not used to delicate food and dainties; their daily food consists of porridge, turnips, cabbage, and cucumbers, fresh and pickled, and in Moscow mostly of big salt fish which stink badly, because of the thrifty use of salt, yet are eaten with relish. . . .

The Russians can endure extreme heat. In the bathhouse they stretch out on benches and let themselves be beaten and rubbed with bunches of birch twigs and wisps of bast (which I could not stand); and when they are hot and red all over and so exhausted that they can bear it no longer in the bathhouse, men and women rush outdoors naked and pour cold water over their bodies; in winter they even wallow in the snow and rub their skin with it as if it were soap; then they go back into the hot bathhouse. And since bathhouses are usually near rivers and brooks, they can throw themselves straight from the hot into the cold bath. . . .

● **The brutality of serfdom is shown in this illustration from Olearius's *Travels in Muscovy*.**
(University of Illinois Library, Champaign)

Generally noble families, even the small nobility, rear their daughters in secluded chambers, keeping them hidden from outsiders; and a bridegroom is not allowed to have a look at his bride until he receives her in the bridal chamber. Therefore some happen to be deceived, being given a misshapen and sickly one instead of a fair one, and sometimes a kinswoman or even a maidservant instead of a daughter; of which there have been examples even among the highborn. No wonder therefore that often they live together like cats and dogs and that wife-beating is so common among Russians. . . .

In the Kremlin and in the city there are a great many churches, chapels, and monasteries, both within and without the city walls, over two thousand in all. This is so because every nobleman who has some fortune has a chapel built for himself, and most of them are of stone. The stone churches are round and vaulted inside. . . . They allow neither organs nor any other musical instruments in their churches, saying: Instruments that have neither souls nor life cannot praise God. . . .

In their churches there hang many bells, sometimes five or six, the largest not over two hundredweights. They ring these bells to summon people to church, and also when the priest during mass raises the chalice. In Moscow, because of the multitude of churches and chapels, there are several thousand bells, which during the divine service create such a clang and din that one unaccustomed to it listens in amazement. **99**

Source: G. Vernadsky and R. T. Fisher, Jr., eds., *A Source Book for Russian History from Early Times to 1917*, vol. 1 (New Haven: Yale University Press, 1972), pp. 249–251. Reprinted by permission of Yale University Press.

QUESTIONS FOR ANALYSIS

1. How did Olearius characterize the Russians in general? What evidence did he offer for his judgment?

2. How might Olearius's account help explain Stenka Razin's rebellion (page 508)?

3. On the basis of these passages, why do you think Olearius's book was so popular and influential in central and western Europe?

Peter the Great This compelling portrait by Grigory Musikiysky captures the strength and determination of the warrior-tsar in 1723, after more than three decades of personal rule. In his hand Peter holds the scepter, symbol of royal sovereignty, and across his breastplate is draped an ermine fur, a mark of honor. In the background are the battleships of Russia's new Baltic fleet and the famous St. Peter and St. Paul Fortress that Peter built in St. Petersburg. Peter the Great commissioned this magnificent new crown (left) for himself for his 1682 joint coronation with his half-brother Ivan. (crown: Bildarchiv Preussischer Kulturbesitz/Kremlin Museums, Moscow/The Bridgeman Art Library; portrait: Bildarchiv Preussischer Kulturbesitz/The Bridgeman Art Library)

toward wild, recently conquered territories to the east and south. There they joined free groups and warrior bands known as **Cossacks**. In the 1580s Ivan's government began to forbid peasants to leave their masters, a first step toward the imposition of serfdom on all peasants. (Formerly only those who could not repay debts to their landlords fell into the category of serfs.)

Simultaneously, Ivan bound urban traders and artisans to their towns and jobs so that he could tax them more heavily. These restrictions checked the growth of the Russian middle classes and stood in sharp contrast to developments in western Europe. From nobles down to merchants and peasants, all the Russian people were thus brought into the tsar's service. Ivan even made use of Cossack armies in forays to the southeast, forging a new alliance between Moscow and the Cossacks.

Following Ivan's death, Russia entered a chaotic period known as the Time of Troubles (1598–1613). While Ivan's relatives struggled for power, the Cossacks and peasants rebelled against nobles and officials. This social explosion from below brought the nobles together. They crushed the Cossack rebellion and elected Ivan's grandnephew, Michael Romanov, the new hereditary tsar (r. 1613–1645).

Although the new tsar successfully reconsolidated central authority, social and religious uprisings continued. One of the largest rebellions was led by the Cossack Stenka Razin, who in 1670 attracted a great army of urban poor and peasants, killing landlords and government officials and proclaiming freedom from oppression. In 1671 this rebellion was defeated.

Despite the turbulence of the period, the Romanov tsars, like their Western counterparts, made several important achievements during the second half of the seventeenth century. After a long war, Russia gained land in Ukraine from Poland in 1667 and completed the conquest of Siberia by the end of the century. Territorial expansion was accompanied by growth of the bureaucracy and the army. The great profits from Siberia's natural resources funded the Romanovs' bid for Russia's status as a Great Power. Thus, Russian imperialist expansion to the east paralleled the Western powers' exploration and conquest of the Atlantic world in the same period.

The Reforms of Peter the Great

Heir to Romanov efforts at state-building, Peter the Great (r. 1682–1725) embarked on a tremendous campaign to accelerate and complete these processes. Possessing enormous energy and willpower, Peter was determined to continue the tsarist tradition of territorial expansion.

In 1697 the tsar, who was fascinated by foreign technology, led a group of 250 Russian officials and young nobles on an eighteen-month tour of western European capitals. Traveling unofficially to avoid lengthy diplomatic ceremonies, Peter met with foreign kings and experts. He was particularly impressed with the growing power of the Dutch and the English, and he considered how Russia could profit from their example. He soon had reason to apply what he had learned.

Suffering initial defeat in war with Sweden in 1701, Peter responded with measures designed to increase state power, strengthen his armies, and gain victory. He required all nobles to serve in the army or in the civil administration — for life. Peter also created schools and universities to produce skilled technicians and experts. Furthermore, he established an interlocking military-civilian bureaucracy with fourteen ranks, and he decreed that all had to start at the bottom and work toward the top. Drawing on his experience abroad, Peter sought talented foreigners and placed them in his service. These measures gradually combined to make the army and government more powerful and efficient.

Peter also greatly increased the service requirements of commoners. He established a regular standing army of more than two hundred thousand peasant-soldiers commanded by officers from the nobility. Taxes on peasants to fund the military and other government spending increased threefold during Peter's reign. Serfs were arbitrarily assigned to work in the growing number of factories and mines that supplied the military.

In 1709 Peter's new war machine was able to crush the army of Sweden in Ukraine at Poltava in one of the most significant battles in Russian history. Russia's victory against Sweden was conclusive in 1721, and Estonia and present-day Latvia came under Russian rule for the first time. The cost was high: warfare consumed 80 to 85 percent of all revenues. But Russia became the dominant power in the Baltic and very much a great European power.

After his victory at Poltava, Peter channeled enormous resources into building a new Western-style capital on the Baltic to rival the great cities of Europe. Originally a desolate and swampy Swedish outpost, the magnificent city of St. Petersburg was designed to reflect modern urban planning with wide, straight avenues, buildings set in a uniform line, and large parks.

Each summer, twenty-five to forty thousand peasants were sent to provide construction labor in St. Petersburg without pay.

There were other important consequences of Peter's reign. For Peter, modernization meant westernization, and both Westerners and Western ideas flowed into Russia for the first time. He required nobles to shave their heavy beards and wear Western clothing. He also required them to attend parties where young men and women would mix together and freely choose their own spouses, in defiance of the traditional pattern of strictly controlled marriages. From these efforts a new elite class of Western-oriented Russians began to emerge.

Peter's reforms were unpopular with many Russians. For nobles, one of Peter's most detested reforms was the imposition of unigeniture — inheritance of land by one son alone — cutting off daughters and other sons from family property. For peasants, the reign of the tsar saw a significant increase in the bonds of serfdom, and the gulf between the enserfed peasantry and the educated nobility increased.

Peter's reforms were in some ways a continuation of Russia's distinctive history. He built on the service obligations of Ivan the Terrible and his successors, and his monarchical absolutism can be seen as the culmination of the long development of a unique Russian civilization.

Alternatives to Absolutism in England and the Dutch Republic

☐ Why and how did the constitutional state triumph in England and the Dutch Republic?

While France, Prussia, Russia, and Austria developed absolutist states, England and the Netherlands evolved toward **constitutionalism**, which is the limitation of government by law. Constitutionalism also implies a balance between the authority and power of the government, on the one hand, and the rights and liberties of the subjects, on the other.

- **Cossacks** Free groups and outlaw armies originally comprising runaway peasants living on the borders of Russian territory from the fourteenth century onward. By the end of the sixteenth century they had formed an alliance with the Russian state.

- **constitutionalism** A form of government in which power is limited by law and balanced between the authority and power of the government, on the one hand, and the rights and liberties of the subject or citizen, on the other; it includes constitutional monarchies and republics.

A nation's constitution may be written or unwritten. It may be embodied in one basic document, like the Constitution of the United States. Or it may be only partly formalized and include parliamentary statutes, judicial decisions, and a body of traditional procedures and practices, like the English and Dutch constitutions.

Despite their common commitment to constitutional government, England and the Dutch Republic represented significantly different alternatives to absolute rule. After decades of civil war and an experiment with **republicanism**, the English opted for a constitutional monarchy in 1688. Under this system of government, England retained a monarch as the titular head of government but vested sovereignty in an elected parliament. For their part, the Dutch rejected monarchical rule in 1648, when their independence from Spain was formally recognized. Instead, they adopted a republican form of government in which elected estates (assemblies) held supreme power.

Absolutist Claims in England

Queen Elizabeth I of England (r. 1558–1603) exercised very great personal power. A rare female monarch, she was able to maintain control over her realm in part by refusing to marry and submit to a husband. Elizabeth was immensely popular with her people but left no immediate heir to continue her legacy.

In 1603 Queen Elizabeth's Scottish cousin James Stuart succeeded her as James I (r. 1603–1625). King James was well educated and had thirty-five years' experience as king of Scotland. But he was not as interested in displaying the majesty of monarchy as Elizabeth had been. Urged to wave at the crowds who waited to greet their new ruler, James complained that he was tired and threatened to drop his breeches "so they can cheer at my arse."[11]

James's greatest problem stemmed from his absolutist belief that a monarch has a divine right to his authority and is responsible only to God. James went so far as to lecture the House of Commons (part of the English Parliament): "There are no privileges and immunities which can stand against a divinely appointed

> **❝** There are no privileges and immunities which can stand against a divinely appointed King. **❞**
>
> **KING JAMES I**

King." Such a view ran counter to the long-standing English idea that a person's property could not be taken away without due process of law. James I and his son Charles I (r. 1625–1649) considered such constraints a threat to their divine-right prerogative. Consequently, at every meeting of Parliament between 1603 and 1640, bitter squabbles erupted between the Crown and the House of Commons. Charles I's attempt to govern without Parliament (1629–1640) and to finance his government by emergency taxes brought the country to a crisis.

Religious Divides and Civil War

Religious issues also embittered relations between the king and the House of Commons. In the early seventeenth century increasing numbers of English people felt dissatisfied with the Church of England established by Henry VIII and reformed by Elizabeth. Many **Puritans** believed that the Reformation had not gone far enough. They wanted to "purify" the Anglican Church of Roman Catholic elements — elaborate vestments and ceremonials, bishops, and even the giving and wearing of wedding rings.

James I responded to such ideas by declaring, "No bishop, no king." For James, bishops were among the chief supporters of the throne. His son and successor, Charles I, further antagonized subjects with opposing religious views. Not only did Charles marry a Catholic princess, but he also supported the policies of Archbishop of Canterbury William Laud (1573–1645). In 1637 Laud attempted to impose two new elements on church organization in Scotland: a new prayer book, modeled on the Anglican *Book of Common Prayer*, and bishoprics. The Presbyterian Scots rejected these elements and revolted. To finance an army to put down the Scots, King Charles was compelled to summon Parliament in November 1640.

Charles had ruled from 1629 to 1640 without Parliament, financing his government through extraordinary stopgap levies considered illegal by most English people. Most members of Parliament believed that such taxation without consent amounted to despotism. Consequently, they were not willing to trust the king with an army. Moreover, many supported the Scots' resistance to Charles's religious innovations. Accordingly, this Parliament, called the Long Parliament because it sat from 1640 to 1660, enacted legislation that limited the power of the monarch and made government without Parliament impossible.

In 1641 the House of Commons passed the Triennial Act, which compelled the king to summon Parlia-

---

- **republicanism** A form of government in which there is no monarch and power rests in the hands of the people as exercised through elected representatives.

- **Puritans** Members of a sixteenth- and seventeenth-century reform movement within the Church of England that advocated purifying it of Roman Catholic elements, such as bishops, elaborate ceremonials, and wedding rings.

ment every three years. The Commons also impeached Archbishop Laud and then threatened to abolish bishops. King Charles, fearful of a Scottish invasion — the original reason for summoning Parliament — reluctantly accepted these measures. The next act in the conflict was precipitated by the outbreak of rebellion in Ireland, where English governors and landlords had long exploited the people. In 1641 the Catholic gentry of Ireland led an uprising in response to a feared invasion by anti-Catholic forces of the British Long Parliament.

Without an army, Charles I could neither come to terms with the Scots nor respond to the Irish rebellion. After a failed attempt to arrest parliamentary leaders, Charles left London for the north of England, where he recruited an army. In response, Parliament formed its own army, the New Model Army. During the spring of 1642 both sides prepared for war.

The English civil war (1642–1649) pitted the power of the king against that of the Parliament. After three years of fighting, Parliament's New Model Army defeated the king's armies at the battles of Naseby and Langport in the summer of 1645. Charles refused to concede defeat. Both sides jockeyed for position, waiting for a decisive event. This arrived in the form of the army under the leadership of Oliver Cromwell, a member of the House of Commons and a devout Puritan. In 1647 Cromwell's forces captured the king and dismissed members of the Parliament who opposed Cromwell's actions. In 1649 the remaining representatives, known as the Rump Parliament, put Charles on trial for high treason. Charles was found guilty and beheaded

The English Civil War, 1642–1649

Puritan Occupations
These twelve engravings depict typical Puritan occupations and show that the Puritans came primarily from the artisan and lower middle classes. The governing classes and peasants made up a much smaller percentage of Puritans, and most generally adhered to the traditions of the Church of England.
(Visual Connection Archive)

on January 30, 1649, an act that sent shock waves around Europe.

The Puritan Protectorate

With the execution of Charles, kingship was abolished. The question then became how the country would be governed. One answer was provided by philosopher Thomas Hobbes (1588–1679). Hobbes held a pessimistic view of human nature and believed that, left to themselves, humans would compete violently for power and wealth. The only solution, as he outlined in his 1651 treatise *Leviathan*, was a social contract in which all members of society placed themselves under the absolute rule of a monarch who would maintain peace and order. Hobbes imagined society as a human body in which the monarch served as head and individual subjects together made up the body. Just as the body cannot sever its own head, so Hobbes believed that society could not, having accepted the contract, rise up against its king. For this reason he was deeply shocked by Charles's execution.

Hobbes's longing for a benevolent absolute monarch was not widely shared in England. Instead, a commonwealth, or republican government, was proclaimed. Theoretically, legislative power rested in the surviving members of Parliament, and executive power was lodged in a council of state. In fact, the army that had defeated the king controlled the government, and Oliver Cromwell controlled the army. Though called the **Protectorate**, the rule of Cromwell (1653–1658) was a form of military dictatorship.

The army prepared a constitution, the Instrument of Government (1653), that invested executive power in a lord protector (Cromwell) and a council of state. It provided for triennial parliaments and gave Parliament the sole power to raise taxes. But after repeated disputes, Cromwell dismissed Parliament in 1655, and the instrument was never formally endorsed. Cromwell continued the standing army and proclaimed quasi-martial law. He divided England into twelve military districts, each governed by a major general. Reflecting Puritan ideas of morality, Cromwell's state forbade sports, kept the theaters closed, and rigorously censored the press.

On the issue of religion, Cromwell favored some degree of toleration, and the Instrument of Government gave all Christians except Roman Catholics the right

to practice their faith. Cromwell had long associated Catholicism in Ireland with sedition and heresy, and he led an army there to reconquer the country in August 1649. One month later, his forces crushed a rebellion at Drogheda and massacred the garrison. Following Cromwell's reconquest, the English banned Catholicism in Ireland, executed priests, and confiscated land from Catholics for English and Scottish settlers. These brutal acts left a legacy of Irish hatred for England and had little success in discouraging Catholicism.

The Protectorate collapsed when Cromwell died in 1658 and his ineffectual son succeeded him. Fed up with military rule, the English longed for a return to civilian government and, with it, common law and social stability. By 1660 they were ready to restore the monarchy.

Restoration of the English Monarchy

The Restoration of 1660 brought to the throne Charles II (r. 1660–1685), eldest son of Charles I, formerly exiled in the Netherlands. Both houses of Parliament were also restored, together with the established Anglican Church. The Restoration failed to resolve two serious problems, however. What was to be the attitude of the state toward Puritans, Catholics, and dissenters from the established church? And what was to be the relationship between the king and Parliament?

To answer the first question, Parliament enacted the **Test Act** of 1673 against those outside the Church of England, denying them the right to vote, hold public office, preach, teach at or attend the universities, or even assemble for meetings. In politics Charles II set out to work with Parliament, but this resolve did not last. Finding that Parliament did not grant him an adequate income, in 1670 Charles entered into a secret agreement with his cousin Louis XIV. Under this pact, the French king would give Charles two hundred thousand pounds annually, and in return Charles would relax the laws against Catholics, gradually re-Catholicize England, and convert to Catholicism himself. When the details of this treaty leaked out, a great wave of anti-Catholic sentiment swept England.

When James II (r. 1685–1688) succeeded his brother, the worst fears of English anti-Catholics were realized. In violation of the Test Act, James appointed Roman Catholics to positions in the army, the universities, and local government. And he went further; attempting to broaden his base of support with Protestant dissenters and nonconformists, James granted religious freedom to all.

Seeking to prevent the return of Catholic absolutism, a group of eminent persons in Parliament and the Church of England offered the English throne to James's

---

• **Protectorate** The English military dictatorship established by Oliver Cromwell following the execution of Charles I (1653–1658).

• **Test Act** Legislation passed by the English parliament in 1673 to secure the position of the Anglican Church by stripping Puritans, Catholics, and other dissenters of the right to vote, preach, assemble, hold public office, and attend or teach at the universities.

The Massacre at Drogheda In September 1749 English forces under Oliver Cromwell laid siege to Drogheda, a town on the east coast of Ireland and killed approximately three thousand soldiers and civilians when they entered the town. The Drogheda massacre long fostered hatred of Cromwell and English rule in Ireland. (The Granger Collection, New York)

Protestant daughter Mary and her Dutch husband, Prince William of Orange. In December 1688 James II, his queen, and their infant son fled to France. Early in 1689 William and Mary were crowned king and queen of England.

Constitutional Monarchy

The English call the events of 1688 and 1689 the Glorious Revolution because it replaced one king with another with a minimum of bloodshed. It also represented the destruction, once and for all, of the idea of divine-right monarchy. The revolution established the principle that sovereignty, the ultimate power in the state, was divided between king and Parliament and that the king ruled with the consent of the governed.

The men who brought about the revolution framed their intentions in the Bill of Rights, which was formulated in direct response to the attempts by the Stuart kings to impose absolute rule on England. Law was to be made in Parliament; once made, it could not be suspended by the Crown. Parliament had to be called at least once every three years, and no taxes could be im-

posed without its approval. The independence of the judiciary was also established, and there was to be no standing army in peacetime. In terms of laws regarding religion, Protestants could possess arms, but the Catholic minority could not. No Catholic could ever inherit the throne. Additional legislation granted freedom of worship to Protestant dissenters, but not to Catholics.

The Glorious Revolution and the concept of representative government found its best defense in political philosopher John Locke's *Second Treatise of Civil Government* (1690). Locke (1632–1704) maintained that a government that oversteps its proper function—protecting the natural rights of life, liberty, and property—becomes a tyranny. (See "Viewpoints: The Debate over the Extent of Royal Power in England," page 514.) By "natural rights" Locke meant rights basic to all men because all have the ability to reason. Under a tyrannical government, he argued, the people have the natural right to rebellion.

Although the events of 1688 and 1689 brought England closer to Locke's ideal, they did not constitute a democratic revolution. The Glorious Revolution placed sovereignty in Parliament, and Parliament represented

Viewpoints

The Debate over the Extent of Royal Power in England

• In 1688 King James II of England, fearing a revolution like the one that led to the trial and execution of his grandfather, Charles I, fled to France. The crisis was resolved when Parliament invited James's daughter Mary and her husband, William of Orange, to take the throne. Although the Glorious Revolution shed little blood, it did generate furious debate over the extent of royal power in England. Thomas Cartwright, a bishop of the Church of England, spoke out in defense of James and his God-given right to rule. Taking the opposite side, John Locke argued that sovereign power resided in the people, who could reject a monarch if he set himself above the law. In 1689 William and Mary settled the debate by signing the Petition of Right, which enshrined the rights of Parliament and limited the authority of the monarch.

Thomas Cartwright, A Sermon Preached upon the Anniversary Solemnity of the Inauguration of Our Dread Sovereign Lord King James II

❝Our religion will never suffer us to dispense with our loyalty, to serve any worldly interest or advantage; no, not for its own defense. It sets the crown fast and easy upon the King's head, without catechizing him: for be his heart inclinable to any religion, or none, it leaves him no rival, none to insult or lord it over him. It disclaims all usurpation, popular or papal; neither pope nor presbyter may control him; none but the great God, the only ruler of princes, can over-rule him; to whom 'tis his duty, glory and happiness to be subject. Though the King should not please or humor us; though he should rend off the mantle from our bodies (as Saul did from Samuel) nay though he should sentence us to death (of which, blessed be God and the King, there is no danger), yet if we are living members of the Church of England, we must neither open our mouths, nor lift our hands against him; but honor him before the people and elders of Israel.❞

John Locke, *Two Treatises of Government*

❝But government into whosesoever hands it is put, being as I have before shown, entrusted with this condition, and for this end, that men might have and secure their properties, the prince or senate, however it may have power to make laws for the regulation of property between the subjects one amongst another, yet can never have a power to take to themselves the whole, or any part of the subjects' property without their own consent. For this would be in effect to leave them no property at all.

. . . The constitution of the legislative is the first and fundamental act of society, whereby provision is made for the continuation of their union, under the direction of persons, and bonds of laws, made by persons authorized thereunto, by the consent and appointment of the people, without which no one man, or number of men, amongst them, can have authority of making laws that shall be binding to the rest. When any one, or more, shall take upon them to make laws, whom the people have not appointed so to do, they make laws without authority, which the people are not therefore bound to obey; by which means they come again to be out of subjection, and may constitute to themselves a new legislative, as they think best, being in full liberty to resist the force of those, who, without authority, would impose any thing upon them.❞

Source: Steven C. A. Pincus, *England's Glorious Revolution, 1688–1689: A Brief History with Documents* (Boston: Bedford/St. Martin's, 2006), pp. 71–72 (Cartwright), 161–164 (Locke).

QUESTIONS FOR ANALYSIS

1. How does Cartwright justify James's right to rule England? Are there any limitations on royal authority according to Cartwright?

2. What is the reason for people forming a government, according to Locke? What would be the justification for disobeying laws and rejecting the authority of government?

MAP 17.4 Seventeenth-Century Dutch Commerce Dutch wealth rested on commerce, and commerce depended on the huge Dutch merchant marine, manned by perhaps forty-eight thousand sailors. The fleet carried goods from all parts of the globe to the port of Amsterdam.

the upper classes. Aristocratic government lasted in England at least until 1832 and in many ways until 1928, when women received full voting rights.

The Dutch Republic in the Seventeenth Century

In the late sixteenth century the seven northern provinces of the Netherlands fought for and won their independence from Spain. The independence of the Republic of the United Provinces of the Netherlands was recognized in 1648 in the treaty that ended the Thirty Years' War. In this period, often called the "golden age of the Netherlands," Dutch ideas and attitudes played a profound role in shaping a new and modern worldview. At the same time, the United Provinces developed its own distinctive model of a constitutional state.

Rejecting the rule of a monarch, the Dutch established a republic, a state in which power rests in the hands of the people and is exercised through elected representatives. Other republics of the time included the Swiss Confederation and several autonomous city-states of Italy and the Holy Roman Empire. Among the Dutch, an oligarchy of wealthy businessmen called regents handled domestic affairs in each province's estates, or assemblies. The provincial estates held virtually all the power. A federal assembly, or States General, handled foreign affairs and war, but it did not possess sovereign authority. All issues had to be referred back to the local estates for approval, and each of the seven provinces could veto any proposed legislation.

In each province, the estates appointed an executive officer, known as the **stadholder**, who carried out ceremonial functions and was responsible for military defense. Although in theory freely chosen by the estates, in practice the reigning prince of Orange usually held the office of stadholder in several of the seven provinces of the republic. Tensions persisted between supporters of the House of Orange and those of the staunchly

• **stadholder** The executive officer in each of the United Provinces of the Netherlands, a position often held by the princes of Orange.

republican estates, who suspected the princes of harboring monarchical ambitions. When one of them, William III, took the English throne in 1689 with his wife, Mary, the republic simply continued without stadholders for several decades.

The political success of the Dutch rested on their commercial prosperity. The moral and ethical bases of that commercial wealth were thrift, frugality, and religious toleration. Jews enjoyed a level of acceptance and assimilation in Dutch business and general culture unique in early modern Europe. (See "Individuals in Society: Glückel of Hameln," page 517.) In the Dutch Republic, toleration paid: it attracted a great deal of foreign capital and investment.

The Dutch came to dominate the shipping business by putting profits from their original industry—herring fishing—into shipbuilding. They boasted the lowest shipping rates and largest merchant marine in Europe, allowing them to undersell foreign competitors (Map 17.4). Trade and commerce brought the Dutch the highest standard of living in Europe, perhaps in the world.

Colonialism in the Americas

☐ How did European nations compete to build new colonies in the Americas?

Absolutist or constitutional, European powers deeply envied the fabulous wealth and glory Spain acquired from her American colonies. As Spain's power began to weaken in the early seventeenth century, the Dutch, English, and French seized their opportunity, ruthlessly vying to claim their own territories in the New World. Competition among them was encouraged by mercantilist economic doctrine, which dictated that foreign trade was a zero-sum game in which one country's gains necessarily entailed another's loss. Conflicts over access to trade mounted in the seventeenth century, but by the early eighteenth century England had won a series of concessions that enabled it to dominate trade across the Atlantic.

Life in the colonies was shaped by many factors, including the absence or presence of European women. Complex ethnic and cultural identities emerged due to the mixing of European, indigenous, and African peoples.

Colonial Expansion of Northern European Powers

For a century after the fall of the Mexica (Aztec) capital of Tenochtitlán, the Spanish and Portuguese domi-

nated colonization of the Americas (see Chapter 16). In the early seventeenth century, however, England, France, and the Netherlands profited from Spain's weakness to challenge its dominion. Unlike Spain, where the royal government financed exploration and directly ruled the colonies, England, France, and the Netherlands left colonization largely to chartered companies endowed with monopolies over settlement and trade in a given area.

The first English colony was founded at Roanoke (in what is now North Carolina) in 1585. After a three-year loss of contact with England, the settlers were found to have disappeared; their fate remains a mystery. The colony of Virginia, founded at Jamestown in 1607, had better luck and gained a steady hold, producing tobacco for a growing European market. Indentured servants obtained free passage to the colony in exchange for several years of work and the promise of greater opportunity than in England. In the 1670s Carolina was settled by English colonists from the Caribbean island of Barbados, who found conditions suitable for large rice plantations. During the late seventeenth century enslaved Africans replaced indentured servants as laborers on tobacco and rice plantations, and a harsh racial divide was imposed.

For the first settlers on the coast of New England, the reasons for seeking a new life in the colonies were more religious than economic. Many of these colonists were radical Protestants escaping Anglican repression. The small and struggling outpost of Plymouth Colony (1620) was followed by Massachusetts Bay Colony (1630), which grew into a prosperous settlement. Religious disputes in Massachusetts led to the dispersion of settlers into the new communities of Providence, Connecticut, Rhode Island, and New Haven. Because New England lacked the conditions for plantation agriculture, slavery was always a minor element of life there.

Whereas the Spanish established wholesale dominance over Mexico and Peru, English settlements hugged the Atlantic coastline. This did not prevent conflict with the indigenous inhabitants over land and resources. The haphazard nature of English colonization also led to conflicts of authority within the colonies. As the English crown grew more interested in colonial expansion, efforts were made to acquire the territory between New England in the north and Virginia in the south. The goal was to unify English holdings and minimize French and Dutch competition on the Atlantic seaboard. The results of these efforts were the mid-Atlantic colonies: the Catholic settlement of Maryland (1632); New York, captured from the Dutch in 1664; and the Quaker colony of Pennsylvania (1681).

The French established colonies in present-day Canada and then moved farther south. In 1608 Samuel de Champlain founded the first permanent French

Individuals in Society

Glückel of Hameln

IN 1690 A JEWISH WIDOW IN THE SMALL
German town of Hameln in Lower Saxony sat down to write her autobiography. She wanted to distract her mind from the terrible grief she felt over the death of her husband and to provide her twelve children with a record "so you will know from what sort of people you have sprung, lest today or tomorrow your beloved children or grandchildren came and know naught of their family." Out of her pain and heightened consciousness, Glückel (1646–1724) produced an invaluable source for scholars.

She was born in Hamburg two years before the end of the Thirty Years' War. In 1649 the merchants of Hamburg expelled the Jews, who moved to nearby Altona, then under Danish rule. When the Swedes overran Altona in 1657–1658, the Jews returned to Hamburg "purely at the mercy of the Town Council." Glückel's narrative unfolds against a background of the constant harassment to which Jews were subjected—special papers, permits, bribes—and in Hameln she wrote, "And so it has been to this day and, I fear, will continue in like fashion."

When Glückel was "barely twelve," her father betrothed her to Chayim Hameln, and they married when she was fourteen. She describes him as "the perfect pattern of the pious Jew," a man who stopped his work every day for study and prayer, fasted, and was scrupulously honest in his business dealings. Only a few years older than Glückel, Chayim earned his living dealing in precious metals and in making small loans on pledges (pawned goods). This work required constant travel to larger cities, markets, and fairs, often in bad weather, always over dangerous roads. Chayim consulted his wife about all his business dealings. As he lay dying, a friend asked if he had any last wishes. "None," he replied. "My wife knows everything. She shall do as she has always done." For thirty years Glückel had been his friend, full business partner, and wife. They had thirteen children, twelve of whom survived their father, eight then unmarried. As Chayim had foretold, Glückel succeeded in launching the boys in careers and in providing dowries for the girls.

Glückel's world was her family, the Jewish community of Hameln, and the Jewish communities into which her children married. Her social and business activities took her across Europe, from Amsterdam to Berlin,

from Danzig to Vienna; thus her world was far from narrow or provincial. She took great pride that Prince Frederick of Cleves, later king of Prussia, danced at the wedding of her eldest daughter. The rising prosperity of Chayim's businesses allowed the couple to maintain up to six servants.

Glückel was deeply religious, and her culture was steeped in Jewish literature, legends, and mystical and secular works. Above all, she relied on the Bible. Her language, heavily sprinkled with scriptural references, testifies to a rare familiarity with the Scriptures.

Students who wish to learn about seventeenth-century business practices, the importance of the dowry in marriage, childbirth, Jewish life, birthrates, family celebrations, and even the meaning of life can gain a good deal from the memoirs of this extraordinary woman who was, in the words of one of her descendants, the poet Heinrich Heine, "the gift of a world to me."

Source: *The Memoirs of Glückel of Hameln* (New York: Schocken Books, 1977).

QUESTIONS FOR ANALYSIS

1. Consider the ways in which Glückel of Hameln was both an ordinary and an extraordinary woman of her times. Would you call her a marginal or a central person in her society? Why?
2. How might Glückel's successes be attributed to the stabilizing force of absolutism in the seventeenth century?

• Although no images of Glückel exist, Rembrandt's *The Jewish Bride* suggests the mutual devotion of Glückel and her husband for one another. (Rijksmuseum-Stichting Amsterdam)

The Fur Trade In the early seventeenth century, European fur traders relied on Native Americans' expertise and experience, leading to the equal relations depicted in this scene from the colony of New Sweden (in modern-day Pennsylvania). The action in the background shows violence among indigenous groups, rivalries exacerbated by contact with Europeans and their trade goods. Hudson's Bay Company, the English colonial trading company, issued its own tokens as currency in the fur trade. This token, dating from the mid-nineteenth century, displays the company's crest, which says "a skin for a skin" in Latin. Two stags face each other, with a fox at the top and four beavers on the shield. Traders received tokens for the pelts they sold and could use them to purchase goods from the company's store. European demand for beaver hats, made from the felted pelts of beavers, drove the tremendous expansion of the North American fur trade in the beginning of the seventeenth century. (engraving: Fur trade in New Sweden in the early 1600s, Peter Lindestrom, artist. From *Geographia Americae with An Account of the Delaware Indians, Based on Surveys and Notes Made 1654–1656*, by Peter Lindestrom, published by The Swedish Colonial Society; token: © National Maritime Museum/The Image Works; hat: Picture Research Consultants and Archives)

settlement at Quebec as a post for trading beaver pelts with local Algonquin and Huron peoples. Settlement of Ville-Marie, later named Montreal, followed in 1642. Louis XIV's capable economic minister, Jean-Baptiste Colbert, established direct royal control over New France (Canada) and sent colonists to enlarge its population. Although the population of the French settlements was always minuscule compared with that of British North America, the French were energetic and industrious traders and explorers. Following the waterways of the St. Lawrence River, the Great Lakes, and the Mississippi River, they ventured into much of North America in the 1670s and 1680s. In 1673 the Jesuit Jacques Marquette and the merchant Louis Joliet

sailed down the Mississippi and claimed possession of the land on both sides of the river as far south as present-day Arkansas. In 1682 Robert de La Salle traveled the Mississippi to the Gulf of Mexico, opening the way for French occupation of Louisiana.

In the first decades of the seventeenth century, English and French captains also defied Spain's hold over the Caribbean Sea (see Map 18.2 on page 548). The English seized control of Bermuda (1612), Barbados (1627), and a succession of other islands. The French took Cayenne (1604), St. Christophe (1625), Martinique and Guadeloupe (1635), and, finally, Saint-Domingue (1697) on the western half of Spanish-occupied Hispaniola. These islands acquired new importance after

1640, when the Portuguese brought sugar plantations to Brazil. Sugar and slaves quickly followed in the West Indies (see pages 479–480), making the Caribbean plantations the most lucrative of all colonial possessions.

Not content with challenging the Portuguese in the Indian Ocean (see page 481), the Dutch also aspired to a role in the Americas. Founded in 1621 in a period of war with Spain, the Dutch West India Company aggressively sought to open trade with North and South America and to take possession of Spanish territories there. The company captured or destroyed hundreds of Spanish ships, seized a fleet carrying Spanish silver in 1628, and gained control of portions of Brazil and the Caribbean. The Dutch also successfully interceded in the transatlantic slave trade, bringing much of the west coast of Africa under their control.

Dutch efforts to colonize North America were less successful. The colony of New Netherland, governed from New Amsterdam (modern-day New York City), was hampered by lack of settlement and weak governance and was easily captured by the English.

Mercantilism and Colonial Wars

European powers in the seventeenth century shared a mercantilist view of economics (see page 498). In England the desire to increase both military power and private wealth resulted in the mercantile system of the **Navigation Acts**. Oliver Cromwell established the first of these laws in 1651, and the restored monarchy of Charles II extended them in 1660 and 1663. The acts required most goods imported into England and Scotland (Great Britain after 1707) to be carried on British-owned ships with British crews or on ships of the country producing the article. Moreover, these laws gave British merchants and shipowners a virtual monopoly on trade with British colonies. The colonists were required to ship their products on British (or American) ships and to buy almost all European goods from Britain. It was believed that these economic regulations would eliminate foreign competition, thereby helping British merchants and workers as well as colonial plantation owners and farmers. It was hoped, too, that the emerging British Empire would develop a shipping industry with a large number of experienced seamen who could serve when necessary in the Royal Navy.

European Claims in North America, 1714

The Navigation Acts were a form of economic warfare. Their initial target was the Dutch, who were far ahead of the English in shipping and foreign trade in the mid-seventeenth century. In conjunction with three Anglo-Dutch wars between 1652 and 1674, the Navigation Acts seriously damaged Dutch shipping and commerce. By the late seventeenth century the Netherlands was falling behind England in shipping, trade, and settlement.

Thereafter France was England's most serious rival in the competition for overseas empire. Rich in natural resources, allied with Spain, and home to a population three or four times that of England, France was continental Europe's leading military power. It was already building a powerful fleet and a worldwide system of rigidly monopolized colonial trade. But the War of the Spanish Succession, the last of Louis XIV's many wars (see page 500), tilted the balance in favor of England. The 1713 Peace of Utrecht forced France to cede its North American holdings in Newfoundland, Nova Scotia, and the Hudson Bay territory to Britain. Spain was compelled to give Britain control of its West African slave trade—the so-called *asiento* (ah-SYEN-toh)—and to let Britain send one ship of merchandise into the Spanish colonies annually. These acquisitions primed Britain to take a leading role in the growing Atlantic trade of the eighteenth century, including the transatlantic slave trade (discussed in Chapter 19).

Life in the Colonies

Many factors helped shape life in European colonies, including locations of settlements, indigenous cultures and practices, and the cultural attitudes and official policies of the European colonizers. Women played a crucial role in the creation of new identities and the continuation of old ones. The first explorers formed unions with native women, through coercion or consent, and relied on them as translators, guides, and intermediaries in the formation of alliances with indigenous powers. As settlement developed, the character of each colony was influenced by the presence or absence of European women. Where women and children accompanied male colonists, as in the British colonies

---

• **Navigation Acts** Mid-seventeenth-century English mercantilist laws that greatly restricted other countries' rights to trade with England and its colonies.

and the Spanish mainland colonies, new settlements took on European languages, religion, and ways of life that have endured, with input from local cultures, to this day. Where European women did not accompany male settlers, as on the west coast of Africa and most European outposts in Asia, local populations largely retained their own cultures, to which male Europeans acclimatized themselves.

Most women who crossed the Atlantic were Africans, who constituted four-fifths of the female newcomers before 1800.[12] Wherever slavery existed, masters profited from their power to engage in sexual relations with enslaved women. One important difference among European colonies was in the status of children born of such unions. In some colonies, mostly those dominated by the Portuguese, Spanish, or French,

▫ Picturing the Past

Mulatto Painting The caption in the upper left corner of this mid-eighteenth-century painting identifies the family as being composed of a Spanish father and a black mother, and their child is described as "mulatto." The painting was number six in a series of sixteen images by the painter José de Alcibar, each showing a different racial and ethnic combination. The series belonged to a popular genre in the Spanish Americas known as *castas* paintings, which commonly depicted sixteen different forms of racial mixing. (Attrib. Jose de Alcibar, 6, De *Espano y Negra, Mulato,* ca. 1760–1770. Denver Art Museum: Collection of Frederick and Jan Mayer. Photo © James O. Milmoe)

ANALYZING THE IMAGE How would you characterize the relations among mother, father, and child as shown in this painting? Does the painter suggest power relations within the family? What attitude does the painter seem to have toward the family?

CONNECTIONS Why do you think such paintings were so popular? Who do you think the audience might have been, and why would viewers be fascinated by such images?

substantial populations of free blacks descended from the freed children of the unions. In English colonies, masters were less likely to free children they fathered with female slaves.

The mixing of indigenous people with Europeans and Africans created whole new populations and ethnicities and complex self-identities. In Spanish America the word *mestizo—métis* in French— described people of mixed Native American and European descent. The blanket terms "mulatto" and "people of color" were used for those of mixed African and European origins. With its immense slave-based plantation system, large indigenous population, and relatively low Portuguese immigration, Brazil developed a particularly complex racial and ethnic mosaic.

CONNECTIONS

The seventeenth century represented a difficult passage between two centuries of dynamism and growth in Europe. On one side lay the sixteenth century's religious enthusiasm and strife, overseas discoveries, rising populations, and vigorous commerce. On the other side stretched the eighteenth century's renewed population growth, economic development, and cultural flourishing. The first half of the seventeenth century was marked by the spread of religious and dynastic warfare across Europe, resulting in death and widespread suffering. Recurring crop failure, famine, and epidemic disease contributed to a stagnant economy and population loss. In the middle decades of the seventeenth century, the very survival of the European monarchies established in the Renaissance appeared in doubt.

With the re-establishment of order in the second half of the century, maintaining stability was of paramount importance to European rulers. While a few nations placed their trust in constitutionally limited governments, many more were ruled by monarchs proclaiming their absolute and God-given authority. The ability to actually assume such power depended on cooperation from local elites, who acquiesced to state authority in exchange for privileges and payoffs. In this way, both absolutism and constitutionalism relied on political compromises forged from decades of strife.

As Spain's power weakened, other European nations bordering the Atlantic Ocean sought their own profits and glory from overseas empires. Henceforth, war among European powers would include high-stakes conflicts over territories and trade in the colonies. European rulers' increased control over their own subjects thus went hand in glove with the expansion of European power in the world.

The eighteenth century was to see these power politics thrown into question by new Enlightenment aspirations for human society, which themselves derived from the inquisitive and self-confident spirit of the scientific revolution. These movements—both of which would have long-lasting influence worldwide—are explored in the next chapter. By the end of the eighteenth century, demands for real popular sovereignty, colonial self-rule, and slave emancipation challenged the very bases of order so painfully achieved in the seventeenth century. Chapter 22 recounts the revolutionary movements that swept the late-eighteenth-century Atlantic world, while Chapters 25, 26, and 27 follow the story of European imperialism and the resistance of colonized peoples into the nineteenth century.

▫ CHAPTER REVIEW

▫ **What were the common crises and achievements of seventeenth-century European states? (p. 492)**

Most parts of Europe experienced the seventeenth century as a period of severe economic, social, and military crisis. Across the continent, rulers faced popular rebellions from desperate subjects, who were pushed to the brink by poor harvests, famine, disease, poor wages, high prices, and more. In eastern Europe, lords addressed labor shortages by increasing peasants' work burdens and reducing their rights. The Thirty Years' War also had devastating consequences, drastically reducing urban and rural populations and harming trade and agriculture. Despite these obstacles, both absolutist and constitutional European states emerged from the seventeenth century with increased powers and more centralized control. Whether they ruled through monarchical fiat or parliamentary negotiation, European governments strengthened their bureaucracies, raised more taxes, and significantly expanded their armies.

▫ **Why and how did the French absolutist state arise under Louis XIV, and why did absolutist Spain experience decline in the same period? (p. 496)**

Louis XIV rose to power in the wake of noble rebellion and popular riots that left the French wishing for a strong monarch to reimpose order. Using the doctrine of the divine right of kings to justify his hold on power, Louis ruled France by securing the collaboration of high nobles in exchange for confirmation of their ancient privileges. To build armies and fight wars, Louis relied on the wealth brought in through mercantilist policies. In Spain, where monarchs made similar claims to absolute power, the seventeenth century witnessed economic catastrophe and a decline in royal capacities. This decline resulted from a fall in colonial trade revenue, massive state debt, and a decline in manufacturing and agricultural productivity. Adding to these problems were internal conflicts and military defeats.

▫ **How did Austrian, Prussian, and Russian rulers transform their nations into powerful absolutist monarchies? (p. 501)**

Within a framework of resurgent serfdom and entrenched nobility, Austrian and Prussian monarchs fashioned strong absolutist states in the seventeenth and early eighteenth centuries. These monarchs won absolutist control over standing armies, taxation, and representative bodies, but left intact the underlying social and economic relationships between the nobles and their peasants. In exchange, nobles cooperated with the growth of state power. In Russia, Mongol conquest and rule set the stage for absolutism, and a harsh tsarist autocracy was firmly in place by the time of the reign of Ivan the Terrible in the sixteenth century. Ivan's brutal rule brought all segments of Russian society into state service, sparking resentment and revolt. The reign of Ivan and his successors saw a great expansion of Russian territory, laying the foundations for a huge multiethnic empire. More than a century later, Peter the Great succeeded in modernizing Russia's traditional absolutism by reforming the army and the bureaucracy.

▫ **Why and how did the constitutional state triumph in England and the Dutch Republic? (p. 509)**

England and the Netherlands defied the general trend toward absolute monarchy. In England, opposition arose against the monarchy for a number of reasons, including the Crown's resistance to religious reform, its skirting of parliamentary oversight, and its levying of taxes that most people considered illegal. Civil war resulted, and the country eventually came under what amounted to a military dictatorship. Eventually, however, England emerged with a constitutional monarchy. After the Glorious Revolution of 1688–1689, power was divided between king and Parliament, Parliament had to be called at least once every three years, and the independence of the judiciary was established. By contrast, the Dutch rejected monarchical rule after winning independence from Spain. Instead, the United Provinces of the Netherlands adopted a decentralized republican government in which local affairs were run by provincial estates and the national States General handled foreign affairs and war.

□ How did European nations compete to build new colonies in the Americas? (p. 516)

As Spain's power weakened in the early seventeenth century, England, France, and the Netherlands competed with one another to gain territories in and wealth from the Americas. English settlement took on distinct characteristics in different regions, with religious dissenters establishing colonies in New England, while plantations with slave labor dominated in the South. New France had a small population, but its industrious traders explored and claimed for France vast territories along the waterways of the interior. In the early seventeenth century the Dutch successfully rivaled Spain's control of trade by disrupting shipping and by seizing portions of territories in Brazil and the Caribbean. Mercantilist competition among European powers led to conflict, with England emerging in the early eighteenth century as the most advantaged power. Life in the colonies was shaped by many factors, especially by the extent of immigration by European women. Throughout the Americas, new ethnic identities were formed by the mixing of European, indigenous, and African populations.

SUGGESTED READING

Benedict, Philip, and Myron P. Gutmann, eds. *Early Modern Europe: From Crisis to Stability*. 2005. A helpful introduction to the many facets of the seventeenth-century crisis.

Burke, Peter. *The Fabrication of Louis XIV*. 1992. Explains the use of architecture, art, medals, and other symbols to promote the king's image.

Clark, Christopher. *Iron Kingdom: The Rise and Downfall of Prussia, 1600–1947*. 2006. A fascinating long-term account tracing Prussia's emergence as an international power and the impact of Prussian history on later political developments in Germany.

Collins, James B. *The State in Early Modern France*. 1995. A detailed and well-argued survey of French administration from Louis XIII to Louis XVI.

Elliott, John H. *Imperial Spain, 1469–1716*, 2d ed. 2002. An authoritative account of Spain's rise to imperial greatness and its slow decline.

Gaunt, Peter, ed. *The English Civil War: The Essential Readings*. 2000. A collection showcasing leading historians' interpretations of the civil war.

Hagen, William W. *Ordinary Prussians: Brandenburg Junkers and Villagers, 1500–1840*. 2002. A fascinating look at the people of a Prussian estate, with first-person accounts.

Hughes, Lindsey, ed. *Peter the Great and the West: New Perspectives*. 2001. Essays by leading scholars on the reign of Peter the Great and his opening of Russia to the West.

Ingrao, Charles W. *The Habsburg Monarchy, 1618–1815*, 2d ed. 2000. An excellent synthesis of the political and social development of the Habsburg empire in the early modern period.

Parker, Geoffrey. *The Thirty Years' War*, 2d ed. 1997. The standard account of the Thirty Years' War.

Schama, Simon. *The Embarrassment of Riches: An Interpretation of Dutch Culture in the Golden Age*. 1987. A lengthy but vivid and highly readable account of Dutch culture in the seventeenth century, including a chapter on the mania for speculation on the tulip market.

NOTES

1. Theodore K. Rabb, *The Struggle for Stability in Early Modern Europe* (Oxford: Oxford University Press, 1975).

2. Quoted in Cecile Hugon, *Social France in the XVII Century* (London: McMilland, 1911), p. 189.

3. H. Kamen, "The Economic and Social Consequences of the Thirty Years' War," *Past and Present* 39 (April 1968): 44–61.

4. Quoted in John A. Lynn, *Giant of the Grand Siècle: The French Army, 1610–1715* (Cambridge, U.K.: Cambridge University Press, 1997), p. 74.

5. F. Arkwright, ed., *The Memoirs of the Duke de Saint-Simon*, vol. 5 (New York: Brentano's, n.d.), p. 276.

6. John A. Lynn, "Recalculating French Army Growth," in *The Military Revolution Debate: Readings on the Military Transformation of Early Modern Europe*, ed. Clifford J. Rogers (Boulder, Colo.: Westview Press, 1995), p. 125.

7. J. H. Elliott, *Imperial Spain, 1469–1716* (New York: Mentor Books, 1963), pp. 306–308.

8. H. Rosenberg, *Bureaucracy, Aristocracy, and Autocracy: The Prussian Experience, 1660–1815* (Boston: Beacon Press, 1966), p. 43.

9. Cited in Giles MacDonogh, *Frederick the Great: A Life in Deed and Letters* (New York: St. Martin's, 2001), p. 23.

10. Rosenberg, *Bureaucracy, Aristocracy, and Autocracy*, p. 40.

11. For a revisionist interpretation, see J. Wormald, "James VI and I: Two Kings or One?" *History* 62 (June 1983): 187–209.

12. Geoffrey Vaughn Scammel, *The First Imperial Age: European Overseas Expansion, c. 1400–1715* (London and New York: Routledge, 2002), p. 432.

For practice quizzes and other study tools, visit the **Online Study Guide** at bedfordstmartins.com/mckayworld.

For primary sources from this period, see *Sources of World Societies*, **Second Edition**.

For Web sites, images, and documents related to topics in this chapter, visit **Make History** at bedfordstmartins.com/mckayworld.

• **Free People of Color** A sizable mixed-race population emerged in many European colonies in the Americas, often descendants of unions between masters and enslaved African women. The wealthiest of the free people of color, as they were called, were plantation owners with slaves of their own. (Unknown artist, *Portrait of a Young Woman*, late 18th century, pastel, 16 × 12 inches, Saint Louis Art Museum, Museum Purchase 186:1951)

18

Intellectual developments of the sixteenth through eighteenth centuries created the modern worldview that the West continues to hold — and debate — to this day. Beginning in the sixteenth century, European scholars developed fundamentally new ways of understanding the natural world, later characterized as a "scientific revolution." Whereas medieval scholars looked to classical works and the Bible, seventeenth-century natural philosophers, as they called themselves, performed experiments and relied on complex mathematical calculations. The resulting conception of the universe and its laws remained in force until Albert Einstein's discoveries in the first half of the twentieth century.

New Worldviews and Ways of Life
1540–1790

Eighteenth-century philosophers extended the use of reason from nature to human society. Self-proclaimed members of an "Enlightenment" movement, they wished to bring the same progress to human affairs that their predecessors brought to the understanding of the natural world. While the scientific revolution ushered in modern science, the Enlightenment created concepts of human rights, equality, progress, and tolerance that still guide Western societies. At the same time, some Europeans used their new understanding of reason to explain their own superiority, thus rationalizing attitudes now regarded as racist and sexist.

The expression of new ideas was encouraged by changes in the material world. With the growth of population, the revitalization of industry and growing world trade, Europeans began to consume at a higher level. Feeding the growth of consumerism was the expansion of transatlantic trade and lower prices for colonial goods, often produced by slaves. During the eighteenth century, ships crisscrossing the Atlantic circulated commodities, ideas, and people to all four continents bordering the ocean. As trade became more integrated and communication intensified, an Atlantic world of mixed identities and shared debates emerged. •

The Scientific Revolution
☐ What was revolutionary in the new attitudes toward the natural world?

The Enlightenment
☐ How did a new spirit of critical and rational thinking affect ideas about society and human relations?

Enlightened Absolutism
☐ What impact did new ways of thinking have on monarchical absolutism and those under its rule?

The Growth of Consumerism and the Atlantic World
☐ How did the growth of consumerism and the Atlantic economy interact with Enlightenment ideas?

The Scientific Revolution

☐ What was revolutionary in the new attitudes toward the natural world?

A noted historian has said that the scientific revolution, which lasted roughly from 1540 to 1690, was "the real origin both of the modern world and the modern mentality."[1] Through new methods of investigating the physical world, Western society began to come to a new understanding of astronomy, physics, and medicine based on both experimentation and reasoning.

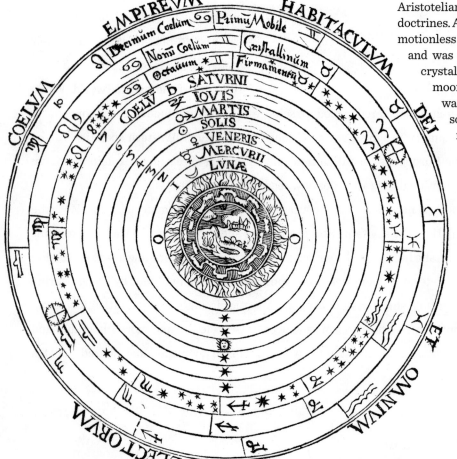

Scientific Thought Through the Early 1500s

The term *science* as we use it today came into use only in the nineteenth century. Prior to the scientific revolution, many different scholars and practitioners were involved in aspects of what came together to form science. One of the most important disciplines was **natural philosophy**, which focused on fundamental questions about the nature of the universe, its purpose, and how it functioned. In the early 1500s natural philosophy was still based primarily on the ideas of Aristotle, the great Greek philosopher of the fourth century B.C.E. Medieval theologians such as Thomas Aquinas brought Aristotelian philosophy into harmony with Christian doctrines. According to the revised Aristotelian view, a motionless earth was fixed at the center of the universe and was encompassed by ten separate concentric crystal spheres in which were embedded the moon, sun, planets, and stars. Beyond the spheres was Heaven, with the throne of God and the souls of the saved. Angels kept the spheres moving in perfect circles.

Aristotle's cosmology made intellectual sense, but it could not account for the observed motions of the stars and planets and, in particular, provided no explanation for the apparent backward motion of the planets (which we now know

The Aristotelian Universe as Imagined in the Sixteenth Century
A round earth is at the center, surrounded by spheres of water, air, and fire. Beyond this small nucleus, the moon, the sun, and the five planets were embedded in their own rotating crystal spheres, with the stars sharing the surface of one enormous sphere. Beyond, the heavens were composed of unchanging ether. (Image Select/Art Resource, NY)

occurs as planets closer to the sun periodically overtake the earth on their faster orbits). The great second-century Greek scholar Ptolemy offered a theory for this phenomenon. According to Ptolemy, the planets moved in small circles, called epicycles, each of which moved in turn along a larger circle or deferent. Ptolemaic astronomy was less elegant than Aristotle's neat nested circles and required complex calculations, but it provided a surprisingly accurate model for predicting planetary motion.

Aristotle's views, revised by medieval philosophers, also dominated thinking about physics and motion on earth. Aristotle had distinguished sharply between the world of the celestial spheres and that of the earth — the sublunar world. The sublunar realm was made up of four imperfect, changeable elements: air, fire, water, and earth. The spheres, however, consisted of a perfect, incorruptible "quintessence," or fifth essence. Aristotle and his followers also believed that a uniform force moved an object at a constant speed and that the object would stop as soon as that force was removed. Both of these views would be challenged based on new observations and analysis of the physical world.

Origins of the Scientific Revolution

Why did Aristotelian teachings give way to new views about the universe? The first important driver of the scientific revolution was the medieval university. By the thirteenth century permanent universities had been established in western Europe. In the fourteenth and fifteenth centuries leading universities established new professorships of mathematics, astronomy, and physics (natural philosophy) within their faculties of philosophy. Although the prestige of the new fields was low, a permanent community of scholars was now focused on investigating scientific problems

Medieval scholarship in the universities was based on the study of ancient texts, whose wisdom was considered authoritative. Contact with Muslims in Spain and Sicily brought awareness of many ancient texts that survived only in Arabic versions, and these were translated into Latin in the twelfth century. In some instances, such as mathematics and astronomy, the translations were accompanied by learned commentaries that went beyond ancient learning. Arabic and Persian mathematicians, for example, invented algebra, the

concept of the algorithm, and decimal point notation, while Arabic astronomers improved on measurements recorded in ancient works.

Second, the Renaissance also stimulated scientific progress. Renaissance patrons played a role in funding scientific investigations, as they did art and literature. The goal of exploration in late fifteenth and sixteenth centuries was not only to find wealth and Christian converts, but also to increase Europeans' knowledge about the wider world. In addition, Renaissance artists' turn toward realism and their use of geometry to convey three-dimensional perspective encouraged scholars to practice close observation and to use mathematics to describe the natural world. Furthermore, the Renaissance rise of printing provided a faster and less expensive way to circulate knowledge across Europe.

The navigational problems of long sea voyages in the age of overseas expansion were a third factor in the scientific revolution. To help solve these problems, inventors developed many new scientific instruments, such as the telescope, barometer, thermometer, pendulum clock, microscope, and air pump. Better instruments, which permitted more accurate observations, often led to important new knowledge.

* **natural philosophy** An early modern term for the study of the nature of the universe, its purpose, and how it functioned; it encompassed what we call "science" today.

Finally, recent historical research has focused on the contribution of practices now regarded as far beyond the realm of science. For most of human history, interest in astronomy was inspired by the belief that the changing relationships between planets and stars influenced events on earth. Many of the most celebrated astronomers were also astrologers. Used as a diagnostic tool in medicine, astrology formed a regular part of the curriculum of medical schools. Centuries-old practices of magic and alchemy also remained important traditions for participants in the scientific revolution. The idea that objects possessed hidden or "occult" qualities that allowed them to affect other objects was a particularly important legacy of the magical tradition. Such hidden qualities helped inspire an important new law of physics (see page 530).

Copernican Hypothesis

The first great departure from the medieval understanding of the physical world system was the work of the Polish cleric Nicolaus Copernicus (1473–1543). After studying at the university of Kraków, Copernicus departed for Italy, where he studied astronomy, medicine, and church law at the famed universities of Bologna, Padua, and Ferrara. In the course of his study of astronomy, Copernicus came to believe that Ptolemy's cumbersome and occasionally inaccurate rules detracted from the majesty of a perfect creator. He preferred an ancient Greek idea: that the sun, rather than the earth, was at the center of the universe.

Finishing his university studies and returning to a church position in East Prussia, Copernicus worked on his hypothesis from 1506 to 1530. Without questioning the Aristotelian belief in crystal spheres or the idea that circular motion was divine, Copernicus theorized that the stars and planets, including the earth, revolved around a fixed sun. Fearing the ridicule of other astronomers, Copernicus did not publish his *On the Revolutions of the Heavenly Spheres* until 1543, the year of his death.

The **Copernican hypothesis** presented a revolutionary view of the universe and brought sharp attacks from religious leaders, especially Protestants, who objected to the idea that the earth moved but the sun did not. Protestant leaders John Calvin and Martin Luther condemned Copernicus. Luther noted that the theory was counter to the Bible: "as the Holy Scripture tells us, so did Joshua bid the sun stand still and not the earth."[2] Catholic reaction was milder at first. The Catholic Church had never held to literal interpretations of the Bible, and not until 1616 did it officially declare the Copernican hypothesis false.

Other events were almost as influential in creating doubts about traditional astronomical ideas. In 1572 a new star appeared and shone very brightly for almost two years. The new star, which was actually a distant exploding star, seemed to contradict the idea that the heavenly spheres were unchanging and therefore perfect. In 1577 a new comet suddenly moved through the sky, cutting a straight path across the supposedly impenetrable crystal spheres. It was time, as a sixteenth-century scientific writer put it, for "the radical renovation of astronomy."[3]

Proving Copernicus Right

One astronomer who agreed with Copernicus was the Danish astronomer Tycho Brahe (TEE-koh BRAH-hee; 1546–1601). Brahe established himself as Europe's leading astronomer with his detailed observations of the new star of 1572. Aided by grants from the king of Denmark, Brahe built the most sophisticated observatory of his day.

Upon the king's death, Brahe acquired a new patron in the Holy Roman emperor Rudolph II and built a new observatory in Prague. In return for the emperor's support, he pledged to create new and improved tables of planetary motions, dubbed the *Rudolfine Tables*. For twenty years Brahe observed the stars and planets with his naked eye, compiling much more complete and accurate data than ever before. His limited understanding of mathematics and his sudden death in 1601, however, prevented him from making much sense out of his mass of data.

It was left to Brahe's young assistant, Johannes Kepler (1571–1630), to rework Brahe's mountain of observations. A brilliant mathematician, Kepler was inspired by his belief that the universe was built on mystical mathematical relationships and a musical harmony of the heavenly bodies.

Kepler's examination of his predecessor's findings convinced him that they could not be explained by Ptolemy's astronomy. Abandoning the notion of epicycles and deferents, Kepler developed three revolutionary laws of planetary motion. First, he demonstrated that the orbits of the planets around the sun are elliptical rather than circular. Second, he demonstrated that the planets do not move at a uniform speed in their orbits. When a planet is close to the sun it moves more rapidly, and it slows as it moves farther away from the sun. Finally, Kepler's third law stated that the time a planet takes to make its complete orbit is precisely related to its distance from the sun.

• **Copernican hypothesis** The idea that the sun, not the earth, was the center of the universe.

• **law of inertia** A law formulated by Galileo that states that motion, not rest, is the natural state of an object, and that an object continues in motion forever unless stopped by some external force.

Kepler's contribution was monumental. Whereas Copernicus had speculated, Kepler proved mathematically the precise relations of a sun-centered (solar) system. His work demolished the old system of Aristotle and Ptolemy, and in his third law he came close to formulating the idea of universal gravitation (see page 530). In 1627 he also fulfilled Brahe's pledge by completing the *Rudolfine Tables* begun so many years earlier. These tables were used by astronomers for many years.

Kepler was not, however, the consummate modern scientist that his achievements suggest. His duties as court mathematician included casting horoscopes, and his own diary was based on astrological principles. He also wrote at length on cosmic harmonies and explained, for example, elliptical motion through ideas about the beautiful music created by the combined motion of the planets. His career exemplifies the complex interweaving of rigorous empirical observations and mystical beliefs in the emerging science of his day.

While Kepler was unraveling the mysteries of planetary motion, a young Florentine named Galileo Galilei (1564–1642) was challenging old ideas about motion on earth. Galileo's achievement was the elaboration and consolidation of the experimental method. That is, rather than speculate about what might or should happen, Galileo conducted controlled experiments to find out what actually did happen.

In some of his experiments Galileo measured the movement of a rolling ball across a surface, repeating the action again and again to verify his results. In his famous acceleration experiment, he showed that a uniform force—in this case, gravity—produced a uniform acceleration. Through another experiment, he formulated the **law of inertia**. According to this law, rest is not the natural state of objects. Rather, an object continues in motion forever unless stopped by some external force,

such as friction. His discoveries thus proved Aristotelian physics wrong.

Galileo also applied the experimental method to astronomy. On hearing details about the invention of the telescope in Holland, Galileo made one for himself. He quickly discovered the first four moons of Jupiter, which clearly suggested that Jupiter could not possibly be embedded in an impenetrable crystal sphere as Aristotle and Ptolemy maintained. This discovery provided new evidence for the Copernican theory, in which Galileo already believed. Galileo then pointed his telescope at the moon. He wrote in 1610 in *Siderus Nuncius*:

> By the aid of a telescope anyone may behold [the Milky Way] in a manner which so distinctly appeals to the senses that all the disputes which have tormented philosophers through so many ages are exploded by the irrefutable evidence of our eyes, and we are freed from wordy disputes upon the subject.[4]

Galileo's Telescopic Observations of the Moon Among the many mechanical devices Galileo invented was a telescope that could magnify objects twenty times (other contemporary telescopes could magnify objects only three times). Using this telescope, he obtained the empirical evidence that proved the Copernican system. He sketched many illustrations of his observations, including the six phases of the moon, two of which are shown here. (Scala/Art Resource, NY)

Reading these famous lines, one feels a crucial corner in Western civilization being turned. A new method of learning and investigating was being developed, in which scholars relied more on observable evidence and critical thinking than on established authority. This method proved useful in any field of inquiry. A historian investigating documents of the past, for example, is not so different from a Galileo studying stars and rolling balls.

As early as 1597, when Johannes Kepler sent Galileo an early publication defending Copernicus, Galileo wrote back agreeing with his position and confessing he lacked the courage to follow Kepler's example. Within the Catholic world, expressing public support for Copernicus was increasingly dangerous. In 1616 the Holy Office placed the works of Copernicus and his supporters, including Kepler, on a list of books Catholics were forbidden to read.

Out of caution Galileo silenced his beliefs for several years, until in 1623 he saw new hope with the ascension of Pope Urban VIII, a man sympathetic to developments in the new science. However, Galileo's 1632 *Dialogue on the Two Chief Systems of the World* went too far. Published in Italian and widely read, this work openly lampooned the traditional views of Aristotle and Ptolemy and defended those of Copernicus. In 1633 Galileo was tried for heresy by the papal Inquisition. Imprisoned and threatened with torture, the aging Galileo recanted, "renouncing and cursing" his Copernican errors.

Newton's Synthesis

Despite the efforts of the church, by about 1640 the work of Brahe, Kepler, and Galileo had been largely accepted by the scientific community. But the new findings failed to explain what forces controlled the movement of the planets and objects on earth. That challenge was taken up by English scientist Isaac Newton (1642–1727).

Although he was a genius who united the experimental and theoretical-mathematical sides of modern science, Newton — like Kepler and other practitioners of the scientific revolution — was far from being the perfect rationalist so glorified by writers in the eighteenth and nineteenth centuries. For example, he was intensely religious and also fascinated by alchemy, whose practitioners believed (among other things) that base metals could be turned into gold.

Nevertheless, Newton dedicated himself to scientific pursuits from a young age. Born into the lower English gentry, he enrolled at Cambridge University in 1661. He arrived at some of his most basic ideas about physics in 1666 at age twenty-four but was unable to prove them mathematically. In 1684, after years of studying optics, Newton returned to physics for eighteen extraordinarily intensive months. The result was his towering accomplishment, a single explanatory system that integrated the astronomy of Copernicus, as corrected by Kepler's laws, with the physics of Galileo and his predecessors. Newton did this through a set of mathematical laws that explain motion and mechanics. These laws were published in 1687 in Newton's *Mathematical Principles of Natural Philosophy* (also known as the *Principia*). Because of their complexity, it took scientists and engineers two hundred years to work out all their implications.

The key feature of the Newtonian synthesis was the **law of universal gravitation**. According to this law, each body in the universe attracts every other body in a precise mathematical relationship, whereby the force of attraction is proportional to the quantity of matter of the objects and inversely proportional to the square of the distance between them. The whole universe — from Kepler's elliptical orbits to Galileo's rolling balls — was unified in one majestic system. Newton's synthesis prevailed until the twentieth century.

Bacon, Descartes, and the Scientific Method

One of the keys to achieving a better understanding of the world was the development of better ways of obtaining knowledge. Two important thinkers, Francis Bacon (1561–1626) and René Descartes (day-KAHRT; 1596–1650), were influential in describing and advocating for improved scientific methods based, respectively, on experimentation and mathematical reasoning.

The English politician and writer Francis Bacon was the greatest early propagandist for the new experimental method. Rejecting the Aristotelian and medieval method of using speculative reasoning to build general theories, Bacon argued that new knowledge had to be pursued through empirical research. The researcher who wants to learn more about leaves or rocks, for example, should not speculate about the subject but should rather collect a multitude of specimens and then compare and analyze them to derive general principles. Bacon's contribution was to formalize the empirical method, which had already been used by Brahe and Galileo, into the general theory of inductive reasoning known as **empiricism**.

• **law of universal gravitation** Newton's law that all objects are attracted to one another and that the force of attraction is proportional to the object's quantity of matter and inversely proportional to the square of the distance between them.

• **empiricism** A theory of inductive reasoning that calls for acquiring evidence through observation and experimentation rather than reason and speculation.

• **Cartesian dualism** Descartes's view that all of reality could ultimately be reduced to mind and matter.

On the continent, more speculative methods retained support. In 1619, as a twenty-three-year-old soldier serving in the Thirty Years' War (1618–1648), the French philosopher René Descartes experienced a life-changing intellectual vision one night. Descartes saw that there was a perfect correspondence between geometry and algebra and that geometrical spatial figures could be expressed as algebraic equations and vice versa. A major step forward in the history of mathematics, Descartes's discovery of analytic geometry provided scientists with an important new tool.

Descartes used mathematics to elaborate a highly influential vision of the workings of the cosmos. Drawing on ancient Greek atomist philosophies, Descartes developed the idea that matter was made up of identical "corpuscles" (tiny particles) that collided together in an endless series of motions. All occurrences in nature could be analyzed as matter in motion, and, according to Descartes, the total "quantity of motion" in the universe was constant. Descartes's mechanistic view of the universe depended on the idea that a vacuum was impossible, so that every action had an equal reaction, continuing in an eternal chain reaction. Although Descartes's hypothesis about the vacuum was proved wrong, his notion of a mechanistic universe intelligible through the physics of motion proved highly influential.

Descartes's greatest achievement was to develop his initial vision into a whole philosophy of knowledge and science. The Aristotelian cosmos was appealing in part because it corresponded with the evidence of the human senses. However, Descartes acknowledged that impressions of the world gained through the senses can sometimes be proved wrong. Thus, they can be doubted. Only things about which there can be no doubt should be accepted as truths, Descartes argued, and from these truths, or general principles, people can arrive at additional truths. This process of moving from general principles to specific truths is known as deductive reasoning. Descartes's reasoning ultimately reduced all substances to "matter" and "mind" — that is, to the physical and the spiritual. Descartes believed that God had endowed man with reason for a purpose and that rational speculation could provide a path to the truths of creation. His view of the world as consisting of two fundamental entities is known as **Cartesian dualism**. Descartes's thought was highly influential in France and the Netherlands but less so in England, where an emphasis on experimentation won the day.

Both Bacon's inductive experimentalism and Descartes's deductive mathematical reasoning had faults. Bacon's inability to appreciate the importance of mathematics and his obsession with practical results clearly showed the limitations of antitheoretical empiricism. Likewise, some of Descartes's positions — he believed, for example, that it was possible to deduce

the whole science of medicine from a set of foundational first principles — demonstrated the inadequacy of rigid, dogmatic rationalism. Although insufficient on their own, Bacon's and Descartes's extreme approaches are combined in the modern scientific method, which began to crystallize in the late seventeenth century.

☐ MAJOR CONTRIBUTORS TO THE SCIENTIFIC REVOLUTION

Nicolaus Copernicus (1473–1543)	Published *On the Revolutions of the Heavenly Spheres* (1543); theorized that the sun, rather than the earth, was the center of the galaxy
Paracelsus (1493–1541)	Pioneered the use of chemicals and drugs to address perceived chemical imbalances
Andreas Vesalius (1514–1564)	Published *On the Structure of the Human Body* (1543)
Tycho Brahe (1546–1601)	Built observatories and compiled data for the *Rudolfine Tables*, a new table of planetary data
Francis Bacon (1561–1626)	Advocated experimental method, formalizing theory of inductive reasoning known as empiricism
Galileo Galilei (1564–1642)	Used telescopic observation to provide evidence for Copernican hypothesis; experimented to formulate laws of physics, such as inertia
Johannes Kepler (1571–1630)	Used Brahe's data to mathematically prove the Copernican hypothesis; his new laws of planetary motion united for the first time natural philosophy and mathematics; completed the *Rudolfine Tables* in 1627
William Harvey (1578–1657)	Discovered blood circulation (1628)
René Descartes (1596–1650)	Used deductive reasoning to formulate theory of Cartesian dualism
Robert Boyle (1627–1691)	Founded the modern science of chemistry; created the first vacuum; discovered Boyle's law on the properties of gases
Isaac Newton (1642–1727)	Introduced the law of universal gravitation, synthesizing the theories of Copernicus and Galileo

Medicine, the Body, and Chemistry

The scientific revolution, which began with the study of the cosmos, soon inspired renewed study of the microcosm of the human body. For many centuries the ancient Greek physician Galen's explanation of the body carried the same authority as Aristotle's account of the universe. According to Galen, the body contained four humors: blood, phlegm, black bile, and yellow bile. Illness was believed to result from an imbalance of these humors.

Swiss physician and alchemist Paracelsus (1493–1541) was an early proponent of the experimental method in medicine and pioneered the use of chemicals and drugs to address what he saw as chemical,

Frontispiece to *De Humani Corporis Fabrica* (*On the Structure of the Human Body*) The frontispiece to Vesalius's pioneering work, published in 1643, shows him dissecting a corpse before a crowd of students. This was a revolutionary new hands-on approach for physicians, who usually worked from a theoretical, rather than a practical, understanding of the body. Based on direct observation, Vesalius replaced ancient ideas drawn from Greek philosophy with a much more accurate account of the structure and function of the body. (© SSPL/Science Museum/The Image Works)

rather than humoral, imbalances. Another experimentalist, Flemish physician Andreas Vesalius (1514–1564), studied anatomy by dissecting human bodies. In 1543, the same year Copernicus published *On the Revolutions of the Heavenly Spheres*, Vesalius issued *On the Structure of the Human Body*. Its two hundred precise drawings revolutionized the understanding of human anatomy. The experimental approach also led English royal physician William Harvey (1578–1657) to discover the circulation of blood through the veins and arteries in 1628. Harvey was the first to explain that the heart worked like a pump and to explain the function of its muscles and valves.

Irishman Robert Boyle (1627–1691) founded the modern science of chemistry. Following Paracelsus's lead, he undertook experiments to discover the basic elements of nature, which he believed was composed of infinitely small atoms. Boyle was the first to create a vacuum, thus disproving Descartes's belief that a vacuum could not exist in nature, and he discovered Boyle's law (1662), which states that the pressure of a gas varies inversely with volume.

Science and Society

The rise of modern science had many consequences. First, it led to the rise of a new and expanding social group — the international scientific community. Members of this community were linked together by common interests and shared values as well as by journals and learned scientific societies. The personal success of scientists and scholars depended on making new discoveries, and as a result science became competitive. Second, as governments intervened to support and sometimes direct research, the new scientific community became closely tied to the state and its agendas. National academies of science were created under state sponsorship in London in 1662, Paris in 1666, Berlin in 1700, and later across Europe. At the same time, some scientists developed a critical attitude toward established authority that would inspire thinkers to question traditions in other domains as well, such as politics and religion.

Some things did not change in the scientific revolution. For example, new "rational" methods for approaching nature did not question traditional inequalities between the sexes — and may have worsened them in some ways. When Renaissance courts served as centers of learning, talented noblewomen could find niches in study and research. But the rise of a professional scientific community raised barriers for women because the new academies that furnished professional credentials did not accept female members.

There were, however, a number of noteworthy exceptions. In Italy, universities and academies did offer posts to women. Moreover, women across Europe were allowed to work as makers of wax anatomical models and as botanical and zoological illustrators. They were also very much involved in informal scientific communities, attending salons (see page 539), participating in scientific experiments, and writing learned treatises. Some female intellectuals were recognized as full-fledged participants in the philosophical dialogue.

The scientific revolution had few consequences for economic life and the living standards of the masses until the late eighteenth century, when its insights helped create new manufacturing technologies. Instead, it was first and foremost an intellectual revolution. For more than a hundred years its greatest impact was on how people thought and believed.

Finally, there is the question of the role of religion in the development of science. All Western religious authorities — Catholic, Protestant, and Jewish — opposed the Copernican system to a greater or lesser extent until about 1630, by which time the scientific revolution was definitely in progress. The Catholic Church was initially less hostile than Protestant and Jewish religious leaders, and Italian scientists played a crucial role in scientific progress right up to the trial of Galileo in 1633. Thereafter, the Counter-Reformation church became more hostile to science, a change that helped account for the decline of science in Italy (but not in Catholic France) after 1640. At the same time, Protestant countries — especially those lacking a strong religious authority capable of imposing religious orthodoxy on scientific questions — became quite "pro-science." Such countries included the Netherlands, Denmark, and England.

The Enlightenment

☐ How did a new spirit of critical and rational thinking affect ideas about society and human relations?

The scientific revolution was the single most important factor in the creation of the new worldview of the eighteenth-century **Enlightenment**. This worldview grew out of a rich mix of diverse and often conflicting ideas. For the writers who espoused them, the ideas competed vigorously for the attention of a growing public of well-educated readers, who remained a minority of the population.

Despite the diversity, three concepts stand at the core of Enlightenment thinking. The most important and original idea was that the methods of natural science could and should be used to examine and understand all aspects of life. This was what intellectuals meant by *reason*, a favorite word of Enlightenment thinkers. Nothing was to be accepted on faith; every-

Popularizing Science The frontispiece illustration of Fontenelle's *Conversations on the Plurality of Worlds* (1686) invites the reader to share the pleasures of astronomy with an elegant lady and an entertaining teacher. The drawing shows the planets revolving around the sun. (© Roger-Viollet/The Image Works)

thing was to be submitted to rationalism, a secular, critical way of thinking. A second important Enlightenment concept was that the scientific method was capable of discovering the laws of human society as

• **Enlightenment** The influential intellectual and cultural movement of the late seventeenth and eighteenth centuries that introduced new ways of thinking based on the use of reason, the scientific method, and progress.

Metamorphoses of the Caterpillar and Moth Maria Sibylla Merian (1647–1717), the stepdaughter of a Dutch painter, became a celebrated scientific illustrator in her own right. Her finely observed pictures of insects in the South American colony of Surinam introduced many new species. For Merian, science was intimately tied with art: she not only painted but also bred caterpillars and performed experiments on them. Her two-year stay in Surinam, where she was accompanied by a teenage daughter, was a daring feat for a seventeenth-century woman. (Bildarchiv Preussischer Kulturbesitz/Art Resource, NY)

well as those of nature. This second concept led to the third key idea, that of progress: the goal of creating better societies and better people by discarding outmoded traditions and embracing rationalism.

The Emergence of the Enlightenment

An intellectual movement based on the core concepts just mentioned, the European Enlightenment (ca. 1690–1789) gained strength gradually and did not reach maturity until about 1750. Yet it was the generation that came of age between the publication of Newton's *Principia* in 1687 and the death of French king Louis XIV in 1715 that tied the crucial knot between the scientific

revolution and a new outlook on life. Talented writers of that generation popularized hard-to-understand scientific achievements for the educated elite.

This new generation came to believe that the human mind itself is capable of making great progress. Medieval and Reformation thinkers had been concerned primarily with the abstract concepts of sin and salvation. The humanists of the Renaissance had emphasized worldly matters (especially art and literature), but their inspiration came from the classical past. By contrast, Enlightenment thinkers came to believe that their era had gone far beyond antiquity and that fresh intellectual progress was possible.

The excitement of the scientific revolution also generated doubt and uncertainty, as Europeans of the late seventeenth century began to question long-standing religious assumptions and practices. In the wake of the devastation wrought by the Catholic-Protestant struggle of the Thirty Years' War, some people asked whether ideological conformity in religious matters was really necessary. Others skeptically asked if religious truth could ever be known with absolute certainty and concluded that it could not.

The most famous of these skeptics was the French Huguenot Pierre Bayle (1647–1706). Bayle critically examined the religious beliefs and persecutions of the past in his *Historical and Critical Dictionary* (1697). Demonstrating that human beliefs had been extremely varied and often mistaken, he concluded that nothing can ever be known beyond all doubt, a view known as skepticism.

Some Jewish scholars participated in the early Enlightenment movement. The philosopher Baruch Spinoza (1632–1677) was excommunicated by the relatively large Jewish community of Amsterdam for his controversial religious ideas. Spinoza believed that mind and body are united in one substance and that God and nature were two names for the same thing. He envisioned a deterministic universe in which good and evil were merely relative values. Few of Spinoza's radical writings were published during his lifetime, but he is now recognized as among the most original thinkers of the early Enlightenment.

Out of this period of intellectual turmoil came John Locke's *Essay Concerning Human Understanding* (1690), often viewed as the first major text of the Enlightenment. In this work Locke (1632–1704) set forth a new theory about how human beings learn and form their ideas. Whereas Descartes based his deductive logic on the conviction that certain first premises, or innate ideas, are imbued in all humans by God, Locke insisted that all ideas are derived from experience. According to Locke, the human mind at birth is like a blank tablet, or tabula rasa, on which the environment writes the individual's understanding and beliefs. Human development is therefore determined by education and social institutions, for good or for evil. Locke's essay contributed to the theory of sensationalism, the idea that all human ideas and thoughts are produced as a result of sensory impressions. The *Essay Concerning Human Understanding* passed through many editions and translations and, along with Newton's *Principia*, was one of the dominant intellectual inspirations of the Enlightenment.

The rapidly growing literature about non-European lands and cultures was another cause of questioning among thinkers. In the wake of the great discoveries, Europeans were learning that the peoples of the world had their own very different beliefs and customs. Whereas Europeans shaved their faces and let their hair grow, Turks shaved their heads and let their beards grow. In Europe a man bowed before a woman to show respect, while in Siam (now Thailand) a man turned his back on a woman when he met her because it was disrespectful to look directly at her. Countless similar examples discussed in travel accounts helped change the perspective of educated Europeans. They began to look at truth and morality in relative, rather than absolute, terms. If anything was possible, who could say what was right or wrong?

The Influence of the Philosophes

By the time Louis XIV died in 1715, many of the ideas that would soon coalesce into the new worldview had been assembled. Yet Christian Europe was still strongly attached to its established political and social structures and its traditional spiritual beliefs. By 1775, however, a large portion of western Europe's educated elite had embraced many of the new ideas. This acceptance was largely the work of the **philosophes**, a group of influential intellectuals in France who proudly proclaimed that they were bringing the light of knowledge to their ignorant fellow creatures.

To appeal to the public and get around the censors, the philosophes wrote novels and plays, histories and philosophies, dictionaries and encyclopedias, all filled with satire and double meanings to spread their message. One of the greatest philosophes, the baron de Montesquieu (mahn-tuhs-KYOO; 1689–1755), pioneered this approach in *The Persian Letters*, an extremely influential social satire published in 1721. This work consisted of letters supposedly written by two Persian travelers, Usbek and Rica, who as outsiders see European customs in unique ways and thereby allow Montesquieu a vantage point for criticizing existing practices and beliefs.

Having gained fame by using wit as a weapon against cruelty and superstition, Montesquieu settled down on his family estate to study history and politics. Disturbed by royal absolutism under Louis XIV and inspired by the example of the physical sciences, Montesquieu set out to apply the critical method to the problem of government in *The Spirit of Laws* (1748).

> **"** I would reform an abuse which cuts off, so to speak, half the human race. I would make women participate in all the rights of humankind, and above all in those of the intellect. **"**
>
> **MADAME DU CHÂTELET**

Showing that forms of government were shaped by history, geography, and customs, Montesquieu identified three main types: monarchies, republics, and despotisms. Admiring greatly the English balance of power among the king, the houses of Parliament, and the independent courts, he argued for a separation of powers, with political power divided among a variety of classes and legal estates holding unequal rights and privileges. Montesquieu was no democrat; he was apprehensive about the uneducated poor, and he did not question the overarching sovereignty of the French monarch. But he was concerned that royal rule in France was drifting into tyranny and believed that strengthening the influence of intermediary powers was the best way to prevent it. Decades later, his theory of separation of powers had a great impact on the constitutions of the young United States in 1789 and of France in 1791.

The most famous philosophe was François-Marie Arouet, who was known by the pen name Voltaire (1694–1778). In his long career, Voltaire wrote more than seventy witty volumes, hobnobbed with kings and queens, and died a millionaire because of shrewd business speculations. His early career, however, was turbulent, and he was arrested on two occasions for insulting noblemen. To avoid a prison term in France, Voltaire moved to England for three years, and there he came to share Montesquieu's enthusiasm for English liberties and institutions.

Returning to France, Voltaire met Gabrielle-Emilie Le Tonnelier de Breteuil, marquise du Châtelet (1706–1749), a gifted woman from the high aristocracy. Madame du Châtelet invited Voltaire to live in her country house at Cirey in Lorraine and became his long-time companion (under the eyes of her tolerant husband). Passionate about science, she studied physics and mathematics and published scientific articles and translations, including the first French translation of Newton's *Principia*. Excluded from the Royal Academy of Sciences because she was a woman, Madame du Châtelet had no doubt that women's limited role in science was due to their unequal education. She once wrote that if she were a ruler, "I would reform an abuse which cuts off, so to speak, half the human race. I would

---

• **philosophes** A group of French intellectuals who proclaimed that they were bringing the light of knowledge to their fellow creatures in the Age of Enlightenment.

Voltaire and Philosophes This painting belongs to a series commissioned by Catherine the Great to depict daily life at the philosopher's retreat at Ferney in Switzerland. It shows Voltaire seated at the dinner table surrounded by his followers, including *Encyclopedia* editors Diderot and d'Alembert. The scene is imaginary, for Diderot never visited Ferney. (Photo by permission of the Voltaire Foundation, University of Oxford)

make women participate in all the rights of humankind, and above all in those of the intellect."[5]

While living at Cirey, Voltaire wrote works praising England and popularizing English scientific progress. Yet, like almost all of the philosophes, Voltaire was a reformer, not a revolutionary, in social and political matters. He pessimistically concluded that the best form of government was a good monarch, since human beings "are very rarely worthy to govern themselves." (For a discussion of monarchs influenced by Enlightenment ideals, see page 540.) Nor did Voltaire believe in social and economic equality. The only realizable equality, Voltaire thought, was that "by which the citizen only depends on the laws which protect the freedom of the feeble against the ambitions of the strong."[6]

Voltaire's philosophical and religious positions were much more radical than his social and political beliefs. Voltaire believed in God, but his was a distant, noninterventionist, deistic God. Drawing on Newton, he envisioned a mechanistic universe in which God acted like a great clockmaker who built an orderly system and then stepped aside and let it run. Above all, Voltaire and most of the philosophes hated all forms of religious intolerance, which they believed often led to fanaticism and savage, inhuman action.

The ultimate strength of the philosophes lay in their number, dedication, and organization. Their greatest and most representative intellectual achievement was a group effort—the seventeen-volume *Encyclopedia: The Rational Dictionary of the Sciences, the Arts, and the Crafts*, edited by Denis Diderot (1713–1784) and Jean le Rond d'Alembert (1717–1783). The two men set out in 1751 to find coauthors who would examine the rapidly expanding whole of human knowledge. Even more fundamentally, they set out to teach people how to think critically and objectively about all matters.

The *Encyclopedia* survived initial resistance from the French government and the Catholic Church. Completed in 1765, it contained hundreds of thousands of articles by leading scientists, writers, skilled workers, and progressive priests, and it treated every aspect of life and knowledge. Science and the industrial arts were exalted, religion and immortality questioned. Intoler-

• **economic liberalism** The theory that the pursuit of self-interest in a competitive market suffices to improve living conditions, rendering government intervention unnecessary and undesirable, associated with Adam Smith.

ance, legal injustice, and out-of-date social institutions were openly criticized. The *Encyclopedia* also included thousands of articles describing non-European cultures and societies, including acknowledgment of Muslim scholars' contribution to the development of Western science. Summing up the new worldview of the Enlightenment, the *Encyclopedia* was widely read, especially in less-expensive reprint editions, and it was extremely influential.

Enlightenment Across Europe

Enlightenment thought took on distinctive forms in different European countries. Even within each nation, reform-minded philosophers and writers formed their own societies and cliques with contrasting interests and points of view. Overall, England and the Netherlands were the most accepting of philosophical ideas, and they served as a beacon of tolerance and limited government for the rest of Europe.

The Scottish Enlightenment, centered in Edinburgh, was marked by an emphasis on pragmatic and scientific reasoning. Intellectual revival there was stimulated by the creation of the first public educational system in Europe. A key figure in Edinburgh was David Hume (1711–1776), whose carefully argued religious skepticism had a powerful impact at home and abroad. Building on Locke's teachings on learning, Hume argued that the human mind is really nothing but a bundle of impressions. These impressions originate only in sense experiences and our habits of joining these experiences together. Since our ideas ultimately reflect only our sense experiences, our reason cannot tell us anything about questions that cannot be verified by sense experience, such as questions about the origin of the universe or the existence of God. Paradoxically, Hume's rationalistic inquiry ended up undermining the Enlightenment's faith in the power of reason.

Another Scottish philosopher, Adam Smith (1723–1790), was a pioneer of the new field of political economy. Inspired by the possibilities of growing world trade, Smith developed the general idea of freedom of enterprise and established the basis for modern economics in his groundbreaking work, *Inquiry into the Nature and Causes of the Wealth of Nations* (1776). In keeping with his deep-seated fear of political oppression and with the "system of natural liberty" that he advocated, Smith argued that government should limit itself to "only three duties": defending against foreign invasion, maintaining civil order with courts and police protection, and sponsoring certain indispensable public works and institutions that private investors would never fund because such ventures would not be profitable. He believed that the pursuit of self-interest in a competitive market would be sufficient to improve the living conditions of citizens, a

☐ MAJOR FIGURES OF THE ENLIGHTENMENT

Baruch Spinoza (1632–1677)	Early Enlightenment thinker excommunicated from the Jewish community for his concept of a deterministic universe
John Locke (1632–1704)	*Essay Concerning Human Understanding* (1690)
Gottfried Leibniz (1646–1716)	Early German rational philosopher and scientist
Pierre Bayle (1647–1706)	*Historical and Critical Dictionary* (1697)
Montesquieu (1689–1755)	*The Persian Letters* (1721); *The Spirit of Laws* (1748)
Voltaire (1694–1778)	Renowned French philosophe and author of more than seventy works
Gabrielle-Emilie Le Tonnelier de Breteuil, marquise du Châtelet (1706–1749)	French scholar and supporter of equal education for women
David Hume (1711–1776)	Central figure of the Scottish Enlightenment
Jean-Jacques Rousseau (1712–1778)	*The Social Contract* (1762)
Denis Diderot (1713–1784) and Jean le Rond d'Alembert (1717–1783)	Editors of *Encyclopedia: The Rational Dictionary of the Sciences, the Arts, and the Crafts* (1765)
Adam Smith (1723–1790)	Pioneering political economist and author of *Inquiry into the Nature and Causes of the Wealth of Nations* (1776)
Immanuel Kant (1724–1804)	*What Is Enlightenment?* (1784); *On the Different Races of Man* (1775)

view that quickly emerged as the classic argument for **economic liberalism**.

In most of central and eastern Europe, reform-minded thinkers rejected the deism of Voltaire and the skepticism of Hume. Instead, they tried to integrate the findings of the scientific revolution with the teachings of established churches. In Germany, Gottfried Leibniz (GAHT-freed LIGHB-nuhtz; 1646–1716) was a founding father of the Enlightenment. His work spanned many disciplines, including mathematics, physics, history, and rationalist philosophy. Leibniz attempted to

The French Book Trade
Book consumption surged in the eighteenth century and along with it, new bookstores. This appealing bookshop in France with its intriguing ads for the latest works offers to put customers "Under the Protection of Minerva," the Roman goddess of wisdom. Large packets of books sit ready for shipment to foreign countries. (Musée des Beaux-Arts, Dijon/Art Resource, NY)

reconcile philosophy with faith by arguing that God allowed evil to exist as a means of allowing imperfect humans to exercise free will. He further argued that, despite the existence of pain and suffering, our world must be the best of all possible worlds since it was created by an omnipotent and benevolent God, a position later mocked as naively optimistic by Voltaire. Leibniz's last years were overshadowed by a dispute over whether he or Newton had invented calculus. Leibniz's opponents argued, probably incorrectly, that he had plagiarized Newton's work.

Immanuel Kant (1724–1804), a professor in East Prussia and the greatest German philosopher of his day, took up the question of the age when he published a pamphlet in 1784 titled *What Is Enlightenment?* Kant answered, "*Sapere Aude* (dare to know)! 'Have the courage to use your own understanding' is therefore the motto of enlightenment." He argued that if serious thinkers were granted the freedom to exercise their reason publicly in print, enlightenment would almost surely follow. Kant nonetheless epitomized the cautious eastern European attitude toward state authority. He insisted that in their private lives, individuals must obey all laws, no matter how unreasonable, and should

be punished for "impertinent" criticism. Kant thus tried to reconcile absolute monarchical authority with a critical public sphere.

Urban Culture and Life in the Public Sphere

A major stimulant to Enlightenment thought was urbanization. More and more people migrated to the city, especially after 1750. London and Paris swelled to over 500,000 people, while Naples and Amsterdam had populations of more than 100,000. Urban life gave rise to new institutions and practices that encouraged the spread of Enlightenment ideas. From about 1700 to 1789, the production and consumption of books grew significantly, and the types of books people read changed dramatically. The proportion of religious and devotional books published in Paris declined after 1750; history and law held constant; the arts and sciences surged.

Reading more books on many more subjects, the educated public increasingly approached reading in a new way. The result was what some scholars have called a reading revolution. The old style of reading was centered on a core of sacred texts. Reading was patriarchal and communal, with the father of the family slowly reading texts aloud. Now reading involved a broader field of books that constantly changed. Reading became individual and silent, and texts could be

---

• **salons** Regular social gatherings held by talented and rich Parisian women in their homes, where philosophes and their followers met to discuss literature, science, and philosophy.

questioned. Subtle but profound, the reading revolution ushered in new ways of relating to the written word.

The conversation, discussion, and debate encouraged by an urban milieu also played a critical role in the Enlightenment. Paris set the example that other French and European cities followed. In Paris from about 1740 to 1789, a number of talented, wealthy women presided over regular social gatherings named after their elegant private drawing rooms, or **salons**. There they encouraged the exchange of observations on literature, science, and philosophy with great aristocrats, wealthy middle-class financiers, high-ranking officials, and noteworthy foreigners. Talented hostesses, or *salonnières* (sah-lahn-ee-EHRZ), mediated the public's examination of Enlightenment thought. As one philosophe described his Enlightenment hostess and her salon:

> She could unite the different types, even the most antagonistic, sustaining the conversation by a well-aimed phrase, animating and guiding it at will. . . . Politics, religion, philosophy, news: nothing was excluded. Her circle met daily from five to nine. There one found men of all ranks in the State, the Church, and the Court, soldiers and foreigners, and the leading writers of the day.[7]

▫ Picturing the Past

Enlightenment Culture An actor performs the first reading of a new play by Voltaire at the salon of Madame Geoffrin in this painting from 1755. Voltaire, then in exile, is represented by a bust statue. (Réunion des Musées Nationaux/Art Resource, NY)

ANALYZING THE IMAGE Which of these people do you think is the hostess, Madame Geoffrin, and why? Using details from the painting to support your answer, how would you describe the status of the people shown?

CONNECTIONS What does this image suggest about the reach of Enlightenment ideas to common people? To women? Does the painting of the bookstore on page 538 suggest a broader reach? Why?

Elite women also exercised great influence on artistic taste. Soft pastels, ornate interiors, sentimental portraits, and starry-eyed lovers protected by hovering cupids were all hallmarks of the style they favored. This style, known as rococo, was popular throughout Europe from 1720 to 1780. During this period, women were also closely associated with the rise of the novel as a literary genre, both as authors and readers. The novel helped popularize a new cult of sensibility, which celebrated strong emotions and intimate family love. Some philosophes championed greater rights and expanded education for women, claiming that the position and treatment of women were the best indicators of a society's level of civilization and decency.[8]

While salon membership and artistic pursuits were largely restricted to the well-born and the exceptionally talented, a number of institutions emerged for the rest of society. Lending libraries served an important function for people who could not afford their own books. The coffeehouses that first appeared in the late seventeenth century became meccas of philosophical discussion. In addition, book clubs, Masonic lodges (groups of Freemasons, a secret egalitarian society that existed across Europe), and journals all played a part in creating a new **public sphere** that celebrated open debate informed by critical reason. The public sphere was an idealized space where members of society came together to discuss the social, economic, and political issues of the day.

What of the common people? Did they participate in the Enlightenment? Enlightenment philosophes did not direct their message to peasants or urban laborers. They believed that the masses had no time or talent for philosophical speculation and that elevating them would be a slow and potentially dangerous process.

There is some evidence, however, that ordinary people were not immune to the words of the philosophes. At a time of rising literacy, book prices were dropping in cities and towns, and many philosophical ideas were popularized in cheap pamphlets. Moreover, even illiterate people had access to written material through the practice of public reading. Although they were barred from salons and academies, ordinary people were nonetheless exposed to the new ideas in circulation.

Late Enlightenment

After about 1770 a number of thinkers and writers began to attack the Enlightenment's faith in reason and progress. The most famous of these was the Swiss intellectual Jean-Jacques Rousseau (1712–1778). Rousseau was both one of the most influential voices of the Enlightenment and, in his rejection of rationalism and social discourse, a harbinger of reaction against En-

lightenment ideas. Like other Enlightenment thinkers, Rousseau was passionately committed to individual freedom. Unlike them, however, he attacked rationalism and civilization as destroying, rather than liberating, the individual. Warm, spontaneous feeling, Rousseau believed, had to complement and correct cold intellect. Moreover, he asserted, the basic goodness of the individual and the unspoiled child had to be protected from the cruel refinements of civilization. Rousseau's ideals greatly influenced the early romantic movement, which rebelled against the culture of the Enlightenment in the late eighteenth century.

Rousseau also called for a rigid division of gender roles, arguing that women and men were radically different beings. According to Rousseau, because women were destined by nature to assume a passive role in sexual relations, they should also be passive in social life. Additionally, he believed that women's love for displaying themselves in public, attending salons, and pulling the strings of power was unnatural and had a corrupting effect on both politics and society. Rousseau thus rejected the sophisticated way of life of Parisian elite women. His criticism led to broader calls for privileged women to renounce what he regarded as frivolous behavior and stay at home to care for their children.

Rousseau's contribution to political theory in *The Social Contract* (1762) was based on two fundamental concepts: the general will and popular sovereignty. According to Rousseau, the **general will** is sacred and absolute, reflecting the common interests of all people, who have displaced the monarch as the holder of sovereign power. The general will is not necessarily the will of the majority, however. At times the general will may be the authentic, long-term needs of the people as correctly interpreted by a farseeing minority. Little noticed before the French Revolution, Rousseau's concept of the general will appealed greatly to democrats and nationalists after 1789.

Enlightened Absolutism

☐ What impact did new ways of thinking have on monarchical absolutism and those under its rule?

Although Enlightenment thinkers were often critical of untrammeled despotism and eager for reform, their impact on politics was mixed. Outside of England and the Netherlands, especially in central and eastern Europe, most believed that political change could best come from above — from the ruler — rather than from below. Nevertheless, government officials' daily involvement in complex affairs of state made them natu-

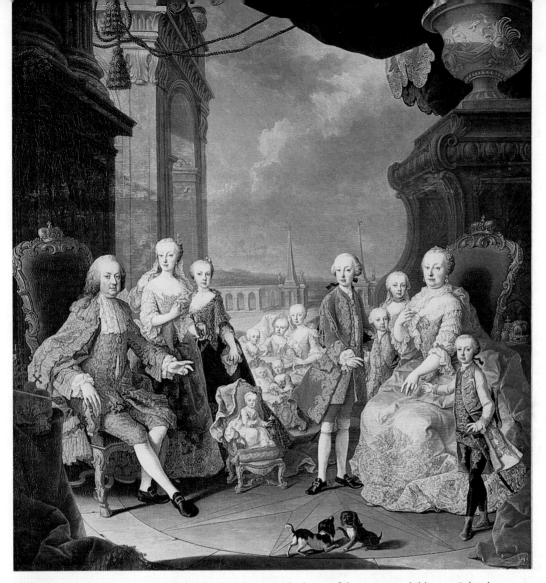

Maria Theresa The empress and her husband pose with eleven of their sixteen children at Schönbrunn palace in this family portrait by court painter Martin Meytens (1695–1770). Joseph, the heir to the throne, stands at the center of the star on the floor. Wealthy women often had very large families, in part because they, unlike poor women, seldom nursed their babies. (Réunion des Musées Nationaux/Art Resource, NY)

rally attracted to ideas for improving human society. Encouraged and instructed by these officials, some absolutist rulers tried to reform their governments in accordance with Enlightenment ideals. The result was what historians have called the **enlightened absolutism** of the later eighteenth century.

Reforms in Prussia, Russia, and Austria

Frederick II (r. 1740–1786) of Prussia, known as Frederick the Great, sought to improve the standing of his nation within Europe (see page 503). In 1740 he initiated the War of the Austrian Succession (1740–1748) to contest the right of a woman, Maria Theresa, to inherit the Habsburg throne. After a bold military victory, Frederick the Great acquired almost all of the

province of Silesia from Austria, albeit without unseating Maria Theresa from her throne. Influenced by the philosophes, Frederick tolerantly allowed his subjects to believe as they wished in religious and philosophical matters. He promoted the advancement of knowledge, improving his country's schools and

- **public sphere** An idealized intellectual space that emerged in Europe during the Enlightenment. Here, the public came together to discuss important social, economic, and political issues.

- **general will** A concept associated with Rousseau, referring to the common interests of all the people, who have replaced the power of the monarch.

- **enlightened absolutism** Term coined by historians to describe the rule of eighteenth-century monarchs who, without renouncing their own absolute authority, adopted Enlightenment ideals of rationalism, progress, and tolerance.

> "I must enlighten my people, cultivate their manners and morals, and make them as happy as human beings can be, or as happy as the means at my disposal permit."
>
> **FREDERICK THE GREAT**

permitting scholars to publish their findings. He also sought to improve life for ordinary people with innovations in agriculture and industry. As he wrote to his friend Voltaire, "I must enlighten my people, cultivate their manners and morals, and make them as happy as human beings can be, or as happy as the means at my disposal permit."

Frederick's most fundamental reforms were to the legal system. Under his reign, Prussia's laws were simplified, torture of prisoners was abolished, and judges decided cases quickly and impartially. Prussian officials became famous for their hard work and honesty. However, Frederick did not free the serfs of Prussia; instead, he extended the privileges of the nobility over them.

Frederick's reputation as an enlightened prince was rivaled by that of Catherine the Great of Russia (r. 1762–1796), one of the most remarkable rulers of her time. When she was fifteen years old Catherine's family ties to the Romanov dynasty made her a suitable bride for the heir to the Russian throne. Catherine profited from her husband's unpopularity, having him murdered so that she could be declared empress of Russia.

The War of Austrian Succession, 1740–1748

Never questioning that absolute monarchy was the best form of government, Catherine set out to rule in an enlightened manner. She had three main goals. First, she worked hard to continue Peter the Great's efforts to bring the culture of western Europe to Russia (see page 509). To do so, she patronized Western architects, sculptors, musicians, and philosophes and encouraged Russian nobles to follow her example. Catherine's second goal was domestic reform. She restricted the practice of torture and allowed limited religious toleration. She also tried to improve education and strengthen local government. The philosophes applauded these measures and hoped more would follow.

These hopes were dashed by a massive uprising of serfs in 1733 under the leadership of a common Cossack soldier named Emelian Pugachev. Although Pugachev was ultimately captured and executed, his rebellion shocked Russian rulers and put an end to any intentions Catherine might have had about reforming the system. After 1775 Catherine gave the nobles absolute control of their serfs and extended serfdom into new areas. In 1785 she formally freed nobles from taxes and state service. Therefore, under Catherine the Russian nobility attained its most exalted position, and serfdom entered its most oppressive phase.

Catherine's third goal was territorial expansion, and in this respect she was extremely successful. Her armies subjugated the last descendants of the Mongols and the Crimean Tartars, and began the conquest of the Caucasus, on the border between Europe and Asia. Her greatest coup was the partition of Poland, which took place in stages from 1772 to 1795 (Map 18.1).

Maria Theresa (r. 1740–1780) of Austria also established reforms in her nation, although traditional power politics was a more important motivation for her than were Enlightenment teachings. Her more radical son, Joseph II (r. 1780–1790), drew on Enlightenment ideals, earning the title of "revolutionary emperor." Most notably, Joseph abolished serfdom in 1781, and in 1789 he decreed that peasants could pay landlords in cash rather than through compulsory labor. This measure was rejected not only by the nobility but also by the peasants it was intended to help, because they lacked the necessary cash. When Joseph died at forty-nine, the Habsburg empire was in turmoil. His brother Leopold II (r. 1790–1792) canceled Joseph's radical edicts in order to reestablish order.

Jewish Life and the Limits of Enlightened Absolutism

Perhaps the best example of the limitations of enlightened absolutism are the debates surrounding the possible emancipation of the Jews. Europe's small Jewish populations lived under highly discriminatory laws. For the most part, Jews were confined to tiny, overcrowded ghettos, excluded by law from most business and professional activities, and could be ordered out of a kingdom at a moment's notice. Still, a very few did manage to succeed and to obtain the right of permanent settlement, usually by performing some special service for the state, such as money lending. Also, because of their large and closely knit communities, Jewish merchants and traders were prominent in international trade.

Individuals in Society

Moses Mendelssohn and the Jewish Enlightenment

IN 1743 A SMALL, HUMPBACKED JEWISH BOY with a stammer left his poor parents in Dessau in central Germany and walked eighty miles to Berlin, the capital of Frederick the Great's Prussia. According to one story, when the boy reached the Rosenthaler Gate, the only one through which Jews could pass, he told the inquiring watchman that his name was Moses and that he had come to Berlin "to learn." The watchman laughed and waved him through. "Go Moses, the sea has opened before you."*

In Berlin the young Mendelssohn studied Jewish law and eked out a living copying Hebrew manuscripts in a beautiful hand. But he was soon fascinated by an intellectual world that had been closed to him in the Dessau ghetto. There, like most Jews throughout central Europe, he had spoken Yiddish— a mixture of German, Polish, and Hebrew. Now, working mainly on his own, he mastered German; learned Latin, Greek, French, and English; and studied mathematics and Enlightenment philosophy. Word of his exceptional abilities spread in Berlin's Jewish community (the dwelling of 1,500 of the city's 100,000 inhabitants). He began tutoring the children of a wealthy Jewish silk merchant, and he soon became the merchant's clerk and later his partner. But his great passion remained the life of the mind and the spirit, which he avidly pursued in his off-hours.

Gentle and unassuming in his personal life, Mendelssohn was a bold thinker. Reading eagerly in works of Western philosophy dating back to antiquity, he was, as a pious Jew, soon convinced that Enlightenment teachings need not be opposed to Jewish thought and religion. He concluded that reason could complement and strengthen religion, although each would retain its integrity as a separate sphere.† Developing this idea in his first great work, "On the Immortality of the Soul" (1767), Mendelssohn used the neutral setting of a philosophical dialogue between Socrates and his followers in ancient Greece to argue that the human soul lived forever. In refusing to bring religion and critical thinking into conflict, he was strongly influenced by contemporary German philosophers who argued similarly on behalf of Christianity. He reflected the way the German Enlightenment generally supported established religion, in contrast to the French Enlightenment, which attacked it.

Mendelssohn's treatise on the human soul captivated the educated German public, which marveled that a Jew could have written a philosophical masterpiece. In the excitement, a Christian zealot named Lavater challenged Mendelssohn in a pamphlet to accept Christianity or to demonstrate how the Christian faith was not "reasonable." Replying politely but pas-

sionately, the Jewish philosopher affirmed that his studies had only strengthened him in his faith, although he did not seek to convert anyone not born into Judaism. Rather, he urged toleration in religious matters and spoke up courageously against Jewish oppression.

Orthodox Jew and German philosophe, Moses Mendelssohn serenely combined two very different worlds. He built a bridge from the ghetto to the dominant culture over which many Jews would pass, including his novelist daughter Dorothea and his famous grandson, the composer Felix Mendelssohn.

QUESTIONS FOR ANALYSIS

1. How did Mendelssohn seek to influence Jewish religious thought in his time?
2. How do Mendelssohn's ideas compare with those of the French Enlightenment?

Lavater (right) attempts to convert Mendelssohn, in a painting of an imaginary encounter by Moritz Oppenheim. (akg-images)

---

*H. Kupferberg, *The Mendelssohns: Three Generations of Genius* (New York: Charles Scribner's Sons, 1972), p. 3.

†D. Sorkin, *Moses Mendelssohn and the Religious Enlightenment* (Berkeley: University of California Press, 1996), pp. 8 ff.

Legend:
- Poland in 1772
- Austria in 1795
- Prussia in 1795
- Russia in 1795
- 1772 Year territory seized

□ Mapping the Past

MAP 18.1 The Partition of Poland, 1772–1795 In 1772 the threat of war between Russia and Austria arose over Russian gains from the Ottoman Empire. To satisfy desires for expansion without fighting, Prussia's Frederick the Great proposed dividing parts of Poland among Austria, Prussia, and Russia. In 1793 and 1795 the three powers partitioned the remainder, and Poland ceased to exist as an independent nation.

ANALYZING THE MAP Of the three powers that divided the kingdom of Poland, which benefited the most? How did the partition affect the geographical boundaries of each state, and what was the significance? What border with the former Poland remained unchanged? Why do you think this was the case?

CONNECTIONS Why was Poland vulnerable to partition in the later half of the eighteenth century? What does it say about European politics at the time that a country could simply cease to exist on the map? Could that happen today?

The Pale of Settlement, 1791

In the eighteenth century, an Enlightenment movement known as the **Haskalah** emerged from within the European Jewish community. This movement was led by the Prussian philosopher Moses Mendelssohn (1729–1786). Christian and Jewish Enlightenment philosophers, including Mendelssohn, began to advocate for freedom and civil rights for European Jews. In an era of growing reason and tolerance, they argued, restrictions on religious grounds could not stand. (See "Individuals in Society: Moses Mendelssohn and the Jewish Enlightenment," page 543.)

Arguments for tolerance won some ground, especially under Joseph II of Austria. Most monarchs, however, refused to entertain the idea of emancipation. In 1791 Catherine the Great established the Pale of Settlement, a territory including modern-day Belarus, Lithuania, Latvia, Moldava, Ukraine, and parts of Poland, in which most Jews were required to live until the Russian Revolution of 1917.

The Growth of Consumerism and the Atlantic World

☐ How did the growth of consumerism and the Atlantic economy interact with Enlightenment ideas?

The new practices of debate and sociability brought by the Enlightenment took place within a rapidly evolving material world. A rising European population in the eighteenth century furnished more skilled hands to produce finished goods as well as more consumers to purchase these products. Scientific instruments for making discoveries, and books and newspapers for publicizing them; coffee and tea for stimulating thought; hats, ribbons, and stockings for embellishing sociable urbanites — material goods like these set the stage for the lively exchange of ideas.

Consumerism in the eighteenth century was fed by an increasingly integrated Atlantic economy that circulated finished European products, raw materials from the colonies, and enslaved peoples from Africa. Over time, distinctive Atlantic communities and identities were constituted by the peoples, goods, and ideas that crisscrossed the ocean.

In turn, the contents of Enlightenment thought were shaped by the material world in which they emerged. Enlightenment thinkers drew inspiration from accounts of New World encounters as well as from the economic possibilities of colonial trade. As Adam Smith himself declared, "The discovery of America and that of a passage to the East Indies by the Cape of Good Hope, are the two greatest and most important events recorded in the history of mankind."[9] Enlightenment thinkers also used science and reason to establish a racial hierarchy that placed whites at the top, helping to justify slavery.

A Revolution in Consumption and Daily Life

One of the most important developments of eighteenth-century Europe was the emergence of a fledgling consumer culture. Many purchasers of consumer goods were from the upper and upper-middle classes, but a boom in cheap reproductions of luxury items provided affordable goods for people of modest means. From food to ribbons and from coal stoves to umbrellas, the material worlds of city dwellers grew richer and more diverse. This "consumer revolution," as it has been called, created new expectations for comfort and self-expression, dramatically changing European daily life in the eighteenth century.

Food was one of the chief areas of advance. Using Enlightenment techniques of observation and experimentation, a group of scientists, government officials, and a few big landowners devised new agricultural practices and tools that raised crop yields dramatically, especially in England and the Netherlands. These included new forms of crop rotation, better equipment, and selective breeding of livestock. The controversial process of **enclosure**, fencing off common land to create privately owned fields, allowed a break with traditional methods, but at the cost of reducing poor farmers' access to land.

Colonial plants also provided new sources of calories and nutrition. Introduced into Europe from the Americas — along with corn, squash, tomatoes, and many other useful plants — the humble potato provided an excellent new food source. Containing a good supply of carbohydrates and vitamins A and C, the potato offset the lack of fresh vegetables and fruits in common people's winter diet. After initial resistance, the potato became an important dietary supplement in much of Europe by the end of the eighteenth century. Together, these improvements in agriculture led to a rapid growth of population, especially after 1750.

> "The discovery of America and that of a passage to the East Indies by the Cape of Good Hope, are the two greatest and most important events recorded in the history of mankind."
>
> **ADAM SMITH**

One of the most remarkable dietary changes in the eighteenth century was the greater consumption of sugar, tea, coffee, tobacco, and chocolate. Previously expensive and rare luxury items, they became dietary staples for people of all social classes, especially in Britain. This was possible because new surpluses in production provided by slave labor in the New World lowered the price of many of these items.

No commodities grew as quickly in popularity as sugar and tea. There were significant class distinctions in the consumption of tea. Whereas the gentry took tea as a leisurely and genteel ritual, the lower classes usually drank it at work to fight monotony or fatigue. With the widespread adoption of these products (which turned out to be mildly to extremely addictive), working people in Europe became increasingly dependent on faraway colonial economies and slave labor. What they now saw as daily necessities linked them to global trade networks beyond their ability to shape or control.

- **Haskalah** A Jewish Enlightenment movement led by Prussian philosopher Moses Mendelssohn.
- **enclosure** The controversial process of fencing off common land to create privately owned fields that increased agricultural production at the cost of reducing poor farmers' access to land.

The Consumer Revolution From the mid-eighteenth century on, the cities of western Europe witnessed a new proliferation of consumer goods. Items once limited to the wealthy few—such as fans (lower right), watches, snuffboxes, umbrellas, ornamental containers (right), and teapots—were now reproduced in cheaper versions for middling and ordinary people. The fashion for wide hoopskirts was so popular that the armrests of the chairs of the day, known as Louis XV chairs (left), were specially designed to accommodate them. (fan: Scala/White Images/Art Resource, NY; jar: Victoria & Albert Museum, London/The Bridgeman Art Library; chair: Louvre/Réunion des Musées Nationaux/Art Resource, NY)

Greater demand for manufactured clothing was another major factor behind the growth of consumption. Shrewd entrepreneurs made fashionable clothing seem more desirable, while legions of women entering the textile and needle trades made it ever cheaper. As a result, eighteenth-century western Europe witnessed a dramatic rise in the consumption of clothing, particularly in large cities. One historian has documented a large growth in the size and value of Parisians' wardrobes from 1700 to 1789, as well as a new level of diversity in garments and accessories, colors, and fabrics.[10] Colonial economies again played an important role in lowering the cost of materials, such as cotton and vegetable dyes, largely due to the unpaid toil of enslaved Africans. Cheaper copies of elite styles made it possible for working people to as-

pire to follow fashion for the first time. Elite onlookers were bemused by the sight of lower-class people in fashionable dress. In 1784 Mrs. Fanny Cradock described encountering her milkman during an evening stroll "dressed in a fashionable suit, with an embroidered waistcoat, silk knee-breeches and lace cuffs."[11]

Mrs. Cradock's milkman notwithstanding, the spread of fashion was primarily a female phenomenon. Parisian women significantly out-consumed men, acquiring larger and more expensive wardrobes than those of their husbands, brothers, and fathers. Whereas traditionally fashion had belonged as much to men as to women, henceforth it was increasingly identified with women and the perceived frivolity of the "fair sex."

Changes in outward appearances were reflected in inner spaces as new attitudes about privacy and individuality also emerged. In 1700 the cramped home of a modest family consisted of a few rooms, each of which had multiple functions. For example, the same room might be used for sleeping, receiving friends, and working. In the eighteenth century rents rose sharply, making it impossible to gain more space, but families began attributing specific functions to specific rooms and putting barriers up to divide rooms into separate spaces.

New levels of comfort and convenience accompanied this trend toward more individualized ways of life. In 1700 a meal might be served in a common dish, with each person dipping his or her spoon into the pot. By the end of the eighteenth century even humble households contained a much greater variety of cutlery and dishes, making it possible for each person to eat from his or her own plate. More books and prints, now available at lower prices, decorated the shelves and walls. Improvements in glassmaking provided more transparent glass, which allowed daylight to penetrate into gloomy rooms. Cold and smoky hearths were replaced by more efficient and cleaner coal stoves, which also eliminated the backache of cooking over an open fire. All these changes made rooms warmer, better lit, more comfortable, and more personalized.

The scope of the new consumer economy should not be exaggerated. These developments were concentrated in large cities in northwestern Europe and in the colonial cities of North America. Even in these centers elites benefited the most from new modes of life. This was not yet the society of mass consumption that emerged toward the end of the nineteenth century with the full expansion of the Industrial Revolution. The eighteenth century did, however, lay the foundations for one of the most distinctive features of modern Western life: societies based on the consumption of goods and services obtained through global markets in which many individuals' identities and self-worth are shaped through the goods they consume.

The Atlantic Economy

The consumer revolution fed on the dynamic growth of trade across the Atlantic Ocean. Commercial exchange in the Atlantic is often referred to as the triangle trade, designating a three-way transport of goods: European commodities, like guns and textiles, to Africa; enslaved Africans to the colonies; and colonial goods, such as cotton, tobacco, and sugar, back to Europe. This model highlights some of the most important flows of trade but significantly oversimplifies the picture. For example, a brisk intercolonial trade also existed, with the

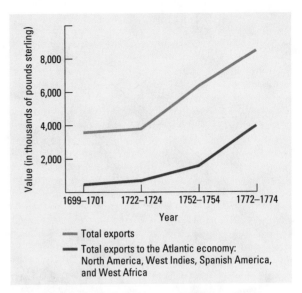

FIGURE 18.1 Exports of English Manufactured Goods, 1700–1774 While trade between England and Europe stagnated after 1700, English exports to Africa and the Americas boomed and greatly stimulated English economic development. (Source: Data from R. Davis, "English Foreign Trade, 1700–1774," *Economic History Review*, 2nd ser., 15 [1962]: 302–303.)

Caribbean slave colonies importing food in the form of fish, flour, and livestock from the northern colonies and rice from the south, in exchange for sugar and slaves (Map 18.2).

Moreover, the Atlantic economy was inextricably linked to trade with the Indian and Pacific Oceans. An outstanding example is the trade in cowrie shells. These seashells, originating in the Maldives in the Indian Ocean, were used as a form of currency in West Africa. European traders obtained them in Asia, packing them alongside porcelains, spices, and silks for the journey home. The cowries were then brought from European ports to the West African coast to be traded for slaves. Indian cotton cloth was also prized in Africa and played a similar role in exchange. The rising economic and political power of Europeans in the eighteenth century thus drew on the connections they established between the long-standing Asian and Atlantic trade worlds.

Across the eighteenth century the economies of European nations bordering the Atlantic Ocean relied more and more on colonial exports. In England, sales to the mainland colonies of North America and the West Indian sugar islands — with an important assist from West Africa and Latin America — soared from £500,000 to £4 million (Figure 18.1). Exports to England's colonies in Ireland and India also rose substantially from 1700 to 1800.

At the core of this Atlantic world was the misery and profit of the Atlantic slave trade (see pages 572–582). The brutal practice intensified dramatically after 1700 and especially after 1750 with the growth of

MAP 18.2 The Atlantic Economy in 1701 The growth of trade encouraged both economic development and military conflict in the Atlantic basin. Four continents were linked together by the exchange of goods and slaves.

trade and demand for slave-produced goods. English dominance of the slave trade provided another source of large profits to the home country.

The French also profited enormously from colonial trade in the eighteenth century, even after losing their vast North American territories to England in 1763. The Caribbean colonies of Saint-Domingue (modern-day Haiti), Martinique, and Guadeloupe, which remained in French hands, provided immense fortunes in plantation agriculture and slave trading. By 1789 the population of Saint-Domingue (sehn daw-MEHNG) included five hundred thousand slaves, whose labor had allowed the colony to become the world's leading producer of coffee and sugar and the most profitable plantation colony in the New World.[12] The wealth generated from colonial trade fostered the confidence of the merchant classes in Nantes, Bordeaux, and other large cities, and merchants soon joined other elite groups clamoring for more political power.

The third major player in the Atlantic economy, Spain, also saw its colonial fortunes improve during the eighteenth century. Its mercantilist goals were boosted by a recovery in silver production, which had dropped significantly in the seventeenth century. Spanish territory in North America expanded significantly in the second half of the eighteenth century. At the close of the Seven Years' War (1756–1763), Spain gained Louisiana from the French, and its influence extended westward all the way to northern California through the efforts of Spanish missionaries and ranchers.

Plantation Zones, ca. 1700

Identities and Communities of the Atlantic World

As contacts among the Atlantic coasts of the Americas, Africa, and Europe became more frequent, and as European settlements grew into well-established colonies, new identities and communities emerged. The term *Creole* referred to people of Spanish ancestry born in the Americas. Wealthy Creoles and their counterparts throughout the Atlantic colonies prided themselves on following European ways of life. In addition to their agricultural estates, they maintained townhouses in colonial cities built on the European model, with theaters, central squares, churches, and coffeehouses. They purchased luxury goods made in Europe, and their children were often sent to be educated in the home country.

Over time, however, the colonial elite came to feel that their circumstances gave them different interests

> ❝A turn of mind peculiar to the planter, occasioned by a physical difference of constitution, climate, customs, and education, tends . . . to repress the remains of his former attachment to his native soil.❞
>
> **EUROPEAN OBSERVER**

and characteristics from those of their home population. As one observer explained, "a turn of mind peculiar to the planter, occasioned by a physical difference of constitution, climate, customs, and education, tends . . . to repress the remains of his former attachment to his native soil."[13] Colonial elites became "Americanized" by adopting native foods, like chocolate and potatoes, and sought relief from tropical disease in native remedies. Also, they began to turn against restrictions from their home countries: Creole traders and planters increasingly resented the regulations and taxes imposed by colonial bureaucrats, and such resentment would eventually lead to revolutions against colonial powers (discussed in Chapter 27).

Enlightenment ideas thrived in the colonies, although with as much diversity and disagreement as in Europe. The colonies of British North America were deeply influenced by the Scottish Enlightenment, with its emphasis on pragmatic approaches to the problems of life. Following the Scottish model, leaders in the colonies adopted a moderate, "common-sense" version of the Enlightenment that emphasized self-improvement and ethical conduct. In most cases, this version of the Enlightenment was perfectly compatible with religion and was chiefly spread through the growing colleges and universities of the colonies, which remained church-based institutions.

Some thinkers went even further in their admiration for Enlightenment ideas. Benjamin Franklin's writings and political career provide an outstanding example of the combination of the pragmatism and economic interests of the Scottish Enlightenment with the constitutional theories of Locke, Montesquieu, and Rousseau. Franklin was privately a lifelong deist, but he continued to attend church and respect religious proprieties, a cautious pattern followed by fellow deist Thomas Jefferson and other leading thinkers of the American Enlightenment.

Northern Enlightenment thinkers often depicted the Spanish American colonies as the epitome of the

Viewpoints

Malachy Postlethwayt and Olaudah Equiano on the Abolition of Slavery

• *As Britain took control of transatlantic commerce during the eighteenth century, debate arose over the morality of the slave trade and the country's involvement in it. Malachy Postlethwayt, an economist, rejected criticism of slavery by arguing that African nations treated their subjects much worse than slave traders did and that the benefits of Christianity by far outstripped any disadvantages slaves might endure. In his famous autobiography, former slave Olaudah Equiano emphasized the cruelties of slavery. He argued, against authors like Postlethwayt, that trade with free peoples in Africa promised much more economic benefit to Britain than did slavery.*

Malachy Postlethwayt, *The National and Private Advantages of the African Trade Considered*

"Many are prepossessed against this trade, thinking it a barbarous, inhuman and unlawful traffic for a Christian country to trade in Blacks; to which I would beg leave to observe; that though the odious appellation of slaves is annexed to this trade, it being called by some the slave-trade, yet it does not appear from the best enquiry I have been able to make, that the state of those people is changed for the worse, by being servants to our British planters in America; they are certainly treated with great lenity and humanity: and as the improvement of the planter's estates depends upon due care being taken of their healths and lives, I cannot but think their condition is much bettered to what it was in their own country.

Besides, the negro princes in Africa, 'tis well known, are in perpetual war with each other, and since before they had this method of disposing of their prisoners of war to Christian merchants, they were wont not only to be applied to inhuman sacrifices, but to extreme torture and barbarity, their transportation must certainly be a melioration [improvement] of their condition; provided living in a civilized Christian country, is better than living among savages; Nay, if life be preferable to torment and cruel death, their state cannot, with any color or reason, be presumed to be worsened."

Olaudah Equiano, Appeal for the Abolition of Slavery

"Tortures, murder, and every other imaginable barbarity and iniquity, are practiced upon the poor slaves with impunity. I hope the great slave trade will be abolished. I pray it may be an event at hand. The great body of manufacturers, uniting in the cause, will considerably facilitate and expedite it; and as I have already stated, it is most substantially their interest and advantage, and as such the nation's at large (except those persons concerned in the manufacturing neck yokes, collars, chains, handcuffs, leg bolts, drags, thumb screws, iron muzzles, and coffins; cats, scourges, and other instruments of torture used in the slave trade). In a short time one sentiment will alone prevail, from motives of interest as well as justice and humanity. . . . If the blacks were permitted to remain in their own country, they would double themselves every fifteen years. In proportion to such increase will be the demand for manufactures. Cotton and indigo grow spontaneously in most parts of Africa; a consideration this of no small consequence to the manufacturing towns of Great Britain. It opens a most immense, glorious and happy prospect—the clothing, &c. of a continent ten thousand miles in circumference, and immensely rich in productions of every denomination in return for manufactures."

Sources: Malachy Postlethwayt, *The National and Private Advantages of the African Trade Considered* (London: Jon and Paul Knapton, 1746), pp. 4–5; Olaudah Equiano, *The Interesting Narrative of the Life of Olaudah Equiano*, Second Edition, ed. Robert J. Allison (Boston: Bedford/St. Martin's, 2007), pp. 194–195.

QUESTIONS FOR ANALYSIS

1. What contrast does Postlethwayt draw between the treatment of African people under slavery and in their home countries? What conclusion does he draw from this contrast?

2. To whom does Equiano address his appeal for abolition of the slave trade? What economic reasons does he provide for trading goods rather than slaves with Africa?

---

superstition and barbarity they contested. The Catholic Church strictly controlled the publication of books there, just as it did on the Iberian Peninsula. Nonetheless, educated elites were well aware of the new currents of thought, and the universities, newspapers, and salons of Spanish America produced their own reform ideas. The establishment of a mining school in Mexico City in 1792, the first in the Spanish colonies, illumi-

nates the practical achievements of reformers. In all European colonies, one effect of Enlightenment thought was to encourage colonists to criticize the policies of the mother country and aspire toward greater autonomy.

Not all Europeans in the colonies were wealthy or well-educated. Numerous poor and lower-middle-class whites worked as clerks, shopkeepers, craftsmen, and plantation managers. Whether rich or poor, however, white Europeans usually made up a small proportion of the population. Since most European migrants were men, much of the colonial population of the Atlantic world descended from unions — forced or through consent — of European men and indigenous or African women. Colonial attempts to establish and systematize racial categories greatly influenced developing Enlightenment thought on racial differences (see below).

In the Spanish and French Caribbean, as in Brazil, many masters acknowledged and freed their mixed-race children, leading to sizable populations of free people of color. Advantaged by their fathers, some became wealthy landowners and slaveholders in their own right. In the second half of the eighteenth century, the prosperity of some free people of color brought a backlash from the white population of Saint-Domingue in the form of new race laws prohibiting nonwhites from marrying whites and forcing them to adopt distinctive attire. In the British colonies of the Caribbean and the southern mainland, by contrast, masters tended to leave their mixed-race progeny in slavery, maintaining a stark discrepancy between free whites and enslaved people of color.[14] British colonial law forbade marriage between Englishmen and women and Africans or Native Americans.

Some mixed-race people sought to enter Creole society and obtain its many official and unofficial privileges by passing as white. Where they existed in any number, though, free people of color established their own proud social hierarchies based on wealth, family connections, occupation, and skin color.

Restricted from owning land and holding many occupations in Europe, Jews were eager participants in the new Atlantic economy and established a network of mercantile communities along its trade routes. As in the Old World, Jews in European colonies faced discrimination; for example, restrictions existed on the number of slaves they could own in Barbados in the early eighteenth century.[15] Jews were considered to be white Europeans and thus ineligible to be slaves, but they did not enjoy equal status with Christians. The status of Jews adds one more element to the complexity of Atlantic identities.

Race and the Enlightenment

Encounters in the Atlantic world — either personal or experienced through memoirs, travel literature, and other sources — had a strong impact on Enlightenment philosophers' views on race. Although most Europeans had little direct contact with Africans, educated writers were well aware of the growth of the slave trade and may have come across the increasing numbers of individuals of African descent living in European cities. Some Enlightenment thinkers took part in the slave trade. John Locke invested significant sums in slaving enterprises and served for many years as an administrator to colonial trade bodies. Among other activities, he coauthored the constitution for the Carolina colony, which included a clause dictating that Christian baptism would not endow freedom on slaves. Scholars still debate how this champion of freedom from tyranny could be personally involved in slavery.

Alongside intensified interaction with non-European peoples, another primary catalyst for new ideas about race was the urge to classify nature unleashed by the scientific revolution and its insistence on empirical observation. As scientists developed more elaborate taxonomies of plant and animal species, they also began to classify humans into hierarchically ordered "races" and to investigate the origins of race. The French naturalist Georges-Louis Leclerc, Comte de Buffon (1707–1788), argued that humans originated with one species that then developed into distinct races due largely to climatic conditions. Enlightenment thinkers such as David Hume and Immanuel Kant (see page 537) helped popularize these ideas.

In *On the Different Races of Man* (1775), Kant claimed that there were four human races, each of which had derived from a supposedly original race of "white brunette" people. According to Kant, the closest descendants of the original race were the white inhabitants of northern Germany. As they acquired new physical characteristics from their local climate and geography, the other races had degenerated both physically and culturally from this origin.

Using the word *race* to designate biologically distinct groups of humans was new. Previously, Europeans grouped other peoples into "nations" based on their historical, political, and cultural affiliations, rather than on supposedly innate physical differences. Unsurprisingly, when European thinkers drew up a hierarchical classification of human species, their own "race" was placed at the top. Europeans had long believed they were culturally superior. The new idea that racial difference was physical and innate rather than cultural taught them they were biologically superior as well. In turn, scientific racism helped legitimate and justify the tremendous growth of slavery that occurred during the eighteenth century. If one race of humans was fundamentally different and inferior, its members could be seen as particularly fit for enslavement. (See "Viewpoints: Malachy Postlethwayt and Olaudah Equiano on the Abolition of Slavery," page 550.)

Racist ideas did not go unchallenged. *Encyclopedia* editor Denis Diderot penned a scathing critique of European arrogance and exploitation in the voice of Tahitian villagers. (See "Listening to the Past: Denis Diderot's 'Supplement to Bougainville's Voyage,'" page 552.) Scottish philosopher James Beattie (1735–1803) responded directly to claims of white superiority by

Listening to the Past

Denis Diderot's "Supplement to Bougainville's Voyage"

Denis Diderot (1713–1784) was born in a provincial town in eastern France and educated in Paris. Rejecting careers in the church and the law, he devoted himself to literature and philosophy. In 1749, sixty years before Charles Darwin's birth, Diderot was jailed by Parisian authorities for publishing an essay questioning God's role in the creation and suggesting the autonomous evolution of species. Following these difficult beginnings, Diderot's editorial work and writing on the Encyclopedia *were the crowning intellectual achievements of his life and, according to some, of the Enlightenment itself.*

Like other philosophes, Diderot disseminated Enlightenment ideas through various types of writing, ranging from scholarly articles in the Encyclopedia *to philosophical treatises, novels, plays, book reviews, and erotic stories. His "Supplement to Bougainville's Voyage" (1772) was a fictional account of a European voyage to Tahiti inspired by the writings of traveler Louis-Antoine de Bougainville. In this passage, Diderot expresses his own loathing of colonial conquest and exploitation through the voice of an elderly Tahitian man. The character's praise for his own culture allows Diderot to express his Enlightenment idealization of natural man, free from the vices of civilized societies.*

“He was the father of a large family. When the Europeans arrived he looked upon them with scorn, showing neither astonishment, nor fear, nor curiosity. On their approach he turned his back and retired into his hut. Yet his silence and anxiety revealed his thoughts only too well; he was inwardly lamenting the eclipse of his countrymen's happiness. When Bougainville was leaving the island, as the natives swarmed on the shore, clutching his clothes, clasping his companions in their arms and weeping, the old man made his way forward and proclaimed solemnly, “Weep, wretched natives of Tahiti, weep. But let it be for the coming and not the leaving of these ambitious, wicked men. One day you will know them better. One day they will come back, bearing in one hand the piece of wood you see in that man's belt, and, in the other, the sword hanging by the side of that one, to enslave you, slaughter you, or make you captive to their follies and vices. One day you will be subject to them, as corrupt, vile and miserable as they are. . . .”

Then turning to Bougainville, he continued, “And you, leader of the ruffians who obey you, pull your ship away swiftly from these shores. We are innocent, we are content, and you can only spoil that happiness. We follow the pure instincts of nature, and you have tried to erase its impression from our hearts. Here, everything belongs to everyone, and you have preached I can't tell what distinction between ‘yours’ and ‘mine.’ . . . If a Tahitian should one day land on your shores and engrave on one of your stones or on the bark of one of your trees, *This land belongs to the people of Tahiti,* what would you think then? You are stronger than we are, and what does that mean? When one of the miserable trinkets with which your ship is filled was taken away, what an uproar you made, what revenge you exacted! At that moment, in the depths of your heart, you were plotting the theft of an entire country! You are not a slave, you would rather die than be one, and yet you wish to make slaves of us. Do you suppose, then, that a Tahitian cannot defend his own liberty and die for it as well? This inhabitant of Tahiti, whom you wish to ensare like an

pointing out that Europeans had started out as savage as nonwhites and that many non-European peoples in the Americas, Asia, and Africa had achieved high levels of civilization. German thinker Johann Gottfried von Herder (1744–1803) criticized Kant, arguing that humans could not be classified into races based on skin color and that each culture was as intrinsically worthy as any other.

One popular idea, among Rousseau and others, was that indigenous peoples of the Americas represented prime examples of "natural man," the being who embodied the essential goodness of humanity uncorrupted by decadent society. Other popular candidates for uto-pian natural man were the Pacific Island societies explored by Captain James Cook and others from the 1770s on (see pages 834–835).

There are clear parallels between the use of science to propagate racial hierarchies and to defend social inequalities between men and women. As we have noted, French philosopher Jean-Jacques Rousseau used women's "natural" passivity to argue for their passive role in society, just as other thinkers used non-Europeans' "natural" inferiority to defend slavery and colonial domination. The new powers of science and reason were thus marshaled to imbue traditional stereotypes with the force of natural law.

animal, is your brother. You are both children of Nature. What right do you have over him that he does not have over you? You came; did we attack you? Have we plundered your ship? Did we seize you and expose you to the arrows of our enemies? Did we harness you to work with our animals in the fields? We respected our own image in you.

"Leave us our ways; they are wiser and more decent than yours. We have no wish to exchange what you call our ignorance for your useless knowledge. Everything that we need and is good for us we already possess. Do we merit contempt because we have not learnt how to acquire superfluous needs? When we are hungry, we have enough to eat. When we are cold, we have enough to wear. You have entered our huts; what do you suppose we lack? Pursue as far as you wish what you call the comforts of life, but let sensible beings stop when they have no more to gain from their labours than imaginary benefits. If you persuade us to go beyond the strict bounds of necessity, when will we finish our work? When will we enjoy ourselves? We have kept our annual and daily labours within the smallest possible limits, because in our eyes nothing is better than rest. Go back to your own country to agitate and torment yourselves as much as you like. But leave us in peace. Do not fill our heads with your factitious needs and illusory virtues." **"**

Source: Edited excerpts from pages 41–43 in Denis Diderot, *Political Writings*, translated and edited by John Hope Mason and Robert Wokler. © 1992 by Cambridge University Press.

QUESTIONS FOR ANALYSIS

1. On what grounds does the speaker argue for the Tahitians' basic equality with the Europeans?

2. What is the good life, according to the speaker, and how does it contrast with the European way of life? Which do you think is the better path, and why?

3. In what ways could Diderot's thoughts here be seen as representative of Enlightenment ideas? Are there ways in which they are not?

4. How realistic do you think this account is? Does it matter? How might defenders of colonial expansion respond to Diderot's criticism?

• This image depicts the meeting of French explorer Louis-Antoine de Bougainville with Tahitians in April 1768. Of his stay on the island, Bougainville wrote: "I felt as though I had been transported to the Garden of Eden. . . . Everywhere reigned hospitality, peace, joy, and every appearance of happiness." Diderot's philosophical tract was a fictional sequel to Bougainville's account. (Unknown artist, Tahitians presenting fruit to Bougainville attended by his officers. PIC T2996 NK5066 LOC7321, National Library of Australia)

CONNECTIONS

Hailed as the origin of modern thought, the scientific revolution must also be seen as a product of its past. Borrowing in part from Arabic translators and commentators, medieval universities gave rise to important new scholarship. In turn, the ambition and wealth of Renaissance patrons nurtured intellectual curiosity and encouraged scholarly research and foreign exploration. Religious faith also influenced the scientific revolution, inspiring some thinkers to understand the glory of God's creation, while bringing censure and personal tragedy to others. Natural philosophers following Copernicus pioneered new methods of observing and explaining nature while drawing on centuries-old traditions of mysticism, astrology, alchemy, and magic.

Enlightenment ideas of the eighteenth century were a similar blend of past and present, progressive and traditional, homegrown and influenced by other cultures. Enlightenment thinkers advocated universal rights and liberties but also preached the biological inferiority of non-Europeans. Their principles served as much to bolster authoritarian regimes as to inspire revolutionaries to fight for human rights. Although the Enlightenment fostered critical thinking about everything from science to religion, most Europeans, including many prominent thinkers, remained devout Christians.

Key Western values of rationalism, human rights, and open-mindedness were born from the scientific revolution and the Enlightenment. With their new notions of progress and social improvement, Europeans would embark on important revolutions in politics and industry (see Chapters 22 and 23). Nonetheless, some critics have seen a darker side. For them, the mastery over nature permitted by the scientific revolution now threatens to overwhelm the earth's fragile equilibrium, and the Enlightenment belief in the universal application of reason can lead to intolerance of other people's spiritual, cultural, and political values. Such vivid debate about the legacy of these intellectual and scientific developments testifies to their continuing importance in today's world.

As the era of European exploration and conquest gave way to empire-building, the eighteenth century witnessed increased consolidation of global markets and bitter competition among Europeans. The eighteenth-century Atlantic world thus tied the shores of Europe, the Americas, and Africa in a web of commercial and human exchange, including the tragedy of slavery, discussed in Chapter 19. The Atlantic world maintained strong ties with trade in the Pacific and the Indian Ocean.

☐ CHAPTER REVIEW

KEY TERMS

natural philosophy (p. 526)
Copernican hypothesis (p. 528)
law of inertia (p. 529)
law of universal gravitation (p. 530)
empiricism (p. 530)
Cartesian dualism (p. 531)
Enlightenment (p. 533)

philosophes (p. 535)
economic liberalism (p. 537)
salons (p. 539)
public sphere (p. 540)
general will (p. 540)
enlightened absolutism (p. 541)
Haskalah (p. 544)
enclosure (p. 545)

☐ What was revolutionary in the new attitudes toward the natural world? (p. 526)

Decisive breakthroughs in astronomy and physics in the seventeenth century demolished the medieval synthesis of Aristotelian philosophy and Christian theology. One of the most notable discoveries was that the sun, not the earth, was the center of the universe. Although the early scientists considered their ideas to be in line with religion, their discoveries ran counter to long-held beliefs about the design of the universe by a creator; therefore, the findings of Copernicus, Kepler, Galileo, and others were opposed by religious authorities, and Galileo was tried for heresy. Meanwhile, Bacon promoted an experimental method that drew conclusions based on empirical evidence, and Descartes championed deductive reasoning, which speculated truths based on known principles. These two important methods eventually combined to form the modern scientific method, which relies on both experimentation and reason. Following these early innovators, Newton devised the law of universal gravitation, which for the first time synthesized the orbiting planets of the solar system with the motion of objects on earth. The impact of these scientific breakthroughs on intellectual life was enormous, nurturing a new critical attitude in many disciplines. In addition, an international scientific community arose, and state-sponsored academies, which were typically closed to women, advanced scientific research.

☐ How did a new spirit of critical and rational thinking affect ideas about society and human relations? (p. 533)

Interpreting scientific findings in a manner that questioned long-standing traditions and religious beliefs, Enlightenment philosophes extolled the superiority of rational, critical thinking. This new method, they believed, promised not just increased knowledge but

even the discovery of the fundamental laws of human society. Believing that all aspects of life were open to question and skepticism, Enlightenment thinkers opened the doors to religious tolerance, representative government, and general intellectual debate. Among the influential Enlightenment thinkers were Locke, who asserted that all human ideas are produced as a result of sensory impressions; Montesquieu, who argued for the separation of powers based on a critical and comparative study of governments; Voltaire, who drew on Newton to envision a mechanistic universe; Hume, who through rationalistic inquiry concluded that reason can be applied only to phenomena that can be verified by the human senses; and Rousseau, who described a general will reflecting the common interests of all people.

☐ What impact did new ways of thinking have on monarchical absolutism and those under its rule? (p. 540)

The ideas of the Enlightenment were an inspiration for monarchs, particularly absolutist rulers in central and eastern Europe, who saw in them important tools for reform. In Prussia and Russia, rulers became more religiously tolerant and made efforts to improve education and government, among other changes. However, conditions for serfs worsened under their rule. In

Austria, Joseph II abolished serfdom, but his reform efforts were ultimately unsuccessful. All in all, the influence of Enlightenment ideas on monarchies was limited, as perhaps is best illustrated by most rulers' refusal to support emancipation of the Jews.

◻ **How did the growth of consumerism and the Atlantic economy interact with Enlightenment ideas? (p. 545)**

The eighteenth century witnessed rising levels of consumption and increased comfort and privacy within the home, particularly in the cities and towns of northwestern Europe and British North America. These achievements were made possible in part by the expansion of transatlantic trade and the lowering of prices on colonial goods due to the growth of slave labor. Atlantic trade involved the exchange of commodities among Europe, Africa, and the Americas, but it was also linked in important ways with trade in the Indian and Pacific Oceans. The movement of people and ideas across the Atlantic in the eighteenth century helped shape the identities of colonial inhabitants. At first colonial elites prided themselves on following European ways of life. With time, however, they developed customs and attitudes apart from those of their homeland. Enlightenment ideas circulated in the colonies with as much diversity as in the mother countries. In turn, Enlightenment thinkers drew inspiration from the new peoples and cultures Europeans encountered. One important development was new ideas about race, defined as biologically distinct groups of people with innate differences and inequalities. When European thinkers created a hierarchical classification of humans, they placed their own race at the top, helping to justify the enslavement of peoples they saw as their inferiors.

SUGGESTED READING

Alexander, John T. *Catherine the Great: Life and Legend.* 1989. The best biography of the famous Russian tsarina.

Delbourgo, James, and Nicholas Dew, eds. *Science and Empire in the Atlantic World.* 2008. A collection of essays examining the relationship between the scientific revolution and the imperial expansion of European powers across the Atlantic.

Ellis, Markman. *The Coffee-House: A Cultural History.* 2004. An engaging study of the rise of the coffeehouse and its impact on European cultural and social life.

Eze, E. Chukwudi, ed. *Race and the Enlightenment: A Reader.* 1997. A pioneering source on the origins of modern racial thinking in the Enlightenment.

Goodman, Dena. *The Republic of Letters: A Cultural History of the Enlightenment.* 1994. An innovative study of the role of salons and salon hostesses in the rise of the Enlightenment.

MacDonogh, Giles. *Frederick the Great.* 2001. An outstanding biography of the Prussian king.

Mannin, Susan, and Francis D. Cogliano. *The Atlantic Enlightenment.* 2008. A series of essays examining the

exchange of Enlightenment ideas, authors, and texts across the Atlantic Ocean.

Osler, Margaret J., ed. *Rethinking the Scientific Revolution.* 2000. A collection of essays focusing on new historical approaches to the scientific revolution.

Outram, Dorinda. *The Enlightenment*, 2d ed. 2006. An outstanding and accessible introduction to Enlightenment debates that emphasizes the Enlightenment's social context and global reach.

Shapin, Steven. *The Scientific Revolution.* 2001. A concise and well-informed general introduction to the scientific revolution.

Sorkin, David. *Moses Mendelssohn and the Religious Enlightenment.* 1996. A brilliant study of the Jewish philosopher and of the role of religion in the Enlightenment.

NOTES

1. H. Butterfield, *The Origins of Modern Science* (New York: Macmillan, 1951), p. viii.
2. Quoted in A. G. R. Smith, *Science and Society in the Sixteenth and Seventeenth Centuries* (New York: Harcourt Brace Jovanovich, 1972), p. 97.
3. Quoted in Butterfield, *The Origins of Modern Science*, p. 47.
4. Ibid., p. 120.
5. L. Schiebinger, *The Mind Has No Sex? Women in the Origins of Modern Science* (Cambridge, Mass.: Harvard University Press, 1989), p. 64.
6. Quoted in G. L. Mosse et al., eds., *Europe in Review* (Chicago: Rand McNally, 1964), p. 156.
7. Quoted in G. P. Gooch, *Catherine the Great and Other Studies* (Hamden, Conn.: Archon Books, 1966), p. 149.
8. See E. Fox-Genovese, "Women in the Enlightenment," in *Becoming Visible: Women in European History*, 2d ed., ed. R. Bridenthal, C. Koonz, and S. Stuard (Boston: Houghton Mifflin, 1987), esp. pp. 252–259, 263–265.
9. R. Heilbroner, *The Essential Adam Smith* (New York: W. W. Norton, 1986), p. 281.
10. Daniel Roche, *The Culture of Clothing: Dress and Fashion in the Ancien Regime*, trans. Jean Birrell (Cambridge, U.K.: Cambridge University Press, 1996).
11. Quoted in Cissie Fairchilds, "The Production and Marketing of Populuxe Goods in Eighteenth-Century Paris," in *Consumption and the World of Goods*, ed. John Brewer and Roy Porter (London: Routledge, 1993), p. 228.
12. Laurent Dubois and John D. Garrigus, *Slave Revolution in the Caribbean, 1789–1904* (New York: Palgrave, 2006), p. 8.
13. Pierre Marie François Paget, *Travels Round the World in the Years 1767, 1768, 1769, 1770, 1771* (London, 1793), vol. 1, p. 262.
14. Orlando Patterson, *Slavery and Social Death* (Cambridge, Mass.: Harvard University Press, 1982), p. 255.
15. Erik R. Seeman, "Jews in the Early Modern Atlantic: Crossing Boundaries, Keeping Faith," in *The Atlantic in Global History, 1500–2000*, ed. Jorge Canizares-Esguerra and Erik R. Seeman (Upper Saddle River, N.J.: Pearson Prentice-Hall, 2007), p. 43.

For practice quizzes and other study tools, visit the **Online Study Guide** at bedfordstmartins.com/mckayworld.

For primary sources from this period, see *Sources of World Societies*, **Second Edition**.

For Web sites, images, and documents related to topics in this chapter, visit **Make History** at bedfordstmartins.com/mckayworld.

• **Waist Pendant of Benin Worn by Royalty** European intrusion in Africa during the early modern period deeply affected the diverse societies of Africa. The facial features, the beard, and the ruffled collar on this Edo peoples' artifact dating from the sixteenth to the nineteenth centuries are clearly Portuguese, but the braided hair is distinctly African, probably signifying royalty. (Image copyright © The Metropolitan Museum of Art/Art Resource, NY)

19

African states and societies of the early modern period — from the fifteenth through the eighteenth centuries — comprised a wide variety of languages, cultures, and kinds of economic and political development. Kingdoms and stateless societies coexisted throughout Africa, from the small villages of the Senegambia to the kingdom of Songhai and its renowned city of Timbuktu in West Africa, and from the Christian state of Ethiopia to the independent city-states of the Swahili coast in East Africa. So too by the fifteenth century had Africans developed a steady rhythm of contact and exchange. Across the great Sahara, trade goods and knowledge passed back and forth from West Africa to North Africa and beyond to Europe and the Middle East. The same was true in East Africa, where Indian Ocean traders touched up and down the African coast to deliver goods from Arabia, India, and Asia and to pick up the ivory, gold, spices, and other products representing Africa's rich natural wealth. In the interior as well, extensive trading networks linked African societies across the vast continent.

Africa and the World
1400–1800

Modern European intrusion into Africa beginning in the fifteenth century profoundly affected these diverse societies and ancient trading networks. The intrusion led to the trans-atlantic slave trade, one of the greatest forced migrations in world history, through which Africa made a substantial, though involuntary, contribution to the building of the West's industrial civilization. In the seventeenth century an increasing desire for sugar in Europe resulted in an increasing demand for slave labor in South America and the West Indies. In the eighteenth century Western technological changes created a demand for cotton and other crops that required extensive human labor, thus intensifying the West's "need" for African slaves. •

West Africa in the Fifteenth and Sixteenth Centuries
□ What different types of economic, social, and political structures were found in the kingdoms and states along the west coast and in the Sudan?

Cross-Cultural Encounters Along the East African Coast
□ How did the arrival of Europeans and other foreign cultures impact the East African coast, and how did Ethiopia and the Swahili city-states respond to these incursions?

The African Slave Trade
□ What role did slavery play in African societies before the transatlantic slave trade began, and what was the effect of European involvement?

West Africa in the Fifteenth and Sixteenth Centuries

□ What different types of economic, social, and political structures were found in the kingdoms and states along the west coast and in the Sudan?

In mid-fifteenth-century Africa, Benin and a number of other kingdoms flourished along the two-thousand-mile west coast between Senegambia and the northeastern shore of the Gulf of Guinea. Because much of that coastal region is covered by tropical rain forest, in contrast to the western Sudan, it is called the West African Forest Region (Map 19.1). Further inland, in the region of the Sudan, the kingdoms of Songhai, Kanem-Bornu, and Hausaland benefited from the trans-Saharan caravan trade, which along with goods brought Islamic culture to the region. These West African kingdoms maintained their separate existences for centuries. Stateless societies such as those in the region of Senegambia (modern-day Senegal and the Gambia) existed alongside these more centralized states. Despite their political differences and whether they were agricultural, pas-

toral, or a mixture of both, the cultures of West Africa equally faced the challenges presented by famine, disease, and the slave trade.

The West Coast: Senegambia and Benin

The Senegambian states possessed a homogeneous culture and a common history. For centuries Senegambia—named for the Senegal and Gambia Rivers—served as an important entrepôt for desert caravan contact with North African and Middle Eastern Islamic civilizations. Through the transatlantic slave trade, Senegambia came into contact with Europe and the Americas. Thus Senegambia felt the impact of Islamic culture to the north and of European influences from the maritime West.

The Senegambian peoples spoke Wolof, Serer, and Pulaar, which all belong to the West African language group. Both the Wolof-speakers and the Serer-speakers had clearly defined social classes: royalty, nobility, warriors, peasants, low-caste artisans such as blacksmiths and leatherworkers, and enslaved persons. This enslaved class consisted of individuals who were pawned for debt, house servants who could not be sold, and people who were acquired through war or purchase. Senegambian slavery varied from society to society but generally was not a benign institution. In some places, slaves were considered chattel property and were treated as harshly as they would be later in the Western Hemisphere.

The word **chattel** originally comes from a Latin word meaning head, as in "so many head of cattle." It

The Oba of Benin The oba's palace walls were decorated with bronze plaques that date from about the sixteenth to the eighteenth centuries. This plaque vividly conveys the oba's power, majesty, and authority. The necklace (or choker) is his symbol of royalty. His warrior attendants surround and protect him and carry his royal regalia. (Museum für Völkerkunde/Kunsthistorisches Museum, Vienna)

reflects the notion that enslaved people are not human, but subhuman, like beasts of burden, like animals. Thus, they can be treated like animals—whipped, beaten, worked to exhaustion, and forced to live in conditions no better than those provided for animals. But in Senegambia and other parts of Africa, many enslaved people were not considered chattel property. That is, unlike livestock or other common property, they could not be bought and sold. Some even served as royal advisers and enjoyed great power and prestige.[1] What is more, unlike in the Americas, where slave status passed forever from one generation to the next, in Africa the enslaved person's descendants were sometimes considered free, although the stigma of slave could attach to the family.

Senegambia was composed of stateless societies, culturally homogeneous ethnic societies where kinship and lineage groups tended to fragment communities. These societies comprised small groups of villages without a central capital. Among these stateless societies **age-grade systems** evolved. Age-grades were groups of teenage males and females whom the society initiated into adulthood at the same time. Age-grades cut across family ties, created community-wide loyalties, and provided a means of local law enforcement, because each age-grade was responsible for the behavior of all its members.

The typical Senegambian community was a small, self-supporting agricultural village of closely related families. Fields were cut from the surrounding forest, and the average six- to eight-acre farm supported a moderate-size family. Millet and sorghum were the staple grains in northern Senegambia; farther south, forest dwellers cultivated yams as a staple. Senegambians supplemented their diet with plantains, beans, bananas, fish, oysters, and small game such as rabbits and monkeys. Village markets for produce exchange offered opportunities for receiving outside news and for social diversion. Social life was centered around the family, and government played a limited role, interceding mostly to resolve family disputes and conflicts between families.

Alongside West African stateless societies like the Senegambia were kingdoms and states ruled by kings who governed defined areas through bureaucratic hierarchies. The great forest kingdom of Benin emerged in the fifteenth and sixteenth centuries in what is now

CHRONOLOGY

1400–1600s	Salt trade dominates West African economy
ca. 1464–1591	Songhai kingdom dominates the western Sudan
1485	Portuguese and other Europeans first appear in Benin
1492–1528	Muhammad Toure governs and expands kingdom of Songhai
1498	Portuguese explorer Vasco da Gama sails around Africa
ca. 1500–1900	Era of transatlantic slave trade
1502–1507	Portuguese erect forts at Kilwa, Zanzibar, and Sofala on Swahili coast
1529	Adal defeats Ethiopian emperor and begins systematic devastation of Ethiopia
1543	Portuguese defeat Muslims in Ethiopia
1571–1603	Idris Alooma governs kingdom of Kanem-Bornu
1591	Moroccan army defeats Songhai
1658	Dutch allow importation of slaves into Cape Colony
1680s	Famine from Senegambian coast to Upper Nile
1738–1756	Major famine in West Africa
1789	Olaudah Equiano publishes autobiography

southern Nigeria (see Map 19.1). Over time the position of its **oba**, or king, was exalted, bringing stability to the state. In the later fifteenth century the oba Ewuare, a great warrior himself, strengthened his army and pushed Benin's borders as far as the Niger River in the east, westward into Yoruba country, and south to the Gulf of Guinea. During the late sixteenth and seventeenth centuries the office of the oba evolved from a warrior-kingship to a position of spiritual leadership.

At its height in the late sixteenth century, Benin controlled a vast territory, and European visitors described a sophisticated society. A Dutch visitor in the early 1600s, possibly Dierick Ruiters, described the capital, Benin City, as possessing a great, wide, and straight main avenue down the middle, with many side streets crisscrossing it. The visitor entered the city through a high, well-guarded gate framed on each side

- **chattel** An item of personal property; a term used in reference to enslaved people that conveys the idea that they are subhuman, like animals, and therefore may be treated like animals.
- **age-grade systems** Among the societies of Senegambia, groups of men and women whom the society initiated into adulthood at the same time.
- **oba** The title of the king of Benin.

□ Mapping the Past

MAP 19.1 West African Societies, ca. 1500–1800

The coastal region of West Africa witnessed the rise of a number of kingdoms in the sixteenth century.

ANALYZING THE MAP What geographical features defined each of the kingdoms shown here? Consider rivers, lakes, oceans, deserts, and forests. How might they have impacted the size and shape of these kingdoms?

CONNECTIONS Compare this map to the spot map of the slave coast of West Africa on page 576. Consider the role that rivers and other geographical factors played in the development of the West African slave trade. Why were Luanda and Benguela the logical Portuguese sources for slaves?

	Songhai, ca. 1500
	Kanem-Bornu, ca. 1500
	Benin, ca. 1625
	Kongo, ca. 1625
	Area occupied by Fulani people

by a very tall earthen bulwark, or wall, with an accompanying moat. There was also an impressive royal palace, with at least four large courtyards surrounded by galleries leading up to it. William Bosman, another Dutch visitor writing a hundred years later, in 1702, described the prodigiously long and broad streets "in which continual Markets are kept, either of Kine [cattle], Cotton, Elephants Teeth, European Wares; or, in short, whatever is to be come at in this Country."[2] Visitors also noted that Benin City was kept scrupulously clean and had no beggars and that public security was so effective that theft was unknown. The period also witnessed remarkable artistic creativity in ironwork, carved ivory, and especially bronze portrait busts. Over nine hundred brass plaques survive, providing important information about Benin court life, military triumphs, and cosmological ideas.

In 1485 Portuguese and other Europeans began to appear in Benin in pursuit of trade, and over the next couple of centuries Benin grew rich from the profits made through the slave trade and the export of tropical products, particularly pepper and ivory. Its main European trading partners along this stretch of the so-called slave coast were the Dutch and Portuguese. In the early eighteenth century tributary states and stronger neighbors nibbled at Benin's frontiers, challenging its power. Benin, however, survived as an independent entity until the British conquered and burned Benin City in 1898 as part of the European imperialist seizure of Africa (discussed in Chapter 25).

The Sudan: Songhai, Kanem-Bornu, and Hausaland

The Songhai kingdom, a successor state of the kingdoms of Ghana (ca. 900–1000) and Mali (ca. 1200–1450), dominated the whole Niger region of the western and central Sudan (see Map 19.1). The imperial expansion of Songhai (song-GUY) began during the reign of the Songhai king Sonni Ali (r. ca. 1464–1492) and continued under his eventual successor, Muhammad Toure (r. 1493–1528). From his capital at Gao, Toure extended his rule as far north as the salt-mining center at **Taghaza** in the western Sahara and as far east as Agades and Kano. A convert to Islam, Toure returned from a pilgrimage to Mecca impressed by what he had seen there. He tried to bring about greater centralization in his own territories by building a strong army, improving taxation procedures, and replacing local Songhai officials with more efficient Arabs in an effort to substitute royal institutions for ancient kinship ties.

We know little about daily life in Songhai society because of the paucity of written records and surviving artifacts. Some information is provided by Leo Africanus (ca. 1465–1550), a Moroccan captured by pirates and given as a slave to Pope Leo X. Leo Africanus became a Christian, taught Arabic in Rome, and in 1526 published an account of his many travels, including a stay in the Songhai kingdom.

As a scholar, Africanus was naturally impressed by Timbuktu, the second city of the empire, which he visited in 1513. "Here [is] a great store of doctors, judges, priests, and other learned men, that are bountifully maintained at the King's court," he reported.[3] Many of these Islamic scholars had studied in Cairo and other centers of Muslim learning. They gave Timbuktu a reputation for intellectual sophistication, religious piety, and moral justice. (See "Viewpoints: European Descriptions of Timbuktu and Jenne," page 562.)

Songhai under Muhammad Toure seems to have enjoyed economic prosperity. Leo Africanus noted the abundant food supply, which was produced in the southern savanna and carried to Timbuktu by a large fleet of canoes. The elite had large amounts of money to spend, and expensive North African and European luxuries — clothes, copperware, glass and stone beads, perfumes, and horses — were much in demand. The existence of many shops and markets implies the development of an urban culture. At Timbuktu, merchants, scholars, judges, and artisans constituted a distinctive bourgeoisie. The presence of many foreign merchants, including Jews and Italians, gave the city a cosmopolitan atmosphere. Jews largely controlled the working of gold.

Slavery played an important role in Songhai's economy. On the royal farms scattered throughout the kingdom, enslaved people produced rice — the staple crop — for the royal granaries. Slaves could possess their own slaves, land, and cattle, but they could not bequeath any of this property; the king inherited all of it. Muhammad Toure greatly increased the number of royal slaves. He gave slaves to favorite Muslim scholars, who thus gained a steady source of income. Slaves were also sold at the large market at Gao, where traders from North Africa bought them in order to resell them in Cairo, Constantinople, Lisbon, Naples, Genoa, and Venice.

Despite its considerable economic and cultural strengths, Songhai had serious internal problems. Islam never took root in the countryside, and Muslim officials alienated the king from his people. Muhammad Toure's reforms were a failure. He governed diverse peoples — Tuareg, Malinke, and Fulani as well as Songhai — who were often hostile to one another, and no cohesive element united them. Finally, the Songhai never developed an effective method of transferring power. Revolts, conspiracies, and palace intrigues followed the death of every king, and only three of the nine rulers in the dynasty begun by Muhammad Toure died natural deaths. Muhammad Toure himself was

> "The Sultan was intent on the clear path laid down by the Qur'an . . . in all his affairs and actions."
>
> **IBN-FARTURA**

murdered by one of his sons. His death began a period of political instability that led to the kingdom's slow disintegration.

In 1582 the Moroccan sultanate began to press southward in search of a greater share of the trans-Saharan trade. The Songhai people, lacking effective leadership and believing the desert to be sure protection against invasion, took no defensive precautions. In 1591 a Moroccan army of three thousand soldiers — many of whom were slaves of European origin equipped with European muskets — crossed the Sahara and inflicted a crushing defeat on the Songhai at Tondibi, spelling the end of the Songhai Empire.

East of Songhai lay the kingdoms of Kanem-Bornu and Hausaland (see Map 19.1). Under the dynamic military leader Idris Alooma (r. 1571–1603), Kanem-Bornu subdued weaker peoples and gained jurisdiction over an extensive area. Well-drilled and equipped with firearms, camel-mounted cavalry and a standing army decimated warriors fighting with spears and arrows. Idris Alooma perpetuated a form of feudalism by granting land to able fighters in return for loyalty and the promise of future military assistance. Meanwhile, agriculture occupied most people, peasants and slaves alike. Kanem-Bornu shared in the trans-Saharan trade, shipping eunuchs and young girls to North Africa in return for horses and firearms. A devout Muslim, Idris Alooma elicited high praise from ibn-Fartura, who wrote a history of his reign called *The Kanem Wars*:

> So he made the pilgrimage and visited Medina with delight. . . . Among the benefits which God . . . conferred upon the Sultan Idris Alooma was the acquisition of Turkish musketeers and numerous household slaves who became skilled in firing muskets. . . .
>
> Among the most surprising of his acts was the stand he took against obscenity and adultery, so that no such thing took place openly in his time. Formerly the people had been indifferent to such offences. . . . In fact he was a power among his people and from him came their strength.
>
> The Sultan was intent on the clear path laid down by the Qur'an . . . in all his affairs and actions.[4]

Idris Alooma built mosques at his capital city of N'gazargamu and substituted Muslim courts and

• **Taghaza** A settlement in the western Sahara, the site of the main salt-mining center.

Viewpoints

European Descriptions of Timbuktu and Jenne

> • Timbuktu and Jenne were important cities in the West African empires of Ghana, Mali, and Songhai. The writings of Al-Hassan ibn Muhammad al-Wezaz al-Fasi, also known as Leo Africanus (ca. 1493–ca. 1554?), provide the most authoritative accounts of West Africa between the writings of Ibn Battuta in the 1300s and the writings of European travelers in the 1800s. The Tarikh al-Sudan (History of the Sudan), written by Abd-al-Rahman al-Sadi (1594– after 1656), is one of the most important histories of the Mali and Songhai empires in the fifteenth, sixteenth, and seventeenth centuries.

Leo Africanus, On Timbuktu

❝This name was . . . imposed upon this kingdome from the name of a certain towne so called, which (they say) king *Mense Suleiman* founded in the yeere of the Hegeira 610, and it is situate within twelve miles of a certaine branch of Niger, all the houses whereof are now changed into cottages built of chalke, and covered with thatch. Howbeit there is a most stately temple to be seene, the wals thereof are made of stone and lime; and a princely palace also built by a most excellent workeman of Granada. Here are many shops of artificiers, and merchants, and especially of such as weave linen and cotton cloth. And hither do the Barbarie-merchants bring cloth of Europe. All the women of this region except maid-servants go with their faces covered, and sell all necessarie victuals.

The inhabitants, & especially strangers there residing, are exceeding rich, insomuch, that the king that now is, married both his daughters unto two rich merchants. Here are many wels, containing most sweete water; and so often as the river Niger overfloweth, they conveigh the water thereof by certaine sluces into the towne.

Corne, cattle, milke, and butter this region yeeldeth in great abundance: but salt is verie scarce here; for it is brought hither by land from Tegaza, which is five hundred miles distant. When I myself was here, I saw one camels loade of salt sold for 80 ducates. The rich king of Tombuto hath many plates and scepters of gold, some whereof weigh 1300 pounds: and he keeps a magnificent and well furnished court. . . .

Here are great store of doctors, judges, priests, and other learned men, that are bountifully maintained at the kings cost and charges. And hither are brought divers manuscripts or written books out of Barbarie, which are sold for more money than any other merchandize.❞

Al-Sadi, On Jenne

❝Jenne is a large, well-favoured, and blessed city, characterized by prosperity, good fortune and compassion. God bestowed these things upon that land as innate characteristics. It is the nature of Jenne's inhabitants to be kind and charitable, and solicitous for one another. . . .

Jenne is one of the great markets of the Muslims. Those who deal in salt from the mine of Taghaza meet there with those who deal in gold from the mine of Bitu. These two blessed mines have no equal in the entire world. People discovered their great blessing through going to them for business, amassing such wealth as only God—Sublime is He—could assess. This blessed city of Jenne is the reason why caravans come to Timbuktu from all quarters—north, south, east and west. Jenne is situated to the south and west of Timbuktu beyond the two rivers. . . .

Jenne was founded as a pagan town in the middle of the second century of the *hijira* of the Prophet [150 A.H. = 767– 768 C.E.]. . . . Its people became Muslims at the end of the sixth century. First, Sultan Kunburu became a Muslim, then people followed his example. When he made up his mind to embrace Islam he ordered that all the Muslim scholars within the city should be assembled. They totaled 4,200, and he made a profession of Islam before them, and told them to call upon God Most High to grant the city three things: firstly, that anyone who fled there from his homeland in poverty and distress should have this translated by God into luxury and ease, so that he may forget his homeland; secondly, that more strangers than local folk should settle there; and thirdly, that those who came to trade there should lose patience and grow weary over selling their goods, and so dispose of them cheaply, allowing the people of Jenne to make a profit.❞

Sources: Al-Hassan ibn-Mohammad al-Wezaz al-Fasi, *The History and Description of Africa*. Done into English in 1600 by John Pory. Robert Brown, ed. (London: Hakluyt Society, 1896), vol. III, pp. 824–825; John O. Hunwick, *Timbuktu and the Songhay Empire: Al-Sadi's Tarikh al-Sudan Down to 1613 and Other Contemporary Documents* (Leiden: Brill, 1999), pp. 17–19. Used by permission of Koninklijke Brill NV.

QUESTIONS FOR ANALYSIS

1. During the colonial era, and even to the present day, Africa and its inhabitants were described in the most denigrating terms, such as *pagan*, *savage*, *illiterate*, *poor*, and *uncivilized*. How do the descriptions of these two African market and learning centers sync with those characterizations?

2. How important was Islam to the success of these two cities? In what ways?

Islamic law for African tribunals and ancient customary law. His eighteenth-century successors lacked his vitality and military skills, however, and the empire declined.

Between Songhai and Kanem-Bornu were the lands of the Hausa, an agricultural people who lived in small villages. Hausa merchants carried on a heavy trade in slaves and kola nuts with North African communities across the Sahara, and obscure trading posts evolved into important Hausa city-states like Kano and Katsina, through which Islamic influences entered the region. Kano and Katsina became Muslim intellectual centers and in the fifteenth century attracted scholars from Timbuktu. The Muslim chronicler of the reign of King Muhammad Rimfa of Kano (r. 1463–1499) records that the king introduced the Muslim practices of purdah, or seclusion of women; of the *idal-fitr*, the festival after the fast of Ramadan; and of assigning eunuchs to high state offices.[5] As in Songhai and Kanem-Bornu, however, Islam made no strong imprint on the Hausa masses until the nineteenth century.

The Lives of the People of West Africa

The negative effects of the transatlantic slave trade (see page 580) on West Africa's population profoundly affected marriage patterns and family structure. Wives and children were highly desired because they could clear and cultivate the land and because they brought prestige, social support, and security in old age. The result was intense competition for women, inequality of access to them, an emphasis on male virility and female fertility, and serious tension between male generations. Polygyny was almost universal; as recently as the nineteenth century two-thirds of rural wives were in polygynous marriages.

Men acquired wives in two ways. First, some couples simply eloped and began their union. More commonly, a man's family gave bride wealth to the bride's family as compensation for losing the fruits of her productive and reproductive abilities. She was expected to produce children, to produce food through her labor, and to pass on the culture in the raising of her children. Because it took time for a young man to acquire the bride wealth, all but the richest men delayed marriage until about age thirty. Women married at about the onset of puberty.

The easy availability of land in Africa reduced the kinds of generational conflict that occurred in western Europe, where land was scarce. Competition for wives between male generations, however, was fierce. On the one hand, myth and folklore stressed respect for the elderly, and the older men in a community imposed their authority over the younger ones by including painful rites of initiation into adulthood, such as circumcision. On the other hand, West African societies were not based on rule by elders, as few people lived much beyond forty. Young men possessed the powerful asset of their labor, which could easily be turned into independence where so much land was available.

"Without children you are naked" goes a Yoruba proverb, and children were the primary goal of marriage. Just as a man's virility determined his honor, so barrenness damaged a woman's status. A wife's infidelity was considered a less serious problem than her infertility. A woman might have six widely spaced pregnancies in her fertile years; the universal practice of breast-feeding infants for two, three, or even four years may have inhibited conception. Long intervals between births due to food shortages also may have limited pregnancies and checked population growth. The harsh

Queen Mother and Attendants As in Ottoman, Chinese, and European societies, the mothers of African rulers sometimes exercised considerable political power because of their influence on their sons. African kings granted the title Queen Mother as a badge of honor. In this figure, the long beaded cap, called "chicken's beak," symbolizes the mother's rank, as do her elaborate neck jewelry and attendants. (Image copyright © The Metropolitan Museum of Art/Art Resource, NY)

climate, poor nutrition, and infectious diseases also contributed to a high infant mortality rate.

Both nuclear and extended families were common in West Africa. Nuclear families averaged only five or six members, but the household of a Big Man (a local man of power) included his wives, married and unmarried sons, unmarried daughters, poor relations, dependents, and scores of children. Extended families were common among the Hausa and Malinke peoples. On the Gold Coast in the seventeenth century, a well-to-do man's household might number 150 people, in the Kongo region several hundred. Where one family cultivated extensive land, a large household of young adults, children, and slaves probably proved most efficient. Still, although many children might be born, many also died. Families rarely exceeded five or six people; high infant mortality rates and short life spans kept the household numbers low.

In agriculture men did the heavy work of felling trees and clearing the land; women then planted, weeded, and harvested. Between 1000 and 1400, cassava (manioc), bananas, and plantains came to West Africa from Asia. Cassava required little effort to grow and became a staple food, but it had little nutritional value. In the sixteenth century the Portuguese introduced maize (corn), sweet potatoes, and new varieties of yams from the Americas. Fish supplemented the diets of people living near bodies of water. According to Olaudah Equiano (oh-lah-OO-dah ay-kwee-AH-noh), the Ibo people in the mid-eighteenth century ate plantains, yams, beans, and Indian corn, along with stewed poultry, goat, or bullock (castrated steer) seasoned with peppers.[6] Such a protein-rich diet was probably exceptional.

Disease posed perhaps the biggest obstacle to population growth. Malaria, spread by mosquitoes and rampant in West Africa (except in cool, dry Cameroon), was the greatest killer, especially of infants. West Africans developed a relatively high degree of immunity to malaria and other parasitic diseases, including hookworm (which enters the body through shoeless feet and attaches itself to the intestines), yaws (contracted by nonsexual contact and recognized by ulcerating lesions), sleeping sickness (the parasite enters the blood through the bite of the tsetse [SEHT-see] fly; symptoms are enlarged lymph nodes and, at the end, a comatose state), and a mild nonsexual form of syphilis. Acute strains of smallpox introduced by Europeans certainly did not help population growth, nor did venereal syphilis, which possibly originated in Latin America. As in Chinese and European communities in the early modern period,

the sick depended on folk medicine. African medical specialists, such as midwives, bonesetters, exorcists using religious methods, and herbalists, administered a variety of treatments, including herbal medications like salves, ointments, and purgatives. Still, disease was common where the diet was poor and lacked adequate vitamins.

The devastating effects of famine, often mentioned in West African oral traditions, represented another major check on population growth. Drought, excessive rain, swarms of locusts, and rural wars that prevented the cultivation of land all meant later food shortages. In the 1680s famine extended from the Senegambian coast to the Upper Nile, and many people sold themselves into slavery for food. In the eighteenth century "slave exports" reached their peak in times of famine, and ships could fill their cargo holds simply by offering food. The worst disaster occurred from 1738 to 1756, when, according to one chronicler, the poor were reduced to cannibalism, an African metaphor for the complete collapse of civilization.[7]

Because the Americas had been isolated from the Eurasian-African landmass for thousands of years, parasitic diseases common in Europe, Africa, and Asia were unknown in the Americas before the arrival of the Europeans. Enslaved Africans taken to the Americas brought with them the diseases common to tropical West Africa, such as yellow fever, dengue fever, malaria, and hookworm. Thus, the hot, humid disease environment in the American tropics, where the majority of enslaved Africans lived and worked, became more "African." On the other hand, cold-weather European diseases, such as chicken pox, mumps, measles, and influenza, prevailed in the northern temperate zone in North America and the southern temperate zone in South America. This difference in disease environment partially explains why Africans made up the majority of the unskilled labor force in the tropical areas of the Americas, and Europeans made up the majority of the unskilled labor force in the temperate zones of the Western Hemisphere, such as the northern United States and Canada.

Trade and Industry

As in all premodern societies, West African economies rested on agriculture. There was some trade and industry, but population shortages encouraged local self-sufficiency, slowed transportation, and hindered exchange. There were very few large markets, and their relative isolation from the outside world and failure to attract large numbers of foreign merchants limited technological innovation.

For centuries, black Africans had exchanged goods with North African merchants in centers such as Gao and Timbuktu. That long-distance trans-Saharan trade was conducted and controlled by Muslim-Berber mer-

• **Tuareg** Along with the Moors, warriors who controlled the north-south trans-Saharan trade in salt.

• **cowrie shells** Imported from the Maldives, they served as the medium of exchange in West Africa.

chants using camels. The two primary goods exchanged were salt, which came from salt mines in North Africa, and gold, which came mainly from gold mines in modern-day Mali.

As elsewhere around the world, water was the cheapest method of transportation, and many small dugout canoes and larger trading canoes plied the Niger and its delta region (see Map 19.1). On land West African peoples used pack animals (camels or donkeys) rather than wheeled vehicles; south of the Sahara, only a narrow belt of land was suitable for animal-drawn carts. When traders reached an area infested with tsetse flies, they transferred each animal's load to human porters. Such difficulties in transport severely restricted long-distance trade, so most people relied on the regional exchange of local specialties.

West African communities had a well-organized market system. At informal markets on riverbanks, fishermen bartered fish for local specialties. More formal markets existed within towns and villages or on neutral ground between them. Markets also rotated among neighboring villages on certain days. People exchanged cotton cloth, thread, palm oil, millet, vegetables, and small articles for daily living. Local sellers were usually women; traders from afar were men.

Salt had long been one of Africa's most critical trade items. Salt is essential to human health; the Hausa language has more than fifty words for it. The salt trade dominated the West African economies in the fifteenth, sixteenth, and seventeenth centuries. The main salt-mining center was at Taghaza (see Map 19.1) in the western Sahara. In the most wretched conditions, slaves dug the salt from desiccated lakes and loaded heavy blocks onto camels' backs. **Tuareg** warriors and later Moors (peoples of Berber and Arab descent) traded their salt south for gold, grain, slaves, and kola nuts, which were used by Muslims as stimulants or aphrodisiacs. **Cowrie shells**, imported from the Maldives in the Indian Ocean by way of Gujarat (see page 609) and

West African Trade Routes

North Africa, served as the medium of exchange (and continued to do so long after European intrusion). Gold continued to be mined and shipped from Mali until South American bullion flooded Europe in the sixteenth century (see page 480). Thereafter, its production in Africa steadily declined. In the late twentieth and early twenty-first centuries gold mining revived in Mali, to the point that gold briefly was Mali's number-one export in 2002. Mali is now Africa's third largest gold producer, after South Africa and Ghana.

West African peoples engaged in many crafts, such as basket weaving and pottery making. Ironworking, a specialized skill producing articles useful to hunters, farmers, and warriors, became hereditary in individual families; such expertise was regarded as family property. The textile industry had the greatest level of specialization. The earliest fabric in West Africa was made of vegetable fiber. Muslim traders introduced cotton

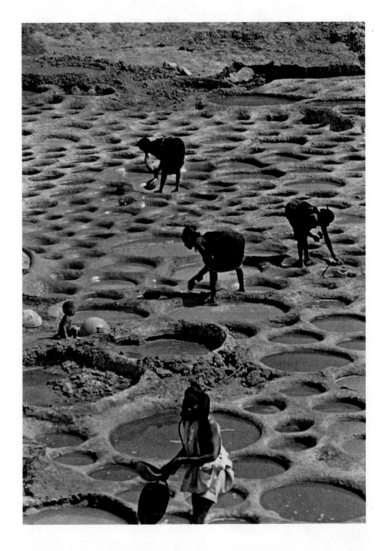

Salt Making in the Central Sahara For centuries camel caravans transported salt south across the Sahara to the great West African kingdoms, where it was exchanged for gold. Here at Tegguida-n-Tessum, Niger, in the central Sahara, salt is still collected by pouring spring water into small pools dug out of the saline soil. The water leaches out the salt before evaporating in the desert sun, leaving deposits of pure salt behind, which are then shaped into blocks for transport. (Afrique Photo, Cliché Naud/ Visual Connection Archive)

MAP 19.2 East Africa in the Sixteenth Century In early modern times, the Christian kingdom of Ethiopia, first isolated and then subjected to Muslim and European pressures, played an insignificant role in world affairs. But the East African city-states, which stretched from Sofala in the south to Mogadishu in the north, had powerfully important commercial relations with Mughal India, China, the Ottoman world, and southern Europe.

and its weaving in the ninth century, as the fine-quality fabrics found in Mali reveal. By the fifteenth century the Wolof and Malinke regions had professional weavers producing beautiful cloth, but this cloth was too expensive to compete in the Atlantic and Indian Ocean markets after 1500. Women who spun cotton used only a spindle and not a wheel, which slowed output. Women wove on inefficient broadlooms, men on less clumsy but narrow looms. Although the relatively small quantities of cloth produced on these narrow looms (one to two inches wide) could not compete in a world market, they are the source of the famous multicolored African kente cloth made from threads of cotton, or cotton and silk, by the Akan people of Ghana and the Ivory Coast. The area around Kano, in northern Nigeria, was famous for the deeply dyed blue cloth produced on the narrowest looms in the world and favored by the Tuareg Berber peoples of North Africa.

Cross-Cultural Encounters Along the East African Coast

☐ How did the arrival of Europeans and other foreign cultures impact the East African coast, and how did Ethiopia and the Swahili city-states respond to these incursions?

East Africa in the early modern period faced repeated incursions from foreign powers. At the beginning of the sixteenth century Ethiopia faced challenges from the Muslim state of Adal, and then from Europeans. Jesuit attempts to substitute Roman liturgical forms met with fierce resistance and ushered in a centuries-long period of hostility to foreigners. The wealthy Swahili city-states along the southeastern coast of Africa also resisted European intrusions in the sixteenth century, with even more disastrous results. Cities such as Mogadishu, Kilwa, and Sofala used Arabic as the language of communication, and their commercial economies had long been tied to the trade of the Indian Ocean. The arrival of the Portuguese in 1498 proved catastrophic for those cities, and the Swahili coast suffered economic decline as a result.

Muslim and European Incursions in Ethiopia, ca. 1500–1630

At the beginning of the sixteenth century the powerful East African kingdom of Ethiopia extended from Massawa in the north to several tributary states in the south (Map 19.2), but the ruling Solomonic dynasty in Ethiopia, in power since the thirteenth century, faced

Saint George in Ethiopian Art This wall painting of Saint George slaying a dragon resides in the stone-carved Church of St. George at Lalibela, Ethiopia, and attests to the powerful and pervasive Christian influence on Ethiopian culture. (Galen R. Frysinger)

serious external threats. Alone among the states in northeast and eastern Africa, Ethiopia was a Christian kingdom that practiced **Coptic Christianity**, an orthodox form of the Christian faith that originated in Egypt in 451. Christianity had first come to Ethiopia from Egypt when the archbishop in Alexandria appointed Saint Frumentius the first bishop of Ethiopia in 328. By the early 1500s Ethiopia was an island of Christianity surrounded by a sea of Muslim states.

Adal, a Muslim state along the southern base of the Red Sea, began incursions into Ethiopia, and in 1529 the Adal general Ahmad ibn-Ghazi inflicted a disastrous defeat on the Ethiopian emperor Lebna Dengel (r. 1508–1540). Ahmad followed up his victory with systematic devastation of the land; destruction of many Ethiopian artistic and literary works, churches, and monasteries; and the forced conversion of thousands to Islam. Lebna Dengel fled to the mountains and appealed to Portugal for assistance. A Portuguese force of four hundred men under Christovao da Gama came to his aid, but Dengel was killed in battle before the Portuguese arrived. The Muslim occupation of Christian Ethiopia, which began around 1531, ended in 1543, after a joint Ethiopian and Portuguese force defeated a larger Muslim army at the battle of Wayna Daga on February 21. During the battle Ahmad ibn-Ghazi was killed by a Portuguese musketeer, leaving a horrific legacy of destruction and death that continues to resonate in Ethiopia today.

In the late twelfth century tales of Prester John, rumored to be a powerful Christian monarch ruling a vast and wealthy African empire, reached western Europe. The search for Prester John, as well as for gold and

spices, spurred the Portuguese to undertake a series of trans-African expeditions that reached Timbuktu and Mali in the 1480s and the Ethiopian court by 1508. Although Prester John was a totally mythical figure, Portuguese emissaries triumphantly but mistakenly identified the Ethiopian emperor as Prester John.[8] Desirous of converting Ethiopians from Coptic Christianity to Roman Catholicism, the Portuguese responded to Lebna Dengel's request for help with a force of musketeers. In 1543 they decisively defeated the Muslims near Lake Tana.

No sooner had the Muslim threat ended than Ethiopia encountered three more dangers. The Galla, Cushitic-speaking peoples, moved northward in great numbers, occupying portions of Harar, Shoa, and Amhara. The Ethiopians could not defeat them militarily, and the Galla were not interested in assimilation. For the next two centuries the two peoples lived together in an uneasy truce. Simultaneously, the Ottoman Turks seized Massawa and other coastal cities. Then the Jesuits arrived and attempted to force Roman Catholicism on a proud people whose Coptic form of Christianity long antedated the European version. The overzealous Jesuit missionary Alphonse Mendez tried to revamp the Ethiopian liturgy, rebaptize the people, and

• **Coptic Christianity** Orthodox form of Christianity from Egypt practiced in Ethiopia.

replace ancient Ethiopian customs and practices with Roman ones. Since Ethiopian national sentiment was closely tied to Coptic Christianity, violent rebellion and anarchy ensued.

In 1633 the Jesuit missionaries were expelled. For the next two centuries, hostility to foreigners, weak political leadership, and regionalism characterized Ethiopia. Civil conflicts between Galla and Ethiopia erupted continually. The Coptic Church, though lacking strong authority, survived as the cornerstone of Ethiopian national identity.

The Swahili City-States and the Arrival of the Portuguese, ca. 1500–1600

The word **Swahili** means "People of the Coast" and refers to the people living along the East African coast and on the nearby islands. Although predominantly a Bantu-speaking people, the Swahili have incorporated significant aspects of Arabic culture. The Arabic alphabet was used for the first written works in Swahili (although the Latin alphabet is now standard), and roughly 35 percent of Swahili words come from Arabic. Surviving texts in Swahili—from the earliest known Swahili documents dating from 1711—provide historians with a glimpse of early Swahili history that is not possible when studying early nonliterate African societies. By the eleventh century the Swahili had accepted Islam, which provided a common identity and unifying factor for all the peoples along coastal East Africa. Living on the Indian Ocean coast, the Swahili also felt the influences of Indians, Indonesians, and Persians.

Swahili civilization was overwhelmingly maritime. A fertile, well-watered, and intensely cultivated stretch of land extending down the coast yielded rice, grains, citrus fruit, and cloves. The region's considerable prosperity, however, rested on trade and commerce. The Swahili acted as middlemen in an Indian Ocean–East African economy that might be described as early capitalism. They exchanged ivory, rhinoceros horn, tortoise shells, inlaid ebony chairs, copra (dried coconut meat that yields coconut oil), and inland slaves for Arabian and Persian perfumes, toilet articles, ink, and paper and for Indian textiles, beads, and iron tools. In the fifteenth century the cosmopolitan city-states of Mogadishu, Pate, Lamu, Mombasa, and especially Kilwa enjoyed a worldwide reputation for commercial prosperity and high living standards.[9]

The arrival of the Portuguese explorer Vasco da Gama (see Map 16.2 on page 469) in 1498 spelled the end of the Swahili cities' independence. Lured by the spice trade, da Gama wanted to build a Portuguese maritime empire in the Indian Ocean. Swahili rulers responded in different ways to Portuguese intrusion. Some, such as the sultan of Malindi, quickly agreed to a trading alliance with the Portuguese. Others, such as the sultan of Mombasa, were tricked into commercial agreements. Still other Swahili rulers totally rejected Portuguese overtures, and their cities were subjected to bombardment. To secure alliances made between 1502 and 1507 the Portuguese erected forts at the southern port cities of Kilwa, Zanzibar, and Sofala. These fortified markets and trading posts served as the foundation of Portuguese commercial power on the Swahili coast. (See "Listening to the Past: Duarte Barbosa on the Swahili City-States," page 570.) The better-fortified northern cities, such as Mogadishu, survived as important entrepôts for goods to India.

The Portuguese presence in the south did not yield the expected commercial fortunes. Rather than accept Portuguese commercial restrictions, the residents deserted the towns, and the town economies crumbled. Large numbers of Kilwa's people, for example, immigrated to northern cities. The gold flow from inland mines to Sofala slowed to a trickle. Swahili noncooperation successfully prevented the Portuguese from gaining control of the local coastal trade.

In 1589 Portugal finally won an administrative stronghold near Mombasa. Called Fort Jesus, it remained a Portuguese base for over a century. In the late seventeenth century pressures from the northern European maritime powers—the Dutch, French, and English, aided greatly by Omani Arabs—combined with local African rebellions to bring about the collapse of Portuguese influence in Africa. A Portuguese presence remained only at Mozambique in the far south and Angola on the west coast.

The Portuguese had no religious or cultural impact on the Swahili cities. Their sole effect was the cities' economic decline.

The African Slave Trade

▢ What role did slavery play in African societies before the transatlantic slave trade began, and what was the effect of European involvement?

The exchange of peoples captured in local and ethnic wars within sub-Saharan Africa, the trans-Saharan slave trade with the Mediterranean Islamic world beginning in the seventh century, and the slave traffic across the Indian Ocean all testify to the long tradition and continental dimensions of the African slave trade before European intrusion. The enslavement of human beings was practiced in some form or another all over

● **Swahili** Meaning "People of the Coast," the term used for the people living along the East African coast and on nearby islands.

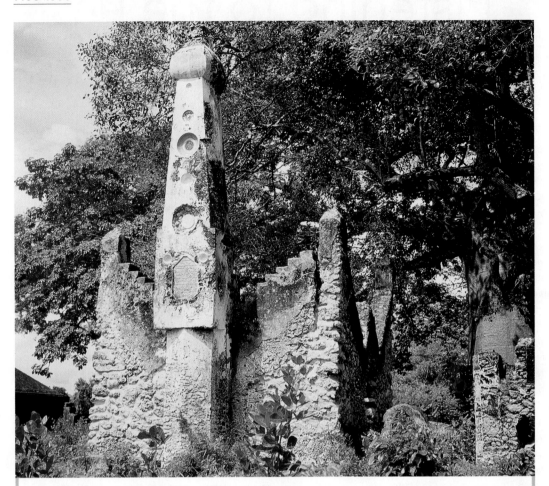

◻ Picturing the Past

Chinese Porcelain Plates Embedded in an eighteenth-century Kunduchi pillar tomb, these Chinese plates testify to the enormous Asian-African trade that flourished in the fourteenth to sixteenth centuries. Kunduchi, whose ruins lie north of Dar es Salaam in present-day Tanzania, was one of the Swahili city-states. (Werner Forman/Art Resource, NY)

ANALYZING THE IMAGE How many Chinese plates can you identify? What features identify this as a tomb?

CONNECTIONS Why would a Muslim African want a Chinese plate embedded in his tomb? What does this suggest about his status, occupation, and wealth?

Africa — indeed, all over the world. Sanctioned by law and custom, enslaved people served critical and well-defined roles in the social, political, and economic organization of many African societies. Domestically these roles ranged from concubines and servants to royal guards and advisers. As later in the Americas, some enslaved people were common laborers. Economically, slaves were commodities for trade, more or less important than other trade items, such as gold and ivory.

The trans-Saharan slave trade became less important than the transatlantic trade, which witnessed an explosive growth during the seventeenth and eighteenth centuries. The millions of enslaved Africans forcibly exported to the Americas would have a lasting impact on African society and would lead ultimately to a wider use of slaves within Africa itself.

The Institution of Slavery in Africa

Islamic practices strongly influenced African slavery. African rulers justified enslavement with the Muslim argument that prisoners of war could be sold and that

Listening to the Past

Duarte Barbosa on the Swahili City-States

The Portuguese writer, government agent, and traveler Duarte Barbosa made two voyages to India. Arriving first in 1500, he acted for five years as interpreter and translator in Cochin and Cananor in Kerala (in southwestern India on the Malabar Coast), returning to Lisbon in 1506. On his second trip to India in 1511, he served the Portuguese government as chief scribe in the factory of Cananor (a factory was a warehouse for the storage of goods, not a manufacturing center) and as the liaison with the local Indian rajah (prince). Barbosa returned to Portugal around 1516. In September 1519 he began his greatest adventure, setting off with Ferdinand Magellan to circumnavigate the globe. Magellan was killed in a battle with native forces in the Philippines. Barbosa then took joint command of the expedition, but was himself killed in the Philippines less than a week after Magellan, on May 1, 1521.

On the basis of his trips around the Indian Ocean in 1518, Barbosa completed his Libro de Duarte Barbosa (The Book of Duarte Barbosa), *a geographical and ethnographic survey of peoples, lands, and commerce from the Cape of Good Hope to China. It was based largely on his personal observations. First published in Italian, the book won wide acclaim in Europe, and modern scholars consider its geographical information very accurate. The excerpts below describe some of the city-states along the East African coast of Swahili.*

Sofala

And the manner of their traffic was this: they came in small vessels named *zambucos* from the kingdoms of Kilwa, Mombasa, and Malindi, bringing many cotton cloths, some spotted and others white and blue, also some of silk, and many small beads, grey, red, and yellow, which things come to the said kingdoms from the great kingdom of Cambaya [in northwest India] in other greater ships. And these wares the said Moors who came from Malindi and Mombasa paid for in gold at such a price that those merchants departed well pleased; which gold they gave by weight.

The Moors of Sofala kept these wares and sold them afterwards to the Heathen of the Kingdom of Benametapa, who came thither laden with gold which they gave in exchange for the said cloths without weighing it. These Moors collect also great store of ivory which they find hard by Sofala, and this also they sell in the Kingdom of Cambaya at five or six cruzados the quintal. They also sell some ambergris, which is brought to them from the Hucicas, and is exceeding good. These Moors are black, and some of them tawny; some of them speak Arabic, but the more part use the language of the country. They clothe themselves from the waist down with cotton and silk cloths, and other cloths they wear over their shoulders like capes, and turbans on their heads. Some of them wear small caps dyed in grain in chequers and other woollen clothes in many tints, also camlets and other silks.

Their food is millet, rice, flesh and fish. In this river as far as the sea are many sea horses, which come out on the land to graze, which horses always move in the sea like fishes; they have tusks like those of small elephants in size, and the ivory is better than that of elephants, being whiter and harder, and it never loses colour. In the country near Sofala are many wild elephants, exceeding great (which the country-folk know not how to tame) ounces, lions, deer and many other wild beasts. It is a land of plains and hills with many streams of sweet water. . . . "

Kilwa

"Going along the coast from this town of Mozambique, there is an island hard by the mainland which is called Kilwa, in which is a Moorish town with many fair houses of stone and mortar, with many windows after our fashion, very well arranged in streets, with many flat roofs. The doors are of wood, well carved, with excellent joinery. Around it are streams and orchards and fruit-gardens with many channels of sweet water. It has a Moorish king over it. From this place they trade with Sofala, whence they bring back gold, and from here they spread all over . . . the seacoast [which] is well-peopled with villages and abodes of Moors.

Before the King our Lord sent out his expedition to discover India the Moors of Sofala, Cuama, Angoya and Mozambique

captured people were considered chattel, or personal possessions, to be used any way the owner saw fit. Between 650 and 1600, black as well as white Muslims transported perhaps as many as 4.82 million black slaves across the trans-Saharan trade route.[10] In the fourteenth and fifteenth centuries the rulers and elites of Mali and Benin imported thousands of white Slavic slave women, symbols of wealth and status, who had been seized in slave raids from the Balkans and Caucasus regions of the eastern Mediterranean by Turks, Mongols, and others.[11] In 1444, when Portuguese caravels landed 235 slaves at Algarve in southern Portugal, a contemporary observed that they seemed "a marvelous (extraordinary) sight, for, amongst them, were some were all subject to the King of Kilwa, who was the most mighty king among them. And in this town was great plenty of gold, as no ships passed towards Sofala without first coming to this island. . . .

This town was taken by force from its king by the Portuguese, as, moved by arrogance, he refused to obey the King our Lord. There they took many prisoners and the king fled from the island, and His Highness ordered that a fort should be built there, and kept it under his rule and governance. Afterwards he ordered that it should be pulled down, as its maintenance was of no value nor profit to him, and it was destroyed by Antonio de Saldanha. . . . "

Malindi

" . . . Journeying along the coast towards India, there is a fair town on the mainland lying along a strand, which is named Malindi. It pertains to the Moors and has a Moorish king over it; the which place has many fair stone and mortar houses of many storeys, with great plenty of windows and flat roofs, after our fashion. The place is well laid out in streets. The folk are both black and white; they go naked, covering only their private parts with cotton and silk cloths. Others of them wear cloths folded like cloaks and waist-bands, and turbans of many rich stuffs on their heads.

They are great barterers, and deal in cloth, gold, ivory, and divers other wares with the Moors and Heathen of the great kingdom of Cambaya; and to their haven come every year many ships with cargoes of merchandize, from which they get great store of gold, ivory and wax. In this traffic the Cambay merchants make great profits, and thus, on one side and the other, they earn much money. There is great plenty of food in this city (rice, millet, and some wheat which they bring from Cambaya), and divers sorts of fruit, inasmuch as there is here abundance of fruit-gardens and orchards. Here too are plenty of round-tailed sheep, cows and other cattle and great store of oranges, also of hens.

The king and people of this place ever were and are friends of the King of Portugal, and the Portuguese always find in them great comfort and friendship and perfect peace, "and there the ships, when they chance to pass that way, obtain supplies in plenty." "

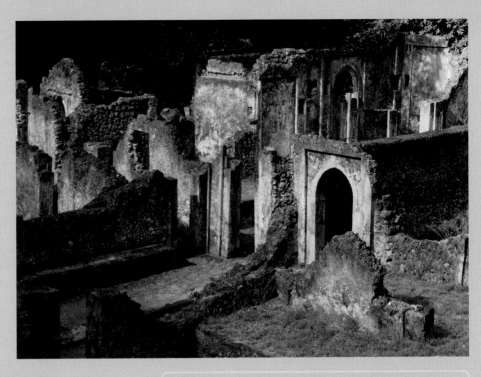

• The walls of the sultan's palace sit silently amidst the ruins at Gedi, a historic Swahili site a few miles south of Malindi on the Kenyan coast. Founded in the late thirteenth or early fourteenth century, it survived as a thriving trading community until the early seventeenth century. Although it was not a major Swahili town, excavations have uncovered iron lamps from India, scissors from Spain, a Chinese Ming vase, Persian stoneware, and Venetian beads. Some homes had bathrooms with running water and flush toilets, and the streets had drainage gutters. The dated tomb in the cemetery has 1399 incised in its plaster wall. (Ariadne Van Zandbergen/Lonely Planet Images)

Source: Dames, Mansel Longworth, trans., *The Book of Duarte Barbosa, Volume 1* (London: Bedford Press, 1918).

QUESTIONS FOR ANALYSIS

1. What seems to have impressed Barbosa? What was his attitude toward the various peoples he saw? What Portuguese or Western prejudices do you discern?
2. What was the Portuguese relationship to the Swahili city-states at the time Barbosa saw them?
3. What was the source of Sofala's gold? Of Sofala's and Malindi's ivory? What did the Indian kingdom of Cambaya use ivory for?

white enough, fair enough, and well-proportioned; others were less white, like mulattoes; others again were black as Ethiops."[12]

Meanwhile, the flow of black people to Europe, begun during the Renaissance, continued. In the seventeenth and eighteenth centuries as many as two hundred thousand Africans entered European societies.

Some arrived as slaves, others as servants; the legal distinction was not always clear. Eighteenth-century London, for example, had more than ten thousand blacks, most of whom arrived as sailors on Atlantic crossings or as personal servants brought from the West Indies. In England most were free, not slaves. Initially, a handsome black was a fashionable accessory, a rare status symbol. Later, English aristocrats considered black servants too ordinary. The duchess of Devonshire offered her mother an eleven-year-old boy, explaining that the duke did not want a Negro servant because "it was more original to have a Chinese page than to have a black one; everybody had a black one."[13] London's black population constituted a well-organized, self-conscious subculture, with black pubs, black churches, and black social groups assisting the black poor and unemployed. Some black people attained wealth and position, the most famous being Francis Barber, manservant of the sixteenth-century British literary giant Samuel Johnson and heir to Johnson's papers and to most of his sizable fortune. Barber had helped Johnson in revising Johnson's famous *Dictionary of the English Language*, published in 1755, and he is frequently mentioned in the celebrated biography of Johnson by James Boswell. He was a contemporary of another well-known African who lived in London for a while, Olaudah Equiano.

In 1658 the Dutch East India Company (see page 481) began to allow the importation of slaves into the Cape Colony, which the company had founded on the southern tip of Africa in 1652. Over the next century and a half about 75 percent of the slaves brought into the colony came from Dutch East India Company colonies in India and Southeast Asia or from Madagascar; the remaining 25 percent came from Africa. Some of those enslaved at the Cape served as domestic servants or as semiskilled artisans, but most worked long and hard as field hands and at any other menial or manual forms of labor needed by their European masters.

The Dutch East India Company was the single largest slave owner in the Cape Colony, employing its slaves on public works and company farms. Initially, individual company officials collectively owned the most slaves, working them on their wine and grain estates, but by about 1740 urban and rural free burghers owned the majority of the slaves. In 1780 half of all white men at the Cape had at least one slave, as slave ownership fostered a strong sense of racial and economic solidarity in the white master class.

The slave population at the Cape was never large, although from the early 1700s to the 1820s it outnumbered the European free burgher population. When the British ended slavery in the British Empire in 1834, there were around thirty-six thousand slaves in

Cape Colony, ca. 1750

> "It was more original to have a Chinese page than to have a black one; everybody had a black one."
>
> — **DUCHESS OF DEVONSHIRE**

the Cape Colony. In comparison, over three hundred thousand enslaved Africans labored on the Caribbean island of Jamaica, also a British slaveholding colony at the time.

Although in the seventeenth and eighteenth centuries Holland enjoyed a Europe-wide reputation for religious toleration and intellectual freedom (see page 515), in the Cape Colony the Dutch used a strict racial hierarchy and heavy-handed paternalism to maintain control over enslaved native and foreign-born peoples. Early accounts of slavery at the Cape often gave the impression that it was a relatively benign institution in comparison with slavery in the Americas. Modern scholars, however, consider slavery in the Cape Colony in many ways as oppressive as slavery in the Americas and the Muslim world. In Muslim society, the offspring of a freeman and an enslaved woman were free, but in southern Africa such children remained enslaved. Because enslaved males greatly outnumbered enslaved females in the Cape Colony, marriage and family life were almost nonexistent. Because there were few occupations requiring special skills, those enslaved in the colony lacked opportunities to earn manumission. And in contrast with North and South America and with Muslim societies, in the Cape Colony only a very small number of those enslaved won manumission; most of them were women, suggesting sexual or close personal relationships with their owners.[14]

The savanna and Horn regions of East Africa experienced a great expansion of the slave trade in the late eighteenth century and the first half of the nineteenth century. Exports of slaves from these areas and from the eastern coast of Africa amounted to perhaps thirty thousand a year. Why this demand? Merchants and planters wanted slaves to work the sugar plantations on the Mascarene Islands, located east of Madagascar, the clove plantations on Zanzibar and Pemba, and the food plantations along the Kenyan coast. The eastern coast also exported enslaved people to the Americas, particularly to Brazil. In the late eighteenth and early nineteenth centuries, precisely when the slave trade to North America and the Caribbean declined, the Arabian and Asian markets expanded. Only with colonial conquest of Africa by Great Britain, Germany, and Italy after 1870 did suppression of the trade begin. Enslavement, of course, persists even today. (See "Global Trade: Slaves," page 574.)

The Transatlantic Slave Trade

Although the trade in African people was a worldwide phenomenon, the transatlantic slave trade involved the largest number of enslaved Africans. This forced

Below Stairs The prints and cartoons of Thomas Rowlandson (1756–1827) testify to the sizable numbers of blacks in eighteenth-century London, where they worked in naval and military as well as domestic service. Here the household cook, maid, and footman relax before the kitchen fire. Interracial marriages were not uncommon. (Courtesy of the Trustees of the British Museum)

migration of millions of human beings, extending from the early sixteenth to the late nineteenth centuries, represents one of the most inhumane, unjust, and shameful tragedies in human history. It also immediately provokes a troubling question: Why Africa? Why, in the seventeenth and eighteenth centuries, did enslavement in the Americas become exclusively African?

European settlers first enslaved indigenous peoples, the Amerindians, to mine the silver and gold discovered in the New World (see page 480). When they proved ill suited to the harsh rigors of mining, the Spaniards brought in Africans. Although the Dutch had transported Indonesian peoples to work as slaves in the Cape Colony in South Africa, the cost of transporting Chinese or Pacific island peoples to the Americas was far too great.

One scholar has argued that a pan-European insider-outsider ideology prevailed across Europe. This cultural attitude permitted the enslavement of outsiders but made the enslavement of white Europeans taboo. Europeans could not bear the sight of other Europeans doing plantation slave labor. According to this theory, a similar pan-African ideology did not exist, as Africans had no problem with selling Africans to Europeans.[15] Several facts argue against the validity of this theory. English landlords exploited their Irish peasants with merciless severity; French aristocrats often looked on their peasantry with cold contempt; and Russian boyars treated their serfs with casual indifference and harsh brutality. These and other possible examples contradict the existence of a pan-European ideology or culture that opposed the enslavement of white Europeans. Moreover, the flow of white enslaved Slavic peoples from the Balkans into the eastern Mediterranean continued unabated during the same period.

Another theory holds that in the Muslim and Arab worlds by the tenth century, an association had developed between blackness and menial slavery. The Arab word *abd*, or "black," had become synonymous with *slave*. Although the great majority of enslaved persons in the Islamic world were white, a racial element existed in Muslim perceptions: not all slaves were black, but blacks were identified with slavery. In Europe, after the arrival of tens of thousands of sub-Saharan Africans in the Iberian Peninsula during the fifteenth century, Christian Europeans also began to make a strong association between slavery and black Africans. Therefore, Africans seemed the "logical" solution to the labor shortage in the Americas.[16]

Another important question relating to the African slave trade is this: Why were African peoples enslaved in a period when serfdom was declining in western Europe, and when land was so widely available and much of the African continent had a labor shortage? The answer seems to lie in a technical problem related to African agriculture. Partly because of the tsetse fly, which causes sleeping sickness and other diseases, and partly because of easily leached lateritic soils (containing high concentrations of oxides), farmers had great difficulty using draft animals. Tropical soils responded poorly to plowing, and most work had to be done with the hoe. Productivity, therefore, was low. Economists maintain that in most societies, the value of a worker's productivity determines the value of his or her labor. In precolonial Africa, the individual's agricultural productivity was low, so his or her economic value to society was less than the economic value of a European peasant in Europe. Enslaved persons in the Americas were more productive than free producers in Africa. And European slave dealers were very willing to pay a price higher than the value of an African's productivity in Africa.

The incidence of disease in the Americas also helps explain African enslavement. Smallpox took a terrible toll on Native Americans (see page 577), and between 30 and 50 percent of Europeans exposed to malaria succumbed to that sickness. Africans had developed some

Global Trade

Slaves

Slaves are people who are bound to servitude and often traded as property or as a commodity. The traffic in human persons bought and sold for the profits of their labor cannot decently be compared to the buying and selling of other commodities; people are not goods. But most societies, with the remarkable exception of the Aborigines in Australia, have treated people as goods and have engaged in the slave trade. Those who have been enslaved include captives in war, persons convicted of crimes, persons sold for debt, and persons bought and sold for sex. The ancient Greek philosophers, notably Aristotle, justified slavery as "natural." The Middle Eastern monotheistic faiths—Judaism, Christianity, and Islam—while professing the sacred dignity of each individual, and the Asian religious and sociopolitical ideologies of Buddhism and Confucianism, while stressing an ordered and harmonious society, all tolerated slavery and urged slaves' obedience to established authorities. Until the Enlightenment of the eighteenth century, most people everywhere accepted slavery as a "natural phenomenon." It is not without irony that the Thirteenth Amendment to the U.S. Constitution (ratified in 1865), popularly interpreted as abolishing slavery, allows slavery "as a punishment for crime whereof the party shall have been duly convicted."

Between 1500 and 1900 the transatlantic African slave trade accounted for the largest number of people bought and sold. As such, and because of ample documentation, it has attracted much of the attention of scholars, and it also has tended to identify the institution of slavery with African blacks. From a global perspective, however, the trade was far broader.

MAP 19.3 The International Slave Trade

The revolting conditions on slave ships sailing to Caribbean and North American ports pale in barbarity beside conditions on the southern route to Brazil, where slaves were literally packed like sardines in a can. (Visual Connection Archive)

Slaves came from all over the world and included people of all races. The steady flow of white women and children from the Crimea, the Caucasus, and the Balkans in the fourteenth to eighteenth centuries for domestic, military, or sexual services in Ottoman lands, Italy, and sub-Saharan Africa; the use of convicts as galley slaves in the Venetian, French, Spanish, and Turkish navies; the enslavement of peoples defeated in war by Aztec, Inca, Sioux, Navajo, and other indigenous peoples of the Americas; the various forms of debt slavery in China and in Russia (where the legal distinction between serf and slave before 1861 was very hazy); the traffic of Indonesian and Pacific island peoples for slave labor in Dutch South Africa; and the trans-Saharan stream of Africans to Mediterranean ports that continued at medieval rates into the late nineteenth century—all were different forms of a worldwide practice. Although these forms sometimes had little in common with one another, they all involved the buying and selling of human beings who could not move about freely or enjoy the fruits of their labor.

The price of slaves varied widely over time and from market to market, according to age, sex, physical appearance, buyers' perceptions of the social characteristics of each slave's ethnic background, and changes in supply and demand. The Mediterranean and Indian Ocean markets preferred women for domestic service; the Atlantic markets wanted strong young men for mine and plantation work, for example. We have little solid information on prices for slaves in the Balkans, Caucasus, or Indian Ocean region. Even in the Atlantic trade, it is difficult to determine, over several centuries, the value of currencies, the cost and insurance on transported slaves, and the cost of goods exchanged for slaves. Yet the gold-encrusted cathedrals of Spain and the elegant plantation houses of the southern United States stand as testimony to the vast fortunes made in the slave trade.

How is the human toll of slavery measured? Transformations within societies occurred not only because of local developments but also because of interactions among regions. For example, the virulent racism that in so many ways defines the American experience resulted partly from medieval European habits of dehumanizing the enemy (English versus Irish, German versus Slav, Christian versus Jew and Muslim) and partly from the movement of peoples and ideas all over the globe. American gold prospectors in the 1850s carried the bigotry they had heaped on blacks in the Americas to Australia, where it conditioned attitudes toward Asians and other peoples of color. Racism, like the slave trade, is a global phenomenon.

For all the cries for human rights today, the slave trade continues on a broad scale. The ancient Indian Ocean traffic in Indian girls and boys for "service" in the Persian Gulf oil kingdoms persists, as does the sale of African children for work in Asia. In 2011 an estimated 12 to 27 million people globally are held in one form of slavery or another. The U.S. State Department estimates that 15,000 to 18,000 enslaved foreign nationals are brought to the United States each year and, conservatively, perhaps as many as 50,000 people, mostly women and children, are in slavery in America at any given time. They have been bought, sold, tricked, and held in captivity, and their labor, often as sex slaves, has been exploited for the financial benefit of masters in a global enterprise.

immunity to both diseases, and in the Americas they experienced the lowest mortality rate of any people, making them, ironically, the most suitable workers for the environment.

In 1500 a Portuguese fleet en route to India around Africa sailed too far west into the Atlantic and made landfall on the coast of modern Brazil. Although its commander, Pedro Cabral, did not know where he was, he followed the common practice (see page 465) and immediately claimed the land for King Manuel I, the Portuguese monarch. Colonization began in the early 1530s, and in 1551 the Portuguese founded a sugar colony at Bahia. Between 1551 and 1575, before the North American slave traffic began, the Portuguese delivered more African slaves to Brazil than would ever reach British North America (see Figure 19.1). Portugal essentially monopolized the slave trade until 1600 and continued to play a large role in the seventeenth century, though the trade was in-

The Slave Coast of West Africa

creasingly taken over by the Dutch, French, and English. From 1690 until the British House of Commons abolished the slave trade in 1807, England was the leading carrier of African slaves.

Population density and supply conditions along the West African coast and the sailing time to New World markets determined the sources of slaves. As the demand for slaves rose, slavers moved down the West African coast from Senegambia to the more densely populated hinterlands of the Bight of Benin and the Bight of Biafra. The abundant supply of Africans to enslave in Angola, the region south of the Congo River, and the quick passage from Angola to Brazil and the Caribbean established that region as the major coast for Portuguese slavers.

Transatlantic wind patterns partly determined exchange routes. Shippers naturally preferred the swiftest crossing — that is, from the African port nearest the latitude of the intended American destination. Thus Portuguese shippers carried their cargoes from Angola to Brazil, and British merchants sailed from the Bight of Benin to the Caribbean. The great majority of enslaved Africans were intended for the sugar and coffee plantations extending from the Caribbean islands to Brazil. Angola produced 26 percent of all African slaves and 70 percent of all Portuguese slaves. Trading networks extending deep into the interior culminated at two major ports on the Angolan coast, Luanda and Benguela. The Portuguese acquired a few slaves through warfare but secured the vast majority through trade with African dealers. Whites did not participate in the inland markets, which were run solely by Africans.

Almost all Portuguese shipments went to satisfy the virtually insatiable Brazilian demand for slaves. The so-called **Middle Passage** was the horrific journey experienced by Africans from freedom to enslavement in the Americas. Here is an excerpt from a Portuguese doctor's 1793 report on conditions in Luanda before the voyage across the Atlantic had begun. Be sure to note in this and subsequent quotations how the enslaved peoples are clearly considered, and treated, as chattel:

> The dwelling place of the slave is simply the dirt floor of the compound, and he remains there exposed to harsh conditions and bad weather, and at night there are only a lean-to and some sheds . . . which they are herded into like cattle.
>
> Their food continues scarce as before . . . limited at times to badly cooked beans, at other times to corn. . . .

FIGURE 19.1 Estimated Slave Imports by Destination, 1501–1866 Brazil was the single largest importer of African slaves from 1501 to 1866. But when taken cumulatively, the British, French, Dutch, and Danish colonies of the Caribbean rivaled the much larger colony of Brazil for numbers of slaves imported from Africa. (Source: Data from Emory University. "Assessing the Slave Trade: Estimates," in *Voyages: The Trans-Atlantic Slave Trade Database.* 2009. http://www.slavevoyages.org.)

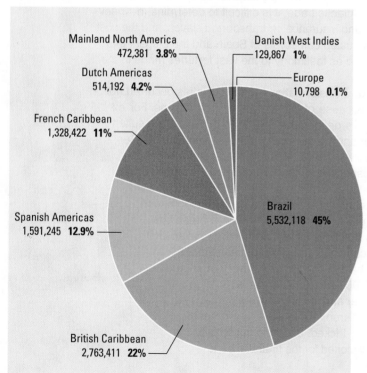

And when they reach a port . . . , they are branded on the right breast with the coat of arms of the king and nation, of whom they have become vassals. . . . This mark is made with a hot silver instrument in the act of paying the king's duties, and this brand mark is called a *carimbo*. . . .

In this miserable and deprived condition the terrified slaves remain for weeks and months, and the great number of them who die is unspeakable. With some ten or twelve thousand arriving at Luanda each year, it often happens that only six or seven thousand are finally transported to Brazil.[17]

Conditions during the Middle Passage were even worse. Olaudah Equiano (see "Individuals in Society: Olaudah Equiano," page 578) describes the experience of his voyage as a captured slave from Benin to Barbados in the Caribbean:

At last, when the ship we were in had got in all her cargo [of slaves], they made ready with many fearful noises, and we were all put under deck so that we could not see how they managed the vessel. . . . The stench of the hold while we were on the coast was so intolerably loathsome that it was dangerous to remain there for any time, and some of us had been permitted to stay on the deck for the fresh air; but now that the whole ship's cargo were confined together it became absolutely pestilential. The closeness of the place and the heat of the climate, added to the number in the ship, which was so crowded that each had scarcely room to turn himself, almost suffocated us. This produced copious perspirations, so that the air soon became unfit for respiration from a variety of loathsome smells, and brought on a sickness among the slaves, of which many died, thus falling victims to the improvident avarice, as I may call it, of their purchasers. This wretched situation was again aggravated by the galling of the chains, now become insupportable, and the filth of the necessary tubs [of human waste], into which the children often fell and were almost suffocated. The shrieks of the women and the groans of the dying rendered the whole a scene of horror almost inconceivable.[18]

Although the demand was great, Portuguese merchants in Angola and Brazil sought to maintain only a steady trickle of slaves from the African interior to Luanda and across the ocean to Bahia and Rio de Janeiro: a flood of slaves would have depressed the American market. Rio, the port capital through which most enslaved Africans passed, commanded the Brazilian trade. Planters and mine operators from the provinces traveled to Rio to buy slaves. Between 1795 and 1808, approximately 10,000 Angolans per year stood in the Rio slave market. In 1810 the figure rose to 18,000; in 1828 it reached 32,000.[19]

The English ports of London, Bristol, and particularly Liverpool dominated the British slave trade. In the eighteenth century Liverpool was the world's greatest slave-trading port. In all three cities, small and cohesive merchant classes exercised great public influence. The cities also had huge stores of industrial products for export, growing shipping industries, and large amounts of ready cash for investment abroad. Merchants generally formed partnerships to raise capital and to share the risks; each voyage was a separate enterprise or venture.

Slaving ships from Bristol plied back and forth along the Gold Coast, the Bight of Benin, Bonny, and Calabar looking for African traders who were willing to supply them with slaves. Liverpool's ships drew enslaved people from Gambia, the Windward Coast, and the Gold Coast. British ships carried textiles, gunpowder and flint, beer and spirits, British and Irish linens, and woolen cloth to Africa. A collection of goods was grouped together into what was called the **sorting**. An English sorting might include bolts of cloth, firearms, alcohol, tobacco, and hardware; this batch of goods would be traded for an enslaved individual or a quantity of gold, ivory, or dyewood.[20]

European traders had two systems for exchange. First, especially on the Gold Coast, they established factory-forts (for more on factory-forts, see page 608). These fortified trading posts were expensive to maintain but proved useful for fending off European rivals. Second, they used **shore trading**, in which European ships sent boats ashore or invited African dealers to bring traders and enslaved Africans out to the ships. The English captain John Adams, who made ten voyages to Africa between 1786 and 1800, described the shore method of trading at Bonny:

This place is the wholesale market for slaves, as not fewer than 20,000 are annually sold here; 16,000 of whom are natives of one nation called Ibo. . . . Fairs where the slaves of the Ibo nation are obtained are held every five or six weeks at several villages, which are situated on the banks of the rivers and creeks in the interior, and to which the African traders of Bonny resort to purchase them.

. . . The traders augment the quantity of their merchandise, by obtaining from their friends, the captains of the slave ships, a considerable quantity

- **Middle Passage** African slaves' voyage across the Atlantic to the Americas, a long and treacherous journey during which slaves endured appalling and often deadly conditions.
- **sorting** A collection or batch of British goods that would be traded for a slave or for a quantity of gold, ivory, or dyewood.
- **shore trading** A process for trading goods in which European ships sent boats ashore or invited African dealers to bring traders and slaves out to the ships.

Olaudah Equiano

THE TRANSATLANTIC SLAVE TRADE WAS A MASS movement involving millions of human beings. It was also the sum of individual lives spent partly or entirely in slavery. Most of those lives remain hidden to us. Olaudah Equiano (1745–1797) represents a rare ray of light into the slaves' obscurity; he is probably the best-known African slave.

In his autobiography, *The Interesting Narrative of the Life of Olaudah Equiano* (1789), Equiano says that he was born in Benin (modern Nigeria) of Ibo ethnicity.* His father, one of the village elders (or chieftains), presided over a large household that included "many slaves," prisoners captured in local wars. All people, slave and free, shared in the cultivation of family lands. One day, when all the adults were in the fields, two strange men and a woman broke into the family compound, kidnapped the eleven-year-old Olaudah and his sister, tied them up, and dragged them into the woods. Brother and sister were separated, and Olaudah was sold several times to various dealers before reaching the coast. As it took six months to walk there, his home must have been far inland. The sea, the slave ship, and the strange appearance of the white crew terrified the boy (see page 577). Equiano's master took him to Jamaica, to Virginia, and then to England, where he placed him in the custody of a kind family. They gave him the rudiments of an education, and he was baptized a Christian.

Equiano soon went to sea as a captain's boy (servant), serving in the Royal Navy during the Seven Years' War. On shore at Portsmouth, England, after one battle, Equiano was urged by his master to read, study, and learn basic mathematics. This education served him well, for after a voyage to the West Indies, his master sold him to a Philadelphia Quaker, Robert King, who was a rum and sugar merchant. Equiano worked as a clerk in King's warehouse, as a longshoreman loading and unloading cargo ships, and at sea where he developed good navigational skills; King paid him for his work. Equiano became an entrepreneur himself, buying and selling small goods in the islands and mainland ports. Determined to buy his freedom, Equiano had amassed enough money by 1766, and King signed the deed of manumission. Equiano was twenty-one years old; he had been a slave for ten years.

Equiano returned to London and used his remaining money to hire tutors to teach him hairdressing, mathematics, and how to play the French horn. When money was scarce, he found work as a merchant seaman, traveling to Portugal, Nice, Genoa, Naples, and Turkey. He even participated in an Arctic expedition.

Equiano's *Narrative* reveals a complex and sophisticated man. He had a strong constitution and an equally strong character. His Christian faith undoubtedly sustained him. On the title page of his book, he cited a verse from Isaiah (12:2): "The Lord Jehovah is my strength and my song." The very first thought that came to his mind the day he was freed was a passage from Psalm 126: "I glorified God in my heart, in whom I trusted."

Equiano loathed the brutal slavery he saw in the West Indies and the vicious racism he experienced in the North American colonies. He respected the fairness of Robert King, admired British navigational and industrial technologies, and had many close white friends. He once described himself as "almost an Englishman." He was also involved in the black communities in the West Indies and in London. Equiano's *Narrative* is a well-documented argument for the abolition of slavery and a literary classic that went through nine editions before his death.

Olaudah Equiano's *Narrative*, with its horrific descriptions of slavery, proved influential, and after its publication Equiano became active in the abolition movement. He spoke to large crowds in the industrial cities of Manchester and Birmingham in England, arguing that it was in the business interests of manufacturers to support abolition, as Africa was a huge, virtually untapped market for English cloth. Though he died in 1797, ten years before its passage, Equiano significantly advanced the abolitionist cause that led to the Slave Trade Act of 1807.

Source: *Equiano's Travels: The Interesting Narrative of the Life of Olaudah Equiano*, ed. Paul Edwards (Portsmouth, N.H.: Heinemann, 1996).

• **Olaudah Equiano, 1789, dressed as an elegant Englishman, his Bible open to the book of Acts.** (National Portrait Gallery, Smithsonian Institution/Art Resource, NY)

*Recent scholarship has re-examined Equiano's life and raised some questions about his African origins and his experience of the Middle Passage. To explore the debate over Equiano's authorship of the African and Middle Passage portions of his autobiography, see Vincent Carretta, *Equiano, the African: Biography of a Self-Made Man* (New York: Penguin, 2007).

QUESTIONS FOR ANALYSIS

1. How typical was Olaudah Equiano's life as a slave? How atypical?
2. Describe Equiano's culture and his sense of himself.

Peddlers in Rio de Janeiro A British army officer sketched this early-nineteenth-century scene of everyday life in Rio de Janeiro, Brazil. The ability to balance large burdens on the head meant that the person's hands were free for other use. Note the player (on the left) of a musical instrument originating in the Congo. On the right a woman gives alms to the man with the holy image in return for being allowed to kiss the image as an act of devotion. We do not know whether the peddlers were free and self-employed or were selling for their owners. (From "Views and Costumes of the City and Neighborhood of Rio de Janeiro, Brazil," in *Drawings Taken by Lieutenant Henry Chamberlain, During the Years 1819 and 1820* [London: Columbian Press, 1822])

of goods on credit. . . . Evening is the period chosen for the time of departure, when they proceed in a body, accompanied by the noise of drums, horns, and gongs. At the expiration of the sixth day, they generally return bringing with them 1,500 or 2,000 slaves, who are sold to Europeans the evening after their arrival, and taken on board the ships. . . .

It is expected that every vessel, on her arrival at Bonny, will fire a salute the instant the anchor is let go, as a compliment to the black monarch who soon afterwards makes his appearance in a large canoe, at which time, all those natives who happen to be alongside the vessel are compelled to proceed in their canoes to a respectful distance, and make way for his Majesty's barge. After a few compliments to the captain, he usually enquires after brother George, meaning the King of England, George III, and hopes he and his family are well. He is not pleased unless he is regaled with the best the ship affords. . . . His power is absolute; and the surrounding country, to a considerable distance, is subject to his dominion.[21]

The shore method of buying slaves allowed the ship to move easily from market to market. The final prices of those enslaved depended on their ethnic origin, their availability when the shipper arrived, and their physical health when offered for sale in the West Indies or the North or South American colonies.

Supplying slaves for the foreign market was controlled by a small, wealthy African merchant class, or it was a state monopoly. By contemporary standards, slave raiding was a costly operation: gathering a band of raiders and the capital for equipment, guides, tolls, and supplies involved considerable expense. Only black African entrepreneurs with sizable capital and labor could afford to finance and direct raiding drives. They exported enslaved men and women because the profits on exports were greater than the profits to be made from using labor in the domestic economy.

The transatlantic slave trade that the British, as well as the Dutch, Portuguese, French, Americans, and others, participated in was part of a much larger trading network that is known in history as the "triangle trade." European merchants sailed to Africa on the first leg of the voyage to trade European manufactured goods for enslaved Africans. When they had filled their ships' holds with enslaved peoples, they headed across the Atlantic on the second leg of the voyage, the Middle Passage. When they reached the Americas the merchants unloaded and sold their human cargoes and used the profits to purchase raw materials — cotton, sugar, indigo — that they then transported back to Europe, completing the third leg of the commercial triangle.

Enslaved African people had an enormous impact on the economics of the Portuguese and Spanish colonies of South America and in the Dutch, French, and British colonies of the Caribbean and North America. For example, on the sugar plantations of Mexico and the Caribbean; on the cotton, rice, and tobacco plantations of North America; and in the silver and gold mines of

The African Slave Trade Enslaved African men, women, and children, captured in the interior, are marched to the coast by their African captors. The guards carry guns obtained from Europeans in the slave trade. The enslaved men are linked together by heavy wooden yokes, making it impossible to escape. (The Granger Collection, New York)

Peru and Mexico, enslaved Africans not only worked in the mines and fields but also filled skilled, supervisory, and administrative positions and performed domestic service. In the United States, enslaved Africans and their descendants influenced many facets of American culture, such as language, music (ragtime and jazz), dance, and diet. Even the U.S. Capitol building, where Congress meets, was built partly by slave labor.[22] But the importance of the slave trade extended beyond the Atlantic world. The expansion of capitalism, as well as the industrialization of Western societies, Egypt, and the nations of West, Central, and South Africa — all related in one way or another to the traffic in African people.

Impact on African Societies

What economic impact did European trade have on African societies? Africans possessed technology well suited to their environment. Over the centuries, they had cultivated a wide variety of plant foods; developed plant and animal husbandry techniques; and mined, smelted, and otherwise worked a great variety of metals. Apart from firearms, American tobacco and rum, and the cheap brandy brought by the Portuguese, European goods presented no novelty to Africans. They found foreign products desirable because of their low prices.

Traders of handwoven Indian cotton textiles, Venetian imitations of African beads, and iron bars from European smelters could undersell African manufacturers. Africans exchanged slaves, ivory, gold, pepper, and animal skins for those goods. African states eager to expand or to control commerce bought European firearms, although the difficulty of maintaining guns often gave gun owners only marginal superiority over skilled bowmen.[23] The kingdom of Dahomey (modern-day Benin in West Africa), however, built its power on the effective use of firearms.

The African merchants who controlled the production of exports gained the most from foreign trade. Dahomey's king, for example, had a gross income in 1750 of £250,000 (almost U.S. $33 million today) from the overseas export of his fellow Africans. A portion of his profit was spent on goods that improved his people's living standard. Slave-trading entrepôts, which provided opportunities for traders and for farmers who supplied foodstuffs to towns, caravans, and slave ships, prospered. But such economic returns did not spread very far.[24] International trade did not lead to Africa's economic development. Africa experienced neither technological growth nor the gradual spread of economic benefits in early modern times.

As in the Islamic world, women in sub-Saharan Africa also engaged in the slave trade. In Guinea these

Queen Njiga Mbandi Ana de Sousa
Njiga (also known as Nzinga) of Ndongo (r. 1624–1629) is the most important female political figure in the history of early modern Angola. She used military force in her expansionist policy and participated fully in the slave trade, but she fiercely resisted Portuguese attempts to control that trade. Here she sits enthroned, wearing her crown (the cross a sign of her Christian baptism) and bracelets, giving an order. She has become a symbol of African resistance to colonial rule. (Courtesy, Luigi Araldi, Modena)

women slave merchants and traders were known as *nhara*, a corruption of the Portuguese term *senhora*, a title used for a married woman. They acquired considerable riches, often by marrying the Portuguese merchants and serving as go-betweens for these outsiders who were not familiar with the customs and languages of the African coast. One of them, Mae Aurélia Correia (1810?–1875?), led a life famous in the upper Guinea coastal region for its wealth and elegance. Between the 1820s and 1840s she operated her own trading vessels and is said to have owned several hundred slaves. Some of them she hired out as skilled artisans and sailors. She and her sister (or aunt) Julia amassed a fortune in gold, silver jewelry, and expensive cloths while living in European-style homes. Julia and her husband, a trader from the Cape Verde Islands, also owned their own slave estates where they produced peanuts.

The intermarriage of French traders and Wolof women in Senegambia created a métis, or mulatto, class. In the emerging urban centers at Saint-Louis, members of this small class adopted the French language, the Roman Catholic faith, and a French manner of life, and they exercised considerable political and economic power. However, European cultural influences did not penetrate West African society beyond the seacoast.

The political consequences of the slave trade varied from place to place. The trade enhanced the power and wealth of some kings and warlords in the short run but promoted conditions of instability and collapse over the long run. In the Kongo kingdom, which was located in parts of modern Angola, the Republic of the Congo, and the Democratic Republic of the Congo, the perpetual Portuguese search for Africans to enslave undermined the monarchy, destroyed political unity, and led to constant disorder and warfare; power passed to the village chiefs. Likewise in Angola, which became a Portuguese

proprietary colony (a territory granted to one or more individuals by the Crown for them to govern at their will), the slave trade decimated and scattered the population and destroyed the local economy. By contrast, the military kingdom of Dahomey, which entered into the slave trade in the eighteenth century and made it a royal monopoly, prospered enormously. Dahomey's economic strength rested on the slave trade. The royal army raided deep into the interior, and in the late eighteenth century Dahomey became one of the major West African sources of slaves. When slaving expeditions failed to yield sizable catches and when European demand declined, the resulting depression in the Dahomean economy caused serious political unrest. Iboland, inland from the Niger Delta, from whose great port cities of Bonny and Brass the British drained tens of thousands of enslaved Africans, experienced minimal political effects. A high birthrate kept pace with the incursions of the slave trade, and Ibo societies remained demographically and economically strong.

What demographic impact did the slave trade have on Africa? Between approximately 1501 and 1866, more than 12 million Africans were forcibly exported to the Americas, 6 million were traded to Asia, and 8 million were retained as slaves within Africa. Figure 19.2 shows the estimated number of slaves shipped to the Americas in the transatlantic slave trade. Export figures do not include the approximately 10 to 15 percent who died during procurement or in transit.

The early modern slave trade involved a worldwide web of relationships among markets in the Middle East,

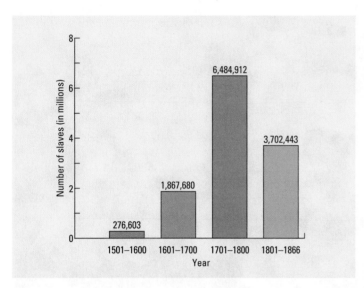

FIGURE 19.2 The Transatlantic Slave Trade, 1501–1866
The volume of slaves involved in the transatlantic slave trade peaked during the eighteenth century. These numbers show the slaves who embarked from Africa, and do not reflect the 10 to 15 percent of enslaved Africans who died in transit. (Source: Data from Emory University. "Assessing the Slave Trade: Estimates," in *Voyages: The Trans-Atlantic Slave Trade Database*. 2009. http://www.slavevoyages.org.)

Africa, Asia, Europe, and the Americas. But Africa was the crucible of the trade. There is no small irony in the fact that Africa, which of all the continents was most desperately in need of population because of its near total dependence on labor-intensive agriculture and pastoralism, lost so many millions to the trade. Although the British Parliament abolished the slave trade in 1807 and traffic in Africans to Brazil and Cuba gradually declined, within Africa the trade continued at the levels of the peak years of the transatlantic trade, 1780–1820. In the later nineteenth century, developing African industries, using slave labor, produced a variety of products for domestic consumption and export. Again, there is irony in the fact that in the eighteenth century European demand for slaves expanded the trade (and wars) within Africa, yet in the nineteenth century European imperialists defended territorial aggrandizement by arguing that they were "civilizing" Africans by abolishing slavery. But after 1880 European businessmen (and African governments) did not push abolition; they wanted cheap labor.

Markets in the Americas generally wanted young male slaves. Asian and African markets preferred young females. Women were sought for their reproductive value, as sex objects, and because their economic productivity was not threatened by the possibility of physical rebellion, as might be the case with young men. Consequently, two-thirds of those exported to the Americas were male, one-third female. As a result, the population on the western coast of Africa became predominantly female; the population in the East African savanna and Horn regions was predominantly male. The slave trade therefore had significant consequences for the institutions of marriage, the local trade in enslaved people (as these local populations became skewed with too many males or too many females), and the sexual division of labor. Although Africa's overall population may have shown modest growth from roughly 1650 to 1900, that growth was offset by declines in the Horn and on the eastern and western coasts. While Europe and Asia experienced considerable demographic and economic expansion in the eighteenth century, Africa suffered a decline.[25]

Sapi-Portuguese Saltcellar Contact with the Sapi people of present-day Sierra Leone in West Africa led sixteenth-century Portuguese traders to commission this ivory saltcellar, for which they brought Portuguese designs. But the object's basic features—a spherical container and separate lid on a flat base, with men, women, and supporting beams below—are distinctly African. An executioner, holding an ax with which he has beheaded five men, stands on the lid. This piece was probably intended as an example of Sapi artistic virtuosity, rather than for practical table use. (Courtesy, Museo Nazionale Preistorico ed Etnografico, Rome)

CONNECTIONS

During the period from 1400 to 1800 many parts of Africa experienced a profound transition with the arrival of Europeans all along Africa's coasts. Ancient trade routes, such as those across the Sahara Desert or up and down the East African coast, were disrupted. In West Africa trade routes that had been purely internal now connected with global trade networks at European coastal trading posts. Along Africa's east coast, the Portuguese attacked Swahili city-states in their effort to take control of the Indian Ocean trade nexus.

The most momentous consequence of the European presence along Africa's coast, however, was the introduction of the transatlantic slave trade. For more than three centuries Europeans, with the aid of African slave traders, enslaved millions of Africa's healthiest and strongest men and women. Although many parts of Africa were untouched by the transatlantic slave trade, at least directly, areas where Africans were enslaved experienced serious declines in agricultural production, little progress in technological development, and significant increases in violence.

As we will see in Chapters 20 and 21, early European commercial contacts with the empires of the Middle East and of South and East Asia were similar in many ways to those with Africa. Initially, the Portuguese, and then the English, Dutch, and French, did little more than establish trading posts at port cities and had to depend on the local people to bring them trade goods from the interior. Tropical diseases, particularly in India and in Southeast Asia, took heavy death tolls on the Europeans as they did in tropical Africa. What is more, while it was possible for the Portuguese to attack and conquer the individual Swahili city-states, Middle Eastern and Asian empires — such as the Ottomans in Turkey, the Safavids in Persia, the Mughals in India, and the Ming and Manchu Dynasties in China — were, like the West African kingdoms, economically and militarily powerful enough to dictate terms of trade with the Europeans.

Resistance to enslavement took many forms on both sides of the Atlantic. In Haiti, as discussed in Chapter 22, resistance led to revolution and independence, marking the first successful uprising of non-Europeans against a colonial power. At the end of the nineteenth century, as described in Chapter 25, Europeans used the ongoing Arab-Swahili slave raids from Africa's eastern coast far into the interior as an excuse to invade and eventually colonize much of central and eastern Africa. The racial discrimination that accompanied colonial rule in Africa would set the stage for a struggle for equality that would lead to eventual independence after World War II.

☐ CHAPTER REVIEW

☐ What different types of economic, social, and political structures were found in the kingdoms and states along the west coast and in the Sudan? (page 558)

In the early modern world, kingdoms and stateless societies in West Africa existed side by side. Stateless societies like the Senegambia were oriented around a single village or group of villages without a central capital. Age-grade systems, which passed on societal norms to successive generations and unified communities, were a common feature of many of these societies. Benin and other kingdoms were ruled by obas, kings who governed defined areas through bureaucratic hierarchies. The economies of both the kingdoms and the stateless societies were predominantly agricultural.

KEY TERMS

chattel (p. 558)
age-grade systems (p. 559)
oba (p. 559)
Taghaza (p. 560)
Tuareg (p. 565)
cowrie shells (p. 565)
Coptic Christianity (p. 567)
Swahili (p. 568)
Middle Passage (p. 576)
sorting (p. 577)
shore trading (p. 577)

Village markets served as sites for the exchange of produce and news and for social interaction. The transatlantic slave trade, along with disease and famine, had a negative effect on population throughout West Africa, resulting in intense competition for women.

The Sudanic empires immediately south of the Sahara, such as Songhai, Kanem-Bornu, and Hausaland, controlled the north-south trans-Saharan trade in gold, salt, cloth, and other items. The rulers of the kingdoms of the Sudan were predominantly Muslim. Being part of the Islamic world gave these societies not only commercial links to Europe, the Middle East, and beyond, but also access to some of the most advanced scholarship in the world at the time. As a result, Timbuktu became a Muslim intellectual center, as did Kano and Katsina. Still, although West African societies experienced strong Islamic influences, Muslim culture affected primarily the royal and elite classes and seldom reached the masses.

▢ How did the arrival of Europeans and other foreign cultures impact the East African coast, and how did Ethiopia and the Swahili city-states respond to these incursions? (page 566)

Europeans came to believe that the Christian kingdom of Ethiopia was ruled by a wealthy (mythical) Christian monarch named Prester John. The Prester John fable attracted Europeans to Ethiopia for centuries. The myth partly explains why, when the Ethiopians called for European assistance in fighting off Muslim incursions by the Red Sea state of Adal in the sixteenth century, the Portuguese came to their aid, soundly defeating a Muslim force at Lake Tana in 1543. Jesuit missionaries soon followed and tried to convert Ethiopians to Roman Catholicism, but the Ethiopians fiercely resisted, expelling the Jesuits in 1633.

The wealthy Swahili city-states on the southeastern coast of Africa possessed a Muslim and mercantile culture. The Swahili acted as middlemen in the East African–Indian Ocean trade network, and had long felt the influence of Indians, Indonesians, Persians, and Arabs. When the Portuguese arrived in the Indian Ocean in the late fifteenth and early sixteenth centuries, they sought to conquer and control this network. Some Swahili rulers agreed to form trading alliances with the Portuguese, while others refused and faced bombardment. Although the Portuguese had little effect on Swahili culture or religion, their presence caused the economic decline and death of many Swahili cities as people along the coast deserted their cities rather than face Portuguese control.

▢ What role did slavery play in African societies before the transatlantic slave trade began, and what was the effect of European involvement? (page 568)

Many African societies had long used some form of slavery. Generally, slaves were obtained as payment for debt, in war, or through simple purchase. Slaves were treated relatively benignly in some societies, serving as wives, house servants, royal guards, or even royal

advisers. But other slaves were considered chattel possessions, little more than animals, and suffered under harsh and brutal treatment as field hands, common laborers, sex objects, or miners. European involvement in the slave trade began around 1550 with the Portuguese importation of slaves to work in Brazil. The Dutch East India Company used enslaved Africans to work Cape Colony, supplemented with slaves from Southeast Asia. As the labor demands in the colonies of the New World grew, the transatlantic slave trade run by Europeans exploited millions of Africans to work in the often harsh conditions of the New World. African entrepreneurs and merchants played an important role in the slave trade, capturing and selling slaves from the interior to the Portuguese in Angola and to the British along the Gold Coast of West Africa. Africans exchanged slaves for firearms and inexpensive foreign products. Influences were variable, with some kingdoms experiencing a rise of wealth and power, though over time the influence was largely destabilizing. As a result of the demand in the New World for young male slaves, the West African population became predominately female, further destabilizing African society and leading to economic decline.

SUGGESTED READING

Berger, Iris, E. Frances White, and Cathy Skidmore-Heiss. *Women in Sub-Saharan Africa: Restoring Women to History.* 1999. Necessary reading for a complete understanding of African history.

Cooper, Frederick. *Plantation Slavery on the East Coast of Africa.* 1997. Useful study of slavery as practiced in Africa.

Fredrickson, G. M. *Racism: A Short History.* 2002. Contains probably the best recent study of the connection between African slavery and Western racism.

Klein, Martin, and Claire C. Robertson. *Women and Slavery in Africa.* 1997. From the perspective that most slaves in Africa were women.

Law, Robin. *Oyo Empire, c. 1600–c. 1836: A West African Imperialism in the Era of the Atlantic Slave Trade.* 1977. Remains the definitive study of the powerful Oyo Empire in what is today southwestern Nigeria.

Lovejoy, Paul E. *Transformation in Slavery: A History of Slavery in Africa.* 2d ed. 2000. Essential for an understanding of slavery in an African context.

Middleton, J. *The World of Swahili: An African Mercantile Civilization.* 1992. Introduction to East Africa and the Horn region.

Northrup, D. *Africa's Discovery of Europe, 1450–1850.* 2002. Offers a unique perspective on African-European contact.

Oliver, Roland, and Anthony Atmore. *Medieval Africa, 1250–1800.* 2001. A history of premodern Africa by two renowned historians of the continent.

Pearson, Michael N. *Port Cities and Intruders: The Swahili Coast, India, and Portugal in the Early Modern Era.* 2002. Comprehensive introduction to the Swahili coast and the Indian Ocean trade network.

Powell, Eve Troutt, and John O. Hunwick. *The African Diaspora in the Mediterranean Lands of Islam.* 2002. Important study of Islam and the African slave trade.

Robinson, David. *Muslim Societies in African History.* 2004. Valuable introduction to Islam in Africa by a renowned Africanist.

Shell, R. *Children of Bondage: A Social History of the Slave Society at the Cape of Good Hope, 1652–1938.* 1994. A massive study of Cape slave society filled with much valuable statistical data.

Shillington, K. *History of Africa.* 2005. Provides a soundly researched, highly readable, and well-illustrated survey.

Thorton, J. *Africa and Africans in the Making of the Atlantic World, 1400–1680.* 1992. Places African developments in an Atlantic context.

NOTES

1. P. D. Curtin, *Economic Change in Precolonial Africa: Senegambia in the Era of the Slave Trade* (Madison: University of Wisconsin Press, 1975), pp. 34–35; J. A. Rawley, *The Transatlantic Slave Trade: A History* (Lincoln: University of Nebraska Press, 2005).

2. Pieter de Marees, *Description of the Gold Kingdom of Guinea* (Dantzig, 1602), Albert van Dantzig and Adam Jones, trans. and eds. (Oxford, U.K.: Oxford University Press, 1987), pp. 226–228; William Bosman, *A New Description of the Coast of Guinea*, ed. John Ralph Willis (London: Frank Cass, 1967), p. 461.

3. Quoted in R. Hallett, *Africa to 1875* (Ann Arbor: University of Michigan Press, 1970), p. 151.

4. A. ibn-Fartura, "The Kanem Wars," in *Nigerian Perspectives*, ed. T. Hodgkin (London: Oxford University Press, 1966), pp. 111–115.

5. "The Kano Chronicle," quoted in *Nigerian Perspectives*, ed. T. Hodgkin (London: Oxford University Press, 1966), pp. 89–90.

6. *Equiano's Travels: The Interesting Narrative of the Life of Olaudah Equiano*, ed. P. Edwards (Portsmouth, N.H.: Heinemann, 1996), p. 4.

7. J. Iliffe, *Africans: The History of a Continent* (Cambridge, U.K.: Cambridge University Press, 2007), p. 68.

8. See A. J. R. Russell-Wood, *The Portuguese Empire: A World on the Move* (Baltimore: Johns Hopkins University Press, 1998), pp. 11–13.

9. Ibid., pp. 35–38.

10. P. E. Lovejoy, *Transformations in Slavery: A History of Slavery in Africa* (Cambridge, U.K.: Cambridge University Press, 1992), p. 25, Table 2.1, "Trans-Saharan Slave Trade, 650–1600."

11. Iliffe, *Africans*, p. 77.

12. Quoted in H. Thomas, *The Slave Trade* (New York: Simon and Schuster, 1997), p. 21.

13. G. Gerzina, *Black London: Life Before Emancipation* (New Brunswick, N.J.: Rutgers University Press, 1995), pp. 29–66, passim; quotation from p. 53.

14. C.-H. Shell, *Children of Bondage: A Social History of the Slave Society at the Cape of Good Hope, 1652–1838* (Hanover, N.H.: University Press of New England, 1994), pp. 285–289.

15. See D. Eltis, *The Rise of African Slavery in the Americas* (Cambridge, U.K.: Cambridge University Press, 2000), Chap. 3; and the review/commentary by J. E. Inikori, *American Historical Review* 106, no. 5 (December 2001): 1751–1753.

16. R. Blackburn, *The Making of New World Slavery: From the Baroque to the Modern, 1492–1800* (New York: Verso, 1998), pp. 79–80.

17. R. E. Conrad, *Children of God's Fire: A Documentary History of Black Slavery in Brazil* (Princeton, N.J.: Princeton University Press, 1983), pp. 20–23.

18. *Equiano's Travels*, pp. 23–26.

19. Rawley, *The Transatlantic Slave Trade*, pp. 45–47.

20. Robert W. July, *A History of the African People* (Prospect Heights, Ill.: Waveland Press, 1998), p. 171.

21. J. Adams, "Remarks on the Country Extending from Cape Palmas to the River Congo," *Nigerian Perspectives*, ed. T. Hodgkin (London: Oxford University Press, 1966), pp. 178–180.

22. J. Thornton, *Africa and Africans in the Making of the Atlantic World* (New York: Cambridge University Press, 1992), pp. 138–142.

23. Robert W. July, *Precolonial Africa: An Economic and Social History* (New York: Scribner's, 1975), pp. 269–270.

24. A. G. Hopkins, *An Economic History of West Africa* (New York: Columbia University Press, 1973), p. 119.

25. P. Manning, *Slavery and African Life: Occidental, Oriental, and African Slave Trades* (New York: Cambridge University Press, 1990), pp. 22–23 and Chap. 3, pp. 38–59.

For practice quizzes and other study tools, visit the **Online Study Guide** at bedfordstmartins.com/mckayworld.

For primary sources from this period, see *Sources of World Societies*, **Second Edition**.

For Web sites, images, and documents related to topics in this chapter, visit **Make History** at bedfordstmartins.com/mckayworld.

• **Persian Princess** The ruling houses of the Islamic empires were great patrons of art and architecture. This depiction of a princess in a garden is from an early-seventeenth-century palace built by Shah Abbas of the Safavid Dynasty in Persia. (Giraudon/The Bridgeman Art Library)

20

The Islamic World Powers

1300–1800

After the decline of the Mongol Empire in the mid-fourteenth century, powerful new Islamic states emerged in south and west Eurasia. By the sixteenth century the Ottoman Empire, centered in Anatolia; the Safavid (sah-FAH-weed) Empire in Persia; and the Mughal (MOO-guhl) Empire in India controlled vast territories from West Africa to Central Asia, from the Balkans to the Bay of Bengal.

Lasting more than six centuries (1299–1922), the Ottoman Empire was one of the largest, best-organized, and most enduring political entities in world history. In Persia (now Iran) the Safavid Dynasty created a Shi'a state and presided over a brilliant culture. In India the Mughal leader Babur and his successors gained control of much of the Indian subcontinent. Mughal rule inaugurated a period of radical administrative reorganization in India and the flowering of intellectual and architectural creativity. Although these three states were often at war with each other, they shared important characteristics and challenges. For instance, their ruling houses all emerged from Turkish tribal organizations, and they all had to adapt their armies to the introduction of firearms. Over time, they became strongly linked culturally, as merchants, poets, philosophers, artists, and military advisers moved relatively easily across their political boundaries. Before the end of this period, Europeans were also active in trade in these empires, especially in India. •

The Turkish Ruling Houses: The Ottomans, Safavids, and Mughals

☐ How were the three Islamic empires established, and what sorts of governments did they set up?

Cultural Flowering

☐ What cultural advances occurred under the rule of the Ottoman, Safavid, and Mughal empires?

Non-Muslims Under Muslim Rule

☐ How did Christians, Jews, Hindus, and other non-Muslims fare under these Islamic states?

Shifting Trade Routes and European Penetration

☐ How were the Islamic empires affected by the gradual shift toward trade routes that bypassed their lands?

Political Decline

☐ Did any common factors lead to the decline of central power in the Islamic empires in the seventeenth and eighteenth centuries?

The Turkish Ruling Houses: The Ottomans, Safavids, and Mughals

☐ How were the three Islamic empires established, and what sorts of governments did they set up?

Before the Mongols arrived in Central Asia and Persia, another nomadic people from the region of modern Mongolia, the Turks, had moved west, gained control over key territories from Anatolia to Delhi in north India, and contributed to the decline of the Abbasid caliphate in the thirteenth century. The Turks had been quick to join the Mongols and were important participants in the armies and administrations of the Mongol states in Persia and Central Asia. In these regions, Turks far outnumbered ethnic Mongols.

As Mongol strength in Persia and Central Asia deteriorated in the late thirteenth to mid-fourteenth centuries, the Turks resumed their expansion. In the late fourteenth century the Turkish leader Timur (1336–1405), also called Tamerlane, built a Central Asian em-

Empire of Timur, ca. 1405

pire from his base in Samarkand that reached into India and through Persia to the Black Sea. Timur campaigned continuously from the 1360s until his death in 1405, his goal to repeat the achievements of Chinggis Khan. He did not get involved in administering the new territories but rather appointed lords and let them make use of existing political structures. His conquests were exceptionally destructive and benefited only Samarkand, where craftsmen and other specialists were forced to move to work for the new rulers. After his death his sons and grandson fought each other for succession. By 1450 his empire was in rapid decline, and power devolved to the local level. Meanwhile, Sufi orders (groups of Islamic mystics) thrived, and Islam became the most important force integrating the region. It was from the many small Turkish chiefs that the founders of the three main empires emerged.

The Ottoman Turkish Empire's Expansion

The **Ottomans** took their name from Osman (r. 1299–1326), the chief of a band of seminomadic Turks that had migrated into western **Anatolia** while the Mongols still held Persia. The Ottomans gradually expanded at the expense of other small Turkish states and the Byzantine Empire (Map 20.1). The Ottoman ruler called himself "border chief," or leader of the *ghazis* (GAH-zeez), frontier raiders. Although temporarily slowed by defeat at the hands of Timur in 1402, the Ottomans quickly reasserted themselves after Timur's death in 1405.

Osman's campaigns were intended to subdue, not to destroy. The Ottomans built their empire by absorbing the Muslims of Anatolia and by becoming the protector of the Orthodox Church and of the millions of Greek Christians in Anatolia and the Balkans. In 1326 they took Bursa in western Anatolia, and in 1352 they gained a foothold in Europe by seizing Gallipoli. Their victories led more men, including recent converts, to join them as ghazis. In 1389 at Kosovo in the Balkans, the Ottomans defeated a combined force of Serbs and Bosnians. And in 1396 on the Danube River in modern Bulgaria, they crushed King Sigismund of Hungary, who was supported by French, German, and English knights. After the victories in the Balkans, the Ottomans added to their military strength by obtaining slave troops. These troops were outfitted with guns and artillery and trained to use them effectively.

In 1453, during the reign of Sultan Mehmet II (r. 1451–1481), the Ottomans conquered Constantinople, capital of the Byzantine Empire, which had lasted a thousand years. The Byzantine emperor, Constantine IX Palaeologus (r. 1449–1453), with only about ten thousand men, relied on Constantinople's magnificent system of circular walls and stone fortifications for defense. Although Mehmet II had more than a hundred thousand men and a large fleet, iron chains spanning the city's harbor kept him out. Nevertheless, Turkish ingenuity and up-to-date technology eventually decided the battle. Mehmet's army carried boats over steep hills to come in behind the chains blocking the harbor and then bombarded the city from the rear. A Transylvanian cannon maker who had deserted the Greeks for the Turks cast huge bronze cannon on the spot (bringing raw materials to the scene of military action was easier than moving guns long distances), and these guns were used to weaken the defensive walls.

Once Constantinople was theirs, the Ottoman **sultans** considered themselves successors of both the Byzantine and Seljuk Turk emperors, and they quickly absorbed the rest of the Byzantine Empire. In the sixteenth century they continued to expand through the Middle East and into North Africa.

To begin the transformation of Constantinople (renamed Istanbul) into an imperial Ottoman capital, Mehmet ordered the city cleaned up and the walls repaired. He appointed officials to adapt the city administration to Ottoman ways and ordered wealthy residents to participate in building mosques, markets, fountains, baths, and other public facilities. The city's

□ CHRONOLOGY

1299–1326 Reign of Osman, founder of the Ottoman Dynasty

1299–1922 Ottoman Empire

1336–1405 Life of Timur

ca. mid-1400s Coffeehouses become center of Islamic male social life

1453 Ottoman conquest of Constantinople

1501–1524 Reign of Safavid Shah Isma'il

1501–1722 Safavid empire

1520–1558 Hürrem wields influence in the Ottoman Empire as Suleiman's concubine and then wife

1520–1566 Reign of Ottoman sultan Suleiman I; period of artistic flowering in Ottoman Empire

1521 Piri Reis produces *Book of the Sea*, a navigational map book

1526–1857 Mughal Empire

1556–1605 Reign of Akbar in Mughal Empire

1570 Ottomans take control of Cyprus

1571 First major Ottoman defeat by Christians, at Lepanto

1587–1629 Reign of Shah Abbas; height of Safavid power; carpet weaving becomes major Persian industry

1631–1648 Construction of Taj Mahal under Shah Jahan in India

1658–1707 Reign of Aurangzeb; Mughal power begins to decline

1763 Treaty of Paris recognizes British control over much of India

population had declined in the decades before the conquest, and warfare, flight, and the sale of many survivors into slavery had decreased it further. Therefore, Mehmet transplanted inhabitants of other territories to the city, granting them tax remissions and possession of empty houses. He wanted them to start businesses, make Istanbul prosperous, and transform it into a microcosm of the empire.

Gunpowder, which was invented by the Chinese and adapted to artillery use by the Europeans, played an influential role in the expansion of the Ottoman

- **Ottomans** Ruling house of the Turkish empire that lasted from 1299 to 1922.
- **Anatolia** The region of modern Turkey.
- **sultan** An Arabic word originally used by the Seljuk Turks to mean authority or dominion; it was used by the Ottomans to connote political and military supremacy.

□ Mapping the Past

MAP 20.1 The Ottoman Empire at Its Height, 1566 The Ottomans, like their great rivals the Habsburgs, rose to rule a vast dynastic empire encompassing many different peoples and ethnic groups. The army and the bureaucracy served to unite the disparate territories into a single state.

ANALYZING THE MAP Trace the coastlines of the Ottoman Empire. What were the major port cities of the empire? Which regions were encompassed within the empire at its height?

CONNECTIONS If the Ottoman Empire is compared to Europe of the same period (see Map 17.1 on page 495), which had more of its territory near the sea? How did proximity to the Mediterranean shape the politics of Ottoman-European relations in this period?

state. In the first half of the sixteenth century, thanks to the use of this technology, the Ottomans gained control of shipping in the eastern Mediterranean, eliminated the Portuguese from the Red Sea and the Persian Gulf, and supported Andalusian and North African Muslims in their fight against the Christian reconquest of Muslim Spain. In 1514, under the superb military leadership of Selim (r. 1512–1520), the Ottomans turned the Safavids back from Anatolia. In addition, the Ottomans added Syria and Palestine (1516) and Egypt (1517) to their empire, giving them control of

the holy cities of Islam. Next they extended their rule across North Africa to Tunisia and Algeria. Selim's rule marks the beginning of four centuries when most Arabs were under Ottoman rule.

Suleiman (r. 1520–1566) extended Ottoman dominion to its widest geographical extent (see Map 20.1). Suleiman's army crushed the Hungarians at Mohács in 1526, killing the king and thousands of his nobles. Three years later the Turks besieged the Habsburg capital of Vienna. This target proved impossible to attain, however, perhaps because the Ottomans had reached the logistical limit of their expansion, as some scholars argue.

From the late fourteenth to the early seventeenth centuries, the Ottoman Empire was a key player in European politics. In 1525 Francis I of France and Suleiman struck an alliance; both believed that only their collaboration could prevent Habsburg domination of Europe. The Habsburg emperor Charles V retaliated by seeking an alliance with Safavid Persia. Suleiman renewed the French agreement with Francis's son, Henry II (r. 1547–1559), and this accord became the cornerstone of Ottoman policy in western Europe. Suleiman also allied with the German Protestant princes, forcing the Catholic Habsburgs to grant concessions to the Protestants. Ottoman pressure thus contributed to the official recognition of Lutheran Prot-

estants at the Peace of Augsburg in 1555 and the consolidation of the national monarchy in France.

In eastern Europe to the north of Ottoman lands stood the Grand Duchy of Moscow. In the fifteenth century Ottoman rulers did not regard it as a threat; in 1497 they even gave Russian merchants freedom of trade within the empire. But in 1547 Ivan IV (the Terrible) brought the entire Volga region under Russian control (see Map 20.1). In 1557 Ivan's ally, the Cossack chieftain Dimitrash, tried to take Azov, the northernmost Ottoman fortress. Ottoman plans to recapture the area succeeded in uniting Russia, Persia, and the pope against the Turks.

Though usually victorious on land, the Ottomans did not enjoy complete dominion on the seas. Competition with the Habsburgs and pirates for control of the

Battle of Mohács The *Süleymanname* (Book of Suleiman), a biography, contains these wonderful illustrations of the battle that took place in Hungary on August 29, 1526. In the right panel, Suleiman in a white turban sits on a black horse surrounded by his personal guard, while janissaries fire cannon at the enemy. In the left panel, the Europeans are in disarray, in contrast to the Turks' discipline and order. Suleiman inflicted a crushing defeat and absorbed Hungary into the Ottoman Empire. (Private Collection/Archives Charmet/The Bridgeman Art Library)

Mediterranean led the Ottomans to conquer Cyprus in 1570 and settle thousands of Turks from Anatolia there. (Thus began the large Turkish presence on Cyprus that continues to the present day.) In response, Pope Pius V organized a Holy League against the Turks, which had a victory in 1571 at Lepanto off the west coast of Greece with a squadron of more than two hundred Spanish, Venetian, and papal galleys. Still, the Turks remained supreme on land and quickly rebuilt their entire fleet.

To the east, war with Safavid Persia occupied the sultans' attention throughout the sixteenth century. Several issues lay at the root of the long and exhausting conflict: religious antagonism between the Sunni Ottomans and the Shi'a Persians, competition to expand at each other's expense in Mesopotamia, desire to control trade routes, and European alliances. (For more on the Shi'a faith, see page 595.) Finally, in 1638 the Ottomans captured Baghdad, and the treaty of Kasr-I-Shirim established a permanent border between the two powers.

The Ottoman political system reached its classic form under Suleiman I. All authority flowed from the sultan to his public servants: provincial governors, police officers, military generals, heads of treasuries, and **viziers**. In Turkish history, Suleiman is known as "the Lawgiver" because of his profound influence on the civil law. He ordered Lütfi Paşa (d. 1562), a poet and juridical scholar of slave origin, to draw up a new general code of laws that prescribed penalties for routine criminal acts such as robbery, adultery, and murder. It also sought to reform bureaucratic and financial corruption, such as foreign merchants' payment of bribes to avoid customs duties, imprisonment without trial, and promotion in the provincial administration because of favoritism rather than ability. The legal code also introduced the idea of balanced government budgets. The head of the religious establishment was given the task of reconciling sultanic law with Islamic law. Suleiman's legal acts influenced many legal codes, including that of the United States. Today, Suleiman's image appears in the chamber of the U.S. House of Representatives, along with the images of the Athenian lawmaker Solon, Moses, and Thomas Jefferson.

- **viziers** Chief assistants to caliphs.
- **devshirme** A process whereby the sultan's agents swept the provinces for Christian youths to become slaves.
- **janissaries** Turkish for "recruits"; they formed the elite army corps.
- **concubine** A woman who is a recognized spouse but of lower status than a wife.
- **shah** Persian word for "king."
- **Safavid** The dynasty that encompassed all of Persia and other regions; its state religion was Shi'ism.
- **Qizilbash** Nomadic Sufi tribesmen who were loyal to and supportive of the early Safavid state.

The Ottomans ruled their more distant lands, such as those in North Africa, relatively lightly. Governors of distant provinces collected taxes and maintained trade routes, but their control did not penetrate deeply into the countryside.

The Ottoman Empire's Use of Slaves

The power of the Ottoman central government was sustained through the training of slaves. Slaves were purchased from Spain, North Africa, and Venice; captured in battle; or drafted through the system known as **devshirme**, by which the sultan's agents compelled Christian families in the Balkans to sell their boys. As the Ottoman frontier advanced in the fifteenth and sixteenth centuries, Albanian, Bosnian, Wallachian, and Hungarian slave boys filled Ottoman imperial needs. The slave boys were converted to Islam and trained for the imperial civil service and the standing army. The brightest 10 percent entered the palace school, where they learned to read and write Arabic, Ottoman Turkish, and Persian in preparation for administrative jobs. Other boys were sent to Turkish farms, where they acquired physical toughness in preparation for military service. Known as **janissaries** (Turkish for "recruits"), they formed the elite army corps. Thoroughly indoctrinated and absolutely loyal to the sultan, the janissary slave corps threatened the influence of fractious old Turkish families. They played a central role in Ottoman military affairs in the sixteenth century, adapting easily to the use of firearms. The devshirme system enabled the Ottomans to apply merit-based recruitment to military and administrative offices at little cost and provided a means of assimilating Christians living in Ottoman lands. Some Muslims, however, doubted whether janissary converts could be viewed as reliably Muslim.

The Ottoman ruling class consisted partly of descendants of Turkish families that had formerly ruled parts of Anatolia and partly of people of varied ethnic origins who rose through the bureaucratic and military ranks, many beginning as the sultan's slaves. All were committed to the Ottoman way: Islamic in faith, loyal to the sultan, and well versed in the Turkish language and the culture of the imperial court. In return for their services to the sultan, they held landed estates for the duration of their lives. The ruling class had the legal right to use and enjoy the profits, but not the ownership, of the land. Because all property belonged to the sultan and reverted to him on the holder's death, Turkish nobles, unlike their European counterparts, did not have a local base independent of the ruler. The absence of a hereditary nobility and private ownership of agricultural land differentiates the Ottoman system from European feudalism.

Music in a Garden This illustration of a courtly romance depicts several women in a garden, intently listening to a musician, with cups of a beverage in their hands. (Biblioteca Vaticana Apostolica)

Another distinctive characteristic of the Ottomans was the sultan's failure to marry. From about 1500 on, the sultans did not contract legal marriages but perpetuated the ruling house through concubinage. A slave **concubine** could not expect to exert power the way a local or foreign noblewoman could (with a notable exception; see "Individuals in Society: Hürrem," page 594). When one of the sultan's concubines became pregnant, her status and her salary increased. If she delivered a boy, she raised him until the age of ten or eleven. Then the child was given a province to govern under his mother's supervision. She accompanied him there, was responsible for his good behavior, and worked through imperial officials and the janissary corps to promote his interests. Because succession to the throne was open to all the sultan's sons, fratricide often resulted upon his death, and the losers were blinded or executed.

Slave concubinage paralleled the Ottoman development of slave soldiers and slave viziers. All held positions entirely at the sultan's pleasure, owed loyalty solely to him, and thus were more reliable than a hereditary nobility, as existed in Europe. Great social prestige, as well as the opportunity to acquire power and wealth, was attached to being a slave of the imperial household. Suleiman even made it a practice to marry his daughters to top-ranking slave-officials.

The Safavid Empire in Persia

With the decline of Timur's empire after 1450, Persia was controlled by Turkish lords, with no single one dominant until 1501, when fourteen-year-old Isma'il (1487–1524) led a Turkish army to capture Tabriz and declared himself **shah** (king).

The strength of the early **Safavid** state rested on three crucial features. First, it had the loyalty and military support of Turkish Sufis known as **Qizilbash** (KIH-zil-bahsh; a Turkish word meaning "redheads" that was applied to these people because of the red hats they wore). The shah secured the loyalty of the Qizilbash by granting them vast grazing lands, especially on the troublesome Ottoman frontier. In return, the Qizilbash supplied him with troops. Second, the Safavid state utilized the skills of urban bureaucrats and made them an essential part of the civil machinery of government.

The third source of Safavid strength was the Shi'a faith, which became the compulsory religion of the

Individuals in Society

Hürrem

HÜRREM (1505?–1558) WAS BORN IN THE western Ukraine (then part of Poland), the daughter of a Ruthenian priest, and was given the Polish name Aleksandra Lisowska. When Tartars raided, they captured and enslaved her. In 1520 she was given as a gift to Suleiman on the occasion of his accession to the throne. The Venetian ambassador (probably relying on secondhand or thirdhand information) described her as "young, graceful, petite, but not beautiful." She was given the Turkish name Hürrem, meaning "joyful."

Hürrem apparently brought joy to Suleiman. Their first child was born in 1521. By 1525 they had four sons and a daughter; sources note that by that year Suleiman visited no other woman. But he waited eight or nine years before breaking Ottoman dynastic tradition by making Hürrem his legal wife, the first slave concubine so honored. For the rest of her life, Hürrem played a highly influential role in the political, diplomatic, and philanthropic life of the Ottoman state. First, great power flowed from her position as mother of the prince, the future sultan Selim II (r. 1566–1574). Then, as the intimate and most trusted adviser of the sultan, she was Suleiman's closest confidante. During his frequent trips to the far-flung corners of his multi-ethnic empire, Hürrem wrote him long letters filled with her love and longing for him and her prayers for his safety in battle. She also shared political information about affairs in Istanbul, the activities of the grand vizier, and the attitudes of the janissaries. At a time when some people believed that the sultan's absence from the capital endangered his hold on the throne, Hürrem acted as his eyes and ears for potential threats.

Hürrem was the sultan's contact with her native Poland, which sent more embassies to Istanbul than any other power. Through her correspondence with King Sigismund I, peace between Poland and the Ottomans was maintained. When Sigismund II succeeded his father in 1548, Hürrem sent congratulations on his accession, along with two pairs of pajamas (originally a Hindu garment but commonly worn in southwestern Asia) and six handkerchiefs. Also, she sent the shah of Persia gold-embroidered sheets and shirts that she had sewn herself, seeking to display the wealth of the sultanate and to keep peace between the Ottomans and the Safavids.

The enormous stipend that Suleiman gave Hürrem permitted her to participate in his vast building program. In Jerusalem (in the Ottoman province of Palestine), she founded a hospice for fifty-five pilgrims that included a soup kitchen that fed four hundred pilgrims a day. In Istanbul Suleiman built and Hürrem endowed the Haseki (meaning "royal favorite concubine") mosque complex and a public bath for women near the Women's Market.

Perhaps Hürrem tried to fulfill two functions hitherto distinct in Ottoman political theory: those of the sultan's favorite and of mother of the prince. She also performed the conflicting roles of slave concubine and imperial wife. Many Turks resented Hürrem's interference at court. They believed she was behind the execution of Suleiman's popular son Mustafa on a charge of treason to make way for her own son to succeed as sultan.

Source: Leslie P. Pierce, *The Imperial Harem: Women and Sovereignty in the Ottoman Empire* (New York: Oxford University Press, 1993).

QUESTIONS FOR ANALYSIS

1. How does Hürrem compare to powerful women in other places, such as Empress Wu in China, Isabella of Castile, Catherine de' Medici of France, Elizabeth I of England, Mary Queen of Scots, or any other you know about?

2. What was Hürrem's "nationality"? What role did it play in her life?

Hürrem and her ladies in the harem.
(Bibliothèque nationale de France)

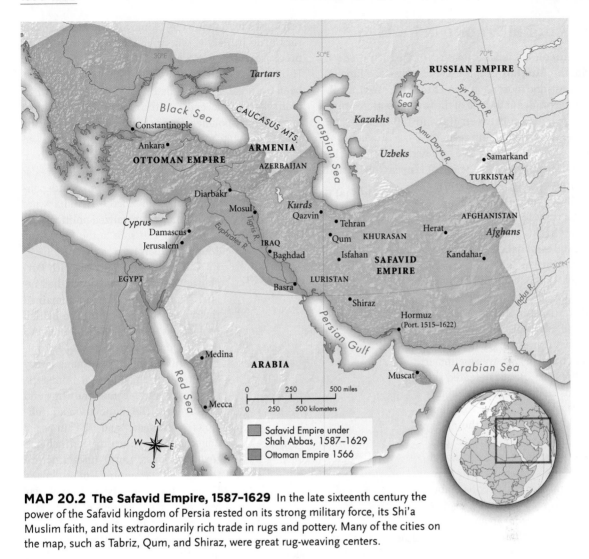

MAP 20.2 The Safavid Empire, 1587–1629 In the late sixteenth century the power of the Safavid kingdom of Persia rested on its strong military force, its Shi'a Muslim faith, and its extraordinarily rich trade in rugs and pottery. Many of the cities on the map, such as Tabriz, Qum, and Shiraz, were great rug-weaving centers.

empire. The Shi'a believed that leadership among Muslims rightfully belonged to the Prophet Muhammad's descendants. Because Isma'il claimed descent from a line of twelve infallible imams (leaders) beginning with Ali (Muhammad's cousin and son-in-law), he was officially regarded as their representative on earth. Isma'il's own beliefs were messianic and not mainstream, but he took steps that ended up promoting standard Shi'ism. For example, he recruited Shi'a scholars outstanding in learning and piety from other lands to instruct and guide his people, and he persecuted and exiled Sunni **ulama**. To this day, Iran remains the only Muslim state in which Shi'ism is the official religion.

Safavid power reached its height under Shah Abbas (r. 1587–1629), who moved the capital from Qazvin to Isfahan. His military achievements, support for trade and commerce, and endowment of the arts earned him the epithet "the Great." In the military realm, he adopted the Ottoman practice of building an army of slaves, primarily captives from the Caucuses (especially Armenians and Georgians), who could serve as a counterweight to the Qizilbash, who had come to be considered a threat. He also increased the use of gunpowder weapons and made alliances with European powers against the Ottomans and Portuguese. In his campaigns against the Ottomans, Shah Abbas captured Baghdad, Mosul, and Diarbakr in Mesopotamia (Map 20.2).

Conflict between the Ottomans and the Safavids was not an even match. The Safavids did not have as many people or as much wealth as the Ottomans and continually had to defend against encroachments on their western border. Still, they were able to attract some of the Turks in Ottoman lands who felt that their government had shifted too far from its nomadic roots. After Shah Abbas, Safavid power was sapped by civil war between tribal factions vying for control of the court.

• **ulama** Religious scholars whom Sunnis trust to interpret the Qur'an and the Sunna, the deeds and sayings of Muhammad.

The Mughal Empire in India

Of the three great Islamic empires of the early modern world, the **Mughal** Empire of India was the largest, wealthiest, and most populous. Extending over 1.2 million square miles at the end of the seventeenth century, with a population between 100 and 150 million, and with fabulous wealth and resources, the Mughal Empire surpassed the other two by a wide margin. In the sixteenth century, only the Ming Dynasty in China could compare.

In 1504 Babur (r. 1483–1530), a Turkish ruler forced out of a small territory in Central Asia, captured Kabul and established a kingdom in Afghanistan. An adventurer who claimed descent from Chinggis Khan and Timur, Babur moved southward in search of resources to restore his fortunes. In 1526, with a force that was small (twelve thousand in number) but was equipped with firearms, Babur defeated the sultan of Delhi at Panipat. Babur's capture of the cities of Agra and Delhi, key fortresses of the north, paved the way for further conquests in northern India. Although many of his soldiers wished to return north with their spoils, Babur decided to stay in India. A gifted writer, Babur wrote an autobiography in Turkish that recounts his military campaigns, describes places and people he encountered, recounts his difficulties giving up wine, and shows his wide-ranging interests in everything from fruit and swimming to a Turkish general who excelled at leapfrog. He was not particularly impressed by India, as can be inferred from this description in his memoirs:

> Hindustan is a country which has few pleasures to recommend it. The people are not handsome. They have no idea of the charms of friendly society, of frankly mixing together, or familiar discourse. They have no genius, no comprehension of mind, no politeness of manner, no kindness or fellow-feeling, no ingenuity or mechanical invention in planning or executing their handicraft works, no skill or knowledge in design or architecture; they have no horses, no good flesh, no grapes or muskmelons, no good fruits, no ice or cold water, no good food or bread in their bazaars, no baths or colleges, no candles, no torches, not a candlestick.[1]

During the reign of Babur's son Humayun (r. 1530–1540 and 1555–1556), the Mughals lost most of their territories in Afghanistan. Humayun went into temporary exile in Persia, where he developed a deep appreciation for Persian art and literature. The reign of Humayun's son Akbar (r. 1556–1605) may well have been the greatest in the history of India. A boy of thirteen when he succeeded to the throne, Akbar pursued expansionist policies. Under his dynamic leadership, the Mughal state took definitive form and encompassed most of the subcontinent north of the Godavari River. No kingdom or coalition of kingdoms could long resist Akbar's armies. The once independent states of northern India were forced into a centralized political system under the sole authority of the Mughal emperor.

Akbar replaced Turkish with Persian as the official language of the Mughal Empire, and Persian remained the official language until the British replaced it with English in 1835. To govern this vast region, Akbar developed an administrative bureaucracy centered on four co-equal ministers: for finance and revenue; the army and intelligence; the judiciary and religious patronage; and the imperial household, whose jurisdiction included roads, bridges, and infrastructure throughout the empire. Under Akbar's Hindu finance minister, Raja Todar Mal, a uniform system of taxes was put in place. In the provinces, imperial governors, appointed by and responsible solely to the emperor, presided over administrative branches modeled on those of the central government. The government, however, rarely interfered in the life of village communities. Whereas the Ottoman sultans and Safavid shahs made extensive use of slaves acquired from non-Muslim lands for military and administrative positions, Akbar used the services of royal princes, nobles, and warrior-aristocrats. Initially these men were Muslims from Central Asia, but to reduce their influence, Akbar vigorously recruited Persians and Hindus. No single ethnic or religious faction could challenge the emperor.

Akbar's descendants extended the Mughal Empire further. His son Jahangir (r. 1605–1628) lacked his father's military abilities and administrative genius, but he did succeed in consolidating Mughal rule in Bengal. Jahangir's son Shah Jahan (r. 1628–1658) launched fresh territorial expansion. Faced with dangerous revolts by the Muslims in Ahmadnagar and the resistance of the newly arrived Portuguese in Bengal, Shah Jahan not only crushed this opposition but also strengthened his northwestern frontier. Shah Jahan's son Aurangzeb (r. 1658–1707), unwilling to wait for his

The Mughal Empire, 1526–1857

Mughal territory
- In 1525
- Added, by 1539
- Added, by 1605
- Added, by 1707
- Lost, by 1707

HIMALAYA MTS.

Panipat
Delhi
Agra

Arabian Sea

Bay of Bengal

Persian "Ardabil" Carpet, ca. 1540 The Persians were among the first carpet weavers of ancient times and perfected the art over thousands of years. This wool carpet, reputably from the Safavid shrine at Ardabil, is one of only three signed and dated carpets from the Safavid period, when Persian carpet making was at its zenith. Hand-knotted and hand-dyed, it was royally commissioned with a traditional medallion design, consisting of a central sunburst medallion surrounded by radiating pendants. Mosque lamps project from the top and bottom of the medallion. Inscribed on the carpet is an ode by the fourteenth-century poet Hafiz: "I have no refuge in this world other than thy threshold / My head has no resting place other than this doorway." (Victoria & Albert Museum/The Art Archive)

father to die, deposed him and confined him for years in a small cell. A puritanically devout and strictly orthodox Muslim, as well as a skillful general and a clever diplomat, Aurangzeb ruled more of India than did any previous Mughal emperor, having extended the realm deeper into south India. His reign, however, also marked the beginning of the empire's decline. His non-Muslim subjects were not pleased with his religious zealotry, and his military campaigns were costly. In the south resistance to Mughal rule led to major uprisings. (For more on Aurangzeb's rule, see page 607.)

Cultural Flowering

☐ What cultural advances occurred under the rule of the Ottoman, Safavid, and Mughal empires?

All three Islamic empires presided over an extraordinary artistic and intellectual flowering in everything from carpet making to architecture and gardening, from geography and astronomy to medicine. At the same time, new religious practices (and conflicts) emerged,

and new gathering places — coffeehouses — became popular outlets for socializing and exchanging ideas. Artistic and intellectual advances spread from culture to culture, probably because of the common Persian influence on the Turks since the tenth century. This exchange was also aided by common languages. Persian was used as the administrative language by the Mughals in India, and Arabic was a lingua franca of the entire region because of its centrality in Islam. In Ottoman lands both Persian and Arabic were literary languages, but Turkish slowly became the lingua franca of the realm. (For Ottoman perceptions of the other major Islamic empires, see "Viewpoints: Ottoman Travelers in Mughal and Safavid Lands," page 598.)

The Arts

One of the arts all three empires shared was carpet making. Carpet designs and weaving techniques demonstrate both cultural integration and local

● **Mughal** A term meaning "Mongol," used to refer to the Muslim empire of India, although its founders were primarily Turks, Afghans, and Persians.

Viewpoints

Ottoman Travelers in Mughal and Safavid Lands

• *As the Ottoman Empire expanded, soldiers, officers, and administrators were dispatched to distant lands. Just as European travelers wrote of their adventures and the unusual customs they encountered, so too did Ottoman travelers.*

The first excerpt from such travel writing comes from Sidi Ali Reis (1498–1563), an Ottoman admiral whose ship was blown off course and shipwrecked in northwest India. With the winds against him, he returned overland through India, Afghanistan, and Persia, the journey taking three years (1554–1556). The second excerpt is from Mustafa Ali's "Description of Cairo," written in 1599. Ali was a career official who held a series of posts as a financial administrator and worked on a history of the world. Although he had requested an assignment in Egypt, thinking it would help him with his world history, he found much of which he did not approve there. The final excerpt is from the lengthy travel writings of Evilya Celebi (1611–1682). In this passage he reports on Tabriz, then under Safavid control, which he visited in 1640 in the entourage of an envoy. This region was predominantly Shi'a, which attracted Celebi's attention.

Sidi Ali Reis on His Journey Across India, 1554–1556

"The Sultan offered to give me an escort by the way of Lahore, warning me to be on my guard against the Djats, a hostile tribe which had its abode there. But whichever route I chose I should have to wait a while yet, and as a matter of fact I waited for a whole month. One night in my dream I saw my mother, who told me that she had seen her highness Fatima in a dream, and had learned from her the glad news that I should soon be coming home, safe and sound.

When next morning I told this dream to my companions they were full of good courage. Sultan Mahmud, when he heard of it, at once consented to my departure. He gave me a beautiful horse, a team of camels, a large and a small tent, and money for the journey. He also provided me with a letter of recommendation to Humayun, and an escort of 250 mounted camel-drivers from Sind. . . . On the second day we came to the spring, but found no water, and many of my companions nearly succumbed with heat and thirst. I gave them some Teriak [opium], of the very best quality, and on the second day they were recovered. After this experience we deemed it advisable to leave the desert and to return to Mav, for the proverb says truly, "A stranger is an ignorant man."

The people of Sind gave us permission to proceed as far as the Machvara, and this river was crossed by boats. On the other side we found 500 Djats awaiting us, but our firearms frightened them and they did not attack. We advanced unmolested, and reached the town of Multan on the fifteenth of Ramazan."

Mustafa Ali's Description of Cairo, 1599

"Their women, all of them, ride donkeys! Even the spouses of some notables ride on donkeys to the Bulak promenade. Week after week they mount their donkeys and dismount like soldiers. Moreover, when they marry a daughter off they let her ride on a donkey and seventy or eighty women ride [with her], while the only things visible in terms of weapons are their shields. People of intelligence find that this unbecoming behavior constitutes a serious defect for the city of Cairo, because in other lands they put prostitutes on a donkey as a punishment. In Cairo the women mount donkeys by their own free will and expose themselves [to the eyes of the public]; therefore it appears appropriate that for punishment they be put on camels."

Evilya Celebi on His 1640 Visit to Tabriz

"Painters, architects, goldsmiths, and tailors are nowhere to be found so perfect as here. Precious stuffs manufactured here go all over the world; the velvet is much renowned. . . . Among the abundance of delicious fruits are particularly the pears and exquisite apricots; they are not found in such perfection even at Constantinople.

On New Year's day or the beginning of spring, battles are fought in this place by horses trained in the dark during forty or fifty days, by camels, buffaloes, sheep, asses, dogs, and cocks. These fights are peculiar to Persia. Every year on the tenth of the first month, being the feast of A'ashura, all the population of the town assemble under tents. . . . The finest show is in the variegated tent of the Khân, where all the great men of Tabriz are assembled, and where a Hymn on the death of Hussein is recited, in the same manner as the Hymn on the Prophet's birthday is in the Turkish mosques. The hearers listen, sighing and lamenting, but when the reciter arrives at the passage where Hussein is killed by accursed Shabr, a curtain opens behind him, and a severed head and trunk of a body, representing that of the Imam when dead, is thrown on the ground, when there rises such an uproar of cries and lamentations that everybody loses his wits. At this moment some hundred men mingle in the crowd with razors, with which they cut the arms and breasts of all loving believers, who desire to shed their blood on this day in remembrance of the blood shed by the Imam; they make such deep incisions and scars, that the ground appears as if it was blooming with tulips."

Sources: Ármin Vámbéry, trans., *The Travels and Adventures of the Turkish Admiral Sidi Ali Reïs in India, Afghanistan, Central Asia, and Persia, During the Years 1553–1556* (London: Luzac, 1899); Andreas Tietze, trans., *Mustafa Ali's Description of Cairo of 1599* (Vienna: Verlag der Österreichischen Akademie der Wissenschaften, 1975), p. 41; Evliya Effendi, *Narrative of Travels in Europe, Asia, and Africa in the Seventeenth Century*, trans. Joseph von Hammer (London: William H. Allen, 1834), pp. 137–138, slightly modified.

QUESTIONS FOR ANALYSIS

1. Why do you think these authors wrote about their experiences? Who was their likely audience?
2. Do you see any common themes or issues in these writings?

distinctiveness. Turkic migrants carried their weaving traditions with them as they moved but also readily adopted new motifs, especially from Persia. In Anatolia the town of Usak began its rise as a center of commercial carpet production in the fifteenth century. In Safavid Persia Shah Abbas was determined to improve his country's export trade and built the small cottage business of carpet weaving into a national industry. In the capital city of Isfahan alone, factories employed more than twenty-five thousand weavers who produced woolen carpets, brocades, and silks of brilliant color, design, and quality. Women and children often were employed as weavers, especially of the most expensive rugs, because their smaller hands could tie tinier knots.

Another art that spread from Persia to both Ottoman and Mughal lands was miniature painting, especially for book illustration. This tradition had been enriched by the many Chinese artists brought to Persia during the Mongol period. There was also an interplay between carpets and miniature painting. Naturalistic depictions of lotus blossoms, peonies, chrysanthemums, tulips, carnations, birds, and even dragons appear in both book illustrations and carpets.

Akbar enthusiastically supported artists who produced magnificent paintings and books in the Indo-Persian style. In Mughal India, as throughout the Muslim world, books were regarded as precious objects. Time, talent, and expensive materials went into their production, and they were highly coveted because they reflected wealth, learning, and power. Akbar reportedly possessed twenty-four thousand books when he died. Abu-l-Fazl describes Akbar's library and love of books:

> His Majesty's library is divided into several parts. . . . Prose works, poetical works, Hindi, Persian, Greek, Kashmirian, Arabic, are all separately placed. In this order they are also inspected. Experienced people bring them daily and read them before His Majesty, who hears every book from beginning to end . . . and rewards the readers with presents of cash either in gold or silver, according to the number of leaves read out by them. . . . There are no historical facts of past ages, or curiosities of science, or interesting points of philosophy, with which His Majesty, a leader of impartial sages, is unacquainted.[2]

City and Palace Building

In all three empires strong rulers built capital cities and imperial palaces as visible expressions of dynastic majesty. Europeans called Suleiman "the Magnificent" because of the grandeur of his court. With annual state revenues of about $80 million (at a time when

> "There are no historical facts of past ages, or curiosities of science, or interesting points of philosophy, with which His Majesty, a leader of impartial sages, is unacquainted."
>
> **ABU-L-FAZL**

Elizabeth I of England could expect $150,000 and Francis I of France perhaps $1 million) and thousands of servants, he had a lifestyle no European monarch could begin to rival. He used his fabulous wealth to adorn Istanbul with palaces, mosques, schools, and libraries, and the city reached about a million in population. The building of hospitals, roads, and bridges and the reconstruction of the water systems of the great pilgrimage sites at Mecca and Jerusalem benefited his subjects. Safavid Persia and Mughal India produced rulers with similar ambitions.

The greatest builder under the Ottomans was Mimar Sinan (1491–1588), a Greek-born devshirme recruit who rose to become imperial architect under Suleiman. A contemporary of Michelangelo, Sinan designed 312 public buildings, including mosques, schools, hospitals, public baths, palaces, and burial chapels. His masterpieces, the Shehzade and Suleimaniye mosques in Istanbul, which rivaled the Byzantine church of Hagia Sophia, were designed to maximize the space under the dome. His buildings expressed the discipline, power, and devotion to Islam that characterized the Ottoman Empire under Suleiman.

Shah Abbas made his capital, Isfahan, the jewel of the Safavid Empire. He had his architects place a polo ground in the center and surrounded it with palaces, mosques, and bazaars. A seventeenth-century English visitor described one of Isfahan's bazaars as "the surprisingest piece of Greatness in Honour of commerce the world can boast of." Besides splendid rugs, stalls displayed pottery and fine china, metalwork of exceptionally high quality, and silks and velvets of stunning weave and design. A city of perhaps 750,000 people, Isfahan also contained 162 mosques, 48 schools where future members of the ulama learned the sacred Muslim sciences, 273 public baths, and the vast imperial palace. Mosques were richly decorated with blue tile. Private houses had their own garden courts, and public gardens, pools, and parks adorned the wide streets. Tales of the beauty of Isfahan circulated worldwide, attracting thousands of tourists annually in the seventeenth and eighteenth centuries.

Akbar in India was also a great builder. The birth of a long-awaited son, Jahangir, inspired Akbar to build a new city, Fatehpur-Sikri, to symbolize the regime's

Islamic foundations. He personally supervised the construction of the city, which combined the Muslim tradition of domes, arches, and spacious courts with the Hindu tradition of flat stone beams, ornate decoration, and solidity. According to the historian Abu-l-Fazl, "His Majesty plans splendid edifices, and dresses the work of his mind and heart in the garment of stone and clay."[3] Completed in 1578, the city included an imperial palace, a mosque, lavish gardens, and a hall of worship, as well as thousands of houses for ordinary people. Unfortunately because of its bad water supply, the city was soon abandoned.

Of Akbar's successors, Shah Jahan had the most sophisticated interest in architecture. Because his capital at Agra was cramped, in 1639 he decided to found a new capital city at Delhi. In the design and layout of the buildings, Persian ideas predominated, an indication of the number of Persian architects and engineers who had flocked to the subcontinent. The walled palace-fortress alone extended over 125 acres. Built partly of red sandstone, partly of marble, it included private chambers for the emperor; mansions for the wives, widows, and concubines of the imperial household; huge audience rooms for the conduct of public business (treasury, arsenal, and military); baths; and vast gardens filled with flowers, trees, and thirty silver fountains spraying water. In 1650, with living quarters for guards, military officials, merchants, dancing girls, scholars, and hordes of cooks and servants, the palace-fortress housed 57,000 people. It also boasted a covered public bazaar (comparable to a modern mall), 270 feet long and 27 feet wide, with arcaded shops. It was probably the first roofed shopping center in India, although such centers were common in western Asia. The sight of the magnificent palace left contemporaries speechless. Shah Jahan had a Persian poetic couplet inscribed on the walls:

> If there is a paradise on the face of the
>   earth,
> It is this, it is this.

Two Masterpieces of Islamic Architecture
Istanbul's Suleimaniye Mosque, designed by Sinan and commissioned by Suleiman I, was finished in 1557. Its interior (left), is especially spacious. The Taj Mahal (above), built about a century later in Agra in northern India, is perhaps the finest example of Mughal architecture. Its white marble exterior is decorated with Arabic inscriptions and floral designs. (mosque: Flirt/SuperStock; Taj Mahal: John Elk/Stock, Boston)

Beyond the walls, princes and aristocrats built mansions and mosques on a smaller scale. With its fine architecture and its population of between 375,000 and 400,000, Delhi gained the reputation of being one of the great cities of the Muslim world.

For his palace, Shah Jahan ordered the construction of the Peacock Throne. This famous piece, encrusted with emeralds, diamonds, pearls, and rubies, took seven years to fashion and cost the equivalent of $5 million. It served as the imperial throne of India until 1739, when the Persian warrior Nadir Shah seized it as plunder and carried it to Persia.

Shah Jahan's most enduring monument is the Taj Mahal. Between 1631 and 1648 twenty thousand workers toiled over the construction of this memorial in Agra to Shah Jahan's favorite wife, who died giving birth to their fifteenth child. One of the most beautiful structures in the world, the Taj Mahal is both an expression of love and a superb architectural blending of Islamic and Indian culture.

Gardens

Many of the architectural masterpieces of this age had splendid gardens attached to them as well. Gardens represent a distinctive and highly developed feature of Persian culture. They commonly were walled, with a pool in the center and geometrically laid-out flowering plants, especially roses. Identified with paradise in Arabic tradition, gardens served not only as centers of prayer and meditation but also as places of leisure and revelry. A ruler might lounge near his pool as he watched the ladies of his harem bathe in it. Although first limited to the ruler's court, gardening soon spread among the wealthy citizens.

After the incorporation of Persia into the caliphate in the seventh century, formal gardening spread west and east through the Islamic world, as illustrated by the magnificent gardens of Muslim Spain, southern Italy, and later southeastern Europe. The Mongol followers of Timur took landscape architects from Persia back to Samarkand and adapted their designs to nomad encampments. In 1396 Timur ordered the construction of a garden in a meadow, called House of Flowers. When Timur's descendant Babur established the Mughal Dynasty in India, he adapted the Persian garden to the warmer southern climate. Gardens were laid out near palaces, mosques, shrines, and mausoleums, including the Taj Mahal, which had four water channels symbolizing the four rivers of paradise.

Because it evoked paradise, the garden played a large role in Muslim literature. Some scholars hold that to understand Arabic poetry, one must study Arabic gardening. The literary subjects of flowers and gardens provided basic themes for Hispano-Arab poets. The secular literature of Muslim Spain, rife with references

Isfahan Tiles The embellishment of Isfahan under Shah Abbas I created an unprecedented need for tiles, as had the rebuilding of imperial Istanbul after 1453, the vast building program of Suleiman the Magnificent, and a huge European demand. Persian potters learned their skills from the Chinese. By the late sixteenth century Italian and Austrian potters had imitated the Persian and Ottoman tile makers. (© Victoria & Albert Museum, London/ V&A Images)

Polo Two teams of four on horseback ride back and forth on a grass field measuring 200 by 400 yards, trying to hit a 4½-ounce wooden ball with a 4-foot mallet through the opponents' goal. Because a typical match involves many high-speed collisions among the horses, each player has to maintain a string of expensive ponies in order to change mounts several times during the game. Students of the history of sports believe the game originated in Persia, as shown in this eighteenth-century miniature, whence it spread to India, China, and Japan. Brought from India to England, where it became very popular among the aristocracy in the nineteenth century, polo is a fine example of cross-cultural influences. (Private Collection)

such as "a garland of verses," influenced the lyric poetry of southern France, the troubadours, and the courtly love tradition.

Gardens, of course, are seasonal. To remind themselves of paradise during the cold winter months, rulers, city people, and nomads ordered Persian carpets, most of which use floral patterns and have formal garden designs.

Intellectual Advances and Religious Trends

Between 1400 and 1800, the culture of the Islamic empires underwent many changes. Particularly notable were new movements within Islam as well as advances in mathematics, geography, astronomy, and medicine. Building on the knowledge of earlier Islamic writers and

stimulated by Ottoman naval power, the geographer and cartographer Piri Reis produced a map incorporating Islamic and Western knowledge that showed all the known world (1513); another of his maps detailed Columbus's third voyage to the New World. Piri Reis's *Book of the Sea* (1521) contained 129 chapters, each with a map incorporating all Islamic (and Western) knowledge of the seas and navigation and describing harbors, tides, dangerous rocks and shores, and storm areas. In the field of astronomy, Takiyuddin Mehmet (1521–1585), who served as the sultan's chief astronomer, built an observatory at Istanbul. He also produced *Instruments of the Observatory*, which catalogued astronomical instruments and described an astronomical clock that fixed the location of heavenly bodies with greater precision than ever before.

There were also advances in medicine. Under Suleiman the imperial palace itself became a center of medical science, and the large number of hospitals established in Istanbul and throughout the empire testifies to his support for medical research and his concern for the sick. Abi Ahmet Celebi (1436–1523), the chief physician of the empire, produced a study on kidney and bladder stones. He also founded the first Ottoman medical school, which served as a training institution for physicians of the empire.

Recurrent outbreaks of the plague posed a challenge for physicians in Muslim lands. Muhammad had once said not to go to a country where an epidemic existed but also not to leave a place because an epidemic broke out. As a consequence, when European cities began enforcing quarantines to control the spread of the plague, early Muslim rulers dismissed such efforts. By the sixteenth century, however, a better understanding of contagion led to a redefinition of the proper response to a plague epidemic and allowed for leaving the city in search of clean air.

In the realm of religion, the rulers of all three empires drew legitimacy from their support for Islam, at least among their Muslim subjects. The Sunni-Shi'a split between the Ottomans and Safavids led to efforts to define and enforce religious orthodoxy on both sides. For the Safavids this entailed suppressing Sufi movements and Sunnis, even marginalizing—sometimes massacring—the original Qizilbash warriors, who had come to be seen as politically disruptive. Sectarian conflicts within Islam were not as pronounced in Mughal lands, perhaps because even though the Mughals ruled over both Sunni and Shi'a subjects, these subjects were greatly outnumbered by non-Muslims, mostly Hindus.

Sufi fraternities thrived throughout the Muslim world in this era, even when the states tried to limit them. In India, Sufi orders also influenced non-Muslims. The mystical Bhakti movement among Hindus involved dances, poems, and songs reminiscent of Sufi practice. The development of the new religion of the Sikhs (seeks) also was influenced by Sufis. The Sikhs traced themselves back to a teacher in the sixteenth century who argued that God did not distinguish between Muslims and Hindus but saw everyone as his children. Sikhs rejected the caste system (division of society into hereditary groups) and forbade alcohol and tobacco, and men did not cut their hair (covering it instead with a turban). The Sikh movement was most successful in northwest India, where Sikh men armed themselves to defend their communities.

Despite all the signs of cultural vitality in the three Islamic empires, none of them adopted the printing press or went through the sorts of cultural expansion associated with it in China and Europe. Until 1729 the Ottoman authorities prohibited printing books in Turkish or Arabic (Jews, Armenians, and Greeks could establish presses and print in their own languages). Printing was not banned in Mughal India, but neither did the technology spread, even after Jesuit missionaries printed Bibles in Indian languages beginning in the 1550s. The Islamic authorities in each of these empires did not want to see writings circulate that might unsettle society and religious teachings. Nevertheless, the copying of manuscripts was permitted, and those who made their living this way sometimes organized to keep competition at bay.

Coffeehouses and Their Social Impact

In the mid-fifteenth century a new social convention spread throughout the Islamic world — drinking coffee. Arab writers trace the origins of coffee drinking to Yemen Sufis, who sought a trancelike concentration on God to the exclusion of everything else and found that coffee helped them stay awake (similarly, Buddhist monks drank tea to stay awake during long meditation sessions, a practice responsible for the spread of tea in East Asia). Most Sufis were not professional holy men but were employed as tradesmen and merchants. Therefore, the use of coffee for pious purposes led to its use as a business lubricant — an extension of hospitality to a potential buyer in a shop. Merchants carried the Yemenite practice to Mecca in about 1490. From Mecca, where pilgrims were introduced to it, coffee drinking spread to Egypt and Syria. In 1555 two Syrians opened a coffeehouse in Istanbul.

Coffeehouses provided a place for conversation and male sociability; there a man could entertain his friends

▢ Picturing the Past

Turkish Coffeehouse This sixteenth-century miniature depicts a crowded coffeehouse. (Reproduced by kind permission of the Trustees of the Chester Beatty Library, Dublin, Ms 439, folio 9)

ANALYZING THE IMAGE What activities are people engaged in? How does the artist convey differences in the ages of those drinking coffee?

CONNECTIONS Why would religious and political authorities have worried about what went on in coffeehouses?

Listening to the Past

Katib Chelebi on Tobacco

Katib Chelebi (1609–1657) was an Ottoman civil servant who spent much of his time as an accountant for the Turkish army, accompanying it on several important campaigns. Over time he became passionate about learning and pursued not only Islamic law but also ancient Greek philosophy, geography, and modern European sciences. He wrote several important books, including a bibliographical encyclopedia. The book of essays from which the following extract comes also discusses such contemporary issues as coffee, singing, opium, shaking hands, bowing, and bribery.

"Sometime in the latter half of the ninth century of the Hijra, after some Spanish ships had discovered the New World, the Portuguese and English were exploring its shores to find a passage from the Eastern to the Western Ocean. They came to an island close to the mainland, called in the Atlas "Gineya." A ship's doctor, who had been smitten with a lymphatic disorder, due to the influence of the sea air on his natural temperament, decided to try and cure it with hot and dry things, in accordance with the laws of treatment by opposites. When his ship reached that island, he noticed a kind of leaf was burning. He smelled it, and as it was hot of scent he began to inhale it, using an instrument resembling a pipe. It did him good, so he took a large quantity of the leaf and used it throughout their stay. The ship's company saw this and, regarding it as a beneficial medicine, followed the doctor's example and loaded themselves up with the leaf. One saw another and they all began to smoke. When the ship arrived in England, the habit spread, through France to the other lands. People tried it, not knowing its origin, and not considering that it was smoked for a serious purpose. Many became addicts, putting it in the category of stimulating drugs. It has become a thing common to East and West, and no one has succeeded in suppressing it.

From its first appearance in Turkey, which was about the year 1010/1601, to the present day, various preachers have spoken against it individually, and many of the Ulema [ulama] have written tracts concerning it, some claiming that it is a thing forbidden, some that it is disapproved. Its addicts have replied to the effect that it is permissible. After some time had elapsed, the eminent surgeon Ibrāhīm Efendi devoted much care and attention to the matter, conducting great debates in the Abode of the Sultanate, that is, in the city of Istanbul, giving warning talks at a special public meeting in the mosque of Sultan Mehmed, and sticking copies of fetwas [fatwas] onto walls. He troubled himself to no purpose. The more he spoke, the more people persisted in smoking. Seeing that it was fruitless, he abandoned his efforts. After that, the late Sultan Murad IV, towards the end of his reign, closed down the coffeehouses in order to shut the gate of iniquity, and also banned smoking, in consequence of certain outbreaks of fire. People being undeterred, the imperial anger necessitated the chastisement of those who, by smoking, committed the sin of disobedience to the imperial command. Gradually His Majesty's severity in suppression increased, and so did people's desire to smoke, in accordance with the saying, "Men desire what is forbidden," and many thousands of men were sent to the abode of nothingness.

When the Sultan was going on the expedition against Baghdad, at one halting-place fifteen or twenty leading men of the Army were arrested on a charge of smoking, and were put to death with the severest torture in the imperial presence. Some of the soldiers carried short pipes in their sleeves, some in their pockets, and they found an opportunity to smoke even during the executions. At Istanbul, no end of soldiers used to go into the barracks and smoke in the privies. Even during this rigorous prohibition, the number of smokers exceeded that of the non-smokers.

After that Sultan's death, the practice was sometimes forbidden and sometimes allowed, until the Sheykh al-Islam, the late Baha'i Efendi, gave a fetwa ruling that it was permissible, and the practice won renewed popularity among the people of the world. Occasional reprimands from the Throne to smokers have generally been disregarded, and smoking is at present practiced all over the habitable globe. Such are the vicissitudes undergone by tobacco.

Now there are a number of possible ways of considering the subject, which we shall briefly set forth.

(1) The first possibility is that the people may be effectively prevented from smoking and may give it up. This possibility must be set aside, for custom is second nature. Addicts are not made to give up in this way...."

cheaply and more informally than at home. But coffeehouses encountered religious and governmental opposition based on the following arguments: (1) because of its composition, coffee is intoxicating, making it analogous to wine, prohibited to Muslims; (2) coffee drinking was an innovation and therefore a violation of Islamic law; (3) coffeehouses encouraged political discussions, facilitating sedition; (4) coffeehouses attracted unemployed soldiers and other low types, encouraging immoral behavior, such as gambling, using drugs, and soliciting prostitutes; and (5) music at coffeehouses encouraged debauchery. Thus coffeehouses drew the attention of government officials, who considered themselves the guardians of public morality.

A man is smoking a long pipe in one of the stalls in a bazaar depicted in this seventeenth-century Turkish painting. (The Granger Collection, New York)

(2) Is this tobacco found to be good or bad by the intelligence? If we set aside the fact that addicts think it good, common sense judges it to be bad. . . .

(3) Its good and harmful effects. As to its harmful effects there is no doubt. It ends by becoming a basic need of the addict, who does not consider its evil consequences. Its harmful physical effect too is established, for tobacco is medically noxious in that it makes turbid the aerial essence. . . .

(4) Is it innovation? It may be conceded that it is innovation in the eyes of the sacred law, for it appeared in recent times, nor is it possible to class it as "good innovation." That it is innovation in the light of intelligence is sure, for it is not a thing that has been seen or heard of by the intelligent ever since the time of Adam. . . .

(5) Is it abominable? There is no word of justification for this, in reason or in law. . . . It is perhaps not irrelevant to point out that the scent of burning tobacco has curative uses as an inhalant. But an evil odor arises in the mouth of the heavy smoker. . . .

(6) Is it canonically forbidden? It is written in the manuals of jurisprudence that in any particular matter where there is no decisive ruling in the law, the jurisconsult may exercise his own discretion. He may, according to one point of view, bring together all relevant circumstances, consider them, and make his own deductions. Yet the following course is preferable: not to declare things forbidden, but always to have recourse to any legal principle that justifies declaring them permitted, thus preserving the people from being laden with sins and persisting in what has been prohibited.

(7) Is it canonically indifferent? As the rise of smoking is of recent occurrence, there is no explicit treatment or mention of it in the legal manuals. This being so, some say that in accordance with the principle that permissibility is the norm—i.e., that in the absence of a clear prohibition things are permitted— smoking is permitted and lawful. "

Source: Katib Chelebi, *The Balance of Truth*, trans. G. L. Lewis (London: George Allen and Unwin, 1957), pp. 50–58.

QUESTIONS FOR ANALYSIS

1. What do you learn about social life in the Ottoman Empire from this essay?

2. What can you infer about the sorts of arguments that were made by Islamic jurists in Katib Chelebi's day?

3. How open-minded was Katib Chelebi? What evidence from the text led you to your conclusion?

On the other hand, the coffee trade was a major source of profit that local notables sought to control.

Although debate over the morality of coffeehouses continued through the sixteenth century, their eventual acceptance represented a revolution in Islamic life: socializing was no longer confined to the home. Ultimately, because the medical profession remained divided on coffee's harmful effects and because religious authorities could not prove that coffeehouses violated religious law, coffee drinking could not be forbidden. In the seventeenth century coffee and coffeehouses spread to Europe. (For reaction to another new product that spread quickly despite opposition, see "Listening to the Past: Katib Chelebi on Tobacco," above.)

Non-Muslims Under Muslim Rule

☐ How did Christians, Jews, Hindus, and other non-Muslims fare under these Islamic states?

Drawing on Qur'anic teachings, Muslims had long practiced a religious toleration unknown in Christian Europe. Muslim rulers for the most part guaranteed the lives and property of Christians and Jews on their promise of obedience and the payment of a poll tax. In the case of the Ottomans, this tolerance was extended not only to the Christians and Jews who had been living under Muslim rule for centuries but also to the Serbs, Bosnians, Croats, and other Orthodox Christians in the newly conquered Balkans. The Ottoman conqueror of Constantinople, Mehmet, nominated the Greek patriarch as official representative of the Greek population. This and other such appointments recognized non-Muslims as functioning parts of the Ottoman society and economy. In 1454 Rabbi Isaac Sarfati sent a letter to the Jews in the Rhineland, Swabia, Moravia, and Hungary, urging them to move to Turkey because of the good conditions for Jews there. A massive migration to Ottoman lands followed. When Ferdinand and Isabella of Spain expelled the Jews in 1492 and later, many immigrated to the Ottoman Empire.

The Safavid authorities made efforts to convert Armenian Christians in the Caucuses, and many seem to have embraced Islam, some more voluntarily than others. Nevertheless, the Armenian Christian Church retained its vitality, and under the Safavids Armenian Christians were prominent merchants in long-distance trade (see page 610).

Babur and his successors acquired even more non-Muslim subjects with their conquests in India, which had not only Hindus but also substantial numbers of Jains, Zoroastrians, Christians, and Sikhs. Over time, the number of Indians who converted to Islam increased, but the Mughal rulers did not force conversion. The Ganges plain, the area of the Indian subcontinent most intensely exposed to Mughal rule and for the longest span of time, had, when the first reliable census was taken in 1901, a Muslim population of only 10 to 15 percent. Accordingly, some scholars have argued that in the Indian subcontinent there was an inverse relationship between the degree of Muslim political penetration and conversion to Islam.

Akbar went the furthest in promoting Muslim-Hindu accommodation. He celebrated important Hindu festivals, such as Diwali, the festival of lights, and he wore his uncut hair in a turban as a concession to Indian practice. Also, Akbar twice married Hindu princesses, one of whom became the mother of his heir, Jahangir, and he appointed the Spanish Jesuit Antonio Monserrate (1536–1600) as tutor to his second son, Prince Murad. Eventually, Hindus totaled 30 percent of the imperial bureaucracy. In 1579 Akbar abolished the **jizya**, the poll tax on non-Muslims that guaranteed their protection. These actions, especially the abolition

Emperor Akbar in the City of Fatehpur-Sikri In 1569 Akbar founded the city of Fatehpur-Sikri (the City of Victory) to honor the Muslim holy man Shaykh Salim Chishti, who had foretold the birth of Akbar's son and heir Jahangir. Akbar is shown here seated on the cushion in the center overseeing the construction of the city. The image is contained in the *Akbarnama*, a book of illustrations Akbar commissioned to officially chronicle his reign. (Victoria & Albert Museum/The Bridgeman Art Library)

of the jizya, infuriated the ulama, and serious conflict erupted between them and the emperor. Ultimately, Akbar issued an imperial decree declaring that the Mughal emperor had supreme authority, even above the ulama, in all religious matters. This statement, resting on a policy of benign toleration, represented a severe defeat for the Muslim religious establishment.

Some of Akbar's successors, above all Aurangzeb, sided more with the ulama. Aurangzeb appointed censors of public morals in important cities to enforce Islamic laws against gambling, prostitution, drinking, and the use of narcotics. He forbade sati—the self-immolation of widows on their husbands' funeral pyres—and the castration of boys to be sold as eunuchs. He also abolished all taxes not authorized by Islamic law. This measure led to a serious loss of state revenues. To replace them, in 1679 Aurangzeb reimposed the tax on non-Muslims. Aurangzeb's reversal of Akbar's religious toleration and cultural cosmopolitanism extended further. He ordered the destruction of some Hindu temples and tried to curb Sikhism. He also required Hindus to pay higher customs duties than Muslims. Out of fidelity to Islamic law, he even criticized his mother's tomb, the Taj Mahal: "The lawfulness of a solid construction over a grave is doubtful, and there can be no doubt about the extravagance involved."[4] Aurangzeb's attempts to enforce rigid Islamic norms proved highly unpopular with the majority of his subjects and aroused resistance that weakened Mughal rule. Aurangzeb himself died on an unsuccessful military campaign in 1707 to suppress a rebellion by the Marathas in the southern highlands.

Shifting Trade Routes and European Penetration

☐ How were the Islamic empires affected by the gradual shift toward trade routes that bypassed their lands?

It has widely been thought that a decline in the wealth and international importance of the Muslim empires could be directly attributed to the long-term shift in trading patterns that resulted from the discoveries of Columbus, Magellan, and other European explorers. The argument is that new sea routes enabled Europeans to acquire goods from the East without using Muslim intermediaries, so that the rise of Europe associated with exploration and the creation of colonial powers beginning in the sixteenth century led directly and indirectly to the eclipse of the Ottomans, Safavids, and Mughals. Recent scholars have challenged these

> "It is true that there does exist a common right to all to navigate the seas and in Europe we recognize the rights which others hold against us; but the right does not extend beyond Europe."
>
> **PORTUGUESE HISTORIAN BARRÕES**

ideas as too simplistic. Turkish, Persian, and Indian merchants remained very active as long-distance traders into the eighteenth century and opened up many new routes themselves. Moreover, it was not until the eighteenth century that there were many signs of political decline in the three Islamic empires. As well, government revenue came more from taxes on farmers than from trade.

Agriculture benefited from the spread of new crops, such as coffee and sugar, from elsewhere in the Old World, but New World crops like potatoes and sweet potatoes played a relatively minor role in the economy and do not seem to have fueled population increases as rapid as those in western Europe and East Asia. By 1800 the population of India was about 190 million, that of Safavid lands about 8 million, and that of Ottoman lands about 24 million. (By comparison, China's population stood at about 300 million in 1800, greater than that of all three Islamic empires put together.)

Still, the importance of trade to the economies of the three Islamic empires should not be discounted. Over the centuries covered in this chapter, trading patterns and practices evolved, and European penetration increased.

European Rivalry for Trade in the Indian Ocean

Shortly before Babur's invasion of India, the Portuguese had opened the subcontinent to Portuguese trade. In 1510 they established the port of Goa on the west coast of India as their headquarters and through an aggressive policy took control of Muslim shipping in the Indian Ocean and Arabian Sea, charging high fees to let ships through. The Portuguese historian Barrões attempted to justify Portugal's seizure of commercial traffic that the Muslims had long dominated:

> It is true that there does exist a common right to all to navigate the seas and in Europe we recognize the rights which others hold against us; but the right does not extend beyond Europe and therefore the Portuguese as Lords of the Sea are justified in confiscating the goods of all those who navigate the seas without their permission.[5]

jizya A poll tax on non-Muslims.

Northern limit of Mughal Empire in 1707
- Muslim land in 1765
- Muslim land in 1805
- Area controlled by Hindus in 1805
- Land under British East India Company rule in 1805
- Site of important battle

MAP 20.3 India, 1707–1805 In the eighteenth century Mughal power gradually yielded to the Hindu Marathas and to the British East India Company.

In short, the Portuguese decided that Western principles of international law should not restrict them in Asia. As a result, they controlled the spice trade over the Indian Ocean for almost a century.

In 1602 the Dutch formed the Dutch East India Company with the stated goal of wresting the enormously lucrative spice trade from the Portuguese. In 1685 they supplanted the Portuguese in Ceylon (Sri Lanka). The scent of fabulous profits also attracted the English. With a charter signed by Queen Elizabeth, eighty London merchants organized the British East India Company. In 1619 Emperor Jahangir granted a British mission important commercial concessions. Soon, by offering gifts, medical services, and bribes to Indian rulers, the British East India Company was able to set up twenty-eight coastal forts/trading posts. By 1700 the company had founded the cities that became Madras and Calcutta (today called Chennai and Kolkata) and had taken over Bombay (today Mumbai), which had been a Portuguese possession (Map 20.3).

The British called their trading posts **factory-forts**. The term *factory* did not signify manufacturing; it designated the walled compound containing the residences, gardens, and offices of British East India Company officials and the warehouses where goods were stored before being shipped to Europe. The company president exercised political authority over all residents.

Factory-forts existed to make profits from Asian-European trade, which was robust due to the popularity of Indian and Chinese wares in Europe in the late seventeenth and early eighteenth centuries. The European middle classes wanted Indian textiles, which were colorful, durable, cheap, and washable. The upper classes desired Chinese wallpaper and porcelains and Indian silks and brocades. Other Indian goods in demand included pepper and other spices, sugar, and opium. To pay for these goods, the British East India Company sold silver, copper, zinc, lead, and fabrics to the Indians. Profits grew even larger after 1700, when the company began to trade with China.

Merchant Networks in the Islamic Empires

The shifting trade patterns associated with European colonial expansion brought no direct benefit to the Ottomans and the Safavids, whose merchants could now be bypassed by Europeans seeking goods from India, Southeast Asia, or China. Yet merchants from these

• **factory-forts** A term first used by the British for their trading post at Surat that was later applied to all European walled settlements in India.

English Factory-Fort at Surat
The factory-fort began as a storage place for goods before they were bought and transported abroad; it gradually expanded to include merchants' residences and some sort of fortification. By 1650 the English had twenty-three factory-forts in India. Surat, in the Gujarat region, was the busiest factory-fort and port until it was sacked by the Marathas in 1664. (Mansell Collection/Getty Images)

Islamic empires often proved adaptable, finding ways to benefit from the new trade networks.

In the case of India, the appearance of European traders led to a rapid increase in overall trade, helping Indian merchants and the Indian economy. Some Indian merchants in Calcutta and Bombay, for instance, made gigantic fortunes from trade within Asia carried on European ships. Block-printed cotton cloth, produced by artisans working at home, was India's chief export. Through an Islamic business device involving advancing payment to artisans, banker-brokers supplied the material for production and money for the artisans to live on while they worked; the cloth brokers specified the quality, quantity, and design of the finished products. This procedure resembles the later English "domestic" or "putting-out" system (see page 687), for the very good reason that the English took the idea from the Indians.

Within India, the demand for cotton cloth, as well as for food crops, was so great that Akbar had to launch a wide-scale road-building campaign. From the Indian region of Gujarat, Indian merchant bankers shipped their cloth worldwide: across the Indian Ocean to Aden and the Muslim-controlled cities on the east coast of Africa; across the Arabian Sea to Muscat and Hormuz and up the Persian Gulf to the cities of Persia; up the Red Sea to the Mediterranean; by sea also to Malacca, Indonesia, China, and Japan; by land across Africa to Ghana on the west coast; and to Astrakhan, Poland, Moscow, and even the Russian cities on the distant Volga River. Indian businessmen had branch offices in many of these places, and all this activity produced fabulous wealth for some Indian merchants. Some scholars have compared India's international trade in

English Dress Made of Indian Printed Cotton Cloth Early British traders in India were impressed with the quality of the textiles made there and began ordering designs that would be popular with the English. This dress, created around 1770–1780 in England, is made of printed cotton (chintz) from the southeastern part of India. Chintz became so popular in England that it was eventually banned because it was threatening local textile industries. (© Victoria and Albert Museum, London/V&A Images) the sixteenth century with that of Italian firms, such as the Medici. Indian trade actually extended over a far wider area, however. Indian merchants were often devout Hindus, Muslims, Buddhists, or Jains, evidence that undermines the argument of some Western writers, notably Karl Marx (see page 721), that religion retarded Asia's economic development.

Throughout Muslim lands both Jews and Christians were active in commerce. A particularly interesting case involves the Armenian Christians in the Safavid empire in the sixteenth to eighteenth centuries. Armenian merchants had been trading from their base in Armenia for centuries and were especially known for their trade in Persian silk. When the Portuguese first appeared on the western coast of India in 1498 and began to settle in south India, they found many Armenian merchant communities already there. A few decades later Akbar invited Armenians to settle in his new capital, Agra. In 1603 Shah Abbas captured much of Armenia, taking it from the Ottomans. Because defending this newly acquired border area was difficult, he forced the Armenians to move more deeply into Persia. Among them was the merchant community of Julfa, which was moved to a new suburb of Isfahan that was given the name New Julfa. The old city of Julfa was burned down so that they could not return. Shah Abbas made use of the Armenian merchants as royal merchants and financiers, but their economic mainstay continued to be long-distance trade.

Surviving letters and account books have allowed scholars to reconstruct the expanding trading networks of the Armenian merchants — networks that stretched from Venice and Amsterdam in western Europe, Moscow in Russia, Ottoman-controlled Aleppo and Smyrna, to all the major trading cities of India and even regions farther east, including Guangzhou in southern China and Manila in the Philippines. Many Armenian communities in these cities became quite substantial, built churches, and recruited priests. Kinship connections were regularly used to cement commercial relations, and members of the community living in these scattered cities would return to New Julfa to marry, creating new kinship connections. Business, though, was conducted through contracts. The merchant about to take a journey would borrow a sum of money to purchase goods and would contract to pay it back with interest on his return. Using couriers, these Armenian merchants sent long letters describing the trade environment and the prices that could be realized for given goods. These letters were written in a dialect of Armenian known to few outside their community, making it easier to maintain confidentiality in reports on trade conditions.

The Armenian merchants would sail on whatever ships were available, including Dutch and Italian ones. The goods they dealt in included silver, gold, precious stones, indigo and other dyestuffs, silk, cotton cloth, and tea. The merchants often could speak half a dozen languages and were comfortable in both Islamic and Christian lands. In India Armenian merchants reached an agreement with the British East India Company that recognized their rights to live in company cities and observe their own religion. By the 1660s they had settled in Manila, and a few decades later they entered what is now Malaysia and Indonesia. By the end of the seventeenth century a small group of Armenian merchants had crossed the Himalayas from India and established themselves in Lhasa, Tibet. By the mid-eighteenth century they had also settled in the Dutch colony of Batavia (Indonesia). Clearly the Armenian merchants were able to operate profitably in cities European powers dominated.

In the mid-eighteenth century the Armenian community lost its center in New Julfa because of religious

Armenian Brass Bowl The inscription on this bowl dates it to 1616 and places it in New Julfa, the Armenian quarter of Isfahan. It would have been used by an Armenian Christian priest to wash his hands. (© Ana A. Melikian 2007)

persecution by a zealous shah, and the community scattered. Still, Armenian merchants remained prominent in many trading centers, including Russia, the Mediterranean, and especially India, well into the nineteenth century.

From the British East India Company to the British Empire in India

Britain's presence in India began with the British East India Company and its desire to profit from trade. Managers of the company in London discouraged all unnecessary expenses and financial risks and thus opposed missionary activities or interference in local Indian politics. Nevertheless, the company responded to political instability in India in the early eighteenth century by extending political control. When warlords appeared or an uprising occurred, people from the surrounding countryside flocked into the company's factory-forts, which gradually came to exercise political authority over the territories around them. The company's factories evolved into defensive installations manned by small garrisons of native troops—known as **sepoys**—trained in Western military weapons and tactics.

Britain eventually became the dominant foreign presence in India, despite challenges from the French. The French arrived in India in the 1670s and established factories in Bengal, Pondicherry, and elsewhere. They made allies of Indian princes and built an army of native troops who were trained as infantrymen. From 1740 to 1763, Britain and France were engaged in a tremendous global struggle, and India, like North America in the Seven Years' War, became a battlefield and a prize. The French won land battles, but English sea power proved decisive by preventing the landing of French reinforcements. The Treaty of Paris of 1763 recognized British control of much of India, marking the beginning of the British Empire in India.

How was Britain to govern so large a territory? Eventually, the East India Company was pushed out of its governing role because the English Parliament distrusted the company, believing it was corrupt. The Regulating Act of 1773 created the office of governor general to exercise political authority over the territory controlled by the company. The India Act of 1784 required that the governor general be chosen from outside the company, and it made company directors subject to parliamentary supervision.

Implementation of these reforms fell to three successive governors, Warren Hastings, (r. 1774–1785), Lord Charles Cornwallis (r. 1786–1794), and the marquess Richard Wellesley (r. 1797–1805). Hastings sought allies among Indian princes, laid the foundations for the first Indian civil service, abolished tolls to facilitate internal trade, placed the salt and opium trades under government control, and planned a codification of Muslim and Hindu laws. Cornwallis introduced the British style of property relations, in effect converting a motley collection of former Mughal officers, tax collectors, and others into English-style landlords. The result was a new system of landholding in which the rents of tenant farmers supported the landlords. Wellesley was victorious over local rulers who resisted British rule, vastly extending British influence in India. Like most nineteenth-century British governors of India, Wellesley believed that British rule strongly benefited the Indians. With supreme condescension, he wrote that British power should be established over the Indian princes in order

> to deprive them of the means of prosecuting any measure or of forming any confederacy hazardous to the security of the British empire, and to enable us to preserve the tranquility of India by exercising a general control over the restless spirit of ambition and violence which is characteristic of every Asiatic government.[6]

Political Decline

☐ Did any common factors lead to the decline of central power in the Islamic empires in the seventeenth and eighteenth centuries?

By the end of the eighteenth century, all three of the major Islamic empires were on the defensive and losing territory (Map 20.4). They faced some common problems—succession difficulties, financial strain, and loss of military superiority—but their circumstances differed in significant ways as well.

The first to fall was the Safavid empire. Persia was exceptionally difficult to govern, and it did not have the revenue base to maintain the sort of standing armies that the Ottomans and the Mughals had. Decline in the strength of the army encouraged increased foreign aggression. In 1722 the Afghans invaded from the east, seized Isfahan, and were able to repulse an Ottoman invasion from the west. In Isfahan thousands of officials and members of the shah's family were executed. In the following century some potential leaders emerged, but none were able to reunite all of Persia. In this political vacuum, Shi'a religious institutions grew stronger.

• **sepoys** The native Indian troops who were trained as infantrymen.

MAP 20.4 The Muslim World, ca. 1700 The three great Islamic empires were adjacent to each other and of similar physical size. Many of their other neighbors were Muslim as well.

The Ottoman Empire also suffered from poor leadership. Early Ottoman practice had guaranteed that the sultans would be forceful men. The sultan's sons gained administrative experience as governors of provinces and military experience on the battlefield as part of their education. After the sultan died, any son who wanted to succeed had to contest his brothers to claim the throne, after which the new sultan would have his defeated brothers executed. Although bloody, this system led to the succession of capable, determined men. After Suleiman's reign, however, the tradition was abandoned. To prevent threats of usurpation, sons of the sultan were brought up in the harem and confined there as adults, denied roles in government. The result was a series of rulers who were incompetent or minor children, leaving power in the hands of high officials and the mothers of the heirs. Political factions formed around viziers, military leaders, and palace women. In the contest for political favor, the devshirme was abandoned, and political and military ranks were filled by Muslims.

The Ottoman Empire's military strength also declined. The defeat of the Turkish fleet by the Spanish off the coast of Greece at Lepanto in 1571 marked the loss of Ottoman dominance in the Mediterranean, and the empire's political and military setbacks continued. By the terms of a peace treaty with Austria signed at Karlowitz (1699), the Ottomans lost the major European provinces of Hungary and Transylvania, along with the tax revenues they had provided. Also, the Ottoman armies were depending more on mercenaries, and they did not keep up with the innovations in drill, command, and control that were then transforming European armies. From the late seventeenth century Ottoman armies began losing wars and territory along both northern and eastern borders. In 1730 the empire gave up territory along its eastern border. And in 1774 it lost the lands on the northern bank of the Black Sea to Russia. In North Africa the local governors came to act more independently, sometimes starting hereditary dynasties.

In Mughal India the old Turkish practice of letting heirs fight for the throne persisted, leading to frequent struggles over succession, but also to strong rulers. Yet military challenges proved daunting there as well. After defeating his father and brothers, Aurangzeb pushed the conquest of the south. The stiffest opposition came from the Marathas, a militant Hindu group centered in the western Deccan. From 1681 until his death in 1707, Aurangzeb led repeated sorties through the Deccan. He took many forts and won several battles, but total destruction of the Maratha guerrilla bands eluded him.

Aurangzeb's death led to thirteen years of succession struggles, shattering the empire. His eighteenth-century successors were less successful than the Ottomans in making the dynasty the focus of loyalty. Mughal provincial governors began to rule independently, giving only minimal allegiance to the throne at Delhi. Meanwhile, the Marathas pressed steadily northward, constituting the gravest threat to Mughal authority. In 1857 the Mughal Dynasty came to an end.

In 1739 the Persian adventurer Nadir Shah invaded India, defeated the Mughal army, looted Delhi, and after a savage massacre carried off a huge amount of treasure, including the Peacock Throne. When Nadir Shah withdrew to Afghanistan, he took with him the Mughal government's prestige. Constant skirmishes between the Afghans and the Marathas for control of the Punjab and northern India ended in 1761 at Panipat, where the Marathas were crushed by the Afghans. At that point, India no longer had a state strong enough to impose order on the subcontinent or check the penetration of the Europeans.

In all three empires economic difficulties also put strain on the state. A long period of peace in the late sixteenth century and again in the mid-eighteenth century, as well as a decline in the frequency of visits of the plague, led to a doubling of the population. Increased population, coupled with the "little ice age" of the mid-seventeenth century, meant that the land could not sustain so many people; nor could the towns provide jobs for the thousands of agricultural workers who fled to them. The return of demobilized soldiers aggravated the problem. Inflation, famine, and widespread revolts resulted. The economic center of gravity shifted from the capital to the provinces, and politically the empire began to decentralize as well. Power was seized by local notables and military strongmen at the expense of central government officials. There was a positive side to increasing provincial autonomy, however, because it drew more people into political participation, thus laying a foundation for later nationalism. At the time, however, it was perceived in negative terms.

CONNECTIONS

From 1300 to 1800 and from North Africa to India, Islamic civilization thrived under three dynastic houses: the Ottomans, the Safavids, and the Mughals. All three empires had a period of expansion when territory was enlarged, followed by a high point politically and culturally, and later a period of contraction, when territories broke away. Two of the empires had large non-Muslim populations. India, even under Mughal rule, remained a predominantly Hindu land, and the Ottomans, in the process of conquering the Balkans, acquired a population that was predominantly Greek Orthodox Christians. Though all three states supported Islam, the Safavids took Shi'a teachings as orthodox, and the other two favored Sunni teachings. At the cultural level, the borders of these three states were porous, and people, ideas, art motifs, languages, and trade flowed back and forth.

In East Asia the fifteenth through eighteenth century also saw the creation of strong, prosperous, and expanding states, though in the case of China (under the Qing Dynasty) and Japan (under the Tokugawa Shogunate) the eighteenth century was a cultural high point, not a period of decline. The Qing emperors were Manchus, from the region northeast of China proper, reminiscent of the Mughals, who began in Afghanistan. As in the Islamic lands, during these centuries the presence of European powers became an issue in East Asia, though the details were quite different. Although one of the commodities that the British most wanted was the tea produced in China, Britain did not extend political control in China the way it did in India. Japan managed to refuse entry to most European traders after finding their presence and their support for missionary activity disturbing. The next chapter takes up these developments in East Asia.

☐ CHAPTER REVIEW

☐ **How were the three Islamic empires established, and what sorts of governments did they set up? (p. 588)**

After the decline of the Mongols in Central Asia and Persia, many small Turkic-ruled states emerged. Three of them went on to establish large empires: the Ottomans in Anatolia, the Safavids in Persia, and the Mughals in India. The Ottoman Empire's political system reached its classic form under Suleiman I. All authority flowed from the sultan to his public servants: provincial governors, police officers, military generals, heads of treasuries, and viziers. In Persia power was held for some time by Turkish lords, no single one dominant until 1501, when a fourteen-year-old military leader declared himself shah. The strength of the Safavid state rested in part on the skills of urban bureaucrats, who were an essential part of the civil machinery of government. One of the great leaders of the Mughal Empire, Akbar, developed an administrative bureaucracy centered on four co-equal ministers: for finance and revenue; the army and intelligence; the judiciary and religious patronage; and the imperial household. Whereas the Ottoman sultans and Safavid shahs made extensive use of slaves acquired from non-Muslim lands for military and administrative positions, Akbar used the services of royal princes, nobles, and warrior-aristocrats. All three empires responded to the shift in military technology away from the mounted archer toward the use of gunpowder weapons. The Ottomans in particular made effective use of guns and artillery.

☐ **What cultural advances occurred under the rule of the Ottoman, Safavid, and Mughal empires? (p. 597)**

All three Islamic empires presided over an extraordinary artistic and intellectual flowering in everything from carpet making and book illustration to architecture and gardening, from geography and astronomy to medicine. At the same time, new religious practices and conflicts emerged, and new gathering places — coffeehouses — became popular outlets for socializing and exchanging ideas. In the realm of religion, the rulers of all three empires drew legitimacy from their support for Islam, at least among their Muslim subjects; however, there were key differences: the Ottomans and Mughals supported the Sunni tradition, the Safavids the Shi'a tradition.

☐ **How did Christians, Jews, Hindus, and other non-Muslims fare under these Islamic states? (p. 606)**

All the Islamic empires had a substantial number of non-Muslim subjects. Drawing on Qur'anic teachings, Muslims had long practiced a religious toleration unknown in Christian Europe. Most Muslim rulers guaranteed the lives and property of Christians and Jews who promised obedience and paid a poll tax. The Ottomans ruled over the Balkans, where most of the people were Christian, and Muslims in India were greatly outnumbered by Hindus. Although the Safavid authorities made efforts to convert Armenian Christians in the Caucuses, the Armenian Christian Church retained its vitality.

☐ **How were the Islamic empires affected by the gradual shift toward trade routes that bypassed their lands? (p. 607)**

European exploration and colonization of foreign lands opened new trade routes and enabled Europeans to acquire goods from the East without using Muslim intermediaries. Nevertheless, enterprising merchants from India and Persia frequently found ways to profit from the new trade relations, showing considerable adaptability. Within India, British merchants took on more and more political control in politically unstable areas, leading before the end of the eighteenth century to a colonial empire in India recognized by the British Parliament.

☐ **Did any common factors lead to the decline of central power in the Islamic empires in the seventeenth and eighteenth centuries? (p. 611)**

By the end of the eighteenth century all three of the major Islamic empires were on the defensive and losing territory. Common challenges included succession difficulties, economic problems, and loss of military superiority. The first to fall was the Safavid Empire, which did not have the revenue base to maintain the sort of standing armies that the Ottomans and the Mughals had. Decline in the strength of its armies encouraged increased foreign aggression. The Ottoman Empire suffered from weakened leadership and military strength. From the late seventeenth century, Ottoman armies began losing wars and territory along both the northern and eastern borders, eventually giving up northern and eastern territories entirely. Military challenges proved daunting in Mughal India as well. The stiffest opposition came from the Marathas, a militant Hindu group in the south. India also suffered from succession struggles that shattered the empire. All three empires faced decentralization of authority. Power was seized by local notables and military strongmen at the expense of central government officials.

SUGGESTED READING

Atil, Esin. *The Age of Sultan Suleyman the Magnificent*. 1987. A splendidly illustrated celebration of the man and his times.

Barkey, Karen. *Empire of Difference*. 2008. Places the history of the Ottomans in comparative perspective.

Bridge, Antony. *Suleiman the Magnificent*. 1983. Lively, accessible account of the sultan's impact.

Dale, Stephen Frederic. *The Garden of the Eight Paradises: Babur and the Culture of Empire in Central Asia, Afghanistan and India, 1483–1750*. 2004. A scholarly biography that draws on and analyzes Babur's autobiography.

Dale, Stephen Frederic. *The Muslim Empires of the Ottomans, Safavids, and Mughals*. 2010. A comparative study of the three empires, with much on religion and culture.

Findley, Carter Vaughn. *The Turks in World History*. 2005. Takes a macro look at the three Islamic empires as part of the history of the Turks.

Finkel, Caroline. *Osman's Dream: A History of the Ottoman Empire*. 2006. A new interpretation that views the Ottomans from their own perspective.

Inalcik, Halil, and Renda Günsel. *Ottoman Civilization*. 2002. A huge, beautifully illustrated, government-sponsored overview, with an emphasis on the arts and culture.

Jackson, Peter, and Lawrence Lockhart, eds. *The Cambridge History of Iran*, Vol. 6, *The Timurid and Safavid Periods*. 1986. A set of essays by leading scholars on the social and cultural as well as the political and economic history of Iran.

Keay, John. *India: A History*. 2000. A comprehensive history, rich in insights.

Lapidus, Ira M. *A History of Islamic Societies*, 2d ed. 2002. A comprehensive, yet lucid survey.

Mukhia, Harbans. *The Mughals of India: A Framework for Understanding*. 2004. A short but thoughtful analysis of the Mughal society and state.

Pierce, Leslie. *The Imperial Harem: Women and Sovereignty in the Ottoman Empire*. 1993. A fresh look at the role of elite women under the Ottomans.

Richards, John F. *The Mughal Empire*. 1993. A coherent narrative history of the period 1526–1720.

Ruthven, Malise, and Azim Nanji. *Historical Atlas of Islam*. 2004. Provides numerous maps illustrating the shifting political history of Islamic states.

NOTES

1. *Memoirs of Zehir-Ed-Din Muhammed Baber: Emperor of Hindustan*, trans. John Leyden and William Erskine (London: Longman and Cadell, 1826), p. 333.
2. Quoted in M. C. Beach, *The Imperial Image: Paintings for the Mughal Court* (Washington, D.C.: Freer Gallery of Art, Smithsonian Institution, 1981), pp. 9–10.
3. Quoted in V. A. Smith, *The Oxford History of India* (Oxford, U.K.: Oxford University Press, 1967), p. 398.
4. Quoted in S. K. Ikram, *Muslim Civilization in India* (New York: Columbia University Press, 1964), p. 202.
5. Quoted in K. M. Panikkar, *Asia and Western Domination* (London: George Allen & Unwin, 1965), p. 35.
6. Quoted in W. Bingham, H. Conroy, and F. W. Iklé, *A History of Asia*, vol. 2 (Boston: Allyn and Bacon, 1967), p. 74.

For practice quizzes and other study tools, visit the **Online Study Guide** at bedfordstmartins.com/mckayworld.

For primary sources from this period, see *Sources of World Societies*, **Second Edition**.

For Web sites, images, and documents related to topics in this chapter, visit **Make History** at bedfordstmartins.com/mckayworld.

• **Kabuki Actor** Urban entertainment flourished in Japan under the rule of the Tokugawa shoguns. This late-eighteenth-century woodblock print was made for the many fans of the Kabuki actor Matsumoto Yonesaburo, who specialized in performing female roles. (Private Collection/Photo © Boltin Picture Library/ The Bridgeman Art Library)

21

The four centuries from 1400 to 1800 were a time of growth and dynamic change throughout East Asia. Although both China and Japan suffered periods of war, each ended up with expanded territories. The age of exploration brought New World crops to the region, leading to increased agricultural output and population growth. It also brought new opportunities for foreign trade and new religions. Another link between these countries was the series of massive Japanese invasions of Korea in the late sixteenth century, which led to war between China and Japan.

Continuity and Change in East Asia
1400–1800

In China, the native Ming Dynasty brought an end to Mongol rule. Under the Ming, China saw agricultural reconstruction, commercial expansion, and the rise of a vibrant urban culture. In the early seventeenth century, after the Ming Dynasty fell into disorder, the non-Chinese Manchus founded the Qing Dynasty (1644–1911) and added Taiwan, Mongolia, Tibet, and Xinjiang to their realm. The Qing Empire thus was comparable to the other multiethnic empires of the early modern world, such as the Ottoman, Russian, and Habsburg empires. In China itself the eighteenth century was a time of peace and prosperity.

In the Japanese islands the fifteenth century saw the start of civil war that lasted a century. At the end of the sixteenth century the world seemed to have turned upside down when a commoner, Hideyoshi (HEE-deh-YOH-shee), became the supreme ruler. He did not succeed in passing on his power to an heir, however. Power was seized by Tokugawa Ieyasu (toe-koo-GAH-wuh ee-yeh-YAH-soo). Under the Tokugawa Shogunate (1603–1867), Japan restricted contact with the outside world and social mobility among its own people. Yet Japan thrived, as agricultural productivity increased and a lively urban culture developed. ●

Ming China, 1368-1644

☐ What sort of state and society developed in China after the Mongols were ousted?

The story of Ming China begins with the rise of a poor boy to emperor of a new dynasty. This individual, Zhu Yuanzhang (JOO-yoowan-JAHNG) — known as Taizu as emperor — proved to be one of the most despotic emperors in Chinese history. Still, peace brought prosperity and a lively urban culture. By the beginning of the seventeenth century, however, the Ming government was beset by fiscal, military, and political problems.

The Rise of Zhu Yuanzhang and the Founding of the Ming Dynasty

The founder of the **Ming Dynasty**, Zhu Yuanzhang (1328-1398), began life in poverty during the last decades of the Mongol Yuan Dynasty. His home region was hit by drought and then plague in the 1340s, and when he was only sixteen years old, his father, oldest brother, and that brother's wife all died, leaving two penniless boys with three bodies to bury. With no relatives to turn to, Zhu Yuanzhang asked a monastery to accept him as a novice. The monastery itself was short of funds, and the monks soon sent Zhu out to beg for food. For three or four years he wandered through central China. Only after he returned to the monastery did he learn to read.

A few years later, in 1351, members of a religious sect known as the Red Turbans rose in rebellion against the government. Red Turban teachings drew on Manichaean ideas about the incompatibility of the forces of good and evil as well as on the cult of the Maitreya Buddha, who according to believers would in the future bring his paradise to earth to relieve human suffering. The Red Turbans met with considerable success, even defeating Mongol cavalry. When the temple where Zhu Yuanzhang was living was burned down in the fighting, Zhu joined the rebels and rose rapidly.

Zhu and his followers developed into brilliant generals, and gradually they defeated one rival after another. In 1356 Zhu took the city of Nanjing and made it his base. In 1368 his armies took Beijing, which the Mongol emperor and his closest followers had vacated just days before. Then forty years old, Zhu Yuanzhang declared himself emperor of the Ming ("Bright") Dynasty. As emperor, he was known as Taizu (TIGH-dzoo) or the Hongwu emperor.

Taizu started his reign wanting to help the poor. To lighten the weight of government taxes and compulsory labor, he ordered a full-scale registration of cultivated land and population so that these burdens could be assessed more fairly. He also tried persuasion. He issued instructions to be read aloud to villagers, telling them to be obedient to their parents, live in harmony with their neighbors, work contentedly at their occupations, and refrain from evil.

Although in many ways anti-Mongol, Taizu retained some Yuan practices. One was setting up provinces as the administrative layer between the central government and the prefectures (local governments a step above counties). Another was hereditary service obligations for both artisan and military households. Any family classed as a military household had to supply a soldier at

Ming China, ca. 1600

all times, replacing those who were injured, who died, or who deserted.

Garrisons were concentrated along the northern border and near the capital at Nanjing. Each garrison was allocated a tract of land that the soldiers took turns cultivating to supply their own food. Although in theory this system should have supplied the Ming with a large but inexpensive army, the reality was less satisfactory. Garrisons were rarely self-sufficient. Furthermore, men compelled to become soldiers did not necessarily make good fighting men, and desertion was difficult to prevent. Consequently, like earlier dynasties, the Ming turned to non-Chinese northerners for much of its armed forces. Many of the best soldiers in the Ming army were Mongols in Mongol units. Taizu did not try to conquer the Mongols, and Ming China did not extend into modern Inner Mongolia.

Taizu had deeply ambivalent feelings about men of education and sometimes brutally humiliated them in open court, even having them beaten. His behavior was so erratic that it is most likely that he suffered from some form of mental illness. As Taizu became more literate, he realized that scholars could criticize him in covert ways, using phrases that had double meanings or that sounded like words for "bandit," "monk," or the like. Even poems in private circulation could be used as evidence of subversive thoughts. When literary men began to avoid official life, Taizu made it illegal to turn down appointments or to resign from office. He began falling into rages that only the empress could stop, and after her death in 1382 no one could calm him. In 1376 Taizu had thousands of officials killed because they were found to have taken shortcuts in their handling of paperwork for the grain tax. In 1380 Taizu concluded that his chancellor was plotting to assassinate him, and thousands only remotely connected to the chancellor were executed. From then on, Taizu acted as his own chancellor, dealing directly with the heads of departments and ministries.

The next important emperor, called Chengzu or the Yongle emperor (r. 1403–1425), was also a military man. One of Taizu's younger sons, he took the throne by force from his nephew and often led troops into battle against the Mongols. Like his father, Chengzu was willing to use terror to keep government officials in line.

Early in his reign, Chengzu decided to move the capital from Nanjing to Beijing, which had been his own base as a prince and the capital during Mongol times. Constructed between 1407 and 1420, Beijing was a planned city. Like Chang'an in Sui-Tang times (581–

907), it was arranged like a set of boxes within boxes built on a north-south axis. The main outer walls were forty feet high and nearly fifteen miles around, pierced by nine gates. Inside was the Imperial City, with government offices, and within that the palace itself, called the Forbidden City, with close to ten thousand rooms. Because the Forbidden City survives today, people can still see the series of audience halls with vast courtyards between them where attending officials would stand or kneel.

The areas surrounding Beijing were not nearly as agriculturally productive as those around Nanjing. To supply Beijing with grain, the Yuan Grand Canal connecting the city to the rice basket of the Yangzi River regions was broadened, deepened, and supplied with more locks and dams. The 15,000 boats and the 160,000 soldiers of the transport army who pulled loaded barges from the towpaths along the canal became the lifeline of the capital.

Problems with the Imperial Institution

Taizu had decreed that succession should go to the eldest son of the empress or to the son's eldest son if the son predeceased his father, the system generally

---

• **Ming Dynasty** The Chinese dynasty in power from 1368 to 1644; it marked a period of agricultural reconstruction, foreign expeditions, commercial expansion, and a vibrant urban culture.

Forbidden City The palace complex in Beijing, commonly called the Forbidden City, was built in the early fifteenth century when the capital was moved from Nanjing to Beijing. Audience halls and other important state buildings are arranged on a north-south axis with huge courtyards between them, where officials would stand during ceremonies. (Vincent Loy, photographer)

followed by earlier dynasties. In Ming times, the flaws in this system became apparent as one mediocre, obtuse, or erratic emperor followed another. There were emperors who refused to hold audiences, who fell into irrational fits, and who let themselves be manipulated by palace ladies.

Because Taizu had abolished the position of chancellor, emperors turned to secretaries and eunuchs to manage the paperwork. Eunuchs were essentially slaves. Many boys and young men were acquired by dubious means, often from non-Chinese areas in the south, and after they were castrated they had no option but to serve the imperial family. Zheng He, for instance (see page 639), was taken from Yunnan as a boy of ten by a Ming general assigned the task of securing boys to be castrated. Society considered eunuchs the basest of servants, and Confucian scholars heaped scorn on them. Yet Ming emperors, like rulers in earlier dynasties, often preferred the always compliant eunuchs to high-minded, moralizing civil service officials.

In Ming times the eunuch establishment became huge. By the late fifteenth century the eunuch bureaucracy had grown as large as the civil service, each with roughly twelve thousand positions. After 1500 the eunuch bureaucracy grew even more rapidly, and by the mid-sixteenth century seventy thousand eunuchs were in service throughout the country, ten thousand in the capital. Tension between the two bureaucracies was high. In 1420 Chengzu set up a eunuch-run secret service to investigate cases of suspected corruption and sedition in the regular bureaucracy. Eunuch control over vital government processes, such as appointments, became a severe problem.

In hope of persuading emperors to make reforms, many Ming officials risked their careers and lives by speaking out. In 1376, when Taizu asked for criticism, one official criticized harsh punishment of officials for minor lapses. Incensed, Taizu had him brought to the capital in chains and let him starve to death in prison. In 1519, when an emperor announced plans to make a tour of the southern provinces, over a hundred officials staged a protest by kneeling in front of the palace. The emperor ordered the officials to remain kneeling for three days, then had them flogged; eleven died. The Confucian tradition celebrated these acts of political protest as heroic. Rarely, however, did they succeed in moving an emperor to change his mind.

Although the educated public complained about the performance of emperors, no one proposed or even imagined alternatives to imperial rule. High officials were forced to find ways to work around uncooperative emperors, but they were not able to put in place institutions that would limit the damage an emperor could do. Knowing that strong emperors often acted erratically, many high officials came to prefer weak emperors who let them take care of the government. Emperors, of course, resented the way officials tried to keep them busy doing harmless activities.

The Mongols and the Great Wall

The early Ming emperors held Mongol fighting men in awe and feared they might form another great military machine of the sort Chinggis Khan (ca. 1162–1227) had put together two centuries earlier. Although in Ming times the Mongols were never united in a pan-Mongol federation, groups of Mongols could and did raid. Twice they threatened the dynasty: in 1449 the khan of the western Mongols captured the Chinese emperor, and in 1550 Beijing was surrounded by the forces of the khan of the Mongols in Inner Mongolia. Fearful of anything that might strengthen the Mongols, Ming officials were reluctant to grant any privileges to Mongol leaders, such as trading posts along the borders. Instead, they wanted the different groups of Mongols to trade only through the formal tribute system. When trade was finally liberalized in 1570, friction was reduced.

Two important developments shaped Ming-Mongol relations: the construction of the Great Wall, and closer relations between Mongolia and Tibet. The Great Wall, much of which survives today, was built as a compromise when Ming officials could agree on no other way to manage the Mongol threat. The wall extends about 1,500 miles from northeast of Beijing into Gansu province. In the eastern 500 miles, the wall averages about 35 feet high and 20 feet across, with lookout towers every half mile. Much of the way, the wall is faced with brick, which gives it an imposing appearance that greatly impressed the first Westerners who saw it.

Whether the wall did much to protect Ming China from the Mongols is still debated. Perhaps of more significance was the spread of Tibetan Buddhism among the Mongols. Tibet in this period was largely ruled by the major Buddhist monasteries. When Tibetan monasteries needed military assistance, they asked competing Mongol leaders for help, and many struggles were decided by Mongol military intervention. The Tibetan Buddhist Tsong-kha-pa (1357–1419) founded the Yellow Hat or Gelug-pa sect, whose heads later became known as the Dalai Lamas. In 1577 the third Dalai Lama accepted the invitation of Altan Khan to visit Mongolia, and the khan declared Tibetan Buddhism to be the official religion of all the Mongols. The Dalai Lama gave the khan the title "King of Religion," and the khan swore that the Mongols would renounce blood sacrifice. When the third Dalai Lama's reincarnation was found to be the great-grandson of Altan Khan, the ties between Tibet and Mongolia, not sur-

prisingly, became even stronger. From the perspective of Ming China, the growing influence of Buddhism among the Mongols seemed a positive development, as Buddhist emphasis on nonviolence was expected to counter the Mongols' love of war.

The Examination Life

In sharp contrast to Europe in this era, Ming China had few social barriers. It had no hereditary aristocracy that could have limited the emperor's absolute power. Although China had no titled aristocracy, it did have an elite whose status was based above all on government office acquired through education. Agricultural land remained the most highly prized form of wealth, but antiques, books, paintings and calligraphies, and urban real estate also brought status. Unlike in many European countries of the era, China's merchants did not become a politically articulate bourgeoisie. Instead, the politically active class was that of the scholars who Confucianism taught should aid the ruler in running the state. With the possible exception of the Jewish people, no people have respected learning as much as the Chinese. Merchants tried to marry into the scholar class in order to rise in the world.

Thus, despite the harsh and arbitrary ways in which the Ming emperors treated their civil servants, educated men were eager to enter the government. Reversing the policies of the Mongol Yuan Dynasty, the Ming government recruited almost all of its officials through **civil service examinations**. Candidates had to study the Confucian classics and the interpretations of them by the twelfth-century Neo-Confucian scholar Zhu Xi (joo shee; 1130–1200), whose teachings were declared orthodox. To become officials, candidates had to pass examinations at the prefecture, the provincial, and the capital levels. To keep the wealthiest areas from dominating the exams, quotas were established for the number of candidates that each province could send on to the capital.

Of course, boys from well-to-do families had a significant advantage because their families could start their education with tutors at age four or five, though less costly schools were becoming increasingly available as well. Families that for generations had pursued other careers — for example, as merchants or physicians (see "Individuals in Society: Tan Yunxian, Woman Doctor," page 622) — had more opportunities than ever for their sons to become officials through the exams. Clans sometimes operated schools for their members because the clan as a whole would enjoy the prestige of a successful clansman. Most of those who attended school stayed

---

• **civil service examinations** A highly competitive series of tests held at the prefecture, province, and capital levels to select men to become officials.

Tan Yunxian, Woman Doctor

THE GRANDMOTHER OF TAN YUNXIAN

(Tahn Yunshyen) (1461–1554) was the daughter of a physician, and her husband had married into her home to learn medicine himself. At least two of their sons—including Yunxian's father—passed the civil service examination and became officials, raising the social standing of the family considerably. The grandparents wanted to pass their medical knowledge down to someone, and because they found Yunxian very bright, they decided to teach it to her.

Yunxian married and raised four children but also practiced medicine, confining her practice to women. At age fifty she wrote an autobiographical account, *Sayings of a Female Doctor*. In the preface she described how, under her grandmother's tutelage, she had first memorized the *Canon of Problems* and the *Canon of the Pulse*. Then when her grandmother had time, she asked her granddaughter to explain particular passages in these classic medical treatises.

Yunxian began the practice of medicine by treating her own children, asking her grandmother to check her diagnoses. When her grandmother was old and ill, she gave Yunxian her notebook of prescriptions and her equipment for making medicines, telling her to study them carefully. Later, Yunxian herself became seriously ill and dreamed of her grandmother telling her on what page of which book to find the prescription that would cure her. When she recovered, she began her medical career in earnest.

Yunxian's book records the cases of thirty-one patients she treated, most of them women with chronic complaints rather than critical illnesses. Many of the women had what the Chinese classed as women's complaints, such as menstrual irregularities, repeated miscarriages, barrenness, and postpartum fatigue. Some had ailments that men too could suffer, such as coughs, nausea, insomnia, diarrhea, rashes, and swellings. Like other literati physicians, Yunxian regularly prescribed herbal medications. She also practiced moxibustion, the technique of burning moxa (dried artemisia) at specified points on the body with the goal of stimulating the circulation of *qi* (life energy). Because the physician applying the moxa had to touch the patient, male physicians could not perform moxibustion on women.

Yunxian's patients included working women, and Yunxian seems to have thought that their problems often sprang from overwork. One woman came to her because she had had vaginal bleeding for three years. When questioned, the woman told Yunxian that she worked all day with her husband at their kiln making bricks and tiles. Yunxian's diagnosis was overwork, and she gave the woman pills to replenish her yin. A boatman's wife came to her complaining of numbness in her hands. When the woman told Yunxian that she worked in the wind and rain

handling the boat, the doctor advised some time off. In another case Yunxian explained to a servant girl that she had gone back to work too soon after suffering a wind damage fever.

By contrast, when patients came from upper-class families, Yunxian believed negative emotions were the source of their problems, particularly if a woman reported that her mother-in-law had scolded her or that her husband had recently brought a concubine home. Yunxian told two upper-class women who had miscarried that they lost their babies because they had hidden their anger, causing fire to turn inward and destabilize the fetus.

Tan Yunxian herself lived a long life, dying at age ninety-three.

Source: Based on Charlotte Furth, *A Flourishing Yin: Gender in China's Medical History, 960–1665* (Berkeley: University of California Press, 1999), pp. 285–295.

QUESTIONS FOR ANALYSIS

1. Why do you think Tan Yunxian treated only women? Why might she have been more effective with women patients than a male physician would have been?

2. What do you think of Yunxian's diagnoses? Do you think she was able to help many of her patients?

• Tan Yunxian would have consulted traditional herbals, like this one, with sketches of plants of medicinal value and descriptions of their uses. (Wellcome Library, London)

Portrait of a Scholar-Official The official Jiang Shunfu arranged to have his portrait painted wearing an official robe and hat and followed by two boy attendants, one holding a lute wrapped in cloth. During Ming and Qing times, the rank of an official was made visible by the badges he wore on his robes. The pair of cranes on Jiang's badge shows he held a first-rank post in the civil service hierarchy. (From *Mingqing renwuxiaoxiang huaxuan* [Nanjing: Nanjing Bowuguan], pl 16)

only a few years, but students who seemed most promising moved on to advanced schools where they would practice essay writing and study the essays of men who had succeeded in the exams.

The examinations at the prefecture level lasted a day and drew hundreds if not thousands of candidates. The government compound would be taken over to give all candidates places to sit and write. The provincial and capital examinations were given in three sessions spread out over a week. In the first session, candidates wrote essays on passages from the classics. In the second and third sessions, candidates had to write essays on practical policy issues and on a passage from the *Classic of Filial Piety* (a brief text celebrating devotion to parents and other superiors). In addition, they had to show that they could draft state papers such as edicts, decrees, and judicial rulings. Reading the dynastic histories was a good way to prepare for policy questions and state paper exercises.

The provincial examinations were major local events. From five thousand to ten thousand candidates descended on the city and filled up its hostels. Candidates would show up a week in advance to present their credentials and gather the paper, ink, brushes, candles, blankets, and food they needed to survive in their small exam cells. To prevent cheating, no written material could be taken into the cells, and candidates were searched before being admitted. Anyone caught wearing a cheat-sheet (an inner gown covered with the classics in minuscule script) was thrown out of the exam and banned from the next session as well. Clerks used horns and gongs to begin and end each two-day session. During the sessions candidates had time to write rough drafts of their essays, correct them, and then copy neat final versions. The whole time tension was high. Sometimes rumors that the examiners had been bribed to leak the questions led to riots in the exam quarters, and knocked-over candles occasionally caused fires.

After the papers were handed in, clerks recopied them and assigned them numbers to preserve anonymity. Proofreaders checked the copying before handing the papers to the assembled examiners, who divided them up to grade. The grading generally took about twenty days, and most candidates stayed in the vicinity to await the results. Those few who passed (generally from 2 to 10 percent) were invited to the governor's compound for a celebration. By the time they reached home, most of their friends, neighbors, and relatives had already heard their good news. They could not spend long celebrating, however, because they had to begin preparing for the capital exams, less than a year away.

Everyday Life in Ming China

For civil servants and almost everyone else, everyday life in Ming China followed patterns established in earlier periods. The family remained central to most people's lives, and almost everyone married. Beyond the family, people's lives were shaped by the type of work they did and where they lived.

Large towns and cities proliferated in Ming times and became islands of sophistication in the vast sea of rural villages. In these urban areas small businesses manufactured textiles, paper, and luxury goods such as silks and porcelains. The southeast became a center for the production of cotton and silks; other areas specialized in the grain and salt trades and in silver. Merchants could make fortunes moving these goods across the country.

Printing was invented in Tang times (618–907) and had a great impact on the life of the educated elite in Song times (960–1279), but not until Ming times did it transform the culture of the urban middle classes. By the late Ming period publishing houses were putting out large numbers of books aimed at general audiences. These included fiction, reference books of all sorts, and popular religious tracts, such as ledgers for calculating the moral value of one's good deeds and subtracting the demerits from bad deeds. To make

their books attractive in the marketplace, entrepreneurial book publishers commissioned artists to illustrate them. By the sixteenth century more and more books were being published in the vernacular language (the language people spoke), especially short stories, novels, and plays. Ming vernacular short stories depicted a world much like that of their readers, full of shop clerks and merchants, monks and prostitutes, students and matchmakers.

The full-length novel made its first appearance during the Ming period. The plots of the early novels were heavily indebted to story cycles developed by oral storytellers over the course of several centuries. *Water Margin* is the episodic tale of a band of bandits, while *The Romance of the Three Kingdoms* is a work of historical fiction based on the exploits of the generals and statesmen contending for power at the end of the Han Dynasty. *The Journey to the West* is a fantastic account of the Tang monk Xuanzang's travels to India; in this book he is accompanied by a pig and a monkey with supernatural powers. *Plum in the Golden Vase* is a novel of manners about a lustful merchant with a wife and five concubines. Competing publishers brought out

Popular Romance Literature Women were among the most avid readers of the scripts for plays, especially romantic ones like *The Western Chamber*, a story of a young scholar who falls in love with a well-educated girl he encounters by chance. In this scene, the young woman looks up at the moon as her maid looks at its reflection in the pond. Meanwhile, her young lover scales the wall. This multicolor woodblock print, made in 1640, was one of twenty-one created to illustrate the play. (Museum für Ostasiatische Kunst, Köln, Inv.-No. R 61,2 [No. 11]. Photo: Rheinisches Bildarchiv, Köln)

their own editions of these novels, sometimes adding new illustrations or commentaries.

The Chinese found recreation and relaxation in many ways besides reading. The affluent indulged in an alcoholic drink made from fermented and distilled rice, and once tobacco was introduced from the Americas, both men and women took up pipes. Plays were also very popular. The Jesuit missionary Matteo Ricci, who lived in China from 1583 to 1610, described resident troupes in large cities and traveling troupes that "journey everywhere throughout the length and breadth of the country" putting on plays. The leaders of the troupes would purchase young children and train them to sing and perform. Ricci thought too many people were addicted to these performances:

> These groups of actors are employed at all imposing banquets, and when they are called they come prepared to enact any of the ordinary plays. The host at the banquet is usually presented with a volume of plays and he selects the one or several he may like. The guests, between eating and drinking, follow the plays with so much satisfaction that the banquet at times may last for ten hours.[1]

People not only enjoyed play performances but also avidly read the play scripts. The love stories and social satires of Tang Xianzu, the greatest of the Ming playwrights, were very popular. One of his plays tells the story of a young man who falls asleep while his meal is cooking. In his dream he sees his whole life: he comes in first in the civil service examinations, rises to high office, is unfairly slandered and condemned to death, and then is cleared and promoted. At the point of death, he wakes up, sees that his dinner is nearly ready, and realizes that life passes as quickly as a dream.

More than bread in Europe, rice supplied most of the calories of the population in central and south China. (In north China, wheat, made into steamed or baked bread or into noodles, served as the dietary staple.) In the south, terracing and irrigation of mountain slopes, introduced in the eleventh century, had increased rice harvests. Other innovations also brought good results. Farmers began to stock the rice paddies with fish, which continuously fertilized the rice fields, destroyed malaria-bearing mosquitoes, and enriched the diet. Farmers also developed commercial cropping in cotton, sugar cane, and indigo. New methods of crop rotation allowed for continuous cultivation and for more than one harvest per year from a single field.

The Ming rulers promoted the repopulation and colonization of war-devastated regions through reclamation of land and massive transfers of people. Immigrants to these areas received large plots and exemption from taxation for many years. Reforestation played a dramatic role in the agricultural revolution. In 1391 the Ming government ordered 50 million trees planted

> "The guests, between eating and drinking, follow the plays with so much satisfaction that the banquet at times may last for ten hours."
>
> **MATTEO RICCI**

in the Nanjing area to produce lumber for the construction of a maritime fleet. In 1392 each family holding colonized land in Anhui province had to plant two hundred mulberry, jujube, and persimmon trees. In 1396 peasants in the present-day provinces of Hunan and Hubei in central China planted 84 million fruit trees. Historians have estimated that 1 billion trees were planted during Taizu's reign.

Increased food production led to steady population growth and the multiplication of markets, towns, and small cities. Larger towns had permanent shops; smaller towns had periodic markets — some every five days, some every ten days, some only once a month. They sold essential goods — such as pins, matches, oil for lamps, candles, paper, incense, and tobacco — to country people from the surrounding hamlets. Markets usually included moneylenders, pawnbrokers, a tearoom, and sometimes a wine shop where tea and rice wine were sold and entertainers performed. Tradesmen carrying their wares on their backs and craftsmen — carpenters, barbers, joiners, locksmiths — moved constantly from market to market. Itinerant salesmen depended on the city market for their wares.

Ming Decline

Beginning in the 1590s the Ming government was beset by fiscal, military, and political problems. The government went nearly bankrupt helping defend Korea against a Japanese invasion (see pages 642–643). Then came a series of natural disasters: floods, droughts, locusts, and epidemics ravaged one region after another. At the same time, a "little ice age" brought a drop in average temperatures that shortened the growing season and reduced harvests. In areas of serious food shortages, gangs of army deserters and laid-off soldiers began scouring the countryside in search of food. Once the gangs had stolen all their grain, hard-pressed farmers joined them just to survive. The Ming government had little choice but to try to increase taxes to deal with these threats, but the last thing people needed was heavier taxes.

Adding to the hardship was a sudden drop in the supply of silver. In place of the paper money that had circulated in Song and Yuan times, silver ingots came into general use as money in Ming times. Even agricultural taxes came to be paid in silver rather than in grain. Much of this silver originated in either Japan or the

New World and entered China as payment for the silk and porcelains exported from China (see pages 482–483). When events in Japan and the Philippines led to disruption of trade, silver imports dropped. This led to deflation in China, which caused real rents to rise. Soon there were riots among urban workers and tenant farmers. In 1642 a group of rebels cut the dikes on the Yellow River, causing massive flooding. A smallpox epidemic soon added to the death toll. In 1644 the last Ming emperor, in despair, took his own life when rebels entered Beijing, opening the way for the start of a new dynasty.

The Manchus and Qing China, to 1800

☐ Did the return of alien rule with the Manchus have any positive consequences for China?

The next dynasty, the **Qing Dynasty** (1644–1911), was founded by the Manchus, a non-Chinese people who were descended from the Jurchens who had ruled north China during the Jin Dynasty (1127–1234), when south China was controlled by the Song. Manchu men shaved the front of their heads and wore their hair in a long braid called a queue. In the late sixteenth century the Manchus began expanding their territories, and in 1644 they founded the Qing Dynasty, which brought peace and in time prosperity. Successful Qing military campaigns extended the borders into Mongol, Tibetan, and Uighur regions, creating a multiethnic empire that was larger than any earlier Chinese dynasty.

The Rise of the Manchus

In the Ming period the Manchus lived in dispersed communities in what is loosely called Manchuria (the northeast of modern-day China). In the more densely populated southern part of Manchuria, the Manchus lived in close contact with Mongols, Koreans, and Chinese (Map 21.1). They were not nomads but rather hunters, fishers, and farmers. Like the Mongols, they also were excellent horsemen and archers and had a strongly hierarchical social structure, with elites and slaves. Slaves, often Korean or Chinese, were generally acquired through capture. A Korean visitor described many small Manchu settlements, most no larger than twenty households, supported by fishing, hunting for pelts, collecting pine nuts or ginseng, or growing crops such as wheat, millet, and barley. Villages were often at odds with each other over resources, and men did not leave their villages without arming themselves with bows and arrows or swords. Interspersed among these Manchu settlements were groups of nomadic Mongols who lived in tents.

The Manchus credited their own rise to Nurhaci (1559–1626). Over several decades, he united the Manchus and expanded their territories. Like Chinggis Khan, who had reorganized the Mongol armies to reduce the importance of tribal affiliations, Nurhaci created a new social basis for his armies in units called **banners**. Each banner was made up of a set of military companies and included the families and slaves of the soldiers. Each company had a hereditary captain, often from Nurhaci's own lineage. Over time new companies and new banners were formed, and by 1644 there were eight each of Manchu, Mongol, and Chinese banners. When new groups were defeated, their members were distributed among several banners to lessen their potential for subversion.

The Manchus entered China by invitation of the distinguished Ming general Wu Sangui, himself a native of southern Manchuria, who was near the eastern end of the Great Wall when he heard that the rebels had captured Beijing. The Manchus proposed to Wu that they join forces and liberate Beijing. Wu opened the gates of the Great Wall to let the Manchus in, and within a couple of weeks they occupied Beijing. When the Manchus made clear that they intended to conquer the rest of the country and take the throne themselves, Wu and many other Chinese generals joined forces with them. Before long, China was again under alien rule.

In the summer of 1645 the Manchus ordered all Chinese serving in Manchu armies to shave the front of their heads in the Manchu fashion, presumably to make it easier to recognize whose side they were on. Soon this order was extended to all Chinese men. Because so many of those newly conquered by the Qing refused to shave off their hair, Manchu commanders felt justified in ordering the slaughter of defiant cities. After quelling resistance, the Qing put in place policies and institutions that gave China a respite from war and disorder. However, most of the political institutions of the Ming Dynasty were taken over relatively unchanged, including the examination system.

After peace was achieved, population growth took off. Between 1700 and 1800 the Chinese population seems to have nearly doubled, from about 150 million to over 300 million. Population growth during the eighteenth century has been attributed to many factors: global warming that extended the growing season, expanded use of New World crops, slowing of the spread of new diseases that had accompanied the sixteenth-century expansion of global traffic, and the efficiency

• **Qing Dynasty** The dynasty founded by the Manchus that ruled China from 1644 to 1911.

• **banners** Units of the Qing army, composed of soldiers, their families, and slaves.

▢ Mapping the Past

MAP 21.1 The Qing Empire, ca. 1800 The sheer size of the Qing Empire in China almost inevitably led to its profound cultural influence on the rest of Asia.

ANALYZING THE MAP How many different cultural groups are depicted? Which occupied the largest territories? Where was crop agriculture most prevalent?

CONNECTIONS What geographical and political factors limited the expansion of the Qing Empire?

of the Qing government in providing relief in times of famine.

Some scholars have recently argued that China's overall standard of living in the mid-eighteenth century was comparable to Europe's and that the standards of China's most developed regions, such as the lower Yangzi region, compared favorably to the most developed regions of Europe at the time, such as England and the Netherlands. Life expectancy, food consumption, and even facilities for transportation were at similar levels.

Competent and Long-Lived Emperors

For more than a century, China was ruled by only three rulers, each of them hard-working, talented, and com-

mitted to making the Qing Dynasty a success. Two, the Kangxi and Qianlong emperors, had exceptionally long reigns.

Kangxi (r. 1661–1722) proved adept at meeting the expectations of both the Chinese and the Manchu elites. At age fourteen he announced that he would begin ruling on his own and had his regent imprisoned. Kangxi (KAHNG-shee) could speak, read, and write Chinese and made efforts to persuade educated Chinese that the Manchus had a legitimate claim to rule, even trying to attract Ming loyalists who had been unwilling to serve the Qing. He undertook a series of tours of the south, where Ming loyalty had been strongest, and he held a special exam to select men to compile the official history of the Ming Dynasty.

Kangxi's son and heir, the Yongzheng emperor (r. 1722–1735), was also a hard-working ruler who took an interest in the efficiency of the government. Because his father had lived so long, he did not come to the throne until his mid-forties and reigned only thirteen years. His successor, however, the Qianlong emperor (r. 1736–1796), like Kangxi had a reign of sixty years, with the result that China had only three rulers in 135 years.

Qianlong (chyan-loong) put much of his energy into impressing his subjects with his magnificence. He understood that the Qing's capacity to hold the multiethnic empire together rested on their ability to appeal to all those they ruled. Besides speaking Manchu and Chinese, Qianlong learned to converse in Mongolian, Uighur, Tibetan, and Tangut, and he addressed envoys in their own languages. He became as much a patron of Tibetan Buddhism as of Chinese Confucianism. He initiated a massive project to translate the Tibetan Buddhist canon into Mongolian and Manchu and had huge multilingual dictionaries compiled.

To demonstrate to the Chinese scholar-official elite that he was a sage emperor, Qianlong worked on affairs of state from dawn until early afternoon and then turned to reading, painting, and calligraphy. He was ostentatious in his devotion to his mother, visiting her daily and tending to her comfort with all the devotion of the most filial Chinese son. He took several tours down the Grand Canal to the southeast, in part to emulate his grandfather, in part to entertain his mother, who accompanied him on these tours.

Despite these displays of Chinese virtues, the Qianlong emperor was not fully confident that the Chinese supported his rule, and he was quick to act on any suspicion of anti-Manchu thoughts or actions. During a project to catalogue nearly all the books in China, he began to suspect that some governors were holding back books with seditious content. He ordered full searches for books with disparaging references to the Manchus or to previous alien conquerors like the Jurchens and Mongols. Sometimes passages were deleted or rewritten, but when an entire book was offensive, it was destroyed. So thorough was this book-burning that no copies survive of more than two thousand titles.

Through Qianlong's reign, China remained an enormous producer of manufactured goods and led the way in assembly-line production. The government operated huge textile factories, but some private firms were even larger. Hangzhou had a textile firm that gave work to four thousand weavers, twenty thousand spinners, and ten thousand dyers and finishers. The porcelain kilns at Jingdezhen employed the division of labor on a large scale and were able to supply porcelain to much of the world. The growth of the economy benefited the Qing state, and the treasury became so full that the Qianlong emperor was able to cancel taxes on several occasions. When he abdicated in 1796, his treasury had 400 million silver dollars in it.

Imperial Expansion

The Qing Dynasty put together a multiethnic empire that was larger than any earlier Chinese dynasty. Taiwan was acquired in 1683 after Qing armies pursued a rebel there. Mongolia was acquired next. In 1696 Kangxi led an army of eighty thousand men into Mongolia, and within a few years Manchu supremacy was accepted there. Cannon and muskets gave Qing forces military superiority over the Mongols, who were armed only with bows and arrows. Thus the Qing could dominate the steppe cheaply, effectively ending two thousand years of Inner Asian military advantage.

Presenting a Horse to the Emperor This detail from a 1757 hand scroll shows the Qianlong emperor, seated, receiving envoys from the Kazakhs. Note how the envoy, presenting a pure white horse, is kneeling to the ground performing the kowtow, which involved lowering his head to the ground as an act of reverence. The artist was Guiseppe Castiglione (1688–1768), an Italian who worked as a painter in Qianlong's court. (Qing, 1757. Handscroll, ink and colors on paper [45 cm × 2.67 m]. Musée Guimet, Paris/Art Resource, NY)

In the 1720s the Qing established a permanent garrison of banner soldiers in Tibet. By this time, the expanding Qing and Russian empires were nearing each other. In 1689 the Manchu and the Russian rulers approved a treaty — written in Russian, Manchu, Chinese, and Latin — defining their borders in Manchuria and regulating trade. Another treaty in 1727 allowed a Russian ecclesiastical mission to reside in Beijing and a trade caravan to make a trip from Russia to Beijing once every three years.

The last region to be annexed was Chinese Turkestan (the modern province of Xinjiang). Both the Han and the Tang Dynasties had stationed troops in the region, exercising loose overlordship, but neither Song nor Ming had tried to control the area. The Qing won the region in the 1750s through a series of campaigns against Uighur and Dzungar Mongol forces.

Both Tibet and Turkestan were ruled lightly. The local populations kept their own religious leaders and did not have to wear the queue.

Japan's Middle Ages, ca. 1400–1600

☐ How did Japan change during this period of political instability?

In the twelfth century Japan entered an age dominated by military men, an age that can be compared to Europe's feudal age. The Kamakura Shogunate (1185–1333) had its capital in the east, at Kamakura. It was succeeded by the Ashikaga Shogunate (1336–1573), which returned the government to Kyoto (KYOH-toh) and helped launch, during the fifteenth century, the great age of Zen-influenced Muromachi culture. The sixteenth century brought civil war over succession to the shogunate, leading to the building of massive castles and the emergence of rulers of obscure origins who eventually unified the realm.

Muromachi Culture

The headquarters of the Ashikaga shoguns were on Muromachi Street in Kyoto, and the refined and elegant style that they promoted is often called Muromachi culture. The shoguns patronized Zen Buddhism, the school of Buddhism associated with meditation and mind-to-mind transmission of truth. Because Zen monks were able to read and write Chinese, they often assisted the shoguns in handling foreign affairs. Many of the Kyoto Zen temples in this period had rock gardens, seen as aids to Zen meditation.

Zen ideas of simplicity permeated the arts. The Silver Pavilion built by the shogun Yoshimasa (r. 1449–1473) epitomizes Zen austerity. A white sand cone constructed in the temple garden was designed to reflect moonlight. Yoshimasa was also influential in the development of the tea ceremony, practiced by warriors, aristocrats, and priests, but not by women. Aesthetes celebrated the beauty of imperfect objects, such as plain or misshapen cups or pots. Spare monochrome paintings fit into this aesthetic, as did simple asymmetrical flower arrangements.

The shoguns were also patrons of the **Nō theater**. Nō drama originated in popular forms of entertainment, including comical skits and dances directed to the gods. It was transformed into high art by Zeami (1363–1443), an actor and playwright who also wrote on the aesthetic theory of Nō. Nō was performed on a bare stage with a pine tree painted across the backdrop. One or two actors wearing brilliant brocade robes would perform, using stylized gestures and stances. One actor would wear a mask indicating whether the character he was portraying was male or female, old or young, a god, a ghost, or a demon. The actors would be accompanied by a chorus and a couple of musicians playing drums and flute. Many of the stories concerned ghosts consumed by jealous passions or the desire for revenge. Zeami argued that the most meaningful moments came during silence, when the actor's spiritual presence allowed the audience to catch a glimpse of the mysterious and inexpressible.

Civil War

Civil war began in Kyoto in 1467 as a struggle over succession to the shogunate. Rival claimants and their followers used arson as their chief weapon and burned down temples and mansions, destroying much of the city and its treasures. In the early phases defeated opponents were exiled or allowed to retire to monasteries. As the conflict continued, violence escalated; hostages and prisoners were slaughtered and corpses mutilated. Once Kyoto was laid waste, war spread to outlying areas. When the shogun could no longer protect cities, merchants banded together to hire mercenaries. In the political vacuum, the Lotus League, a commoner-led religious sect united by faith in the saving power of the Lotus Sutra, set up a commoner-run government that collected taxes and settled disputes. In 1536, during eight days of fighting, the powerful Buddhist monastery Enryakuji attacked the League and its temples, burned much of the city, and killed men, women, and children thought to be believers.

• **Nō theater** A type of Japanese theater in which performers convey emotions and ideas as much through gestures, stances, and dress as through words.

In these confused and violent circumstances, power devolved to the local level, where warlords, called **daimyo** (DIGH-mee-oh), built their power bases. Unlike earlier power holders, these new lords were not appointed by the court or shogunate and did not send taxes to absentee overlords. Instead they seized what they needed and used it to build up their territories and recruit more samurai. To raise revenues they surveyed the land and promoted irrigation and trade. Many of the most successful daimyo were self-made men who rose from obscurity.

The violence of the period encouraged castle building. The castles were built not on mountaintops but on level plains, and they were surrounded by moats and walls made from huge stones. Inside a castle was a many-storied keep. Though relatively safe from incendiary missiles, the keeps were vulnerable to Western-style cannon, introduced in the 1570s. Many of the castles had splendid living quarters for the daimyo; leading painters embellished interior sliding doors and screens.

The Victors: Nobunaga and Hideyoshi

The first daimyo to gain a predominance of power was Oda Nobunaga (1534–1582). A samurai of the lesser daimyo class, he recruited followers from masterless

Hideyoshi's Campaigns in Japan and Korea, 1537–1598

MING CHINA

KOREA

Sea of Japan

JAPAN

Edo

Kyoto

Takamatsu

Kagoshima

→ Reunification campaign
→ Campaign against Korea

samurai who had been living by robbery and extortion. After he won control of his native province in 1559, he immediately set out to extend his power through central Japan. A key step was destroying the military power of the great monasteries. To increase revenues, he minted coins, the first government-issued money in Japan since 958. Also to raise revenues, he promoted trade by eliminating customs barriers and opening the little fishing village of Nagasaki to foreign commerce; it soon became Japan's largest port.

In 1582, in an attempted coup, Nobunaga was forced by one of his vassals to commit suicide. His general and staunchest adherent, Toyotomi Hideyoshi (1537–1598), avenged him and continued the drive toward unification of the daimyo-held lands.

Like the Ming founder, Hideyoshi was a peasant's son who rose to power through military talent. Hideyoshi succeeded in bringing northern and western Japan under his control. In 1582 he attacked the great fortress at Takamatsu. When direct assault failed, his troops flooded the castle to force its surrender. A successful siege of the town of Kagoshima then brought the southern island of Kyushu (KYOO-shoo) under his domination. Hideyoshi soothed the vanquished daimyo as Nobunaga had done—with lands and military positions—but he also required them to swear allegiance and to obey him down to the smallest particular. For

Matsumoto Castle Hideyoshi built Matsumoto Castle between 1594 and 1597. Designed to be impregnable, it was surrounded by a moat and had a base constructed of huge stones. In the sixteenth and early seventeenth centuries Spanish and Portuguese missionaries compared Japanese castles favorably to European castles of the period. (Adina Tovy/Robert Harding World Imagery)

MAP 21.2 Tokugawa Japan, 1603–1867 The lands that the shogunate directly controlled were concentrated near its capital at Edo. The daimyo of distant places, such as the island of Kyushu, were required to make long journeys to and from Edo every year.

the first time in over two centuries, Japan had a single ruler.

Hideyoshi did his best to ensure that future peasants' sons would not be able to rise as he had. His great sword hunt of 1588 collected weapons from farmers, who were no longer allowed to wear swords. Restrictions were also placed on samurai; they were prohibited from leaving their lord's service or switching occupations. To improve tax collection, Hideyoshi ordered a survey of the entire country. His agents collected detailed information about each daimyo's lands and about towns, villages, agricultural produce, and industrial output all over Japan. His surveys not only tightened tax collection, but also registered each peasant household, tied the peasants to the land, and tightened the collection of the land tax. With the country pacified, Hideyoshi embarked on an ill-fated attempt to conquer Korea and China that ended only with his death, discussed below (see page 643).

The Tokugawa Shogunate, to 1800

☐ What was life like in Japan during the Tokugawa peace?

On his deathbed, Hideyoshi set up a council of regents to govern during the minority of his infant son. The strongest regent was Hideyoshi's long-time supporter

Tokugawa Ieyasu (1543–1616), who ruled vast territories around Edo (AY-doh; modern-day Tokyo). In 1600 at Sekigahara, Ieyasu smashed a coalition of daimyo defenders of the heir and began building his own government. In 1603 he took the title "shogun." The **Tokugawa Shogunate** that Ieyasu fashioned lasted until 1867. This era is also called the Edo period after the location of the shogunate, starting Tokyo's history as Japan's most important city (Map 21.2). Peace brought many benefits. Towns and cities thrived and became centers for the theater and publishing.

Tokugawa Government

In the course of the seventeenth century the Tokugawa shoguns worked to consolidate relations with the daimyo. In a scheme resembling the later residency requirements imposed by Louis XIV in France (see page 497) and Peter the Great in Russia (see page 509), Ieyasu set up the **alternate residence system**, which compelled the lords to live in Edo every other year and to leave their wives and sons there—essentially as hostages. This arrangement had obvious advantages:

- **daimyo** Regional lords in Japan; many had built their power by seizing what they needed and promoting irrigation and trade to raise revenues.
- **Tokugawa Shogunate** The Japanese government founded by Tokugawa Ieyasu that lasted from 1603 until 1867; it is also called the Edo period because the shogunate was located at Edo.
- **alternate residence system** Arrangement in which lords lived in Edo every other year and left their wives and sons there as hostages.

Daimyo Procession The system of alternate residence meant that some daimyo were always on the road. Daimyo's travel with their attendants between their domains and Edo, the shogun's residence, stimulated construction of roads, inns, and castle towns. (Tokugawa Art Museum, © The Togugawa Art Museum Image Archives/DNPartcom)

the shogun could keep tabs on the daimyo, control them through their wives and children, and weaken them financially with the burden of maintaining two residences.

The peace imposed by the Tokugawa Shogunate brought a steady rise in population to about 30 million people by 1800 (making Tokugawa Japan about one-tenth the size of Qing China). To maintain stability, the early Tokugawa shoguns froze social status. Laws rigidly prescribed what each class could and could not do. Nobles, for example, were strictly forbidden to go sauntering, whether by day or by night, through the streets or lanes in places where they had no business to be. Daimyo were prohibited from moving troops outside their frontiers, making alliances, and coining money. As intended, these rules protected the Tokugawa shoguns from daimyo attack and helped ensure a long era of peace.

The early Tokugawa shoguns also restricted the construction and repair of castles — symbols, in Japan as in medieval Europe, of feudal independence. Continuing Hideyoshi's policy, the Tokugawa regime enforced a policy of complete separation of samurai and peasants. Samurai were defined as those permitted to carry swords. They had to live in castles (which evolved into castle-towns), and they depended on stipends from their lords, the daimyo. Samurai were effectively prevented from establishing ties to the land, so they could not become landholders. Likewise, merchants and artisans had to live in towns and could not own land. Japanese castle-towns evolved into bustling, sophisticated urban centers.

After 1639 Japan limited its contacts with the outside world because of concerns about both the loyalty of subjects converted to Christianity by European missionaries and about the imperialist ambitions of European powers (discussed below). However, China remained an important trading partner and source of ideas. For example, Neo-Confucianism gained a

stronger hold among the samurai-turned bureaucrats, and painting in Chinese styles enjoyed great popularity. The Edo period also saw the development of a school of native learning that rejected Buddhism and Confucianism as alien and tried to identify a distinctly Japanese sensibility.

Commercialization and the Growth of Towns

During the civil war period, warfare seems to have promoted social and economic change, much as it had in China during the Warring States Period (403–221 B.C.E.). Trade grew, and greater use was made of coins imported from Ming China. Markets began appearing at river crossings, at the entrances to temples and shrines, and at other places where people congregated. Towns and cities sprang up all around the country, some of them around the new castles. Traders and artisans dealing in a specific product — such as comb makers, sesame oil producers, or metalworkers — began forming guilds. Money-lending was a very profitable business — annual interest rates reached 300 percent. In Kyoto the powerful monastery Enryakuji licensed the moneylenders, in essence running a lucrative protection racket. Foreign trade also flourished, despite chronic problems with pirates who raided the Japanese, Korean, and Chinese coasts (see pages 642–643).

Recent scholarship demonstrates that the Tokugawa era witnessed the foundations of modern Japanese capitalism: the development of a cash economy, the use of money to make more money, the accumulation of large amounts of capital for investment in factory or technological enterprises, the growth of business ventures operating over a national network of roads, and the expansion of wage labor. That these developments occurred simultaneously with, but entirely independent of, similar changes in Europe fascinates and challenges historians.

In most cities, merchant families with special privileges from the government controlled the urban economy. Frequently, a particular family dominated the trade in a particular product and then branched out into other businesses. The family of Kōnoike Shinroku is an example. In 1600 he established a sake (SAH-kee) brewery in the village of Kōnoike (sake is an alcoholic beverage made from fermented rice). By 1604 he had opened a branch office in Edo, and in 1615 he opened an office in Osaka and began shipping tax-rice (taxes paid in rice) from western Japan to Osaka. In 1656 one of Shinroku's sons founded a banking or money-changing business in Osaka. Forty years later the Kōnoike family was doing business in thirty-two daimyo domains. Eventually, the Kōnoike banking house made loans to and handled the tax-rice for 110 daimyo families. In 1705, with the interest paid from daimyo loans, the Kōnoike bought a tract of ponds and swampland, turned the land into rice paddies, and settled 480 households on the land. (Land reclamation under merchant supervision became a typical feature of Tokugawa business practices.) Involved by this time in five or six business enterprises, the house of Kōnoike had come a long way from brewing sake.

Japanese merchant families also devised distinct patterns and procedures for their business operations. What today is called "family-style management principles" determined the age of apprenticeship (between eleven and thirteen); the employee's detachment from past social relations and adherence to the norms of a particular family business; salaries; seniority as the basis of promotion, although job performance at the middle rungs determined who reached the higher ranks; and the time for retirement. All employees in a family business were expected to practice frugality, resourcefulness, self-denial, and careful accounting. These values formed the basis of what has been called the Japanese "industrious revolution." They help to explain how, after the Meiji (MAY-jee) Restoration of 1867 (see page 797), Japan was able to industrialize rapidly and compete successfully with the West. (In both Japan and China, there was a market for books giving advice on how to get ahead. See "Viewpoints: Chinese and Japanese Financial Advice," page 634.)

In the seventeenth century underemployed farmers and samurai, not to mention the ambitious and adventurous, thronged to the cities. As a result, Japan's cities grew tremendously. Kyoto became the center for the manufacture of luxury goods like lacquer, brocade, and fine porcelain. Osaka was the chief market, especially for rice. Edo was a center of consumption by the daimyo, their vassals, and government bureaucrats. Both Osaka and Edo reached about a million residents.

Two hundred fifty towns came into being in this period. Most ranged in size from 3,000 to 20,000 people, but a few, such as Hiroshima, Kagoshima, and Nagoya, had populations of between 65,000 and 100,000. In addition, perhaps two hundred towns along the main road to Edo emerged to meet the needs of men traveling on the alternate residence system. In the eighteenth century perhaps 4 million people, 15 percent of the Japanese population, resided in cities or towns.

Interior of Nijo Castle To assert control over the imperial court and the city of Kyoto, Tokugawa Ieyasu built palace-like Nijo Castle there in 1601–1603. He had the sliding doors painted by leading artists of the period, making the castle as elegant as the imperial palace. (From Fujioka Michio, *Genshoku Nihon no Bijutsu*, Vol. 12: Shiro to Shoin [Tokyo: Shogakkan, 1968])

Viewpoints

Chinese and Japanese Financial Advice

> • *The two passages below offer advice on how to prosper and avoid common mistakes. The first is a short passage from a longer work by a Chinese official, Zhang Ying (1638–1708), addressed to his son. The second, also from a longer work, is by his Japanese contemporary, Ihara Saikaku (1642–1693), and is aimed as much to entertain as to inform its audience.*

Zhang Ying, *On Permanent Property*

66 All worldly things that once were new will eventually age. A house that has stood for a long time will decay; clothes worn for a long time will become shabby. Cattle, slaves, and horses are costly when purchased, yet ten years later they are no longer the same, and after another ten years they do not even exist. Only land remains new through hundreds and thousands of years. Even if, due to negligence, the soil becomes barren, once fertilizer is applied, it becomes rich again. With cultivation desolate land becomes productive; with irrigation dry land becomes arable; with weeding neglected soil becomes fertile. Since time immemorial man has not had to worry about the land becoming worn out or ruined, nor about its running away or becoming scarce. Indeed, land is truly precious.

Nowadays the young heirs of large estates wear fancy clothes, ride strong horses, and seek pleasure to their hearts' content in song and dance. A fur garment easily costs scores of gold taels; a feast, several taels. The price of grain in our area has been low for the past decade so that now ten piculs of grain will barely pay for a feast and a hundred piculs will scarcely buy a fur garment; but the young heirs act ignorant of this. They do not wish to know that the peasants, bodies soaked and feet muddy, toil all year round to produce a hundred piculs of grain. 99

Ihara Saikaku, *This Scheming World*

66 When a man becomes rich, people always say he's lucky. But this is merely a conventional expression, for in reality he becomes rich and his household thrives solely on account of his own ability and foresight. Even Ebisu, the god of wealth, is unable at will to exercise power over riches.

But be that as it may, our wealthy merchants, for whom the discussion of a pending loan to a feudal lord is a far more engaging pastime than carousing or any other form of merry-making, have recently organized themselves into the Daikoku Club. Shunning a rendezvous in the red-light district, they gather in the guest room of the Buddhist temple in Shimotera, Ikutama. There they meet every month to discuss the financial condition of each individual applicant for a loan. Though they are all well along in years, they take pleasure only in ever-increasing interest and in mounting capital, utterly heedless of the life to come. Although it's quite true that there's nothing more desirable than plenty of money, the proper way for a man to get along in the world should be this: in his youth until the age of twenty-five to be ever alert, in his manly prime up to thirty-five to earn a lot of money, in the prime of discretion in his fifties to pile up his fortune, and at last in his sixties—the year before his sixty-first birthday—to turn over all his business to his eldest son. Thereafter it is proper for him to retire from active affairs and devote the remainder of his days to visiting temples for the sake of his soul. 99

Sources: Zhang Ying from Patricia Buckley Ebrey, *Chinese Civilization: A Sourcebook*, 2nd ed., Revised and Enlarged. Reprinted with the permission of The Free Press, a Division of Simon & Schuster, Inc. Copyright © 1993 by Patricia Buckley Ebrey. Copyright © 1981 by The Free Press. All rights reserved; Ihara Saikaku, *This Scheming World*, trans. Masanori Takatsuka and David C. Stubbs (Rutland, Vt.: Tuttle, 1965), p. 42. Copyright © 1965 by Charles E. Tuttle Publishing Co., Inc. Used by permission of Tuttle Publishing, a member of the Periplus Publishing Group.

QUESTIONS FOR ANALYSIS

1. How does the advice of these two authors reflect the ways one could get ahead in their respective societies?

2. Do you see any common elements in the advice offered in these two passages?

3. Do you think the difference in intended audience explains some of the differences in these two passages?

Life in the Japanese Entertainment Quarters This detail from a seventeenth-century six-panel Japanese screen depicts men and women playing instruments and enjoying games. The women are probably professional entertainers (geisha). (Courtesy, Hikone Castle Museum)

The Life of the People in the Edo Period

The Tokugawa shoguns brought an end to civil war by controlling the military. Stripped of power and required to spend alternate years at Edo, many of the daimyo and samurai passed their lives in idle pursuit of pleasure. They spent extravagantly on fine silks, paintings, concubines, boys, the theater, and the redecoration of their castles. Around 1700 one scholar observed that the entire military class was living "as in an inn, that is, consuming now and paying later."[2] Eighteenth-century Japanese novels, plays, and histories portray the samurai engrossed in tavern brawls and sexual orgies. These temptations, as well as more sophisticated pleasures and the heavy costs of maintaining alternate residences at Edo, gradually bankrupted the warrior class.

All major cities contained places of amusement for men — teahouses, theaters, restaurants, and houses of prostitution. Desperately poor parents sometimes sold their daughters to entertainment houses (as they did in China and medieval Europe), and the most attrac-

tive or talented girls, trained in singing, dancing, and conversational arts, became courtesans, later called geishas (GAY-shuhz), "accomplished persons."

Another form of entertainment in the cities was **kabuki theater**, patronized by both merchants and samurai. An art form created by townspeople, kabuki originated in crude, bawdy skits dealing with love and romance. Performances featured elaborate costumes, song, dance, and poetry. Because actresses were thought to corrupt public morals, the Tokugawa government banned them from the stage in 1629. From that time on, men played all the parts. Male actors in female dress and makeup performed as seductively as possible to entice the burly samurai who thronged the theaters. Homosexuality, long accepted in Japan, was widely practiced among the samurai, who pursued the actors and spent profligately on them. Some moralists and bureaucrats complained from time to time, but the

• **kabuki theater** A popular form of Japanese drama that brings together dialogue, dance, and music to tell stories. The actors wear colorful costumes and dramatic makeup.

◻ Picturing the Past

Interior View of a Theater Complex kabuki plays, which dealt with heroes, loyalty, and tragedy and which included music and dance, became the most popular form of entertainment in Tokugawa Japan for all classes. Movable scenery and lighting effects made possible the staging of storms, fires, and hurricanes. (Tokyo National Museum/image: TNM Image Archives)

ANALYZING THE IMAGE How many people are performing in this scene? Are there more men or women in the audience? How do you distinguish them? Are any of the men samurai?

CONNECTIONS What connections do you see between the popularity of kabuki plays and other aspects of Japanese life in this period?

Tokugawa government decided to accept kabuki and prostitution as necessary evils. The samurai paid for their costly pleasures in the way their European counterparts did — by fleecing the peasants and borrowing from the merchants.

Cities were also the center for commercial publishing. As in contemporary China, the reading public eagerly purchased fiction and the scripts for plays. Ihara Saikaku (1642–1693) wrote stories of the foibles of townspeople in such books as *Five Women Who Loved Love* and *The Life of an Amorous Man*. One of the

puppet plays of Chikamatsu Monzaemon (1653–1724) tells the story of the son of a business owner who, caught between duty to his family and love of a prostitute, decides to resolve the situation by double suicide. The art of color woodblock printing also was perfected during this period. Many of the surviving prints, made for a popular audience, depict the theater and women of the entertainment quarters.

Almost as entertaining was watching the long processions of daimyo, their retainers, and their luggage as they passed back and forth to and from Edo twice a year. The shogunate prohibited travel by commoners, but they could get passports to take pilgrimages, visit relatives, or seek the soothing waters of medicinal hot springs. Setting out on foot, groups of villagers would travel to such shrines as Ise, often taking large detours to visit Osaka or Edo to sightsee or attend the theater. Older women with daughters-in-law to run their households were among the most avid pilgrims.

According to Japanese tradition, farmers deserved respect. In practice, however, peasants were often treated callously. It was government policy to tax them to the level of bare subsistence, and official legislation repeatedly redefined their duties. In 1649 every village in Japan received these regulations:

> Peasants are people without sense or forethought. Therefore they must not give rice to their wives and children at harvest time, but must save food for the future. They should eat millet, vegetables, and other coarse food instead of rice. Even the fallen leaves of plants should be saved as food against famine. . . . During the seasons of planting and harvesting, however, when the labor is arduous, the food taken may be a little better. . . .
>
> They must not buy tea or sake to drink nor must their wives. The husband must work in the fields, the wife must work at the loom. Both must do night work. However good-looking a wife may be, if she neglects her household duties by drinking tea or sightseeing or rambling on the hillsides, she must be divorced.
>
> Peasants must wear only cotton or hemp — no silk. They may not smoke tobacco. It is harmful to health, it takes up time, and costs money. It also creates a risk of fire.[3]

During the seventeenth and eighteenth centuries the extravagant lifestyles of the daimyo and upper-level samurai were paid for by raising taxes on their subordinate peasants, from 30 or 40 percent of the rice crop to 50 percent. Not surprisingly, this angered peasants, and peasant protests became chronic during the eighteenth century. For example, oppressive taxation provoked eighty-four thousand farmers in the province of Iwaki to revolt in 1739; after widespread burning and destruction, their demands for lower taxes were met. Natural disasters also added to the peasants' misery. In 1783 Mount Asama erupted, spewing volcanic ash that darkened the skies all summer; the resulting crop failures led to famine. When famine recurred again in 1787, commoners rioted for five days in Edo, smashing merchants' stores and pouring sake and rice into the muddy streets. The shogunate responded by trying to control the floating population of day laborers without families in the city. At one point they were rounded up and transported to work the gold mines in an island off the

> "Peasants must wear only cotton or hemp — no silk. They may not smoke tobacco. It is harmful to health, it takes up time, and costs money. It also creates a risk of fire."
>
> **JAPANESE VILLAGE REGULATIONS, 1649**

north coast, where most of them died within two or three years.

This picture of peasant hardship tells only part of the story. Agricultural productivity increased substantially during the Tokugawa period. Peasants who improved their lands and increased their yields continued to pay the same assessed tax and could pocket the surplus as profit. As those without land drifted to the cities, peasants left in the countryside found ways to improve their livelihoods. At Hirano near Osaka, for example, 61.7 percent of all arable land was sown in cotton. The peasants ginned the cotton locally before transporting it to wholesalers in Osaka. In many rural places, as many peasants worked in the manufacture of silk, cotton, or vegetable oil as in the production of rice.

In comparison to farmers, merchants had a much easier life, even if they had no political power. By contemporary standards anywhere in the world, the Japanese mercantile class lived well. In 1705 the shogunate confiscated the property of a merchant in Osaka "for conduct unbecoming a member of the commercial class." In fact, the confiscation was at the urging of influential daimyo and samurai who owed the merchant gigantic debts. The government seized 50 pairs of gold screens, 360 carpets, several mansions, 48 granaries and warehouses scattered around the country, and hundreds of thousands of gold pieces. Few merchants possessed such fabulous wealth, but many lived in comfort, if not luxury.

Within a village, some families would be relatively well-off, others barely able to get by. The village headman generally came from the richest family, but he consulted a council of elders on important matters. Women in better-off families were much more likely to learn to read than women in poor families. Daughters of wealthy peasants studied penmanship, the Chinese classics, poetry, and the proper forms of correspondence, and they rounded out their education with travel. By contrast, girls from middle-level peasant families might have had from two to five years of formal schooling, but they were thought incapable of learning the difficult Chinese characters, so their education focused on moral instruction intended to instill virtue.

By the fifteenth and sixteenth centuries Japan's family and marriage systems had evolved in the

Edo Craftsmen at Work Less than 3 inches tall, the ivory figure below shows a parasol maker seated on the floor (the typical Japanese practice) eating his lunch, his tools by his side. The painting on the left shows a family of dyers, with men, women, and children all sharing the labor. (ivory: Private Collection/Photo © Boltin Picture Library; painting: Werner Forman/Art Resource, NY)

direction of a patrilocal, patriarchal system more like China's, and Japanese women had lost the prominent role in high society that they had occupied during the Heian period. It became standard for women to move into their husbands' homes, where they occupied positions subordinate to both their husbands and their mothers-in-law. In addition, elite families stopped dividing their property among all of their children; instead they retained it for the sons alone or increasingly for a single son who would continue the family line. Marriage, which now had greater consequence, also had a more public character and was marked by greater ceremony. Wedding rituals involved both the exchange of betrothal gifts and the movement of the bride from her parents' home to her husband's home. She brought with her a trousseau that provided her with clothes and other items she would need for daily life, but not with

land, which would have given her economic autonomy. On the other hand, her position within her new family was more secure, for it became more difficult for a husband to divorce his wife. She also gained authority within the family. If her husband was away, she managed family affairs. If her husband fathered children with concubines, she was their legal mother.

A peasant wife shared responsibility for the family's economic well-being with her husband. If of poor or middling status, she worked alongside her husband in the fields, doing the routine work while he did the heavy work. If they were farmhands and worked for wages, the wife invariably earned a third or a half less than her husband. Wives of prosperous farmers never worked in the fields, but they reeled silk, wove cloth, helped in any family business, and supervised the maids. When cotton growing spread to Japan in the sixteenth century, women took on the jobs of spinning and weaving it. Whatever their economic status, Japanese women, like women everywhere in the world, tended the children. Families were growing smaller in this period in response to the spread of single-heir inheritance. From studies of household registers, demographic historians have shown that Japanese families restricted the number of children they had by practicing abortion and infanticide, turning to adoption when no heir survived.

How was divorce initiated, and how frequent was it? Customs among the upper class differed considerably from peasant practices. Among the elite, the husband alone could initiate divorce; all he had to do was order his wife to leave or send her possessions to her parents' home. For the wife, divorce carried a stigma, but she could not prevent it or insist on keeping her children. Widows and divorcées of the samurai elite—where female chastity was the core of fidelity—were expected not to remarry. Among the peasant classes, by contrast, divorce seems to have been fairly common—at least 15 percent in the villages near Osaka in the eighteenth century. A poor woman wanting a divorce could simply leave her husband's home. It was also possible to secure divorce through a temple. If a married woman entered the temple and performed rites there for three years, her marriage bond was dissolved. Sometimes Buddhist temple priests served as divorce brokers: they went to the village headman and had him force the husband to agree to a divorce. News of the coming of temple officials was usually enough to produce a letter of separation.

Maritime Trade, Piracy, and the Entry of Europe into the Asian Maritime Sphere

☐ How did the sea link the countries of East Asia, and what happened when Europeans entered this maritime sphere?

In the period 1400–1800, maritime trade and piracy connected China and Japan to each other and also to Korea, Southeast Asia, and Europe. All through the period China and Japan traded extensively with each other as well as with Korea. Both Korea and Japan relied on Chinese coinage, and China relied on silver from Japan. During the fifteenth century China launched overseas expeditions. Japan was a major source of pirates. In the sixteenth century European traders appeared, eager for Chinese porcelains and silks. Christian missionaries followed, but despite initial suc-

cesses, they were later banned, first by the Japanese government and then by the Chinese government. Political changes in Europe changed the international makeup of the European traders in East Asia, with the dominant groups first the Portuguese, next the Dutch, and then the British.

Zheng He's Voyages

Early in the Ming period the Chinese government tried to revive the tribute system of the Han (202–220 C.E.) and Tang Dynasties (618–907), when China had dominated East Asia and envoys had arrived from dozens of distant lands. To invite more countries to send missions, the third Ming emperor (Chengzu or Yongle) authorized an extraordinary series of voyages to the Indian Ocean under the command of the Muslim eunuch Zheng He (1371–1433; see also the "Individuals in Society" feature on page 463).

Zheng He's father had made the trip to Mecca, and the seven voyages that Zheng led between 1405 and 1433 followed old Arab trade routes. The first of the seven was made by a fleet of 317 ships, of which 62 were huge, 440 feet long. Each expedition involved from twenty thousand to thirty-two thousand men. Their itineraries included stops in Vietnam, Malaysia, Indonesia, Sri Lanka, India, and, in the later voyages, Hormuz (on the coast of Persia) and East Africa (see Map 16.1 on page 462). At each stop Zheng He went ashore to visit rulers, transmit messages of China's peaceful intentions, and bestow lavish gifts. Rulers were invited to come to China or send envoys and were offered accommodation on the return voyages. Near the Straits of Malacca, Zheng He's fleet battled Chinese pirates, bringing them under control. Zheng He made other shows of force as well, deposing rulers deemed unacceptable in Java, Sumatra, and Sri Lanka.

On the return of these expeditions, the Ming emperor was delighted by the exotic things the fleet brought back, such as giraffes and lions from Africa, fine cotton cloth from India, and gems and spices from Southeast Asia. Ma Huan, an interpreter who accompanied Zheng He, collected data on the plants, animals, peoples, and geography that they encountered and wrote a book titled *The Overall Survey of the Ocean's Shores*. Still, these expeditions were not voyages of discovery; they followed established routes and pursued diplomatic rather than commercial goals.

Why were these voyages abandoned? Officials complained about their cost and modest returns. As a consequence, after 1474, all of the remaining ships with three or more masts were broken up and used for lumber. Chinese did not pull back from trade in the South China Sea and Indian Ocean, but the government no longer promoted trade, leaving the initiative to private merchants and migrants.

Keinen's Poetic Diary of the Korea Campaign

The Buddhist priest Keinen (1534?–1611) was ordered in 1597 to accompany the local daimyo on Hideyoshi's second campaign in Korea and spent seven months there. As a Buddhist, he did not revel in military feats but rather deplored the death and suffering that he observed. Adopting the time-honored form of the poetic diary, Keinen ends each day's entry with a short poem. The excerpt quoted here begins about six weeks after he left home.

66 Eighth month, 4th day. Every one is trying to be the first off the ship; no one wants to lag behind. They fall over each other in trying to get at the plunder, to kill people. It is a sight I cannot bear to see.

> A hubbub rises
> as from roiling clouds and mist
> where they swarm about
> in their rage for the plunder
> of innocent people's goods.

VIII.5.
They are burning the houses. As I watched them go up in smoke, I thought that my own existence was like this and was seized by sympathy.

> The "Red Country" is
> what they call it, but black is
> the smoke that rises
> from the burning houses
> where you see flames flying high.

VIII.6.
The very fields and hillsides have been put to the fire, not to speak of the forts. People are put to the sword, or they are shackled with chains and bamboo tubes choking the neck. Parents sobbing for their children, children searching for their parents—never before have I seen such a pitiable sight.

> The hills are ablaze
> with the cries of soldiers
> intoxicated
> with their pyrolatry—
> the battleground of demons.

VIII.7.
Looking at the various kinds of plunder amassed by them all, I formed a desire for such things. Could I really be like this, I thought, and felt ashamed. How can I attain salvation like this, I thought.

> How ashamed I am!
> For everything that I see
> I form desires—

a creature of delusions,
my mind full of attachments.

On the same day, as I exerted myself in reflections on my spiritual state, I felt myself more and more ashamed. And yet the Buddha has vowed not to give weight to the weightiest of evil deeds, not to abandon the most abandoned and intemperate!

> Unless it be through
> reliance on the vow of
> Amida Buddha,
> who could obtain salvation
> with such wicked thoughts as mine?

VIII.8.
They are carrying off Korean children and killing their parents. Never shall they see each other again. Their mutual cries—surely this is like the torture meted out by the fiends of hell.

> It is piteous;
> when the four fledglings parted,*
> it must have been thus—
> I see the parents' lament
> over their sobbing children.

VIII.11.
As night fell, I saw people's houses go up in smoke. They have lost everything to the fire, all their grain and all their property.

> How wretched it is!
> Smoke lingers still where the grain
> was burned and wasted;
> so that is where I lay my
> head tonight: on the scorched earth.

VIII.13.
His lordship has set up camp about five leagues this side of Namwon. Unless this fortress is taken, our prospects are dubious; so we are to close in and invest it this evening. The word is that fifty or sixty thousand soldiers from Great Ming are garrisoning the place.

> We'll solve the challenge
> posed even by this fortress
> of the Red Country!—
> The troops rejoice to hear this,
> and they rest their weary feet.

*An allusion to the proverbial tale of a mother bird's sorrow at her fledglings' departure to the four directions.

VIII.14.

Rain has been falling steadily since the evening. It comes down in sheets, like a waterfall. We have put up a makeshift tent covered with oil paper only, and it is frightening how the rain pours in. It is impossible to sleep. I had to think of the story "The Devil at One Gulp" in *Tales of Ise*.† The night described in that tale must have been just like this.

> Inexorably,
> fearsome torrents beating down
> remind me of that
> dreadful night when the devil
> at one gulp ate his victim.

VIII.15.

The fortress is to be stormed before dawn tomorrow. Fascines of bamboo have been distributed to the assault troops. The sun was about to set as they worked their way close in, right up against the edge of the castle's bulwarks, and gunfire opened up from the several siege detachments, accompanied by arrows shot from short-bows. Unthinkable numbers of men were killed. As I saw them dying:

> From the fortress, too,
> from their short-bows, too.
> How many killed? Beyond count
> is the number of the dead.

The castle fell to the assault in the course of the night. Lord Hishu's troops were the first inside the walls. Needless to say, he is to get a vermilion-seal letter of commendation.

VIII.16.

All in the fortress were slaughtered, to the last man and woman. No prisoners were taken. To be sure, a few were kept alive for exchange purposes.

> How cruel! This world
> of sorrow and inconstancy
> does have one constant—
> men and women, young and old
> die and vanish; are no more.

VIII.17.

Until yesterday they did not know that they would have to die; today, they are transformed into the smoke of impermanence, as is the way of this world of constant change. How can I be unaffected by this!

> Look! Everyone, look!
> Is this, then, to be called the human condition?—
> a life with a deadline,
> a life with a limit: today. "

†This is a story of an abduction that ends badly. The lady in question, sequestered in a broken-down storehouse to keep her safe from the elements on a dark and stormy night, is devoured "at one gulp" by an ogre who dwells there.

● Although the Japanese invasion failed, some of the warriors who fought in it were celebrated, like Kato Kiyomasa, shown here fighting a tiger in the hills of Korea. (Courtesy, Stephen Turnbull)

Source: *Sources of Japanese Tradition*, by Wm. Theodore de Bary, Donald Keene, George Tanabe, and Paul Varley. Copyright © 2001 by Columbia University Press. Reproduced with permission of the publisher.

QUESTIONS FOR ANALYSIS

1. Buddhism teaches the impermanence of phenomena, the need to let go of attachments, and it opposes the taking of life. Can any of Keinen's responses be identified as specifically Buddhist?

2. Does Keinen's use of poetry seem natural, or do you think it seems forced?

3. What would be the purpose of bringing a Buddhist priest opposed to killing on a military campaign?

Piracy and Japan's Overseas Adventures

One goal of Zheng He's expeditions was to suppress piracy, which had become a problem all along the China coast. Already in the thirteenth century social disorder and banditry in Japan had expanded into seaborne banditry, some of it within the Japanese islands around the Inland Sea (Map 21.3), but also in the straits between Korea and Japan. Japanese "sea bandits" would raid the Korean coast, seizing rice and other goods to take home. In the sixteenth century bands several hundred strong would attack and loot Chinese coastal cities or hold them hostage for ransom. As maritime trade throughout East Asia grew more lively, sea bandits also took to attacking ships to steal their cargo. Although the pirates were called the "Japanese pirates" by both the Koreans and the Chinese, pirate gangs in fact recruited from all countries. The Ryūkyū (ryoo-kyoo) Islands and Taiwan became major bases.

Possibly encouraged by the exploits of these bandits, Hideyoshi, after his victories in unifying Japan, decided to extend his territory across the seas. In 1590, after receiving congratulations from Korea on his victories, Hideyoshi sent a letter asking the Koreans to allow his armies to pass through their country, declaring that his real target was China: "Disregarding the distance of the sea and mountain reaches that lie in between, I shall in one fell swoop invade Great Ming. I have in mind to introduce Japanese customs and values to the four hundred and more provinces of that country and bestow upon it the benefits of imperial rule and culture for the coming hundred million years."[4] He also sent demands for submission to countries of Southeast Asia and to the Spanish governor of the Philippines.

In 1592 Hideyoshi mobilized 158,000 soldiers and 9,200 sailors for his invasion, and equipped them with muskets and cannon, which had recently been introduced into Japan. His forces overwhelmed Korean defenders and reached Seoul within three weeks and Pyongyang in two months. A few months later, in the middle of winter, Chinese armies arrived to help defend Korea, and Japanese forces were pushed back

MAP 21.3 East Asia, ca. 1600 Pirates and traders often plied the same waters as seaborne trade grew in the sixteenth century. The Portuguese were especially active in setting up trading ports.

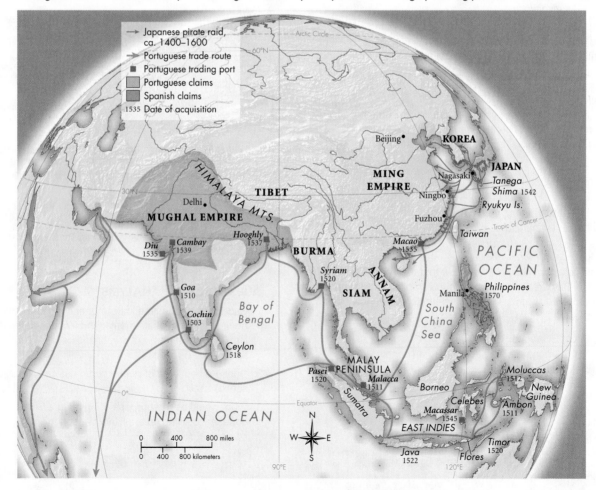

from Pyongyang. A stalemate lasted till 1597; when Hideyoshi sent new troops. This time the Ming army and the Korean navy were more successful in resisting the Japanese. For years the Korean navy had to defend against Japanese pirates, and it was able to keep the Japanese from supplying or reinforcing their troops. In 1598, after Hideyoshi's death, the Japanese army withdrew, but Korea was left devastated. (See "Listening to the Past: Keinen's Poetic Diary of the Korea Campaign," page 640.)

After recovering from the setbacks of these invasions, Korea began to advance socially and economically. During the Choson Dynasty (1392–1910), the Korean elite (the yangban) turned away from Buddhism and toward strict Neo-Confucian orthodoxy. As agricultural productivity improved, the population grew from about 4.4 million in 1400, to about 8 million in 1600, 10 million in 1700, and 14 million in 1810 (or about half as big as Japan's population and one-twentieth as big as China's). With economic advances slavery declined. When slaves ran away, landowners found that it was less expensive to replace them with sharecroppers than to recapture them. Between 1750 and 1790 the

> **❝**I have in mind to introduce Japanese customs and values to the four hundred and more provinces of that country [China] and bestow upon it the benefits of imperial rule and culture for the coming hundred million years.**❞**
>
> **HIDEYOSHI**

slave population dropped from 30 percent to 5 percent of the population. The hold of the yangban elite, however, remained strong. Through the eighteenth century about two dozen yangban families dominated the civil service examinations, leaving relatively few slots for commoners to rise to through study.

Europeans Enter the Scene

In the sixteenth century Portuguese, Spanish, and Dutch merchants and adventurers began to participate in the East Asian maritime world. The trade between Japan, China, and Southeast Asia was very profitable,

Dutch in Japan The Japanese were curious about the appearance, dress, and habits of the Dutch who came to the enclave of Deshima to trade. In this detail from a long hand scroll, Dutch traders are shown interacting with a Japanese samurai in a room with Japanese tatami mats on the floor. Note also the Western musical instruments. (Private Collection/The Bridgeman Art Library)

and the European traders wanted a share of it. They also wanted to develop trade between Asia and Europe.

The Portuguese and Dutch were not reluctant to use force to gain control of trade, and they seized many outposts along the trade routes, including Taiwan. Moreover, they made little distinction between trade, smuggling, and piracy. In 1521 the Ming tried to ban the Portuguese from China. Two years later an expeditionary force commissioned by the Portuguese king to negotiate a friendship treaty defeated its mission by

Missionary Publication To appeal to a Chinese audience, the Jesuits illustrated some of their publications in a distinctly Chinese style. This book illustration shows Mary during the annunciation in a Chinese-style room with a Chinese landscape painting on the wall, and the descent from Heaven of the angel Gabriel signaled in Chinese fashion by stylized clouds. (Courtesy, Archivum Romanum Societatis Iesu [ARSI], Rome)

firing on Chinese warships near Guangzhou. In 1557, without informing Beijing, local Chinese officials decided that the way to regulate trade was to allow the Portuguese to build a trading post on uninhabited land near the mouth of the Pearl River. The city they built there — Macao — became the first destination for Europeans going to China until the nineteenth century, and it remained a Portuguese possession until 1999.

European products were not in demand in China, but silver was. Japan had supplied much of China's silver, but with the development of silver mines in the New World, European traders began supplying large quantities of silver to China, allowing the expansion of China's economy.

Chinese were quick to take advantage of the new trading ports set up by European powers. In Batavia harbor (now Jakarta, Indonesia) Chinese ships outnumbered those from any other country by two or three to one. Manila, under Spanish control, and Taiwan and Batavia, both under Dutch control, all attracted thousands of Chinese colonists. Local people felt the intrusion of Chinese more than of Europeans, and riots against Chinese led to massacres on several occasions.

A side benefit of the appearance of European traders was New World crops. Sweet potatoes, maize, peanuts, tomatoes, chili peppers, tobacco, and other crops were quickly adopted in East Asia. Sweet potatoes and maize in particular facilitated population growth because they could be grown on land previously thought too sandy or too steep to cultivate. Sweet potatoes became a common poor people's food.

Christian Missionaries

The Spanish and Portuguese kings supported missionary activity, and merchant vessels soon brought Catholic missionaries to East Asia. The first to come were Jesuits, from the order founded by Ignatius Loyola in 1534 to promote Catholic scholarship and combat the Protestant Reformation.

The Jesuit priest Francis Xavier had worked in India and the Indies before China and Japan attracted his attention. In 1549, after many misadventures, he landed on Kyushu, Japan's southernmost island (see Map 21.2). After he was expelled by the local lord, he traveled throughout western Japan as far as Kyoto, proselytizing wherever warlords allowed. He soon made many converts among the poor and even some among the daimyo. Xavier then set his sights on China but died on an uninhabited island off the China coast in 1552.

Other missionaries carried on his work, and by 1600 there were three hundred thousand baptized Christians in Japan. Most of them lived on Kyushu, where the shogun's power was weakest and the loyalty of the daimyo most doubtful. In 1615 bands of Christian samurai supported Tokugawa Ieyasu's enemies at the fierce Battle of Osaka. A couple of decades later, thirty thousand peasants in the heavily Catholic area of northern Kyushu revolted. The Tokugawa shoguns thus came to associate Christianity with domestic disorder and insurrection. Accordingly, what had been mild persecution of Christians became ruthless repression after 1639. Foreign priests were expelled or tortured, and thousands of Japanese Christians suffered crucifixion.

Meanwhile, in China the Jesuits concentrated on gaining the linguistic and scholarly knowledge they would need to convert the educated class. The Jesuit Matteo Ricci studied for years in Macao before setting himself up in Nanjing and trying to win over members of the educated class. In 1601 he was given permission to reside in Beijing, where he made several high-placed conversions. He also interested educated Chinese men in Western geography, astronomy, and Euclidean mathematics.

Ricci and his Jesuit successors believed that Confucianism was compatible with Christianity. Both shared similar concerns for morality and virtue, and they viewed making food offerings to ancestors as an expression of filial reverence rather than as a form of worship. The Franciscan and Dominican mendicant orders that arrived in China in the seventeenth century disagreed with the Jesuit position. In 1715 religious and political quarrels in Europe led the pope to decide that the Jesuits' accommodating approach was heretical. Angry at this insult, the Kangxi emperor forbade all Christian missionary work in China.

Porcelain Vase Among the objects produced in China that were in high demand in Europe in the seventeenth and eighteenth centuries were colorful porcelains. In this period Chinese potters perfected the use of overglaze enamels, which allowed the application of many colors to a single object. Blue, green, yellow, orange, and red all appear on this 18-inch-tall (45.7 cm) vase. (Image copyright © The Metropolitan Museum/Art Resource, NY)

Learning from the West

Although both China and Japan ended up prohibiting Christian missionary work, other aspects of Western culture were seen as impressive and worth learning. The closed-country policy that Japan instituted in 1639 restricted Japanese from leaving the country and kept European merchants in small enclaves. Still, Japanese interest in Europe did not disappear. Through the Dutch enclave of Deshima on a tiny island in Nagasaki harbor, a stream of Western ideas and inventions trickled into Japan in the eighteenth century. Western writings, architectural illustrations, calendars, watches, medicine, weapons, and paintings deeply impressed the Japanese. Western portraits and other paintings introduced the Japanese to perspective, shading, and other strategies for bringing more realism to art.

In China, too, both scholars and rulers showed an interest in Western learning. The Kangxi emperor frequently discussed scientific and philosophical questions with the Jesuits at court. When he got malaria, he accepted the Jesuits' offer of the medicine quinine. In addition, he had translations made of a collection of Western works on mathematics and the calendar. The court was impressed with the Jesuits' skill in astronomy and quickly appointed them to the Board of Astronomy. In 1674 the emperor asked them to re-equip the observatory with European instruments. In the visual arts the emperor and his successors employed Italian painters to make imperial portraits. Qianlong also took a fancy to European-style gardens and palaces. Firearms and mechanical clocks also were widely admired. The court established its own clock and watch factory, and in 1673 the emperor insisted that the Jesuits manufacture cannon for him and supervise gunnery practice.

Admiration was not one-sided. In the early eighteenth century China enjoyed a positive reputation in Europe. Voltaire wrote of the rationalism of Confucianism and saw advantages to the Chinese political system because the rulers did not put up with parasitical aristocrats or hypocritical priests. Chinese medical practice also drew

European interest. One Chinese practice that Europeans adopted was "variolation," an early form of smallpox inoculation.

The Shifting International Environment in the Eighteenth Century

The East Asian maritime world underwent many changes from the sixteenth to the eighteenth centuries. As already noted, the Japanese pulled back their own traders and limited opportunities for Europeans to trade in Japan. In China the Qing government limited trading contacts with Europe to Guangzhou in the far south in an attempt to curb piracy. Portugal lost many of its bases to the Dutch, and by the eighteenth century the British had become as active as the Dutch. In the seventeenth century the British and Dutch sought primarily porcelains and silk, but in the eighteenth century tea became the commodity in most demand. By the end of the century tea made up 80 percent of Chinese exports to Europe.

By the late eighteenth century Britain had become a great power and did not see why China should be able to dictate the terms of trade. Wanting to renegotiate its relations with China, in the 1790s King George III sent Lord George Macartney on a mission there. Macartney was instructed to secure a place for British traders to live near the tea-producing areas, negotiate a commercial treaty, create a desire for British products, arrange

for diplomatic representation in Beijing, and open Japan and Southeast Asia to British commerce. He traveled with an eighty-four-person entourage and six hundred cases packed with British goods that he hoped would impress the Chinese court and attract trade: clocks, telescopes, knives, globes, plate glass, Wedgwood pottery, landscape paintings, woolen cloth, and carpets. The only member of the British party able to speak Chinese, however, was a twelve-year-old boy who had learned a bit of the language by talking with Chinese passengers on the long voyage.

After Lord Macartney arrived in Guangzhou in 1793, he proceeded overland. Because he would not perform the **kowtow** (kneeling on both knees and bowing his head to the ground), he was denied a formal audience in the palace. He was permitted to meet more informally with the Qianlong emperor at his summer retreat, but no negotiations followed this meeting because Qianlong saw no merit in Macartney's requests. As he pointed out in his formal reply, the Qing Empire "possesses all things in prolific abundance and lacks no product within its own borders"; thus trading with Europe was a kindness, not a necessity.[5] The Qing court was as intent on maintaining the existing system of regulated trade as Britain was intent on doing away with it.

Several members of the Macartney mission wrote books about China on their return, updating European understanding of China. These books, often illustrated, described many elements of Chinese culture and social customs — accounts less rosy than the reports written by the Jesuits a century or two earlier. The British writers, for instance, introduced the idea that Chinese women were oppressed, unable even to sit at the same table with their husbands to eat dinner.

• **kowtow** The ritual of kneeling on both knees and bowing one's head to the ground performed by children to their parents and by subjects to the Chinese ruler.

CONNECTIONS

During the four centuries from 1400 to 1800, the countries of East Asia became increasingly connected. On the oceans trade and piracy linked them, and for the first time a war involved all three East Asian countries. In all three this was a time of economic advance. At the same time, their cultures and social structures were in no sense converging. The elites of the three countries were very different: in both Korea and Japan elite status was hereditary, while in China the key route to status and power involved doing well on a written examination. In Japan the samurai elite were expected to be skilled warriors, but in China and Korea the highest prestige went to men of letters. The Japanese woodblock prints that capture many features of the entertainment quarters in Japanese cities show a world distinct from anything in China and Korea.

By the end of this period, East Asian countries found themselves in a rapidly changing international environment, mostly because of revolutions occurring far from their shores. The next two chapters take up the story of these revolutions, first the political ones in America, France, and Haiti, and then the Industrial Revolution that began in Britain. In time these revolutions would profoundly alter East Asia as well.

◻ CHAPTER REVIEW

◻ **What sort of state and society developed in China after the Mongols were ousted?** (p. 618)

After the fall of the Mongols, China was ruled by the native Ming Dynasty for nearly three centuries. The dynasty's founder, who knew poverty firsthand, ruled for thirty years, becoming more paranoid and despotic over time. Very few of his successors were particularly good rulers, yet China thrived in many ways. Population grew as food production increased. Educational levels were high as more and more men prepared for the civil service examinations. Urban culture was lively, and publishing houses put out novels, short stories, and plays in the vernacular language for large audiences.

◻ **Did the return of alien rule with the Manchus have any positive consequences for China?** (p. 626)

The Ming suffered a series of disasters, beginning with a Japanese invasion of Korea at the end of the sixteenth century, and in 1644 the dynasty fell to a force from beyond the Great Wall, the Manchus. The Manchu rulers proved more competent than the Ming emperors and were able to both maintain peace and expand the empire to its maximum extent, bringing in Mongolia, Tibet, and Central Asia. Population grew steadily under Manchu rule, probably reaching around 300 million.

◻ **How did Japan change during this period of political instability?** (p. 629)

During the fifteenth and sixteenth centuries Japan was fragmented by civil war. New power holders emerged in the daimyo, who built stone castles to defend their territories. As daimyo attacked and defeated each other, power was gradually consolidated, until Hideyoshi gained control of most of the country. Japan also saw many cultural developments during this period, including the increasing influence of Zen ideas on the arts and the rise of Nō theater.

◻ **What was life like in Japan during the Tokugawa peace?** (p. 631)

After Hideyoshi's death, power was seized by Tokugawa Ieyasu, the founder of the Tokugawa Shogunate. In this shogunate's first two centuries (the seventeenth and eighteenth centuries), Japan reaped the rewards of peace. Steady economic growth and increased agri-

KEY TERMS

Ming Dynasty (p. 619)
civil service
  examinations
  (p. 621)
Qing Dynasty (p. 626)
banners (p. 626)
Nō theater (p. 629)

daimyo (p. 630)
Tokugawa Shogunate
  (p. 631)
alternate residence
  system (p. 631)
kabuki theater (p. 635)
kowtow (p. 646)

cultural productivity swelled the population to approximately 30 million. But as the wealth of the business classes grew, the samurai, now dependent on fixed stipends, became progressively poorer. Samurai and others in search of work and pleasure fled to cities, where amusements of many kinds flourished.

◻ **How did the sea link the countries of East Asia, and what happened when Europeans entered this maritime sphere?** (p. 639)

Between 1400 and 1800 maritime trade connected the countries of Asia, in particular China and Japan. Piracy was a perpetual problem. Early in this period China sent out seven naval expeditions looking to promote diplomatic contacts, and these went as far as Africa. In the sixteenth century European traders arrived in China and Japan. The first European traders often acted like pirates, but profitable trading relationships soon developed. The Chinese economy became so dependent on huge imports of silver acquired through this trade that when supplies were cut off, it caused severe hardship. Trade with Europe also brought New World crops and new ideas. The Catholic missionaries who began to arrive in Asia introduced Western science and learning as well as Christianity, until they were banned in both Japan and China. Although the shogunate severely restricted trade, some Western scientific ideas and technology entered Japan through the port of Nagasaki. Chinese, too, took an interest in those elements of Western technology and science that seemed advanced, such as firearms, clockwork, astronomy, and oil painting. Because Europeans saw much to admire in East Asia in this period, ideas also flowed from East to West.

SUGGESTED READING

Berry, Mary Elizabeth. *The Culture of Civil War in Kyoto*. 1994. Uses diaries and other records to examine how people made sense of violence and social change.

Crossley, Pamela. *The Manchus*. 2002. A lively account that lets one think about Qing history from the rulers' point of view.

Elman, Benjamin. *A Cultural History of Civil Examinations in Late Imperial China.* 2000. Provides fascinating detail on how the examination system worked.

Elvin, Mark. *The Pattern of the Chinese Past.* 1973. Offers an explanation of China's failure to maintain its technological superiority in terms of a "high-level equilibrium trap."

Handley, Susan B. *Everyday Things in Premodern Japan.* 1999. Shows that the standard of living during the Edo period was comparable to that in the West at the same time.

Hegel, Robert E., trans. *True Crimes in Eighteenth-Century China: Twenty Case Histories.* 2009. Describes various crimes (including neighborhood feuds, murder, and sedition) and how the Chinese government dealt with them at several levels.

Keene, Donald. *Yoshimasa and the Silver Pavilion: The Creation of the Soul of Japan.* 2003. A lively introduction to the aesthetic style associated with Zen and its connection to shogunate patrons.

Mann, Susan. *Precious Records: Women in China's Long Eighteenth Century.* 1997. A well-written analysis of women's lives in the educated class.

McDermott, Joseph. *A Social History of the Chinese Book: Books and Literati Culture in Late Imperial China.* 2006. Places Chinese printing in a comparative perspective.

Mote, Frederic. *Imperial China.* 1999. An overview that analyzes the strengths and weaknesses of both the Ming and Qing Dynasties.

Mungello, David. *The Great Encounter of China and the West, 1500–1800.* 1999. A short but stimulating examination of the various dimensions of the first phase of Chinese-European relations.

Pomeranz, Kenneth. *The Great Divergence: China, Europe, and the Making of the Modern World Economy.* 2000. Argues that the most advanced areas of China were on a par with the most advanced regions of Europe through the eighteenth century.

Rowe, William T. *China's Last Empire: The Great Qing.* 2009. An up-to-date and thoughtful narrative of the Manchu rulers and the empire over which they presided.

Totman, Conrad. *A History of Japan.* 2000. An excellent, well-balanced survey.

Vaporis, Constantine Komitos. *Breaking Barriers: Travel and the State in Early Modern Japan.* 1994. An examination of recreational and religious travel.

Waldron, Arthur. *The Great Wall of China: From History to Myth.* 1990. Places the construction of the current Great Wall in the context of Ming-Mongol relations.

NOTES

1. L. J. Gallagher, trans., *China in the Sixteenth Century: The Journals of Matthew Ricci: 1583–1610* (New York: Random House, 1953), p. 23.
2. Quoted in D. H. Shively, "Bakufu Versus Kabuki," in *Studies in the Institutional History of Early Modern Japan,* ed. J. W. Hall (Princeton, N.J.: Princeton University Press, 1970), p. 236.
3. Quoted in G. B. Sansom, *A History of Japan, 1615–1867,* vol. 3 (Stanford, Calif.: Stanford University Press, 1978), p. 99.
4. W. T. de Bary et al., eds., *Sources of Japanese Tradition from Earliest Times to 1600* (New York: Columbia University Press, 2001), p. 467.
5. Pei-kai Cheng and M. Lestz, with J. Spence, ed., *The Search for Modern China: A Documentary History* (New York: W.W. Norton, 1999), p. 106.

For practice quizzes and other study tools, visit the **Online Study Guide** at bedfordstmartins.com/mckayworld.

For primary sources from this period, see *Sources of World Societies*, **Second Edition**.

For Web sites, images, and documents related to topics in this chapter, visit **Make History** at bedfordstmartins.com/mckayworld.

• **Liberty** The figure of Liberty bears a copy of the Declaration of the Rights of Man and of the Citizen in one hand and a pike to defend them in the other in this painting by the female artist Nanine Vallain. The painting hung in France's Jacobin club until its fall from power. (Nanine Vallain, *La Liberté*, oil on canvas, 1794/Musée de la revolution française de Vizille, © Conseil général de l'Isère/Domaine de Vizille)

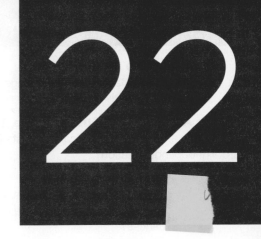

A great wave of revolution rocked the Atlantic world in the last decades of the eighteenth century. As trade goods, individuals, and ideas circulated in ever greater numbers across the Atlantic Ocean, debates and events in one locale soon influenced those in another. Enlightenment ideals of freedom and equality flourished, inspiring reformers in many places to demand an end to the old ways. At the same time, wars fought for dominance of the Atlantic economy left European governments weakened by crushing debts, making them vulnerable to calls for reform.

Revolutions in the Atlantic World 1775–1815

The revolutionary era began in North America in 1775. Then in 1789 France became the leading revolutionary nation. It established first a constitutional monarchy, then a radical republic, and finally a new empire under Napoleon that would last until 1815. During this period of constant domestic turmoil, French armies violently exported revolution throughout much of Europe. Inspired both by the ideals of the revolution on the continent and by internal colonial conditions, the slaves in the French colony of Saint-Domingue rose up in 1791. Their rebellion would eventually lead to the creation of the independent nation of Haiti in 1804. The relationship between Europe and its colonies was fundamentally altered by this wave of revolution and by subsequent independence movements in Spanish North America. In Europe and its colonies abroad, the world of modern politics was born. •

Background to Revolution

☐ What were the factors behind the age of revolution in the Atlantic world?

The American Revolutionary Era, 1775–1789

☐ Why and how did American colonists forge a new, independent nation?

Revolution in France, 1789-1791

☐ How did the events of 1789 result in a constitutional monarchy in France, and what were the consequences?

World War and Republican France, 1791–1799

☐ Why and how did the French Revolution take a radical turn entailing terror at home and war with European powers?

Napoleon's Europe, 1799–1815

☐ Why did Napoleon Bonaparte assume control of France and much of Europe, and what factors led to his downfall?

The Haitian Revolution, 1791–1804

☐ How did slave revolt on colonial Saint-Domingue lead to the creation of the independent state of Haiti in 1804?

The Three Estates French inhabitants were legally divided into three orders, or estates: the clergy, the nobility, and everyone else. In this political cartoon from 1789 a peasant of the third estate struggles under the weight of a happy clergyman and a plumed nobleman. The caption—"Let's hope this game ends soon"—sets forth a program of reform that any peasant could understand. (Réunion des Musées Nationaux/Art Resource, NY)

Background to Revolution

☐ What were the factors behind the age of revolution in the Atlantic world?

The origins of the revolutions in the Atlantic world were complex. No one cause lay behind them, nor was revolution inevitable or foreordained. However, certain important factors helped set the stage for reform. Among them were fundamental social and economic changes and political crises that eroded state authority. Another significant cause of revolutionary fervor was the impact of political ideas derived from the Enlightenment. Even though major intellectuals of the Enlightenment, the philosophes, were usually cautious about political reform themselves, the confidence in reason and progress that they fostered helped inspire a new generation to fight for greater freedom from repressive governments. Perhaps most important, financial crises generated by war expenses brought European states to their knees and allowed abstract discussions of reform to become pressing realities.

Social Change

Eighteenth-century European society was still legally divided into groups with special privileges, such as the nobility and the clergy, and groups with special burdens, such as the peasantry. Nobles in France enjoyed not only exemption from taxation but also exclusive rights to hunt game, bear swords, and wear gold ribbon in their clothing. In most countries, various middle-class groups—professionals, merchants, and guild masters—enjoyed privileges that allowed them to monopolize all sorts of economic activity.

Traditional privileges persisted in societies undergoing dramatic and destabilizing change. Due to increased agricultural production, Europe's population rose rapidly after 1750, and its cities and towns swelled in size. Inflation kept pace with demography, making it ever more difficult for urban people to find affordable food and living space. One way they kept up, and even managed to participate in the new consumer revolution (see pages 545–547), was by working harder and for longer hours. More women and children entered the paid labor force. In another change, men and women in jostling European cities were freer from the constraints of village life, and the rate of illegitimate births soared. A more positive development was increased schooling and a rise in literacy rates, particularly among urban men.

The growth of the economy created new inequalities between rich and poor. While the poor struggled with rising prices, investors who sponsored overseas trade or the spread of manufacture in the countryside reaped great profits. Old distinctions between landed aristocracy and city merchant began to fade as enterprising nobles put money into trade and rising middle-class bureaucrats and merchants bought landed estates and noble titles. Marriages between proud nobles and wealthy, educated commoners (often called the *bourgeoisie* [boorzh-wah-ZEE] in France) served both groups' interests, and a mixed-caste elite began to take shape. In the context of these changes, ancient privileges seemed to pose an intolerable burden to many observers.

Another social change involved the racial regimes established in European colonies to enable and protect slavery. By the late eighteenth century European law accepted that only Africans and people of African descent were subject to slavery. Even free people of color — a term for non-slaves of African or mixed African-European descent — were subject to special laws restricting the property they could own, whom they could marry, and what clothes they could wear. Racial privilege conferred a new dimension of entitlement on European settlers in the colonies, and they used extremely brutal methods to enforce it. The contradiction between slavery and the Enlightenment ideals of liberty and equality was all too evident to slaves and free people of color.

Growing Demands for Liberty and Equality

In addition to destabilizing social changes, the ideals of liberty and equality helped fuel revolutions in the Atlantic world. What did these concepts mean to eighteenth-century politicians and other people, and why were they so radical and revolutionary in their day?

The call for liberty was first of all a call for individual human rights. Before the revolutionary period, even the most enlightened monarchs believed they needed to regulate what people wrote and believed. Opposing this long-standing practice, supporters of the cause of individual liberty (who became known as "liberals" in the early nineteenth century) demanded freedom to worship according to the dictates of their consciences, an end to censorship, and freedom from arbitrary laws and from judges who simply obeyed orders from the government. The Declaration of the Rights of Man and of the Citizen, issued at the beginning of the French Revolution, proclaimed that "Liberty consists in being able to do anything that does not harm another person." In the context of the monarchical and absolutist forms of government then dominating Europe, this was a truly radical idea.

The call for liberty was also a call for a new kind of government. Reformers believed that the people had sovereignty — that is, that the people alone had the

> "Liberty consists in being able to do anything that does not harm another person."
>
> **DECLARATION OF THE RIGHTS OF MAN**

authority to make laws limiting an individual's freedom of action. In practice, this system of government meant choosing legislators who represented the people and were accountable to them. Monarchs might retain their thrones, but their rule should be constrained by the will of the people.

Equality was a more ambiguous idea. Eighteenth-century liberals argued that, in theory, all citizens should have identical rights and liberties and that the nobility had no right to special privileges based on birth. However, they accepted a number of distinctions. First, most eighteenth-century liberals were men of their times, and they generally believed that equality between men and women was neither practical nor desirable. Women played an important political role in the French Revolution at several points, but the men of the French Revolution limited formal political rights — the right to vote, to run for office, to participate in government — to men. Second, few questioned the inequality between blacks and whites. Even those who believed that the slave trade was unjust and should be abolished, such as Thomas Jefferson, usually felt that abolition was so socially and economically dangerous that it needed to be indefinitely postponed.

Finally, liberals never believed that everyone should be equal economically. Although Jefferson wrote in an early draft of the American Declaration of Independence that everyone was equal in "the pursuit of property," liberals certainly did not expect equal success in that pursuit. (Jefferson later changed "property" to the more noble-sounding "happiness.") Great differences in wealth and income between rich and poor were perfectly acceptable. The essential point was that every free male should have a legally equal chance at economic gain. However limited they appear to modern eyes, these demands for liberty and equality were revolutionary, given that a privileged elite had long existed with little opposition.

The two most important thinkers to use Enlightenment goals of personal freedom and legal equality to justify liberal self-government were John Locke and the baron de Montesquieu. Locke maintained that England's long political tradition rested on "the rights of Englishmen" and on representative government through Parliament. He argued that if a government oversteps its proper function of protecting the natural rights of life, liberty, and private property, it becomes a tyranny. Montesquieu was also inspired by English constitutional history and the Glorious Revolution, which placed sovereignty in Parliament (see pages 510–515). He, too, believed that powerful "intermediary groups" — such as the judicial nobility of which he

was a proud member — offered the best defense of liberty against despotism.

The belief that representative institutions could defend their liberty and interests appealed powerfully to the bourgeoisie. Yet liberal ideas about individual rights and political freedom also appealed to members of the hereditary nobility, at least in western Europe and as formulated by Montesquieu. Representative government did not mean democracy, which liberal thinkers tended to equate with mob rule. Rather, they envisioned voting for representatives as being restricted to men who owned property — those with "a stake in society." The blurring of practical distinctions between landed aristocrats and wealthy commoners meant that there was no clear-cut opposition between nobles and non-nobles on political issues. The poor themselves usually had little time to plan for reform, given the challenges of earning their daily bread.

Revolutions thus began with aspirations for equality and liberty among the social elite. Soon, however, dissenting voices emerged as some revolutionaries became frustrated with the limitations of classical liberal notions of equality and liberty and clamored for a fuller realization of these concepts. Depending on location, their demands included political rights for women and free people of color, the emancipation of slaves, and government regulation to guarantee fair access to resources and to impose economic equality. The age of revolution was thus characterized as much by conflicts over how far reform should go as by the arguments for change that launched this age in the first place.

The Seven Years' War

The roots of revolutionary ideology could be found in the writings of Locke or Montesquieu, but it was by no means inevitable that their ideas would result in revolution. Many members of the educated elite were satisfied with the status quo or too intimidated to challenge it. Instead, events — political, economic, and military — created crises that opened the door for radical action. One of the most important was the global conflict known as the Seven Years' War (1756–1763).

The war's battlefields stretched from central Europe to India to North America (where the conflict was known as the French and Indian War), pitting a new alliance of England and Prussia against the French and Austrians. Its origins were in conflicts left unresolved at the end of the War of the Austrian Succession in 1748 (see pages 502–503). In central Europe, Austria's Maria Theresa vowed to win back Silesia, which Prussia took in the war of succession, and to crush Prussia, thereby re-establishing the Habsburgs' traditional leadership in German affairs. By the end of the Seven Years' War Maria Theresa had almost succeeded, but Prussia survived with its boundaries intact.

• **Treaty of Paris** The 1763 peace treaty that ended the Seven Years' War, according vast French territories in North America and India to Britain and Louisiana to Spain.

Unresolved tensions also lingered in North America, particularly regarding the border between the French and British colonies. The encroachment of English settlers into territory claimed by the French in the Ohio Valley resulted in skirmishes that soon became war. Although the inhabitants of New France were greatly outnumbered — Canada counted fifty-five thousand inhabitants, compared to 1.2 million in the thirteen English colonies — French forces achieved major victories until 1758. Then, the British diverted resources from the war in Europe, using superior sea power to destroy the French fleet and choke off French commerce around the world. In 1759 the British laid siege to Quebec for four long months, finally defeating the French in a battle that sealed the fate of France in North America.

British victory on all colonial fronts was ratified in the 1763 **Treaty of Paris**. Canada and all French territory east of the Mississippi River passed to Britain, and France ceded Louisiana to Spain as compensation for Spain's loss of Florida to Britain. France also gave up most of its holdings in India, opening the way to British dominance on the subcontinent (Map 22.1).

By 1763 Britain had realized its goal of monopolizing a vast trading and colonial empire, but at a tremendous cost in war debt. France emerged from the conflict humiliated and broke, but with its profitable Caribbean colonies intact. In the aftermath of war, both British and French governments had to raise taxes to repay loans, raising a storm of protest and demands for fundamental reform. Since the Caribbean colony of Saint-Domingue remained French, revolutionary turmoil in

MAP 22.1 European Claims in North America and India Before and After the Seven Years' War, 1755–1763 As a result of the war, France lost its vast territories in North America and India. In an effort to avoid costly conflicts with Native Americans living in the newly conquered territory, the British government in 1763 prohibited colonists from settling west of the Appalachian Mountains. One of the few remaining French colonies in the Americas, Saint-Domingue (on the island of Hispaniola) was the most profitable plantation in the New World.

the mother country would directly affect its population. The seeds of revolutionary conflict in the Atlantic world were thus sown.

The American Revolutionary Era, 1775–1789

☐ Why and how did American colonists forge a new, independent nation?

Increased taxes were one factor behind colonial protests in the New World, where the era of liberal political revolution began. After revolting against their home country, the thirteen mainland colonies of British North America succeeded in establishing a new unified government. Participants in the revolution believed they were demanding only the traditional rights of English men and women. But those traditional rights were liberal rights, and in the American context they had very strong democratic and popular overtones. Thus the American Revolution was fought in the name of ideals that were still quite radical for their time. In founding a government firmly based on liberal principles, the Americans set an example that would have a forceful impact on France and its colonies.

The Origins of the Revolution

The high cost of the Seven Years' War doubled the British national debt. Anticipating further expenses to defend newly conquered territories, the government in London imposed bold new administrative measures. Breaking with tradition, the British announced that they would maintain a large army in North America and tax the colonies directly. In 1765 Parliament passed the Stamp Act, which levied taxes on a long list of commercial and legal documents, diplomas, newspapers, almanacs, and playing cards. A stamp glued to each article indicated that the tax had been paid.

These measures seemed perfectly reasonable to the British, for a much heavier stamp tax already existed in Britain, and proceeds from the tax were to fund the defense of the colonies. Nonetheless, the colonists vigorously protested the Stamp Act by rioting and by boycotting British goods. Thus Parliament reluctantly repealed it.

This dispute raised important political questions. To what extent could the British government reassert its power while limiting the authority of elected colonial bodies? Who had the right to make laws for Americans? The British government replied that Americans were represented in Parliament, albeit indirectly (like most British people), and that Parliament ruled throughout the empire. Many Americans felt otherwise. In the words of John Adams, a major proponent of colonial independence, "A Parliament of Great Britain can have no more rights to tax the colonies than a Parliament of Paris." Thus British colonial administration and parliamentary supremacy came to appear as grave threats to existing American liberties.

Americans' resistance to these threats was fed by the great degree of independence they had long enjoyed. In British North America, unlike in England and Europe, no powerful established church existed, and religious freedom was taken for granted. Colonial assemblies made the important laws, which were seldom overturned by the British government. Also, the right to vote was much more widespread than in England. In many parts of colonial Massachusetts, for example, as many as 95 percent of adult males could vote.

Moreover, greater political equality was matched by greater social and economic equality, at least for the free population. No hereditary nobility exercised privileges over peasants and other social groups. Instead, independent farmers dominated colonial society. This was particularly true in the northern colonies, where the revolution originated.

In 1773 disputes over taxes and representation flared up again. Under the Tea Act of that year, the British government permitted the financially hard-pressed East India Company to ship tea from China directly to its agents in the colonies rather than through London middlemen, who sold to independent merchants in the colonies. Thus the company secured a profitable monopoly on the tea trade, and colonial merchants were excluded. The price on tea was actually lowered for colonists, but the act generated a great deal of opposition because of the monopoly it gave to the East India Company.

Commemorative Teapot Manufacturers were quick to bring products to the market celebrating weighty political events, like this British teapot heralding "Stamp Act Repeal'd." By purchasing such items, ordinary people could champion political causes of the day and bring public affairs into their private lives. (Gift of Richard C. Manning/Peabody Essex Museum, Salem, Massachusetts. Acquired 9/16/1933)

In protest, Boston men disguised as Native Americans had a rowdy Tea Party in which they boarded East India Company ships and threw tea from them into the harbor. In response, the so-called Coercive Acts of 1774 closed the port of Boston, curtailed local elections, and expanded the royal governor's power. County conventions in Massachusetts urged that such measures be "rejected as the attempts of a wicked administration to enslave America." Other colonial assemblies joined in the denunciations. In September 1774, the First Continental Congress—consisting of colonial delegates who sought at first to peacefully resolve conflicts with Britain—met in Philadelphia. The more radical members of this assembly argued successfully against concessions to the English crown. The British Parliament also rejected compromise, and in April 1775 fighting between colonial and British troops began at Lexington and Concord.

Independence from Britain

As fighting spread, the colonists moved slowly toward open calls for independence. The uncompromising attitude of the British government and its use of German mercenaries did much to dissolve loyalties to the home country and to unite the separate colonies. *Common Sense* (1775), a brilliant attack by the recently arrived English radical Thomas Paine (1737–1809), also mobilized public opinion in favor of independence. A runaway bestseller with sales of 120,000 copies in a few months, Paine's tract ridiculed the idea of a small island ruling a great continent. In his call for freedom and republican government, Paine expressed Americans' growing sense of separateness and moral superiority.

On July 4, 1776, the Second Continental Congress adopted the **Declaration of Independence**. Written by Thomas Jefferson and others, this document boldly listed the tyrannical acts committed by George III (r. 1760–1820) and confidently proclaimed the natural rights of mankind and the sovereignty of the American states. The Declaration of Independence in effect universalized the traditional rights of English people and made them the rights of all mankind. It stated that "all Men are created equal, that they are endowed by their Creator with certain unalienable Rights, that among these are Life, Liberty, and the Pursuit of Happiness." No other American political document has ever caused such excitement, either at home or abroad.

□ KEY EVENTS OF THE AMERICAN REVOLUTION	
1765	Britain passes the Stamp Act
1773	Britain passes the Tea Act
1774	Britain passes the Coercive Acts in response to the Tea Party in the colonies; the First Continental Congress refuses concessions to the English crown
April 1775	Fighting begins between colonial and British troops
July 4, 1776	The Second Continental Congress adopts the Declaration of Independence
1777–1780	The French, Spanish, and Dutch side with the colonists against Britain
1783	The Treaty of Paris recognizes the independence of the American colonies
1787	The U.S. Constitution is signed
1791	The first ten amendments to the Constitution are ratified (the Bill of Rights)

Loyalist stronghold
Patriot stronghold
Strongly contested area

Québec
Montréal
VT.
N.H.
MASS.
Boston
N.Y.
Newport
R.I.
CONN.
Philadelphia
PA.
N.J.
New York
DEL.
MD.
VA.
Norfolk
N.C.
ATLANTIC OCEAN
S.C.
Wilmington
GA.
Charleston
Savannah

Loyalist Strength in the Colonies, ca. 1774–1776

After the Declaration of Independence, the conflict often took the form of a civil war pitting patriots against Loyalists, those who maintained an allegiance to the Crown. The Loyalists tended to be wealthy and politically moderate. Many patriots—such as John Hancock and George Washington—were also wealthy, but they willingly allied themselves with farmers and artisans in a broad coalition. This coalition harassed the Loyalists and confiscated their property to help pay for the war, causing more than thirty thousand of them to flee, mostly to Canada. The broad social base of the revolutionaries tended to make the revolution democratic. State governments extended the right to vote to many more men, including free African American men in many cases, but not to women.

On the international scene, the French wanted revenge against the British for the humiliating defeats of the Seven Years' War. Thus they sympathized with the rebels and supplied guns and gunpowder from the

• **Declaration of Independence** The 1776 document in which the American colonies declared independence from Great Britain and recast traditional English rights as universal human rights.

The Signing of the Declaration of Independence, July 4, 1776 John Trumbull's famous painting shows the dignity and determination of America's revolutionary leaders. An extraordinarily talented group, they succeeded in rallying popular support without losing power to more radical forces in the process. (Photo © Boltin Picture Library/The Bridgeman Art Library)

beginning of the conflict. By 1777 French volunteers were arriving in Virginia, and a dashing young nobleman, the marquis de Lafayette (1757–1834), quickly became one of the most trusted generals of George Washington, who was commanding American troops. In 1778 the French government offered a formal alliance to the American ambassador in Paris, Benjamin Franklin, and in 1779 and 1780 the Spanish and Dutch declared war on Britain. Catherine the Great of Russia helped organize the League of Armed Neutrality to protect neutral shipping rights and succeeded in hampering Britain's naval power. Thus by 1780 Britain was engaged in an imperial war against most of Europe as well as the thirteen colonies. In these circumstances, and in the face of severe reverses in India, in the West Indies, and at Yorktown in Virginia, a new British government decided to cut its losses and end the war.

American officials in Paris were receptive to negotiating a deal with England alone, for they feared that France wanted a treaty that would bottle up the new United States east of the Allegheny Mountains and give British holdings west of the Alleghenies to France's ally, Spain. Thus the American negotiators deserted their French allies and accepted the extraordinarily favorable terms Britain offered.

Under the Treaty of Paris of 1783, Britain recognized the independence of the thirteen colonies and ceded all its territory between the Allegheny Mountains and the Mississippi River to the Americans. Out of the bitter rivalries of the Old World, the Americans snatched dominion over a vast territory.

Framing the Constitution

The liberal program of the American Revolution was consolidated by the federal Constitution, the Bill of Rights, and the creation of a national republic. Assembling in Philadelphia in the summer of 1787, the

• **Antifederalists** Opponents of the American Constitution who felt it diminished individual rights and accorded too much power to the federal government at the expense of the states.

delegates to the Constitutional Convention were determined to end the period of economic depression, social uncertainty, and leadership under a weak central government that had followed independence. The delegates thus decided to grant the federal, or central, government important powers: regulation of domestic and foreign trade, the right to tax, and the means to enforce its laws.

Strong rule would be placed squarely in the context of representative self-government. Senators and congressmen would be the lawmaking delegates of the voters, and the president of the republic would be an elected official. The central government would operate in Montesquieu's framework of checks and balances, under which authority was distributed across three different branches — the executive, legislative, and judicial branches — that would systematically balance one another, preventing one interest from gaining too much power. The power of the federal government would in turn be checked by that of the individual states.

When the results of the secret deliberations of the Constitutional Convention were presented to the states for ratification, a great public debate began. The opponents of the proposed Constitution — the **Antifederalists** — charged that the framers of the new document had taken too much power from the individual states and made the federal government too strong. Moreover, many Antifederalists feared for the individual freedoms for which they had fought. To overcome these objections, the Federalists promised to spell out these basic freedoms as soon as the new Constitution was adopted. The result was the first ten amendments to the Constitution, which the first Congress passed shortly after it met in New York in March 1789. These amendments, ratified in 1791, formed an effective Bill of Rights to safeguard the individual. Most of them — trial by jury, due process of law, the right to assemble, freedom from unreasonable search — had their origins in English law and the English Bill of Rights of 1689. Other rights — the freedoms of speech, the press, and religion — reflected natural-law theory and the strong value colonists had placed on independence from the start.

Like the French republic that was soon to emerge, the early American republic also sought to advance the rights of African Americans, and many free people of color voted in elections to ratify the Constitution. Congress banned slavery in federal territory in 1789, then the export of slaves from any state, and finally, in 1808, the import of slaves to any state. These early measures, along with voting rights for free people of color, were eroded in the early nineteenth century as abolitionist fervor waned.

The American Constitution and the Bill of Rights exemplified the great strengths and the limits of what came to be called classical liberalism. Liberty meant individual freedoms and political safeguards. Liberty also meant representative government but did not necessarily mean democracy, with its principle of one person, one vote. Equality meant equality before the law, not equality of political participation or wealth. It did not mean equal rights for women, slaves, or indigenous peoples.

Revolution in France, 1789–1791

☐ How did the events of 1789 result in a constitutional monarchy in France, and what were the consequences?

No country felt the consequences of the American Revolution more deeply than France. Hundreds of French officers served in America and were inspired by the experience. The most famous of these, the young and impressionable marquis de Lafayette, left home as a great aristocrat determined to fight France's traditional foe, England. He returned with a love of liberty and firm republican convictions. French intellectuals and publicists engaged in passionate analysis of the federal Constitution as well as the constitutions of the various states of the new United States. The American Revolution undeniably fueled dissatisfaction with the old monarchical order in France. Yet the French Revolution did not mirror the American example. It was more radical and more complex, more influential and more controversial, more loved and more hated. For Europeans and most of the rest of the world, it was the great revolution of the eighteenth century, the revolution that opened the modern era in politics.

Breakdown of the Old Order

As did the American Revolution, the French Revolution had its immediate origins in the financial difficulties of the government. The efforts of the ministers of King Louis XV (r. 1715–1774) to raise taxes to meet the expenses of the War of the Austrian Succession and the Seven Years' War were thwarted by the high courts, known as the parlements. The noble judges of the parlements resented this threat to their exemption from taxation and decried the government's actions as a form of royal despotism.

When renewed efforts to reform the tax system met a similar fate in 1776, the government was forced to finance its enormous expenditures during the American war with borrowed money. As a result, the national debt soared. By the 1780s fully 50 percent of France's annual budget went to interest payments on the ever-increasing debt. Another 25 percent went to maintain the military, while 6 percent was absorbed by the royal family and the court at Versailles. Less than 20 percent of the national budget was available for the productive functions of the state, such as transportation and general administration. This was an impossible financial situation.

Nor could the king and his ministers print money and create inflation to cover their deficits, as modern governments do. Unlike England and Holland, which had far larger national debts relative to their populations, France had no central bank, no paper currency, and no means of creating credit. Therefore, when a depressed economy and a lack of public confidence made it increasingly difficult for the government to obtain new loans in 1786, it had no alternative but to try increasing taxes. Because France's tax system was unfair and out-of-date, increased revenues were possible only through fundamental reforms. Such reforms, which would affect all groups in France's complex and fragmented society, were guaranteed to create social and political unrest.

These crises struck a monarchy that had lost much of its mantle of royal authority. Kings had always maintained mistresses, who were invariably chosen from the court nobility. Louis XV broke that pattern with Madame de Pompadour, daughter of a disgraced bourgeois financier. As the king's favorite mistress from 1745 to 1750, Pompadour exercised tremendous influence that continued even after their love affair ended. She played a key role, for example, in bringing about France's break with Prussia and its new alliance with Austria in the mid-1750s. Pompadour's low birth and hidden political influence generated a stream of resentful and illegal pamphleteering. The king was being stripped of the sacred aura of God's anointed on earth (a process called desacralization) and was being reinvented in the popular imagination as a degenerate.

Despite the progressive desacralization of the monarchy, Louis XV would probably have prevailed had he lived longer, but he died in 1774. The new king, Louis XVI (r. 1774–1792), was a shy twenty-year-old with good intentions. Taking the throne, he is reported to have said, "What I should like most is to be loved."[1] The eager-to-please monarch Louis waffled on political reform and the economy, and he proved unable to quell the rising storm of opposition.

The Formation of the National Assembly

Spurred by a depressed economy and falling tax receipts, Louis XVI's minister of finance revived old proposals to impose a general tax on all landed property as well as to form provincial assemblies to help administer the tax, and he convinced the king to call an assembly of notables in 1787 to gain support for the idea. The assembled notables, mainly important noblemen and high-ranking clergy, declared that such sweeping tax changes required the approval of the **Estates General**, the representative body of all three estates, which had not met since 1614.

Facing imminent bankruptcy, the king tried to reassert his authority. He dismissed the notables and established new taxes by decree. In stirring language, the judges of the Parlement of Paris promptly declared the royal initiative null and void. When the king tried to exile the judges, a tremendous wave of protest swept the country. Frightened investors refused to advance more loans to the state. Finally in July 1788, a beaten Louis XVI bowed to public opinion and called for a spring session of the Estates General. Absolute monarchy was collapsing.

As its name indicates, the Estates General was a legislative body with representatives from the three orders of society: the clergy, nobility, and commoners. Following centuries-old tradition each order met separately to elect delegates, first at a local and then at a regional level. Results of the elections reveal the mindset of each estate on the eve of the revolution. The local assemblies of the clergy, representing the first estate, elected mostly parish priests rather than church leaders, demonstrating their dissatisfaction with the church hierarchy. The nobility, or second estate, voted in a majority of conservatives, primarily from the provinces, where nobles were less wealthy and more numerous. Nonetheless, fully one-third of noble representatives were liberals committed to major changes. Commoners of the third estate, who constituted over 95 percent of the population, elected primarily lawyers and government officials to represent them, with few delegates representing business and the poor.

The petitions for change drafted by the newly elected assemblies showed a surprising degree of consensus about the key issues confronting the realm. In all three estates, voices spoke in favor of replacing absolutism with a constitutional monarchy in which laws and taxes would require the consent of the Estates General in regular meetings. There was also the strong feeling that individual liberties would have to be guaranteed by law and that economic regulations should be loosened.

On May 5, 1789, the twelve hundred delegates of the three estates gathered in Versailles for the opening ses-

• **Estates General** Traditional representative body of the three estates of France that met in 1789 in response to imminent state bankruptcy.

• **National Assembly** French representative assembly formed in 1789 by the delegates of the third estate and some members of the clergy, the second estate.

sion of the Estates General. Despite widespread hopes for serious reform, the Estates General was almost immediately deadlocked due to arguments about voting procedures. Controversy had begun during the electoral process itself, when the government confirmed that, following precedent, each estate should meet and vote separately. During the lead-up to the Estates General, critics had demanded a single assembly dominated by the third estate. In his famous pamphlet "What Is the Third Estate?" the abbé Emmanuel Joseph Sieyès (himself a member of the first estate) argued that the nobility was a tiny, overprivileged minority and that the neglected third estate constituted the true strength of the French nation. (See "Listening to the Past: Abbé de Sieyès, 'What Is the Third Estate?'" page 664.) The government conceded that the third estate should have as many delegates as the clergy and the nobility combined, but then upheld a system granting one vote per estate instead of one vote per person. This meant that the two privileged estates could always outvote the third, even if the third estate had a majority by head count.

The issue came to a crisis in June 1789 when delegates of the third estate refused to meet until the king ordered the clergy and nobility to sit with them in a single body. Finally, after six weeks, a few parish priests began to go over to the third estate, which on June 17 voted to call itself the **National Assembly**. On June 20 the delegates of the third estate, excluded from their hall because of "repairs," moved to a large indoor tennis court where they swore the famous Oath of the Tennis Court, pledging not to disband until they had been recognized as a national assembly and had written a new constitution.

The king's response was disastrously ambivalent. On June 23 he made a conciliatory speech to a joint session in which he urged reforms, and four days later he ordered the three estates to meet together. At the same time, Louis apparently followed the advice of relatives and court nobles who urged him to dissolve the National Assembly by force. The king called an army of eighteen thousand troops toward the capital to bring the delegates under control, and on July 11 he dismissed his finance minister and other more liberal ministers. It appeared that the monarchy was prepared to renege on its promises for reform and to use violence to restore its control.

Popular Uprising and the Rights of Man

While delegates at Versailles were pressing for political rights, economic hardship gripped common people in the towns and countryside. Conditions were already tough, due to the disastrous financial situation of the Crown. A poor grain harvest in 1788 caused the price of

☐ KEY EVENTS OF THE FRENCH REVOLUTION

May 5, 1789	Estates General meets at Versailles
June 17, 1789	Third estate declares itself the National Assembly
June 20, 1789	Oath of the Tennis Court
July 14, 1789	Storming of the Bastille
July–August 1789	Great Fear
August 4, 1789	National Assembly abolishes feudal privileges
August 27, 1789	National Assembly issues Declaration of the Rights of Man
October 5, 1789	Women march on Versailles; royal family returns to Paris
November 1789	National Assembly confiscates church lands
July 1790	Civil Constitution of the Clergy establishes a national church; Louis XVI agrees to a constitutional monarchy
June 1791	Royal family is arrested while attempting to flee France
August 1791	Austria and Prussia issue the Declaration of Pillnitz
April 1792	France declares war on Austria
August 1792	Mob attacks the palace, and Legislative Assembly takes Louis XVI prisoner
September 1792	National Convention declares France a republic and abolishes monarchy
January 21, 1793	Louis XVI is executed
February 1793	France declares war on Britain, Holland, and Spain; revolts take place in some provinces
March 1793	Struggle between Girondists and the Mountain
June 1793	Sans-culottes invade the National Convention; Girondist leaders are arrested
September 1793	Price controls are instituted to aid the poor
1793–1794	Reign of Terror
Spring 1794	French armies are victorious on all fronts
July 1794	Robespierre is executed; Thermidorian reaction begins
1795	Economic controls are abolished, and suppression of the sans-culottes begins
1795–1799	Directory rules
1798	Austria, Britain, and Russia form the Second Coalition against France
1799	Napoleon Bonaparte overthrows the Directory and seizes power

The Tennis Court Oath, June 20, 1789 Painted two years after the event shown, this dramatic painting by Jacques-Louis David depicts a crucial turning point in the early days of the Revolution. On June 20 delegates of the third estate arrived at their meeting hall in the Versailles palace to find the doors closed and guarded. Fearing the king was about to dissolve their meeting by force, the deputies reassembled at a nearby indoor tennis court and swore a solemn oath not to disperse until they had been recognized as the National Assembly. (Musée de la Ville de Paris, Musée Carnavalet, Paris/Giraudon/The Bridgeman Art Library)

bread to soar suddenly and inflation spread quickly through the economy. As a result, demand for manufactured goods collapsed, and many artisans and small traders lost work. In Paris perhaps 150,000 of the city's 600,000 people were unemployed by July 1789.

Against this background of poverty and political crisis, the people of Paris entered decisively onto the revolutionary stage. They believed that, to survive, they should have steady work and enough bread at fair prices. They also feared that the dismissal of the king's liberal finance minister would put them at the mercy of aristocratic landowners and grain speculators. At the beginning of July, knowledge spread of the massing of troops near Paris. On July 14, 1789, several hundred people stormed the Bastille (ba-STEEL), a royal prison, to obtain weapons and gunpowder for the city's defense. Faced with popular violence, Louis soon announced the reinstatement of his finance minister and the withdrawal of troops from Paris. The National Assembly

was now free to continue its work without the threat of royal military intervention.

Just as the laboring poor of Paris had been roused to a revolutionary fervor, the struggling French peasantry had also reached a boiling point. In the summer of 1789, throughout France peasants began to rise in insurrection against their lords, ransacking manor houses and burning feudal documents that recorded their obligations. In some areas peasants reoccupied common lands enclosed by landowners and seized forests. Fear of marauders and vagabonds hired by vengeful landlords — called the Great Fear by contemporaries — seized the rural poor and fanned the flames of rebellion.

Faced with chaos, the National Assembly responded to peasant demands with a surprise maneuver on the night of August 4, 1789. By a decree of the assembly, all the old noble privileges — peasant serfdom where it still existed, exclusive hunting rights, fees for having legal cases judged in the lord's court, the right to make peasants work on the roads, and a host of other dues — were abolished along with the tithes paid to the church. From this point on, French peasants would seek mainly to protect and consolidate this victory.

Having granted new rights to the peasantry, the National Assembly moved forward with its mission of reform. On August 27, 1789, it issued the Declaration of the Rights of Man and of the Citizen. This clarion call of the liberal revolutionary ideal guaranteed equality before the law, representative government for a sovereign people, and individual freedom. This revolutionary credo, only two pages long, was disseminated throughout France, the rest of Europe, and around the world.

The National Assembly's declaration had little practical effect for the poor and hungry people of Paris. The economic crisis worsened after the fall of the Bastille, as aristocrats fled the country and the luxury market collapsed. Foreign markets also shrank, and unemployment among the urban working class grew. In addition, women — the traditional managers of food and resources in poor homes — could no longer look to the church, which had been stripped of its tithes, for aid.

On October 5 some seven thousand women marched the twelve miles from Paris to Versailles to demand action. This great crowd, "armed with scythes, sticks and pikes," invaded the National Assembly. Interrupting a delegate's speech, an old woman defiantly shouted into the debate, "Who's that talking down there? Make the chatterbox shut up. That's not the point: the point is that we want bread."[2] Hers was the genuine voice of the people, essential to any understanding of the French Revolution.

The women invaded the royal apartments, killed some of the royal bodyguards, and searched for the queen, Marie Antoinette, who was widely despised for her frivolous and supposedly immoral behavior. "We are going to cut off her head, tear out her heart, fry her liver, and that won't be the end of it," they shouted. It seems likely that only the intervention of Lafayette and the National Guard saved the royal family. But the only way to calm the disorder was for the king to live closer to his people in Paris, as the crowd demanded.

Liberal elites brought the revolution into being and continued to lead politics. Yet the people of France were now roused and would henceforth play a crucial role in the unfolding of events.

A Constitutional Monarchy and Its Challenges

The day after the women's march on Versailles, the National Assembly followed the king to Paris, and the next two years, until September 1791, saw the consolidation of the liberal revolution. In June 1790 the

The Women of Paris March to Versailles On October 5, 1789, a large group of poor Parisian women marched to Versailles to protest the price of bread. For the people of Paris, the king was the baker of last resort, responsible for feeding his people during times of scarcity. The angry women forced the royal family to return with them and to live in Paris, rather than remain isolated from their subjects at court. (Erich Lessing/Art Resource, NY)

Abbé de Sieyès, "What Is the Third Estate?"

In the flood of pamphlets that appeared after Louis XVI's call for a meeting of the Estates General, the most influential was written in 1789 by a Catholic priest named Emmanuel Joseph Sieyès. In "What Is the Third Estate?" the abbé Sieyès vigorously condemned the system of privilege that lay at the heart of French society. The term privilege *combined the Latin words for "private" and "law." In Old Regime France, no one set of laws applied to all; over time, the monarchy had issued a series of particular laws, or privileges, that enshrined special rights and entitlements for select individuals and groups. Noble privileges were among the weightiest.*

Sieyès rejected this entire system of legal and social inequality. Deriding the nobility as a foreign parasite, he argued that the common people of the third estate, who did most of the work and paid most of the taxes, constituted the true nation. His pamphlet galvanized public opinion and played an important role in convincing representatives of the third estate to proclaim themselves a National Assembly in June 1789. Sieyès later helped bring Napoleon Bonaparte to power, abandoning the radicalism of 1789 for an authoritarian regime.

" 1. What is the Third Estate? Everything.
2. What has it been until now in the political order? Nothing.
3. What does it want? To become something.

. . . What is a Nation? A body of associates living under a *common* law and represented by the same *legislature*.

Is it not more than certain that the noble order has privileges, exemptions, and even rights that are distinct from the rights of the great body of citizens? Because of this, it [the noble order] does not belong to the common order, it is not covered by the law common to the rest. Thus its civil rights already make it a people apart inside the great Nation. It is truly *imperium in imperio* [a law unto itself].

As for its *political* rights, the nobility also exercises them separately. It has its own representatives who have no mandate from the people. Its deputies sit separately, and even when they assemble in the same room with the deputies of the ordinary citizens, the nobility's representation still remains essentially distinct and separate: it is foreign to the Nation by its very principle, for its mission does not emanate from the people, and by its purpose, since it consists in defending, not the general interest, but the private interests of the nobility.

The Third Estate therefore contains everything that pertains to the Nation and nobody outside of the Third Estate can claim to be part of the Nation. What is the Third Estate? EVERYTHING. . . .

By Third Estate is meant the collectivity of citizens who belong to the common order. Anybody who holds a legal privilege of any kind leaves that common order, stands as an exception to the common law, and in consequence does not belong to the Third Estate. . . . It is certain that the moment a citizen acquires privileges contrary to common law, he no longer belongs to the common order. His new interest is opposed to the general interest; he has no right to vote in the name of the people. . . .

In vain can anyone's eyes be closed to the revolution that time and the force of things have brought to pass; it is none the less real. Once upon a time the Third Estate was in bondage and the noble order was everything that mattered. Today the Third is everything and nobility but a word. Yet under the cover of this word a new and intolerable aristocracy has slipped in, and the people has every reason to no longer want aristocrats. . . .

What is the will of a Nation? It is the result of individual wills, just as the Nation is the aggregate of the individuals who com-

National Assembly abolished the nobility and in July the king swore to uphold the as-yet-unwritten constitution, effectively enshrining a constitutional monarchy. The king remained the head of state, but all lawmaking power now resided in the National Assembly, elected by the wealthiest half of French males. The constitution finally passed in September 1791 and, reluctantly recognized by Louis XVI, was the first in French history. It broadened women's rights to seek divorce, to inherit property, and to obtain financial support for illegitimate children from fathers, but excluded women from political office and voting.

This decision was attacked by a small number of men and women who believed that the rights of man should be extended to all French citizens. Olympe de Gouges (1748–1793), a self-taught writer and woman of the people, protested the evils of slavery as well as the injustices done to women. In September 1791 she published her "Declaration of the Rights of Woman." This pamphlet echoed its famous predecessor, the Declaration of the Rights of Man and of the Citizen, proclaiming, "Woman is born free and remains equal to man in rights." De Gouges's position found little sympathy among leaders of the revolution, however.

pose it. It is impossible to conceive of a legitimate association that does not have for its goal the common security, the common liberty, in short, the public good. No doubt each individual also has his own personal aims. He says to himself, "protected by the common security, I will be able to peacefully pursue my own personal projects, I will seek my happiness where I will, assured of encountering only those legal obstacles that society will prescribe for the common interest, in which I have a part, and with which my own personal interest is so usefully allied." . . .

Advantages which differentiate citizens from one another lie outside the purview of citizenship. Inequalities of wealth or ability are like the inequalities of age, sex, size, etc. In no way do they detract from the *equality* of citizenship. These individual advantages no doubt benefit from the protection of the law; but it is not the legislator's task to create them, to give privileges to some and refuse them to others. The law grants nothing; it protects what already exists until such time that what exists begins to harm the common interest. These are the only limits on individual freedom. I imagine the law as being at the center of a large globe; we the citizens without exception, stand equidistant from it on the surface and occupy equal places; all are equally dependent on the law, all present it with their liberty and their property to be protected; and this is what I call the *common rights* of citizens, by which they are all alike. All these individuals communicate with each other, enter into contracts, negotiate, always under the common guarantee of the law. If in this general activity somebody wishes to get control over the person of his neighbor or usurp his property, the common law goes into action to repress this criminal attempt and puts everyone back in their place at the same distance from the law. . . .

It is impossible to say what place the two privileged orders [the clergy and the nobility] ought to occupy in the social order: this is the equivalent of asking what place one wishes to assign to a malignant tumor that torments and undermines the strength of the body of a sick person. It must be *neutralized*. We must re-establish the health and working of all organs so thoroughly that they are no longer susceptible to these fatal schemes that are capable of sapping the most essential principles of vitality. 🙶

Source: *The French Revolution and Human Rights: A Brief Documentary History*, pp. 65, 67, 68–70. Edited, Translated, and with an Introduction by Lynn Hunt. © 1996 by Bedford/St. Martin's. Reprinted by permission of the publisher.

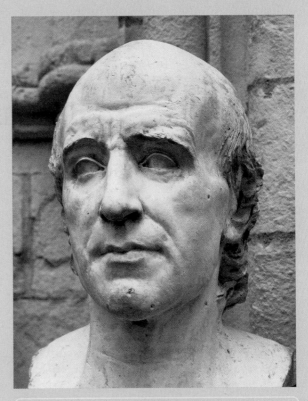

● **This bust, by the sculptor Pierre Jean David d'Angers, shows an aged and contemplative Sieyès reflecting, perhaps, on his key role in the outbreak and unfolding of the French Revolution.** (Erich Lessing/Art Resource, NY)

QUESTIONS FOR ANALYSIS

1. What criticism of noble privileges does Sieyès offer? Why does he believe nobles are "foreign" to the nation?

2. How does Sieyès define the nation, and why does he believe that the third estate constitutes the nation?

3. What relationship between citizens and the law does Sieyès envision? What limitations on the law does he propose?

In addition to ruling on women's rights, the National Assembly replaced the complicated patchwork of historic provinces with eighty-three departments of approximately equal size, a move toward more rational and systematic methods of administration. Monopolies, guilds, and workers' associations were prohibited, and barriers to trade within France abolished in the name of economic liberty. Thus the National Assembly applied the spirit of the Enlightenment in a thorough reform of France's laws and institutions.

The National Assembly also imposed a radical reorganization on religious life. It granted religious freedom to the small minority of French Jews and Protestants. (See "Viewpoints: The Question of Jewish Citizenship in France," page 666.) Furthermore, in November 1789 it nationalized the Catholic Church's property and abolished monasteries. The government used all former church property as collateral to guarantee a new paper currency, the assignats (A-sihg-nat), and then sold the property in an attempt to put the state's finances on a solid footing.

Imbued with the rationalism and skepticism of the eighteenth-century philosophes, many delegates distrusted popular piety and "superstitious religion." Thus

Viewpoints

The Question of Jewish Citizenship in France

• *In August 1789 the legislators of the French Revolution adopted the Declaration of the Rights of Man and of the Citizen, enshrining full legal equality under the law for French citizens. Who exactly could become a citizen and what rights they might enjoy quickly became contentious issues. After granting civil rights to Protestants in December 1789, the National Assembly began to consider the smaller but more controversial population of French Jews. Eager to become citizens, the Jews of Paris, Alsace, and Lorraine presented a joint petition to the National Assembly in January 1790. Their appeal was met with negative reactions in some quarters, including from the bishop of Nancy in Lorraine, a province on France's eastern border with a relatively large Jewish population.*

Jewish Petition to the National Assembly, January 28, 1790

❝A great question is pending before the supreme tribunal of France. *Will the Jews be citizens or not?* . . .

In general, civil rights are entirely independent from religious principles. And all men of whatever religion, whatever sect they belong to, whatever creed they practice, provided that their creed, their sect, their religion does not offend the principles of a pure and severe morality, all these men, we say, equally able to serve the fatherland, defend its interests, contribute to its splendor, should all equally have the title and the rights of citizen.

. . . Reflect, then, on the condition of the Jews. Excluded from all the professions, ineligible for all the positions, deprived even of the capacity to acquire property, not daring and not being able to sell openly the merchandise of their commerce, to what extremity are you reducing them? You do not want them to die, and yet you refuse them the means to live; you refuse them the means, and you crush them with taxes. . . .

. . . Everything is changing; the lot of the Jews must change at the same time; and the people will not be more surprised by this particular change than by all those which they see around them everyday. This is therefore the moment, the true moment to make justice triumph: attach the improvement of the lot of the Jews to the revolution.❞

La Fare, Bishop of Nancy, On the Admissibility of Jews to Full Civil and Political Rights, Spring 1790

❝Thus, Sirs, assure each Jewish individual his liberty, security, and the enjoyment of his property. You owe it to this individual who has strayed into our midst; you owe him nothing more. He is a foreigner to whom, during the time of this passage and his stay, France owes hospitality, protection and security. But it cannot and should not admit to public posts, to the administration, to the prerogatives of the family a tribe that, regarding itself everywhere as foreign, never exclusively embraces any region; a tribe whose religion, customs, and physical and moral regime essentially differ from that of all other people; a tribe whose eyes turn constantly toward the common fatherland that should one day reunite its dispersed members. . . .

There are also moral and local considerations that should, if not guide, then at least enlighten the legislation regarding the Jewish nation. . . .

The prejudices of the people against the Jews are only too well-known. From time to time, they explode into violence: recently in Alsace, some people committed the most criminal excesses against the Jews. A few months ago, similar misfortunes menaced them in Nancy. . . .

From this account it is easy to understand the habitual disposition of the people; it is a fire always ready to be lit. Any extension that a decree of the National Assembly would hasten to give to the civil existence of the Jews, before opinion has been prepared in advance and led by degrees to this change, could occasion great disaster.❞

Source: *The French Revolution and Human Rights: A Brief Documentary History*, pp. 93–96 (Jewish petition) and pp. 97–98 (La Fare). Edited, Translated, and with an Introduction by Lynn Hunt. © 1996 by Bedford/St. Martin's. Reprinted by permission of the publisher.

QUESTIONS FOR ANALYSIS

1. On what basis do the Jews of Paris, Alsace, and Lorraine argue for their inclusion in citizenship rights? How do they describe the constraints of the Jewish population prior to the Revolution?

2. How does the Bishop of Nancy characterize the Jews' relationship to the French nation, and why does it disqualify them for citizenship? What dangers does he see in granting citizenship to French Jews?

in July 1790, with the Civil Constitution of the Clergy, they established a national church with priests chosen by voters. The National Assembly then forced the Catholic clergy to take an oath of loyalty to the new government. The pope formally condemned this attempt to subjugate the church, and only half the priests of France swore the oath. Many sincere Christians, especially those in the countryside, were also upset by these changes in the religious order. The attempt to remake the Catholic Church, like the abolition of guilds and workers' associations, sharpened the conflict between the educated classes and the common people that had been emerging in the eighteenth century.

World War and Republican France, 1791–1799

☐ Why and how did the French Revolution take a radical turn entailing terror at home and war with European powers?

When Louis XVI accepted the National Assembly's constitution in September 1791, a young provincial lawyer and delegate named Maximilien Robespierre (1758–1794) concluded that "The Revolution is over." Robespierre was right in the sense that the most constructive and lasting reforms were in place. Yet he was wrong in suggesting that turmoil had ended, for a much more radical stage lay ahead, one that would bring war with foreign powers, terror at home, and a transformation in France's government.

The International Response

The outbreak and progress of revolution in France produced great excitement and a sharp division of opinion in Europe and the United States. On the one hand, liberals and radicals saw a mighty triumph of liberty over despotism. On the other hand, conservative leaders such as British statesman Edmund Burke (1729–1797) were troubled by the aroused spirit of reform. In 1790 Burke published *Reflections on the Revolution in France*, in which he defended inherited privileges. He glorified Britain's unrepresentative Parliament and predicted that reform like that occurring in France would lead only to chaos and tyranny.

One passionate rebuttal came from a young writer in London, Mary Wollstonecraft (1759–1797). Incensed by Burke's book, Wollstonecraft (WOOL-stuhn-kraft) wrote a blistering, widely read attack, *A Vindication of the Rights of Man* (1790). Two years later, she published her masterpiece, *A Vindication of the Rights of Woman* (1792). As de Gouges had one year before her, Wollstonecraft demanded equal rights for women. She also advocated coeducation out of the belief that it would make women better wives and mothers, good citizens, and economically independent. Considered very radical for the time, the book became a founding text of the feminist movement.

The kings and nobles of continental Europe, who had at first welcomed the revolution in France as weakening a competing power, now feared its impact. In June 1791 Louis XVI and Marie Antoinette were arrested

The Capture of Louis XVI, June 1791
This painting commemorates the midnight arrest of Louis XVI and the royal family as they tried to flee France in disguise and reach counter-revolutionaries in the Austrian Netherlands. Recognized and stopped at Varennes, just forty miles from the border, the king still nearly succeeded, telling municipal officers that dangerous mobs controlled Paris and securing promises of safe passage. But within hours the local leaders reversed themselves, and by morning Louis XVI was headed back to Paris. (Bibliothèque nationale de France)

and returned to Paris after trying unsuccessfully to slip out of France. To supporters of the revolution, the attempted flight was proof that the king was treacherously seeking foreign support for an invasion of France. To the monarchs of Austria and Prussia, the arrest of a crowned monarch was unacceptable. Two months later they issued the Declaration of Pillnitz, which professed their willingness to intervene in France to restore Louis XVI's rule if necessary. It was expected to have a sobering effect on revolutionary France without causing war.

But the crowned heads of Europe misjudged the situation. The new French representative body, called the Legislative Assembly, that convened in October 1791 had completely new delegates and a different character. Still prosperous, well-educated middle-class men, the delegates were younger and less cautious than their predecessors. Many of the them belonged to the political **Jacobin club**. Such clubs had proliferated in Parisian neighborhoods since the beginning of the revolution, drawing men and women to debate the political questions of the day.

The Jacobins and other deputies reacted with patriotic fury to the Declaration of Pillnitz. They said that if the kings of Europe were attempting to incite war against France, then "we will incite a war of people against kings. . . . Ten million Frenchmen, kindled by the fire of liberty, armed with the sword, with reason, with eloquence would be able to change the face of the world and make the tyrants tremble on their thrones."[3] In April 1792 France declared war on Francis II, the Habsburg monarch.

France's crusade against tyranny went poorly at first. Prussian forces joined Austria against the French, who broke and fled at their first military encounter with this First Coalition of the foreign powers united against the revolution. The Legislative Assembly declared the country in danger, and volunteers rallied to the capital. In this wartime atmosphere, rumors of treason by the king

Areas of French Insurrection, 1793

Caen • Paris
BRITTANY
VENDÉE   FRANCE
Lyons •
Bordeaux •
Marseilles •
SPAIN
Mediterranean Sea
▪ Vendée Rebellion
▪ Counter-revolutionary insurrections

and queen spread in Paris. On August 10, 1792, a revolutionary crowd attacked the royal palace at the Tuileries (TWEE-luh-reez), while the king and his family fled for their lives to the nearby Legislative Assembly. Rather than offering refuge, the Assembly suspended the king from all his functions, imprisoned him, and called for a legislative and constitutional assembly to be elected by universal male suffrage.

The Second Revolution and the New Republic

The fall of the monarchy marked a rapid radicalization of the revolution, a phase that historians often call the second revolution. In late September 1792 the new, popularly elected National Convention, which replaced the Legislative Assembly, proclaimed France a republic, a nation in which the people, instead of a monarch, held sovereign power.

All the members of the National Convention were republicans, and at the beginning almost all belonged to the Jacobin club of Paris. But the Jacobins themselves were increasingly divided into two bitterly opposed groups — the **Girondists** and the **Mountain**, led by Robespierre and another young lawyer, Georges Jacques Danton.

This division emerged clearly after the National Convention overwhelmingly convicted Louis XVI of treason. The Girondists accepted his guilt but did not wish to put the king to death. By a narrow majority, the Mountain carried the day, and Louis was executed on January 21, 1793, by guillotine, which the French had recently perfected. Marie Antoinette would be put to death later that year. But both the Girondists and the Mountain were determined to continue the "war against tyranny." The Prussians had been stopped at the Battle of Valmy on September 20, 1792, one day before the republic was proclaimed. French armies then invaded Savoy and captured Nice, moved into the German Rhineland, and by November 1792 were occupying the entire Austrian Netherlands (modern Belgium).

Everywhere they went, French armies of occupation chased princes, abolished feudalism, and found support among some peasants and middle-class people. But French armies also lived off the land, requisitioning food and supplies and plundering local treasures. The liberators therefore looked increasingly like foreign invaders. Meanwhile, international tensions mounted. In February 1793 the National Convention, at war with

• **Jacobin club** A political club during the French Revolution to which many of the deputies of the Legislative Assembly belonged.

• **Girondists** A moderate group that fought for control of the French National Convention in 1793.

• **Mountain** Led by Robespierre, the French National Convention's radical faction, which seized legislative power in 1793.

• **sans-culottes** The laboring poor of Paris, so called because the men wore trousers instead of the knee breeches of the aristocracy and middle class; the term came to refer to the militant radicals of the city.

Austria and Prussia, declared war on Britain, Holland, and Spain as well. Republican France was now at war with almost all of Europe.

Groups within France added to the turmoil. Peasants in western France revolted against being drafted into the army, with the Vendée region of Brittany emerging as the epicenter of revolt. Devout Catholics, royalists, and foreign agents encouraged their rebellion, and the counter-revolutionaries recruited veritable armies to fight for their cause.

In March 1793 the National Convention was locked in a life-and-death political struggle between members of the Mountain and the more moderate Girondists. With the middle-class delegates so bitterly divided, the laboring poor of Paris once again emerged as the decisive political factor. The laboring poor and the petty traders were often known as the **sans-culottes** (san-koo-LAHT, "without breeches") because their men wore trousers instead of the knee breeches of the aristocracy and the solid middle class. They demanded radical political action to guarantee them their daily bread. The Mountain, sensing an opportunity to outmaneuver the Girondists, joined with sans-culottes activists to engineer a popular uprising. On June 2, 1793,

▫ Picturing the Past

Contrasting Visions of the Sans-Culottes These two images offer profoundly different representations of a sans-culotte woman. The image on the left was created by a French artist, while the image on the right is English. The French words above the image on the right read in part, "Heads! Blood! Death! . . . I am the Goddess of Liberty! . . . Long Live the Guillotine!" (Bibliothèque nationale de France)

ANALYZING THE IMAGE How would you describe the woman on the left? What qualities does the artist seem to ascribe to her, and how do you think these qualities relate to the sans-culottes and the Revolution? How would you characterize the facial expression and attire of the woman on the right? How does the inclusion of the text contribute to your impressions of her?

CONNECTIONS What does the contrast between these two images suggest about differences between French and English perceptions of the sans-culottes and of the French Revolution? Why do you think the artists have chosen to depict women?

armed sans-culottes invaded the Convention and forced its deputies to arrest twenty-nine Girondist deputies for treason. All power passed to the Mountain.

The Convention also formed the Committee of Public Safety in April 1793 to deal with the threats from within and outside France. The committee, which Robespierre led, held dictatorial power to deal with the national emergency, allowing it to use whatever force necessary to defend the Revolution. Moderates in leading provincial cities revolted against the committee's power and demanded a decentralized government. Counter-revolutionary forces in the Vendée won significant victories, and the republic's armies were driven back on all fronts. By July 1793 only the areas around Paris and on the eastern frontier were firmly held by the central government. Defeat seemed imminent.

> ❝Terror is nothing more than prompt, severe inflexible justice.❞
>
> **ROBESPIERRE**

Total War and the Terror

A year later, in July 1794, the central government had reasserted control over the provinces, and the Austrian Netherlands and the Rhineland were once again in French hands. This remarkable change of fortune was due to the revolutionary government's success in harnessing the explosive forces of a planned economy, revolutionary terror, and modern nationalism in a total war effort.

Robespierre and the Committee of Public Safety advanced on several fronts in 1793 and 1794, seeking to impose republican unity across the nation. First, they collaborated with the sans-culottes, who continued pressing the common people's case for fair prices and a moral economic order and who distrusted most wealthy capitalists and all aristocrats. Thus in September 1793 Robespierre and his coworkers established a planned economy with egalitarian social overtones. Rather than let supply and demand determine prices, the government set maximum allowable prices for key products. Though the state was too weak to enforce all its price regulations, it did fix the price of bread in Paris at levels the poor could afford.

The people were also put to work, mainly producing arms and munitions for the war effort. The government told craftsmen what to produce, nationalized many small workshops, and requisitioned raw materials and grain. Through these economic reforms the

second revolution produced an emergency form of socialism, which thoroughly frightened Europe's propertied classes and greatly influenced the subsequent development of socialist ideology.

Second, while radical economic measures supplied the poor with bread and the armies with weapons, the **Reign of Terror** (1793–1794) enforced compliance with republican beliefs and practices. Special revolutionary courts responsible only to Robespierre's Committee of Public Safety tried "enemies of the nation" for political crimes. As a result, some forty thousand French men and women were executed or died in prison. Robespierre's Reign of Terror is therefore one of the most controversial phases of the French Revolution. Presented as a necessary measure to save the republic, the Terror was a weapon directed against all suspected of opposing the revolutionary government. As Robespierre himself put it, "Terror is nothing more than prompt, severe inflexible justice."[4] For many Europeans of the time, however, the Reign of Terror represented a frightening perversion of the ideals of 1789.

In their efforts to impose unity, the Jacobins took actions to suppress women's participation in political debate, which they perceived as disorderly and a distraction from women's proper place in the home. On October 30, 1793, the National Convention declared that "The clubs and popular societies of women, under whatever denomination are prohibited." Among those convicted of sedition was writer Olympe de Gouges, who was sent to the guillotine in November 1793.

Beyond imposing political unity by force, the Terror also sought to bring the revolution into all aspects of everyday life. The government sponsored revolutionary art and songs as well as a new series of secular holidays and open-air festivals to celebrate republican virtue and a love of nation. Moreover, the government attempted to rationalize French daily life by adopting the decimal system for weights and measures and a new calendar based on ten-day weeks. Another important element of this cultural revolution was the campaign of de-Christianization, which aimed to eliminate Catholic symbols and beliefs. Fearful of the hostility aroused in rural France, however, Robespierre called for a halt to de-Christianization measures in mid-1794.

The third and perhaps most decisive element in the French republic's victory over the First Coalition was its ability to draw on the power of patriotic dedication to a national state and a national mission. An essential part of modern nationalism, which would fully emerge throughout Europe in the nineteenth century, this commitment was something new in history. With a common language and a common tradition newly reinforced by the ideas of popular sovereignty and democ-

- **Reign of Terror** The period from 1793 to 1794, during which Robespierre's Committee of Public Safety tried and executed thousands suspected of treason and a new revolutionary culture was imposed.

- **Thermidorian reaction** A reaction to the violence of the Reign of Terror in 1794, resulting in the execution of Robespierre and the loosening of economic controls.

racy, large numbers of French people were stirred by a common loyalty. They developed an intense emotional commitment to the defense of the nation, and they saw the war against foreign opponents as a life-and-death struggle between good and evil.

The all-out mobilization of French resources under the Terror combined with the fervor of modern nationalism to create an awesome fighting machine. After August 1793 all unmarried young men were subject to the draft, and by January 1794 French armed forces outnumbered those of their enemies almost four to one.[5] Well-trained, well-equipped, and constantly indoctrinated, the enormous armies of the republic were led by young, impetuous generals. These generals often had risen from the ranks, and they personified the opportunities the revolution offered gifted sons of the people. By spring 1794 French armies were victorious on all fronts. The republic was saved.

The Thermidorian Reaction and the Directory

The success of the French armies led Robespierre and the Committee of Public Safety to relax the emergency economic controls, but they extended the political Reign of Terror. In March 1794 Robespierre's Terror wiped out many of his critics. Two weeks later Robespierre sent long-standing collaborators whom he believed had turned against him, including Danton, to the guillotine. A group of radicals and moderates in the Convention, knowing that they might be next, organized a conspiracy. They howled down Robespierre when he tried to speak to the National Convention on July 27, 1794 — a date known as 9 Thermidor according to France's newly adopted republican calendar. The next day it was Robespierre's turn to be guillotined.

As Robespierre's closest supporters followed their leader to the guillotine, the respectable middle-class lawyers and professionals who had led the liberal revolution of 1789 reasserted their authority. This period of **Thermidorian reaction**, as it was called, harkened back to the beginnings of the Revolution, rejecting the radicalism of the sans-culottes in favor of moderate policies that favored property owners. In 1795 the National Convention abolished many economic controls, let prices rise sharply, and severely restricted the local political organizations through which the sans-culottes exerted their strength.

The collapse of economic controls, coupled with runaway inflation, hit the working poor very hard. After the Convention used the army to suppress the sans-culottes' protests, the urban poor lost their revolutionary fervor. Excluded and disillusioned, they would have little interest in and influence on politics until 1830.

In 1795 the middle-class members of the National Convention wrote yet another constitution to guaran-

tee their economic position and political supremacy. As in previous elections, the mass of the population voted only for electors, whose number was cut back to men of substantial means. Electors then voted for members of a reorganized Legislative Assembly to replace the National Convention and for key officials throughout France. The new assembly also chose a five-man executive body called the Directory.

The Directory continued to support French military expansion abroad. War was no longer so much a crusade as a response to economic problems. Large, victorious French armies reduced unemployment at home. However, the French people quickly grew weary of the corruption and ineffectiveness that characterized the Directory. This general dissatisfaction revealed itself clearly in the national elections of 1797, which returned a large number of conservative and even monarchist deputies who favored peace at almost

The Execution of Robespierre Completely wooden except for the heavy iron blade, the guillotine was painted red for Robespierre's execution, a detail not captured in this black-and-white engraving of the 1794 event. Large crowds witnessed the execution in a majestic public square in central Paris, then known as the Place de la Revolution and now called the Place de la Concorde (Harmony Square). (Snark/Art Resource, NY)

any price. The members of the Directory, fearing for their skins, used the army to nullify the elections and began to govern dictatorially. Two years later Napoleon Bonaparte ended the Directory in a coup d'état (koo day-TAH) and substituted a strong dictatorship for a weak one.

Napoleon's Europe, 1799–1815

☐ Why did Napoleon Bonaparte assume control of France and much of Europe, and what factors led to his downfall?

For almost fifteen years, from 1799 to 1814, France was in the hands of a keen-minded military dictator of exceptional ability. Napoleon Bonaparte (1769–1821) realized the need to put an end to civil strife in France in order to create unity and consolidate his rule. And he did. But Napoleon saw himself as a man of destiny, and the glory of war and the dream of universal empire proved irresistible.

Napoleon's Rule of France

Born on the Mediterranean island of Corsica into an impoverished noble family, Napoleon left home and became a lieutenant in the French artillery in 1785. After a brief and unsuccessful adventure fighting for Corsican independence in 1789, he returned to France as a French patriot and a revolutionary. Rising rapidly in the new army, Napoleon was placed in command of French forces in Italy and won brilliant victories there in 1796 and 1797. His next campaign, in Egypt, was a failure, but Napoleon returned to France before the fiasco was generally known, and his reputation remained intact.

Napoleon soon learned that some prominent members of the legislature were plotting against the Directory. The dissatisfaction of these plotters stemmed not so much from the fact that the Directory was a dictatorship as from the fact that it was a weak dictatorship. To these disillusioned revolutionaries, ten years of upheaval and uncertainty had made firm rule much more appealing than liberty and popular politics.

The flamboyant thirty-year-old Napoleon, nationally revered for his heroism, was an ideal choice for the strong ruler the conspirators were seeking. Thus they and Napoleon organized a takeover. On November 9,

1799, they ousted the Directors, and the following day soldiers disbanded the legislature. Napoleon was named first consul of the republic, and a new constitution consolidating his position was overwhelmingly approved in a plebiscite in December 1799.

The essence of Napoleon's domestic policy was to use his popularity and charisma to maintain order and end civil strife. He did so by working out unwritten agreements with powerful groups in France whereby the groups received favors in return for loyal service. Napoleon's bargain with the middle class was codified in the famous Civil Code of March 1804, also known as the **Napoleonic Code**, which reasserted two of the fundamental principles of the revolution of 1789: equality of all male citizens before the law and absolute security of wealth and private property.

At the same time, Napoleon built on the bureaucracy inherited from the Revolution and the former monarchy to create a thoroughly centralized state. He consolidated his rule by recruiting disillusioned revolutionaries for the network of government officials; they depended on him and came to serve him well. Nor were members of the old nobility slighted. In 1800 and again in 1802 Napoleon granted amnesty to one hundred thousand noble émigrés on the condition that they return to France and take a loyalty oath. Members of this returning elite soon ably occupied many high posts in the expanding centralized state.

Furthermore, Napoleon applied his diplomatic skills to healing the Catholic Church in France so that it could serve as a bulwark of social stability. Napoleon and Pope Pius VII (pontificate 1800–1823) signed the Concordat of 1801. Under this agreement the pope gained the right for French Catholics to practice their religion freely, but Napoleon gained political power: his government now nominated bishops, paid the clergy, and exerted great influence over the church in France.

The domestic reforms of Napoleon's early years were his greatest achievement, and much of his legal and administrative reorganization has survived in France to this day. More generally, Napoleon's domestic initiatives gave the great majority of French people a sense of stability and national unity.

But order and unity had a price: authoritarian rule. Women, who had often participated in revolutionary politics without having legal equality, lost many of the gains they made in the 1790s. Under the new Napoleonic Code, women were regarded as dependents of either their fathers or their husbands, and they could not make contracts or have bank accounts in their own names. Napoleon aimed at re-establishing a family monarchy, where the power of the husband and father was as absolute over the wife and the children as that of Napoleon over his subjects. In other restrictions, free speech and freedom of the press were curtailed, and the occasional elections were thoroughly controlled by

• **Napoleonic Code** French civil code promulgated in 1804 that reasserted the 1789 principles of the equality of all male citizens before the law and the absolute security of wealth and private property.

The Coronation of Napoleon, 1804 In this detail from a grandiose painting by Jacques-Louis David, Napoleon, instead of the pope, prepares to crown his wife, Josephine, in an elaborate ceremony in Notre Dame Cathedral. Napoleon, the ultimate upstart, also crowned himself. Pope Pius VII, seated glumly behind the emperor, is reduced to being a spectator. (Louvre/Réunion des Musées Nationaux/Art Resource, NY)

Napoleon and his government. After 1810 political suspects were held in state prisons, as they had been during the Terror.

Napoleon's Expansion in Europe

After coming to power in 1799 Napoleon sent peace feelers to Austria and Britain, the two remaining members of the Second Coalition that had been formed against France in 1798. When these overtures were rejected, French armies led by Napoleon decisively defeated the Austrians. In the Treaty of Lunéville (1801), Austria accepted the loss of almost all its Italian possessions, and German territory on the west bank of the Rhine was incorporated into France. The British agreed to the Treaty of Amiens in 1802, allowing France to remain in control of Holland, the Austrian Netherlands, the west bank of the Rhine, and most of the Italian peninsula.

In 1802 Napoleon was secure but still driven to expand his power. Aggressively redrawing the map of Germany so as to weaken Austria and encourage the secondary states of southwestern Germany to side with France, Napoleon tried to restrict British trade with all of Europe. He then plotted to attack Britain, but his Mediterranean fleet was destroyed by Lord Nelson at the Battle of Trafalgar on October 21, 1805. Renewed fighting had its advantages, however, for the first consul used his high status as a military leader to have himself proclaimed emperor in late 1804.

Austria, Russia, and Sweden joined with Britain to form the Third Coalition against France shortly before the Battle of Trafalgar. Yet the Austrians and the Russians were no match for Napoleon, who scored a brilliant victory over them at the Battle of Austerlitz in December 1805. Russia decided to pull back, and Austria accepted large territorial losses in return for peace as the Third Coalition collapsed.

German Confederation of the Rhine, 1806

Francisco Goya, *The Third of May 1808* Spanish master Francisco Goya created a passionate and moving indictment of the brutality of war in this painting from 1814, which depicts the close-range execution of Spanish rebels by Napoleon's forces in May 1808. Goya's painting evoked the bitterness and despair of many Europeans who suffered through Napoleon's invasions. (Erich Lessing/Art Resource, NY)

Napoleon then reorganized the German states to his liking. In 1806 he abolished many tiny German states as well as the Holy Roman Empire and established by decree the German Confederation of the Rhine, a union of fifteen German states minus Austria, Prussia, and Saxony. Naming himself "protector" of the confederation, Napoleon firmly controlled western Germany.

Napoleon's intervention in German affairs alarmed the Prussians, who mobilized their armies. In October 1806 Napoleon attacked them and won two more brilliant victories at Jena and Auerstädt, where the Prussians were outnumbered two to one. The war with Prussia, now joined by Russia, continued into the following spring. After Napoleon's larger armies won another victory, Alexander I of Russia was ready to negotiate for peace. In the treaties of Tilsit in 1807, Prussia lost half of its population through land concessions, while Russia accepted Napoleon's reorganization of western and central Europe and promised to enforce Napoleon's economic blockade against British goods.

The Grand Empire and Its End

Increasingly, Napoleon saw himself as the emperor of Europe, not just of France. The so-called **Grand Empire** he built had three parts. The core, or first part, was an ever-expanding France, which by 1810 included Belgium, Holland, parts of northern Italy, and much German territory on the east bank of the Rhine (Map 22.2). The second part consisted of a number of dependent satellite kingdoms. The third part comprised the independent but allied states of Austria, Prussia, and Russia. After 1806 both satellites and allies were expected to support Napoleon's **Continental System**, a

• **Grand Empire** The empire over which Napoleon and his allies ruled, encompassing virtually all of Europe except Great Britain and Russia.

• **Continental System** A blockade imposed by Napoleon to halt all trade between continental Europe and Britain, thereby weakening the British economy and military.

Legend:
- French empire
- Dependent states
- Allied with Napoleon
- ✴ French victory
- ✴ French defeat

KINGDOM OF NORWAY AND DENMARK

KINGDOM OF SWEDEN

Stockholm

St. Petersburg

Napoleon's invasion of Russia, June–Sept. 1812

Borodino 1812

Moscow

North Sea

Baltic Sea

Copenhagen

SWEDISH POMERANIA

Königsberg

Tilsit

Vilna

Smolensk

Maloyaroslavets 1812

GREAT BRITAIN

Hamburg

Lübeck

PRUSSIA

Danzig

Friedland 1807

French retreat, Oct.–Dec. 1812

Neman R.

RUSSIAN EMPIRE

London

Bremen

Berlin

Rhine

Elbe R.

WESTPHALIA

Auerstädt 1806

SAXONY

GRAND DUCHY OF WARSAW

Kiev

Brussels

Waterloo 1815

Jena 1806

Amiens

Paris

CONFEDERATION OF THE RHINE

Austerlitz 1805

Wagram 1804

Vienna

Pressburg

Lunéville

BAVARIA

ATLANTIC OCEAN

FRANCE

WÜRTTEMBERG

Zurich

BADEN

Buda

Pest

AUSTRIAN EMPIRE

ILLYRIAN PROVINCES

Marengo 1800

Milan

KINGDOM OF ITALY

Genoa

Danube R.

Black Sea

PORTUGAL

Marseilles

Elba

Corsica

Lisbon

Madrid

SPAIN

Rome

OTTOMAN EMPIRE

Naples

Trafalgar 1805

Sardinia

GIBRALTAR (Gr. Br.)

KINGDOM OF NAPLES

Mediterranean Sea

Palermo

KINGDOM OF SICILY

Ionian Is. (Gr. Br.)

Athens

Malta (Gr. Br.)

0   100   200 miles
0   100   200 kilometers

▢ Mapping the Past

MAP 22.2 Napoleonic Europe in 1812 At the height of the Grand Empire in 1810, Napoleon had conquered or allied with every major European power except Britain. But in 1812, angered by Russian repudiation of his ban on trade with Britain, Napoleon invaded Russia with disastrous results. Compare this map with Map 17.2 (page 500), which shows the division of Europe in 1715.

ANALYZING THE MAP How had the balance of power shifted in Europe from 1715 to 1812? What changed, and what remained the same? What was the impact of Napoleon's wars on Germany, the Italian peninsula, and Russia?

CONNECTIONS Why did Napoleon achieve vast territorial gains where Louis XIV did not?

blockade in which no ship coming from Britain or her colonies was permitted to dock at any port that was controlled by the French. The blockade was intended to halt all trade between Britain and continental Europe, thereby destroying the British economy and its military force.

The impact of the Grand Empire on the peoples of Europe was considerable. In the areas incorporated into France and in the satellites, Napoleon abolished feudal dues and serfdom. Yet he had to put the prosperity and special interests of France first in order to safeguard his power base. Levying heavy taxes in money and men for his armies, Napoleon came to be regarded more as a conquering tyrant than as an enlightened liberator. Thus French rule sparked patriotic upheavals and encouraged the growth of reactive nationalism.

The first great revolt occurred in Spain. In 1808 a coalition of Catholics, monarchists, and patriots rebelled against Napoleon's attempts to make Spain a French satellite. French armies occupied Madrid, but the foes of Napoleon fled to the hills and waged uncompromising guerrilla warfare. Events in Spain sent a clear warning: resistance to French imperialism was growing.

Yet Napoleon pushed on. In 1810, when the Grand Empire was at its height, Britain still remained at war with France, helping the guerrillas in Spain and Portugal. The Continental System was a failure. Instead of harming Britain, the system provoked this foe to set up a counter-blockade, which created hard times for French artisans and the middle class. Perhaps looking for a scapegoat, Napoleon turned on Alexander I of Russia, who in 1811 openly repudiated Napoleon's war of prohibitions against British goods.

Napoleon's invasion of Russia began in June 1812. Originally, he planned to winter in the Russian city of Smolensk if Alexander did not sue for peace. However, after reaching Smolensk Napoleon recklessly pressed on toward Moscow (see Map 22.2). The Battle of Borodino that followed was a draw, and the Russians retreated in good order. Alexander ordered the evacuation of Moscow, which the Russians then burned in part, and he refused to negotiate. Finally, after five weeks in the scorched and abandoned city, Napoleon ordered a disastrous retreat. The Russian army, the Russian winter, and starvation cut Napoleon's army to pieces.

Leaving his troops to their fate, Napoleon raced to Paris to raise another army. Possibly he might still have saved his throne if he had been willing to accept a France reduced to its historical size — the proposal offered by Austria's foreign minister, Prince Klemens von Metternich. But Napoleon refused. Consequently, Austria and Prussia deserted Napoleon and joined Russia and Britain in the Treaty of Chaumont in March 1814, by which the four powers pledged allegiance to defeat the French emperor.

All across Europe patriots called for a "war of liberation" against Napoleon's oppression. Less than a month later, on April 4, 1814, a defeated Napoleon abdicated his throne. After this unconditional abdication, the victorious allies granted Napoleon the island of Elba off the coast of Italy as his own tiny state.

The allies also agreed to the restoration of the Bourbon dynasty under Louis XVIII (r. 1814–1824) and promised to treat France with leniency in a peace settlement. The new monarch tried to consolidate support among the people by issuing the Constitutional Charter, which accepted many of France's revolutionary changes and guaranteed civil liberties.

Yet Louis XVIII lacked the glory and magnetism of Napoleon. Hearing of political unrest in France and diplomatic tensions in Vienna, Napoleon staged a daring escape from Elba in February 1815. Landing in France, he issued appeals for support and marched on Paris. French officers and soldiers who had fought so long for their emperor responded to the call. Louis XVIII fled, and once more Napoleon took command. But Napoleon's gamble was a desperate long shot, for the allies were united against him. At the end of a frantic period known as the Hundred Days, they crushed his forces at Waterloo on June 18, 1815, and imprisoned him on the island of St. Helena, off the western coast of Africa. Louis XVIII returned to the throne, and the allies dealt more harshly with the French. As for Napoleon, he took revenge by writing his memoirs, nurturing the myth that he had been Europe's revolutionary liberator, a hero whose work had been undone by oppressive reactionaries.

The Haitian Revolution, 1791–1804

☐ How did slave revolt on colonial Saint-Domingue lead to the creation of the independent nation of Haiti in 1804?

The events that led to the creation of the independent nation of Haiti constitute the third, and perhaps most extraordinary, chapter of the revolutionary era in the Atlantic world. Prior to 1789 Saint-Domingue, the French colony that was to become Haiti, reaped huge profits through a ruthless system of slave-based plantation agriculture. News of revolution in France lit a powder keg of contradictory aspirations among white

Saint-Domingue Slave Life Although the brutal conditions of plantation slavery left little time or energy for leisure, slaves on Saint-Domingue took advantage of their day of rest on Sunday to engage in social and religious activities. The law officially prohibited slaves of different masters from mingling together, but such gatherings were often tolerated if they remained peaceful. This image depicts a fight between two slaves, precisely the type of unrest and violence feared by authorities. (Musée du Nouveau Monde, La Rochelle/Photo12.com—ARJ)

planters, free people of color, and slaves. While revolutionary authorities debated how far to extend the rights of man on Saint-Domingue, slaves took matters into their own hands, rising up to claim their freedom. Their revolt succeeded, despite invasion by the British and Spanish and Napoleon Bonaparte's bid to reimpose French control. In 1804 Haiti became the first nation in history to claim its freedom through slave revolt.

Revolutionary Aspirations in Saint-Domingue

On the eve of the French Revolution, Saint-Domingue — the most profitable of all Caribbean colonies — was even more rife with social tensions than France itself. The colony, which occupied the western third of the island of Hispaniola, was inhabited by a variety of social groups who resented and mistrusted one another.

The European population included French colonial officials, wealthy plantation owners and merchants, and poor immigrants. Vastly outnumbering the white population were the colony's five hundred thousand slaves, along with a sizable population of free people of African and mixed African and European descent. Members of this last group referred to themselves as "free coloreds" or free people of color.

The 1685 Code Noir (Black Code) that set the parameters of slavery had granted free people of color the same legal status as whites: they could own property, live where they wished, and pursue any education or career they desired. From the 1760s on, however, colonial administrators began rescinding these rights, and by the time of the French Revolution, myriad aspects of free coloreds' lives were ruled by discriminatory laws.

The political and intellectual turmoil of the 1780s, with its growing rhetoric of liberty, equality, and

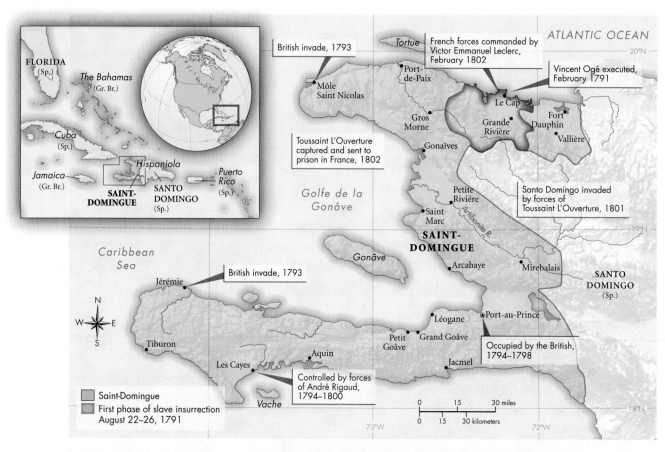

MAP 22.3 The War of Haitian Independence, 1791–1804 Neighbored by the Spanish colony of Santo Domingo, Saint-Domingue was the most profitable European colony in the Caribbean. In 1791 slave revolts erupted in the north near Le Cap, which had once been the capital. In 1770 the French had transferred the capital to Port-au-Prince, which in 1804 became capital of the newly independent Haiti.

fraternity, raised new challenges and possibilities for each of Saint-Domingue's social groups. For slaves, who constituted approximately 90 percent of the population, news of abolitionist movements in France led to hopes that the mother country might grant them freedom. Free people of color looked to reforms in Paris as a means of gaining political enfranchisement and reasserting equal status with whites. The white elite, not surprisingly, saw matters very differently. Infuriated by talk of abolition and determined to protect their way of life, they looked to revolutionary ideals of representative government for the chance to gain control of their own affairs, as had the American colonists before them.

The National Assembly frustrated the hopes of all these groups. Cowed by colonial representatives who claimed that support for free people of color would result in slave insurrection and independence, the Assembly refused to extend French constitutional safeguards to the colonies. After dealing this blow to the aspirations of slaves and free coloreds, the committee

also reaffirmed French monopolies over colonial trade, thereby angering planters as well. Like the American settlers before them, the colonists chafed under the rule of the mother country.

In July 1790 Vincent Ogé (aw-ZHAY; ca. 1750–1791), a free man of color, returned to Saint-Domingue from Paris determined to win rights for his people. He raised an army of several hundred and sent letters to the new Provincial Assembly of Saint-Domingue demanding political rights for all free citizens. But Ogé's demands were refused, so he and his followers turned to armed insurrection. After initial victories, his army was defeated, and Ogé was tortured and executed by colonial officials. Revolutionary leaders in Paris were more sympathetic to Ogé's cause. In May 1791, responding to what it perceived as partly justified grievances, the National Assembly granted political rights to free people of color born to two free parents who possessed sufficient property. When news of this legislation arrived in Saint-Domingue, the white elite was furious, and the colonial governor refused to enact it. Violence now erupted between groups of whites and free coloreds in parts of the colony.

The Outbreak of Revolt

Just as the sans-culottes helped push forward more radical reforms in France, the second stage of revolution in Saint-Domingue also resulted from decisive action from below. In August 1791 slaves, who had witnessed the confrontation between whites and free coloreds for over a year, took events into their own hands. Groups of slaves held a series of nighttime meetings to plan a mass insurrection.

Revolts began on a few plantations on the night of August 22. Within a few days the uprising had swept much of the northern plain, creating a slave army estimated at around 2,000 individuals. By August 27 it was described by one observer as "10,000 strong, divided into 3 armies, of whom 700 or 800 are on horseback, and tolerably well-armed."[6] During the next month slaves attacked and destroyed hundreds of sugar and coffee plantations.

On April 4, 1792, as war loomed with the European states, the National Assembly issued a decree extending full citizenship rights, including the right to vote, to free blacks and free people of color. As in France, voting rights and the ability to hold public office applied to men only. The Assembly hoped this measure would win the loyalty of free blacks and their aid in defeating the slave rebellion.

Warfare in Europe soon spread to Saint-Domingue (Map 22.3). Since the beginning of the slave insurrection, the Spanish colony of Santo Domingo, just to the east of Saint-Domingue, had supported rebel slaves. In early 1793 the Spanish began to bring slave leaders and their soldiers into the Spanish army. Toussaint L'Ouverture (TOO-sahn LOO-vair-toor; 1743–1803), a freed slave who had joined the revolt, was named a Spanish officer. In September the British navy blockaded the colony, and invading British troops captured French territory on the island. For the Spanish and British, revolutionary chaos provided a tempting opportunity to capture a profitable colony.

Desperate for forces to oppose France's enemies, commissioners sent by the newly elected National Convention promised freedom to slaves who fought for France. By October 1793 they had abolished slavery throughout the colony. On February 4, 1794, the Convention ratified the abolition of slavery and extended it to all French territories, including the Caribbean colonies of Martinique and Guadeloupe.

The tide of battle began to turn when Toussaint L'Ouverture switched sides, bringing his military and political skills, along with four thousand well-trained soldiers, to support the French war effort. By 1796

□ KEY EVENTS OF THE HAITIAN REVOLUTION	
1760s	Colonial administrators begin rescinding the rights of free people of color
July 1790	Vincent Ogé leads a failed rebellion to gain rights for free people of color
August 1791	Slave revolts begin
April 4, 1792	National Assembly enfranchises all free blacks and free people of color
September 1793	British troops invade Saint-Domingue
February 4, 1794	National Convention ratifies the abolition of slavery and extends it to all French territories
May 1796	Toussaint L'Ouverture is named commander of Saint-Domingue
1800	After invading the south of Saint-Domingue, L'Ouverture gains control of the entire colony
1802	French general Charles-Victor-Emmanuel Leclerc arrests L'Ouverture and deports him to France
1803	L'Ouverture dies
1804	After defeating French forces, Jean Jacques Dessalines declares the independence of Saint-Domingue and the creation of the sovereign nation of Haiti

the French had regained control of the colony, and L'Ouverture had emerged as the key leader of the combined slave and free colored forces. (See "Individuals in Society: Toussaint L'Ouverture," page 680.) In May 1796 he was named commander of the western province of Saint-Domingue (see Map 22.3). The increasingly conservative nature of the French government during the Thermidorian reaction, however, threatened to undo the gains made by former slaves and free people of color.

The War of Haitian Independence

With Toussaint L'Ouverture acting increasingly as an independent ruler of the western province of Saint-Domingue, another general, André Rigaud (1761–1811), set up his own government in the southern peninsula. Tensions mounted between L'Ouverture and Rigaud. While L'Ouverture was a freed slave of African descent, Rigaud belonged to the free colored elite. This elite resented the growing power of former slaves like

Individuals in Society

Toussaint L'Ouverture

LITTLE IS KNOWN OF THE EARLY LIFE OF Saint-Domingue's brilliant military and political leader Toussaint L'Ouverture. He was born in 1743 on a plantation outside Le Cap owned by the Count de Bréda. According to tradition, L'Ouverture was the eldest son of a captured African prince from modern-day Benin. Toussaint Bréda, as he was then called, occupied a privileged position among slaves. Instead of performing backbreaking labor in the fields, he served his master as a coachman and livestock keeper. He also learned to read and write French and some Latin, but he was always more comfortable with the Creole dialect.

During the 1770s the plantation manager emancipated L'Ouverture, who subsequently leased his own small coffee plantation, worked by slaves. He married Suzanne Simone, who already had one son, and the couple had another son during their marriage. In 1791 he joined the slave uprisings that swept Saint-Domingue, and he took on the *nom de guerre* ("war name") L'Ouverture, meaning "the opening." L'Ouverture rose to prominence among rebel slaves allied with Spain and by early 1794 controlled his own army. A devout Catholic who led a frugal and ascetic life, L'Ouverture impressed others with his enormous physical energy, intellectual acumen, and air of mystery. In 1794 he defected to the French side and led his troops to a series of victories against the Spanish. In 1795 the National Convention promoted L'Ouverture to brigadier general.

Over the next three years L'Ouverture successively eliminated rivals for authority on the island. First he freed himself of the French commissioners sent to govern the colony. With a firm grip on power in the northern province, L'Ouverture defeated General André Rigaud in 1800 to gain control in the south. His army then marched on the capital of Spanish Santo Domingo on the eastern half of the island, meeting little resistance. The entire island of Hispaniola was now under his command.

With control in his hands, L'Ouverture was confronted with the challenge of building a post-emancipation society, the first of its kind. The task was made even more difficult by the chaos wreaked by war, the destruction of plantations, and bitter social and racial tensions. For L'Ouverture the most pressing concern was to re-establish the plantation economy. Without revenue to pay his army, the gains of the rebellion could be lost. He therefore encouraged white planters to return and reclaim their property. He also adopted harsh policies toward former slaves, forcing them back to their plantations and restricting their ability to acquire land. When they resisted, he sent troops across the island to enforce submission. L'Ouverture's 1801 constitution reaffirmed his draconian labor policies and named L'Ouverture governor for life, leaving Saint-Domingue as a colony in name alone. In June 1802 French forces arrested L'Ouverture and jailed him at Fort de Joux in France's Jura Mountains near the Swiss border. He died of pneumonia on April 7, 1803, leaving his lieutenant, Jean Jacques Dessalines, to win independence for the new Haitian nation.

QUESTIONS FOR ANALYSIS

1. Toussaint L'Ouverture was both slave and slave owner. How did each experience shape his life and actions?
2. What did L'Ouverture and Napoleon Bonaparte have in common? How did they differ?

Equestrian portrait of Toussaint L'Ouverture.
(Réunion des Musées Nationaux/Art Resource, NY)

L'Ouverture, who in turn accused them of adopting the racism of white settlers. Civil war broke out between the two sides in 1799, when L'Ouverture's forces, led by his lieutenant, Jean Jacques Dessalines (1758–1806), invaded the south. Victory over Rigaud in 1800 gave L'Ouverture control of the entire colony.

This victory was soon challenged by Napoleon, who had his own plans for re-establishing slavery and using the profits as a basis for expanding French power. Napoleon ordered his brother-in-law, General Charles-Victor-Emmanuel Leclerc (1772–1802), to lead an expedition to the island to crush the new regime. In 1802 Leclerc landed in Saint-Domingue and ordered the arrest of Toussaint L'Ouverture. The rebel leader was deported to France, along with his family, where he died in 1803.

It was left to L'Ouverture's lieutenant, Jean Jacques Dessalines, to unite the resistance, and he led it to a crushing victory over French forces. On January 1, 1804, Dessalines formally declared the independence of Saint-Domingue and the creation of the new sovereign nation of Haiti, the name used by the pre-Columbian inhabitants of the island.

Haiti, the second independent state in the Americas and the first in Latin America, was born from the first successful large-scale slave revolt in history. Fearing the spread of slave rebellion to the United States, President Thomas Jefferson refused to recognize Haiti. The liberal proponents of the American Revolution thus chose to protect slavery at the expense of revolutionary ideals of universal human rights. Yet Haitian independence had fundamental repercussions for world history, helping spread the idea that liberty, equality, and fraternity must apply to all people. The next phase of Atlantic revolution soon opened in the Spanish American colonies.

CONNECTIONS

The Atlantic world was the essential context for the great revolutionary wave of the late eighteenth century. The movement of peoples, commodities, and ideas across the Atlantic Ocean in the eighteenth century created a world of common debates, conflicts, and aspirations. Moreover, the high stakes of colonial empire heightened competition among European states, leading to a series of wars that generated crushing costs for overburdened treasuries. For both the British in their North American colonies and the French at home, the desperate need for new taxes weakened government authority and opened the door to revolution. In turn, the ideals of the French Revolution inspired slaves and free people of color in Saint-Domingue, thus opening the promise of liberty, equality, and fraternity to people of all races.

The chain reaction did not end with the birth of an independent Haiti in 1804. The next chapter of liberation movements took place in Spanish America in the following decades (see Chapter 27). On the European continent throughout the nineteenth and early twentieth centuries, periodic convulsions occurred as successive generations struggled over political rights first proclaimed by the generation of 1789 (see Chapter 24). Meanwhile, as dramatic political events unfolded, a parallel economic revolution was gathering steam. This was the Industrial Revolution, originating around 1750 and accelerating through the end of the eighteenth century (see Chapter 23). After 1815 the twin forces of industrialization and democratization would combine to transform Europe and the world.

☐ CHAPTER REVIEW

☐ **What were the factors behind the age of revolution in the Atlantic world? (p. 652)**

The origins of revolutions in the Atlantic world were varied and complex. They included long-term social and economic changes, such as greater inequalities between rich and poor, that challenged the traditional privileges held by elites. Enlightenment ideals of liberty and equality inspired liberal reformers to insist on limited governments, universal human rights, and equality of opportunity under the law. However, liberals' understanding of liberty and equality often excluded women and nonwhites. The huge expenses of the Seven Years' War also opened the door to revolution by forcing the British and French governments to raise taxes and thereby provoke violent protest.

☐ **Why and how did American colonists forge a new, independent nation? (p. 656)**

British efforts to raise taxes to meet debts from the Seven Years' War aroused violent protest in the American colonies. In 1774 the First Continental Congress met and rejected compromise with the home government. When the British also refused to back down, fighting broke out between the two sides. Two years later the Second Continental Congress issued the Declaration of Independence, a document that made the traditional rights of English people into universal human rights. Conflict ensued between Loyalists, who wished to remain within the British Empire, and American patriots. Eager to profit from the weakness of a mighty empire, the French, Spanish, and Dutch declared war on Britain. In 1783 the British recognized the independence of the thirteen colonies. The Constitutional Convention drafted a constitution for the new nation, but controversy soon erupted over the balance between federal and state power and the status of individual freedoms. To protect such freedoms, Congress passed the first ten amendments to the Constitution, a Bill of Rights safeguarding the individual. However, the new government did not grant women, slaves, or indigenous peoples equal rights.

☐ **How did the events of 1789 result in a constitutional monarchy in France, and what were the consequences? (p. 659)**

When the Estates General gathered in 1789, delegates from the third estate, representing the common people, refused to accept the old system of one vote per estate. Instead, they declared themselves a National Assembly. Popular revolts prevented the king from intervening, and he was forced to accept the situation. The National

Assembly promulgated France's first constitution in 1791, leaving the king as head of state but limited by the powers of the National Assembly. The nobility was abolished, but only the wealthiest half of the male population could vote in elections for the National Assembly and women were not allowed to vote or hold political office. Also, to the horror of the pope and devout French Catholics, the government seized church property and imposed an oath of loyalty on priests.

☐ **Why and how did the French Revolution take a radical turn entailing terror at home and war with European powers? (p. 667)**

Support for the constitutional monarchy ended with the royal family's attempted flight in June 1791. The new Legislative Assembly, comprising younger and more radical delegates led by members of the Jacobin club, declared war on Austria (which wanted Louis XVI and his queen kept in power) and proclaimed France a republic. With the execution of the royal couple and the declaration of terror as the order of the day, the French Revolution took an increasingly radical turn from the end of 1792. France was largely victorious, mostly because of the total war effort undertaken by the Jacobin leadership. To defend the Revolution against its perceived internal enemies, Jacobins eliminated political opponents and then factions within their own party. They also attempted to bring about a cultural revolution, in part by attacking Christianity and substituting secular republican festivals. The Directory that took power after the fall of Robespierre restored political equilibrium at the cost of the radical platform of social equality he had pursued.

☐ **Why did Napoleon Bonaparte assume control of France and much of Europe, and what factors led to his downfall? (p. 672)**

Wearied by the weaknesses of the Directory, a group of conspirators joined forces with Napoleon Bonaparte to oust the Directors and give Napoleon control of France. His reputation as a brilliant military leader and his charisma and determination made him seem ideal to lead the country to victory over its enemies. However, Napoleon's relentless ambitions ultimately led to his downfall. Not satisfied with his successes throughout Europe, and struggling to maintain his hold on Spain and Portugal, Napoleon made the fatal mistake of attempting to invade Russia in the summer of 1812. After a disastrous retreat from Moscow, he was eventually forced to abdicate the throne in 1814.

◻ How did slave revolt on colonial Saint-Domingue lead to the creation of the independent nation of Haiti in 1804? (p. 676)

The outbreak of revolution in France raised new and contradictory possibilities for the people in the French colony of Saint-Domingue. On the one hand, slaves and free people of color hoped that reforms in the mother country might lead to more rights for them. On the other hand, the white elite hoped that a representative government would help them gain more control. The revolutionary government in France waffled disastrously on colonial affairs, succeeding only in infuriating all sides. After a failed uprising by free men of color, slaves took matters into their own hands in August 1791. Their revolt, combined with the outbreak of war and the radicalization of the revolution in France, led to the enfranchisement of free men of color, the emancipation of slaves who fought for France, and the abolition of slavery throughout the colony in late 1793. Like Napoleon Bonaparte, Toussaint L'Ouverture was an unknown soldier who emerged into the political limelight out of the chaos of revolution, only to endure exile and defeat. Unlike Napoleon's quest to expand his empire, L'Ouverture's cause ultimately prevailed. After his exile, war between the French forces and the armies he had led resulted in French defeat and independence for Haiti in 1804.

SUGGESTED READING

Bell, David A. *The Cult of the Nation in France: Inventing Nationalism, 1680–1800.* 2001. Traces early French nationalism through its revolutionary culmination.

Blanning, T. C. W. *The French Revolutionary Wars (1787–1802).* 1996. A masterful account of the revolutionary wars that also places the French Revolution in its European context.

Broers, Michael. *Europe Under Napoleon.* 2002. Probes Napoleon's impact on the territories he conquered.

Calloway, Colin G. *The Scratch of a Pen: 1763 and the Transformation of North America.* 2006. A study of the dramatic impact of the Seven Years' War on the British and French colonies of North America.

Connelly, Owen. *The French Revolution and Napoleonic Era.* 1991. An excellent introduction to the French Revolution and Napoleon.

Desan, Suzanne. *The Family on Trial in Revolutionary France.* 2004. Studies the effects of revolutionary law on the family, including the legalization of divorce.

Dubois, Laurent. *Avengers of the New World: The Story of the Haitian Revolution.* 2004. An excellent and highly readable account of the revolution that transformed the French colony of Saint-Domingue into the independent state of Haiti.

Englund, Steven. *Napoleon: A Political Life.* 2004. A good biography of the French emperor.

Goulda, Eliga H., and Peter Onuf, eds. *Empire and Nation: The American Revolution in the Atlantic World.* 2005. A collection of essays placing the American Revolution in its wider Atlantic context, including studies of its impact on daily life in the new republic and the remaining British Empire.

Hunt, Lynn. *Politics, Culture, and Class in the French Revolution,* 2d ed. 2004. A pioneering examination of the French Revolution as a cultural phenomenon that generated new festivals, clothing, and songs, and even a new calendar.

Landes, John B. *Visualizing the Nation: Gender, Representation, and Revolution in Eighteenth-Century France.* 2001. Analyzes images of gender and the body in revolutionary politics.

Sutherland, Donald. *France, 1789–1815.* 1986. An overview of the French Revolution that emphasizes its many opponents as well as its supporters.

Tackett, Timothy. *When the King Took Flight.* 2003. An exciting re-creation of the royal family's doomed effort to escape from Paris.

NOTES

1. Quoted in G. Wright, *France in Modern Times,* 4th ed. (New York: W. W. Norton, 1987), p. 34.
2. G. Pernoud and S. Flaisser, eds., *The French Revolution* (Greenwich, Conn.: Fawcett, 1960), p. 61.
3. Quoted in L. Gershoy, *The Era of the French Revolution, 1789–1799* (New York: Van Nostrand, 1957), p. 150.
4. Cited in Wim Klooster, *Revolutions in the Atlantic World: A Comprehensive History* (New York and London: New York University Press, 2009), p. 74.
5. T. Blanning, *The French Revolutionary Wars, 1787–1802* (London: Arnold, 1996), pp. 116–128.
6. Quoted in Laurent Dubois, *Avengers of the New World: The Story of the Haitian Revolution* (Cambridge, Mass.: Harvard University Press, 2004), p. 97.

For practice quizzes and other study tools, visit the **Online Study Guide** at bedfordstmartins.com/mckayworld.

For primary sources from this period, see *Sources of World Societies,* **Second Edition.**

For Web sites, images, and documents related to topics in this chapter, visit **Make History** at bedfordstmartins.com/mckayworld.

• **Young Factory Worker** Children composed a substantial element of the workforce in early factories, where they toiled long hours in dangerous and unsanitary conditions. Until a mechanized process was invented at the end of the nineteenth century, boys working in glass-bottle factories, like the youth pictured here, stoked blazing furnaces with coal and learned to blow glass. (© Boume Gallery, Reigate, Surrey, UK/The Bridgeman Art Library)

While the revolutions of the Atlantic world and in France were opening a new political era, another revolution was beginning to transform economic and social life. The Industrial Revolution began in Great Britain around the 1780s and started to influence continental Europe after 1815. Quite possibly only the development of agriculture during Neolithic times had a comparable impact and significance. Non-European nations began to industrialize after 1860, with the United States and Japan taking an early lead.

The Industrial Revolution profoundly modified much of human experience. It changed patterns of work, transformed the social class structure and the way people thought about class, and eventually altered the international balance of political power. The Industrial Revolution also helped ordinary people gain a higher standard of living as the widespread poverty of the preindustrial world was gradually reduced.

Unfortunately, improvement in the European standard of living was limited until about 1850 for at least two reasons. First, even in Britain, only a few key industries experienced a technological revolution. Many more industries continued to use old methods. Second, rapid growth in population, which began in the eighteenth century, threatened to eat up the growth in production and to leave most individuals poorer than ever. Industrialization drew on British profits from Atlantic trade, including slavery. Even more important were the consequences of early industrialization in Britain and on the European continent, which allowed Europeans to increase their economic and political dominance over other nations. •

The Revolution in Energy and Industry
1760–1850

The Industrial Revolution in Britain

□ What were the origins of the Industrial Revolution in Britain, and how did it develop between 1780 and 1850?

Industrialization Beyond Britain

□ How after 1815 did countries outside of Britain respond to the challenge of industrialization?

Relations Between Capital and Labor

□ How did the Industrial Revolution affect people of all social classes, and what measures were taken to improve the conditions of workers?

The Industrial Revolution in Britain

□ What were the origins of the Industrial Revolution in Britain, and how did it develop between 1780 and 1850?

The Industrial Revolution began in Britain, the nation created by the formal union of Scotland, Wales, and England in 1707. The transformation in industry was something new in history, and it was unplanned. With no models to copy and no idea of what to expect, Britain pioneered not only in industrial technology but also in social relations and urban living. Just as France was the trailblazer in political change, Britain was the leader in economic development, and it must therefore command special attention.

Origins of the British Industrial Revolution

Although many aspects of the origins of the British Industrial Revolution are still matters for scholarly debate, it is generally agreed that industrial changes grew out of a long process of development. The scientific revolution and Enlightenment fostered a new worldview that embraced progress and the role of research and experimentation in understanding and mastering the natural world. In the economic realm, the seventeenth-century expansion of English woolen cloth exports throughout Europe brought commercial profits and high wages to the detriment of traditional

Industrial areas
▪ Coal deposit
○ Metal goods
▪ Woolen cloth
— Canals, 1800
— Navigable rivers

Cottage Industry and Transportation in Eighteenth-Century England

producers in Flanders and Italy. By the eighteenth century the expanding Atlantic economy was also serving Britain well. The mercantilist colonial empire Britain aggressively built, augmented by a strong position in Latin America and in the African slave trade, provided raw materials like cotton and a growing market for British manufactured goods (see Chapter 18).

Agriculture also played an important role in bringing about the Industrial Revolution in Britain. English farmers were second only to the Dutch in productivity in 1700, and they were continually adopting new methods of farming. The result, especially before 1760, was a period of bountiful crops and low food prices. The ordinary English family no longer had to spend almost everything it earned just to buy bread. Thus the family could spend more on manufactured goods — a razor for the man or a shawl for the woman. Moreover, in the eighteenth century the members of the average British family were redirecting their labor away from unpaid work for household consumption toward work for wages that they could spend on goods, a trend reflecting the increasing commercialization of the entire European economy. In Britain, rising urbanization and high wages both reflected these developments and spurred them forward.

As manufacturing expanded to supply both foreign and British customers, the domestic market for raw materials was well-positioned to meet the growing demands of manufacturers. In an age when it was much cheaper to ship goods by water than by land, no part of England was more than fifty miles from navigable water. Beginning in the 1770s a canal-building boom enhanced this advantage. Rivers and canals provided easy movement of England's and Wales's enormous deposits of iron and coal, resources that would be critical raw materials in Europe's early industrial age. Nor were there any tariffs within the country to hinder trade, as there were in France before 1789 and in politically fragmented Germany.

Finally, Britain had long had a large class of hired agricultural laborers, rural proletarians whose numbers were further increased by the second great round of enclosures (the division of common lands into privately held and managed properties) in the late eighteenth century. These rural wage earners were relatively mobile — compared to village-bound peasants in France and western Germany, for example — and along with cottage workers they formed a potential industrial labor force for capitalist entrepreneurs.

All these factors combined to initiate the **Industrial Revolution**, a term first coined by awed contemporaries in the 1830s to describe the burst of major inventions and technical changes they had witnessed in certain industries. This technical revolution went hand in hand with an impressive quickening in the annual rate of industrial growth in Britain. Whereas industry had grown at only 0.7 percent between 1700 and 1760 (before the Industrial Revolution), it grew at the much higher rate of 3 percent between 1801 and 1831 (when industrial transformation was in full swing).[1]

The great economic and political revolutions that shaped the modern world occurred almost simultaneously, though they began in different countries. But the Industrial Revolution was a longer process than the political upheavals of the French Revolution. It was not complete in Britain until 1850 at the earliest, and it had no real impact on continental countries until after the end of the Napoleonic wars in 1815. It spread beyond Europe in the second half of the nineteenth century.

The First Factories

The pressures to produce more goods for a growing market and to reduce the labor costs of manufacturing were directly related to the first decisive breakthrough of the Industrial Revolution: the creation of the world's first large factories in the British cotton textile industry. Technological innovations in the manufacture of cotton cloth led to a new system of production and social relationships. The putting-out system involved a merchant who loaned, or "put out," raw materials to cottage workers who processed the raw materials in their own homes and returned the finished products to the merchant.

During the eighteenth century this system was used across Europe, but most extensively in Britain. There, pressured by growing demand, the system's limitations began to outweigh its advantages for the first time. This was especially true in the British textile industry after about 1760. There was always a serious imbalance in textile production based on cottage industry: the work of four or five spinners was needed to keep one weaver steadily employed. Cloth weavers constantly had to try to find more thread and more spinners.

□ **CHRONOLOGY**

ca. 1765 Hargreaves invents spinning jenny; Arkwright creates water frame

1769 Watt patents modern steam engine

ca. 1780–1850 Industrial Revolution and accompanying population boom in Great Britain

1799 Combination Acts passed in England

1805 Egypt begins process of modernization

1810 Strike of Manchester, England, cotton spinners

ca. 1815 Industrial gap between continental Europe and England widens

1824 British Combination Acts repealed

1830 Stephenson's *Rocket*; first important railroad

1830s Industrial banks promote rapid industrialization of Belgium

1833 Factory Act passed in England

1834 German *Zollverein* created

1842 Mines Act passed in England

1844 Engels, *The Condition of the Working Class in England*

1850s Japan begins to adopt Western technologies; industrial gap widens between the West and the world

1851 Great Exhibition held at Crystal Palace in London

1860s Germany and the United States begin to rapidly industrialize

Moreover, deep-seated conflicts existed between merchants who put out materials and the workers who processed them. In "The Clothier's Delight, or the Rich Men's Joy and the Poor Men's Sorrow," an English popular song written about 1700, a merchant boasts of the countless tricks he used to "beat down wages":

> We heapeth up riches and treasure great store
> Which we get by griping and grinding the poor.
> And this is a way for to fill up our purse
> Although we do get it with many a curse.[2]

There were constant disputes over the weights of materials and the quality of the cloth. Merchants accused workers of stealing raw materials, and weavers complained that merchants delivered underweight bales.

• **Industrial Revolution** A term first coined in the 1830s to describe the burst of major inventions and economic expansion that took place in certain industries, such as cotton textiles and iron, between 1780 and 1850.

Woman Working a Spinning Jenny The loose cotton strands on the slanted bobbins shown in this illustration of Hargreave's spinning jenny passed up to the sliding carriage and then on to the spindles (inset) in back for fine spinning. The worker, almost always a woman, regulated the sliding carriage with one hand, and with the other she turned the crank on the wheel to supply power. By 1783 one woman could spin a hundred threads at a time. (spinning jenny: Mary Evans Picture Library/The Image Works; spindle: Picture Research Consultants & Archives)

Both were right; each tried to cheat the other, even if only in self-defense.

There was another problem, at least from the merchant-capitalist's point of view. Scattered rural labor was extremely difficult to control. Cottage workers tended to work in spurts. After they got paid on Saturday afternoon, the men in particular tended to drink and carouse for two or three days. Productivity suffered, and by the end of the week many weavers had to work feverishly to make their quota. If they did not succeed, there was little the merchant could do. The merchant-capitalist's search for more efficient methods of production intensified.

Many a tinkering worker knew that a better spinning wheel promised rich rewards. It proved hard to spin the traditional raw materials — wool and flax — with improved machines, but cotton was different. Cotton textiles had first been imported into Britain from India by the East India Company as a rare and delicate luxury for the upper classes, and by 1760 a tiny domestic cotton industry had emerged in northern England. After many experiments over a generation, a gifted carpenter and jack-of-all-trades, James Hargreaves, in-

vented his cotton-spinning jenny about 1765. At almost the same moment, a barber-turned-manufacturer named Richard Arkwright invented (or possibly pirated) another kind of spinning machine, the water frame. These breakthroughs produced an explosion in the infant cotton textile industry in the 1780s, when it was increasing the value of its output at an unprecedented rate of about 13 percent each year. By 1790 the new machines were producing ten times as much cotton yarn as had been made in 1770.

Hargreaves's **spinning jenny** was simple, inexpensive, and powered by hand. In early models from six to twenty-four spindles were mounted on a sliding carriage, and each spindle spun a fine, slender thread. The woman moved the carriage back and forth with one hand and turned a wheel to supply power with the other. Now it was the male weaver who could not keep up with the vastly more efficient female spinner.

Arkwright's **water frame** employed a different principle. It quickly acquired a capacity of several hundred spindles and demanded much more power — waterpower. The water frame thus required large specialized mills, factories that employed as many as one

A Pioneering Silk Mill In the 1600s Italians invented a machine to spin the thread for the silk that rich people loved. Their carefully guarded secret was stolen in 1717 by John Lombe, who then built this enormous silk mill in England. But the factory production of textiles only took off when the spinning of cotton — a fabric for all classes — was mechanized in the later eighteenth century. (© The Art Gallery Collection/Alamy)

thousand workers from the very beginning. It did not completely replace cottage industry, however, for the water frame could spin only a coarse, strong thread, which was then put out for respinning on hand-powered cottage jennies. Around 1790 a hybrid machine invented by Samuel Crompton proved capable of spinning very fine and strong thread in large quantities. Gradually, all cotton spinning was concentrated in large-scale factories.

The first consequences of these revolutionary developments in the textile industry were more beneficial than is generally believed. Cotton goods became much cheaper, and they were increasingly bought by all classes. Families using cotton in cottage industry were freed from their constant search for adequate yarn from scattered part-time spinners, since all the thread needed could be spun in the cottage on the jenny or obtained from a nearby factory. The wages of weavers, now hard-pressed to keep up with the spinners, rose markedly until about 1792. They were among the best-paid workers in England. As a result, large numbers of agricultural laborers became hand-loom weavers, while mechanics and capitalists sought to invent a power loom to save on labor costs. This Edmund Cartwright achieved in 1785. But the power looms of the factories worked poorly at first, and hand-loom weavers continued to receive good wages until at least 1800.

Unfortunately, working conditions in the early cotton factories were less satisfactory than those of cottage weavers and spinners, and adult workers were reluctant to work in them. Therefore, factory owners often turned to young children who had been abandoned by their parents and put in the care of local parishes. Parish officers often "apprenticed" such

- **spinning jenny** A simple, inexpensive, hand-powered spinning machine created by James Hargreaves in 1765.
- **water frame** A spinning machine created by Richard Arkwright that had a capacity of several hundred spindles and used waterpower; it therefore required a larger and more specialized mill — a factory.

unfortunate foundlings to factory owners. The parish thus saved money, and the factory owners gained workers over whom they exercised almost the authority of slave owners. Apprenticed as young as five or six years of age, boy and girl workers were forced by law to labor for their "masters" for as many as fourteen years. Housed, fed, and locked up nightly in factory dormitories, the young workers labored thirteen or fourteen hours a day for little or no pay. Harsh physical punishment maintained brutal discipline. Hours were appalling—commonly thirteen or fourteen hours a day, six days a week. To be sure, poor children typically worked long hours and frequently outside the home for brutal masters, but the wholesale coercion of orphans as factory apprentices constituted exploitation on a truly unprecedented scale.

The creation of the world's first modern factories in the British cotton textile industry in the 1770s and 1780s, which grew out of the putting-out system of cottage production, was a major historical development. Both symbolically and substantially, the big new cotton mills marked the beginning of the Industrial Revolution in Britain. By 1831 the largely mechanized cotton textile industry accounted for fully 22 percent of the country's entire industrial production.

The Steam Engine Breakthrough

Human beings have long used their toolmaking abilities to construct machines that convert one form of energy into another for their own benefit. In the medieval period Europeans began to adopt water mills to grind their grain and windmills to pump water and drain swamps. More efficient use of water and wind in the sixteenth and seventeenth centuries enabled them to accomplish more. Nevertheless, even into the eighteenth century European society, like other areas of the world, continued to rely mainly on wood for energy, and human beings and animals continued to perform most work. This dependence meant that Europe and the rest of the world remained poor in energy and power.

The shortage of energy had become particularly severe in Britain by the eighteenth century. Wood, a basic raw material and the primary source of heat for all homes and industries, was in ever-shorter supply. Processed wood (charcoal) was the fuel that was mixed with iron ore in the blast furnace to produce pig iron. The iron industry's appetite for wood was enormous, and by 1740 the British iron industry was stagnating. Vast forests enabled Russia in the eighteenth century

to become the world's leading producer of iron, much of which was exported to England.

As this early energy crisis grew worse, Britain looked to coal as an alternative to its vanishing wood. Coal was first used in Britain in the late Middle Ages as a source of heat. By 1640 most homes in London were heated with coal, and it was also used in industry to provide heat for making beer, glass, soap, and other products. The breakthrough came when industrialists began to use coal to produce mechanical energy and to power machinery.

As more coal was produced, mines were dug deeper and deeper and were constantly filling with water. Mechanical pumps, usually powered by animals walking in circles at the surface, had to be installed. Such power was expensive and bothersome. In an attempt to overcome these disadvantages, Thomas Savery in 1698 and Thomas Newcomen in 1705 invented the first primitive **steam engines**. Both engines burned coal to produce steam, which was then used to operate a pump. Although both models were extremely inefficient, by the early 1770s many of the Savery engines and hundreds of the Newcomen engines were operating successfully in English and Scottish mines.

In 1763 a gifted young Scot named James Watt (1736–1819) was drawn to a critical study of the steam engine. Watt was employed at the time by the University of Glasgow as a skilled craftsman making scientific instruments. The Scottish universities were pioneers in practical technical education, and in 1763 Watt was called on to repair a Newcomen engine being used in a physics course. After a series of observations, Watt saw that the Newcomen engine's waste of energy could be reduced by adding a separate condenser. This splendid invention, patented in 1769, greatly increased the efficiency of the steam engine.

To invent something is one thing; to make it a practical success is quite another. Watt needed skilled workers, precision parts, and capital, and the relatively advanced nature of the British economy proved essential. A partnership in 1775 with Matthew Boulton, a wealthy English industrialist, provided Watt with adequate capital and exceptional skills in salesmanship that equaled those of the renowned pottery king, Josiah Wedgwood. (See "Individuals in Society: Josiah Wedgwood," page 692.) In the craft tradition of locksmiths, tinsmiths, and millwrights, Watt found mechanics who could install, regulate, and repair his sophisticated engines. From ingenious manufacturers such as the cannonmaker John Wilkinson, Watt was gradually able to purchase precision parts. By the late 1780s the firm of Boulton and Watt had made the steam engine a practical and commercial success in Britain.

The coal-burning steam engine of Watt and his followers was the Industrial Revolution's most fundamental advance in technology. For the first time in history,

---

• **steam engines** A breakthrough invention by Thomas Savery in 1698 and Thomas Newcomen in 1705 that burned coal to produce steam, which was then used to operate a pump; the early models were superseded by James Watt's more efficient steam engine, patented in 1769.

James Nasmyth's Mighty Steam Hammer Nasmyth's invention was the forerunner of the modern pile driver, and its successful introduction in 1832 epitomized the rapid development of steam power technology in Britain. In this painting by the inventor himself, workers manipulate a massive iron shaft being hammered into shape at Nasmyth's foundry near Manchester. (Science & Society Picture Library, London)

humanity had, at least for a few generations, almost unlimited power at its disposal. For the first time, inventors and engineers could devise and implement all kinds of power equipment to aid people in their work.

The steam engine was quickly put to use in several industries in Britain. It drained mines and made possible the production of ever more coal to feed steam engines elsewhere. The steam-power plant began to replace waterpower in the cotton-spinning mills during the 1780s, contributing greatly to that industry's phenomenal rise. Steam also took the place of waterpower in flour mills, in the malt mills used in breweries, in the flint mills supplying the pottery industry, and in the mills exported by Britain to the West Indies to crush sugar cane.

Coal and steam power promoted important breakthroughs in other industries. The British iron industry was radically transformed. Originally, the smoke and fumes of coal burning meant that it could not be substituted for charcoal (derived from limited supplies of wood) in smelting iron. Starting around 1710, ironmakers began to use coke — a smokeless and hot-burning fuel produced by heating coal to rid it of water and impurities — to smelt pig iron. After 1770 the adoption of steam-driven bellows in blast furnaces allowed for great increases in the quantity of pig iron produced by British ironmakers. In the 1780s Henry Cort developed the puddling furnace, which allowed pig iron to be refined in turn with coke.

Cort also developed steam-powered rolling mills, which were capable of spewing out finished iron in every shape and form. The economic consequence of these technical innovations was a great boom in the British iron industry. In 1740 annual British iron production was only 17,000 tons. With the spread of coke smelting and the impact of Cort's inventions,

Individuals in Society

Josiah Wedgwood

AS THE MAKING OF CLOTH AND IRON WAS revolutionized by technical change and factory organization, so too were the production and consumption of pottery. Acquiring beautiful tableware became a craze for eighteenth-century consumers, and continental monarchs often sought prestige in building royal china works. But the grand prize went to Josiah Wedgwood, who wanted to "astonish the world."

The twelfth child of a poor potter, Josiah Wedgwood (1730–1795) grew up in the pottery district of Staffordshire in the English Midlands, where many tiny potteries made simple earthenware utensils for sale in local markets. Having grown up as an apprentice in the family business inherited by his oldest brother, Wedgwood struck off on his own in 1752. Soon manager of a small pottery, Wedgwood learned that new products recharged lagging sales. Studying chemistry and determined to succeed, Wedgwood spent his evenings experimenting with different chemicals and firing conditions.

In 1759, after five years of tireless efforts, Wedgwood perfected a beautiful new green glaze. Now established as a master potter, he opened his own factory and began manufacturing teapots and tableware finished in his green and other unique glazes, or adorned with printed scenes far superior to those being produced by competitors. Wedgwood's products caused a sensation among consumers, and his business quickly earned substantial profits. Subsequent breakthroughs, including ornamental vases imitating classical Greek models and jasperware for jewelry, contributed greatly to Wedgwood's success.

Competitors were quick to copy Wedgwood's new products and sell them at lower prices. Thus Wedgwood and his partner Thomas Bentley sought to cultivate an image of superior fashion, taste, and quality in order to develop and maintain a dominant market position. They did this by first capturing the business of the trend-setting elite. In one brilliant coup the partners first sold a very large cream-colored dinner set to Britain's queen, which they quickly christened "Queen's ware" and sold as a very expensive, must-have luxury to English aristocrats. Equally brilliant was Bentley's suave expertise in the elegant

London showroom selling Wedgwood's imitation Greek vases, which became the rage after the rediscovery of Pompeii and Herculaneum in the mid-eighteenth century.

Above all, once Wedgwood had secured his position as the luxury market leader, he was able to successfully extend his famous brand to the growing middle class, capturing an enormous mass market for his "useful ware." Thus when sales of a luxury good grew "stale," Wedgwood made tasteful modifications and sold it to the middling classes for twice the price his competitors could charge. This unbeatable combination of mass appeal and high prices brought Wedgwood great fame all across Europe and enormous wealth.

A workaholic with an authoritarian streak, Wedgwood contributed substantially to the development of the factory system. In 1769 he opened a model factory on a new canal he had promoted. With two hundred workers in several departments, Wedgwood exercised tremendous control over his workforce, imposing fines for many infractions, such as being late, drinking on the job, or wasting material. He wanted, he said, to create men who would be like "machines" that "cannot err." Yet Wedgwood also recognized the value in treating workers well. He championed a division of labor that made most workers specialists who received ongoing training. He also encouraged employment of family groups, who were housed in company row houses with long narrow backyards suitable for raising vegetables and chickens. Paying relatively high wages and providing pensions and some benefits, Wedgwood developed a high-quality labor force that learned to accept his rigorous discipline and carried out his ambitious plans.

• Josiah Wedgwood (top right) perfected jasperware, a fine-grained pottery usually made in "Wedgwood blue" with white decoration. This elegant cylindrical vase (right), decorated in the form of a miniature Roman household altar, was destined for the luxury market. (portrait: Down House, Kent, Darwin Heirlooms Trust; vase: Image copyright © The Metropolitan Museum of Art/ Art Resource, NY)

QUESTIONS FOR ANALYSIS

1. How and why did Wedgwood succeed?
2. Was Wedgwood a good boss or a bad one? Why?
3. How did Wedgwood exemplify the new class of factory owners?

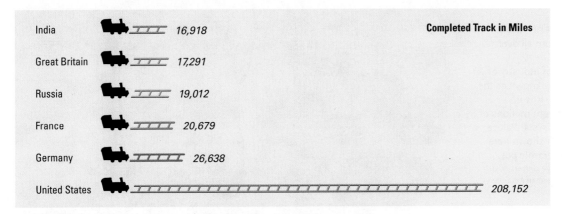

	Completed Track in Miles
India	16,918
Great Britain	17,291
Russia	19,012
France	20,679
Germany	26,638
United States	208,152

FIGURE 23.1 Railroad Track Mileage, 1890 Steam railroads were first used by the general public for shipping in England in the 1820s, and they quickly spread to other countries. The United States was an early adopter of railroads and by 1890 had surpassed all other countries in miles of track, as shown in this figure.

production had reached 260,000 tons by 1806. In 1844 Britain produced 3 million tons of iron. Once scarce and expensive, iron became the cheap, basic, indispensable building block of the economy.

The Coming of the Railroads

The coal industry had long been using plank roads and rails to move coal wagons within mines and at the surface. Rails reduced friction and allowed a horse or a human being to pull a heavier load. Thus, once a rail capable of supporting a heavy locomotive was developed in 1816, all sorts of experiments with steam engines on rails went forward. In 1825, after ten years of work, George Stephenson built an effective locomotive. In 1830 his ***Rocket*** sped down the track of the just-completed Liverpool and Manchester Railway at sixteen miles per hour. The line from Liverpool to Manchester was a financial as well as a technical success, and many private companies were quickly organized to build more rail lines. Within twenty years they had completed the main trunk lines of Great Britain (Map 23.1). Other countries were quick to follow, with the first steam-powered trains operating in the United States in the 1830s and in Brazil, Chile, Argentina, and the British colonies of Canada, Australia, and India in the 1850s (Figure 23.1).

The significance of the railroad was tremendous. It dramatically reduced the cost and uncertainty of shipping freight over land. This advance had many economic consequences. Previously, markets had tended to be small and local; as the barrier of high transportation costs was lowered, markets became larger and even nationwide. Larger markets encouraged larger factories with more sophisticated machinery in a growing number of industries. Such factories could make goods more cheaply and gradually subjected most cottage workers and many urban artisans to severe competi-

tive pressures. In all countries, the construction of railroads created a strong demand for unskilled labor and contributed to the growth of a class of urban workers.

The railroad changed the outlook and values of the entire society. The last and culminating invention of the Industrial Revolution, the railroad dramatically revealed the power and increased the speed of the new age. Racing down a track at sixteen miles per hour or by 1850 at a phenomenal fifty miles per hour was a new and awesome experience. As a French economist put it after a ride on the Liverpool and Manchester in 1833, "There are certain impressions that one cannot put into words!" Some great painters, notably Joseph M. W. Turner (1775–1851) and Claude Monet (1840–1926), succeeded in expressing this sense of power and awe. So did the massive new train stations, the cathedrals of the industrial age. Leading railway engineers such as Isambard Kingdom Brunel and Thomas Brassey, whose tunnels pierced mountains and whose bridges spanned valleys, became public idols — the astronauts of their day. Everyday speech absorbed the images of railroading. After you got up a "full head of steam," you "highballed" along. And if you didn't "go off the track," you might "toot your own whistle." The railroad fired the imagination.

Industry and Population

In 1851 London hosted an industrial fair called the Great Exhibition in the newly built **Crystal Palace**. For visitors, one fact stood out: Britain was the "workshop of the world." Britain alone produced two-thirds

- ***Rocket*** The name given to George Stephenson's effective locomotive that was first tested in 1830 on the Liverpool and Manchester Railway at sixteen miles per hour.
- **Crystal Palace** The location of the Great Exhibition in 1851 in London, an architectural masterpiece made entirely of glass and iron.

Crystal Palace Souvenir More than 6 million visitors from all over Europe marveled at the Great Exhibition of the Works of Industry of All the Nations, popularly known as the Crystal Palace Exhibition. It is no surprise that people bought millions of souvenirs picturing the Crystal Palace. The handsome depiction shown here brightened the lid of a ceramic pot. (Fitzwilliam Museum, Cambridge University, UK/ Bridgeman Giraudon/The Bridgeman Art Library)

MAP 23.1 The Industrial Revolution in England, ca. 1850 Industry concentrated in the rapidly growing cities of the north and the center of England, where rich coal and iron deposits were close to one another.

of the world's coal and more than half of its iron and cotton cloth. More generally, in 1860 Britain produced a remarkable 20 percent of the entire world's output of industrial goods, whereas it had produced only about 2 percent of the world total in 1750.[3] Experiencing revolutionary industrial change, Britain became the first industrial nation (see Map 23.1).

As the British economy significantly increased its production of manufactured goods, the gross national product (GNP) rose roughly fourfold at constant prices between 1780 and 1851. At the same time, the population of Britain boomed, growing from about 9 million in 1780 to almost 21 million in 1851. Thus, growing numbers consumed much of the increase in total production.

Although the question is still debated, many economic historians believe that rapid population growth in Great Britain was not harmful because it facilitated industrial expansion. More people meant a more mobile labor force, with a wealth of young workers in need of employment and ready to go where the jobs were. Contemporaries were much less optimistic. In his *Essay on the Principle of Population* (1798), Thomas Malthus (1766–1834) examined the dynamics of human populations. He argued that

> there are few states in which there is not a constant effort in the population to increase beyond the means of subsistence. This constant effort as constantly tends to subject the lower classes of society to distress, and to prevent any great permanent melioration of these conditions.[4]

Since, in his opinion, population would always tend to grow faster than the food supply, Malthus concluded

French Train Poster
The International Sleeping-Car Company was founded in 1872, inspired by the model of the American Pullman night trains. It quickly became the most important operator of sleeping and dining cars in Europe. The company's posters, like the one pictured here, appealed to wealthy and middle-class customers by emphasizing the luxury and spaciousness of its accommodations. The company's most famous line was the Orient Express (1883–2009), which ran from Paris to Istanbul. (Kharbine-Tapabor/The Art Archive)

that the only hope of warding off such "positive checks" to population growth as war, famine, and disease was "prudential restraint." That is, young men and women had to limit the growth of population by marrying late in life. But Malthus was not optimistic about this possibility. The powerful attraction of the sexes would cause most people to marry early and have many children.

Economist David Ricardo (1772–1823) spelled out the pessimistic implications of Malthus's thought. Ricardo's depressing **iron law of wages** posited that because of the pressure of population growth, wages would always sink to subsistence level. That is, wages would be just high enough to keep workers from starving.

Malthus, Ricardo, and their followers were proved wrong in the long run. However, until the 1820s, or even the 1840s, contemporary observers might reasonably have concluded that the economy and the total population were racing neck and neck, with the outcome very much in doubt. There was another problem as well. Perhaps workers, farmers, and ordinary people did not get their rightful share of the new wealth. Perhaps only the rich got richer, while the poor got poorer or made no progress. We turn to this great issue after looking at the process of industrialization outside of Britain.

Industrialization Beyond Britain

☐ How after 1815 did countries outside of Britain respond to the challenge of industrialization?

As new technologies and organization of labor began to revolutionize production in Britain, other countries took notice and began to emulate its example. Imitating Britain's success was hampered by the particular economic and social conditions of each country, many of whose peoples resisted attempts at drastic change. Yet by the end of the nineteenth century, several European countries as well as the United States and Japan had industrialized their economies to a considerable, but variable, degree.

The process of industrialization proceeded gradually, with uneven jerks and national and regional variations. Scholars are still struggling to explain these variations as well as the dramatic gap that emerged for the first time in history between Western and non-Western levels of economic production. These

• **iron law of wages** Theory proposed by English economist David Ricardo suggesting that the pressure of population growth prevents wages from rising above the subsistence level.

• TABLE 23.1 Per Capita Levels of Industrialization, 1750–1913

	1750	1800	1830	1860	1880	1900	1913
Great Britain	10	16	25	64	87	100	115
Belgium	9	10	14	28	43	56	88
United States	4	9	14	21	38	69	126
France	9	9	12	20	28	39	59
Germany	8	8	9	15	25	52	85
Austria-Hungary	7	7	8	11	15	23	32
Italy	8	8	8	10	12	17	26
Russia	6	6	7	8	10	15	20
China	8	6	6	4	4	3	3
India	7	6	6	3	2	1	2

Note: All entries are based on an index value of 100, equal to the per capita level of industrialization in Great Britain in 1900. Data for Great Britain include Ireland, England, Wales, and Scotland.

Source: P. Bairoch, "International Industrialization Levels from 1750 to 1980," *Journal of European Economic History* 11 (Spring 1982): 294, U.S. Journals at Cambridge University Press. Reprinted by permission.

questions are especially important because they may offer valuable lessons for poor countries that today are seeking to improve their material condition through industrialization and economic development. The latest findings on the nineteenth-century experience are encouraging. They suggest that there were alternative paths to the industrial world and that there was and is no need to follow a rigid, predetermined British model.

National and International Variations

Comparative data on industrial production in different countries over time help give us an overview of what happened. One set of data, the work of a Swiss scholar, compares the level of industrialization on a per capita basis in several countries from 1750 to 1913. These data are far from perfect, but they reflect basic trends and are presented in Table 23.1 for closer study.

Table 23.1 presents a comparison of how much industrial product was produced, on average, for each person in a given country in a given year. All the numbers expressed in terms of a single index number of 100, which equals the per capita level of industrial goods in Great Britain (and Ireland) in 1900. Every number in the table is thus a percentage of the 1900 level in Britain and is directly comparable with other numbers. The countries are listed in roughly the order that they began to use large-scale, power-driven technology.

What does this overview tell us? First, one sees in the first column that in 1750 all countries were fairly close together, including non-Western areas such as China and India. Both China and India had been extremely important players in early modern world trade, earning high profits from exporting their luxury goods.

However, the column headed 1800 shows that Britain had opened up a noticeable lead over all countries by 1800, and that gap progressively widened as the British Industrial Revolution accelerated to 1830 and reached full maturity by 1860.

Second, the table shows that the countries of continental Europe and the United States began to emulate the British model successfully over the nineteenth century, with significant variations in the timing and in the extent of industrialization. Belgium, achieving independence from the Netherlands in 1831 and rich in iron and coal, led in adopting Britain's new technology, and it experienced a truly revolutionary surge between 1830 and 1860. France developed factory production more gradually, and most historians now detect no burst in French mechanization and no acceleration in the growth of overall industrial output that may accurately be called revolutionary. Its slow but steady growth was overshadowed by the spectacular rise of Germany and the United States after 1860 in what has been termed the "second industrial revolution." In general, eastern and southern Europe began the process of modern industrialization later than northwestern and central Europe. Nevertheless, these regions made real progress in the late nineteenth century, as growth after 1880 in Austria-Hungary, Italy, and Russia suggests.

Finally, the late but substantial industrialization in eastern and southern Europe meant that all European states as well as the United States managed to raise per capita industrial levels in the nineteenth century. These increases stood in stark contrast to the decreases that occurred at the same time in many non-Western countries, most notably in China and India as Table 23.1 shows. European countries industrialized to a greater or lesser extent even as most of the non-Western world stagnated. Japan, which is not included in this table, stands out as an exceptional area of non-Western industrial growth in the second half of the nineteenth century. After the forced opening of the country to the West in the 1850s, Japanese entrepreneurs began to adopt Western technology and manufacturing methods, resulting in a production boom by the late nineteenth century (see Chapter 26). Differential rates of wealth- and power-creating industrial development, which heightened disparities within Europe, also greatly magnified existing inequalities between Europe and the rest of the world (see Chapter 25).

The Challenge of Industrialization in Continental Europe

The different patterns of industrial development suggest that the process of industrialization was far from automatic. To be sure, throughout Europe the eighteenth century was an era of agricultural improvement, population increase, expanding foreign trade, and growing cottage industry. Thus, when the pace of British industry began to accelerate in the 1780s, continental businesses began to adopt the new methods as they proved their profitability. British industry enjoyed clear superiority, but at first the European continent was close behind.

By 1815, however, the situation was quite different. No wars in the early industrial period had been fought on British soil, so Britain did not experience nearly as much physical destruction or economic dislocation as Europe did. Rather, British industry maintained the momentum of the 1780s and continued to grow and improve between 1789 and 1815. On the European continent, by contrast, the upheavals that began with the French Revolution disrupted trade, created runaway inflation, and fostered social anxiety. War severed normal communications with Britain, severely handicapping continental efforts to use new British machinery and technology. Thus France and the rest of Europe were further behind Britain in 1815 than in 1789.

This widening gap made it more difficult, if not impossible, for other countries to follow the British pattern in energy and industry after peace was restored in 1815. Above all, in the newly mechanized industries, British goods were being produced very economically, and these goods had come to dominate world markets completely. In addition, British technology had become so advanced and complicated that very few engineers or skilled technicians outside England understood it. Moreover, the technology of steam power had grown much more expensive. It involved large investments in the iron and coal industries and, after 1830, required the existence of railroads. Continental businesspeople had great difficulty finding the large sums of money the new methods demanded, and laborers bitterly resisted the move to working in factories. All these factors slowed the spread of modern industry (Map 23.2).

After 1815, however, European countries had at least three important advantages. First, most had a rich tradition of putting-out enterprise, merchant capitalists, and skilled urban artisans. Such a tradition gave their firms the ability to adapt and survive in the face of new market conditions. Second, continental capitalists did not need to develop their own advanced technology. Instead, they could simply "borrow" the new methods developed in Great Britain, as well as the engineers and some of the financial resources they lacked. European countries such as France and Russia also had a third asset that many non-Western areas lacked in the nineteenth century: they had strong, independent governments that did not fall under foreign political control. These governments would eventually use the power of the state to promote industry and catch up with Britain.

Agents of Industrialization

The British realized the great value of their technical discoveries and tried to keep their secrets to themselves. Until 1825 it was illegal for artisans and skilled mechanics to leave Britain; until 1843 the export of textile machinery and other equipment was forbidden. Many talented, ambitious workers, however, slipped out of the country illegally and introduced the new methods abroad.

One such man was William Cockerill, a Lancashire carpenter. He and his sons began building cotton-spinning equipment in French-occupied Belgium in 1799. In 1817 the most famous son, John Cockerill, built a large industrial enterprise in Liège in southern Belgium, which produced machinery, steam engines, and then railway locomotives. He also established modern ironworks and coal mines.

Cockerill's plants in the Liège area became an industrial nerve center for the gathering and transmitting of industrial information across Europe. Many skilled British workers came to work for Cockerill, and some went on to found their own companies throughout Europe. Newcomers brought the latest industrial plans and secrets from Britain, so Cockerill could boast that ten days after an industrial advance occurred in Britain, he knew all about it in Belgium.

Thus British technicians and skilled workers were a powerful force in the spread of early industrialization. A second agent of industrialization consisted of talented entrepreneurs such as Fritz Harkort (1793–1880), a pioneer in the German machinery industry. Serving in England as a Prussian army officer during the Napoleonic wars, Harkort was impressed and enchanted with what he saw. He concluded that Germany had to match all these English achievements as

◻ Mapping the Past

MAP 23.2 Continental Industrialization, ca. 1850 Although continental countries were beginning to make progress by 1850, they still lagged far behind Britain. For example, continental railroad building was still in an early stage, whereas the British rail system was essentially complete (see Map 23.1). Coal played a critical role in nineteenth-century industrialization both as a power source for steam engines and as a raw material for making iron and steel.

ANALYZING THE MAP Locate the major exposed (that is, known) coal deposits in 1850. Which countries and areas appear rich in coal resources, and which appear poor? Is there a difference between northern and southern Europe?

CONNECTIONS What is the relationship between known coal deposits and emerging industrial areas in continental Europe? In England (see Map 23.1)?

quickly as possible. Setting up shop in the Ruhr Valley, Harkort felt an almost religious calling to build steam engines.

Lacking skilled laborers, Harkort turned to England for experienced, though expensive, mechanics. Getting materials was also difficult. He had to import the thick iron boilers that he needed from England at great cost. In spite of all these problems, Harkort succeeded in building and selling engines. His ambitious efforts over sixteen years also resulted in large financial losses for

himself and his partners. His career illustrates both the great efforts of a few important business leaders to duplicate the British achievement and the difficulty of the task.

Entrepreneurs like Harkort were obviously exceptional. Most continental businesses adopted factory technology slowly, and handicraft methods lived on. Indeed, continental industrialization usually brought substantial but uneven expansion of handicraft industry in both rural and urban areas for a time. Artisan production of luxury items grew in France as the rising income of the international middle class created increased foreign demand for silk scarves, embroidered needlework, perfumes, and fine wines.

Government Support and Corporate Banking

Another major force in the spread of industrialization throughout Europe was government, which often helped business people in continental countries to overcome some of their difficulties. **Tariff protection** was one such support, and it proved to be important. For example, after Napoleon's wars ended in 1815, France was suddenly flooded with cheaper and better British goods. The French government responded by laying high tariffs on many British imports in order to protect the French economy. After 1815 continental governments bore the cost of building roads and canals to improve transportation. They also bore to a significant extent the cost of building railroads. Belgium led the way in the 1830s and 1840s. Built rapidly as a unified network, Belgium's state-owned railroads stimulated the development of heavy industry and made the country an early industrial leader.

The Prussian government provided another kind of invaluable support. It guaranteed that the state treasury would pay the interest and principal on railroad bonds if the closely regulated private companies in Prussia were unable to do so. In France the state shouldered all the expense of acquiring and laying roadbed, including bridges and tunnels. In short, governments helped pay for railroads, the all-important leading sector in continental industrialization.

The career of German journalist and thinker Friedrich List (1789–1846) reflects government's greater role in industrialization on the European continent than in England. List considered the growth of modern industry of the utmost importance because manufacturing was a primary means of increasing people's well-being and relieving their poverty. Moreover, List was a dedicated nationalist. He wrote that the "wider the gap between the backward and advanced nations becomes, the more dangerous it is to remain behind." To promote industry was to defend the nation.

The practical policies that List focused on were railroad building and the tariff. List supported the formation of a customs union, or *Zollverein* (TSOL-fehrign), among the separate German states. Such a tariff union came into being in 1834, allowing goods to move between the German member states without tariffs, while erecting a single uniform tariff against other nations. List wanted a high protective tariff, which would encourage infant industries, allowing them to develop and eventually hold their own against their more ad-

> "The wider the gap between the backward and advanced nations becomes, the more dangerous it is to remain behind."
>
> **FRIEDRICH LIST**

vanced British counterparts. He denounced the British doctrine of free trade as part of Britain's attempt to dominate the entire world:

> At no other epoch has the world seen a manufacturing and commercial power possessing such immense resources as those in the hands of the power which now holds sway [Britain] so consistently selfish. It is absorbing with untiring energy the manufacturing and commercial industries of the world and the important colonies, and it is making the rest of the world, like the Hindus, its serfs in all industrial and commercial relations.[5]

By the 1840s List's **economic nationalism**, designed to protect and develop the national economy, had become increasingly popular in Germany and elsewhere.

Finally, banks, like governments, also played a larger and more creative role on the continent than in Britain. Previously, almost all banks in Europe had been private. Because of the possibility of unlimited financial loss, the partners of private banks tended to be conservative and were content to deal with a few rich clients and a few big merchants. They generally avoided industrial investment as being too risky.

In the 1830s two important Belgian banks pioneered in a new direction. They received permission from the growth-oriented government to establish themselves as corporations enjoying limited liability. That is, if the bank went bankrupt, stockholders could now lose only their original investments in the bank's common stock, and they could not be forced by the courts to pay for any additional losses out of other property they owned. Limited liability helped these Belgian banks attract investors. They mobilized impressive resources for investment in big companies, became industrial banks, and successfully promoted industrial development.

Similar corporate banks became important in France and Germany in the 1850s and 1860s. Usually working in collaboration with governments, corporate

---

- **tariff protection** A government's way of supporting and aiding its own economy by laying high taxes on imported goods from other countries, as when the French responded to cheaper British goods flooding their country by imposing high tariffs on some imported products.
- **economic nationalism** Policies aimed at protecting and developing a country's economy.

A German Ironworks, 1845 The Borsig ironworks in Berlin mastered the new British method of smelting iron ore with coke. Germany, especially the state of Prussia, was well endowed with both iron and coal, and the rapid exploitation of these resources after 1840 transformed a poor agricultural country into an industrial powerhouse. (akg-images)

banks established and developed many railroads and many companies working in heavy industry, which were also increasingly organized as limited liability corporations.

The combined efforts of skilled workers, entrepreneurs, governments, and industrial banks meshed successfully between 1850 and the financial crash of 1873. In Belgium, Germany, and France, key indicators of modern industrial development — such as railway mileage, iron and coal production, and steam-engine capacity — increased at average annual rates of 5 to 10 percent. As a result, rail networks were completed in western and much of central Europe, and the leading continental countries mastered the industrial technologies that had first been developed in Great Britain. In the early 1870s Britain was still Europe's most industrial nation, but a select handful of countries were closing the gap that had been opened by the Industrial Revolution.

The Situation Outside of Europe

The Industrial Revolution did not extend outside of Europe prior to the 1870s, with the exception of the United States and Japan, both early adopters of British practices. In many countries, national governments and pioneering entrepreneurs did make efforts to adopt the technologies and methods of production that had proved so successful in Britain, but they fell short of transitioning to an industrial economy. For example, in Russia the imperial government brought steamships to the Volga River and a railroad to the capital, St. Petersburg, in the first decades of the nineteenth century. By mid-century ambitious entrepreneurs had established steam-powered cotton factories using imported British machines. However, these advances did not lead to overall industrialization of the country, most of whose people remained mired in rural servitude. Instead, Russia confirmed its role as provider of raw materials, especially timber and grain, to the hungry West.

Egypt similarly began an ambitious program of modernization in the first decades of the nineteenth century, which included the use of imported British technology and experts in textile manufacture and other industries (see page 770). These industries, however, could not compete with lower-priced European imports. Like Russia, Egypt fell back on agricultural exports to European markets, like sugar and cotton.

Such examples of faltering efforts at industrialization could be found in many other places in the Middle East, Asia, and Latin America. Where European governments maintained direct or indirect control, they acted to maintain colonial markets as sources for their own products, rather than encouraging the spread of industrialization. In India millions of poor textile workers lost their livelihood because they could not compete with industrially produced British cottons. The arrival of railroads in India in the mid-nineteenth century served the purpose of agricultural rather than industrial development. Latin American countries (discussed in Chapter 27) were distracted from economic concerns by the early-nineteenth-century wars of independence. By the mid-nineteenth century they had adopted steam power for sugar and coffee processing, but as elsewhere these developments led to increased reliance on agricultural crops for export, not a rise in industrial production. As in India, the arrival of cheap British cottons destroyed the pre-existing textile industry that had employed many men and women.

Relations Between Capital and Labor

☐ How did the Industrial Revolution affect people of all social classes, and what measures were taken to improve the conditions of workers?

In Britain, industrial development brought new social relations and intensified long-standing problems between capital and labor. A new group of factory owners and industrial capitalists arose. These men and women and their families strengthened the wealth and size of the middle class, which had previously been made up mainly of merchants and professional people. The demands of modern industry also created a much larger group, the factory workers.

The growth of new occupational groups in industry stimulated thinking about social relations. Often combined with reflections on the French Revolution, this thinking led to the development of a new overarching interpretation—a new paradigm—regarding social relationships. Briefly, this paradigm argued, with considerable success, that individuals were members of economically determined classes that had conflicting interests. Accordingly, the comfortable, well-educated "public" of the eighteenth century came increasingly to see itself as the middle class, and the "people" gradually transformed themselves into the modern working class. And if the new class interpretation was more of a deceptive simplification than a fundamental truth for some critics, it appealed to many because it seemed to explain what was happening. Therefore, conflicting classes existed, in part, because many individuals came to believe they existed and developed an appropriate sense of class feeling—what Marxists call **class-consciousness** (see page 721).

The New Class of Factory Owners

Early industrialists operated in a highly competitive economic system. As the careers of Watt and Harkort illustrate, there were countless production problems, and success and large profits were by no means certain. Manufacturers therefore waged a constant battle to cut their production costs and stay afloat. Much of the profit had to go back into the business for new and better machinery.

Most early industrialists drew upon their families and friends for labor and capital, but they came from a variety of backgrounds. Many, such as Harkort, were from well-established merchant families with rich networks of contacts and support. Others, such as Watt, Wedgwood, and Cockerill, were of modest means, especially in the early days. Artisans and skilled workers of exceptional ability had unparalleled opportunities. Members of ethnic and religious groups who had been discriminated against in the traditional occupations controlled by the landed aristocracy jumped at the new chances and often helped each other. Scots, Quakers, and other Protestant dissenters were tremendously important in Britain; Protestants and Jews dominated banking in Catholic France.

As factories and firms grew larger, opportunities declined, at least in well-developed industries. It became considerably harder for a gifted but poor young mechanic to start a small enterprise and end up as a wealthy manufacturer. Formal education became more important for young men as a means of success and advancement, and formal education at the advanced level was expensive. In Britain by 1830 and in France and Germany by 1860, leading industrialists were more likely to have inherited their well-established enterprises, and they were financially much more secure than their struggling parents had been. They also had a greater sense of class-consciousness; they were fully aware that ongoing industrial development had widened the gap between themselves and their workers.

The wives and daughters of successful businessmen also found fewer opportunities for active participation in Europe's business world. Rather than contributing as vital partners in a family-owned enterprise, as so many middle-class women had done, these women were increasingly valued for their ladylike gentility. By 1850 some influential women writers and most businessmen assumed that middle-class wives and daughters should steer clear of work in offices and factories. Rather, a middle-class lady should concentrate on her proper role as wife and mother, preferably in an elegant residential area far removed from ruthless commerce and the volatile working class.

• **class-consciousness** An individual's sense of class differentiation.

◻ Picturing the Past

Ford Maddox Brown, *Work* This midcentury painting provides a rich and realistic visual representation of the new concepts of social class that became common by 1850. (Birmingham Museums and Art Gallery/ The Bridgeman Art Library)

ANALYZING THE IMAGE Describe the different types of work shown. What different social classes are depicted, and what kinds of work and leisure are the members of the different social classes engaged in?

CONNECTIONS What does this painting and its title suggest about the artist's opinion of the work of common laborers?

The New Factory Workers

The social consequences of the Industrial Revolution have long been hotly debated. The condition of British workers during the transformation has always generated the most controversy among historians because Britain was the first country to industrialize and because the social consequences seemed harshest there.

From the beginning, the Industrial Revolution in Britain had its critics. Among the first were the romantic poets. William Blake (1757–1827) called the early factories "satanic mills" and protested against the hard life of the London poor. William Wordsworth (1770–1850) lamented the destruction of the rural way of life and the pollution of the land and water. Some

handicraft workers—notably the **Luddites**, who attacked factories in northern England in 1812 and after—smashed the new machines, which they believed were putting them out of work. Doctors and reformers wrote of problems in the factories and new towns, while Malthus and Ricardo concluded that workers would earn only enough to stay alive.

This pessimistic view was accepted and reinforced by Friedrich Engels (1820–1895), the future revolutionary and colleague of Karl Marx. After studying conditions in northern England, this young middle-class German published in 1844 *The Condition of the Working Class in England*, a blistering indictment of the middle classes. "At the bar of world opinion," he wrote, "I charge the English middle classes with mass murder, wholesale robbery, and all the other crimes in the calendar." The new poverty of industrial workers was worse than the old poverty of cottage workers and agricultural laborers, according to Engels. The culprit was industrial capitalism, with its relentless competition and constant technical change. Engels's extremely influential charge of middle-class exploitation and increasing worker poverty was embellished by Marx and later socialists.

Meanwhile, other observers believed that conditions were improving for the working people. In 1835 in his study of the cotton industry, Andrew Ure wrote that conditions in most factories were not harsh and were even quite good. Edwin Chadwick, a government official well acquainted with the problems of the working population, concluded that the "whole mass of the laboring community" was increasingly able "to buy more of the necessities and minor luxuries of life."[6] Nevertheless, those who thought conditions were getting worse for working people were probably in the majority.

Historians' studies of statistics from this period have weakened the idea that the condition of the working class got much worse with industrialization. But the most recent scholarship also confirms the view that the early years of the Industrial Revolution were hard ones for British workers. There was little or no increase in the purchasing power of the average British worker from about 1780 to about 1820. Only after 1820, and especially after 1840, did real wages rise substantially, so that the average worker earned and consumed roughly 50 percent more in real terms in 1850 than in 1770.[7] In short, there was considerable economic improvement for workers throughout Great Britain by 1850, but that improvement was hard won and slow in coming.

This important conclusion must be qualified, however. First, the number of hours in the average workweek increased. Thus, to a large extent, workers earned more because they worked more. In England nonagricultural workers labored about 250 days per year in 1760 as compared to 300 days per year in 1830, while the normal workday remained an exhausting eleven hours throughout the entire period. In 1760 nonagricultural workers still observed many religious and public holidays by not working, and many workers took Monday off. These days of leisure and relaxation declined rapidly after 1760, and by 1830 nonagricultural workers had joined landless agricultural laborers in toiling six rather than five days a week.[8]

Second, the wartime decline in the average worker's real wages and standard of living from 1792 to 1815 had a powerful negative impact on workers. These difficult war years, with more unemployment and sharply higher prices for bread, were formative years for the new factory labor force, and they colored the early experience of modern industrial life in somber tones.

Another way to consider the workers' standard of living is to look at the goods that they purchased. Again the evidence is somewhat contradictory. Speaking generally, workers ate somewhat more food of higher nutritional quality as the Industrial Revolution progressed. Diets became more varied; people ate more potatoes, dairy products, fruits, and vegetables. Clothing improved, but housing for working people probably deteriorated somewhat. In short, per capita use of specific goods supports the position that the standard of living of the working classes rose, at least moderately, after the long wars with France.

Work in Early Factories

What about working conditions? Did workers eventually earn more only at the cost of working longer and harder? Were workers exploited harshly by the new factory owners?

The first factories were cotton mills, which began functioning in the 1770s along fast-running rivers and streams and were often located in sparsely populated areas. Cottage workers in the vicinity, accustomed to the putting-out system, were reluctant to work in the new factories even when they received relatively good wages because factory work was unappealing. In a factory, workers had to keep up with the machine and follow its relentless tempo. Moreover, they had to show up every day, on time, and work long, monotonous hours under the constant supervision of demanding overseers, and they were punished systematically if they broke the work rules. For example, if a worker was late to work, or accidentally spoiled material, or nodded off late in the day, the employer imposed fines that were deducted from the weekly pay. Children and adolescents were often beaten for their infractions.

Cottage workers were not used to that kind of life and discipline. All members of the family worked hard and long, but in spurts, setting their own pace. They could interrupt their work when they wanted to. Women and children could break up their long hours of spinning with other tasks. On Saturday afternoon the head of the family delivered the week's work to the merchant manufacturer and got paid. Saturday night was a time of relaxation and drinking, especially for the men.

Also, early factories resembled English poorhouses, where totally destitute people went to live at public expense. Some poorhouses were industrial prisons, where the inmates had to work in order to receive their food and lodging. The similarity between large brick factories and large stone poorhouses increased the cottage workers' fear of factories and their hatred of factory discipline. It was cottage workers' reluctance to work in factories that prompted the early cotton mill owners

• **Luddites** Group of handicraft workers who attacked factories in northern England in 1812 and after, smashing the new machines that they believed were putting them out of work.

Workers at a U.S. Mill Female workers at a U.S. cotton mill in 1890 take a break from operating belt-driven weaving machines to pose for this photograph, accompanied by their male supervisor. The first textile mills, established in the 1820s in Massachusetts, employed local farm girls. As competition intensified, conditions deteriorated and the mills increasingly relied on immigrant women who had few alternatives to the long hours, noise, and dangers of factory work. By 1900, more than one million women worked in factories in the United States. (Courtesy of George Eastman House, International Museum of Photography and Film, GEH neg. 14250)

to turn to abandoned and pauper children for their labor. As we have seen, these owners contracted with local officials to employ large numbers of such children, who had no say in the matter. In the eighteenth century semi-forced child labor seemed necessary and was socially accepted. From our modern point of view, it was cruel exploitation and a blot on the record of the new industrial system.

Working Families and Children

By the 1790s the early pattern was rapidly changing. The use of pauper apprentices was in decline, and in 1802 it was forbidden by Parliament. Many more textile factories were being built, mainly in urban areas,

where they could use steam power rather than water-power and attract a workforce more easily than in the countryside. As a result, people came from near and far to work in the cities, both as factory workers and as laborers, builders, and domestic servants. Yet as they took these new jobs, working people did not simply give in and accept the highly disciplined system of labor. Rather, they helped modify the system by carrying over old, familiar working traditions.

For one thing, workers often came to the mills and the mines as family units. This was how they had worked on farms and in the putting-out system. The mill or mine owner bargained with the head of the family and paid him or her for the work of the whole family. In the cotton mills, children worked for their mothers or fathers, collecting scraps and "piecing" broken threads together. In the mines, children sorted coal and worked the ventilation equipment. Their mothers hauled coal in the tunnels below the surface, while their fathers hewed with pick and shovel at the face of the seam.

The preservation of the family as an economic unit in the factories from the 1790s on made the new surroundings more tolerable, both in Great Britain and in other countries, during the early stages of industrialization. Parents disciplined their children, making firm measures socially acceptable, and directed their upbringing. The presence of the whole family meant that children and adults worked the same long hours (twelve-hour shifts were normal in cotton mills in 1800). Adult workers were not particularly interested in limiting the minimum working age or hours of their children as long as family members worked side by side. Only when technical changes threatened to place control and discipline in the hands of impersonal managers and overseers did adult workers protest against inhuman conditions in the name of their children.

Some enlightened employers and social reformers in Parliament definitely felt otherwise. They argued that more humane standards were necessary, and they used widely circulated parliamentary reports to influence public opinion. For example, Robert Owen (1771–1858), a successful manufacturer in Scotland, testified in 1816 before an investigating committee on the basis of his experience. He argued that employing children under ten years of age as factory workers was "injurious to the children, and not beneficial to the proprietors."[9] Workers also provided graphic testimony at such hearings as the reformers pressed Parliament to pass corrective laws. They scored some important successes.

Their most significant early accomplishment was the **Factory Act of 1833**. It limited the factory workday of children between nine and thirteen to eight hours and that of adolescents between fourteen and eighteen to twelve hours. Children under nine were to be enrolled in the elementary schools that factory owners were required to establish. The employment of children declined rapidly. Thus the Factory Act broke the pattern of whole families working together in the factory because efficiency required standardized shifts for all workers.

Ties of blood and kinship were important in other ways in Great Britain in the formative years between about 1790 and 1840. Many manufacturers and builders hired workers through subcontractors. They paid the subcontractors on the basis of what the subcontractors and their crews produced. Subcontractors in turn hired and fired their own workers, many of whom were friends and relations. The subcontractor might be as harsh as the greediest capitalist, but the relationship between subcontractor and work crew was close

and personal. This kind of personal relationship had traditionally existed in cottage industry and in urban crafts, and it was more acceptable to many workers than impersonal factory discipline.

Ties of kinship were particularly important for newcomers, who often traveled great distances to find work. Many urban workers in Great Britain were from Ireland. Forced out of rural Ireland by population growth and deteriorating economic conditions from 1817 on, Irish in search of jobs took what they could get. As early as 1824 most of the workers in the Glasgow cotton mills were Irish; in 1851 one-sixth of the population of Liverpool was Irish. Like many other immigrant groups held together by ethnic and religious ties, the Irish worked together, formed their own neighborhoods, and not only survived but also thrived.

The Sexual Division of Labor

The era of the Industrial Revolution witnessed major changes in the sexual division of labor. In preindustrial Europe most people worked in family units. By tradition, certain jobs were defined by gender, but many tasks might go to either sex. Family employment carried over into early factories and subcontracting, but by the 1830s it was collapsing as child labor was restricted and new attitudes emerged. A different sexual division of labor gradually arose to take its place. By 1850 the man was emerging as the family's primary wage earner, while the married woman found only limited job opportunities. Generally denied good jobs at high wages in the growing urban economy, women were expected to concentrate on housework, raising the children, and some craftwork at home.

This new pattern of **separate spheres** had several aspects. First, all studies agree that married women from the working classes were much less likely to work full-time for wages outside the house after the first child arrived, although they often earned small amounts doing putting-out handicrafts at home and taking in boarders. Second, when married women did work for wages outside the house, they usually came from the poorest families, where the husbands were poorly paid, sick, unemployed, or missing. Third, these poor married or widowed women were joined by legions of young unmarried women, who worked full-time but only in certain jobs, of which textile factory work, laundering, and domestic service were particularly important. Fourth, all women were generally confined to

- **Factory Act of 1833** English law that led to a sharp decline in the employment of children by limiting the hours that children over age nine could work and requiring younger children to attend factory-run elementary schools.
- **separate spheres** A gender division of labor with the wife at home as mother and homemaker and the husband as wage earner.

Viewpoints

Women's Role in Industrialized Europe

• *Higher wages for men during the Industrial Revolution contributed to social changes that encouraged the nineteenth-century ideology of separate spheres, which emphasized the importance of women's role of caretaker of the domestic realm. Sarah Stickney Ellis's "The Women of England: Their Social Duties and Domestic Habits," excerpted below, was one of a flood of publications offering middle-class women household advice. For the vast majority of European women and children, however, life still included hard toil. As middle-class reformers began to investigate working-class living conditions, they were shocked by what they found. The second document comes from an 1845 interview of doctors by a reformer in a German industrial city.*

Sarah Stickney Ellis, "The Women of England: Their Social Duties and Domestic Habits," 1839

❝ "What shall I do to gratify myself—to be admired—or to vary the tenor of my existence?" are not the questions which a woman of right feelings asks awaking to the avocations of the day. Much more congenial to the highest attributes of woman's character, are inquiries such as these: "How shall I endeavor through this day to turn the time, the health, and the means permitted me to enjoy, to the best account? Is any one sick, I must visit their chamber without delay, and try to give their apartment an air of comfort, by arranging such things as the wearied nurse may not have thought of. Is any one about to set off on a journey, I must see that the early meal is spread, to prepare it with my own hands, in order that the servant, who was working late last night, may profit by unbroken rest. Did I fail in what was kind or considerate to any of the family yesterday; I will meet her this morning with a cordial welcome, and show, in the most delicate way I can, that I am anxious to atone for the past. Was any one exhausted by the last day's exertion, I will be an hour before them this morning, and let them see that their labor is so much in advance. Or, if nothing extraordinary occurs to claim my attention, I will meet the family with a consciousness that, being the least engaged of any member of it, I am consequently the most at liberty to devote myself to the general good of the whole, by cultivating cheerful conversation, adapting myself to the prevailing tone of feeling, and leading those who are least happy, to think and speak of what will make them more so." ❞

1845 Interview Concerning the Lives of Women and Children in a German Industrial City

❝ Question: What is your usual experience regarding the cleanliness of these classes?

Dr. Bluemner: Bad! Mother has to go out to work, and can therefore pay little attention to the domestic economy, and even if she makes an effort, she lacks time and means. A typical woman of this kind has four children, of whom she is still suckling one, she has to look after the whole household, to take food to her husband at work, perhaps a quarter of a mile away on a building site; she therefore has no time for cleaning and then it is such a small hole inhabited by so many people. The children are left to themselves, crawl about the floor or in the streets, and are always dirty; they lack the necessary clothing to change more often, and there is no time or money to wash these frequently. There are, of course, gradations; if the mother is healthy, active and clean, and if the poverty is not too great, then things are better.

Question: What is the state of health among the lower class? . . .

Dr. Kalckstein: . . . The dwellings of the working classes mostly face the yards and courts. The small quantity of fresh air admitted by the surrounding buildings is vitiated by the emanations from stables and middens [garbage heaps]. Further, because of the higher rents, people are forced to share their dwellings and to overcrowd them. The adults escape the worst influences by leaving the dwellings during the day, but the children are exposed to it with its whole force. ❞

Sources: Sarah Stickney Ellis, "The Women of England: Their Social Duties and Domestic Habits," in Walter Arnstein, ed., *The Past Speaks*, 2d ed. (Lexington, Mass.: D. C. Heath, 1993), 2:172–175; Laura L. Frader, ed., *The Industrial Revolution: A History in Documents* (Oxford, U.K.: Oxford University Press, 2006), p. 85.

QUESTIONS FOR ANALYSIS

1. What daily tasks and duties does Sarah Stickney Ellis prescribe for the mother of the family?

2. Based on the second document, what obstacles to achieving the ideals prescribed by Stickney Ellis existed for working-class women? To what extent do the doctors seem to blame the women themselves for their situation?

low-paying, dead-end jobs. Evolving gradually, but largely in place by 1850, the new sexual division of labor in Britain constituted a major development in the history of women and of the family. (See "Viewpoints: Women's Role in Industrialized Europe," page 706.)

If the reorganization of paid work along gender lines is widely recognized, there is no agreement on its causes. One school of scholars sees little connection with industrialization and finds the answer in the deeply ingrained sexist attitudes that predated the economic transformation. These scholars stress the role of male-dominated craft unions in denying working women access to good jobs and relegating them to unpaid housework. Other scholars, stressing that the gender roles of women and men can vary enormously with time and culture, look more to a combination of economic and biological factors in order to explain the emergence of a sex-segregated division of labor.

Three ideas stand out in this more recent interpretation. First, the new and unfamiliar discipline of the clock and the machine was especially hard on married women of the laboring classes. Above all, relentless factory discipline conflicted with child care in a way that labor on the farm or in the cottage had not. A woman operating earsplitting spinning machinery could mind a child of seven or eight working beside her (until such work was outlawed), but she could no longer pace herself through pregnancy or breast-feed her baby on the job. Thus a working-class woman had strong incentives to concentrate on child care within her home if her family could afford it.

Second, running a household in conditions of primitive urban poverty was an extremely demanding job in its own right. There were no supermarkets or public transportation. Shopping and feeding the family constituted a never-ending challenge. Taking on a brutal job outside the house — a "second shift" — had limited appeal for the average married woman from the working class. Thus many women might well have accepted the emerging division of labor as the best available strategy for family survival in the industrializing society.[10]

Third, why were the young, generally unmarried women who did work for wages outside the home segregated and confined to certain "women's jobs"? No doubt the desire of males to monopolize the best opportunities and hold women down provides part of the answer. Yet as some feminist scholars have argued, sex-segregated employment was also a collective response to the new industrial system. Previously, at least in theory, young people worked under a watchful parental eye. The growth of factories and mines brought unheard-of opportunities for girls and boys to mix on the job, free of familial supervision. Such opportunities led to more unplanned pregnancies and fueled the illegitimacy explosion that had begun in the late eigh-

teenth century and that gathered force until at least 1850. Thus segregation of jobs by gender was partly an effort by older people to help control the sexuality of working-class youths.

Investigations into the British coal industry before 1842 provide a graphic example of this concern. (See "Listening to the Past: The Testimony of Young Mine Workers," page 708.) The middle-class men leading the inquiry, who expected their daughters and wives to pursue ladylike activities, often failed to appreciate the physical effort of the girls and women who dragged with belt and chain the heavy carts of coal along narrow underground passages. But they professed horror at the sight of girls and women working without shirts, which was a common practice because of the heat, and they quickly assumed the prevalence of licentious sex with the male miners, who also wore very little clothing. In fact, most girls and married women worked for related males in a family unit that provided considerable protection and restraint. Yet many witnesses from the working class also believed that the mines were inappropriate and dangerous places for women and girls. Some miners stressed particularly the danger of sexual aggression for girls working past puberty. As one explained, "I consider it a scandal for girls to work in the pits. Till they are 12 or 14 they may work very well but after that it's an abomination. . . . The work of the pit does not hurt them, it is the effect on their morals that I complain of."[11] The **Mines Act of 1842** prohibited underground work for all women and girls as well as for boys under ten.

Some women who had to support themselves protested against being excluded from coal mining, which paid higher wages than most other jobs open to working-class women. But provided they were part of families that could manage economically, the girls and the women who had worked underground were generally pleased with the law. In explaining her satisfaction in 1844, one mother of four provided real insight into why many married working women accepted the emerging sexual division of labor:

> While working in the pit I was worth to my [miner] husband seven shillings a week, out of which we had to pay 2½ shillings to a woman for looking after the younger children. I used to take them to her house at 4 o'clock in the morning, out of their own beds, to put them into hers. Then there was one shilling a week for washing; besides, there was mending to pay for, and other things. The house was not guided. The other children broke things; they did not go to school when they were sent; they would be playing about,

---

• **Mines Act of 1842** English law prohibiting underground work for all women and girls as well as for boys under ten.

Listening to the Past

The Testimony of Young Mine Workers

The use of child labor in British industrialization quickly attracted the attention of humanitarians and social reformers. This interest led to investigations by parliamentary commissions, which resulted in laws limiting the hours and the ages of children working in large factories. Designed to build a case for remedial legislation, parliamentary inquiries gave large numbers of workers a rare chance to speak directly to contemporaries and to historians.

The moving passages that follow are taken from testimony gathered in 1841 and 1842 by the Ashley Mines Commission. Interviewing employers and many male and female workers, the commissioners focused on the physical condition of the youth and on the sexual behavior of workers far underground. The subsequent Mines Act of 1842 sought to reduce immoral behavior and sexual bullying by prohibiting underground work for all women and girls (and for boys younger than ten).

Mr. Payne, Coal Master

❝That children are employed generally at nine years old in the coal pits and sometimes at eight. In fact, the smaller the vein of coal is in height, the younger and smaller are the children required; the work occupies from six to seven hours per day in the pits; they are not ill-used or worked beyond their strength; a good deal of depravity exists but they are certainly not worse in morals than in other branches of the Sheffield trade, but upon the whole superior; the morals of this district are materially improving; Mr. Bruce, the clergyman, has been zealous and active in endeavoring to ameliorate their moral and religious education. . . .❞

Ann Eggley, Hurrier, 18 Years Old

❝I'm sure I don't know how to spell my name. We go at four in the morning, and sometimes at half-past four. We begin to work as soon as we get down. We get out after four, sometimes at five, in the evening. We work the whole time except an hour

for dinner, and sometimes we haven't time to eat. I hurry [move coal wagons underground] by myself, and have done so for long. I know the corves [small coal wagons] are very heavy, they are the biggest corves anywhere about. The work is far too hard for me; the sweat runs off me all over sometimes. I am very tired at night. Sometimes when we get home at night we have not power to wash us, and then we go to bed. Sometimes we fall asleep in the chair. Father said last night it was both a shame and a disgrace for girls to work as we do, but there was naught else for us to do. I began to hurry when I was seven and I have been hurrying ever since. I have been 11 years in the pits. The girls are always tired. I was poorly twice this winter; it was with headache. I hurry for Robert Wiggins; he is not akin to me. . . . We don't always get enough to eat and drink, but we get a good supper. I have known my father go at two in the morning to work . . . and he didn't come out till four. I am quite sure that we work constantly 12 hours except on Saturdays. We wear trousers and our shifts in the pit and great big shoes clinkered and nailed. The girls never work naked to the waist in our pit. The men don't insult us in the pit. The conduct of the girls in the pit is good enough sometimes and sometimes bad enough. I never went to a day-school. I went a little to a Sunday-school, but I soon gave it over. I thought it too bad to be confined both Sundays and week-days. I walk about and get the fresh air on Sundays. I have not learnt to read. I don't know my letters. I never learnt naught. I never go to church or chapel; there is no church or chapel at Gawber, there is none nearer than a mile. . . . I have never heard that a good man came into the world who was God's son to save sinners. I never heard of Christ at all. Nobody has ever told me about him, nor have my father and mother ever taught me to pray. I know no prayer; I never pray.❞

Patience Kershaw, Age 17

❝My father has been dead about a year; my mother is living and has ten children, five lads and five lasses; the oldest is about thirty, the youngest is four; three lasses go to mill; all the lads are colliers, two getters and three hurriers; one lives

and get ill-used by other children, and their clothes torn. Then when I came home in the evening, everything was to do after the day's labor, and I was so tired I had no heart for it; no fire lit, nothing cooked, no water fetched, the house dirty, and nothing comfortable for my husband. It is all far better now, and I wouldn't go down again.[12]

The Early Labor Movement in Britain

Many kinds of employment changed slowly during and after the Industrial Revolution in Great Britain. In 1850 more British people still worked on farms than in any other occupation. The second-largest occupation was domestic service, with more than one million at home and does nothing; mother does nought but look after home.

All my sisters have been hurriers, but three went to the mill. Alice went because her legs swelled from hurrying in cold water when she was hot. I never went to day-school; I go to Sunday-school, but I cannot read or write; I go to pit at five o'clock in the morning and come out at five in the evening; I get my breakfast of porridge and milk first; I take my dinner with me, a cake, and eat it as I go; I do not stop or rest any time for the purpose; I get nothing else until I get home, and then have potatoes and meat, not every day meat. I hurry in the clothes I have now got on, trousers and ragged jacket; the bald place upon my head is made by thrusting the corves; my legs have never swelled, but sisters' did when they went to mill; I hurry the corves a mile and more under ground and back; they weigh 300 cwt.;* I hurry 11 a day; I wear a belt and chain at the workings to get the corves out; the putters [miners] that I work for are *naked* except their caps; they pull off all their clothes; I see them at work when I go up; sometimes they beat me, if I am not quick enough, with their hands; they strike me upon my back; the boys take liberties with me, sometimes, they pull me about; I am the only girl in the pit; there are about 20 boys and 15 men; all the men are naked; I would rather work in mill than in coal-pit. 99

Isabel Wilson, Coal Putter, 38 Years Old

66 When women have children thick [fast] they are compelled to take them down early. I have been married 19 years and have had 10 bairns [children]; seven are in life. When on Sir

John's work was a carrier of coals, which caused me to miscarry five times from the strains, and was gai [very] ill after each. Putting is no so oppressive; last child was born on Saturday morning, and I was at work on the Friday night.

Once met with an accident; a coal brake my cheek-bone, which kept me idle some weeks. I have wrought below 30 years, and so has the guid man; he is getting touched in the breath now.

None of the children read, as the work is no regular. I did read once, but no able to attend to it now; when I go below lassie 10 years of age keeps house and makes the broth or stir-about. 99

Source: *Voices of the Industrial Revolution: Selected Readings from the Liberal Economists and Their Critics*, pp. 87–90, edited by J. Bowditch and C. Ramsland. Copyright © 1961, 1989 by the University of Michigan. Reprinted by permission of the publisher.

QUESTIONS FOR ANALYSIS

1. How does Payne's testimony compare with that of Ann Eggley and Patience Kershaw?

2. Describe the work of Eggley, Kershaw, and Wilson. What strikes you most about the testimonies of these workers?

3. The witnesses were responding to questions from middle-class commissioners. What did the commissioners seem interested in? Why?

*An old English unit of weight equaling 112 pounds.

household servants, 90 percent of whom were women. Thus many old, familiar jobs outside industry lived on and provided alternatives for individual workers. This helped ease the transition to industrial civilization.

Within industry itself, the pattern of artisans working with hand tools in small shops remained unchanged in many trades, even as others were revolutionized by technological change. For example, the British iron in-

dustry was completely dominated by large-scale capitalist firms by 1850. Many large ironworks had more than one thousand people on their payrolls. Yet the firms that fashioned iron into small metal goods, such as tools, tableware, and toys, employed on average fewer than ten wage workers who used handicraft skills. Only gradually after 1850 did some owners find ways to reorganize some handicraft industries with new machines

Union Membership Certificate This handsome membership certificate belonged to Arthur Watton, a properly trained and certified papermaker of Kings Norton in Birmingham, England. Members of such unions proudly framed their certificates and displayed them in their homes, showing that they were skilled workers. (Courtesy, Sylvia Waddell)

• **Combination Acts** English laws passed in 1799 that outlawed unions and strikes, favoring capitalist business people over skilled artisans. Bitterly resented and widely disregarded by many craft guilds, the acts were repealed by Parliament in 1824.

and new patterns of work. The survival of small workshops gave many workers an alternative to factory employment.

Working-class solidarity and class-consciousness developed in small workshops as well as in large factories. In the northern factory districts, anticapitalist sentiments were frequent by the 1820s. Commenting in 1825 on a strike in the woolen center of Bradford and the support it had gathered from other regions, one paper claimed with pride that "it is all the workers of England against a few masters of Bradford."[13] Modern technology and factory organization had created a few versus the many.

The transformation of some traditional trades by organizational changes, rather than technological innovations, could by themselves also create ill will and class feeling. The classical liberal concept of economic freedom and laissez faire emerged in the late eighteenth century, and it continued to gather strength in the early nineteenth century. In 1799 Parliament passed the **Combination Acts**, which outlawed unions and strikes. In 1813 and 1814 Parliament repealed the old and often disregarded law of 1563 regulating the wages of artisans and the conditions of apprenticeship. As a result of these and other measures, certain skilled artisan workers, such as bootmakers and high-quality tailors, found aggressive capitalists ignoring traditional work rules and trying to flood their trades with unorganized women workers and children to beat down wages.

The capitalist attack on artisan guilds and work rules was bitterly resented by many craftworkers, who subsequently played an important part in Great Britain and in other countries in gradually building a modern labor movement. The Combination Acts were widely disregarded by workers. Printers, papermakers, carpenters, tailors, and other such craftsmen continued to take collective action, and societies of skilled factory workers also organized unions. Unions sought to control the number of skilled workers, to limit apprenticeship to members' own children, and to bargain with owners over wages.

They were not afraid to strike; there was, for example, a general strike of adult cotton spinners in Manchester in 1810. In the face of widespread union activity, Parliament repealed the Combination Acts in 1824, and unions were tolerated, though not fully accepted, after 1825. The next stage in the development of the British trade-union movement was the attempt to create a single large national union. This effort was led not so much by working people as by social reformers such as Robert Owen. Owen, a self-made cotton manufacturer (see page 705), had pioneered in industrial relations by combining firm discipline with concern for the health, safety, and hours of his workers. After 1815 he experimented with cooperative and socialist communities, including one at New Harmony, Indiana. Then in 1834 Owen organized one of the largest and most visionary of the early national unions, the Grand National Consolidated Trades Union.

When Owen's and other grandiose schemes collapsed, the British labor movement moved once again after 1851 in the direction of craft unions. The most famous of these was the Amalgamated Society of Engineers, which represented skilled machinists. These unions won real benefits for members by fairly conservative means and thus became an accepted part of the industrial scene.

British workers also engaged in direct political activity in defense of their own interests. After the collapse of Owen's national trade union, many working people went into the Chartist movement, which sought political democracy. The key Chartist demand — that all men be given the right to vote — became the great hope of millions of aroused people. Workers were also active in campaigns to limit the workday in factories to ten hours and to permit duty-free importation of wheat into Great Britain to secure cheap bread. Thus working people developed a sense of their own identity and played an active role in shaping the new industrial system. They were neither helpless victims nor passive beneficiaries.

The Impact of Slavery

Another mass labor force of the Industrial Revolution was made up of the millions of enslaved men, women, and children who toiled in European colonies in the Caribbean and in North and South America. Historians have long debated the extent to which revenue from slavery contributed to Britain's achievements in the Industrial Revolution. They now agree that profits from colonial plantations and slave trading were a small portion of British income in the eighteenth century and were probably more often invested in land than in industry.

Nevertheless, the impact of slavery on Britain's economy was much broader than direct profits alone. In the mid-eighteenth century the need for items to exchange for colonial cotton, sugar, tobacco, and slaves stimulated demand for British manufactured goods in the Caribbean, North America, and West Africa. Britain's dominance in the slave trade also led to the development of finance and credit institutions that would help early industrialists obtain capital for their businesses. The British Parliament abolished the slave trade in 1807 and freed all slaves in British territories in 1833, but by 1850 most of the cotton processed by British mills was supplied by the coerced labor of slaves in the southern United States. Thus, the Industrial Revolution cannot be detached from the Atlantic world and the misery of slavery it included.

CONNECTIONS

For much of its history, Europe lagged behind older and more sophisticated civilizations in China and the Middle East. There was little reason to predict that the West would one day achieve world dominance. And yet by 1800 Europe had broken ahead of the other regions of the world in terms of wealth and power, a process historians have termed "the Great Divergence."[14]

One important prerequisite for the rise of Europe was its growing control over world trade, first in the Indian Ocean in the sixteenth and seventeenth centuries and then in the eighteenth-century Atlantic world. Acquisition of New World colonies — itself the accidental result of explorers seeking direct access to the rich Afroeurasian trade world — brought Europeans new sources of wealth and raw materials as well as guaranteed markets for their finished goods. A second crucial factor in the rise of Europe was the Industrial Revolution, which by dramatically increasing the pace of production and distribution while reducing their cost, allowed Europeans to control other countries first economically and then politically. Britain dominated this process at first, but was soon followed by other European nations. By the middle of the nineteenth century the gap between Western industrial production and standards of living and those of the non-West had grown dramatically, bringing with it the economic dependence of non-Western nations, meager wages for their largely impoverished populations, and increasingly aggressive Western imperial ambitions (see Chapter 25). In the late nineteenth century non-Western countries began to experience their own processes of industrialization. Today's world is witnessing a surge in productivity in China, India, and other non-Western nations, leading some to question how long Western superiority will endure.

□ CHAPTER REVIEW

□ **What were the origins of the Industrial Revolution in Britain, and how did it develop between 1780 and 1850? (p. 686)**

As markets for manufactured goods increased both domestically and overseas, Britain was able to respond with increased production, largely because of its stable government, abundant natural resources, and flexible labor force. The first factories arose as a result of technical innovations in spinning cotton, thereby revolutionizing the textile industry. The widespread availability and affordability of cotton provided benefits for many, but also resulted in the brutal forced labor of orphaned children on a large scale. The demand for improvements in energy led to innovations and improvements in the steam engine, which transformed the iron industry, among others. In the early nineteenth century transportation of goods was greatly enhanced when railroads were built.

□ **How after 1815 did countries outside of Britain respond to the challenge of industrialization? (p. 695)**

For reasons including warfare on home soil and barriers to trade, continental Europe lagged behind England in industrialization in 1815. After 1815 some continental countries, especially France, Belgium, and Germany, gradually built on England's technical breakthroughs, such as textile machinery and steam engines. Entrepreneurs set up their own factories and hired skilled urban workers from the area along with English immigrants experienced in the new technologies. England tried to limit the spread of trade secrets, and financing was difficult for early continental capitalists, but government interventions, such as tariff protection and infrastructure, were a great boon to industrialization on the European continent. In addition, newly established corporate banks worked in conjunction with governments to invest heavily in railroads and other industries. Beginning around 1850 Japan and the United States also began to rapidly industrialize, but generally the Industrial Revolution spread more slowly outside of Europe, as many countries were confined to producing agricultural goods and other

KEY TERMS	
Industrial Revolution (p. 687)	class-consciousness (p. 701)
spinning jenny (p. 688)	Luddites (p. 702)
water frame (p. 688)	Factory Act of 1833 (p. 705)
steam engines (p. 690)	separate spheres (p. 705)
Rocket (p. 693)	
Crystal Palace (p. 693)	Mines Act of 1842 (p. 707)
iron law of wages (p. 695)	Combination Acts (p. 710)
tariff protection (p. 699)	
economic nationalism (p. 699)	

raw materials to serve European markets. As a result, the gap between the industrialized West and the rest of the world widened.

□ **How did the Industrial Revolution affect people of all social classes, and what measures were taken to improve the conditions of workers? (p. 701)**

The rise of modern industry had a profound impact on people and their lives, beginning in Britain in the late eighteenth century. Industrialization led to the growing size and wealth of the middle class, as factory owners took their place beside successful merchants and professional people. These early entrepreneurs at first came from diverse backgrounds, providing economic opportunities for religious and ethnic minorities, but by the middle of the nineteenth century wealthy industrial families controlled large enterprises, and it was difficult for the poor but talented person to break in. The modern industrial working class also developed during this time, filling the need for vast quantities of labor power. Rigid rules, stern discipline, and long hours weighed heavily on factory workers, and improvements in the standard of living came slowly, but they were substantial by 1850. Workers often labored as family units in early factories, but as restrictions were placed on child labor, married women withdrew increasingly from wage work and concentrated on child care and household responsibilities. At the same time many young women worked before they were married, and jobs for young workers were often separated by gender in an attempt to control sexual behavior. The era of industrialization also fostered new attitudes toward child labor, encouraged protective factory legislation, and called forth a new sense of class feeling and an assertive labor movement.

SUGGESTED READING

Cameron, Rondo, and Larry Neal. *A Concise Economic History of the World*, 4th ed. 2003. Provides an introduction to key issues related to the Industrial Revolution and has a carefully annotated bibliography.

Davidoff, Leonore, and Catherine Hall. *Family Fortunes: Men and Women of the English Middle Class, 1750–1850*, rev. ed. 2003. Examines both economic activities and cultural beliefs with great skill.

Dolan, Brian. *Wedgwood: The First Tycoon*. 2004. A comprehensive study of the famous entrepreneur.

Fuchs, Rachel G. *Gender and Poverty in Nineteenth-Century Europe*. 2005. Provides a broad comparative perspective.

Gaskell, Elizabeth. *Mary Barton*. 1848. Gaskell's famous novel offers a realistic portrayal of the new industrial society.

Goodman, Jordan, and Katrina Honeyman. *Gainful Pursuits: The Making of Industrial Europe, 1600–1914*. 1988. An excellent general treatment of European industrial growth.

Horn, Jeff. *Understanding the Industrial Revolution: Milestones in Business History*. 2007. Clear, concise, and engaging; an excellent work for students.

Kemp, Tom. *Industrialization in Europe*, 2d ed. 1985. A useful overview.

Landes, David. *Dynasties: Fortunes and Misfortunes of the World's Great Family Businesses*. 2006. A collection offering fascinating and insightful histories of famous enterprises and leading capitalists.

Pomeranz, Kenneth. *The Great Divergence: China, Europe, and the Making of the Modern World Economy*. 2000. A sophisticated reconsideration of why western Europe underwent industrialization and China did not.

Stearns, Peter N. *The Industrial Revolution in World History*, 3d ed. 2007. A useful brief survey.

Thompson, E. P. *The Making of the English Working Class*. 1963. A fascinating book in the Marxist tradition that is rich in detail and early working-class lore.

Valenze, Deborah. *The First Industrial Woman*. 1995. A gender study that reinvigorates the debate between optimists and pessimists about the consequences of industrialization in Britain.

Walton, Whitney. *France and the Crystal Palace: Bourgeois Taste and Artisan Manufacture in the 19th Century*. 1992. Examines the gradual transformation of handicraft techniques and their persistent importance in the international economy.

NOTES

1. N. F. R. Crafts, *British Economic Growth During the Industrial Revolution* (Oxford, U.K.: Oxford University Press, 1985), p. 32.
2. Quoted in P. Mantoux, *The Industrial Revolution in the Eighteenth Century* (New York: Harper & Row, 1961), p. 75.
3. P. Bairoch, "International Industrialization Levels from 1750 to 1980," *Journal of European Economic History* 11 (Spring 1982): 269–333.
4. Quoted by J. Bowditch and C. Ramsland, eds., *Voices of the Industrial Revolution* (Ann Arbor: University of Michigan Press, 1961), p. 55, from the fourth edition of Thomas Malthus, *Essay on the Principle of Population* (1807).
5. Friedrich List, *The National System of Political Economy*, trans. G. A. Matile (Philadelphia: J. B. Lippincott, 1856), p. 61; edited slightly.
6. Quoted in W. A. Hayek, ed., *Capitalism and the Historians* (Chicago: University of Chicago Press, 1954), p. 126.
7. Crafts, *British Economic Growth*, p. 95.
8. H.-J. Voth, *Time and Work in England, 1750–1830* (Oxford, U.K.: Oxford University Press, 2000), pp. 268–270; also pp. 118–133.
9. Quoted in E. R. Pike, *"Hard Times": Human Documents of the Industrial Revolution* (New York: Praeger, 1966), p. 109.
10. See especially J. Brenner and M. Rama, "Rethinking Women's Oppression," *New Left Review* 144 (March–April 1984): 33–71, and sources cited there.
11. J. Humphries, ". . . 'The Most Free from Objection' . . . : The Sexual Division of Labor and Women's Work in Nineteenth-century England," *Journal of Economic History* 47 (December 1987): 941; Pike, *"Hard Times,"* p. 266.
12. Quoted in Pike, *"Hard Times,"* p. 208.
13. Quoted in D. Geary, ed., *Labour and Socialist Movements in Europe Before 1914* (Oxford, U.K.: Berg, 1989), p. 29.
14. Kenneth Pomeranz, *The Great Divergence: China, Europe, and the Making of the Modern World Economy* (Princeton, N.J.: Princeton University Press, 2000).

For practice quizzes and other study tools, visit the **Online Study Guide** at bedfordstmartins.com/mckayworld.

For primary sources from this period, see *Sources of World Societies*, **Second Edition**.

For Web sites, images, and documents related to topics in this chapter, visit **Make History** at bedfordstmartins.com/mckayworld.

• **Christabel Pankhurst, Militant Suffragette** Christabel Pankhurst led the British Women's Social and Political Union, whose motto was "deeds, not words." This photo was taken in 1912 in Paris, where Pankhurst was living to avoid arrest for her increasingly violent actions to obtain the vote for women, including bombing the home of the future prime minister. Women in Britain and many other countries gained the right to vote in the years immediately after World War I. (Hulton-Deutsch Collection/Corbis)

24

Europe's momentous economic and political transformation of modern times began in the late eighteenth century with the Industrial Revolution in England and then the French Revolution. Until about 1815 these economic and political revolutions were separate, involving different countries and activities and proceeding at very different paces. After peace returned in 1815, economic and political changes tended to fuse, reinforcing each other and bringing about what historian Eric Hobsbawm has incisively called the dual revolution. For instance, the growth of the industrial middle class encouraged the drive for representative government, and the demands of French workers in 1793 and 1794 eventually inspired socialists in many countries. Gathering strength, the dual revolution transformed Europe and had a powerful impact on the rest of the world.

Ideologies of Change in Europe 1815-1914

The dual revolution also posed a tremendous intellectual challenge. The changes that were occurring fascinated observers and stimulated the growth of new ideas and powerful ideologies. The most important of these were revitalized conservatism and three ideologies of change—liberalism, nationalism, and socialism. All played critical roles in the political and social battles of the era and the great popular upheaval that eventually swept across Europe in the revolutions of 1848. These revolutions failed, however, and gave way to more sober—and more successful—nation building in the 1860s. Redrawing the political geography of central Europe and uniting first Italy and then Germany, European political leaders and middle-class nationalists also began to deal effectively with some of the problems posed by the burgeoning of urban society. Additionally, European leaders encouraged their peoples to put their faith in a responsive national state. At the same time, the triumph of nationalism promoted bitter rivalries between states and peoples, and in the twentieth century it brought an era of tragedy and decline in Europe. •

A Conservative Peace Gives Way to Radical Ideas

□ How did the allies fashion a peace settlement in 1815, and what radical ideas emerged between 1815 and 1848?

The triumph of revolutionary economic and political forces was by no means certain as the Napoleonic era ended. The conservative aristocratic monarchies of Russia, Prussia, Austria, and Great Britain — known as the Quadruple Alliance — had finally defeated France (see Chapter 22) and reaffirmed their determination to hold France in line. But many other international questions were outstanding, and the allies agreed to meet at the **Congress of Vienna** to fashion a general peace settlement. The great challenge for political leaders in

Adjusting the Balance The Englishman below on the left uses his money to counterbalance the people that the Prussian and the fat Metternich are gaining in Saxony and Italy. Alexander I sits happily on his prize, Poland. This cartoon captures the essence of how the educated public thought about the balance-of-power diplomacy resulting in the Treaty of Vienna, the last page of which was signed and sealed in 1815 by the representatives of the various European states (left). (cartoon: Bibliothèque nationale de France; treaty: The "Final Act" of the Treaty of Vienna, established at the Congress of Vienna, 9 June 1815 [pen & ink on paper]/Archives du Ministère des Affaires Étrangères, Paris, France/Archives Charmet/The Bridgeman Art Library)

LA BALANCE POLITIQUE.

1814 was to construct a settlement that would last and not sow the seeds of another war. Their efforts were largely successful and contributed to a century unmarred by destructive generalized war (Map 24.1).

In the years following the peace settlement intellectuals and social observers sought to understand the revolutionary changes that had occurred and were still taking place. Almost all of these basic ideas were radical. In one way or another, the new ideas rejected conservatism, with its stress on tradition, a hereditary monarchy, and a strong landowning aristocracy. Radical thinkers developed and refined alternative visions — alternative ideologies — and tried to convince society to act on them.

The European Balance of Power

With the French agreeing to the restoration of the Bourbon dynasty (see Chapter 22), the allies were lenient toward that nation after Napoleon's abdication. The first Peace of Paris gave France the boundaries it possessed in 1792, which were larger than those of 1789, and France did not have to pay any war reparations.

When the four allies of the Quadruple Alliance met together at the Congress of Vienna they also agreed to raise a number of barriers against renewed French aggression. The Low Countries — Belgium and Holland — were united under an enlarged Dutch monarchy capable of opposing France more effectively. Prussia received considerably more territory along France's eastern border to stand as a "sentinel on the Rhine" against renewed French aggression. In these ways, the Quadruple Alliance combined leniency toward France with strong defensive measures.

In their moderation toward France, the allies were motivated by self-interest and traditional ideas about the balance of power. To the peacemakers, especially to Klemens von Metternich (1773–1859), Austria's foreign minister, the balance of power meant an international equilibrium of political and military forces that would discourage aggression by any combination of states or, worse, the domination of Europe by any single state. The Quadruple Alliance members, therefore, did not just sign the treaty and go home. They agreed to meet periodically to discuss their common interests and to consider appropriate measures to maintain peace in Europe. This agreement marked the beginning of the

European "congress system," which lasted long into the nineteenth century.

Coerced Conservatism After 1815

The peace settlement's domestic side was much less moderate. In 1815, under Metternich's leadership, Austria, Prussia, and Russia embarked on a crusade against the ideas and politics of the **dual revolution**. Metternich's policies dominated the entire German Confederation of thirty-eight independent German states, which the Vienna peace settlement had called into being (see Map 24.1). It was through the German

- **Congress of Vienna** A meeting of the Quadruple Alliance — Russia, Prussia, Austria, and Great Britain — and France held in 1814–1815 to fashion a general peace settlement that attempted to redraw Europe's political map after the defeat of Napoleonic France.
- **dual revolution** A term that historian Eric Hobsbawm used for the economic and political changes that tended to fuse and reinforce each other after 1815.

◻ Mapping the Past

MAP 24.1 Europe in 1815 In 1815 Europe contained many different states, but after the defeat of Napoleon international politics was dominated by the five Great Powers: Russia, Prussia, Austria, Great Britain, and France. (The number rises to six if one includes the Ottoman Empire.)

ANALYZING THE MAP Trace the political boundaries of each Great Power, and compare their geographical strengths and weaknesses. What territories did Prussia and Austria gain as a result of the war with Napoleon?

CONNECTIONS How did Prussia's and Austria's territorial gains contribute to the balance of power established at the Congress of Vienna? What other factors enabled the Great Powers to achieve such a long-lasting peace?

Confederation that Metternich had the repressive Carlsbad Decrees issued in 1819. These decrees required the member states to root out subversive ideas in their universities and newspapers, and a permanent committee was established to investigate and punish any liberal or radical organizations.

Born into the landed nobility, Metternich zealously defended his class and its privileges. Like many European conservatives of his time, he believed that liberalism (see page 719), as embodied in revolutionary America and France, had been responsible for a generation of war with untold bloodshed and suffering. He blamed liberal revolutionaries for stirring up the lower classes, which he believed desired nothing more than peace and quiet.

Because liberals believed that each national group had a right to establish its own independent government, the quest for national self-determination posed a grave threat to the Habsburgs' vast Austrian Empire. It was a dynastic state dominated by Germans but containing many other national groups, including Magyars (Hungarians), Czechs, Italians, Poles, Ukrainians, Slovenes, Croats, Serbs, Ruthenians, and Romanians. As a result, the multinational state that Metternich served was both strong and weak. It was strong because of its large population and vast territories; it was weak because of its many and potentially dissatisfied nationalities. In these circumstances, Metternich virtually had to oppose liberalism and nationalism, for Austria was unable to accommodate those ideologies of the dual revolution.

Liberalism and the Middle Class

The principal ideas of **liberalism** — liberty and equality — were by no means defeated in 1815. (This form of liberalism is often called "classical liberalism" and should not be confused with modern American liberalism, which usually favors government programs to meet social needs and to regulate the economy.) First realized successfully in the American Revolution and then achieved in part in the French Revolution, liberalism demanded representative government and equality before the law. The idea of liberty also meant specific individual freedoms: freedom of the press, freedom of speech, freedom of assembly, and freedom from arbitrary arrest. In Europe only France, with Louis XVIII's Constitutional Charter, and Great Britain, with its Parliament and historic rights of English men and women, had realized much of the liberal program in 1815. Even in those countries, liberalism had not fully succeeded.

Liberalism faced more radical ideological competitors in the early nineteenth century. Opponents of liberalism especially criticized its economic principles, which called for unrestricted private enterprise and no government interference in the economy. This philosophy was popularly known as the doctrine of **laissez faire** (lay-say FEHR).

Scottish philosopher Adam Smith (see page 537) posited the idea of a free economy in 1776 in opposition to mercantilism and its attempt to regulate trade. Smith argued that freely competitive private enterprise would give all citizens a fair and equal opportunity to do what they did best and would result in greater income for everyone. In early-nineteenth-century Britain this economic liberalism was embraced most en-

thusiastically by business groups and thus became a doctrine associated with business interests.

In the early nineteenth century liberal political ideals also became more closely associated with narrow class interests. Early-nineteenth-century liberals favored representative government, but they generally wanted property qualifications attached to the right to vote. In practice this meant limiting the vote to well-to-do males.

As liberalism became increasingly identified with the middle class after 1815, some intellectuals and foes of conservatism felt that liberalism did not go nearly far enough. Inspired by memories of the French Revolution and the young American republic, they called for universal voting rights, at least for males, and for democracy. These democrats and republicans were more radical than the liberals, and they were more willing to endorse violent upheaval to achieve goals.

The Growing Appeal of Nationalism

Nationalism was a second radical ideology in the years after 1815 — an idea destined to have an enormous influence in the modern world. In 1808, in an address to a German audience in French-occupied Berlin, the German philosopher Johann Gottlieb Fichte called on all Germans "to have that organic unity in which no member regards the fate of another as the fate of a stranger."[1] Fichte and other early advocates of the "national idea" argued that the members of each ethnic group (although the term *ethnic group* was not used at the time) had its own genius and its own cultural unity, which were manifested especially in a common language, history, and territory. In fact, such cultural unity was more a dream than a reality as local dialects abounded, historical memory divided the inhabitants of the different states as much as it unified them, and a variety of ethnic groups shared the territory of most states.

Nevertheless, European nationalists sought to make the territory of each people coincide with well-defined boundaries in an independent nation-state. It was this

---

- **liberalism** A philosophy whose principal ideas were equality and liberty; liberals demanded representative government and equality before the law as well as such individual freedoms as freedom of the press, freedom of speech, freedom of assembly, and freedom from arbitrary arrest.

- **laissez faire** A doctrine of economic liberalism that believed in unrestricted private enterprise and no government interference in the economy.

- **nationalism** The idea that each people had its own genius and its own specific unity, which manifested itself especially in a common language and history, and often led to the desire for an independent political state.

Building German Nationalism As popular upheaval in France spread to central Europe in March 1848, Germans from the solid middle classes came together in Frankfurt to draft a constitution for a new united Germany. (akg-images)

political goal that made nationalism so explosive in central and eastern Europe after 1815, when there were either too few states (Austria, Russia, and the Ottoman Empire) or too many (the Italian peninsula and the German Confederation), and when different peoples overlapped and intermingled.

The nationalist vision triumphed in the long run partly because the development of complex industrial and urban society required better communication between individuals and groups.[2] The development of a standardized national language that was spread through mass education created at least a superficial cultural unity. Nation-states also emerged because those who believed in the new ideology wanted to create "imagined communities," communities seeking to bind inhabitants around the abstract concept of an all-embracing national identity. Thus nationalists and leaders brought citizens together with emotionally charged symbols and ceremonies, such as ethnic festivals and flag-waving parades that celebrated the imagined nation of spiritual equals.[3]

Many of the African and Asian colonies that gained their independence in the twentieth century are ex-

amples of the imagined communities concept. During the colonial era European powers established a single language — English, French, or German, for example — as a common language of communication in their respective colonies. Many local nationalist leaders, who came from different ethnic groups within a colony, attended Christian mission schools or other schools run by the colonizer and learned a European language while adopting numerous elements of the European culture. This allowed them to communicate and plan common strategies for independence under the banner of a generally superficial national identity. Many of these leaders, such as India's Mohandas Gandhi (see page 890), even lived in Europe and witnessed the creation and promotion of national identities there firsthand.

Between 1815 and 1850 most people who believed in nationalism also believed in either liberalism or radical democratic republicanism. A common faith in the creativity and nobility of the people was perhaps the single most important reason for the linking of these two concepts. Liberals and especially democrats saw the people as the ultimate source of all good government. Early nationalists usually believed that every nation, like every citizen, had the right to exist in freedom and to develop its character and spirit. Yet early nationalists also stressed the differences among peoples, and they developed a strong sense of "we" and "they"; the "they" was often viewed as the enemy. Thus while European nationalism's main thrust was liberal and democratic, below the surface lurked ideas of national superiority and national mission that eventually led to aggression and conflict against supposedly inferior peoples in Africa and Asia, and to the great world wars of the twentieth century.

The Birth of Socialism

Socialism, the new radical doctrine after 1815, began in France. Early French socialist thinkers were acutely aware that the political revolution in France, the rise of laissez faire, and the emergence of modern industry in England were transforming society. They were disturbed because they saw these trends as fomenting selfish individualism and division within communities. There was, they believed, an urgent need for a further reorganization of society to establish cooperation and a new sense of community.

Early French socialists believed in economic planning. Inspired by the price controls and other emergency measures implemented in revolutionary France (see Chapter 22), they argued that the government should rationally organize the economy and help the poor. Socialists also believed that government should regulate private property or that private property should be abolished and replaced by state or community ownership.

One of the most influential early socialist thinkers was Henri de Saint-Simon (1760–1825). Saint-Simon optimistically proclaimed the tremendous possibilities of industrial development: "The age of gold is before us!" In his view the key to progress was proper social organization that required the "parasites"—the royal court, the aristocracy, lawyers, churchmen—to give way, once and for all, to the "doers"—the leading scientists, engineers, and industrialists. The doers would carefully plan the economy, guide it forward, and improve conditions for the poor.

Charles Fourier (1772–1837), another influential French thinker, envisaged a socialist utopia of self-sufficient communities. An early proponent of the total emancipation of women, Fourier also called for the abolition of marriage, free unions based only on love, and sexual freedom. To many people, these ideas were shocking and made the socialist program appear doubly dangerous and revolutionary.

It was left to Karl Marx (1818–1883) to establish firm foundations for modern socialism. Marx had studied philosophy at the University of Berlin before turning to journalism and economics. In 1848 the thirty-year-

> "The history of all previously existing society is the history of class struggles."
>
> **KARL MARX AND FRIEDRICH ENGELS**

old Karl Marx and the twenty-eight-year-old Friedrich Engels (1820–1895; see page 702) published *The Communist Manifesto*, which became the bible of socialism.

Early French socialists often appealed to the middle class and the state to help the poor. Marx ridiculed such appeals as naive. He argued that middle class interests and those of the industrial working class were inevitably opposed to each other. According to the *Manifesto*, the "history of all previously existing society is the history of class struggles." In Marx's view one class had always exploited the other, and, with the advent of modern industry, society was split more clearly than ever before: between the middle class—the **bourgeoisie** (boor-ZHWAH-zee)—and the modern working class—the **proletariat**.

Just as the bourgeoisie had triumphed over the feudal aristocracy, Marx predicted that the proletariat would conquer the bourgeoisie in a violent revolution. For Marx, class identity trumped national identity. While a tiny majority owned the means of production and grew richer, the ever-poorer proletariat was constantly growing in size and in class-consciousness. Marx believed that the critical moment when class conflict would result in revolution was very near, as the last lines of *The Communist Manifesto* make clear:

> Germany . . . is on the eve of a bourgeois revolution, that is bound to be . . . the prelude to an immediately following proletarian revolution. . . .
>
> Let the ruling classes tremble at a Communist revolution. The proletarians have nothing to lose but their chains. They have a world to win. WORKING MEN OF ALL COUNTRIES, UNITE!

Marx was strongly influenced by England's classical economists, who taught that labor was the source of all value. He went on to argue that profits were really wages stolen from the workers. Moreover, Marx incorporated Friedrich Engels's account of the terrible oppression of the new class of factory workers in England. Thus Marx pulled together powerful ideas and insights to create one of the great secular religions out of the intellectual ferment of the early nineteenth century.

- **socialism** A backlash against the emergence of individualism and the fragmentation of society, and a move toward international cooperation and a sense of community; the key ideas were economic planning, greater economic equality, and state regulation of property.
- **bourgeoisie** The well-educated, prosperous, middle-class groups.
- **proletariat** The Marxist term for the modern working class.

Reforms and Revolutions, 1815–1850

☐ Why in 1848 did revolutions triumph briefly throughout most of Europe, and why did they fail?

As liberal, national, and socialist forces battered the conservatism of 1815, pressure built up. In some countries change occurred gradually and peacefully, but in 1848 revolutionary political and social ideologies combined with economic crisis to produce a vast upheaval. Great Britain, France, Austria, and Prussia all experienced variations on this basic theme between 1815 and 1848.

Liberal Reform in Great Britain

The landowning aristocracy dominated eighteenth-century British society, but that class was neither closed nor rigidly defined. Basic civil rights were guaranteed, but only about 8 percent of the population could vote for representatives to Parliament. By the 1780s there was growing interest in some sort of reform, but the French Revolution threw the British aristocracy into a panic, and after 1815 it was determined to defend its ruling position.

Only in 1832 did a surge of popular protest convince the king and lords to give in. The Reform Bill of 1832 had profound significance. First, the bill moved British politics in a democratic direction and allowed the House of Commons to emerge as the all-important legislative body. Second, the new industrial areas of the country gained representation in the Commons. Third, the number of voters increased by about 50 percent. Comfortable middle-class urban groups, as well as some substantial farmers, received the vote. Thus the pressures building in Great Britain were temporarily released without revolution or civil war.

A major reform had been achieved peacefully, and continued reform within the system appeared difficult but not impossible. In 1847 the Tories passed the Ten Hours Act, which limited the workday for women and young people in factories to ten hours. Tory aristocrats continued to champion legislation regulating factory conditions. They were competing vigorously with the middle class for working-class support. This healthy competition was a crucial factor in Great Britain's peaceful evolution in the nineteenth century.

The people of Ireland did not benefit from this political competition. Long ruled as a conquered people, most of the population was made up of Irish Catholic peasants who rented their land from a tiny minority of Church of England Protestants. Ruthlessly exploited and growing rapidly in numbers, the Irish peasantry around 1800 lived under abominable conditions. The novelist Sir Walter Scott wrote:

> The poverty of the Irish peasantry is on the extreme verge of human misery; their cottages would scarce serve for pig styes even in Scotland; and their rags seem the very refuse of a sheep, and are spread over their bodies with such an ingenious variety of wretchedness that you would think nothing but some sort of perverted taste could have assembled so many shreds together.[4]

A compassionate French traveler agreed, writing that Ireland was " pure misery, naked and hungry. . . . I saw the American Indian in his forests and the black slave in his chains, and I believed that I was seeing the most extreme form of human misery; but that was before I knew the lot of poor Ireland."[5]

In spite of terrible conditions, Ireland's population continued to increase, caused in part by the extensive cultivation of the potato. The potato crop failed in 1845, 1846, 1848, and 1851 in Ireland and throughout much of Europe. Blight attacked the young plants, and the tubers rotted. The general result in Europe was high food prices, suffering, and, frequently, social upheaval. In Ireland the result was widespread starvation and mass fever epidemics. Total population losses were staggering. Fully one million emigrants fled the famine between 1845 and 1851, going primarily to the United States and Great Britain. The Great Famine, as this tragedy came to be known, intensified anti-British feeling and promoted Irish nationalism.

Revolutions in France

Louis XVIII's Constitutional Charter of 1814 protected the economic and social gains made by sections of the middle class and the peasantry in the French Revolution, and it permitted great intellectual and artistic freedom. The charter was anything but democratic, however. Only a tiny minority of males had the right to vote for the legislative deputies who, with the king and his ministers, made the nation's laws.

Although Louis Philippe (r. 1830–1848) accepted the Constitutional Charter of 1814 and titled himself merely the "king of the French people," the situation in France remained fundamentally unchanged. The vote was extended only from 100,000 to 170,000 citizens. Republicans, democrats, social reformers, and the poor of Paris were bitterly disappointed. The government's stubborn refusal to consider electoral reform heightened a sense of class injustice among shopkeepers and urban working people, and it eventually touched off a popular revolt in Paris in February 1848. Barricades went up, and Louis Philippe quickly abdicated.

The revolutionaries were firmly committed to a truly popular and democratic republic so that the common

□ Picturing the Past

The Triumph of Democratic Republics This French illustration offers an opinion of the initial revolutionary breakthrough in 1848. The peoples of Europe, joined together around their respective national banners, are achieving republican freedom, which is symbolized by the Statue of Liberty and the discarded crowns. The woman wearing pants at the base of the statue—very radical attire—represents feminist hopes for liberation. (Musée de la Ville, Paris/Giraudon/The Bridgeman Art Library)

ANALYZING THE IMAGE How many different flags can you count and/or identify? How would you characterize the types of people marching and the mood of the crowd?

CONNECTIONS What do the angels, Statue of Liberty, and discarded crowns suggest about the artist's view of the events of 1848? Do you think this illustration was created before or after the collapse of the revolution in France? Why?

people—the peasants and the workers—could reform society with wise legislation. In practice, building such a republic meant giving the right to vote to every adult male, and this was quickly done. Revolutionary compassion and sympathy for freedom were expressed in the freeing of all slaves in French colonies, the abolition of the death penalty, and the establishment of national workshops as an alternative to capitalist employment for unemployed Parisian workers.

Yet there were profound differences within the revolutionary coalition in Paris, and the socialism promoted by radical republicans frightened not only the middle and upper classes but also the peasants, many of whom owned land. When the French masses voted for delegates to the new Constituent Assembly in late April 1848, they elected a majority of moderate republicans who opposed any further radical social measures.

After the elections this clash of ideologies—of liberal capitalism and socialism—became a clash of classes and arms. When the government dissolved the national workshops in Paris, workers rose in a spontaneous and violent uprising. Working people fought with courage, but the government had the army and the support of peasant France. After three terrible "June Days" and the death or injury of more than ten thousand people, the republican army stood triumphant in a sea of working-class blood and hatred.

The revolution in France thus ended in spectacular failure. The February coalition of the middle and working classes had in four short months become locked in mortal combat. In place of a generous democratic republic, the Constituent Assembly completed a constitution featuring a strong executive. This allowed Louis Napoleon, nephew of Napoleon Bonaparte, to win a landslide victory in the December 1848 election.

President Louis Napoleon at first shared power with a conservative National Assembly. But in 1851 Louis Napoleon dismissed the Assembly and seized power in a coup d'état. A year later he called on the French to make him hereditary emperor, and 97 percent voted to do so in a national plebiscite. Louis Napoleon — proclaimed Emperor Napoleon III — then ruled France until 1870. Gradually his government became less authoritarian as he liberalized his empire. In 1870, on the eve of a disastrous war with Prussia (see page 729), Louis Napoleon was still seeking with some success to reconcile a strong national state with universal male suffrage and an independent National Assembly with real power.

The Revolutions of 1848 in Central Europe

Throughout central Europe the news of the upheaval in France evoked excitement and eventually revolution. Liberals demanded written constitutions, representative government, and greater civil liberties from authoritarian regimes. When governments hesitated,

Street Fighting in Berlin, 1848 This contemporary lithograph portrays a street battle on March 18, 1848, between Prussian troops loyal to King Frederick William IV and civilian men and women demonstrators. The king withdrew his troops the following day rather than kill anymore of his "beloved Berliners." Revolutionaries across Europe often dug up paving stones and used them as weapons. The tricolor flag achieved prominence during the revolution as the symbol of a united and democratic Germany. (akg-images)

popular revolts followed. Urban workers and students served as the shock troops, but they were allied with middle-class liberals and peasants. In the face of this united front, monarchs collapsed and granted almost everything. The popular revolutionary coalition then broke down as it had in France.

The revolution in the Austrian Empire began in 1848 in Hungary, where nationalistic Hungarians demanded national autonomy, full civil liberties, and universal suffrage. When Viennese students and workers also took to the streets and peasant disorders broke out, the Habsburg emperor Ferdinand I (r. 1835–1848) capitulated and promised reforms and a liberal constitution. The coalition of revolutionaries was not stable, however. When the monarchy abolished serfdom, the newly free peasants lost interest in the political and social questions agitating the cities.

The revolutionary coalition was also weakened and ultimately destroyed by conflicting national aspirations. In March the Hungarian revolutionary leaders pushed through an extremely liberal, almost democratic, constitution. But the Hungarian revolutionaries also sought to create a unified, centralized Hungarian nation. To the minority groups that formed half of the population — the Croats, Serbs, and Romanians — such unification was completely unacceptable. Each felt entitled to political autonomy and cultural independence. Likewise, Czech nationalists based in Bohemia and the city of Prague came into conflict with German nationalists. Thus conflicting national aspirations within the Austrian Empire enabled the monarchy to play off one ethnic group against the other.

The monarchy's first breakthrough came in June when the army crushed a working-class revolt in Prague. In October the predominantly peasant troops of the regular Austrian army attacked the student and working-class radicals in Vienna and retook the city. Thus the determination of Austria's aristocracy and the loyalty of its army were the final ingredients in the triumph of reaction and the defeat of revolution.

When Ferdinand I abdicated in favor of his young nephew, Franz Joseph (see page 743), only Hungary had yet to be brought under control. Another determined conservative, Nicholas I of Russia (r. 1825–1855), obligingly lent his iron hand. In June 1849, 130,000 Russian troops poured into Hungary and subdued the country. For a number of years the Habsburgs ruled Hungary as a conquered territory.

After Austria, Prussia was the largest and most influential German kingdom. Prior to 1848, the goal of middle-class Prussian liberals had been to reshape Prussia into a liberal constitutional monarchy, which would transform the German Confederation into a unified nation. The agitation following Louis Philippe's fall in France encouraged Prussian liberals to press their demands. When the artisans and factory workers in Berlin exploded in March 1848 and joined with the middle-class liberals in the struggle against the monarchy, Prussian King Frederick William IV (r. 1840–1861) caved in. On March 21 he promised to grant Prussia a liberal constitution and to merge Prussia into a new national German state.

A self-appointed committee of liberals from various German states met in Frankfurt in May 1848 and began writing a federal constitution for a unified German state. This National Assembly completed drafting a liberal constitution in March 1849 and elected King Frederick William of Prussia emperor of the new German national state. By early 1849, however, Frederick William had reasserted his royal authority, contemptuously refusing to accept the "crown from the gutter." When Frederick William tried to get the small monarchs of Germany to elect him emperor with authoritarian power, Austria balked. Supported by Russia, Austria forced Prussia to renounce all its unification schemes in late 1850. The German Confederation was re-established. Attempts to unite the Germans — first in a liberal national state and then in a conservative Prussian empire — had failed completely.

Nation Building in Italy, Germany, and Russia

☐ How did strong leaders and nation building transform Italy, Germany, and Russia?

Louis Napoleon's triumph in 1848 and his authoritarian rule in the 1850s provided Europe's old ruling classes with a new model in politics. To what extent might the expanding urban middle classes and even portions of the working classes rally to a strong and essentially conservative national state that also promised change? This was one of the great political questions in the 1850s and 1860s. In central Europe, a resounding answer came with the national unification of Italy and Germany.

The Russian empire also experienced profound political crises in this period, but they were unlike those in Italy or Germany because Russia was already a vast multinational state built on long traditions of military conquest and absolutist rule by elites from the dominant ethnic group — the Russians. It became clear to the Russian leaders that they had to embrace the process of **modernization**, defined narrowly as the changes that enable a country to compete effectively with the leading countries at a given time.

• **modernization** The changes that enable a country to compete effectively with the leading countries at a given time.

MAP 24.2 The Unification of Italy, 1859–1870 The leadership of Sardinia-Piedmont, nationalist fervor, and Garibaldi's attack on the kingdom of the Two Sicilies were decisive factors in the unification of Italy.

Victor Emmanuel, king of independent Sardinia, retained the moderate liberal constitution granted under duress in March 1848. To the Italian middle classes Sardinia (see Map 24.2) appeared to be a liberal, progressive state ideally suited to achieve the goal of national unification.

Sardinia had the good fortune of being led by Count Camillo Benso di Cavour. Cavour came from a noble family and embraced the economic doctrines and business activities associated with the prosperous middle class. Cavour's national goals were limited and realistic. Until 1859 he sought unity only for the states of northern and perhaps central Italy in a greatly expanded kingdom of Sardinia.

In the 1850s Cavour worked to consolidate Sardinia as a liberal constitutional state capable of leading northern Italy. He worked out a secret diplomatic alliance with Napoleon III, and in July 1858 he goaded Austria into attacking Sardinia. The combined Franco-Sardinian forces were victorious, but Napoleon III decided on a compromise peace with the Austrians in July 1859. Sardinia would receive only Lombardy, the area around Milan. Cavour resigned in a rage.

Popular revolts and Italian nationalism salvaged Cavour's plans. While the war against Austria raged in the north, dedicated nationalists in central Italy had risen and driven out their rulers. Nationalist fervor seized the urban masses, and the leaders of the nationalist movement called for fusion with Sardinia. Cavour returned to power in early 1860, and the people of cen-

Cavour, Garibaldi, and the Unification of Italy

Italy had never been a united nation prior to 1850. A battleground for the Great Powers after 1494, Italy was reorganized in 1815 at the Congress of Vienna. Austria received the rich northern provinces of Lombardy and Venetia. Sardinia and Piedmont fell under the rule of an Italian monarch, and Tuscany shared north-central Italy with several smaller states. The papacy ruled over central Italy and Rome, while a branch of the Bourbons ruled Naples and Sicily. Metternich was not wrong in dismissing Italy as "a geographical expression" (Map 24.2).

After 1815 the goal of a unified Italian nation captured the imaginations of many Italians, but there was no agreement on how it could be achieved. In 1848 revolutionary efforts to form a democratic Italian republic failed, and after he was temporarily driven from Rome during the upheavals of 1848, a frightened Pope Pius IX (r. 1846–1878) turned against most modern trends, including national unification. At the same time, tral Italy voted overwhelmingly to join a greatly enlarged kingdom of Sardinia. Cavour had achieved his original goal of a north Italian state (see Map 24.2).

For superpatriots such as Giuseppe Garibaldi (1807–1882), the job of unification was still only half done. A poor sailor's son, Garibaldi personified the romantic revolutionary nationalism of 1848. Having led a unit of volunteers to several victories over Austrian troops in 1859, Garibaldi emerged in 1860 as an independent force in Italian politics. (See "Individuals in Society: Giuseppe Garibaldi," page 728.)

Secretly supported by Cavour, Garibaldi conceived a bold plan to "liberate" the kingdom of the Two Sicilies. Landing on the shores of Sicily in May 1860, Garibaldi's guerrilla band of a thousand Red Shirts captured the imagination of the Sicilian peasantry, which rose in rebellion. Outwitting the royal army, Garibaldi captured Palermo, crossed to the mainland, and prepared to attack Rome and the pope. But Cavour quickly sent Sardinian forces to occupy most of the Papal States (but not Rome) and to intercept Garibaldi. When Garibaldi and Victor Emmanuel rode through Naples to cheering crowds, they symbolically sealed the union of north and south, of monarch and people.

The new kingdom of Italy, which did not include Venice until 1866 or Rome until 1870, was a parliamentary monarchy under Victor Emmanuel, neither radical nor democratic. Only a small minority of Italian males had the franchise. Despite political unity, the propertied classes and the common people were divided. A great social and cultural gap separated the progressive industrializing north from the stagnant agrarian south.

Bismarck and German Unification

In the aftermath of 1848, the German states, particularly Austria and Prussia, were locked in a political stalemate, each seeking to block the power of the other within the German Confederation. At the same time, powerful economic forces were undermining the political status quo. Modern industry was growing rapidly within the German customs union, or *Zollverein*, founded in 1834 to stimulate trade. By 1853 all the German states except Austria had joined the customs union, and a new Germany excluding Austria was becoming an economic reality.

Prussia had emerged from the upheavals of 1848 with a parliament of sorts, which was in the hands of the liberal middle class by 1859. The national uprising in Italy in 1859, however, convinced Prussia's tough-minded William I (r. 1861–1888) that political change and even war with Austria or France was possible. William I pushed to raise taxes and increase the defense budget to double the army's size. The Prussian

> "The great questions of the day will not be decided by speeches and resolutions . . . but by blood and iron."
>
> **OTTO VON BISMARCK**

parliament, reflecting the middle class's desire for a less militaristic society, rejected the military budget in 1862, and the liberals triumphed in new elections. King William then called on Count Otto von Bismarck to head a new ministry and defy the parliament.

The most important figure in German history between Martin Luther and Adolf Hitler, Otto von Bismarck (1815–1898) was above all a master of politics. Born into the Prussian landowning aristocracy, Bismarck loved power, but he was also extraordinarily flexible and pragmatic in pursuing his goals. When Bismarck took office as chief minister in 1862, he declared that the government would rule without parliamentary consent. He lashed out at the middle-class opposition: "The great questions of the day will not be decided by speeches and resolutions . . . but by blood and iron." Bismarck had the Prussian bureaucracy go right on collecting taxes even though the parliament refused to approve the budget, and he reorganized the army. For their part, the voters of Prussia continued to express their opposition by sending large liberal majorities to the parliament from 1862 to 1866.

In 1866 Bismarck launched the Austro-Prussian War with the intent of expelling Austria from German politics. The war lasted only seven weeks, and the reorganized Prussian army defeated Austria decisively at the Battle of Sadowa in Bohemia. Bismarck forced Austria to withdraw from German affairs. The mainly Protestant states north of the Main River were grouped in the new North German Confederation, led by an expanded Prussia (Map 24.3). Each state retained its own local government, but the federal government — William I and Bismarck — controlled the army and foreign affairs.

Long convinced that the old order should make peace with the liberal middle class and the nationalist movement, Bismarck asked the Prussian parliament to approve after the fact all of the government's "illegal" spending between 1862 and 1866. Most of the liberals jumped at the chance to cooperate. With German unity in sight, they legalized the government's spending. The constitutional struggle in Prussia was over, and the German middle class was accepting respectfully the monarchical authority and aristocratic superiority that Bismarck represented.

The final act in the drama of German unification followed quickly with a patriotic war with France. The apparent issue — whether a distant relative of Prussia's William I might become king of Spain — was only

Individuals in Society

Giuseppe Garibaldi

WHEN GIUSEPPE GARIBALDI (1807–1882) visited England in 1864, he received the most triumphant welcome ever given to any foreigner. Honored and feted by politicians and high society, he also captivated the masses. An unprecedented crowd of a half-million people cheered his carriage through the streets of London. These ovations were no fluke. In his time, Garibaldi was probably the most famous and most beloved figure in the world.* How could this be?

A rare combination of wild adventure and extraordinary achievement partly accounted for his demigod status. Born in Nice, Garibaldi went to sea at fifteen and sailed the Mediterranean for twelve years. At seventeen his travels took him to Rome, and he was converted in an almost religious experience to the "New Italy, the Italy of all the Italians." As he later wrote in his best-selling *Autobiography*, "The Rome that I beheld with the eyes of youthful imagination was the Rome of the future— the dominant thought of my whole life."

Sentenced to death in 1834 for his part in a revolutionary uprising in Genoa, Garibaldi barely escaped to South America. For twelve years he led a guerrilla band in Uruguay's struggle for independence from Argentina. "Shipwrecked, ambushed, shot through the neck," he found in a tough young woman, Anna da Silva, a mate and companion in arms. Their first children nearly starved in the jungle while Garibaldi, clad in his long red shirt, fashioned a legend as a fearless freedom fighter.

After he returned to Italy in 1848, the campaigns of his patriotic volunteers against the Austrians in 1848 and 1859 mobilized democratic nationalists. The stage was set for his volunteer army to liberate Sicily against enormous odds, astonishing the world and creating a large Italian state. Garibaldi's achievement matched his legend.

A brilliant fighter, the handsome and inspiring leader was an uncompromising idealist of absolute integrity. He never drew personal profit from his exploits, continuing to milk his goats and rarely possessing more than one change of clothing. When Victor Emmanuel offered him lands and titles after his great victory in 1861, even as the left-leaning volunteers were disbanded and humiliated, Garibaldi declined, saying he could not be bought off. Returning to his farm on a tiny rocky island, he denounced the government without hesitation when he concluded that it was betraying the dream of unification with its ruthless rule in the south. Yet even after a duplicitous Italian government caused two later attacks on Rome to fail, his faith in the generative power of national unity never wavered. Garibaldi showed that ideas and ideals count in history.

Above all, millions of ordinary men and women identified with Garibaldi because they believed that he was fighting for them. They recognized him as one of their own and saw that he remained true to them in spite of his triumphs, thereby ennobling their own lives and aspirations. Welcoming runaway slaves as equals in Latin America, advocating the emancipation of women, introducing social reforms in the south, and pressing for free education and a broader suffrage in the new Italy, Garibaldi the national hero fought for freedom and human dignity. The common people understood and loved him for it.

*Denis Mack Smith, *Garibaldi: A Great Life in Brief* (New York: Alfred A. Knopf, 1956), pp. 136–147; and Denis Mack Smith, "Giuseppe Garibaldi," *History Today*, August 1991, pp. 20–26.

QUESTIONS FOR ANALYSIS

1. Why was Garibaldi so famous and popular?
2. Nationalism evolved and developed in the nineteenth century. How did Garibaldi fit into this evolution? What kind of a nationalist was he?

● **Giuseppe Garibaldi, the charismatic leader, shown in an 1856 engraving based on a photograph.** (Bettmann/Corbis)

MAP 24.3 The Unification of Germany, 1866–1871 This map shows how Prussia expanded and a new German Empire was created through two wars, the Austro-Prussian War of 1866 and the Franco-Prussian War of 1870–1871.

a diplomatic pretext. By 1870, alarmed by their powerful new neighbor on the Rhine, French leaders had decided on a war to teach Prussia a lesson.

As soon as war against France began in 1870, Bismarck had the wholehearted support of the south German states. German forces under Prussian leadership defeated Louis Napoleon's armies at Sedan on September 1, 1870. Three days later French patriots in Paris proclaimed yet another French republic and vowed to continue fighting. But after five months, in January 1871, a starving Paris surrendered, and France accepted Bismarck's harsh peace terms. By this time the south German states had agreed to join a new Ger-

man Empire. As in the 1866 constitution, the Prussian king and his ministers had ultimate power in the new German Empire, and the lower house of the legislature was elected by universal male suffrage.

The Franco-Prussian War released an enormous surge of patriotic feeling in Germany. The new German Empire had become Europe's most powerful state, and most Germans were enormously proud, blissfully imagining themselves the fittest and best of the European species. Semi-authoritarian nationalism and a "new conservatism," which was based on an alliance of the propertied classes and sought the active support of the working classes, had triumphed in Germany.

The Modernization of Russia

In the 1850s Russia was a poor agrarian society with a rapidly growing population. Almost 90 percent of the population lived off the land, and serfdom was still the basic social institution. Then the Crimean War of 1853 to 1856, arising out of a dispute with France over who should protect certain Christian shrines in the Ottoman Empire, brought crisis. France and Great Britain, aided by Sardinia and the Ottoman Empire, inflicted a humiliating defeat on Russia.

Military defeat showed that Russia had fallen behind western Europe in many areas. Russia needed railroads, better armaments, and reorganization of the army if it was to maintain its international position. Moreover, the war had caused hardship and raised the specter of massive peasant rebellion. Military disaster thus forced the new tsar, Alexander II (r. 1855–1881), and his ministers along the path of rapid social change and general modernization.

The first and greatest of the reforms was the freeing of the serfs in 1861. The emancipated peasants received, on average, about half of the land. Yet they had to pay fairly high prices for their land, which was owned collectively by peasant villages. Thus the effects of the reform were limited. More successful was reform of the legal system, which established independent courts and equality before the law. Education was also liberalized somewhat, and censorship was relaxed but not removed.

Russia's greatest strides toward modernization were economic rather than political. Rapid railroad construction to 1880 enabled agricultural Russia to export grain and thus earn money for further industrialization. Industrial suburbs grew up around Moscow and St. Petersburg, and a class of modern factory workers began to take shape.

In 1881 a small group of terrorists assassinated Alexander II, and the reform era came to an abrupt end. Political modernization remained frozen until 1905, but economic modernization sped forward in the massive industrial surge of the 1890s. The key leader was Sergei Witte (suhr-GAY VIH-tuh), the energetic minister of finance. Under Witte's leadership the government doubled Russia's railroad network by the end of the century and promoted Russian industry with high protective tariffs.

By 1900 a fiercely independent Russia was catching up with western Europe and expanding its empire in Asia. By 1903 Russia had established a sphere of influence in Chinese Manchuria and was eyeing northern Korea. When the diplomatic protests of equally impe-

The Crimean War, 1853–1856

The Fruits of Terrorism
In the late 1870s a small group of revolutionaries believed that killing the tsar could destroy the Russian state. Succeeding in blowing up the reforming Alexander II after several near misses, the five assassins, including one woman, were quickly caught and hanged. Russia entered an era of reaction and harsh authoritarian rule. (Visual Connection Archive)

rialistic Japan were ignored, the Japanese launched a surprise attack on Russian forces in Manchuria in February 1904. After Japan scored repeated victories, to the amazement of self-confident Europeans, Russia was forced in September 1905 to accept a humiliating defeat.

Military disaster in East Asia brought political upheaval at home. On January 22, 1905, workers protesting for improved working conditions and higher wages were attacked by the tsar's troops outside the Winter Palace. Over one hundred were killed and around three hundred wounded. This event, known as Bloody Sunday, set off a wave of strikes, peasant uprisings, and troop mutinies across Russia. The revolutionary surge culminated in October 1905 in a paralyzing general strike, which forced the government to capitulate. The tsar, Nicholas II (r. 1894–1917), issued the **October Manifesto**, which granted full civil rights and promised a popularly elected Duma (DOO-muh; parliament) with real legislative power.

Under the new constitution Nicholas II retained great powers and the Duma had only limited authority. The middle-class liberals, the largest group in the newly elected Duma, were badly disappointed, and efforts to cooperate with the tsar's ministers soon broke down. In 1907 Nicholas II and his reactionary advisers rewrote the electoral law so as to increase greatly the weight of the propertied classes. When elections were held, the tsar could count on a loyal majority in the Duma. On the eve of World War I, Russia was partially modernized, a conservative constitutional monarchy with a peasant-based but industrializing economy.

Life in the Emerging Urban Society

☐ What was the impact of urban growth on cities, social classes, families, and ideas?

After 1850, as identification with the nation-state was becoming a basic organizing principle in Europe, urban growth rushed forward with undiminished force. In 1900 western Europe was urban and industrial as surely as it had been rural and agrarian in 1800. Rapid urban growth worsened long-standing overcrowding and unhealthy living conditions. Government leaders, city planners, reformers, and scientists worked tirelessly to address these challenges, and eventual success

The Russian Revolution of 1905

☐ Area of peasant unrest
• Major strikes and mutinies

with urban problems encouraged people to put their faith in a responsive national state.

Taming the City

Since the Middle Ages European cities had been centers of government, culture, and large-scale commerce. They had also been congested, dirty, and unhealthy. The Industrial Revolution revealed these conditions more starkly than ever before. The steam engine freed industrialists from dependence on the energy of fast-flowing streams and rivers so that by 1800 there was every incentive to build new factories in cities, which had better shipping facilities and a large and ready workforce. Therefore, as industry grew, there was also a rapid expansion of already overcrowded and unhealthy cities.

In the 1820s and 1830s people in Britain and France began to worry about the condition of their cities. Except on the outskirts, each town or city was using every scrap of land to the full extent. Parks and open areas were almost nonexistent, and narrow houses were usually built wall to wall in long rows. Highly concentrated urban populations lived in extremely unsanitary and unhealthy conditions, with open drains and sewers flowing alongside or down the middle of unpaved streets. "Six, eight, and even ten occupying one room is anything but uncommon," wrote a Scottish doctor for a government investigation in 1842.

The urban challenge eventually brought an energetic response from a generation of reformers. The most famous early reformer was Edwin Chadwick, a British official. Chadwick was a follower of radical British philosopher Jeremy Bentham (1748–1832), whose approach to social issues, called utilitarianism, had taught that public problems ought to be dealt with on a rational, scientific basis and according to the "greatest good for the greatest number." Chadwick became convinced that disease and death actually caused poverty and that disease could be prevented by cleaning up the urban environment.

Collecting detailed reports from local officials and publishing his findings in 1842, Chadwick correctly believed that the stinking excrement of communal outhouses could be carried off by water through sewers at less than one-twentieth the cost of removing it by hand. In 1848 Chadwick's report became the basis of Great Britain's first public health law, which created a

• **October Manifesto** The result of a great general strike in Russia in October 1905, it granted full civil rights and promised a popularly elected Duma (parliament) with real legislative power.

King Cholera This 1852 drawing from *Punch* tells volumes about the unhealthy living conditions of the urban poor. In the foreground children play with a dead rat and a woman scavenges a dung heap. Cheap rooming houses provide shelter for the frightfully overcrowded population. Such conditions and contaminated water spread deadly cholera epidemics from India throughout Europe in the 1800s. The doctor's medicine chest seen here could provide patients only with opium mixtures to relieve pain and reduce intestinal swelling. (drawing: © British Library Board, P.P. 5270 vol. 23, 139; chest: Science & Society Picture Library)

national health board and gave cities broad authority to build modern sanitary systems. Such sanitary movements won dedicated supporters in the United States, France, and Germany from the 1840s on. By the 1860s and 1870s European cities were making real progress toward adequate water supplies and sewerage systems, and city dwellers were beginning to reap the reward of better health.

Early sanitary reformers were seriously handicapped by the prevailing miasmatic theory of disease — the belief that people contract disease when they breathe the bad odors of decay and putrefying excrement. In the 1840s and 1850s keen observation by doctors and public health officials suggested that contagion was spread through filth and not caused by it, thus weakening the miasmatic idea. The breakthrough was the development of the **germ theory** of disease by Louis Pasteur (1822–1895), a French chemist who began studying fermentation for brewers in 1854. Pasteur found that the growth of living organisms in a beverage could be suppressed by heating it — by pasteurization.

By 1870 the work of Pasteur and others had clearly demonstrated the connection between germs and disease. When, in the middle of the 1870s, Robert Koch and his German coworkers developed pure cultures of harmful bacteria and described their life cycles, the dam broke. Over the next twenty years researchers identified the organisms responsible for disease after disease. These discoveries led to the development of a number of effective vaccines. Surgeons also applied the germ theory in hospitals, sterilizing not only the wound but everything else — hands, instruments, clothing — that entered the operating room.

The achievements of the bacterial revolution coupled with the public health movement saved millions of lives, particularly after about 1890. In England, France, and Germany death rates declined dramatically, and the awful death sentences of the past — diphtheria, typhoid, typhus, cholera, yellow fever — became vanishing diseases in the industrializing nations.

More effective urban planning after 1850 also improved the quality of urban life. France took the lead during the rule of Napoleon III (1848–1870), who believed that rebuilding much of Paris would provide employment, improve living conditions, and glorify his empire. In the baron Georges Haussmann (1809–1884), an aggressive, impatient Alsatian whom he placed in charge of Paris, Napoleon III found an authoritarian planner capable of bulldozing both buildings and opposition. In twenty years Paris was transformed by slum clearance, new streets and housing, parks and open spaces, and good fresh water. The rebuilding of Paris stimulated modern urbanism throughout Europe, particularly after 1870.

The development of mass public transportation was also of great importance in the improvement of urban living conditions. In the 1870s many European cities authorized private companies to operate horse-drawn streetcars, which had been developed in the United States. Then in the 1890s countries in North America and Europe adopted another American transit innovation, the electric streetcar. Electric streetcars were cheaper, faster, more dependable, and more comfortable than their horse-drawn counterparts. Millions of riders hopped on board during the workweek. On weekends and holidays streetcars carried city people on outings to parks and the countryside, racetracks, and music halls.[6] Electric streetcars also gave people of modest means access to improved housing, as the still-crowded city was able to expand and become less congested.

New Social Hierarchies and the Middle Classes

By 1850 at the latest, working conditions were improving. Moreover, real wages were rising for the mass of the population, and they continued to do so until 1914. With increased wages, the rigid class structures of Old Regime Europe began to break down and, theoretically at least, open the way for social equality. Greater economic rewards for the average person did not eliminate hardship and poverty, however, nor did they significantly narrow the gap between rich and the poor. In almost every industrialized country around 1900, the richest 20 percent of households received anywhere from 50 to 60 percent of all national income, whereas the bottom 30 percent of households received 10 percent or less of all income. Thus the gap between rich and poor remained enormous and was probably almost as great in 1900 as it had been in the age of agriculture and aristocracy before the Industrial Revolution.

The great gap between rich and poor endured, in part, because industrial and urban development made society more diverse and less unified. Society had not split into two sharply defined opposing classes, as Marx had predicted. Instead, economic specialization created more new social groups than it destroyed. There

developed an almost unlimited range of jobs, skills, and earnings; one group or subclass blended into another in a complex, confusing hierarchy.

The diversity and range within the urban middle class were striking as the twentieth century opened, and it is meaningful to think of a confederation of middle classes loosely united by occupations requiring mental, rather than physical, skill. As the upper middle class, composed mainly of successful business families, gained in income and progressively lost all traces of radicalism after the trauma of 1848, they were almost irresistibly drawn toward the aristocratic lifestyle. Next came the much larger, much less wealthy, and increasingly diversified middle middle class. Here one found moderately successful industrialists and merchants, professionals in law and medicine, and mid-level managers of large public and private institutions. The expansion of industry and technology created a growing demand for experts with specialized knowledge, and the most valuable of the specialties became solid middle-class professions. Engineers, architects, chemists, accountants, and surveyors first achieved professional standing in this period. At the bottom were independent shopkeepers, small traders, and tiny manufacturers — the lower middle class. Industrialization and urbanization also diversified the lower middle class and expanded the number of white-collar employees. White-collar employees were propertyless, but generally they were fiercely committed to the middle class and to the ideal of moving up in society.

Well fed and well served, the middle classes were also well housed by 1900 and were quite clothes conscious. Education was another growing expense as middle-class parents tried to provide their children with ever-more-crucial advanced education. The keystones of culture and leisure were books, music, and travel.

The middle classes were loosely united by a shared code of expected behavior and morality. This code stressed hard work, self-discipline, and personal achievement. Men and women who fell into crime or poverty were generally assumed to be responsible for their own circumstances. In short, the middle-class person was supposed to know right from wrong and to act accordingly.

The People and Occupations of the Working Classes

About four out of five Europeans belonged to the working classes at the turn of the twentieth century. Many of them were small landowning peasants and

• **germ theory** The idea that disease is caused by the spread of living organisms that can be controlled.

A Summer's Day in Hyde Park, **1858** John Ritchie's famous painting of Victorian England portrays the mixing of the social classes in London's Hyde Park. Middle class (bourgeoisie) ladies display their conspicuous finery, while representatives of the upper classes ride by in a fine carriage. (© Museum of London, UK/The Bridgeman Art Library)

hired farm hands. This was especially true in eastern Europe.

The urban working classes were even less unified and homogeneous than the middle classes. In the first place, economic development and increased specialization expanded the traditional range of working-class skills, earnings, and experiences. In the second place, skilled, semiskilled, and unskilled workers developed widely divergent lifestyles and cultural values, and their differences contributed to a keen sense of social status and hierarchy within the working classes.

Highly skilled workers, who made up about 15 percent of the working classes, became known as the labor aristocracy. The most "aristocratic" of the highly skilled workers were construction bosses and factory foremen, men who had often risen from the ranks and were fiercely proud of their achievement. The labor aristocracy also included members of the traditional highly skilled handicraft trades that had not yet been placed in factories, as well as new kinds of skilled workers such as shipbuilders and railway locomotive engineers. Thus the labor elite remained in a state of flux as individuals and whole crafts moved in and out of it.

Below the labor aristocracy stood the complex world of semiskilled and unskilled urban workers. A large number of the semiskilled were factory workers who earned good wages and whose relative importance in the labor force was increasing. Below the semiskilled workers was a larger group of unskilled workers that included day laborers such as longshoremen, wagon-driving teamsters, and maids. Many of these people had real skills and performed valuable services, but they were unorganized and divided, united only by the common fate of meager earnings. The same lack of unity characterized street vendors and market people — self-employed workers who competed savagely with each other and with the established lower middle class shopkeepers.

To make ends meet, many working-class wives had to join the broad ranks of working women in the "sweated industries." These industries resembled the old putting-out and cottage industries of earlier times, and they were similar to what we call sweatshops today. The women, sometimes unskilled and nearly always unorganized labor, normally worked at home and were paid by the piece. Sweating became a catch-all word denoting meager wages, hard labor, unsanitary and dangerous working conditions, and harsh treatment, often by a middleman who had subcontracted the work.

The urban working classes sought fun and recreation, and they found both. Across the face of Europe drinking remained unquestionably the favorite working class leisure-time activity. Generally, however, heavy problem drinking declined in the late nineteenth century as drinking became more public and social. Cafés and pubs became increasingly bright, friendly places.

The two other leisure-time passions of the working classes were sports and music halls. A great decline in cruel sports, such as bullbaiting and cockfighting, led to the rise of modern spectator sports, of which racing and soccer were the most popular. There was a great deal of gambling on sports events. Music halls and vaudeville theaters, the working-class counterparts of middle-class opera and classical theater, were enormously popular throughout Europe.

The Changing Family

Industrialization and the growth of modern cities also brought great changes to women's lives. These changes were particularly consequential for married women, and most women did marry in the nineteenth century.

After 1850 the work of most wives continued to become increasingly distinct and separate from that of their husbands. Husbands became wage earners in factories and offices; wives tended to stay home, manage households, and care for children. As economic conditions improved, only married women in poor families tended to work outside the home. The ideal became separate spheres (see page 705), the strict division of labor by sex. This rigid division meant that married women faced great obstacles if they needed or wanted to move into the men's world of paid employment outside the home. Well-paying jobs were off-limits to women, and a woman's wage was almost always less than a man's, even for the same work.

Middle-class women lacked legal rights and faced discrimination in education and employment. Thus organizations founded by middle-class feminists campaigned for legal equality as well as for access to higher education and professional employment. In the later nineteenth century middle-class women scored some significant victories, such as the 1882 law giving English married women full property rights. Socialist women leaders usually took a different path. They argued that the liberation of working-class women would come only with the liberation of the entire working class through revolution. In the meantime, they championed the cause of working women and won some practical improvements. In a general way these different approaches to women's issues reflected the diversity of classes in urban society.

As the ideology and practice of rigidly separate spheres narrowed women's horizons, their control and influence in the home became increasingly strong throughout Europe in the later nineteenth century. Among the English working classes, for example, the wife generally determined how the family's money was spent. All the major domestic decisions, from the children's schooling and religious instruction to the selection of new furniture or a new apartment, were hers. (See "Listening to the Past: Mrs. Beeton's Guide for Running a Victorian Household," page 736.)

The woman's guidance of the household went hand in hand with the increased emotional importance of home and family. The home she ran was idealized as a warm shelter in a hard and impersonal urban world. Husbands and wives were expected to have emotional ties to each other, and mothers were expected to have powerful feelings toward their children. Among the middle and upper classes, marriages in the late nineteenth century were increasingly based on sentiment and sexual attraction, as money, family pressures, and financial calculation gradually declined in importance. Among the working classes, young people often began working or left home when they reached adolescence, so they had greater independence in their decisions about who to marry.

Ideas about sexuality within marriage varied. Many French marriage manuals of the late 1800s stressed that women had legitimate sexual needs, such as the "right to orgasm." In the more puritanical United States, however, sex manuals recommended sexual abstinence for unmarried men and limited sexual activity for married men. Respectable women were thought to experience no sexual pleasure at all from sexual activity, and anything vaguely sexual was to be removed from their surroundings; even the legs of pianos should be covered.

Medical doctors in both Europe and the United States began to study sexual desires and behavior more closely, and to determine what was considered "normal" and "abnormal." Same-sex attraction, labeled "homosexuality" for the first time, was identified as a "perversion." Governments seeking to promote a healthy society as a way of building up their national strength increasingly regulated prostitution, the treatment of venereal disease, and access to birth control in ways that were shaped by class and gender hierarchies. Masturbation, termed the "secret vice," became a matter of public concern in this era of growing nationalism because doctors and officials worried that it would weaken boys and men, making them incapable of defending the nation or engaging in industrial work.

Medical science also turned its attention to motherhood, and a wave of specialized books on child

Listening to the Past

Mrs. Beeton's Guide for Running a Victorian Household

The growth of the middle class in the second half of the nineteenth century resulted in sharper divisions of labor according to sex. More and more husbands were now going off each morning to their jobs in factories and offices, while their wives remained at home to manage the household. But life in a middle-class Victorian household was often quite different from the homes in which these women had been raised. Many a wife faced a steep learning curve as she learned to manage servants, purchase and use new gadgets and appliances, handle large household budgets, and present herself, her children, and her home in a comfortable and respectable middle class light.

Fortunately, there were many how-to manuals and guides that these wives could refer to for answers about nearly anything related to the home. One of the most popular of these how-to manuals in England was Mrs. Beeton's Book of Household Management. *Compiled and edited by Isabella Mary Beeton (1836–1865), this book offered advice on such wide-ranging topics as the management of children, dealing with servants, making a will, emergencies and doctors, taxes, fashion, animal husbandry, and shopkeepers. The book was also popularly referred to as "Mrs. Beeton's Cookbook" because over 900 of the 1,100 plus pages contained recipes. The excerpt that follows comes from the section on "The Mistress."*

1. As With the Commander of an Army, or the leader of any enterprise, so is it with the mistress of a household. Her spirit will be seen through the whole establishment; and just in proportion as she performs her duties intelligently and thoroughly, so will her domestics follow in her path. Of all those requirements, which more particularly belong to the feminine character, there are none which take a higher rank, in our estimation, than such as enter into a knowledge of household duties; for on these are perpetually dependent the happiness, comfort, and well-being of a family. . . .

2. Early Rising is One Of The Most Essential Qualities which enter into good Household Management, as it is not only the parent of health, but of innumerable other advantages. Indeed, when a mistress is an early riser, it is almost certain that her house will be orderly and well-managed. On the contrary, if she remain in bed till a late hour, then the domestics, who, as we have before observed, invariably partake somewhat of their mistress's character, will surely become sluggards. . . .

4. Cleanliness Is Also Indispensable To Health, and must be studied both in regard to the person and the house, and all that it contains. Cold or tepid baths should be employed every morning, unless, on account of illness or other circumstances, they should be deemed objectionable. . . .

5. Frugality And Economy Are Home Virtues, without which no household can prosper. . . . We must always remember that it is a great merit in housekeeping to manage a little well. . . . Economy and frugality must never, however, be allowed to degenerate into parsimony and meanness. . . .

14. Charity And Benevolence Are Duties which a mistress owes to herself as well as to her fellow-creatures. . . . Visiting the houses of the poor is the only practical way really to understand the actual state of each family; and although there may be difficulties in following out this plan in the metropolis and other large cities, yet in country towns and rural districts these objections do not obtain. Great advantages may result from visits paid to the poor; for there being, unfortunately, much ignorance, generally, amongst them with respect to all household knowledge, there will be opportunities for advising and instructing them, in a pleasant and unobtrusive manner, in cleanliness, industry, cookery, and good management.

15. In Marketing, That The Best Articles Are The Cheapest, may be laid down as a rule; and it is desirable, unless an experienced and confidential housekeeper be kept, that the mistress should herself purchase all provisions and stores needed for the house. If the mistress be a young wife, and not accustomed to order "things for the house," a little practice and experience will soon teach her who are the best trades people

rearing and infant hygiene instructed middle-class women on how to be better mothers. Social reformers, some of them women, attempted to instruct working-class women in this new "science of motherhood," but, often working at a "sweated" trade or caring for boarders within their own homes, poorer women had little time for new mothering practices. Similarly, when Europeans established colonial empires, the wives of missionaries and officials sometimes tried to change child-rearing practices of local peoples. They were rarely successful, and different child-rearing practices became yet another sign of colonial people's inferiority in European eyes.

Women in industrializing countries also began to limit the number of children they bore. This revolutionary reduction in family size, in which the comfortable and well-educated classes took the lead, was founded on the parents' desire to improve their ecoto deal with, and what are the best provisions to buy.

16. A Housekeeping Account-book should invariably be kept, and kept punctually and precisely. . . . The housekeeping accounts should be balanced not less than once a month; so that you may see that the money you have in hand tallies with your account of it in your diary. . . .

18. In Obtaining A Servant's Character, it is not well to be guided by a written one from some unknown quarter; but it is better to have an interview, if at all possible, with the former mistress. By this means you will be assisted in your decision of the suitableness of the servant for your place, from the appearance of the lady and the state of her house. Negligence and want of cleanliness in her and her household generally, will naturally lead you to the conclusion, that her servant has suffered from the influence of the bad example.

19. The Treatment Of Servants is of the highest possible moment, as well to the mistress as to the domestics themselves. On the head of the house the latter will naturally fix their attention; and if they perceive that the mistress's conduct is regulated by high and correct principles, they will not fail to respect her. If, also, a benevolent desire is shown to promote their comfort, at the same time that a steady performance of their duty is exacted, then their respect will not be unmingled with affection, and they will be still more solicitous to continue to deserve her favour. . . .

48. Of The Manner Of Passing Evenings At Home, there is none pleasanter than in such recreative enjoyments as those which relax the mind from its severer duties, whilst they stimulate it with a gentle delight. Where there are young people forming a part of the evening circle, interesting and agreeable pastime should especially be promoted. It is of incalculable benefit to them that their homes should possess all the attractions of healthiest amusement, comfort, and happiness; for if they do not find pleasure there, they will seek it elsewhere. It ought, therefore, to enter into the domestic policy of every parent, to make her children feel that home is the happiest place in the world; that to imbue them with this delicious home-feeling is one of the choicest gifts a parent can bestow. . . .

54. Such Are The Onerous Duties which enter into the position of the mistress of a house, and such are, happily, with a slight but continued attention, of by no means difficult performance. She ought always to remember that she is the first and the last, the Alpha and the Omega in the government of her establishment; and that it is by her conduct that its whole internal policy is regulated. "

Source: Isabella Mary Beeton, ed., *Beeton's Book of House Management* (London: S.O. Beeton, 1863), pp. 1–2, 5–7, 17, 18–19.

QUESTIONS FOR ANALYSIS

1. In what ways might the mistress of the household be considered like the commander of an army?

2. How important is outward appearance—to guests, servants, and the outside world—for the Victorian mistress of a household?

3. What advice does Mrs. Beeton give for the well-being and happiness of children?

4. Some scholars consider Mrs. Beeton a feminist. Do you agree with that assessment? Why?

---

nomic and social position and that of their children. By having fewer youngsters, parents could give those they had advantages, from music lessons to expensive university education. A young German skilled worker with one child spoke for many in his class when he said, "We want to get ahead, and our daughter should have things better than my wife and sisters did."[7]

The working classes probably had more avenues of escape from such tensions than did the middle classes.

Unlike their middle-class counterparts who remained economically dependent on their families until a long education was finished or a proper marriage secured, working-class boys and girls went to work when they reached adolescence. Earning wages on their own, they could bargain with their parents for greater independence within the household, or they could leave home to live cheaply as paying lodgers in other working-class homes. Thus the young person from the working classes broke away from the family more easily when emotional ties became oppressive.

Science for the Masses

The intellectual achievements of the scientific revolution (see Chapter 18) had resulted in few practical benefits, and theoretical knowledge had also played a relatively small role in the Industrial Revolution in England. But breakthroughs in industrial technology stimulated basic scientific inquiry as researchers sought to explain how such things as steam engines and blast furnaces actually worked. The result from the 1830s onward was an explosive growth of fundamental scientific discoveries that were increasingly transformed into material improvements for the general population.

A perfect example of the translation of better scientific knowledge into practical human benefits was the work of Louis Pasteur and his followers in biology and the medical sciences (see page 732). Another was the development of the branch of physics known as thermodynamics, the relationship between heat and mechanical energy. By midcentury physicists had formulated the fundamental laws of thermodynamics, which were then applied to mechanical engineering, chemical processes, and many other fields.

The triumph of science and technology had at least three significant consequences. First, though ordinary citizens continued to lack detailed scientific knowledge, everyday experience and innumerable articles in newspapers and magazines impressed the importance of science on the popular mind. Second, as science became more prominent in popular thinking, the philosophical implications of science formulated in the Enlightenment spread to broad sections of the population. Natural processes appeared to be determined by rigid laws, leaving little room for either divine intervention

Madrid in 1900 This wistful painting of a Spanish square on a rainy day, by Enrique Martínez Cubells y Ruiz (1874–1917), includes a revealing commentary on how scientific discoveries transformed urban life. Coachmen wait atop their expensive hackney cabs for a wealthy clientele, while modern electric streetcars that carry the masses converge on the square from all directions. In this way the development of electricity brought improved urban transportation and enabled the city to expand to the suburbs. (Museo Municipal, Madrid/The Bridgeman Art Library)

or human will. Third, the methods of science acquired unrivaled prestige after 1850. For many, the union of careful experiment and abstract theory was the only reliable route to truth and objective reality.

Living in an era of rapid change, nineteenth-century thinkers in Europe were fascinated with the idea of evolution and dynamic development. The most influential of all nineteenth-century evolutionary thinkers was Charles Darwin (1809–1882). Darwin came to doubt the general belief in a special divine creation of each species of animal. (A species is generally defined as a group of organisms that can interbreed with one another and produce fertile offspring of both sexes.) Instead, he concluded, all life had gradually evolved from a common ancestral origin in an unending "struggle for survival." Darwin's theory of **evolution** is summarized in the title of his work *On the Origin of Species by the Means of Natural Selection* (1859). He argued that small variations within individuals in one species allowed them to acquire more food and better living conditions and made them more successful in reproducing, thus passing their genetic material to the next generation. When a number of individuals within a species became distinct enough that they could no longer interbreed successfully with others, they became a new species.

Ever since humans began shaping the world around them tens of thousands of years ago, they have engaged in intentional selection and selective breeding in plants and animals to produce, for example, a new color of rose, a faster racehorse, or chickens that lay more eggs. Natural selection is not intentional; it results when random variations give some individuals an advantage in passing on their genetic material. Combined with the groundbreaking work in genetics carried out by the Augustinian priest and scientist Gregor Johann Mendel (1822–1884), Darwin's theory has become one of the fundamental unifying principles of modern biology.

Darwin's theory of natural selection provoked, and continues to provoke, resistance, particularly because he extended the theory to humans. Despite the criticism, however, Darwin's theory had a powerful and many-sided influence on European thought and the European middle classes. His findings reinforced the teachings of secularists such as Marx, who scornfully dismissed religious belief in favor of agnostic or atheistic materialism. Many writers also applied the theory of biological evolution to human affairs. Herbert Spencer (1820–1903), an English philosopher, saw the human race as driven forward to ever-greater specialization and progress by a brutal economic struggle that efficiently determines the "survival of the fittest." The idea that human society also evolves, and that the stronger will become powerful and prosperous while the weaker will be conquered or remain poor became known as **Social Darwinism**. Powerful nations used this ideology to justify nationalism and expansion, and colonizers to justify imperialism. Not surprisingly, Spencer and other Social Darwinists were especially popular with the upper middle class.

Not only did science shape society, but society also shaped science. As nations asserted their differences from one another, they sought "scientific" proof for those differences, which generally meant proof of their own superiority. European and American scientists, anthropologists, and physicians measured skulls, brains, and facial angles to prove that whites were more intelligent than other races, and that northern Europeans were more advanced than southern Europeans, perhaps even a separate "Nordic race" or "Aryan race." Africans were described and depicted as "missing links" between chimpanzees and Europeans, and they were occasionally even displayed as such in zoos and fairs. This scientific racism extended to Jews, who were increasingly described as a separate and inferior race, not a religious group. In the late nineteenth century a German author coined the term "anti-Semitism" to provide a more scientific-sounding term for hostility toward Jews, describing Jews as a separate "Semitic" race (see page 744).

Cultural Shifts

The French Revolution kindled the belief that radical reconstructions of politics and society were also possible in cultural and artistic life. The most significant expression of this belief in the early nineteenth century was the romantic movement. In part a revolt against classicism and the Enlightenment, romanticism was characterized by a belief in emotional exuberance, unrestrained imagination, and spontaneity in both art and personal life. Romanticism crystallized fully in the 1790s, primarily in England and Germany, and gained strength until the 1840s. Many romantic artists of the early nineteenth century lived lives of tremendous emotional intensity. They typically led bohemian lives, wearing their hair long and uncombed in preference to powdered wigs, and rejecting the materialism of refined society. Great individualists, they believed the full development of each person's unique human potential to be the supreme purpose in life.

One of the greatest and most moving romantic painters in France, Eugène Delacroix (oe-ZHEHN

- **evolution** The idea, applied by Charles Darwin, that concluded that all life had gradually evolved from a common origin; as applied by thinkers in many fields, the idea stressed gradual change and continuous adjustment.

- **Social Darwinism** The application of the theory of biological evolution to human affairs, it sees the human race as driven to ever-greater specialization and progress by an unending economic struggle that determines the survival of the fittest.

> "Beethoven's music sets in motion the lever of fear, of awe, of horror, of suffering, and awakens just that infinite longing which is the essence of Romanticism."
>
> **ERNST HOFFMANN**

deh-luh-KWAH; 1798–1863), was a romantic master of dramatic, colorful scenes that stirred the emotions. He was fascinated with remote and exotic subjects (see *Massacre at Chios*, below). Yet he was also a passionate spokesman for freedom.

It was in music that romanticism realized most fully and permanently its goals of free expression and emotional intensity. Abandoning well-defined structures, the great romantic composers used a wide range of forms to create musical landscapes and evoke powerful emotion. The first great romantic composer is among the most famous today, Ludwig van Beethoven

(1770–1827). As one contemporary admirer wrote, "Beethoven's music sets in motion the lever of fear, of awe, of horror, of suffering, and awakens just that infinite longing which is the essence of Romanticism."

Nowhere was the break with classicism more apparent than in romanticism's general conception of nature. Classicism was not particularly interested in nature. The romantics, in contrast, were enchanted by nature. For some it was awesome and tempestuous, while others saw nature as a source of spiritual inspiration.

The study of history became a romantic passion. History was the key to a universe that was now perceived to be organic and dynamic, not mechanical and static as the Enlightenment thinkers had believed. Historical studies supported the development of national aspirations and encouraged entire peoples to seek in the past their special destinies.

Romanticism found a distinctive voice in poetry. William Wordsworth (1770–1850) was the towering

Delacroix, *Massacre at Chios*
The Greek struggle for freedom and independence won the enthusiastic support of liberals, nationalists, and romantics. The Ottoman Turks were portrayed as cruel oppressors who were holding back the course of history, as in this moving masterpiece by Delacroix. (Réunion des Musées Nationaux/Art Resource, NY)

leader of English romanticism. In 1798 Wordsworth and his fellow romantic poet Samuel Taylor Coleridge (1772–1834) published their *Lyrical Ballads*, which abandoned flowery classical conventions for the language of ordinary speech. Wordsworth described his conception of poetry as the "spontaneous overflow of powerful feeling recollected in tranquility."

Victor Hugo (1802–1885) was France's greatest romantic master in both poetry and prose. His powerful novels exemplified the romantic fascination with fantastic characters, strange settings, and human emotions. The hero of Hugo's famous *Hunchback of Notre Dame* (1831) is the great cathedral's deformed bell-ringer, a "human gargoyle" overlooking the teeming life of fifteenth-century Paris.

In central and eastern Europe, literary romanticism and early nationalism often reinforced each other. Like modern anthropologists, romantics turned their attention to peasant life and transcribed the folk songs, tales, and proverbs that the cosmopolitan Enlightenment had disdained. The brothers Jacob and Wilhelm Grimm were particularly successful at rescuing German fairy tales from oblivion. In the Slavic lands romantics played a decisive role in converting spoken peasant languages into modern written languages. The greatest of all Russian poets, Aleksander Pushkin (1799–1837), used his lyric genius to mold the modern literary language of Russia.

Beginning in the 1840s, romanticism gave way to a new artistic genre, realism, which continued to dominate Western culture and style until the 1890s. Realist writers believed that literature should depict life exactly as it is. Forsaking poetry for prose and the personal, emotional viewpoint of the romantics for strict scientific objectivity, the realists simply observed and recorded.

The major realist writers focused on creating fiction based on contemporary everyday life. Beginning with a dissection of the middle classes, from which most of them sprang, many realists eventually focused on the working classes, especially the urban working classes, which had been neglected in literature before this time. The realists put a microscope to many unexplored and taboo subjects — sex, strikes, violence, alcoholism — shocking many middle-class critics. *Madame Bovary*, by Gustave Flaubert (1821–1880), for example, describes the heroine's adulterous affairs and lavish spending as she seeks to escape a dull husband and dull existence in a small provincial village. Now considered one of the greatest novels ever written, public prosecutors charged Flaubert with obscenity when it first appeared in 1856.

The realists' claims of objectivity did not prevent the elaboration of a definite worldview. Realists such as the famous French novelist Emile Zola (1840–1902) and English novelist Thomas Hardy (1840–1928) were strict determinists. They believed that human beings, like atoms, are components of the physical world and that all human actions are caused by unalterable natural laws: heredity and environment determine human behavior; good and evil are merely social conventions.

Nationalism and Socialism, 1871–1914

☐ How did nationalism and socialism shape European politics in the decades before the Great War?

After 1871 Europe's heartland was organized into strong national states. Only on Europe's borders — in Ireland and Russia, in Austria-Hungary and the Balkans — did people still strive for national unity and independence. Nationalism served, for better or worse, as a new unifying principle. At the same time, socialist parties grew rapidly. Many prosperous and conservative citizens were troubled by the socialist movement. Governing elites manipulated national feeling to create a sense of unity to divert attention from underlying class conflicts, and increasingly channeled national sentiment in an antiliberal and militaristic direction, tolerating anti-Semitism and waging wars in non-Western lands. This policy helped manage domestic conflicts, but only at the expense of increasing the international tensions that erupted in World War I.

Trends in Suffrage

There were good reasons why ordinary people — the masses of an industrializing, urbanizing society — felt increasing loyalty to their governments in central and western Europe. More people could vote. By 1914 universal male suffrage had become the rule rather than the exception. This development had as much psychological as political significance. Ordinary men felt they were becoming "part of the system."

Women also began to demand the right to vote. The women's suffrage movement achieved its first success in the western United States, and by 1913 women could vote in twelve states. In Europe, Norway gave the vote to most women in 1914. Suffragettes had little success elsewhere before 1914, but they prepared the way for getting the vote in many countries immediately after World War I.

As the right to vote spread, politicians and parties in national parliaments usually represented the people more responsively. The multiparty system prevailing in most countries meant that parliamentary majorities were built on shifting coalitions, which gave political parties leverage to obtain benefits for their supporters. Governments also passed laws to alleviate general problems, thereby acquiring greater legitimacy and appearing more worthy of support.

The German Empire

The new German Empire was a federal union of Prussia and twenty-four smaller states. The separate states conducted much of the everyday business of government. Unifying the whole was a strong national government with a chancellor — Bismarck until 1890 — and a popularly elected parliament called the Reichstag. Although Bismarck refused to be bound by a parliamentary majority, he pragmatically sought the backing of whichever coalition of political parties would support his policies.

As for socialism, Bismarck tried to stop its growth in Germany because he feared its revolutionary language and allegiance to a movement transcending the nation-state. In 1878 he pushed through a law outlawing the Social Democrats, but he was unable to force socialism out of existence. Bismarck's essentially conservative nation-state then pioneered social measures designed to win working-class support. In 1883 the Reichstag approved a national social security system that was the first of its kind anywhere.

Under Kaiser William I (r. 1861–1888), Bismarck had, in effect, managed the domestic and foreign policies of the state. In 1890 the new emperor, William II (r. 1888–1918), eager to rule in his own right and to earn the workers' support, forced Bismarck to resign. Following Bismarck's departure, the Reichstag passed new laws to aid workers and to legalize socialist political activity. German foreign policy changed most profoundly as well, and mostly for the worse (see pages 845–846).

Although William II was no more successful than Bismarck in getting workers to renounce socialism, in the years before World War I the Social Democratic party broadened its base and adopted a more patriotic tone. German socialists identified increasingly with the German state and concentrated on gradual social and political reform.

Republican France

Although Napoleon III's reign made some progress in reducing antagonisms between classes, the Franco-Prussian war undid these efforts, and in 1871 France seemed hopelessly divided once again. The republicans who proclaimed the Third Republic in Paris refused to admit defeat. They defended Paris with great heroism for weeks, until they were starved into submission by German armies in January 1871. When na-

tional elections then sent a large majority of conservatives and monarchists to the National Assembly, France's leaders decided they had no choice but to surrender Alsace and Lorraine to Germany. The traumatized Parisians exploded in patriotic frustration and proclaimed the Paris Commune in March 1871.

Commune leaders wanted to govern Paris without interference from the conservative French countryside. The National Assembly, led by aging conservative politician Adolphe Thiers, would hear none of it. The Assembly ordered the French army into Paris and brutally crushed the Commune. Twenty thousand people died in the fighting. As in June 1848, it was Paris against the provinces, French against French. Out of this tragedy France slowly formed a new national unity before 1914.

The moderate republicans sought to preserve their creation by winning the loyalty of the next generation. Trade unions were fully legalized, and France acquired a colonial empire. More important, a series of laws between 1879 and 1886 established free compulsory elementary education for both girls and boys, thereby greatly reducing the role of parochial Catholic schools that had long been hostile to republics and to much of secular life. In France and throughout the world the general expansion of public education served as a critical nation- and nationalism-building tool in the late nineteenth century.

Although the educational reforms of the 1880s disturbed French Catholics, many of them rallied to the republic in the 1890s, and tensions between church and state eased. Unfortunately, the **Dreyfus affair** changed all that. In 1894 Alfred Dreyfus, a Jewish captain in the French army, was falsely accused and convicted of treason. In 1898 and 1899 the case split France apart. On one side was the army, which had manufactured evidence against Dreyfus, joined by anti-Semites and most of the Catholic establishment. On the other side stood the civil libertarians and most of the more radical republicans.

This battle, which eventually led to Dreyfus's being declared innocent, revived militant republican feeling against the church. Between 1901 and 1905 the government severed all ties between the state and the Catholic Church after centuries of close relations. In France only the growing socialist movement, with its very different but thoroughly secular ideology, stood in opposition to patriotic republican nationalism.

Great Britain and the Austro-Hungarian Empire

The development of Great Britain and Austria-Hungary, two leading but quite different powers, throws a powerful light on the dynamics of national-

The Traitor: Degradation of Alfred Dreyfus After being arrested and convicted in a secret court martial for treason, Captain Dreyfus bravely stood at attention during a public degradation ceremony. While the officer on duty tore off his stripes, ripped off his honors, and broke his sword in two, Dreyfus shouted out, "You are degrading an innocent man! Long live France! Long live the army!" (Private Collection/The Bridgeman Art Library)

LE TRAITRE

ism in Europe before 1914. At home Britain made more of its citizens feel a part of the nation by passing consecutive voting rights bills that gave solid middle-class males the right to vote in 1832, all middle-class males and the best-paid male workers the right in the Second Reform Bill of 1867, and finally every adult male through the Third Reform Bill of 1884. Moreover, extensive social welfare measures, slow to come to Great Britain, were passed in a spectacular rush between 1906 and 1914. The Liberal Party then substantially raised taxes on the rich as part of the so-called People's Budget to pay for national health insurance, unemployment benefits, old-age pensions, and a host of other social measures. The state was integrating the urban masses socially as well as politically.

On the eve of World War I, however, the unanswered question of Ireland brought Great Britain to the brink of civil war. The terrible Irish famine fueled an Irish revolutionary movement. Thereafter the English slowly granted concessions, but refused to give Ireland self-government. In 1910 Irish nationalists in the British Parliament supported the Liberals in their battle for the People's Budget. In 1913 they received a home-rule bill for Ireland in return.

Ireland and Britain, however, still faced the prospect of civil war. The Irish Catholic majority in the southern counties wanted home rule, but the Irish Protestants in the northern counties of Ulster vowed to resist it. Unable to resolve the conflict as World War I started in August 1914, the British government postponed indefinitely the whole question of Irish home rule.

The dilemma of conflicting nationalisms in Ireland helps one appreciate how desperate the situation in the Austro-Hungarian Empire had become by the early twentieth century. Following the savage defeat of the

Hungarian republic (see page 503), Hungary was ruled as a conquered territory, and Emperor Franz Joseph (r. 1848–1916) and his bureaucracy tried hard to centralize the state and Germanize the language and culture of the different nationalities.

Following its defeat by Prussia in 1866, a weakened Austria was forced to establish the so-called dual monarchy. The empire was divided in two, and the nationalistic Magyars gained virtual independence for Hungary. The two states were joined only by a shared monarch and common ministries for finance, defense, and foreign

> • **Dreyfus affair** A divisive case in which Alfred Dreyfus, a Jewish captain in the French army, was falsely accused and convicted of treason. The Catholic Church sided with the anti-Semites against Dreyfus; after Dreyfus was declared innocent, the French government severed all ties between the state and the church.

affairs. Still, the disintegrating force of competing nationalisms continued unabated, and the Austro-Hungarian Empire was progressively weakened and eventually destroyed by the conflicting national aspirations of its different ethnic groups. It was these ethnic conflicts in the Balkans, the "powder keg of Europe," that touched off the Great War in 1914 (see Chapter 28).

Jewish Emancipation and Modern Anti-Semitism

Revolutionary changes in political principles and the triumph of the nation-state brought equally revolutionary changes in Jewish life in western and central Europe. Beginning in France in 1791, Jews gradually gained their civil rights, although progress was slow and uneven. In the 1850s and 1860s liberals in Austria, Italy, and Prussia pressed successfully for legal equality. In 1871 the constitution of the new German Empire abolished all restrictions on Jewish marriage, choice of occupation, place of residence, and property ownership. Exclusion from government employment and discrimination in social relations remained, however, in central Europe.

The process of emancipation presented Jews with challenges and opportunities. Traditional Jewish occupations, such as court financial agent, village moneylender, and peddler, were undermined by free-market reforms, but careers in business, the professions, and the arts were opening to Jewish talent. By 1871 a majority of Jews in western and central Europe had improved their economic situations and entered the middle classes. Most Jews identified strongly with their respective nation-states and considered themselves patriotic citizens.

Vicious anti-Semitism reappeared after the stock market crash of 1873, beginning in central Europe. Drawing on long traditions of religious intolerance, ghetto exclusion, and periodic anti-Jewish riots and expulsions, this hostility also drew on modern ideas about Jews as a separate race. Modern anti-Semitism whipped up resentment against Jewish achievement and Jewish "financial control," while fanatics claimed that the Jewish race posed a biological threat to the German people. Anti-Semitic beliefs were particularly popular among conservatives, extremist nationalists, and people who felt threatened by Jewish competition.

Anti-Semites also created modern political parties. In Austrian Vienna in the early 1890s, Karl Lueger (LOO-guhr) and his "Christian socialists" won striking electoral victories. Lueger, the popular mayor of Vienna from 1897 to 1910, combined fierce anti-Semitic rhetoric with municipal ownership of basic services. He appealed especially to the German-speaking lower middle class—and to an unsuccessful young artist named Adolf Hitler. In response to spreading anti-Semitism, a Jewish journalist named Theodor Herzl (1860–1904) turned from German nationalism to advocate Jewish political nationalism, or **Zionism**, and the creation of a Jewish state.

Before 1914 anti-Semitism was most oppressive in eastern Europe, where Jews also suffered from terrible poverty. In the Russian empire, where there was no Jewish emancipation and 4 million of Europe's 7 million Jewish people lived in 1880, officials used anti-Semitism to channel popular discontent away from the government. In 1881–1882 a wave of violent pogroms commenced in southern Russia. The police and the army stood aside for days while peasants assaulted Jews and looted and destroyed their property. Official harassment continued in the following decades, and some Russian Jews turned toward self-emancipation and the vision of a Zionist settlement in the Ottoman province of Palestine. Large numbers also emigrated to western Europe and the United States.

The Socialist Movement

Socialism appealed to large numbers of working men and women in the late nineteenth century, and the growth of socialist parties after 1871 was phenomenal. (See "Viewpoints: Socialist and Anti-Socialist Perspectives," page 745.) By 1912 the German Social Democratic Party, which espoused Marxist ideology, had millions of followers and was the Reichstag's largest party. Socialist parties also grew in other countries, and Marxist socialist parties were linked together in an international organization. In 1864 Karl Marx played an important role in founding the First International of socialists.

The First International collapsed in 1872, but in 1889 socialist leaders came together to form the Second International, which lasted until 1914. Every three years delegates from the different parties met to interpret Marxist doctrines and plan coordinated action. Yet socialism was not as radical and revolutionary in these years as it sometimes appeared. As socialist parties grew and attracted large numbers of members, they looked more and more toward gradual change and steady improvement for the working class and less and less toward revolution. Workers themselves were progressively less inclined to follow radical programs for several reasons. As workers gained the right to vote and won real benefits, their attention focused more on elections than on revolutions. Workers were also not

• **Zionism** The movement toward Jewish political nationhood started by Theodor Herzl.

Viewpoints

Socialist and Anti-Socialist Perspectives

• *Socialism as an ideology gained a passionate following across Europe in the middle and late 1800s. Just as ardent were the laissez-faire anti-socialists, who opposed any government interference in a country's economic or social systems.*

The following documents represent the views of a socialist and an anti-socialist. In the first, from an English socialist magazine, are present many of the key words and concepts driving the socialist movement: class, labor theory of value, the rich produce nothing, a call to foreign brethren (fellow workers), and a new social order to replace the class system. The second document comes from William Graham Sumner, a widely read Yale College professor. An ardent supporter of laissez-faire economics and of the "survival of the fittest" beliefs of Social Darwinists, he vehemently opposed socialism and communism. Here he argues against government or private efforts to help society's poor or weak.

"The Meaning of Socialism," January 1885

❝ Fellow Citizens, We come before you as Revolutionists, that is, as men and women who wish to see the basis of society changed.

Why is this?

Because in the society which now exists the majority of the people is miserable and oppressed.... [T]he "labourers," including all those who are engaged in ... producing food for the community, are scarcely raised above starvation, or are punished for the crime of being born poor....

Those poor persons ... are a *class*, necessary, with all its poverty and misery, to the existence, as a class, of that other *class* of rich men: for all society is based upon labour and could not exist without it; and those of its members who *do not* produce wealth must necessarily live on the labours of those who *do* produce it. Those poor people ... form a class which ... has one interest common to all its members, the enjoyment of the fruits of its labour, and one enemy in common, namely the *class* of rich men who produce nothing, and if they work, work only at fleecing the poor class.

So then there are two *classes*; one producing and governed, the other non-producing and governing; one the means of wealth, the other the consumers of wealth: one *Rich*, the other *Poor*.

Fellow Workers, Is it necessary that this miserable state of things should last forever?

We bid you hope ... for the establishment of a new order of things, the Social Order, in which there will be no poor and, therefore, no rich; in which there will be no classes.

English fellow-workmen! . . . Decent and happy life for all lies ahead of us, while all around is mere squalor, disorder, discontent, and the failure of all the hopes of civilization. Come out from these dreary ruins of decaying systems, and march with us toward the new Social Order of the World. ❞

William Graham Sumner, "On a New Philosophy: That Poverty Is the Best Policy," 1883

❝ It is very popular to pose as a "friend of humanity," or a "friend of the working classes." Anything which has a charitable sound and a kind-hearted tone generally passes without investigation, because it is disagreeable to assail it. Sermons, essays, and orations assume a conventional standpoint with regard to the poor, the weak, etc.; and it is allowed to pass as ... unquestioned doctrine ... that "the rich" ought to "care for the poor." ...

The humanitarians, philanthropists, and reformers ... find enough which is sad and unpromising in the condition of many members of society. They see wealth and poverty side by side. They note great inequality of social position and social chances. They eagerly set about ... to account for what they see, and to devise schemes for remedying what they do not like. In their eagerness to recommend the less fortunate classes to pity and consideration they forget all about the rights of other classes; they gloss over all the faults of the classes in question, and they exaggerate their misfortunes and their virtues. They invent new theories of property, distorting rights and perpetrating injustice, as any one is sure to do who sets about the re-adjustment of social relations with the interests of one group distinctly before his mind, and the interests of all other groups thrown into the background.

Here it may suffice to observe that, on the theories of the social philosophers to whom I have referred, we should get a new maxim of judicious living: Poverty is the best policy. If you get wealth, you will have to support other people; if you do not get wealth, it will be the duty of other people to support you. ❞

Sources: The Executive Council of the Social-Democratic Federation, "The Meaning of Socialism," *To-day: The Monthly Magazine of Scientific Socialism* III (January-June 1885): 1–5, 10; William Graham Sumner, *What Social Classes Owe to Each Other* (New York and London: Harper & Brothers, 1883, 1920), pp. 16–17, 21–22, 24.

QUESTIONS FOR ANALYSIS

1. What are the positions taken by the authors? Are these positions still current today?

2. How do you think Sumner would feel about modern government programs like Social Security and Medicare? What might be his argument for or against such programs?

"The Expulsion of the Jews from Russia" So reads this postcard, correctly suggesting that Russian government officials often encouraged popular anti-Semitism and helped drive many Jews out of Russia in the late nineteenth century. The road signs indicate that these poor Jews are crossing into Germany, where they will find a grudging welcome and a meager meal at the Jolly Onion Inn. Other Jews from eastern Europe settled in France and Britain, thereby creating small but significant Jewish populations in both countries for the first time since they had expelled most of their Jews in the Middle Ages. (Alliance Israelite Universelle, Paris/Archives Charmet/ The Bridgeman Art Library)

immune to nationalistic patriotism, even as they loyally voted for socialists. Nor were workers a unified social group. Perhaps most important of all, workers' standard of living rose steadily after 1850, and the quality of life improved substantially in urban areas. Thus workers tended to become militantly moderate: they demanded gains, but they were less likely to take to the barricades in pursuit of them.

The growth of labor unions reinforced this trend toward moderation. In the early stages of industrialization, modern unions were considered subversive bodies and were generally prohibited by law. In Great Britain new unions that formed for skilled workers after 1850 avoided radical politics and concentrated on winning better wages and hours for their members through collective bargaining and compromise. Af-

ter 1890 unions for unskilled workers developed in Britain.

German unions were not granted important rights until 1869, and until the anti-socialist law was repealed in 1890 the government frequently harassed them as socialist fronts. But after most legal harassment was eliminated, union membership skyrocketed from only about 270,000 in 1895 to roughly 3 million in 1912. Genuine collective bargaining, long opposed by socialist intellectuals as a "sellout," was officially recognized as desirable by the German Trade Union Congress in 1899.

The German trade unions and their leaders were thoroughgoing revisionists. **Revisionism** was an effort by various socialists to update Marxist doctrines to reflect the realities of the time. The socialist Eduard Bernstein (1850–1932) argued in his *Evolutionary Socialism* in 1899 that Marx's predictions of ever-greater poverty for workers had been proved false. Therefore, Bernstein suggested, socialists should re-

• **revisionism** An effort by various socialists to update Marxist doctrines to reflect the realities of the time.

form their doctrines and win gradual evolutionary gains for workers through legislation, unions, and further economic development. The Second International denounced these views as heresy. Yet the revisionist gradualist approach continued to gain the tacit acceptance of many German socialists, particularly in the trade unions.

Moderation found followers elsewhere. In France the great socialist leader Jean Jaurès (1859–1914) formally repudiated revisionist doctrines in order to establish a unified socialist party, but he remained at heart a gradualist. Questions of revolutionary versus gradualist policies split Russian Marxists.

Socialist parties in other countries had clear-cut national characteristics. Russians and socialists in the Austro-Hungarian Empire tended to be the most radical. In Great Britain the socialist but non-Marxist Labour Party formally committed to gradual reform. In Spain and Italy anarchism, seeking to smash the state rather than the bourgeoisie, dominated radical thought and action.

In short, socialist policies and doctrines varied from country to country. Socialism itself was to a large extent "nationalized." This helps explain why almost all socialist leaders supported their governments when war came in 1914.

CONNECTIONS

Much of world history in the past two centuries can be seen as the progressive unfolding of the dual revolution. Europe in the nineteenth century, and Asia, Latin America, and Africa more recently, underwent interrelated economic and political transformations. Although defeated in 1848, the new political ideologies associated with the French Revolution triumphed after 1850. Nationalism, with its commitment to the nation-state, became the most dominant of the new ideologies. National movements brought about the creation of unified nation-states in two of the most fractured regions in Europe, Germany and Italy.

After 1870 nationalism and militarism, its frequent companion, touched off increased competition between the major European powers for raw materials and markets for manufactured goods. As discussed in the next chapter, during the last decades of the nineteenth century Europe colonized nearly all of Africa and large areas in Asia. In Europe itself nationalism promoted a bitter, almost Darwinian competition between states, threatening the very progress and unity it had helped to build. In 1914 the power of unified nation-states turned on itself, unleashing an unprecedented conflict among Europe's Great Powers. Chapter 28 tells the story of this First World War.

Nationalism also sparked worldwide challenges to European dominance by African and Asian leaders who fought to liberate themselves from colonialism, and it became a rallying cry in nominally independent countries like China and Japan, whose leaders sought complete independence from European and American influence and a rightful place among the world's leading nations. Chapters 25, 26, 32, and 33 explore these developments. Likewise, Chapter 34 discusses how the problems of rapid urbanization and the huge gaps between rich and poor caused by economic transformations in America and Europe in the 1800s are now the concern of policy makers in Africa, Asia, and Latin America.

Another important ideology of change, socialism, remains popular in Europe, but never accomplished more than democratically electing socialist parties to office in some countries. Marxist revolutions that took absolute control of entire countries, as in Russia, China, and Cuba, had to wait until the twentieth century.

CHAPTER REVIEW

□ How did the allies fashion a peace settlement in 1815, and what radical ideas emerged between 1815 and 1848? (p. 716)

In 1814 the victorious allied powers sought to restore peace and stability in Europe. Dealing moderately with France and wisely settling their own differences, they laid the foundations for beneficial international cooperation throughout much of the nineteenth century. Led by Metternich of Austria, the conservative powers used intervention and repression as they sought to prevent the spread of subversive ideas and radical changes in domestic politics. After 1815 ideologies of liberalism, nationalism, and socialism all developed to challenge the existing order. The principal ideas of liberalism were equality and liberty, which were expressed in representative government and civil rights. Nationalism was based on the notion that each people had its own genius and cultural unity; to this was added the idea that each people deserved its own political entity and government. The key ideas of socialism were economic planning, greater economic equality, and the state regulation of property.

□ Why in 1848 did revolutions triumph briefly throughout most of Europe, and why did they fail? (p. 722)

The growth of liberal, nationalist, and socialist forces culminated in the liberal and nationalistic revolutions of 1848. Monarchies panicked and crumbled in the face of popular uprisings and widespread opposition that cut across class lines, and the revolutionaries triumphed, first in France and then across the continent. Very few revolutionary goals were realized. The moderate, nationalistic middle classes were unable to consolidate their initial victories. Instead, they drew back when artisans, factory workers, and radical socialists rose up to present their own, much more revolutionary demands. This retreat facilitated a resurgence of conservative forces that crushed revolution across Europe.

□ How did strong leaders and nation building transform Italy, Germany, and Russia? (p. 725)

In Italy Cavour joined traditional diplomacy and war against Austria with nationalist uprising in central Italy to expand the constitutional monarchy in Sardinia-Piedmont. He then succeeded in merging the south and the north together in a conservative nation-state under Victor Emmanuel. In Prussia Bismarck also combined traditional statecraft with

KEY TERMS

Congress of Vienna (p. 716)
dual revolution (p. 717)
liberalism (p. 719)
laissez faire (p. 719)
nationalism (p. 719)
socialism (p. 721)
bourgeoisie (p. 721)
proletariat (p. 721)
modernization (p. 725)

October Manifesto (p. 731)
germ theory (p. 732)
evolution (p. 739)
Social Darwinism (p. 739)
Dreyfus affair (p. 742)
Zionism (p. 744)
revisionism (p. 746)

national feeling. Ruling without the consent of parliament and reorganizing the army, Bismarck succeeded in making Prussia the dominant German state. War with France completed the unification process, expanding the power of Prussia and its king in a new German Empire, and instilling in all Germans a strong sense of national pride. In autocratic Russia, defeat in the Crimean War posed a regime-threatening crisis, which led to the emancipation of the serfs and economic modernization that featured railroad building, military improvements, and industrialization. Political reform was limited, however, and even after the revolution of 1905 led to a popularly elected Duma, the tsar retained great power.

□ What was the impact of urban growth on cities, social classes, families, and ideas? (p. 731)

As new industrial factories and offices were built in urban areas, urban populations grew at unprecedented rates. Living conditions sharply declined until the mid-nineteenth century, when governments finally began to clean up the cities. Society also benefited from scientific advancements, including germ control and new public transportation systems that relieved overcrowding. Major changes in the class structure and family life accompanied urban growth. Family life became more stable and more loving, although a sharp separation of gender roles tended to lock women into subordinate and stereotypical roles. The class structure became more complex and diversified. The upper and middle classes expanded and gained income, and their occupations became more diverse. Ordinary people gained a new awareness and appreciation of science, and ideas such as Darwin's theory of natural selection challenged the traditional religious understanding of the world. In the realm of literature and the arts, the romantic movement reinforced the spirit of change. The movement was characterized by a belief in self-expression, imagination, and spontaneity in art as well in personal life. Romanticism gave way to realism in the 1840s, reflecting Western society's growing faith in science, material progress, and evolutionary thinking.

□ How did nationalism and socialism shape European politics in the decades before the Great War? (p. 741)

Western society became increasingly nationalistic as well as urban and industrial in the late nineteenth century. Nation-states became more responsive, and they enlisted widespread support as peaceful political participation expanded, educational opportunities increased, and social security systems took shape. More broadly, nation-states may be seen as providing a stabilizing response to the profoundly unsettling challenges of the dual revolution. Even socialism became increasingly national in orientation, gathering strength as a champion of working-class interests in domestic politics. Yet even though nationalism served to unite peoples, it also drove them apart — not only in Austria-Hungary and Ireland but also throughout Europe and the rest of the world. The national faith, which reduced social tensions within states, promoted a bitter, almost Darwinian competition between states — often most clearly visible in greatly enlarged armies and navies — and thus threatened the progress and unity it had helped to build.

SUGGESTED READING

Anderson, Bonnie S., and Judith P. Zinsser. *A History of Their Own: Women in Europe from Prehistory to the Present*, vol. 2, rev. ed. 2000. An excellent, wide-ranging survey.

Baycroft, Timothy, and Mark Hewitson, eds. *What Is a Nation? Europe 1789–1914*. 2009. A sweeping study of nationalism in all its forms and all the processes that affected its evolution.

Berend, Ivan T. *History Derailed: Central and Eastern Europe in the Long Nineteenth Century*. 2003. Focuses on industrialization and its consequences.

Berger, Stefan, ed. *A Companion to Nineteenth-Century Europe, 1789–1914*. 2006. A useful study with an up-to-date bibliography.

Clark, Linda L. *Women and Achievement in Nineteenth-Century Europe*. 2008. Examines the activities of women who sought recognition for work at home and opportunity for work outside the home.

Coontz, Stephanie. *Marriage, A History: From Obedience to Intimacy, or How Love Conquered Marriage*. 2005. A lively inquiry into the historical background to current practice.

Gildea, Robert. *Barricades and Borders: Europe, 1800–1914*, 2d ed. 1996. A recommended general study.

Kertzer, David I., and Marzio Barbagli, eds. *Family Life in the Nineteenth Century, 1789–1913*. 2002. A broad exploration of European family life and the forces that shaped it in the nineteenth century.

Malia, Martin, and Terrence Emmons. *History's Locomotives: Revolutions and the Making of the Modern World*. 2006. An ambitious comparative work of high quality.

Mann, Thomas. *Buddenbrooks*. 1901. A wonderful historical novel that traces the rise and fall of a prosperous German family over three generations.

Otis, Laura. *Literature and Science in the Nineteenth Century: An Anthology*. 2009. A fascinating selection of writings from a time when humanities and science were not considered separate disciplines.

Rapport, Mike. *1848: Year of Revolution*. 2008. A stimulating account of the revolutions that swept across Europe in 1848.

Rubinstein, W. D. *Britain's Century: Political and Social History, 1815–1905*. 1998. An excellent history with strong coverage of social questions.

Tombs, Robert. *France, 1814–1914*. 1996. An impressive survey with a useful bibliography.

Winks, Robin W., and Joan Neuberger. *Europe and the Making of Modernity: 1815–1914*. 2005. Grand narrative of the forces that shaped modern Europe from the Congress of Vienna to the Great War.

NOTES

1. J. G. Fichte, *Addresses to the German Nation*, trans. R. F. Jones and G. H. Turnbull (Chicago and London: Open Court Publishing Company, 1922), p. 4.

2. E. Gellner, *Nations and Nationalism* (Oxford, U.K.: Basil Blackwell, 1983), pp. 19–39.

3. B. Anderson, *Imagined Communities: Reflections on the Origins and Spread of Nationalism*, rev. ed. (London and New York: Verso, 1991).

4. Quoted by G. O'Brien, *The Economic History of Ireland from the Union to the Famine* (London: Longmans, Green, 1921), p. 21.

5. Ibid., pp. 23–24.

6. J. McKay, *Tramways and Trolleys: The Rise of Urban Mass Transport in Europe* (Princeton, N.J.: Princeton University Press, 1976), p. 81.

7. Quoted in R. P. Neuman, "The Sexual Question and Social Democracy in Imperial Germany," *Journal of Social History* 7 (Winter 1974): 281.

For practice quizzes and other study tools, visit the **Online Study Guide** at bedfordstmartins.com/mckayworld.

For primary sources from this period, see *Sources of World Societies*, **Second Edition**.

For Web sites, images, and documents related to topics in this chapter, visit **Make History** at bedfordstmartins.com/mckayworld.

• **Sengbe Pieh** Enslaved in 1839, Pieh (later known as Joseph Cinqué) led a famous revolt on the slave ship *Amistad*. He and his fellow slaves were charged with mutiny and murder, but in March 1840 the U.S. Supreme Court found them innocent because they had been illegally captured and sold. They returned to their native Sierra Leone as free men. (New Haven Colony Historical Society)

25

While industrialization and nationalism were transforming society in Europe and the neo-European countries (the United States, Canada, Australia, New Zealand, and, to an extent, South Africa), Western society itself was reshaping the world. European commercial interests went in search of new sources of raw materials and markets for their manufactured goods. At the same time, millions of Europeans and Asians picked up stakes and emigrated abroad. What began as a relatively peaceful exchange of products with Africa and Asia in the early nineteenth century had transformed by the end of the century into a frenzy of imperialist occupation and domination that had a profound impact on both the colonizers and the colonized.

Africa, Southwest Asia, and the New Imperialism
1800-1914

The political annexation of territory in the 1880s—the "new imperialism," as it is often called by historians—was the capstone of Western society's underlying economic and technological transformation. More directly, Western imperialism rested on a formidable combination of superior military might and strong authoritarian rule, and it posed a brutal challenge to African and Asian peoples. Different societies met this Western challenge in different ways and with changing tactics, as we shall see. Nevertheless, by 1914 non-Western elites in many lands were rallying their peoples and leading an anti-imperialist struggle for dignity and genuine independence that would triumph after 1945. •

Africa: From the Slave Trade to European Colonial Rule

□ What were the most significant changes in Africa during the nineteenth century, and why did they occur?

From the beginning of the nineteenth century to the global depression of the 1930s, the different regions of Africa experienced gradual but monumental change. The long-standing transatlantic slave trade declined and practically disappeared by the late 1860s. In the early nineteenth century Islam expanded its influence in a long belt south of the Sahara, but Africa generally remained free of European political control. After about 1880 further Islamic expansion to the south stopped, but the pace of change accelerated as France and Britain led European nations in the "scramble for Africa." Africa was divided and largely conquered by Europeans, and by 1900 the foreigners were consolidating their authoritarian empires.

Trade and Social Change

The most important development in West Africa before the European conquest was the decline of the Atlantic slave trade and the simultaneous rise of the export of **palm oil** and other commodities. A major break with the past, the shift in African foreign trade marked the beginning of modern economic development in sub-Saharan Africa.

Although the trade in African people was a worldwide phenomenon, the transatlantic slave trade between Africa and the Americas became the most extensive and significant portion of it (see pages 572–580). The forced migration of millions of Africans — so cruel, unjust, and tragic — intensified after 1700, and especially after 1750 (see Figure 19.2, page 582). Increasing demand for labor resulted in rising prices for African slaves in the eighteenth century. Some African merchants and rulers who controlled exports profited, but in the long run the slave trade resulted in instability and warfare, decimated the population, and destroyed local economies.

Until 1700, and perhaps even 1750, most Europeans considered the African slave trade a legitimate business activity. After 1775 a broad campaign to abolish slavery developed in Britain. This campaign grew into one of the first peaceful mass political movements based on the mobilization of public opinion in British history. British women played a critical role in this movement, denouncing the immorality of human bondage and stressing the cruel treatment of female slaves and slave families. The abolitionist movement also argued for a transition to legitimate (non-slave) trade, to end both the transatlantic slave trade and the internal African slave systems. In 1807 Parliament declared the slave trade illegal. Britain then established the anti-slavery West Africa Squadron, using its navy to seize the ships of the slave runners, liberating the captives, and settling them in the British port of Freetown, in Sierra Leone, as well as in Liberia (Map 25.1). Freed American slaves — with the help of the American Colonization Society, a group devoted to returning freed slaves to Africa — had established the colony of Liberia in 1821–1822. They named their capital Monrovia, after America's fifth president, James Monroe, who prominently supported the enterprise.

British action had a limited impact at first. The transatlantic slave trade regained its previous massive level after Napoleon was defeated and peace returned to Europe in 1815, and the worldwide trade in enslaved

---

• **palm oil** A West African tropical product often used to make soap; the British encouraged its cultivation as an alternative to the slave trade.

Africans declined only gradually. Britain's West Africa squadron intercepted fewer than 10 percent of all slave ships, and the demand for slaves remained high on the expanding and labor-intensive sugar and coffee plantations of Cuba and Brazil until the 1850s and 1860s. In the United States the Constitution (1787) prohibited the banning of the importation of slaves before 1808, which was a twenty-year concession to the southern states for their agreeing to join the new union. By 1807 there was a passionate, sometimes violent national debate over the moral and commercial questions surrounding slavery. On March 2, 1807 President Thomas Jefferson signed into law an act that banned the importation of slaves from January 1, 1808. From that time on, natural increase (slaves having children) accounted mainly for the subsequent growth of the African American slave population before the Civil War. Strong financial incentives remained, however, for Portuguese and other European slave traders, as well as for those African rulers who relied on profits from the trade for power and influence.

As more nations joined Britain in outlawing the slave trade, the shipment of human cargo slackened along the West African coast. The decline began on the long stretch from Guinea and Senegal to the Gold Coast and present-day Nigeria by the 1830s and occurred thereafter in west-central Africa in present-day Congo and Angola (see Map 25.1). At the same time the ancient but limited shipment of slaves across the Sahara and from the East African coast into the Indian Ocean and through the Red Sea expanded dramatically. Only in the 1860s did this trade begin to decline rapidly. As a result of these shifting currents, exports of slaves from all of West Africa across the Atlantic declined from an estimated 6.5 million persons in the eighteenth century to 3.9 million in the nineteenth century. Yet total exports of slaves from all regions of sub-Saharan Africa declined less than half as fast in the same years, from 7.4 million to 6.1 million.[1] The abolitionist vision of "legitimate" commerce in tropical products quickly replacing illegal slave exports was not realized.

Nevertheless, beginning in West Africa, trade in tropical products did make steady progress, for several reasons. First, with Britain encouraging palm tree cultivation as an alternative to the slave trade, palm oil sales from West Africa to Britain surged from only one thousand tons in 1810 to more than forty thousand tons in 1855. Second, the sale of palm oil admirably served the self-interest of industrializing Europe. Manufacturers used palm oil to lubricate their giant machines, and from palm oil they made the first good, cheap soap and other cosmetics. Products made from new processes in petroleum refining supplanted palm oil in the mid- to late 1800s, but contemporary brand names like Palmolive and Lever Brothers are vestiges of the days when palm oil was king. Third, the production of peanuts for export also grew rapidly, in part because both small, independent African farmers and their families and large-scale enterprises could produce peanuts for the substantial American and European markets.

Finally, powerful West African rulers and warlords who had benefited from the Atlantic slave trade succeeded in redirecting some of their slaves into the production of legitimate goods for world markets. This was possible because slavery and slave markets remained strong in sub-Saharan Africa, as local warfare and

☐ Picturing the Past

Pears' Soap Advertisement Andrew Pears began making his transparent soap in London in 1789. Starting in the late 1800s, it was marketed worldwide as a product symbolizing progress in advancing Europe's "civilizing mission." In 1910 the Lever brothers, William and James, bought Pears's company and sold Pears' Soap along with their own brands, including Sunlight, Lifebuoy, and Lux. These soaps were made with palm oil from Lever plantations in the Congo and the Solomon Islands. Pears' Soap is still made today, in India. (North Wind Picture Archives/Alamy)

ANALYZING THE IMAGE Which elements or words in this advertisement suggest the Western ideal of "civilization"? Which elements or words are used to describe non-Europeans?

CONNECTIONS How might the English phrase "Cleanliness is next to Godliness" relate to this advertisement? How can Pears' Soap "lighten the white man's burden" and brighten "the dark corners of the earth"?

The first step towards lightening

The White Man's Burden

is through teaching the virtues of cleanliness.

Pears' Soap

is a potent factor in brightening the dark corners of the earth as civilization advances, while amongst the cultured of all nations it holds the highest place—it is the ideal toilet soap.

---

slave raiding continued to enslave large numbers of men, women, and children. While some enslaved captives were still sold abroad to places, like Brazil, where the slave trade remained legal, women might be kept as wives, concubines, or servants. Men were often used to transport goods, mine gold, grow crops, and serve in slave armies. For example, after the collapse of the Oyo empire in the nineteenth century, Yoruba warlords in present-day Nigeria developed palm oil plantations worked by slaves. By the 1860s and 1870s, 104 families in the city of Ibadan owned fifty thousand slaves, an average of five hundred per family.[2] As the experience of the Yoruba suggests, the slow decline of the transatlantic slave trade coincided with the most intensive use of slaves within Africa.

At the same time, a new group of African merchants—including liberated slaves from Freetown and

Monrovia who had received some Western education—did rise to handle legitimate trade, and some grew rich. Women were among the most successful of these merchants. Although there is a long tradition of the active involvement in trade of West African women, the arrival of Europeans provided new opportunities. The African wife of a European trader served as her husband's interpreter and learned all aspects of his business. When the husband died, as European men invariably did in the hot, humid, and mosquito-infested areas of tropical West Africa, the African wife inherited his commercial interests, including his inventory and his European connections. Many such widows used their considerable business acumen to make small fortunes.

By the 1850s and 1860s legitimate African traders, flanked by Western-educated African lawyers, teachers, and journalists, formed an emerging middle class in the coastal towns of West Africa. This tiny middle class provided new leadership that augured well for the region's future. Unfortunately for West Africans, in the 1880s and 1890s African business leadership gave way to imperial subordination.

Islamic Revival and Expansion in Africa

By the early eighteenth century Islam had been practiced throughout the Sudanic Savanna — the vast belt of flat grasslands across Africa below the southern fringe of the Sahara, stretching from Senegal and Gambia in the west to the mountains of Ethiopia in the east — for five hundred to a thousand years, depending on the area. The cities, political rulers, and merchants in many small states were Muslim. Yet the peasant farmers and migratory cattle raisers — the vast majority of the population — generally remained true to traditional animist practices, worshipping ancestors, local shrines, and protective spirits. Many Muslim rulers shared some of these beliefs and did not try to convert their subjects in the countryside or enforce Islamic law.

Beginning in the eighteenth century and gathering strength in the early nineteenth century, a powerful Islamic revival brought reform and revolutionary change from within to the western and eastern Sudan, until this process was halted by European military conquest at the end of the nineteenth century. In essence, Muslim scholars and fervent religious leaders arose to wage successful **jihads**, or religious wars, against both animist rulers and Islamic states that they deemed corrupt. The new reformist rulers believed that African cults and religious practice could no longer be tolerated, and they often effected mass conversions of animists to Islam.

The most important of these revivalist states, the enormous **Sokoto caliphate**, illustrates the pattern of Islamic revival in Africa. It was founded by Usuman dan Fodio (1754–1817), an inspiring Muslim teacher who first won zealous followers among both the Fulani herders and the Hausa peasants in the Muslim state of Gobir in the northern Sudan. After his religious community was attacked by Gobir's rulers, Usuman launched the jihad of 1804, one of the most important events in nineteenth-century West Africa. Usuman claimed that the Hausa rulers of Muslim Gobir "worshipped many places of idols, and trees, and rocks, and sacrificed to them," killing and plundering their subjects without any regard for Islamic law.[3] Young religious students and discontented Fulani cattle raisers formed the backbone of the fighters, who succeeded in overthrowing the Hausa rulers and inspired more jihads in the Sudan. In 1809 Usuman established the new Sokoto caliphate, which was ably consolidated by his son Muhammad Bello as a vast and enduring decentralized state (see Map 25.1).

The triumph of the Sokoto caliphate had profound consequences for Africa and the Sudan. First, the caliphate was based on Islamic history and law, which gave sub-Saharan Africa a sophisticated written constitution that earlier preliterate states had never achieved. This government of laws, rather than men, provided stability and made Sokoto one of the most prosperous regions in tropical Africa. Second, because of Sokoto and other revivalist states, Islam became much more widely and deeply rooted in sub-Saharan Africa than ever before. By 1880 the entire western and central Sudan was united in Islam. In this vast expanse Islam became an unquestioned part of everyday life and culture. Women gained greater access to education, even as veiling and seclusion became more common. Finally, Islam had always approved of slavery for non-Muslims and Muslim heretics, and "the *jihads* created a new slaving frontier on the basis of rejuvenated Islam."[4] In 1900 the Sokoto caliphate had at least 1 million and perhaps as many as 2.5 million slaves. Among all modern slave societies, only the American South had more slaves, about 4 million in 1860.

Islam also expanded in East Africa, in large part because of the efforts of Sayyid Said (r. 1804–1856), the energetic imam of Oman. Reviving his family's lordship of the African island of Zanzibar and eventually moving his capital from southern Arabia to Zanzibar in 1840, Sayyid Said (sa-EED sa-EED) and his Baluchi mercenaries (from present-day Pakistan) gained control of most of the Swahili-speaking East African coast. Said concentrated the shipment of slaves to the Ottoman Empire and Arabia through Zanzibar. In addition, he successfully encouraged Indian merchants to develop slave-based clove plantations in his territories. Thus, from the 1820s on Arab merchants and adventurers pressed far into the interior in search of slaves and ivory, converting and intermarrying with local Nyamwezi (nyahm-WAY-zee) elites and establishing small Muslim states. The Arab immigrants brought literacy, administrative skills, and increased trade and international contact, as well as the intensification of slavery, to East Africa. In 1870, before Christian missionaries and Western armies began to arrive in force, it appeared that most of the East African population would accept Islam within a generation.[5]

The Scramble for Africa, 1880–1914

Between 1880 and 1914 Britain, France, Germany, Belgium, Spain, and Italy, worried that they would not get

---

- **jihad** Religious war waged by Muslim scholars and religious leaders against both animist rulers and Islamic states that they deemed corrupt.
- **Sokoto caliphate** Founded in 1809 by Usuman dan Fodio, this African state was based on Islamic history and law.

Colonial presence, 1914

☐ British	☐ Belgian
☐ French	☐ Spanish
☐ German	☐ Independent African
☐ Italian	states
☐ Portuguese	☐ Afrikaner republic

Colonial presence, 1878

☐ Mapping the Past

MAP 25.1 The Partition of Africa The European powers carved up Africa after 1880 and built vast political empires.

ANALYZING THE MAP What European countries were leading imperialist states in Africa, and what lands did they hold? What countries maintained political independence?

CONNECTIONS The late nineteenth century was the high point of European imperialism. What were the motives behind the rush for land and empire in Africa?

"a piece of that magnificent African cake" (in King Leopold II of Belgium's graphic phrase), scrambled for African possessions as if their national livelihoods were at stake. By 1914 only Ethiopia in northeast Africa and Liberia on the West African coast remained independent (see Map 25.1).

In addition to the general causes underlying Europe's imperialist burst after 1880 (see pages 763–767), certain events and individuals stand out. First, as the antislavery movement succeeded in shutting down the Atlantic slave trade by the late 1860s, the persistence of slavery elsewhere attracted growing attention in western Europe and the Americas. Through the publications of Protestant missionaries such as David Livingstone from Scotland and the fiery eyewitness accounts of the Catholic White Fathers missionary society (named for their white robes), antislavery activists learned of the horrors of slave raids and the suffering of thousands of innocent victims sold within Africa and through East African ports. The public was led to believe that European conquest and colonization would end this human tragedy by bringing, in Livingstone's famous phrase, "Commerce, Christianity, and Civilization" to Africa.

Leopold II of Belgium (r. 1865–1909) also played a crucial role. His agents signed treaties with African chiefs and planted Leopold's flag along the Congo River. In addition, Leopold intentionally misled leaders of the other European nations to gain their support by promising to promote Christianity and civilization in his proposed Congo Free State. By 1883 Europe had caught "African fever," and the race for territory was on.

To lay down some rules for this imperialist competition, Premier Jules Ferry of France and Chancellor Otto von Bismarck of Germany arranged a European conference on Africa in Berlin in 1884–1885. The **Berlin Conference**, to which Africans had not been invited, established the principle that European claims to African territory had to rest on "effective occupation" in order to be recognized by other states. This meant that Europeans would push relentlessly into interior regions from all sides and that no single European power would be able to claim the entire continent. A nation could establish a colony only if it had effectively taken possession of the territory through signed treaties with local leaders and had begun to develop it economically. The representatives at the conference recognized Leopold's rule over a neutral Congo state and agreed to work to stop slavery and the slave trade in Africa.

In addition to developing rules for imperialist competition, participants at the Berlin Conference also promised to end slavery and to bring Christianity and civilization to Africa. In truth, however, these ideals ran a distant second to, and were not allowed to interfere with, their primary goal of commerce — holding on

> "They shall, without distinction of creed or nation, protect and favour all religious, scientific or charitable institutions . . . which aim at instructing the natives and bringing home to them the blessings of civilization."
>
> **BERLIN CONFERENCE**

to their old markets and exploiting new ones:

> All the Powers exercising sovereign rights or influence in the aforesaid territories bind themselves to watch over the preservation of the native tribes, and to care for the improvement of the conditions of their moral and material well-being, and to help in suppressing slavery, and especially the slave trade.
>
> They shall, without distinction of creed or nation, protect and favour all religious, scientific or charitable institutions and undertakings created and organized for the above ends, or which aim at instructing the natives and bringing home to them the blessings of civilization.[6]

The Berlin Conference coincided with Germany's emergence as an imperial power. In 1884 and 1885 Bismarck's Germany established **protectorates** over a number of small African kingdoms and societies in Togoland, Kamerun, southwest Africa, and, later, East Africa (see Map 25.1). In acquiring colonies, Bismarck cooperated with France's Jules Ferry against the British. (See "Listening to the Past: A French Leader Defends Imperialism," page 764.) The French expanded into West Africa and formed a protectorate on the Congo River. As for the British, they began enlarging their West African enclaves and pushed northward from the Cape Colony and westward from the East African coast.

Pushing southward from Egypt, which the British had seized control of in 1882 (see page 772), the British were blocked in the eastern Sudan by fiercely independent Muslims, who had felt the full force of Islamic revival. In 1881 a pious local leader, Muhammad Ahmad (1844–1885), led a revolt against foreign control of Egypt. In 1885 his army massacred a British force and took the city of Khartoum, forcing the British to retreat to Cairo. Ten years later a British force returned, building a railroad to supply arms and reinforcements as it went. Finally, in 1898 these troops met their foe at Omdurman, where Sudanese Muslims armed with spears charged time and time again, only to be cut down by the

---

• **Berlin Conference** A meeting of European leaders held in 1884–1885 to lay down basic rules for imperialist competition in sub-Saharan Africa.

• **protectorate** An autonomous state or territory partly controlled and protected by a stronger outside power.

Brutality in the Congo No Africans suffered more violent and brutal treatment under colonial rule than those living in Belgian King Leopold the II's Congo Free State. When not having their hands, feet, or heads cut off as punishment, Africans were whipped with *chicottes*, whips made of dried hippopotamus hide. Some Congolese were literally whipped to death. (Courtesy, Anti-Slavery International, London)

recently invented machine gun. In the end eleven thousand brave but poorly armed Muslim fighters lay dead. Only twenty-eight Britons had been killed.

All European nations resorted to some violence in their colonies to retain control, subdue the population, appropriate land, and force African laborers to work long hours at physically demanding, and often dangerous, jobs. In no colony, however, was the violence and brutality worse than in Leopold II's Congo Free State. Rather than promoting Christianity and civilization as Leopold had promised, the European companies operating in the Congo Free State introduced slavery, unimaginable savagery, and terror. Missionaries and other religious leaders were not even allowed into the colony, for fear of their reporting the horrors they would witness there.

Profits in the Congo Free State came first from the ivory trade, but in the 1890s, when many of the elephant herds in the Congo had been decimated, a new cash crop arose to take ivory's place. In the mid-1880s a northern Irishman named John Dunlop developed a process to make inflatable rubber tires for his son's tricycle. Other scientific developments soon followed, and new uses for rubber were found, which caused a worldwide boom in the demand for raw rubber. As it happened, more than half of the Congo Free State possessed wild rubber vines growing thickly in the equatorial rain forest. By the mid-1890s rubber had surpassed ivory as the colony's major income producer, and Leopold and the companies he allowed to make profits in the Congo soon could not get enough of it. Violence and brutality increased exponentially as the European appetite for rubber became insatiable. Europeans and their well-armed mercenaries terrorized

entire regions, cutting off hands, feet, and heads and wiping out whole villages to make it clear to the Africans that they must either work for the Europeans or die. The African blood that was shed is recalled in the colony's frightening nickname—the "red rubber colony." In the early 1900s, human rights activists such as Edmund Morel exposed the truth about the horrific conditions in the Congo Free State, and in 1908 Leopold was forced to turn over his private territory to Belgium as a colony, the Belgian Congo. (See "Viewpoints: The Congo Free State," page 759.)

Southern Africa in the Nineteenth Century

The development of southern Africa diverged from the rest of sub-Saharan Africa in important ways. Whites settled in large numbers, modern capitalist industry took off, and British imperialists had to wage all-out war.

In 1652 the Dutch East India Company established a supply station at Cape Town for Dutch ships sailing between Amsterdam and Indonesia. The healthy, temperate climate and the sparse Khoisan population near the Cape resulted in the colony's gradual expansion. When the British took possession of the colony in the Napoleonic wars, the Cape Colony included about twenty thousand free Dutch citizens and twenty-five thousand African slaves, with substantial mixed-race communities on the northern frontier of white settlement.

After 1815 powerful African chiefdoms, Dutch settlers—first known as Boers, and then as **Afrikaners**—and British colonial forces waged a complicated three-

• **Afrikaners** Descendants of the Dutch settlers in the Cape Colony in southern Africa.

Viewpoints

The Congo Free State

• One historian estimates that between 1890 and 1910 the African population of the Congo Free State declined by nearly 10 million souls.* The public learned of the brutal conditions in the Congo through the efforts of reformers and journalists. George Washington Williams (1849–1891), an African American Baptist minister, lawyer, and historian, was dazzled, as were many others, by the noble humanitarian goals that Leopold II claimed to have for the Congo, but when he visited the Congo in 1890 he was sickened by what he saw. His public letter to King Leopold, excerpted below, offers one of the earliest firsthand accounts of the horrors of Congo. Edmund Morel (1873–1924), a British clerk, was similarly galvanized to undertake a campaign against Leopold after noticing that nearly 80 percent of the goods that his shipping firm sent to the Congo were weapons, shackles, and ammunition, while arriving ships were filled with cargoes of rubber, ivory, and other high-value goods.

George Washington Williams, "An Open Letter to His Serene Majesty Leopold II," 1890

❝ Your Majesty's Government has been, and is now, guilty of waging unjust and cruel wars against natives, with the hope of securing slaves and women, to minister to the behests of the officers of your Government. . . . I have no adequate terms with which to depict to your Majesty the brutal acts of your soldiers upon such raids as these. The soldiers who open the combat are usually the bloodthirsty cannibalistic Bangalas, who give no quarter to the aged grandmother or nursing child at the breast of its mother. There are instances in which they have brought the heads of their victims to their white officers on the expeditionary steamers, and afterwards eaten the bodies of slain children. In one war two Belgian Army officers saw, from the deck of their steamer, a native in a canoe some distance away. He was not a combatant and was ignorant of the

---

*Adam Hochschild, *King Leopold's Ghost* (Boston: Houghton Mifflin, 1999), pp. 225–234.

---

conflict . . . upon the shore, some distance away. The officers made a wager of £5 that they could hit the native with their rifles. Three shots were fired and the native fell dead, pierced through the head, and the trade canoe was transformed into a funeral barge and floated silently down the river. ❞

Edmund Morel, from *King Leopold's Rule in Africa*, 1904

❝ One of the most atrocious features of the persistent warfare of which year in year out the Congo territories are the scene, is the mutilation both of the dead and of the living which goes on under it. . . . The first intimation that Congo State troops were in the habit of cutting off the hands of men, women, and children in connection with the rubber traffic reached Europe through the Rev. J. B. Murphy, of the American Baptist Missionary Union, in 1895. He described how the State soldiers had shot some people on Lake Mantumba . . . , "cut off their hands and took them to the Commissaire." The survivors of the slaughter reported the matter to a missionary at Irebu, who went down to see if were true, and was quickly convinced by ocular demonstration. Among the mutilated victims was a little girl, not quite dead, who subsequently recovered. In a statement which appeared in the [London] *Times*, Mr. Murphy said, "These hands—the hands of men, women, and children—were placed in rows before the Commissary, who counted them to see that the soldiers had not wasted cartridges." ❞

Sources: George Washington Williams, "An Open Letter to Leopold II, King of the Belgians and Sovereign of the Independent State of Congo, July 18, 1890," in John Hope Franklin, *George Washington Williams: A Biography* (Chicago: University of Chicago Press, 1985), pp. 245–246, 250–251; Edmund D. Morel, *King Leopold's Rule in Africa* (New York: Funk and Wagnalls, 1905), pp. 110–111.

QUESTIONS FOR ANALYSIS

1. What factors might have allowed such horrible atrocities to be committed without greater public awareness and outcry?

2. How do these two readings exemplify the theory that the colonial experience brutalized both colonized and colonizer?

---

cornered battle to build strong states in southern Africa. Of critical importance, the talented Zulu leader Shaka (r. 1818–1828) revolutionized African warfare and managed to create the largest and most powerful African society in southern Africa in the nineteenth century. Drafted by age groups and placed in highly disciplined regiments, Shaka's warriors perfected the use of a short stabbing spear in deadly hand-to-hand combat. The Zulu armies often destroyed their African enemies completely, sowing chaos and sending refugees fleeing in all directions. Shaka's wars also led to the consolidation of the Zulu, Tswana, Swazi, and Sotho peoples into stronger states in southern Africa. By 1880 these states were largely subdued by Dutch and British invaders, but only after many hard-fought frontier wars.

Beginning in 1834 the British gradually abolished slavery in the Cape Colony and introduced color-blind legislation (whites and blacks were equal before the law) to protect African labor. In 1836 about ten thousand Afrikaner cattle ranchers and farmers, who resented the British colonial officials and missionaries treating blacks as equals after abolishing slavery, began to make their so-called Great Trek northward into the interior. In 1845 another group of Afrikaners joined them north of the Orange River. Over the next thirty years Afrikaner and British settlers, who often fought and usually detested each other, reached a mutually advantageous division of southern Africa. The British ruled strategically valuable coastal colonies, and the Afrikaners controlled their ranch-land republics in the interior. The Zulu, the Xhosa, and other African peoples lost much of their land but remained the majority — albeit an exploited majority.

The discovery of incredibly rich deposits of diamonds in 1867 and of gold in the 1880s revolutionized the economy of southern Africa, making possible large-scale industrial capitalism and transforming the lives of all its peoples. Small-scale white and black diamond diggers soon gave way to Cecil Rhodes (1853–1902) and the powerful financiers behind his De Beers mining company. Rhodes came from a large middle-class British family and at seventeen went to southern Africa to seek his fortune. Extraction of the deep-level gold deposits discovered in 1886 in the Afrikaners' Transvaal republic required big foreign investment, European engineering expertise, and an enormous labor force. By 1888 Rhodes's firm monopolized the world's diamond industry and earned him fabulous profits.

The "color bar" system of the diamond fields gave whites — often English-speaking immigrants — the well-paid skilled positions and put black Africans in the dangerous, low-wage jobs far below the earth's surface. Whites lived with their families in subsidized housing. African workers lived in all-male prison-like dormitories, closely watched by company guards. Southern Africa became the world's leading gold producer, pulling in black migratory workers from all over the region (as it does to this day).

The mining bonanza whetted the appetite of British imperialists led by the powerful Rhodes. Between 1889 and 1893 Rhodes used missionaries and a front company chartered by the British government to force African chiefs to accept British protectorates, and he managed to add Southern and Northern Rhodesia (modern-day Zimbabwe and Zambia) to the British

Diamond Mining in South Africa At first, both black and white miners could own and work claims at the diamond diggings, as this early photo suggests. However, as the industry expanded and was monopolized by European financial interests, white workers claimed the supervisory jobs, and blacks were limited to dangerous low-wage labor. (Hulton Archive/Corbis)

Empire. Rhodes and the imperialist clique then succeeded in starting the South African War of 1899–1902 (also known as the Anglo-Boer War), Britain's greatest imperial campaign on African soil. The British needed 450,000 troops to crush the Afrikaners, who never had more than 30,000 men in the field. Estimates of Africans who were sometimes forced and sometimes volunteered to work for one side or the other range from 15,000 to 40,000 for each side; they did everything from scouting and guard duty to heavy manual labor, driving wagons, and guarding the livestock.

The long and bitter war divided whites in South Africa, but South Africa's blacks were the biggest losers. The British had promised the Afrikaners representative government in return for surrender in 1902, and they made good on their pledge. In 1910 the Cape Colony; the former Afrikaner colony Natal (nuh-TAL), which had been annexed by the British in 1843; and the two Afrikaner republics formed a new self-governing Union of South Africa. After the peace settlement, because whites — 21.5 percent of the total population in 1910 — held almost all political power in the new union and because the Afrikaners outnumbered the English-speakers, the Afrikaners began to regain what they had lost on the battlefield. South Africa, under a joint British-Afrikaner government within the British Empire, began the creation of a modern segregated society that culminated in an even harsher system of racial separation, or apartheid, after World War II.

Colonialism's Impact After 1900

By 1900 much of black Africa had been conquered — or, as Europeans preferred to say, "pacified" — and a system of colonial administration was taking shape. In general, this system weakened or shattered the traditional social order and challenged accepted values.

The self-proclaimed political goal of the French and the British — the principal foreign powers — was to provide good government for their African subjects, especially after World War I. "Good government" meant, above all, law and order. It meant strong, authoritarian government, which maintained a small army and built up an African police force to put down rebellion, suppress ethnic warfare, and protect life and property. Good government required a modern bureaucracy capable of taxing and governing the population. Many African leaders and their peoples had chosen not to resist the invaders' superior force, and others stopped fighting and turned to other, less violent means of resisting co-

The Struggle for South Africa, 1878

lonial rule. Thus the goal of law and order was widely achieved.

Colonial governments demonstrated much less interest in providing basic social services. Expenditures on education, public health, hospitals, and other social services increased after the First World War but still remained small. Europeans feared the political implications of mass education and typically relied instead on the modest efforts of state-subsidized mission schools. Moreover, they tried to make even their poorest colonies pay for themselves. Thus salaries of government workers normally absorbed nearly all tax revenues.

Economically, the colonial goal was to draw the African interior into the world economy on terms favorable to the dominant Europeans. The key was railroads linking coastal trading centers to outposts hundreds of miles in the interior. Cheap, dependable transportation facilitated easy shipment of raw materials out and manufactured goods in. Most African railroads, generally direct lines from sources of raw materials in the interior to coastal ports, were built after 1900; fifty-two hundred miles were in operation by 1926, when attention turned to building roads for trucks. Railroads and roads had two other important outcomes: they allowed the quick movement of troops to put down local unrest, and they allowed many African peasants to earn wages for the first time.

The focus on economic development and low-cost rule explained why colonial governments were reluctant to move decisively against slavery within Africa. Officials feared that an abrupt abolition of slavery where it existed would disrupt production and lead to costly revolts by powerful slaveholding elites, especially in Muslim areas. Thus colonial regimes settled for halfway measures designed to satisfy humanitarian groups in Europe and also make all Africans, free or enslaved, participate in a market economy and work for wages. Even this cautious policy was enough for many slaves to boldly free themselves by running away, and it facilitated a rapid decline of slavery within Africa. At the same time, colonial governments often imposed head or hut taxes, payable in labor or European currency, to compel Africans to work for their white overlords. No aspect of colonialism was more despised by Africans than forced labor, widespread until about 1920. In some regions, particularly in West Africa, African peasants continued to respond freely to the new economic opportunities by voluntarily shifting to export crops on their own farms. Overall, the result of these developments was an increase in wage work and production geared to the world market and a decline in nomadic

A Missionary School A Swahili schoolboy leads his classmates in a reading lesson in Dar es Salaam in German East Africa before 1914, as portraits of Emperor William II and his wife look down on the classroom. Europeans argued that they were spreading the benefits of a superior civilization with schools like this one, which is unusually well-built and furnished because of its strategic location in the capital city. (Ullstein Bilderdienst/The Granger Collection, New York)

herding and traditional self-sufficient farming of sustainable crops.

In sum, the imposition of bureaucratic Western rule and the gradual growth of a world-oriented cash economy after 1900 had a revolutionary impact on large parts of Africa. The experiences of the Gold Coast and British East Africa, two very different African colonies, dramatically illustrate variations on the general pattern.

The British established the beginnings of the Gold Coast colony in 1821. Over the remainder of the century they extended their territorial rule inland from the coast and built up a fairly complex economy. This angered the powerful Asante kingdom in the interior, which also wanted control of the coast. After a series of Anglo-Asante wars beginning in 1824, British troops finally forced the Asante kingdom to accept British protectorate status in 1902. The large territory the British then controlled is essentially today's nation of Ghana.

Precolonial local trade was vigorous and varied, and palm oil exports were expanding. Into this sophisticated economy British colonists subsequently introduced the production of cocoa beans for the world's chocolate. Output rose spectacularly from a few hundred tons in the 1890s to 305,000 tons in 1936. Independent peasants and energetic African businessmen and businesswomen were mainly responsible for the spectacular success of cocoa-bean production. Creative African entrepreneurs even built their own roads, and they sometimes reaped big profits.

The Gold Coast also showed the way politically and culturally. The westernized black elite — relatively prosperous and well-educated lawyers, professionals, and journalists — and businesspeople took full advantage of opportunities provided by the fairly enlightened colonial regime. The black elite was the main presence in the limited local elections permitted by the British, for few permanent white settlers ventured to hot and densely populated West Africa.

Across the continent in the colony of British East Africa (modern Kenya), events unfolded differently. In West Africa Europeans had been establishing trading posts since the 1400s and carried on a complex slave trade for centuries. In East Africa there was very little European presence, other than some Portuguese, until after the scramble for Africa in the 1880s. Thus the peoples of East Africa generally remained more isolated from the Europeans than did Africans in the Gold Coast. Once the British started building their strategic railroad from the Indian Ocean across British East Africa in 1901, however, foreigners from Great Britain and India moved in to exploit the situation. Indian settlers became shopkeepers, clerks, and laborers in the towns. British settlers dreamed of turning the cool, beautiful, and fertile highlands of East Africa into a "white man's country" like Southern Rhodesia or the Union of South Africa. They dismissed the local population of peasant farmers as barbarians, fit only to toil as cheap labor on their large estates and plantations. British East Africa's blacks thus experienced much harsher colonial rule than did their fellow Africans in the Gold Coast.

The New Imperialism, 1880–1914

☐ What were the causes and consequences of European empire building after 1880?

Western expansion into Asia and Africa reached its apex between about 1880 and 1914. In those years the leading European nations continued to send streams of money and manufactured goods to both continents, and they also rushed to create or enlarge vast political empires abroad. This frantic political empire building contrasted sharply with the economic penetration of non-Western territories between 1816 and 1880, which, albeit by naked military force, had left a China or a Japan "opened" but politically independent (see Chapter 26). By contrast, the empires of the late nineteenth century recalled the old European colonial empires of the seventeenth and eighteenth centuries and led contemporaries to speak of the **new imperialism**.

Characterized by a frantic rush to plant the flag over as many people and as much territory as possible, the most spectacular manifestation of the new imperialism was the seizure of almost all of Africa, which broke sharply with previous patterns and fascinated contemporary Europeans and Americans. Although the sudden division of Africa was more striking, Europeans also extended their political control in Asia. The British expanded from their base in India, and in the 1880s the French took Indochina (modern Vietnam, Cambodia, and Laos). India and China also experienced a profound imperialist impact (see Chapter 26).

Causes of the New Imperialism

Many factors contributed to the West's late-nineteenth-century rush for territory in Africa and Asia, and it

> "[The] strongest nation has always been conquering the weaker . . . and the strongest tends to be best."
>
> **ENGLISH ECONOMIST**

is little wonder that controversies have raged over interpretation of the new imperialism. But despite complexity and controversy, basic causes are clearly identifiable.

Economic motives played an important role in the extension of political empires, especially of the British Empire. By the late 1870s France, Germany, and the United States were industrializing rapidly behind rising tariff barriers. Great Britain was losing its industrial leadership and facing increasingly tough competition in foreign markets. In this new economic situation Britain came to more highly value its old possessions, especially its vast colony in India, which it had exploited most profitably for more than a century. When in the 1880s European continental powers began to grab unclaimed territories, the British followed suit immediately. They feared that France and Germany would seal off their empires with high tariffs and that future economic opportunities would be lost forever.

The overall economic gains of the new imperialism proved limited before 1914. The new colonies were too poor to buy much, and they offered few immediately profitable investments. Nonetheless, colonies became important for political and diplomatic reasons. Each leading European country saw them as crucial to national security, military power, and international prestige. (See "Listening to the Past: A French Leader Defends Imperialism," page 764.)

Colonial rivalries reflected the increasing aggressiveness of Social Darwinian theories of brutal competition among races (see page 739). As one prominent English economist argued in 1873, the "strongest nation has always been conquering the weaker . . . and the strongest tend to be best." Thus European nations, which were seen as racially distinct parts of the dominant white race, had to seize colonies to show they were strong and virile. Moreover, since racial struggle was nature's inescapable law, the conquest of "inferior" peoples was just. Social Darwinism and harsh racial doctrines fostered imperialist expansion.

So did the industrial world's unprecedented technological and military superiority. Three aspects were crucial. First, the rapidly firing machine gun, so lethal at Omdurman in Sudan, was an ultimate weapon in many another unequal battle. Second, newly discovered

---

• **new imperialism** The late-nineteenth-century drive by European countries to create vast political empires abroad.

Listening to the Past

A French Leader Defends Imperialism

Although Jules Ferry (1832–1893) first gained political prominence as an ardent champion of secular public education, he was most famous for his empire building. While he was French premier in 1880–1881 and again in 1883–1885, France occupied Tunisia, extended its rule in Indonesia, seized Madagascar, and penetrated the Congo. Criticized by conservatives, socialists, and some left-wing republicans for his colonial expansion, Ferry defended his policies before the French National Assembly and also elaborated a philosophy of imperialism in his writings.

In a speech to the Assembly on July 28, 1883, portions of which follow, Ferry answered his critics and summarized his three main arguments with brutal honesty. Note that Ferry adamantly insisted that imperial expansion did not weaken France in its European struggle with Germany, as some opponents charged, but rather that it increased French grandeur and power. Imperialists needed the language of patriotic nationalism to be effective.

❝ *M. Jules Ferry*: Gentlemen, . . . I believe that there is some benefit in summarizing and condensing, in the form of arguments, the principles, the motives, and the various interests by which a policy of colonial expansion may be justified; it goes without saying that I will try to remain reasonable, moderate, and never lose sight of the major continental interests which are the primary concern of this country. What I wish to say, to support this proposition, is that in fact, just as in word, the policy of colonial expansion is a political and economic system; I wish to say that one can relate this system to three orders of ideas: economic ideas, ideas of civilization in its highest sense, and ideas of politics and patriotism.

In the area of economics, I will allow myself to place before you, with the support of some figures, the considerations which justify a policy of colonial expansion from the point of view of that need, felt more and more strongly by the industrial populations of Europe and particularly those of our own rich and hard working country: the need for export markets. Is this some kind of chimera? Is this a view of the future or is it not rather a pressing need, and, we could say, the cry of our industrial population? I will formulate only in a general way what each of you, in the different parts of France, is in a position to confirm. Yes, what is lacking for our great industry, drawn irrevocably on to the path of exportation by the [free trade] treaties of 1860, what it lacks more and more is export markets. Why? Because next door to us Germany is surrounded by barriers, because beyond the ocean, the United States of America has become protectionist, protectionist in the most extreme sense. . . .

Gentlemen, there is a second point, . . . the humanitarian and civilizing side of the question. On this point the honorable M. Camille Pellatan has jeered in his own refined and clever manner; he jeers, he condemns, and he says "What is this civilization which you impose with cannonballs? What is it but another form of barbarism? Don't these populations, these inferior races, have the same rights as you? Aren't they masters of their own houses? Have they called upon you? You come to them against their will, you offer them violence, but not civilization." There, gentlemen, is the thesis; I do not hesitate to say that this is not politics, nor is it history: it is political metaphysics. (*"Ah, Ah" on far left.*)

. . . Gentlemen, I must speak from a higher and more truthful plane. It must be stated openly that, in effect, superior races have rights over inferior races. (*Movement on many benches on the far left.*)

M. Jules Maigne: Oh! You dare to say this in the country which has proclaimed the rights of man!

M. de Guilloutet: This is a justification of slavery and the slave trade! . . .

M. Jules Ferry: I repeat that superior races have a right, because they have a duty. They have the duty to civilize inferior

---

quinine proved effective in controlling attacks of malaria, which had previously decimated Europeans in the tropics whenever they left breezy coastal enclaves and dared to venture into mosquito-infested interiors. Third, the introduction of steam power and the international telegraph permitted Western powers to quickly concentrate their firepower in a given area when it was needed. Steamships with ever-larger cargos made round-trip journeys to far-flung colonies much more quickly and economically. Small steamboats could travel back and forth along the coast and also carry goods up and down Africa's great rivers, as portrayed in the classic American film *The African Queen*. Likewise, train cars pulled by powerful steam engines — immune to disease, unlike animals and humans —

• **quinine** An agent that proved effective in controlling attacks of malaria, which had previously decimated Europeans in the tropics.

races. . . . (*Approval from the left. New interruptions from the extreme left and from the right.*)

. . . M. Pelletan . . . then touched upon a third point, more delicate, more serious, and upon which I ask your permission to express myself quite frankly. It is the political side of the question. The honorable M. Pelletan, who is a distinguished writer, always comes up with remarkably precise formulations. I will borrow from him the one which he applied the other day to this aspect of colonial policy.

"It is a system," he says, "which consists of seeking out compensations in the Orient with a circumspect and peaceful seclusion which is actually imposed upon us in Europe."

I would like to explain myself in regard to this. I do not like this word, "compensation," and, in effect, not here but elsewhere it has often been used in a treacherous way. If what is being said or insinuated is that any government in this country, any Republican minister could possibly believe that there are in any part of the world compensations for the disasters which we have experienced [in connection with our defeat in the Franco-Prussian War of 1870–1871], an injury is being inflicted . . . and an injury undeserved by that government. (*Applause at the center and left.*) I will ward off this injury with all the force of my patriotism! (*New applause and bravos from the same benches.*)

Gentlemen, there are certain considerations which merit the attention of all patriots. The conditions of naval warfare have been profoundly altered. ("Very true! Very true!")

At this time, as you know, a warship cannot carry more than fourteen days' worth of coal, no matter how perfectly it is organized, and a ship which is out of coal is a derelict on the surface of the sea, abandoned to the first person who comes along. Thence the necessity of having on the oceans provision stations, shelters, ports for defense and revictualling. (*Applause at the center and left. Various interruptions.*) And it is for this that we needed Tunisia, for this that we needed Saigon and the Mekong Delta, for this that we need Madagascar, that we are at Diégo-Suarez and Vohemar [two Madagascar ports]

• **Jules Ferry, French politician and ardent imperialist.** (Bettmann/Corbis)

and will never leave them! (*Applause from a great number of benches.*) Gentlemen, in Europe as it is today, in this competition of so many rivals which we see growing around us, some by perfecting their military or maritime forces, others by the prodigious development of an ever growing population; in a Europe, or rather in a universe of this sort, a policy of peaceful seclusion or abstention is simply the highway to decadence! Nations are great in our times only by means of the activities which they develop; it is not simply "by the peaceful shining forth of institutions" (*interruptions on the extreme left and right*) that they are great at this hour.

. . . [The Republican Party] has shown that it is quite aware that one cannot impose upon France a political ideal conforming to that of nations like independent Belgium and the Swiss Republic; that something else is needed for France: that she cannot be merely a free country, that she must also be a great country, exercising all of her rightful influence over the destiny of Europe, that she ought to propagate this influence throughout the world and carry everywhere that she can her language, her customs, her flag, her arms, and her genius. (*Applause at center and left.*)

Source: Speech before the French National Assembly, July 28, 1883. Reprinted in R. A. Austen, ed., *Modern Imperialism: Western Overseas Expansion and Its Aftermath, 1776–1965* (Lexington, Mass.: D. C. Heath, 1969), pp. 70–73.

QUESTIONS FOR ANALYSIS

1. What was Jules Ferry's economic argument for imperial expansion? Why had colonies recently gained greater economic value?
2. How did Ferry's critics attack the morality of foreign expansion? How did Ferry try to claim the moral high ground in his response?
3. What political arguments did Ferry advance? How would you characterize his philosophy of politics and national development?

replaced the thousands of African porters hitherto responsible for carrying raw materials from the interior to the coast. Never before — and never again after 1914 — would the technological gap between the West and the non-Western regions of the world be so great.

Social tensions and domestic political conflicts also contributed to overseas expansion. Conservative political leaders often manipulated colonial issues in order to divert popular attention from domestic conflicts and to create a false sense of national unity. Thus imperial propagandists relentlessly stressed that colonies benefited workers as well as capitalists, and they encouraged the masses to savor foreign triumphs and glory in the supposed increase in national prestige.

Finally, special-interest groups in each country were powerful agents of expansion. Shipping companies wanted lucrative subsidies. White settlers wanted more land, and missionaries and humanitarians wanted to spread religion and stop the slave trade. Military men and colonial officials foresaw rapid advancement and high-paid positions in growing empires. The actions of such groups pushed the course of empire forward.

A "Civilizing Mission"

Imperialists did not rest the case for empire solely on naked conquest and a Darwinian racial struggle or on power politics and the need for navy bases on every ocean. They developed additional arguments to satisfy their consciences and answer their critics.

A favorite idea was that Europeans and Americans could and should "civilize" supposedly primitive non-Western peoples. According to this view, Africans and Asians would receive the benefits of modern economies, cities, advanced medicine, and higher standards of living and eventually might be ready for self-government and Western democracy.

Another argument was that imperial government protected colonized peoples from ethnic warfare and the slave trade within Africa, as well as from cruder forms of exploitation by white settlers and business people. Thus the French spoke of their sacred "civiliz-

ing mission." In 1899 Rudyard Kipling (1865–1936), who wrote extensively on Anglo-Indian life and was perhaps the most influential British writer of the 1890s, exhorted Westerners to unselfish service in distant lands in his poem "The White Man's Burden":

> Take up the White Man's Burden —
> Send forth the best ye breed —
> Go bind your sons to exile
> To serve your captives' need,
> To wait in heavy harness,
> On fluttered folk and wild —
> Your new-caught, sullen peoples
> Half-devil and half-child.[7]

Written in response to America's seizure of the Philippines after the Spanish-American War, Kipling's poem and his concept of a **white man's burden** won wide acceptance among those who supported America's imperial ambitions. It was an important factor in the decision to rule, rather than liberate, the Philippines after the Spanish-American War (see page 826). Like their European counterparts, these Americans believed that their civilization had reached unprecedented heights and that they had unique benefits to bestow on all "less-advanced" peoples.

Imperialists claimed that peace and stability under European control would permit the spread of Christianity. In Africa Catholic and Protestant missionaries competed with Islam south of the Sahara, seeking converts and building schools. Many Africans' first real contact with Europeans and Americans was in mis-

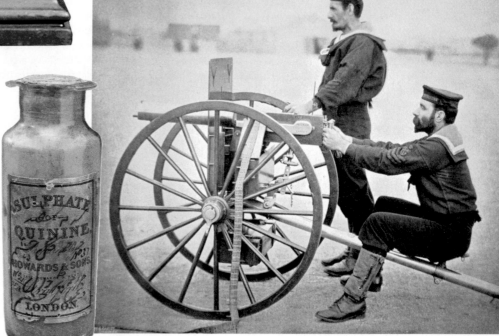

Tools for Empire Building
Western technological advances aided imperialist ambitions in Africa. The Maxim gun was highly mobile and could lay down a continuous barrage that would decimate charging enemies, as in the slaughter of Muslim tribesman at the Battle of Omdurman in the Sudan. Quinine, first taken around 1850 to prevent the contraction of malaria, enabled Europeans to move safely into the African interior and overwhelm native peoples. And the development of the electromagnetic telegraph in the 1840s permitted rapid long-distance communications for the first time in history. (gun: Private Collection/Peter Newark Military Pictures/The Bridgeman Art Library; quinine: Wellcome Library, London; telegraph: John D. Jenkins, www.sparksmuseum.com)

sion schools. Some peoples, such as the Ibo in Nigeria, became highly Christianized. Such occasional successes in black Africa contrasted with the general failure of missionary efforts in the Islamic world and in much of Asia.

Critics of Imperialism

The expansion of empire aroused sharp, even bitter, critics. A forceful attack was delivered in 1902, after the unpopular South African War, by radical English economist J. A. Hobson (1858–1940) in his *Imperialism*, a work that influenced Lenin (see Chapter 28) and others. Hobson contended that the rush to acquire colonies was due to the economic needs of unregulated capitalism. Moreover, Hobson argued, the quest for empire diverted popular attention away from domestic reform and the need to reduce the great gap between rich and poor at home. These and similar arguments had limited appeal because most people were sold on the idea that imperialism was economically profitable for the homeland.

Hobson and many Western critics struck home, however, with their moral condemnation of whites imperiously ruling nonwhites. Kipling and his kind were lampooned as racist bullies whose rule rested on brutality, racial contempt, and the Maxim machine gun. Polish-born novelist Joseph Conrad (1857–1924), in *Heart of Darkness* (1902), castigated the "pure selfishness" of Europeans in "civilizing" Africa. The main character in the novel, once a liberal European scholar, is corrupted by power in Africa and turns into a savage brute.

Critics charged Europeans with applying a degrading double standard and failing to live up to their own noble ideals. At home Europeans had won or were winning representative government, individual liberties, and a certain equality of opportunity. In their empires Europeans imposed military dictatorships on Africans and Asians, forced them to work involuntarily, and discriminated against them shamelessly. Only by renouncing imperialism and giving captive peoples the freedom idealized in Western society would Europeans be worthy of their traditions.

African and Asian Resistance

To peoples in Africa and Asia, Western expansion represented a profoundly disruptive assault with many consequences. Everywhere it threatened traditional ruling classes, economies, and ways of life. Christian missionaries and European secular ideologies challenged established beliefs and values. African and Asian societies experienced crises of identity and a general pattern of reassertion, although the details of each people's story varied substantially.

Often the initial response of African and Asian rulers was to try to drive the unwelcome foreigners away, as in China and Japan (see Chapter 26). Violent antiforeign reactions exploded elsewhere again and again, but the superior military technology of the industrialized West almost invariably prevailed. In addition, European rulers gave special powers and privileges to some individuals and groups from among the local population, including traditional leaders such as chiefs, landowners, and religious figures and Western-educated professionals and civil servants. These local elites recognized the imperial power realities in which they were enmeshed, and used them to maintain or gain authority over the masses. Some concluded that the West was superior in certain ways and that it was therefore necessary to reform and modernize their societies by copying some European achievements. This process of maintaining domination through providing advantages to a select few is referred to as hegemony, and it explains why relatively small numbers of Europeans were able to maintain control over much larger populations without constant rebellion and protest. European empires were won by force, but they were maintained by cultural as well as military and political means.

Nevertheless, imperial rule was in many ways an imposing edifice built on sand. Support for European rule among the conforming and accepting millions was shallow and weak. Thus the conforming masses followed with greater or lesser enthusiasm a few determined personalities who came to oppose the Europeans. Such leaders always arose, both when Europeans ruled directly and when they manipulated native governments, for at least two basic reasons.

First, the nonconformists—the eventual anti-imperialist leaders—developed a burning desire for human dignity. They came to feel that such dignity was incompatible with foreign rule. Second, potential leaders found in the Western world the ideologies and justification for their protest. Thus they discovered liberalism, with its credo of civil liberty and political self-determination. They echoed the demands of anti-imperialists in Europe and America that the West live up to its own ideals. Above all, they found themselves attracted to the nineteenth-century Western ideology of nationalism, which asserted that every people—or at least every European people—had the right to control its own destiny (see Chapter 24). After 1917 anti-imperialist revolt would find another weapon in Lenin's version of Marxist socialism.

• **white man's burden** The idea that Europeans could and should civilize more primitive nonwhite peoples and that imperialism would eventually provide nonwhites with modern achievements and higher standards of living.

The Islamic Heartland Under Pressure

☐ How did the Ottoman Empire and Egypt try to modernize themselves, and what were the most important results?

Stretching from West Africa into southeastern Europe and across Southwest Asia all the way to the East Indies, Islamic civilization competed successfully and continuously with western Europe for centuries. But beginning in the late seventeenth century, the rising absolutist states of Austria and Russia began to challenge the greatest Muslim state, the vast Ottoman Empire, and gradually to reverse Ottoman rule in southeastern Europe. In the nineteenth century European industrialization and nation building further altered the long-standing balance of power, and Western expansion eventually posed a serious challenge to Muslims everywhere.

In close contact with Europe and under constant European pressure, the ruling elites both in the Ottoman Empire and in Egypt, a largely independent Ottoman province, led the way in trying to generate the strength to survive. The ongoing military crisis required, first of all, wrenching army reforms on Western lines in order to defend and preserve the state. These military reforms then snowballed into a series of innovations in education, which had a powerful cultural impact on Ottoman and Egyptian elites.

The results of all these pressures and the momentous changes they brought were profound and paradoxical. On the one hand, the Ottoman Empire and Egypt achieved considerable modernization on Western lines. On the other hand, these impressive accomplishments never came fast enough to offset the growing power and appetite of the West. The Islamic heartland in Southwest Asia and North Africa increasingly fell under foreign control.

Decline and Reform in the Ottoman Empire

Although the Ottoman Empire began to decline slowly after Suleiman the Magnificent in the sixteenth century (see page 592), the relationship between the Ottomans and the Europeans in about 1750 was still one of

roughly equal strength. In the later eighteenth century this situation began to change quickly and radically. The Ottomans fell behind western Europe in science, industrial skill, and military technology. Absolutist Russia pushed southward between 1768 and 1774. The danger that the Great Powers of Europe would gradually conquer the Ottoman Empire and divide up its vast territories was real.

Caught up in the Napoleonic wars and losing more territory to Russia, the Ottomans were forced to grant Serbia local autonomy in 1816. In 1821 the Greeks revolted against Ottoman rule, and in 1830 they won their national independence. Facing uprisings by their Christian subjects in Europe, the Ottomans also failed to defend their Islamic provinces in North Africa. In 1830 French armies began their long and bloody conquest of the Arabic-speaking province of Algeria. By 1860 two hundred thousand French, Italian, and Spanish colonists had settled among the Muslim majority, whose number had been reduced to about 2.5 million by the war against the French and related famines and epidemics.

Ottoman weakness reflected the decline of the sultan's "slave army," the so-called janissary corps (see page 592). With time, the janissaries — boys and other slaves raised in Turkey as Muslims, then trained to serve in the elite corps of the Ottoman infantry — became a corrupt and privileged hereditary caste. They zealously pursued their own interests and refused any military innovations that might undermine their high status.

A transformation of the army was absolutely necessary to battle the Europeans more effectively and enhance the sultanate's authority within the empire. The empire was no longer a centralized military state. Instead, local governors were becoming increasingly independent, pursuing their own interests and even seeking to establish their own governments and hereditary dynasties.

The energetic sultan Selim III (r. 1789–1807) understood these realities, but when he tried to reorganize the army, the janissaries refused to use any "Christian" equipment. In 1807 they revolted, and Selim was quickly executed in a palace revolution, one of many that plagued the Ottoman state. The reform-minded Mahmud II (r. 1808–1839) proceeded cautiously, picking loyal officers and building his dependable artillery corps. In 1826 his council ordered the janissaries to drill in the European manner. As expected, the janis-

Ottoman Decline in the Balkans, 1818–1830

Belgrade

SERBIA (Autonomous, 1816)

Danube R.

OTTOMAN EMPIRE

Ionian Is. (Gr. Br.)

GREECE (Independent, 1830)

Athens

Navarino Bay 1827

Mediterranean Sea

Crete

Pasha Halim Receiving Archduke Maximilian of Austria As this painting suggests, Ottoman leaders became well versed in European languages and culture. They also mastered the game of power politics, playing one European state against another and securing the Ottoman Empire's survival. The black servants on the right may be slaves from the Sudan. (Miramare Palace Trieste/Dagli Orti/The Art Archive)

saries revolted and charged the palace, where they were mowed down by the waiting artillery corps.

The destruction and abolition of the janissaries cleared the way for building a new army, but it came too late to stop the rise of Muhammad Ali, the Ottoman governor in Egypt. In 1831 his French-trained forces occupied the Ottoman province of Syria and appeared ready to depose Mahmud II. The Ottoman sultan survived, but only by begging Europe for help. Britain, Russia, and Austria intervened and negotiated a peace settlement. Having reestablished direct rule over the province of Iraq, the overconfident Ottomans were saved again in 1839 after their forces were routed trying to drive Muhammad Ali from Syria. In the last months of 1840 Russian diplomatic efforts, British and Austrian naval blockades, and threatened military action convinced Muhammad Ali to return Syria to the Ottomans. European powers preferred a weak and dependent Ottoman state to a strong and revital-

ized Muslim entity under a dynamic leader such as Muhammad Ali.

Realizing their precarious position, in 1839 liberal Ottoman statesmen launched an era of radical reforms, which lasted with fits and starts until 1876 and culminated in a constitution and a short-lived parliament. Known as the **Tanzimat** (literally, regulations or orders), these reforms were designed to remake the empire on a western European model. The new decrees called for the equality of Muslims, Christians, and Jews before the law and in business, security of life and property, and a modernized administration and military. New commercial laws allowed free importation of foreign goods, as British advisers demanded, and permitted foreign merchants to operate freely throughout an economically dependent empire. Under heavy British

• **Tanzimat** A set of radical reforms designed to remake the Ottoman Empire on a western European model.

pressure, slavery in the empire was drastically curtailed, though not abolished completely. Of great significance, growing numbers among the elite and the upwardly mobile embraced Western education, adopted Western manners and artistic styles, and accepted secular values to some extent.

Intended to bring revolutionary modernization such as that experienced by Russia under Peter the Great (see page 509) and by Japan in the Meiji era (see page 797), the Tanzimat permitted partial recovery. Yet the Ottoman state and society failed to regain its earlier strength for several reasons. First, implementation of the reforms required a new generation of well-trained and trustworthy officials, and that generation did not exist. Second, the liberal reforms failed to halt the growth of nationalism among Christian subjects in the Balkans (see Chapter 28), which resulted in crises and defeats that undermined all reform efforts. Third, the Ottoman initiatives did not curtail the appetite of Western imperialism, and European bankers gained a usurious stranglehold on Ottoman finances. In 1875 the Ottoman state had to declare partial bankruptcy and place its finances in the hands of European creditors.

Finally, the elaboration — at least on paper — of equal rights for citizens and religious communities did not create greater unity within the state. Religious disputes increased, worsened by the relentless interference of the Great Powers. This development embittered relations between the religious communities, distracted the government from its reform mission, and split Muslims into secularists and religious conservatives. Many conservative Muslims detested the religious reforms, which they saw as an irreverent departure from Islamic tradition and holy law. These Islamic conservatives became the most dependable supporters of Sultan Abdülhamid (r. 1876–1909), who abandoned the model of European liberalism in his long and repressive reign.

The combination of declining international power and conservative tyranny eventually led to a powerful resurgence of the modernizing impulse among idealistic Turkish exiles in Europe and young army officers in Istanbul. These fervent patriots, the so-called **Young Turks**, seized power in the revolution of 1908, and they forced the sultan to implement reforms. Failing to stop the rising tide of anti-Ottoman nationalism in the Balkans, the Young Turks helped to prepare the way for the birth of modern secular Turkey after the defeat and collapse of the Ottoman Empire in World War I (see pages 863–864).

• **Young Turks** Fervent patriots who seized power in the revolution of 1908, forcing the conservative sultan to implement reforms; they helped pave the way for the birth of modern secular Turkey.

Egypt: From Reform to British Occupation

The ancient land of the pharaohs had been ruled by a succession of foreigners since 525 B.C.E. and was most recently conquered by the Ottoman Turks in the early sixteenth century. In 1798 French armies under the young general Napoleon Bonaparte invaded Egypt and occupied the territory for three years as part of France's war with Britain. Into the power vacuum left by the French withdrawal stepped an extraordinary Albanian-born Turkish general, Muhammad Ali (1769–1849).

First appointed governor of Egypt by the Turkish sultan, Muhammad Ali set out to build his own state on the strength of a large, powerful army organized along European lines. In 1820–1822 the Egyptian leader conquered much of the Sudan to secure slaves for his army, and thousands of African slaves were brought to Egypt during his reign. Because many slaves died in Egyptian captivity, Muhammad Ali turned to drafting Egyptian peasants. He also reformed the government and promoted modern industry. (See "Individuals in Society: Muhammad Ali," page 771.) For a time Muhammad Ali's ambitious strategy seemed to work, but it eventually foundered when his armies occupied Syria and he threatened the Ottoman sultan Mahmud II. In the face of European military might and diplomatic entreaties, Muhammad Ali agreed to peace with his Ottoman overlords and withdrew. In return he was given unprecedented hereditary rule over Egypt and Sudan. By the time of his death in 1849, Muhammad Ali had established a strong and virtually independent Egyptian state within the Turkish empire.

To pay for a modern army and industrialization, Muhammad Ali encouraged the development of commercial agriculture geared to the European market. This development had profound social implications. Egyptian peasants had been poor but largely self-sufficient, growing food on state-owned land allotted to them by tradition. Offered the possibility of profits from export agriculture, high-ranking officials and members of Muhammad Ali's family began carving large private landholdings out of the state domain, and they forced the peasants to grow cash crops for European markets. Ownership of land became very unequal. By 1913, 12,600 large estates owned 44 percent of the land, and 1.4 million peasants owned only 27 percent. Estate owners "modernized" agriculture, to the detriment of the peasants' well-being.

Muhammad Ali's policies of modernization attracted growing numbers of Europeans to the banks of the Nile. By 1863, when Muhammad Ali's grandson Ismail began his sixteen-year rule as Egypt's khedive (kuh-DEEV), or prince, the port city of Alexandria had more than fifty thousand Europeans. Europeans served as army

Individuals in Society

Muhammad Ali

THE DYNAMIC LEADER MUHAMMAD ALI (1769–1849) stands across the history of modern Egypt like a colossus. Yet the essence of the man remains a mystery, and historians vary greatly in their interpretations of him. Sent by the Ottomans, with Albanian troops, to oppose the French occupation of Egypt in 1799, Muhammad Ali maneuvered skillfully after the French withdrawal in 1802. In 1805 he was named pasha, or Ottoman governor, of Egypt. Only the Mamluks remained as rivals. Originally an elite corps of Turkish slave-soldiers, the Mamluks had become a semifeudal military ruling class living off the Egyptian peasantry. In 1811 Muhammad Ali offered to make peace, and he invited the Mamluk chiefs and their retainers to a banquet in Cairo's Citadel. As the unsuspecting guests processed through a narrow passage, his troops opened fire, slaughtering all the Mamluk leaders.

After eliminating his foes, Muhammad Ali embarked on a program of radical reforms. He reorganized agriculture and commerce, reclaiming most of the cultivated land for the state domain, which he controlled. He also established state agencies to monopolize, for his own profit, the sale of agricultural goods. Commercial agriculture geared to exports to Europe developed rapidly, especially after the successful introduction of high-quality cotton in 1821. Canals and irrigation systems along the Nile were rebuilt and expanded.

Muhammad Ali used his growing revenues to recast his army along European lines. He recruited French officers to train the soldiers. As the military grew, so did the need for hospitals, schools of medicine and languages, and secular education. Young Turks and some Egyptians were sent to Europe for advanced study. The ruler boldly financed factories to produce uniforms and weapons, and he prohibited the importation of European goods so as to protect Egypt's infant industries. In the 1830s state factories were making one-fourth of Egypt's cotton into cloth. Above all, Muhammad Ali drafted Egyptian peasants into the military for the first time, thereby expanding his army to 100,000 men. It was this force that conquered the Ottoman province of Syria, threatened the sultan in Istanbul, and triggered European intervention. Grudgingly recognized by his Ottoman overlord as Egypt's hereditary ruler in 1841, Muhammad Ali nevertheless had to accept European and Ottoman demands to give up Syria and abolish his monopolies and protective tariffs. The old ruler then lost heart; his reforms languished, and his factories disappeared.

In the attempt to understand Muhammad Ali and his significance, many historians have concluded that he was a national hero, the "founder of modern Egypt." His ambitious state-building projects—hospitals, schools, factories, and the army—were the basis for an Egyptian reawakening and eventual independence from the Ottomans' oppressive foreign rule. Similarly, state-sponsored industrialization promised an escape from poverty and Western domination, which was foiled only by European intervention and British insistence on free trade.

A growing minority of historians question these views. They see Muhammad Ali primarily as an Ottoman adventurer. In their view, he did not aim for national independence for Egypt, but rather "intended to carve out a small empire for himself and for his children after him."* Paradoxically, his success, which depended on heavy taxes and brutal army service, led to Egyptian nationalism among the Arabic-speaking masses, but that new nationalism was directed against Muhammad Ali and his Turkish-speaking entourage. Continuing research into this leader's life will help to resolve these conflicting interpretations.

QUESTIONS FOR ANALYSIS

1. Which of Muhammad Ali's actions support the interpretation that he was the founder of modern Egypt? Which actions support the opposing view?
2. After you have studied Chapter 26, compare Muhammad Ali and the Meiji reformers in Japan. What accounts for the similarities and differences?

*K. Fahmy, *All the Pasha's Men: Mehmed Ali, His Army, and the Making of Modern Egypt* (Cambridge, U.K.: Cambridge University Press, 1997), p. 310.

Muhammad Ali, the Albanian-born ruler of Egypt, in 1839 (Mary Evans Picture Library/The Image Works)

> **"**History confirms and demonstrates that the status of women is inseparably tied to the status of a nation.**"**
>
> **QASIM AMIN**

officers, engineers, doctors, government officials, and police officers. Others worked in trade, finance, and shipping. Above all, Europeans living in Egypt combined with landlords and officials to continue the development of commercial agriculture geared to exports. By 1900 about two hundred thousand Europeans lived in Egypt and accounted for 2 percent of the population. As throughout the Ottoman Empire, Europeans enjoyed important commercial and legal privileges and formed an economic elite.

Ismail (r. 1863–1879) was a westernizing autocrat. Educated at France's leading military academy, he dreamed of using European technology and capital to modernize Egypt and build a vast empire in northeastern Africa. He promoted cotton production, and exports to Europe soared. Ismail also borrowed large sums, and with his support the Suez Canal was completed by a French company in 1869, shortening the voyage from Europe to Asia by thousands of miles. Cairo acquired modern boulevards and Western hotels. As Ismail proudly declared, "My country is no longer in Africa, we now form part of Europe."[8]

Major cultural and intellectual changes accompanied the political and economic ones. The Arabic of the masses, rather than the Turkish of the conquerors, became the official language, and young Egyptians educated in Europe helped spread new skills and ideas in the bureaucracy. A host of writers, intellectuals, and religious thinkers responded to the novel conditions with innovative ideas that had a powerful impact in Egypt and other Muslim societies.

Three influential figures who represented broad families of thought were especially significant. The teacher and writer Jamal al-Din al-Afghani (1838/39–1897) preached Islamic regeneration and defense against Western Christian aggression. Regeneration, he argued, required the purification of religious belief, the unity of all Muslim peoples, and a revolutionary overthrow of corrupt Muslim rulers and foreign exploiters. The more moderate Muhammad Abduh (1849–1905) also searched for Muslim rejuvenation and launched the modern Islamic reform movement, which became very important in the twentieth century. Abduh concluded that Muslims should return to the purity of the earliest, most essential doctrines of Islam and reject later additions that could limit Muslim creativity. This would permit a flexible, reasoned approach to change, social questions, and foreign ideas.

Finally, the writer Qasim Amin (1863–1908) represented those who found inspiration in the West in the late nineteenth century. In his influential book *The Liberation of Women* (1899), Amin argued forcefully that superior education for European women had contributed greatly to the Islamic world's falling far behind the West. The rejuvenation of Muslim societies required greater equality for women:

> History confirms and demonstrates that the status of women is inseparably tied to the status of a nation. Where the status of a nation is low, reflecting an uncivilized condition for that nation, the status of women is also low, and when the status of a nation is elevated, reflecting the progress and civilization of that nation, the status of women in that country is also elevated.[9]

Egypt changed rapidly during Ismail's rule, but his projects were reckless and enormously expensive. By 1876 the Egyptian government could not pay the interest on its colossal debt. Rather than let Egypt go bankrupt and repudiate its loans, France and Great Britain intervened politically to protect the European investors who held the Egyptian bonds. They forced Ismail to appoint French and British commissioners to oversee Egyptian finances so that the Egyptian debt would be paid in full. This meant that Europeans were going to determine the state budget and in effect rule Egypt.

Foreign financial control evoked a violent nationalistic reaction among Egyptian religious leaders, intellectuals, and army officers. In 1879, under the leadership of Colonel Ahmed Arabi, they formed the Egyptian Nationalist Party. Continuing diplomatic pressure, which forced Ismail to abdicate in favor of his weak son, Tewfiq (r. 1879–1892), resulted in bloody anti-European riots in Alexandria in 1882. A number of Europeans were killed, and Tewfiq and his court had to flee to British ships for safety. The British fleet then bombarded Alexandria, and a British expeditionary force decimated Arabi's forces and occupied all of Egypt.

The Suez Canal, 1869

Egyptian Travel Guide Ismail's efforts to transform Cairo were fairly successful. As a result European tourists could more easily visit the country that their governments dominated. Ordinary Europeans were lured to exotic lands by travel books like this colorful "Official Guide" to an exhibition on Cairo held in Berlin. (Private Collection/Archives Charmet/The Bridgeman Art Library)

The British said that their occupation was temporary, but British armies remained in Egypt until 1956. They maintained the façade of the khedive's government as an autonomous province of the Ottoman Empire, but the khedive was a mere puppet. The British consul, General Evelyn Baring, later Lord Cromer, ruled the country after 1883. Baring was a paternalistic reformer, and his rule resulted in tax reforms and somewhat better conditions for peasants. Foreign bondholders received their interest payments, and Egyptian nationalists chafed under foreign rule.

In Egypt the British abandoned what some scholars have called the "imperialism of free trade," which was based on economic penetration and indirect rule. They accepted a new model for European expansion in the densely populated lands of Africa and Asia. Such expansion was based on military force, political domination, and a self-justifying ideology of beneficial reform. This model, which was also adopted in varying ways by other European colonial powers in the age of the new imperialism, was to predominate in the British colonies from the 1880s until 1914.

The Expanding World Economy

☐ What were the global consequences of European industrialization between 1800 and 1914?

The Industrial Revolution created, first in Great Britain and then in continental Europe and North America, a growing and dynamic economic system. In the course of the nineteenth century that system expanded and transformed economic relations across the face of the earth. As a result the world's total income grew as never before, and international trade boomed. Western nations used their superior military power to force non-Western nations to open their doors to Western economic interests, and the largest share of the ever-increasing gains from trade flowed to the West, resulting in a stark division between rich and poor countries.

The Rise of Global Inequality

From a global perspective, the ultimate significance of the Industrial Revolution was that it allowed those regions of the world that industrialized in the nineteenth century to increase their wealth and power enormously in comparison with those that did not. A gap between the industrializing regions and the nonindustrializing or **Third World** regions (mainly Africa, Asia, and Latin America) opened and grew steadily throughout the nineteenth century. Moreover, this pattern of uneven global development became institutionalized, built into the structure of the world economy. Thus evolved a world of haves and have-nots, with the have-not peoples and nations far outnumbering the haves.

Figure 25.1 depicts the gap between the industrializing regions (mainly Europe and North America) and the nonindustrializing Third World that opened up in the late eighteenth and the nineteenth centuries. In 1750 the average standard of living was no higher in Europe as a whole than in the rest of the world. By 1914 the average person in the wealthiest countries had an income four or five times as great (and in Great Britain nine or ten times as great) as the income of the average person in the poorest countries of Africa and Asia. The rise in average income and well-being, first in Great Britain and then in the other developed countries,

• **Third World** A term that refers to the nonindustrialized nations of Africa, Asia, and Latin America as a single unit.

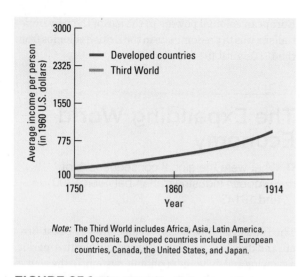

Note: The Third World includes Africa, Asia, Latin America, and Oceania. Developed countries include all European countries, Canada, the United States, and Japan.

FIGURE 25.1 The Growth of Average Income per Person Worldwide, 1750–1914 (Source of data: P. Bairoch and M. Lévy-Leboyer, eds., *Disparities in Economic Development Since the Industrial Revolution*, published 1981, Macmillan Publishers.)

reflected the rising level of industrialization in these countries before World War I.

The reasons for these enormous income disparities, which are poignant indicators of disparities in food and clothing, health and education, life expectancy, and general material well-being, have generated a great deal of debate. One school of interpretation stresses that the West used science, technology, capitalist organization, and even its critical worldview to create its wealth and greater physical well-being. Another school argues that the West used its political and economic power to steal much of its riches, continuing its rapacious colonialism in the nineteenth and twentieth centuries.

These issues are complex, and there are few simple answers. As noted in Chapter 23, the wealth-creating potential of technological improvement and more intensive capitalist organization was great. At the same time, the initial breakthroughs in the late eighteenth century rested in part on Great Britain's having already used political force to dominate a substantial part of the world economy. In the nineteenth century other industrializing countries joined with Britain to extend Western dominion over the entire world economy. Unprecedented wealth was created, but the lion's share of that new wealth flowed to the West and its propertied classes and to a tiny non-Western elite of cooperative rulers, landowners, and merchants.

The World Market

World trade was a powerful stimulus to economic development in the nineteenth century. In 1913 the value of world trade was about twenty-five times what it had been in 1800, even though prices of manufactured goods

and raw materials were lower in 1913 than in 1800. In a general way, the enormous increase in international commerce summed up the growth of an interlocking world economy centered in Europe.

Great Britain played a key role in using trade to tie the world together economically. In 1815 Britain had a colonial empire, with India, Canada, Australia, and other scattered areas remaining British possessions after American independence. The technological breakthroughs of the Industrial Revolution encouraged British manufacturers to seek export markets around the world. After Parliament repealed laws restricting the importation of grain in 1846, Britain also became the world's leading importer of foreign goods. Free access to Britain's market stimulated the development of mines and plantations in Africa and Asia.

The growth of trade was facilitated by the conquest of distance. The earliest railroad construction occurred in Europe and in America north of the Rio Grande; other parts of the globe saw the building of rail lines after 1860. By 1920 about a quarter of the world's railroads were in Latin America, Asia, Africa, and Australia. Wherever railroads were built, they drastically reduced transportation costs, opened new economic opportunities, and called forth new skills and attitudes.

Much of the railroad construction undertaken in Africa, Asia, and Latin America connected seaports with inland cities and regions, as opposed to linking and developing cities and regions within a country. Thus railroads dovetailed with Western economic interests, facilitating the inflow and sale of Western manufactured goods and the export and development of local raw materials.

The power of steam also revolutionized transportation by sea. Steam power, long used to drive paddle wheelers on rivers, particularly in Russia and North America, finally began to supplant sails on the oceans of the world in the late 1860s. Lighter, stronger, cheaper steel replaced iron, which had replaced wood. Passenger and freight rates tumbled, and the shipment of low-priced raw materials from one continent to another became feasible.

The revolution in land and sea transportation helped European settlers take vast, thinly populated territories and produce agricultural products and raw materials for sale in Europe. Improved transportation enabled Asia, Africa, and Latin America to export not only the traditional tropical products — spices, dyes, tea, sugar, coffee — but also new raw materials for industry, such as jute, rubber, cotton, and coconut oil. (See "Global Trade: Indigo," page 776.)

Intercontinental trade was enormously facilitated by the Suez Canal and the Panama Canal (see page 819). Of great importance, too, was large and continual investment in modern port facilities, which made loading and unloading cheaper, faster, and more dependable. Finally, transoceanic telegraph cables inaugurated rapid communications among the financial centers of the world and linked world commodity prices in a global network.

The growth of trade and the conquest of distance encouraged Europeans to make massive foreign investments beginning about 1840. Most of the capital exported did not go to European colonies or protectorates in Asia and Africa. About three-quarters of total European investment went to other European countries, the United States and Canada, Australia and New Zealand, and Latin America. Europe found its most profitable opportunities for investment in construction of the railroads, ports, and utilities that were necessary to settle and develop the lands of extensive European expansion. Much of this investment was peaceful and mutually beneficial for lenders and borrowers. The victims were Native American Indians and Australian Aborigines, who were displaced and decimated by the diseases, liquor, and weapons of an aggressively expanding Western society (see Chapter 27).

The Great Global Migration

□ What fueled migration, and what was the general pattern of this unprecedented movement of people?

A poignant human drama was interwoven with this worldwide economic expansion: millions of people pulled up stakes and left their ancestral lands in one of history's greatest migrations: the so-called **great migration**. In the early eighteenth century the world's population entered a period of rapid growth that continued unabated through the nineteenth and twentieth centuries. The population of Europe (including Asiatic Russia) more than doubled during the nineteenth century, from approximately 188 million in 1800 to roughly 432 million in 1900.

Between 1750 and 1900 the population of Asia followed the same general trend. China, by far the world's most populous country in the middle of the eighteenth century, increased from about 143 million in 1741 to a little more than 400 million in the 1840s, although total numbers grew more slowly in the turbulent late nineteenth century. Since population increased more slowly in Africa and Asia than in Europe, Europeans and peoples of predominately European origin jumped from about 22 percent of the world's total in 1850 to a high of about 38 percent in 1930.

The growing number of Europeans was a driving force behind emigration and Western expansion. The rapid increase in numbers led to relative overpopula-

British East African Railway Poster Europeans constructed railroads in most of their African colonies to haul raw materials from the interior to coastal ports and to transport colonial officials, white settlers, and foreign tourists. Britain's East African railroad line from Kampala, Uganda, to the Kenyan port city of Mombasa was one of the most famous and most romanticized. Indians from British India did much of the construction and then remained in Kenya to form substantial Indian communities. U.S. President Theodore Roosevelt rode this train while on his 1909 African safari. (National Archives, London/HIP/Art Resource, NY)

tion in area after area in Europe. Thus millions of country folk went abroad as well as to nearby cities in search of work and economic opportunity. Some governments encouraged their excess populations to immigrate, even paying some of their expenses. Wars, famine, poverty, and, particularly in the case of Jews in Russia and

• **great migration** The mass movement of people from Europe in the nineteenth century; one reason that the West's impact on the world was so powerful and many-sided.

Global Trade

Indigo is the oldest and most important natural colorant, and it serves as an illustrative example of the prodigious growth of world trade in the nineteenth century. Indigo is made from the leaves of a small bush that are carefully fermented in vats; the extract is then processed into cakes of pigment. It has been highly prized since antiquity. It dyes all fabrics, does not fade with time, and yields tints ranging from light blue to the darkest purple-blue. Used primarily today as a dye for blue jeans, indigo has been used throughout history as a dye for textiles, as a pigment for painting, and for medicinal and cosmetic purposes.

Widely grown and used in Asia, indigo trickled into Europe from western India in the High Middle Ages but was very expensive. Woad—an inferior homegrown product—remained Europe's main blue dye until the opening of a direct sea route to India by the Portuguese in 1498 reconfigured the intercontinental trade in indigo, as it did for many Asian products. Bypassing Muslim traders in the Indian Ocean, first Portuguese and then Dutch and English merchants and trading companies supplied European dyers and consumers with cheaper, more abundant indigo.

In the early seventeenth century indigo became one of the British East India Company's chief articles of trade, and it was exported from India to Europe more than ever before. As European governments adopted mercantilist policies, they tried to control trade and limit the flow of gold and silver abroad for products like indigo. The result was a second transformation in the global trade in indigo.

MAP 25.2 The Indigo Trade

Europeans established indigo plantations in their American colonies, and by the first half of the eighteenth century only small quantities of indigo continued to reach Europe from peasant producers in western India. Indigo plantations in Brazil, Guatemala, Haiti and the Caribbean, and South Carolina were big capitalistic operations and frequently very profitable. They depended on slaves brought from Africa, as did the entire Atlantic economy in the eighteenth century.

In the late eighteenth century the geography of the indigo trade shifted dramatically once again: production returned to India, now largely controlled by the British. Why

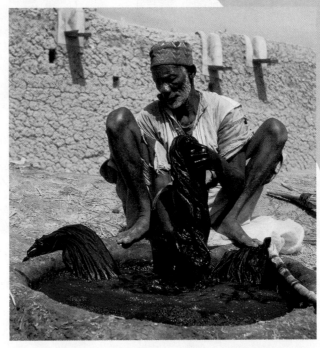

Squatting next to a dye pit in northern Nigeria, a man soaks clothing in natural indigo dye, which is still used locally in parts of Africa and South Asia. (Lawrence Manning/Corbis)

did this happen? Political upheaval in the revolutionary era played a key role. American independence left South Carolina outside Britain's mercantilist system; the slave rebellion in Haiti in 1791 decimated some of the world's richest indigo producers; and Britain's continental blockades cut off Spain and France from their colonies. On the economic side, the takeoff in the British textile industry created surging demand for indigo. Thus in the 1780s the British East India Company hired experienced indigo planters from the West Indies to develop indigo production in Bengal. Leasing lands from Indian *zemindars* (landlords who doubled as tax collectors), British planters coerced Bengali peasants into growing indigo, which the planters processed in their "factories." Business expanded rapidly, as planters made—and lost—fortunes in the boom-and-bust cycles characteristic of commodity production in the nineteenth century.

In 1859 Bengali peasants revolted and received unexpected support from British officials advocating free-market contracts and recourse to the courts to settle disputes. As peasants pressed their case against the outraged planters, Indian professionals and intellectuals joined their cause. Winning freer and more equitable contracts, the rural-urban alliance created in the "Indigo Disturbances" marked a key step in the growth of nationalism in Bengal, a leading force in the subsequent drive for Indian independence.

Even as the Indigo Disturbances agitated Bengal, industrializing Europe discovered on its doorstep a completely new source of colorants: thick, black coal tar. This residue, a noxious byproduct of the destructive distillation of soft coal for the gas used in urban lighting and heating, was emerging as the basic material for the chemistry of carbon compounds and a new synthetic dye industry. British, German, and French chemists synthesized a small number of dyes between 1856 and 1869, when the first synthetic dye replaced a natural dye. Thereafter, German researchers and Germany's organic chemical companies built an interlocking global monopoly that produced more than 90 percent of the world's synthetic dyes.

Indigo was emblematic of this resounding success. Professor Adolf Bayer first synthesized indigo in 1880. But an economically viable process required many years of costly, systematic research before two leading German companies working together achieved their objective in 1897. Producers' groups in India slashed indigo prices drastically, but to no avail. Indian exports of natural indigo plummeted from nineteen thousand tons in 1895 to only one thousand tons in 1913. Synthetic indigo claimed the global market, German firms earned super profits, and Indian peasants turned to different crops. Today, nearly all the indigo produced in the world is synthetic, although limited production of natural indigo still occurs in India, as well as in parts of Africa and South America.

Steerage Passengers, 1902 Conditions for steerage passengers traveling from Europe to the Americas were cramped, as evidenced by this photo from 1902. (The Granger Collection, New York)

eastern Europe, bigotry and discrimination were also leading causes for immigrants to leave their ancestral homelands. More than 60 million people left Europe over the course of the nineteenth century, primarily for the rapidly growing "areas of European settlement" — North and South America, Australia, New Zealand, and Siberia (see Chapter 27). European emigration crested in the first decade of the twentieth century, when more than five times as many men and women departed as in the 1850s.

The European migrant was most often a small peasant landowner or a village craftsman whose traditional way of life was threatened by too little land, estate agri-culture, and cheap factory-made goods. Determined to maintain or improve their precarious status, the vast majority of migrants were young and often unmarried. Many European migrants returned home after some time abroad. One in two migrants to Argentina and probably one in three to the United States eventually returned to their native lands.

Ties of family and friendship played a crucial role in the movement of peoples. Many people from a given province or village settled together in rural enclaves or tightly knit urban neighborhoods thousands of miles away. Very often a strong individual — a businessman, a religious leader — would blaze the way, and others would follow, forming a **migration chain**.

Many young European men and women were spurred to leave by a spirit of revolt and independence. In Sweden and Norway, in Jewish Russia and Italy, these young people felt frustrated by the small privi-leged classes that often controlled both church and

- **migration chain** The movement of peoples in which one strong individual blazes the way and others follow.
- **great white walls** Discriminatory laws built by Americans and Australians to keep Asians from settling in their countries in the 1880s.

government and resisted demands for change and greater opportunity. Migration slowed when the economic situation improved at home, particularly as countries industrialized and many more occupational opportunities became available. People also stayed put when they began to win basic political and social reforms, such as the right to vote and social security.

A substantial number of Asians — especially Chinese, Japanese, Indians, and Filipinos — also responded to population pressure and rural hardship with temporary or permanent migration. At least 3 million Asians moved abroad before 1920. Most went as indentured laborers to work under incredibly difficult conditions on the plantations or in the gold mines of Latin America, southern Asia, Africa, California, Hawaii, and Australia (see Chapter 26). White estate owners often used Asians to replace or supplement blacks after the suppression of the Atlantic slave trade.

Such migration from Asia would undoubtedly have grown to much greater proportions if planters and mine owners in search of cheap labor had had their way. But usually they did not. Asians fled the plantations and gold mines as soon as possible, seeking greater opportunities in trade and towns. There they came into conflict with white settlers in areas of European

settlement. These settlers demanded a halt to Asian immigration. By the 1880s Americans and Australians were building **great white walls**—discriminatory laws designed to keep Asians out.

The general policy of "whites only" in the lands of large-scale European settlement meant that Europeans and people of European ancestry reaped the main benefits of the great migration. By 1913 people in Australia, Canada, and the United States all had higher average incomes than did people in Great Britain, still Europe's wealthiest nation. This, too, was part of Western dominance in the increasingly lopsided world.

Within Asia and Africa the situation was different. Migrants from south China frequently settled in Dutch, British, and French colonies of Southeast Asia, where they established themselves as peddlers and small shopkeepers (see Chapter 26). These "overseas Chinese" gradually emerged as a new class of entrepreneurs and officeworkers. Traders from India and modern-day Lebanon performed the same function in much of sub-Saharan Africa after the European seizure in the late nineteenth century. Thus in some parts of Asia and Africa the business class was both Asian and foreign, protected and tolerated by Western imperialists who found these business people useful.

CONNECTIONS

By the end of the nineteenth century broader industrialization across Europe increased the need for raw materials and markets, and with it came a rush to create or enlarge vast political empires abroad. The new imperialism was aimed primarily at Africa and Asia, and in the years before 1914 the leading European nations not only created empires abroad, but also continued to send massive streams of migrants, money, and manufactured goods around the world. (The impact of this unprecedented migration is taken up in the next two chapters.) This political empire building contrasted sharply with the economic penetration of non-Western territories between 1816 and 1880, which had left China and Japan "opened" but politically independent, as Chapter 26 will show.

European influence also grew in the Middle East. Threatened by European military might, modernization, and Christianity, Turks and Arabs tried to implement reforms that would assure their survival and independence but also to retain key aspects of their cultures, particularly Islam. Although they made important advances in the modernization of their economies and societies, their efforts were not enough to overcome Western imperialism. With the end of World War I and the collapse of the Ottoman Empire, England and France divided much of the Middle East into colonies and established loyal surrogates as rulers in other, nominally independent countries. Chapter 29 will take up the story of these developments.

Easy imperialist victories over weak states and poorly armed non-Western peoples encouraged excessive pride and led Europeans to underestimate the fragility of their accomplishments. Imperialism also made nationalism more aggressive and militaristic. As European imperialism was dividing the world after the 1880s, the leading European states were also dividing themselves into two opposing military alliances. As Chapter 28 will show, when the two armed camps stumbled into war in 1914, the results were disastrous. World War I set the stage for a new anti-imperialist struggle in Africa and Asia for equality and genuine independence (see Chapters 32 and 33).

☐ CHAPTER REVIEW

☐ What were the most significant changes in Africa during the nineteenth century, and why did they occur? (p. 752)

European pressure in Africa contributed to the reorientation of the economy, which gradually turned from a focus on the transatlantic slave trade to the production of commodities for export. As a result, the slave trade declined steeply. A legitimate trade in African goods, including palm oil, proved profitable and led to the emergence of a small black middle class. Islam revived and expanded until about 1870. The European conquest of Africa after 1880 led to colonial empires that improved internal security and built bureaucracies, but also treated Africans as racial inferiors.

☐ What were the causes and consequences of European empire building after 1880? (p. 763)

After 1880 a handful of Western nations seized most of Africa and parts of Asia and rushed to build authoritarian empires. The reasons for this empire building included trade rivalries, competitive nationalism in Europe, and self-justifying claims of a civilizing mission. Above all, European states had acquired unprecedented military superiority, which they used to crush resistance and impose their will.

☐ How did the Ottoman Empire and Egypt try to modernize themselves, and what were the most important results? (p. 768)

The Ottoman Empire and Egypt introduced reforms to improve the military, provide technical and secular education, and expand personal liberties. In so doing, both countries prepared the way for modern nation-states in the twentieth century, but they failed to defend themselves from Western imperialism. The Ottoman Empire lost territory, but survived in a weakened condition. Faced with resistance by Christian nationalists and conservative Muslims, and economically hindered by Western imperialism, the modernization efforts failed to salvage the Ottoman sultan's progressive regime. Muhammad Ali was more successful, reforming the government and promoting modern industry, but Egypt went bankrupt and was conquered and ruled by Britain. Western domination was particularly bitter for most Muslims because they saw it as profaning their religion as well as taking away their political independence.

KEY TERMS

palm oil (p. 752)	white man's burden
jihad (p. 755)	(p. 766)
Sokoto caliphate	Tanzimat (p. 769)
(p. 755)	Young Turks (p. 770)
Berlin Conference	Third World (p. 773)
(p. 757)	great migration (p. 775)
protectorate (p. 757)	migration chain
Afrikaners (p. 758)	(p. 778)
new imperialism	great white walls
(p. 763)	(p. 779)
quinine (p. 764)	

☐ What were the global consequences of European industrialization between 1800 and 1914? (p. 773)

Between 1800 and 1914 European industrialization caused a growing gap in average income between people in the West and people in Africa, Asia, and Latin America. This new world of rich lands and poor lands experienced a prodigious increase in international trade, but most of the gains went to the Western nations, which profitably subordinated many lands to their own economic interests. Great Britain, with its colonies in Asia, Africa, and the Americas, played a key role in using trade to tie the world's markets together. Railroad construction and the development of steam power facilitated trade and made moving goods easier, and transoceanic telegraph cables allowed for rapid communication between far-flung financial centers.

☐ What fueled migration, and what was the general pattern of this unprecedented movement of people? (p. 775)

In response to population pressures at home and economic opportunities abroad, Western nations sent forth millions of emigrants to the sparsely populated areas of European settlement in North and South America, Australia, and Asiatic Russia. Some migrants were motivated by a desire to escape oppression, though migration generally slowed when the economic situation improved at home or when social or political reform occurred. Migration from Asia was much more limited, mainly because European settlers raised high barriers to prevent the settlement of Asian immigrants.

SUGGESTED READING

Bagachi, Amiya Kumar. *Perilous Passage: Mankind and the Ascendancy of Capital.* 2005. A spirited radical critique of Western imperialism.

Conklin, Alice. *A Mission to Civilize: The French Republican Ideal and West Africa, 1895–1930.* 1997. An outstanding examination of French imperialism.

Cook, Scott B. *Colonial Encounters in the Age of High Imperialism.* 1996. A stimulating and very readable overview.

Coquery-Vidrovitch, Catherine. *Africa and the Africans in the Nineteenth Century: A Turbulent History.* 2009. English translation of a highly regarded history by a premier African scholar.

Findley, C. *The Turks in World History.* 2005. An exciting reconsideration of the Turks in long-term perspective.

Harper, Marjory, and Stephen Constantine. *Migration and Empire.* 2010. A comparative study of migration throughout the British Empire.

Headrick, D. *Tools of Empire.* 1991. Stresses technological superiority in Western expansion.

Hochschild, Adam. *King Leopold's Ghost: A Story of Greed, Terror, and Heroism in Colonial Africa.* 1999. The definitive account of King Leopold's Congo and the human rights crusaders who exposed its horrors.

Hourani, A. *A History of the Arab Peoples,* 2d ed. 2010. Brilliant on developments in the nineteenth century.

Law, Robin, ed. *From Slave Trade to "Legitimate" Commerce: The Commercial Transition in Nineteenth-Century West Africa.* 2002. Leading scholars describe the transition to legitimate trade from an African perspective.

Lovejoy, P. *Transformation in Slavery: A History of Slavery in Africa,* 2d ed. 2000. A fine synthesis of current knowledge.

Mahfouz, H. *Palace of Desire.* 1991. A great novelist's portrait of an Egyptian family before 1914.

Medard, Henri, and Shane Doyle. *Slavery in the Great Lakes Region of East Africa.* 2007. A significant contribution to the understudied story of slavery in East Africa, mainly in the nineteenth and early twentieth centuries.

Nugent, Walter. *Crossings: The Great Transatlantic Migrations, 1870–1914.* 1992. A classic study of migration history.

Wright, John. *The Trans-Saharan Slave Trade.* 2007. A well-researched study of slavery in a long-neglected region of Africa.

NOTES

1. P. Lovejoy, *Transformations in Slavery: A History of Slavery in Africa,* 2d ed. (Cambridge, U.K.: Cambridge University Press, 2000), p. 142.
2. Ibid., p. 179.
3. Quoted in J. Iliffe, *Africans: The History of a Continent* (Cambridge, U.K.: Cambridge University Press, 1995), p. 169.
4. Lovejoy, *Transformations in Slavery,* p. 15.
5. R. Oliver, *The African Experience* (New York: Icon Editions, 1991), pp. 164–166.
6. Quoted in H. Wheaton, *Elements of International Law* (London: Stevens & Sons, Limited, 1889), p. 804.
7. Rudyard Kipling, *The Five Nations* (London, 1903).
8. Quoted in Earl of Cromer, *Modern Egypt* (London, 1911), p. 48.
9. Qasim Amin, *The Liberation of Women and The New Woman* (The American University of Cairo Press, 2000), p. 6.

For practice quizzes and other study tools, visit the **Online Study Guide** at bedfordstmartins.com/mckayworld.

For primary sources from this period, see *Sources of World Societies*, **Second Edition**.

For Web sites, images, and documents related to topics in this chapter, visit **Make History** at bedfordstmartins.com/mckayworld.

Rammohun Roy The expansion of British power in India posed intellectual and cultural challenges to the native elite. Among those who rose to this challenge was writer and reformer Rammohun Roy, depicted here. (V&A Images, London/Art Resource, NY)

26

During the nineteenth century the societies of Asia underwent enormous changes as a result of population growth, social unrest, and the looming presence of Western imperialist powers. At the beginning of the century Spain, the Netherlands, and Britain had colonies in the Philippines, modern Indonesia, and India, respectively. By the end of the century much more land—most of the southern tier of Asia, from India to the Philippines—had been made colonies of Western powers. Most of these colonies became tied to the industrializing world as exporters of agricultural products or raw materials, including timber, rubber, tin, sugar, tea, cotton, and jute. The Western presence brought benefits, especially to educated residents of major cities, where the colonizers often introduced modern public health, communications, and educational systems. Still, cultural barriers between the colonizers and the colonized were huge, and the Western presence rankled. The West relied on force to conquer and rule, and it treated non-Western peoples as racial inferiors.

Asia in the Era of Imperialism
1800-1914

Not all the countries in Asia were reduced to colonies. Although Western powers put enormous pressures on China and exacted many concessions from it, China remained politically independent. Much more impressively, Japan became the first non-Western country to use an ancient love of country to transform itself and thereby meet the many-sided challenge of Western expansion. Japan emerged from the nineteenth-century crisis stronger than any other Asian nation, becoming the first non-Western country to industrialize successfully. By the end of this period Japan had become an imperialist power itself, making Korea and Taiwan its colonies. •

India and the British Empire in Asia

□ In what ways did India change as a consequence of British rule?

Arriving in India on the heels of the Portuguese in the seventeenth century, the British East India Company outmaneuvered French and Dutch rivals and was there to pick up the pieces as the Mughal Empire decayed during the eighteenth century (see pages 611–613). By 1757 the company had gained control over much of India. During the nineteenth century the British gov-ernment replaced the company, progressively unified the subcontinent, and harnessed its economy to British interests.

Travel and communication between Britain and India became much faster, safer, and more predictable in this period. Clipper ships with their huge sails cut the voyage from Europe to India from six to three months. By the 1850s steamships were competing with clipper ships, and they made ocean travel more predictable. After the 1869 opening of the Suez Canal, which connected the Mediterranean and Red Seas, the voyage by steamship from England to India took only three weeks. Another advance was the cables that were laid on the ocean floor in the 1860s, allowing telegrams to be sent

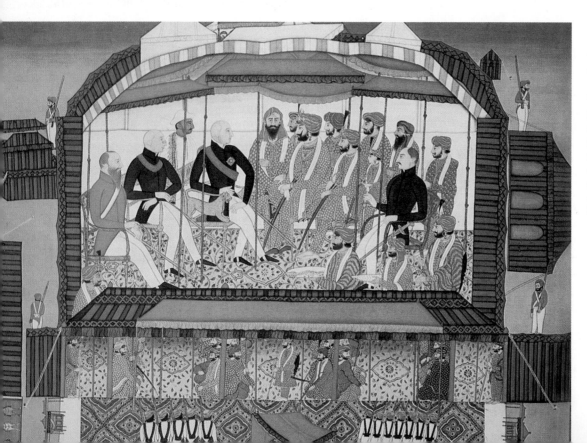

British and Sikh Leaders at Lahore The Sikh kingdom in the Punjab fell to the British in a brief war in 1845–1846. This painting depicts the British and Sikh representatives who negotiated the resulting treaty, which gave Britain control of the region. (Courtesy of the Trustees of the British Museum)

The Great Revolt/Great Mutiny, 1857

from England to India. Whereas at the beginning of the nineteenth century someone in England had to wait a year or more to get an answer to a letter sent to India, by 1870 it took only a couple of months—or, if the matter was urgent, only a few hours by telegraph. Faster travel and communication aided the colonial government and foreign merchants, but they did not keep Indians from resenting British rule.

The Evolution of British Rule

In 1818 the British East India Company controlled territory occupied by 180 million Indians—more people than lived in all of western Europe and fifty times the number of people the British had lost in 1783 when the thirteen American colonies successfully overthrew British colonial control. In India the British ruled with the cooperation of local princely allies, whom they could not afford to offend. To assert their authority, the British disbanded and disarmed local armies, introduced simpler private property laws, and enhanced the powers of local princes and religious leaders, both Hindu and Muslim. The British administrators, backed by British officers and native troops, were on the whole competent and concerned about the welfare of the Indian peasants. Slavery was outlawed and banditry suppressed, and new laws designed to improve women's position in society were introduced. Sati (widow suicide) was outlawed in 1829, legal protection of widow remarriage was extended in 1856, and infanticide (disproportionately of female newborns) was banned in 1870.

The last armed resistance to British rule occurred in 1857. By that date the British military presence in India had grown to include two hundred thousand Indian sepoy troops and thirty-eight thousand British officers. The sepoys were well trained and armed with modern rifles. In 1857 groups of them, especially around Delhi, revolted in what the British called the **Great Mutiny** and the Indians called the **Great Revolt**. The sepoys' grievances were many, ranging from the use of fat from cows (sacred to Hindus) and pigs (regarded as filthy by Muslims) to grease rifle cartridges to high tax rates and the incorporation of low-caste soldiers into the army. The insurrection spread rapidly throughout northern and central India before it was finally crushed, primarily by native troops from other parts of India loyal to the British. Thereafter, although princely states

• **Great Mutiny/Great Revolt** The terms used by the British and the Indians, respectively, to describe the last armed resistance to British rule in India, which occurred in 1857.

were allowed to continue, Britain ruled India much more tightly. Moreover, the British in India acted more like an occupying power and mixed less with the Indian elite.

After 1858 India was ruled by the British Parliament in London and administered by a civil service in India, the upper echelons of which were all white. In 1900 this elite consisted of fewer than thirty-five hundred top officials for a population of 300 million. In 1877 Queen Victoria adopted the title empress of India, and her image became a common sight in India.

The Socioeconomic Effects of British Rule

The impact of British rule on the Indian economy was multifaceted. In the early stages, the British East India Company expanded agricultural production, creating large plantations. Early crops were opium to export to China (see page 793) and tea to substitute for imports from China. India gradually replaced China as the leading exporter of tea to Europe. During the nineteenth century India also exported cotton fiber, silk, sugar, jute, coffee, and other agricultural commodities to be processed elsewhere. Clearing land for tea and coffee plantations, along with massive commercial logging operations, led to extensive deforestation.

To aid the transport of goods, people, and information, the colonial administration invested heavily in India's infrastructure. By 1855 India's major cities had all been linked by telegraph and railroads, and postal service was being extended to local villages. By 1870 India had the fifth-largest rail network in the world — 4,775 miles, carrying more than 18 million passengers

a year. By 1900 the rail network had increased fivefold to 25,000 miles, and the number of passengers had increased tenfold to 188 million. By then over 370,000 Indians worked for the railroads. Irrigation also received attention, and by 1900 India had the world's most extensive irrigation system.

At the same time, Indian production of textiles suffered a huge blow. Britain imported India's raw cotton but exported machine-spun yarn and machine-woven cloth, displacing millions of Indian hand-spinners and hand-weavers. By 1900 India was buying 40 percent of Britain's cotton exports. Not until 1900 were small steps taken toward industrializing India. Local Gujaratis set up textile mills in Bombay, and the Tata family started the first steel mill in Bihar in 1911. By 1914 about a million Indians worked in factories.

As the economy expanded the standard of living of the poor did not see much improvement. Tenant farming and landlessness increased with the growth in plantation agriculture. Increases in production were eaten up by increases in population, which, as noted, had reached approximately 300 million by 1900. There was also a negative side to improved transportation. As Indians traveled more widely on the convenient trains, disease spread, especially cholera, which is transmitted by exposure to contaminated water. Pilgrims' bathing in and drinking from sacred pools and rivers worsened this problem. New sewerage and water supply systems were installed in Calcutta in the late 1860s, and the death rate there decreased, but in 1900 four out of every one thousand residents of British India still died of cholera each year.

Wooden Model of a Colonial Courtroom The judge, an officer with the British East India Company who is seated on a chair with his top hat on the table, presides over a courtroom filled with Indian assistants seated on the floor and the plaintiffs and defendants in the case standing. Notice the attention the Indian craftsman paid to the details of the dress and hats of each of the figures in this 20-inch-long wooden model. (© Victoria and Albert Museum, London/V&A Images)

The British and the Indian Educated Elite

The Indian middle class probably gained more than the poor from British rule, because they were the ones to benefit from the English-language educational system Britain established in India. (See "Viewpoints: Rammohun Roy and Thomas Babington Macauley on Education for Indians," page 788.) Missionaries also established schools with Western curricula, and 790,000 Indians were attending some 24,000 schools by 1870. High-caste Hindus came to form a new elite profoundly influenced by Western thought and culture.

By creating a well-educated, English-speaking Indian elite and a bureaucracy aided by a modern communication system, the British laid the groundwork for a unified, powerful state. Britain placed under the same general system of law and administration the various Hindu and Muslim peoples of the subcontinent who had resisted one another for centuries. It was as if Europe, with its many states and varieties of Christianity, had been conquered and united in a single great empire. University graduates tended to look on themselves as Indians more than as residents of separate states and kingdoms, a necessary step for the development of Indian nationalism.

Some Indian intellectuals sought to reconcile the values of the modern West and their own traditions. Rammohun Roy (1772–1833), who had risen to the top of the native ranks in the British East India Company, founded a college that offered instruction in Western languages and subjects. He also founded a society to reform traditional customs, especially child marriage, the caste system, and restrictions on widows. He espoused a modern Hinduism founded on the *Upanishads* (oo-PAH-nih-shahds), the ancient sacred texts of Hinduism.

The more that Western-style education was developed in India, the more the inequalities of the system became apparent to educated Indians. Indians were eligible to take the examinations for entry into the elite **Indian Civil Service**, the bureaucracy that administered the Indian government, but the exams were given in England. Since few Indians could travel such a long distance to take the test, in 1870 only 1 of the 916 members of the service was Indian. In other words, no matter how Anglicized educated Indians became, they could never become the white rulers' equals. The top jobs, the best clubs, the modern hotels, and even certain railroad compartments were sealed off to brown-skinned men and women. Most of the British elite considered the jumble of Indian peoples and castes to be racially inferior. For example, when the British Parliament in 1883 was considering a bill to allow Indian judges to try white Europeans in India, the British community rose in protest and defeated the measure.

> "However well educated and clever a native may be, and however brave he may prove himself, I believe that no rank we can bestow on him would cause him to be considered an equal of the British officer."
>
> **LORD KITCHENER**

As Lord Kitchener, one of the most distinguished British military commanders in India, stated:

> It is this consciousness of the inherent superiority of the European which has won for us India. However well educated and clever a native may be, and however brave he may prove himself, I believe that no rank we can bestow on him would cause him to be considered an equal of the British officer.[1]

The peasant masses might accept such inequality as the latest version of age-old class and caste hierarchies, but the well-educated, English-speaking elite eventually could not. They had studied not only Milton and Shakespeare but also English traditions of democracy, liberty, and national pride.

In the late nineteenth century the colonial ports of Calcutta, Bombay, and Madras, now all linked by railroads, became centers of intellectual ferment. In these and other cities, newspapers in English and in regional languages gained influence. Lawyers trained in English law began agitating for Indian independence. By 1885, when a group of educated Indians came together to found the **Indian National Congress**, demands were increasing for the equality and self-government that Britain enjoyed and had already granted white-settler colonies such as Canada and Australia (see Chapter 27). The Congress Party called for more opportunities for Indians in the Indian Civil Service and reallocation of the government budget from military expenditures to the alleviation of poverty. They advocated unity across religious and caste lines, but most members were upper-caste, Western-educated Hindus.

Defending British possessions in India became a key element of Britain's foreign policy during the nineteenth century and led to steady expansion of the territory Britain controlled in Asia. The kingdom of Burma, to India's east, also was trying to expand, which led the British to annex Assam (located between India and Burma) in 1826, then all of Burma by 1852. Burma was

• **Indian Civil Service** The bureaucracy that administered the government of India. Entry into its elite ranks was by examinations that Indians were eligible to take but that were offered only in England.

• **Indian National Congress** A political association formed in 1885 that worked for Indian self-government.

Viewpoints

Rammohun Roy and Thomas Babington Macauley on Education for Indians

• *Opinion was divided among both British administrators and Indian intellectuals about the sort of education the colonial government should offer to Indians. In 1823 the leading Indian intellectual, Rammohun Roy (1772–1833), well-educated in both traditional Indian subjects and in English, responded negatively to a British proposal to establish a school teaching Sanskrit and Hindu literature. The matter of higher education in India was not settled until 1835, when Thomas Babington Macauley (1800–1859), in his capacity as a colonial officer, came out strongly for Western education.*

Rammohun Roy, 1823

"When this Seminary of learning was proposed, we understood that the Government in England had ordered a considerable sum of money to be annually devoted to the instruction of its Indian Subjects. We were filled with sanguine hopes that this sum would be laid out in employing European Gentlemen of talents and education to instruct the natives of India in Mathematics, Natural Philosophy, Chemistry, Anatomy, and other useful Sciences, which the Nations of Europe have carried to a degree of perfection that has raised them above the inhabitants of other parts of the world....

We now find that the Government are establishing a Sanskrit school under Hindu Pundits to impart such knowledge as is already current in India. This Seminary (similar in character to those which existed in Europe before the time of Lord Bacon) can only be expected to load the minds of youth with grammatical niceties and metaphysical distinctions of little or no practicable use to the possessors or to society. The pupils will there acquire what was known two thousand years ago, with the addition of vain and empty subtleties since produced by speculative men, such as is already commonly taught in all parts of India.

The Sanskrit language, so difficult that almost a life time is necessary for its perfect acquisition, is well known to have been for ages a lamentable check on the diffusion of knowledge; and the learning concealed under this almost impervious veil is far from sufficient to reward the labour of acquiring it."

Thomas Babington Macauley, 1835

"What then shall that language [of instruction] be? One half of the committee maintain that it should be the English. The other half strongly recommend the Arabic and Sanskrit. The whole question seems to me to be which language is the best worth knowing? ...

It will hardly be disputed, I suppose, that the department of literature in which the Eastern writers stand highest is poetry. And I certainly never met with any orientalist who ventured to maintain that the Arabic and Sanskrit poetry could be compared to that of the great European nations. But when we pass from works of imagination to works in which facts are recorded and general principles investigated, the superiority of the Europeans becomes absolutely immeasurable....

It is taken for granted by the advocates of oriental learning that no native of this country can possibly attain more than a mere smattering of English.... They assume it as undeniable that the question is between a profound knowledge of Hindu and Arabian literature and science on the one side, and superficial knowledge of the rudiments of English on the other. This is not merely an assumption, but an assumption contrary to all reason and experience.... There are in this very town natives who are quite competent to discuss political or scientific questions with fluency and precision in the English language. I have heard the very question on which I am now writing discussed by native gentlemen with a liberality and an intelligence which would do credit to any member of the Committee of Public Instruction....

In one point I fully agree with the gentlemen to whose general views I am opposed. I feel with them that it is impossible for us, with our limited means, to attempt to educate the body of the people. We must at present do our best to form a class who may be interpreters between us and the millions whom we govern, a class of persons Indian in blood and color, but English in tastes, in opinions, in morals and in intellect. To that class we may leave it to refine the vernacular dialects of the country, to enrich those dialects with terms of science borrowed from the Western nomenclature, and to render them by degrees fit vehicles for conveying knowledge to the great mass of the population."

Source: Bureau of Education. *Selections from Educational Records, Part I (1781–1839)*, edited by H. Sharp (Calcutta: Superintendent Government Printing, 1920; reprint: Delhi: National Archives of India, 1965), pp. 98–101, 107–117.

QUESTIONS FOR ANALYSIS

1. Are the reasons that Roy and Macauley prefer instruction in English similar?

2. What can you infer about the views of the other side? What would be the strongest reasons for establishing colleges using Indian languages?

MAP 26.1 Asia in 1914 India remained under British rule, while China precariously preserved its political independence. The Dutch Empire in modern-day Indonesia was old, but French control of Indochina was a product of the new imperialism.

ANALYZING THE MAP Consider the colonies of the different powers on this map. What European countries were leading imperialist states, and what lands did they hold? Can you see places where colonial powers were likely to come into conflict with each other?

CONNECTIONS Do the sizes of the various colonial territories as seen on this map adequately reflect their importance to the countries that possessed them? If not, what else should be taken into account in thinking about the value of these sorts of colonial possessions?

then administered as a province of India. British trade between India and China went through the Strait of Malacca, making that region strategically important. Britain had taken over several Dutch territories in this region, including Java, during the Napoleonic occupation of the Netherlands (Map 26.1). After returning them to the Netherlands in 1814, Britain created its own base in the area at Singapore, later expanding into

Malaya (now Malaysia) in the 1870s and 1880s. In both Burma and Malaya, Britain tried to foster economic development, building railroads and promoting trade. Burma became a major exporter of timber and rice, Malaya of tin and rubber. So many laborers were brought into Malaya for the expanding mines and plantations that its population came to be approximately one-third Malay, one-third Chinese, and one-third Indian.

Competition for Southeast Asia

☐ Why were most but not all Southeast Asian societies reduced to colonies?

At the beginning of the nineteenth century only a small part of Southeast Asia was under direct European control. Spain administered the Philippines, and the Dutch controlled Java. By the end of the century most of the region would be in foreign hands.

The Dutch East Indies

Although Dutch forts and trading posts in the East Indies dated back to the seventeenth century, in 1816 the Dutch ruled little more than the island of Java. Thereafter they gradually brought almost all of the 3,000-mile-long archipelago under their political authority. In extending their rule, the Dutch, like the British in India, brought diverse peoples with different languages and distinct cultural traditions into a single political entity (see Map 26.1). Thus they inadvertently created the foundations of modern-day Indonesia—the world's fourth most populous nation.

Taking over the Dutch East India Company in 1799, the Dutch government modified the company's loose control of Java and gradually built a modern bureaucratic state. Javanese resistance to Dutch rule led to the bloody **Java War** (1825–1830). In 1830, after the war, the Dutch abolished the combination of tribute from rulers and forced labor from peasants that they had used to obtain spices, and they established instead a particularly exploitive policy called the Culture System. Under this system, Indonesian peasants were forced to plant a fifth of their land in export crops, especially coffee and sugar, to turn over to the Dutch as tax. The Culture System proved highly profitable for the Dutch and brought Dutch shipping and intercontinental commerce back to life. In 1870 Dutch liberals succeeded in eliminating some of the system's most coercive elements, but the practical effects were limited because Dutch and Javanese officials still worked together to make sure the flow of goods continued.

At the end of the nineteenth century the Dutch began to encourage Western education in the East Indies. The children of local rulers and privileged elites, much like their counterparts in India, encountered new ideas in Dutch-language schools. They began to question the long-standing cooperation of local elites with Dutch colonialism, and they searched for a new national identity. Thus anticolonial nationalism began to take shape in the East Indies in the early twentieth century, and it would blossom after World War I.

Mainland Southeast Asia

Unlike India and Java, mainland Southeast Asia had escaped European rule during the eighteenth century. In 1802 the **Nguyen Dynasty** came to power in Vietnam, putting an end to thirty years of peasant rebellion and civil war. For the first time in the country's history, a single Vietnamese monarchy ruled the entire country, and Vietnam's future appeared bright. Working through a centralizing scholar bureaucracy fashioned on the Chinese model, the Nguyen (gwin) Dynasty energetically built irrigation canals, roads and bridges, and impressive palaces in Hue (hway), the new capital city. In 1821 a European who had lived in India, Java, and Siam (Thailand) wrote that Hue had a "neatness, magnitude, and perfection" that made other Asian achievements look "like the works of children."[2] Yet construction placed a heavy burden on the peasants drafted to do the work, and it contributed to a resurgence of peasant uprisings.

The French Governor General and the Vietnamese Emperor The twelfth emperor of the Nguyen Dynasty, Khai Dinh (1885–1925) had to find ways to get along with the French governor general (in this picture, Albert Sarraut) if he wished to preserve his dynasty. Seen here in 1917 or 1918, he had adopted Western leather shoes but otherwise tried to keep a distinct Vietnamese identity in his dress. (Roger Viollet/Getty Images)

Roman Catholic missionaries from France posed a second, more dangerous threat to Vietnam's Confucian ruling elite. The king and his advisers believed that Christianity would undermine Confucian moral values and the unity of the Vietnamese state. In 1825 King Minh Mang (r. 1820–1841) outlawed the teaching of Christianity, and soon his government began executing Catholic missionaries and Vietnamese converts. As many as thirty thousand Vietnamese Christians were executed in the 1850s. In response, in 1859–1860 a French naval force seized Saigon and three surrounding provinces in southern Vietnam, making that part of Vietnam a French colony. In 1884–1885 France launched a second war against Vietnam and conquered the rest of the country. Laos and Cambodia were added to form French Indochina in 1887. In all three countries the local rulers were left on their thrones, but France dominated and tried to promote French culture.

After the French conquest, Vietnamese patriots continued to resist the colonial occupiers with a combination of loyalty to Confucian values and intense hatred of foreign rule. After Japan's victory over Russia in 1905 (see page 802), a new generation of nationalists saw Japan as a model for Vietnamese revitalization and freedom. They went to Japan to study and planned for anticolonial revolution in Vietnam.

In all of Southeast Asia, only Siam succeeded in preserving its independence. Siam was sandwiched between the British in Burma and the French in Indochina. Siam's very able King Chulalongkorn (r. 1868–1910) took advantage of this situation to balance the two competitors against each other and to escape the smothering embrace of both. Chulalongkorn had studied Greek and Latin and Western science and kept up with Western news by reading British newspapers from Hong Kong and Singapore. He outlawed slavery and implemented modernizing reforms that centralized the government so that it could more effectively control outlying provinces coveted by the imperialists. Independent Siam gradually developed a modern centralizing state similar to those constructed by Western imperialists in their Asian possessions.

The Philippines

The United States became one of the imperialist powers in Asia when it took the Philippines from Spain in 1898. When the Spanish established rule in the Philippines in the sixteenth century, the islands had no central government or literate culture; order was maintained by village units dominated by local chiefs. Under the Spanish, Roman Catholic churches were established, and Spanish priests able to speak the local languages became the most common intermediaries between local populations, who rarely could speak Spanish, and the new rulers. The government of Spain encouraged Spaniards to colonize the Philippines through the *encomienda* system (see page 477): Spaniards who had served the Crown were rewarded with grants giving them the exclusive right to control public affairs and collect taxes in a specific locality of the Philippines. A local Filipino elite also developed, aided by the Spanish introduction of private ownership of land. Given the great distance between Madrid and Manila, the capital of the Philippines, the local governor general, appointed by Spain, had almost unlimited powers over the courts and the military. Manila developed into an important entrepôt in the galleon trade between Mexico and China, and this trade also attracted a large Chinese community, which handled much of the trade within the Philippines.

Spain did not do much to promote education in the Philippines. In the late nineteenth century, however, wealthy Filipinos began to send their sons to study abroad, and a movement to press Spain for reforms emerged among those who had been abroad. When the Spanish cracked down on critics, a rebellion erupted in 1896 (see "Individuals in Society: José Rizal," page 792). It was settled in 1897 with Spanish promises to reform.

In 1898 war between Spain and the United States broke out in Cuba (see page 825), and in May the American naval officer Commodore George Dewey sailed into Manila Bay and sank the Spanish fleet anchored there. Dewey called on the Philippine rebels to help defeat the Spanish forces, but when the rebels declared independence, the U.S. government refused to recognize them, despite protests by American anti-imperialists. U.S. forces fought the Philippine rebels, and by the end of the insurrection in 1902 the war had cost the lives of 5,000 Americans and about 200,000 Filipinos. In the following years, the United States introduced a form of colonial rule that included public works and economic development projects, improved education and medicine, and in 1907 an elected legislative assembly.

China Under Pressure

☐ Was China's decline in the nineteenth century due more to internal problems or to Western imperialism?

In 1800 most Chinese had no reason to question the conception of China as the central kingdom. No other country had so many people; Chinese products were in great demand in foreign countries; and the borders had recently been expanded. A century later China's world standing had sunk precipitously. In 1900 foreign troops

- **Java War** The 1825–1830 war between the Dutch government and the Javanese, fought over the extension of Dutch control of the island.
- **Nguyen Dynasty** The last Vietnamese ruling house, which lasted from 1802 to 1945.

Individuals in Society

José Rizal

IN THE MID-SEVENTEENTH CENTURY, A CHINESE merchant immigrated to the Philippines and married a woman who was half Chinese, half Philippine. Because of anti-Chinese animosity, he changed his name to Mercado, Spanish for "merchant."

Mercado's direct patrilineal descendant, José Rizal (1861–1896), was born into a well-to-do family that leased a plantation from Dominican friars. Both of his parents were educated, and he was a brilliant student himself. In 1882, after completing his studies at the Jesuit-run college in Manila, he went to Madrid to study medicine. During his ten years in Europe he not only earned a medical degree in Spain and a Ph.D. in Germany but he also found time to learn several European languages and make friends with scientists, writers, and political radicals.

While in Europe, Rizal became involved with Philippine revolutionaries and contributed numerous articles to their newspaper, *La Solidaridad*, published in Barcelona. Rizal advocated making the Philippines a province of Spain, giving it representation in the Spanish parliament, replacing Spanish friars with Filipino priests, and making Filipinos and Spaniards equal before the law. He spent a year at the British Museum doing research on the early phase of the Spanish colonization of the Philippines. He also wrote two novels.

The first novel, written in Spanish, was fired by the passions of nationalism. In satirical fashion, it depicts a young Filipino of mixed blood who studies for several years in Europe before returning to the Philippines to start a modern secular school in his hometown and to marry his childhood sweetheart. The church stands in the way of his efforts, and the colonial administration proves incompetent. The novel ends with the hero being gunned down after the friars falsely implicate him in a revolutionary conspiracy. Rizal's own life ended up following this narrative surprisingly closely.

In 1892 Rizal left Europe, stopped briefly in Hong Kong, and then returned to Manila to help his family with a lawsuit. Though he secured his relatives' release from jail, he ran into trouble himself. Because his writings were critical of the power of the church, he made many enemies, some of whom had him arrested. He was sent into exile to a Jesuit mission town on the relatively primitive island of Mindanao. There he founded a school and a hospital, and the Jesuits tried to win him back to the church. He kept busy during his four years in exile, not only teaching English, science, and self-defense, but also maintaining his correspondence with scientists in Europe. When a nationalist secret society rose in revolt in 1896, Rizal, in an effort to distance himself, volunteered to go to Cuba to help in an outbreak of yellow fever. Although he had no connections with the secret society and was on his way across the ocean, Rizal was arrested and shipped back to Manila.

Tried for sedition by the military, Rizal was found guilty. When handed his death certificate, Rizal struck out the words "Chinese half-breed" and wrote "pure native." He was publicly executed by a firing squad in Manila at age thirty-five, making him a martyr of the nationalist cause.

QUESTIONS FOR ANALYSIS

1. Did Rizal's comfortable family background contribute to his becoming a revolutionary?
2. How would Rizal's European contemporaries have reacted to his opposition to the Catholic Church?

• **After Rizal's death, his portrait was used to inspire patriotism.** (Cover of "The Filipino Teacher," December 1908. Courtesy, Museo Santisima Trinidad)

marched into China's capital to protect foreign nationals, and more and more Chinese had come to think that their government, society, and cultural values needed to be radically changed.

The Opium War

Seeing little to gain from trade with European countries, the Qing (Manchu) emperors, who had been ruling China since 1644 (see pages 626–629), permitted Europeans to trade only at the port of Guangzhou (Canton) and only through licensed Chinese merchants. Initially, the balance of trade was in China's favor. Great Britain and the other Western nations used silver to pay for tea, since they had not been able to find anything that Chinese wanted to buy. By the 1820s, however, the British had found something the Chinese would buy: opium. Grown legally in British-occupied India, opium was smuggled into China, where its use and sale were illegal. Huge profits and the cravings of addicts led to rapid increases in sales, from 4,500 chests a year in 1810 to 10,000 in 1830 and 40,000 in 1838. At this point it was China that suffered a drain of silver, since it was importing more than it was exporting.

To deal with this crisis, the Chinese government dispatched Lin Zexu to Guangzhou in 1839. He dealt harshly with Chinese who purchased opium and seized the opium stores of British merchants. Lin even wrote to Queen Victoria: "Suppose there were people from another country who carried opium for sale to England and seduced your people into buying and smoking it;

> "Suppose there were people from another country who carried opium for sale to England and seduced your people into buying and smoking it; certainly your honorable ruler would deeply hate it and be bitterly aroused."
>
> **LIN ZEXU**

certainly your honorable ruler would deeply hate it and be bitterly aroused."[3] When Lin pressured the Portuguese to expel the uncooperative British from their trading post at Macao, the British settled on the barren island of Hong Kong.

Although for years the little community of foreign merchants had accepted Chinese rules, by 1839 the British, the dominant group, were ready to flex their muscles. British merchants wanted to create a market for their goods in China and get tea more cheaply by trading closer to its source in central China. They also wanted a European-style diplomatic relationship with China, with envoys and ambassadors, commercial treaties, and published tariffs. With the encouragement of their merchants in China, the British sent an expeditionary force from India with forty-two warships, many of them leased from the major opium trader, Jardine, Matheson, and Company.

With its control of the seas, the British easily shut down key Chinese ports and forced the Chinese to negotiate. Dissatisfied with the resulting agreement, the

Treaty of Nanjing The settlement reached by Britain and China in 1842 was written in both English and Chinese. The chief negotiators of both sides signed the document, and the seals of both countries were placed on it. The Chinese seal was impressed with red ink in the traditional way, while the British used wax. (The National Archives, UK)

British sent a second, larger force, which took even more coastal cities, including Shanghai. This **Opium War** was settled at gunpoint in 1842. The resulting treaties opened five ports to international trade, fixed the tariff on imported goods at 5 percent, imposed an indemnity of 21 million ounces of silver on China to cover Britain's war expenses, and ceded the island of Hong Kong to Britain. Through the clause on **extraterritoriality**, British subjects in China became answerable only to British law, even in disputes with Chinese. The treaties also had a "most-favored nation" clause, which meant that whenever one nation extracted a new privilege from China, it was extended automatically to Britain.

The treaties satisfied neither side. China continued to refuse to accept foreign diplomats at its capital in Beijing, and the expansion of trade fell far short of Western expectations. Between 1856 and 1860 Britain and France renewed hostilities with China. Seventeen thousand British and French troops occupied Beijing and set the emperor's summer palace on fire. Another round of harsh treaties gave European merchants and missionaries greater privileges and forced the Chinese to open several more cities to foreign trade. Large areas in some of the treaty ports were leased in perpetuity to foreign powers; these were known as **concessions**.

Internal Problems

China's problems in the nineteenth century were not all of foreign origin. By 1850 China, for centuries the world's most populous country, had more than 400 million people. As the population grew, farm size shrank, forests were put to the plow, and surplus labor suppressed wages. When the best parcels of land were all occupied, conflicts over rights to water and tenancy increased. Hard times also led to increased female infanticide, as families felt that they could not afford to raise more than two or three children and

Chinese Rebellions, 1851–1911

Nanjing
Shanghai
CHINA
Guangzhou
Macao   Hong Kong
(Port.)   (Gr. Br.)

☐ Taiping Rebellion, 1851–1864
☐ Boxer uprising, 1900
■ Revolt of 1911

saw sons as necessities. A shortage of marriageable women resulted, reducing the incentive for young men to stay near home and do as their elders told them. Some became bandits, others boatmen, carters, sedan-chair carriers, and, by the end of the century, rickshaw pullers.

These economic and demographic circumstances led to some of the most destructive rebellions in China's history. The worst was the **Taiping Rebellion** (1851–1864), in which some 20 million people lost their lives, making it one of the bloodiest wars in world history.

The Taiping (TIGH-ping) Rebellion was initiated by Hong Xiuquan (hong show-chwan; 1814–1864), a man from South China who had studied for the civil service examinations but never passed. His career as a religious leader began with visions of an old golden-bearded man and a middle-aged man who addressed him as younger brother and told him to annihilate devils. After reading a Christian tract given to him by a missionary, Hong interpreted his visions to mean he was Jesus's younger brother. He soon gathered followers, whom he instructed to destroy idols and ancestral temples, give up opium and alcohol, and renounce foot binding and prostitution. In 1851 he declared himself king of the Heavenly Kingdom of Great Peace (Taiping), an act of open insurrection.

By 1853 the Taiping rebels, as Hong's followers were known, had moved north and established their capital at the major city of Nanjing, which they held onto for a decade. From this base they set about creating a utopian society based on the equalization of landholdings and the equality of men and women. This utopia required men and women to live separately:

> It is a matter of course that we should attend to our parents and look after our wives and children, but when one first creates a new rule, the state must come first and the family last, public interests first and private interests last. . . . There must be no common mixing of the male and female groups, which would cause debauchery and violation of Heaven's command. Although to pay respects to parents and to visit wives and children occasionally are in keeping with human nature and not prohibited, yet it is only proper to converse before the door, stand a few steps apart and speak in a loud voice; one must not enter the sisters' camp or permit the mixing of men and women. Only thus, by complying with rules and commands, can we become sons and daughters of Heaven.[4]

- **Opium War** The 1839–1842 war between the British and the Chinese over limitations on trade and the importation of opium into China.

- **extraterritoriality** The legal principle that exempts individuals from local law, applicable in China because of the agreements reached after China's loss in the Opium War.

- **concessions** Large areas of Chinese treaty ports that were leased in perpetuity to foreign powers.

- **Taiping Rebellion** A massive rebellion by believers in the religious teachings of Hong Xiuquan, begun in 1851 and not suppressed until 1864.

China's First Railroad Soon after this 15-mile-long railroad was constructed near Shanghai in 1876 by the British firm of Jardine and Matheson, the provincial governor bought it in order to tear it out. Many Chinese of the period saw the introduction of railroads as harmful not only to the balance of nature but also to people's livelihoods, since the railroads eliminated jobs in transport like dragging boats along canals or driving pack horses. (Private Collection)

Christian missionaries quickly concluded that the Christian elements in Taiping doctrines were heretical and did not help the rebels. To suppress the Taipings, the Manchus had to turn to Chinese scholar-officials, who raised armies on their own, revealing that the Manchus were no longer the mighty warriors they had been when they had conquered China two centuries earlier.

The Self-Strengthening Movement

After the various rebellions were suppressed, forward-looking reformers began addressing the Western threat. Under the slogan "self-strengthening," they set about modernizing the military along Western lines, establishing arsenals and dockyards. Recognizing that guns and ships were merely the surface manifestations of the Western powers' economic strength, some of the most progressive reformers also initiated new industries, which in the 1870s and 1880s included railway lines, steam navigation companies, coal mines, telegraph lines, and cotton spinning and weaving factories. These were the same sorts of initiatives that the British were introducing in India, but China lagged behind, especially in railroads.

These measures drew resistance from conservatives, who thought copying Western practices was compounding defeat. The highly placed Manchu official Woren objected that "from ancient down to modern times" there had never been "anyone who could use mathematics to raise a nation from a state of decline or to strengthen it in times of weakness."[5] Yet knowledge of the West gradually improved with more translations and travel in both directions. Newspapers covering world affairs began publication in Shanghai and Hong Kong. By 1880 China had embassies in London, Paris, Berlin, Madrid, Washington, Tokyo, and St. Petersburg.

Despite the enormous effort put into trying to catch up, China was humiliated yet again at the end of the nineteenth century. First came the discovery that Japan had so successfully modernized that it posed a threat to China (see pages 787–802). Then, in 1894 Japanese efforts to separate Korea from Chinese influence led to the brief Sino-Japanese War in which China was decisively defeated even though much of its navy had been purchased abroad at great expense. In the peace negotiations, China ceded Taiwan to Japan, agreed to a huge indemnity (compensation for war expenses), and gave Japan the right to open factories in China. China's helplessness in the face of aggression led to a scramble among the European powers for concessions and protectorates in China. At the high point of this rush in 1898, it appeared that the European powers might actually divide China among themselves, the way they had recently divided Africa.

Republican Revolution

China's humiliating defeat in the Sino-Japanese War in 1895 led to a renewed drive for reform. In 1898 a group of educated young reformers gained access to the twenty-seven-year-old Qing emperor. They warned him of the fate of Poland (divided by the European powers in the eighteenth century; see pages 541–542) and regaled him with the triumphs of the Meiji reformers in Japan. They proposed redesigning China as a

Hong Kong Tailors In 1872 the newspaper *Shenbao* was founded in Shanghai, and in 1884 it added an eight-page weekly pictorial supplement. Influenced by the pictorial press then popular in Europe, it depicted both news and human interest stories, both Chinese and foreign. This scene shows a tailor shop in Hong Kong where Chinese tailors use sewing machines and make women's clothes in current Western styles. To Chinese readers, men making women's clothes and placing them on bamboo forms would have seemed as peculiar as the style of the dresses. (From *Dianshizhai huabao*, a Shanghai picture magazine, 1885 or later)

constitutional monarchy with modern financial and educational systems. For three months the emperor issued a series of reform decrees. But the Manchu establishment and the empress dowager, who had dominated the court for the last quarter century, felt threatened and not only suppressed the reform movement but imprisoned the emperor as well. Hope for reform from the top was dashed.

A period of violent reaction swept the country, reaching its peak in 1900 with the uprising of a secret society that foreigners dubbed the **Boxers**. The Boxers blamed China's ills on foreigners, especially the missionaries who traveled throughout China telling the Chinese that their beliefs were wrong and their customs backward. After the Boxers laid siege to the foreign legation quar-

ter in Beijing, a dozen nations including Japan sent twenty thousand troops to lift the siege. In the negotiations that followed, China had to accept a long list of penalties, including cancellation of the civil service examinations for five years (punishment for gentry collaboration) and a staggering indemnity of 450 million ounces of silver, almost twice the government's annual revenues.

After this defeat, gradual reform lost its appeal. More and more Chinese were studying abroad and learning about Western political ideas, including democracy and revolution. The most famous was Sun Yatsen (1866–1925). Sent by his peasant family to Hawai'i, he learned English and then continued his education in Hong Kong. From 1894 on, he spent his time abroad organizing revolutionary societies and seeking financial support from overseas Chinese. He later joined forces with Chinese student revolutionaries studying in Japan, and together they attempted several times to spark rebellion. The plot that finally triggered the collapse of China's imperial system is known as the **1911 Revolution**. Army officers fearful that their connections to the revolutionaries would be exposed staged a coup and persuaded the provincial governments to secede. The powers behind the child emperor (who had as-

• **Boxers** A Chinese secret society that blamed the country's ills on foreigners, especially missionaries, and rose in rebellion in 1900.

• **1911 Revolution** The uprising that brought China's monarchy to an end.

• **gunboat diplomacy** The imposition of treaties and agreements under threat of military violence, such as the opening of Japan to trade after Commodore Perry's demands.

• **Meiji Restoration** The 1867 ousting of the Tokugawa Shogunate that "restored" the power of the Japanese emperors.

cended to the throne at the age of three in 1908) agreed to his abdication, and at the beginning of 1912 China's long history of monarchy came to an end, to be replaced by a republic modeled on Western political ideas. China had escaped direct foreign rule but would never be the same.

Japan's Rapid Transformation

☐ How was Japan able to quickly master the challenges posed by the West?

During the nineteenth century, while China's standing in the world plummeted, Japan's was rising. European traders and missionaries first arrived in Japan in the sixteenth century, but in the early seventeenth century, in part because of the remarkable success of Catholic missionaries (see pages 644–645), the Japanese government expelled them. During the eighteenth century Japan much more effectively than China kept foreign merchants and missionaries at bay. It limited trade to a single port (Nagasaki), where only the Dutch were allowed, and forbade Japanese to travel abroad. Because Japan's land and population were so much smaller than China's, the Western powers never expected much from Japan as a trading partner and did not press it as urgently. Still, the European threat was part of what propelled Japan to modernize.

The "Opening" of Japan

Wanting to play a greater role in the Pacific, the United States decided to force the Japanese to share their ports and behave as a "civilized" nation. In 1853 Commodore Matthew Perry steamed into Edo (now Tokyo) Bay and demanded diplomatic negotiations with the emperor. Some Japanese samurai (members of the warrior class) urged resistance, but senior officials knew what had happened in China and how defenseless their cities would be against naval bombardment. Under threat of **gunboat diplomacy**, and after consulting with the daimyo (major lords), the officials signed a treaty with the United States that opened two ports and permitted trade.

Japan at this time was a complex society. The emperor in Kyoto had no effective powers. For more than two hundred years real power had been in the hands of the Tokugawa shogun in Edo (see pages 631–632). The country was divided into numerous domains, each under a daimyo. Each daimyo had under him samurai, who had hereditary stipends and privileges, such as the right to wear a sword. Peasants and merchants were also le-

gally distinct classes, and in theory social mobility from peasant to merchant or merchant to samurai was impossible. After two centuries of peace, there were many more samurai than were needed to administer or defend the country, and many lived very modestly. They were proud, however, and felt humiliated by the sudden American intrusion and the unequal treaties that the Western countries imposed. Some began agitating against the shogunate under the slogan "Revere the emperor and expel the barbarians."

When foreign diplomats and merchants began to settle in Yokohama after 1858, radical samurai reacted with a wave of antiforeign terrorism and antigovernment assassinations. The Western response was swift and unambiguous. Much as the Western powers had sent troops to Beijing a few years before, they now sent an allied fleet of American, British, Dutch, and French warships to demolish key Japanese forts, further weakening the power and prestige of the shogun's government.

The Meiji Restoration

In 1867 a coalition of reform-minded daimyo led a coup that ousted the Tokugawa Shogunate. The samurai who led this coup declared a return to direct rule by the emperor, not practiced in Japan for more than six hundred years. This emperor was called the Meiji (MAY-jee) emperor and this event the **Meiji Restoration**, a great turning point in Japanese history.

The domain leaders who organized the coup, called the Meiji Oligarchs, moved the boy emperor to Tokyo castle (previously the seat of the shogun, now the imperial palace). They used the young sovereign to win over both the lords and the commoners. During the emperor's first decade on the throne, the leaders carried him around in hundreds of grand imperial processions so that he could see his subjects and they him. The emerging press also worked to keep its readers informed of the young emperor's actions and their obligations to him. Real power remained in the hands of the oligarchs.

The battle cry of the Meiji reformers had been "strong army, rich nation." How were these goals to be accomplished? In an about-face that is one of history's most remarkable chapters, the determined but flexible leaders of Meiji Japan dropped their antiforeign attacks. Convinced that they could not beat the West until they had mastered the secrets of its military and industrial might, they initiated a series of measures to reform Japan along modern Western lines. One reformer even proposed that "Japan must be reborn with America its mother and France its father."[6] In 1868 an imperial declaration promised that "Deliberative assemblies shall be widely established and all matters decided by public discussion" and that "Knowledge shall

Japan's Modernized Army A set of woodblock prints depicting the new sights of Tokyo included this illustration of a military parade ground. The soldiers' brightly colored Western-style uniforms undoubtedly helped make this a sight worth seeing. (Laurie Platt Winfrey/ The Granger Collection, New York)

First the samurai's stipends were reduced; then in 1876 the stipends were replaced by one-time grants of income-bearing bonds. Most samurai had to find work or start businesses, as the value of the bonds declined with inflation. Furthermore, samurai no longer were to wear their swords, long the symbols of their status. Even their monopoly on the use of force was eliminated: the new army recruited commoners along with samurai. Not surprisingly, some samurai rose up against their loss of privileges. In one extreme case, the rebels refused to use guns in a futile effort to retain the mystique of the sword. None of these uncoordinated uprisings made any difference.

Several leaders of the Meiji Restoration, in France on a fact-finding mission during the Franco-Prussian War of 1870–1871, were impressed by the active participation of French citizens in the defense of Paris. This contrasted with the indifference of most Japanese peasants during the battles that led to the Meiji Restoration. For Japan to survive in the hostile international environment, they concluded, ordinary people had to be trained to fight. Consequently, a conscription law, modeled on the French law, was issued in 1872. Like French law, it exempted first sons. To improve the training of soldiers, the new War College was organized along German lines, and German instructors were recruited to teach there. Young samurai were trained to form the new professional officer corps. The success of this approach was demonstrated first in 1877, when the professionally led army of draftees crushed a major rebellion by samurai.

Many of the new institutions established in the Meiji period reached down to the local level. Schools open to all were rapidly introduced after 1872. Teachers were trained in newly established teachers' colleges, where they learned to inculcate discipline, patriotism, and morality. Another modern institution that reached the local level was a national police force. In 1884 police training schools were established in every prefecture, and within a few years one- or two-man police stations were set up throughout the country. These policemen came to act as local agents of the central government. They not only dealt with crime but also enforced public health rules, conscription laws, and codes of behavior.

In time these new laws and institutions brought benefits, but at the local level they were often perceived as oppressive. Protests became very common against everything from conscription and the Western calendar to the new taxes to pay for the new schools.

In 1889 Japan became the first non-Western country to adopt the constitutional form of government. Prefectural assemblies, set up in the 1870s and 1880s, gave local elites some experience in debating political issues. The constitution, however, was handed down from above, drafted by the top political leaders and issued in the name of the emperor. A commission sent abroad to study European constitutional governments had come

be sought throughout the world so as to strengthen the foundations of imperial rule."[7] Within four years a delegation was traveling the world to learn what made the Western powers strong. Its members examined everything from the U.S. Constitution to the factories, shipyards, and railroads that made the European landscape so different from Japan's.

Japan under the shoguns had been decentralized, with most of the power over the population in the hands of the daimyos. By elevating the emperor, the oligarchs were able to centralize the government. In 1871 they abolished the domains and merged the domain armies. Following the example of the French Revolution, they dismantled the four-class legal system and declared everyone equal. This amounted to stripping the samurai (7 to 8 percent of the population) of their privileges.

to the conclusion that the German constitutional monarchy would provide the best model for Japan, rather than the more democratic governments of the British, French, and Americans. Japan's new government had a two-house parliament, called the Diet. The upper house of lords was drawn largely from former daimyo and nobles, and the lower house was elected by a limited electorate (about 5 percent of the adult male population in 1890). Although Japan now had a government based on laws, it was authoritarian rather than democratic. The emperor was declared "sacred and inviolable." He had the right to appoint the prime minister and cabinet. He did not have to ask the Diet for funds because wealth assigned to the imperial house was entrusted to the Imperial Household Ministry, which was outside the government's control.

Cultural change during the Meiji period was as profound as political change. For more than a thousand years China had been the major source of ideas and technologies introduced into Japan, ranging from the writing system to Confucianism and Buddhism, tea and silk, chopsticks and soy sauce. But in the late nineteenth century China, beset by Western pressure, had become an object lesson on the dangers of stagnation rather than a model to follow. The influential author Fukuzawa Yukichi began urging Japan to pursue "civilization and enlightenment," by which he meant Western civilization. (See "Listening to the Past: Fukuzawa Yukichi, Escape from Asia," page 800.) Fukuzawa advocated learning Western languages and encouraged Japan to learn from the West in order to catch up with it. Soon Japanese were being told to conform to Western taste, eat meat, wear Western-style clothes, and drop customs that Westerners found odd, such as married women blackening their teeth.

□ Picturing the Past

Japan's First Skyscraper Meiji Japan's fascination with things Western led to the construction of Western-style buildings. Japan's first elevator made possible this twelve-story tower built in Tokyo in 1890. Situated in the entertainment district, it was filled with shops, theaters, bars, and restaurants. (Edo-Tokyo Museum. Image: TNM Image Archives/Tokyo Metropolitan Foundation for History and Culture Image Archives)

ANALYZING THE IMAGE Locate all the people in this picture. How are they dressed? What are they doing?

CONNECTIONS Keeping in mind that the building in this picture was built in 1890, what connections would you draw between the politics of the period and this visual celebration of a new style of architecture?

Industrialization

The leaders of the Meiji Restoration, wanting to strengthen Japan's military capacity, promoted industrialization. The government paid large salaries to attract foreign experts to help with industrialization, and Japanese were encouraged to go abroad to study science and engineering.

Listening to the Past

Fukuzawa Yukichi, Escape from Asia

Fukuzawa Yukichi was one of the most prominent intellectuals and promoters of westernization in Meiji Japan. His views on domestic policy were decidedly liberal, but he took a hard-line approach to foreign affairs. His ruthless criticism of Korea and China published on March 16, 1885, can be read as inviting colonialism. In 1895, ten years after writing this call to action, he rejoiced at Japan's victory over China in their conflict over Korea.

"Civilization is like an epidemic of measles. The current measles in Tokyo, which has advanced eastwards from Nagasaki in western Japan, seems to have begun to claim more victims with the arrival of springtime. Will we be able now to find a means of checking this epidemic? It is obvious that we have no way to do so. We cannot put up effective resistance, even against an epidemic that carries with it only harm; much less against civilization, which is always accompanied by both harm and good, but by more good than harm.

Though our land of Japan is situated on the Eastern edge of Asia, the spirit of its people has already shaken off the backwardness of Asia to accept the civilization of the West. Unfortunately, however, we have two neighboring countries, one being called China, the other called Korea. The people of these two countries are no different from us Japanese people in having been brought up since olden times in the Asian culture and customs, and yet, whether because they are of another racial origin, or because, while similar in culture and customs, differ from us in the main lines of their traditional education, a comparison of the three countries, Japan, China, and Korea, reveals that the latter two resemble each other more closely than they do Japan. The people of those two countries do not know how to go about reforming and making progress, whether individually or as a country. It is not that they have not seen or heard of civilized things in the present world of facile communication; yet what their eyes and ears perceive have failed to stimulate their minds, and their emotional attachment to ancient manners and customs has changed little for the past hundreds and thousands of years. In this lively theater of civilization, where things change daily, they still speak of education in terms of Confucianism, cite humanity, justice, civility, and wisdom as their principles of school education, are completely obsessed only with outward appearance, are in reality not only ignorant of truths and principles but so extreme in their cruelty and shamelessness that for them morality is completely nonexistent, and yet are as arrogant as if they never gave a thought to self-examination.

In our view, these countries have no likelihood of maintaining their independence in the current tide of civilization's eastward advance. Let there not be the slightest doubt that, unless they are fortunate enough to have motivated men appear in their lands who, as a first step to improve the condition of their countries will plan such a great enterprise of overall reform of their governments as our Restoration was, and succeed in altering their people's minds through political reforms, those countries will meet their doom in but a few years, with their territories divided among the civilized countries of the world. The reason is that China and Korea, confronted by an epidemic of civilization comparable to measles, are impossibly trying to ward it off, despite its inevitability, by shutting themselves up in a room, with the result being that they are cutting off their supply of fresh air and asphyxiating themselves. Though mutual help

The government played an active role in getting railroads, mines, and factories started. Japan's coal mines had produced only 390,000 tons in 1860, but by 1900 this output had risen to 5 million tons. Early on the Japanese government decided to compete with China in the export of tea and silk to the West. Introducing the mechanical reeling of silk gave Japan a strong price advantage in the sale of silk, and Japan's total foreign trade increased tenfold from 1877 to 1900. The next stage was to develop heavy industry. The huge indemnity exacted from China in 1895 was used to establish the Yawata Iron and Steel Works. The third stage of Japan's industrialization would today be called import substitution. Factories such as cotton mills were set up to help cut the importation of Western consumer goods. By 1912 factory output accounted for 13 percent of the national product, even though only 3 percent of the labor force worked in factories, mostly small ones with fewer than fifty workers.

Most of the great Japanese industrial conglomerates known as *zaibatsu* (zigh-BAHT-dzoo), such as Mitsubishi, got their start in this period, often founded by men with government connections. Sometimes the government set up plants that it then sold to private investors at bargain prices. Successful entrepreneurs were treated as patriotic heroes.

As in Europe, the early stages of industrialization brought hardship to the countryside. Farmers often ribetween neighboring countries has been likened to the relationship between the lips and the teeth, China and Korea of today cannot be of any assistance at all to our country of Japan.

Civilized western man is not without a tendency to regard all three countries as identical because of their geographic proximity and to apply his evaluation of China and Korea to Japan also. For example, when he finds that the governments of China and Korea are old-fashioned autocracies without abiding laws, the western man will suppose Japan too to be a lawless country. When he finds that the gentlemen of China and Korea are too deeply infatuated to know what science is, the western scholar will think that Japan too is a land of Yin-Yang and the Five Elements. When the Chinese display their servility and shamelessness, they obscure the chivalrous spirit of the Japanese. When the Koreans employ cruel means of physical punishment, the Japanese too are surmised to be just as inhuman. Such examples are too numerous to count. This may be compared to the case in which most of those in a string of houses within a village or town are foolish, lawless, cruel, and inhuman; an occasional family that heeds what is just and right will be eclipsed by the other's evil and its virtue will never be noticed. It is indeed not infrequent that something similar happens in our foreign relations and indirectly interferes with them. This should be regarded a great misfortune for our country of Japan.

To plan our course now, therefore, our country cannot afford to wait for the enlightenment of our neighbors and to cooperate in building Asia up. Rather, we should leave their ranks to join the camp of the civilized countries of the West. Even when dealing with China and Korea, we need not have special scruples simply because they are our neighbors, but should behave toward them as the westerners do. One who befriends an evil person cannot avoid being involved in his notoriety. In spirit, then, we break with our evil friends of Eastern Asia. "

Source: Centre for East Asian Cultural Studies, comp., *Meiji Japan Through Contemporary Sources*, Vol. 3, 1869–1894 (Tokyo: Centre for East Asian Cultural Studies, 1972), pp. 129–133, modified.

Fukuzawa Yukichi. (Fukuzawa Memorial Center for Modern Japanese Studies, Keio University)

QUESTIONS FOR ANALYSIS

1. What does Fukuzawa mean by "civilization"?
2. How does Fukuzawa's justification of colonialism compare to Europeans' justification of it during the same period?

oted as their incomes failed to keep up with prices or as their tax burdens grew. Workers in modern industries were no happier, and in 1898 railroad workers went on strike for better working conditions and overtime pay. Still, rice production increased, death rates dropped as public health was improved, and the population grew from about 33 million in 1868 to about 45 million in 1900.

Japan as an Imperial Power

During the course of the Meiji period, Japan became an imperial power, making Taiwan and Korea into its colonies. Taiwan had been a part of China for two centuries; Korea had been an independent country with a unified government since 668. The conflicts that led to Japanese acquisition of both of them revolved around Korea.

The Choson Dynasty had been on the throne in Korea since 1392. Chinese influence had grown over this period as the Korean elite enthusiastically embraced Confucian teachings and studied for Chinese-style civil service examinations. In the second half of the nineteenth century Korea found itself caught between China, Japan, and Russia, each trying to protect or extend its sphere of influence. Westerners also began demanding that Korea be "opened." Korea's first response was to insist that its foreign relations be handled through Beijing. Matters were complicated by the rise in the 1860s of a religious cult, the Tonghak movement, that had strong xenophobic elements. Although the government executed the cult founder in 1864, this cult continued to gain support, especially among impoverished peasants. Thus, like China in the same period, the Korean government faced simultaneous internal and external threats.

In 1871 the U.S. minister to China took five warships to try to open Korea, but left after exchanges of fire resulted in 250 Koreans dead without any progress in getting the Korean government to make concessions. Japan tried next and in 1876 forced the Korean government to sign an unequal treaty and open three ports to Japanese trade. On China's urging, Korea also signed treaties with the European powers in an effort to counterbalance Japan.

Over the next couple of decades reformers in China and Japan tried to encourage Korea to adopt its own self-strengthening movement, but Korean conservatives, including the queen (serving as regent for the child king), did their best to undo reform efforts. In 1894, when the religious cult rose in a massive revolt, both China and Japan sent military forces, claiming to come to the Korean government's aid. They ended up fighting each other instead in what is known as the Sino-Japanese War (see page 795). With Japan's decisive victory, it gained Taiwan from China and was able to make Korea a protectorate. Japan also arranged the assassination of the Korean queen in 1895.

As already noted, five years later Japan participated with the European powers in occupying Beijing to suppress the Boxer Rebellion. In this period Japan was competing aggressively with the leading European powers for influence and territory in China, particularly in the northeast (Manchuria). There Japanese and Russian imperialism met and collided. In 1904 Japan attacked Russian forces and, after its 1905 victory in the bloody **Russo-Japanese War**, emerged with a valuable foothold in China—Russia's former protectorate over Port Arthur (see Map 26.1).

Japan also steadily gained more control over Korea. In 1907, when the Korean king proved less than fully compliant, the Japanese forced him to abdicate in favor of his feeble-minded son. Korean resistance to Japan's actions was suppressed in bloody fighting, and in 1910 Korea was formally annexed as a province of Japan.

Japanese Expansion, 1875–1914

RUSSIA

MANCHURIA

Sea of Japan

JAPAN

KOREA

Tokyo
Yokohama

Nagasaki

PACIFIC OCEAN

CHINA

Ryukyu Is.

Taiwan

■ Japan in 1875
□ Territory acquired by 1910
□ Sphere of Japanese influence

Japan's victories over China and Russia changed the way European nations looked at Japan. Through negotiations Japan was able to eliminate extraterritoriality in 1899 and gain control of its own tariffs in 1911. Within Japan, the success of the military in raising Japan's international reputation added greatly to its political influence.

The Movement of Peoples

☐ Why did people move much more in this period, and where did they go?

The nineteenth century was marked by extensive movement of people into, across, and out of Asia. In no earlier period had so many Europeans lived in Asia or so many Asians taken up residence in other countries. This vast migration both resulted from and helped accelerate the increasing integration of the world economy (see pages 773–775). Crossing oceans became faster and safer with the digging of the Suez and Panama Canals, which greatly shortened journeys. Foreigners had died at a high rate in tropical zones because of diseases they were not immune to; in the nineteenth century the survival rate improved as doctors found new treatments. Knowledge of foreign cultures improved. More and more people studied foreign languages. Translations of works from Western to Asian languages and vice versa made knowledge of other cultures easier to acquire, at least for the literate.

Westerners to Asia

Imperialism brought Europeans to Asia in unprecedented numbers. By the early 1900s significant expatriate communities of European and American businessmen, missionaries, and colonial civil servants had formed in most Asian countries—the largest in India. By 1863 there were already sixty-five thousand British troops in India and many more British in the civil service and commercial companies. Especially after the opening of the Suez Canal in 1869, British working in India were accompanied by their wives and children, who would return to Britain every few years on leave. By the eve of World War I, hundreds of thousands of expatriates lived in India, many since birth.

Beginning in 1809 British recruits to the British East India Company and subsequently to the Indian Civil Service were required to learn at least one Indian language fluently, but that did not mean that they mixed freely with Indians. The trend, especially after the Great Revolt of 1857 (see page 785), was for the British to live

MAP 26.2 Emigration Out of Asia, 1820–1914 As steamships made crossing oceans quicker and more reliable, many people in Asia left their home countries to find new opportunities elsewhere. European imperialism contributed to this flow, especially by recruiting workers for newly established plantations or mines. Many emigrants simply wanted to work a few years to build their savings and planned to return home. Often, however, they ended up staying in their new countries and forming families there.

separately from the Indians in their own enclaves. The Indian servants who tended colonists' houses and grounds, minded their children, and did their shopping handled most of colonists' dealings with local Indians. British residents who were curious about India and wanted to make Indian friends found social intercourse difficult, especially with Muslims and higher-caste Hindus, whose social contact with outsiders was restricted by traditional rules.

China was not under colonial occupation and so did not have as many foreign civil servants and soldiers in its cities, but it did attract more missionaries than any other Asian country. After 1860, when China agreed to allow missionaries to proselytize throughout the country, missionaries came in large numbers. Unlike the British civil servants in India, missionaries had no choice but to mix with the local population, finding the best opportunities for conversion among ordinary poor Chinese. Although most missionaries devoted them-

selves to preaching, over the course of the nineteenth century more and more worked in medicine and education. By 1905 about 300 fully qualified physicians were doing medical missionary work, and 250 mission hospitals and dispensaries served about 2 million patients. Missionary hospitals in Hong Kong also ran a medical school, which trained hundreds of Chinese as physicians.

Missionaries helped spread Western learning at their schools. For their elementary schools, missionaries produced textbooks in Chinese on a full range of subjects. They also translated dozens of standard works into Chinese, especially in the natural sciences, mathematics, history, and international law. By 1906 nearly 60,000 Chinese students were attending 2,400

Russo-Japanese War The 1904–1905 war between Russia and Japan fought over imperial influence and territory in northeast China (Manchuria).

Christian schools. Most of this activity was supported by contributions sent from America and Britain.

Missionaries in China had more success in spreading Western learning than in gaining converts. By 1900 fewer than a million Chinese were Christians. Ironically, although Western missionaries paid much less attention to Korea—the first missionary arrived there in 1884—Christianity took much stronger root there, and today about 25 percent of the Korean population is Christian. Catholic missionaries also had some success in Vietnam after the French occupied the country and extended protection to them.

Asian Emigration

In the nineteenth century Asians, like Europeans, left their native countries in unprecedented numbers (Map 26.2). As in Europe, both push and pull factors prompted people to leave home. Between 1750 and 1900 world population grew rapidly, in many places tripling. China and India were extremely densely populated countries—China with more than 400 million people in the mid-nineteenth century, India with more than 200 million. Not surprisingly, these two giants were the leading exporters of people in search of work or land. On the pull side were the new opportunities created by the flow of development capital into previously underdeveloped areas. In many of the European colonies in Asia and Africa the business class came to consist of both Asian and European migrants, the Asians protected and tolerated by the Western imperialists who found them useful. Asian diasporas formed in many parts of the world, with the majority in Asia itself, especially Southeast Asia.

For centuries people had emigrated from China in search of new opportunities. Chinese from the southern coastal regions came to form key components of mercantile communities throughout Southeast Asia, from Siam south to Java and east to the Philippines. Chinese often assimilated in Siam and Vietnam, but they rarely did so in Muslim areas such as Java, Catholic areas such as the Philippines, and primitive tribal areas such as northern Borneo. In these places, distinct Chinese communities emerged, usually dominated by speakers of a single Chinese dialect.

With the growth in trade that accompanied the European expansion, Chinese began to settle in the islands of Southeast Asia in larger numbers. After Singapore was founded by the British in 1819, Chinese rapidly poured in, soon to become the dominant ethnic group. In British-controlled Malaya, some Chinese built great fortunes in the tin business, while others worked in the mines. There the Chinese community included old overseas families, Malay speakers who had long lived in the Portuguese city of Malacca, and a much larger number of more recent immigrants, most of whom spoke Cantonese. Chinese also settled in the Spanish-controlled Philippines and in Dutch-controlled Indonesia, but there they suffered repeated persecutions. In Borneo early in the nineteenth century, the Dutch expropriated the mines that the Chinese had worked for generations. Elsewhere, however, the Dutch made use of the Chinese. In Java, for instance, Chinese merchants were used as tax collectors. Moreover, after the Dutch conquered southern Sumatra in 1864, Chinese were recruited to work in the sugar and tobacco plantations. By 1900 more than five hundred thousand Chinese were living in the Dutch East Indies.

Discovery of gold in California in 1848, Australia in 1851, and Canada in 1858 encouraged Chinese to book passage to those places (see Chapter 27). In California few arrived soon enough to strike gold, but they soon found other work. Thousands laid railroad tracks, and others took up mining in Wyoming and Idaho. In 1880 more than a hundred thousand Chinese men and three thousand Chinese women were living in the western United States.

Indian entrepreneurs were attracted by the burgeoning commerce of Southeast Asia, though not in quite as large numbers as the Chinese. Indians also moved outside Asia, especially to areas under British control. The bulk of Indian emigrants were **indentured laborers**, recruited under contract. The rise of indentured labor from Asia was a direct result of the outlawing of the African slave trade in the early nineteenth century by Britain and the United States. Sugar plantations in the Caribbean and elsewhere needed new sources of workers, and planters in the British colonies discovered that they could recruit Indian laborers to replace blacks. By 1870 more than half a million Indians had migrated to Mauritius (in the southern Indian Ocean, east of Madagascar) and to the British Caribbean, especially Trinidad. After the French abolished slavery in 1848, they recruited workers from India as well, with nearly eighty thousand Indians making the trip to the French Caribbean over the next half century. Later in the century, many Indians emigrated to British colonies in Africa, the largest numbers to South Africa. Indentured Indian laborers built the railroad in East Africa. Malaya, Singapore, and Fiji also received many emigrants from India.

Indentured laborers secured as substitutes for slaves were often treated little better than slaves both on the ships that delivered them and on the plantations and in the mines where they worked. After abuses of this sort were exposed, the Indian colonial government established regulations stipulating a maximum indenture period of five years, after which the migrant would be entitled to passage home. Even though government "protectors" were appointed at the ports of embarka-

Canadian Immigration Certificate This certificate proved that the eleven-year-old boy in the photograph had a legal right to be in Canada, as the $500 head tax required for immigration of Chinese had been paid. The head tax on Chinese immigrants introduced in 1885 started at $50, but it was raised to $100 in 1900 and to $500 in 1903. Equal to about what a laborer could earn in two years, the tax succeeded in its goal of slowing the rate of Asian immigration to Canada. (Library and Archives Canada)

tion, exploitation of indentured workers continued largely unchecked. Still, many of the migrants stayed on after their indenture.

In areas outside the British Empire, China offered the largest supply of ready labor. Starting in the 1840s contractors arrived at Chinese ports to recruit labor for plantations and mines in Cuba, Peru, Hawai'i, Sumatra, South Africa, and elsewhere. In the 1840s, for example, the Spanish government actively recruited Chinese laborers for the plantations of Cuba. These workers were placed under eight-year contracts, were paid about twenty-five cents a day, and were fed potatoes and salted beef. Between 1853 and 1873 more than 130,000 Chinese laborers went to Cuba, the majority spending their lives as virtual slaves.

Chinese laborers did not have the British government to protect them and seem to have suffered even more than Indian workers. Some of the worst abuses were in Peru, where nearly a hundred thousand Chinese had arrived by 1875, lured by promoters who prom-

ised them easy riches. Instead, they were set to laying railroad tracks or working on cotton plantations or in dangerous guano pits. Those who tried to flee were forced to work in chains.

India and China sent more people abroad than any other Asian countries during this period, but they were not alone. As Japan started to industrialize, its cities could not absorb all those forced off the farms, and people began emigrating in significant numbers, many to Hawai'i and later to South America. Emigration from the Philippines also was substantial, especially after it became a U.S. territory in 1898.

Asian migration to the United States, Canada, and Australia—the primary destinations of European emigrants—would undoubtedly have been greater if it had not been so vigorously resisted by the white settlers in those regions. On the West Coast of the

• **indentured laborers** Laborers who in exchange for passage agreed to work for a number of years, specified in a contract.

> "Passive resistance is a method of securing rights by personal suffering; it is the reverse of resistance by arms."
>
> **MOHANDAS GANDHI**

The Countries of Asia in Comparative Perspective

☐ What explains the similarities and differences in the experiences of Asian countries in this era?

United States, friction between Chinese and white settlers was fed by racist rhetoric that depicted Chinese as opium-smoking heathens. In 1882 Chinese were barred from becoming American citizens, and the immigration of Chinese laborers was suspended. In 1888 President Grover Cleveland declared the Chinese "impossible of assimilation with our people, and dangerous to our peace and welfare."[8]

Most of the Asian migrants discussed so far were illiterate peasants or business people, not members of traditional educated elites. By the beginning of the twentieth century, however, another group of Asians was going abroad in significant numbers: students. Indians and others in the British colonies usually went to Britain, Vietnamese and others in the French colonies to France, and so on. Chinese eager to master modern learning most commonly went to Japan, but others went to Europe and the United States, as did Japanese students. Most of these students traveled abroad to learn about Western science, law, and government in the hope of strengthening their own countries. On their return they contributed enormously to the intellectual life of their societies, increasing understanding of the modern Western world and also becoming the most vocal advocates of overthrowing the old order and driving out the colonial masters.

Among the most notable of these foreign-educated radicals were Mohandas Gandhi (1869–1948) and Sun Yatsen (see page 796). Sun developed his ideas about the republican form of government while studying in Hawai'i and Hong Kong. Gandhi, after studying law in Britain, took a job in South Africa, where he became involved in trying to defend the interests of the Indians who lived and worked there. He started a periodical, *Indian Opinion*, in which he gradually elaborated his idea of passive resistance. In 1909 he wrote:

> Passive resistance is a method of securing rights by personal suffering; it is the reverse of resistance by arms. When I refuse to do a thing that is repugnant to my conscience, I use soul-force. For instance, the Government of the day has passed a law which is applicable to me. I do not like it. If by using violence I force the Government to repeal the law, I am employing what may be termed body-force. If I do not obey the law and accept the penalty for its breach, I use soul-force. It involves sacrifice of self.[9]

The European concept of Asia encourages us to see commonalities among the countries from India east. Although to Westerners it may seem natural to think about Japan and Indonesia as part of the same region, the world looked very different from the perspective of the peoples of these countries. The concept of Asia is handy, but we should be careful not to let it keep us from recognizing the very real differences in the historical experiences of the countries we label "Asian."

At the start of the nineteenth century the societies in this region varied much more than those of any other part of the world. In the temperate zones of East Asia the old established monarchies of China, Japan, and Korea were all densely populated and boasted long literary traditions and traditions of unified governments. They had ties to each other that dated back many centuries and shared many elements of their cultures. South of them, in the tropical and subtropical regions, cultures were more diverse. India was just as densely populated as China, Japan, and Korea, but politically and culturally less unified, with several major languages and dozens of independent rulers reigning in kingdoms large and small, not to mention the growing British presence. In both India and Southeast Asia, Islam was much more important than it was in East Asia, although there was a relatively small Muslim minority in China. All of the countries with long written histories and literate elites were at a great remove from the thinly populated and relatively primitive areas without literate cultures and sometimes even without agriculture, such as some of the islands of the Philippines and Indonesia.

The nineteenth century gave the societies of Asia more in common in that all of them in one way or another had come into contact with the expanding West (an experience that linked them to societies across the Middle East, Africa, and Latin America as well). Still, the Western powers did not treat all of the countries the same way. Western powers initially wanted manufactured goods such as Indian cotton textiles and Chinese porcelains from the more developed Asian societies. At the beginning of the nineteenth century Britain had already gained political control over large parts of India and was intent on forcing China to trade on terms more to its benefit. It paid virtually no attention to Korea and Japan, not seeing in them the same potential for profit. The less developed parts of Asia also attracted increasing Western interest, not because they could provide manufactured goods, but because they offered opportunities for Western development, much as the Americas had earlier.

The West that the societies of Asia faced during the nineteenth century was itself rapidly changing, and the steps taken by Western nations to gain power in Asia naturally also changed over time. Western science and technology were making rapid advances, which gave European armies progressively greater advantages in weaponry. The Industrial Revolution made it possible for countries that industrialized early, such as Britain, to produce huge surpluses of goods for which they had to find markets, shifting their interest in Asia from a place to buy goods to a place to sell goods. Britain had been able to profit from its colonization of India, and this profit both encouraged it to consolidate its rule and invited its European rivals to look for their own colonies. For instance, rivalry with Britain led France to seek colonies in Southeast Asia not only for its own sake but also as a way to keep Britain from extending its sphere of influence any farther.

There were some commonalities in the ways Asian countries responded to pressure from outside. In the countries with long literary traditions, often the initial response of the established elite was to try to drive the unwelcome foreigners away. This was the case in China, Japan, and Korea in particular. Violent antiforeign re-actions exploded again and again, but the superior military technology of the industrialized West almost invariably prevailed. After suffering humiliating defeats, some Asian leaders insisted on the need to preserve their cultural traditions at all costs. Others came to the opposite conclusion that the West was indeed superior in some ways and that they would have to adopt European ideas or techniques for their own purposes. This can be seen both among Indians who acquired education in English and in many of the Meiji reformers in Japan. The struggles between the traditionalists and the westernizers were often intense. As nationalism took hold in the West, it found a receptive audience among the educated elites in Asia. How could the assertion that every people had the right to control its own destiny not appeal to the colonized?

Whether they were colonized or not, most countries in Asia witnessed the spread of new technologies between 1800 and 1914. Railroads, telegraphs, modern sanitation, and a wider supply of inexpensive manufactured goods brought fundamental changes in everyday life not only to lands under colonial rule, such as India and Vietnam, but also, if less rapidly, to places that managed to remain independent, such as China and Japan. In fact, the transformation of Japan between 1860 and 1900 was extraordinary. By 1914 Japan had urban conveniences and educational levels comparable to those in Europe.

CONNECTIONS

The nineteenth century brought Asia change on a much greater scale than did any earlier century. Much of the change was political — old political orders were ousted or reduced to tokens by new masters, often European colonial powers. Old elites found themselves at a loss when confronted by the European powers with their modern weaponry and modern armies. Cultural change was no less dramatic as the old elites pondered the differences between their traditional values and the ideas that seemed to underlie the power of the European states. In several places ordinary people rose in rebellion, probably in part because they felt threatened by the speed of cultural change. Material culture underwent major changes as elites experimented with Western dress and architecture and ordinary people had opportunities to travel on newly built railroads. Steamships, too, made long-distance travel easier, facilitating the out-migration of people seeking economic opportunities far from their countries of birth.

In the Americas, too, the nineteenth century was an era of unprecedented change and movement of people. Colonial empires were being overturned there, not imposed as they were in Asia in the same period. Another sharp contrast is that the Americas and Australia (discussed in the next chapter) were on the receiving end of the huge migrations taking place, while Asia, like Europe, was much more an exporter of people. The Industrial Revolution brought change to all these areas, though in the old countries of Asia the negative effects of this revolution were more often felt as traditional means of making a living disappeared. Intellectually, in both Asia and the Americas the ideas of nationalism and nation building shaped how people, especially the more educated, thought about the changes they were experiencing.

◻ CHAPTER REVIEW

◻ **In what ways did India change as a consequence of British rule? (p. 784)**

In the nineteenth century Britain extended its rule to all of India, though often the British ruled indirectly through local princes. Britain brought many modern advances to India, such as railroads and schools. Slavery was outlawed, as was widow suicide and infanticide. Resistance to British rule took several forms. In 1857 Indian soldiers in the employ of the British rose in a huge revolt, and after Britain put down this rebellion it ruled India much more tightly. Indians who received English education turned English ideas of liberty and representative rule against the British and founded the Indian National Congress, which called for Indian independence.

◻ **Why were most but not all Southeast Asian societies reduced to colonies? (p. 790)**

By the end of the nineteenth century most Southeast Asian countries, from Burma to the Philippines, had been made colonies of Western powers, which developed them as exporters of agricultural products or raw materials including rubber, tin, sugar, tea, cotton, and jute. The principal exception was Siam (Thailand), whose king was able to play the English and French off against each other and institute centralizing reforms. In the Philippines more than three centuries of Spanish rule came to an end in 1898, but Spain was only replaced by another colonial power: the United States.

◻ **Was China's decline in the nineteenth century due more to internal problems or to Western imperialism? (p. 791)**

In the nineteenth century China's world standing declined as a result of both foreign intervention and internal unrest. The government's efforts to suppress opium imports from Britain led to military confrontation with the British and to numerous concessions that opened China to trade on Britain's terms. Within its borders, China faced unprecedented population pressure and worsening economic conditions that resulted in uprisings in several parts of the country. These rebellions proved very difficult to suppress. Further humiliations by the Western powers led to concerted efforts to modernize the military and learn other secrets of Western success, but China never quite caught up. Inspired by Western ideas of republican government, revolutionaries tried to topple the dynasty, finally succeeding in 1911–1912.

KEY TERMS

Great Mutiny/Great Revolt (p. 785)
Indian Civil Service (p. 787)
Indian National Congress (p. 787)
Java War (p. 790)
Nguyen Dynasty (p. 790)
Opium War (p. 794)
extraterritoriality (p. 794)
concessions (p. 794)
Taiping Rebellion (p. 794)
Boxers (p. 796)
1911 Revolution (p. 796)
gunboat diplomacy (p. 797)
Meiji Restoration (p. 797)
Russo-Japanese War (p. 802)
indentured laborers (p. 804)

◻ **How was Japan able to quickly master the challenges posed by the West? (p. 797)**

Japan was the one Asian country to quickly transform itself when confronted by the military strength of the West. It did this by overhauling its power structure. The Meiji centralized and strengthened Japan's power by depriving the samurai of their privileges, writing a constitution, instituting universal education, and creating a modern army. At the same time they guided Japan toward rapid industrialization. By the early twentieth century Japan had become an imperialist power with colonies in Korea and Taiwan.

◻ **Why did people move much more in this period, and where did they go? (p. 802)**

The rapid pace of political and economic change in the nineteenth century led people to move across national borders much more frequently than before. By the early 1900s significant expatriate communities of Westerners had formed in many cities in Asia. Asian students traveled to Europe, Japan, or the United States to continue their educations. Millions more left in search of work. With the end of the African slave trade, recruiters from the Americas and elsewhere went to India and China to secure indentured laborers. In other cases, ambitious young men who heard of gold strikes or other chances to get rich funded their own travels. Emigrants from China, one of the major exporters of people, sought work in such Southeast Asian territories as Malaya, Singapore, the Philippines, and Indonesia. As a consequence, Asian diasporas formed in many parts of the world.

◻ **What explains the similarities and differences in the experiences of Asian countries in this era?** (p. 806)

The differences between the countries of Asia at the turn of the twentieth century can be explained in several ways. The countries did not start with equivalent circumstances. Some had long traditions of unified rule; others did not. Some had manufactured goods that Western powers wanted; others offered raw materials or cheap labor. The timing of the arrival of Western powers also made a difference, especially because Western military superiority increased over time. European Great Power rivalry had a major impact, especially after 1860. Similarities in the experiences of Asian countries are also notable and include many of the benefits (and costs) of industrialization seen elsewhere in the world, such as modernizations in communication and transportation, extension of schooling, and the emergence of radical ideologies.

SUGGESTED READING

Bayly, C. A. *Indian Society and the Making of the British Empire*. 1990. A synthesis of recent research that provides a complex portrait of the interaction of Indian society and British colonial administration.

Bose, Sugata, and Ayesha Jalal. *Modern South Asia: History, Culture, Political Economy*. 1998. Incorporates recent scholarship with postcolonial perspective in a wide-ranging study.

Duus, Peter. *The Abacus and the Sword: The Japanese Penetration of Korea, 1895–1910*. 1995. Analyzes the interplay of business interests (the abacus) and military interests (the sword) in Japan's push for colonial possessions.

Fairbank, John King, and Merle Goldman. *China: A New History*, 2d ed. 2006. A treatment of China's experiences in the nineteenth century that is rich in interesting detail.

Hane, Mikiso. *Peasants, Rebels, Women and Outcastes: The Underside of Modern Japan*, 2d ed. 2003. Draws on wide-ranging sources to provide a fuller picture of Japanese history.

Hopper, Helen. *Fukuzawa Yukichi: From Samurai to Capitalist*. 2005. A brief account of the life of a key westernizing intellectual.

Irokawa, Daiichi. *The Culture of the Meiji Period*. 1988. Makes excellent use of letters, diaries, and songs to probe changes in the ways ordinary people thought during a crucial period of political change.

Kuhn, Philip A. *Chinese Among Others: Emigration in Modern Times*. 2008. A history of Chinese emigration that is global in scope and vividly written.

Masselos, Jim. *Indian Nationalism: A History*, 5th ed. 2004. A detailed account of the political movement for independence in nineteenth- and twentieth-century India.

Pruitt, Ida. *A Daughter of Han: The Autobiography of a Chinese Working Woman*. 1967. A highly revealing glimpse of Chinese society fashioned by journalist Ida Pruitt in the 1930s based on what a Chinese woman born in 1867 told Pruitt of her life.

Rowe, William T. *China's Last Empire: The Great Qing*. 2009. An overview of the Qing Empire by a major historian.

Spence, Jonathan. *God's Chinese Son*. 1997. Tells the story of the Taipings as much as possible from their own perspective.

Steinberg, David Joel, ed. *In Search of Southeast Asia: A Modern History*, rev. ed. 1987. An impressive work on Southeast Asia by seven specialists.

Walthall, Anne. *Japan: A Cultural, Social, and Political History*. 2006. A concise overview with good coverage of local society and popular culture.

NOTES

1. Quoted in K. M. Panikkar, *Asia and Western Dominance: A Survey of the Vasco da Gama Epoch of Asian History* (London: George Allen & Unwin, 1959), p. 116.
2. Quoted in D. J. Steinberg, ed., *In Search of Southeast Asia: A Modern History*, rev. ed. (Honolulu: University of Hawaii Press, 1987), p. 129.
3. Ssu-yu Teng and J. K. Fairbank, *China's Response to the West: A Documentary Survey* (New York: Atheneum, 1971), p. 26.
4. Wm. Theodore de Bary and Richard Lufrano, eds., *Sources of Chinese Tradition*, vol. 2: *From 1600* (New York: Columbia University Press, 2001).
5. Teng and Fairbank, p. 76, modified.
6. Quoted in J. W. Hall, *Japan, from Prehistory to Modern Times* (New York: Delacorte Press, 1970), p. 289.
7. R. Tsunoda, W. T. de Bary, and D. Keene, eds., *Sources of Japanese Tradition*, vol. 2 (New York: Columbia University Press, 1964), p. 137.
8. Quoted in J. D. Spence, *The Search for Modern China* (New York: W. W. Norton, 1990), p. 215.
9. Homer A. Jack, ed., *The Gandhi Reader: A Sourcebook of His Life and Writings* (Bloomington: Indiana University Press, 1956), p. 112.

For practice quizzes and other study tools, visit the **Online Study Guide** at bedfordstmartins.com/mckayworld.

For primary sources from this period, see *Sources of World Societies*, **Second Edition**.

For Web sites, images, and documents related to topics in this chapter, visit **Make History** at bedfordstmartins.com/mckayworld.

• **Ute Indian** Native Americans found their world under assault during the nineteenth century, as the United States expanded its territory and encouraged settlers to farm lands where Indians had long lived. The Ute Indian depicted here was photographed by William Gunnison Chamberlain, probably in his Denver studio in 1868. (The Granger Collection, New York)

27

In the Americas and in Australia, as in Europe, the nineteenth century was a period of nation building and industrial and commercial growth. Unlike in Europe, the century was also a time of geographical expansion and large-scale in-migration.

At the end of the eighteenth century Canada and the countries of South America remained colonies. Their European mother countries looked on the democratic experiment of the infant United States with suspicion and scorn. The island continent of Australia, remote from Europe and economically undeveloped, served as a dumping ground for English criminals. The nineteenth century brought revolutions, civil wars, and foreign invasions, among other challenges. In some countries abolishing slavery was achieved with great difficulty. Yet by 1914 all the countries were not only politically independent but also stronger and richer than they had been in 1800.

Many issues cross-cut the histories of all these countries in the long nineteenth century: nation building, nationalism, urbanization, racism, regional separatism, new technologies, new lands to put to the plow, new trading patterns, and new constitutional governments, to name just a few. Yet the outcomes by 1914 were strikingly different. The United States had become a major industrial power and a stable democracy with a standard of living comparable to that of western Europe. Canada and Australia also had stable democratic governments and high standards of living, but their economies remained predominantly agricultural. Most of the countries of Latin America suffered political instability, and their economies did not fare as well in the emerging world trade system. •

Nation Building in the Americas and Australia

1770–1914

Latin America, 1800–1914

□ Why and how did the Spanish and Portuguese colonies of North and South America shake off European domination and develop into national states?

The United States, 1789–1914

□ How did the United States build a large but unified nation?

Canada, from French Colony to Nation

□ What geographical, economic, and political conditions shaped the development of Canada?

Australia, from Penal Colony to Nation

□ What circumstances shaped the development of Australia?

The New Countries from a Comparative Perspective

□ How and why did the new countries treated in this chapter develop differently?

Latin America, 1800–1914

□ Why and how did the Spanish and Portuguese colonies of North and South America shake off European domination and develop into national states?

In 1800 the Spanish Empire in the Americas stretched from the headwaters of the Mississippi River in present-day Minnesota to the tip of Cape Horn in the Antarctic (see Map 27.1). In addition to large regions of South America, it encompassed large parts of the present-day United States from California to Texas. Mexico's silver mines were the richest in the world, and Mexico City had a larger population than any city in Spain. Spain believed that the great wealth of the Americas existed for its benefit, a stance that fostered bitterness and the desire for independence in the colonies. Between 1806 and 1825 the Spanish colonies in Latin America were convulsed by upheavals that ultimately resulted in their separation from Spain. Until 1898 Spain did, however, retain Cuba and Puerto Rico, its colonies in the Caribbean.

The **Creoles** — people of European descent born in the Americas (see page 549) — resented the economic and political dominance of the **peninsulares** (puh-nihn-suh-LUHR-ayz), as the colonial officials and other natives of Spain or Portugal were called. In 1800 there

Don Juan Joachin Gutierrez Altamirano Velasco, ca. 1752 In this painting by Miguel Cabrera, the pleated cuffs on Velasco's shirt, the richly embroidered and very expensive coat, the knee breeches, the tricorn hat, the plaque of titles, and the coat of arms on the wall all attest to the proud status of this member of the peninsulares, the most powerful element in colonial Mexican society. (Miguel Cabrera, Mexican, 1695–1768, oil on canvas, 81 5/16 x 53½. Brooklyn Museum of Art, Museum Collection Fund, and the Dick S. Ramsay Fund 52.166.1) were about thirty thousand peninsulares and 3.5 million Creoles. Peninsulares controlled the rich export-import trade, intercolonial trade, and mining industries. The Creoles wanted to supplant the peninsulares as the ruling class and, more generally, to free themselves from Spain and Portugal. They had little interest in improving the lot of the Indians, the mestizos (meh-STEE-zohz) of mixed Spanish and Indian background, or the mulattos of mixed Spanish and African heritage.

Over the course of the nineteenth century, the countries of Latin America developed into national states. The predominant factors in this evolution were the heritage of colonial exploitation, a neo-colonial economic structure, massive emigration from Europe and Asia, and the fusion of Amerindian, Caucasian, African, and Asian peoples.

The Origins of the Revolutions Against Colonial Powers

The Latin American movements for independence drew strength from unfair taxation and trade policies, Spain's declining control over its Latin American colonies, racial and class discrimination, and the spread of revolutionary ideas. By the eighteenth century the Spanish colonies had become self-sufficient producers of foodstuffs, wine, textiles, and consumer goods, though Spain maintained monopolies on alcohol and tobacco and the colonies traded with each other. In Peru, for example, domestic agriculture supported the large mining settlements, and the colony did not have to import food. Craft workshops owned by the state or by private individuals produced consumer goods for the working class; what was not manufactured locally was bought from Mexico and transported by the Peruvian merchant marine.

Spain's humiliating defeat in the War of the Spanish Succession (1701–1713; see page 501) prompted demands for sweeping reform of all of Spain's institutions, including its colonial policies and practices. To improve administrative efficiency, the enlightened monarch Charles III (r. 1759–1788) carved the region of modern Colombia, Venezuela, and Ecuador out of the vast viceroyalty of Peru; it became the new viceroyalty of New Granada with its capital at Bogotá. The Crown also created the viceroyalty of Rio de la Plata (present-day Argentina) with its capital at Buenos Aires (Map 27.1).

CHRONOLOGY

1770	James Cook lands in Australia and claims land for British crown
1774	Quebec Act grants religious freedom to French Canadians
1778–1788	Height of Spain's trade with its colonies
1780	Tupac Amaru II leads rebellion in Peru
1786	British government establishes a penal colony at Botany Bay, Australia
1791	Constitution Act in Canada divides the province of Quebec in two
1803	United States purchases Louisiana Territory from France
1804	Haiti achieves independence from France and becomes the first black republic
1815–1825	Wars of independence in Latin America
1845	First use of term *manifest destiny* in United States; Texas and Florida admitted into United States
1861–1865	U.S. Civil War
1865–1877	U.S. Reconstruction
1867	Dominion of Canada formed
1883–1894	Mexican land laws put most land into the hands of a few individuals
1898	Spanish-American War
1901	Commonwealth of Australia formed
1904	United States secures the rights to build and control the Panama Canal
1914	Panama Canal completed

Additionally, Spain adopted free-trade policies (allowing trade without government interference) in order to compete with Great Britain and Holland in the great eighteenth-century struggle for empire. In Latin America these actions stimulated the production of crops that were in demand in Europe: coffee in Venezuela; sugar in the Caribbean; hides, leather, and salted beef in the Rio de la Plata viceroyalty. Between 1778 and 1788 the volume of Spain's trade with the colonies soared, possibly by as much as 700 percent.[1]

Colonial manufacturing, which had been growing steadily, suffered a heavy blow under free trade. Colonial textiles, china, and wine, for example, could not

---

- **Creoles** People of Spanish descent born in the Americas.
- **peninsulares** A term for natives of Spain and Portugal.

Before independence

Spanish colonies

- Viceroyalty of New Spain
- Viceroyalty of New Granada
- Viceroyalty of Peru and Audencia of Chile
- Viceroyalty of Rio de la Plata

Portuguese colonies

- Viceroyalty of Brazil

✕ Silver mine

Effective frontier of Spanish settlement

NEW FRANCE (Conquered by England, 1760)

ENGLISH COLONIES (Independence declared, 1776)

COAHUILA

Gulf of Mexico

VICEROYALTY OF NEW SPAIN
BAJIO LEÓN (1535)
✕ Zacatecas
✕ Guanajuato
Guadalajara
Mexico City
Veracruz

FLORIDA (Ceded to England, 1763–1783)

Havana

HAITI [SAINT-DOMINGUE] (Ceded to France, 1697)

PUERTO RICO

BRITISH HONDURAS

JAMAICA (Conquered by England, 1655)

Guatemala

SANTO DOMINGO

Caribbean Sea

ATLANTIC OCEAN

Caracas

Bogotá

VICEROYALTY OF NEW GRANADA (Separated from Viceroyalty of Peru, 1717, 1739)

GUIANA

Quito

Equator

VICEROYALTY OF PERU (1590s)
Lima
Cuzco

VICEROYALTY OF BRAZIL (1720)

Salvador

La Paz

Chuquisaca (La Plata; Sucre)
✕ Potosí

São Paulo
Rio de Janeiro (Capital, 1763)

PACIFIC OCEAN

AUDIENCIA OF CHILE (Retained by Viceroyalty of Peru, 1776)

VICEROYALTY OF RIO DE LA PLATA (Separated from Viceroyalty of Peru, 1776)
Santiago
Buenos Aires
Montevideo

Claimed but not settled by Spain

Islas Malvinas (Falkland Islands)

Cape Horn

0   500   1,000 miles
0   500   1,000 kilometers

In 1830

1811 Year independence gained

Colony

OREGON COUNTRY (Joint U.S.-British occupation)

BRITISH NORTH AMERICA (CANADA) (Gr. Br.)

UNITED STATES 1783

MEXICO 1821

San Antonio

ATLANTIC OCEAN

Gulf of Mexico

Mexico City
Veracruz

BAHAMA IS. (Gr. Br.)
Havana
CUBA (Spain)
HAITI 1804
PUERTO RICO (Spain)

BRITISH HONDURAS
JAMAICA (Gr. Br.)

Guatemala City
GUATEMALA
Caribbean Sea

UNITED PROVINCES OF CENTRAL AMERICA 1823–1839

Panama
Caracas
VENEZUELA
Socorro
Bogotá
GRAN COLOMBIA 1819–1830

TRINIDAD (Gr. Br.)
BR. GUIANA (Gr. Br.)
DUTCH GUIANA (Neth.)
FRENCH GUIANA (France)

Quito
ECUADOR

Equator
Galápagos Islands

PACIFIC OCEAN

PERU 1824
Lima

BOLIVIA 1825
La Paz
Sucre

EMPIRE OF BRAZIL 1822

Salvador

PARAGUAY 1811

UNITED PROVINCES OF THE RIO DE LA PLATA 1816

CHILE 1817
Santiago

URUGUAY 1828

ARGENTINA
Buenos Aires
Montevideo

Rio de Janeiro
São Paulo

PATAGONIA (Disputed between Argentina and Chile)

Islas Malvinas (Falkland Islands)

0   500   1,000 miles
0   500 1,000 kilometers

▢ Mapping the Past

MAP 27.1 Latin America in ca. 1780 and 1830 By 1830 almost all of Central America, South America, and the Caribbean islands had won independence. Note that the many nations that now make up Central America were unified when they first won independence from Mexico. Similarly, modern Venezuela, Colombia, and Ecuador were still joined in Gran Colombia.

ANALYZING THE MAP Compare the boundaries of the Spanish and Portuguese colonies in ca. 1780 with the boundaries of the independent states in 1830. How did these boundaries change, and which regions experienced the most breakup?

CONNECTIONS Why did Pan-Americanism fail?

compete with cheap Spanish products. In the Rio de la Plata region heavy export taxes and light import duties shattered the wine industry. Madrid's tax reforms also aggravated discontent. Like Great Britain, Spain believed its colonies should bear some of the costs of their own defense. Accordingly, Madrid raised the prices of its monopoly products—tobacco and liquor—and increased sales taxes on many items. As a result, protest movements in Latin America, like those in the thirteen North American colonies a decade earlier, claimed that the colonies were being unfairly taxed.

Political conflicts beyond the colonies also helped to drive aspirations for independence. The French Revolution and Napoleonic wars, which involved France's occupation of Spain and Britain's domination of the seas, isolated Spain from Latin America. As Spain's control over its Latin American colonies diminished, foreign traders, especially from the United States, swarmed into Spanish-American ports. In 1796 the Madrid government made exceptions to its trade restrictions for countries not engaged in the Napoleonic wars, such as the United States, thus acknowledging Spain's inability to supply the colonies with needed goods and markets.

Racial, ethnic, and class privileges also fueled discontent. At the end of the eighteenth century colonists complained bitterly that only peninsulares were appointed to the colonies' highest judicial bodies and to other positions in the colonial governments. From 1751 to 1775 only 13 percent of appointees to the judicial bodies were Creoles.[2] According to the nineteenth-century Mexican statesman and historian Lucas Alamán (1792–1853):

> This preference shown to Spaniards in political offices and ecclesiastical benefices has been the principal cause of the rivalry between the two classes; add to this the fact that Europeans possessed great wealth, which although it may have been the just reward of effort and industry, excited the envy of Americans and was considered as so much usurpation from them; consider that for all these reasons the Spaniards had obtained a decided preponderance over those born in the country; and it will not be difficult to explain the increasing jealousy and rivalry between the two groups which culminated in hatred and enmity.[3]

From a racial standpoint, the makeup of Latin American societies is one of the most complicated in the world. Because few European women immigrated to the colonies, Spanish men formed relationships with Indian and African women, while African men deprived of black women sought Indian women. The result was a population composed of every possible combination of Indian, Spanish, and African blood. Demographers

estimate that Indians still accounted for between 60 and 75 percent of the population of Latin America at the end of the colonial period, in spite of the tremendous population losses caused by the introduction of diseases in the sixteenth and seventeenth centuries. The colonies that became Peru and Bolivia had Indian majorities; the regions that became Argentina and Chile had European majorities.

Indians and black slaves toiled in the silver and gold mines of Mexico, Colombia, and Peru; in the wheat fields of Chile; in the humid, mosquito-ridden canebrakes of Mexico and the Caribbean; and in the diamond mines and coffee and sugar plantations of Brazil. Almost 40 percent of all slaves shipped from Africa went to the Caribbean, where the white elite formed a tiny minority. Also, Indians faced other difficulties. Many of them were still subject to the *repartimiento* and the *mit'a*. The law of repartimiento required Indians to buy goods solely from local tax collectors. *Mit'a* means a turn or rotation; the practice was that every seventh household in the region between Huancavelica and Potosí in the Andes took a turn working in the silver mines, with the duration of service varying.

Spanish theories of racial purity rejected people of mixed blood, particularly those of African descent. Peninsulares and Creoles reinforced their privileged status by showing contempt for people who were not white. Moreover, owners of mines, plantations, and factories had a vested interest in keeping blacks and Indians in servile positions. Nevertheless, nonwhites in Latin America did experience some social mobility in the colonial period, certainly more than nonwhites in the North American colonies experienced. A few mulattos rose in the army, some as high as the rank of colonel. The army and the church seem to have offered the greatest opportunities for social mobility. Many black slaves gained their freedom by fleeing to the jungles or mountains, where they established self-governing communities. Around the year 1800 Venezuela counted 2,400 fugitive slaves in a total population of 87,000.

A final factor contributing to rebellion were the Enlightenment ideas of Voltaire, Rousseau, and Montesquieu, which had been trickling into Latin America for decades (see Chapter 18). North American ships calling at South American ports introduced the subversive writings of Thomas Paine and Thomas Jefferson. In 1794 the Colombian Antonio Nariño translated and published the French Declaration of the Rights of Man and the Citizen. (Spanish authorities sentenced him to ten years in an African prison, but he lived to become the father of Colombian independence.) By 1800 the Creole elite throughout Latin America was familiar with liberal Enlightenment political thought, and the Creoles wanted the "rights of man" extended to themselves.

Resistance, Rebellion, and Independence

The mid-eighteenth century witnessed frequent Andean Indian rebellions against the Spaniards' harsh exploitation. In 1780, under the leadership of a descendant of the Inca rulers who took the name Tupac Amaru II, a massive insurrection exploded. Indian chieftains from the Cuzco region (see Map 27.1) gathered a powerful force of Indians and people of mixed race. Rebellion swept across highland Peru, where many Spanish officials were executed. Before peace was restored two years later, a hundred thousand people lay dead, and vast amounts of property were destroyed. Although Spanish rule was not ended, the government abolished the repartimiento system and established assemblies of local representatives in Cuzco. The revolts also raised elite fears of racial and class warfare.

As news of the rebellion of Tupac Amaru II trickled northward, it helped stimulate the 1781 Comunero Revolution in the New Granada viceroyalty (see

Triumph of Bolívar Bolívar was treated as a hero everywhere he went in South America. (akg-images)

Map 27.1). In this revolution an Indian peasant army commanded by Creole captains marched on Bogotá. Dispersed by the ruling Spanish, who made promises they did not intend to keep, the revolt in the end did little to improve the Indians' lives.

Much more than the revolts in Peru and New Granada, the successful revolution led by Toussaint L'Ouverture (1743–1803) in Haiti aroused elite fears of black revolt and class warfare (see pages 676–681 and Map 22.3). In 1804 Haiti declared its independence, becoming the second nation (after the United States) in the Western Hemisphere to achieve self-rule. The revolt was also the first successful uprising of a non-European people against a colonial power, and it sent waves of fear through the upper classes in both Europe and Latin America.

In 1808 Napoleon Bonaparte deposed the Spanish king Ferdinand VII and placed his own brother on the Spanish throne (see page 676). Since everything in Spanish America was done in the name of the king, the Creoles in Latin America argued that the removal of the legitimate king shifted sovereignty to the people — that is, to themselves. The Creoles who led the various movements for independence did not intend a radical redistribution of property or a reconstruction of society. They merely rejected the authority of the Spanish crown.

The great hero of the movement for independence was Simón Bolívar (1783–1830), a very able general who is considered the Latin American George Washington. In a letter to the governor of Jamaica in 1815, he explained his objections to Spanish rule:

> Americans today, and perhaps to a greater extent than ever before, who live within the Spanish system, occupy a position in society no better than that of serfs destined for labor, or at best they have no more status than that of mere consumers. Yet even this status is surrounded with galling restrictions, such as being forbidden to grow European crops, or to store products which are royal monopolies, or to establish factories of a type the [Iberian] Peninsula itself does not possess. To this add the exclusive trading privileges, even in articles of prime necessity, and the barriers between American provinces, designed to prevent all exchange of trade, traffic, and understanding. In short, do you wish to know what our future held? Simply the cultivation of the fields of indigo, grain, coffee, sugar cane, cacao, and cotton; cattle raising on the broad plains; hunting wild game in the jungles; digging in the earth to mine its gold which can never sate that greedy nation [Spain].[4]

Bolívar's victories over the royalist armies won him the presidency of Gran Colombia (formerly the New Granada viceroyalty) in 1819. He dreamed of a continental union and in 1826 summoned a conference of the American republics at Panama. The meeting achieved little, however. The territories of Gran Colombia splintered (see Map 27.1), and a sadly disillusioned Bolívar went into exile, saying, "America is ungovernable." Under Spain, Mexico had been united with Central America as the Viceroyalty of New Spain. In the 1830s, after independence, regional separatism resulted in New Spain's breakup into five separate countries. In South America, too, the old colonies were divided, not amalgamated. The failure of Pan-Americanism isolated individual countries, prevented collective action, and later paved the way for the political and economic intrusion of the United States and other powers.

Brazil followed a different path to independence from Portugal. When Napoleon's troops entered Portugal, the royal family fled to Brazil and made Rio de Janeiro the capital of the Portuguese Empire. The new government immediately lifted the old mercantilist restrictions and opened Brazilian ports to the ships of all friendly nations. The king returned to Portugal in 1821, leaving his son Pedro in Brazil as regent. Under popular pressure, Pedro proclaimed Brazil's independence in 1822, issued a constitution, and even led resistance against Portuguese troops. He accepted the title Emperor Pedro I (r. 1822–1834). Even though Brazil was a monarchy, Creole elites dominated society as they did elsewhere in Latin America. The reign of his successor, Pedro II (r. 1831–1889), witnessed the expansion of the coffee industry, the beginnings of the rubber industry, and massive immigration.

The Aftermath of Independence

The Latin American wars of independence, over by 1825, differed from the American Revolution in important ways. First, they lasted much longer, and outside powers provided no help, leaving those involved weary and divided. Second, many of the peninsulares returned to Europe instead of remaining in Latin America to build new nations, as most North American colonists had. Also, although the Creole elites followed the example of the United States by writing constitutions for the new Latin American governments, these governments excluded much of the population from political participation. To a large degree the local elites took over exploiting the peasantry from the old colonial elites. Small independent farmers of the sort who became common in the United States and Canada did not gain a comparable place in Latin America. The new governments also largely confirmed the wealth of the Roman Catholic Church and its authority over the people, not adopting separation of church and state.

The newly independent nations had difficulty achieving political stability when the wars of independence

□ LATIN AMERICA, CA. 1760-1900	
1759-1788	Reign of Spain's Charles III, who instituted administrative and economic reforms
1781	Comunero Revolution in New Granada
1791-1804	Haitian Revolution
1806-1825	Latin American wars of independence against Spain
1822	Proclamation of Brazil's independence by Portugal
1826	Call by Simón Bolívar for Panama conference on Latin American union
ca. 1870-1929	Latin American neocolonialism
1876-1911	Porfirio Díaz's control of Mexico
1880-1914	Massive emigration from Europe and Asia to Latin America
1888	Emancipation of slaves in Brazil; final abolition of slavery in Western Hemisphere
1898	Spanish-American War; end of Spanish control of Cuba; transfer of Puerto Rico and the Philippines to the United States

ended. Between 1836 and 1848 Mexico lost half of its territory to the United States, and other countries, too, had difficulty defending themselves from their neighbors. (See "Viewpoints: Mexican and American Perspectives on the U.S.-Mexican War," page 818.) The Creole leaders of the revolutions had no experience in government, and the wars left a legacy of military, not civilian, leadership.

In many Latin American countries, generals ruled. In Argentina, Juan Manuel de Rosas (r. 1835–1852) assumed power amid widespread public disorder and ruled as dictator. In Mexico, liberals declared a federal republic, but incessant civil strife led to the rise of the dictator Antonio López de Santa Anna (1794–1876) in the mid-nineteenth century. Likewise in Venezuela, strongmen, dictators, and petty aristocratic oligarchs governed from 1830 to 1892. Some countries suffered constant coups d'état; in the course of the century, Bolivia had sixty and Venezuela fifty-two.

On occasion, the ruling generals were charismatic military leaders who were able to attract mass support for their governments. In Venezuela, José Antonio Páez (1790–1873) was able to present himself as a patron of the common man and maintain his popularity even though his economic policies favored the elite and he built up a personal fortune. Some rulers were of common origins. In Mexico, Benito Juarez (1806–1872) was

Viewpoints

Mexican and American Perspectives on the U.S.-Mexican War

• *In the mid-nineteenth century the United States acquired large tracts of land from Mexico, including Texas, New Mexico, Arizona, and California. The wars that were settled with these transfers were controversial even in their day, and in both Mexico and the United States some people justified government policies while others condemned them. Newspapers, which covered the events in both Mexico and the United States, played an important part in shaping opinion. Other Americans, especially those opposed to slavery and its expansion, were dubious about the war from the start.*

President of Mexico, José Joaquín de Herrera, to the Governors of the Mexican States Asking for Their Support in Accepting the Loss of Texas, December 1845

In order to start a war, politicians agree that three questions must be examined: 1st, that of justice, 2nd, that of availability of resources, 3rd, that of convenience. . . . If, for launching war, one would only have to consider our justice, any hesitation in this matter would be either a crime or a lack of common sense. But next come the questions of feasibility and convenience for starting and maintaining hostilities with firmness and honor and all the consequences of a war of this nature.

A foreign war against a powerful and advanced nation that possesses an impressive navy and a . . . population that increases every day because of immigrants attracted to its great . . . prosperity, would imply immense sacrifices of men and money—not to assure victory, but simply to avoid defeat. Are such sacrifices possible for the Mexican Republic in her present state of exhaustion, after so many years of error and misadventure?

Manuel Crescencio Rejón, Minister of the Interior and Foreign Affairs Under Two Mexican Presidents, Arguing Against Ratification of the Treaty of Guadalupe Hidalgo, 1848

The social advantages which would accrue to us by accepting a peace now have been exaggerated, as well as the ease with which we would be able to maintain our remaining territories. It would be necessary, in order to sustain such illusions, to underestimate the spirit of enterprise of the North American people in industrial and commercial pursuits, to misunderstand their history and their tendencies, and also to presuppose in our own spirit less resistance than we have already shown toward the sincere friends of progress. Only through such illusions might one maintain that the treaty would

bring a change that would be advantageous to us—as has been claimed.

Walt Whitman, Editorial in the *Brooklyn Daily Eagle*, May 11, 1846

We are justified in the face of the world, in having treated Mexico with more forbearance than we have ever yet treated an enemy—for Mexico, though contemptible in many respects, is an enemy deserving a vigorous "lesson." . . . Let our arms now be carried with a spirit which shall teach the world that, while we are not forward for a quarrel, America knows how to crush, as well as how to expand!

Ulysses S. Grant in 1885 Looking Back on His Participation in the War

Generally the officers of the army were indifferent whether the annexation was consummated or not; but not so all of them. For myself, I was bitterly opposed to the measure, and to this day regard the war, which resulted, as one of the most unjust ever waged by a stronger against a weaker nation. It was an instance of a republic following the bad example of European monarchies, in not considering justice in their desire to acquire additional territory. . . . The occupation, separation and annexation [of Mexico] were, from the inception of the movement to its final consummation, a conspiracy to acquire territory out of which slave states might be formed for the American Union.

Sources: Carol and Thomas Christensen, *The U.S. Mexican War* (San Francisco: Bay Books, 1998), p. 50; Ernesto Chávez, *The U.S. War with Mexico: A Brief History with Documents* (Boston: Bedford/St. Martin's, 2008), pp. 127, 83; Ulysses S. Grant, *Memoirs*, chap. 3, accessed through Project Gutenberg, http://www.gutenberg.org/files/5860/5860-h/5860-h.htm.

QUESTIONS FOR ANALYSIS

1. What issues do the Mexican politicians raise? Do they agree on anything?

2. How does the knowledge that Whitman's piece was a newspaper editorial shape your reading of it?

3. What might the implications have been for the U.S. forces if many officers disapproved of the war the way Grant did?

something of an exception to the generalization that Creoles had a tight hold on power. A Zapotec Indian who did not learn Spanish until he was twelve, Juarez became a strong advocate of democracy. He led efforts to reduce the power of the Catholic Church and later led resistance to the "emperor" imposed by Napoleon III in 1862. Between 1858 and his death in 1872 Juarez served five terms as president of Mexico.

The economic lives of most Latin American countries were disrupted during the years of war. Mexico and Venezuela in particular suffered great destruction of farmland and animals. Armies were frequently recruited by force, and when the men were demobilized, many did not return home. The consequent population dislocation hurt agriculture and mining. Guerrilla warfare disrupted trade and communications, and the seizure of private property for military use ruined many people.

On the positive side, the push for independence speeded abolition of slavery. The destruction of agriculture in countries such as Mexico and Venezuela caused the collapse of the plantation system, and fugitive slaves could not be recaptured. Generals on both sides offered slaves their freedom in exchange for military service. Still, Cuba and Brazil, which had large slave populations, did not free their slaves until 1886 and 1888, respectively.

Although the edifice of racism persisted in the nineteenth century, Latin America offered blacks greater economic and social mobility than did the United States. One reason is that the Creole elite in Latin America approved of "whitening" — that is, they viewed race mixture as a civilizing process that diminished and absorbed the dark and "barbarous" blood of Africans and Indians. In Latin America, light-skinned people of color could rise economically and socially in a way not available to those with darker skins. (See "Listening to the Past: Mary Seacole on Her Early Life," page 822.)

Neocolonialism and Its Socioeconomic Effects

At first, political instability discouraged foreign investment in Latin America's newly independent nations. But with the general expansion of world trade after 1870 and the development of stable dictatorships, foreign investors turned to Latin America for raw materials and basic commodities to supply industrializing Europe and the United States. Modern business enterprises, often owned by foreign capitalists, led the way. These firms usually specialized in a single product that could be shipped through the growing international network of railroads, ports, and ocean freighters.

In Mexico, for example, North American capital supported the production of hemp, sugar, bananas, and rubber, frequently on American-owned plantations, and British and American interests backed the development of tin, copper, and gold mining. British capital financed Argentina's railroads, meatpacking industry, and utilities; Chile's copper and nitrate industries (nitrate is used in the production of pharmaceuticals and fertilizers); and Brazil's coffee, cotton, and sugar production. By 1904 Brazil produced 76 percent of the world's coffee. The extension of railroads also attracted outside entrepreneurs. (See "Individuals in Society: Henry Meiggs, Promoter and Speculator," page 820.)

Thus, by the turn of the century, the Latin American nations were active participants in the international economic order, but foreigners controlled most of their industries, and their governments used force when they felt their economic interests were threatened. This form of economic domination is often called **neocolonialism**. Perhaps the best example was the U.S.-financed building of the Panama Canal. In 1904 Americans secured the rights to control the Panama Canal, connecting the Atlantic and Pacific Oceans, on their own terms. This monumental construction project wasn't completed until 1914 and took the lives of thousands of workers. The United States retained control of the Panama Canal Zone until 1999. In 1912 and 1926 U.S. Marines interfered in Nicaragua to bolster conservative governments; the Marines who were sent to Haiti in 1915 to protect American property stayed until 1934; and those sent to the Dominican Republic in 1916 stayed until 1924.

Another distinctive feature of neocolonialism was that each country's economy revolved around only one or two products: sugar in Cuba, nitrates and copper in Chile, meat in Argentina, coffee in Brazil. Consequently, a sharp drop in world demand for a product could devastate the export sector and with it the nation's economic well-being. For example, the outbreak of the First World War in 1914 drastically reduced exports of Latin American raw materials and imports of European manufactured goods, provoking a general economic crisis.

Many of the workers on the plantations producing export products were Indians or mestizos. In the United States and Canada, Indians were pushed out of the way when their land was taken from them. In Latin America, by contrast, many more of them were kept in place and incorporated into the social system as subordinated workers, especially on large plantations called **haciendas** (ah-see-EN-dahz).

- **neocolonialism** Term referring to the political and economic systems that perpetuated Western economic domination of nations after their political independence.
- **haciendas** Large landed estates.

Individuals in Society

Henry Meiggs, Promoter and Speculator

ALL THROUGHOUT THE AMERICAS IN THE nineteenth century opportunities beckoned. Henry Meiggs, born in upstate New York in 1811, responded to several of them, building and losing fortunes in Brooklyn, San Francisco, Chile, and Peru.

Meiggs, with only an elementary school education, began work at his father's shipyard. He soon started his own lumber business and did well until he lost everything in the financial panic of 1837. He rebuilt his business, and when gold was discovered in California in 1848, he filled a ship with lumber and sailed around Cape Horn to San Francisco, where he sold his cargo for $50,000, twenty times what he had paid for it. He then entered the lumber business, organizing crews of five hundred men to fell huge Californian redwoods and bring them to his steam sawmills. As his business flourished, he began speculating in real estate, which led to huge debts when the financial crisis of 1854 hit. In an attempt to save himself and his friends, Meiggs forged warrants for more than $900,000; when discovery of the fraud seemed imminent, he sailed with his wife and children for South America.

Although at one point Meiggs was so strapped for cash that he sold his watch, within three years of arriving in Chile, he had secured his first railway contract, and by 1867 he had built about 200 miles of rail lines in that country. In 1868 he went to Peru, which had less than 60 miles of track at the time. In the next nine years he would add 700 more.

Meiggs was not an engineer, but he was a good manager. He recruited experienced engineers from abroad and arranged purchase of foreign rolling stock, rails, and ties, acting as a promoter and developer. Much of the funding came from international investors in Peruvian bonds.

The most spectacular of the rail lines Meiggs built was Peru's Callao-Lima-Oroya line, which crosses the Andes at about seventeen thousand feet above sea level, making it the highest standard gage railway in the world. Because water was scarce in many areas along the construction site, it had to be transported up to workers, who were mostly local people. Dozens of bridges and tunnels had to be built, and casualties were high. Eight hundred people were invited to the banquet that marked the beginning of work on the Oroya Railway. Meiggs drummed up enthusiasm at the event by calling the locomotive the "irresistible battering ram of modern civilization."

In Peru Meiggs became known for his extravagance and generosity, and some charged that he bribed Peruvian officials on a large scale to get his projects approved. He was a good speaker and loved to entertain lavishly. In one example of his generosity, he distributed thousands of pesos and soles to the victims of the earthquake of 1868. He also contributed to the beautification of Lima by tearing down an old wall and putting a seven-mile-long park in its place.

Always the speculator, in 1877 Meiggs died poor, his debts exceeding his assets. He was beloved, however, and more than twenty thousand Peruvians, many of whom had labored on his projects, attended his funeral at a Catholic church in Lima.

QUESTIONS FOR ANALYSIS

1. What accounts for the changes in fortune that Meiggs experienced?
2. Were the Latin American governments that awarded contracts to Meiggs making reasonable decisions?
3. Should it matter whether Meiggs had to bribe officials to get the railroads built? Why?

• The challenges in building the Callo-Lima-Oroya railroad across the Andes can be imagined from this picture of one of its many bridges.
(From Elio Galessio, *Ferrocarriles del Perú: Un viaje a través de su Historia.* Reproduced with permission of the author)

Diego Rivera, *The Exploiters* The Mexican painter Diego Rivera (1886–1957) painted many large murals, using his art to convey messages of social protest. This mural was painted in 1926 for the wall of a chapel at an agricultural college in Mexico City. (*Los Explotadores*, 1926 © Banco de Mexico, Diego Rivera and Frida Kahlo Museums/2011 Artists Rights Society [ARS], New York)

The late nineteenth century witnessed ever-greater concentrations of land in ever fewer hands. In places like the Valley of Mexico in southern Mexico, a few large haciendas controlled all the land. Under the 1876–1911 dictatorship of General Porfirio Díaz, the Mexican government in 1883 passed a law allowing real estate companies (controlled by Díaz's political cronies) to survey public and "vacant" lands and to retain one-third of the land they surveyed. An 1894 law provided that land could be declared vacant if legal title to it could not be produced. Since few Indians had deeds to the land that their ancestors had worked for centuries, the door swung open to wholesale expropriation of small landholdings and entire villages. Indians who dared armed resistance were crushed by government troops and carried off to virtual slave labor. As a result of the policies of Díaz (who was overthrown in the Mexican Revolution that started in 1910), vast stretches of land — in one case, 12 million acres — came into the hands of private individuals. Debt peonage also became common: landowners paid their laborers not in cash but in vouchers redeemable only at the landowner's store, where high prices and tricky bookkeeping kept the **peons** permanently in debt.

The Impact of Immigrants from Europe, Asia, and the Middle East

In 1852 the Argentine political philosopher Juan Bautista Alberdi published *Bases and Points of Departure for Argentine Political Organization,* arguing that the development of his country depended on immigration. Indians and blacks, Alberdi maintained, lacked basic skills, and it would take too long to train them. Thus he pressed for massive immigration from the "advanced" countries of northern Europe and the United States. Alberdi's ideas won immediate acceptance and were even incorporated into the Argentine constitution, which declared that "the Federal government will encourage European immigration." Other Latin American countries adopted similar policies promoting immigration.

Although Europe was a significant source of immigrants to Latin America, so were Asia and the Middle East. For example, in the late nineteenth and early twentieth centuries large numbers of Japanese arrived in Brazil, most settling in urban areas, especially in São

peons Low-status laborers.

Listening to the Past

Mary Seacole on Her Early Life

Mary Seacole was born in Jamaica in 1805, the daughter of a Scottish soldier and a local Jamaican Creole woman. She learned folk medical treatment from her mother, who ran a boarding house, and gradually took to running hotels and to working as a nurse herself. During the Crimean War she volunteered to go to the Crimea to treat wounded soldiers. Shortly afterward, in 1857, she wrote an autobiography, an excerpt of which follows.

❝I was born in the town of Kingston, in the island of Jamaica, some time in the present century. . . . I am a Creole, and have good Scotch blood coursing in my veins. My father was a soldier, of an old Scotch family; and to him I often trace my affection for a camp-life, and my sympathy with what I have heard my friends call "the pomp, pride, and circumstance of glorious war." Many people have also traced to my Scotch blood that energy and activity which are not always found in the Creole race, and which have carried me to so many varied scenes: and perhaps they are right. I have often heard the term "lazy Creole" applied to my country people; but I am sure I do not know what it is to be indolent. . . .

My mother kept a boarding-house in Kingston, and was, like very many of the Creole women, an admirable doctress; in high repute with the officers of both services, and their wives, who were from time to time stationed at Kingston. It was very natural that I should inherit her tastes; and so I had from early youth a yearning for medical knowledge and practice which has never deserted me. . . .

[After returning to Kingston from a trip in 1825], I nursed my old indulgent patroness in her last long illness. After she died, in my arms, I went to my mother's house, where I stayed, making myself useful in a variety of ways, and learning a great deal of Creole medicinal art, until I couldn't find courage to say "no" to a certain arrangement timidly proposed by Mr. Seacole, but married him, and took him down to Black River, where we established a store. Poor man! He was very delicate; and before

I undertook the charge of him, several doctors had expressed most unfavorable opinions of his health. I kept him alive by kind nursing and attention as long as I could; but at last he grew so ill that we left Black River, and returned to my mother's house at Kingston.

Within a month of our arrival there he died. This was my first great trouble, and I felt it bitterly. For days I never stirred—lost to all that passed around me in a dull stupor of despair. If you had told me that the time would soon come when I should remember this sorrow calmly, I should not have believed it possible: and yet it was so. I do not think that we hot-blooded Creoles sorrow less for showing it so impetuously; but I do think that the sharp edge of our grief wears down sooner than theirs who preserve an outward demeanor of calmness, and nurse their woe secretly in their hearts. . . .

In the year 1850, the cholera swept over the island of Jamaica with terrible force. . . . While the cholera raged, I had but too many opportunities of watching its nature, and from a Dr. B—, who was then lodging in my house, received many hints as to its treatment which I afterwards found invaluable.

Early in the same year my brother had left Kingston for the Isthmus of Panama, then the great high-road to and from golden California, where he had established a considerable store and hotel. Ever since he had done so, I had found some difficulty in checking my reviving disposition to roam, and at last persuading myself that I might be of use to him (he was far from strong), I resigned my house into the hands of a cousin, and made arrangements to journey to Chagres. . . .

All my readers must know—a glance at the map will show it to those who do not—that between North America and the envied shores of California stretches a little neck of land, insignificant-looking enough on the map, dividing the Atlantic from the Pacific. By crossing this, the travellers from America avoided a long, weary, and dangerous sea voyage round Cape Horn, or an almost impossible journey by land.

But that journey across the Isthmus, insignificant in distance as it was, was by no means an easy one. It seemed as if

Paulo. By 1920 Brazil had the largest Japanese community in the world outside of Japan. From the Middle East, Lebanese, Turks, and Syrians also entered Brazil. Between 1850 and 1880, 144,000 South Asian laborers went to Trinidad, 39,000 to Jamaica, and smaller numbers to the islands of St. Lucia, Grenada, and St. Vincent as indentured servants under five-year contracts. Perhaps one-third returned to India, but the rest stayed, saved money, and bought small businesses or land. Cuba, the largest of the Caribbean islands (about the size of

Pennsylvania), had received 500,000 African slaves between 1808 and 1865. When slavery was abolished in 1886, some of the work in the sugar-cane fields was done by Chinese indentured servants, who followed the same pattern as the South Asian migrants who had gone to Trinidad. Likewise, the abolition of slavery in Mexico led to the arrival of thousands of Chinese bonded servants.

Immigration helped fuel urbanization, and Portuguese, Italian, French, Chinese, and Japanese imminature had determined to throw every conceivable obstacle in the way of those who should seek to join the two great oceans of the world....

When, after passing Chagres, an old-world, tumble-down town, for about seven miles, the steamer reached Navy Bay, I thought I had never seen a more luckless, dreary spot.... It seemed as capital a nursery for ague and fever as Death could hit upon anywhere, and those on board the steamer who knew it confirmed my opinion. As we arrived a steady down-pour of rain was falling from an inky sky; the white men who met us on the wharf appeared ghostly and wraith-like, and the very negroes seemed pale and wan. The news which met us did not tempt me to lose any time in getting up the country to my brother. According to all accounts, fever and ague, with some minor diseases, especially dropsy, were having it all their own way at Navy Bay, and, although I only stayed one night in the place, my medicine chest was called into requisition. But the sufferers wanted remedies which I could not give them—warmth, nourishment, and fresh air. Beneath leaky tents, damp huts, and even under broken railway wagons, I saw men dying from sheer exhaustion. Indeed, I was very glad when, with the morning, the crowd, as the Yankees called the bands of pilgrims to and from California, made ready to ascend to Panama....

It was not so easy to hire a boat as I had been led to expect. The large crowd had made the boatmen somewhat exorbitant in their demands.... There were several reasons why I should engage one for my own exclusive use, instead of sharing one with some of my traveling companions. In the first place, my luggage was somewhat bulky; and, in the second place, my experience of travel had not failed to teach me that Americans (even from the Northern States) are always uncomfortable in the company of colored people, and very often show this feeling in stronger ways than by sour looks and rude words. I think, if I have a little prejudice against our cousins across the Atlantic—and I do confess to a little—it is not unreasonable. I have a few shades of deeper brown upon my skin which shows me related—and I am proud of the relationship—to those poor mortals whom you once held enslaved, and whose bodies America still owns. And having this bond, and knowing what slavery is; having seen with my eyes and heard with my ears proof positive enough of its horrors—let others affect to doubt them if they will—is it surprising that I should be somewhat impatient of the airs of superiority which many Americans have endeavored to assume over me? Mind, I am not speaking of all. I have met with some delightful exceptions. 99

The first edition of Mary Seacole's *Wonderful Adventures* appeared in London in 1857 with her picture on the cover.
(© Museum of London)

Source: Mary Seacole, *Wonderful Adventures of Mrs. Seacole in Many Lands* (London: Blackwood, 1857), pp. 1–17.

QUESTIONS FOR ANALYSIS

1. How does Mary Seacole understand race?
2. How does she understand disease? What were the health problems that she saw as most serious?
3. What audience do you think Seacole is attempting to address in her autobiography?

grants gave an international flavor and a more vigorous tempo to Latin American cities. Thanks to the influx of new arrivals Rio de Janeiro, Mexico City, Montevideo, Santiago, Havana, and Buenos Aires experienced spectacular growth.

By 1914 Buenos Aires in particular had emerged as one of the most cosmopolitan cities in the world, with a population of 3.6 million. As Argentina's political capital, the city housed all its government bureaucracies and agencies. The meatpacking, food-processing, flour-milling, and wool industries were concentrated there as well. Half of all overseas tonnage passed through the city, which was also the heart of the nation's railroad network. Elegant shops near the Plaza de Mayo catered to the expensive tastes of the elite upper classes, who constituted about 5 percent of the population. By contrast, the thousands of immigrants who toiled twelve hours a day, six days a week, on docks and construction sites and in meatpacking plants were crowded into the city's one-room tenements,

Buenos Aires, 1894 When this photo was taken, Buenos Aires was already a cosmopolitan city, with a population of more than 600,000, and its streets looked much like streets in European cities of the time. (Archivo General de la Nación, Buenos Aires)

furnished with a few iron cots, a table and chairs, and maybe an old trunk.

Despite such difficult living conditions, immigrants' dreams of rapid economic success in the New World often came true. The first generation almost always did manual labor, but its sons often advanced to upper-blue-collar or white-collar jobs. The sons of successful Genoese or Neapolitan immigrants typically imitated the dress, manners, and values of the Creole elite.

Immigrants brought wide-ranging skills that helped develop industry and commerce. In Argentina, Italian and Spanish settlers stimulated the expansion of the cattle industry and the development of the wheat and shoe industries. In Brazil, Swiss immigrants built the cheese business, Italians gained a leading role in the coffee industry, and Japanese pioneered the development of the cotton industry. In Peru, Italians became influential in banking and the restaurant business, while the French dominated dressmaking as well as the jewelry and pharmaceutical businesses. Chinese laborers built the railroads, and in sections of large cities such as Lima, the Chinese came to dominate the ownership of shops and restaurants. European immigrants also brought anarchist and socialist ideas and became involved in union organizing.

The vast majority of migrants were unmarried males; seven out of ten people who landed in Argentina between 1857 and 1924 were single males between thirteen and forty years old. There, as in other South American countries, many of those who stayed sought Indian or other low-status women, leading to further racial mixing.

The creation of independent nations in Latin America did little to improve the position of the poor.

Neocolonialism had a modernizing influence on commerce and industry, but it further concentrated wealth. Spanish and Portuguese merchants who returned to the Iberian Peninsula were replaced by British and U.S. businessmen. Just as the United States waged wars against the Indians (see pages 825–827) and pushed its frontier westward, so Brazil, Venezuela, Ecuador, Peru, and Bolivia expanded into the Amazonian frontier at the expense of indigenous peoples. Likewise, Mexico, Chile, and Argentina had their "Indian wars" and frontier expansion. Racial prejudice kept most of the South American black population in a wretched socioeconomic position until well past 1914. European immigrants, rather than black plantation workers, gained the urban jobs. In 1893, 71.2 percent of the working population of São Paulo was foreign-born. Blacks continued to work cutting sugar cane and picking coffee.

The United States, 1789–1914

☐ How did the United States build a large but unified nation?

The American Revolution (see page 656) seemed to validate the Enlightenment idea that a better life on earth was possible. Americans carried an unbounded optimism about the future into the nineteenth and twentieth centuries. Until 1860 most eastern states limited voting rights to property holders or taxpayers, but suffrage was gradually expanded to include most adult white males. The movement toward popular democracy accelerated as the young nation, confident of its "manifest destiny," pushed relentlessly across the continent. As settlers moved into new territories, the industrializing North and the agricultural South came into conflict over extending slavery into these lands. The ensuing Civil War (1861–1865) cost six hundred thousand American lives — more than any other war the nation has fought. Yet the victory of the North preserved the federal system and strengthened the United States as a nation.

The years between 1865 and 1917 witnessed the transformation of the United States into a major industrial power. Immigrants settled much of the West, put the prairies to the plow, provided the labor to exploit the country's mineral resources, turned small provincial towns into sophisticated centers of ethnic and cultural diversity, and built the railroads that tied the country together. Most of the social and cultural phenomena seen in western Europe in this period (see Chapter 24) — such as improved sanitation, mass transit, faith in science, and strong identification with the nation — occurred also in the United States.

Manifest Destiny and Its Consequences for Native Americans

In an 1845 issue of the *United States Magazine and Democratic Review*, editor John L. O'Sullivan boldly declared that foreign powers were trying to prevent American annexation of Texas in order to impede "the fulfillment of our manifest destiny to overspread the continent allotted by Providence for the free development of our yearly multiplying millions." O'Sullivan was articulating a sentiment prevalent in the United States since early in its history: that God had foreordained the nation to cover the entire continent. After a large-circulation newspaper picked up the phrase **manifest destiny**, it was used on the floor of Congress and soon entered the language as a catchword for and justification of expansion.

When George Washington became president in 1789, fewer than 4 million people inhabited the thirteen states on the eastern seaboard. By the time Abraham Lincoln became the sixteenth president in 1861, the United States stretched across the continent and had 31 million inhabitants. During the colonial period, pioneers pushed westward to the Appalachian Mountains. After independence, westward movement accelerated. The eastern states claimed all the land from the Atlantic Ocean to the Mississippi River, but two forces blocked immediate expansion. The Indians, trying to save their lands, allied with the British in Canada to prevent further American encroachment. In 1794 Brit-

> ❝The fulfillment of our manifest destiny [is] to overspread the continent allotted by Providence for the free development of our yearly multiplying millions.❞
>
> **JOHN L. O'SULLIVAN**

ain agreed to evacuate border forts in the Northwest Territory, roughly the area north of the Ohio River and east of the Mississippi, and thereby end British support for the Indians. A similar treaty with Spain paved the way for southeastern expansion.

Events in Europe and the Caribbean led to a massive increase in American territory. In 1800 Spain ceded the Louisiana Territory — the land between the Mississippi River and the Rocky Mountains — to France. Three years later Napoleon sold it to the United States for only $12 million. Spain, preoccupied with rebellions in South America, sold the Florida Territory to the U.S. government, and beginning in 1821 American settlers poured into the Mexican territory of Texas, whose soil proved excellent for the production of cotton and sugar. Southern politicians, fearing that Texas would become a refuge for fugitive slaves, pressured President John Tyler to admit Texas to the United States. The admission of Florida as the twenty-seventh state and Texas as the twenty-eighth state in 1845 meant the absorption of large numbers of Hispanic people into the United States. Many of them had lived in those regions since the sixteenth century, long before Anglo immigration.

The acquisition of Texas's 267,339 square miles (making it a fifth larger than France) whetted American appetites for the rest of the old Spanish Empire in North America. Some expansionists even dreamed of taking Cuba and Central America.

Exploiting Mexico's political instability, President James Polk goaded Mexico into war. Mexico suffered total defeat and in the 1848 **Treaty of Guadalupe Hidalgo** surrendered its remaining claims to Texas, yielded New Mexico and California to the United States, and recognized the Rio Grande as the international border. A treaty with Great Britain in 1846 had already recognized the American settlement in the Oregon Territory, so with the new lands from Mexico the continent had been acquired. Then, in 1898 a revolt in Cuba against an incompetent Spanish administration had consequences beyond "manifest destiny." Inflamed by press reports of Spanish atrocities, public opinion swept

- **manifest destiny** The belief that God had foreordained Americans to cover the entire continent.
- **Treaty of Guadalupe Hidalgo** The 1848 treaty between the United States and Mexico in which Mexico ceded large tracts of land to the United States in exchange for $15 million.

> "We are deprived of membership in the human family! We have neither land, nor home, nor resting place, that can be called our own."
>
> **CHEROKEE CHIEF JOHN ROSS**

the United States into war. The Spanish-American War—the "splendid little war," as Secretary of State John Hay called it—lasted just ten weeks and brought U.S. control over Cuba, the Philippines, and Puerto Rico. The United States had become a colonial power.

The people who were native to this vast continent fared poorly under manifest destiny. Government officials sometimes manipulated the Indians by gathering a few chiefs, plying them with cheap whiskey, and then inducing them to hand over the tribes' hunting grounds. Sometimes officials exploited rivalries among tribes or used bribes. By these methods, William Henry Harrison, superintendent of the Indians of the Northwest Territory and a future president, got some Native Americans to cede 48 million acres (Map 27.2). He had the full backing of President Jefferson.

The policy of pushing the Indians westward across the Mississippi accelerated during Andrew Jackson's presidency (1829–1837). Thousands of Delawares, Shawnees, and Wyandots, tricked into moving from east of the Mississippi River to reservations west of Missouri, died of cholera and measles during the journey. The survivors found themselves hopelessly in debt for supplies and farming equipment. The state of Georgia, meanwhile, was nibbling away at Cherokee lands, which were theoretically protected by treaty with the U.S. government. When gold was discovered on the Cherokee lands, a gold rush took place. The Creek, Cherokee, and other tribes were rounded up, expelled, and sent beyond the western boundaries of Missouri and Arkansas. Cherokee Chief John Ross, in a 1935 letter to Congress, movingly appealed, "We are deprived of membership in the human family! We have neither land, nor home, nor resting place, that can be called our own."[5]

The mid-nineteenth century saw a steady flow of white settlers westward past the Mississippi River into the Great Plains, home to many Indians who hunted on horseback using rifles. The U.S. Army, in the name of protecting the migrants, fought the Indians, destroyed

MAP 27.2 Indian Cession of Lands to the United States, 1784–1890 Forced removal of the Creeks, Cherokees, and Chickasaws to reservations in Oklahoma led to the deaths of thousands of Native Americans on the Trail of Tears, as well as to the destruction of their cultures.

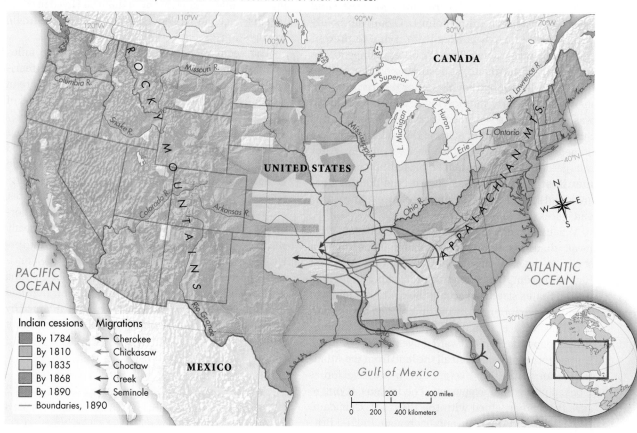

their lodges and horses, and slaughtered the buffalo on which they depended for food, shelter, and clothing. The federal government's policy was to confine indigenous people to reservations, where malnutrition and disease took a terrible toll.

Cultural differences aggravated conflict between white settlers and Native Americans. Unlike the whites, Indians did not think of land in terms of private property; they believed that land, like other resources such as air and water, belonged to everyone, that individuals or groups might hold temporary stewardship over the land but that it should be respected and treasured for future generations. In another cultural difference, white Americans, because they had a commander in chief (the president) who could give orders and expect them to be carried out, assumed that a respected Native American chief could make agreements binding on all tribes. But no chief could command all the Sioux, let alone all the Plains Indians. When a tribe or group of tribes opposed or disregarded a treaty made by a particular chief, the whites claimed that the Indians as a whole had broken the treaty.

In 1868, after pursuing a policy of total war on the Plains Indians, General W. T. Sherman brokered the Treaty of Fort Laramie. This treaty promised that the United States would close western forts and grant the Sioux and Cheyenne permanent control of their ancestral lands in the Dakotas: the Black Hills as well as the area between the Platte River and the Bighorn Mountains. A few chiefs signed; many did not. In 1874 gold was discovered in the Black Hills, and prospectors flooded into the area. By 1875 whites outnumbered Indians there, violating the terms of the treaty. During the course of the nineteenth century, while the number of white residents skyrocketed from 4.3 million to 66.8 million, the number of Indians steadily declined to a recorded 237,196 in 1900.

Women's Roles in White Settlements

Generally speaking, the settlers' lives blurred sex roles. It fell to women to make homes out of crude log cabins that had no windows or doors or out of tarpaper shacks with mud floors. Lacking cookstoves, they prepared food over open fireplaces, using all kinds of substitutes for ingredients easily available back east. To wash clothes, women had to make soap out of lye and carefully saved household ashes.

Considered the carriers of "high culture," women organized whatever educational, religious, musical, and recreational activities the settlers' society possessed. Women also had to defend their homes against prairie fires and Indian attacks. These burdens were accompanied by frequent pregnancies and, often, the need to give birth without medical help or even the support of other women. The death rate for infants and young children ran as high as 30 percent in the mid-nineteenth century. Even so, the women had large families.

Influenced by ideas then circulating in England, some women began promoting rights for women. At the Seneca Falls Convention in 1848, they demanded equal political and economic rights. Others promoted women's education and opened women's colleges. It was not until 1920, however, that women in the United States got the right to vote.

England remained an important cultural influence in other spheres besides women's rights and abolition. Many books published in London were quickly reprinted in the United States once copies arrived, and favorite English novelists such as Charles Dickens became popular in the United States as well. Education beyond the elementary level usually involved reading classics of English literature. Meanwhile, in the American South, rights to an education and other freedoms were withheld from another group of citizens: blacks.

Black Slavery in the South

In 1619, as one solution to the chronic labor shortage in North America, Dutch traders brought the first black people to Virginia as prisoners (white indentured servants who worked for a term of years was another solution). In the early eighteenth century, with the expansion of rice cultivation in the Carolinas and tobacco farming in Virginia and Maryland, planters demanded more laborers. Between 1720 and 1770, black prisoners poured into the Southern colonies, and in South Carolina they came to outnumber whites by almost two to one. From 1730 through 1760, white fears of black revolts pushed colonial legislatures to pass laws that established blacks' legal position as property of whites, enshrining the slave system in law. Racist arguments of blacks' supposed inferiority were used to justify slavery.

The American Revolution did not bring liberty to slaves. The framers of the Constitution treated private property as sacrosanct and viewed slaves as property. Antislavery sentiment was growing, however, and states from Delaware north eventually outlawed slavery. In 1809 the United States followed Britain's lead in outlawing the importation of slaves. Nevertheless, white planters and farmers had a material and psychological interest in maintaining black bondage, which brought financial profit and conferred social status and prestige.

Between 1820 and 1860, as new lands in the South and West — in Arkansas, Mississippi, Texas, and Louisiana — were put to the production of cotton and sugar, the demand for labor skyrocketed. The upper South — Maryland and Virginia — where decades of tobacco farming had reduced the fertility of the soil, supplied the slaves. Slave traders worked either independently

▫ Picturing the Past

Slave Auction, 1850s In a scene outside a country tavern near a river with a Mississippi-type steamer on it, an auctioneer extols a biracial girl's qualities to a group of planters (center), while another dealer with a whip (left) brutally separates a mother from her children. The picture was intended to send an abolitionist message. (Carnegie Museum of Art, Pittsburgh. Gift of Mrs. W. Fitch Ingersoll)

ANALYZING THE IMAGE Look at the clothing the various people are wearing. What social distinctions do they convey? Is there anything else about the picture that lets you know it was intended to send an abolitionist message?

CONNECTIONS Can you think of other examples of art with social or political messages? How would this painting compare in its effectiveness?

or from firms in Charleston, Natchez, and New Orleans, the largest slave market in the United States. This period witnessed the forced migration of about 650,000 people, in many cases causing the breakup of slave families.

Despite such threats to black families, a study of the entire adult slave population of North Carolina in 1860 has shown that most slave women spent their entire adult lives in settled unions with the same hus-

band. Planters encouraged slave marriages because large slave families were in their economic interest, especially after the end of the Atlantic slave trade. As one owner put it, "marriage adds to the comfort, happiness, and health of those entering upon it, besides insuring a greater increase."[6] Evidence from all parts of the South reveals that, in spite of illiteracy, separated spouses tried to remain in touch with one another and, once slavery had been abolished, went to enormous

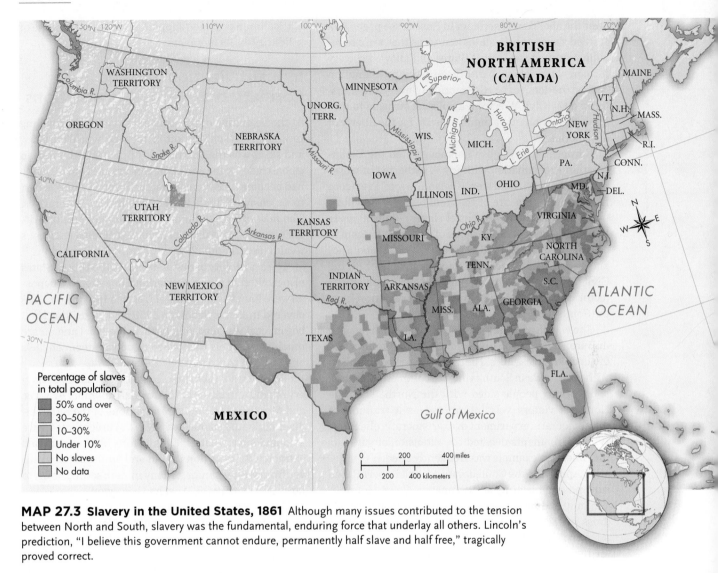

MAP 27.3 Slavery in the United States, 1861 Although many issues contributed to the tension between North and South, slavery was the fundamental, enduring force that underlay all others. Lincoln's prediction, "I believe this government cannot endure, permanently half slave and half free," tragically proved correct.

lengths to reunite their families. Typically, a slave woman had her first child around the age of nineteen. On the Good Hope plantation in South Carolina, 80 percent of slave couples had at least four children.

Blacks who were freed by their masters often went north in search of better opportunities. James Forten, a free black man (d. 1842) from Philadelphia, built a large sail-making business that employed an integrated workforce. He had a reputation as a businessman of integrity and acquired considerable wealth. But most whites of the city refused to accept him as a citizen and subjected him to verbal and physical assaults.[7]

The Civil War and Its Impact

In the 1850s westward expansion, not moral outrage, brought the controversy over slavery to a head. As Congress created new territories, the question of whether slavery would be extended to them arose again and again (Map 27.3). For years elaborate compromises were worked out, but tensions rose, fueled by increasing differences between the North and South. On the eve of the Civil War the South was overwhelmingly agricultural, while the North controlled 90 percent of the country's industrial capacity.

Abraham Lincoln, committed to checking the spread of slavery, was elected president in 1860. To protest his victory, South Carolina seceded from the Union in December of that year. Ten Southern states soon followed South Carolina's example and formed the **Confederacy**. Its capital was at Richmond, Virginia.

Lincoln declared the seceding states' actions illegal and declared war on them to preserve the Union. The years of fighting that followed took a huge toll on both sides. Thinking that it might help end the war more quickly, Lincoln issued the Emancipation Proclamation, which became effective on January 1, 1863 (two years

• **Confederacy** The eleven Southern states that seceded from the United States and bonded together with a capital at Richmond, Virginia.

after the abolition of serfdom in Russia; see page 730). It freed slaves only in states and areas that were in rebellion against the United States and allowed slavery for convicted felons. Nevertheless, the proclamation spelled the doom of North American slavery and transformed the Civil War from a political struggle to preserve the Union into a moral crusade for the liberty of all Americans.

European and English liberals greeted the Emancipation Proclamation with joy. A gathering of working people in Manchester, England, wrote President Lincoln: "The erasure of that foul blot upon civilization and Christianity — chattel slavery — during your Presidency will cause the name of Abraham Lincoln to be honoured and revered by posterity."[8] As Lincoln acknowledged, this was a magnanimous statement, for the Civil War hurt working people in Manchester, whose factories had closed when importation of cotton from the South stopped.

The war also had important political consequences in Europe. In 1861 British and European opinion had divided along class lines. The upper classes sympathized with the American South, while the commercial classes and working people sided with the North. Thus the Northern victory was interpreted as a triumph of the democratic experiment over aristocratic oligarchy. When parliaments debated the extension of suffrage, the American example was frequently cited.

In April 1865 the Confederate general Robert E. Lee surrendered his army at Appomattox Court House in Virginia, ending the war. In his second inaugural address in 1864 Lincoln had called for "malice toward none and charity for all." Those who came to power after Lincoln was assassinated in April 1865 were less inclined to be generous toward the South.

During Reconstruction (1865–1877), the vanquished South had to adjust to a new social and economic order without slavery. Former slaves wanted land to farm, but, lacking cash, they soon accepted the sharecropping system: sharecroppers paid landowners about half of a year's crops at harvest time in return for a cabin, food, mules, seed, tools, and land.

The Fifteenth Amendment to the U.S. Constitution outlawed denying anyone the vote "on account of race, color, or previous condition of servitude," and in the early years of Reconstruction, when Northerners were in charge, many former slaves voted. However, between 1880 and 1920, after Southerners returned to power, so-called Jim Crow laws were passed to prevent blacks from voting and to enforce rigid racial segregation.

In these racist circumstances, no institution played a more positive role in the construction of a black community than the black Protestant churches. Black preachers esteemed for their oratorical skill, organizational ability, and practical judgment became leaders of the black community. Throughout the South the black church provided support, security, and a sense of solidarity for its members.

Industrialization and the Formation of Large Corporations

At the beginning of the nineteenth century, providing raw materials such as cotton, tobacco, whale oil, pelts, and skins was the central role of the United States in global trade. By the end of the century the United States had become a major manufacturing power, due in part to extensive British investment in U.S. enterprises. The flow of British funds was a consequence of Britain's own industrialization, which generated enormous wealth (see Chapter 23).

The availability of raw materials in the United States also facilitated industrialization. Huge iron ore deposits were found near the Great Lakes in 1844; oil was discovered in Pennsylvania in 1859, and oil drilling soon began; coal was also widely available. Coal and oil are much better fuels than wood to power steam engines and to smelt iron and other metals.

The West also held precious metals, and the discovery of gold and silver in California, Colorado, Arizona, and Montana and on the reservations of the Sioux Indians of South Dakota (see page 827) precipitated huge gold and silver rushes. Even before 1900 miners had extracted $1.24 billion in gold and $901 million in silver from western mines. Many miners settled down to farm, and by 1912 the West had been won.

The federal government contributed to industrialization by turning over vast amounts of land and mineral resources to industry for development. The railroads — the foundation of industrial expansion — received 130 million acres. By 1900 the U.S. railroad system was 193,000 miles long, connected every part of the nation, and represented 40 percent of the railroad mileage of the entire world.

Between 1880 and 1920 industrial production soared. By the 1890s the United States was producing twice as much steel as Britain. Large factories replaced small ones, and Henry Ford of Detroit set up assembly lines in the automobile industry. Each person working on the line performed only one task instead of assembling an entire car. In 1910 Ford sold 10,000 cars; in 1914, a year after he inaugurated the first moving assembly line, he sold 248,000 cars. Other new machines also had a pervasive impact. Sewing machines made cheap, varied mass-produced clothing available for city people to purchase in department stores and country people through mail-order catalogues.

Even food production was industrialized. Grain elevators, introduced in 1850, made it possible to store much more grain, which could be transported by the growing rail system as needed. The new practice of canning meant that food did not have to be eaten immedi-

Oklahoma Homesteaders Beginning in 1889, Indian land in Oklahoma was offered to white settlers, who had to build a dwelling and cultivate the land for five years to gain full title to it. With trees scarce, settlers often built their houses of sod, which provided insulation but could be damaged by heavy rain. This picture of three generations of a family outside their sod house was taken in 1901. (Western History Collection, University of Oklahoma Libraries)

ately, and the development of refrigeration meant that meat could be shipped long distances. Factories turned out crackers, cookies, and breakfast cereals.

The national economy experienced repeated cycles of boom and bust in the late nineteenth century. Serious depressions in 1873, 1884, and 1893 slashed prices and threw many people out of work. Leading industrialists responded by establishing larger corporations and consolidating companies into huge conglomerates. As a result of the merger of several small oil companies, John D. Rockefeller's Standard Oil Company controlled 84 percent of the nation's oil and most American pipelines in 1898. J. P. Morgan's United States Steel monopolized the iron and steel industries, and Swift & Co. of Chicago controlled the meat-processing industry.

Immigrants and Their Reception

Immigrants were an important source of workers for the new American industries, and the United States attracted these newcomers from its founding. Before the Civil War most immigrants came from England, Ireland, and Germany. When the Irish potato crop was destroyed by a fungal disease leading to a horrific famine in 1845–1859, a million people fled overseas, the majority heading to the United States. Immigrants who arrived with nothing had to work as laborers for years, but in time many were able to acquire farms, especially if they were willing to move west as the country expanded. The Homestead Act of 1862 made land available to anyone willing to work it. From then until the end of the century, 500 million acres were put into production.

Between 1860 and 1900, 14 million additional immigrants arrived in the United States, and during the peak years between 1900 and 1914, another 14 million immigrants passed through the U.S. customs inspection station at Ellis Island in New York City. Industrial America developed on the sweat and brawn of these people. Chinese, Scandinavian, and Irish immigrants laid thirty thousand miles of railroad tracks between 1867 and 1873 and another seventy-three thousand miles in the 1880s. At the Carnegie Steel Corporation, Slavs and Italians produced one-third of the world's total steel supply in 1900. Lithuanians, Poles, Croats, Scandinavians, Irish, and blacks entered the Chicago stockyards and built the meatpacking industry. Irish immigrants continued to operate the spinning frames and knitting machines of New England's textile mills.

As in South America, immigration fed the growth of cities. In 1790 only 5.1 percent of Americans were living in centers of twenty-five hundred or more people. By 1860 this figure had risen to 19.9 percent, and by 1900 almost 40 percent were living in cities. Also by 1900, three of the largest cities in the world were in the United States — New York City with 3.4 million people, Chicago with 1.7 million, and Philadelphia with 1.4. As in Europe (see Chapter 24), cities themselves were being transformed. By the early twentieth century they had electricity, sewer systems that curbed the spread of infectious diseases, and streetcars that allowed them to expand, thus reducing crowding.

Still, the working conditions that new immigrants found were often deplorable. Industrialization had created a vast class of wage workers who depended totally on their employers for work. To keep labor costs low, employers paid workers piecemeal for the number of articles they made, and they hired women and children who could be paid much less than men. Some women textile workers earned as little as $1.56 for seventy hours of work, while men received from $7 to $9 for the same work. Because business owners fought in legislatures and courts against the installation of costly safety devices, working conditions in mines and mills were frightful. In 1913 alone, even after some safety measures had been taken, twenty-five thousand people died in industrial accidents. Between 1900 and 1917 seventy-two thousand railroad worker deaths occurred. Workers responded with strikes, violence, and, gradually, unionization.

In *How the Other Half Lives* (1890), Jacob Riis, a newspaper reporter and recent immigrant from Denmark, drew national attention to what he called "the foul core of New York's slums." Riis estimated that three hundred thousand people inhabited a single square mile on New York's Lower East Side. Overcrowding, poor sanitation, and lack of health services caused frequent epidemics. The blight of slums also increased crime, prostitution, alcoholism, and other addictions.

Nationalism carried different meanings in the United States than it did in Europe (see pages 719–721). It did not refer to an ancient people whose unique culture was tied to its language, as it did in Europe. Immigrants were expected to switch their loyalties to their new country and learn English. As in Europe, much was done to promote patriotism and bring people together through flag-waving parades and other emotionally charged symbols and ceremonies. The negative side of identification with the nation was nativist sentiment — that is, hostility to foreign and "un-American" looks, behavior, and loyalties — among native-born Americans. Some of this antagonism sprang from racism, some from old Protestant suspicions of Roman Catholicism, the faith of many of the new arrivals. Long-standing anti-Semitism also played a part. A great deal of the dislike of the foreign-born sprang from fear of economic competition. To most Americans, the Chinese with their exotic looks and willingness to work for very little seemed especially dangerous. Increasingly violent agitation against Asians

Racist Cartoon from *Harper's Weekly*, 1869 Nineteenth-century immigrants encountered terrible prejudice, as even "respectable" magazines and newspapers spewed out racism, such as this cartoon from an 1869 issue of *Harper's Weekly* that satirizes both the Irish and the Chinese as "uncivilized." The Irishman is identified by his shillelagh, a blackthorn club, here used to imply a tendency toward violence, and the Chinese man is identified by his long pigtail and his bowing, seen as a sign of his devious obsequiousness. Well into the twentieth century, being American meant being of Anglo-Saxon descent. (*Harper's Weekly*, August 28, 1869. Private Collection)

THE COMING MAN — JOHN CHINAMAN.
Uncle Sam introduces Eastern Barbarism to Western Civilization.

led to race riots in California and finally culminated in the Chinese Exclusion Act of 1882, which denied Chinese laborers entrance to the country.

The severe economic depression of the 1890s also fed resentment toward immigrants. Faced with overproduction, the rich and politically powerful owners of mines, mills, and factories fought the organization of labor unions, laid off thousands of workers, slashed wages, and ruthlessly exploited their workers. Workers in turn feared that immigrant labor would drive salaries lower.

Canada, from French Colony to Nation

◻ What geographical, economic, and political conditions shaped the development of Canada?

In 1608 the French explorer Samuel de Champlain (1567–1635) sailed down the St. Lawrence River (see Map 27.4) and established a trading post on the site of present-day Quebec. Thus began the permanent colony of New France. The fur-trading monopolies subsequently granted to Champlain by the French crown attracted settlers, and Jesuit missionaries to the Indians further increased the French population. The British, however, vigorously challenged French control of the lucrative fur trade. The mid-eighteenth-century global struggle for empire between the British and the French, known in Europe as the Seven Years' War (see pages 654–656), spilled into North America, where it was known as the French and Indian Wars. In 1759, on a field next to the city of Quebec, the English defeated the French and ended the French empire in North America. By the Treaty of Paris of 1763, France ceded Canada to Great Britain.

For the French Canadians, who in 1763 numbered about ninety thousand, the British conquest was a tragedy. British governors replaced the French, and English-speaking merchants from Britain and the thirteen American colonies to the south took over the colony's economic affairs. The Roman Catholic Church remained, however, and played a powerful role in the political and cultural, as well as the religious, life of French Canadians. Most French Canadians were farmers, though a small merchant class sold furs and imported manufactured goods.

In 1774 the British Parliament passed the Quebec Act, which granted religious freedom to French Canadians and recognized French law in civil matters, but it denied Canadians a legislative assembly, a traditional feature of British colonial government. Instead, Parliament placed power in the hands of an appointed governor and an appointed council composed of both English and French Canadians. English Canadian businessmen protested that they were being denied a basic right of Englishmen — representation.

During the American Revolution, about forty thousand Americans demonstrated their loyalty to Great Britain and its empire by moving to Canada. These "loyalists" not only altered the French-English ratio in the population but also pressed for a representative assembly. In 1791 Parliament responded with the Constitution Act, which divided the province of Quebec in two and provided for an elective assembly in each province.

Not wanting to repeat the errors made in 1776, when failure to grant the thirteen colonies autonomy provoked them to declare independence, the British gradually extended home rule to Canada, beginning in 1840. During the American Civil War (1861–1865), English-American relations were severely strained, and fear of American aggression led to **confederation**, a loose union of the provinces, each with substantial powers. In 1867 the provinces of New Brunswick and Nova Scotia joined Ontario and Quebec to form the Dominion of Canada (Map 27.4). The Dominion Cabinet was given jurisdiction over internal affairs, while Britain retained control over foreign policy. (In 1931 the British Statute of Westminster officially recognized Canadian autonomy in foreign affairs.)

Believing that the U.S. Constitution left the states too strong and helped to bring on the Civil War, the framers of the Canadian constitution created a powerful central government. The first prime minister, John A. Macdonald, vigorously pushed Canada's "manifest destiny" to absorb the entire northern part of the continent. In 1870 his government purchased the vast Northwest Territories of the Hudson's Bay Company for $1.5 million. Fearful that the sparsely settled colony of British Columbia would join the United States, Macdonald lured British Columbia into the confederation with a subsidy to pay its debts and the promise of a transcontinental railroad. Likewise, the tiny, debt-ridden maritime province of Prince Edward Island was drawn into the confederation with a large subsidy. In the five short years between 1868 and 1873, through Macdonald's imagination and drive, Canadian sovereignty stretched from coast to coast. The completion of the Canadian Pacific Railroad in 1885 led to the formation of two new prairie provinces, Alberta and Saskatchewan, which in 1905 entered the Dominion. (Only in 1949 did the island of Newfoundland renounce colonial status and join the Dominion.)

Canada was thinly populated in the nineteenth century, and by 1900 still had only a little over 5 million

---

• **confederation** A relatively loose form of union, leaving the parts with substantial powers.

MAP 27.4 The Dominion of Canada, 1871 Shortly after the Dominion of Canada came into being as a self-governing nation within the British Empire in 1867, new provinces were added. Vast areas of Canada were too sparsely populated to achieve provincial status. Alberta and Saskatchewan did not become part of the Dominion until 1905, Newfoundland only in 1949.

people (as compared to 76 million in the United States). As in the United States, the native peoples were pushed aside by Canada's development plans, and their population dropped by half or more during the century, many succumbing to the newcomers' diseases. There were only about 127,000 left in 1900. French Canadians remained the largest minority in the population. Distinctively different in language, law, and religion and fiercely proud of their culture, they resisted assimilation.

Immigration picked up in the 1890s. Between 1897 and 1912, 961,000 people entered Canada from the British Isles, 594,000 from Europe, and 784,000 from the United States. Some immigrants went to work in the urban factories of Hamilton, Toronto, and Montreal. However, most immigrants from continental Europe — Poles, Germans, Scandinavians, and Russians — flooded the midwestern plains and soon transformed the prairies into one of the world's greatest grain-growing regions. Between 1891 and 1914, wheat production rocketed from 2 million bushels per year to 150 million bushels. Mining also was expanded, and British Columbia, Ontario, and Quebec produced large quantities of wood pulp, much of it sold to the United States. Canada's great rivers were harnessed to supply hydroelectric power for industrial and domestic use. But Canada remained a predominantly agricultural country, with less than 10 percent of its population engaged in manufacturing (and a third of them processing timber or food).

Australia, from Penal Colony to Nation

☐ What circumstances shaped the development of Australia?

In April 1770 James Cook, the English explorer, navigator, and captain of HMS *Endeavor*, dropped anchor in a wide bay about ten miles south of the present city of Sydney on the coast of eastern Australia. Because the young botanist on board the ship, Joseph Banks, subsequently discovered thirty thousand specimens of plant life in the bay, sixteen hundred of them unknown to European science, Captain Cook called the place

• **Botany Bay** A bay on the coast of eastern Australia in which numerous specimens of plant life were discovered. It later became home to a penal colony.

• **New South Wales** The name given to Australia by James Cook, the English explorer; today it is the name of the most populous of the six states of Australia.

Russian Immigrant Women in Saskatchewan These women were Doukhobors, members of a Christian religious sect who came to Canada from Russia seeking religious freedom from tsarist persecution. While most of the men took railroad jobs, the women planted the vast plains with rye, wheat, oats, and flax. Their farms and orchards flourished, and the Doukhobors played an important role in the development of western Canada. (Saskatchewan Archives Board, photo no. R-B 1964)

Botany Bay. Totally unimpressed by the flat landscape and its few naked inhabitants — the Aborigines, or native people — Cook sailed north along the coast (Map 27.5). On August 21, on a rock later named Possession Island, Cook formally claimed the entire land south of where he stood for King George III, sixteen thousand miles away. Cook called the land **New South Wales**. In accepting possession, the British crown acted on the legal fiction that Australia was *Terra Nullius*, completely unoccupied, thus entirely ignoring the native people.

Britain populated the new land with prisoners, and their labor — as well as the efforts of their descendants and new arrivals — transformed Australia into an economically viable and increasingly independent nation. Like the other nations discussed in this chapter, Australia was not free of racial discrimination.

A Distant Land Turned Penal Colony

The world's smallest continent, Australia is about half the size of Europe and almost as large as the United States (excluding Alaska and Hawai'i). It has a temperate climate and little intense cold. Three topographical zones (see Map 27.5) roughly divide the continent. The Western Plateau, a vast desert and semidesert region, covers almost two-thirds of the continent. The Central Eastern Lowlands extend from the Gulf of Carpentaria in the north to western Victoria in the south. The Eastern Highlands are a complex belt of tablelands.

When Cook arrived in Australia, about three hundred thousand Aborigines lived there. A peaceful and nomadic people who had emigrated from southern Asia millennia earlier, the Aborigines lived entirely by food gathering, fishing, and hunting. They had no agriculture. Although they used spears, bows, and arrows in hunting, they never practiced warfare as it was understood by more technologically advanced peoples such as the Mexica (Aztecs) of Mexico or the Mandinke of West Africa. When the white settlers arrived, they occupied the Aborigine lands unopposed. Like the Indians of Central and South America, the Aborigines fell victim to the white peoples' diseases and to a spiritual malaise caused by the breakdown of their tribal life. Today only about forty-five thousand pureblood Aborigines survive.

The victory of the thirteen North American colonies in 1783 inadvertently contributed to the establishment of a colony in Australia five years later. Crime in England was increasing in the 1770s and 1780s, and the transportation of felons "beyond the seas" seemed the answer to the problem of overcrowded prisons. Until the founding of the United States in 1776, the British government had shipped about one thousand convicts annually to the North American colony of Georgia. After that became impossible, the British Cabinet approved the establishment of a penal colony at Botany Bay in 1786 to serve as "a remedy for the evils likely to result from the late alarming and numerous increase of felons in this country, and more particularly in the metropolis (London)."[9] The name "Botany Bay" became

Governor Arthur's Proclamation In 1830, to communicate to Aborigines the idea of equal justice for all, the governor of Van Dieman's land (modern Tasmania) had picture boards displayed. This one shows an Aborigine being hung for killing a settler with a spear, and a settler being hung for shooting an Aborigine with a rifle. (Mitchell Library, State Library of New South Wales)

a byword for the forced and permanent exile of criminals. In May 1787 a fleet of eleven ships packed with a thousand felons and their jailers sailed for Australia. On January 28, 1788, after an eight-month voyage, it landed in Sydney Cove.

Mere survival in an alien world was the first challenge. Because the land at Botany Bay proved completely unsuited for agriculture and lacked decent wa-

ter, the first governor, Arthur Phillip, moved the colony ten miles north to Port Jackson, later called Sydney. Announcing that those who did not work would not eat, Phillip set the prisoners to planting seeds. But coming from the slums of London, the convicts knew nothing of agriculture, and some were too ill or too old to work. Moreover, the colony lacked draft animals and plows. Consequently, the colony of New South Wales tottered on the brink of starvation for years.

Until the penal colony system was abolished in 1869, a total of 161,000 convicts were transported to Australia. Transportation rested on two premises: that criminals should be punished and that they should not be a financial burden on the state. Convicts became free when their sentences expired or were remitted, but few returned to England.

For the first thirty years of the penal colony, men far outnumbered women. Because the British government refused to allow wives to accompany their convict-husbands, prostitution flourished. Many women convicts, if not professional prostitutes when they left England, became such during the long voyage south. Army officers, government officials, and free immigrants chose favorite convicts as mistresses.

Officers and jailers, though descended from the middle and lower middle classes, tried to establish a colonial gentry and to impose the rigid class distinctions that they had known in England. Known as **exclusionists**, these self-appointed members of the colonial gentry tried to exclude from polite society all freed people, called **emancipists**. Deep and bitter class feeling took root.

An Economy Built on Wool, Gold, and Immigrant Labor

Governor Phillip and his successors urged the British Colonial Office to send free settlers, not just prisoners, to Australia. After the end of the Napoleonic wars in 1815 a steady stream of people relocated there. The end of the European wars also released capital for potential investment. But investment in what? What commodity could be developed and exported to England?

Immigrants explored several possibilities. Sealing seemed a good prospect, but the seal population was quickly depleted. Credit for the development of the product that was to be Australia's staple commodity for export — wool — goes to John Macarthur (1767–1834). Granted a large tract of Crown lands and assigned thirty convicts to work for him, Macarthur conducted experiments in the production of fine merino wool. In 1800 he sent sample fleeces to England to determine their quality and to attract the financial support of British manufacturers.

The report of J. T. Bigge, an able lawyer sent out in 1819 to evaluate the colony, proved decisive. Persuaded

MAP 27.5 Australia Because of the vast deserts in western Australia, cities and industries developed mainly in the east. Australia's early geographical and cultural isolation bred a sense of inferiority. Air travel, the communications revolution, and the massive importation of Japanese products and American popular culture have changed that.

by large landowners like Macarthur, Bigge reported that wool was the country's future staple. He recommended that convicts be removed from the temptations of towns and seaports and dispersed to work on the estates of men of capital. He also urged the suspension of British duties on colonial wool. The Colonial Office accepted this advice, and the pastoral economy of Australia, as the continent was beginning to be called, began.

Australia's temperate climate is ideally suited to sheep farming. Moreover, wool production requires much land and little labor — precisely the situation in Australia. In 1830 the sheep population reached a half million. After 1820 the commercial importance of Australia exceeded its significance as a penal colony, and wool exports steadily increased, from 75,400 pounds in 1821, to 2 million pounds in 1830, to 24 million pounds in 1845.

Settlers also experimented with wheat farming. Soil deficiencies and the dry climate slowed early production, but farmers eventually developed a successful white-grained winter variety, and by 1900 wheat was Australia's second most valuable crop.

Population shortage remained a problem through the nineteenth century. In its quest for British immigrants, Australia could not compete with North America. The twelve-thousand-mile journey to Australia cost between £20 and £25 and could take five weary months. By contrast, the trip to Canada or the United States cost only £5 and lasted just ten weeks. To reduce the financial disincentives, the government offered immigrants free passage. Still, in the nineteenth century over 2.5 million British immigrants went to North America and only 223,000 to Australia.

In the early nineteenth century Australia's population was concentrated on the eastern coast of the

- **exclusionists** The officers and jailers who tried to establish a colonial gentry and impose rigid class distinctions from England.
- **emancipists** The lower strata of the Australian social order in the mid-nineteenth century, made up of former convicts.

continent, but the growth of sheep farming led to the opening of the interior. The Ripon Land Regulation Act of 1831, which provided land grants, attracted free settlers, and by 1850 Australia had five hundred thousand inhabitants. The discovery of gold in Victoria in 1851 quadrupled that number in a few years. Although the government charged prospectors a very high license fee, men and women from all parts of the globe flocked to Australia to share in the fabulous wealth.

The gold rush led to an enormous improvement in transportation within Australia. People customarily traveled by horseback or on foot and used two-wheel ox-drawn carts to bring wool from inland ranches to coastal cities. Then two newly arrived Americans, Freeman Cobb and James Rutherford, built sturdy four-wheel coaches capable of carrying heavy cargo and of negotiating the bush tracks. Railroad construction, financed by British investors, began in the 1870s, and by 1890 nine thousand miles of track had been laid. The improved transportation offered by railways stimulated agricultural production.

The gold rush also provided financial backing for educational and cultural institutions. Public libraries, museums, art galleries, and universities opened in the thirty years following 1851. In keeping with the overwhelmingly British ethnic origin of most immigrants to Australia, these institutions dispensed a distinctly British culture, though a remote and provincial version.

On the negative side, the large numbers of Asians in the goldfields — in Victoria in 1857, one adult male in seven was Chinese — sparked bitter racial prejudice. Scholars date the "white Australia policy" (discussed below) to whites' hostility toward and resentment and fear of the Chinese. Although Americans numbered only about five thousand in Victoria and Asians forty thousand, Americans — with their California gold-rush experience, aggressive ways, and "democratic" frontier outlook — exercised an influence on Australian society far out of proportion to their numbers. On the U.S. Fourth of July holiday in 1852, 1854, and 1857, anti-Chinese riots occurred in the goldfields of Victoria.

"Colored peoples" (as nonwhites were called in Australia) adapted more easily than the British to the warm climate and worked for lower wages. Thus they proved essential to the country's economic development in the nineteenth century. Chinese and Japanese built the railroads and ran the market gardens near, and the shops in, the towns. Filipinos and Pacific Islanders labored in the sugar-cane fields. Afghanis and their camels controlled the carrying trade in some areas. But fear that colored labor would lower living standards and undermine Australia's distinctly British culture triumphed. The Commonwealth Immigration Restriction Act of 1901 closed immigration to Asians and established the "white Australia policy," which remained on the books until the 1970s.

The Shaping of a Government and a National Identity

In 1850 the British Parliament passed the Australian Colonies Government Act, which allowed the four most populous colonies — New South Wales, Tasmania, Victoria, and South Australia — to establish colonial legislatures, determine voting rights, and frame their own constitutions. By 1859 all but one colony was self-governing. The provincial parliament of South Australia was probably the most democratic in the world, in that it was elected by universal manhood suffrage (that is, by all adult males) and by secret ballot. Other colonies soon adopted the secret ballot. In 1902 Australia became one of the first countries in the world to give women the vote.

The Commonwealth of Australia came into existence on January 1, 1901. From the British model, Australia adopted the parliamentary form of government in which a cabinet is responsible to the House of Com-

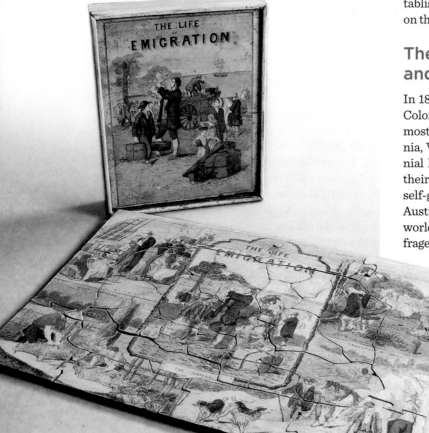

The "Life of Emigration" Puzzle Some of the advertising designed to attract people to move to Australia was aimed at children. The 38-piece wooden puzzle depicts the life of a family moving from Britain to Australia, from their departure to clearing ground and sheering sheep. It dates to about 1840. (Photograph Courtesy of the State Library of South Australia, S.A. Memory website)

mons. From the American system, Australia took the concept of decentralized government, whereby the states and the federal government share power.

The New Countries from a Comparative Perspective

☐ How and why did the new countries treated in this chapter develop differently?

Looked at from the perspective of world history, the new countries of the Americas and Australia had much in common. All of them began as European colonies. All had indigenous populations who suffered from the arrival of Europeans. For all of them the nineteenth century was a period of nation building, and all had achieved self-rule by the end of the century. In all cases the languages of the colonial powers — English, French, Spanish, and Portuguese — became the languages of government after independence. All the new nations provided European financiers with investment opportunities, not only in the expansion of agricultural enterprises, but also in mines, transportation, and manufacturing. And by the end of the nineteenth century they all had become connected to the rest of the world through global trade. Another global current they all felt was nationalism, which in these countries meant mass identification with the country rather than with an ancient people and its language. All at one time or another allowed or encouraged immigration, and many had also imported slaves from Africa. Discrimination on the basis of ethnic origin and race was pervasive in all of them.

Despite so many similarities, the countries covered in this chapter were already very different by 1914. By then the United States had become one of the half-dozen richest and most powerful countries in the world. That could not be said of any of the others. While the United States had built a strong industrial base, the economies of most of the other countries were still predominantly agricultural. While the three English-speaking countries had established strong democratic traditions, most of the countries of Latin America were controlled by narrow elites or military strongmen, with much of the population excluded from the political process. Of the countries of Latin America, only Argentina, with its temperate climate, fertile prairies, and large influx of European immigrants approached the prosperity of the United States, Canada, or Australia.

What accounts for these differences in outcomes? That the three countries that began as British colonies ended up as stable democracies strongly suggests that their common origins mattered. Even though they obtained independence in different ways, the British tradition of representative government shaped the political culture of each of the new states. By the time they achieved independence, their citizens were already accustomed to elections and local self-government. That was not true of former Spanish or Portuguese colonies.

The United States also benefited from its size. That a single country was formed by the original thirteen colonies in North America and preserved through the Civil War gave the United States the advantages of substantial size from the beginning. In addition it had room to expand west into territory with many advantages — a temperate climate, navigable rivers, and abundant arable land and mineral resources. The expansion of the United States was made possible by the willingness of France and Spain to sell it large territories in the early years and its own willingness to aggressively pursue expansion at the expense of the Indians and Mexico. As a consequence of its original size and subsequent expansion, the United States became the largest of the new countries in population. The only country that had more land was Canada, and much of Canada's land was too far north for agriculture. If Simón Bolívar had succeeded in forming a union of the Spanish-speaking countries of South America, it might have shared some of the advantages of size that the United States had.

It was important that the United States did not long remain a supplier for Europe of raw materials and basic commodities, but was quick to industrialize. Why did the United States industrialize in the nineteenth century much more rapidly than any of the other countries of the Western Hemisphere or Australia? Many reasons can be suggested. It had ample resources such as iron, coal, petroleum, and fertile land. Also, its government put few obstacles in the way of those who built the great enterprises. At the same time, through much of the nineteenth century, the United States placed high tariffs on imports to discourage the importing of European goods and to foster its own industries. To support these industries it had no difficulty attracting both capital and immigrants from abroad. Furthermore, the United States developed a social structure that rewarded self-made men and encouraged innovation. At the beginning of the nineteenth century the most crucial advances in industrial technology were made in Europe, but by the beginning of the next century they were just as likely to come from the United States. It was the United States that introduced streetcars and Henry Ford who developed the assembly line.

Once the United States became an industrialized country, its economic advantages accelerated; its citizens had more money to buy the products of its industries, its capitalists had more income to invest, educational levels rose as the advantages of learning became clearer, it attracted more immigrants, and so on. Countries further behind could not easily catch up. In other words, by diversifying its economy early, the United States escaped the neocolonial situation.

CONNECTIONS

In the Americas and Australia the century or so leading up to World War I was a time of nation building. Colonial governments were overthrown, new constitutions were written, settlement was extended, slavery was ended, and immigrants were welcomed. On the eve of World War I, there was reason to be optimistic about the future of all these countries. Although wealth was very unevenly distributed, in most of them it was not hard to point to signs of progress: growing cities, expanding opportunities for education, modern conveniences.

World War I, the topic of the next chapter, affected these countries in a variety of ways. Those most deeply involved were Canada and Australia, which followed Britain into the war in 1914 and sent hundreds of thousands of men to fight (over 600,000 from Canada and over 300,000 from Australia), losing many in some of the bloodiest battles of the war. The United States did not join the war until 1917, but quickly mobilized several million men and in 1918 began sending soldiers and materials in huge numbers. Even countries that maintained neutrality, as all the Latin American countries other than Brazil did, felt the economic impact of the war, especially the increased demand for food and manufactured goods. For them, the war had a positive side. How the war was started, expanded, and finally concluded are the topics of the next chapter.

◻ CHAPTER REVIEW

◻ **Why and how did the Spanish and Portuguese colonies of North and South America shake off European domination and develop into national states? (p. 812)**

In Latin America dissatisfaction with Spanish colonial rule grew over the course of the eighteenth century, both on the part of the Indians and mestizos and on the part of the Creoles of European ancestry who resented the privileges granted those from Spain. The wars of independence that lasted from 1806 to 1825 ended colonial rule but also led to fragmentation of Latin America into more than a dozen separate countries. Frequently, military dictators gained political power. Many Indians and mestizos worked on haciendas, often constrained by debt peonage. Many of the large plantations produced basic commodities for the international market, dominated by foreign powers.

◻ **How did the United States build a large but unified nation? (p. 824)**

The United States was the first of the European colonies in the New World to gain its independence, and it remained a step ahead during the nineteenth century both in attracting immigrants and in industrializing. After achieving independence from British rule, settlers in the United States pushed relentlessly across the continent to fulfill their "manifest destiny," making their homes on land taken from Native Americans. Eventually, the industrializing North and the agricultural South came into conflict over extending slavery into new territories. The North's victory in the bloody Civil War assured the permanence of the Union, but

the racial inequality that had been at the core of slavery remained, and blacks continued to face discrimination. Domestic matters preoccupied the United States through most of the nineteenth century, as the country subdued the continent, tied it together with railroads, and built gigantic steel, oil, textile, food-processing, and automobile industries. Nationalist sentiment grew, and with it discrimination against immigrants.

◻ **What geographical, economic, and political conditions shaped the development of Canada? (p. 833)**

Canada's political system was shaped by the emergence of the United States to its south. Many English loyalists fled to Canada during the American Revolution, and they and other Canadians were wary about U.S. intentions. Britain, not wanting to repeat its experience with its earlier American colonies, gradually extended home rule in Canada. Adopting the British model of cabinet government and utilizing rich natural resources and immigrant labor, the provinces of Canada formed a strong federation with close eco-

KEY TERMS

Creoles (p. 812)
peninsulares (p. 812)
neocolonialism (p. 819)
haciendas (p. 819)
peons (p. 821)
manifest destiny (p. 825)
Treaty of Guadalupe Hidalgo (p. 825)
Confederacy (p. 829)
confederation (p. 833)
Botany Bay (p. 835)
New South Wales (p. 835)
exclusionists (p. 836)
emancipists (p. 836)

nomic ties to the United States. French Canadians, however, were never entirely satisfied with their situation as a minority.

☐ What circumstances shaped the development of Australia? (p. 834)

Australia is much farther from Britain than North America is, and it was colonized later. The first European settlers were forcibly transported to Australia as convicts, but by the mid-nineteenth century Australia was attracting large numbers of Irish and English immigrants and smaller numbers from other countries. As in the United States and Canada, the discovery of gold quickened the pace of immigration. Because of Australia's dry climate, agriculture concentrated on sheep raising and wheat farming. After 1850 Australia was largely self-governing, and in 1901 it established itself as a commonwealth, adopting a parliamentary system from the British and a decentralized form of government from the United States.

☐ How and why did the new countries treated in this chapter develop differently? (p. 839)

Of all the new countries of the Americas and Australia, only the United States had become a great power by 1914. Like the other countries that had begun as British colonies, the United States developed a stable democracy based on representative government. Political stability aided its rapid industrialization, which was also fostered by its rich endowment of natural resources and its ability to attract capital and immigrants. By the beginning of the twentieth century many of the countries of Latin America, by contrast, seemed trapped in neocolonial systems that kept much of their population poor.

SUGGESTED READING

Bayly, C. A. *The Birth of the Modern World.* 2003. Useful for viewing the countries of the Americas in the context of global developments.

Bender, Thomas. *A Nation Among Nations: America's Place in World History.* 2006. Shows that key events in American history are best seen in global context.

Berlin, Ira. *Many Thousands Gone: The First Two Centuries of Slavery in North America.* 1998. An excellent study that shows how varied slavery was in different times and places.

Burkholder, Mark A., and Lyman Johnson. *Colonial Latin America,* 6th ed. 2007. A broad, comprehensive survey of Latin American history in the colonial period.

Fernandez-Armesto, Felipe. *The Americas: A Hemispheric History.* 2003. Provocative and engagingly written.

Foner, Eric. *Reconstruction: America's Unfinished Revolution, 1863–1877.* 1988. A lucidly written social history that gives attention to the role of former slaves in remaking their world.

Howe, Irving. *World of Our Fathers.* 1976. A brilliant account of the lives of Jews and other immigrants in American cities.

Hughes, Robert. *The Fatal Shore.* 1987. A beautifully written account of the origins of Australia as a penal colony, drawing on diaries and letters.

Lesser, Jeffrey. *Negotiating National Identity: Immigrants, Minorities, and the Struggle for Ethnicity in Brazil.* 1999. A broad-ranging social history.

Macintyre, Stuart. *A Concise History of Australia.* 2009. A masterful work by an Australian historian.

Morton, Desmond. *A Short History of Canada,* 6th ed. 2006. A well-written popular history.

Rodriguez O., J. E. *The Independence of Spanish America.* 1998. An up-to-date treatment focusing on nation building.

Stampp, K. M. *America in 1857: A Nation on the Brink.* 1990. The best comprehensive treatment of the pre–Civil War years.

Terrill, Ross. *The Australians.* 1987. An appreciation of the Australian people and the society they made, from the first settlers to the present.

White, Richard. *"It's Your Misfortune and None of My Own": A History of the American West.* 1991. Includes environmental, urban, ethnic, and women's history, as well as the more familiar story.

NOTES

1. See B. Keen and M. Wasserman, *A Short History of Latin America* (Boston: Houghton Mifflin, 1980), pp. 109–115.
2. M. Burkholder and D. S. Chandler, *From Impotence to Authority: The Spanish Crown and the American Audiencias, 1687–1808* (Columbia: University of Missouri Press, 1977), p. 145.
3. Quoted in J. Lynch, *The Spanish-American Revolutions, 1808–1826* (New York: Norton, 1973), p. 18.
4. Simón Bolívar, *The Hope of the Universe,* trans. J. L. Salcedo-Bastardo (Paris: Unesco, 1983), p. 105. Copyright © 1983 UNESCO for the English translation. Used by permission of UNESCO.
5. Gary E. Moulton, ed., *The Papers of Chief John Ross,* vol. 1, 1807–1839 (Norman: University of Oklahoma Press, 1985).
6. H. G. Gutman, *The Black Family in Slavery and Freedom, 1750–1925* (New York: Random House, 1977).
7. See J. Winch, *A Gentleman of Color: The Life of James Forten* (New York: Oxford University Press, 2002), passim.
8. Quoted in S. E. Morison, *The Oxford History of the American People* (New York: Oxford University Press, 1965), p. 654.
9. Quoted in R. Hughes, *The Fatal Shore* (New York: Knopf, 1987), p. 66.

For practice quizzes and other study tools, visit the **Online Study Guide** at bedfordstmartins.com/mckayworld.

For primary sources from this period, see *Sources of World Societies*, **Second Edition**.

For Web sites, images, and documents related to topics in this chapter, visit **Make History** at bedfordstmartins.com/mckayworld.

• **Senegalese Soldier** A *tirailleur* (literally, "skirmisher") from French West Africa who fought in Europe during the Great War. Across the bottom of this post card image from the era, the soldier proclaimed his loyalty with the phrase "Glory to the Greater France," meaning France and its colonies. Note the two German *pickelhaube* (spike helmets) he wears on his head. (Private Collection/Archives Charmet/The Bridgeman Art Library)

In the summer of 1914 the nations of Europe went willingly to war. They believed they had no other choice. Both peoples and governments confidently expected a short war leading to a decisive victory. Such a war, they believed, would "clear the air," and then European society could go on as before. They were wrong. The First World War was long, indecisive, and tremendously destructive. It quickly degenerated into a senseless military stalemate lasting four years. To the shell-shocked generation of survivors, it became simply the Great War.

World War and Revolution

1914–1929

In the midst of the war, in March 1917, the war-weary Russian people rebelled against their tsar, Nicholas II, forcing him to abdicate. Moderate reformists established a provisional government, but made the fatal decision to continue the war against Germany. In November Vladimir Lenin and his communist Bolshevik party staged a second revolution, promising an end to the war. The Germans forced on the Russians a harsh peace, but for Lenin this was a small price to pay for the establishment of the first communist state in history. Few then could have realized how profoundly this event would shape the remainder of the twentieth century.

When the victorious allies, led by Great Britain, France, and the United States, gathered in Paris in 1919 to write the peace, they were well-aware of the importance of their decisions. Some came to Paris seeking revenge, some came looking for the spoils of war, and others promoted nationalist causes or sought an idealistic end to war. The process was massive and complex and in the end, few left Paris satisfied with the results. The peace and prosperity the delegates had so earnestly sought lasted barely a decade.   •

The First World War, 1914–1918

□ How did Europe's system of alliances contribute to the outbreak of World War I, and how did the conflict become a global war?

The First World War clearly marked a great break in the course of world history. The war accelerated the growth of nationalism in Asia (see Chapter 29), and it consolidated America's position as a global power. Yet the war's greatest impact was on Europe. Drawn into war by a complicated system of alliances, the Allied and Central Powers soon found themselves in a prolonged and destructive war. Imperialism would further expand the conflict into the Middle East, Africa, and Asia, making this a global war of unprecedented scope. The young soldiers who went to war believed in the pre-1914 world of order, progress, and patriotism. Then, in soldier and writer Erich Remarque's words, the "first bombardment showed us our mistake, and under it the world as they had taught it to us broke in pieces."

MAP 28.1 European Alliances at the Outbreak of World War I, 1914 By the time war broke out, Europe was divided into two opposing alliances; the Triple Entente of Britain, France, and Russia, and the Triple Alliance of Germany, Austria-Hungary, and Italy. Italy switched sides and joined the Entente in 1915.

The Bismarckian System of Alliances

The Franco-Prussian War (see page 729) and the unification of Germany opened a new era in international relations. By 1871 France was defeated and Bismarck had made Prussia-Germany the most powerful nation in Europe. Bismarck declared Germany a "satisfied" power, having no territorial ambitions within Europe and desiring only peace.

But how to preserve the peace? Bismarck's first concern was to keep France diplomatically isolated and without military allies. His second concern was the threat to peace posed by the conflicting interests of Austria-Hungary and Russia, particularly in the Balkans, where the Ottoman Empire was losing its grip, leaving a power vacuum. To avoid Germany's being dragged into a great war between the two rival empires, Bismarck devised an alliance system to restrain both Russia and Austria-Hungary, to prevent conflict between them, and to isolate a hostile France.

Bismarck's balancing efforts infuriated Russian nationalists, leading Bismarck to conclude a defensive military alliance with Austria against Russia in 1879. Motivated by tensions with France, Italy joined Germany and Austria to form the Triple Alliance in 1882.

Bismarck's foreign policy accomplishments after 1871 were impressive, but his alliance system broke down in the 1890s. For two decades he maintained good relations with Britain and Italy while encouraging France in Africa but keeping France isolated in Europe. In 1890 the new emperor William II forced Bismarck to resign. William then refused to renew Bismarck's nonaggression pact with Russia, by which both states promised neutrality if the other was attacked. This prompted France to court Russia, offering loans, arms, and friendship. As a result, continental Europe was divided into two rival blocs (Map 28.1).

Great Britain's foreign policy became increasingly crucial. After 1891 Britain was the only uncommitted Great Power. Many Germans and some Britons felt that the racially related Germanic and Anglo-Saxon peoples were natural allies. However, the good relations that had prevailed between Prussia and Great Britain since the mid-eighteenth century gave way after 1890 to a bitter Anglo-German rivalry.

There were several reasons for this development. Commercial rivalry between Germany and Great Brit-

ain in world markets and Germany's pursuit of colonies unsettled the British. Above all, Germany's decision in 1900 to expand greatly its battle fleet challenged Britain's long-standing naval supremacy. This decision coincided with the South African War (see page 761) between the British and the Afrikaners, which revealed widespread anti-British feeling around the world. Thus British leaders prudently set about shoring up their exposed position with alliances and agreements. Britain improved its relations with the United States, concluded an alliance with Japan in 1902, and in the Anglo-French Entente of 1904 settled all outstanding colonial disputes with France.

Frustrated by Britain's closer relationship with France, Germany's leaders decided to test the entente's strength. Rather than accept the typical territorial payoff of imperial competition—a slice of French jungle somewhere in Africa or a port in Morocco—in return for French primacy in Morocco, in 1905 the Germans insisted on an international conference on the whole Moroccan question. Germany's crude bullying

MAP 28.2 The Balkans, 1878–1914 The Ottoman Empire suffered large territorial losses after the Congress of Berlin in 1878, but remained a power in the Balkans. By 1914 ethnic boundaries that did not follow political boundaries had formed, and Serbian national aspirations threatened Austria-Hungary.

forced France and Britain closer together, and Germany left the conference empty-handed.

The Moroccan crisis was something of a diplomatic revolution. Britain, France, Russia, and even the United States began to view Germany as a potential threat. At the same time, German leaders began to suspect sinister plots to encircle Germany and block its development as a world power. In 1907 Russia, battered by its disastrous war with Japan and the 1905 revolution, agreed to settle its territorial quarrels with Great Britain in Persia and Central Asia and signed the Anglo-Russian Agreement. Thus the treaty served as a catalyst for the **Triple Entente**, the alliance of Great Britain, France, and Russia in the First World War (see Map 28.1).

Germany's decision to add an enormously expensive fleet of big-gun battleships to its already expanding navy also heightened tensions. German nationalists saw a large navy as the legitimate mark of a great world power. But British leaders considered it a military challenge that forced them to spend the "People's Budget" (see page 743) on battleships rather than on social welfare. By 1909 Britain was psychologically, if not officially, in the Franco-Russian camp. Europe's leading nations were divided into two hostile blocs, both ill-prepared to deal with upheaval in the Balkans.

The Outbreak of War

In the early twentieth century a Balkans war seemed inevitable. The reason was simple: nationalism was destroying the Ottoman Empire in Europe and threatening to break up the Austro-Hungarian Empire. Western intervention in 1878 had forced the Ottoman Empire to cede most of its territory in Europe, but it retained important Balkan holdings (Map 28.2).

By 1903 Balkan nationalism was asserting itself again. Serbia led the way, becoming openly hostile to both Austria-Hungary and the Ottoman Empire. The Slavic Serbs looked to Slavic Russia for support of their national aspirations. In 1908, to block Serbian ex-

• **Triple Entente** The alliance of Great Britain, France, and Russia in the First World War.

Nationalist Opposition in the Balkans This band of well-armed and determined guerrillas from northern Albania was typical of groups fighting against Ottoman rule in the Balkans. Balkan nationalists succeeded in driving the Ottoman Turks out of most of Europe, but their victory increased tensions with Austria-Hungary and among the Great Powers. (Roger-Viollet/Getty Images)

pansion, Austria formally annexed Bosnia and Herzegovina, with their large Serbian, Croatian, and Muslim populations. Serbia erupted in rage but could do nothing without support from its ally Russia.

Then two nationalist wars, the First and Second Balkan Wars in 1912 and 1913, finally destroyed the centuries-long Ottoman presence in Europe (see Map 28.2). This sudden but long-awaited event elated the Balkan nationalists and dismayed Austria-Hungary's multinational leaders. The former hoped and the latter feared that Austria might next be broken apart.

Within this tense context, Archduke Francis Ferdinand, heir to the Austro-Hungarian throne, and his wife, Sophie, were assassinated by Serbian revolutionaries on June 28, 1914, during a state visit to the Bosnian capital of Sarajevo. Austria-Hungary's leaders held Serbia responsible and presented Serbia with an unconditional ultimatum on July 23, including demands that amounted to Austrian control of the Serbian state. When Serbia replied moderately but evasively, Austria began to mobilize and declared war on Serbia on July 28.

Of prime importance in Austria-Hungary's fateful decision was Germany's unconditional support. Emperor William II and his chancellor, Theobald von Bethmann-Hollweg, realized that war between Austria and Russia was likely, for Russia could not stand by and watch the Serbs be crushed. Yet Bethmann-Hollweg hoped that while Russia (and its ally France) would go to war, Great Britain would remain neutral.

Military plans and timetables, rather than diplomacy, soon began to dictate policy. On July 28, as Austrian armies bombarded Belgrade, Tsar Nicholas II ordered a partial mobilization against Austria-Hungary, but almost immediately found this was impossible. Russia had assumed a war with both Austria and Germany, and it could not mobilize against one without mobilizing against the other. Therefore, on July 29 Russia ordered full mobilization and in effect declared general war. The German general staff had also prepared for a two-front war. Its Schlieffen plan called for first knocking out France with a lightning attack through neutral Belgium to capture Paris before turning on Russia. On August 3 German armies invaded Belgium. Great Britain declared war on Germany the following day. In each country the great majority of the population rallied

The Schlieffen Plan

- ← – – Planned German offensive
- ← Actual German offensive
- Neutral nations

GREAT BRITAIN   NETHERLANDS   BELGIUM   Brussels   GERMANY   Rhine R.   LUX.   Reims   Metz   Paris   Seine R.   Marne R.   FRANCE   SWITZ.

0   100   200 mi.
0   100   200 km

Legend (inset, top right):
- Triple Entente and allies
- Central Powers and allies
- Greatest extent of territory gained by Germany-Austria
- German submarine war zone
- Neutral nations
- Farthest advance by Central Powers on date marked
- Farthest advance by Entente Powers on date marked
- British naval blockade
- Major battle

Main map labels:

NORWAY · SWEDEN · FINLAND · Helsinki · Petrograd (St. Petersburg) · ESTONIA · LATVIA · Riga · COURLAND · LITHUANIA · Vilnius · Masurian Lakes 1914 · RUSSIA · Moscow · BELARUS · Tannenberg 1914 · Warsaw · Brest-Litovsk · KINGDOM OF POLAND (Russia) · Kiev · GALICIA · Dnieper R.

North Sea · Jutland 1916 · Kiel · DENMARK · Baltic Sea · Farthest Russian advance, 1914 · E. PRUSSIA · Vistula R. · Elbe R.

GREAT BRITAIN · Lusitania 1915 · London · NETHERLANDS · Rhine R. · GERMANY · Berlin · Armistice line, November 1918 · BELGIUM · LUXEMBOURG · Armistice line, December 1917 · March 1918 · Treaty of Brest-Litovsk, March 1918 · Farthest German military advance

See inset map · Paris · Seine R. · ALSACE-LORRAINE · May 1915 · Western front · SWITZERLAND · AUSTRIA-HUNGARY · Vienna · Budapest · TRANSYLVANIA

Bordeaux · FRANCE · Garonne R. · Rhône R. · Aug. 1917 · Mar. 1918 · Caporetto 1917 · Po R. · Italian front · ROMANIA · Bucharest · Danube R. · March 1918 · Black Sea · Caspian Sea

SPAIN · Ebro R. · Corsica · Elba · Rome · ITALY · Adriatic Sea · Sarajevo · SERBIA · MONTENEGRO · BULGARIA · Constantinople · Nov. 1917 · PERSIA · Mar. 1918

Balearic Is. · Sardinia · ALBANIA · 1917–1918 · 1916 · 1915 · Dardanelles · Gallipoli 1915 · OTTOMAN EMPIRE · IRAQ · Al Kut 1915 1916 1917 · Basra

Balkan front · GREECE · Oct. 1918 · Baghdad · Middle Eastern front · SYRIA

ALGERIA (Fr.) · Tunis · TUNISIA (Fr.) · Sicily · Malta · Crete · Mediterranean Sea · Cyprus · Damascus

LIBYA (It.) · EGYPT (Gr. Br.) · Red Sea · Al Aqabah 1917

Compass: N W E S

Scale: 0 200 400 miles · 0 200 400 kilometers

The Western Front (inset, lower left)

NETHERLANDS · Ruhr R. · Dover · Ostend · Antwerp · FLANDERS · Ghent · Cologne · Ypres · Calais · Louvain · Liège · Scheldt R. · Brussels · BELGIUM · Rhine R. · Armistice line, November 1918 · Meuse R. · Coblenz · English Channel · Arras · ARDENNES · Somme R. · St. Quentin · LUX. · GERMANY · Amiens · Somme · Sedan · Aisne R. · Moselle R. · ARGONNE FOREST · LORRAINE · Saar R. · Compiègne · Reims · Belleau Wood · Marne R. · Verdun · St. Mihiel · Marne I · Château-Thierry · Châlons-sur-Marne · Nancy · Paris · Marne II · Seine R. · Strasbourg · ALSACE · FRANCE · Epinal · Mulhouse · Basel · SWITZ.

Western Front legend:
- Germany, 1914
- Greatest extent of territory gained by Germany, Sept. 1914
- Front at beginning of 1915
- German offensive, Summer 1918
- Major battle

Scale: 0 25 50 miles · 0 25 50 kilometers

MAP 28.3 The First World War in Europe
The trench war on the western front was concentrated in Belgium and northern France (inset), while the war in the east encompassed an enormous territory.

to defend its nation and enthusiastically embraced war in August 1914. Patriotic nationalism brought unity in the short run.

Stalemate and Slaughter

When the Germans invaded Belgium in August 1914, everyone believed the war would be short: "The boys will be home by Christmas." The Belgian army defended its homeland, however, and then fell back to join a rapidly landed British army corps near the Franco-Belgian border. Instead of quickly capturing Paris in a vast encircling movement, by the end of August German soldiers were advancing along an enormous front in the scorching summer heat. On September 6 the French attacked a gap in the German line at the Battle of the Marne. For three days, France threw everything into the attack. At one point, the French government desperately requisitioned all the taxis of Paris to rush reserves to the troops at the front. Finally, the Germans fell back. France had been miraculously saved (Map 28.3).

The two stalled armies now dug in behind rows of trenches, mines, and barbed wire to protect themselves from machine-gun fire. Eventually an unbroken line of parallel trenches stretched over four hundred miles from the Belgian coast to the Swiss frontier. By November 1914 the slaughter on the western front had begun in earnest. Ceaseless shelling by heavy artillery supposedly "softened up" the enemy in a given area. Then young soldiers went "over the top" of the trenches in frontal attacks on the enemy's line.

German writer Erich Remarque, who fought on the western front, described a typical attack in his great novel *All Quiet on the Western Front* (1929):

> We see men living with their skulls blown open; we see soldiers run with their two feet cut off. . . . Still the little piece of convulsed earth in which we lie is held. We have yielded no more than a few hundred yards of it as a prize to the enemy. But on every yard there lies a dead man.

The human cost of **trench warfare** was staggering; territorial gains were minuscule. The massive French and British offensives during 1915 never gained more than three miles of blood-soaked earth from the enemy. In the Battle of the Somme in the summer of 1916, the British and French gained an insignificant 125 square miles at the cost of 600,000 dead or wounded, and the Germans lost 500,000 men. In that same year the unsuccessful German campaign against Verdun cost 700,000 lives on both sides. British poet Siegfried Sassoon (1886–1967) wrote of the Somme offensive, "I am staring at a sunlit picture of Hell." (See "Viewpoints: Poetry of the Great War," page 850.) The year 1917 was equally terrible.

On the eastern front, the slaughter did not degenerate into suicidal trench warfare. With the outbreak of war, the "Russian steamroller" immediately moved into eastern Germany but suffered appalling losses against the Germans at the Battles of Tannenberg and the Masurian Lakes in August and September 1914 (see Map 28.3). With the help of German forces, the Austrians reversed the Russian advances of 1914 and forced the Russians to retreat deep into their own territory in the 1915 eastern campaign. A staggering 2.5 million Russians were killed, wounded, or taken prisoner.

These changing tides of victory and hopes of territorial gains brought neutral countries into the war. Italy, a member of the Triple Alliance since 1882, had declared its neutrality in 1914 on the grounds that Austria had launched a war of aggression. Then, in May 1915 Italy joined the Triple Entente of Great Britain, France, and Russia in return for promises of Austrian territory. In October 1914 the Ottoman Empire joined with Austria and Germany, by then known as the Central Powers. The following September Bulgaria followed the Ottoman Empire's lead in order to settle old scores with Serbia.

The War Becomes Global

In late 1914 the Ottoman Turks joined forces with Germany and Austria-Hungary. The Young Turks (see page 770) were pro-German because the Germans had helped reform the Ottoman armies before the war and had built important railroads, like the one to Baghdad. Alliance with Germany permitted the Turks to renounce the limitations on Ottoman sovereignty that the Europeans had imposed in the nineteenth century and also to settle old scores with Russia, the Turks' historic enemy.

The entry of the Ottoman Turks pulled the entire Middle East into the war and made it truly a global conflict. While Russia attacked the Ottomans in the Caucasus, the British protected their rule in Egypt. In 1915, at the Battle of Gallipoli, British forces tried to take the Dardanelles and Constantinople from the Ottoman Turks but were badly defeated. Casualties were high on both sides and included thousands of Australians and New Zealanders. Deep loyalty to the mother country led Australia to send 329,000 men and vast economic aid to Britain during the war. Over 100,000 New Zealanders also served in the war, almost a tenth of New Zealand's entire population, and they suffered a 58 percent casualty rate — one of the highest of any country in the war. Nearly 4,000 native New Zealand Maori soldiers also fought at Gallipoli and on

> • **trench warfare** Fighting behind rows of trenches, mines, and barbed wire; used in World War I with a staggering cost in lives and minimal gains in territory.

Viewpoints

Poetry of the Great War

• *Some of the finest and most memorable literature and poetry of the twentieth century came from the generation who experienced the Great War. These are three of the most famous poems of the Great War, all written by soldiers during the war. Rupert Brooks's "The Soldier" is the most famous of a series of sonnets he wrote in 1914. Brooks died on April 23, 1915, at the age of twenty-seven while traveling with the British Mediterranean Expeditionary Force to Gallipoli. John McCrae, a Canadian doctor, published "In Flanders Fields" in December 1915. He died of pneumonia while serving at a Canadian field hospital in northern France on January 28, 1918. British poet Wilfred Owen wrote "Dulce et Decorum Est" in 1917. He was killed in battle a week before the armistice on November 4, 1918.*

Rupert Brooks, "The Soldier"

If I should die, think only this of me:
    That there's some corner of a foreign field
That is for ever England. There shall be
    In that rich earth a richer dust concealed;
A dust whom England bore, shaped, made aware,
    Gave, once, her flowers to love, her ways to roam,
A body of England's, breathing English air,
    Washed by the rivers, blest by suns of home.

And think this heart, all evil shed away,
    A pulse in the eternal mind, no less
        Gives somewhere back the thoughts by England given;
Her sights and sounds; dreams happy as her day;
    And laughter, learnt of friends; and gentleness,
        In hearts at peace, under an English heaven.

John McCrae, "In Flanders Fields"

In Flanders fields the poppies blow
    Between the crosses, row on row,
    That mark our place; and in the sky
    The larks, still bravely singing, fly
Scarce heard amid the guns below.

We are the Dead. Short days ago
We lived, felt dawn, saw sunset glow,
    Loved and were loved, and now we lie
            In Flanders Fields.

Take up our quarrel with the foe:
To you from falling hands we throw
    The torch; be yours to hold it high.
    If ye break faith, with us who die
We shall not sleep, though poppies grow
            In Flanders Fields.

Wilfred Owen, "Dulce et Decorum Est"

Bent double, like old beggars under sacks,
Knock-kneed, coughing like hags, we cursed through sludge,
Till on the haunting flares we turned our backs
And towards our distant rest began to trudge.
Men marched asleep. Many had lost their boots
But limped on, blood-shod. All went lame; all blind;
Drunk with fatigue, deaf even to the hoots
Of gas shells dropping softly behind.

Gas! Gas! Quick, boys!—An ecstasy of fumbling,
Fitting the clumsy helmets just in time;
But someone still was yelling out and stumbling,
And floundering like a man in fire or lime . . .
Dim, through the misty panes and thick green light,
As under a green sea, I saw him drowning.

In all my dreams, before my helpless sight,
He plunges at me, guttering, choking, drowning.

If in some smothering dreams you too could pace
Behind the wagon that we flung him in,
And watch the white eyes writhing in his face,
His hanging face, like a devil's sick of sin;
If you could hear, at every jolt, the blood
Come gargling from the froth-corrupted lungs,
Obscene as cancer, bitter as the cud
Of vile, incurable sores on innocent tongues—
My friend, you would not tell with such high zest
To children ardent for some desperate glory,
The old Lie: Dulce et decorum est [It is sweet and fitting
    to die]
Pro patria mori. [For one's country.]

Source: Jon Silkin, ed., *The Penguin Book of First World War Poetry*, 2d ed. revised (New York: Penguin Putnam, 1996): pp. 81–82, 85, 192–193.

QUESTIONS FOR ANALYSIS

1. Which of these poems would you describe as the most idealistic and patriotic?

2. What do you think explains the obvious antiwar nature of Owen's poem compared to the poems of Brooks and McCrae?

Henri de Groux, *The Assault, Verdun* An eerie portrayal by Belgian artist Henri de Groux (1867–1930) of French troops moving forward in a thick haze of smoke and perhaps clouds of diphosgene, a poisonous gas first used by the Germans at Verdun on June 22, 1916. (Musée des Deux Guerres Mondiales, Paris/The Bridgeman Art Library)

the western front. A highly decorated New Zealand infantryman named Ormond Burton, who served in Gallipoli and then in France, later observed that "somewhere between the landing at Anzac [a cove on the peninsula of Gallipoli] and the end of the battle of the Somme, New Zealand very definitely became a nation."[1]

The British were more successful at inciting the Arabs to revolt against their Turkish overlords. The foremost Arab leader was Hussein ibn-Ali (1856–1931), who governed much of the Ottoman Empire's territory along the Red Sea, an area known as the Hejaz (see Map 29.1, page 880). In 1915 Hussein won vague British commitments for an independent Arab kingdom. The next year he revolted against the Turks, proclaiming himself king of the Arabs. He joined forces with the British under T. E. Lawrence, who in 1917 led Arab tribesmen and Indian soldiers in a successful guerrilla war against the Turks on the Arabian peninsula. In the Ottoman province of Iraq, Britain occupied Basra in 1914 and captured Baghdad in 1917. In 1918 British armies totally smashed the old Ottoman state, drawing

primarily on imperial forces from Egypt, India, Australia, and New Zealand. Thus war brought revolutionary change to the Middle East (see pages 881–889).

Japan, allied with the British since 1902, used the war as an opportunity to seize Germany's holdings on the Shandong (Shantung) Peninsula and in 1915 forced China to accept Japanese control of Shandong and southern Manchuria. China had declared its neutrality in 1914, and these actions infuriated Chinese patriots and heightened long-standing tensions between China and Japan.

War also spread to colonies in Africa and East Asia. Instead of revolting as the Germans hoped, French and British colonial subjects generally supported the allied powers. Colonized peoples provided critical supplies and fought in Europe and in the Ottoman Empire. They also helped local British and French commanders seize Germany's colonies around the globe. More than a million Africans and Asians served in the various armies of the warring powers, with more than double that number serving as porters to carry equipment. Some of the

> "We black African soldiers were very sorrowful about the white man's war. . . . The reason for war was never disclosed to any soldier. . . . We just fought and fought until we got exhausted and died."
>
> **INFANTRYMAN KANDE KAMARA**

most famous and bravest of these colonial troops were the Senegalese Tirailleurs (colonial riflemen). Drawn from Senegal and French West Africa, over 140,000 fought on the western front, and 31,000 of them died there.

Many of these men joined up to get clothes (uniforms), food, and money for enlisting. Others did so because colonial recruiters promised them better lives when they returned home. Most were illiterate and had no idea of why they were going or what they would experience. As one West African infantryman, Kande Kamara, later wrote:

We black African soldiers were very sorrowful about the white man's war. . . . I didn't really care who was right — whether it was the French or the Germans — I went to fight with the French army and that was all I knew. The reason for war was never disclosed to any soldier. . . . We just fought and fought until we got exhausted and died.[2]

The war had a profound impact on these colonial troops. Fighting against and killing Europeans destroyed the impression, encouraged in the colonies, that the Europeans were superhuman. New concepts like nationalism and individual freedoms — ideals for which the Europeans were supposedly fighting — were carried home to become rallying cries for future liberation struggles.

Another crucial development in the expanding conflict came in April 1917 when the United States declared war on Germany. American intervention grew out of the war at sea and sympathy for the Triple Entente. At the beginning of the war Britain and France

Indian Soldiers Convalescing in England Over 130,000 Indian soldiers served on the Western Front during the Great War, mostly during the first year of battle before being transferred to the Middle East to fight at Gallipoli and in the Mesopotamian campaign. Wounded Indian troops convalesced at the Royal Pavilion at Brighton, a former royal residence built in a faux-Oriental style that drew on several elements of Indian and Islamic architecture. In this posed piece, one of a series of photos of the Indian "martial races" distributed as postcards and used for slide-show lectures, some men sit playing cards, while others watch. Such photos reassured British and Indians alike that Britain took good care of its loyal imperial soldiers. (Royal Pavilion, Museums & Libraries, Brighton & Hove, photo ID 742)

established a naval blockade to strangle the Central Powers. No neutral cargo ship was permitted to sail to Germany. In early 1915 Germany launched a counter-blockade using the new and murderously effective submarine. In May a German submarine sank the British passenger liner *Lusitania.* More than a thousand people, including 139 U.S. citizens died. President Woodrow Wilson protested vigorously. Germany was forced to restrict its submarine warfare for almost two years, or face almost certain war with the United States.

Early in 1917 the German military command—confident that improved submarines could starve Britain into submission before the United States could come to its rescue—resumed unrestricted submarine warfare. This was a reckless gamble, and the United States declared war on Germany. The United States eventually tipped the balance in favor of the Triple Entente and its allies.

The Home Front

☐ How did total war impact the home fronts of the major combatants?

The war's impact on civilians was no less massive than on the men crouched in the trenches. Total war mobilized entire populations, led to increased state power, and promoted social equality. It also led to dissent and a growing antiwar movement.

Mobilizing for Total War

In August 1914 most Europeans greeted the outbreak of hostilities enthusiastically, believing that their own nation was in the right and defending itself from aggression. Yet by mid-October generals and politicians had begun to realize that victory would require more than patriotism. Combatant countries desperately needed men and weapons. Change had to come, and fast, to keep the war machine from sputtering to a stop.

The change came through national unity governments that began to plan and control economic and social life in order to wage **total war**. Governments imposed rationing, price and wage controls, and even restrictions on workers' freedom of movement. These total war economies involved entire populations, blurring the old distinction between soldiers on the battlefield and civilians at home. (See "Listening to the Past: The Experience of War," page 854.) The ability of central governments to manage and control highly complicated economies increased and strengthened their powers, often along socialist lines.

Germany went furthest in developing a planned economy to wage total war. As soon as war began, the

Hair for the War Effort Blockaded and cut off from overseas supplies, Germany mobilized effectively to find substitutes at home. This poster calls on German women—especially young women with long, flowing tresses—to donate their hair, which was used to make rope. Children were organized by their teachers into garbage brigades to collect every scrap of useful material. (akg-images)

Jewish industrialist Walter Rathenau convinced the German government to set up the War Raw Materials Board to ration and distribute raw materials. Under Rathenau's direction, every useful material from foreign oil to barnyard manure was inventoried and rationed. Moreover, the board launched successful attempts to produce substitutes, such as synthetic rubber and synthetic nitrates, for scarce war supplies. Food was also rationed.

Following the terrible Battles of Verdun and the Somme in 1916, military leaders forced the Reichstag to accept the Auxiliary Service Law, which required all males between seventeen and sixty to work only at jobs considered critical to the war effort. Women also

• **total war** Practiced by countries fighting in World War I, a war in which the government plans and controls all aspects of economic and social life in order to make the greatest possible military effort.

Listening to the Past

The Experience of War

World War I was a total war: it enlisted the efforts of male and female adults and children, both at home and on the battle-field. It was a terrifying and painful experience for all those involved, not the romantic endeavor it was purported to be. The documents below offer two different wartime experiences. The first is from a letter written by a German soldier fighting in the trenches. The second is from the diary of a Viennese woman. As you read both passages, think about the different ways war and its consequences were made real for these two people.

A German Soldier Writes from the Trenches, March 1915

❝*Souchez, March 11th, 1915*

"So fare you well, for we must now be parting," so run the first lines of a soldier-song which we often sang through the streets of the capital. These words are truer than ever now, and these lines are to bid farewell to you, to all my nearest and dearest, to all who wish me well or ill, and to all that I value and prize.

Our regiment has been transferred to this dangerous spot, Souchez. No end of blood has already flowed down this hill. A week ago the 142nd attacked and took four trenches from the French. It is to hold these trenches that we have been brought here. There is something uncanny about this hill-position. Already, times without number, other battalions of our regiment have been ordered here in support, and each time the company came back with a loss of twenty, thirty or more men. In the days when we had to stick it out here before, we had 22 killed and 27 wounded. Shells roar, bullets whistle; no dugouts, or very bad ones; mud, clay, filth, shell-holes so deep that one could bathe in them.

This letter has been interrupted no end of times. Shells began to pitch close to us—great English 12-inch ones—and we had to take refuge in a cellar. One such shell struck the next house and buried four men, who were got out from the ruins horribly mutilated. I saw them and it was ghastly!

Everybody must be prepared now for death in some form or other. Two cemeteries have been made up here, the losses have been so great. I ought not to write that to you, but I do so all the same, because the newspapers have probably given you quite a different impression. They tell only of our gains and say nothing about the blood that has been shed, of the cries of agony that never cease. The newspaper doesn't give any description either of *how* the "heroes" are laid to rest, though it talks about "heroes' graves" and writes poems and such-like about them. Certainly in Lens I have attended funeral-parades where a number of dead were buried in one large grave with pomp and circumstance. But up here it is pitiful the way one throws the dead bodies out of the trench and lets them lie there, or scatters dirt over the remains of those which have been torn to pieces by shells.

I look upon death and call upon life. I have not accomplished much in my short life, which has been chiefly occupied with study. I have commended my soul to the Lord God. It bears His seal and is altogether His. Now I am free to dare anything. My future life belongs to God, my present one to the Fatherland, and I myself still possess happiness and strength.❞

A Viennese Woman Remembers Home Front Life

❝Ten dekagrammes [3½ ounces] of horse-flesh per head are to be given out to-day for the week. The cavalry horses held in reserve by the military authorities are being slaughtered for lack of fodder, and the people of Vienna are for a change to get a few mouthfuls of meat of which they have so long been deprived. Horse-flesh! I should like to know whether my instinctive repugnance to horse-flesh as food is personal, or whether my dislike is shared by many other housewives. My loathing of it is based, I believe, not on a physical but on a psychological prejudice.

I overcame my repugnance, rebuked myself for being sentimental, and left the house. A soft, steady rain was falling,

---

worked in war factories, mines, and steel mills. Thus in Germany total war led to history's first "totalitarian" society.

As mature liberal democracies, France, Great Britain, and the United States were much less authoritarian in August 1914 than autocratic Russia, Germany, and Austria-Hungary. France and Great Britain also tended to mobilize economically for total war less rapidly and less completely than Germany, as they could import materials from their colonies and from the United States. When it became apparent that the war was not going to end quickly, however, the western allies all began to pass laws that gave their governments sweeping powers over all areas of the nation's daily life — including industrial and agricultural production, censorship, education, health and welfare, the curtailment of civil liberties, labor, and foreign aliens.

In June 1915, for example, a serious shortage of shells led the British to establish a Ministry of Munitions that organized private industry to produce for the from which I tried to protect myself with galoshes, waterproof, and umbrella. As I left the house before seven o'clock and the meat distribution did not begin until nine o'clock, I hoped to get well to the front of the queue.

No sooner had I reached the neighbourhood of the big market hall than I was instructed by the police to take a certain direction. I estimated the crowd waiting here for a meagre midday meal at two thousand at least. Hundreds of women had spent the night here in order to be among the first and make sure of getting their bit of meat. Many had brought with them improvised seats—a little box or a bucket turned upside down. No one seemed to mind the rain, although many were already wet through. They passed the time chattering, and the theme was the familiar one: What have you had to eat? What are you going to eat? One could scent an atmosphere of mistrust in these conversations: they were all careful not to say too much or to betray anything that might get them into trouble.

At length the sale began. Slowly, infinitely slowly, we moved forward. The most determined, who had spent the night outside the gates of the hall, displayed their booty to the waiting crowd: a ragged, quite freshly slaughtered piece of meat with the characteristic yellow fat. [Others] alarmed those standing at the back by telling them that there was only a very small supply of meat and that not half the people waiting would get a share of it. The crowd became very uneasy and impatient, and before the police on guard could prevent it, those standing in front organized an attack on the hall which the salesmen inside were powerless to repel. Everyone seized whatever he could lay his

hands on, and in a few moments all the eatables had vanished. In the confusion stands were overturned, and the police forced back the aggressors and closed the gates. The crowds waiting outside, many of whom had been there all night and were soaked through, angrily demanded their due, whereupon the mounted police made a little charge, provoking a wild panic and much screaming and cursing. At length I reached home, depressed and disgusted, with a broken umbrella and only one galosh.

We housewives have during the last four years grown accustomed to standing in queues; we have also grown accustomed to being obliged to go home with empty hands and still emptier stomachs. Only very rarely do those who are sent away disappointed give cause for police intervention. On the other hand, it happens more and more frequently that one of the pale, tired women who have been waiting for hours collapses from exhaustion. The turbulent scenes which occurred to-day inside and outside the large market hall seemed to me perfectly natural. In my dejected mood the patient apathy with which we housewives endure seemed to me blameworthy and incomprehensible. **99**

Sources: Alfons Ankenbrand, in *German Students' War Letters*, ed. A. F. Wedd (London: Methuen, 1929), pp. 72–73; *Blockade: The Diary of an Austrian Middle-Class Woman*, 1914–1924, trans. Winifred Ray (New York: Ray Long & Richard Smith, 1932), pp. 63–68.

QUESTIONS FOR ANALYSIS

1. What is the soldier's view of the war? Would you characterize it as an optimistic or pessimistic letter?

2. What similarities and differences do you see in the experience of the Viennese woman as compared to the soldier's experience?

3. Why does the Viennese woman describe the housewives as "blameworthy" or "incomprehensible"?

war, controlled profits, allocated labor, fixed wage rates, and settled labor disputes. By December 1916 the British economy was largely planned and regulated directly by the state. The Espionage Act of June 1917 and the Sedition Act of May 1918 allowed the United States government to keeps groups like labor unions, political parties, and ethnic organizations under surveillance. Welfare systems of various kinds were also adopted in most of the belligerent countries. Many of these laws were revoked at war's end. Still, they set precedents and

would be turned to again in response to the economic depressions of the 1920s and 1930s and World War II.

The Social Impact

The social impact of total war was no less profound than the economic impact, though again there were important national variations. The military's insatiable needs—nearly every belligerent power resorted to conscription to put soldiers in the field—created a

> " I am going into a munitions factory to make shells. The job will not be as well paid as domestic service . . . but it will be my bit, and every time you fire your gun you can remember I am helping to make the shells. "

PARLOR MAID TO HER BOYFRIEND LEAVING FOR THE FRONT

tremendous demand for workers. This situation — seldom, if ever, seen before 1914 — brought about momentous changes.

One such change was greater power and prestige for labor unions. Unions cooperated with war governments in return for real participation in important decisions. This entry of labor leaders into policymaking councils paralleled the entry of socialist leaders into the war governments.

Women's roles also changed dramatically. In every country, large numbers of women left home and domestic service to work in industry, transportation, and offices. As one former parlor maid is reported to have told her boyfriend as he prepared to leave for France:

> While you are at the front firing shells, I am going into a munitions factory to make shells. The job will not be as well paid as domestic service, it will not be as comfortable as domestic service; it will be much harder work, but it will be my bit, and every time you fire your gun you can remember I am helping to make the shells.[3]

Moreover, women became highly visible — not only as munitions workers but as bank tellers, mail carriers, even police officers. Women also served as nurses and doctors at the front. (See "Individuals in Society: Vera Brittain," page 857.) In general, the war greatly expanded the range of women's activities and changed attitudes toward women. Although most women were quickly let go and their jobs given back to the returning soldiers, their many-sided war effort caused Britain, Germany, and Austria to grant them the right to vote immediately after the war.

Recent scholarship has shown, however, that traditional views of gender — of male roles and female roles — remained remarkably resilient and that there was a significant conservative backlash in the postwar years. Even as the war progressed, many men, particularly soldiers, grew increasingly hostile toward women. Some were angry at mothers, wives, and girlfriends for urging them to enlist and fight in the horrible war. Suggestive posters of scantily clad women were used to remind men of the rewards they would receive for enlisting and fighting, while soldiers with wives and girlfriends back home grew increasingly convinced that they were

cheating on them. Others worried that factory or farm jobs had been taken by women and that they would have no work when they returned home. Men were also concerned that if women received the vote at war's end, they would vote themselves into power. These concerns are reflected in a letter from Private G. F. Wilby, serving in East Africa, to his fiancée in London, Ethel Baxter, in August 1918:

> Whatever you do, don't go in Munitions or anything in that line — just fill a Woman's position and remain a woman. . . . I want to return and find the same loveable little woman that I left behind — not a coarse thing more of a man than a woman.[4]

War promoted social equality, blurring class distinctions and lessening the gap between rich and poor. Greater equality was reflected in full employment, rationing according to physical needs, and a sharing of hardships. Society became more uniform and more egalitarian, in spite of some war profiteering.

Growing Political Tensions

During the war's first two years many soldiers and civilians supported their governments. Belief in a just cause and patriotic nationalism united peoples behind their various national leaders. Each government employed censorship and propaganda to maintain popular support.

By spring 1916, however, people were beginning to crack under the strain of total war. In April Irish nationalists in Dublin unsuccessfully tried to take advantage of this situation and rose up against British rule in the Easter Rebellion. Strikes and protest marches over inadequate food flared up on every home front. Besides the massive mutiny of Russian soldiers in 1917 that supported the revolution, nearly half of the French infantry divisions mutinied for two months after the army suffered enormous losses in the Second Battle of the Aisne in April 1917.

The Central Powers experienced the most strain. In October 1916 a young socialist assassinated Austria's chief minister. Conflicts among nationalities grew, and both Czech and Yugoslav leaders demanded autonomous democratic states for their peoples. The strain of total war was also evident in Germany. By 1917 national political unity was collapsing and prewar social conflicts re-emerging. A coalition of socialists and Catholics in the Reichstag called for a compromise "peace without annexations or reparations." Conservatives and military leaders found such a peace unthinkable. Thus militaristic Germany, like its ally Austria-Hungary and its enemy France, began to crack in 1917. But it was Russia that collapsed first and saved the Central Powers — for a time.

Individuals in Society

Vera Brittain

ALTHOUGH THE GREAT WAR UPENDED MILLIONS of lives, it struck Europe's young people with the greatest force. For Vera Brittain (1893–1970), as for so many in her generation, the war became life's defining experience, which she captured forever in her famous autobiography, *Testament of Youth* (1933).

Brittain grew up in a wealthy business family in northern England, bristling at small-town conventions and discrimination against women. Very close to her brother Edward, two years her junior, Brittain read voraciously and dreamed of being a successful writer. Finishing boarding school and beating down her father's objections, she prepared for Oxford's rigorous entry exams and won a scholarship to its women's college. Brittain also fell in love with Roland Leighton, an equally brilliant student from a literary family and her brother's best friend. All three, along with two more close friends, Victor Richardson and Geoffrey Thurlow, confidently prepared to enter Oxford in late 1914.

When war suddenly approached in July 1914, Brittain shared with millions of Europeans a thrilling surge of patriotic support for her government, a prowar enthusiasm she later played down in her published writings. She wrote in her diary that her "great fear" was that England would declare its neutrality and commit the "grossest treachery" toward France.* She seconded Roland's decision to enlist, agreeing with her sweetheart's glamorous view of war as "very ennobling and very beautiful." Later, exchanging anxious letters in 1915 with Roland in France, Vera began to see the conflict in personal, human terms. She wondered if any victory or defeat could be worth Roland's life.

Struggling to quell her doubts, Brittain redoubled her commitment to England's cause and volunteered as an army nurse. For the next three years she served with distinction in military hospitals in London, Malta, and northern France, repeatedly torn between the vision of noble sacrifice and the reality of human tragedy. She lost her sexual inhibitions caring for mangled male bodies, and she longed to consummate her love with Roland. Awaiting his return on leave on Christmas Day in 1915, she was greeted instead with a telegram: Roland had been killed two days before.

Roland's death was the first of the devastating blows that eventually overwhelmed Brittain's idealistic patriotism. In 1917, first Geoffrey and then Victor died from gruesome wounds. In early 1918, as the last great German offensive covered the floors of her war-zone hospital with maimed and dying German prisoners, the bone-weary Vera felt a common humanity and saw only more victims. A few weeks later brother Edward—her last hope—died in action. When the war ended, she was, she said, a "complete automaton," with "my deepest emotions paralyzed if not dead."

Returning to Oxford and finishing her studies, Brittain gradually recovered. She formed a deep, restorative friendship with another talented woman writer, Winifred Holtby, published novels and articles, and became a leader in the feminist campaign for gender equality. She also married and had children. But her wartime memories were always there. Finally, Brittain succeeded in coming to grips with them in *Testament of Youth*, her powerful antiwar autobiography. The unflinching narrative spoke to the experiences of an entire generation and became a runaway bestseller. Above all, perhaps, Brittain captured the ambivalent, contradictory character of the war, when millions of young people found excitement, courage, and common purpose but succeeded only in destroying their lives with their superhuman efforts and futile sacrifices. Becoming ever more committed to pacifism, Brittain opposed England's entry into World War II.

QUESTIONS FOR ANALYSIS

1. What were Brittain's initial feelings toward the war? How and why did they change as the conflict continued?

2. Why did Brittain volunteer as a nurse, as many women did? How might wartime nursing have influenced women of her generation?

3. In portraying the ambivalent, contradictory character of World War I for Europe's youth, was Brittain describing the contradictory character of all modern warfare?

● **Vera Brittain was marked forever by her wartime experiences.** (Vera Brittain Archive, William Ready Division of Archives and Research Collections, McMaster University Library)

*Quoted in the excellent study by P. Berry and M. Bostridge, *Vera Brittain: A Life* (London: Virago Press, 2001), p. 59; additional quotations are from pp. 80 and 136.

"Never Forget!" This 1915 French poster with a passionate headline dramatizes Germany's brutal invasion of Belgium in 1914. The "rape of Belgium" featured prominently—and effectively—in anti-German propaganda. (Mary Evans Picture Library/The Image Works)

ANALYZING THE IMAGE How is neutral Belgium personified? What do you think the artist's purpose was?

CONNECTIONS How did governments use propaganda and other means to unite people for the war effort?

The Russian Revolution

□ What factors led to the Russian Revolution, and what was its outcome?

The 1917 Russian Revolution, directly related to the Great War, had a significance far beyond the wartime agonies of a single Allied or Central Power nation. The Russian Revolution opened a new era with a radically new prototype of state and society.

The Fall of Imperial Russia

Like their allies and their enemies, Russians had embraced war with patriotic enthusiasm in 1914. At the Winter Palace, while kneeling throngs sang "God Save the Tsar," Tsar Nicholas II (r. 1894–1917) vowed never to make peace as long as the enemy stood on Russian soil. For a moment Russia was united, but soon the war began to take its toll.

Unprecedented artillery barrages quickly exhausted Russia's supplies of shells and ammunition, and better-equipped German armies inflicted terrible losses — one and a half million casualties and nearly another million captured in 1915 alone. Russian soldiers were sent to the front without rifles; they were told to find their arms among the dead. The Duma, Russia's lower house of the parliament, and local governments led the effort toward full mobilization on the home front. These efforts improved the military situation, but overall Russia mobilized less effectively for total war than did the other warring nations.

The great problem was leadership. Under the constitution resulting from the 1905 revolution (see page 731), the tsar retained complete control over the bureaucracy and the army. A kindly, slightly dull-witted man, Nicholas distrusted the moderate Duma and rejected popular involvement. As a result, the Duma, the educated middle classes, and the masses became increasingly critical of the tsar's leadership. In response,

Nicholas announced in September 1915 that he was traveling to the front to lead Russia's armies.

His departure was a fatal turning point. His German-born wife, Tsarina Alexandra, took control of the government. She tried to rule absolutely in her husband's absence with an uneducated Siberian preacher, Rasputin, as her most trusted adviser. Rasputin gained her trust by claiming that he could stop the bleeding of her hemophiliac son Alexis, heir to the throne. In this atmosphere of unreality, the government slid steadily toward revolution.

In a desperate attempt to right the situation, three members of the high aristocracy murdered Rasputin in December 1916. In the meantime, food shortages worsened and morale declined. On March 8 a women's bread march in Petrograd (formerly St. Petersburg) started riots, which spread throughout the city. The tsar ordered troops to restore order, but discipline broke down, and the soldiers joined the revolutionary crowd. The Duma declared a provisional government on March 12, 1917. Three days later, Nicholas abdicated.

The Provisional Government

The **March Revolution** was joyfully accepted throughout the country. After generations of authoritarianism, the provisional government established equality before the law; freedom of religion, speech, and assembly; the right of unions to organize and strike; and other classic liberal measures. But both moderate socialist and liberal leaders of the provisional government rejected social revolution. A new government formed in May 1917, which included the socialist Alexander Kerensky, refused to confiscate large landholdings and give them to peasants, fearing that such drastic action in the countryside would only complete the disintegration of Russia's peasant army. For the patriotic Kerensky, who became prime minister in July, as for other moderate socialists, the continuation of war was still the all-important national duty.

From its first day, the provisional government had to share power with a formidable rival — the **Petrograd Soviet** (or council) of Workers' and Soldiers' Deputies. Modeled on the revolutionary soviets of 1905, the Petrograd Soviet comprised two to three thousand workers, soldiers, and socialist intellectuals. This counter- or half-government issued its own radical orders, further weakening the provisional government. Most famous of these was Army Order No. 1, issued in March 1917, which stripped officers of their authority and gave power to elected committees of common soldiers.

The order led to a total collapse of army discipline. Peasant soldiers began "voting with their feet," to use Lenin's graphic phrase. They returned to their villages

"The Russian Ruling House" This wartime cartoon captures the ominous, spellbinding power of Rasputin over Tsar Nicholas II and his wife, Alexandra. Rasputin's manipulations disgusted Russian public opinion and contributed to the monarchy's collapse. (Stock Montage)

to get a share of the land, which peasants were simply seizing from landowners in a great agrarian upheaval. Liberty was turning into anarchy in the summer of 1917, offering an unparalleled opportunity for the most radical and most talented of Russia's many socialist leaders, Vladimir Ilyich Lenin (1870–1924).

- **March Revolution** The first phase of the Russian Revolution of 1917, in which unplanned uprisings led to the abdication of the tsar and the establishment of a transitional democratic government that was then overthrown in November by Lenin and the Bolsheviks.
- **Petrograd Soviet** A counter-government that was a huge, fluctuating mass meeting of two to three thousand workers, soldiers, and socialist intellectuals.

Lenin and His Supporters Vladimir Lenin (center) with two other major figures of the Russian Revolution, Joseph Stalin (left) and Mikhail Kalinin (right). After Lenin's death in January 1924, Stalin moved to seize power and ruled the Soviet Union until his death in 1953. Kalinin was one of Lenin's earliest followers and then supported Stalin in the power struggle after Lenin's death. He was one of the few "old Bolsheviks" to survive Stalin's purges and received a large state funeral following his death from natural causes in 1946. (Gamma-Keystone/Getty Images)

Lenin and the Bolshevik Revolution

Born into the middle class, Lenin became an enemy of imperial Russia when his older brother was executed for plotting to kill the tsar in 1887. As a law student Lenin studied Marxist doctrines with religious ferocity. Exiled to Siberia for three years because of socialist agitation, after his release Lenin lived in western Europe for seventeen years and developed his own revolutionary interpretations of Marxist thought.

Three interrelated ideas were central for Lenin. First, he stressed that only violent revolution could destroy capitalism. Second, Lenin believed that a socialist revolution was possible even in a country like Russia, where capitalism was not fully developed. There the industrial working class was small, but the poor peasants were also potential revolutionaries.

Third, Lenin believed that at a given moment revolution was determined more by human leadership than by vast historical laws. He called for a highly disciplined workers' party, strictly controlled by a dedicated elite of intellectuals and full-time revolutionaries like him. This elite would not stop until revolution brought it to power.

Lenin's ideas did not go unchallenged by other Russian Marxists. At a Social Democratic Labor Party congress in London in 1903, Lenin demanded a small, disciplined, elitist party; his opponents wanted a more democratic party with mass membership. The Russian Marxists split into two rival factions. Lenin's camp was called **Bolsheviks**, or "majority group"; his opponents were Mensheviks, or "minority group."

From exile in neutral Switzerland, Lenin saw the war as a product of imperialistic rivalries and an opportunity for socialist revolution. After the March Revolution of 1917, the German government provided safe passage for Lenin across Germany and back into Russia, hoping he would undermine Russia's sagging war effort. They were not disappointed. Arriving in Petrograd on April 3, Lenin attacked at once. To the great astonishment of the local Bolsheviks, he rejected all cooperation with what he called the "bourgeois" provisional government. His slogans were radical in the extreme: "All power to the soviets"; "All land to the peasants"; "Stop the war now." Lenin was a superb tactician, and throughout the summer the Bolsheviks markedly increased their popular support, while Prime Minister Kerensky's unwavering support for the war lost him all credit with the army, the only force that might have saved him and democratic government in Russia.

In October the Bolsheviks gained a fragile majority in the Petrograd Soviet. It was Lenin's supporter Leon

• **Bolsheviks** The majority group; this was Lenin's camp of the Russian party of Marxist socialism.

Trotsky (1879–1940), an independent radical Marxist and later commander of the Red Army, who brilliantly executed the Bolshevik seizure of power. On November 6 militant Trotsky followers joined with trusted Bolshevik soldiers to seize government buildings and arrest provisional government members. At the congress of soviets a Bolshevik majority then declared that all power had passed to the soviets and named Lenin head of the new government.

The Bolsheviks came to power for three key reasons. First, by late 1917 democracy had given way to anarchy. Second, in Lenin and Trotsky the Bolsheviks had an utterly determined and truly superior leadership. Third, the Bolsheviks appealed to soldiers and urban workers who were exhausted by war and eager for socialism.

Dictatorship and Civil War

The true accomplishment of the Bolsheviks was not taking power but keeping it and conquering the chaos they had helped create. Lenin had the genius to profit from developments over which he and the Bolsheviks had no control. Since summer 1917 an unstoppable peasant revolution had swept across Russia, as peasants divided among themselves the estates of the landlords and the church. Thus Lenin's first law, which supposedly gave land to the peasants, actually merely approved what peasants were already doing. Lenin then met urban workers' greatest demand with a decree in November giving direct control of individual factories to local workers' committees.

The Bolsheviks proclaimed their regime a "provisional workers' and peasants' government," promising that a freely elected Constituent Assembly would draw up a new constitution. But after Bolshevik delegates won fewer than one-fourth of the seats in free elections in November, the Constituent Assembly met for only one day, on January 18, 1918. Bolshevik soldiers acting under Lenin's orders then permanently disbanded it.

Lenin acknowledged that Russia had lost the war with Germany and that the only realistic goal was peace at any price. That price was very high. Germany demanded that the Soviet government give up all its western territories, and a third of old Russia's population was surrendered in the Treaty of Brest-Litovsk (BREHST lih-TAWFSK), signed with Germany in March 1918. With peace, Lenin escaped the disaster of continued war and could pursue his goal of absolute political power for the Bolsheviks — now renamed Communists — within Russia.

The war's end, along with the destruction of the democratically elected Constituent Assembly, revealed Bolshevik rule as dictatorship from the capital. For the next three years "Long live the [democratic] soviets; down with the Bolsheviks" was a popular slogan. Offi-

☐ KEY EVENTS OF THE RUSSIAN REVOLUTION

1914	Russia enters the war
1916–1917	Tsarist government in crisis
March 1917	March Revolution; Duma declares a provisional government; tsar abdicates; Petrograd Soviet issues Army Order No. 1
April 1917	Lenin returns from exile
October 1917	Bolsheviks gain a majority in the Petrograd Soviet
November 7, 1917	Bolsheviks seize power; Lenin named head of new communist government
March 1918	Treaty of Brest-Litovsk; Trotsky becomes head of the Red Army
1918–1922	Civil war
1922	Civil war ends; Lenin and the Bolshevik-Communists take control of Russia

cers of the old army organized the so-called White opposition to the Bolsheviks in southern Russia, Ukraine, Siberia, and west of Petrograd, and by the summer of 1918 the country was plunged into civil war. The Whites came from many social groups and were united only by their hatred of the Bolsheviks — the Reds. By the end of the year, White armies were on the attack. In October 1919 it appeared they might triumph as they closed in on Lenin's government from three sides. Yet they did not. The Red Army under Trotsky's command captured Vladivostok in October 1922 and that effectively marked the end of the civil war.

Lenin and the Red Army won for several reasons. Strategically, the Bolsheviks controlled the center, while the disunited Whites attacked from the fringes. Moreover, the poorly defined political program of the Whites did not unite all the foes of the Bolsheviks under a progressive democratic banner. Most important, the Communists developed a better army, an army for which the divided Whites were no match.

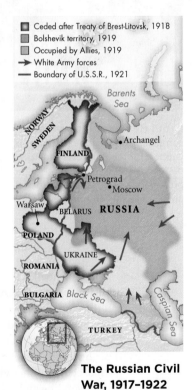

☐ Ceded after Treaty of Brest-Litovsk, 1918
☐ Bolshevik territory, 1919
☐ Occupied by Allies, 1919
→ White Army forces
— Boundary of U.S.S.R., 1921

The Russian Civil War, 1917–1922

"You! Have You Volunteered?" A Red Army soldier makes a compelling direct appeal to the ordinary citizen and demands all-out support for the Bolshevik cause in this 1920 poster by Dmitri Moor, a popular Soviet artist. Lenin recognized the importance of visual propaganda in a vast country with limited literacy, and mass-produced posters like this one were everywhere during the civil war of 1918–1922. (Stephen White, University of Glasgow)

The Bolsheviks also mobilized the home front. Establishing **war communism** — the application of the total-war concept to a civil conflict — they seized grain from peasants, introduced rationing, nationalized all banks and industry, and required everyone to work. Although these measures contributed to a breakdown of normal economic activity, they also served to maintain labor discipline and to keep the Red Army supplied.

Revolutionary terror also contributed to the Communist victory. The old tsarist secret police was reestablished as the Cheka, which hunted down and executed thousands of real or supposed foes, including the tsar and his family. During the so-called Red Terror of 1918–1920 the Cheka sowed fear, silenced opposition, and killed tens of thousands of "class enemies."

Finally, foreign military intervention in the civil war ended up helping the Communists. The Allies sent troops to prevent war materiel that they had sent to the provisional government from being captured by the Germans. After the Soviet government nationalized all foreign-owned factories without compensation and refused to pay foreign debts, Western governments began to support White armies. While these efforts did little to help the Whites' cause, they did permit the Communists to appeal to the patriotic nationalism of ethnic Russians.

The War's Consequences

☐ What were the global consequences of the First World War?

In spring 1918 the Germans launched their last major attack against France. It failed, and Germany was defeated. Austria-Hungary and the Ottoman Empire broke apart and ceased to exist. Then, as civil war spread in Russia and as chaos engulfed much of eastern Europe, the victorious Western Allies came together in Paris to establish a lasting peace.

Laboring intensively, the allies soon worked out terms for peace with Germany and for the creation of the peacekeeping League of Nations. The 1919 peace settlement, however, turned out to be a failure. Surely this was the ultimate tragedy of the Great War that cost $332 billion and left 10 million people dead and another 20 million wounded.

The End of the War

Victory over revolutionary Russia temporarily boosted sagging German morale, and in the spring of 1918 the German army under General Ludendorff fell on France once more. For a time German armies pushed forward, coming within thirty-five miles of Paris, but they never broke through. They were stopped in July at the second Battle of the Marne, where 140,000 fresh American soldiers saw action. Adding 2 million men in arms to the war effort by August, the late but massive American intervention decisively tipped the scales in favor of Allied victory.

By September British, French, and American armies were advancing steadily on all fronts. On October 4 the German emperor formed a new, more liberal German government to sue for peace. As negotiations over an armistice dragged on, the frustrated German people rose up. On November 3 sailors in Kiel (keel) mutinied, and throughout northern Germany soldiers and workers established revolutionary councils on the Russian soviet model. Austria-Hungary surrendered to the Allies the same day. With army discipline collapsing, the German emperor abdicated and fled to Holland. Socialist leaders in Berlin proclaimed a German republic on November 9, and agreed to tough Allied terms of surrender. The armistice went into effect on November 11, 1918.

The German Revolution of November 1918 resembled the Russian Revolution of March 1917. In both countries a popular uprising toppled an authoritarian monarchy, and moderate socialists took control of the government. But when Germany's radical socialists tried to seize power, the moderate socialists called on the army to crush the attempted coup. Thus Germany had a political revolution, but without a communist second installment.

Military defeat brought political revolution to Austria-Hungary, as it had to Germany, Russia, and the Ottoman Empire (see pages 879–886). The independent states of Austria, Hungary, Czechoslovakia, and a larger Romania were created out of the Austro-Hungarian Empire (Map 28.4). A greatly expanded Serbian monarchy united the Slavs in the western Balkans and took the name Yugoslavia.

The Treaty of Versailles

The peace conference opened in the Versailles Palace near Paris in January 1919 with seventy delegates from twenty-seven nations. There were great expectations. A young British diplomat later wrote that the victors "were journeying to Paris . . . to found a new order in Europe. We were preparing not Peace only, but Eternal Peace."[5]

This idealism was strengthened by President Wilson's January 1918 peace proposal, the Fourteen Points, which stressed national self-determination and the rights of small countries and called for the creation of the **League of Nations**, a permanent international organization designed to protect member states from aggression and avert future wars.

The real powers at the conference were the United States, Great Britain, and France. Germany and Russia were excluded, and Italy's role was limited. Almost immediately the three Allies began to quarrel. President Wilson insisted that the first order of business be the creation of the League of Nations. Wilson had his way, although prime ministers Lloyd George of Great Britain and especially Georges Clemenceau of France were unenthusiastic. They were primarily concerned with punishing Germany.

The "Big Three" were soon in a stalemate over what do to with Germany. Although personally inclined to make a somewhat moderate peace with Germany, Lloyd George felt pressured for a victory worthy of the sacrifices of total war. As Rudyard Kipling summed up the general British feeling at war's end, the Germans were "a people with the heart of beasts."[6] Clemenceau also wanted revenge and lasting security for France, which, he believed, required the creation of a buffer state between France and Germany, the permanent demili-

tarization of Germany, and vast German reparations. Wilson, supported by Lloyd George, would hear none of this, and by April the conference was deadlocked on the German question.

In the end, Clemenceau agreed to a compromise. He gave up the French demand for a Rhineland buffer state in return for a formal defensive alliance with the United States and Great Britain. Both Wilson and Lloyd George also promised that their countries would come to France's aid if attacked. Thus Clemenceau appeared to win his goal of French security, as Wilson had won his of a permanent international organization.

The **Treaty of Versailles** was the first step toward re-establishing international order. Germany's colonies were given to France, Britain, and Japan as League of Nations mandates. Germany's territorial losses within Europe were minor: Alsace-Lorraine was returned to France, and parts of Germany were ceded to the new Polish state (see Map 28.4). The treaty limited Germany's army to one hundred thousand men and allowed no new military fortifications in the Rhineland.

More harshly, the Allies declared that Germany (with Austria) was responsible for the war and had therefore to pay reparations equal to all civilian damages caused by the war. These much-criticized "war-guilt" and "reparations" clauses expressed inescapable popular demands for German blood. The actual reparations figure was not set, however, and there was the clear possibility that it might be set at a reasonable level when tempers had cooled in the future.

When presented with the treaty, the German government protested vigorously, but there was no alternative. On June 28, 1919, German representatives of the ruling moderate Social Democrats and the Catholic Party signed the treaty.

The Allies concluded separate peace treaties with the other defeated powers — Austria, Hungary, Bulgaria, and Turkey. For the most part these treaties merely ratified the existing situation in east-central Europe following the breakup of the Austro-Hungarian Empire (see Map 28.4). The Ottoman Empire was broken up, and, controversially, Britain and France extended their power in the Middle East.

Despite strong French objections, Hussein ibn-Ali's son Faisal (1885–1933) attended the Versailles Peace Conference, but his efforts to secure Arab independence

---

- **war communism** The application of the total-war concept to a civil conflict; the Bolsheviks seized grain from peasants, introduced rationing, nationalized all banks and industry, and required everyone to work.

- **League of Nations** A permanent international organization established during the 1919 Paris peace conference to protect member states from aggression and avert future wars.

- **Treaty of Versailles** The 1919 peace settlement that ended World War I; it declared Germany responsible for the war; limited Germany's army to one hundred thousand men, and forced Germany to pay huge reparations.

□ Mapping the Past

MAP 28.4 Territorial Changes in Europe After World War I The Great War brought tremendous changes to eastern Europe. Empires were shattered, new nations were established, and a dangerous power vacuum was created by the relatively weak states established between Germany and Soviet Russia.

ANALYZING THE MAP What territory did Germany lose, and to whom? What new independent states were formed from the old Russian empire?

CONNECTIONS How were the principles of national self-determination applied to the redrawing of Europe after the war? Did this theory work out?

came to nothing. President Wilson wanted to give the Arab case serious consideration, but the British and the French were determined to rule Syria, Iraq, and Palestine as League of Nations mandates and to accept only the independence of Hussein's kingdom of Hejaz. Brushing aside Arab opposition, France received Lebanon and Syria. Britain took Iraq and Palestine, which was to include a Jewish national homeland first promised by Britain in 1917 in the Balfour Declaration (see page 882). Officially League of Nations mandates, these Allied acquisitions were one of the most imperialistic elements of the peace settlement. Another was mandating Germany's holdings in China to Japan (see page 894). The mandates system left colonial peoples in the Middle East and Asia bitterly disappointed (see Chapter 29) and demonstrated that the age of Western, and Eastern, imperialism lived on.

American Rejection of the Versailles Treaty

The 1919 peace settlement was not perfect, but for war-shattered Europe it was an acceptable beginning. Germany was punished but not dismembered. A new world organization complemented a traditional defensive alliance of victorious powers. The remaining problems could be worked out in the future. Moreover, Allied leaders wanted a quick settlement for another reason: they detested Lenin and feared his Bolshevik Revolution might spread.

There were, however, two great interrelated obstacles to such peace: Germany and the United States. Plagued by communist uprisings, reactionary plots, and popular disillusionment with losing the war, Germany's moderate socialists and their liberal and Catholic supporters faced an enormous challenge. They needed time (and luck) if they were to establish a peaceful and democratic republic. Progress in this direction required understanding yet firm treatment of Germany by the victorious Western Allies.

In the United States, there was a quick reversion to prewar preferences for isolationism, and the U.S. Senate rejected the treaty. Republican senators led by Henry Cabot Lodge believed that the treaty gave away Congress's constitutional right to declare war. In failing health, Wilson rejected all attempts at compromise and thereby ensured the treaty would never be ratified by the United States in any form and that the United States would never join the League of Nations. Moreover, the Senate refused to ratify Wilson's defensive alliance with France and Great Britain. America turned its back on Europe. Using U.S. action as an excuse, Great Britain also refused to ratify its defensive alliance with France. Betrayed by its allies, France stood alone, and the great hopes of early 1919 had turned to ashes by year's end.

The Search for Peace and Political Stability, 1919–1929

☐ How did leaders deal with the political dimensions of uncertainty and try to re-establish peace and prosperity in the interwar years?

The Versailles settlement had established a shaky truce, not a solid peace, and the pursuit of real and lasting peace in the first half of the interwar years proved difficult for many reasons. Germany hated the Treaty of Versailles. France was fearful and isolated. Britain was undependable, and the United States had turned its back on European problems. Eastern Europe was in ferment, and no one could predict the future of communist Russia. Moreover, the international economic situation was poor and was greatly complicated by war debts and disrupted patterns of trade. Yet for a time, from 1925 to late 1929, it appeared that peace and stability were within reach.

Germany and the Western Powers

Germany held the key to lasting peace, yet all Germans believed that the Treaty of Versailles represented a harsh dictated peace and should be revised or repudiated as soon as possible. Moreover, France and Great Britain disagreed over Germany. By the end of 1919 France wanted to stress the harsh elements in the Treaty of Versailles. Most of the war on the western front had been fought on French soil, and the expected costs of reconstruction, as well as of repaying war debts to the United States, were staggering. Thus the French believed that reparations from Germany were an economic necessity. Large reparation payments could hold Germany down indefinitely, and France would realize its goal of security.

The British soon felt differently. Prewar Germany had been Great Britain's second-best market, and after the war a healthy, prosperous Germany appeared to be essential to the British economy. The British were also suspicious of France's army—the largest in Europe—and the British and French were also at odds over their League of Nations mandates in the Middle East.

While France and Britain drifted in different directions, the Allied reparations commission completed its work. In April 1921 it announced that Germany had to pay the enormous sum of 132 billion gold marks ($33 billion) in annual installments of 2.5 billion gold marks. The young German republic—known as the Weimar Republic—made its first payment in 1921. Then in 1922, wracked by rapid inflation and political assassinations and motivated by hostility and arrogance as well, the Weimar Republic announced its inability to pay more and proposed a reparations moratorium for three years.

The British were willing to accept a moratorium, but the French were not. Led by their prime minister, Raymond Poincaré (1860–1934), they decided they had to either call Germany's bluff or see the entire peace settlement dissolve to France's great disadvantage.

French Occupation of the Ruhr, 1923–1925

North Sea

NETHERLANDS

Occupied by French forces, 1923–1925

Berlin

GERMANY

BELGIUM

RUHR

RHINELAND

Demilitarized under Treaty of Versailles, 1920–1935

LUX.

SAAR

Rhine R.

Occupied under Treaty of Versailles, 1920–1935

SWITZ.

"Hands Off the Ruhr" The French occupation of the Ruhr to collect reparations payments raised a storm of patriotic protest in Germany. This anti-French poster of 1923 turns Marianne, the personification of French virtue, into a vicious harpy. (Photo: International Institute of Social History. Collection: Imperial War Museum)

So in January 1923 armies of France and its ally Belgium occupied the Ruhr district, industrial Germany's heartland, creating the most serious international crisis of the 1920s.

Strengthened by a wave of patriotism, the German government ordered the people of the Ruhr to stop working and to nonviolently resist the French occupation. The French responded by sealing off not only the Ruhr but also the entire Rhineland from the rest of Germany, letting in only enough food to prevent starvation.

By the summer of 1923 France and Germany were engaged in a great test of wills. French armies could not collect reparations from striking workers at gun-

point. But French occupation was paralyzing Germany and its economy. Needing to support the striking Ruhr workers and their employers, the German government began to print money to pay its bills. Prices soared, and German money rapidly lost all value. Many retired and middle-class people saw their savings wiped out. Catastrophic inflation cruelly mocked the old middle-class virtues of thrift, caution, and self-reliance. Many Germans felt betrayed. They hated and blamed the Western governments, their own government, big business, the Jews, the workers, and the Communists for their misfortune. The crisis left them psychologically prepared to follow radical right-wing leaders including Adolf Hitler and the new Nazi Party.

In August 1923, as the mark fell and political unrest grew throughout Germany, Gustav Stresemann (1878–1929) became German chancellor. Stresemann adopted a compromising attitude. He called off the peaceful resistance campaign in the Ruhr and in October agreed in principle to pay reparations, but asked for a re-examination of Germany's ability to pay. Poincaré accepted. Thus, after five years of hostility and tension, Germany and France, with the help of the British and the Americans, decided to try compromise and cooperation.

Hope in Foreign Affairs

In 1924 an international committee of financial experts headed by American banker Charles G. Dawes met to re-examine reparations. The resulting **Dawes Plan** (1924) was accepted by France, Germany, and Britain. Germany's yearly reparations were reduced and linked to the level of German economic prosperity. Germany would also receive large loans from the United States to promote German recovery. In short, Germany would get private loans from the United States and pay reparations to France and Britain, thus enabling those countries to repay the large sums they owed the United States.

This circular flow of international payments was complicated and risky, but it worked for a while. Germany experienced a spectacular economic recovery. With continual inflows of American capital, Germany paid about $1.3 billion in reparations in 1927 and 1928, enabling France and Britain to pay the United States. Thus, the Americans belatedly played a part in the general economic settlement that facilitated the worldwide recovery of the late 1920s.

This economic settlement was matched by a political settlement. In 1925 European leaders met in Locarno, Switzerland. Germany and France solemnly pledged to accept their common border, and both Britain and Italy agreed to fight either France or Germany if one invaded the other. Stresemann also agreed to settle boundary disputes with Poland and Czechoslovakia by peaceful means, and France promised those countries military aid if Germany attacked them. For years a "spirit of Locarno" gave Europeans a sense of growing security and stability in international affairs.

Other developments also strengthened hopes for international peace. In 1926 Germany joined the League of Nations, and in 1928 fifteen countries signed the Kellogg-Briand Pact, initiated by French prime minister Aristide Briand and U.S. secretary of state Frank B. Kellogg. The signing states "condemned and renounced war as an instrument of national policy." The pact fostered the cautious optimism of the late 1920s and also encouraged the hope that the United States would accept its international responsibilities.

Hope in Democratic Government

European domestic politics also offered reason to hope. During the Ruhr occupation and the great inflation, Germany's republican government appeared ready to collapse. In 1923 Communists momentarily entered provincial governments, and in November an obscure politician named Adolf Hitler proclaimed a "national socialist revolution" in a Munich beer hall. Hitler's plot to seize government control was poorly organized and easily crushed. Hitler was sentenced to prison, where he outlined his theories and program in his book ***Mein Kampf*** (My Struggle, 1925). Throughout the 1920s, Hitler's National Socialist Party attracted support from only a few fanatical anti-Semites, ultranationalists, and disgruntled former servicemen.

The moderate businessmen who tended to dominate the various German coalition governments believed that economic prosperity demanded good relations with the Western Powers, and they supported parliamentary government at home. Elections were held regularly, and as the economy boomed, republican democracy appeared to have growing support among a majority of Germans. There were, however, sharp political divisions in the country. Many unrepentant nationalists and monarchists populated the right and the army. Members of Germany's Communist Party received directions from Moscow, and they accused the Social Democrats of betraying the revolution. The working classes were divided politically, but a majority supported the socialist, but nonrevolutionary Social Democrats.

The situation in France was similar to that in Germany. Communists and socialists battled for the workers' support. After 1924 the democratically elected government rested mainly in the hands of moderate coalitions, and business interests were well represented. France's great accomplishment was rapid rebuilding of its war-torn northern region, and good times prevailed until 1930.

Britain, too, faced challenges after 1920. The wartime trend toward greater social equality continued, however, helping maintain social harmony. The great problem was unemployment, which hovered around 12 percent throughout the 1920s. The state provided unemployment benefits and supplemented those payments with subsidized housing, medical aid, and increased old-age pensions. These and other measures kept living standards from seriously declining, defused class tensions, and pointed the way to the welfare state Britain established after World War II.

Relative social harmony was accompanied by the rise of the Labour Party. Committed to moderate, "revisionist" socialism (see page 746), the Labour Party under Ramsay MacDonald (1866–1937) governed the country in 1924 and 1929. Labour moved toward socialism gradually and democratically, so that the middle classes were not overly frightened as the working classes won new benefits.

The British Conservatives under Stanley Baldwin (1867–1947) showed the same compromising spirit on social issues, and Britain experienced only limited social unrest in the 1920s and 1930s. In 1922 Britain granted southern, Catholic Ireland full autonomy after a bitter guerrilla war, thereby removing another source of prewar friction. Thus developments in both international relations and domestic politics gave the leading democracies cause for cautious optimism in the late 1920s.

The Age of Anxiety

☐ In what ways were the anxieties of the postwar world expressed or heightened by revolutionary ideas in modern thought, art, and science and new forms of communication?

When Allied diplomats met in Paris in early 1919 with their optimistic plans for building a lasting peace, most people looked forward to happier times and a return to the familiar prewar terms of peace, prosperity, and progress. These hopes were in vain. The First World War and the Russian Revolution had mangled too many things beyond repair. Great numbers of men and women felt themselves increasingly adrift in an age of anxiety and continual crisis.

• **Dawes Plan** The product of the reparations commission, accepted by Germany, France, and Britain, that reduced Germany's yearly reparations, made payment dependent on German economic prosperity, and granted Germany large loans from the United States to promote recovery.

• ***Mein Kampf*** Adolf Hitler's autobiography, published in 1925, which also contains Hitler's political ideology.

Uncertainty in Philosophy and Religion

Before 1914 most people in the West still believed in Enlightenment philosophies of progress, reason, and individual rights. At the turn of the century progress was a daily reality, apparent in the rising standard of living, the taming of the city, the spread of political rights to women and workers, and the growth of state-supported social programs. Just as there were laws of science, many thinkers felt, there were laws of society that rational human beings could discover and wisely act on. The German philosopher Friedrich Nietzsche (NEE-chuh; 1844–1900) was particularly influential. In the first of his *Untimely Meditations* (1873), he argued that ever since classical Athens, the West had overemphasized rationality and stifled the passion and animal instinct that drive human activity and true creativity.

Nietzsche went on to question the values of Western society. He believed that reason, democracy, progress, and respectability were outworn social and psychological constructs that suffocated self-realization and excellence. Rejecting religion, Nietzsche claimed that Christianity embodied a "slave morality" that glorified weakness, envy, and mediocrity. Little read during his lifetime, Nietzsche attracted growing attention in the early twentieth century.

The First World War accelerated the revolt against established certainties in philosophy. Logical positivism, often associated with Austrian philosopher Ludwig Wittgenstein (VIT-guhn-shtighn; 1889–1951), rejected most concerns of traditional philosophy — from God's existence to the meaning of happiness — as nonsense, and argued that life must be based on facts and observation. Others looked to **existentialism** for answers. Highly diverse and even contradictory, existential thinkers were loosely united in a search for moral values in a world of anxiety and uncertainty. Often inspired by Nietzsche, they did not believe that a supreme being had established humanity's fundamental nature and had given life its meaning. In the words of the famous French existentialist Jean-Paul Sartre (ZHAWN-pawl SAHR-truh; 1905–1980), human beings simply exist.

The loss of faith in human reason and in continual progress led to a renewed interest in Christianity. After World War I several thinkers and theologians began to revitalize Christian fundamentals. Sometimes

described as Christian existentialists because they shared the loneliness and despair of atheistic existentialists, they stressed human beings' sinful nature, the need for faith, and the mystery of God's forgiveness.

As a result, religion became much more relevant and meaningful than it had been before the war, and intellectuals turned to religion between about 1920 and 1950. Though often of a despairing, existential variety, it was one meaningful answer to terror and anxiety. In the words of a famous Roman Catholic convert, English novelist Graham Greene, "One began to believe in heaven because one believed in hell."[7]

The New Physics

By the late nineteenth century science was one of the main pillars supporting Western society's optimistic and rationalistic worldview. Unchanging natural laws seemed to determine physical processes and permit useful solutions to more and more problems. All this was comforting, especially to people no longer committed to traditional religious beliefs. And all this was challenged by the new physics.

An important first step toward the new physics was the discovery at the end of the nineteenth century that atoms were not stable and unbreakable. Polish-born physicist Marie Curie (1867–1934) and her French husband Pierre (1859–1906) discovered that radium constantly emits subatomic particles and thus does not have a constant atomic weight. Building on this, German physicist Max Planck (1858–1947) showed in 1900 that subatomic energy is emitted in uneven little spurts, which Planck called "quanta," and not in a steady stream, as previously believed.

In 1905 the German-Jewish genius Albert Einstein (1879–1955) further undermined Newtonian physics. His theory of special relativity postulated that time and space are relative to the observer's viewpoint and that only the speed of light is constant for all frames of reference in the universe. In addition, Einstein's theory stated that matter and energy are interchangeable and that even a particle of matter contains enormous levels of potential energy.

The 1920s opened the "heroic age of physics," in the apt words of one of its leading pioneers, Ernest Rutherford (1871–1937). Breakthrough followed breakthrough. In 1919 Rutherford first split the atom. By 1944 seven subatomic particles had been identified, the most important of which was the neutron. The neutron's capacity to pass through other atoms allowed for even more intense experimental bombardment of matter, leading to chain reactions of unbelievable force. The implications of the new theories and discoveries were disturbing to millions of people in the 1920s and 1930s. The new universe was strange and troubling, and, more-

---

• **existentialism** The name given to a highly diverse and even contradictory philosophy that stresses the meaningless of existence and the search for moral values in a world of terror and uncertainty.

• **id, ego, superego** Freudian terms for the primitive, irrational unconscious (id), the rationalizing conscious that mediates what a person can do (ego), and the ingrained moral values, which specify what a person should do (superego).

over, science appeared distant from human experience
and human problems.

Freudian Psychology

With physics presenting an uncertain universe so unrelated to ordinary human experience, questions about
the power and potential of the human mind assumed
special significance. The findings and speculations of
psychologist Sigmund Freud (1856–1939) were particularly disturbing.

Before Freud, most psychologists assumed that
human behavior was the result of rational thinking
by the conscious mind. By analyzing dreams and hysteria, Freud developed a very different view of the human psyche. Freud concluded that human behavior

was, governed by three parts of the self: the **id**, **ego**, and
superego. The irrational unconscious, which he called
the id, was driven by sexual, aggressive, and pleasure-
seeking desires and was locked in constant battle with
the mind's two other parts: the rationalizing conscious—
the ego—which mediates what a person can do, and ingrained moral values—the superego—which specify
what a person should do. Thus, for Freud human behavior was a product of a fragile compromise between
instinctual drives and the controls of rational thinking
and moral values. The danger for individuals was that
unacknowledged drives might overwhelm the control
mechanisms, leading to sexual repression, guilt, neu-
rotic fears, and even violence.

Freudian psychology and clinical psychiatry had
become an international movement by 1910, but only

after 1918 did they receive popular attention. Many interpreted Freud as saying that the first requirement for mental health was an uninhibited sex life. After World War I this popular interpretation reflected and encouraged growing sexual experimentation.

Twentieth-Century Literature

Western literature was also influenced by the general intellectual climate of pessimism, relativism, and alienation. Nineteenth-century novelists had typically written as all-knowing narrators, describing realistic characters in an understandable, if sometimes harsh, society. In the twentieth century many writers adopted the limited, often confused viewpoint of a single individual. Like Freud, these novelists focused on the complexity and irrationality of the human mind.

Some novelists used the stream-of-consciousness technique with its reliance on internal monologues to explore the psyche. The most famous stream-of-consciousness novel is *Ulysses*, published by Irish novelist James Joyce (1882–1941) in 1922. Into an account of a single day in the life of an ordinary man, Joyce weaves an extended ironic parallel between his hero's aimless wanderings through Dublin's streets and pubs and the adventures of Homer's hero Ulysses on his way home from Troy. Abandoning conventional grammar and blending foreign words, puns, bits of knowledge, and scraps of memory together in bewildering confusion, the language of *Ulysses* was intended to mirror modern life itself.

Creative writers rejected the idea of progress; some even described "anti-utopias," nightmare visions of things to come. In 1918 Oswald Spengler (1880–1936) published *The Decline of the West*, in which he argues that Western civilization was in its old age and would soon be conquered by East Asia. Likewise, T. S. Eliot (1888–1965) depicts a world of growing desolation in his famous poem *The Waste Land* (1922). Franz Kafka's (1883–1924) novels *The Trial* (1925) and *The Castle* (1926) portray helpless individuals crushed by inexplicably hostile forces.

Modern Architecture, Art, and Music

Like scientists and intellectuals, creative artists rejected old forms and old values after the war. **Modernism** in architecture, art, and music meant constant experimentation and a search for new kinds of expression.

The United States, with its rapid urban growth and lack of rigid building traditions, pioneered in the new architecture. In the 1890s the Chicago School of architects, led by Louis H. Sullivan (1856–1924), used cheap steel, reinforced concrete, and electric elevators to build skyscrapers and office buildings lacking almost any exterior ornamentation. The buildings of Frank Lloyd Wright (1867–1959), another visionary American architect, were renowned for their sometimes radical design, their creative use of wide varieties of materials, and their appearance of being part of the landscape.

In Europe architectural leadership centered in German-speaking countries. In 1919 Walter Gropius (1883–1969) merged the schools of fine and applied arts at Weimar into a single interdisciplinary school, the Bauhaus. Throughout the 1920s the Bauhaus, with its stress on **functionalism** and good design for everyday life, attracted enthusiastic students from all over the world.

After 1905 art increasingly took on a nonrepresentational, abstract character. New artistic styles grew out of a revolt against French impressionism, which was characterized by an overall feeling, or impression, of light falling on a real-life scene before the artist's eyes, rather than an exact copy of objects. Though individualistic in their styles, "postimpressionists" and "expressionists" were united in their desire to depict unseen inner worlds of emotion and imagination. Artists such as the Dutch expressionist Vincent van Gogh (1853–1890) painted the moving vision of the mind's eye. Paul Gauguin (1848–1903), a French expressionist, moved to the South Pacific, where he found inspiration in Polynesian forms, colors, and legends.

In 1907 in Paris the famous Spanish painter Pablo Picasso (1881–1973), along with other artists, established cubism—an artistic approach concentrated on a complex geometry of zigzagging lines and sharply angled overlapping planes. Since the Renaissance artists had represented objects from a single viewpoint and had created unified human forms. In his first great cubist work, *Les Demoiselles d'Avignon* (1907), Picasso's figures resemble large wooden African masks, presenting a radical new view of reality with a strikingly non-Western depiction of the human form. The influence of Polynesian art on Gauguin and of carved African masks on Picasso reflected the growing importance of non-Western artistic traditions in Europe in the late nineteenth and early twentieth centuries.

About 1910 came the ultimate stage in the development of abstract, nonrepresentational art. Artists such as the Russian-born Wassily Kandinsky (1866–1944) turned away from nature completely. "The observer," said Kandinsky, "must learn to look at [my] pictures . . .

• **modernism** A variety of cultural movements at the end of the nineteenth century and beginning of the twentieth that rebelled against traditional forms and conventions of the past.

• **functionalism** The principle that buildings, like industrial products, should serve the purpose for which they were made as well as possible.

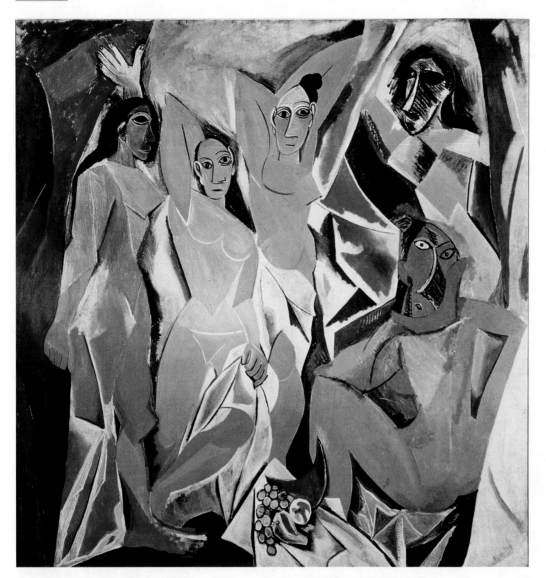

Picasso, *Les Demoiselles d'Avignon* Originating in memories of a brothel scene in Barcelona, this is one of the twentieth century's more influential paintings. Picasso abandoned unified perspective and depicted instead fragmented figures and distorted forms in his search for the magical violence of a pictorial breakthrough. The three faces on either side were inspired by African masks. (Digital image © The Museum of Modern Art/Licensed by Scala/Art Resource, NY/© 2011 Estate of Pablo Picasso/Artists Rights Society [ARS], New York)

as form and color combinations . . . as a representation of mood and not as a representation of *objects*."[8]

Radicalization accelerated after World War I. The most notable new developments were Dadaism and surrealism. Dadaism attacked all accepted standards of art and behavior, delighting in outrageous conduct. After 1924 many Dadaists were attracted to surrealism. Surrealists, such as Salvador Dalí (1904–1989), painted fantastic worlds of wild dreams and complex symbols.

Developments in modern music were strikingly parallel to those in painting. Composers, too, were attracted by the emotional intensity of expressionism. The pulsating, dissonant rhythms and the dancers'

earthy representation of lovemaking in the ballet *The Rite of Spring* by composer Igor Stravinsky (1882–1971) practically caused a riot when first performed in Paris in 1913. Likewise, modernism in opera and ballet flourished. Led by Viennese composer Arnold Schönberg (SHUHN-buhrg; 1874–1951), some composers turned their backs on long-established musical conventions. As abstract painters arranged lines and color but did not draw identifiable objects, so modern composers arranged sounds without creating recognizable harmonies. Accustomed to the harmonies of classical and romantic music, audiences generally resisted modern atonal music.

Movies and Radio

Cinema and radio became major industries after World War I, and standardized commercial entertainment began to replace the traditional arts and amusements of people in villages and small towns. Moving pictures were first shown as a popular novelty in naughty peepshows and penny arcades in the 1890s, especially in Paris. The first movie houses, dating from an experiment in Los Angeles in 1902, showed short silent action films.

During the First World War the United States became the dominant force in the rapidly expanding silent-film industry, and Charlie Chaplin (1889–1978), an Englishman working in Hollywood, was unquestionably the king of the "silver screen." In his enormously popular role as a lonely tramp, complete with baggy trousers, battered derby, and an awkward, shuffling walk, Chaplin symbolized the "gay spirit of laughter in a cruel, crazy world."[9] Chaplin also demonstrated that in the hands of a genius the new medium could combine mass entertainment and artistic accomplishment.

Motion pictures also became powerful tools of indoctrination, especially in countries with dictatorial regimes. Lenin encouraged the development of Soviet film making, and beginning in the mid-1920s a series of

The International Appeal of Cinema A movie house in Havana, Cuba, in 1933 showing two American films made in 1932: *El Rey de la Plata* (*Silver Dollar*) starring Edward G. Robinson, and *6 horas de Vida* (*Six Hours to Live*) featuring Warner Baxter. The partially visible poster in the upper right is advertising *El último varon sobre la Tierra* (*The Last Man on Earth*), an American-produced Spanish-language movie staring Raul Roulien, first released in Spain in January 1933. (Image copyright © The Metropolitan Museum of Art, Gift of Arnold H. Crane, 1971(1971.646.12). © Walker Evans Archive The Metropolitan Museum Of Art/Art Resource, NY)

epic films, the most famous of which were directed by Sergei Eisenstein (1898–1948), dramatized the communist view of Russian history. In Germany Hitler turned to a talented woman filmmaker, Leni Riefenstahl (1902–2003), for a masterpiece of documentary propaganda, *The Triumph of the Will,* based on the 1934 Nazi Party rally at Nuremberg. Her film was a brilliant and all-too-powerful depiction of Germany's Nazi rebirth.

Whether foreign or domestic, motion pictures became the main entertainment of the masses worldwide until after the Second World War. Featuring glittering stars such as Ginger Rogers and Fred Astaire and the fanciful cartoons of Mickey Mouse, motion pictures offered ordinary people a temporary escape from the hard realities of international tensions, uncertainty, unemployment, and personal frustrations.

Radio also dominated popular culture after the war. The work of Guglielmo Marconi (1874–1937) in 1901 and the development of the vacuum tube in 1904 permitted the transmission of speech and music. Only in 1920, however, were the first major public broadcasts made in Great Britain and the United States. Every major country quickly established national broadcasting networks. In the United States these were privately owned and financed by advertising, as was LOR Radio Argentina, which became the first formal radio station in the world when it made its first broadcast in August 1920. In Europe, China, Japan, India, and elsewhere the typical pattern was direct government control. By the late 1930s more than three-fourths of the households in both democratic Great Britain and dictatorial Germany had at least one cheap, mass-produced radio.

Like the movies, radio was well suited for political propaganda. Dictators such as Mussolini and Hitler controlled the airwaves and could reach enormous national audiences with their frequent, dramatic speeches. In democratic countries politicians such as President Franklin Roosevelt and Prime Minister Stanley Baldwin effectively used informal "fireside chats" to bolster support.

CONNECTIONS

The Great War has continued to influence global politics and societies more than ninety years after the guns went silent in November 1918. Anyone seeking to understand the origins of many modern world conflicts must study first the intrigues and treaties and the revolutions and upheavals that were associated with this first truly world war.

The war's most obvious consequences were felt in Europe, where three empires collapsed and new states were created out of the ruins. Old European antagonisms and mistrust made the negotiation of fair and just treaties ending the war impossible, despite the best efforts of an outsider, American President Wilson, to make this a war to end all wars. In Chapter 30 we will see how the conflict contributed to a worldwide depression, the rise of totalitarian dictatorships, and a Second World War more global and destructive than the first. In the Middle East the five-hundred-year-old Ottoman Empire came to an end, allowing France and England to carve out mandated territories — including modern Iraq, Palestine/Israel, and Lebanon — that remain flashpoints for violence and political instability in the twenty-first century. Nationalism, the nineteenth-century European ideology of change, took root in Asia, partly driven by Wilson's promise of self-determination. In Chapter 29 the efforts of various nationalist leaders — Atatürk in Turkey, Gandhi in India, Mao Zedong in China, Ho Chi Minh in Vietnam, and others — to throw off colonial domination will be examined. Included there also will be a discussion of how the rise of ultranationalism in Japan led it into World War II and ultimate defeat.

America's entry into the Great War placed it on the world stage, a place it has not relinquished as a superpower in the twentieth and twenty-first centuries. Russia too eventually became a superpower, but this outcome was not so clear in 1919 as its leaders fought for survival in a vicious civil war. By the outbreak of World War II Joseph Stalin had solidified Communist power, and the Soviet Union and the United Sates would play leading roles in the defeat of totalitarianism in Germany and Japan. But at war's end, as explained in Chapter 31, the two superpowers found themselves opponents in a Cold War that lasted for much of the rest of the twentieth century.

☐ CHAPTER REVIEW

☐ How did Europe's system of alliances contribute to the outbreak of World War I, and how did the conflict become a global war? (p. 844)

Following the Franco-Prussian War of 1870–1871, German Chancellor Otto van Bismarck sought to maintain peace in Europe by negotiating a series of alliances among the various nations. When Kaiser William II became German emperor in 1888, he forced Bismarck to resign, refused to renew the Russian-German nonaggression pact, and raised tensions across Europe. He caused France and Russia to join together against the Triple Alliance of Germany, Austria, and Italy, and he also alienated Great Britain, which later joined France and Russia in an alliance known as the Triple Entente. The assassination of the heir to the Austro-Hungarian throne by a Serbian nationalist in 1914 set these alliances in motion and drew the two rival blocs into war. The war in Europe was dominated by trench warfare, and stalemate and slaughter defined both the western and eastern fronts. Imperialistic ties would broaden the war's scope significantly, bringing countries in the Middle East, Asia, and Africa into the conflict.

☐ How did total war impact the home fronts of the major combatants? (p. 853)

The war caused an administrative revolution born of the need to mobilize entire societies and economies for total war. As a result, government power greatly increased in the West. The war effort's need for workers led to greater social equality, particularly for women who entered the workplace to fill jobs vacated by men away at the front. Labor unions grew and enjoyed greater power and prestige. Thus, even in European countries where a Communist takeover never came close to occurring, society experienced a great revolution, and socialism became a realistic economic blueprint that many countries adopted. Total war also led to increased strain at home and was manifested in strikes and a growing antiwar movement.

☐ What factors led to the Russian Revolution, and what was its outcome? (p. 858)

After three years of horrible slaughter on the eastern front, the Russian people were tired of the ineffective autocratic rule of Tsar Nicholas II and wanted change. In March 1917 the tsar abdicated, and the reins of government were taken over by a provisional government.

Controlled by moderate social democrats, the provisional government refused to pull Russia out of the war, and the massive waste of Russian lives continued until army discipline completely collapsed in resistance to the war. This opened the way for a second Russian revolution, this one led by Vladimir Lenin and his Communist Bolshevik Party in November 1917. The Bolsheviks established a radical regime, smashed existing capitalist institutions, and stayed in power with a new kind of authoritarian rule that posed a powerful ongoing challenge to Europe and its colonial empires.

☐ What were the global consequences of the First World War? (p. 862)

The "war to end war" brought not peace but only a fragile truce. Over the protests of the United States, France and Great Britain viewed the Versailles treaty as an opportunity to take revenge on Germany for the war. The treaty denied Germany an empire by taking away its colonies, forced Germany to destroy its army and navy, and demanded exorbitant war reparations. It also redrew the map of Europe, dissolving the Austro-Hungarian and Ottoman Empires. But the Allies failed to maintain their wartime solidarity, and Germany remained unrepentant, setting the stage for World War II. Globally, the European powers refused to extend the right of self-determination to their colonies in the Middle East, Africa, and Asia, and the mandate system created after the war would sow bitter discontent among colonized peoples.

☐ How did leaders deal with the political dimensions of uncertainty and try to re-establish peace and prosperity in the interwar years? (p. 865)

The death and destruction caused by World War I led to political and economic disruption across Europe in the years following the war. The question of German war reparations left the Allies divided. In the 1920s moderate political leaders replaced the World War I generation and compromised to create an enduring peace and rebuild prewar prosperity. The Dawes Plan was one example of how Europe and America worked to create financial stability in Europe. For a brief period late in the decade they seemed to have succeeded: Germany experienced an economic recovery, France rebuilt its war-torn regions, and Britain's Labour Party expanded social services. Ultimately though, these measures were short-lived.

☐ In what ways were the anxieties of the postwar world expressed or heightened by revolutionary ideas in modern thought, art, and science and new forms of communication? (p. 867)

The horrors of the Great War and, particularly, the turning of new technologies to the slaughter of millions shattered the ideals of the Enlightenment and caused widespread anxiety. Beginning in the interwar years philosophers, artists, and writers portrayed these anxieties in their work — such as existentialism in philosophy, cubism and surrealism in art, functionalism in architecture, literature that explored alienation and relativism, and atonal music. Freudian psychology gained popularity and sought to prove that human behavior was basically irrational, while Einstein's new universe was "relative," containing no absolute objective reality. The new forms of communication — movies and the radio — were initially forms of escape from the world's cares, but soon became powerful tools of indoctrination for modern dictators.

SUGGESTED READING

Andelman, David A. *A Shattered Peace: Versailles 1919 and the Price We Pay Today.* 2007. Clearly written history of the Versailles Peace Conference and how it has shaped world history to the present day.

Camus, Albert. *The Stranger* and *The Plague,* 1942 and 1947. The greatest existential novelist at his unforgettable best.

Ecksteins, Modris. *Rites of Spring: The Great War and the Birth of the Modern Age.* 1989. An imaginative cultural investigation that has won critical acclaim.

Fromkin, David. *Europe's Last Summer: Who Started the Great War?* 2004. Well-argued, compulsively readable discussion of responsibility for the war by a master historian.

Fromkin, David. *A Peace to End All Peace: The Fall of the Ottoman Empire and the Creation of the Modern Middle East,* 2d ed. 2009. A brilliant account of the Middle East in the critical years between 1914 and 1922.

Gay, Peter. *Modernism: The Lure of Heresy.* 2007. A personal perspective on twentieth-century high culture by a leading intellectual and cultural historian.

Gilbert, Martin. *The First World War: A Complete History.* 1994. Comprehensive study in one volume by a major military historian.

Gorham, Deborah. *Vera Brittain: A Feminist Life.* 1996. A major study of Brittain's life.

Issacson, Walter. *Einstein: His Life and Universe.* 2007. Well-received introduction to Einstein's life and work.

Macmillan, Margaret. *Paris, 1919: Six Months That Changed the World.* 2001. A masterful account of the negotiations and the issues at the Paris Peace Conference.

Massie, Raymond. *Nicholas and Alexandra.* 1971. A moving popular biography of Russia's last royal family and the terrible health problem of the heir to the throne.

Reed, John. *Ten Days That Shook the World.* 1919. The classic eyewitness account of the Russian Revolution by a young, pro-Bolshevik American.

Smith, Bernard. *Modernism's History: A Study in Twentieth-Century Thought and Ideas.* 1998. Admirably straightforward with a global perspective.

Wade, Rex. *The Russian Revolution, 1917.* 2000. Comprehensive and accessible history of the revolution.

Young, Louise. *Japan's Total Empire: Manchuria and the Culture of Wartime Imperialism.* 1998. A fascinating pioneering work on Japanese imperialism.

NOTES

1. Quoted in Keith Sinclair, *The Growth of New Zealand Identity, 1890–1980* (Auckland, N.Z.: Longman Paul, 1987), p. 24.
2. Svetlana Palmer and Sarah Wallis, eds., *Intimate Voices from the First World War* (New York: William Morrow, 2003), p. 221.
3. Ethel Alec-Tweedie, *Women and Soldiers,* 2d ed. (London: John Lane, 1918), p. 29.
4. Janet S. K. Watson, "Khaki Girls, VADS, and Tommy's Sisters: Gender and Class in First World War Britain," *The International History Review* 19 (1997): 49.
5. Quoted in H. Nicolson, *Peacemaking 1919* (New York: Grosset & Dunlap Universal Library, 1965), pp. 8, 31–32.
6. Quoted ibid., p. 24.
7. G. Greene, *Another Mexico* (New York: Viking Press, 1939), p. 3.
8. Quoted in A. H. Barr, Jr., *What Is Modern Painting?* 9th ed. (New York: Museum of Modern Art, 1966), p. 25.
9. R. Graves and A. Hodge, *The Long Week End: A Social History of Great Britain, 1918–1939* (New York: Macmillan, 1941), p. 131.

For practice quizzes and other study tools, visit the **Online Study Guide** at bedfordstmartins.com/mckayworld.

For primary sources from this period, see *Sources of World Societies,* **Second Edition**.

For Web sites, images, and documents related to topics in this chapter, visit **Make History** at bedfordstmartins.com/mckayworld.

• **Kasturba Gandhi** Wife of Indian political leader Mohandas Gandhi, she was barely fourteen and he thirteen years old when the marriage took place. Kasturba (1869–1944) supported Gandhi through decades of struggle for Indian independence. Here she spins cotton on a *charkha*, or spinning wheel, part of Gandhi's campaign for Indians to become self-sufficient by making their own cloth and freeing themselves from imported British goods. (© Dinodia Photo Library/The Image Works)

29

From Asia's perspective the First World War was largely a European civil war that shattered Western imperialism's united front, underscored the West's moral bankruptcy, and convulsed prewar relationships throughout Asia. Most crucially, the war sped the development of modern nationalism in Asia. Before 1914 the nationalist gospel of anti-imperialist political freedom and racial equality had already won converts among Asia's westernized, educated elites. In the 1920s and 1930s it increasingly won the allegiance of the masses. As in nineteenth-century Europe, nationalism in Asia between 1914 and 1939 became a mass movement with potentially awesome power.

Nationalism in Asia

1914–1939

The modern nationalism movement was never monolithic. In Asia especially, where the new and often narrow ideology of nationalism was grafted onto old, rich, and complex civilizations, the shape and eventual outcome of nationalist movements varied enormously. Between the outbreak of the First and Second World Wars each Asian country developed a distinctive national movement rooted in its own unique culture and history. Each nation's people created their own national reawakening, which renovated thought and culture as well as politics and economics. And as in Europe, nationalist movements gave rise to conflict both within large, multiethnic states and against other independent states in Asia.

The Asian nationalist movement witnessed the emergence of two of the true giants of the twentieth century. Mohandas Gandhi in India and Mao Zedong in China both drew their support from the peasant masses in the two most populous countries in the world. Gandhi successfully used campaigns of peaceful nonviolent resistance to British colonial rule to gain Indian independence. Mao on the other hand used weapons of war to defeat his opponents and established a modern Communist state. •

The First World War's Impact on Nationalist Trends

□ Why did modern nationalism develop in Asia between the First and Second World Wars, and what was its appeal?

Nationalist Movements in the Middle East

□ How did the collapse of the Ottoman Empire in World War I shape nationalist movements in the Middle East?

Toward Self-Rule in India

□ What role did Gandhi and his campaign of militant nonviolence play in leading India to independence from the British?

Nationalist Struggles in East and Southeast Asia

□ How did nationalism shape political developments in East and Southeast Asia?

The First World War's Impact on Nationalist Trends

□ Why did modern nationalism develop in Asia between the First and Second World Wars, and what was its appeal?

Every Asian national movement sought genuine freedom from foreign imperialism. The First World War profoundly affected these aspirations by altering relations between Asia and Europe. For four years Asians watched Kipling's haughty bearers of "the white man's burden" (see page 766) vilifying and destroying each other. Japan's defeat of imperial Russia in 1905 (see page 731) had shown that an Asian power could beat a European Great Power; now for the first time Asians saw the entire West as divided and vulnerable.

Asian Reaction to the War in Europe

In China and Japan few people particularly cared who won the distant war in Europe. In British India and French Indochina enthusiasm was also limited, but the war's impact was unavoidably greater. Total war required the British and the French to draft their colonial subjects into the conflict, uprooting hundreds of thousands of Asians to fight the Germans and the Ottoman Turks. This too had major consequences. An Indian or Vietnamese soldier who fought in France and

Prince Faisal and His British Allies On board a British warship on route to the Versailles Peace Conference in 1919, Prince Faisal is flanked on his right by British officer T. E. Lawrence, popularly known as Lawrence of Arabia because of his daring campaign against the Turks. Faisal failed to win political independence for the Arabs because the British backed away from the vague pro-Arab promises they had made during the war. (Courtesy, Paul Atterbury)

came in contact there with democratic and republican ideas was less likely to accept foreign rule when he returned home.

The British and the French had made rash promises to gain the support of colonial peoples during the war. French representatives suggested to Syrian nationalists in 1917 that Syria would have self-government after the war. British leaders promised Europe's Jewish nationalists a homeland in Palestine, while promising Arab nationalists independence from the Ottoman Empire. In India the British were forced in 1917 to announce a new policy of self-governing institutions in order to counteract Indian popular unrest fanned by wartime inflation and heavy taxation. After the war the nationalist genie the colonial powers had called on refused to slip meekly back into the bottle.

U.S. President Wilson's war aims had also raised the hopes of peoples under imperial rule. In January 1918 Wilson proposed his Fourteen Points (see page 863), whose key idea was national self-determination for the peoples of Europe and the Ottoman Empire. Wilson also recommended that in all colonial questions "the interests of native populations be given equal weight with the desires of European governments," and he seemed to call for national self-rule. This subversive message had enormous appeal for educated Asians, fueling their hopes of freedom.

□ CHRONOLOGY

1904–1905 Russo-Japanese War ends in Russia's defeat

1916 Sykes-Picot Agreement divides Ottoman Empire; Lucknow Pact forms alliance between Hindus and Muslims in India; New Culture Movement in China begins

1917 Balfour Declaration establishes Jewish homeland in Palestine

1919 Amritsar Massacre in India; May Fourth Movement in China; Treaty of Versailles; Afghanistan achieves independence

1920 King of Syria deposed by French; Gandhi launches campaign of nonviolent resistance against British rule in India

1920s–1930s Large numbers of European Jews immigrate to Palestine; Hebrew becomes common language

1923 Sun Yatsen allies Nationalist Party with Chinese Communists; Treaty of Lausanne ends war in Turkey; Mustafa Kemal begins to modernize and secularize Turkey

1925 Reza Shah Pahlavi proclaims himself shah of Persia and begins modernization campaign

1927 Jiang Jieshi, leader of Chinese Nationalist Party, purges his Communist allies

1930 Gandhi leads Indians on march to the sea to protest the British salt tax

1931 Japan occupies Manchuria

1932 Iraq gains independence in return for military alliance with Great Britain

1934 Mao Zedong leads Chinese Communists on Long March; Philippines gain self-governing commonwealth status from United States

1937 Japanese militarists launch attack on China; Rape of Nanjing

The Mandates System

After winning the war, the Allies tried to re-establish or increase their political and economic domination in the colonial states of Asia and Africa. Although fatally weakened, Western imperialism remained very much alive in 1918, partly because President Wilson was no revolutionary. At the Versailles Peace Conference he compromised on colonial questions in order to achieve some of his European goals and the creation of the League of Nations. Also, Allied statesmen and ordinary French and British citizens quite rightly believed that their colonial empires had contributed to their ultimate victory over the Central Powers. They would not give up such valuable possessions voluntarily. If pressed, Europeans said their administration was preparing colonial subjects for eventual self-rule, but only in the distant future.

The compromise at Versailles between Wilson's vague, moralistic idealism and the European preoccupation with "good administration" was a system of League of Nations mandates over Germany's former colonies and the old Ottoman Empire. Article 22 of the League of Nations Covenant, which was part of the Treaty of Versailles, assigned territories "inhabited by peoples incapable of governing themselves" to various "developed nations." "The well-being and development of such peoples" was declared "a sacred trust of civilization." The **Permanent Mandates Commission**, whose members came from European countries with colonies, was created to oversee the developed

---

• **Permanent Mandates Commission** A commission created by the League of Nations to oversee the developed nations' fulfillment of their international responsibility toward their mandates.

□ Mapping the Past

MAP 29.1 The Partition of the Ottoman Empire, 1914–1923 By 1914 the Ottoman Turks had been pushed out of the Balkans, and their Arab provinces were on the edge of revolt. That revolt erupted in the First World War and contributed greatly to the Ottomans' defeat. When the Allies then attempted to implement their plans, including independence for the Armenian people, Mustafa Kemal arose to forge in battle the modern Turkish state.

ANALYZING THE MAP What new countries were established as a result of the partition of the Ottoman Empire? Where were mandates established?

CONNECTIONS How might the collapse of the Ottoman Empire in World War I have contributed to the current situation in the Middle East?

nations' fulfillment of their international responsibility. Thus the League elaborated a new principle—development toward the eventual goal of self-government—but left its implementation to the colonial powers themselves.

The mandates system demonstrated that Europe was determined to maintain its imperial power and influence. Bitterly disappointed patriots throughout Asia saw France, Great Britain, and other nations—industrialized Japan was the only Asian state to obtain mandates—as grabbing Germany's colonies as spoils of war and extending the existing system of colonial rule in Muslim North Africa into the territories of the old Ottoman Empire. Yet Asian patriots did not give up. They preached national self-determination and struggled to build mass movements capable of achieving freedom and independence.

In this struggle Asian nationalists were encouraged by Soviet communism. After seizing power in 1917, Lenin declared that the Asian inhabitants of the new Soviet Union were complete equals of the Russians with a right to their own development. (In actuality this equality hardly existed, but the propaganda was effective nonetheless.) The Communists also denounced European and American imperialism and pledged to support revolutionary movements in colonial countries, even when they were primarily movements of national independence led by middle-class intellectuals instead of by revolutionary workers. Foreign political and economic exploitation was the immediate enemy, they said, and socialist revolution could wait until Western imperialism had been defeated. The example, ideology, and support of Soviet communism exerted a powerful influence in the 1920s and 1930s, particularly in China and French Indochina (see page 894).

Nationalism's Appeal

There were at least three reasons for the upsurge of nationalism in Asia. First and foremost, nationalism provided the most effective means of organizing anti-imperialist resistance both to direct foreign rule and to indirect Western domination. Second, nationalism called for fundamental changes and challenged old political and social practices and beliefs. As in Russia after the Crimean War, in Turkey after the collapse of the Ottoman Empire, and in Japan after the Meiji Restoration, the nationalist creed after World War I went hand in hand with acceptance of modernization by the educated elites. Modernization promised changes that would enable old societies to compete effectively with the world's leading nations. Educated elites thus used modernization to contest the influence and power of conservative traditionalists. Third, nationalism offered a vision of a free and prosperous future, and provided

an ideology to ennoble the sacrifices the struggle would require.

Nationalism also had a dark side. As in Europe (see page 721), Asian nationalists developed a strong sense of "we" and "they." "They" were often the enemy. European imperialists were just such a "they," and nationalist feeling generated the will to destroy European empires and challenge foreign economic domination. But, as in Europe, Asian nationalism also stimulated bitter conflicts and wars between peoples, in two different ways.

First, nationalism stimulated conflicts between relatively homogeneous peoples in large states, rallying, for example, Chinese against Japanese and vice versa. Second, it often heightened tensions between ethnic or religious groups within states, especially states with diverse populations like British India and the Ottoman Empire. Such states had been formed by authoritarian rulers and their armies and bureaucracies, very much like the Austro-Hungarian and Russian empires before 1914. When their rigid rule declined or snapped, the different nationalistic peoples might easily quarrel, seeking to divide the existing state or to dominate the enemy "they" within its borders.

Nationalism's appeal in Asia was not confined to territories under direct European rule. The extraordinary growth of international trade after 1850 had drawn millions of Asian peasants and shopkeepers into the Western-dominated world economy, disrupting local markets and often creating hostility toward European businessmen. Moreover, Europe and the United States had forced even the most solid Asian states, China and Japan, to accept unequal treaties and humiliating limitations on their sovereignty. Thus the nationalist promise of genuine economic independence and true political equality with the West appealed as powerfully in old but weak states like China as in colonial territories like British India.

Nationalist Movements in the Middle East

☐ How did the collapse of the Ottoman Empire in World War I shape nationalist movements in the Middle East?

The most flagrant attempt to expand Western imperialism occurred in the Middle East, or, more accurately, in Southwest Asia—the vast expanse that stretches eastward from the Suez Canal and Turkey's Mediterranean shores across the Tigris-Euphrates Valley and the Persian (Iranian) Plateau to the Arabian Sea and the Indus Valley (Map 29.1). There the British and the French successfully encouraged an Arab revolt in 1916 and destroyed the Ottoman Empire. Europeans then sought to replace Turks as principal rulers throughout the region, even in Turkey itself. Turkish, Arab, and Persian nationalists, as well as Jewish nationalists arriving from Europe, reacted violently. They struggled to win dignity and nationhood, and as the Europeans were forced to make concessions, they sometimes came into sharp conflict with each other, most notably in Palestine.

The Arab Revolt

Long subject to European pressure, the Ottoman Empire failed to reform and modernize in the late nineteenth century (see pages 768–770). Declining international stature and domestic tyranny led to revolutionary activity among idealistic exiles and young army officers who wanted to seize power and save the Ottoman state. These patriots, the so-called Young Turks, succeeded in the 1908 revolution, and subsequently they were determined to hold together the remnants of the vast multiethnic empire. Defeated by Bulgaria, Serbia, and Greece in the Balkan War of 1912, and stripped of practically all territory in Europe, the Young Turks redoubled their efforts in Southwest Asia. The most important of their possessions were Syria — consisting of modern-day Lebanon, Syria, Israel, the West Bank, the Gaza Strip, and Jordan — and Iraq. The Ottoman Turks also claimed the Arabian peninsula but exercised only loose control there.

For centuries the largely Arabic populations of Syria and Iraq had been tied to their Ottoman rulers by their common faith in Islam (though there were Christian Arabs as well). Yet beneath the surface, ethnic and linguistic tensions simmered between Turks and Arabs, who were as different as Chinese and Japanese.

Young Turk actions after 1908 made the embryonic "Arab movement" a reality. The majority of Young Turks promoted a narrow Turkish nationalism. They further centralized the Ottoman Empire and extended the sway of the Turkish language, culture, and race. In 1909 the Turkish government brutally slaughtered thousands of Armenian Christians, a prelude to the wholesale massacre of more than a million Armenians during the First World War. Meanwhile, Arab discontent grew.

During World War I the Turks freely aligned themselves with the Central Powers — Germany and Austria-Hungary (see page 849). As a result, the Young Turks drew all of the Middle East into what had been up to that point a European war. Arabs opposed to Ottoman rule found themselves allied with the British, who encouraged the alliance with vague promises of an independent Arab kingdom. After decisive British victories on the Arab peninsula in 1917 and 1918, Arabs rejoiced, and many patriots expected a large, unified Arab state to rise from the dust of the Ottoman collapse. Within two years, however, Arab nationalists felt bitterly betrayed by Great Britain and its allies, and this bitterness left a legacy of distrust and hatred toward the West.

Arab bitterness was partly directed at secret wartime treaties between Britain and France to divide and rule the old Ottoman Empire. In the 1916 **Sykes-Picot Agreement**, Britain and France secretly agreed that France would receive modern-day Lebanon, Syria, and much of southern Turkey, and Britain would receive Palestine, Jordan, and Iraq. The Sykes-Picot Agreement contradicted British (and later Wilsonian) promises concerning Arab independence after the war, and left Arab nationalists feeling cheated and betrayed.

A related source of Arab bitterness was Britain's wartime commitment to a Jewish homeland in Palestine. The **Balfour Declaration** of November 1917, made by the British foreign secretary Arthur Balfour, declared:

> His Majesty's Government views with favor the establishment in Palestine of a National Home for the Jewish People, and will use their best endeavors to facilitate the achievement of this object, it being clearly understood that nothing shall be done which may prejudice the civil and religious rights of existing non-Jewish communities in Palestine, or the rights and political status enjoyed by Jews in any other country.

As a careful reading reveals, the Balfour Declaration made contradictory promises to European Jews and Middle Eastern Arabs.

Some British Cabinet members believed the Balfour Declaration would appeal to German, Austrian, and American Jews and thus help the British war effort. Others sincerely supported the Zionist vision of a Jewish homeland (see page 888), but also believed that this homeland would be grateful to Britain and thus help maintain British control of the Suez Canal.

In 1914 Jews made up about 11 percent of the predominantly Arab population in the Ottoman territory that became, under British control, Palestine. The "National Home for the Jewish People" mentioned in the Balfour Declaration implied to the Arabs — and to the Zionist Jews as well — some kind of Jewish state that would be incompatible with majority rule. Moreover, a state founded on religious and ethnic exclusivity was out of keeping with both Islamic and Ottoman tradition, which had historically been more tolerant of religious diversity and minorities than had the Christian monarchs and nation-states of Europe.

• **Sykes-Picot Agreement** The 1916 secret agreement between Britain and France that divided up the Arab lands of Lebanon, Syria, southern Turkey, Palestine, Jordan, and Iraq.

• **Balfour Declaration** A 1917 statement by British foreign secretary Arthur Balfour that supported the idea of a Jewish homeland in Palestine.

The Armenian Atrocities When in 1915 some Armenians welcomed Russian armies as liberators after years of persecution, the Ottoman government ordered a genocidal mass deportation of its Armenian citizens from their homeland in the empire's eastern provinces. This photo, taken in Kharpert in 1915 by a German businessman from his hotel window, shows Turkish guards marching Armenian men off to a prison, where they will be tortured to death. A million Armenians died from murder, starvation, and disease during World War I. (Armenian Library and Museum of America Archives)

After Faisal bin Hussein's failed efforts at Versailles to secure Arab independence (see page 863), Arab nationalists met in Damascus as the General Syrian Congress in 1919 and unsuccessfully called again for political independence. (See "Listening to the Past: Resolution of the General Syrian Congress at Damascus," page 884.) Ignoring Arab opposition, the British mandate in Palestine formally incorporated the Balfour Declaration and its commitment to a Jewish national home. In March 1920 Faisal's followers met again as the Syrian National Congress and proclaimed Syria independent, with Faisal as king. A similar congress declared Iraq an independent kingdom.

Western reaction to events in Syria and Iraq was swift and decisive. A French army stationed in Lebanon attacked Syria, taking Damascus in July 1920. Faisal fled, and the French took over. Meanwhile, the British put down an uprising in Iraq with bloody fighting and established effective control there. Western imperialism appeared to have replaced Turkish rule in the Middle East (see Map 29.1).

The Turkish Revolution

At the end of the First World War, on November 12 and 13, 1918, French and then British troops entered Con-

stantinople to begin a five-year occupation of the Ottoman capital. A young English official wrote that he found the Ottoman Empire "utterly smashed." The Turks were "worn out" from the war, and without bitterness they awaited the construction of a "new system."[1] The Allies' new system was blatant imperialism, which proved harsher for the defeated Turks than for the "liberated" Arabs. A treaty forced on the helpless sultan dismembered Turkey and reduced it to a puppet state. Great Britain and France occupied parts of Turkey, and Italy and Greece claimed shares as well. There was a sizable Greek minority in western Turkey, and Greek nationalists cherished the "Great Idea" of a modern Greek empire modeled on long-dead Christian Byzantium. In 1919 Greek armies carried by British ships landed on the Turkish coast at Smyrna, met little resistance from the exhausted Turkish troops, and advanced into the interior. Turkey seemed finished.

But Turkey produced a great leader and revived to become an inspiration to the entire Middle East. Mustafa Kemal (1881–1938), considered the father of modern Turkey, was a military man sympathetic to the Young Turk movement. Kemal had distinguished himself in the Great War by directing the successful defense of the Dardanelles against British attack. After the armistice, he watched with anguish the Allies' aggression and the

Listening to the Past

Resolution of the General Syrian Congress at Damascus

Great Britain and France had agreed to divide up the Arab lands, and the British also had made conflicting promises to Arab and Jewish nationalists. However, President Wilson insisted at Versailles that the right of self-determination should be applied to the conquered Ottoman territories, and he sent an American commission of inquiry to Syria, even though the British and French refused to participate. The commission canvassed political views throughout greater Syria, and its long report with many documents reflected public opinion in the region in 1919.

To present their view to the Americans, Arab nationalists from present-day Syria, Lebanon, Israel, the West Bank, the Gaza Strip, and Jordan came together in Damascus as the General Syrian Congress, and they passed the following resolution on July 2, 1919. In addition to the Arab call for political independence, the delegates addressed the possibility of French rule under a League of Nations mandate and the establishment of a Jewish national home.

❝We the undersigned members of the General Syrian Congress, meeting in Damascus on Wednesday, July 2nd, 1919, . . . provided with credentials and authorizations by the inhabitants of our various districts, Moslems, Christians, and Jews, have agreed upon the following statement of the desires of the people of the country who have elected us to present them to the American Section of the International Commission; the fifth article was passed by a very large majority; all the other articles were accepted unanimously.

1. We ask absolutely complete political independence for Syria within these boundaries. [Describes the area including the present-day states of Syria, Lebanon, Israel, the West Bank, the Gaza Strip, and Jordan.]

2. We ask that the Government of this Syrian country should be a democratic civil constitutional Monarchy on broad decentralization principles, safeguarding the rights of minorities, and that the King be the Emir Faisal, who carried on a glorious

struggle in the cause of our liberation and merited our full confidence and entire reliance.

3. Considering the fact that the Arabs inhabiting the Syrian area are not naturally less gifted than other more advanced races and that they are by no means less developed than the Bulgarians, Serbians, Greeks, and Roumanians at the beginning of their independence, we protest against Article 22 of the Covenant of the League of Nations, placing us among the nations in their middle stage of development which stand in need of a mandatory power.

4. In the event of the rejection by the Peace Conference of this just protest for certain considerations that we may not understand, we, relying on the declarations of President Wilson that his object in waging war was to put an end to the ambition of conquest and colonization, can only regard the mandate mentioned in the Covenant of the League of Nations as equivalent to the rendering of economical and technical assistance that does not prejudice our complete independence. And desiring that our country should not fall a prey to colonization and believing that the American Nation is farthest from any thought of colonization and has no political ambition in our country, we will seek the technical and economical assistance from the United States of America, provided that such assistance does not exceed 20 years.

5. In the event of America not finding herself in a position to accept our desire for assistance, we will seek this assistance from Great Britain, also provided that such assistance does not infringe the complete independence and unity of our country and that the duration of such assistance does not exceed that mentioned in the previous article.

6. We do not acknowledge any right claimed by the French Government in any part whatever of our Syrian country and refuse that she should assist us or have a hand in our country under any circumstances and in any place.

7. We oppose the pretensions of the Zionists to create a Jewish commonwealth in the southern part of Syria, known as Palestine, and oppose Zionist migration to any part of our country; for we do not acknowledge their title but consider

sultan's cowardice. In early 1919 he began working to unify Turkish resistance.

The sultan, bowing to Allied pressure, initially denounced Kemal, but the cause of national liberation proved more powerful. The catalyst was the Greek in-

vasion and attempted annexation of much of western Turkey. A young Turkish woman described feelings she shared with countless others:

> After I learned about the details of the Smyrna occupation by Greek armies, I hardly opened my mouth on any subject except when it concerned the sacred struggle. . . . I suddenly ceased to exist as an individual. I worked, wrote and lived as a unit of that magnificent national madness.[2]

• **Treaty of Lausanne** The 1923 treaty that ended the Turkish war and recognized the territorial integrity of a truly independent Turkey.

> Palestinian Arabs protest against large-scale Jewish migration into Palestine.
> (Roger-Viollet/Getty Images)

them a grave peril to our people from the national, economical, and political points of view. Our Jewish compatriots shall enjoy our common rights and assume the common responsibilities.

8. We ask that there should be no separation of the southern part of Syria, known as Palestine, nor of the littoral western zone, which includes Lebanon, from the Syrian country. We desire that the unity of the country should be guaranteed against partition under whatever circumstances.

9. We ask complete independence for emancipated Mesopotamia [today's Iraq] and that there should be no economical barriers between the two countries.

10. The fundamental principles laid down by President Wilson in condemnation of secret treaties impel us to protest most emphatically against any treaty that stipulates the partition of our Syrian country and against any private engagement aiming at the establishment of Zionism in the southern part of Syria; therefore we ask the complete annulment of these conventions and agreements.

The noble principles enunciated by President Wilson strengthen our confidence that our desires emanating from the depths of our hearts, shall be the decisive factor in determining our future; and that President Wilson and the free American people will be our supporters for the realization of our hopes, thereby proving their sincerity and noble sympathy with the aspiration of the weaker nations in general and our Arab people in particular.

We also have the fullest confidence that the Peace Conference will realize that we would not have risen against the Turks, with whom we had participated in all civil, political, and representative privileges, but for their violation of our national rights, and so will grant us our desires in full in order that our political rights may not be less after the war than they were before, since we have shed so much blood in the cause of our liberty and independence.

We request to be allowed to send a delegation to represent us at the Peace Conference to defend our rights and secure the realization of our aspirations. 99

Source: "Resolution of the General Syrian Congress at Damascus, 2 July 1919," from the *King-Crane Commission Report*, in *Foreign Relations of the United States: Paris Peace Conference, 1919*, 12: 780–781.

QUESTIONS FOR ANALYSIS

1. What kind of state did the delegates want?

2. How did the delegates want to modify an unwanted League of Nations mandate to make it less objectionable?

3. Did the delegates view their "Jewish compatriots" and the Zionists in different ways? Why?

Refusing to acknowledge the Allied dismemberment of their country, the Turks battled on through 1920 despite staggering defeats. The next year the Greeks advanced almost to Ankara, the nationalist stronghold in central Turkey. There Mustafa Kemal's forces took the offensive and won a great victory. The Greeks and their British allies sued for peace. The resulting **Treaty of Lausanne** (1923) abolished the hated capitulations, which since the sixteenth century had given Europe-

ans special privileges in the Ottoman Empire (see page 606) and recognized a truly independent Turkey. Turkey lost only its former Arab provinces (see Map 29.1).

Mustafa Kemal believed Turkey should modernize and secularize along Western lines. His first moves were political. Drawing on his prestige as a war hero, Kemal called on the National Assembly to depose the sultan and establish a republic. He had himself elected president and moved the capital from cosmopolitan

Mustafa Kemal Surnamed Atatürk, meaning "father of the Turks," Mustafa Kemal and his supporters imposed revolutionary changes aimed at modernizing and westernizing Turkish society and the new Turkish government. Dancing here with his adopted daughter at her high-society wedding, Atatürk often appeared in public in elegant European dress—a vivid symbol for the Turkish people of his radical break with traditional Islamic teaching and custom. (Hulton Archive/Getty Images)

ligious authorities. Profoundly influenced by the example of western Europe, Mustafa Kemal set out, like the philosophes of the Enlightenment, to limit religious influence in daily affairs. Like Russia's Peter the Great, he employed dictatorial measures rather than reason to reach his goal. Kemal decreed a revolutionary separation of church and state. Secular law codes inspired by European models replaced religious courts. State schools replaced religious schools and taught such secular subjects as science, mathematics, and social sciences.

Mustafa Kemal also struck down many entrenched patterns of behavior. Women, traditionally secluded and inferior to males in Islamic society, received the right to vote. Civil law on a European model, rather than the Islamic code, now governed marriage. Women could seek divorces, and no man could have more than one wife at a time. Men were forbidden to wear the tall red fez of the Ottoman era as headgear; government employees were ordered to wear business suits and felt hats, erasing the visible differences between Muslims and "infidel" Europeans. The old Arabic script was replaced with a new Turkish alphabet based on Roman letters, which facilitated massive government efforts to spread literacy after 1928. Finally, in 1935, family names on the European model were introduced. Before this, while Jewish and Christian citizens of the empire used surnames, Muslim Turks had not. Muslims generally used a simple formulation of "son of" with their father's name. The National Assembly granted Mustafa Kemal the surname Atatürk, which means "father of the Turks."

By his death in 1938, Atatürk and his supporters had consolidated their revolution. Government-sponsored industrialization was fostering urban growth and new attitudes, encouraging Turks to embrace business and science. Poverty persisted in rural areas, as did some religious discontent among devout Muslims. But like the Japanese after the Meiji Restoration, the Turkish people had rallied around the nationalist banner to repulse European imperialism and were building a modern secular nation-state.

Modernization Efforts in Persia and Afghanistan

In Persia (renamed Iran in 1935), strong-arm efforts to build a unified modern nation ultimately proved less successful than in Turkey. In the late nineteenth century Persia had also been subject to extreme foreign pressure, which stimulated efforts to reform the government as a means of reviving Islamic civilization. In 1906 a nationalistic coalition of merchants, religious leaders, and intellectuals revolted. The despotic shah was forced to grant a constitution and establish a national assembly, the **Majlis**. Nationalist hopes ran high.

Constantinople (now Istanbul) to Ankara in the Turkish heartland. Kemal savagely crushed the demands for independence of ethnic minorities like the Armenians and the Kurds, but he realistically abandoned all thought of winning back lost Arab territories. He then created a one-party system—partly inspired by the Bolshevik example—in order to work his will.

Kemal's most radical changes pertained to religion and culture. For centuries most believers' intellectual and social activities had been regulated by Islamic re-

• **Majlis** The national assembly established by the despotic shah of Iran in 1906.

Yet the 1906 Persian revolution was doomed to failure, largely because of European imperialism. Without consulting Iran, Britain and Russia in 1907 divided the country into spheres of influence. Britain's sphere ran along the Persian Gulf; the Russian sphere encompassed the whole northern half of Persia (see Map 29.1). Thereafter Russia intervened constantly. It blocked reforms, occupied cities, and completely dominated the country by 1912. When Russian power collapsed in the Bolshevik Revolution, British armies rushed into the power vacuum. By bribing corrupt Persians, Great Britain in 1919 negotiated a treaty allowing the installation of British "advisers" in every government department.

The Majlis refused to ratify the treaty, and the blatant attempt to make Persia a British satellite aroused the national spirit. In 1921 reaction against the British brought to power a military dictator, Reza Shah Pahlavi (1877–1944), who proclaimed himself shah in 1925 and ruled until 1941.

Inspired by Turkey's Mustafa Kemal, the patriotic, religiously indifferent Reza Shah had three basic goals: to build a modern nation, to free Persia from foreign domination, and to rule with an iron fist. The challenge was enormous. Persia was a vast, undeveloped country of deserts, mountain barriers, and rudimentary communications. The rural population was mostly poor and illiterate, and among the Persian majority were sizable ethnic minorities with their own aspirations. Furthermore, Iran's powerful religious leaders hated Western (Christian) domination but were equally opposed to a more secular, less Islamic society.

To realize his vision of a strong Persia, the energetic shah created a modern army, built railroads, and encouraged commerce. He won control over ethnic minorities such as the Kurds in the north and Arab tribesmen on the Iraqi border. He reduced the privileges granted to foreigners and raised taxes on the powerful Anglo-Persian Oil Company, which had been founded in 1909 to exploit the first great oil strike in the Middle East. Yet Reza Shah was less successful than Atatürk.

Because the European-educated elite in Persia was smaller than the comparable group in Turkey, the idea of re-creating Persian greatness on the basis of a secularized society attracted relatively few determined supporters. Many powerful religious leaders turned against Reza Shah, and he became increasingly brutal, greedy, and tyrannical, murdering his enemies and lining his pockets. His support of Hitler's Nazi Germany (discussed in Chapter 30) also exposed Persia's tenuous and fragile independence to the impact of European conflicts.

Afghanistan, meanwhile, was nominally independent in the nineteenth century, but the British imposed political restrictions and constantly meddled in the country's affairs. In 1919 the violently anti-British emir Amanullah (1892–1960) declared a holy war on the

Afghanistan Under Amanullah Khan

An Afghan Reformer
Amanullah Khan, the ruler of Afghanistan from 1919 to 1929, was inspired by Mustafa Kemal in Turkey, and he too looked to Europe for models of reform and modernization. Shown here arriving in Berlin in 1926 and accompanied by President von Hindenburg on the right, Amanullah's efforts to promote secular education and end polygamy and women's veiling incensed Islamic religious leaders and led to a fearsome backlash and his abdication.
(Hulton Archive/Getty Images)

British government in India and won complete independence for the first time. Amanullah then decreed revolutionary reforms designed to hurl his primitive country into the twentieth century. The result was tribal and religious revolt, civil war, and retreat from reform. Islam remained both religion and law. A powerful but primitive patriotism enabled Afghanistan to win political independence from the West, but not to build a modern society.

Gradual Independence in the Arab States

French and British mandates established at gunpoint forced Arab nationalists to seek independence by gradual means after 1920. Arab nationalists were indirectly aided by Western taxpayers, who wanted cheap — that is, peaceful — empires. As a result, Arabs won considerable control over local affairs in the mandated states, except Palestine, though the mandates remained European satellites in international and economic affairs.

In Iraq, the British chose Faisal bin Hussein, whom the French had deposed in Syria, as king. Faisal obligingly gave British advisers broad behind-the-scenes control. The king also accepted British ownership of Iraq's oil fields, consequently giving the West a stranglehold on the Iraqi economy. Given the severe limitations imposed on him, Faisal (r. 1921–1933) proved to be an able ruler, gaining the support of his people and encouraging moderate reforms. In 1932 he secured Iraqi independence at the price of a restrictive long-term military alliance with Great Britain.

Egypt had been occupied by Great Britain since 1882 (see page 773) and had been a British protectorate since 1914. Following intense nationalist agitation after the Great War, Great Britain in 1922 proclaimed Egypt formally independent but continued to occupy the country militarily and control its politics. In 1936 the British agreed to restrict their troops to their bases in the Suez Canal Zone.

The French compromised less in their handling of their mandated Middle East territories. Following the collapse of the Ottoman Empire after World War I, the French designated Lebanon as one of several ethnic enclaves within a larger area that became part of the French mandate of Syria. They practiced a policy of divide-and-rule and generally played off ethnic and religious minorities against each other. Maronite Catholic Christians made up the majority of Lebanon's population, but there were also significant numbers of Muslims and Druzes. In 1926 Lebanon became a separate republic but remained under the control of the

French mandate. Arab nationalists in Syria finally won promises of Syrian independence in 1936 in return for a treaty of friendship with France.

In short, the Arab states gradually freed themselves from Western political mandates but not from the Western military threat or from pervasive Western influence. Of great importance, large Arab landowners and urban merchants increased their wealth and political power after 1918, and they often supported the Western hegemony, from which they benefited greatly. Western control of the newly discovered Arab oil fields helped to convince radical nationalists that economic independence and genuine freedom had not yet been achieved.

Arab-Jewish Tensions in Palestine

Relations between the Arabs and the West were complicated by the tense situation in the British mandate of Palestine, and that situation deteriorated in the interwar years. Both Arabs and Jews denounced the British, who tried unsuccessfully to compromise with both sides. Arab nationalist anger, however, was aimed primarily at Jewish settlers. The key issue was Jewish migration from Europe to Palestine.

A small Jewish community had survived in Palestine ever since the dispersal of the Jews in Roman times. But Jewish nationalism, known as Zionism, took shape in Europe in the late nineteenth century under the leadership of Theodor Herzl (see page 744). Herzl believed that only a Jewish state could guarantee Jews dignity and security. The Zionist movement encouraged the world's Jews to settle in Palestine, but until 1921 the great majority of Jewish emigrants preferred the United States.

After 1921 the situation changed radically. An isolationist United States drastically limited immigration from eastern Europe, where war and revolution had kindled anti-Semitism. Moreover, the British began honoring the Balfour Declaration despite Arab protests. Thus Jewish immigration to Palestine from turbulent Europe in the interwar years grew rapidly. In the 1930s German and Polish persecution created a mass of Jewish refugees. By 1939 the Jewish population of Palestine had increased almost fivefold since 1914 and accounted for about 30 percent of all inhabitants.

Jewish settlers in Palestine faced formidable difficulties. Although much of the land purchased by the Jewish National Fund was productive, the sellers of such land were often wealthy absentee Arab landowners who cared little for their Arab tenants' welfare. When the new Jewish owners replaced those long-time Arab tenants with Jewish settlers, Arab farmers and intellectuals burned with a sense of injustice. Moreover, most Jewish immigrants came from urban backgrounds and preferred to establish new cities like Tel

• **kibbutz** A Jewish collective farm on which each member shared equally in the work, rewards, and defense.

Kibbutz Children Picking Grapes Many of the early kibbutzim, such as this one at Kfar Blum in Israel's northern Galilee, were agricultural settlements that produced cotton and fruits such as grapes, oranges, and apples that were then packed and shipped around the world. They also produced most of the food eaten by the members. On the kibbutz, as these children illustrate, all did their share of the work. Collection boxes for the Zionist cause (below) date back to 1884, but donations became more standardized after the founding of the Jewish National Fund in 1901. The first Blue Box appeared in 1904, with the suggestion that a box be placed in every Jewish home around the world and contributed to as often as possible. Still in use today, Blue Box donations go for such things as the planting of forests, the establishment of parks, and the building of roads and water reservoirs in the Israeli state. (kibbutz: Courtesy, Kibbutz Kfar Blum Archives; box: Jewish National Fund Photo Archives, Jerusalem)

Aviv or to live in existing towns, where they competed with the Arabs. The land issue combined with economic and cultural friction to harden Arab protest into hatred. Anti-Jewish riots and even massacres ensued.

The British gradually responded to Arab pressure and tried to slow Jewish immigration. This effort satisfied neither Jews nor Arabs, and by 1938 the two communities were engaged in an undeclared civil war. On the eve of the Second World War, the frustrated British proposed an independent Palestine with the number of Jews permanently limited to only about one-third of the total population. Zionists felt themselves in grave danger of losing their dream of an independent Jewish state.

Nevertheless, in the face of adversity Jewish settlers from many different countries gradually succeeded in forging a cohesive community in Palestine. Hebrew, for centuries used only in religious worship, was revived as a living language to bind the Jews in Palestine together. Despite its slow beginnings, rural development achieved often remarkable results. The key unit of agricultural organization was the **kibbutz** (kih-BOOTS), a collective farm on which each member shared equally in the work, rewards, and defense. An egalitarian socialist ideology also characterized industry, which grew rapidly. By 1939 a new but old nation was emerging in the Middle East.

Toward Self-Rule in India

☐ What role did Gandhi and his campaign of militant nonviolence play in leading India to independence from the British?

The national movement in British India grew out of two interconnected cultures, Hindu and Muslim, that came to see themselves as fundamentally different in rising to challenge British rule. Nowhere has modern nationalism's power both to unify and to divide been more strikingly demonstrated than in India.

British Promises and Repression

Indian nationalism had emerged in the late nineteenth century (see page 787), and when the First World War began, the British feared revolt. Instead, Indians supported the war effort. About 1.2 million Indian soldiers and laborers voluntarily served in Europe, Africa, and the Middle East. The British government in India and the native Indian princes sent large supplies of food, money, and ammunition. In return, the British opened more good government jobs to Indians and made other minor concessions.

As the war in distant Europe ground on, however, inflation, high taxes, food shortages, and a terrible influenza epidemic created widespread suffering and discontent. The prewar nationalist movement revived stronger than ever, and moderates and radicals in the Indian National Congress Party (see page 787) joined forces. Moreover, in 1916 Hindu leaders in the Congress Party hammered out an alliance — the **Lucknow Pact** — with India's Muslim League. The League was founded in 1906 to uphold Muslim interests, as, under British rule, the once-dominant Muslim minority had fallen behind the Hindu majority. The Lucknow Pact forged a powerful united front of Hindus and Muslims and called for putting India on equal footing with self-governing British dominions like Canada, Australia, and New Zealand.

The British response was contradictory. On the one hand, the secretary of state for India made the unprecedented announcement in August 1917 that British policy in India called for the "gradual development of self-governing institutions and the progressive realization of responsible government." In late 1919 the British established a dual administration: part Indian and elected, part British and authoritarian. Such uncontroversial activities as agriculture and health were transferred from British to Indian officials who were accountable to elected provincial assemblies. More sensitive matters like taxes, police, and the courts remained solely in British hands.

Old-fashioned authoritarian rule seriously undermined the positive impact of this reform. Despite the unanimous opposition of the elected Indian members, the British in 1919 rammed the repressive Rowlatt Acts through India's Imperial Legislative Council. These acts indefinitely extended wartime "emergency measures" designed to curb unrest and root out "conspiracy." The result was a wave of rioting across India.

Under these tense conditions a crowd of some ten thousand gathered to celebrate a Sikh religious festival in an enclosed square in the Sikh holy city of Amritsar in the northern Punjab province. Unknown to the crowd, the local English commander, General Reginald Dyer, had banned all public meetings that very day. Dyer marched his native Gurkha troops into the square and, without warning, ordered them to fire into the unarmed mass at point-blank range until the ammunition ran out. Official British records of the Amritsar Massacre list 379 killed and 1,137 wounded, but these figures remain hotly contested as being too low. Tensions flared, and India stood on the verge of more violence and repression and, sooner or later, terrorism and guerrilla war. That India took a different path to national liberation was due largely to Mohandas K. Gandhi (1869–1948), the most influential Indian of modern times.

The Roots of Militant Nonviolence

By the time of Gandhi's birth in 1869, the Indian subcontinent was firmly controlled by the British. Part of the country was ruled directly by British (and subor-

British Man Fishing in India British colonial officials, such as this gentleman reposing in a wicker chair while fishing in India around 1925, enjoyed lifestyles that were often much more comfortable than would have been the case back in England. Gardeners, chauffeurs, maids, cooks, and other personal servants, like the three men helping the fisher, were commonly hired to wait on the colonists hand and foot. Some justified the lifestyle as demonstrating the refinements of civilization — part of the white man's burden. (Photograph by Ralph Ponsonby Watts/Mary Evans Picture Library/The Images Works)

dinate Indian) officials, answerable to the British Parliament in London. In each of the so-called protected states, the native prince — usually known as the maharaja — remained the titular ruler, although he was bound to the British by unequal treaties and had to accept the "advice" of the British resident assigned to his court.

Gandhi grew up in one of the small protected states north of Bombay. Gandhi's father was the well-to-do head of a large extended family. Gandhi's mother was devoted but undogmatic in religious matters, and she exercised a strong influence on her son. After his father's death, Gandhi went to study law in England, where he passed the English bar. Upon returning to India, he decided in 1893 to try a case for some wealthy Indian merchants in the colony of Natal (part of modern South Africa). It was a momentous decision.

In Natal, Gandhi took up the plight of the expatriate Indian community. White plantation owners had been importing thousands of poor Indians as indentured laborers on five-year renewable contracts since the 1860s. When Gandhi arrived there were more Indians than whites in Natal. Some of these Indians, after completing their contracts, remained in Natal as free persons and economic competitors. In response, the Afrikaner (of Dutch descent) and British settlers passed brutally discriminatory laws. Poor Indians had to work on plantations or return to India. Rich Indians, who had previously had the vote in Natal, lost that right in 1896. Gandhi undertook his countrymen's legal defense, and in 1897 a white mob almost lynched the "coolie lawyer."

Meanwhile, Gandhi was searching for a spiritual theory of social action. He studied Hindu and Christian teachings, and gradually developed a weapon for the poor and oppressed that he called **satyagraha** (suh-TYAH-gruh-huh). Gandhi conceived of satyagraha, loosely translated as "soul force," as a means of striving for truth and social justice through love and a willingness to suffer the blows of the oppressor, while trying to convert the oppressor to your views of what is true. Its tactic was active nonviolent resistance.

As the undisputed leader of South Africa's Indians before the First World War, Gandhi put his philosophy into action. When South Africa's white government severely restricted Asian immigration and internal freedom of movement, Gandhi organized a nonviolent mass resistance campaign. Thousands of Indian men and women marched in peaceful protest and withstood beatings, arrest, and imprisonment.

In 1914 South Africa's exasperated whites agreed to many of the Indians' demands. They passed a law abolishing discriminatory taxes on Indian traders, recognized the legality of non-Christian marriages, and permitted the continued immigration of free Indians. Satyagraha — militant nonviolence in pursuit of social justice — proved a powerful force in Gandhi's hands.

> "Wherein is courage required — in blowing others to pieces from behind a cannon, or with a smiling face to approach a cannon and be blown to pieces?"
>
> **GANDHI**

Gandhi's Resistance Campaign in India

In 1915 Gandhi returned to India. His reputation had preceded him: the masses hailed him as a mahatma, or "great soul" — a Hindu title of veneration for a man of great knowledge and humanity. Drawing on his South African experience because he knew Indians could not compete militarily against the British, Gandhi in 1920 launched a national campaign of nonviolent resistance to British rule. Denouncing British injustice, he urged his countrymen to boycott British goods, jobs, and honors (such as honorary titles like baron, rai, diwān, and khan, and other awards). He told peasants not to pay taxes or buy English goods, primarily cloth, or the heavily taxed liquor. Gandhi electrified the Indian people, initiating a revolution in Indian politics.

The nationalist movement had previously touched only the tiny, prosperous, Western-educated elite. Now both the illiterate masses of village India and the educated classes heard Gandhi's call for militant nonviolent resistance. It particularly appealed to the masses of Hindus who were not members of the warrior caste or the so-called military races and who were traditionally passive and nonviolent. The British had regarded ordinary Hindus as cowards. Gandhi told them that they could be courageous and even morally superior:

> What do you think? Wherein is courage required — in blowing others to pieces from behind a cannon, or with a smiling face to approach a cannon and be blown to pieces? Who is the true warrior — he who keeps death always as a bosom-friend, or he who controls the death of others? Believe me that a man devoid of courage and manhood can never be a passive resister.[3]

Gandhi made the Indian National Congress into a mass political party, welcoming members from every ethnic group and cooperating closely with the Muslim minority.

In 1922 some Indian resisters turned to violence, murdering twenty-two policemen. Savage riots broke

• **Lucknow Pact** A 1916 alliance between the Hindus leading the Indian National Congress and the Muslim League.

• **satyagraha** Loosely translated as "soul force," which Gandhi believed was the means of striving for truth and social justice through love, suffering, and conversion of the oppressor.

Gandhi Arrives in Delhi, October 1939
A small frail man, Gandhi possessed enormous courage and determination. His campaign of nonviolent resistance to British rule inspired the Indian masses and mobilized a nation. Here he arrives for talks with the British viceroy after the outbreak of World War II. (Hulton Deutsch Collection/Corbis)

India, ca. 1930

out, and Gandhi abruptly called off his campaign. Arrested for fomenting rebellion, Gandhi told the British judge that he had committed "a Himalayan blunder to believe that India had accepted nonviolence." Released from prison after two years, Gandhi set up a commune, established a national newspaper, and set out to reform Indian society and improve the lot of the poor. He welcomed the outcaste untouchables (a caste comprised of people who worked in occupations deemed unclean or "polluting"), worked to help child widows who were denied the right to remarry and suffered discrimination, and promoted native cottage industry production. For Gandhi moral improvement, social progress, and the national movement went hand in hand. Above all, Gandhi nurtured national identity and self-respect. He also tried to instill in India's people the courage to overcome their fear of their colonial rulers and to fight these rulers with nonviolence. (See "Viewpoints: Gandhi and Mao on Revolutionary Means," page 893.)

The 1920–1922 resistance campaign left the British severely shaken, but the commission formed in 1927 to consider further steps toward self-rule included no Indian members. In the meantime, Gandhi had served two years (1922–1924) of a six-year sentence for sedition, and in his absence the Indian National Congress had splintered into various factions. Indian resentment of British rule was intense and growing throughout the 1920s, and Gandhi spent the years after his release from prison quietly trying to unite the different factions. In 1929 the radical nationalists, led by the able and aristocratic Jawaharlal Nehru (1889–1964), pushed

through the National Congress a resolution calling for virtual independence within a year. The British stiffened in their resolve against Indian independence, and Indian radicals talked of a bloody showdown.

Into this tense situation Gandhi masterfully reasserted his leadership, taking a hard line toward the British, but insisting on nonviolent methods. He organized a massive resistance campaign against the tax on salt, which gave the British a veritable monopoly on the salt that was absolutely necessary for survival in India's heat and humidity. As Gandhi shrewdly realized, the tax affected every Indian family. From March 12 to April 6, 1930, Gandhi led fifty thousand people in a spectacular march to the sea, where he made salt in defiance of the law. A later demonstration at the British-run Dharasana salt works resulted in many of the 2,500 nonviolent marchers being beaten senseless by policemen in a brutal and well-publicized encounter. Over the next months the British arrested Gandhi and sixty thousand other protesters for making and distributing salt. But the protests continued, and in 1931 the frustrated and unnerved British released Gandhi from jail and sat down to negotiate with him, as an equal, over Indian self-rule. Negotiations resulted in a new constitution, the Government of India Act, in 1935, which greatly strengthened India's parliamentary representative institutions and gave Indians some voice in the administration of British India. Although there was little Indian involvement in the drafting of the act, and it was never fully implemented, it served as a blueprint for the constitutions of India and Pakistan when they gained independence soon after World War II.

Viewpoints

Gandhi and Mao on Revolutionary Means

• *India's Mohandas Gandhi and China's Mao Zedong successfully led two of the largest and most populous nations to independence in the late 1940s. Both drew much of their support from the peasant masses, among whom they both lived and worked, following very simple lifestyles, as their political power and influence grew.*

Gandhi's and Mao's political philosophies could not have been more different. Gandhi believed that active nonviolent disobedience to British rule was the only way Indians could break free of British rule and gain independence. He explained his views in the following excerpts from articles that he wrote for the journal Young India *in 1921 and 1931. As shown in the second document from Mao's* Little Red Book, *Mao took the exact opposite view. He believed that "power flows from the barrel of a gun" and that violence was the only means by which the Chinese masses could rid themselves of corrupt warlords, cruel landowners, imperialist occupiers, and ruling elites.*

Mohandas Gandhi

Complete civil disobedience is rebellion without the element of violence in it. An out-and-out resister simply ignores the authority of the State. He becomes an outlaw claiming to disregard every unmoral State law. Thus, for instance, he may refuse to pay taxes, he may refuse to recognize the authority in his daily intercourse. . . . In doing all this he never uses force and never resists force when it is used against him. In fact, he invites imprisonment and other uses of force against himself. This he does because and when he finds the bodily freedom he seemingly enjoys to be an intolerable burden. He argues to himself that a State allows personal freedom only in so far as the citizen submits to its regulations. Submission to the State law is the price a citizen pays for his person liberty. Submission, therefore, to a State wholly or largely unjust is an immoral barter for liberty. . . .

A body of civil resisters is, therefore, like an army subject to all the discipline of a soldier. . . . And as a civil resistance army is or ought to be free from passion because free from the spirit of retaliation, it requires the fewest number of soldiers. Indeed, one *perfect* civil resister is enough to win the battle of Right against Wrong. [1921]

You might of course say that there can be no nonviolent rebellion and there has been none known to history. Well, it is my ambition to provide an instance, and it is my dream that my country may win its freedom through nonviolence. And, I would like to repeat to the world times without number, that I will not purchase my country's freedom at the cost of nonviolence. My marriage to nonviolence is such an absolute thing that I would rather commit suicide than be deflected from my position. I have not mentioned truth in this connection, simply because truth cannot be expressed except by nonviolence. [1931]

Mao Zedong

War is the highest form of struggle for resolving contradictions, when they have developed to a certain state, between classes, nations, states, or political groups, and it has existed ever since the emergence of private property and of classes.

The seizure of power by armed force, the settlement of the issue by war, is the central task and the highest form of revolution. This Marxist-Leninist principle of revolution holds good universally, for China and for all other countries.

According to the Marxist theory of the state, . . . whoever wants to seize and retain state power must have a strong army. Some people ridicule us as advocates of the "omnipotence of war." Yes, we are advocates of the omnipotence of revolutionary war; that is good, not bad, it is Marxist. Experience in the class struggle in the era of imperialism teaches us that it is only by the power of the gun that the working class and the laboring masses can defeat the armed bourgeoisie and landlords; in this sense we may say that only with guns can the whole world be transformed.

Sources: Mahatma Gandhi, "Young India, November 10, 1921" and "Young India, November 12, 1931," in *All Men Are Brothers: Autobiographical Reflections*, ed. Krishna Kripalani (New York: Continuum, 1997), pp. 81, 135–136. Reprinted by permission of the Navajivan Trust; Mao Tsetung, *Quotations from Chairman Mao Tsetung* (Peking: Foreign Languages Press, 1972), pp. 58, 61–63.

QUESTIONS FOR ANALYSIS

1. According to Gandhi, when should someone resort to nonviolent disobedience in opposing one's rulers?

2. According to Mao, what is the highest form of revolution? What theory does he draw on for this conclusion?

Despite his best efforts, Gandhi failed to heal a widening split between Hindus and Muslims. Indian nationalism, based largely on Hindu symbols and customs, increasingly disturbed the Muslim minority. Tempers mounted, and both sides committed atrocities. By the late 1930s Muslim League leaders were calling for the creation of a Muslim nation in British India, a "Pakistan" or "land of the pure." As in Palestine, the rise of conflicting nationalisms based on religion in India would lead to tragedy (see pages 990–993).

Nationalist Struggles in East and Southeast Asia

☐ How did nationalism shape political developments in East and Southeast Asia?

Because of the efforts of the Meiji reformers, nationalism and modernization were well developed in Japan by 1914. Japan competed politically and economically with the world's leading nations, building its own empire and proclaiming its special mission in Asia. China lagged behind initially, but after 1912 the pace of nationalist development there began to quicken.

In the 1920s the Chinese nationalist movement managed to win a large measure of political independence from the imperialist West and promoted extensive modernization. These achievements were soon undermined, however, by internal conflict and war with an expanding Japan. Nationalism also flourished elsewhere in Asia, scoring a major victory in the Philippine Islands.

The Rise of Nationalist China

The 1911 revolution that overthrew the Qing Dynasty (see page 796) opened an era of unprecedented change for Chinese society. Before the revolution many progressive Chinese realized that fundamental technological and political reforms were necessary to save the Chinese state, but most hoped to preserve the traditional core of Chinese civilization and culture. The fall of the ancient dynastic system shattered such hopes. If the emperor himself was no longer sacred, what was?

The central figure in the revolution was a seasoned and cunning military man, Yuan Shigai (Yüan Shih-k'ai). Called out of retirement to save the dynasty, Yuan (1859–1916) betrayed the Manchu leaders of the Qing Dynasty and convinced the revolutionaries that he could unite the country peacefully and prevent foreign intervention. Once elected president of the republic,

however, Yuan concentrated on building his own power. In 1913 he used military force to dissolve China's parliament and ruled as a dictator. China's first modern revolution had failed.

The extent of the failure became apparent only after Yuan's death in 1916, when the central government in Beijing almost disintegrated. For more than a decade power resided in a multitude of local military leaders, the so-called warlords. Their wars, taxes, and corruption created terrible suffering.

Foreign imperialism intensified the agony of warlordism. Japan's expansion into Shandong and southern Manchuria during World War I (see page 851) angered China's growing middle class and enraged China's young patriots (Map 29.2). On May 4, 1919, five thousand students in Beijing exploded against the decision of the Versailles Peace Conference to leave the Shandong Peninsula in Japanese hands. This famous incident launched the **May Fourth Movement**, which opposed both foreign domination and warlord government.

The May Fourth Movement, which was both strongly pro-Marxist and passionately anti-imperialist, looked to the October 1917 Bolshevik Revolution in Russia as a model for its own nationalist revolution. In 1923 revolutionary leader Sun Yatsen (1866–1925) decided to ally his Nationalist Party, or Guomindang, with the Communist Third International and the newly formed Chinese Communist Party. The result was the first of many so-called national liberation fronts, in keeping with Lenin's blueprint for temporarily uniting all anticonservative, anti-imperialist forces in a common revolutionary struggle.

Sun, however, was no Communist. In his *Three Principles of the People*, elaborating on the official Nationalist Party ideology—nationalism, democracy, and people's livelihood—nationalism remained of prime importance:

> Compared to the other peoples of the world we have the greatest population and our civilization is four thousand years old; we should be advancing in the front rank with the nations of Europe and America. But the Chinese people have only family and clan solidarity, they do not have national spirit. . . . If we do not earnestly espouse nationalism and weld together our four hundred million people into a strong nation, there is a danger of China's being lost and our people being destroyed. If we wish to avert this catastrophe, we must espouse nationalism and bring this national spirit to the salvation of the country.[4]

Democracy, in contrast, had a less exalted meaning. Sun equated it with firm rule by the Nationalists, who would improve people's lives through land reform and welfare measures.

Students Demonstrating in Tiananmen Square, Beijing, Summer 1919 The news that the Versailles Peace Conference left China's Shandong Peninsula in Japanese hands brought an explosion of student protest on May 4, 1919. Student demonstrations in the capital's historic Tiananmen Square continued through June, as the May Fourth Movement against foreign domination took root and grew. (Photo from Kautz Family YMCA Archives. Reproduced with permission.)

Sun planned to use the Nationalist Party's revolutionary army to crush the warlords and reunite China under a strong central government. When Sun unexpectedly died in 1925, Jiang Jieshi (traditionally called Chiang Kai-shek; 1887–1975), the young Japanese-educated director of the party's army training school, took his place. In 1926 and 1927 Jiang led Nationalist armies in a successful attack on warlord governments in central and northern China. In 1928 the Nationalists established a new capital at Nanjing (Nanking). Foreign states recognized the Nanjing government, and superficial observers believed China to be truly reunified.

In fact, national unification was only skin-deep. China remained a vast agricultural country plagued by foreign concessions, regional differences, and a lack of modern communications. Moreover, the uneasy alliance between the Nationalist Party and the Chinese Communist Party had turned into a bitter, deadly rivalry. Justifiably fearful of Communist subversion of the Nationalist government, Jiang decided in April 1927 to liquidate his left-wing "allies" in a bloody purge. Chinese Communists went into hiding and vowed revenge.

China's Intellectual Revolution

Nationalism was the most powerful idea in China between 1911 and 1929, but it was only one aspect of a complex intellectual revolution, generally known as the **New Culture Movement**, that hammered at

- **May Fourth Movement** A Chinese nationalist movement against foreign imperialists; it began as a student protest against the decision of the Versailles Peace Conference to leave the Shandong Peninsula in the hands of Japan.
- **New Culture Movement** An intellectual revolution, sometimes called the Chinese Renaissance, that attacked traditional Chinese, particularly Confucian, culture and promoted Western ideas of science, democracy, and individualism, from around 1916 to 1923.

MAP 29.2 The Chinese Communist Movement and the War with Japan, 1927–1938
After urban uprisings ordered by Stalin failed in 1927, Mao Zedong succeeded in forming a self-governing Communist soviet in mountainous southern China. Relentless Nationalist attacks between 1930 and 1934 finally forced the Long March to Yan'an, where the Communists were well positioned for guerrilla war against the Japanese.

traditional Chinese thought and custom, advocated cultural renaissance, and pushed China into the modern world. The New Culture Movement was founded around 1916 by young Western-oriented intellectuals in Beijing, some of whom were later involved in the May Fourth movement in 1919. These intellectuals fiercely attacked China's ancient Confucian ethics, which subordinated subjects to rulers, sons to fathers, and wives to husbands. As modernists, they provocatively advocated new and anti-Confucian virtues: individualism, democratic equality, and the critical scientific method. They also promoted the use of simple, understandable written language as a means to clear thinking and mass education. China, they said, needed a whole new culture, a radically different worldview.

Many intellectuals thought the radical worldview China needed was Marxist socialism. It too was Western in origin, "scientific" in approach, and materialist in its denial of religious belief and Confucian family ethics. But while liberalism and individualism reflected the bewildering range of Western thought since the Enlightenment, Marxist socialism offered the certainty of a single all-encompassing creed. As one young Communist intellectual exclaimed, "I am now able to impose order on all the ideas which I could not reconcile; I have found the key to all the problems which appeared to me self-contradictory and insoluble."[5]

Though undeniably Western, Marxism provided a means of criticizing Western dominance, thereby salving Chinese pride. Chinese Communists could blame

□ Picturing the Past

The Fate of a Chinese Patriot On May 30, 1925, Shanghai police opened fire on a group of Chinese demonstrators who were protesting unfair labor practices and wages and the foreign imperialist presence in their country. The police killed nine people and wounded many others, touching off nationwide and international protests and attacks on foreign offices and businesses. This political cartoon shows the fate of the Chinese patriots at the hands of warlords and foreign imperialists. (© Library of Congress, LC-USZ62-99451)

ANALYZING THE IMAGE Which figures represent Chinese warlords, foreign imperialists, and Chinese patriots? What does the cartoon suggest about the fate of the Chinese demonstrators?

CONNECTIONS Why might foreign imperialists and Chinese warlords work together to put down the demonstrations?

China's pitiful weakness on rapacious foreign capitalistic imperialism. Thus Marxism, as modified by Lenin and applied by the Bolsheviks in the Soviet Union, appeared as a means of catching up with the hated but envied West. For Chinese believers, it promised salvation soon.

Chinese Communists could and did interpret Marxism-Leninism to appeal to the masses—the peasants. Mao Zedong (Mao Tse-tung) in particular quickly recognized the impoverished Chinese peasantry's enormous revolutionary potential. (See "Viewpoints: Gandhi and Mao on Revolutionary Means," page 893.) A member of a prosperous, hard-working peasant family, Mao (1893–1976) converted to Marxist socialism in 1918. He began his revolutionary career as an urban labor organizer. In 1925 protest strikes by Chinese textile workers against their Japanese employers unexpectedly spread from the big coastal cities to rural China, prompting Mao to reconsider the peas-

ants. Investigating the rapid growth of radical peasant associations in Hunan province, Mao argued passionately in a 1927 report that

> the force of the peasantry is like that of the raging winds and driving rain. It is rapidly increasing in violence. No force can stand in its way. The peasantry will tear apart all nets which bind it and hasten along the road to liberation. They will bury beneath them all forces of imperialism, militarism, corrupt officialdom, village bosses and evil gentry.[6]

Mao's first experiment in peasant revolt—the Autumn Harvest Uprising of September 1927—was not successful, but Mao learned quickly. He advocated equal distribution of land and broke up his forces into small guerrilla groups. After 1928 he and his supporters built up a self-governing Communist soviet, centered at Ruijin (Juichin) in southeastern China, and dug in against Nationalist attacks.

Japanese Suffragists In the 1920s Japanese women pressed for political emancipation in demonstrations like this one, but they did not receive the right to vote until 1946. Like these suffragists, some young Japanese women adopted Western fashions. Most workers in modern Japanese textile factories were women. (Time Life Pictures/Getty Images)

China's intellectual revolution also stimulated profound changes in popular culture and family life. After the 1911 revolution Chinese women enjoyed increasingly greater freedom and equality. Foot binding was outlawed and attacked as cruel and uncivilized. Arranged marriages and polygamy declined. Women gradually gained unprecedented educational and economic opportunities. Thus rising nationalism and the intellectual revolution interacted with monumental changes in Chinese family life. (See "Individuals in Society: Ning Lao, a Chinese Working Woman," page 899.)

From Liberalism to Ultranationalism in Japan

The efforts of the Meiji reformers (see page 797) to build a powerful nationalistic state and resist Western imperialism were spectacularly successful and deeply impressed Japan's fellow Asians. The Japanese, alone among Asia's peoples, had mastered modern industrial technology by 1910 and had fought victorious wars against both China and Russia. The First World War brought more triumphs. In 1915 Japan easily seized Germany's Asian holdings and held on to most of them as League of Nations mandates. The Japanese economy expanded enormously. Profits soared as Japan won new markets that wartime Europe could no longer supply.

In the early 1920s Japan made further progress on all fronts. Most Japanese nationalists believed that Japan had a semidivine mission to enlighten and protect Asia, but some were convinced that they could achieve their goal peacefully. In 1922 Japan signed a naval arms limitation treaty with the Western powers and returned some of its control over the Shandong Peninsula to China. These conciliatory moves reduced tensions in East Asia. At home Japan seemed headed toward genuine democracy. The electorate expanded twelvefold between 1918 and 1925 as all males over twenty-five won the vote. Two-party competition was intense. Japanese living standards were the highest in Asia. Literacy was universal.

Japan's remarkable rise was accompanied by serious problems. Japan had a rapidly growing population, but scarce natural resources. As early as the 1920s Japan was exporting manufactured goods in order to pay for imports of food and essential raw materials. Deeply enmeshed in world trade, Japan was vulnerable to every boom and bust. These economic realities broadened support for Japan's colonial empire. Before World War I Japanese leaders saw colonial expansion primarily in terms of international prestige and national defense. They believed that control of Taiwan, Korea, and Manchuria provided an essential "outer ring of defense" to protect the home islands from Russian attack and Anglo-American imperialism. Now, in the 1920s, Japan's colonies also seemed essential for markets, raw materials, and economic growth.

Japan's rapid industrial development also created an imbalanced "dualistic" economy. The modern sector

Individuals in Society

Ning Lao, a Chinese Working Woman

THE VOICE OF THE POOR AND UNEDUCATED IS often muffled in history. Thus *A Daughter of Han*, a rare autobiography of an illiterate working woman as told to an American friend, offers unforgettable insights into the evolution of ordinary Chinese life and family relations.

Ning Lao was born in 1867 to poor parents in the northern city of Penglai on the Shandong Peninsula. Her foot binding was delayed to age nine, "since I loved so much to run and play." When the bandages were finally drawn tight, "my feet hurt so much that for two years I had to crawl on my knees."* Her arranged marriage at age fourteen was a disaster. She found that her husband was a drug addict ("in those days everyone took opium to some extent") who sold everything to pay for his habit. Yet "there was no freedom then for women," and "it was no light thing for a woman to leave her house" and husband. Thus Ning Lao endured her situation until her husband sold their four-year-old daughter to buy opium. Taking her remaining baby daughter, she fled.

Taking off her foot bandages, Ning Lao became a beggar. Her feet began to spread, quite improperly, but she walked without pain. And the beggar's life was "not the hardest one," she thought, for a beggar woman could go where she pleased. To better care for her child, Ning Lao became a servant and a cook in prosperous households. Some of her mistresses were concubines (secondary wives taken by rich men in middle age), and she concluded that concubinage resulted in nothing but quarrels and heartache. Hot tempered and quick to take offense and leave an employer, the hard-working woman always found a new job quickly. In time she became a peddler of luxury goods to wealthy women confined to their homes.

The two unshakable values that buoyed Ning Lao were a tough, fatalistic acceptance of life—"Only fortune that comes of itself will come. There is no use to seek for it"—and devotion to her family. She eventually returned to her husband, who had mellowed, seldom took opium, and was "good" in those years. "But I did not miss him when he died. I had my newborn son and I was happy. My house was established. . . . Truly all my life I spent thinking of my family." Her lifelong devotion was reciprocated by her son and granddaughter, who cared for her well in her old age.

Ning Lao's remarkable life story encompasses both old and new Chinese attitudes toward family life. Her son moved to the capital city of Beijing, worked in an office, and had only one wife. Her granddaughter, Su Teh, studied in missionary schools and became a college teacher and a determined foe of arranged marriages. She personified the trend toward greater freedom for Chinese women.

Generational differences also highlighted changing political attitudes. When the Japanese invaded China and occupied Beijing in 1937, Ning Lao thought that "perhaps the Mandate of Heaven had passed to the Japanese . . . and we should listen to them as our new masters." Her nationalistic granddaughter disagreed. She urged resistance and the creation of a new China, where the people governed themselves. Leaving to join the guerrillas in 1938, Su Teh gave her savings to her family and promised to continue to help them. One must be good to one's family, she said, but one must also work for the country.

QUESTIONS FOR ANALYSIS

1. Compare the lives of Ning Lao and her granddaughter. In what ways were they different and similar?

2. In a broader historical perspective, what do you find most significant about Ning Lao's account of her life? Why?

The tough and resilient Ning Lao (right) with Ida Pruitt.
(Reproduced with permission of Eileen Hsu-Belzer)

*Ida Pruitt, *A Daughter of Han: The Autobiography of a Chinese Working Woman* (New Haven, Conn.: Yale University Press, 1945), p. 22. Other quotations are from pages 83, 62, 71, 182, 166, 235, and 246.

> "Our seven hundred million brothers in China and India have no other path to independence than that offered by our guidance and protection."
>
> **JAPANESE ULTRANATIONALIST KITA IKKI**

consisted of a handful of giant conglomerate firms, the **zaibatsu**, or "financial combines." Zaibatsu firms like Mitsubishi employed thousands of workers and owned banks, mines, steel mills, cotton factories, shipyards, and trading companies, all of them closely interrelated. Zaibatsu firms wielded enormous economic power and dominated the other sector of the economy, an unorganized multitude of peasant farmers and craftsmen. The result was financial oligarchy, corruption of government officials, and a weak middle class.

Behind the façade of party politics, the old and new elites — the emperor, high government officials, big businessmen, and military leaders — were jockeying savagely for the real power. Cohesive leadership, which had played such an important role in Japan's modernization by the Meiji reformers, had ceased to exist. By far the most serious challenge to peaceful progress was fanatical nationalism. As in Europe, ultranationalism first emerged in Japan in the late nineteenth century but did not flower fully until the First World War and the 1930s.

Though often vague, Japan's ultranationalists shared several fundamental beliefs. They were violently anti-Western. They rejected democracy, big business, and Marxist socialism, which they blamed for destroying the older, superior Japanese practices they wanted to restore. Reviving old myths, they stressed the emperor's godlike qualities and the samurai warrior's code of honor and obedience. Despising party politics, they assassinated moderate leaders and plotted armed uprisings to achieve their goals. Above all else, the ultranationalists preached foreign expansion. Like Western imperialists shouldering "the white man's burden," Japanese ultranationalists thought their mission was a noble one. "Asia for the Asians" was their anti-Western rallying cry. As the famous ultranationalist Kita Ikki wrote in 1923, "Our seven hundred million brothers in China and India have no other path to independence than that offered by our guidance and protection."[7]

The ultranationalists were noisy and violent in the 1920s, but it took the Great Depression of the 1930s to tip the scales decisively in their favor. The worldwide depression, which had dire consequences for many countries (see Chapter 30), hit Japan like a tidal wave in 1930. Exports and wages collapsed; unemployment and raw suffering soared. Starving peasants ate the bark off trees and sold their daughters to brothels. The ultranationalists blamed the system, and people listened.

Japan Against China

Among those who listened with particular care were young Japanese army officers in Manchuria, the underpopulated, resource-rich province of northeastern China controlled by the Japanese army since its victory over Russia in 1905. Many junior Japanese officers in Manchuria came from the peasantry and were distressed by the stories of rural suffering they heard from home. They also knew the Japanese army's budget and prestige had declined in the prosperous 1920s.

The rise of Chinese nationalism worried the young officers most. This new political force, embodied in the Guomindang unification of China, challenged Japanese control over Manchuria. In response, junior Japanese officers in Manchuria, in cooperation with top generals in Tokyo, secretly manufactured an excuse for aggression in late 1931. They blew up some Japanese-owned railroad tracks near the city of Shenyang (Mukden) and then, with reinforcements rushed in from Korea, quickly occupied all of Manchuria in "self-defense."

In 1932 Japan proclaimed Manchuria an independent state and installed Puyi (1906–1967), the last emperor of the old Qing Dynasty, as puppet emperor. When the League of Nations condemned its aggression in Manchuria, Japan resigned in protest. Japanese aggression in Manchuria proved that the army, though reporting directly to the Japanese emperor, was an independent force subject to no outside control.

The Japanese puppet state named Manchukuo in northeast China became the model for the subsequent conquest and occupation of China and then Southeast Asia. Throughout the 1930s the Japanese worked to integrate Manchuria, along with Korea and Taiwan, into a large, self-sufficient economic bloc that provided resources, markets, and investment opportunities safe from Western power in East Asia. While exporting raw materials, state-sponsored Japanese companies in Manchuria also built steel mills and heavy industry to supply vital military goods. At home, newspapers and newsreels glorified Japan's efforts and mobilized public support for colonial empire.

For China the Japanese conquest of Manchuria was disastrous. Japanese aggression in Manchuria drew attention away from modernizing efforts. The Nationalist government promoted a massive boycott of Japanese goods but lost interest in social reform. Above all, the Nationalist government after 1931 completely neglected land reform and the Chinese peasants' grinding poverty.

- **zaibatsu** Giant conglomerate firms in Japan.
- **Long March** The 6,000-mile retreat of the Chinese Communist army to a remote region on the northwestern border of China, during which tens of thousands lost their lives.

As in many poor agricultural societies throughout history, Chinese peasants paid roughly half of their crops to their landlords as rent. Land ownership was very unequal. One study estimated that a mere 4 percent of families, usually absentee landlords living in cities, owned fully half the land. Poor peasants and farm laborers — 70 percent of the rural population — owned only one-sixth of the land. As a result, peasants were heavily in debt and chronically underfed. A contemporaneous Chinese economist spelled out the revolutionary implications: "It seems clear that the land problem in China today is as acute as that of eighteenth-century France or nineteenth-century Russia." Mao Zedong agreed.

Having abandoned land reform, partly because they themselves were often landowners, the Nationalists under Jiang Jieshi devoted their energies between 1930 and 1934 to great campaigns of encirclement and extermination of the Communists' rural power base in southeastern China. In 1934 they closed in for the kill, but, in one of the most incredible sagas of modern times, the main Communist army broke out, beat off attacks, and retreated 6,000 miles in twelve months to a remote region on the northwestern border (see Map 29.2). Of the estimated 100,000 men and women who began the **Long March**, only 8,000 to 10,000 reached the final destination. There Mao built up his forces once again, established a new territorial base, and won local peasant support by undertaking land reform.

In Japan politics became increasingly chaotic. In 1937 the Japanese military and the ultranationalists were in command. Unable to force China to cede more territory in northern China, they used a minor incident near Beijing as a pretext for a general attack. This marked the beginning of what became World War II in Asia, although Japan issued no declaration of war. The Nationalist government, which had just formed a united front with the Communists, fought hard, but Japanese troops quickly took Beijing and northern China. Taking the great port of Shanghai after ferocious combat, the Japanese launched an immediate attack up the Yangzi River (see Map 29.2).

Foretelling the horrors of World War II, the Japanese air force bombed Chinese cities and civilian populations with unrelenting fury. Nanjing, the capital, fell in December 1937. Entering the city, Japanese soldiers went berserk and committed dreadful atrocities over seven weeks. They brutally murdered an estimated

Japanese Atrocities in China In December 1937, after the fall of the Chinese capital Nanjing, Japanese soldiers went on a horrifying rampage. These Japanese recruits are using Chinese prisoners of war as live targets in a murderous bayonet drill. Other Chinese prisoners were buried alive by their Japanese captors. (Hulton Archive/Getty Images)

200,000 to 300,000 Chinese civilians and unarmed soldiers, and raped 20,000 to 80,000 Chinese women. The "Rape of Nanjing" combined with other Japanese atrocities to outrage world opinion. The Western Powers denounced Japanese aggression but, with tensions rising in Europe, took no action.

By late 1938 Japanese armies occupied sizable portions of coastal China (see Map 29.2). But the Nationalists and the Communists had retreated to the interior, and both refused to accept defeat. In 1939, as Europe edged toward another great war, China and Japan were bogged down in a savage stalemate. This undeclared war — called by historians the Second Sino-Japanese War (1937–1945) — provided a spectacular example of conflicting nationalisms.

Striving for Independence in Southeast Asia

The tide of nationalism was also rising in Southeast Asia. Like their counterparts in India, China, and Japan, nationalists in French Indochina, the Dutch East Indies, and the Philippines urgently wanted genuine political independence and freedom from foreign rule. In both French Indochina and the Dutch East Indies, they ran up against an imperialist stone wall. The obstacle to Filipino independence came from America and Japan.

The French in Indochina, as in all their colonies, refused to export the liberal policies contained in the stirring words of their own Declaration of the Rights of Man and the Citizen: liberty, equality, and fraternity (see page 653). This uncompromising attitude stimulated the growth of an equally stubborn Communist opposition under Ho Chi Minh (1890–1969), which despite ruthless repression emerged as the dominant anti-French force in Indochina.

In the East Indies — modern Indonesia — the Dutch made some concessions after the First World War, establishing a people's council with very limited lawmaking power. But in the 1930s the Dutch cracked down hard, jailing all the important nationalist leaders. Like the French, the Dutch were determined to hold on.

In the Philippines, however, a well-established nationalist movement achieved greater success. As in colonial Latin America, the Spanish in the Philippines had been indefatigable missionaries. By the late nineteenth century the Filipino population was 80 percent Catholic. Filipinos shared a common cultural heritage and a common racial origin. Education, especially for girls, was advanced for Southeast Asia, and already in 1843 a higher percentage of people could read in the Philippines than in Spain itself. Economic development helped to create a westernized elite, which turned first to reform and then to revolution in the 1890s. As in Egypt and Turkey, long-standing intimate contact with Western civilization created a strong nationalist movement at an early date.

Filipino nationalists were bitterly disillusioned when the United States, having taken the Philippines

Uncle Sam as Schoolmaster In this cartoon that first appeared on the cover of *Harper's Weekly* in August 1898, unruly students identified as a "Cuban Ex-patriot" and a "Guerilla" are being disciplined with a switch by a stern Uncle Sam as he tries to teach them self-government. The gentleman to the left reading a book is Jose Miguel Gomez, one of Cuba's revolutionary heroes, while the Filipino insurrectionist Emilio Aguinaldo is made to wear a dunce hat and stand in the corner. The two well-behaved girls to the right represent Hawai'i and Puerto Rico. (The Granger Collection, New York)

from Spain in the Spanish-American War of 1898, ruthlessly beat down a patriotic revolt and denied the universal Filipino desire for independence. The Americans claimed the Philippines were not ready for self-rule and might be seized by Germany or Britain if they could not establish a stable, secure government. As the imperialist power in the Philippines, the United States encouraged education and promoted capitalistic economic development. And as in British India, an elected legislature was given some real powers. In 1919 President Wilson even promised eventual independence, though subsequent Republican administrations saw it as a distant goal.

As in India and French Indochina, demands for independence grew. One important contributing factor was American racial attitudes. Americans treated Filipinos as inferiors and introduced segregationist practices borrowed from the American South. American racism made passionate nationalists of many Filipinos. However, it was the Great Depression that had the most radical impact on the Philippines.

The Spanish-American War in the Philippines, 1898

As the United States collapsed economically in the 1930s, the Philippines suddenly appeared to be a liability rather than an asset. American farm groups lobbied for protection from cheap Filipino sugar. To protect American jobs, labor unions demanded an end to Filipino immigration. Responding to public pressure, in 1934 Congress made the Philippines a self-governing commonwealth and scheduled independence for 1944. Sugar imports were reduced, and immigration was limited to only fifty Filipinos per year.

Like Britain and France in the Middle East, the United States was determined to hold on to its big military bases in the Philippines even as it permitted increased local self-government and promised eventual political independence. Some Filipino nationalists denounced the continued presence of U.S. fleets and armies. Others were less certain that the American presence was the immediate problem. Japan was fighting in China and expanding economically into the Philippines and throughout Southeast Asia. By 1939 a new threat to Filipino independence would come from Japan itself.

CONNECTIONS

Just as nationalism drove politics and state building in Europe in the nineteenth century, so it took root across Asia in the late nineteenth and early twentieth centuries. While nationalism in Europe developed out of a desire to turn cultural unity into political reality and create imagined communities out of millions of strangers, in Asia nationalist sentiments drew their greatest energy from opposition to European imperialism and domination. Asian modernizers, aware of momentous advances in science and technology and of politics and social practices in the West, also pressed the nationalist cause by demanding an end to outdated conservative traditions that they argued only held back the development of modern, independent nations capable of throwing off Western domination and existing as equals with the West.

The nationalist cause in Asia took many forms and produced some of the most remarkable leaders of the twentieth century. In Chapter 32 we will discuss how nationalist leaders across Asia shaped the freedom struggle and the resulting independence according to their own ideological and personal visions. China's Mao Zedong is the giant among the nationalist leaders who emerged in Asia, but he replaced imperialist rule with one-party Communist rule. Gandhi's dream of a unified India collapsed with the partition of British India into Hindu India and Muslim Pakistan and Bangladesh. India and Pakistan remain bitter, and nuclear-armed, enemies today, as we will see in Chapter 34. Egypt assumed a prominent position in the Arab world after World War II under the leadership of Gamal Nasser and, after a series of wars with Israel, began to play a significant role in efforts to find a peaceful resolution to the Israeli-Palestinian conflict. That conflict, however, continues unabated as nationalist and religious sentiments inflame feelings on both sides. Ho Chi Minh eventually forced the French colonizers out of Vietnam, only to face another Western power, the United States, in a long and deadly war. As described in Chapter 32, a unified Vietnam finally gained its independence in 1975, but like China, under one-party Communist control.

Japan remained an exception to much of what happened in the rest of Asia. After a long period of isolation, the Japanese implemented an unprecedented program of modernization and westernization in the late 1800s. Japan continued to model itself after the West when it took control of former German colonies as mandated territories after the Great War and occupied territory in China, Korea, Vietnam, Taiwan, and elsewhere. In the next chapter we will see how ultranationalism drove national policy in the 1930s, ultimately leading to Japan's defeat in World War II.

◼ CHAPTER REVIEW

◻ **Why did modern nationalism develop in Asia between the First and Second World Wars, and what was its appeal? (p. 878)**

The Asian nationalist revolt against the West began before the First World War, but only after 1914 did Asian nationalist movements broaden their bases sufficiently to challenge Western domination effectively. Nationalists in Asia were roused to action by broken promises of independence, exposure to democratic and republican ideas while fighting for their colonial overlords, and the mandate system, which showed that Western imperialists did not plan to give up their colonial territories. Nationalism's appeal lay in its usefulness as a way to organize anti-imperialist resistance, its challenge to old-fashioned political and social beliefs, and its offer of a prosperous free future. Mass nationalist movements sought human dignity as well as political freedom. Generally speaking, Asian nationalists favored modernization and adopted Western techniques and ideas even as they rejected Western rule. Asian nationalists had to fight long and hard, though their struggle gained momentum from growing popular support and the encouragement of the Soviet Union.

◻ **How did the collapse of the Ottoman Empire in World War I shape nationalist movements in the Middle East? (p. 881)**

The collapse of the Ottoman Empire in World War I left a power vacuum that both Western imperialists and Turkish, Arab, Persian, Jewish, and other nationalists sought to fill. The Turks, who had ruled the old Ottoman Empire, created the modern secular state of Turkey under the leadership of Mustafa Kemal. Strong leadership also played a role in the successful nationalist movements in Persia and Afghanistan. The British and French maintained various degrees of control over the League of Nations–mandated Arab states of Iraq, Syria, Lebanon, and Egypt, but lost much of their influence over the next two decades as Arab national-

ists pushed for complete independence. While political independence was achieved, the concessions that Arab rulers had to make in return for independence meant continuing Western influence and the ever-present threat of military action to secure Western economic interests in the regions. The British made promises to both the Palestinians and the Jewish Zionists regarding independent homelands in Palestine, creating an impasse that deteriorated in the interwar year as European Jews migrated in ever greater numbers to Palestine.

◻ **What role did Gandhi and his campaign of militant nonviolence play in leading India to independence from the British? (p. 889)**

Gandhi knew that the Indian people were not capable of fighting a military campaign against the mighty British Empire without suffering hundreds of thousands, perhaps millions, of deaths. But he realized that a few thousand British could do nothing if millions of Indians refused to cooperate or obey British laws. By employing active, nonviolent resistance, which he called satyagraha, Gandhi and his millions of Hindu and Muslim followers were able to bring British colonial rule in India to a standstill, leading to Indian independence in 1947. Regrettably, however, Gandhi was not able to control the extreme religious nationalism of the Muslims and Hindus following independence, and by the end of the 1930s Muslim separatists threatened to split off from predominantly Hindu India.

◻ How did nationalism shape political developments in East and Southeast Asia? (p. 894)

Asia's nationalist movements arose out of separate historical experiences and distinct cultures. The 1911 revolution in China successfully ended the ancient dynastic system, only to see dictators and warlords seize control. The May Fourth Movement of 1919 renewed nationalist hopes, and by 1928 nationalist armies had defeated the warlords. But the direction of unified China was bitterly contested by the Nationalist Party and the Communists led by Mao Zedong. Japan, unlike China, had industrialized early and by the 1920s seemed headed toward genuine democracy. But a growing population and lack of natural resources gave rise to ultranationalists who rejected big business and Marxist socialism in favor of aggressive foreign expansion based on "Asia for Asians." Nationalist movements in Indochina and the East Indies met with little success. The Philippines did achieve independence from the United States, but as was the case for the states of the Middle East, it came at the price of long-term concessions to the U.S. military. The diversity of these nationalist movements helps explain why Asian peoples became defensive in their relations with one another while rising against Western rule. Like earlier nationalists in Europe, Asian nationalists developed a strong sense of "we" and "they"; "they" included other Asians as well as Europeans. Nationalism meant freedom, modernization, and cultural renaissance, but it nonetheless proved to be a mixed blessing.

SUGGESTED READING

Chang, Jung, and Jon Halliday. *Mao: The Unknown Story*. 2006. Very controversial biography of the Chinese leader.

Chow, Tse-tung. *The May Fourth Movement: Intellectual Revolution in Modern China*. 1960. The classic study of the Chinese intellectual revolution that began in 1919.

Erikson, Eric. *Gandhi's Truth: On the Origins of Militant Nonviolence*. 1969. A classic study of Gandhi's life and the origins of satyagraha.

Fromkin, David. *A Peace to End All Peace: The Fall of the Ottoman Empire and the Creation of the Modern Middle East*. 2001. A thorough but readable introduction to the Middle East in the early twentieth century.

Hourani, Albert, and Malise Ruthven. *History of the Arab Peoples*. 2003. One of the best single-volume histories of the Arab peoples.

Hsü, Immanuel C. Y. *The Rise of Modern China*, 6th ed. 1999. Sixth edition of a classic history of modern China.

Irokawa, Daikichi. *The Age of Hirohito: In Search of Modern Japan*. 1995. An excellent brief account by a leading Japanese historian.

Lacqueur, Walter. *A History of Zionism. From the French Revolution to the Establishment of the State of Israel*. 1972. Good general history of Zionism and the founding of Israel.

Mango, Andrew. *Atatürk*. 2000. Rich, well-researched biography of this complex Turkish leader.

Myers, Ramon H., and M. Peattie, eds. *The Japanese Colonial Expansion, 1895–1945*. 1984. Broad collection of essays covering all of Japan's colonial empire, both formal and informal.

Osborne, Milton. *Southeast Asia: An Introductory History*, 9th ed. 2005. Ninth edition of the classic introduction to the region's history.

Owen, Norman, David Chandler, and William R. Roff. *The Emergence of Southeast Asia: A New History*. 2004. Newer history looking at both individual countries and social and economic themes, including gender and ecology.

Reischauer, Edwin O. *Japan: The Story of Nation*, 4th ed. 1991. The classic history in its fourth edition by America's leading historian on Japan.

Spence, Jonathan. *The Search for Modern China*. 1990. Important study of modern China by a leading Chinese scholar.

Wolpert, Stanley. *India*. 2005. An excellent introduction to India's history.

Young, Louise. *Japan's Total Empire: Manchuria and the Culture of Wartime Imperialism*. 1998. A fascinating pioneering work on Japanese imperialism.

NOTES

1. H. Armstrong, *Turkey in Travail: The Birth of a New Nation* (London: John Lane, 1925), p. 75.

2. Quoted in Lord Kinross, *Atatürk: A Biography of Mustafa Kemal, Father of Modern Turkey* (New York: Morrow, 1965), p. 181.

3. Quoted in E. Erikson, *Gandhi's Truth: On the Origins of Militant Nonviolence* (New York: W. W. Norton, 1969), p. 225.

4. Quoted in W. T. deBary, W. Chan, and B. Watson, *Sources of Chinese Tradition* (New York: Columbia University Press, 1964), pp. 768–769.

5. Quoted in J. F. Fairbank, E. O. Reischauer, and A. M. Craig, *East Asia: Tradition and Transformation* (Boston: Houghton Mifflin, 1973), p. 774.

6. Quoted in B. I. Schwartz, *Chinese Communism and the Rise of Mao* (Cambridge, Mass.: Harvard University Press, 1951), p. 74.

7. Quoted in W. T. deBary, R. Tsunoda, and D. Keene, *Sources of Japanese Tradition*, vol. 2 (New York: Columbia University Press, 1958), p. 269.

For practice quizzes and other study tools, visit the **Online Study Guide** at bedfordstmartins.com/mckayworld.

For primary sources from this period, see *Sources of World Societies*, **Second Edition**.

For Web sites, images, and documents related to topics in this chapter, visit **Make History** at bedfordstmartins.com/mckayworld.

• **Jewish Boy in Nazi-Controlled France** Israel Lichtenstein, wearing a Jewish star, was born in Paris in 1932. His father was one of an estimated one million Jews who died in the Auschwitz concentration camp. Israel and his mother were also sent to a concentration camp, but they escaped and survived the Holocaust by going into hiding until the end of the war. Israel later immigrated to the nation of Israel. (United States Holocaust Memorial Museum, courtesy of Israel Lichtenstein)

The years of anxiety and political maneuvering in Europe that followed World War I were made much worse when a massive economic depression spread around the world following the American stock market crash of October 1929. A global economy that had become ever more interconnected now collapsed. As people everywhere looked to their leaders for relief, popularly elected governments and basic civil liberties declined drastically. In Europe on the eve of the Second World War, liberal democratic governments were surviving only in Great Britain, France, the Low Countries, the Scandinavian nations, and neutral Switzerland. Worldwide, in countries such as Brazil, Japan, the Soviet Union, and others, as well as in Europe, dictatorships seemed the wave of the future.

The mid-twentieth-century era of dictatorship is a highly disturbing chapter in the history of civilization. The key development was not only the resurgence of authoritarian rule but also the rise of a particularly ruthless brand of totalitarianism that reached its full realization in the Soviet Union, Nazi Germany, and Japan in the 1930s. Stalin, Hitler, and Japan's military leaders intervened radically in society and ruled with unprecedented severity. Hitler's mobilization was ultimately directed toward racial aggression and territorial expansion, and his sudden attack on Poland in 1939 started World War II. Hitler's successes then encouraged the Japanese to expand their stalemated Chinese campaign into a vast Pacific war by attacking Pearl Harbor, Hawai'i, and advancing into South Asia. Millions died as Stalin imposed communism on the Soviet Union, as a result of the Holocaust, and during Japan's quest to create an "Asia for Asians." Millions more died on the battlefields and in the bombed-out cities of World War II. •

The Great Depression and World War II

1929–1945

The Great Depression, 1929–1939

□ What caused the Great Depression, and what were its consequences?

Like the Great War, the Great Depression must be spelled with capital letters. Beginning in 1929 an exceptionally long and severe economic depression struck the entire world with ever-greater intensity, and recovery was uneven and slow. Only with the Second World War did the depression disappear in much of the world.

The social and political consequences of prolonged economic collapse were enormous and were felt worldwide. Economic depression was a major factor in Japan's aggressive empire building and militarism in the 1930s. Elsewhere in Asia, agricultural depression devastated millions of peasants and small farmers. Agricultural producers in Latin America and Africa also suffered greatly from the collapse in prices, while urban workers faced pay cuts and high unemployment. In West Africa anticolonial nationalism attracted widespread support for the first time in the 1930s, setting the stage for strong independence movements after World War II.

In Europe and the United States the depression shattered the fragile political stability of the mid-1920s. Mass unemployment made insecurity a reality for millions of ordinary people. In desperation, people looked

Louisville Flood Victims, 1937 During the Great Depression, Louisville, Kentucky, was hit by the worst flood in its history. The famous documentary photographer Margaret Bourke-White captured this image of African American flood victims lining up for food. Not only does the billboard message mock the Depression-era conditions, but the smiling white family appears to be driving its car through the line of people, drawing attention to America's race and class differences. (Margaret Bourke-White/Time & Life Pictures/Getty Images)

for leaders who would "do something." They willingly supported radical attempts to deal with the crisis by both democratic leaders and dictators.

The Economic Crisis

Though economic activity was already declining moderately in many countries by early 1929, the U.S. stock market crash in October of that year really started the Great Depression. The American stock market boom, which had seen stock prices double between early 1928 and September 1929, was built on borrowed money. Wealthy investors, speculators, and even people of modest means had bought stocks by paying only a small fraction of the total purchase price and borrowing the remainder from their stockbrokers. Such buying "on margin" was extremely dangerous. When prices started falling, the hard-pressed margin buyers started selling to pay their debts. The result was a financial panic. Countless investors and speculators were wiped out in a matter of days or weeks, and the New York stock market's crash started a domino effect that hit most of the world's major stock exchanges

The financial panic in the United States triggered a worldwide financial crisis, and that crisis resulted in a drastic decline in production in country after country. Throughout the 1920s American bankers and investors had lent large sums to many countries, and as panic broke, New York bankers began recalling their short-term loans. Frightened citizens in Europe, Australia, Canada, several countries in Latin America, and elsewhere began to withdraw their savings from banks, leading to general financial chaos. The recall of American loans also accelerated the collapse in world prices, as business people dumped goods in a frantic attempt to get cash to pay what they owed.

The financial chaos led to a general crisis of production. Between 1929 and 1933 world output of goods fell by an estimated 38 percent. As this happened, countries turned inward and tried to go it alone. Country after country followed the example of the United States, which raised protective tariffs to their highest levels ever in 1930 and tried to seal off shrinking national markets for American producers only.

Although opinions differ, two factors probably best explain the relentless slide to the bottom from 1929 to early 1933. First, the international economy lacked leadership able to maintain stability when the crisis came. Neither the seriously weakened British nor the United States—the world's economic leaders—stabilized the international economic system in 1929. Instead, Britain and the United States cut back international lending and erected high tariffs.

The second factor was that in almost every country, governments cut their budgets and reduced spending when they should have run large deficits to try to stimulate their economies. After World War II such a "counter-cyclical policy," advocated by the British

> "We tell you that great numbers are being rendered distraught through the stress and worry of trying to exist without work. . . . Hungry men are angry men."
>
> **WORKERS IN MANCHESTER, ENGLAND**

economist John Maynard Keynes (1883–1946), became a well-established weapon against depression. But in the 1930s orthodox economists generally regarded Keynes's prescription with horror.

Mass Unemployment

The need for large-scale government spending was tied to mass unemployment. As the financial crisis led to production cuts, workers lost their jobs and had little money to buy goods. This led to still more production cuts, and unemployment soared. In Britain unemployment had averaged 12 percent in the 1920s; between 1930 and 1935 it averaged more than 18 percent. In Germany 25 percent and in Australia 32 percent of the people were out of work in 1932. The worst unemployment was in the United States. In the 1920s unemployment there had averaged only 5 percent; in 1932 it soared to about 33 percent of the entire labor force: 14 million people were out of work.

Mass unemployment created a great social problem. Poverty increased dramatically, although in most industrialized countries unemployed workers generally received some meager unemployment benefits or public aid that prevented starvation. Millions of unemployed people lost their spirit, and homes and ways of life were disrupted in millions of personal tragedies. In 1932 workers in Manchester, England, appealed to their city officials — a typical appeal echoed throughout the Western world:

> We tell you that thousands of people . . . are in desperate straits. We tell you that men, women, and children are going hungry. . . . We tell you that great numbers are being rendered distraught through the stress and worry of trying to exist without work. . . .
>
> If you do not do this — if you do not provide useful work for the unemployed — what, we ask, is your alternative? Do not imagine that this colossal tragedy of unemployment is going on endlessly without some fateful catastrophe. Hungry men are angry men.[1]

Only strong government action could deal with the social powder keg that was preparing to explode.

The New Deal in the United States

The Great Depression and the response to it marked a major turning point in American history. President Herbert Hoover (r. 1929–1933) and his administration initially reacted to the stock market crash and economic decline with dogged optimism but limited action. When the full force of the financial crisis struck Europe in the summer of 1931 and boomeranged back to the United States, banks failed and unemployment soared. In 1932 industrial production fell to about 50 percent of its 1929 level.

In these tragic circumstances Franklin Delano Roosevelt (r. 1933–1945) won a landslide presidential victory in 1932 with promises of a "**New Deal** for the forgotten man." Roosevelt's basic goal was to preserve capitalism by reforming it. Rejecting socialism and government ownership of industry, Roosevelt advocated forceful government intervention in the economy. His commitment to relief programs marked a profound shift from the traditional stress on family support and community responsibility.

Innovative programs promoted agricultural recovery, a top priority. As in Asia, Africa, and Latin America, American farmers were hard hit by the Great Depression. Roosevelt's decision to leave the gold standard and devalue the dollar was designed to raise American prices and save farmers. The Agricultural Adjustment Act (1933) aimed at raising prices and farm income by limiting production. For a while, these measures worked.

Roosevelt then attacked the key problem of mass unemployment. New agencies were created to undertake a vast range of public works projects so that the federal government could employ directly as many people as financially possible. The most famous of these was the Works Progress Administration (WPA), set up in 1935. One-fifth of the entire U.S. labor force worked for the WPA at some point in the 1930s, constructing public buildings, bridges, and highways.

Following the path blazed by Germany's Bismarck in the 1880s (see page 742), the U.S. government in 1935 established a national social security system with old-age pensions and unemployment benefits. The National Labor Relations Act of 1935 declared collective bargaining to be U.S. policy, and union membership more than doubled. In general, between 1935 and 1938 government rulings and social reforms chipped away at the privileges of the wealthy and tried to help ordinary people.

Despite undeniable accomplishments in social reform, the New Deal was only partly successful as a response to the Great Depression. At the height of the recovery in May 1937, 7 million workers were still unemployed (down from a high of 15 million in 1933). The

---

• **New Deal** Franklin Delano Roosevelt's plan to reform capitalism through forceful government intervention in the economy.

economic situation then worsened in the recession of 1937 and 1938, and unemployment was still a staggering 10 million when war broke out in Europe in 1939. The New Deal brought fundamental reform, but it never did pull the United States out of the depression; it took the Second World War to do that.

The European Response to the Depression

The collapse of the American stock market in October 1929 set off a chain of economic downturns that hit Europe, particularly Germany and Great Britain, the hardest. Postwar Europe had come out of the Great War deeply in debt and in desperate need of investment capital to rebuild. The United States became the primary creditor and financier. Germany borrowed, for example, to pay Britain war reparations, and then Britain took that money and paid America back for its war debts and investment loans. When the American economy crashed, the whole system crashed with it.

Of all the Western democracies, the Scandinavian countries under socialist leadership responded most successfully to the challenge of the Great Depression. When the economic crisis struck in 1929, socialist governments in Sweden pioneered the use of large-scale deficits to finance public works projects and thereby maintain production and employment. Scandinavian governments also increased social welfare benefits, from old-age pensions and unemployment insurance to subsidized housing and maternity allowances. All this spending required a large bureaucracy

and high taxes. Yet both private and cooperative enterprise thrived, as did democracy. Some observers saw Scandinavia's welfare socialism as an appealing middle way between sick capitalism and cruel communism or fascism.

In Britain, Ramsay MacDonald's Labour government (1929–1931) and then, after 1931, the Conservative-dominated coalition government followed orthodox economic theory. The budget was balanced, but unemployed workers received barely enough welfare to live. Nevertheless, the economy recovered considerably after 1932. This recovery reflected the gradual reorientation of the British economy. After abandoning the gold standard in 1931 and establishing protective tariffs in 1932, Britain concentrated increasingly on the national, rather than the international, market. Old export industries, such as textiles and coal, continued to decline, but new industries, such as automobiles and electrical appliances, grew. These developments encouraged British isolationism, but often had devastating economic consequences for Britain's far-flung colonies and dominions.

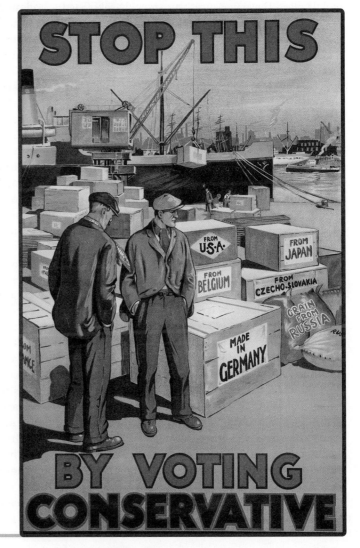

◻ Picturing the Past

British Conservative Party Poster, 1931 This campaign poster from the 1931 British general election portrays crates and bags of goods being unloaded on English docks. (Hulton Archive/Getty Images)

ANALYZING THE IMAGE Where are the goods on the dock from? What do the Conservatives want stopped?

CONNECTIONS Was this attitude toward foreign goods unique to England? What other countries held similar views? What effect did such attitudes have on the worldwide depression?

Because France was relatively less industrialized and more isolated from the world economy, the Great Depression came late. But once the depression hit France, it stayed. Decline was steady until 1935, and a short-lived recovery never brought production or employment back up to predepression levels. Economic stagnation both reflected and heightened an ongoing political crisis. Fascist-type organizations agitated against parliamentary democracy and looked to Mussolini's Italy and Hitler's Germany for inspiration. At the same time, the Communist Party and many workers looked to Stalin's Russia for guidance. Moderate republicanism's vital center was sapped from both sides.

Frightened by the fascists' growing strength at home and abroad, French Communist, Socialist, and Radical parties formed an alliance — the **Popular Front** — for the May 1936 national elections. Following its clear victory, the Popular Front government made the only real attempt to deal with France's social and economic problems of the 1930s. Inspired by Roosevelt's New Deal, the Popular Front launched a far-reaching program of social reform. Popular with workers and the lower middle class, these measures were quickly sabotaged by rapid inflation and cries of revolution from fascists and frightened conservatives. Wealthy people sneaked their money out of the country, labor unrest grew, and France entered a severe financial crisis. In June 1937, with the country hopelessly divided, the Popular Front collapsed.

Worldwide Effects

The Great Depression's magnitude was unprecedented, and its effect rippled well beyond Europe and the United States. As many of the countries and colonies of Africa, Asia, and Latin America were nearly totally dependent on one or two commodities — such as coffee beans, rubber, tin, or cocoa — for income, the implementation of protectionist trade policies by the leading industrial nations had devastating effects. The different colonies and dominions of the British Empire — particularly Australia, India, and Canada — were among the hardest hit by the Great Depression because of their close ties to the economies of Great Britain and the United States.

While Asians were affected by the Great Depression, the consequences varied greatly by country or colony and were not as severe generally as they were elsewhere in the world. That being said, where the depression did hit, it was often severe. The price of rice — Asia's staff of life and main cash crop — fell by two-thirds between 1929 and 1932. Also crippling to the

region's economies was Asia's heavy dependence on raw material exports, such as rubber and tin from Malaya for automobile production. With debts to local moneylenders fixed in value and taxes to colonial governments hardly ever reduced, many Asian peasants in the 1930s struggled under crushing debt and suffered severely.

In Japan the terrible suffering caused by the Great Depression caused ultranationalists and militarists to call for less dependence on global markets and the expansion of a self-sufficient empire. Such expansion began in 1931 when Japan invaded Chinese Manchuria, which became a major source of raw materials feeding Japanese industrial growth (see Chapter 29). Japan recovered more quickly from the Great Depression than any other major industrial power because of prompt action by the civilian democratic government, but the government and large corporations continued to be blamed for the economic downturn. This lack of confidence, combined with the collapsing international economic order, Europe's and America's increasingly isolationist and protectionist policies, and a growing admiration for Nazi Germany and its authoritarian, militaristic model of government, led by the mid-1930s to the military's toppling the civilian authorities and dictating Japan's future.

The Great Depression hit the vulnerable commodities economies of Latin America especially hard. Long dependent on foreign markets, prices and exports of Latin American commodities collapsed as Europe and the United States drastically reduced their purchases and raised tariffs to protect domestic products. Chile's exports fell by nearly 80 percent, for example, while Brazil burned millions of bags of coffee beans for which there was no longer a market. With their foreign sales plummeting, Latin American countries could not buy the industrial goods they needed from abroad. The global depression provoked a profound shift toward economic nationalism after 1930, as popularly based governments worked to reduce foreign influence and gain control of their own economies and natural resources (see page 1008). These efforts were fairly successful. By the late 1940s factories in Argentina, Brazil, and Chile could generally satisfy domestic consumer demand for the products of light industry. But as in Hitler's Germany, the deteriorating economic conditions in Brazil, Guatemala, Nicaragua, Honduras, El Salvador, Argentina, and elsewhere also gave rise to dictatorships, some of them modeled along European Fascist lines (see pages 1008–1017).

The Great Depression was the decisive turning point in the development of African nationalism. For the first time unemployment was widespread among educated Africans. African peasants and small business people who had been drawn into world trade, and who sometimes profited from booms, also felt the agony of the

---

The Spread of Fascism In the 1920s and 1930s most European countries had Fascist sympathizers. The British Union of Fascists, led by Sir Oswald Mosley, modeled itself on Mussolini's nationalist Fascist Party. Its members were highly visible in their black uniforms, but they never numbered more than a few thousand and never elected a member to Parliament. Here Mosley and his Blackshirts prepare to march through London's Jewish East End in October 1936. Anti-Fascist demonstrators attacked Mosley's followers and stopped the march. (Hulton Archive/Getty Images)

decade-long bust, as did urban workers. In some areas the result was unprecedented mass protest. The Gold Coast cocoa holdups of 1930–1931 and 1937–1938 are the most famous examples (see page 1019).

Authoritarian States

> ☐ What was the nature of the new totalitarian dictatorships, and how did they differ from conservative authoritarian states?

Both conservative and radical dictatorships arose in Europe in the 1920s and the 1930s. Although they sometimes overlapped in character and practice, they were profoundly different in essence. Conservative authoritarian regimes were joined in this period by new and frightening radical totalitarian dictatorships.

Conservative Authoritarianism

The traditional form of antidemocratic government in world history was conservative authoritarianism. Like Russia's tsars and China's emperors, the leaders of such governments relied on obedient bureaucracies, vigilant police departments, and trustworthy armies to control society. They forbade or limited popular participation in government, and political opponents were often jailed or exiled. Yet they had neither the ability nor the desire to control many aspects of their subjects' lives. As long as the people did not try to change the system, they often had considerable personal independence.

After the First World War, authoritarianism revived, especially in Latin America and in the less-developed eastern part of Europe. By 1938 in eastern Europe only Czechoslovakia remained true to liberal political ideals. Conservative dictators also took over in Spain and Portugal.

There were several reasons for this development. These lands lacked strong traditions of self-government, and many of the new states, such as Yugoslavia, were torn by ethnic conflicts. Dictatorship appealed to nationalists and military leaders as a way to repress such tensions and preserve national unity. Large landowners and the church were still powerful forces in these predominantly agrarian areas, and they often looked to dictators to save them from progressive land reform or Communist agrarian upheaval. Although some of the conservative authoritarian regimes adopted certain Fascist characteristics in the 1930s, they were concerned more with maintaining the status quo than with mobilizing the masses or forcing society into rapid change or war.

Radical Totalitarian Dictatorships

By the mid-1930s a new kind of radical dictatorship had emerged in the Soviet Union, Germany, and, to a lesser extent, Italy. These dictatorships—termed totalitarian—violently rejected liberal values and exercised unprecedented control over the masses.

Most scholars argue that **totalitarianism** burst on the scene with the total war effort of 1914–1918 (see Chapter 28). World War I called forth a tendency to subordinate all institutions and all classes to the state in order to achieve one supreme objective: victory. As the French thinker Elie Halévy put it in 1936, the varieties of modern totalitarian tyranny—fascism, Nazism, and communism—could be thought of as "feuding brothers" with a common father: the nature of modern war.[2]

During the Russian civil war Lenin showed how a dedicated minority could achieve victory over a less-determined majority and subordinate institutions and human rights to the needs of a single group—the Communist Party—and its leader. Lenin's model of single-party dictatorship inspired imitators, including Adolf Hitler in Germany.

The modern totalitarian state reached maturity in the 1930s in the Stalinist Soviet Union and Nazi Germany. These and other totalitarian states were linked in their use of modern technology, particularly mass communication, to exercise complete political power and control over all aspects of society. Deviation from the norm, even in art or family behavior, could be a crime. This vision of a total state represented a radical revolt against liberalism.

Unlike old-fashioned authoritarianism, modern totalitarianism was based not on an elite seeking to maintain the existing social order, but on people who had become engaged in the political process for change, most notably through commitment to nationalism and socialism. Thus totalitarian societies were fully mobilized societies moving toward a goal. As soon as one goal was achieved, another arose at the leader's command. As a result totalitarianism was an unfinished revolution in which rapid, profound change imposed from above went on forever.

There were major differences between Stalin's Communist U.S.S.R. and Hitler's Nazi Germany. Most notably, Soviet communism seized private property for the state and sought to level society by crushing the middle classes. Nazi Germany also criticized big landowners and industrialists but, unlike the Communists, did not try to nationalize private property, so the middle classes survived. This difference in property and class relations led some scholars to speak of "totalitarianism of the left"—Stalinist Russia—and "totalitarianism of the right"—Nazi Germany.

The aims of Soviet Communists were ultimately international, seeking to unite the workers of the world. Fascist leaders claimed they were interested in changing state and society on a national level only. Mussolini and Hitler used the term **fascism** to describe their movements' supposedly "total" and revolutionary character. Orthodox Marxist Communists argued that the Fascists were powerful capitalists who sought to destroy the revolutionary working class and thus protect their enormous profits. So while Communists and Fascists were both committed to the overthrow of existing society, their ideologies clashed, and they were enemies.

European Fascist movements shared many characteristics, including extreme nationalism; an antisocialism aimed at destroying working-class movements; alliances with powerful capitalists and landowners; a dynamic, charismatic, and violent leader; and glorification of war and the military. Hitler and Stalin, in particular, were masters of the use of propaganda and terror. Fascists, especially in Germany, also embraced racial homogeneity, a fanatical obsession that led to the Holocaust (see page 927).

Although 1930s Japan has sometimes been called a Fascist society, most scholars disagree with this label. There were various ideological forces at work in Japan, including ultranationalism, militarism, reverence for traditional ways, and emperor worship, that contributed to the rise of a totalitarian state before the Second World War. These were all ideas that grew out of events and circumstances beginning with the Meiji Restoration in 1868 (see page 797), not from European philosophies of totalitarian government in the 1920s.

In summary, the concept of totalitarianism remains a valuable tool for historical understanding. It correctly highlights that in the 1930s Germany, the Soviet Union, and Japan made an unprecedented "total claim" on the

- **totalitarianism** A radical dictatorship that exercises complete political power and control over all aspects of society and seeks to mobilize the masses for action.
- **fascism** A movement characterized by extreme, often expansionist nationalism, antisocialism, a dynamic and violent leader, and glorification of war and the military.
- **five-year plan** Launched by Stalin in 1928 and termed the "revolution from above," its goal was to modernize the Soviet Union and generate a Communist society with new attitudes, new loyalties, and a new socialist humanity.
- **New Economic Policy (NEP)** Lenin's 1921 policy re-establishing limited economic freedom in an attempt to rebuild agriculture and industry in the face of economic disintegration.

beliefs and behaviors of their respective citizens.[3] As for fascism, antidemocratic, antisocialist Fascist movements sprang up all over Europe, but only in Italy and Germany (and some would say Spain under Francisco Franco) were they able to take power.

Stalin's Soviet Union

☐ How did Stalin and the Communist Party build a totalitarian order in the Soviet Union?

A master of political infighting, Joseph Stalin (1879–1953) cautiously consolidated his power and eliminated his enemies in the mid-1920s. Then in 1928, as the ruling Communist Party's undisputed leader, he launched the first **five-year plan** — the "revolution from above," as he so aptly termed it. The five-year plan marked the beginning of an attempt to transform Soviet society along socialist lines. Stalin and the Communist Party used constant propaganda, enormous sacrifice, and unlimited violence and state control to establish a dynamic, modern totalitarian state in the 1930s.

From Lenin to Stalin

By spring 1921 Lenin and the Bolsheviks had won the civil war, but they ruled a shattered and devastated land. In the face of economic disintegration, the worst famine in generations, riots by peasants and workers, and an open rebellion by previously pro-Bolshevik sailors at Kronstadt, Lenin changed course. In March 1921 he announced the **New Economic Policy (NEP)**, which re-established limited economic freedom in an attempt to rebuild agriculture and industry. Peasant producers could sell their surpluses in free markets, as could private traders and small handicraft manufacturers. Heavy industry, railroads, and banks, however, remained wholly nationalized.

The NEP was successful both politically and economically. Politically, it was a necessary but temporary compromise with the Soviet Union's overwhelming peasant majority, the only force capable of overturning Lenin's government. Economically, the NEP brought rapid recovery. In 1926 industrial output surpassed prewar levels, and peasants were producing almost as much grain as before the war.

As the economy recovered, an intense power struggle began in the Communist Party's inner circles, for Lenin left no chosen successor when he died in 1924. The principal contenders were Stalin and Leon Trotsky. Stalin was a good organizer but had no experience outside Russia. Trotsky, who had planned the 1917 takeover (see page 861) and created the Red Army, appeared to have all the advantages. Yet Stalin won because he

Soviet Collectivization Poster Soviet leader Joseph Stalin ordered a nationwide forced collectivization campaign from 1928 to 1933. Following communist theory, the government created large-scale collective farms by seizing land and forcing peasants to work on it. In this idealized 1932 poster, farmers are encouraged to complete the five-year plan of collectivization, while Stalin looks on approvingly. The outcome instead was a disaster. Millions of people died in the resulting human-created famine. (Deutsches Plakat Museum, Essen, Germany/Archives Charmet/The Bridgeman Art Library)

gained the support of the party, the only genuine source of power in the one-party state.

With cunning Stalin gradually achieved absolute power between 1922 and 1927. He used the moderates to crush Trotsky, and then turned against the moderates and destroyed them as well. Stalin's final triumph came at the party congress of December 1927, which condemned all "deviation from the general party line" formulated by Stalin.

The Five-Year Plans

The 1927 party congress marked the end of the NEP and the beginning of the era of socialist five-year plans. The first five-year plan had staggering economic objectives. In just five years, total industrial output was to increase by 250 percent and agricultural production by 150 percent, and one-fifth of the peasants were to give up their private plots and join socialist collective farms. By 1930 economic and social change was sweeping the country.

Stalin unleashed his "second revolution" for a variety of reasons. First, like Lenin, Stalin and his militant supporters were deeply committed to socialism as they understood it. Second, there was the old problem of catching up with the advanced and presumably hostile Western capitalist nations. "We are fifty or a hundred years behind the advanced countries," Stalin said in 1931. "We must make good this distance in ten years. Either we do it, or we shall go under."[4]

Domestically, there was the peasant problem. For centuries peasants had wanted to own the land, and finally they had it. Sooner or later, the Communists reasoned, the peasants would become conservative capitalists and threaten the regime. To resolve these issues, Stalin decided on a preventive war against the peasantry in order to bring it under the state's absolute control.

That war was **collectivization** — the forcible consolidation of individual peasant farms into large, state-controlled enterprises. Beginning in 1929 peasants were ordered to give up their land and animals and become members of collective farms. As for the kulaks, the better-off peasants, Stalin instructed party workers to "liquidate them as a class." Stripped of land and livestock, many starved or were deported to forced-labor camps for "re-education."

Since almost all peasants were poor, the term *kulak* soon meant any peasant who opposed the new system. Whole villages were often attacked. One conscience-stricken colonel in the secret police confessed to a foreign journalist:

> I am an old Bolshevik. I worked in the underground against the Tsar and then I fought in the Civil War. Did I do all that in order that I should now surround villages with machine guns and order my men to fire indiscriminately into crowds of peasants? Oh, no, no![5]

Forced collectivization led to disaster. Many peasants slaughtered their animals and burned their crops in protest. Nor were the state-controlled collective farms more productive. Grain output barely increased, and collectivized agriculture made no substantial financial contribution to Soviet industrial development during the first five-year plan.

In Ukraine Stalin instituted a policy of all-out collectivization with two goals: to destroy all expressions of Ukrainian nationalism, and to break the will of the Ukrainian peasants so they would accept collectivization and Soviet rule. Stalin began by purging Ukraine of its intellectuals and political elite, labeling them reactionary nationalists and enemies of socialism. He then set impossibly high grain quotas — up to nearly 50 percent of total production — for the collectivized farms. This grain quota had to be turned over to the government before any peasant could receive a share. The result was a terrible man-made famine in Ukraine in 1932 and 1933, which probably claimed 3 to 5 million lives.

Collectivization was a cruel but real victory for Communist ideologues. By 1938, 93 percent of peasant families had been herded onto collective farms. Regimented as state employees and dependent on the state-owned tractor stations, the collectivized peasants were no longer a political threat.

The industrial side of the five-year plans was more successful. Soviet industry produced about four times as much in 1937 as in 1928. No other major country had ever achieved such rapid industrial growth. Heavy industry led the way, and urban development accelerated: more than 25 million people migrated to cities to become industrial workers during the 1930s.

The sudden creation of dozens of new factories demanded tremendous resources. Funds for industrial expansion were collected from the people by means of heavy hidden sales taxes. Firm labor discipline also contributed to rapid industrialization. Trade unions lost most of their power, and individuals could not move without police permission. When factory managers needed more hands they were sent "unneeded" peasants from collective farms.

Foreign engineers were hired to plan and construct many of the new factories. Highly skilled American engineers, hungry for work in the depression years, were particularly important until newly trained Soviet experts began to replace them after 1932. Siberia's new steel mills were modeled on America's best. Thus Stalin's planners harnessed the skill and technology of capitalist countries to promote the surge of socialist industry.

Life and Culture in Soviet Society

Daily life was hard in Stalin's Soviet Union. Because consumption was reduced to pay for investment, there was no improvement in the average standard of living. There were constant shortages, and scarcity of housing was a particularly serious problem. A relatively lucky family received one room for all its members and

---

• **collectivization** Stalin's forcible consolidation of individual peasant farms into large, state-controlled enterprises.

shared both a kitchen and a toilet with others on the floor. Less fortunate people built scrap-lumber shacks in shantytowns.

Despite the hardships, many Communists saw themselves as heroically building the world's first socialist society while capitalism crumbled and Fascism rose in the West. This optimistic belief in the Soviet Union's future also attracted many disillusioned Westerners to communism in the 1930s.

On a more practical level Soviet workers received some important social benefits, such as old-age pensions, free medical services and education, and day-care centers for children. Unemployment was almost unknown. Finally, there was the possibility of personal advancement. Rapid industrialization required massive numbers of trained experts, such as skilled workers, engineers, and plant managers. Thus the Stalinist state broke with the egalitarian policies of the 1920s and provided tremendous incentives to those who acquired specialized skills. A growing technical and managerial elite joined the political and artistic elites in a new upper class, whose members were rich and powerful.

Soviet society's radical transformation profoundly affected women's lives. The Russian Revolution of 1917 immediately proclaimed complete equality of rights for women. In the 1920s divorce and abortion were made easily available, and women were urged to work outside the home. After Stalin came to power, however, he played down this trend in favor of a return to traditional family values.

The most lasting changes for women involved work and education. Peasant women continued to work on farms, and millions of women now toiled in factories and heavy construction. The more determined women entered the ranks of the better-paid specialists in industry and science. By 1950, 75 percent of all doctors in the Soviet Union were women.

Culture was thoroughly politicized through constant propaganda and indoctrination. Party activists lectured workers in factories and peasants on collective farms, while newspapers, films, and radio broadcasts recounted socialist achievements and capitalist plots. Writers and artists who could effectively combine genuine creativity and political propaganda became the darlings of the regime.

Stalinist Terror and the Great Purges

In the mid-1930s the push to build socialism and a new society culminated in ruthless police terror and a massive purging of the Communist Party. In late 1934 Stalin's number-two man, Sergei Kirov, was mysteriously murdered. Although Stalin himself probably ordered Kirov's murder, he used the incident to launch a reign of terror.

In August 1936 sixteen prominent "Old Bolsheviks" — members of the party before the Russian Revolution of 1917 — confessed to all manner of plots against Stalin in spectacular public show trials in Moscow. Then in 1937 the secret police arrested a mass of lesser party officials and newer members, torturing them and extracting confessions for more show trials. In addition to the party faithful, union officials, managers, intellectuals, army officers, and countless ordinary citizens were struck down. In all, at least 8 million people were arrested, and millions of these were executed or never returned from prisons and forced-labor camps.

Stalin recruited 1.5 million new members to take the place of those purged. Thus more than half of all Communist Party members in 1941 had joined since the purges. These new members were products of the Second Revolution of the 1930s, seeking the opportunities and rewards that party membership offered. This new generation of Stalin-formed Communists served the leader effectively until his death in 1953, and then governed the Soviet Union until the early 1980s.

Stalin's mass purges remain baffling, for most historians believe that those purged posed no threat and confessed to crimes they had not committed. Revisionist historians have challenged the long-standing interpretation that blames the great purges on Stalin's

Women Prisoners Digging a Canal Millions of Soviet citizens were sent to forced-labor prison camps from 1929 to 1953, and over 1.7 million died. Ten to 20 percent of these prisoners were women, many of them found guilty of nothing more than being married to men considered enemies of the state. In this photo women prisoners use picks and shovels to dig the canal bed of the White Sea–Baltic Sea Canal. The canal was 141 miles long, and building it took about twenty months of manual labor between 1931 and 1933. (Photo: Center for History and New Media, George Mason University. Courtesy of Russian State Documentary Film & Photo Archive at Krasnogorsk)

cruelty or madness. They argue that Stalin's fears were exaggerated but genuine and were shared by many in the party and in the general population who were bombarded daily with propaganda. Investigations and trials snowballed into a mass hysteria, a new witch-hunt.[6] In short, a popular but deluded Stalin found large numbers of willing collaborators for crime as well as for achievement.

Mussolini and Fascism in Italy

☐ How did Italian fascism develop?

Mussolini's Fascist movement and his seizure of power in 1922 were important steps in the rise of dictatorships between the two world wars. Mussolini and his supporters were the first to call themselves "fascists" — revolutionaries determined to create a new kind of totalitarian state. His dictatorship was brutal and theatrical, and it contained elements of both conservative authoritarianism and modern totalitarianism.

The Seizure of Power

In the early twentieth century Italy was a liberal state with civil rights and a constitutional monarchy. On the eve of the First World War, the parliamentary regime granted universal male suffrage. But there were serious problems. Poverty was widespread, and many peasants were more attached to their villages and local interests than to the national state. Moreover, the papacy, many devout Catholics, conservatives, and landowners remained opposed to the middle-class lawyers and politicians who ran the country largely for their own benefit. Church-state relations were often tense. Class differences were also extreme, and by 1912 the Socialist Party's radical wing led the powerful revolutionary socialist movement.[7]

World War I worsened the political situation. Having fought on the Allied side almost exclusively for purposes of territorial expansion, the parliamentary government disappointed Italian nationalists with Italy's modest gains at Versailles. Workers and peasants also felt cheated: to win their support during the war, the government had promised social and land reform, which it did not deliver after the war.

The Russian Revolution inspired and energized Italy's revolutionary socialist movement, and radical workers and peasants began occupying factories and seizing land in 1920. These actions scared and mobilized the property-owning classes. Thus by 1921 revolutionary socialists, antiliberal conservatives, and frightened property owners were all opposed — though for different reasons — to the liberal parliamentary government.

Into these crosscurrents of unrest and fear stepped Benito Mussolini (1883–1945). Mussolini began his political career as a Socialist Party leader and radical newspaper editor before World War I. Expelled from the Italian Socialist Party for supporting the war, and wounded on the Italian front in 1917, Mussolini returned home and began organizing bitter war veterans into a band of Fascists — from the Italian word for "a union of forces."

At first Mussolini's program was a radical combination of nationalist and socialist demands, including territorial expansion, workers' benefits, and land reform for peasants. As such, it competed directly with the well-organized Socialist Party and failed to get off the ground. When Mussolini saw that his violent verbal assaults on rival Socialists won him growing support from conservatives and the frightened middle classes, he shifted gears in 1920, exalting nation and race over class.

Mussolini and his private army of **Black Shirts** began to grow violent. Few people were killed, but Socialist newspapers, union halls, and local Socialist Party headquarters were destroyed. A skillful politician, Mussolini convinced his followers that they were not just opposing the "Reds" but were also making a real revolution of the little people against the established interests.

With the government breaking down in 1922, largely because of the chaos created by his Black Shirt bands, Mussolini stepped forward as the savior of order and property, demanding the existing government's resignation and his own appointment by the king. In October 1922 a large group of Fascists marched on Rome to threaten the king and force him to appoint Mussolini prime minister. The threat worked. Victor Emmanuel III (r. 1900–1946) asked Mussolini to form a new cabinet. Thus, after widespread violence and a threat of armed uprising, Mussolini seized power "legally."

The Regime in Action

In 1924 Mussolini declared his desire to "make the nation Fascist" and imposed a series of repressive measures. Press freedom was abolished, elections were fixed, and the government ruled by decree. Mussolini arrested his political opponents, disbanded all independent labor unions, and put dedicated Fascists in con-

• **Black Shirts** A private army under Mussolini that destroyed Socialist newspapers, union halls, and Socialist Party headquarters, eventually pushing Socialists out of the city governments of northern Italy.

• **Lateran Agreement** A 1929 agreement that recognized the Vatican as an independent state, with Mussolini agreeing to give the church heavy financial support in return for the pope's public support.

Mussolini Leading a Parade in Rome Benito Mussolini was a master showman who drew on Rome's ancient heritage to promote Italian fascism. He wanted a grand avenue to stage triumphal marches with thousands of troops, so he had the Way of the Imperial Forums built through the old city. Here Mussolini rides at the head of a grand parade in 1932 to inaugurate the new road, passing the Roman Coliseum, one of the focal points along the route. (Stefano Bianchetti/Corbis)

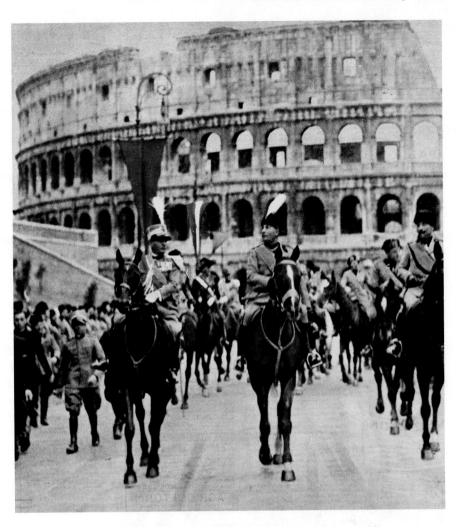

trol of Italy's schools. He created a Fascist youth movement, Fascist labor unions, and many other Fascist organizations. He trumpeted his goal in a famous slogan of 1926: "Everything in the state, nothing outside the state, nothing against the state." By year's end Italy was a one-party dictatorship under Mussolini's unquestioned leadership.

Mussolini did not complete the establishment of a modern totalitarian state. His Fascist Party never destroyed the old power structure. Interested primarily in personal power, Mussolini was content to compromise with the old conservative classes that controlled the army, the economy, and the state. He never tried to purge these classes or even move very vigorously against them. He controlled labor but left big business to regulate itself, profitably and securely. There was no land reform.

Mussolini also drew increasing support from the Catholic Church. In the **Lateran Agreement** of 1929, he recognized the Vatican as a tiny independent state and agreed to give the church heavy financial support. The pope in return urged Italians to support Mussolini's government.

Like Stalin, Hitler, and other totalitarian leaders, Mussolini favored a return of traditional roles for women. He abolished divorce and told women to stay at home and produce children. In 1938 women were limited by law to a maximum of 10 percent of the better-paying jobs in industry and government. Italian women appear not to have changed their attitudes or behavior in any important way under Fascist rule.

Mussolini's government passed no racial laws until 1938 and did not persecute Jews savagely until late in the Second World War, when Italy was under Nazi con-

trol. Nor did Mussolini establish a truly ruthless police state. Only twenty-three political prisoners were condemned to death between 1926 and 1944. Mussolini's Fascist Italy, though repressive and undemocratic, was never really totalitarian.

Hitler and Nazism in Germany

☐ Why were Hitler and his Nazi regime initially so popular, and how did their actions lead to World War II?

The most frightening dictatorship developed in Nazi Germany. A product of Hitler's evil genius as well as of Germany's social and political situation, the Nazi movement shared some of the characteristics of Mussolini's Italian model and fascism. But Nazism asserted an unlimited claim over German society and proclaimed the ultimate power of its aggressive leader, Adolf Hitler. Nazism's aspirations were truly totalitarian.

The Roots of Nazism

Nazism grew out of many complex developments, of which the most influential were extreme nationalism and racism. These two ideas captured the mind of the young Adolf Hitler (1889–1945), and he dominated Nazism until the end of World War II.

The son of an Austrian customs official, Hitler spent his childhood in small towns in Austria. He did poorly in high school and dropped out at age sixteen.

Young People in Hitler's Germany This photo from 1930 shows Hitler admiring a young boy dressed in the uniform of Hitler's storm troopers, a paramilitary organization of the Nazi Party that supported Hitler's rise to power in the 1920s and early 1930s. Only a year after the founding of the storm troopers in 1921, Hitler began to organize Germany's young people into similar paramilitary groups in an effort to militarize all of German society. The young paramilitaries became the Hitler Youth, who eventually numbered in the millions. (Popperfoto/Getty Images)

He then headed to Vienna, where he was exposed to extreme Austro-German nationalists who believed Germans to be a superior people and central Europe's natural rulers. They advocated union with Germany and violent expulsion of "inferior" peoples from the Austro-Hungarian Empire.

From these extremists Hitler eagerly absorbed virulent anti-Semitism, racism, and hatred of Slavs. He developed an unshakable belief in the crudest distortions of Social Darwinism (see page 739), the superiority of Germanic races, and the inevitability of racial conflict. The Jews, he claimed, directed an international conspiracy of finance capitalism and Marxist socialism against German culture, German unity, and the German race. Anti-Semitism and racism became Hitler's most passionate convictions.

Hitler greeted the outbreak of the Great War as a salvation. The struggle and discipline of serving as a soldier in the war gave his life meaning, and when Germany was suddenly defeated in 1918, Hitler's world was shattered. (See "Viewpoints: Hitler, Mussolini, and the Great War, page 921.) Convinced that Jews and Marxists had "stabbed Germany in the back," he vowed to fight on.

In late 1919 Hitler joined a tiny extremist group in Munich called the German Workers' Party, which promised a uniquely German "national socialism" that would abolish the injustices of capitalism and create a mighty "people's community." By 1921 Hitler had gained absolute control of this small but growing party, now renamed the National Socialist German Worker's Party, or Nazi Party. A master of mass propaganda and political showmanship, Hitler worked his audience into a frenzy with wild attacks on the Versailles treaty, the Jews, war profiteers, and Germany's Weimar Republic.

In late 1923 the Weimar Republic seemed on the verge of collapse. In 1925 the old Great War field marshal Paul von Hindenburg (1847–1934) became the second president of the young democratic Germany. Hitler, inspired by Mussolini's recent victory, attempted an armed uprising in Munich. Despite the failure of the poorly organized plot and Hitler's arrest, Nazism had been born.

Hitler's Road to Power

At his trial Hitler violently denounced the Weimar Republic, and he gained enormous publicity. From the unsuccessful revolt, Hitler concluded that he had to come to power legally through electoral competition. He used his brief prison term to dictate *Mein Kampf* (My Struggle). Here he expounded on his basic ideas on race and anti-Semitism, the notion of territorial expansion based on "living space" for Germans, and the role of the leader-dictator, called the *Führer* (FYOUR-uhr).

In the years of relative prosperity and stability between 1924 and 1929, Hitler concentrated on building

Viewpoints

Hitler, Mussolini, and the Great War

• *When the Great War ended, Private Adolf Hitler was in a hospital bed, blinded temporarily by a mustard gas shell. In his infamous autobiography,* Mein Kampf *(My Struggle), Hitler described the agonizing sense of betrayal he felt upon learning of Germany's surrender. Corporal Benito Mussolini, six years Hitler's senior, was also wounded in the war and was discharged in August 1917. Although a revolutionary socialist before the war, as was his father, Mussolini describes in his autobiography how, by war's end, he had turned completely against socialism. Although Italy was on the winning side of World War I, Mussolini felt that Italy's leaders and those who were trying to incite socialist revolution had betrayed his country.*

Adolf Hitler, *My Struggle*

"A few hours later, my eyes had turned into glowing coals, it had grown dark around me. Thus I came to the hospital . . . and there I was fated to experience—the greatest villainy of the century. . . .

On November 10 [1918], the pastor came to the hospital [to inform] us that the House of Hollenzollern should no longer bear the imperial crown; that the fatherland had become a "republic." But when the old gentleman tried to go on, and began to tell us that we must now end the long War, yes, that now that it was lost and we were throwing ourselves upon the mercy of the victors, our fatherland would for the future be exposed to dire oppression, that the armistice should be accepted with confidence in the magnanimity of our previous enemies—I could stand it no longer. It became impossible for me to sit still one minute more. Again everything went black before my eyes; I tottered and groped my way back to the dormitory, threw myself on my bunk and dug my burning head in to my blanket and pillow. . . .

And so it had all been in vain. In vain all the sacrifices and privations; . . . in vain the deaths of two millions who died. Would not the graves . . . open and send the silent mud- and blood-covered heroes back as spirits of vengeance to the homeland which had cheated them with such mockery of the highest sacrifice which a man can make to his people in this world? . . .

Did all this happen only so that a gang of wretched criminals could lay hands on the fatherland? . . .

I, for my part, decided to go into politics."

Benito Mussolini, *My Autobiography*

"Already in January, 1919, the Socialists, slightly checked during the war, began, the moment the ink was drying on the armistice, their work of rebellion and blackmail. . . . We suffered the humiliation of seeing the banners of our glorious regiments returned to their homes without being saluted, without that warm cheer of sympathy owed to those who return from victorious war. . . .

I said then that never in the life of any nation on the day after victory had there been a more odious tragedy. . . . In the first few months of 1919, Italy, led on by politicians . . . had only one frantic wish that I could see—it was to destroy every gain of victorious struggle. Its only dedication was to a denial of the borders and soil extent of the nation. It forgot our 600,000 dead and our 1,000,000 wounded. It made waste of their generous blood. . . . This attempt at matricide of the motherland was abetted by Italians of perverted intellect and by professional socialists. . . .

I wrote . . . Do they want to scrape the earth that was soaked with your blood and to spit on your sacrifice? Fear nothing, glorious spirits! Our task has just begun. No harm shall befall you. We shall defend the dead, and all the dead, even though we put dugouts in the public squares and trenches in the streets of our city."

Sources: Adolph Hitler, excerpts from *Mein Kampf*, translated by Ralph Manheim. Copyright © 1943, renewed 1971 by Houghton Mifflin Harcourt Publishing Company. Also published by Hutchinson. Reprinted by permission of Houghton Mifflin Harcourt Publishing Company and the Random House Group, Ltd. All rights reserved; Benito Mussolini, *My Autobiography* (New York: Charles Scribner's Sons, 1928), pp. 60–63, 65–66. Copyright 1928. Reproduced with permission of ABC-CLIO INC. in the format Textbook and Other Book via Copyright Clearance Center.

QUESTIONS FOR ANALYSIS

1. According to both Hitler and Mussolini, who was betrayed by the war's outcome in their countries?
2. How do both men plan to respond to this betrayal?

---

his Nazi Party. The Nazis remained a small splinter group until the 1929 Great Depression shattered economic prosperity. By the end of 1932 an incredible 43 percent of the labor force was unemployed. Industrial production fell by one-half between 1929 and 1932. No factor contributed more to Hitler's success than the economic crisis. Hitler began promising German voters economic as well as political and international salvation.

Hitler rejected free-market capitalism and advocated government programs to bring recovery. He pitched his speeches to middle- and lower-middle-class groups and to skilled workers. As the economy collapsed, great numbers of these people "voted their

• **Nazism** A movement born of extreme nationalism and racism and dominated by Adolf Hitler from 1933 until the end of World War II in 1945.

pocketbooks"[8] and deserted the conservative and moderate parties for the Nazis. In the 1930 election the Nazis won 6.5 million votes and 107 seats, and in July 1932 they gained 14.5 million votes — 38 percent of the total — and became the largest party in the Reichstag.

Hitler and the Nazis appealed strongly to German youth. Hitler himself was only forty in 1929, and he and most of his top aides were much younger than other leading German politicians. "National Socialism is the organized will of the youth," proclaimed the official Nazi slogan. In 1931 almost 40 percent of Nazi Party members were under thirty, compared with 20 percent of Social Democrats. National recovery, exciting and rapid change, and personal advancement made Nazism appealing to millions of German youths.

Hitler also came to power because of the breakdown of democratic government. Germany's economic collapse in the Great Depression convinced many voters that the country's republican leaders were stupid and corrupt. Disunity on the left was another nail in the republic's coffin. The Communists refused to cooperate with the Social Democrats, even though the two parties together outnumbered the Nazis in the Reichstag.

Finally, Hitler excelled in dirty backroom politics. In 1932 he succeeded in gaining support from key people in the army and big business who thought they could use him to their own advantage. Many conservative and nationalistic politicians thought similarly. Thus in January 1933 President von Hindenburg legally appointed Hitler, leader of Germany's largest party, as German chancellor.

The Nazi State and Society

Hitler quickly established an unshakable dictatorship. When the Reichstag building was partly destroyed by fire in February 1933, Hitler blamed the Communist Party, and he convinced President von Hindenburg, in poor health and displaying signs of senility, to sign dictatorial emergency acts that abolished freedom of speech and assembly and most personal liberties. He also called for new elections in an effort to solidify his political power.

When the Nazis won only 44 percent of the votes, Hitler outlawed the Communist Party and arrested its parliamentary representatives. Then on March 23, 1933, the Nazis forced through the Reichstag the so-called **Enabling Act**, which gave Hitler absolute dictatorial power for four years.

Hitler and the Nazis took over the government bureaucracy intact, installing many Nazis in top positions. Hitler next outlawed strikes and abolished independent labor unions, which were replaced by the Nazi Labor Front. Professional people — doctors and lawyers, teachers and engineers — also saw their independent organizations swallowed up in Nazi associations. Publishing houses and universities were put under Nazi control, and students and professors publicly burned forbidden books. Modern art and architecture were ruthlessly prohibited. Life became violently anti-intellectual. As the cynical Joseph Goebbels, later Nazi minister of propaganda, put it, "When I hear the word 'culture' I reach for my gun."[9] By 1934 a brutal dictatorship characterized by frightening dynamism and total obedience to Hitler was already largely in place.

In June 1934 Hitler ordered his elite personal guard — the SS — to arrest and shoot without trial roughly a thousand long-time Nazi storm troopers. Shortly thereafter army leaders surrendered their independence and swore a binding oath of "unquestioning obedience" to Adolf Hitler. The SS grew rapidly. Under Heinrich Himmler (1900–1945), the SS took over the political police, the Gestapo, and expanded its network of concentration camps.

From the beginning, German Jews were a special object of Nazi persecution. By late 1934 most Jewish lawyers, doctors, professors, civil servants, and musicians had been banned from their professions. In 1935 the infamous Nuremberg Laws classified as Jewish anyone having three or more Jewish grandparents and deprived Jews of all rights of citizenship. By 1938 roughly one-quarter of Germany's half million Jews had emigrated, sacrificing almost all their property in order to leave Germany.

In late 1938 the attack on the Jews accelerated. On November 9 and 10, 1938, the Nazis initiated a series of well-organized attacks against Jews throughout Nazi Germany and some parts of Austria. This infamous event is known as Kristallnacht, or Night of Broken Glass, after the broken glass that littered the streets following the frenzied destruction of Jewish homes, shops, synagogues, and neighborhoods by German civilians and uniformed storm troopers. U.S. Consul David Buffum reported of the Nazis in Leipzig that

> The most hideous phase of the so-called "spontaneous" action, has been the wholesale arrest and transportation to concentration camps of male German Jews between the ages of sixteen and sixty. . . . Having demolished dwellings and hurled most of the effects to the streets, the insatiably sadistic perpetrators threw many of the trembling inmates into a small stream that flows through the Zoological Park, commanding horrified spectators to spit at them, defile them with mud and jeer at their plight.[10]

Many historians consider this night the beginning of Hitler's Final Solution against the Jews (see page 927), and it now became very difficult for Jews to leave Germany.

• **Enabling Act** An act pushed through the Reichstag by the Nazis that gave Hitler absolute dictatorial power for four years.

Some Germans privately opposed these outrages, but most went along or looked the other way. Although this lack of response reflected the individual's helplessness in a totalitarian state, it also reflected the strong popular support Hitler's government enjoyed.

Hitler's Popularity

Hitler had promised the masses economic recovery — "work and bread" — and he delivered. The Nazi Party launched a large public works program to pull Germany out of the depression. Work began on highways, offices, sports stadiums, and public housing. In 1935 Germany turned decisively toward rearmament. Unemployment dropped steadily, and by 1938 the Nazis boasted of nearly full employment. The average standard of living increased moderately. Business profits rose sharply. For millions of people economic recovery was tangible evidence that Nazi promises were more than show and propaganda.

In contrast to those deemed "undesirable" (Jews, Slavs, Gypsies, Jehovah's Witnesses, Communists, and homosexuals), for ordinary German citizens, Hitler's government meant greater equality and more opportunities. In 1933 class barriers in Germany were generally high. Hitler's rule introduced changes that lowered these barriers. For example, stiff educational requirements favoring the well-to-do were relaxed. The new Nazi elite included many young and poorly educated dropouts, rootless lower-middle-class people like Hitler who rose to the top with breathtaking speed. More generally, the Nazis tolerated privilege and wealth only as long as they served party needs.

Yet few historians today believe that Hitler and the Nazis brought about a real social revolution. The well-educated classes held on to most of their advantages, and only a modest social leveling occurred in the Nazi years. Significantly, the Nazis shared with the Italian Fascists the stereotypical view of women as housewives and mothers. Only when facing labor shortages during the war did they reluctantly mobilize large numbers of German women for office and factory work. Yet low unemployment and economic recovery coupled with an aggressive propaganda effort heralding the Nazi state's successes led to broad support for the regime.

Not all Germans supported Hitler, however, and a number of German groups actively resisted him after 1933. Tens of thousands of political enemies were imprisoned, and thousands were executed. In the first years of Hitler's rule, the principal resisters were trade union Communists and Socialists, groups smashed by the expansion of the SS system after 1935. Catholic and Protestant churches produced a second group of opponents. Their efforts were directed primarily at preserving genuine religious life, however, not at overthrowing Hitler. Finally in 1938 and again during the war,

Reaching a National Audience This poster ad promotes the VE-301 receiver, "the world's cheapest radio," and claims that "All Germany listens to the Führer on the people's receiver." Constantly broadcasting official views and attitudes, the state-controlled media also put the Nazis' favorite entertainment — gigantic mass meetings that climaxed with Hitler's violent theatrical speeches — on an invisible stage for millions. (Bundesarchiv Koblenz Plak 003-022-025/Grafiker: Leonid)

some high-ranking army officers, who feared the consequences of Hitler's reckless aggression, plotted, unsuccessfully, against him.

Aggression and Appeasement, 1933–1939

After economic recovery and success establishing Nazi control of society, Hitler turned to the next item on his agenda: aggressive territorial expansion. He camouflaged his plans at first, for the Treaty of Versailles limited Germany's army to only a hundred thousand men. Thus while Hitler loudly proclaimed his peaceful intentions, Germany's withdrawal from

Hitler's Success with Aggression
This biting criticism of appeasing leaders by the cartoonist David Low appeared shortly after Hitler remilitarized the Rhineland. Appeasement also appealed to millions of ordinary citizens in Britain and France who wanted to avoid another great war at any cost.
(Evening Standard/Solo Syndication)

the League of Nations in October 1933 indicated its determination to rearm. When in March 1935 Hitler established a general military draft and declared the "unequal" Versailles treaty disarmament clauses null and void, leaders in Britain, France, and Italy issued a rather tepid joint protest and warned him against future aggressive actions.

But the emerging united front against Hitler quickly collapsed. Britain adopted a policy of appeasement, granting Hitler everything he could reasonably want (and more) in order to avoid war. British appeasement, which practically dictated French policy, was motivated by the pacifism of a population still horrified by the memory of the First World War. As in Germany, many powerful British conservatives underestimated Hitler. They believed that Soviet communism was the real danger and that Hitler could be used to stop it.

In March 1936, Hitler suddenly marched his armies into the demilitarized Rhineland, brazenly violating the Treaties of Versailles and Locarno. France would not move without British support, and Britain refused to act (Map 30.1). As Britain and France opted for appeasement and the So-

Italy's Ethiopian Campaign, 1935–1936

SUDAN (Gr. Br.)
ERITREA (It.)
FRENCH SOMALILAND
BRITISH SOMALILAND
Addis Ababa
ETHIOPIA
ITALIAN SOMALILAND
KENYA (Gr. Br.)
INDIAN OCEAN
→ Italian campaigns, 1935–1936

viet Union watched all developments suspiciously, Hitler found powerful allies. In 1935 the bombastic Mussolini attacked the independent African kingdom of Ethiopia. The Western Powers and the League of Nations condemned Italian aggression, but Hitler supported Italy energetically. In 1936 Italy and Germany established the so-called Rome-Berlin Axis. Japan, which wanted support for its occupation of Manchuria, also joined the Axis alliance (see page 900).

At the same time, Germany and Italy intervened in the Spanish civil war (1936–1939), where their support helped General Francisco Franco's Fascist movement defeat republican Spain. Republican Spain's only official aid in the fight against Franco came from the Soviet Union.

In late 1937 Hitler moved forward with his plans to crush Austria and Czechoslovakia as the first step in his long-contemplated drive to the east for living space. By threatening Austria with invasion, Hitler forced the Austrian chancellor in March 1938 to put local Nazis in control of the government. The next day German armies moved in unopposed, and Austria became two provinces of Greater Germany (see Map 30.1).

Simultaneously, Hitler demanded that the pro-Nazi, German-speaking territory of western Czechoslovakia — the Sudetenland — be turned over to Germany. Democratic Czechoslovakia was prepared to defend itself, but appeasement triumphed again. In September 1938 British prime minister Arthur Neville Chamberlain (1869–1940) flew to Germany three times in fourteen days. In these negotiations, Chamberlain

MAP 30.1 The Growth of Nazi Germany, 1933–1939 Until March 1939 Hitler brought ethnic Germans into the Nazi state; then he turned on the Slavic peoples, whom he had always hated. He stripped Czechoslovakia of its independence and prepared for an attack on Poland in September 1939.

and the French agreed with Hitler that the Sudetenland should be ceded to Germany immediately. Returning to London from the Munich Conference, Chamberlain told cheering crowds that he had secured "peace with honor . . . peace for our time." Sold out by the Western Powers, Czechoslovakia gave in.

Hitler's armies occupied the remainder of Czechoslovakia in March 1939. This time, there was no possible rationale of self-determination for Nazi aggression, because Hitler had seized the Czechs and Slovaks as captive peoples. When Hitler used the question of German minorities in Danzig as a pretext to confront Poland, Chamberlain declared that Britain and France would fight if Hitler attacked his eastern neighbor. Hitler did not take these warnings seriously and pressed on.

In an about-face that stunned the world, sworn enemies Hitler and Stalin signed a nonaggression pact in August 1939. Each dictator promised to remain neutral if the other became involved in war. An attached secret protocol divided eastern Europe into German and Soviet zones "in the event of a political territorial reorganization." Stalin agreed to the pact because he distrusted Western intentions, and Hitler offered territorial gain.

For Hitler, everything was now set. He told his generals on the day of the nonaggression pact, "My only fear is that at the last moment some dirty dog will come up with a mediation plan." On September 1, 1939, the Germans attacked Poland from three sides. Two days later, Britain and France, finally true to their word, declared war on Germany. The Second World War had begun.

The Second World War, 1939–1945

☐ How did Germany and Japan build empires in Europe and Asia, and how did the Allies defeat them?

World war broke out because Hitler's ambitions were essentially unlimited. Nazi soldiers scored enormous successes in Europe until late 1942, establishing a vast empire of death and destruction. Hitler's victories increased tensions in Asia between Japan, whose ambitions in Asia were equally unlimited, and the United States, and prompted Japan to attack the United States. Eventually, the mighty coalition of Britain, the United States, and the Soviet Union, which Winston Churchill called the Grand Alliance, functioned quite effectively in military terms and was determined to halt the aggressors. Thus the Nazi and Japanese empires proved short-lived.

Hitler's Empire in Europe, 1939–1942

Using planes, tanks, and trucks in the first example of a **blitzkrieg**, or "lightning war," Hitler's armies crushed Poland in four weeks. The Soviet Union quickly took its part of the booty — the eastern half of Poland and the Baltic states of Lithuania, Estonia, and Latvia. In the west French and British armies dug in; they expected another war of attrition and economic blockade. But in spring 1940 the Nazi lightning war struck again. After occupying Denmark, Norway, and Holland, German motorized columns broke through southern Belgium and into France.

As Hitler's armies poured into France, aging marshal Henri-Philippe Pétain — a national hero of the Great War — formed a new French government — the so-called Vichy (VIH-shee) government — and accepted defeat. Initially many French supported Pétain, who they believed

Vichy France, 1940

Paris
BELGIUM
LUX.
LORRAINE
ALSACE
FRANCE
SWITZ.
Bay of Biscay
Vichy
VICHY FRANCE
ITALY
SPAIN
Mediterranean Sea

☐ Occupied by Germany
☐ Annexed by Germany

would stand up for them against the Germans, but as the war progressed Pétain increasingly collaborated with the Nazis. By July 1940 Hitler ruled practically all of western continental Europe; Italy was an ally, the Soviet Union a friendly neutral (Map 30.2). Only Britain, led by Winston Churchill (1874–1965), remained unconquered.

To prepare for an invasion of Britain, Germany first needed to gain control of the air. In the Battle of Britain, which began in July 1940, German planes attacked British airfields and key factories, dueling with British defenders high in the skies. In September Hitler began indiscriminately bombing British cities in an attempt to break British morale. British aircraft factories increased production, and the people of London defiantly dug in. By September Britain was beating Germany in the air war, and Hitler gave up his plans for an immediate German invasion of Britain.

Hitler now allowed his lifetime obsession of creating a vast eastern European empire for the "master race" to dictate policy. In June 1941 Germany broke the Nazi-Soviet nonaggression pact and attacked the Soviet Union. By October Leningrad was practically surrounded, Moscow was besieged, and most of Ukraine had been conquered. But the Soviets did not collapse, and when a severe winter struck German armies outfitted in summer uniforms, the invaders were stopped.

Stalled in Russia, Hitler had come to rule an enormous European empire stretching from the outskirts of Moscow to the English Channel. He now began building a **New Order** based on the guiding principle of Nazi totalitarianism: racial imperialism. Within the New Order, the Nordic peoples — the Dutch, Norwegians, and Danes — received preferential treatment, for the Germans believed they were racially related to the German "Aryan" master race. The French, an "inferior" Latin people, occupied the middle position. At the bottom of the New Order were the harshly treated "subhumans," Jews and Slavs.

Hitler envisioned a vast eastern colonial empire where Poles, Ukrainians, and Russians would be enslaved and forced to die out while Germanic peasants would resettle the abandoned lands. Himmler and the elite SS corps, supported by military commanders and German policemen, now implemented a program of destruction in the occupied territories to create a "mass settlement space" for Germans. Many Poles, captured Communists, Gypsies, and Jehovah's Witnesses were murdered in cold blood.

- **blitzkrieg** "Lightning war" using planes, tanks, and trucks, first used by Hitler to crush Poland in four weeks.

- **New Order** Hitler's program, based on the guiding principle of racial imperialism, which gave preferential treatment to the Nordic peoples above "inferior" Latin peoples and, at the bottom, "subhuman" Slavs and Jews.

- **Holocaust** The attempted systematic extermination of all European Jews and other "undesirables" by the Nazi state during World War II.

London Bomb Shelter, 1940
Hitler believed that his relentless terror bombing of London—the "blitz"—could break the will of the British people. He was wrong. The blitz caused enormous destruction, but Londoners went about their business with courage and calm determination, as this unforgettable image of people being entertained in a bomb shelter in the Tube (subway) suggests. (Bettmann/Corbis)

The Holocaust

Finally, the Nazi state condemned all European Jews to extermination in the **Holocaust**. After the fall of Warsaw in 1939 the Nazis began forcing the Jews in the occupied territories to move to urban ghettos. The remaining German Jews were sent to occupied Poland. When war with Russia broke out in 1941, forced expulsion spiraled into extermination. Himmler's SS killing squads and regular army units compelled Soviet Jews to dig giant pits, which became mass graves as the victims were lined up on the edge and cut down by machine guns. Then in late 1941 Hitler and the Nazi leadership, in some still-debated combination, ordered the SS to speed up planning for "the final solution of the Jewish question." Throughout the Nazi empire Jews were systematically arrested, packed like cattle onto freight trains, and dispatched to extermination camps.

Prelude to Murder This photo captures the terrible inhumanity of Nazi racism. Frightened and bewildered families from the soon-to-be-destroyed Warsaw Ghetto are being forced out of their homes by German soldiers for deportation to concentration camps. There they face murder in the gas chambers. (Hulton Archive/Getty Images)

The Holocaust, 1941–1945

Individuals in Society

Primo Levi

MOST JEWS DEPORTED TO AUSCHWITZ WERE murdered as soon as they arrived, but the Nazis made some prisoners into slave laborers, and a few of these survived. Primo Levi (1919–1987), an Italian Jew, became one of the most influential witnesses to the Holocaust and its death camps.

Like many in Italy's small Jewish community, Levi's family belonged to the urban professional classes. The young Primo Levi graduated in 1941 from the University of Turin with highest honors in chemistry. Since 1938, when Italy introduced racial laws, he had faced growing discrimination, and two years after graduation he joined the antifascist resistance movement. Quickly captured, he was deported to Auschwitz with 650 Italian Jews in February 1944. Stone-faced SS men picked only ninety-six men and twenty-nine women to work in their respective labor camps. Levi was one of them.

Nothing had prepared Levi for what he encountered. The Jewish prisoners were kicked, punched, stripped, branded with tattoos, crammed into huts, and worked unmercifully. Hoping for some sign of prisoner solidarity in this terrible environment, Levi found only a desperate struggle of each against all and enormous status differences among prisoners. Many stunned and bewildered newcomers, beaten and demoralized by their bosses—the most privileged prisoners—collapsed and died. Others struggled to secure their own privileges, however small, because food rations and working conditions were so abominable that ordinary Jewish prisoners perished in two to three months.

Sensitive and noncombative, Levi found himself sinking into oblivion. But instead of joining the mass of the "drowned," he became one of the "saved"—a complicated surprise with moral implications that he would ponder all his life. As Levi explained in *Survival in Auschwitz* (1947), the usual road to salvation in the camps was some kind of collaboration with German power.* Savage German criminals were released from prison to become brutal camp guards; non-Jewish political prisoners competed for jobs entitling them to better conditions; and, especially troubling for Levi, a small number of Jewish men plotted and struggled for the power of life and death over other Jewish prisoners. Though not one of these Jewish bosses, Levi believed that he himself, like almost all survivors, had entered the "gray zone" of moral compromise. Only a very few superior individuals, "the stuff of saints and martyrs," survived the death camps without shifting their moral stance.

For Levi, compromise and salvation came from his profession. Interviewed by a German technocrat for the camp's synthetic rubber program, Levi performed brilliantly in scientific German and savored his triumph as a Jew over Nazi racism. Work in the warm camp laboratory offered Levi opportunities to pilfer equipment that could then be traded to other prisoners for food and necessities. Levi also gained critical support from three saintly prisoners who refused to do wicked and hateful acts. And he counted "luck" as essential for his survival: in the camp infirmary with scarlet fever in February 1945 as advancing Russian armies prepared to liberate the camp, Levi was not evacuated by the Nazis and shot to death like most Jewish prisoners.

After the war Primo Levi was forever haunted by the nightmare that the Holocaust would be ignored or forgotten. Always ashamed that so many people whom he considered better than himself had perished, he wrote and lectured tirelessly to preserve the memory of Jewish victims and guilty Nazis. Wanting the world to understand the Jewish genocide in all its complexity so that never again would people tolerate such atrocities, he grappled tirelessly with his vision of individual choice and moral compromise in a hell designed to make the victims collaborate and persecute each other.

QUESTIONS FOR ANALYSIS

1. Describe Levi's experience at Auschwitz. How did camp prisoners treat each other? Why?
2. What does Levi mean by the "gray zone"? How is this concept central to his thinking?
3. Will a vivid historical memory of the Holocaust help prevent future genocide?

*Primo Levi, *Survival in Auschwitz: The Nazi Assault on Humanity*, rev. ed. 1958 (London: Collier Books, 1961), pp. 79–84, and *The Drowned and the Saved* (New York: Summit Books, 1988). These powerful testimonies are highly recommended.

• **Primo Levi, who never stopped thinking, writing, and speaking about the Holocaust.** (Giansanti/Corbis Sygma)

Arriving at their destination, small numbers of Jews were sent to nearby slave labor camps, where they were starved and systematically worked to death. (See "Individuals in Society: Primo Levi," page 928.) Most victims were taken to "shower rooms," which were actually gas chambers. For fifteen to twenty minutes came the terrible screams and gasping sobs of men, women, and children choking to death on poison gas. Then, only silence. Special camp workers quickly yanked the victims' gold teeth from their jaws, and the bodies were cremated. By 1945 about 6 million Jews had been murdered.

Who was responsible for this terrible crime? Some historians lay the guilt on Hitler and the Nazi leadership, arguing that ordinary Germans had little knowledge of the extermination camps, or that those who cooperated had no alternative given the brutality of Nazi terror and totalitarian control. But in recent years many studies have revealed a much broader participation of German people in the Holocaust and popular indifference (or worse) to the Jews' fate.

In most occupied countries, local non-German officials also cooperated in the arrest and deportation of Jews. As in Germany, only a few exceptional bystanders did not turn a blind eye. Catholic and Protestant church leaders protested rarely. Thus some scholars have concluded that the key for most Germans (and most people in occupied countries) was that they felt no personal responsibility for Jews and therefore were not prepared to help them. This meant that many individuals, conditioned by Nazi racist propaganda but also influenced by peer pressure and brutalizing wartime violence, were psychologically prepared to perpetrate ever-greater crimes, from mistreatment to arrest to mass murder.

Japan's Asian Empire

The Nazis did not have a monopoly on racism and brutalizing wartime violence. The Japanese, for their part, encouraged racial hatred of Westerners, giving free rein at home to the anti-Western ultranationalism that had risen in the 1920s and 1930s (see page 900): proclaiming Japan's liberating mission in Asia, glorifying the virtues of honor and sacrifice, and demanding absolute devotion to the semidivine emperor. (See "Listening to the Past: "Ultranationalist Pamphlet for Japanese Students," page 930.)

Abroad, by late 1938, 1.5 million Japanese troops were bogged down in China, holding a great swath of territory but unable to defeat the Nationalists and the Communists (see pages 900–902). In 1939, as war broke out in Europe, the Japanese redoubled their brutal efforts in China to crush peasant support for the Nationalists and the Communists. Implementing a savage

policy of "kill all, burn all, destroy all," Japanese troops committed shocking atrocities, including the so-called Rape of Nanjing (see page 902). During Japan's war in China — the second Sino-Japanese War (1937–1945) — the Japanese are estimated to have killed 4 million Chinese people.

EVENTS LEADING TO WORLD WAR II

1919	Treaty of Versailles is signed
1921	Hitler heads National Socialist German Worker's Party (Nazis)
1922	Mussolini seizes power in Italy
1927	Stalin takes control of the Soviet Union
1929–1939	Great Depression
1931	Japan invades Manchuria
January 1933	Hitler is appointed chancellor of Germany
March 1933	Reichstag passes the Enabling Act, granting Hitler absolute dictatorial power
October 1933	Germany withdraws from the League of Nations
1935	Nuremberg Laws deprive Jews of all rights of citizenship
March 1935	Hitler announces German rearmament
October 1935	Mussolini invades Ethiopia and receives Hitler's support
March 1936	German armies move unopposed into the demilitarized Rhineland
October 1936	Rome-Berlin Axis created
1936–1939	Spanish civil war
1937	Japan invades China
March 1938	Germany annexes Austria
September 1938	Munich Conference: Britain and France agree to German seizure of the Sudetenland from Czechoslovakia
March 1939	Germany occupies the rest of Czechoslovakia; appeasement ends in Britain
August 1939	Nazi-Soviet nonaggression pact is signed
September 1, 1939	Germany invades Poland
September 3, 1939	Britain and France declare war on Germany

Listening to the Past

Ultranationalist Pamphlet for Japanese Students

In August 1941, only four months before Japan's coordinated attack on Pearl Harbor and colonial empires in Southeast Asia, Japan's Ministry of Education issued "The Way of Subjects." Required reading for high school and university students, this twenty-page pamphlet summed up the basic tenets of Japanese ultranationalism, which had become dominant in the 1930s.

As this selection suggests, ultranationalism in Japan combined a sense of mission with intense group solidarity and unquestioning devotion to a semidivine emperor. Thus Japanese expansion into Manchuria and the war in China were part of Japan's sacred calling to protect the throne and to free Asia from Western exploitation and misrule. Of course, an unknown percentage of students (and adults) did not believe that the myths of Japan's state religion were literally true. Nevertheless, they were profoundly influenced by extremist nationalism: Japanese soldiers' determination to fight to the death was a prime indicator of that influence.

66 The way of the subjects of the Emperor issues from the policy of the Emperor and is to guard and maintain the Imperial Throne coexistent with the Heavens and the Earth. This is not an abstract principle but a way of daily practices based on history. The life and activities of the nation are all attuned to the task of strengthening the foundation of the Empire. . . .

Modern history, in a nutshell, has been marked by the formation of unified nations in Europe and their contests for supremacy in the acquisition of colonies. . . . Their march into all parts of the world paved the way for their subsequent world domination politically, economically, and culturally and led them to believe that they alone were justified in their outrageous behavior. . . .

The thoughts that have formed the foundation of Western civilization since the early modern period are individualism, liberalism, materialism, and so on. These thoughts regard the strong preying on the weak as reasonable, unstintedly promote the pursuit of luxury and pleasure, encourage materialism, and stimulate competition for acquiring colonies and securing trade, thereby leading the world to a veritable hell of fighting and bloodshed [in the First World War]. . . . [Thereafter] a vigorous movement was started by Britain, France, and the United States to maintain the status quo by any means. Simultaneously, a movement aiming at social revolution through class conflict on the basis of thoroughgoing materialism like Communism also vigorously developed. On the other hand, Nazism and Fascism arose with great force. The basic principles of the totalitarianism in Germany and Italy are to remove the evils of individualism and liberalism.

That these [totalitarian] principles show great similarity to Eastern culture and spirit is a noteworthy fact that suggests the future of Western civilization and the creation of a new culture. Thus, the orientation of world history has made the collapse of the old world order a certainty. Japan has hereby initiated the construction of a new world order based on moral principles.

The Manchurian Affair [the Japanese invasion of Manchuria in 1931] was a violent outburst of Japanese national life long suppressed. Taking advantage of this, Japan in the glare of all the Powers made a step toward the creation of a world based on moral principles and the construction of a new order. This was a manifestation of the spirit, profound and lofty, embodied in the founding of Empire, and an unavoidable action for its national life and world mission. . . .

The general tendency of world domination by Europe and America has begun to show signs of a change since the Russo-Japanese War of 1904–05. Japan's victory attracted the attention of the entire world, and this caused a reawakening of Asiatic countries, which had been forced to lie prostrate under British and American influence, with the result that an independence movement was started.

Hopes to be free of the shackles and bondage of Europe and America were ablaze among the nations of India, Turkey, Arabia, Thailand, Vietnam, and others. This also inspired a

---

In August 1940 the Japanese announced the formation of a self-sufficient Asian economic zone. Although they spoke of liberating Asia from Western imperialism and of "Asia for the Asians," their true intentions were to eventually rule over a vast Japanese empire. For the moment, however, Japan still depended on imports for essential materials like oil. Thus the Japanese sought alliances that might give them better access to these essential goods and also improve their position in Asia.

Seeking support for its war in China, in September 1940 Japan signed a formal alliance with Germany and Italy, and Vichy France granted the Japanese domination over northern French Indochina — from where they could attack southern China. The United States feared that embattled Britain would collapse if it lost new national movement in China. Amid this stormy atmosphere of Asia's reawakening, Japan has come to be keenly conscious of the fact that the stabilization of East Asia is her mission, and that the emancipation of East Asian nations rests solely on her efforts. . . .

Japan has a political mission to help various regions in the Greater East Asian Co-prosperity Sphere [the Japanese term for Japan's Asian empire], which are reduced to a state of quasi-colony by Europe and America, and rescue them from their control. Economically, this country will have to eradicate the evils of their exploitation and then set up an economic structure for coexistence and co-prosperity. Culturally, Japan must strive to fashion East Asian nations to abandon their following of European and American culture and to develop Eastern culture for the purpose of contributing to the creation of a just world. The East has been left to destruction for the past several hundred years. Its rehabilitation is not an easy task. It is natural that unusual difficulties attend the establishment of a new order and the creation of a new culture. Overcoming these difficulties will do much to help in establishing a world dominated by morality, in which all nations can cooperate and all people can secure their proper positions. . . .

In Japan, the Emperors of a line unbroken for ages eternal govern and reign over it, as the Heavens and the Earth endure, since the Imperial Foundress, Amaterasu-o-Mikami, . . . caused Her grandson Ninigi-no-Mikoto to descend on the eight great countries and She commanded him, saying: "This country, fruitful and abounding in rice, is the land over which Our descendants shall rule. Go you, therefore, down and reign over it. Under you and your offspring it shall prosper as long as the Heavens and the Earth endure." . . .

The Imperial Family is [therefore] the fountain source of the Japanese nation, and national and private lives issue from this. In the past, foreign nationals came to this country only to enjoy the benevolent rule of the Imperial Family, and became Japanese subjects spiritually and by blood. The Imperial virtues are so great and boundless that all are assimilated into one. Here is the reason for the present glorious state, in which the Emperor and his subjects are harmonized into one great unit. That the myriad subjects with one mind are glad to be unified in their devotion to the Throne is the substance of the Imperial subjects.

The way of the subjects is to be loyal to the Emperor in disregard of self. . . . To serve the Emperor is its key point. Our lives will become sincere and true when they are offered to the Emperor and the state. . . . All must be unified under the Emperor. Herein lies the significance of national life in Japan.

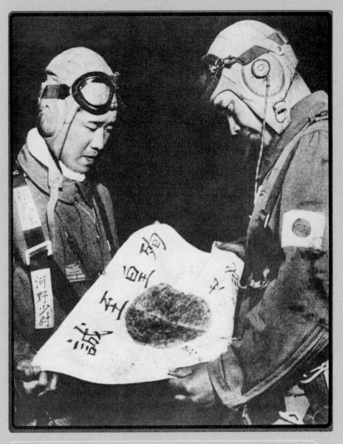

• **Kamikaze pilots ponder the message on the flag that they will take on their suicide mission: "All for the Emperor, we are happy to die for him."** (Photoservice Electa, Milan)

Source: "The Way of Subjects," in *Tokyo Record*, copyright 1943 by Otto D. Tolischus and renewed 1970 by Naya G. Tolischus. Reprinted by permission of Houghton Mifflin Harcourt Publishing Company.

QUESTIONS FOR ANALYSIS

1. How does "The Way of Subjects" interpret modern history? In what ways do Western thought and action threaten Japan?

2. What is Japan's mission in Asia?

3. What is the basis of Japanese sovereignty? What is the individual's proper role in society?

its Asian colonies to Japan. Applying economic sanctions in October 1940, the United States stopped scrap iron sales to Japan and later froze all Japanese assets in the United States.

Japan's invasion of southern Indochina in July 1941 further worsened relations with the United States, which viewed this aggression as a direct threat to the Philippines and the oil-rich Dutch East Indies. The United States responded by cutting off U.S. oil sales to Japan, thereby reducing Japan's oil supplies by 90 percent. Japanese leaders, increasingly convinced that war with the United States was inevitable, because Japan's fleet would run out of fuel in eighteen months, decided after much debate to launch a surprise attack on the U.S. fleet in Pearl Harbor in the Hawaiian Islands. They hoped to cripple their Pacific rival, gain time to build a

MAP 30.2 World War II in Europe and Africa, 1939–1945 The map shows the extent of Hitler's empire at its height, before the Battle of Stalingrad in late 1942 and the subsequent advances of the Allies until Germany surrendered on May 7, 1945.

defensible Asian empire, and eventually win an ill-defined compromise peace.

The Japanese attack at Pearl Harbor was a complete surprise but a limited success. On December 7, 1941, the Japanese sank or crippled every American battleship, but by chance all the American aircraft carriers were at sea and escaped unharmed. More important, Americans were humiliated by this unexpected defeat. Thus Pearl Harbor overwhelmed American isolationism and brought the United States into the war.

Hitler immediately declared war on the United States. Simultaneously, Japanese armies successfully attacked European and American colonies in Southeast Asia. Small but well-trained Japanese armies defeated larger Dutch and British armies to seize the Netherlands East Indies and the British colonies of Hong Kong, Malaya, and Singapore. After American forces surrendered the Philippines in May 1942, Japan held a vast empire in Southeast Asia and the western Pacific (Map 30.3).

□ Mapping the Past

MAP 30.3 World War II in the Pacific Japanese forces overran an enormous amount of territory in 1942, which the Allies slowly recaptured in a long, bitter struggle.

ANALYZING THE MAP Locate the extent of the Japanese empire in 1942, and compare it to the Japanese-controlled territory at surrender in 1945. Where was the fighting in the Pacific concentrated?

CONNECTIONS How was the course of the end of war in Europe different, and what does this suggest about the difficulties that the Allies faced in fighting the Japanese?

The Japanese claimed they were freeing Asians from Western imperialism, and they called their empire the Greater East Asian Co-Prosperity Sphere. By promising to create a mutually advantageous union for Asia's long-term development, the Japanese tapped currents of nationalist sentiment. Most local populations were glad to see the Western powers go, but Asian faith in "co-prosperity" and support for Japan steadily declined as the war went on. Although the Japanese set up anticolonial governments and promised genuine independence, real power always rested with Japanese military commanders and their superiors in Tokyo. The "independent" governments established in the Philippines, French Indochina, Burma, and the Netherlands East

The War in the Philippines U.S. and Philippine forces held out on the Bataan peninsula until April 1942, when seventy-six thousand soldiers surrendered to the Japanese military. Most of the prisoners were sick, wounded, or suffering from malnutrition, and the Japanese systematically executed many of them. Other prisoners, such as those pictured here, were marched to exhaustion without water in the blazing sun on the infamous Bataan Death March, and many were bayoneted or beaten to death. (Bettmann/Corbis)

Indies were basically shams. Moreover, the Japanese never treated local populations as equals, and the occupiers exploited local peoples for Japan's wartime needs. They cut wages, imposed supply quotas on raw materials, and drafted local people for military and labor service.

The Japanese often exhibited great cruelty toward prisoners of war and civilians. After the fall of Hong Kong in December 1941, for example, wounded prisoners were murdered, and there was a mass rape of nurses. Elsewhere Dutch, Indonesian, and perhaps as many as two hundred thousand Korean women were forced to provide sex for Japanese soldiers as "comfort women." Recurring cruel behavior aroused local populations against the invaders.

The Grand Alliance

While the Nazis and the Japanese built their empires, Great Britain, the United States (both vehemently anticommunist), and the Soviet Union (equally anticapitalist) joined together in an unlikely military pact called the Grand Alliance. Chance, rather than choice, had brought them together. Stalin had been cooperating with Hitler between August 1939 and June 1941, and only the Japanese attack on Pearl Harbor had led the United States to enter the war.

As a first step toward building an unshakable alliance, the Grand Alliance agreed on a **Europe first policy** as proposed by Winston Churchill (Chamberlain's successor as British prime minister).

Only after defeating Hitler would the Allies mount an all-out attack on Japan. To further encourage mutual trust, the Allies adopted the principle of the unconditional surrender of Germany and Japan. This policy cemented the Grand Alliance because it denied Germany and Japan any hope of dividing their foes.

The Grand Alliance's military resources were awesome. The United States possessed a unique capacity to wage global war with its large population and mighty industry, which it harnessed in 1943 to outproduce not only the Axis powers but also the rest of the world combined.[11] The British economy was totally and effectively mobilized, and the country became an important staging area for the war in Europe. As for the Soviet Union, so great was its strength that it might well have defeated Germany without Western help. In the face of the German advance, whole factories and populations were successfully evacuated to eastern Russia and Siberia. There war production was reorganized and expanded, and the Red Army was increasingly well supplied and well led. Above all, Stalin drew on the massive support of the people for what the Soviets called the "Great Patriotic War of the Fatherland."

The War in Europe, 1942–1945

Halted at the gates of Moscow and Leningrad in 1941, the Germans renewed their offensive against the Soviet Union in 1942 and attacked Stalingrad in July. The Soviet armies counterattacked, quickly surrounding the entire German Sixth Army of 300,000 men. By late

The Normandy Invasion, Omaha Beach, June 6, 1944 Airborne paratroopers landed behind German coastal fortifications around midnight, and U.S. and British forces hit several beaches at daybreak as Allied ships and bombers provided cover. U.S. troops secured full control of Omaha Beach by nightfall, but at a price of three thousand casualties. Allied air power prevented the Germans from bringing up reserves and counterattacking. (Bettmann/Corbis)

January 1943 only 123,000 soldiers were left to surrender. Hitler, who had refused to allow a retreat, suffered a catastrophic defeat. In summer 1943 the larger, better-equipped Soviet armies took the offensive and began to push the Germans back (see Map 30.2).

Not yet prepared to attack Germany directly through France, the Western Allies saw heavy fighting in North Africa (see Map 30.2). The French Vichy government allowed Germany to transport war materials and aircraft through Syria to Iraq to use against the British, and in 1941 the British had invaded Syria and Lebanon. In summer 1942 British forces defeated German and Italian armies at the Battle of El Alamein (el a-luh-MAYN) in Egypt. Shortly thereafter an Anglo-American force took control of the Vichy French colonies of Morocco and Algeria.

Having driven the Axis powers from North Africa by spring 1943, Allied forces invaded Italy. War-weary Italians deposed Mussolini, and the new Italian government accepted unconditional surrender in September 1943. Italy, it seemed, was liberated. But German commandos rescued Mussolini in a daring raid and put him at the head of a puppet government. German armies seized Rome and all of northern Italy. The allies' Italian campaign against German forces lasted

another two years and involved, in terms of infantry dead and wounded, the most costly battles of the war in western Europe. The German armies in Italy finally surrendered to the Allies on April 29, 1945. Two days earlier Mussolini — dressed in a German military uniform and trying to escape with the retreating German forces — had been captured by partisan forces. He was executed the next day.

To match the Allied war effort, Germany had applied itself to total war in 1942 and had enlisted millions of German women and millions of prisoners of war and slave laborers to work in the war industry. Between early 1942 and July 1944 German war production tripled in spite of heavy Anglo-American bombing. Terrorized at home and frightened by the prospect of unconditional surrender, the Germans fought on with suicidal stoicism.

On June 6, 1944, American and British forces under General Dwight Eisenhower landed on the beaches of Normandy, France, in history's greatest naval invasion.

• **Europe first policy** The military strategy, set forth by Churchill and adopted by Roosevelt, that called for the defeat of Hitler in Europe before the United States launched an all-out strike against Japan in the Pacific.

A Hiroshima Survivor Remembers Yasuko Yamagata was seventeen when she saw the brilliant blue-white "lightning flash" that became a fiery orange ball consuming everything that would burn. Thirty years later Yamagata painted this scene, her most unforgettable memory of the atomic attack. An incinerated woman, poised as if running with her baby clutched to her breast, lies near a water tank piled high with charred corpses. (GE15-05 drawn by Yasuko Yamagata, Hiroshima Peace Memorial Museum)

More than 2 million men and almost a half million vehicles pushed inland and broke through the German lines. In March 1945 American troops crossed the Rhine and entered Germany.

The Soviets, who had been advancing steadily since July 1943, reached the outskirts of Warsaw by August 1944. On April 25, 1945, the Red Army met American forces on the Elbe River in Germany. The Allies had closed their vise on Nazi Germany and overrun Europe. As Soviet forces fought their way into Berlin, Hitler committed suicide in his bunker, and on May 7 the remaining German commanders capitulated.

The War in the Pacific, 1942–1945

While gigantic armies clashed on land in Europe, the greatest naval battles in history decided the fate of the war in Asia. In April 1942 the Japanese devised a plan to take Port Moresby in New Guinea and also destroy U.S. aircraft carriers in an attack on Midway Island (see Map 30.3). Having broken the secret Japanese code, the Americans skillfully won a series of decisive naval victories. First, in the Battle of the Coral Sea in May 1942, an American carrier force halted the Japanese advance on Port Moresby and relieved Australia from the threat of invasion. Then, in the Battle of Midway in June 1942, American pilots sank all four of the attacking Japanese aircraft carriers and established overall naval equality with Japan in the Pacific.

Badly hampered in the ground war by the Europe first policy, the United States gradually won control of the sea and air as it geared up its war industry. By 1943 the United States was producing one hundred thousand aircraft a year, almost twice as many as Japan produced in the entire war. In July 1943 the Americans and their Australian allies opened an "island-hopping" campaign toward Japan. Pounding Japanese forces on a given island with saturation bombing, Allied units would then hit the beaches and secure victory in vicious hand-to-hand combat. By 1944 hundreds of American submarines were hunting in "wolf packs," decimating shipping and destroying economic links in Japan's far-flung, overextended empire.

The Pacific war was brutal—a "war without mercy"—and atrocities were committed on both sides.[12] Aware of Japanese atrocities in China and the Philippines, the U.S. Marines and Army troops seldom took Japanese prisoners after the Battle of Guadalcanal in August 1942, killing even those rare Japanese soldiers who offered to surrender. American forces moving across the central and western Pacific in 1943 and 1944 faced unyielding resistance, and this resistance hardened soldiers as American casualties kept rising. A product of spiraling violence, mutual hatred, and dehumanizing racial stereotypes, the war without mercy intensified as it moved toward Japan.

In June 1944 U.S. bombers began a relentless bombing campaign of the Japanese home islands. In October 1944 American forces under General Douglas MacArthur landed on Leyte Island in the Philippines. The Japanese believed they could destroy MacArthur's troops and transport ships before the main American fleet arrived. The result was the four-day Battle of Leyte Gulf, the greatest battle in naval history, with 282 ships involved. The Japanese lost 13 large warships, including 4 aircraft carriers, while the Americans lost only 3 small ships. The Japanese navy was practically finished.

In spite of massive defeats, Japanese troops continued to fight with courage and determination. Indeed, the bloodiest battles of the Pacific war took place on Iwo Jima in February 1945 and on Okinawa in June 1945. American commanders believed that the conquest of Japan might cost a million American casualties and possibly 10 to 20 million Japanese lives. In fact, Japan was almost helpless, its industry and cities largely destroyed by intense American bombing. Yet the Japanese seemed determined to fight on, ready to die for a hopeless cause.

On August 6 and 9, 1945, the United States dropped atomic bombs on Hiroshima and Nagasaki in Japan. Mass bombing of cities and civilians, one of the terrible new practices of World War II, had led to the final nightmare—unprecedented human destruction in a single blinding flash. On August 14, 1945, the Japanese announced their surrender. The Second World War, which had claimed the lives of more than 50 million soldiers and civilians, was over.

CONNECTIONS

If anyone still doubted the interconnectedness of all the world's inhabitants following the Great War, those doubts faded as events on a truly global scale touched everyone as never before in the 1930s and 1940s. First a Great Depression shook the financial foundations of the wealthiest capitalist economies and the poorest producers of raw materials and minerals. Another world war followed, bringing global death and destruction at a magnitude beyond the imaginations of even Great War survivors. At war's end, as we shall see in Chapter 34, the world's leaders revived Woodrow Wilson's idea of a League of Nations and formed the United Nations in 1946 to prevent such tragedies from ever reoccurring.

Although the United Nations was an attempt to bring nations together, the postwar world became more divided than ever. Chapter 31 will describe how two new superpowers—the United States and the Soviet Union—emerged from World War II to engage one another in the Cold War for nearly the rest of the century. Then in Chapters 32 and 33 we will see how a political Third World of nations in Asia, Africa, and Latin America emerged after the war. Many of them did so by turning the nineteenth-century European ideology of nationalism against its creators, breaking the bonds of colonialism.

Today we want to believe that the era of totalitarian dictatorship was a terrible accident, that Stalin's slave labor camps, Hitler's gas chambers, and Japan's Rape of Nanjing "can't happen again." But the cruel truth is that horrible atrocities continue to plague the world in our time. The Khmer Rouge inflicted genocide on its people in Cambodia, and civil war led to ethnically motivated atrocities in Bosnia, Rwanda, Burundi, and Sudan, recalling the horrors of the Second World War. Today's dictators, however, are losing control over access to information—historically a cornerstone of dictatorial rule—and are being challenged and even overthrown by citizens with cell phones, cameras, and Internet connections. In 2010 and 2011 ruthless dictatorial regimes in Egypt, Tunisia, Syria, Yemen, Libya, Iran, and elsewhere have found it much harder to brutally impose their will over their people when opponents have the ability to instantly expose their murderous actions to the world.

☐ CHAPTER REVIEW

☐ What caused the Great Depression, and what were its consequences? (p. 908)

The 1929 stock market crash in the United States resulted in a financial panic and run on banks, which in turn triggered a collapse of the international economy. The Great Depression shattered the fragile stability briefly achieved after World War I. As production declined, unemployment affected millions worldwide. Countries turned inward as they sought to cope with massive domestic problems and widespread disillusionment. Western democracies responded with relief programs, many modeled after the U.S. New Deal

KEY TERMS

New Deal (p. 910)
Popular Front (p. 912)
totalitarianism
  (p. 914)
fascism (p. 914)
five-year plan (p. 915)
New Economic Policy
  (NEP) (p. 915)
collectivization
  (p. 916)

Black Shirts (p. 918)
Lateran Agreement
  (p. 919)
Nazism (p. 920)
Enabling Act (p. 922)
blitzkrieg (p. 926)
New Order (p. 926)
Holocaust (p. 927)
Europe first policy
  (p. 934)

program, but success was generally limited. In Asia, Japan's financial woes led to aggressive empire building, as the military leadership looked for colonies that would help supply the resource-poor islands of Japan. The old liberal ideals of individual rights and responsibilities, elected government, and economic freedom, even when they managed to survive, seemed ineffective and outmoded to many, setting the stage for the rise of authoritarian and fascist regimes. In the end, only World War II would end the depression.

□ What was the nature of the new totalitarian dictatorships, and how did they differ from conservative authoritarian states? (p. 913)

The effects of the Great Depression, the lack of a democratic tradition, and unrest and ethnic strife led many of the budding democracies of Europe to return to traditional conservative authoritarianism. A new kind of radical dictatorship also formed in the 1920s and 1930s — specifically in Germany and the Soviet Union, and to a lesser extent in Italy, Spain, Japan, and Portugal. Like conservative authoritarian regimes, all were repressive and profoundly antiliberal. But totalitarian regimes were also exceedingly violent, asserted a total claim on the lives of their citizens, posed ambitious goals, and demanded popular support. Stalin's Russia and Hitler's Germany, in particular, exuded tremendous dynamism and awesome power. That dynamism, however, was channeled in quite different directions. Stalin and the Communist Party aimed at building their kind of socialism and the new socialist personality at home. Hitler and the Fascist Nazi elite aimed at unlimited territorial and racial aggression on behalf of a "master race"; domestic control of state and society was only a means to that end.

□ How did Stalin and the Communist Party build a totalitarian order in the Soviet Union? (p. 915)

After consolidating his power in the 1920s, Stalin launched the first of his five-year plans in 1928. These plans were a critical part of Stalin's efforts to totally control the Russian economy and society. Meant to introduce a "revolution from above," they were extremely ambitious efforts to modernize and industrialize the U.S.S.R. along socialist lines and to create a new socialist society. They set staggering industrial and agricultural objectives and replaced private lands with (often forced) collectivization. Labor unions were severely weakened, and foreign experts from Europe and America were brought in to lend their skill and expertise to the building of new factories and machinery in order to catch up with the more advanced capitalist nations of the West. In the 1930s Stalin implemented mass purges of the Communist Party, leading to the imprisonment and deaths of mil-

lions. In this way Stalin was able to staff the ranks of the Communist Party with young loyalists.

□ How did Italian fascism develop? (p. 918)

Mussolini's hatred of liberalism led him to set up the first Fascist government. Mussolini created a one-party dictatorship by abolishing press freedoms, disbanding independent trade unions, rigging elections, and ruling by decree. Mussolini allowed the old conservative classes to retain control of the economy, the army, and the state bureaucracy. He gained the support of the Roman Catholic Church by recognizing the Vatican as a tiny independent state in 1929. Racial laws were never a very significant aspect of Mussolini's rule, as they were for Hitler, and Jews were not severely persecuted until Italy came under Nazi control toward the end of World War II. Though repressive and undemocratic, Mussolini never destroyed the old power structure and allowed big business to regulate itself. Although brutal in its methods, Mussolini's regime was never truly a totalitarian state on the order of Hitler's Germany or Stalin's Soviet Union, which sought to control all aspects of society.

□ Why were Hitler and his Nazi regime initially so popular, and how did their actions lead to World War II? (p. 919)

Hitler and the Nazi Party drew on the humiliation of World War I and the terms of the Versailles treaty to rally support. He used this discontent to disseminate his racist sentiments about "inferior" peoples and to prey on fears of a Jewish conspiracy to harm German culture, German unity, and the German race. When the Great Depression struck, Hitler appealed to people's economic insecurity, making promises that caused voters to desert the old leaders and turn to this dynamic new voice. Popular support for Hitler's regime was initially very high, abetted by relentless propaganda, a steep drop in unemployment, and a rise in business profits and the standard of living. Hitler initially tried to camouflage his plans for aggressive territorial expansion. After he declared the Versailles treaty disarmament clause null and void, British and French leaders tried to use a policy of appeasement. On September 1, 1939, his unprovoked attack on Poland left no doubt about his intentions, and the British and French declared war, starting World War II.

How did Germany and Japan build empires in Europe and Asia, and how did the Allies defeat them? (p. 926)

Nazi armies used blitzkrieg tactics to quickly seize Poland and Germany's Western neighbors. Hitler then shifted his attention to the east, where he planned to build a New Order based on racial imperialism. The result was the Holocaust, in which millions of Jews and other "undesirables" were systematically exterminated. The Japanese also used aggressive territorial expansion to create what they called the Greater East Asian Co-Prosperity Sphere in the Pacific. As the colonies liberated from Western control soon learned, this was a sham, and "Asia for the Asians" meant nothing more than Japanese domination and brutal control. After Japan attacked Pearl Harbor, the United States entered the war. The Grand Alliance of the United States, Britain, and the Soviet Union harnessed the committed populations of these countries and, in the case of the Soviet Union and the United States, their superior war industry to outproduce and outman the overextended and far-flung empires of Japan and Germany.

SUGGESTED READING

Applebaum, Anne. *Gulag*. 2004. An excellent survey of Stalin's labor camps.

Brendon, Piers. *The Dark Valley: A Panorama of the 1930s*. 2002. Masterful, sweeping account of this tumultuous decade.

Brooker, Paul. *Twentieth Century Dictatorships: The Ideological One-Party State*. 1995. A comparative analysis.

Crowe, David M. *The Holocaust: Roots, History and Aftermath*. 2008. Analyzes the origins and ghastly implementation of Nazi racial politics.

Fitzpatrick, Sheila. *Everyday Stalinism: Ordinary Life in Extraordinary Times*. 1999. Social and cultural history.

Geyer, Michael, and Sheila Fitzpatrick. *Beyond Totalitarianism: Nazism and Stalinism Compared*. 2008. Comparative studies of the two dictatorships based on archival sources that have only recently become available to historians.

Gilbert, Martin. *The Second World War: A Complete History*, rev. ed. 2004. Massively detailed global survey.

Glantz, David M. *When Titans Clashed: How the Red Army Stopped Hitler*. 1995. Authoritative account of the eastern front in World War II.

Hasegawa, Tsuyoshi. *Racing the Enemy: Stalin, Truman and the Surrender of Japan*. 2005. Masterful diplomatic history with a controversial new account of the end of the war.

Hillberg, Raul. *The Destruction of the European Jews, 1933–1945*, rev. ed. 3 vols. 1985. A monumental classic.

Keegan, John. *The Second World War*. 1990. Broad survey by a distinguished military historian.

Kindleberger, Charles P. *The World in Depression, 1929–1939*. 1986. Perhaps the best analytical account of the global origins, events, and aftermath of the Great Depression.

Levi, Primo. *Survival at Auschwitz*. 1947. First published in English as *If This Is a Man*; a memoir and meditation on the meaning of survival.

Weinberg, Gerhard. *World at Arms: A Global History of World War II*. 1994. Global survey with a political-diplomatic emphasis.

Wright, Gordon. *The Ordeal of Total War*, rev. ed. 1997. Explores the scientific, psychological, and economic dimensions of the war.

NOTES

1. Quoted in S. B. Clough et al., eds., *Economic History of Europe: Twentieth Century* (New York: Harper & Row, 1968), pp. 243–245.
2. E. Halévy, *The Era of Tyrannies* (Garden City, N.Y.: Doubleday, 1965), pp. 265–316, esp. p. 300.
3. I. Kershaw, *The Nazi Dictatorship: Problems and Perspectives of Interpretation*, 2d ed. (London: Edward Arnold, 1989), p. 34.
4. Quoted in A. G. Mazour, *Soviet Economic Development: Operation Outstrip, 1921–1965* (Princeton, N.J.: Van Nostrand, 1967), p. 130.
5. Quoted in I. Deutscher, *Stalin: A Political Biography*, 2d ed. (New York: Oxford University Press, 1967), p. 325.
6. M. Malia, *The Soviet Tragedy: A History of Socialism in Russia, 1917–1991* (New York: Free Press, 1995), pp. 227–270.
7. R. Vivarelli, "Interpretations on the Origins of Fascism," *Journal of Modern History* 63 (March 1991): 41.
8. W. Brustein, *The Logic of Evil: The Social Origins of the Nazi Party, 1925–1933* (New Haven, Conn.: Yale University Press, 1996), pp. 52, 182.
9. Quoted in R. Stromberg, *An Intellectual History of Modern Europe* (New York: Appleton-Century-Crofts, 1966), p. 393.
10. Quoted in R. Moeller, *The Nazi State and German Society: A Brief History with Documents* (Boston: Bedford/St. Martin's, 2010), p. 108.
11. H. Willmott, *The Great Crusade: A New Complete History of the Second World War* (New York: Free Press, 1989), p. 255.
12. J. Dower, *War Without Mercy: Race and Power in the Pacific War* (New York: Pantheon, 1986).

For practice quizzes and other study tools, visit the **Online Study Guide** at bedfordstmartins.com/mckayworld.

For primary sources from this period, see *Sources of World Societies*, **Second Edition**.

For Web sites, images, and documents related to topics in this chapter, visit **Make History** at bedfordstmartins.com/mckayworld.

• Soviet Worker Statue An idealized, heroic Soviet worker leans forward into the new Soviet age in this example of socialist realism, an artistic style that promoted socialism and communism. Socialist realism was the only acceptable artistic style in the Soviet Union for over sixty years, as Soviet leaders condemned the art of the West as decadent and bourgeois. Statues like this one were propaganda tools glorifying the achievements of the Soviet state. (© Eduard Talaykov)

After the defeat of the Axis powers in Europe and Asia, recovery from this most devastating war began worldwide. Hopes of world peace quickly faded, however, when differences in Allied economic and political ideologies set aside during wartime came to the fore, pitting the democratic and capitalist countries of the United States and its allies, including Japan, against the Marxist Communist Soviet Union and its allies.

Despite the growing tensions of this global Cold War, the postwar decades witnessed remarkable growth and economic prosperity. A battered western Europe once again dug itself out from under the rubble of war and, with U.S. aid, witnessed an amazing recovery. Having avoided wartime destruction and occupation, the United States quickly converted its economies to peacetime production. After seven years of Allied occupation, Japan experienced a quick recovery that by the 1960s made it one of the world's leading economic powers. In the east, the Soviet Union sought to protect itself from future attacks from the west by occupying eastern Europe and establishing Communist dictatorships there.

Global Recovery and Division Between Superpowers
1945 to the Present

In the early 1970s the global economic boom came to an end, and domestic political stability and social harmony evaporated. The spectacular collapse of communism in eastern Europe in 1989 and the end of the Cold War reinforced global integration. The result was monumental change, especially in postcommunist eastern Europe. A similar though less dramatic transformation also occurred in the nations of western Europe as they moved toward greater unity within the European Union. •

The Division of Europe
☐ What were the causes of the Cold War?

Renaissance and Crisis in Western Europe
☐ How did western Europe recover so successfully after World War II, and how did economic decline in the 1970s and 1980s affect society?

Recovery and Reform in Soviet Eastern Europe, 1945–1991
☐ How did the Soviets try to reform society, and what were the consequences of the anticommunist revolutions of 1989?

The United States: Confrontation and Transformation
☐ What contributed to the social and political transformation of the United States in the second half of the twentieth century?

Japan's Resurgence as a World Power
☐ How did Japan recover so quickly after its total defeat in World War II to become an economic superpower?

The Post–Cold War Era in Europe
☐ What was the nature of postcommunist reconstruction in eastern Europe, and how did Europe as a whole respond to calls for increased unity?

The Division of Europe

☐ What were the causes of the Cold War?

In 1945 triumphant American and Russian soldiers embraced along the Elbe River in the heart of vanquished Germany. At home the soldiers' loved ones erupted in joyous celebration. Yet victory was flawed. The Allies could not cooperate politically in peacemaking. The United States and the Soviet Union soon found themselves at loggerheads. By the end of 1947 Europe was rigidly divided, West versus East, in a Cold War eventually waged around the world.

The Origins of the Cold War

Almost as soon as the unifying threat of Nazi Germany disappeared, the Soviet Union and the United States began to quarrel. Hostility between the Eastern and Western superpowers was the logical outgrowth of military developments, wartime agreements, and long-standing political and ideological differences dating back to World War I.

In the early phases of the Second World War, the Americans and the British made military victory their highest priority. They avoided discussion of Joseph Stalin's war aims and the shape of the eventual peace

The Big Three In 1945 a triumphant Winston Churchill, an ailing Franklin Roosevelt, and a determined Joseph Stalin met at Yalta in southern Russia to plan for peace. Cooperation soon gave way to bitter hostility. (F.D.R. Library)

Postwar Territorial Changes in Eastern Europe

Lost by Germany

Gained by Soviet Union

settlement, fearing that hard bargaining might encourage Stalin to make a separate peace with Hitler. By late 1943 decisions about the shape of the postwar world could no longer be postponed. Franklin Roosevelt, Winston Churchill, and Joseph Stalin met in Teheran, Iran, in November 1943, and there the "Big Three" reaffirmed their determination to crush Germany. Churchill argued that American and British forces should attack Germany's "soft underbelly" through the Balkans. Roosevelt, however, agreed with Stalin that a joint American-British frontal assault through France would be better. Soviet, rather than American and British, armies would then liberate eastern Europe.

When the Big Three met again in February 1945 at Yalta on the Black Sea in southern Russia, the Red Army occupied most of eastern Europe and was within a hundred miles of Berlin. American-British forces had yet to cross the Rhine into Germany. Moreover, the United States was far from defeating Japan. In short, the Soviet Union's position was strong and America's was weak. At Yalta the Big Three agreed that Germany would be divided into zones of occupation and would pay the Soviet Union heavy reparations. Stalin agreed to declare war on Japan after Germany's defeat. As for Poland and eastern Europe, the Big Three reached an ambiguous compromise: eastern European governments were to be freely elected but pro-Russian.

Almost immediately this compromise broke down. Even before the conference, Communists arriving home with the Red Army controlled Bulgaria and Poland. Elsewhere in eastern Europe, pro-Soviet "coalition" governments were formed, but key ministerial posts were reserved for Moscow-trained Communists.

At the postwar Potsdam Conference in July 1945, long-avoided differences over eastern Europe were finally debated. The compromising Roosevelt had died

MAP 31.1 Cold War Europe in the 1950s Europe was divided by an "iron curtain" during the Cold War. None of the Communist countries of eastern Europe were participants in the Marshall Plan.

and had been succeeded by the more assertive Harry Truman (1884–1972), who now demanded free elections throughout eastern Europe. Stalin refused point-blank. "A freely elected government in any of these East European countries would be anti-Soviet," he admitted simply, "and that we cannot allow."[1]

Stalin, who had lived through two enormously destructive German invasions, wanted absolute military security from Germany and its potential eastern European allies once and for all. He believed that only Communist states could be truly dependable allies. By the middle of 1945 the United States had no way to determine political developments in eastern Europe short of war, and war was out of the question. Stalin would have his way.

West Versus East

America's response to Stalin's conception of security was to "get tough." In May 1945 Truman abruptly cut off all aid to the Soviet Union. In October he declared that the United States would never recognize any government established by force against the free will of its

> " A freely elected government in any of these East European countries would be anti-Soviet, and that we cannot allow. "
>
> **JOSEPH STALIN**

people. His declaration, however, applied only to Europe and to countries threatened by communism, not to British and French colonies in Asia and Africa, for example, or to Latin American right-wing dictatorships. America's failure to support Third World anticolonial, or liberation, movements would have tragic consequences later on, particularly in Vietnam. In March 1946 former British prime minister Churchill ominously informed an American audience that an "iron curtain" had fallen across the European continent, dividing Germany and all of Europe into two antagonistic camps (Map 31.1). (See "Viewpoints: The Cold War Begins," page 945.)

Stalin's agents quickly renewed the "ideological struggle against capitalist imperialism." France's and Italy's large, well-organized Communist Parties challenged their own governments with violent criticism and large strikes. The Soviet Union also put pressure on Iran, Turkey, and Greece, and a bitter civil war raged in China (see pages 978–979). By spring 1947 many Americans believed that Stalin was determined to export communism throughout Europe and around the world.

Viewpoints

The Cold War Begins

• On March 5, 1946, former British prime minister Winston Churchill delivered his famous "Sinews of Peace" speech to more than forty thousand people at Westminster College in the small town of Fulton, Missouri. Giving the speech the better known name of the "iron curtain" speech, Churchill for the first time used this famous phrase that soon became ubiquitous throughout the world to describe Russia's iron grip on eastern Europe.

A year later, on March 12, 1947, President Harry S. Truman addressed a joint session of the United States Congress to express his concern over the Soviet occupation of eastern Europe and the threat that communism posed to other countries in Europe, particularly Greece and Turkey. In his speech Truman set forth a new doctrine for American foreign policy, moving from a policy of "détente," or friendship with the Soviet Union, to a policy that aimed to directly confront and contain communism.

Winston Churchill, "Sinews of Peace" Speech, March 5, 1946

A shadow has fallen upon the scenes so lately lighted by the Allied victory. Nobody knows what Soviet Russia and its Communist international organization intends to do in the immediate future, or what are the limits, if any, to their expansive and proselytizing tendencies. . . . We welcome Russia to her rightful place among the leading nations of the world. . . . It is my duty however, . . . to place before you certain facts about the present position in Europe.

From Stettin in the Baltic to Trieste in the Adriatic an iron curtain has descended across the Continent. Behind that line lie all the capitals of the ancient states of Central and Eastern Europe. Warsaw, Berlin, Prague, Vienna, Budapest, Belgrade, Bucharest and Sofia, all these famous cities and the populations around them lie in what I must call the Soviet sphere, and all are subject in one form or another, not only to Soviet influence but to a very high and, in some cases, increasing measure of control from Moscow. Athens alone—Greece with its immortal glories—is free to decide its future at an election under British, American and French observation. The Russian-dominated Polish Government has been encouraged to make enormous and wrongful inroads upon Germany, and mass expulsions of millions of Germans on a scale grievous and undreamed-of are now taking place. The Communist parties, which were very small in all these Eastern States of Europe, have been raised to pre-eminence and power far beyond their numbers and are seeking everywhere to obtain totalitarian control. Police governments are prevailing in nearly every case, and so far, except in Czechoslovakia, there is no true democracy.

President Harry S. Truman, Speech to Congress, March 12, 1947

At the present moment in world history nearly every nation must choose between alternative ways of life. The choice is too often not a free one.

One way of life is based upon the will of the majority, and is distinguished by free institutions, representative government, free elections, guarantees of individual liberty, freedom of speech and religion, and freedom from political oppression.

The second way of life is based upon the will of a minority forcibly imposed upon the majority. It relies upon terror and oppression, a controlled press and radio; fixed elections, and the suppression of personal freedoms.

I believe that it must be the policy of the United States to support free peoples who are resisting attempted subjugation by armed minorities or by outside pressures.

I believe that we must assist free peoples to work out their own destinies in their own way.

I believe that our help should be primarily through economic and financial aid, which is essential to economic stability and orderly political processes.

The world is not static, and the status quo is not sacred. But we cannot allow changes in the status quo in violation of the Charter of the United Nations by such methods as coercion, or by such subterfuges as political infiltration. . . .

The seeds of totalitarian regimes are nurtured by misery and want. They spread and grow in the evil soil of poverty and strife. They reach their full growth when the hope of a people for a better life has died. We must keep that hope alive.

The free peoples of the world look to us for support in maintaining their freedoms.

If we falter in our leadership, we may endanger the peace of the world—and we shall surely endanger the welfare of our own nation.

Sources: Winston Churchill, "Sinews of Peace" (the Iron Curtain Speech), delivered at Westminster College in Fulton, Missouri, March 5, 1946, in Robert Rhodes James, ed., *Winston S. Churchill: His Complete Speeches, 1897–1963*. Vol. VII: *1943–1949*. Reprinted with permission of Curtis Brown Ltd.; Henry Steele Commager and Milton Cantor, *Documents of American History*. Vol. II: *Since 1898*, 10th ed. (Englewood Cliffs, N.J.: Prentice Hall, 1988), pp. 527–528.

QUESTIONS FOR ANALYSIS

1. What does "shadow" refer to in the excerpt from Churchill's speech?
2. How do Churchill's speech and Truman's speech—considered by some scholars to be the opening salvos in the Cold War—use language to persuade their audiences of the Soviet threat? What democratic ideals do they call upon?
3. When Truman proposed to "support free peoples who are resisting subjugation," did he also include peoples living under colonial regimes at the time? What does this suggest about U.S. foreign policy?

The United States responded with the **Truman Doctrine**, aimed at "containing" communism to areas already occupied by the Red Army. Truman told Congress in 1947, "I believe it must be the policy of the United States to support free people who are resisting attempted subjugation by armed minorities or by outside pressure." Truman asked Congress for military aid for Greece and Turkey. Then, in June, Secretary of State George C. Marshall offered Europe economic aid — the **Marshall Plan** — to help it rebuild. Stalin refused Marshall Plan assistance for all of eastern Europe, where he had established Soviet-style Communist dictatorships. The Soviet Union's aid and support for the overthrow of the democratically elected Czechoslovakian government in February 1948 and its replacement by a Communist government shocked the U.S. Congress into action, and on April 2, 1948, it voted for the Marshall Plan.

On July 24, 1948, Stalin blocked all highway traffic through the Soviet zone of Germany to Berlin. The Western allies responded by flying hundreds of planes over the Soviet roadblocks to supply provisions to the West Berliners. After 324 days the Soviets backed down: containment seemed to work. In 1949 the United States formed an anti-Soviet military alliance of Western governments: the North Atlantic Treaty Organization (**NATO**). Stalin countered by tightening his hold on his satellites, later united in the Warsaw Pact. Europe was divided into two hostile blocs.

As tensions rose in Europe, the Cold War spread to Asia. In 1945 Korea, like Germany, was divided into Soviet and American zones of occupation, which in 1948 became Communist North Korea and anticommunist South Korea. In late 1949 the Communists triumphed in China (see page 979), frightening many Americans, who saw new evidence of a powerful worldwide Communist conspiracy. When the Russian-backed Communist forces of North Korea invaded South Korea in spring 1950, Truman sent U.S. troops to lead a twenty-nation UN coalition force.

The Korean War (1950–1953) was bitterly fought. The well-equipped North Koreans conquered most of the peninsula, but the South Korean, American, and UN troops rallied and drove their foes north to the Chinese border. At that point China intervened and pushed the South Koreans and Americans back south. In 1953 a fragile truce was negotiated, and the fighting stopped. Thus the United States extended its policy of containing communism to Asia, but drew back from invading Communist China and possible nuclear war.

The Korean War, 1950–1953

CHINA

Chosin Reservoir

Yalu R.

Farthest UN advance Nov. 1950

SOVIET UNION

NORTH KOREA

Pyongyang

Sea of Japan

Demilitarized zone 1953

38th Parallel

Seoul

Inchon landing Sept. 15, 1950

Yellow Sea

SOUTH KOREA

UN defensive line Sept. 1950

Pusan

JAPAN

→ North Korean invasion, June–Sept. 1950

→ UN offensive, Sept.–Nov. 1950

→ Communist Chinese offensive, Nov. 1950–Jan. 1951

Renaissance and Crisis in Western Europe

☐ How did western Europe recover so successfully after World War II, and how did economic decline in the 1970s and 1980s affect society?

As the Cold War divided Europe into two blocs, the future appeared bleak. Yet western Europe recovered to enjoy unprecedented economic prosperity and peaceful social transformation. Then, in the early 1970s, the cycle turned abruptly, and a downturn in the world economy hit western Europe hard.

The Postwar Challenge

After the war, economic conditions in western Europe were terrible. Runaway inflation and black markets testified to severe shortages and hardships. Many questioned whether Europe would ever recover.

Suffering was most intense in defeated Germany. The major territorial change of the war had moved the Soviet Union's border far to the west. Poland was in turn compensated for this loss to the Soviets with land taken from Germany. Thirteen million people were driven from their homes in eastern Europe and forced to resettle in a greatly reduced Germany. By spring 1947 Germany verged on total collapse and threatened to drag down the rest of Europe.

Yet western Europe began to recover. Progressive Catholics and their Christian Democrat political parties were particularly influential. In Italy Alcide De Gasperi (1881–1954) and in Germany Konrad Adenauer (1876–1967) took power, rejecting the fascism of their predecessors and placing their faith in democracy and cooperation. Socialists and Communists active in the resistance against Hitler emerged from the war with increased power and prestige, especially in France and Italy. In the immediate postwar years welfare measures such as family allowances, health insurance, and increased public housing were enacted throughout much of Europe. Social reform complemented political transformation, creating solid foundations for a great European renaissance.

There were many reasons for this amazing recovery. The United States sped the process through the

Greek Guest Workers in Germany
Thousands of Greeks immigrated to Germany after the signing of a guest worker (*Gastarbeiter*) agreement between Greece and Germany in 1961. In the 1950s and 1960s the Greek government encouraged workers, such as these Greek women working in a bottling factory in Hamburg in 1963, to emigrate because of a weak economy and high unemployment. Unlike some guest workers from countries in North Africa and the Middle East, the Greeks have generally integrated smoothly into German society. An estimated 350,000 Greeks were living in Germany in 2011. (Bildarchiv Preussischer Kulturbesitz/Art Resource, NY)

Marshall Plan, and as aid poured in, western Europe's battered economies began to turn the corner. Europe entered a period of unprecedented economic progress lasting into the late 1960s.

Western European governments also adopted a variety of successful economic and social strategies. Postwar West Germany adopted a free-market economy while maintaining the extensive social welfare network inherited from the Hitler era. The French established a new kind of planning commission that set ambitious but flexible goals for the French economy, using the nationalized banks to funnel money into key industries.

European workers also contributed to the economic turnaround. They worked hard for low wages in hope of a better future. During the Great Depression few Europeans had been able to afford many of the new consumer products. Thus in 1945 the electric refrigerator, the washing machine, and the automobile were rare luxuries, and there was great potential demand, which manufacturers moved to satisfy.

Migrant laborers from the Mediterranean basin (southern Italy, North Africa, Turkey, Greece, and Yugoslavia) also played a key role in Europe's postwar recovery. They accepted the least desirable jobs for the lowest pay. Europeans assumed that rising birthrates among the majority population would eventually fill the labor shortages, so at first they labeled the migrants "guest workers" to signal their temporary status. By the 1980s, however, as millions more migrants arrived from Europe's former colonies, it was clear that their presence would be permanent. Their full integration into European society has been incomplete, creating a backlash against them by the majority populations and a simmering anger within the immigrant communities at what seems to be their second-class citizenship.

Finally, western European nations abandoned protectionism and gradually created a large, unified market. This historic action, which stimulated the economy, was part of a larger search for European unity.

Building Europe and Decolonization

Western Europe's political recovery in the generation after 1945 was unprecedented. Democratic governments took root throughout western Europe and thrived in an atmosphere of civil liberties and individual freedom. The changes in Germany were especially profound. Konrad Adenauer, the first chancellor of postwar West Germany, was largely responsible for West Germany's remarkable recovery from near total devastation in World War II to its becoming the leading economic power in Europe. A fierce opponent of communism, Adenauer brought Germany firmly into the Western capitalist camp by developing close ties with the United States and restoring relations with Great Britain and France. Under his direction, Germany became a leading member of NATO and fully supported efforts at European unity. He also initiated dialogues

- **Truman Doctrine** U.S. policy to contain communism to areas already occupied by the Red Army.
- **Marshall Plan** American plan for providing economic aid to Europe to help it rebuild.
- **NATO** The North Atlantic Treaty Organization, an anti-Soviet military alliance of Western nations.

with important figures in Europe's Jewish community and with Israel to bring about a reconciliation of the Jewish and German peoples following the Holocaust.

A similarly extraordinary achievement was the march toward a united Europe. Many Europeans believed that only unity could forestall future European conflicts and that only a new "European nation" could reassert western Europe's influence in world affairs dominated by the United States and the Soviet Union.

The experience of close cooperation among European states for Marshall Plan aid led European federalists to turn toward economics as a way of attaining genuine unity. On May 9, 1950 (now celebrated as Europe Day), French foreign minister Robert Schuman proposed an international organization to control and integrate all European steel and coal production. France, West Germany, Italy, Belgium, the Netherlands, and Luxembourg joined together in 1952. In 1957 the six nations of the Coal and Steel Community signed the Treaty of Rome, creating the European Economic Community, popularly known as the **Common Market**. A Frenchman, Jean Monnet, was the chief architect of this plan, and he is generally recognized as the Founding Father of European unity. The treaty's primary goal was a gradual reduction of all tariffs among the six in order to create a single market almost as large as that of the United States.

The Common Market was a great success, encouraging hopes of rapid progress toward political as well as economic union. In the 1960s, however, a resurgence of more traditional nationalism in France led by Charles de Gaulle, French president from 1958 to 1969, frustrated these hopes. Viewing the United States as the main threat to genuine French (and European) independence, he withdrew all French military forces from NATO, developed France's own nuclear weapons, and refused to permit majority rule within the Common Market. De Gaulle also thwarted efforts by Denmark, Ireland, Norway, and the United Kingdom to join the Common Market. (All but Norway were finally admitted in 1973 after Georges Pompidou succeeded de Gaulle as French president.) Thus, throughout the 1960s the Common Market thrived economically but remained a union of sovereign states.

As Europe moved toward greater economic unity in the postwar era, its centuries-long overseas expansion was dramatically reversed. Between 1945 and the early 1960s almost every colonial territory gained formal independence. This rolling back of Western expansion — decolonization — marks one of world history's great turning points. The basic cause of imperial collapse was the rising demand by Asian and African peoples for national self-determination and racial equality (see Chapters 32 and 33).

European empires had been sustained by an enormous imbalance of power between the rulers and the ruled. By 1945 that imbalance had almost vanished. Most Europeans viewed their empires after 1945 very differently than they had before 1914. Empires had rested on self-confidence and self-righteousness. The horrors of the Second World War destroyed such complacent arrogance and gave imperialism's opponents much greater influence in Europe. After 1945 many Europeans were willing to let go of their colonies more or less voluntarily and to concentrate on rebuilding at home.

European political and business leaders still wanted some ties with the former colonies, however. As a result, western European countries increased their economic and cultural ties with their former African colonies in the 1960s and 1970s. This situation led many Third World leaders and scholars to charge that western Europe and the United States had imposed a system of neocolonialism designed to perpetuate Western economic domination and undermine political independence, just as the United States had subordinated the new nations of Latin America in the nineteenth century (see pages 819–821).

The Changing Class Structure and Social Reform

A more mobile and more democratic European society developed after World War II as old class barriers relaxed. Most noticeably, the structure of the middle class changed. In the nineteenth and early twentieth centuries members of the middle class were generally independent, self-employed property owners who ran businesses or practiced professions such as law or medicine. After 1945 a new breed of managers and experts required by large corporations and government agencies replaced traditional property owners as leaders of the middle class. Members of this new middle class could give their children access to advanced education, but only rarely could they pass on the positions they had attained. Thus the new middle class, based largely on specialized skills and high levels of education, was more open, democratic, and insecure than the old propertied middle class.

The structure of the lower classes also became more flexible and open. There was a mass exodus from farms and the countryside. Meanwhile, the industrial working class ceased to expand, but job opportunities for white-collar and service employees grew rapidly. Such employees bore a greater resemblance to the new middle class of salaried specialists than to industrial workers, who were also better educated and more specialized.

• **Common Market** The European Economic Community created in 1957.

• **OPEC** The Arab-led organization of countries that export oil that helps set policies and prices on its trade.

□ Picturing the Past

Cover of *John Bull Magazine*, January 1957 Like the *Saturday Evening Post* in America, *John Bull* portrayed English life through images and stories. This cover, published twelve years after the end of World War II, shows an English household that has fully recovered from the war, with the husband coming home to two beautiful children and a lovely wife in a modern and stylish kitchen. (Private Collection/The Advertising Archives/The Bridgeman Art Library)

ANALYZING THE IMAGE What are the members of this family doing? What clothes are they wearing, and what might this suggest about their roles within the family?

CONNECTIONS What does this magazine cover suggest about the availability of consumer goods and the desire for them after the war?

European governments also reduced class tensions with a series of social reforms. Many of these reforms — such as increased unemployment benefits and more extensive old-age pensions — strengthened existing social security measures. Other programs were new, such as state-run, comprehensive national health systems. Most countries introduced family allowances — direct government grants to parents to help them raise their children — that helped many poor families make ends meet. Maternity grants and inexpensive public housing for low-income families and individuals were also common. These and other social reforms provided a humane floor of well-being and promoted greater equality.

Economic and Social Dislocation, 1970–1990

An economic crisis in the 1970s brought the postwar economic recovery to a halt. The earliest cause was the collapse of the postwar international monetary system, which since 1945 had been based on the U.S. dollar. In 1971 the dollar's value fell sharply, and inflation accelerated worldwide. Fixed rates of exchange were abandoned, and uncertainty replaced predictability in international trade and finance.

Even more damaging was the dramatic reversal in the price and availability of energy. Cheap oil fueled the postwar boom. (See "Global Trade: Oil," page 950.) In 1971 the Arab-led Organization of Petroleum Exporting Countries — **OPEC** — decided to reverse a decline in the crude oil price by presenting a united front against the oil companies. After the Arab-Israeli war in October 1973 (see page 995), OPEC placed an embargo on oil exports, and crude oil prices quadrupled in a year.

The rise in energy prices coupled with the upheaval in the international monetary system plunged the world into its worst economic decline since the 1930s. Unemployment rose; productivity and living standards declined. By 1976 a modest recovery was in progress, but when Iranian oil production collapsed during Iran's fundamentalist Islamic revolution in 1979 (see page 995), crude oil prices doubled again. By 1985 unemployment rates in western Europe had risen to their highest levels since the Great Depression. Global recovery was painfully slow until late 1993.

Global Trade

Oil in its crude form is found as a liquid hydrocarbon located in certain rocks below the earth's crust. Although it is found throughout the world, the Persian Gulf and Caspian Sea areas contain about three-quarters of the world's proven reserves. The uses of crude oil are limited, but it may be refined into valuable products such as kerosene, gasoline, and fuel oil.

Oil has been used throughout history, although it did not become a worldwide commodity until the nineteenth century. In antiquity, the Sumerians and Babylonians mixed evaporated oil from tar pits with sand to make asphalt for waterproofing ships and paving roads. Islamic societies in the Middle East used small quantities of oil for lighting, although cooking fires were probably the main source of light.

In Europe, lamp oil—from animal fats and plants—was a luxury. The nineteenth century brought revolutionary changes in lighting, and by the 1840s manufacturers in coal-rich Europe were distilling coal into crude oil and gas for use in lighting. North America followed suit. Thus when E. L. Drake drilled the first successful American oil well in Pennsylvania in 1859, a growing demand for lamp oil already existed. The production of kerosene took off as consumers accepted the bright, clean-burning, and relatively inexpensive oil for use in their lamps.

After the late 1860s the United States exported two-thirds of its kerosene, first in wooden barrels, then in large tin cans, and finally in tankers for bulk distribution. The leading producer was John D. Rockefeller's Standard Oil, which held a monopoly on kerosene until the U.S. government

MAP 31.2 The Oil Trade, ca. 1900–1975

broke the corporation into separate companies in 1911. Most kerosene went to Europe at first, but other markets grew rapidly. In the 1870s the Baku region on the Caspian Sea introduced drilling and created a Russian refining industry. Russian capitalists fought well-publicized "oil wars" with Standard Oil for world kerosene markets.

International differences were significant. In the United States and western Europe kerosene appealed especially to farmers and urban working people, who had previously lacked decent lighting. The affluent urban classes generally continued to use coal-distilled gas until the 1880s, when electricity began to replace gas. In China peasants rejected bulk

"FIRST WE'LL VACATION AT THE SHORE, THEN WE'LL GO TO THE MOUNTAINS, THEN UP TO THE LAKE......"

China's growing middle class is adopting the automobile culture of the West, which is putting more pressure on the world's dwindling supply of fossil fuels. (© 2005 Bog Englehart, The Hartford Courant)

distribution and insisted on kerosene in tin cans, recycling them into valuable all-purpose containers. Russia pioneered in using oil as fuel, as the refining of heavy Baku crude yielded abundant thick "leftovers"—an excellent power source for riverboats, railroads, and factories.

During the twentieth century oil became a major fuel source as kerosene production declined. Until 1941 the explosive growth of automobiles in the United States was easily outpaced by the development of domestic oil fields, enabling the United States to sell one-third of all the oil consumed beyond its borders. In oil-poor Europe (Russia excepted), fuel oil loomed large as a strategic material. After 1919 the British government took control of the two oil companies in Iran and Iraq to guarantee supplies for Britain's military and industrial needs. Germany distilled coal into synthetic gasoline, and Hitler relentlessly pushed production of this very expensive alternative to free his war machine from dependence on foreign oil.

The international oil trade shifted dramatically after 1945. The United States, previously producing half the world's oil, became the world's largest importer. The Middle East, producing very modestly in the 1920s and 1930s, became the world's leading exporter. At the same time, western Europe and Japan shifted from coal to oil to drive their factories and fuel their automobiles. Nevertheless, the American and British oil companies in the Middle East expanded output so rapidly—sixteen times between 1948 and 1972—that the inflation-adjusted price for Middle Eastern oil fell substantially in these years.

Increasingly dissatisfied with their share of the profits, the main exporting countries—Iran, Iraq, Kuwait, Saudi Arabia, and Venezuela—organized the Organization of Petroleum Exporting Countries (OPEC) in 1960 to gain control of their oil resources. In 1973, during the Arab-Israeli war, OPEC engineered a fourfold price increase with enormous global consequences. The exporting states also nationalized their oil industries, reducing foreign companies to simple buyers and transporters. The oil exporters used their financial windfalls to improve health and living standards somewhat, but vast sums went for lavish spending by the elite and for overly ambitious development projects. Above all, the money went for expensive military hardware from the industrialized countries, which increased tensions and prolonged the terrible war between Iraq and Iran in the 1980s (see pages 1001–1002).

A price collapse followed the upward price revolution of the 1970s. In the 1980s and early 1990s conservation, greater efficiency, recession, environmental concerns, and significant new oil discoveries outside the Middle East eliminated much of the inflation-adjusted price increases of the 1970s. By 2002 some argued that oil was really "just another commodity." The outbreak of the Iraq War in 2003, however—followed by natural disasters such as Hurricane Katrina; instability in Nigeria, Venezuela, and other major oil-producing countries; and skyrocketing demands for oil by China and India—sent oil to nearly $150 per barrel by 2008, creating another global energy crisis.

Western Europe's welfare system prevented mass suffering through unemployment benefits and other social programs. But increased government spending was not matched by higher taxes, causing a rapid growth of budget deficits, national debts, and inflation. By the late 1970s a powerful reaction against government's ever-increasing role had set in. Growing voter dissatisfaction helped bring Conservative Margaret Thatcher (b. 1925) to power in Britain in 1979. Prime Minister Thatcher slowed government spending and privatized industry by selling off state-owned companies to private investors. Of great social significance, her government encouraged low- and moderate-income renters in state-owned housing projects to buy their apartments at rock-bottom prices. This step created a whole new class of property owners, thereby eroding the electoral base of Britain's socialist Labour Party. Other Western governments introduced austerity measures to slow the growth of public spending and the welfare state.

Individuals felt the impact of austerity, and the threat of unemployment — or underemployment in dead-end jobs — shaped the outlook of a whole generation. Students in the 1980s were serious, practical, and often conservative. As one young woman at a French university told a reporter in 1985, "Jobs are the big worry now, so everyone wants to learn something practical."[2]

Harder times also meant that more women entered or remained in the workforce after they married. Although attitudes related to personal fulfillment were one reason for the continuing increase — especially for well-educated upper-middle-class women — many wives in poor and middle-class families worked outside the home because of economic necessity.

Recovery and Reform in Soviet Eastern Europe, 1945–1991

☐ How did the Soviets try to reform society, and what were the consequences of the anticommunist revolutions of 1989?

While western Europe surged ahead economically after World War II, postwar economic recovery in eastern Europe proceeded along Soviet lines, and changes in the Soviet Union strongly influenced political and social developments. That trend remained true more than forty years later, when radical reform in the Soviet Union opened the door to popular revolution in the eastern European satellites — and ultimately to the collapse of the Soviet Union itself.

Stalin's Last Years

The "Great Patriotic War of the Fatherland" had fostered Russian nationalism and a relaxation of totalitarian terror. Having made a heroic war effort, the vast majority of the Soviet people hoped in 1945 that a grateful party and government would grant greater freedom and democracy, but even before war's end, Stalin was moving his country back toward rigid dictatorship.

As early as 1944 Communist Party members received a new slogan: "The war on Fascism ends, the war on capitalism begins."[3] Stalin's new foe provided him with an excuse for re-establishing a harsh dictatorship. He purged thousands of returning soldiers and ordinary civilians in 1945 and 1946, and he revived the terrible forced-labor camps of the 1930s. Culture and art were purged of Western influences, Orthodox Christianity again came under attack, and Soviet Jews were accused of being pro-Western and antisocialist.

Stalin reasserted his complete control of the government and society with the reintroduction of five-year plans to cope with the enormous task of economic reconstruction. Once again heavy and military industry were given top priority, and consumer goods, housing, and collectivized agriculture were neglected. Everyday life was very hard. In short, it was the 1930s all over again in the Soviet Union, although police terror was less intense.

Stalin then exported the Stalinist system to eastern Europe. Rigid ideological indoctrination, attacks on religion, and a lack of civil liberties were soon facts of life in the region's one-party states. Industry was nationalized and the middle class stripped of its possessions. Only Yugoslavia's Josip Tito (1892–1980), the popular resistance leader and Communist Party chief, could resist Soviet domination successfully, because there was no Russian army in Yugoslavia.

Limited De-Stalinization and Stagnation

In 1953 the aging Stalin died. Even as his heirs struggled for power, they realized that reforms were necessary because of the widespread fear and hatred of Stalin's political terrorism. They curbed secret police powers and gradually closed many forced-labor camps. Change was also necessary for economic reasons. Agriculture was in bad shape, and shortages of consumer goods were discouraging hard work and initiative. Moreover, Stalin's belligerent foreign policy had led directly to a strong Western alliance, isolating the Soviet Union.

The Communist Party leadership was badly split on just how much change to permit. Reformers, led by Nikita Khrushchev (1894–1971), argued for major innovations and won. Khrushchev spoke out in a "secret speech" against Stalin and his crimes at a closed session of the Twentieth Party Congress in 1956:

> It is clear that . . . Stalin showed in a whole series of cases his intolerance, his brutality, and his abuse of power. Instead of proving his political correctness and mobilizing the masses, he often chose the path of repression and physical annihilation, not only against actual enemies, but also against individuals who had not committed any crimes against the party and the Soviet Government.[4]

The liberalization of the Soviet Union — labeled **de-Stalinization** in the West — was genuine. The Communist Party jealously maintained its monopoly on political power, but Khrushchev shook up the party and brought in new members. Some resources were shifted from heavy industry and the military toward consumer goods and agriculture, and controls over workers were relaxed. The Soviet Union's low standard of living finally began to improve and continued to rise substantially throughout the booming 1960s.

De-Stalinization created great ferment among writers and intellectuals who hungered for cultural freedom. The writer Aleksandr Solzhenitsyn (1918–2008) created a sensation when his *One Day in the Life of Ivan Denisovich* was published in the Soviet Union in 1962. Solzhenitsyn's novel portrays life in a Stalinist concentration camp in grim detail and is a damning indictment of the Stalinist past.

Khrushchev also de-Stalinized Soviet foreign policy. "Peaceful coexistence" with capitalism was possible, he argued. But while Cold War tensions relaxed between 1955 and 1957, de-Stalinization stimulated rebelliousness in the eastern European satellites. Poland won greater autonomy in 1956 when extensive rioting brought in a new Communist government. Led by students and workers, the people of Budapest, Hungary, installed a liberal Communist reformer as their new chief in October 1956. After the new government promised free elections and renounced Hungary's military alliance with Moscow, Russian leaders ordered an invasion and crushed the revolution, killing around 2,700 protesters. When the United States did not come to their aid, Hungarians and most eastern Europeans concluded that their only hope was to strive for small domestic gains while following Russia obediently in foreign affairs.

In August 1961 East Germany began construction of a twenty-seven-mile wall between East and West Berlin. A ninety-mile-long barrier was also constructed between the three allied sectors of West Berlin and East Germany, thereby completely cutting off West Berlin. Officially the wall was called the "Anti-Fascist Protection Wall." In reality the Berlin Wall, which dramatically symbolized the Iron Curtain, was necessary to prevent East Germans from "voting with their feet" by defecting to the West.

By late 1962 party opposition to Khrushchev's policies had gained momentum. De-Stalinization was seen as a dangerous threat to party authority. Moreover, Khrushchev's policy toward the West was erratic and ultimately unsuccessful. When Khrushchev ordered missiles with nuclear warheads installed in Fidel Castro's Communist Cuba in 1962, U.S. president John F. Kennedy countered with a naval blockade of Cuba. After a tense diplomatic crisis Khrushchev agreed to remove the missiles. Increasingly viewed in the colorful language of the time as a bumbling buffoon, Khrushchev was removed in a bloodless coup within two years of the Cuban missile crisis.

After Leonid Brezhnev (1906–1982) and his supporters took over in 1964, they talked quietly of Stalin's "good points," stopped further liberalization, and launched a massive arms buildup, determined never to suffer Khrushchev's humiliation in the face of American nuclear superiority.

The Impact of Reform on Everyday Life

In the wake of Khrushchev's reforms, the 1960s brought modest liberalization and more consumer goods to eastern Europe, as well as somewhat greater national autonomy. In January 1968 reform elements in the Czechoslovakian Communist Party gained a majority and replaced a long-time Stalinist leader with Alexander Dubček (1921–1992), whose new government launched dramatic reforms. Dubček (DOOB-chehk) and his allies called for "socialism with a human face." The determination of the Czech reformers frightened hardline Communists who feared any easing of their totalitarian control. Thus in August 1968, five hundred thousand Russian and eastern European troops occupied Czechoslovakia, and the Czech experiment in humanizing communism came to an end. Shortly afterward, Brezhnev declared the so-called **Brezhnev Doctrine**, according to which the Soviet Union and its allies could intervene in any socialist country whenever they saw the need.

In the aftermath of intervention in Czechoslovakia, free expression and open protest disappeared. Dissidents were blacklisted or quietly imprisoned in jails or mental institutions. Unlike in the Stalinist era, though, dictatorship was collective rather than personal, and coercion replaced uncontrolled terror. This compromise seemed to suit the leaders and a majority of the

- **de-Stalinization** The liberalization of the post-Stalin Soviet Union, led by reformer Nikita Khrushchev during his years as the head of the Soviet Union (1953–1964).
- **Brezhnev Doctrine** Doctrine created by Leonid Brezhnev that held that the Soviet Union had the right to intervene in any socialist country whenever it saw the need.

Czechs Protest Soviet Invasion in 1968 A young Czech girl shouts "Ivan go home" at Russian soldiers sitting on tanks in Prague during the Soviet invasion of Czechoslovakia in August 1968. (Bettmann/Corbis)

people, and the Soviet Union appeared stable in the 1970s and early 1980s.

A rising standard of living for ordinary people contributed to stability, although the economic crisis of the 1970s greatly slowed the rate of improvement, and long lines and shortages persisted. The exclusive privileges enjoyed by the Communist Party elite also reinforced the system. Ambitious individuals had tremendous incentives to do as the state wished in order to gain access to special well-stocked stores, attend superior schools, and travel abroad.

Another source of stability was the enduring nationalism of ordinary Russians. Party leaders successfully identified themselves with Russian patriotism, stressing their role in saving the motherland during the Second World War and protecting it now from foreign foes, including eastern European "counter-revolutionaries." Moreover, the politically dominant Great Russians, only half of the total Soviet population, held the top positions in the Soviet Union's non-Russian republics.

Beneath this stability, however, the Soviet Union was experiencing a social revolution. A rapidly expanding urban population abandoned its old peasant ways, exchanging them for more education, better job skills,

and greater sophistication. The number of highly trained scientists, managers, and specialists expanded prodigiously, jumping fourfold between 1960 and 1985. The education that created expertise helped foster the growth of Soviet public opinion. Educated people read, discussed, and formed definite ideas about social questions ranging from environmental pollution to urban transportation. These changes set the stage for the dramatic reforms of the Gorbachev era.

The Gorbachev Era

When Brezhnev died in 1982, efforts were made to improve economic performance and to combat worker absenteeism and high-level corruption. Elected as leader in 1985, Mikhail Gorbachev (b. 1931) believed in communism, but he realized that Brezhnev's reforms would not be enough to save the failing state. Importantly, Gorbachev realized that success at home required better relations with the West. Thus Gorbachev attempted to save the Soviet system with a series of reform policies he labeled democratic socialism, or "socialism with a democratic face."

The first set of reforms was intended to transform and restructure the economy. This economic restructuring, **perestroika**, permitted freer prices, more independence for state enterprises, and the setting up of some profit-seeking private cooperatives. The reforms were rather timid, however, and when the economy stalled, Gorbachev's popular support gradually eroded.

Gorbachev's bold and far-reaching campaign of openness, or **glasnost**, was much more successful. Where censorship, dull uniformity, and outright lies had long characterized public discourse, the new frankness led rather quickly to something approaching free speech and free expression, a veritable cultural revolution.

Democratization was the third of Gorbachev's reforms, and it led to the first free elections in the Soviet Union since 1917. Gorbachev and the party remained in control, but a minority of critical independents was elected in April 1989 to a revitalized Congress of People's Deputies. Democratization encouraged demands for greater autonomy by non-Russian minorities, especially in the Baltic region and in the Caucasus. These demands went beyond what Gorbachev had envisaged. But whereas China's Communist Party leaders brutally massacred similar pro-democracy demonstrators in Beijing in June 1989 (see page 982), Gorbachev drew back from repression. Thus nationalist demands continued to grow.

Finally, Gorbachev brought "new political thinking" to foreign affairs. He withdrew Soviet troops from Afghanistan in February 1989 and sought to reduce East-West tensions. Of enormous importance, Gorbachev repudiated the Brezhnev Doctrine, pledging to respect the political choices of eastern Europe's peoples. By 1989 it seemed that the Soviet occupation of eastern Europe might gradually wither away.

The Revolutions of 1989

Instead of gradually changing, however, in 1989 a series of largely peaceful revolutions swept across eastern Europe, overturning existing Communist regimes. New governments formed dedicated to democratic elections, human rights, and national rejuvenation. Eastern Europe changed dramatically almost overnight.

The Poles led the way. Poland had from the beginning resisted Soviet-style collectivization and had refused to break with the Roman Catholic Church. Faced with an independent agriculture and a vigorous church, the Communists failed to monopolize society. They also failed to manage the economy effectively and instead sent it into a nosedive by the mid-1970s. When Polish-born Pope John Paul II (1920–2005) returned to his native land to preach the love of Christ and country and the "inalienable rights of man," he electrified the Polish nation, and the economic crisis became a spiritual crisis as well.

In August 1980 scattered strikes snowballed into a working-class revolt. Led by Lech Walesa (lehk vah-LEHN-suh; b. 1943), the workers organized an independent trade union they called **Solidarity**. In response, the Communist leadership proclaimed martial law in December 1981 and arrested Solidarity's leaders. (See "Listening to the Past: A Solidarity Leader Speaks from Prison," page 956.) Though outlawed, Solidarity maintained its organization and strong popular support. By 1988 widespread labor unrest and raging inflation had brought Poland to the brink of economic collapse. Thus Solidarity pressured Poland's Communist Party lead-

ers into legalizing Solidarity and allowing free elections in June 1989 for some seats in the Polish parliament. Solidarity won every contested seat. A month later Tadeusz Mazowiecki (b. 1927), the editor of Solidarity's weekly newspaper, was sworn in as the first noncommunist prime minister in eastern Europe in a generation.

Poland was soon followed by Czechoslovakia, where communism died in just ten days in December 1989 during the so-called Velvet Revolution that peacefully ousted Communist leaders. It grew out of massive street protests led by students and intellectuals, and led to the election of Václav Havel (VAH-slahf HAH-vuhl; b. 1936) as president in 1989. (See the feature "Individuals in Society: Václav Havel," page 958.)

Only in Romania was revolution violent and bloody. There the iron-fisted Communist dictator Nicolae Ceauşescu (chow-SHES-kou; 1918–1989) ordered his

Fall of the Berlin Wall A man stands atop the partially destroyed Berlin Wall flashing the V for victory sign as he and thousands of other Berliners celebrate the opening of the Berlin Wall in November 1989. Within a year the wall was torn down, communism collapsed, and the Cold War ended. (Lionel Cironneau/AP Images)

A Solidarity Leader Speaks from Prison

Solidarity built a broad-based alliance of intellectuals, workers, and the Catholic Church. That alliance was one reason that Solidarity became such a powerful movement in Poland. Another reason was Solidarity's commitment to social and political change through nonviolent action. That commitment enabled Solidarity to avoid a bloodbath in 1981 and thus maintain its structure after martial law was declared, although at the time foreign observers often criticized Lech Walesa's leadership for being too cautious and unrealistic.

Adam Michnik was one of Walesa's closest coworkers. Whereas Walesa was a skilled electrician and a devout Catholic, Michnik was an intellectual and a disillusioned Communist. Their faith in nonviolence and in gradual change bound them together. Trained as a historian but banned from teaching because of his leadership in student strikes in 1968, Michnik earned his living as a factory worker. In 1977 he joined with others to found the Committee for the Defense of Workers (KOR), which supported workers fired for striking. In December 1981 Michnik was arrested with the rest of Solidarity's leadership. While in prison, he wrote his influential Letters from Prison, *from which this essay is taken.*

66 Why did Solidarity renounce violence? This question returned time and again in my conversations with foreign observers. I would like to answer it now. People who claim that the use of force in the struggle for freedom is necessary must first prove that in a given situation it will be effective and that force, when it is used, will not transform the idea of liberty into its opposite.

No one in Poland is able to prove today that violence will help us to dislodge Soviet troops from Poland and to remove the communists from power. The U.S.S.R. has such enormous military power that confrontation is simply unthinkable. In other words, we have no guns. Napoleon, upon hearing a similar reply, gave up asking further questions. However, Napoleon was above all interested in military victories and not building democratic, pluralistic societies. We, by contrast, cannot leave it at that.

In our reasoning, pragmatism is inseparably intertwined with idealism. Taught by history, we suspect that by using force to storm the existing Bastilles we shall unwittingly build new

ones. It is true that social change is almost always accompanied by force. But it is not true that social change is merely a result of the violent collision of various forces. Above all, social changes follow from a confrontation of different moralities and visions of social order. Before the violence of rulers clashes with the violence of their subjects, values and systems of ethics clash inside human minds. Only when the old ideas of the rulers lose this moral duel will the subjects reach for force—sometimes. This is what happened in the French Revolution and the Russian Revolution—two examples cited in every debate as proof that revolutionary violence is preceded by a moral breakdown of the old regime. But both examples lose their meaning when they are reduced to such compact notions, in which the Encyclopedists are paired with the destruction of the Bastille, and the success of radical ideologies in Russia is paired with the storming of the Winter Palace. An authentic event is reduced to a sterile scheme.

In order to understand the significance of these revolutions, one must remember Jacobin and Bolshevik terror, the guillotines of the sans-culottes, and the guns of the commissars. Without reflection on the mechanisms in victorious revolutions that gave birth to terror, it is impossible to even pose the fundamental dilemma facing contemporary freedom movements. Historical awareness of the possible consequences of revolutionary violence must be etched into any program of struggle for freedom. The experience of being corrupted by terror must be imprinted upon the consciousness of everyone who belongs to a freedom movement. [Or], as Simone Weil wrote, freedom will again become a refugee from the camp of the victors. . . .

Solidarity's program and ethos are inextricably tied to this strategy. Revolutionary terror has always been justified by a vision of an ideal society. In the name of this vision, Jacobin guillotines and Bolshevik execution squads carried out their unceasing, gruesome work.

The road to God's Kingdom on Earth led through rivers of blood.

Solidarity has never had a vision of an ideal society. It wants to live and let live. Its ideals are closer to the American Revolution than to the French. . . . The ethics of Solidarity, with its consistent rejection of the use of force, has a lot in common with the idea of nonviolence as espoused by Gandhi and

Martin Luther King, Jr. But it is not an ethic representative of pacifist movements.

Pacifism as a mass movement aims to avoid suffering; pacifists often say that no cause is worth suffering or dying for. The ethics of Solidarity are based on an opposite premise: that there are causes worth suffering and dying for. Gandhi and King died for the same cause as the miners in Wujek who rejected the belief that it is better to remain a willing slave than to become a victim of murder [and who were shot down by police for striking against the imposition of martial law in 1981]. . . .

But ethics cannot substitute for a political program. We must therefore think about the future of Polish-Russian relations. Our thinking about this key question must be open; it should consider many different possibilities. . . .

The Soviet state has a new leader; he is a symbol of transition from one generation to the next within the Soviet elite. This change may offer an opportunity, since Mikhail Gorbachev has not yet become a prisoner of his own decisions. No one can rule out the possibility that an impulse for reform will spring from the top of the hierarchy of power. This is exactly what happened in the time of Alexander II and, a hundred years later, under Khrushchev. Reform is always possible, even in the face of resistance by the old apparatus. . . .

So what can now happen [in Poland]?

The "fundamentalists" say, no compromises. Talking about compromise, dialogue, or understanding demobilizes public opinion, pulls the wool over the eyes of the public, spreads illusions. Walesa's declarations about readiness for dialogue were often severely criticized from this point of view. I do not share the fundamentalist point of view. . . . The logic of fundamentalism precludes any attempt to find compromise, even in the future. It harbors not only the belief that communists are ineducable but also a certainty that they are unable to behave rationally, even in critical situations—that, in other words, they are condemned to suicidal obstinacy.

This is not so obvious to me. Historical experience shows that communists were sometimes forced by circumstances to behave rationally and to agree to compromises. Thus the strategy of understanding must not be cast aside. We should not assume that a bloody confrontation is inevitable and, consequently, rule out the possibility of evolutionary, bloodless change. This should be avoided all the more inasmuch as

democracy is rarely born from bloody upheavals. We should be clear in our minds about this: The continuing conflict may transform itself into either a dialogue or an explosion. The TKK [the underground Temporary Coordinating Committee of outlawed Solidarity] and [Lech] Walesa are doing everything in their power to make dialogue possible. Their chances of success will be greater if the level of self-organization of independent Polish society increases. For street lynchings, angry crowds are enough; compromise demands an organized society. **"**

Source: Adam Michnik, *Letters from Prison and Other Essays*, trans. Maya Latynski (Berkeley and Los Angeles: University of California Press, 1985), pp. 86–89, 92, 95, by permission of the University of California Press. Copyright © 1985 by The Regents of the University of California.

QUESTIONS FOR ANALYSIS

1. Are Michnik's arguments for opposing the government with nonviolent actions convincing?

2. How did Michnik's study of history influence his thinking? What lessons did he learn?

3. Analyze Michnik's attitudes toward the Soviet Union and Poland's Communist leadership. What policies did he advocate? Why?

Individuals in Society

Václav Havel

ON THE NIGHT OF NOVEMBER 24, 1989, THE revolution in Czechoslovakia reached its climax. Three hundred thousand people had poured into Prague's historic Wenceslas Square to continue the massive protests that had erupted a week earlier after the police savagely beat student demonstrators. Now all eyes were focused on a high balcony. There an elderly man with a gentle smile and a middle-aged intellectual wearing jeans and a sports jacket stood arm in arm and acknowledged the cheers of the crowd. "Dubček-Havel," the people roared. "Dubček-Havel!" Alexander Dubček, who represented the failed promise of reform communism in the 1960s (see page 953), was symbolically passing the torch to Václav Havel, who embodied the uncompromising opposition to communism that was sweeping the country. That very evening, the hard-line Communist government resigned, and soon Havel was the unanimous choice to head a new democratic Czechoslovakia. Who was this man to whom the nation turned in 1989?

Born in 1936 into a prosperous, cultured, upper-middle-class family, the young Havel was denied admission to the university because of his class origins. Loving literature and philosophy, he gravitated to the theater, became a stagehand, and emerged in the 1960s as a leading playwright. His plays were set in vague settings, developed existential themes, and poked fun at the absurdities of life and the pretensions of communism. In his private life, Havel thrived on good talk, Prague's lively bar scene, and officially forbidden rock 'n' roll.

In 1968 the Soviets rolled into Czechoslovakia, and Havel watched in horror as a tank commander opened fire on a crowd of peaceful protesters in a small town. "That week," he recorded, "was an experience I shall never forget."* The free-spirited artist threw himself into the intellectual opposition to communism and became its leading figure for the next twenty years. The costs of defiance were enormous. Purged and black-listed, Havel lifted barrels in a brewery and wrote bitter satires that could not be staged. In 1977 he and a few other dissidents publicly protested Czechoslovakian violations of the Helsinki Accords on human rights, and in 1989 this Charter '77 group became the inspiration for Civic Forum, the democratic coalition that toppled communism. Havel spent five years in prison and was constantly harassed by the police.

Havel's thoughts and actions focused on truth, decency, and moral regeneration. In 1975, in a famous open letter to Czechoslovakia's Communist boss, Havel wrote that the people were indeed quiet, but only because they were "driven by

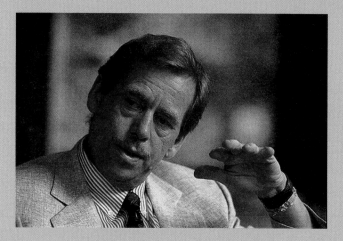

● **Václav Havel, playwright, dissident leader, and the first postcommunist president of the Czech Republic.**
(Chris Niedenthal/Black Star)

fear. . . . Everyone has something to lose and so everyone has reason to be afraid." Havel saw lies, hypocrisy, and apathy undermining and poisoning all human relations in his country: "Order has been established—at the price of a paralysis of the spirit, a deadening of the heart, and a spiritual and moral crisis in society."†

Yet Havel saw a way out of the Communist quagmire. He argued that a profound but peaceful revolution in human values was possible. Such a revolution could lead to the moral reconstruction of Czech and Slovak society, where, in his words, "values like trust, openness, responsibility, solidarity and love" might again flourish and nurture the human spirit. Havel was a voice of hope and humanity who inspired his compatriots with a lofty vision of a moral postcommunist society. As president of his country (1989–2003), Havel continued to speak eloquently on the great questions of our time.

QUESTIONS FOR ANALYSIS

1. Why did Havel oppose Communist rule? How did his goals differ from those of Dubček and other advocates of reform communism?

2. Havel has been called a "moralist in politics." Is this a good description of him? Why? Can you think of a better one?

*Quoted in M. Simmons, *The Reluctant President: A Political Life of Václav Havel* (London: Methuen, 1991), p. 91.

†Quoted ibid., p. 110.

Celebrating Victory, August 1991 A Russian soldier flashes the victory sign in front of the Russian parliament as the last-gasp coup attempt of Communist hardliners is defeated by Boris Yeltsin and an enthusiastic public. The soldier has cut the hammer and sickle out of the Soviet flag, consigning those famous symbols of proletarian revolution to what Trotsky once called the "garbage can of history." (© Filip Horvat)

ruthless security forces to slaughter thousands, thereby sparking an armed uprising. After Ceaușescu's forces were defeated, the tyrant and his wife were captured and executed by a military court.

In Hungary growing popular resistance forced the Communist Party to renounce one-party rule and schedule free elections for early 1990. Hungarians gleefully tore down the barbed-wire "iron curtain" that separated Hungary and Austria (see Map 31.1) and opened their border to refugees from East Germany.

As thousands of dissatisfied East Germans passed through Czechoslovakia and Hungary on their way to thriving West Germany, a protest movement arose in East Germany. Desperately hoping to stabilize the situation, East Germany's Communist Party leaders opened the Berlin Wall in November 1989, then were swept aside. In general elections in March 1990 a conservative-liberal "Alliance for Germany" won and quickly negotiated an economic union with West Germany.

Three factors contributed to the rapid reunification of East and West Germany. First, in the first week after the Berlin Wall was opened, almost 9 million East Germans — roughly half the country's population — poured across the border into West Germany. Almost all returned home, but their experiences in the West aroused long-dormant hopes of unity among ordinary citizens. Second, West German chancellor Helmut Kohl (b. 1930) moved skillfully to reassure American, Soviet, and European leaders they need not fear a reunified Germany. He then promised the citizens of East Germany an im-

mediate economic bonanza — a one-for-one exchange of all East German marks in savings accounts and pensions into much more valuable West German marks. Kohl and Gorbachev signed a historic agreement in July 1990 in which United Germany affirmed its peaceful intentions, and on October 3, 1990, East and West Germany merged, forming a single nation under West Germany's constitution and laws.

The End of the Cold War and Soviet Disintegration

Germany's reunification accelerated the pace of agreements to liquidate the Cold War. In November 1990 delegates from twenty-two European countries joined those from the United States and the Soviet Union in Paris and agreed to scale down their armed forces, recognize all existing borders in Europe, and declare an end to confrontation and division in Europe. The **Charter of Paris for a New Europe** was for all practical purposes a general peace treaty, bringing an end to the Cold War.

Peace in Europe encouraged the United States and the Soviet Union to scrap a significant portion of their nuclear arsenals. In September 1991 President George H. W. Bush (r. 1989–1993) also canceled the around-

• **Charter of Paris for a New Europe** A 1990 general peace treaty that brought an end to the Cold War; it called for a scaling down of all armed forces, acceptance of all existing borders as legal and valid, and an end to all confrontation and division in Europe.

MAP 31.3 Russia and the Successor States After the attempt in August 1991 to depose Gorbachev failed, an anticommunist revolution swept the Soviet Union. Led by Russia and Boris Yeltsin, the republics that formed the Soviet Union declared their sovereignty and independence. Eleven of the fifteen republics then formed a loose confederation called the Commonwealth of Independent States, but the integrated economy of the Soviet Union dissolved into separate national economies, each with its own goals and policies.

the-clock alert status for American bombers outfitted with atomic bombs. Gorbachev quickly followed suit. For the first time in four decades Soviet and American nuclear weapons were not standing ready to destroy capitalism, communism, and life itself.

The great question then became whether the Soviet Union would also experience a popular anticommunist revolution. In February 1990 the Communist Party suffered stunning defeats in local elections throughout the country. Democrats and anticommunists won clear majorities in the Russian Federation's major cities. Breaking definitively from Communist Party hardliners, Gorbachev asked Soviet citizens to ratify a new constitution that formally abolished the Communist Party's monopoly of political power and expanded the

power of the Congress of People's Deputies. Gorbachev then convinced a majority of deputies to elect him president of the Soviet Union.

Gorbachev's eroding power and unwillingness to risk a popular election for the presidency strengthened his rival, Boris Yeltsin (1931–2007). A radical reform Communist, Yeltsin embraced the democratic movement, and in May 1990, as leader of the Russian parliament, Yeltsin announced that Russia would declare its independence from the Soviet Union. This move broadened the base of the anticommunist movement by appealing to the patriotism of ordinary Russians.

In August 1991 Gorbachev survived an attempted coup by Communist Party hardliners who wanted to preserve Communist Party power and the multinational Soviet Union. Instead, an anticommunist revolution swept the Russian Federation as the Communist Party was outlawed and its property confiscated.

• **Civil Rights Act** A 1964 U.S. act that prohibited discrimination in public services and on the job.

Yeltsin and his liberal allies declared Russia independent and withdrew from the Soviet Union. All the other Soviet republics followed suit, and the Soviet Union ceased to exist on December 25, 1991 (Map 31.3).

The United States: Confrontation and Transformation

☐ What contributed to the social and political transformation of the United States in the second half of the twentieth century?

After 1945 members of America's World War II generation had babies, built houses, bought cars, and created the largest economy in the world. They also started to face up to the contradictions inherent in the promotion of democracy abroad and the denial of civil rights at home, and in calling for self-determination in eastern Europe while fighting what many considered a colonial war in Vietnam. As America tried to contain communism around the globe, it underwent an internal transformation that led to new rights for African Americans and women, and the development of a vigorous and active counterculture. The end of the Cold War and the Soviet Union's collapse in 1991 left Americans grappling with questions about the new position of the United States as the world's only superpower.

America's Economic Boom and Civil Rights Revolution

The Second World War ended the Great Depression in the United States, bringing about a great economic boom. Unemployment practically vanished, and Americans' well-being increased dramatically. As in western Europe, the U.S. economy advanced fairly steadily for a generation.

Prosperity helps explain why postwar domestic politics consisted largely of modest adjustments to the status quo until the 1960s. The upset re-election victory in 1948 of President Harry S. Truman (r. 1945–1953) demonstrated that Americans had no interest in undoing Roosevelt's social and economic reforms. In 1952 American voters turned to General Dwight D. Eisenhower (r. 1953–1961), a national hero and self-described moderate. In 1960 young John F. Kennedy (r. 1961–1963) captured the popular imagination. He revitalized the old Roosevelt coalition and modestly expanded existing liberal legislation before being struck down by an assassin's bullet in 1963.

Belatedly and reluctantly, complacent postwar America did experience a genuine social revolution: after a long struggle African Americans (and their white supporters) threw off a deeply entrenched system of segregation and discrimination. This civil rights movement advanced on several fronts. The National Association for the Advancement of Colored People (NAACP) challenged school segregation in the courts. In 1954 it won a landmark decision in the Supreme Court, which ruled in *Brown v. Board of Education* that "separate educational facilities are inherently unequal." Blacks also effectively challenged inequality by using Gandhian methods of nonviolent peaceful resistance (see page 891). In describing his principles for change, the civil rights leader Martin Luther King, Jr. (1929–1968), said that "Christ furnished the spirit and motivation, while Gandhi furnished the method." He told the white power structure, "We will not hate you, but we will not obey your evil laws."[5]

> ❝We will not hate you, but we will not obey your evil laws.❞
>
> **MARTIN LUTHER KING, JR.**

With African American support in key Northern states, Democrat Lyndon Johnson (r. 1963–1969) won the 1964 presidential election in a liberal landslide. He repaid liberals' support by getting enacted the 1964 **Civil Rights Act**, which prohibited discrimination in public services and on the job, and the 1965 Voting Rights Act, which guaranteed all blacks the right to vote.

The March on Washington, August 1963 The march marked a dramatic climax in the civil rights struggle. More than two hundred thousand people gathered at the Lincoln Memorial to hear the young Martin Luther King, Jr., deliver his greatest address, the "I have a dream" speech. (Time & Life Pictures/Getty Images)

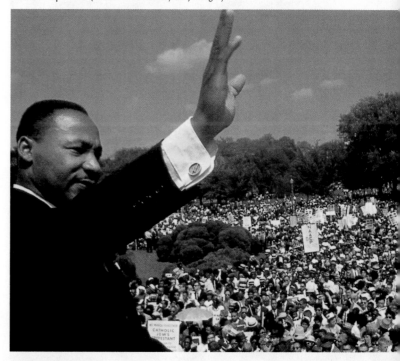

In the mid-1960s President Johnson began an "unconditional war on poverty." With the support of Congress, Johnson's administration created a host of antipoverty projects, such as medical care for the poor and aged, free preschools for poor children, and community-action programs. Thus the United States promoted the kind of fundamental social reform that western Europe had embraced immediately after the Second World War.

Youth and the Counterculture

Economic prosperity and a more democratic class structure had a powerful impact on youth throughout North America and western Europe. The "baby boomers" born after World War II developed a distinctive youth culture that became increasingly oppositional in the 1960s, interacting with leftist thought to create a counterculture that rebelled against parents, authority figures, and the status quo.

Young people in the United States took the lead in what became an international youth culture. American college students in the 1950s were docile and were often dismissed as the "Silent Generation," but some

Duck and Cover American schoolchildren in the 1950s practice the "duck and cover" drill in the event of a nuclear attack by the Soviet Union. (Bettmann/Corbis)

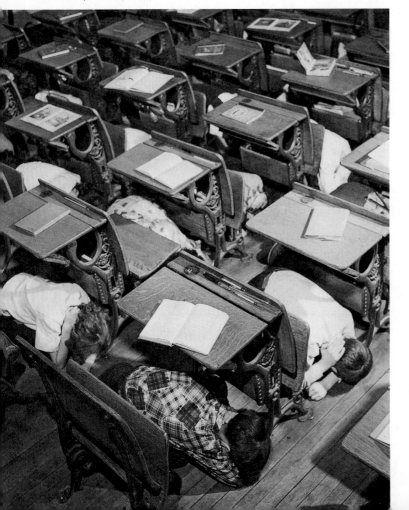

young people did revolt against the conformity of middle-class suburbs. The "beat" movement of the late 1950s expanded on the theme of revolt, and this subculture quickly spread to major American and western European cities.

Rock music helped tie this international subculture together. Rock 'n' roll grew out of the black music culture of rhythm and blues. Artists Elvis Presley and the Beatles, whose music suggested personal and sexual freedom many older people found disturbing, became enormously popular. Bob Dylan, a young folksinger turned rock poet, captured the radical aspirations of some young people when he sang that "the times they are a'changing."

Several factors contributed to the emergence of the international youth culture in the 1960s. First, mass communications and youth travel linked countries and continents together. Second, the postwar baby boom meant that young people formed an unusually large part of the population and therefore exercised exceptional influence on society as a whole. Third, postwar prosperity and greater equality gave young people more purchasing power than ever before. This enabled them to set their own trends and fads in everything from music to fashion to chemical stimulants to sexual behavior.

In the late 1960s student protesters embraced romanticism and revolutionary idealism to oppose the established order. The materialistic West was hopelessly rotten, but better societies were being built in the newly independent countries of Asia and Africa, or so many young radicals believed. Thus the counterculture became linked to the Vietnam War, as politically active students became involved in what became worldwide student opposition to that war.

The Vietnam War

American involvement in Vietnam was a product of the Cold War and the ideology of containment. After Vietnam won independence from France in 1954 (see page 988), the Eisenhower administration refused to sign the Geneva Accords that temporarily divided the country into a socialist north and an anticommunist south pending national unification by means of free elections. When the South Vietnamese government declined to hold elections, Eisenhower provided military aid to help the south resist North Vietnam. President Kennedy later increased the number of American "military advisers." In 1964 President Johnson greatly expanded America's role in the Vietnam conflict, declaring, "I am not going to be the President who saw Southeast Asia go the way China went."[6]

American strategy was to "escalate" the war sufficiently to break the will of the North Vietnamese and their southern allies without resorting to "overkill," which might risk war with the entire Communist bloc. Thus South Vietnam received massive military aid; American forces in the south grew to a half million men; and the United States bombed North Vietnam with ever-greater intensity. But there was no invasion or naval blockade of the north.

The undeclared war in Vietnam, fought nightly on American television, eventually divided the nation. At first, support was strong. Most Americans saw the war as part of a legitimate defense against communism. But an antiwar movement quickly emerged on college campuses. In October 1965 student protesters joined forces with old-line socialists, New Left intellectuals, and pacifists in antiwar demonstrations in fifty American cities. By 1967 a growing number of critics denounced the American presence in Vietnam as a criminal intrusion into a complex and distant civil war.

Criticism reached a crescendo after the Vietcong Tet Offensive in January 1968. This attack on major South Vietnamese cities failed militarily, but it resulted in heavy losses on both sides, and it belied Washington's claims that victory in South Vietnam was in sight. Within months President Johnson announced he would not stand for reelection and called for negotiations with North Vietnam.

Elected in 1968, President Richard Nixon (1913–1994) sought to disengage America gradually from Vietnam. He intensified the continuous bombardment of the enemy while simultaneously pursuing peace talks with the North Vietnamese. He also began a slow process of withdrawal from Vietnam in a process called "Vietnamization." Arguing that the South Vietnamese had to take full responsibility for their country and their security, he cut American forces there from 550,000 to 24,000 in four years. Nixon finally reached a peace agreement with North Vietnam in 1973 that allowed the remaining American forces to complete their withdrawal in 1975.

As Nixon worked to establish peace in Vietnam, the Watergate scandal erupted. Nixon had authorized special units to conduct domestic spying activities that went beyond the law. One such group broke into Democratic Party headquarters in Washington's Watergate building in June 1972 and was promptly arrested. Facing the threat of impeachment for trying to cover up

The Vietnam War, 1964–1975

- → U.S. and South Vietnamese forces
- → Major North Vietnamese supply route into South Vietnam
- ✳ Important battle or action

the affair, Nixon resigned in disgrace in 1974.

Watergate resulted in a major power shift away from the presidency and toward Congress, especially in foreign affairs. When an emboldened North Vietnam attacked South Vietnamese armies in early 1974, Congress refused to permit a military response. After more than thirty-five years of battle, the Vietnamese Communists unified their country in 1975 as a harsh dictatorial state. South Vietnam's fall shook America's postwar confidence and left its citizens divided and uncertain about the proper role of the United States in world affairs.

Détente and a Return to Cold War Tensions

While America was fighting a war, in its eyes, to contain the spread of communism in southeast Asia, relations between the Soviet Union and the United States eased somewhat in the late 1960s and early 1970s. Both sides adopted a policy for the progressive relaxation of Cold War tensions that became known as **détente** (day-TAHNT). The policy of détente reached its high point in 1975 when the United States, Canada, and all European nations (except Albania and Andorra) signed the Helsinki Accords. These nations agreed that Europe's existing political frontiers could not be changed by force, and they guaranteed the human rights and political freedoms of their citizens. Hopes for détente faded quickly, however, when Brezhnev's Soviet Union ignored the human rights provisions of the Helsinki Accords and in December 1979 invaded Afghanistan to save an unpopular Marxist regime. Alarmed, Americans looked to NATO to thwart Communist expansion. President Jimmy Carter (r. 1977–1981) pushed NATO to apply economic sanctions to the Soviet Union, but among the European allies only Great Britain supported Carter's plan. Some observers felt the alliance had lost its cohesiveness.

Yet the Western alliance endured. The U.S. military buildup launched by Jimmy Carter was greatly accelerated by President Ronald Reagan (r. 1981–1989). The Reagan administration deployed nuclear arms in western Europe and built up the navy to preserve American

• **détente** The progressive relaxation of Cold War tensions.

Anti- and Pro-Vietnam War Protesters Clash America became a divided country as the Vietnam War dragged on and American casualties mounted. In May 1970 New York City hardhat construction workers and other prowar sympathizers break up an antiwar demonstration by several hundred young protesters on Wall Street. (Bettmann/Corbis)

power in a renewed crusade against the Soviet Union — the "evil empire" in Reagan's eyes.

Reagan found conservative allies in Britain's strong-willed Margaret Thatcher and in West Germany's distinctly pro-American Helmut Kohl. In the 1980s they gave indirect support to ongoing efforts to liberalize Communist eastern Europe. As rebellions against Soviet domination spread across eastern Europe, the Soviet leader, Mikhail Gorbachev, did little. He was too busy trying, and in the end, failing, to prevent the Soviet economy from crumbling. With the Soviet Union's collapse in 1991, the United States emerged as the world's lone superpower.

In 1991 the United States used its superpower status and military superiority on a grand scale in a quick war in southwestern Asia after Iraq's strongman, Saddam Hussein (1937–2006), invaded Kuwait in August 1990 (see page 1002). With United Nations General Assembly and Security Council consent, a U.S.-led military coalition smashed Iraqi forces in a lightning-quick desert campaign. The Gulf War demonstrated the awesome power of the rebuilt and revitalized U.S. military. In the flush of victory President George H. W. Bush spoke of a "new world order," apparently meaning the United States and a cooperative United Nations working together to impose peace and security throughout the world.

Japan's Resurgence as a World Power

☐ How did Japan recover so quickly after its total defeat in World War II to become an economic superpower?

Japanese aggression had sown extreme misery during World War II and had reaped an atomic whirlwind at Hiroshima and Nagasaki. In 1945 the future looked bleak. Yet Japan under American occupation from 1945 to 1952 turned from military expansion to democracy. It experienced extraordinarily successful economic development until the 1990s and in the process joined the ranks of First World nations both politically and economically.

Japan's American Revolution

When American occupation forces landed in the Tokyo-Yokohama area after Japan's surrender in August 1945, they found only smokestacks and giant steel safes standing amid miles of rubble in what had been the heart of industrial Japan. Japan, like Nazi Germany, was formally occupied by all the Allies, but real power resided in American hands. General Douglas MacArthur (1880–

1964), the five-star hero of the Pacific, exercised almost absolute authority. MacArthur and the Americans had a revolutionary plan for defeated Japan, introducing fundamental reforms designed to make Japan a free, democratic society along American lines.

Japan's sweeping American revolution began with demilitarization and a systematic purge of convicted war criminals and wartime collaborators. The American-dictated constitution of 1946 allowed the emperor to remain the "symbol of the State." Real power resided in the Japanese Diet, whose members were popularly elected. A bill of rights granted basic civil liberties and freed all political prisoners, including Communists. Article 9 of the new constitution also abolished all Japanese armed forces and declared that Japan forever renounced war.

The American occupation left Japan's powerful bureaucracy largely intact and used it to implement fundamental social and economic reforms. The occupation promoted the Japanese labor movement, introduced American-style antitrust laws, and "emancipated" Japanese women, granting them equality before the law. The occupation also imposed revolutionary land reform that strengthened the small, independent peasant, who became a staunch defender of postwar democracy.

America's efforts to remake Japan in its own image were powerful but short-lived. By 1948, as China went Communist, American leaders began to see Japan as a potential ally, not as an object of social reform. The American command began purging leftists and rehabilitating prewar nationalists. The Japanese prime minister during much of the occupation and early post-occupation period was Shigeru Yoshida (1878–1967). Yoshida had served as Japanese ambassador to Italy and the United Kingdom; with his pro-British and pro-American sympathies, he was the ideal leader in Western eyes for postwar Japan. Yoshida adopted a policy that became known as the Yoshida Doctrine. First, he channeled all available resources to promote economic recovery and the rebuilding of Japan's industrial infrastructure. Second, he diluted Japanese sovereignty and independence by allowing the Americans to set Japanese foreign policy. Third, Yoshida left the military defense of the country to the occupying forces.

Hiroshima Railroad Station, 1951 The Hiroshima railroad station, about a mile and a quarter east of ground zero, was destroyed by the atomic bomb dropped on August 6, 1945, but the platforms and railway lines were not. By noon that day relief trains were carrying victims to outlying towns. In this photo taken six years later, two smiling American soldiers serving in Allied-occupied Japan stand in front of a partially restored station while a Japanese schoolgirl in a red hat looks on from a bus whose Japanese characters read "Hiroshima Suburban Bus Company." The sign to the right is advertising "Hiroshima raw oysters" for sale. Life goes on. (Courtesy of the family of Warren Robert Cape)

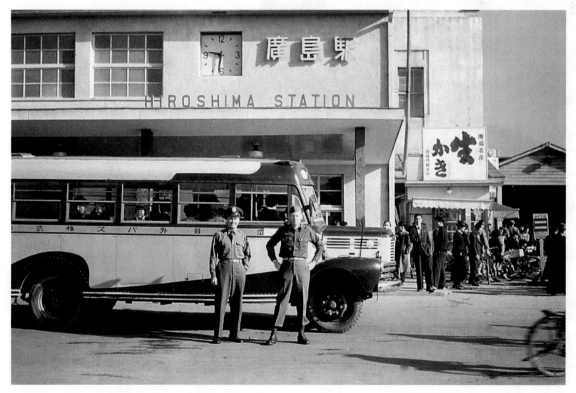

The occupation ended in 1952. Under the treaty terms Japan regained independence, and the United States retained its vast military complex in Japan. Important for the Americans, Japan became the chief Asian ally of the United States in the fight against communism.

"Japan, Inc."

Japan's economic recovery, like Germany's, proceeded slowly after the war. During the Korean War, however, the economy took off and grew with spectacular speed. Japan served as a base for American military operations during the war, and billions of dollars in military contracts and aid poured into the Japanese economy. Between 1950 and 1970 the real growth rate of Japan's economy, adjusted for inflation, averaged a breathtak-

ing 10 percent a year. By the 1960s Japan had the third-largest economy in the world. In 1975 Japan joined France, West Germany, Italy, Great Britain, and the United States to form the G6, the world's six leading industrialized nations. In 1986 Japan's average per capita income exceeded that of the United States for the first time.

Japan's emergence as an economic superpower fascinated outsiders. Many Asians and Africans looked to Japan for the secrets of successful modernization, but some of Japan's Asian neighbors again feared Japanese exploitation. In the 1970s and 1980s some Americans and Europeans bitterly accused **"Japan, Inc."** of an unfair alliance between government and business and urged their own governments to retaliate.

Japan's remarkable economic surge had deep roots in Japanese history and culture. When Commodore Perry arrived in the mid-nineteenth century, Japanese agriculture, education, and material well-being were advanced even by European standards. Moreover, the culturally homogeneous Japanese society put group needs before individual needs. The Meiji reformers who redefined Japan's primary task as catching up with the West had the support of a sophisticated and disciplined people (see pages 797–802). By 1952 the group-centered society had worked out a new national consensus: to build its economy and compete efficiently in world markets. Improved living standards emerged as a related goal after the initial successes of the 1950s.

In a system of managed capitalism, the government decided which industries were important, then made loans and encouraged mergers to create powerful firms in those industries. Antitrust regulations introduced by the Americans were quickly scrapped, and the home market was protected from foreign competition by various measures. Big business was valued and respected because it served the national goal and mir-

Ancient Shinto Practices in Modern Japan Ancient religious practices and modern technology come together as Shinto priests perform a ceremony of purification in front of a reactor pressure chamber in Japan. (Yoshitaka Nakatani/PLUS ONE, Inc., Tokyo) rored Japanese society. Workers were hired for life, and employees' social lives revolved around the company. (Discrimination against women remained severe: their wages and job security were strikingly inferior to men's.) Most unions became moderate, agreeable company unions. The social and economic distance between salaried managers and workers was slight and was often breached. *Efficiency*, *quality*, and *quantity* were the watchwords.

Japan in the Post-Cold War World

The 1990s brought a sharp reversal in Japan's economic performance. From 1990 to 1992 the Japanese stock market dropped by 65 percent. The bursting of the speculative bubble crippled Japanese banks, stymied economic growth, and led to record postwar unemployment of 4.5 percent in 1998. Unemployment remained around that level through 2011. Japan also faced increasingly tough competition from its industrializing neighbors in Asia (see Chapter 32).

The global economic crisis of 2008–2009 had a seriously deleterious effect on most of the leading world economies. The crisis hurt Japan more than other countries, however, because it had still not recovered from the financial reverses of the early 1990s, and, its recovery had been based not on exports but on increased domestic spending. In 2008 the economy shrunk by 1.2 percent and in 2009 by 5 percent. Deflation has become the watchword to describe Japan's economic situation, and domestic spending has dropped dramatically. Meanwhile, Japan has dropped from the world's second largest economy to third—behind the United States and China.

Postwar Japanese society, with its stress on discipline and cooperation rather than individualism and competition, has generally adapted well to meet the challenges of modern industrial urban society. Almost alone among industrial nations, Japan has experienced a marked decrease in crime over the past generation. Since the 1970s the Japanese have addressed such previously neglected problems as industrial pollution and limited energy resources. Unemployment rates, though high by Japanese standards, remain below those of most other industrialized countries. Long-term problems that have to be addressed include a massive government debt, a declining population, the aging of the population, and dependence on foreign sources for the energy, forest products, and minerals needed for modern industry. An earthquake with magnitude 9.0 that struck off Japan's northeast coast on March 11, 2011, followed by a castastrophic tsunami, devastated Japan's already fragile economy and left massive destruction, death, and human misery in their wake.

The Post-Cold War Era in Europe

☐ What was the nature of postcommunist reconstruction in eastern Europe, and how did Europe as a whole respond to calls for increased unity?

The end of the Cold War and the Soviet Union's collapse ended the division of Europe into two opposing camps. Although Europe in the 1990s was a collage of diverse peoples with their own politics, cultures, and histories, the entire continent now shared a commitment to capitalism and democracy.

Common Patterns and Problems

In economic affairs European leaders embraced, or at least accepted, a large part of the neoliberal, free-market vision of capitalist development. This vision differed markedly from western Europe's still-dominant welfare capitalism.

Two factors were particularly important in explaining the shift to tough-minded capitalism. First, Europeans were following practices and ideologies revived and enshrined in the 1980s by Reagan in the United States and Thatcher in Great Britain. Western Europeans especially took free-market prescriptions more seriously during the presidency of Bill Clinton (r. 1993–2001) because U.S. prestige and power were so high after the Cold War ended and because the U.S. economy outperformed its western European counterparts. Second, market deregulation and the privatization of state-controlled enterprises in different European countries were integral parts of the trend toward an open global economy. The rules of this global economy, laid down by powerful Western governments, multinational corporations, and big banks and international financial organizations such as the International Monetary Fund (IMF), called for the free movement of capital, goods, and services; low inflation; and limited government deficits.

The freer global economy had powerful social consequences, and global capitalism and freer markets challenged hard-won social achievements. As in the United States, many Europeans generally opposed corporate downsizing, the efforts to reduce the power of labor unions, and, above all, government plans to reduce social benefits. The reaction was particularly intense in France and Germany, where unions remained strong and

• **"Japan, Inc."** A nickname from the 1980s used to describe the intricate relationship of Japan's business world and government.

socialists championed a minimum amount of change in social policies.

In the 1990s political developments across Europe also shared common patterns and problems. Most obviously, the demise of European communism brought the apparent triumph of liberal democracy everywhere. All countries embraced genuine electoral competition with elected presidents and legislatures, and they guaranteed basic civil liberties. For the first time since before the French Revolution almost all of Europe followed the same general political model, although the variations were endless.

Recasting Russia Without Communism

With Soviet-style communism in ruins, eastern Europeans experienced continued rapid change. In Russia politics and economics were closely intertwined as President Boris Yeltsin (r. 1991–1999) sought to create conditions that would prevent a return to communism and right the faltering economy. Following the example of some postcommunist governments in eastern Europe, in January 1992 Yeltsin opted for breakneck liberalization. This shock therapy freed prices on 90 percent of all Russian goods, with the exception of bread, vodka, oil, and public transportation. The government also launched a rapid privatization of industry and turned thousands of factories and mines over to new private companies.

Yeltsin and his advisers believed shock therapy would revive production and bring prosperity after a brief period of hardship. The results were quite different. Prices soared and production fell sharply. The expected months of hardship stretched into years. By 1996 the Russian economy produced at least one-third and possibly one-half less than in 1991. From 1992 to 2001 the Russian economy fell by almost 30 percent — roughly equivalent to the situation in the United States during the Great Depression. In 2005 Russia's GDP (gross domestic product) was still lower than in 1991, but it grew sharply from 2003 through 2007, averaging around 6.5 to 7 percent a year. The global economic crisis of 2008–2009 hit Russia hard, but by late 2009 Russia's economy was recovering, aided by rising commodity and oil prices. In September 2010 Russian Prime Minister Vladimir Putin predicted a 4.5 percent growth rate for the Russian economy in 2010, after its decline of 8 percent in 2009.

Rapid economic liberalization worked poorly in Russia for several reasons. With privatization, powerful state industrial monopolies became powerful private monopolies that cut production and raised prices in order to maximize profits. Powerful managers forced Yeltsin's government to hand out enormous subsidies and credits to reinforce the positions of big firms or avoid bankruptcies. Finally, the managerial elite worked with criminal elements to intimidate would-be rivals, preventing the formation of new firms.

Runaway inflation and poorly executed privatization brought a profound social revolution to Russia. A new capitalist elite acquired great wealth and power, while the vast majority of people fell into poverty. Managers, former officials, and financiers who came out of the privatization process with large shares of the old state monopolies stood at the top of Russian society.

The quality of public services and health care declined precipitously — to the point that the average Russian male's life expectancy dropped from sixty-nine years in 1991 to fifty-nine years in 2007. In 2003 Russia's per capita income was lower than at any time since 1978, meaning essentially that there had been no economic progress for twenty-five years.

The 2000 election of Yeltsin's handpicked successor, President Vladimir Putin (b. 1952), ushered in a new era of "managed democracy." Putin's stress on public order and economic reform was popular, but during his seven and a half years in office, he became progressively more authoritarian. Significant restrictions were placed on media freedoms, regional elections were abolished, and the distinction between judicial and executive authority collapsed. Putin consolidated the power and authority of the state around himself and his closest advisers, closing off the development of democratic pluralism and an independent legal system in Russia. Putin also supported renationalization of some industries and more state regulation of energy policy and economic planning in general.

Putin's illiberal tendencies were also evident in his brutal military campaign against Chechnya (CHECH-nyuh), a tiny republic of 1 million Muslims in southern Russia (see Map 31.3, inset) that in 1991 declared its independence from Russia. Estimates of the number of Chechen civilians killed between 1994 and 2011 generally range between 100,000 and 200,000. Many more have become refugees, and the country's infrastructure has been destroyed. Chechen resistance to Russian domination continues, often in the form of terrorist attacks, such as a suicide bombing at Moscow's airport in January 2011 that killed scores of travelers.

Putin's increasingly authoritarian rule drew criticism from many quarters, both within and outside Russia. He came under increasing pressure from the European Union countries and even from the United States to back away from some of his most undemocratic positions. Unable to run for reelection in 2008, Putin handpicked a successor, Dmitry Medvedev, to be president, and took the position of Russian prime minister for himself. He remains the power behind the throne in

Russia and an important power broker on the world stage. Though economically now only a middle-tier country, Russia still retains the world's second-largest nuclear arsenal. That requires the rest of the world to acknowledge and negotiate with Russia.

Postcommunist Reconstruction in Eastern Europe

Eastern Europe had many of the same problems as Russia, and developments there were similar. The postcommunist nations worked to replace state planning and socialism with market mechanisms and private property. Western-style electoral politics also took hold, and as in Russia these politics were marked by intense battles between presidents and parliaments and by weak political parties. Ordinary citizens and the elderly were the big losers, while the young and former Communist Party members were the big winners. Regional inequalities persisted. Capital cities such as Warsaw, Prague, and Budapest concentrated wealth, power, and

opportunity; provincial centers stagnated; and industrial areas declined.

Given these challenges, it is perhaps not surprising that some civilians longed for a return to the safety and stability of communism. Most eastern Europeans, however, had never fully accepted communism, primarily because they linked it to Russian imperialism and the loss of national independence. The joyous crowds that toppled Communist regimes believed they were liberating the nation as well as the individual. Thus, when communism died, nationalism was reborn, creating new difficulties in many of the former East Bloc countries.

Poland, the Czech Republic, and Hungary were the most successful in making the transition. They managed to control national and ethnic tensions that might have destroyed their postcommunist reconstruction. The popular goal of "rejoining the West" was a powerful force for moderation in these countries. They hoped to find security in NATO membership, which came in 1997, and prosperity by joining western Europe's economic union (see pages 971–972).

Putin and Democracy After the Soviet Union's collapse in 1991, Russia's new leaders instituted a number of democratic reforms. After taking office in 2000, however, Russian President Vladimir Putin, who worked as a KGB agent during the Soviet era, was accused of rolling back many of these measures, including weakening the power of the Russian parliament, curbing the freedom of the media, restricting individual freedoms, using the war on terrorism to attack opponents, and centralizing and concentrating power in the president's office. Dmitry Medvedev succeeded Putin as president in May 2008 but then appointed Putin as Russian prime minister the day after his inauguration. Putin remains the power behind the throne, with Medvedev rarely challenging any of Putin's policies. (ARIAIL © 2003 Robert Ariail. Reprinted by permission of Universal Uclick for UFS. All rights reserved.)

The great postcommunist tragedy was Yugoslavia, which under Josip Tito had been a federation of republics and regions under Communist rule. After Tito's death in 1980, power passed increasingly to the sister republics, which encouraged a revival of regional and ethnic conflicts made worse by charges of ethnically inspired massacres during World War II and a dramatic economic decline in the mid-1980s.

The revolutions of 1989 accelerated the breakup of Yugoslavia. When Serbian president Slobodan Milosevic (SLOH-buh-dayn muh-LOH-suh-vihch; 1941–2006) attempted to grab land from other republics and unite all Serbs in a "greater Serbia," a civil war broke out that eventually involved Kosovo, Slovenia, Croatia, and Bosnia-Herzegovina. The civil war unleashed ruthless brutality, with murder, rape, the destruction of villages, the herding of refugees into concentration camps,

and charges of "ethnic cleansing"—genocide—against opposing ethnic groups (Map 31.4).

Serbian aggression appalled the Western nations. From March to June 1999 the Western Powers, led by the United States, carried out heavy bombing attacks on the Serbian capital, Belgrade; on Serbian strategic sites; and on Serbian military forces. They demanded that Milosevic withdraw Serbian armies. The impoverished Serbs eventually voted the still-defiant Milosevic out of office in September 2000, and in July 2001 a new pro-Western Serbian government turned him over to a war crimes tribunal in the Netherlands to stand trial for crimes against humanity. The civil wars in the former Yugoslavia were a monument to human cruelty. But ongoing efforts to preserve peace, repatriate refugees, and try war criminals also testified to the regenerative power of liberal values and human rights.

MAP 31.4 The Breakup of Yugoslavia Yugoslavia had the most ethnically diverse population in eastern Europe. The Republic of Croatia had substantial Serbian and Muslim minorities, and Bosnia-Herzegovina had large Muslim, Serbian, and Croatian populations, none of which had a majority. In June 1991 Serbia's brutal effort to seize territory and unite all Serbs in a single state brought a tragic civil war to the region.

Srebrenica When Bosnia officially declared its independence in 1992, a brutal three-year civil war broke out between Bosniaks (predominantly, though not all, Bosnian Muslims) and Croats on the one hand and Bosnian Serbs on the other. Supported by Serbia, Bosnian Serb militias practiced ethnic cleansing in areas under their control. In July 1995 Bosnian Serb militiamen slaughtered more than 8,000 Muslim men and boys in the town of Srebrenica, Bosnia. Here a Bosnian woman weeps over the coffins of 335 bodies found in a mass grave in 2004. (Jon Jones/Sygma/Corbis)

Unity and Identity in Western Europe

The movement toward western European unity received a powerful second wind in the 1990s. French president François Mitterrand (1916–1996) and German chancellor Helmut Kohl took the lead in pushing for the monetary union of European Community members, and the Maastricht Treaty of 1992 created a single EU currency, the euro. In 1993 the European Community proudly rechristened itself the **European Union (EU)** (Map 31.5).

Western European elites generally supported this step toward economic union. They saw monetary union as a means of coping with Europe's ongoing economic problems, imposing financial discipline, cutting costs, and reducing high unemployment. These elites also saw monetary union as a step toward political unity, enabling Europe to take a more prominent role in world politics.

Not all Europeans supported economic union. Many people resented the unending flow of rules handed down by the EU's growing bureaucracy, which sought to standardize everything from cheeses to day care. Moreover, many feared that more power in the hands of distant bureaucrats would undermine popular sovereignty and democratic control. Above all, they feared that the new Europe was being created at their expense. Joining the monetary union required governments to meet stringent fiscal standards and impose budget cuts and financial austerity. The resulting reductions in health care and social benefits hit ordinary citizens and did nothing to reduce western Europe's high unemployment rate.

The movement toward union raised profound questions about the meaning of European unity and identity. Would the EU remain an exclusive Western club, or would it expand to include the postcommunist nations of eastern Europe? If some of them were included, how could Muslim Turkey's long-standing application for membership be ignored? Conversely, how could a union of twenty-five to thirty countries have any real unity? In the face of these questions, western Europeans proceeded cautiously in considering new requests for EU membership.

The highly successful introduction of the euro in January 2002 encouraged the EU to accelerate plans for an ambitious enlargement to the east. On May 1, 2004, the EU started admitting eastern European countries. By 2007 the EU had twenty-seven member states, including most of eastern Europe, and a population of nearly 500 million, making it the world's largest trading bloc. Future candidates for membership include

• **European Union (EU)** An economic and political alliance of twenty-seven European nations.

Croatia, Macedonia, former members of the old Soviet Union, and Turkey.

A proposed EU constitution binding EU member states even closer together was scheduled to go into effect in 2007. First, however, it needed approval by voters in all member countries. In 2005 voters in France and Holland voted overwhelmingly against the constitution and threw the entire process into confusion. The rejected constitution was replaced with the Treaty of Lisbon in 2007. The new treaty kept most of the reforms contained in the original European constitution, but it reformed the political structure of the EU bureaucracy. By November 2009 all members had approved it, and the Lisbon treaty came into force on December 1, 2009, unifying what had been a profoundly divided continent just fifty years earlier.

□ Mapping the Past

MAP 31.5 The European Union, 2011 No longer divided by ideological competition and the Cold War, much of today's Europe has banded together in a European Union.

ANALYZING THE MAP Trace the expansion of membership in the European Union. How would you characterize the most recent members? Whose membership is still pending?

CONNECTIONS Which countries are not part of the Euro Zone? What does this suggest about the euro's success in the European Union?

CONNECTIONS

In 1945 Europe lay in ruins. Two new superpowers emerged to claim the mantle of global leadership: the democratic, capitalistic United States and the communist Soviet Union, each holding diametrically opposing visions of the future world order. As each superpower worked to acquire allies in the new Cold War, other nations, particularly newly independent nations such as China and India, adopted nonaligned positions that denied the right of either the Soviet Union or the United States to determine the world's destiny (see Chapter 32). As western Europe hunkered down to address its domestic problems, the empires created at the end of the nineteenth century crumbled in the face of powerful independence movements in Asia (Chapter 32) and Africa (Chapter 33).

Western Europe and Japan, with massive aid packages from the United States, quickly recovered from the terrible destruction caused by the war and soon surged ahead economically. New industries thrived as they rebuilt infrastructures and supplied the material goods that their citizens had gone without during the global depression and the world war. But as the next chapter discusses, the economic superpower status of the United States, Europe, and Japan faced fierce new competitors from Asia, most notably China.

By the end of the twentieth century the Cold War had ended, democratic governments had replaced the former Soviet Union and its satellite states throughout eastern Europe, and a new European Union had ended the divisions that had plagued Europe for most of the century. New divisions, however, would rise to divide Europe, this time in the form of debate concerning the growing multiethnic European society, as migrants from Africa, Asia, and the economically weaker states of eastern Europe entered the European Union both legally and illegally. Chapter 34 takes up this issue and explores the economic, political, social, and environmental challenges facing the world in the twenty-first century.

☐ CHAPTER REVIEW

☐ What were the causes of the Cold War? (p. 942)

Ideological, political, and security differences going back to the years following the Great War began pulling the United States and the Soviet Union apart before World War II ended. A critical disagreement involved the future of eastern Europe. In his meetings with Churchill, Roosevelt, and Truman, Stalin refused to consider free elections in eastern Europe that might put in place anti-Soviet governments. The Western Allies, and especially the United States, pushed hard for free elections, but there was little they could do to stop the Soviet occupying forces from installing pro-Soviet Communist leaders in these countries. Fearing further Soviet expansion, the United States implemented a policy of containment to try to stem the spread of communism around the world. Forty years of political and military standoffs followed.

KEY TERMS

Truman Doctrine (p. 946)
Marshall Plan (p. 946)
NATO (p. 946)
Common Market (p. 948)
OPEC (p. 949)
de-Stalinization (p. 953)
Brezhnev Doctrine (p. 953)

perestroika (p. 954)
glasnost (p. 954)
Solidarity (p. 955)
Charter of Paris for a New Europe (p. 959)
Civil Rights Act (p. 961)
détente (p. 963)
"Japan, Inc." (p. 966)
European Union (EU) (p. 971)

☐ How did western Europe recover so successfully after World War II, and how did economic decline in the 1970s and 1980s affect society? (p. 946)

Massive aid provided by the Marshall Plan jump-started recovery. Economic policies that encouraged governments to increase spending, even while incurring large deficits, were adopted by most western European countries. Workers, including many migrant laborers from the Mediterranean basin, advanced the economic turnaround by working hard for low wages. Pent-up demand for basic consumer products, like automobiles and refrigerators, encouraged economic production. Efforts to unite western Europe into a single large market helped as well to stimulate European economies. The economic decline of the 1970s brought recovery to a halt, but while unemployment rose eventually to rival that of the Great Depression, welfare systems prevented mass suffering. Increased government spending was not offset by taxes, leading to debt and a political backlash that saw new, more conservative leadership and austerity measures in many countries. To make ends meet, more women entered the workforce.

◻ **How did the Soviets try to reform society, and what were the consequences of the anticommunist revolutions of 1989? (p. 952)**

The Communist system in eastern Europe and the U.S.S.R. underwent tremendous changes after the death of Stalin. Khrushchev implemented a policy of de-Stalinization, which liberalized society, relaxing restrictions on workers and shifting resources from heavy industry and the military to agriculture and consumer goods. As a result, the standard of living rose. After the Cuban Missile crisis, Brezhnev stopped the program of liberalization and launched a heavy military buildup. In the 1980s public opposition to Soviet domination spread throughout the Soviet-bloc countries, fueled by Gorbachev's reform efforts, eventually leading to the revolutions of 1989 and to free elections, the restoration of civil liberties, and the institution of capitalist economies in eastern Europe.

◻ **What contributed to the social and political transformation of the United States in the second half of the twentieth century? (p. 961)**

American leaders generally viewed the Soviet Union and the spread of communism as the greatest dangers they faced and therefore turned their back on Third World liberation movements in order to gain the support of their western European allies in the Cold War. This stance had its most tragic consequences when the United States went to the aid of France in its efforts to hold onto its colony of Vietnam. The Vietnam War divided Americans. Students were active participants in the antiwar movement and the counterculture movement that simultaneously flourished. Liberalism triumphed in the 1960s with important civil rights legislation. The policy of containment gave way to détente in the 1970s, but after the Soviet invasion of Afghanistan and the Soviet refusal to accept the human

rights provisions of the Helsinki Accord, new, more conservative leadership again increased the military buildup. After the dissolution of the Soviet Union, the United States became the world's only superpower.

◻ **How did Japan recover so quickly after its total defeat in World War II to become an economic superpower? (p. 964)**

Before World War II Japan was one of the world's leading industrial nations. By the end of the war Japan lay devastated, facing what seemed like a bleak future. Allied occupation forces under the direction of General Douglas MacArthur set about helping Japan rebuild economically and develop a stable democratic government. Social and economic reforms were pushed through a new, popularly elected Diet (Japanese parliament). Article 9 of the new Japanese constitution abolished the military and renounced war. Eager to have a stable capitalist ally against communism in Asia, the United States guaranteed Japanese security with its own forces. America also poured billions of dollars into the Japanese economy, particularly during the Korean War, when Japan served as a military operations base for American forces. Japan's economic growth skyrocketed in the 1950s and 1960s, surpassing even western Europe's success in postwar recovery.

◻ **What was the nature of postcommunist reconstruction in eastern Europe, and how did Europe as a whole respond to calls for increased unity? (p. 967)**

The collapse of the Soviet Union and of communism there and across eastern Europe led to the adoption of liberal democracy and free market capitalism. Europe was no longer divided, and differences in political organization, human rights, and economic philosophy became less pronounced in the 1990s than at any time since 1914. Eastern Europe struggled to rejoin the West and replace the bankrupt Communist order with efficient capitalist democracies. Results varied greatly, and ordinary citizens often experienced real hardships, but no effort was made to restore economic planning or one-party rule, though a managed democracy in Russia under Putin led to a lessening of freedoms. The knitting together of Europe reached its apex in 1993 with the formation of the European Union. The introduction of a single currency — the euro — in 2002 and the signing of the Treaty of Lisbon in 2009 further solidified the economic and political unification of Europe.

SUGGESTED READING

Ash, Timothy Garton. *The Polish Revolution: Solidarity*, 3d ed. 2002. A definitive account of the role of the Solidarity movement in the Polish revolution and its subsequent fate.

Dobbs, Michael. *Down with Big Brother: The Fall of the Soviet Empire*. 1997. A superb account by a journalist who covered eastern Europe.

Eksteins, Modris. *Walking Since Daybreak: A Story of Eastern Europe, World War II, and the Heart of Our Century*. 1999. A powerful, partly autobiographical account that is highly recommended.

Gaddis, John Lewis. *The Cold War: A New History*. 2005. A concise, authoritative, and accessible account of the Cold War by one of its leading historians.

Grass, Günter. *The Tin Drum*. 1963. Nobel prize winner's exploration of the spiritual dimension of West German recovery in his world-famous novel.

Halberstam, David. *The Coldest Winter: America and the Korean War*. 2007. One of America's finest journalist-historian's last, and perhaps best, history.

Hughes, H. Stuart. *Sophisticated Rebels: The Political Culture of European Dissent, 1968–1987*. 1988. Provocatively analyzes the culture and politics of protest in Europe.

Kagan, Robert. *Of Paradise and Power: America and Europe in the New World Order*. 2004. Controversial but brilliant analysis of the post–Cold War world.

Karnow, Stanley. *Vietnam. A History*, 2d ed. 1997. One of the best and most comprehensive accounts of all sides in the war.

Kingston, Jeffrey. *Japan's Quiet Transformation: Social Change and Civil Society in the 21st Century, Politics, Economics and Society*. 2004. Leading scholar considers Japan's economic problems in the 1990s and their effects on Japanese politics and society.

Lampe, J. *Yugoslavia as History: Twice There Was a Country*, 2d ed. 2000. Judiciously and insightfully considers the history and violent collapse of Yugoslavia.

Laqueur, Walter. *Europe in Our Time: A History, 1945–1992*. 1992. Excellent comprehensive study of postwar Europe, with an extensive bibliography.

Sheehan, Neil. *A Bright and Shining Lie: John Paul Vann and America in Vietnam*. 1988. Classic account of the Vietnam War built around a biography of one of its harshest critics, Lieutenant Colonel Vann.

Urwin, Derek W. *The Community of Europe: A History of European Integration Since 1945*, 2d ed. 1995. Eloquent history of all aspects of European attempts at economic and political union since 1945.

Wapshott, Nicholas. *Ronald Reagan and Margaret Thatcher: A Political Marriage*. 2007. Particularly good analysis of their policies of economic conservatism and anticommunism in the 1980s.

NOTES

1. Quoted in N. Graebner, *Cold War Diplomacy, 1945–1960* (Princeton, N.J.: Van Nostrand, 1962), p. 17.
2. *Wall Street Journal*, June 25, 1985, p. 1.
3. Quoted in D. Treadgold, *Twentieth Century Russia*, 5th ed. (Boston: Houghton Mifflin, 1981), p. 442.
4. *Congressional Record: Proceedings and Debates* of the 84th Congress, 2nd Session (May 22, 1956–June 11, 1956), C11, Part 7 (June 4, 1956), pp. 9389–9403.
5. Regarding Gandhi's methods: see M. L. King, Jr., *Stride Toward Freedom: The Montgomery Story* (New York: Perennial Library, 1964), p. 67. Regarding evil laws: quoted in S. E. Morison et al., *A Concise History of the American Republic* (New York: Oxford University Press, 1977), p. 697.
6. Quoted in Morison, *Concise History*, p. 735.

For practice quizzes and other study tools, visit the **Online Study Guide** at bedfordstmartins.com/mckayworld.

For primary sources from this period, see *Sources of World Societies*, **Second Edition**.

For Web sites, images, and documents related to topics in this chapter, visit **Make History** at bedfordstmartins.com/mckayworld.

• **Iranian Green Revolution Protester** Iranians protest the results of the 2009 presidential election, and a young woman questions whether her vote was counted. Demonstrators returned to the streets of Iran in February 2011, as protests erupted against authoritarian regimes across North Africa and the Middle East. (Getty Images)

32

While the United States and the Soviet Union faced each other in a deadly standoff during the Cold War, most people in the so-called Third World went about their daily lives. The term *Third World* has its origins in the 1950s, when many thinkers, journalists, and politicians viewed Africa, Asia, and Latin America as a single entity, different from both the capitalist, industrialized "First World" and the Communist, industrialized "Second World." Despite differences in history and culture, most Third World countries in Africa, Asia, and Latin America — for a generation — shared many characteristics that encouraged a common consciousness and ideology. This chapter explores the characteristics of the countries in Asia and the Middle East, while Chapter 33 covers the development of the countries of Africa and Latin America.

Nearly all the countries in Asia and the Middle East experienced political or economic domination, nationalist reaction, and a struggle for genuine independence. Their peoples were thus united in their opposition to political and economic oppression in all its forms, particularly colonialism, neocolonialism, and racism. In the mid-twentieth century most Asian and Middle Eastern countries had predominately agricultural economies, earning the majority of their revenues from cash crops or natural resources, particularly oil, whose production was frequently controlled and exploited by First World countries or by multinational agribusinesses. In the second half of the twentieth century a few of these countries — most notably in the oil-rich Middle East and in East Asia, where there has been successful industrialization — became important producers and members of the global economy in their own right. In many cases, however, independence brought ethnic and religious conflict, as between the Muslims and Hindus in India, the Jews and Muslims in Palestine/Israel, the Chinese and Tibetans, and the Persians and Arabs in the Iran-Iraq War. •

Independence, Progress, and Conflict in Asia and the Middle East
1945 to the Present

The Resurgence of East Asia

□ How did the countries of East Asia successfully recover after World War II?

New Nations and Old Rivalries in South Asia

□ How have ethnic and religious rivalries affected the development of stable, independent states in South Asia?

Secularism and Religion at War in the Middle East

□ In what ways has religion played a role in Middle Eastern politics since 1945?

MAP 32.1 The New States in Asia Divided primarily along religious lines into two states, British India led the way to political independence in 1947.

- **Great Leap Forward** Mao Zedong's acceleration of Chinese development in which industrial growth was to be based on small-scale backyard workshops run by peasants living in gigantic self-contained communes.

The Resurgence of East Asia

□ How did the countries of East Asia successfully recover after World War II?

Other than Japan, most Asian countries recovered slowly after World War II. In the early 1950s the two Koreas and China were at war in the Korean peninsula, and the Vietnamese were fighting among themselves and against the French. The Nationalist Chinese in Taiwan were adjusting to life in exile from the mainland. Hong Kong, Singapore, Indonesia, South Korea, and the Philippines were recovering from years of colonial rule and Japanese occupation. Despite these challenges, over the next forty years China and the Asian "economic tigers" developed some of the largest and fastest-growing economies in the world, but liberal democracy remained elusive.

The Communist Victory in China

The Sino-Japanese War of 1937–1945 (see pages 901–902) led to the deaths of millions and created massive Chinese deficits and runaway inflation, hurting morale and ruining lives. The triumph of communism in China was due to many factors. Mao Zedong and the Communists had avoided pitched battles and concentrated on winning peasant support and forming a broad anti-Japanese coalition. By reducing rents, promising land redistribution, enticing intellectuals, and spreading propaganda, they emerged in peasant eyes as the true patriots, the genuine nationalists.

When Japan suddenly collapsed in August 1945, Communists and Nationalists both rushed to seize evacuated territory. In the last months of World War II, the Soviet Union occupied large areas of Manchuria previously held by the Japanese. When the Soviet troops left in March 1946 they allowed the Chinese Communists to seize control of key industrial areas in the north, including stockpiles of weapons left behind by the Japanese. Heavy fighting between the Communists and Nationalists broke out in Manchuria, and civil war began in earnest in April 1946. By 1948 the demoralized Nationalist forces were disintegrating before the better-led, more determined Communists. The following year Nationalist leader Jiang Jieshi and 2 million mainland Chinese fled to Taiwan, and in October 1949 Mao Zedong proclaimed the People's Republic of China (Map 32.1).

Between 1949 and 1954 the Communists consolidated their rule. They seized the vast land holdings of a minority of landlords and rich peasants and distributed the land to 300 million poor peasants. This revolutionary land reform was extremely popular and widely publicized through propaganda campaigns. Meanwhile, as Mao admitted in 1957, mass arrests led to 800,000 "class enemies" being summarily liquidated; the true figure is probably much higher. Millions more were deported to forced labor camps. All visible opposition from the old ruling groups was thus destroyed.

Claiming a new Mandate of Heaven, Mao and the Communists set out to prove that China was once again a great power. This was the real significance of China's participation in the Korean War (see page 946). From 1950 to 1953 the Chinese army's ability to fight the American "imperialists" to a bloody standstill on the Korean peninsula mobilized the masses and increased Chinese self-confidence. Fighting a war in Korea did not prevent the Chinese from also expanding their territory in the west, invading Tibet in 1950 and declaring Chinese sovereignty over the country in 1951. (See "Individuals in Society: The Dalai Lama," page 1040.)

Mao's China

Mao and the party looked to the Soviet Union for inspiration in the early 1950s. Along with the gradual collectivization of agriculture, China adopted a Soviet-style five-year plan to develop large factories and heavy industry rapidly. Russian specialists built many Chinese plants, and Soviet economic aid was considerable. The first five-year plan was successful, as undeniable economic growth followed the Communists' social revolution.

In the cultural and intellectual realms, too, the Chinese followed the Soviet example. Basic civil and political rights, which the Nationalists had seriously curtailed, were now simply abolished. Temples and churches were closed, and press freedom died. Soviet-style puritanism took hold, as the Communists quickly eradicated prostitution and drug abuse, which they had long regarded as marks of exploitation and national decline. They enthusiastically promoted Soviet Marxist ideas concerning women and the family. Full equality, work outside the home, and state-supported child care became primary goals.

In 1958 China broke from the Marxist-Leninist course of development and began to go its own way. Mao proclaimed a **Great Leap Forward** in which in-

☐ CHRONOLOGY

1947 Separation of India and Pakistan

1948 End of British mandate in Palestine; Jews proclaim state of Israel; Mohandas Gandhi assassinated

1949–1954 Mass arrests, forced-labor camps, and Communist propaganda in China

1949–present Harsh restrictions against religion and speech in China

1956 Nasser nationalizes Suez Canal Company

1958 Great Leap Forward in China

1964–1975 Vietnam War

1965 Great Proletarian Cultural Revolution in China

1967 Six-Day War in Israel

1970s–present Revival of Islamic fundamentalism in the Middle East

1975–1990 Civil war in Lebanon

1979 Islamic revolution in Iran

1980–1988 Iran-Iraq War

1987 Palestinians start the intifada

1989 Chinese military puts down student revolt in Tiananmen Square

1990–1991 Persian Gulf War

1991 Congress Party in India embraces Western capitalist reforms

2001 China joins World Trade Organization

2007 Hamas establishes Palestinian Authority government

2009 Mahmoud Ahmadinejad violently suppresses protests in Iran

2010–2011 Populist uprisings and protests across the Middle East

dustrial growth would be based on small-scale backyard workshops and steel mills run by peasants living in gigantic self-contained communes. The creation of a new socialist personality that rejected individualism and traditional Confucian family values, such as filial piety and acceptance of parental authority, was a second goal.

The intended great leap produced an economic disaster, as land in the countryside went untilled when peasants turned to industrial production. As many as 30 million people died in famines that swept the country in 1960–1961, one of the greatest human disasters in world history. When Soviet premier Nikita Khrushchev criticized Chinese policy in 1960, Mao

□ Picturing the Past

Communist China Poster Art One of the most popular art forms in Communist China is poster art, millions of copies of which have been printed to adorn the walls of homes, offices, factories, and businesses. Although related to socialist realism in the Soviet Union (see page 940), this uniquely Chinese version contains neither abstract, modern, or bourgeois elements nor classical Chinese art styles. Like Soviet socialist realism, such posters seek to glorify the state, its leaders, and the heroes of the ongoing revolution. The two young women in this poster wear uniforms and caps bearing the Communist red star, the five points of which represent the five components of Communist society: the youth, the army, the peasants, the workers, and the intellectuals. (Courtesy, Chinese Poster Collection, University of Westminster, London)

ANALYZING THE IMAGE Who is depicted, and what are they doing? What message do you think the artist seeks to convey with this image?

CONNECTIONS What social function or application might posters such as this one have? Is this sort of expression unique to Communist societies, or can you think of examples of other types of art that promote public messages?

condemned him and his Russian colleagues as detestable "modern revisionists." The Russians abruptly cut off economic and military aid, splitting the Communist world apart.

Mao lost influence in the party after the Great Leap Forward fiasco and the Sino-Soviet split, but in 1965 he staged a dramatic comeback. Fearing that China was becoming bureaucratic, capitalistic, and "revisionist" like the Soviet Union, Mao launched the **Great Proletarian Cultural Revolution**. He sought to

purge the party and to recapture the revolutionary fervor of his guerrilla struggle (see pages 897–898). The army and the nation's young people responded enthusiastically, organizing themselves into radical cadres called **Red Guards**. Students denounced their teachers and practiced rebellion in the name of revolution. One Red Guard manifesto exulted that "Revolution is rebellion, and rebellion is the soul of Mao Tse-tung's thought."[1] Mao's thoughts, through his speeches and writings, were collected in the *Little Red Book*, which

Shaming of Enemies During the Cultural Revolution During the Chinese Cultural Revolution in the 1960s, young Chinese militants and Red Guards attacked people identified as enemies of the Communist Party and Chairman Mao. Many of these "enemies" were intellectuals such as teachers and artists, but they could be neighbors and even parents who were considered bourgeois. Here a victim is paraded through the streets wearing a dunce cap with his crimes written on it. (Wide World Photos/AP Images)

became holy scripture to the Red Guards. Here the young Red Guards could gain inspiration from Mao's observation that

> The world is yours, as well as ours, but in the last analysis, it is yours. You young people, full of vigour and vitality, are in the bloom of life, like the sun at eight or nine in the morning. Our hope is placed on you. . . . The world belongs to you. China's future belongs to you.

And here also they could study the underlying maxim of Mao's revolution: "Every communist must grasp the truth, 'Political power grows out of the barrel of a gun.'"[2]

The Red Guards sought to erase all traces of "feudal" and "bourgeois" culture and thought. Ancient monuments and countless works of art, antiques, and books were destroyed. Party officials, professors, and intellectuals were exiled to remote villages to purify themselves with heavy labor. Universities were shut down for years. Thousands of people died, many of them executed, and millions more were sent to rural forced-labor camps. The Red Guards attracted enormous worldwide attention and served as an extreme model for the student rebellions in the West in the late 1960s (see page 962).

The Limits of Reform

Mao and the Red Guards succeeded in mobilizing the masses, shaking up the party, and creating greater so-

cial equality. But the Cultural Revolution also created growing chaos and a general crisis of confidence, especially in the cities. Persecuted intellectuals, technicians, and purged party officials launched a counterattack on the radicals and regained much of their influence by 1969. Thus China shifted to the right at the same time that Europe and the United States did. This shift opened the door to a limited but lasting reconciliation between China and the United States in 1972, facilitated by U.S. president Richard Nixon's visit that year.

After Mao's death in 1976, Deng Xiaoping (1904–1997) and his supporters initiated a series of new policies, embodied in the campaign of the "Four Modernizations": agriculture, industry, science and technology, and national defense. China's 800 million peasants experienced the most beneficial change from what Deng called China's "second revolution." Rigid collectivized agriculture had failed to provide either the peasants or the country with adequate food. Determined to modernize the economy, Deng looked to ally himself with the peasantry. China's peasants were allowed to farm the land in small family units rather than in large

• **Great Proletarian Cultural Revolution** A movement launched by Mao Zedong that attempted to purge the Chinese Communist Party of time-serving bureaucrats and recapture the revolutionary fervor of his guerrilla struggle.

• **Red Guards** Radical cadres formed by young people who would attack anyone identified as an enemy of either the Chinese Communist Party or Chairman Mao.

Chinese Students in 1989 These exuberant demonstrators in Tiananmen Square personify the idealism and optimism of China's prodemocracy movement. After some hesitation the Communist government crushed the student leaders and their supporters with tanks and executions, reaffirming its harsh, authoritarian character. (Erika Lansner/stockphoto.com)

collectives and to "dare to be rich" by producing crops of their choice. Peasants responded enthusiastically, increasing food production by more than 50 percent between 1978 and 1984.

The successful use of free markets in agriculture encouraged further economic experimentation. Foreign capitalists were allowed to open factories in southern China and to export Chinese products around the world. Private enterprise was also permitted in cities, where snack shops and a host of small businesses sprang up. China's Communist Party leaders also drew on the business talent of wealthy "overseas" Chinese in Hong Kong and Taiwan who knew the world market and needed new sources of cheap labor. The Chinese economy grew rapidly between 1978 and 1987, and per capita income doubled in these years.

Most large-scale industry remained state-owned, however, and cultural change proceeded slowly. Above all, the Communist Party zealously preserved its monopoly on political power. When the worldwide movement for greater democracy and political freedom in the late 1980s also took root in China, the government responded by banning all demonstrations and slowing the trend toward a freer economy. Inflation then soared to more than 30 percent a year. The economic reversal, the continued lack of political freedom, and the conviction that Chinese society was becoming more corrupt led China's idealistic university students to spearhead demonstrations in April 1989.

The students evoked tremendous popular support, and on May 17 more than a million people streamed into Beijing's central **Tiananmen Square** in support of their demands. The government declared martial law and ordered the army to clear the students. Masses of courageous Chinese citizens blocked the soldiers' entry into the city for two weeks, but in the early hours of June 4, 1989, tanks rolled into Tiananmen Square. At least seven hundred students died as a wave of repression, arrests, and executions descended on China.

In the months after Tiananmen Square communism fell in eastern Europe, the Soviet Union broke apart, and China's rulers felt vindicated. They believed their action had preserved Communist power, prevented chaos, and demonstrated the limits of reform. After some hesitation Deng and his successor Jiang Zemin (b. 1926) reaffirmed economic liberalization. Private enterprise and foreign investment boomed in the 1990s. Consumerism was encouraged, and the living standard rose. But critics of Communist rule were jailed, and every effort was made to ensure that the People's Army would again crush the people if ordered. Thus China coupled growing economic freedom with continued political repression.

These policies continued into the twenty-first century. In 2001, after long negotiations, China joined the World Trade Organization, giving it all the privileges and obligations of participation in the liberal global economy. Politically Communist, China now has a full-blown capitalist economy. From 1978, when Deng Xiaoping took over and launched economic reforms, through 2010, the Chinese economy grew at an average annual rate of over 9 percent, and foreign trade at an average of 16 percent. When Europe, the United States, Japan, and many other nations faced a severe economic downturn in 2008, China's economy continued to expand. Average per capita income in China has doubled every ten years, and in March 2011 China replaced Japan as the world's second largest economy after that of the United States.

But China continues to have a miserable human rights record. In 2002 current leader Hu Jintao (b. 1942) introduced modest legal reforms. He remains clearly committed, however, to maintaining a strong authoritarian state. There was some hope that, as promised, China's Communist leaders would make significant human rights, labor rights, and press freedom reforms before the 2008 Summer Olympic Games in Beijing began. In spring 2008, however, the Chinese harshly crushed demonstrations in Tibet, sparking worldwide protest. In October 2010 the Nobel Peace Prize committee awarded the prize to Chinese dissident Liu Xiaobo, a professor, literary critic, political essayist, and long-time democracy advocate who was then serving an eleven-year sentence for subversion. China refused to allow Liu, or anyone representing him, to go to Oslo to receive the prize, something that had happened only once before, when Hitler's Nazi Germany refused that right to Nobel Prize–winner and imprisoned pacifist Carl von Ossietzky in 1935. (See "Individuals in Society: Liu Xiaobo," page 984.)

The Asian "Economic Tigers"

China's exploding economy replicated the rapid industrial progress that characterized first Japan (see page 964) and then Asia's economic tigers — Taiwan, Hong Kong, Singapore, and South Korea. Both South Korea and Taiwan were underdeveloped Third World countries in the early postwar years — poor, small, agricultural, densely populated, and lacking natural resources. They also had suffered from Japanese imperialism and from destructive civil wars with Communist foes. Yet they managed spectacular turnarounds by making economic development national missions. First, radical land reform expropriated large landowners and drew small farmers into a competitive market economy. Second, pro-business governments cooperated with capitalists, opposed strikes, and protected businesses from foreign competition while securing access to the large American market. Third, both countries succeeded in preserving many cultural fundamentals even as they accepted and mastered Western technology. Last, tough nationalist leaders — Park Chung Hee (1917–1978) in South Korea and Jiang Jieshi in Taiwan — maintained political stability at the expense of genuine political democracy.

After a military coup overthrew Park in 1980, South Korea suffered under an even more authoritarian regime through the 1980s until democracy was restored at the end of the decade. South Korea's economy, however, continued to grow and expand. By the late 1990s

Asian "Economic Tigers"

South Korea had one of the largest economies in the world and is a world leader in shipbuilding and high-tech products. Its GDP is about twenty times larger than North Korea's.

In 1949, after Jiang Jieshi had fled to Taiwan with his Nationalist troops and around 2 million refugees, he re-established the Republic of China (ROC) in exile. Over the next fifty years Taiwan created one of the world's most highly industrialized capitalist economies, becoming a world leader in high-tech and electronic manufacturing and design.

A large threatening cloud hangs over the island, however. As one of the founding members of the United Nations in 1945, Jiang's ROC government held one of the Security Council's five permanent seats. In 1971 the United Nations expelled the ROC, and its Security Council seat was given to the Communist People's Republic of China (mainland China). This action left Taiwan in political limbo: should it remain the ROC or become an independent Republic of Taiwan? Meanwhile, mainland China claims authority over Taiwan, considers it part of "One China," and has threatened to attack if Taiwan declares its formal independence.

Pro-independence candidate Chen Shui-bian (b. 1950) defeated the Guomindang (Nationalist) candidate in 2000 to become the first non-Guomindang president in Taiwan's postwar history. A moderate, he supported independence and remained defiant toward the mainland. In early 2008, however, the Taiwanese people returned the Guomindang Party and its leader Ma Ying-jeou (b. 1950) to power. Campaigning on the promise of "no reunification, no independence and no war," Ma dropped talk of Taiwanese independence and sought closer relations with China. In 2009, for the first time since 1993, Taiwan did not submit a bid to again become a United Nations member. Thus, the tension surrounding the standoff between China and Taiwan has eased somewhat, and there has been increased contact between the two sides in commerce, communications, and transportation. But China continues to hold to its One China position, and the Chinese military continues to prepare for a possible invasion of the island.

Gaining its sovereignty in 1965 from the Federation of Malaysia, the independent city-state of Singapore is

• **Tiananmen Square** The site of a Chinese student revolt in 1989 at which Communists imposed martial law and arrested, injured, or killed hundreds of students.

Individuals in Society

Liu Xiaobo

AT THE NOBEL PEACE PRIZE CEREMONY IN OSLO on October 8, 2010, the chair reserved for the recipient, Liu Xiaobo (b. 1955) of China, was empty. Liu was serving an eleven-year prison term, and his wife, Liu Xia, was under house arrest. China blocked all news coverage of the event, including Web sites reporting on the ceremony.

Born in 1955, Liu received his Ph.D. in literature from Beijing Normal University in 1988. A highly regarded scholar and teacher, he lectured at Beijing Normal and, in the late 1980s, at Columbia University, the University of Oslo, and the University of Hawai'i. In spring 1989, when Chinese prodemocracy students began to gather in Beijing's Tiananmen Square, Liu was at Columbia. Although he had not previously involved himself in politics, Liu left the United States and returned to China in mid-May to join the students and other demonstrators. He began a hunger strike when rumors of an army crackdown filled the square.

Shortly before the Tiananmen Square massacre on June 4, 1989, Liu began to negotiate with the army to allow the protestors to peacefully leave the square. But at 1 A.M. Chinese troops and tanks moved into the square and attacked the remaining demonstrators. By 5:40 A.M. the square had been cleared. The true number of deaths and injuries in and around the square that night will never be known, but estimates range from a few hundred to a few thousand. Liu and others are widely credited with saving many lives by having negotiated a peaceful withdrawal by the students before the tanks rolled in.

Fearing arrest, Liu initially took asylum in the Australian embassy, but he went into the streets again when the government began going after, arresting, and executing demonstrators. He was arrested on June 8 and spent the next twenty months in prison.

Events at Tiananmen Square had made the previously detached academic a vocal critic of China's human rights poli-

cies. Chinese officials responded by banning all of his publications. Liu continued to write, however, and in Taiwan in 1992 he published a controversial memoir, *The Monologues of a Doomsday's Survivor*, that chronicled his involvement in and criticism of the 1989 popular democracy movement. Now constantly harassed by the government, Liu received a three-year prison sentence in 1996 for involvement in the human rights movement and for disturbing the social order. After his release Liu and his wife lived under constant police surveillance. In 2004 the police raided his home and took his computer and most of his personal papers.

Liu was a founder of the Chinese PEN Centre and served as its president from 2003 to 2007. An international organization of writers, PEN members campaign for freedom of expression and speak on behalf of writers who are being persecuted for their views.

In 2008 Liu helped write Charter 08, a Chinese human rights manifesto signed by over 350 activists and intellectuals. They issued the charter on the sixtieth anniversary of the Universal Declaration of Human Rights, a 1948 United Nations document guaranteeing all human beings certain rights, including the "four freedoms" of speech, of belief, from want, and from fear. On June 23, 2009, Liu was charged with "inciting the subversion of state power" and was sentenced in December to eleven years in prison.

The Nobel Peace Committee awarded Liu the 2010 prize "for his long and non-violent struggle for fundamental human rights in China."* In "I Have No Enemies: My Final Statement," which was read at the award ceremony, Liu wrote:

> But I still want to say to this regime, which is depriving me of my freedom, that . . . I have no enemies and no hatred. . . . I hope that I will be the last victim of China's endless literary inquisitions and that from now on no one will be incriminated because of speech. Freedom of expression is the foundation of human rights, the source of humanity, and the mother of truth. To strangle freedom of speech is to trample on human rights, stifle humanity, and suppress truth.†

QUESTIONS FOR ANALYSIS

1. Why is the Chinese government so afraid of Liu's writings?

2. What do you think Liu meant when he said in his Nobel Peace Prize statement "I have no enemies and no hatred"?

*The Nobel Peace Prize 2010. Nobelprize.org. http://nobelprize.org/nobel_prizes/peace/laureates/2010/.

†Liu Xiaobo-Appell. Nobelprize.org. http://nobelprize.org/nobel_prizes/peace/laureates/2010/xiaobo-lecture.html.

Jailed Chinese dissident and civil rights activist Liu Xiaobo in Beijing, China. (Liu Xia/epa)

Lights in the Night in the Eastern Hemisphere This NASA photo uniquely illustrates differences in wealth between the North and South. Human-made lights shine brightly from developed countries and heavily populated cities. Africa's continent-wide economic poverty is clearly evident, while North Korea sits in stark dark contrast to the blaze of light from South Korea and the other Asian economic tigers. (Image by Craig Mayhew and Robert Simmons, NASA GSFC)

the smallest of the economic tigers. It has prospered on the hard work and inventiveness of its largely Chinese population. Singapore's government promoted education, private enterprise, high technology, and affordable housing for all citizens. The government, dominated by the People's Action Party since independence, forcefully promotes conservative family values and strict social discipline. It also applies a mixture of economic planning and free-market practices, the so-called Singapore model, which has resulted in its enjoying one of the highest per capita incomes in the world since the 1990s. Despite the global economic downturn in 2008 and 2009, Singapore possessed the fastest growing economy in the world in 2010, expanding at nearly 14.7 percent.

One of two Special Administrative Regions (SARs) in China (Macau is the other one), Hong Kong has long played a prominent role in the world economy. The British first occupied Hong Kong in 1841. Primarily a center of oceanic trade in the nineteenth century, Hong Kong turned to finance and manufacturing in the twentieth. On July 1, 1997, the United Kingdom returned Hong Kong to Chinese control. Under the agreement Hong Kong became a Special Administrative Region, and China promised that, under its "one country, two

systems" formula, China's socialist economic system would not be imposed on Hong Kong. Hong Kong is the world's tenth largest trading entity and eleventh largest banking center, and it continues to have one of the world's highest per capita GDPs. Although Hong Kong's economy was hurt by the global downturn in 2008 and 2009, its increasing integration with the Chinese economy has allowed it to recover more quickly than expected.

Political and Economic Progress in Southeast Asia

While many of the countries of Southeast Asia gained independence in the decade after 1945 (see Map 32.1), the attainment of stable political democracy proved a more difficult goal, and authoritarian rule characterized many of the new governments. As ethnic conflicts and Cold War battles divided their countries, governments in the Philippines, Indonesia, North and South Vietnam, Cambodia, and Burma fell to dictatorships or military juntas in an effort to impose order and unity. (See "Listening to the Past: Aung San Suu Kyi, 'Freedom from Fear,'" page 986.) By the early twenty-first

Listening to the Past

Aung San Suu Kyi, "Freedom from Fear"

Aung San Suu Kyi, the Burmese opposition politician, spent fifteen of the last twenty-one years under house arrest between July 20, 1989, and her recent release on November 13, 2010, for her opposition to the military junta that rules Burma. After receiving a Ph.D. at the University of London in 1985, Suu Kyi returned to Burma in 1988 to lead the prodemocracy movement. A Buddhist as well as a follower of Gandhi's philosophy of nonviolence, Suu Kyi was arrested while campaigning for a peaceful transition to a democratic civilian government when Burma's leader General Ne Win retired after twenty-four years in power. In 1991, for her contributions in the struggle for human rights, Suu Kyi received the Nobel Peace Prize and the Sakharov Prize for Freedom of Thought from the European Parliament. This selection is from her "Freedom from Fear" acceptance speech for the Sakharov award.

"It is not power that corrupts but fear. Fear of losing power corrupts those who wield it and fear of the scourge of power corrupts those who are subject to it. Most Burmese are familiar with the four a-gati, the four kinds of corruption. Chanda-gati, corruption induced by desire, is deviation from the right path in pursuit of bribes or for the sake of those one loves. Dosa-gati is taking the wrong path to spite those against whom one bears ill will, and moga-gati is aberration due to ignorance. But perhaps the worst of the four is bhaya-gati, for not only does bhaya fear, stifle and slowly destroy all sense of right and wrong, it so often lies at the root of the other three kinds of corruption.

Just as chanda-gati, when not the result of sheer avarice, can be caused by fear of want or fear of losing the goodwill of those one loves, so fear of being surpassed, humiliated or injured in some way can provide the impetus for ill will. And it would be difficult to dispel ignorance unless there is freedom to pursue the truth unfettered by fear. With so close a relationship between fear and corruption it is little wonder that in any society where fear is rife corruption in all forms becomes deeply entrenched.

It would be difficult to dispel ignorance unless there is freedom to pursue the truth unfettered by fear. With so close a relationship between fear and corruption it is little wonder that in any society where fear is rife corruption in all forms becomes deeply entrenched. . . .

The effort necessary to remain uncorrupted in an environment where fear is an integral part of everyday existence is not immediately apparent to those fortunate enough to live in states governed by the rule of law. Just laws do not merely prevent corruption by meting out impartial punishment to offenders. They also help to create a society in which people can fulfil the basic requirements necessary for the preservation of human dignity without recourse to corrupt practices. Where there are no such laws, the burden of upholding the principles of justice and common decency falls on the ordinary people. It is the cumulative effect on their sustained effort and steady endurance which will change a nation where reason and conscience are warped by fear into one where legal rules exist to promote man's desire for harmony and justice while restraining the less desirable destructive traits in his nature.

In an age when immense technological advances have created lethal weapons which could be, and are, used by the powerful and the unprincipled to dominate the weak and the helpless, there is a compelling need for a closer relationship between politics and ethics at both the national and international levels. The Universal Declaration of Human Rights of the United Nations proclaims that "every individual and every organ of society" should strive to promote the basic rights and freedoms to which all human beings regardless of race, nationality or religion are entitled. But as long as there are governments whose authority is founded on coercion rather than on the mandate of the people, and interest groups which place short-term profits above long-term peace and prosperity, concerted international action to protect and promote human rights will remain at best a partially realized ideal. . . .

The quintessential revolution is that of the spirit, born of an intellectual conviction of the need for change in those mental attitudes and values which shape the course of a nation's development. A revolution which aims merely at changing official policies and institutions with a view to an improvement in material conditions has little chance of genuine success. Without a revolution of the spirit, the forces which produced the iniquities of the old order would continue to be operative,

century all these countries except for Burma have been moving toward more stable governments and growing economies.

The Philippine Islands suffered greatly under Japanese occupation during the Second World War. After the war the United States retained its large military bases (they were finally closed in 1992) but granted the Philippines independence in 1946. The Philippines was an American-style democracy until 1972, when President Ferdinand Marcos (1917–1989) subverted the constitution and ruled as dictator. In 1986 a widespread popular rebellion forced him into exile, and Corazón Aquino (1933–2009) became the first female president. Aquino and the presidents who have followed her have made some progress in improving the economy. Many Filipinos work abroad. Their remit-

At her home in Rangoon, Aung San Suu Kyi sits in front of a portrait of her father, General Aung San, founder of the Burmese independence movement.
(Richard Vogel/AP Images)

posing a constant threat to the process of reform and regeneration. It is not enough merely to call for freedom, democracy and human rights. There has to be a united determination to persevere in the struggle, to make sacrifices in the name of enduring truths, to resist the corrupting influences of desire, ill will, ignorance and fear. . . .

Among the basic freedoms to which men aspire that their lives might be full and uncramped, freedom from fear stands out as both a means and an end. A people who would build a nation in which strong, democratic institutions are firmly established as a guarantee against state-induced power must first learn to liberate their own minds from apathy and fear. . . .

Gandhi, that great apostle of non-violence, and Aung San, the founder of a national army, were very different personalities, but as there is an inevitable sameness about the challenges of authoritarian rule anywhere at any time, so there is a similarity in the intrinsic qualities of those who rise up to meet the challenge.

Fearlessness may be a gift but perhaps more precious is the courage acquired through endeavour, courage that comes from cultivating the habit of refusing to let fear dictate one's actions, courage that could be described as "grace under pressure"—grace which is renewed repeatedly in the face of harsh, unremitting pressure.

Within a system which denies the existence of basic human rights, fear tends to be the order of the day. Fear of imprisonment, fear of torture, fear of death, fear of losing friends, family, property or means of livelihood, fear of poverty, fear of isolation, fear of failure. A most insidious form of fear is that which masquerades as common sense or even wisdom, condemning as foolish, reckless, insignificant or futile the small, daily acts of courage which help to preserve man's self-respect and inherent human dignity. It is not easy for a people conditioned by fear under the iron rule of the principle that might is right to free themselves from the enervating miasma of fear. Yet even under the most crushing state machinery courage rises up again and again, for fear is not the natural state of civilized man.

The wellspring of courage and endurance in the face of unbridled power is generally a firm belief in the sanctity of ethical principles combined with a historical sense that despite all setbacks the condition of man is set on an ultimate course for both spiritual and material advancement. It is his capacity for self-improvement and self-redemption which most distinguishes man from the mere brute. At the root of human responsibility is the concept of perfection, the urge to achieve it, the intelli-

gence to find a path towards it, and the will to follow that path if not to the end at least the distance needed to rise above individual limitations and environmental impediments. It is man's vision of a world fit for rational, civilized humanity which leads him to dare and to suffer to build societies free from want and fear. Concepts such as truth, justice and compassion cannot be dismissed as trite when these are often the only bulwarks which stand against ruthless power. "

Source: Aung San Suu Kyi, *Freedom from Fear and Other Writings*, ed. Michael Aris (New York: Penguin, 2010), pp. 180–185. Copyright © 1991 Aung San Suu Kyi. Reproduced by permission of Penguin Books Ltd.

QUESTIONS FOR ANALYSIS

1. To whom is Aung San Suu Kyi referring when she talks about the fear of losing power?
2. How does Aung San Suu Kyi reconcile her struggle with her Buddhist faith in her reference to the four a-gati?
3. How might Aung San Suu Kyi's words apply to other regimes mentioned in this chapter, such as Egypt, China, or Iran?

tances back home, plus rapid growth in exports to China and strong sales of semiconductor electronics, helped the Philippine economy grow at over 7 percent in 2007. The Philippines weathered the 2008–2009 economic downturn, continuing to show modest gains in economic growth. Despite the growing economy, Communist insurgents and Muslim separatists continue to threaten the Philippines' political stability.

The Netherlands East Indies emerged in 1949 as independent Indonesia under the nationalist leader Achmed Sukarno (1901–1970). Like the Philippines, the populous new nation encompassed a variety of peoples, islands, and religions, with 85 percent of the population practicing Islam (see Map 32.3 on page 995). A military coup led by General Suharto (1921–2008) forced Sukarno out in 1965. Suharto's authoritarian rule concentrated mainly on economic development. Blessed with large oil revenues, Indonesia achieved solid economic growth for a generation. Increasingly tied to the world economy, in 1997 Indonesia was devastated by a financial crisis, and Suharto was forced to resign in 1998.

After Suharto's fall, freely elected governments attacked corruption and reversed the economic decline. In 2000 Indonesia gave East Timor political independence. In 2004, in the first direct presidential elections ever held there, the Indonesians elected Susilo Bambang Yudhoyono (b. 1949) as president. Despite years of militant Islamic terrorist acts and natural disasters — a 2004 Indian Ocean tsunami, earthquakes, severe floods, and outbreaks of avian influenza (bird flu) — the economy grew at over 6 percent in 2007 and 2008, its fastest pace in eleven years. Economic expansion dropped to 4 percent in 2009 during the global economic crisis, but this smaller gain still made Indonesia one of only three of the world's largest economies, along with China and India, to exhibit growth.

The Reunification of Vietnam

French Indochina experienced the bitterest struggle for independence in Southeast Asia. The French tried to reimpose imperial rule there after the Communist and nationalist guerrilla leader Ho Chi Minh (1890–1969) declared an independent republic in 1945, but they were decisively defeated in the 1954 Battle of Dien Bien Phu. At the subsequent international peace conference, French Indochina gained independence. Laos and Cambodia became separate states, and Vietnam was "temporarily" divided into two hostile sections at the seventeenth parallel pending elections to select a single unified government within two years.

The elections were never held, and a civil war soon broke out between the two Vietnamese governments, one Communist and the other anticommunist. (See "Viewpoints: Ho Chi Minh, Lyndon Johnson, and the Vietnam War," page 989.) Despite tremendous military effort in the Vietnam War by the United States in 1964–1975 (see pages 962–963), the Communists proved victorious in 1975 and created a unified Marxist nation. In 1986 Vietnamese Communists began to turn from central planning toward freer markets and private initiative with mixed results. The Vietnamese economy has grown 7 to 8 percent per year since 1990, but these numbers are deceptive because inflation and unemployment are also very high. Vietnam remains one of the poorest countries in the region. Still, Communist officials are committed to a market economy, and Vietnam became the World Trade Organization's 150th member on January 11, 2007. Vietnam's Communist leaders continue to zealously guard their monopoly on political power.

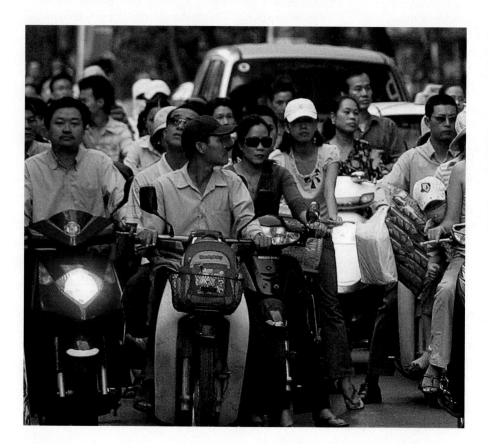

Capitalism in Today's Vietnam
Swarms of "angry bees" in the street of Hanoi, Vietnam, where there are an estimated 4 million people and 2 million bikes. Motorbikes make up 90 percent of all the vehicles on the road in this rapidly modernizing country, and their numbers will only increase as Vietnam adopts market capitalism and its citizens have more disposable income. An accident death rate of over one thousand per month caused the government to mandate safety helmets as of 2008. (Maxim Marmur/Getty Images)

Viewpoints

Ho Chi Minh, Lyndon Johnson, and the Vietnam War

• *On September 2, 1945, after decades of French colonialism and Japanese occupation, Ho Chi Minh, a Marxist revolutionary and North Vietnam's prime minister, read Vietnam's Declaration of Independence to a Hanoi audience. It would be thirty more years, however, before all of Vietnam would be united and independent. For the last ten of those years the United States waged war against Ho and his fellow Communists. On August 5, 1964, U.S. president Lyndon Johnson asked Congress to pass the Gulf of Tonkin Resolution, which authorized U.S. military action against North Vietnam. Seven months later the first U.S. ground forces were sent in, marking the beginning of the Vietnam War.*

Ho Chi Minh, Declaration of Independence of the Democratic Republic of Vietnam, 1945

"All men are created equal. They are endowed by their Creator with certain inalienable rights, among these are Life, Liberty, and the pursuit of Happiness. This immortal statement was made in the Declaration of Independence of the United States of America in 1776. In a broader sense, this means: All the peoples on the earth are equal from birth, all the peoples have a right to live, to be happy and free.

The Declaration of the French Revolution made in 1791 on the Rights of Man and the Citizen also states: "All men are born free and with equal rights and must always remain free and have equal rights." Those are undeniable truths.

Nevertheless, for more than eighty years, the French imperialists, abusing the standard of Liberty, Equality, and Fraternity, have violated our Fatherland and oppressed our fellow-citizens. They have acted contrary to the ideals of humanity and justice. In the field of politics, they have deprived our people of every democratic liberty.

They have enforced inhuman laws. . . . They have built more prisons than schools. They have mercilessly slain our patriots, they have drowned our uprisings in rivers of blood. . . . To weaken our race they have forced us to use opium and alcohol. In the fields of economics, they have fleeced us to the backbone, impoverished our people, and devastated our land. They have robbed us of our rice fields, our mines, our forests, and our raw materials. . . . They have invented numerous unjustifiable taxes and reduced our people, especially our peasantry, to a state of extreme poverty. . . .

A people who have courageously opposed French domination for more than eighty years, a people who have fought side by side with the Allies against the Fascists during these last years, such a people must be free and independent. For these reasons, we . . . solemnly declare to the world that Vietnam has the right to be a free and independent country."

Lyndon Johnson, Address to Congress Regarding the Tonkin Gulf Resolution, 1964

"I . . . ask the Congress for a resolution expressing the unity and determination of the United States in supporting freedom and in protecting peace in southeast Asia.

Our policy in southeast Asia has been consistent and unchanged since 1954. [It has] four simple propositions:

1. *America keeps her word*. Here as elsewhere, we must and shall honor our commitments.

2. *The issue is the future of southeast Asia as a whole.* A threat to any nation in that region is a threat to all, and a threat to us.

3. *Our purpose is peace*. We have no military, political, or territorial ambitions in the area.

4. *This is not just a jungle war, but a struggle for freedom on every front of human activity.*

The North Vietnamese regime has constantly sought to take over South Vietnam and Laos . . . violat[ing] the Geneva accords for Vietnam. It has systematically conducted a campaign of subversion, which includes the direction, training, and supply of personnel and arms for the conduct of guerrilla warfare in South Vietnamese territory. In Laos, the North Vietnamese regime has maintained military forces, used Laotian territory for infiltration into South Vietnam, and most recently carried out combat operations.

As President of the United States I . . . now ask the Congress, to join in affirming the national determination . . . that the United States will continue in its basic policy of assisting the free nations of the area to defend their freedom."

Sources: Ho Chi Minh, *Selected Works* (Hanoi, 1960–1962), 3: pp. 17–21. Reprinted with permission of The Gioi Publishers; Lyndon B. Johnson, "Special Message to the Congress on U.S. Policy in Southeast Asia, August 5, 1964," in *Public Papers of the Presidents of the United States: Lyndon B. Johnson, 1963–1964*. Vol. II: *July 1 to December 31, 1964* (Washington, D.C.: Government Printing Office, 1965), pp. 930–932.

QUESTIONS FOR ANALYSIS

1. What were some of the wrongs that Ho Chi Minh charged the French had committed against his country and people?

2. What were the four basic propositions underlying American policy in Southeast Asia?

New Nations and Old Rivalries in South Asia

☐ How have ethnic and religious rivalries affected the development of stable, independent states in South Asia?

The South Asian subcontinent has transformed itself no less spectacularly than have China, Japan, and the Asian economic tigers. India's national independence movements triumphed decisively over British imperialism after the Second World War. The newly independent nations of India, Pakistan, and Bangladesh exhibited many variations on the dominant themes of national renaissance and modernization, and ethnic and religious rivalries greatly complicated the process of renewal and development.

MAP 32.2 The Partition of British India, 1947 Violence and fighting were most intense where there were large Hindu and Muslim minorities—in Kashmir, the Punjab, and Bengal. The tragic result of partition, which occurred repeatedly throughout the world in the twentieth century, was a forced exchange of populations and greater homogeneity on both sides of the border.

The End of British India

World War II accelerated the drive toward Indian independence begun by Mohandas Gandhi (see page 891). In 1942 Gandhi called on the British to "quit India" and threatened another civil disobedience campaign. He and the other Indian National Congress Party leaders were soon after arrested and were jailed for most of the war. Thus, India's wartime support for Britain was substantial but not always enthusiastic. Meanwhile, the Congress Party's prime political rival skillfully seized the opportunity to increase its influence.

That rival was the **Muslim League**, led by the English-educated lawyer Muhammad Ali Jinnah (1876–1948). Jinnah feared Hindu domination of an independent Indian state led by the Congress Party. Asserting in nationalist terms the right of Muslim areas to separate from the Hindu majority, in March 1940 Jinnah called on the British government to grant the Muslim and Hindu peoples separate homelands by dividing India into autonomous national states:

> The Hindus and Muslims have two different religions, philosophies, social customs, literatures. They neither inter-marry, nor dine together, and indeed, they belong to two different civilizations which are based mainly on conflicting ideas and conceptions. Their aspects on life and of life are different. It is quite clear that Hindus and Mussalmans derive their inspirations from different sources of history. They have different epics, their heroes are different, and they have different episodes. Very often the hero of one is a foe of the other and likewise, their victories and defeats overlap. To yoke together two such nations under a single State, one as a numerical minority and the other as majority, must lead to growing discontent and final destruction of any fabric that may be so built up for the government of such a State.[3]

Gandhi regarded Jinnah's two-nation theory as untrue and as promising the victory of hate over love.

Britain agreed to speedy independence for India after 1945, but conflicting Hindu and Muslim nationalisms and religious hatred led to murderous clashes between the two communities in 1946. When it became clear that Jinnah and the Muslim League would accept nothing less than an independent Pakistan, India's last viceroy—war hero Lord Louis Mountbatten (1900–1979)—proposed partition. Both sides accepted. At midnight on August 14, 1947, India and Pakistan gained political independence (Map 32.2).

In the weeks following independence communal strife exploded into an orgy of massacres and mass expulsions. Perhaps a hundred thousand Hindus and Muslims were slaughtered, and an estimated 5 million be-

> **"**What is there to celebrate? I see nothing but rivers of blood.**"**
>
> **MOHANDAS GANDHI**

came refugees. Congress Party leaders were completely powerless to stop the wave of violence. "What is there to celebrate?" exclaimed Gandhi in reference to independence, "I see nothing but rivers of blood."[4] In January 1948 Gandhi himself was gunned down by a Hindu fanatic.

After the ordeal of independence, relations between India and Pakistan — both members of the British Commonwealth — were, and continue to be, tense. Fighting over the disputed area of Kashmir, a strategically important northwestern border state with a Muslim majority annexed by India, continued until 1949 and broke out again in 1965–1966, 1971, and 1999 (see Map 32.2).

Pakistan and the Creation of Bangladesh

Pakistan's western and eastern provinces shared the Muslim faith but were separated by more than a thousand miles of Indian territory, as well as by language, ethnic background, and social custom. The Bengalis of East Pakistan constituted a majority of Pakistan's population as a whole but were neglected by the central government, which remained in the hands of West Pakistan's elite after Jinnah's death. In essence, East Pakistan remained a colony of West Pakistan.

Tensions came to a head in the late 1960s. Bengali leaders calling for virtual independence were charged with treason, and martial law was proclaimed in East Pakistan. In 1971 the Bengalis revolted and won their independence as the new nation of Bangladesh. For the next twenty years Bangladesh, nominally a secular parliamentary democracy, lurched erratically from one government to the next, experiencing a series of military takeovers, restorations of civilian authority, political assassinations, and charges of official corruption. It also suffered a string of natural calamities, mostly related to the country's straddling the Ganges Delta, a vast, low-lying fertile area of land that is subject to annual monsoon floods, tornados, and cyclones.

Bangladesh is the world's eighth most populous country (around 160 million), one of the most densely populated, and also one of the poorest. It is particularly vulnerable to climate change: should world sea levels rise as predicted over the next few decades, an estimated 20 million Bangladeshis could be forced from their homes. Still, since 1991 Bangladesh's economy

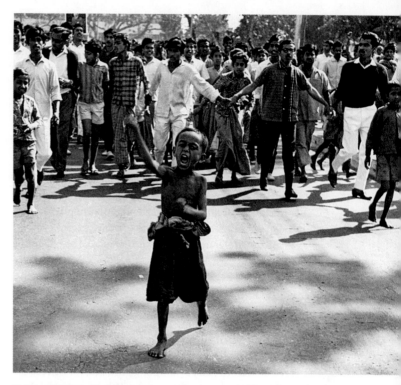

Bengali Revolt, 1969 When India won its independence from British colonial rule in 1947, West Pakistan and East Bengal separated from mainly Hindu India and became the new country of Pakistan. The nearly thousand miles between West and East Pakistan and the location of the capital and the Constituent Assembly in Karachi, West Pakistan, left East Pakistanis feeling marginalized and neglected. In this 1969 photo a child leads an angry street protest against West Pakistan's dominance. In 1971 such popular anger led to the Bangladesh Liberation War between East and West that ended with Bangladesh gaining its independence in December 1971. (Rashid Talukder/Drik Picture Agency)

has grown and diversified with a steady increase in foreign investment, the middle class has expanded, illiteracy rates have fallen, poverty has decreased, and there has been a marked improvement in gender parity in the country's schools. In 2005 the global investment firm Goldman Sachs named Bangladesh one of the "next eleven," believing that it, along with Mexico, Nigeria, Pakistan, and seven other countries, could potentially become some of the world's largest economies in the twenty-first century.

Like Bangladesh, Pakistan has experienced political instability and widespread corruption, alternating between civilian and military rule since independence. Zulfikar Ali Bhutto served as Pakistan's fourth president from 1971 to 1973 and then as prime minister from 1973 to 1977 under a new constitution. He was

> **Muslim League** The rival to the Indian Congress, it argued for separate homelands for Muslims and Indians.

then arrested and executed in 1979, probably at the direction of military strongman General Muhammad Zia-ul-Haq, who ruled Pakistan with a heavy hand from 1977 to 1988. Zia was responsible for aiding neighboring Afghanistan following the Soviet invasion of that country in 1979, and his help eventually led to Soviet withdrawal. During the 1980s Pakistan was a close ally of the United States, but relations between the two countries became chilly in the 1990s when Pakistan refused to abandon its development of nuclear weapons. After the September 11, 2001, al-Qaeda attack on the United States (see page 1045), Pakistan again became an important ally and the recipient of billions of dollars in military aid from the United States.

Although General Pervez Musharraf (b. 1943) did much to revive the Pakistani economy in the early years of his rule, in 2007 he attempted to reshape the country's Supreme Court by replacing the chief justice with one of his close allies, bringing about calls for his impeachment. Benazir Bhutto (1953–2007), who became the first female elected head of a Muslim state when she was elected prime minister in 1988, returned from exile to challenge Musharraf's increasingly repressive military rule. While campaigning, Bhutto was assassinated on December 27, 2007. After being defeated at the polls in 2008, Musharraf resigned and went into exile in London to avoid facing impeachment and possible corruption and mur-

der charges. In the elections that followed, Asif Ali Zardari (b. 1955), the widower of Benazir Bhutto, won the presidency by a landslide.

Pakistan had a population of over 170 million in 2010, a number that is expected to increase to over 250 million by 2030, which will represent the single largest Muslim population in the world, surpassing current leader Indonesia. It has a semi-industrialized economy, the second largest in South Asia after India, with the service sector and telecommunications growing in importance.

Recently, there has been increasing concern about the stability and resolve of the new Pakistani government. As of 2009 around 1.7 million Afghani refugees had settled in northwest and west Pakistan. Many were suspected of being sympathetic to the Taliban and of harboring fugitive Taliban and al-Qaeda members, including the al-Qaeda leader, Osama bin Laden. These suspicions were reinforced when U.S. Special Forces killed bin Laden on May 1, 2011. He had been hiding for several years in a walled compound only thirty miles from the Pakistani capital, Islamabad, and only a few hundred yards from a major Pakistani military academy. Since 2009 the United States has increased missile strikes against supposed Taliban strongholds in Pakistan, leading to large demonstrations against the United States as well as Pakistan's government for its perceived inability to stop the attacks. Massive flooding

Bhutto's Assassination
Pakistani presidential candidate Benazir Bhutto stands up in her campaign van just moments before she was assassinated on December 27, 2007. In the initial confusion it was reported that an assassin fired at her with a pistol and then threw a bomb. Scotland Yard investigators later determined that she died when the force of the bomb explosion slammed her head into part of the open hatch. (Mohammed Javed/AP Images)

in July 2010 and the government's slow response further weakened President Zardari's regime. The United States continues to send Pakistan massive amounts of military aid to fight the insurgents and humanitarian aid to help Pakistan recover from the floods, hoping to keep the country stable and an ally in the war in Afghanistan.

India Since Independence

Jawaharlal Nehru (1889–1964) and the Indian National Congress Party ruled India for a generation after independence and introduced major social reforms. Hindu women were granted legal equality, including the right to vote, to seek divorce, and to marry outside their castes. The constitution abolished the untouchable caste. In practice less-discriminatory attitudes toward women and untouchables evolved slowly — especially in the villages, where 85 percent of the people lived.

The Congress Party leadership tried with modest success to develop the country economically by means of democratic socialism. But population growth of about 2.4 percent per year ate up much of the increase in output. Intense poverty remained the lot of most people and encouraged widespread corruption within the bureaucracy. The Congress Party maintained neutrality in the Cold War and sought to join with newly independent states in Asia and Africa to create a "third force" of nonaligned nations, aiming for economic and cultural cooperation. This effort culminated in the Afro-Asian Conference in Bandung, Indonesia, in 1955.

Nehru's daughter, Indira Gandhi (1917–1984; no relation to Mohandas Gandhi), became prime minister in 1966 and dominated Indian political life for a generation. In 1975 she subverted parliamentary democracy and proclaimed a state of emergency. Attacking dishonest officials, black marketers, and tax evaders, she also threw the weight of the government behind a heavy-handed campaign of mass sterilization to reduce population growth. More than 7 million men were sterilized in 1976.

Many believed that Gandhi's emergency measures marked the end of the parliamentary democracy and Western liberties introduced in the last phase of British rule. But true to the British tradition, Gandhi called for free elections. She suffered a spectacular electoral defeat, largely because of the vastly unpopular sterilization campaign and her subversion of democracy. Her successors fell to fighting among themselves, and in 1980 she won an equally stunning electoral victory.

Separatist ethnic nationalism plagued Indira Gandhi's last years in office. Democratic India remained a patchwork of religions, languages, and peoples, always threatening to further divide the country along ethnic or religious lines. Most notable were the 15 million

Sikhs of the Punjab in northern India (see Map 32.2), with their own religion — founded by Guru Nanak Dev (1469–1538) — and a distinctive culture. Most Sikhs wanted greater autonomy for the Punjab, and by 1984 some Sikh radicals were fighting for independence. Gandhi cracked down hard, and she was assassinated by Sikhs in retaliation. Violence followed as Hindu mobs slaughtered over a thousand Sikhs throughout India.

Elected prime minister in 1984 by a landslide sympathy vote, one of Indira Gandhi's sons, Rajiv Gandhi (1944–1991), showed considerable skill at effecting a limited reconciliation with a majority of the Sikh population. Under his leadership the Congress Party moved away from the socialism of his mother and grandfather and he prepared the way for Finance Minister Manmohan Singh to introduce market reforms, capitalist development, and Western technology and investment from 1991 onward. These reforms were successful, and since the 1990s India's economy has experienced explosive growth.

Holding power almost continuously from 1947, the Congress Party was challenged increasingly by Hindu nationalists in the 1990s. These nationalists argued forcefully that India was based, above all, on Hindu culture and religious tradition and that these values had been badly compromised by the Western secularism of Congress Party leaders and by the historical influence of India's Muslims. Campaigning also for a strong Indian military, the Hindu nationalist party finally gained power in 1998. The new government immediately resumed testing of nuclear devices, asserting its vision of a militant Hindu nationalism. In 2004 the United Progressive Alliance (UPA), a center-left coalition dominated by the Congress Party, regained control of the government and elected Manmohan Singh (b. 1932) as prime minister. In 2009 Singh became only the second Indian prime minister since Jawaharlal Nehru to be re-elected to office after completing a full five-year term.

After Pakistan announced that it had developed nuclear weapons in 1998, relations between Pakistan and India worsened. In December 2001 the two nuclear powers seemed poised for war until intense diplomatic pressure forced them to step back from the abyss. In April 2005 both sides agreed to open business and trade relations and to work to negotiate a peaceful solution to the Kashmir dispute. Islamic and Hindu chauvinism remains strong, however, and tension between the two countries again increased dramatically in November 2008 when a Pakistan-based terrorist organization carried out a widespread shooting and bombing attack across Mumbai, India's largest city, killing 164 and wounding over 300. Tensions remain high, and nationalist and religious extremists in both countries appear willing to carry out such attacks again.

Secularism and Religion at War in the Middle East

☐ In what ways has religion played a role in Middle Eastern politics since 1945?

Throughout the vast umma (world of Islam), nationalism remained the primary political force after 1945 (Map 32.3). Anti-Western and anticommunist in most instances, Muslim nationalism generally combined a strong secular state with deep devotion to Islam. Nationalism in the Arab countries of the Middle East wore two faces. The idealistic side focused on the Pan-Arab dream of uniting all Arabs in a single nation that would be strong enough to resist the West, defeat the new state of Israel, and achieve genuine independence. Despite political and economic alliances like the Arab League, this vision floundered on intense regional, ideological, and personal rivalries. Thus a more practical Arab nationalism focused largely on nation building within former League of Nations mandates and European colonies.

In the very heart of this world of Islam, Jewish nationalists founded the state of Israel following the Second World War. The Zionist claim to a homeland came into sharp, and often violent, conflict with the rights and claims of the Palestinians. Religious differences, territorial claims, and the right to nationhood have been at the heart of the Israeli-Palestinian conflict since the early 1900s.

In the Muslim countries of the Middle East, nation building, often led by westernized elites, almost universally culminated in the creation of one-party dictatorships, corruption, and continued daily hardship for the masses. In the 1970s some Islamic preachers and devoted laypeople charged that the model of modernizing, Western-inspired nationalism had failed. These critics, labeled fundamentalists in the West, urged a return to strict Islamic principles and traditional morality. They evoked a sympathetic response among many educated Muslims as well as among villagers and city dwellers. In countries like Egypt they worked to overthrow the government, which generally resulted in their movements being banned and their leaders arrested. In countries like Lebanon and Turkey they gained some political power within the secular governments. In Iran in 1979 they overthrew the secular government and created an Islamic republic.

• **Palestine Liberation Organization (PLO)** Created in 1964, a loose union of Palestinian refugee groups opposed to Israel and working toward Palestinian home rule.

The Arab-Israeli Conflict

Before the Second World War, Arab nationalists were loosely united in their opposition to the colonial powers and to Jewish migration to Palestine. The British had granted independence to Egypt and Iraq before the war, and the French followed suit with Syria and Lebanon in 1945. In British-mandated Palestine, the situation was volatile. Jewish settlement in Palestine (see pages 888–889) was strenuously opposed by the Palestinian Arabs and the seven independent states of the newly founded Arab League (Egypt, Iraq, Jordan, Lebanon, Saudi Arabia, Syria, and Yemen). Murder and terrorism flourished, nurtured by bitterly conflicting Arab and Jewish nationalisms.

The British announced in early 1947 their intention to withdraw from Palestine in 1948. The insoluble problem of a Jewish homeland was dumped in the lap of the United Nations. In November 1947 the UN General Assembly passed a plan to partition Palestine into two separate states — one Arab and one Jewish (Map 32.4). The Jews accepted, and the Arabs rejected, the partition of Palestine.

By early 1948 an undeclared civil war was raging in Palestine. When the British mandate ended on May 14, 1948, the Jews proclaimed the state of Israel. Arab countries immediately attacked the new Jewish state, but the Israelis drove off the invaders and conquered more territory. Roughly nine hundred thousand Palestinian refugees fled or were expelled from old Palestine. The war left an enormous legacy of Arab bitterness toward Israel and its political allies, Great Britain and the United States.

In Egypt the humiliation of Arab defeat triggered a nationalist revolution. A young army colonel named Gamal Abdel Nasser (1918–1970) drove out the corrupt and pro-Western king Farouk in 1952. Nasser preached the gospel of neutralism in the Cold War, but accepted Soviet aid to demonstrate Egypt's independence of the West. Relations with Israel and the West worsened, and in 1956 Nasser nationalized the European-owned Suez Canal Company, Europe's last vestige of power in the Middle East. Outraged, the British and French joined forces with the Israelis and successfully invaded Egypt. The United States unexpectedly sided with the Soviets and forced the British, French, and Israelis to withdraw from Egypt.

Nasser's victory encouraged anti-Western radicalism, hopes of Pan-Arab political unity, and a vague "Arab socialism." Yet the Arab world remained deeply divided apart from bitter opposition to Israel and support for the right of Palestinian refugees to return to their homeland. In 1964 a loose union of Palestinian refugee groups opposed to Israel joined together, under the leadership of Yasir Arafat (1929–2004) to form the **Palestine Liberation Organization (PLO)**.

MAP 32.3 Modern Islam, ca. 2010 Although the Islamic heartland remains the Middle East and North Africa, Islam is growing steadily in Africa south of the Sahara and is the faith of heavily populated Indonesia.

On June 1, 1967, as Syrian and Egyptian armies massed on their borders, the Israelis formed a national unity government and on June 4 made the decision to go to war. The Israelis launched a surprise air strike early on June 5 and by noon had destroyed most of the Egyptian, Syrian, and Jordanian air forces. Over the next five days Israeli armies defeated Egyptian, Syrian, Jordanian, and Palestinian forces and took control of the Sinai Peninsula and the Gaza Strip from Egypt, the West Bank and East Jerusalem from Jordan, and the Golan Heights from Syria. In the Six-Day War (also known as the 1967 Arab-Israeli War), Israel proved itself to be the pre-eminent military force in the region, and it expanded the territory under its control threefold.

After the war, Israel began to build large Jewish settlements in the Gaza Strip and the West Bank, home to millions of Palestinians. On November 22, 1967, the UN Security Council adopted Resolution 242, which contained a "land for peace" formula by which Israel was called upon to withdraw from the occupied territories, and in return the Arab states were to withdraw all claims to Israeli territory, cease all hostilities, and recognize the sovereignty of the Israeli state. The resolution did not specifically mention the Palestinians, and the PLO and Syria refused to agree to it.

On Yom Kippur on October 6, 1973, the holiest day in Judaism, a coalition of Arab forces led by Syria and Egypt launched a surprise attack on Israel across the Golan Heights and the Sinai Peninsula. Despite initial setbacks, the Israelis successfully counterattacked and were less than sixty miles from Cairo and twenty-five miles from Damascus when a ceasefire ended hostilities on October 25. For the Arab world, the Yom Kippur War (or 1973 Arab-Israeli War) marked a psychological victory because of the Arab states' initial successes. The Israelis, despite having turned back the attack, now felt less invincible than they had following the Six-Day War, and the United States recognized the need to become more actively involved in mediation and peacemaking. Efforts undertaken by U.S. president Jimmy Carter led to the Camp David Accords in 1979 that normalized relations between Egypt and Israel and brokered the return of the Sinai Peninsula to Egypt—the first successful realization of the UN "land for peace" formula.

MAP 32.4 Palestine, Israel, and the Middle East Since the British mandate expired on May 14, 1948, there have been five major wars and innumerable armed clashes in what was formerly Palestine (inset). Through negotiations between Israel and the PLO, Jericho and the Gaza Strip were placed under Palestinian self-rule, and Israeli troops were withdrawn in 1994. In 2010–2011 a series of populist uprisings and protests spread throughout the Middle East, toppling some regimes and leading to both uncertainty and hope for democratic reform.

The Palestinian Quest for Independence

In 1987 young Palestinians in the occupied territories of the Gaza Strip and the West Bank began the **intifada**, a prolonged campaign of rock throwing and civil disobedience against Israeli soldiers. Inspired increasingly by Islamic fundamentalists, the Palestinian uprising eventually posed a serious challenge not only to Israel but also to the secular Palestine Liberation Organization (PLO), long led from abroad by Yasir Arafat. The result was an unexpected and mutually beneficial agreement in 1993 between Israel and the PLO. Israel agreed to recognize Arafat's organization and start a peace process that granted Palestinian self-rule in Gaza and called for self-rule throughout the West Bank in five

Israel's Wall of Separation

A Palestinian man waves as he walks across the hills near Jerusalem, where Israel's wall of separation divides Israeli and Palestinian territory. Israelis argue that the wall, made of concrete and covered with razor wire, protects them from Palestinian militants and suicide bombers. Increasingly it is described by Palestinians and others as a Berlin Wall–like structure, a symbol of Israelis forcing a separation, an Israeli version of apartheid, between the two peoples. (Kevin Frayer/AP Images)

years. In return, Arafat renounced terrorism and abandoned the long-standing demand that Israel must withdraw from all land occupied in the 1967 war.

The peace process increasingly divided Israel. In 1995 a right-wing Jewish extremist assassinated Prime Minister Yitzhak Rabin (1922–1995). In 1996 a coalition of opposition parties won a slender majority, charging the Palestinian leadership with condoning anti-Jewish terrorism. The new Israeli government limited Palestinian self-rule where it existed and expanded Jewish settlements in the West Bank. On the Palestinian side, dissatisfaction with the peace process grew. Between 1993 and 2000 the number of Jewish settlers in the West Bank doubled to two hundred thousand and Palestinian per capita income declined by 20 to 25 percent.

Failed negotiations between Arafat and Israel in 2000 unleashed an explosion of tit-for-tat violence, known as the Second Intifada, in Israel, the West Bank, and the Gaza Strip. In 2003 the Israelis began building a barrier around the West Bank, which has met with opposition from Israelis and Palestinians alike.

The death of Yasir Arafat, the PLO's long-time leader, in November 2004 marked a major turning point in the Israeli-Palestinian dispute. Mahmoud Abbas, Arafat's successor, is viewed as moderate and pragmatic, but peace talks have made very little progress since he took office. In January 2006 Hamas, a radical Sunni Muslim political party, won 72 of the 136 seats in the Pales-

tinian legislature, seizing control from Abbas and the PLO. Considered by many in the West to be a terrorist organization, Hamas had gained widespread support from many Palestinians for the welfare programs it established in the West Bank and Gaza Strip.

Immediately after the Hamas victory, Israel, the United States, the European Union, and several other Western donor nations cut off all aid to the Palestinian Authority, the governing body of the West Bank and Gaza Strip established by the 1994 peace agreement. In June 2007 Hamas seized control of the Gaza Strip. Since then, economic and humanitarian conditions for Palestinians living in the Gaza Strip have deteriorated. In 2010, 63 percent of the 1.5 million citizens of Gaza lived below the United Nations–defined poverty line. When a "Gaza freedom flotilla" attempted to break an Israeli blockade around Gaza in May 2010, the Israeli navy intercepted the flotilla and raided the ships. Nine activists, eight of whom were Turkish nationals, were killed. This set off a worldwide condemnation of Israel's actions and severely strained relations between Israel and Turkey. Under pressure, Israel eased its blockade in 2010, allowing more humanitarian goods and food aid into Gaza, but the movement of people to and from Gaza remains restricted.

• **intifada** A popular uprising by young Palestinians against Israeli rule; the Arabic word *intifada* means "shaking off."

While Gaza remained isolated, Abbas and the Palestinian Authority formed a separate government in the West Bank. In September 2010 Israeli prime minster Benjamin Netanyahu (b. 1949) agreed to hold direct peace talks with President Abbas and the Palestinians, mediated by the U.S. Obama administration, which hoped to broker a two-state solution to the Israeli-Palestinian conflict. The peace talks broke down barely three weeks after they started, as Israel resumed construction of settlement homes in the West Bank and East Jerusalem. Thus, despite years of diplomacy, war, and stalemate, the nature of a future Palestinian state remains unresolved.

Egypt: Arab World Leader

Egypt, with its large military, its anti-imperialist rhetoric, and its support for Arab unity, was recognized as the leader of the Arab world from the time of Nasser's seizure of power in 1956 to the mid-1970s. In late 1977 Egypt's president Anwar Sadat (1918–1981) made a pathbreaking official visit to Israel, leading to a historic, though limited, peace settlement known as the Camp David Accords (see page 995). Each country gained: Egypt got back the Sinai Peninsula, which Israel had taken in the 1967 Six-Day War (see Map 32.4), and Israel obtained peace and normal relations with Egypt. Israel also kept the Gaza Strip, taken from Egypt in 1967 and home to about 1 million Palestinians. Some Arab leaders denounced Sadat's initiative as treason, and Egypt was suspended from the Arab League from 1979 to 1989.

After Sadat's assassination by Islamic radicals in 1981, Egypt's relations with Israel deteriorated, but Egypt and Israel maintained their fragile peace as Sadat's successor as president, Hosni Mubarak (b. 1928), took office in 1981. Mubarak was a consistent supporter of Israel and a mediator for peaceful relations between Israel and the Arab world. His diplomatic efforts were successful in getting Egypt readmitted to the Arab League in 1989 and getting its headquarters moved back to Cairo. Egypt is considered the closest Middle Eastern ally of the United States after Israel, and since the Camp David Accords the United States has given Egypt billions of dollars in development, humanitarian, and military aid.

Egyptian Protesters in Cairo, January 29, 2011 The Tunisian overthrow of the repressive regime of long-serving President Ben Ali on January 14, 2011, set off a wave of popular uprisings against authoritarian regimes across North Africa and the Middle East. Next to go was Egypt's Hosni Mubarak, who had ruled Egypt with an iron hand for nearly thirty years. He stepped down on February 11, 2011, after the army—including the men on the tanks in this image—joined the protesters. (Ahmed Ali/AP Images)

Domestically, however, Mubarak failed to promote significant economic development and ruled with an increasingly dictatorial hand. Prices of basic goods and foodstuffs continued to rise, while the standard of living for many Egyptians remained stagnant. Many of the government's critics charged that massive fraud and corruption funneled Egypt's wealth to a privileged few. Over 40 percent of the total population lived in poverty.

The human rights picture during Mubarak's thirty years in office was no better. Officially Egypt is a republic, but it has been ruled under an emergency law since 1967. The law suspended constitutional rights, limited freedom of expression and assembly, gave the government the right to arrest people without charge and detain prisoners indefinitely, extended police powers, legalized censorship, and allowed for the establishment of a special security court. Mubarak used the emergency law to create a wholly separate justice system in order to silence all opposition and punish, torture, and kill anyone who was perceived as a threat to his rule. Demonstrations, political organizations, and even financial donations that were not approved by the government were banned under the law. Thousands of people were arrested. In May 2010 the parliament approved the law's extension for another two years.

In December 2010 demonstrations broke out in Tunisia against the twenty-three-year authoritarian rule of President Zine Ben Ali (b. 1936), leading to his downfall on January 14, 2011. This populist revolt soon spread across North Africa and the Middle East, including to the streets of Cairo and other cities as Egyptians of all ages united in revolt against Mubarak's dictatorial rule. After three weeks of increasingly large demonstrations, coordinated through Facebook, Twitter, and other electronic communications networks, Mubarak stepped down as president on February 11, 2011.

Libya, located between Tunisia and Egypt, also witnessed a massive uprising against its dictatorial leader of forty-two years, Muammar Gaddafi (b. 1942). Gaddafi reacted much more violently and ruthlessly than either of his neighboring dictators in his effort to remain in power, using his army and air force to attack cities, neighborhoods, and rural areas held by opposition forces. As of June 2011 he retained control over the western part of the country but had lost power over several major cities in the east.

A Fractured Lebanon

With the Vichy French government unable to maintain its control over Lebanon, the mandated territory gained its independence from French rule in 1943. Lebanon prospered until the early 1970s and became a favorite tourist destination and a regional center of banking and trade. When Lebanon became an indepen-

dent nation, the unwritten National Pact included an agreement that the Lebanese president would be a Christian and the prime minister a Muslim. This arrangement was based on a 1932 census that showed a Christian majority. By the late 1960s the Lebanese Muslim population had grown significantly, and Muslims were no longer content with a Christian-controlled government and military. Their long-simmering dissatisfaction and anger over the dispersal of political power came to a head in early 1975, starting with armed scrimmages between Christian and Muslim factions that resulted in the slaughter of many innocent civilians, and the escalating violence and reprisals led to a devastating fifteen-year civil war.

In the course of the war the Lebanese army disintegrated when soldiers switched their allegiance from the national government to various sectarian militias. One of these was a hard-line group known as Hezbollah, or Party of God. Hezbollah condemned the Israeli invasions of Lebanon in 1978 and 1982 aimed at eradicating the Palestine Liberation Organization's control of southern Lebanon, and had as one of its stated objectives the complete destruction of the state of Israel.

The Lebanese civil war was brutal and massively destructive. War crimes and terrorist acts were committed by all sides. Lebanon's entire infrastructure was destroyed, and Beirut in 1990 looked like the bombed-out cities of Europe after World War II. The civil war ended after Lebanon's Maronite Christian and Muslim communities agreed to a more balanced sharing of power, and by 1991 the sectarian violence had generally ceased. Israeli forces finally left Lebanon in 2000, and Syria withdrew its fifteen thousand troops, who had been sent in by the Arab League to maintain peace, in 2005.

By 2004 Hezbollah had established virtual control over much of southern Beirut and southern Lebanon, and in elections held in 2005 it won fourteen seats in the Lebanese legislature. Hezbollah members adhere to a distinct brand of Islamic theology and ideology developed by the Shi'ite

The 2006 Israel-Lebanon War

Ayatollah Ruhollah Khomeini, leader of the Iranian Islamic Revolution in 1979. This connection explains the significant financial and military support that Iran provides and its powerful influence in shaping Hezbollah's policies, particularly toward Israel.

On July 12, 2006, Hezbollah's hostility toward Israel erupted into what became known as the July War in Lebanon and the Second Lebanon War in Israel. Hezbollah's continued shelling of northern Israel and Israel's seeming inability to gain a quick military victory generated mounting discontent among Israeli soldiers and civilians alike about the handling and course of the war. By early August all sides clearly desired a way out, and with the help of the United Nations Security Council, both sides agreed to a cease-fire on August 14, 2006.

Opinions about who won and who lost the war vary, but it was costly to both sides. Hezbollah declared victory, and many in the Muslim world felt pride in Hezbollah's ability to stand up to the Israeli military machine. Although Hezbollah may have won the propaganda war, there can be no doubt that the group paid dearly. It lost the elaborate infrastructure it had taken years to build in the south, and it lost the support of hundreds of thousands of Lebanese whose homes, lives, and livelihoods were destroyed by its actions. For its part, Israel also claimed victory, but it was also no better off. Many Israelis believed that indecisive leadership cost Israel a rare opportunity to destroy Hezbollah. Israelis emerged from the war deeply troubled by a new sense of vulnerability and turned to Israeli hardliners such as Benjamin Netanyahu, who was elected prime minister in the next election.

Meanwhile, efforts to rebuild Lebanon have been ongoing. The majority of Lebanese people appear to want peace, but since 2006 Hezbollah has rearmed and has reemerged as a political and military power. In May 2008 a Christian and former commander of the Lebanese armed forces, Michel Suleiman (b. 1948), became president. He formed a national unity government, which included Hezbollah parliament members, sought equal political relations with Syria, and tried to integrate Hezbollah's militia into the Lebanese army. But in early January 2011 Hezbollah pulled out of the national coalition government, causing it to collapse. In late January Suleiman appointed a Sunni businessman, Najib Mikati, as prime minister-designate. Mikati was supported by Hezbollah and its allies in parliament, leading to widespread rioting by Sunnis across Lebanon, who viewed the action as the next step in the eventual takeover of Lebanon by the Shiite Hezbollah movement.

Challenges to Turkey's Secularism

Through the remainder of the twentieth century, Turkey remained basically true to Atatürk's vision of a thoroughly modernized, secularized, Europeanized state (see pages 883–886). Islam continued to exert less influence in daily life as Turkey joined NATO in 1952 and eventually sought full membership in the European Union (EU). But Turkey remains a country on the border — seeking membership in the European Union of the West, while acknowledging its Islamic heritage and historical connections with the East. Many of its citizens lead Western lifestyles, although the population is overwhelmingly Sunni Muslim. In the twenty-first century Turks have become increasingly divided over the future of the secular state in Turkey.

Turkey is the most secular of Islamic countries. Since the 1920s Turks have maintained a strict separation of state and religion. In the 2002 elections, however, the newly formed Justice and Development Party, or AKP, scored a stunning victory, with Abdullah Gül (b. 1950) becoming president of Turkey and Recep Erdogan (b. 1954), head of the AKP, becoming prime minister. Although the AKP campaigned as a moderate, conservative, pro-Western party, many Turks are concerned that it is intent on doing away with Turkey's secular constitution and establishing an Islamic state. Erdogan has adamantly denied having a secret agenda, but his support for laws such as the banning of alcoholic beverages, the lifting of the headscarf ban in all universities, the placing of anti-secular individuals in government offices, and the awarding of government contracts to Islamic businesses plus the arrest of several secular opponents of the government have been criticized by secular parties.

Despite this opposition the AKP continues to remain popular and win elections. During its rule, the Turkish economy has seen rapid growth, and the hyperinflation that plagued the country for three decades had fallen to around 7 percent in November 2010. Turkey weathered the 2008–2009 global economic downturn better than most countries, and its stock market in 2009 rose the most in the world after Argentina's.

A second major problem facing Turkey is its handling of its minority Kurdish population (see Map 32.5 on page 1002). Many observers view the landslide victory of the AKP in the 2007 elections as having been prompted by a surge in Turkish nationalism and a resurgence of conservative Muslim influence since September 11, 2001, when the West, particularly the George W. Bush administration in the United States, demanded a "with us or against us" position from Turkey, Pakistan, and other allies in the Middle East (see pages 1041–1043). When Turkey refused to participate in the invasion of Iraq in 2003 because it worried about destabilizing fragile relations with its Kurdish citizens, many in the Bush administration labeled the Turks as "against" the United States and the war on terrorism.

As the situation in Iraq continued to deteriorate and as the Kurds in northern Iraq continued to push for more autonomy, Kurdish nationalists in Turkey increased their attacks on Turkish targets. In February and March 2008 the Turkish army began a military of-

Kurdish Woman on Trial in Turkey The Turks have been officially trying to assimilate the Kurds since the 1930s with little success. Since the mid-1980s some Kurdish resistance movements have peacefully campaigned for Kurdish rights in Turkey, while others have violently fought for an independent Kurdistan. This image shows a Kurdish woman suspected of membership in the PKK, or Kurdistan Workers Party, being tried in a Turkish terrorist court. The PKK is a militant separatist organization seeking Kurdish independence. The woman was sentenced to thirteen years in prison. (Ed Kasht/Corbis)

fensive against Kurds in eastern Turkey and also across the border in northern Iraq. In December 2010 the leader of the leading Kurdish independence movement, the Kurdistan Workers' Party, labeled a terrorist organization by the Turks, announced a unilateral cease-fire and suggested that the Kurds would be willing to accept a degree of Kurdish autonomy within Turkey rather than demand a separate Kurdish state.

Despite concerted efforts by leaders to meet the economic, legal, and humanitarian standards set by the EU, Turkey's pace of reform received heavy EU criticism. The 1915–1917 Turkish massacres of Armenians (see page 883) remain a major point of contention. Even if Turkey meets all of the EU's demands, it cannot be admitted into the EU until the next round of EU membership admissions in 2013. In the meantime support for EU membership has weakened as the economy has strengthened and Turkey's role as a regional power broker has grown. In 2010 support for EU membership had dropped to 38 percent, down from 73 percent in 2004.

Revolution and War in Iran and Iraq

After 1945 Iran tried again to follow Turkey's example, as it had before 1939 (see page 886). Once again its success was limited. The new shah—Muhammad Reza Pahlavi (r. 1941–1979), the son of Reza Shah Pahlavi—

angered Iranian nationalists by courting Western powers and Western oil companies. In 1953 the freely elected prime minister Muhammad Mossaddeq (1882–1967) tried to nationalize the British-owned Anglo-Iranian Oil Company, and the shah was forced to flee to Europe. But Mossaddeq's victory was short-lived. Loyal army officers, with the help of the American CIA, quickly restored the shah to his throne.

The shah set out to build a powerful modern nation to ensure his rule, and Iran's gigantic oil revenues provided the necessary cash. The shah undermined the power bases of the traditional politicians—large landowners and religious leaders—by means of land reform, secular education, and increased power for the central government. Modernization surged forward, but at the loss of ancient values, widespread corruption, and harsh dictatorship. The result was a violent reaction against modernization and secular values: an Islamic revolution in 1979 aimed at infusing strict Islamic principles into all aspects of personal and public life. Led by the Islamic cleric Ayatollah Ruholla Khomeini, the fundamentalists deposed the shah and tried to build their vision of a true Islamic state.

Iran's Islamic republic frightened its neighbors. Iraq, especially, feared that Iran—a nation of Shi'ite Muslims—would succeed in getting Iraq's Shi'ite majority to revolt against its Sunni leaders (Map 32.5). Thus in September 1980 Iraq's strongman, Saddam Hussein (1937–2006), launched a surprise attack. With

▢ Mapping the Past

MAP 32.5 Abrahamic Religions in the Middle East and Surrounding Regions Islam, Judaism, and Christianity, which all trace their origins back to the patriarch Abraham, have significant populations in the Middle East. Since the 1979 Iranian revolution Shi'ites throughout the region have become more militant and more strident in their demands for equality and power. One of the largest stateless ethnic groups, the Kurds, who follow various religions, has become a major player in the politics of the region, especially in Iraq and Turkey, where the group seeks Kurdish independence.

ANALYZING THE MAP Which religion dominates? Where are the largest concentrations of Jews and Christians in the Middle East located?

CONNECTIONS How have divisions between Shi'ite and Sunni Muslims contributed to war in the region?

their enormous oil revenues and military machines, Iranians and Iraqis — Persians and Arabs — clashed in a savage eight-year conflict that killed hundreds of thousands of soldiers before finally grinding to a halt in 1988.

Hussein next eyed Kuwait's great oil wealth. In August 1990 he ordered his forces to overrun his tiny southern neighbor and proclaimed its annexation to Iraq. To Saddam's surprise, his aggression resulted in a vigorous international response and touched off the Persian Gulf War. In early 1991 his troops were chased

out of Kuwait by an American-led, United Nations–sanctioned military coalition, which included Arab forces from Egypt, Syria, and Saudi Arabia.

Iran and Iraq went in different directions in the 1990s. The United Nations Security Council imposed stringent economic sanctions on Iraq as soon as it invaded Kuwait, and these sanctions continued after the Gulf War to force Iraq to destroy its weapons of mass destruction. United Nations inspectors destroyed many such weapons, but the United States charged

Iraq with deceit and ongoing weapons development. An American-led invasion of Iraq in 2003 overthrew Saddam Hussein's regime (see pages 1041–1043).

As secular Iraq spiraled downward toward collapse and foreign occupation, Iran appeared to back away from fundamentalism. Following the constitution established by Ayatollah Khomeini, executive power in Iran was divided between a Supreme Leader and twelve-member Guardian Council selected by high Islamic clerics, and a president and parliament elected by universal male and female suffrage. The Supreme Leader was a very conservative religious leader, but a growing reform movement pressed for a relaxation of strict Islamic decrees and elected a moderate, Mohammad Khatami (b. 1943), as president in 1997 and again in 2001. The Supreme Leader, controlling the army and the courts, vetoed many of Khatami's reform measures and jailed some of the religious leadership's most vocal opponents.

In 2005 dubious election returns gave the presidency to an ultraconservative Islamic hardliner, Mahmoud Ahmadinejad (b. 1956). His populist speeches and actions made him popular among some elements of Iranian society. His calls for Israel's destruction; his support of extremist groups in Iraq, Gaza, and Lebanon; and his refusal to suspend Iran's nuclear program, however, have caused much anxiety and anger in the West. Despite this setback, many Iranians believe that moderate, secular reform is inevitable, for, as one Iranian journalist observed, "Fundamentalism is good for protest, good for revolution, and good for war, but not so good for development. No country can organize its society on fundamentalism."[5]

The journalist may be right in the long run, but the Iranian regime under Ahmadinejad has become more brutal in its opposition to internal dissent and more defiant in its relations with the United States and the West. Despite a failed economic policy that continues to rely heavily on oil revenues, Ahmadinejad won re-election as

> "Fundamentalism is good for protest, good for revolution, and good for war, but not so good for development."
>
> **IRANIAN JOURNALIST**

president in 2009 after a strong, and bitterly contested, challenge from more moderate candidates. The government responded quickly and violently to quell massive protests that broke out after news of the election results. The protestors used social-networking Internet sites, such as Twitter and Facebook, to communicate with each other and to send images of the uprising across the globe. The demonstrations lasted for a month, but since the summer of 2009 the Iranian government has silenced much of the opposition, banned rallies, and worked to block Web sites and the cell phone and computer transmissions that proved so effective a revolutionary tool for the protesters.

Iran's continued development of its nuclear program (see page 1047) remains the single greatest concern for leaders in the United States and Europe. They are also troubled by Iran's military and monetary support for the spread of its own Shi'ite brand of Islamic fundamentalism to countries across the Middle East in which the Shi'ite populations are either the majority or make up a large minority of the people, such as Iraq, Syria, Lebanon, Azerbaijan, Pakistan, Yemen, Kuwait, and Bahrain. Iran remains the primary backer of the Hamas party in the Gaza Strip and Hezbollah in Lebanon.

Iranian Nuclear Energy Program
Despite threats of sanctions from the United States, France, Germany, Great Britain, and Russia, Iran continues to develop its nuclear energy program. Here Iranian scientists move a container of radioactive uranium. Whether the uranium is being used for peaceful purposes, as Iran staunchly maintains, or to develop nuclear weapons, as the West argues, remains to be seen. (Behrouz Mehri/AFP/Getty Images)

CONNECTIONS

Since the end of World War II, Asia and the Middle East have undergone tremendous economic, political, and social changes. Japan's defeat and the collapse of European imperial empires allowed nationalist movements in these regions finally to begin to chart their own destinies. As part of the so-called Third World, a term that carried more of a political than an economic meaning in the 1950s and 1960s, the newly independent countries led by China and India declared themselves to be nonaligned in the superpowers' Cold War. Most were concerned with feeding their hungry millions, rebuilding from the destruction of the war and occupation, and creating stable governments — some Communist, some part socialist and part free market, and some copying the Western model of democratic capitalism. In the Middle East, Arab leaders spoke of Pan-Arab unity but set about creating individual nations. Many of them became one-party dictatorships just as oppressive and exploitative of the masses as had been the European colonial powers and the Ottoman Turks. Decolonization in Africa and Latin America followed a similar pattern, as Chapter 33 explores.

As we will see in Chapter 34, in the decades since 1945 the United Nations has grown in importance, and that is in no small part due to the efforts of UN representatives of Asian, African, and Latin American nations who have pushed for greater efforts to deal with global problems that have the most negative impact on them, such as delivering better health services, advancing educational opportunities for boys and girls equally, ending global poverty, and cleaning up the environment. We will also look at how the growth of multinational corporations, the green revolution in agriculture, and mushrooming urbanization have had both positive and harmful effects on the world's populations.

◻ CHAPTER REVIEW

◻ **How did the countries of East Asia successfully recover after World War II? (p. 978)**

With the Japanese defeat in World War II, long-suppressed nationalist movements pushed for political independence across East Asia. Mao Zedong's Communist forces took over in China, and the pro-Western Nationalist leader Jiang Jieshi retreated to Taiwan, where he re-established the Republic of China in exile. After Mao's death, China initiated a second revolution focused on modernization. While cultural change proceeded slowly and has been marked by political repression, the Chinese capitalist-based economy continues to grow rapidly. Meanwhile, thirty-five years of Japanese occupation of the Korean peninsula ended, only to have the country divided. North Korea suffered economically, but South Korea became one of the Asian economic tigers, a modern industrial powerhouse with one of the highest standards of living in the world. The other Asian economic tigers — Taiwan, Hong Kong, and Singapore — also left the war and colonial rule behind them to develop vibrant global economies. In Southeast Asia, Indonesia, Cambodia, and the Philippines suffered under decades of authoritarian rule, but have become more stable and democratic. Vietnam had to fight a long war of independence against the French and then the Americans before beginning an economic recovery.

KEY TERMS

Great Leap Forward (p. 979)

Great Proletarian Cultural Revolution (p. 980)

Red Guards (p. 980)

Tiananmen Square (p. 982)

Muslim League (p. 990)

Palestine Liberation Organization (PLO) (p. 994)

intifada (p. 996)

◻ **How have ethnic and religious rivalries affected the development of stable, independent states in South Asia? (p. 990)**

The Hindu and Muslim populations of India threw off British colonial rule only to go to war among themselves. Mohandas Gandhi was unable to convince the two groups to remain united in an independent India, and the Muslims broke away to create the country of Pakistan in 1947. Pakistan and India have remained at odds ever since, often violently, because of religious hatred and territorial disputes in the Kashmir region of northwest India. Ethnic strife also developed between the Bengalis of East Pakistan and the Pakistanis, leading to the creation of the independent state of Bangladesh in 1971.

☐ In what ways has religion played a role in Middle Eastern politics since 1945? (p. 994)

The Muslim world was rejuvenated after 1945, most notably under Nasser in Egypt. Nasser was respected throughout the Arab world for having stood up to the West. Unable to unite as a single Arab state, nationalist leaders began to form individual nations out of territories that had been League of Nations mandates and European colonies. Common to them all was a deep devotion to Islam. For some people in these countries, however, the secular modern states that were created were too Western and grated against the Islamic fundamentalism that they practiced. Many of the governments were one-party dictatorships that too often seemed to favor the westernized elite rather than to improve the lives of the impoverished masses, leading to civil war in places like Lebanon. Islamic fundamentalist movements arose throughout the Middle East and attempted to overthrow these governments and install their own brand of Islamic rule. In Iran they succeeded. Religion also played a key role in the establishment of the Jewish state of Israel and in the ongoing hostilities between Israel, Palestine, and the rest of the Muslim world.

SUGGESTED READING

Chang, Jung, and Jon Halliday. *Mao: The Unknown Story*. 2005. Controversial new biography of the Chinese Communist leader.

Church, Peter. *A Short History of South-East Asia*, 4th ed. 2005. A concise but comprehensive survey of the region's history.

Cleveland, William, and Martin Bunton. *A History of the Modern Middle East*, 4th ed. 2008. Well-crafted survey introduction to the modern history and politics of the Middle East.

Findley, Carter V. *Turkey, Islam, Nationalism, and Modernity: A History, 1789–2007*. 2010. A comprehensive survey of Turkey and its place between East and West by a pre-eminent scholar of Turkish history.

Gelvin, James L. *The Modern Middle East: A History* 3d ed. 2011. Excellent introduction to modern Middle Eastern history into the twenty-first century.

Guha, Ramachandra. *India After Gandhi: The History of the World's Largest Democracy*. 2007. In-depth study of the last sixty years of Indian history and development.

Jayakar, Pupul. *Indira Gandhi: An Intimate Biography*. 1993. Very readable narrative of the powerful and controversial Indian prime minister.

Kamrava, Mehran. *The Modern Middle East: A Political History Since the First World War*, 2d ed. 2011. A concise overview of modern Middle East history, economics, and politics.

Keddie, Nikki R. *Modern Iran: Roots and Results of Revolution*. 2006. A classic survey of Iranian history and politics by a leading scholar of modern Iran.

Mahbubani, Kishore. *The New Asian Hemisphere: The Irresistible Shift of Global Power to the East*. 2008. A history and analysis of the rise of Asia in world politics and economics by one of Asia's leading intellectuals.

Meredith, Robyn. *The Elephant and the Dragon: The Rise of India and China and What It Means for All of Us*. 2005. Useful and accessible introduction to these two economic giants.

Moaddel, Mansoor. *Islamic Modernism, Nationalism, and Fundamentalism*. 2005. A scholarly historical introduction to society and politics of the Middle East.

Nehru, Jawaharlal. *An Autobiography*. 1962. Classic personal account of India's history in the first half of the twentieth century by its first president.

Osborne, Milton. *Southeast Asia: An Introductory History*, 9th rev. ed. 2005. Classic introduction to the region.

Wasserstrom, Jeffrey N., ed. *Twentieth Century China: New Approaches*. 2002. Collection of essays on cultural and national developments using recently released archives.

NOTES

1. Quoted in P. B. Ebrey, ed., *Chinese Civilization and Society: A Source Book* (New York: Free Press, 1981), p. 393.
2. Mao Zedong, *Quotations from Chairman Mao Tsetung* (Peking: Foreign Language Press, 1972), pp. 288, 61.
3. Syed Sharifuddin Pirzada, ed., *Foundations of Pakistan: All-India Muslim League Documents*. Vol. 2: *1924–1947* (Karachi: National Publishing House, 1970), p. 338.
4. Quoted in K. Bhata, *The Ordeal of Nationhood: A Social Study of India Since Independence, 1947–1970* (New York: Atheneum, 1971), p. 9.
5. Quoted in B. Baktiari and H. Vaziri, "Iran's Liberal Revolution?" *Current History*, January 2002, p. 21.

For practice quizzes and other study tools, visit the **Online Study Guide** at bedfordstmartins.com/mckayworld.

For primary sources from this period, see *Sources of World Societies*, **Second Edition**.

For Web sites, images, and documents related to topics in this chapter, visit **Make History** at bedfordstmartins.com/mckayworld.

• Sandinista Soldier in Nicaragua Street art in Jinotega, Nicaragua, shows an armed female soldier of the Sandinista National Liberation Front picking coffee beans in her military camouflage. The Sandinistas overthrew the U.S.-backed dictator Anastasio Somoza in 1979. After their victory, the Socialist Sandinistas ruled Nicaragua until 1990 and then returned to power in 2006. (Thalia Watmough/aliki image library/Alamy)

There are fifty-five countries in Africa and twenty in Latin America. There is thus room for much variety — economically, politically, and socially — when discussing the history of these two huge continents over the past hundred-plus years. As we discussed in the previous chapter, Latin America and Africa, together with East and South Asia, were considered part of the Third World during the Cold War era. There were sound reasons for this. Most of the countries sought to remain nonaligned, refusing to side with either of the two superpowers. In general they were also economically less developed — meaning less industrialized — than most of the countries in the Northern Hemisphere. Their economies were based primarily on agricultural or other raw material production, such as oil, gold, or hemp.

Most Latin American countries gained their independence in the early 1800s, while sub-Saharan African countries did not break free from their colonial bonds until the 1960s and later. Still, events in many of the countries on both sides of the Atlantic were similar in the last half of the twentieth century and the early twenty-first century. Politically, for example, there was an initial period of democracy followed by years of harsh dictatorships, some military, some civilian with military support. When the Soviet Union collapsed in 1991, a euphoria of democracy swept through many nations of Africa and Latin America as citizens concluded that if the Soviet dictatorship could be overthrown and representative government instituted, it could happen in their countries as well. •

The Global South: Latin America and Africa
1945 to the Present

Latin America: Moving Toward Democracy

□ What kind of government was most prevalent in Latin America during the twentieth century, and how did this change after 1980?

Nationalism in Sub-Saharan Africa

□ What factors influenced decolonization in sub-Saharan Africa after World War II?

Sub-Saharan Africa Since 1960

□ What are some of the common features of independent Africa since 1960?

Interpreting the Experiences of the Emerging World

□ How do contemporary writers seek to understand and represent the common experiences of peoples in the emerging world?

Latin America: Moving Toward Democracy

□ What kind of government was most prevalent in Latin America during the twentieth century, and how did this change after 1980?

After the Second World War Latin America experienced a many-faceted recovery, somewhat similar to that of Europe, though beginning earlier. A generation later, Latin America also experienced its own period of turbulence and crisis similar to the upheaval experienced in the Middle East and Asia. Many Latin American countries responded by establishing authoritarian military regimes. Others, particularly Cuba and Nicaragua, took Marxist paths. In the late 1980s most Latin American countries copied eastern Europe by electing civilian governments and embracing economic liberalism for the first time since the 1920s.

Economic Nationalism in Mexico and Brazil

The growth of **economic nationalism** was a common development throughout Latin America in much of the twentieth century. Just as Spain's Central and South American colonies and Portuguese Brazil won political independence in the early nineteenth century, much of recent history has witnessed a quest for genuine economic independence. To understand the rise of economic nationalism, one must remember that Latin American countries developed as producers of foodstuffs and raw materials exported to Europe and the United States in return for manufactured goods and capital investment. This exchange brought considerable economic development but exacted a heavy price: neocolonialism (see pages 819–821). Latin America became dependent on foreign markets, products, and investments. Industry did not develop, and large landowners profited the most from eco-

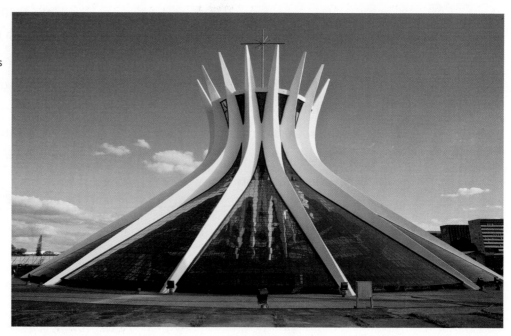

Brasília: Metropolitan Cathedral The Metropolitan Cathedral in Brazil's capital city, Brasília. The cathedral was inaugurated in 1970, ten years after the inauguration of the planned city that replaced Rio de Janeiro as Brazil's capital. (Jane Sweeney/Lonely Planet Images)

nomic development, using their advantage to enhance their social and political power. The Great Depression further hampered development (see page 912) and provoked a shift toward economic nationalism. Economic nationalism and the rise of industry were especially successful in the two largest countries of Latin America, Mexico and Brazil.

The Mexican Revolution of 1910 overthrew the elitist upper-class rule of the tyrant Porfirio Díaz and culminated in a new constitution in 1917. This radical nationalistic document called for universal suffrage, massive land reform, benefits for labor, and strict control of foreign capital. Progress was modest until 1934, when a charismatic young Indian from a poor family, Lázaro Cárdenas (1895–1970), became president and dramatically revived the languishing revolution. Cárdenas belonged to the Institutional Revolutionary Party (PRI), a nationalist, socialist party founded in 1929 that ruled Mexico continuously until 2000. Under Cárdenas many large estates were divided among small farmers or were returned undivided to Indian communities. State-supported Mexican businessmen built many small factories to meet domestic needs. In 1938 Cárdenas nationalized the petroleum industry. The 1930s also saw the flowering of a distinctive Mexican culture that proudly embraced the long-despised Indian past.

Beginning in the 1940s more moderate Mexican presidents used the state's power to promote industrialization, and the Mexican economy grew consistently through the 1970s. During the years of the "Mexican miracle," the economy grew 3 to 4 percent annually, and inflation was low. Agricultural production, which had always formed the basis of Latin American economies, declined as the industrial and service sectors grew. This was a time of rapid urbanization as well, with people leaving the rural areas for jobs in factories or for lower-paying service jobs, such as maids and janitors. While the country's economic health improved, social inequities remained. The upper and middle classes reaped the lion's share of the benefits of this economic growth.

As time went on, successive Mexican governments became more authoritarian, sometimes resorting to violence to quell dissent. Mexico's miracle began to fade

in the mid-1970s when its president, Luis Echeverría (b. 1922), began populist economic and political reform, including nationalizing key industries and redistributing private land to peasants. Echeverría also imposed limits on foreign investments, angering the United States with remarks opposing American "expansionism," and befriending Marxist Chilean president Salvador Allende.

José López Portillo (1920–2004) succeeded Echeverría as president in 1976. During his administration significant oil fields were discovered that made Mexico the world's fourth largest oil producer. Portillo's time in office was characterized by massive corruption and rampant inflation. Before leaving office in 1982, he ordered the nationalization of Mexico's banking system. When a national debt crisis crippled economies

economic nationalism A systematic effort by Latin American nationalists to end neocolonialism and to free their national economies from American and western European influences.

▫ Picturing the Past

Juan O'Gorman, *Credit Transforms Mexico* Emerging as an important architect in the 1930s, O'Gorman championed practical buildings and then led the movement to integrate architecture with art in postrevolutionary Mexico. These panels are from a 1965 fresco for a bank interior. (Photos: Enrique Franco-Torrijos. Courtesy, Banco Bital, S.A., Mexico City)

ANALYZING THE IMAGE What Mexican motifs are shown? How do the two panels differ in terms of lighting and mood, and what message does this imply about prerevolutionary and postrevolutionary life?

CONNECTIONS O'Gorman believed that Mexico had to preserve its cultural values in order to preserve its independence. What did he mean by this?

across Latin America, Mexico was one of the worst affected. There was little improvement in the 1990s, which witnessed a two-week-long armed rebellion against the government by the Zapatista Army of National Liberation (EZLN). Based in the Mexican state of Chiapas, the Zapatistas were primarily rural indigenous peasants who opposed national policies, like the North American Free Trade Agreement (1994), that they believed were harmful to peasant farmers like

themselves. When the Mexican army put down their rebellion, they turned to peaceful protest and continue to seek national and international support to improve their plight.

Mexico's economy reached rock bottom in December 1994 when it completely collapsed and had to be rescued by a financial aid package from the United States. Through the remainder of the 1990s, however, the economy quickly recovered. Mexico's GDP rose significantly for more than a decade until the global economic downturn of 2008–2009. Mexico had a positive growth rate again in 2010 of around 5.2 percent. Some economists believe that Mexico's economy

• **Cuban Revolution** The Communist revolution led by Fidel Castro that overthrew the American-backed Cuban dictator Fulgencio Batista on January 1, 1959.

could have grown 1 to 2 percent more had drug wars and related violence not deterred tourism and foreign investment.

Like Mexico's, Brazil's economy at the turn of the century was controlled by large landowners. Brazilian politics was dominated by the coffee barons and by regional rivalries after the fall of Brazil's monarchy in 1889. Regional rivalries and deteriorating economic conditions allowed a military revolt led by Getúlio Vargas (1882–1954) to seize control of the federal government in 1930. An ardent anticommunist, Vargas established a full-fledged dictatorship known as the "new state," which was modeled somewhat along European Fascist lines, in 1937. His rule lasted until 1945. Despite his harsh treatment of opponents, he was generally popular with the masses, combining effective economic nationalism and moderate social reform. It was a period of rapid industrialization, and Vargas allowed labor to organize and introduced a minimum wage and a wide range of benefits. None of his reforms were extended to the rural poor, however.

After World War II modernization continued for the next fifteen years, and Brazil's economy boomed. Economic nationalism was especially vigorous under the flamboyant president Juscelino Kubitschek (1902–1976). Between 1956 and 1960 Kubitschek's government borrowed heavily from international bankers to promote industry and build the new capital of Brasília in the midst of a wilderness. Kubitschek's slogan was "Fifty Years' Progress in Five."

By the late 1950s economic and social progress seemed to be bringing less violent, more democratic politics to Brazil and other Latin American countries. These expectations were shaken by the Communist Cuban Revolution, and conservative leaders and military officers across Latin America took control of governments in order to block any further spread of communism. In 1961 left-wing candidate João Goulart (1919–1976) became Brazil's president. Goulart introduced a number of social and economic reforms, including the expropriation and redistribution of land, the extension of voting rights to illiterates, the prohibition of private schools, a limit on the amount of profits a multinational corporation could take out of the country, and a requirement that people could own only one house. Goulart also tried to promote a nuclear-free Latin America; much to Washington's displeasure, he established close ties with the new Castro regime in Cuba.

In 1964 the military drove Goulart from office, and over the next twenty years the military installed one right-wing hard-line general-president after another. At the same time, the generals of these repressive military dictatorships oversaw political-economic reforms that promoted an economic miracle in Brazil. A slow return to democracy began in 1974, and in 1985 Brazilians elected the first civilian government in twenty years. The first decade of civilian rule was shaky, with crushingly high inflation, but the election of Fernando Cardoso (b. 1931) in 1994 began a string of four successful peaceful, democratic transitions of power. The election in October 2010 brought to office Brazil's first woman president, Dilma Rousseff (b. 1947).

Communist Revolution in Cuba

Achieving nominal independence in 1898 as a result of the Spanish-American War (see page 903), Cuba was practically an American protectorate until the 1930s, when a series of rulers with Socialist and Communist leanings seized and lost power. Cuba's political institutions were weak and its politicians corrupt. In March 1952 Fulgencio Batista (1901–1973), a Cuban military colonel, staged a coup with American support and instituted a repressive authoritarian regime that favored wealthy Cubans and multinational corporations. Through the 1950s Cuba was one of Latin America's most prosperous countries, although enormous differences remained between rich and poor.

The **Cuban Revolution** led by Fidel Castro (b. 1927) began in 1953. Castro's second in command, the legendary Argentinean Marxist revolutionary Ernesto "Che" Guevara (1928–1967), and a force of guerrilla rebels finally overthrew the Cuban government on New Year's Day 1959. Castro had promised a "real" revolution, and it soon became clear that "real" meant "Communist." Middle-class Cubans began fleeing to Miami, and Cuban relations with the Eisenhower administration deteriorated rapidly. In April 1961 U.S. president John F. Kennedy tried to use Cuban exiles to topple Castro, but Kennedy abandoned the exiles as soon as they landed ashore at the Bay of Pigs in southern Cuba.

After routing the Bay of Pigs forces, Castro moved to build an authoritarian Communist society. He formed an alliance with the Soviet bloc, used prisons and emigration to silence opposition, and expropriated all private property. Like Stalin's Soviet Union, Castro's Communist dictatorship was characterized by a cult of personality, and he played a central role in the exportation of Communist revolutions throughout Latin America. Castro's close ties with the Soviet Union led to the Cuban missile crisis in 1962 (see page 953), a confrontation between the United States and the U.S.S.R. over the placement of Soviet nuclear missiles in Cuba. In 1963 the United States placed a

Cuba

Fidel Castro's March to Havana, 1959 In August 1958 Cuban rebel forces turned back a government offensive planned by Cuban president Fulgencio Batista. On January 1, 1959, after Castro's forces went on the offensive and won two major battles, Batista fled the country to the Dominican Republic. This photo shows cheering throngs of supporters greeting Castro and his men on their triumphal march to the capital. (Bettmann/Corbis)

complete commercial and diplomatic embargo on Cuba that has remained in place ever since.

Under Castro's regime, human rights deteriorated dramatically. Every aspect of Cuban life was closely monitored, and any perceived opposition to the government was quickly repressed. The standard of living declined significantly following the revolution as the U.S. embargo took hold and as the Organization of American States (OAS) followed America's lead and suspended Cuba from the organization. OAS sanctions were lifted in 1975, and in 2009 the OAS voted to allow Cuba to rejoin the organization. Remaining defiant, Cuba's leaders said they were not interested.

Between 1961 and 1991 Cuba was heavily dependent on the Soviet Union for trade, development, commercial, and military aid. Soviet economic support allowed Cuba to assist many less developed countries in Latin America and Africa. Cuba intervened militarily in the civil war in Angola and also supported leftist governments in Mozambique, Zaire, Ethiopia, and Guinea-Bissau, among others. Cuba sent doctors as well as soldiers to many countries, and thousands of Cuban doctors continue to serve in Latin American and African countries where there is great need. Although statistics provided by the Cuban government are thought to be inflated, observers agree that Castro's government has significantly raised the educational level of all of its citizens, provided them with some of the best health care in Latin America, and organized cultural and arts programs that enjoy massive participation rates.

When the Soviet Union collapsed in 1991, Cuba entered what became known as the "special period in peacetime." Foreign economists estimate that Cuba lost 80 percent of its import and export trade and that its GDP dropped by 35 percent. The loss of oil imports from the Soviet Union effectively shut down the economy and plunged Cuba into an economic depression. Famine spread as agricultural production stopped. Cuban leaders were forced to implement a number of free-market reforms, including allowing some private ownership and self-employment. Tourism was promoted, and foreign investment encouraged. By 1999 the new measures had started to take effect. In the mid-1990s Cuba's GDP stood at around $25 billion. By 2010 it had reached an estimated $114 billion. Cuba has replaced Soviet petroleum with an estimated 100,000 barrels per day from Venezuela. Short of cash for foreign imports, Cuba provided Venezuela with 30,000 medical professionals as partial payment for the petroleum. Despite these gains, as much as one-third of Cuba's population lives in poverty.

In 2006 eighty-year-old Fidel Castro temporarily transferred power to his brother, Raúl, the commander of the military, while he recovered from surgery. Two years later a frail Castro announced his resignation as president, and Raúl took his place as Cuba's leader. Raúl Castro (b. 1931) introduced a number of economic and political measures that removed many restrictions limiting daily life, including restrictions on cell phones and purchases of computers, videos, air conditioners,

MAP 33.1 Authoritarian Governments in Latin America Over the past eighty years nearly all the peoples of Latin America, including those living in Caribbean island nations, have suffered at one time or another under some type of authoritarian regime. These governments have varied in form from single individuals ruling as dictators to groups of officers governing as military juntas. Only since the 1990s have the majority of Latin Americans countries rejected authoritarian rule and adopted more or less democratic models of government.

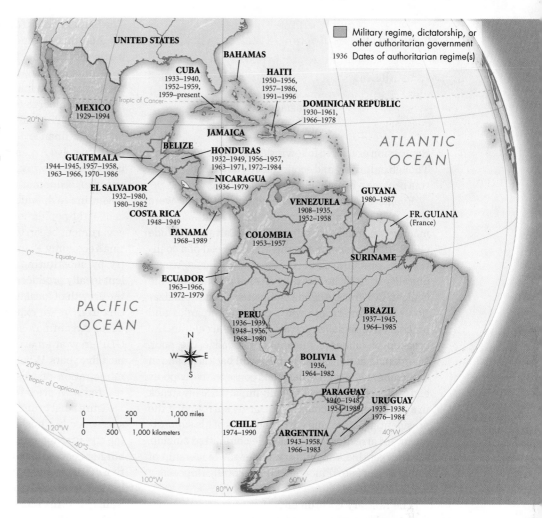

and other electronics. To increase the number of citizens who might be able to afford these items, Castro raised salaries for employees of all state-owned companies. Unused government lands were turned over to private farmers. Raúl Castro also expressed his desire to improve relations with the United States. For his part U.S. president Barack Obama relaxed the travel ban in 2009, allowing Cuban-Americans to freely travel to Cuba. In 2010, however, Obama extended the decades-long embargo for another year, to September 2011.

From Authoritarianism to Democracy in Latin America

Following Castro's seizure of power in Cuba in 1961, the United States feared that he would spread his Communist ideology to the rest of Central and South America. In 1961 the U.S. funded the new hemispheric Alliance for Progress, intended to promote long-term economic development and democratic social reform. U.S. aid contributed modestly to continued Latin American economic development in the 1960s, but democratic social reforms — the other half of the Alliance for Progress formula — stalled. Conflict between leftist

movements and ruling elites grew, won most often by the elites and their military allies, but at the cost of imposing a new kind of conservative authoritarianism. By the late 1970s only Costa Rica, Venezuela, Colombia, and Mexico retained some measure of democratic government (Map 33.1). As in Brazil, military juntas (groups of military officers) seized control of Argentina and Chile, and imposed even more brutal and authoritarian regimes. Oil-rich Venezuela also went through a period of military rule, democracy, and most recently a unique brand of socialism.

In Argentina the dictatorial populist and economic nationalist Juan Perón (1895–1974) began his presidency in 1946 with widespread support, in no small measure because of the extreme adoration the common people held for his wife, Eva Perón. (See "Individuals in Society: Eva Perón," page 1015.) His rule grew increasingly oppressive, however, and when Eva died of cancer in 1953, Perón's opponents' efforts to overthrow him increased. In 1955 the military staged a coup and restored elected democratic government. Then, worried by a Perónist revival and following the Brazilian example, the army took control in 1966 and again in 1976 after a brief civilian interlude.

"First we will kill all the subversives, then we will kill their collaborators, then their sympathizers, then . . . finally we will kill the timid."

IBÉRICO SAINT JEAN

Repression escalated following each military takeover. Though culturally and economically advanced, Argentina became a brutal military dictatorship.

Events in Chile followed a similar path and were truly tragic, given the country's long tradition of democracy and moderate reform. When Salvador Allende (1908–1973), a doctor and the Marxist head of a coalition of Communists, Socialists, and Radicals, won a plurality in 1970, he was duly elected president by the Chilean Congress. Allende completed the nationalization of the American-owned copper companies and proceeded to socialize private industry, accelerate the breakup of landed estates, and radicalize the poor. Marxism in action evoked a powerful backlash, and in September 1973, with widespread conservative support and U.S. backing, the traditionally impartial army struck in a well-organized coup. As the army surrounded the presidential palace, and with thousands of his supporters under arrest or worse, Allende committed suicide. As in Argentina, the military, under the leadership of General Augusto Pinochet (1915–2006), imposed a harsh despotism.

The military governments that revived antidemocratic authoritarianism in Latin America blocked not only Marxist and Socialist programs but most liberal and moderate reforms as well. The new authoritarians were, however, determined modernizers, deeply committed to nationalism, industrialization, technology, and some modest social progress. They even promised free elections in the future. That time came in the 1980s, when another democratic wave gained momentum throughout Latin America. By the late 1980s, 94 percent of Latin Americans lived under regimes that guaranteed elections and civil liberties.

In Argentina General Leopoldo Galtieri (1926–2003) was the last president of a military-ruled government that gradually lost almost all popular support because of its "dirty war" (1976–1983) against its own citizens, in which thousands arbitrarily accused of opposing the regime were imprisoned, tortured, and murdered. One of Galtieri's fellow generals, Ibérico Saint Jean, stated the junta's strategy in blunt terms: "First we will kill all the subversives, then we will kill their collaborators, then their sympathizers, then . . . those who remain indifferent, and finally we will kill the timid."[1]

In 1982, in a desperate gamble to rally the people, Argentina's military rulers seized the Falkland (or Malvinas) Islands (see Map 33.1) from Great Britain.

The British rout of Argentina's poorly led troops forced the humiliated generals to schedule national democratic elections in 1983. The democratically elected government prosecuted the former military rulers for their crimes and laid solid foundations for liberty and political democracy.

In the 1980s and 1990s a succession of presidents and their finance ministers put forward a range of plans to solve Argentina's economic problems. Nothing seemed to work, and in 2002 the country experienced an economic, social, and political crisis, leading Argentina to default on its foreign debt. With 60 percent of the population living below the poverty line, the government began to institute policies to grow Argentina's economy. Plans were set in place to revive industry by substituting imported products with equivalent locally produced goods. This not only encouraged the growth of local industries, but also allowed Argentina to increase exports and pay off its international debts. Argentina's economy began to revive, and real GDP grew at an average 9 percent annually over the next five years. When inflation increased under the administration of Néstor Kirchner (r. 2003–2007), he reacted with price restraints on businesses and other measures that crippled the economy. Cristina Kirchner succeeded her husband as president in 2007, becoming the first woman president in Argentina's history, but her economic policies have been no better. Argentina's GDP dropped dramatically, to 0.5 percent in 2009, made worse by the global economic crisis of 2008–2009. Still, Argentina remains the fourth largest economy in Latin America, after Brazil, Mexico, and Venezuela.

Venezuela's history is closely linked to Simón Bolívar, a revolutionary who led independence movements against Spanish colonial rule in the early 1800s (see page 816). More recently its history has been tied to oil, which was discovered in massive deposits during the World War I. Wealth from the oil gave Venezuela the highest per capita GDP in Latin America by 1935, lifting it from being one of the poorest to one of the richest countries on the continent. The military ruled Venezuela until 1958, except for a brief three-year period of civilian rule (led by the Democratic Action Party) following World War II. In January 1958 a coalition of all the major political parties except the Communists forced out the military dictator Pérez Jiménez (r. 1952–1958). The Social Christian Party of Venezuela (COPEI) and the Democratic Action Party then controlled Venezuelan politics for the next forty years.

While much of the rest of Latin America experienced military dictatorships in the 1960s, 1970s, and 1980s, Venezuela's civilian governments survived coup attempts, riots, massive fraud and corruption, and the unpredictable fluctuations of the international oil markets, and avoided military takeovers. In the 1960s the government also deflected attacks by leftist guerrilla

Eva Perón

EVA PERÓN WAS ONLY THIRTY-THREE WHEN she died of cancer on July 26, 1952, but already many Argentineans considered her a saint. The state radio broadcaster sadly announced that "today at 20:25 Eva Perón, Spiritual Leader of the Nation, entered immortality." Argentina went into official mourning; although Perón had never held an official political office, she was accorded a state funeral. Immediately following her death her corpse was embalmed, with the intention of putting it on public display forever in a planned memorial larger than the Statue of Liberty.

Often called Evita (the Spanish diminutive of Eva), she was one of five illegitimate children born near Buenos Aires to Juan Duarte and Juana Ibarguren. Duarte returned to his legitimate wife and children when Eva was a year old, leaving Juana and her children destitute and dependent on Juana's sewing for their existence. As they grew older all the children had to work, but Eva apparently also dreamed of becoming an actress.

At fifteen Eva Duarte moved to the cosmopolitan city of Buenos Aires. Although she had little formal education and no connections, she possessed great natural beauty, and soon she joined a professional theater group with which she toured nationally. She also modeled, appeared in a few movies, and then got regular employment as a character on a radio series. By 1943, although only twenty-three years old, she was one of the highest paid actresses in the country.

In 1943 Eva met widowed Colonel Juan Perón, then secretary of labor and social welfare in the military government that had seized power that year. Juan Perón had grand ambitions, intending to run for president. Eva Duarte became his partner and confidante, and she won him support among the Argentine masses. In 1945 Juan Perón and Eva Duarte were married.

A year later Perón won the presidency. Eva had gone out on the campaign trail and organized support for her husband from *los descamisados* ("the shirtless ones"), her name for Argentine's poor. When Perón assumed the presidency, Eva, though not officially appointed, became the secretary of labor. Having come from a childhood of poverty herself, she now worked tirelessly for the poor, for the working classes, and with organized labor. She instituted a number of social welfare measures and promoted a new Ministry of Health, which resulted in the creation of new hospitals and disease treatment programs. In 1948 she established the Eva Perón Welfare Foundation, which grew into an immense semiofficial welfare agency, helping the poor throughout Argentina and even contributing to victims of natural disasters in other countries.

From early on, Eva Perón had supported women's suffrage, and in September 1947 Argentine women won the right to vote.

Eva then formed the Female Perónist Party, which by 1951 had five hundred thousand members. Thousands of Argentine women have credited Eva's example as a reason for their becoming involved in politics. In 1951 she seemed ready to run for vice president beside her husband. The huge base of women, the poor, and workers assured them victory. Her declining health, however, forced her to turn down the nomination. Perón won the election by over 30 percent, but when Eva died the following year, Perón's authoritarian rule and bad economic policies lost him support, and a military junta forced him into exile.

Eva Perón's life story is an amazing one, but what happened following her death is just as extraordinary. Before the massive monument intended to hold her embalmed body could be built, the military seized power, and her body disappeared. Seventeen years later the generals finally revealed that it was in a tomb in Milan, Italy. Juan Perón, living in Spain with his third wife, had the body exhumed and brought to Spain, where he kept it in his house. Perón returned to Argentina in 1973 and won the presidential election, but died the following year. His wife, Isabel Perón, succeeded him as president. Juan and Eva's bodies were briefly displayed together at his funeral and then, finally, buried.

QUESTIONS FOR ANALYSIS

1. Why do you think Eva Perón was adored by the Argentine people when she died?
2. What were some of the welfare and government programs that Eva Perón promoted?

Source: Nicholas Fraser and Marysa Navarro, *Evita: The Real Life of Eva Perón* (New York: Norton, 1976).

• **Eva Perón waves to supporters from the balcony of the presidential palace, Casa Rosada, in Buenos Aires, on October 17, 1951.** (Clarin/AP Images)

Justice for the Victims of Chile's General Pinochet
With their faces covered with death masks, demonstrators outside Britain's High Court in 2000 hold up crosses carrying pictures of the "Disappeared"—the thousands kidnapped and allegedly murdered between 1973 and 1988 under the military dictatorship of General Pinochet. The High Court ruled against extraditing Pinochet to Spain to stand trial, but he was finally charged with torture and murder when he returned to Chile. (Dan Chung/Reuters New-Media Inc./ Corbis)

movements that were trying to replicate Fidel Castro's successful revolution in Cuba.

Venezuela's economy grew throughout the twentieth century. By 1970 Venezuela was the wealthiest country in Latin America and one of the twenty richest in the world. Following the 1973 global oil crisis, oil prices skyrocketed, and Venezuela's oil revenues also soared until 1978, when the GDP began to fall. This drop was exacerbated by the collapse of global oil prices in the mid-1980s. There is still much debate over the reason for this decline following seventy years of sustained growth. One answer may be found in the government's massive public spending spree. Venezuela's leaders assumed, like the leaders of many other oil-rich countries such as Nigeria, that the price of oil would never go down. Oil money would always be available to pay off the large external debts they were accumulating. Second, the country did not invest its increased oil revenues in alternative industries that could diversify the economy and pay the bills should oil prices decline. Third, while oil revenues grew, exports of other goods and raw materials declined, leaving Venezuela again more dependent on oil. And fourth, Venezuela cut back oil production, sensing a need to horde its supplies even though new explorations had revealed massive reserves.

In the 1980s and 1990s Venezuela experienced one political crisis after another as the economy declined, poverty and crime rose, and corruption, always a problem in the country, flourished. A succession of events in the late 1980s and early 1990s—including riots in Caracas in February 1989 that left as many as three thousand dead, two attempted military coups in 1992, and the impeachment of then president Carlos Pérez for corruption in 1993—led to the election of Rafael Caldera (1916–2009) as president in 1994. Caldera had served previously as president from 1969 to 1974. One of his first acts in office was to grant a pardon to Hugo Chávez (b. 1954) for his role in the first of the 1992 military coup attempts.

Chávez succeeded Caldera as president in 1998 and immediately launched a "Bolivarian revolution," which included a new constitution, adopted in December 1999, and changed the country's official name to the Bolivarian Republic of Venezuela. The long and complicated new constitution guarantees, among other things, free education to all through college, universal suffrage, social security, free health care, a clean environment, gender equality, the right to property, and the rights of minorities, particularly Venezuela's native peoples, to maintain their traditional cultures, religions, and languages.

Chávez has labeled his efforts "socialism for the twenty-first century," and he refers to his socialist ideology as Bolivarianism. His first action was to rid the government of the old guard and to fill positions of power with his supporters. He then moved to clean up corruption and to redistribute Venezuela's oil revenues to the poor and underprivileged through social programs outlined in the constitution. Despite a 2002 coup attempt, Chávez was re-elected to a second term in December 2006. His power base has changed significantly since his first election victory, and his Bolivarian revolution has alienated most of the upper and middle classes who used to support him. To his credit, the poverty rate in Venezuela has dropped from 55 percent before he took office in 1998 to 28 percent in 2008. It is no wonder that the poorest workers continue to support him.

Since 2006 Chávez has turned more and more toward a socialist agenda and also to a position of absolute power. A referendum in February 2009 eliminated term limits, making it possible for him to remain in office indefinitely. Despite the human rights guarantees in the new constitution, various international organizations have condemned Chávez's human rights record, including the weakening of democratic institutions and the harassment or arrest of political opponents. Economically, Chávez has received much criticism for his overdependence on oil to fund the country's economy. In foreign relations Chávez has sought closer relations with other South American countries, while loudly and frequently condemning the United States, globalization, and open market economies.

The most dramatic developments in Central America occurred in Nicaragua. In 1979 a Socialist political party, the Sandinista National Liberation Front (FSLN), joined with a broad coalition of liberals, Socialists, and Marxist revolutionaries to drive long-time dictator Anastasio Somoza (1925–1980) from power. A multipartisan junta—a coalition of political leaders—then led the country from 1979 to 1985. These leaders wanted genuine political and economic independence from the United States, as well as thoroughgoing land reform, some nationalized industry, and friendly ties with Communist countries. In a general election that was universally described by impartial international observers as free and fair, the FSLN candidate Daniel Ortega (b. 1945) won the presidency for his Sandinista Party with 67 percent of the vote and took office in January 1985.

The Sandinista government and its policies infuriated the Reagan administration in the United States, which sought to overthrow it by creating a counter-revolutionary mercenary army, the Contras, and supplying it with military aid funded illegally through military weapons sales to Iran. After years of civil war, the Nicaraguan economy collapsed, and the Sandinista government's popularity eventually declined. The Sandinistas surrendered power when they were defeated in free elections by a coalition of opposition parties in 1990.

In elections in November 2006 Nicaraguans re-elected Ortega, the FSLN candidate, as president, and he continued to hold that position in 2011. He has remained an outspoken opponent of what he perceives as Western (especially American) imperialism. He has publicly praised controversial leaders such as Iranian president Mahmoud Ahmadinejad (see page 1003) and Venezuela's Hugo Chávez, and observed that capitalism was in its "death throes" during the 2008–2009 global economic crisis.

The Reagan administration also helped engineer a 1986 coup in Haiti, where "Papa Doc" Duvalier, followed by his son, "Baby Doc," had for decades ruled in one of the most repressive dictatorships in the Americas, with U.S. support. Although "Baby Doc" was forced into exile, the country experienced a period of violence and disorder until semi-fair elections were held in 1994 with the help of U.S. military intervention. Over the next ten years, however, Haiti remained unstable with a succession of disputed elections and an increase in violence and human rights abuses. A rebellion broke out in 2004 in the northern part of the country and soon spread to the capital. Then president Jean-Bertrand Aristide (who had previously served as president for eight months in 1991 and again for two years from 1994 to 1996) was forced to flee the country. A United Nations Stabilization Mission was sent to Haiti following the 2004 rebellion to preserve the peace and maintain stability.

Following a round of controversial elections in May 2006, René Préval (b. 1943) became Haiti's president. Préval had some success in improving the economy over the next two years, but in April 2008 widespread food riots broke out across the country. Préval successfully defused the demonstrations by lowering the price of rice. Minor successes in improving the economy or the prices of basic commodities lost all significance when Haiti, already the Western Hemisphere's poorest country, experienced one of the deadliest earthquakes in world history. On January 12, 2010, a catastrophic magnitude 7.0 earthquake rocked the small nation, killing perhaps as many as 316,000 people and leaving 1 to 2 million Haitians homeless. Although the initial reaction from the international community was swift and generous, a year later hundreds of thousands of Haitians continued to live in makeshift tent cities, basic services had not been restored, and there were regular outbreaks of cholera and other diseases due to the lack of clean water and proper sanitation. Widespread corruption, the absence of efficient government services, the inability to dispense relief aid effectively, and the failure of some donor nations to fulfill their monetary pledges for reconstruction have resulted in a slow recovery for this tiny island nation.

Pan–Latin American Unity

In the 1990s Latin America's popularly elected governments relaxed economic relations with other countries, moving decisively from tariff protection and economic nationalism toward free markets and international trade. In so doing, they revitalized their economies and registered solid gains. In 1994 Mexico joined with the United States and Canada in the North American Free Trade Agreement (NAFTA). Hoping to copy the success of the European Union, twelve South American countries (Brazil, Argentina, Paraguay, Uruguay, Venezuela, Bolivia, Colombia, Ecuador, Peru, Guyana, Suriname, and Chile) met in Cuzco, Peru, in December 2004 and signed the Cuzco Declaration, announcing the formation of the Union of South American Nations (UNSAN). The Constitutive Treaty formally establishing the union was signed on May 23, 2008, in Brasília, Brazil. The union is intended to provide a free-trade zone for its members and to compete economically with the United States and the European Community. In March 2011 UNSAN representatives met in Quito, Ecuador, to set in motion the formal operations of the union, electing Colombia's Maria Emma Majia and Venezuelan Ali Rodriguez as co-secretaries general of the organization.

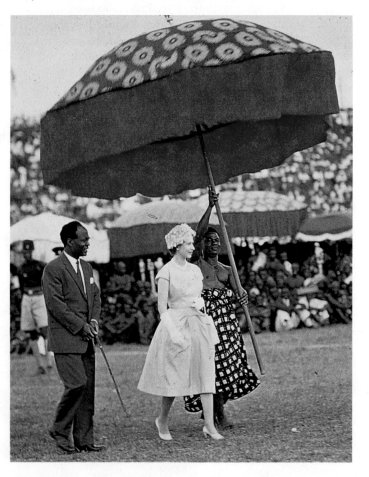

Queen Elizabeth Visits Ghana Britain's Queen Elizabeth II pays an official visit to Ghana, the former Gold Coast colony, in 1961. Accompanying the queen at the colorful welcoming ceremony is Ghana's popular Kwame Nkrumah, who was educated in black colleges in the United States and led Ghana's breakthrough to independence in 1957. (Bettmann/Corbis)

Nationalism in Sub-Saharan Africa

☐ What factors influenced decolonization in sub-Saharan Africa after World War II?

Most of sub-Saharan Africa won political independence fairly rapidly after World War II. By 1964 only Portugal's colonies and white-dominated southern Africa remained beyond the reach of African nationalists. The rise of independent states in sub-Saharan Africa resulted directly from both a reaction against Western imperialism and the growth of African nationalism.

The Growth of African Nationalism

Western intrusion was the critical factor in the development of African nationalism, as it had been in Asia and the Middle East. But two things were different about Africa. First, because the imperial system and Western education did not solidify in Africa until after 1900 (see pages 761–767), national movements began to come of age only in the 1920s and reached maturity after 1945. Second, Africa's multiplicity of ethnic groups, coupled with imperial boundaries that often bore no resemblance to existing ethnic boundaries, greatly complicated the development of political — as distinct from cultural — nationalism. Was a modern national state to be based on ethnic or clan loyalties (as it had been in France and Germany)? Was it to be a continent-wide union of all African peoples? Or would the multiethnic territories arbitrarily carved out by competing European empires become the new African nations? Only after 1945 did a tentative answer emerge.

A few educated West Africans in British colonies had articulated a kind of black nationalism before 1914. But the first real impetus came from the United States and the British West Indies. The most renowned participant in this "black nationalism" was W. E. B. Du Bois (1868–1963). The first black to receive a Ph.D. from Harvard, this brilliant writer and historian organized Pan-African congresses in Paris during the Versailles Peace Conference in 1919 and in Brussels in 1921. **Pan-Africanists** sought black solidarity and, eventually, a vast self-governing union of all African peoples. The flamboyant Jamaican-born Marcus Garvey (1887–1940) was the most influential Pan-Africanist voice in Africa. Young, educated Africans rallied to his call of "Africa for the Africans" and European expulsion from Africa.

In the 1920s many educated French and British Africans experienced a strong surge of pride and cultural nationalism. African intellectuals in Europe formulated and articulated the rich idea of *négritude*, or blackness:

racial pride, self-confidence, and joy in black creativity and the black spirit. This westernized African elite pressed for better access to government jobs, modest steps toward self-government, and an end to humiliating discrimination. They claimed the right to speak for ordinary Africans and denounced the government-supported chiefs as "Uncle Toms," yet their demands remained moderate.

The mass protests that accompanied the deprivations of the Great Depression, in particular the **cocoa holdups** of 1930–1931 and 1937–1938, proved to be the catalyst for the development of African nationalism. Cocoa completely dominated the Gold Coast's economy. As prices plummeted after 1929, cocoa farmers refused to sell their beans to the large British firms that fixed prices and monopolized the export trade. Instead, the farmers organized cooperatives to cut back production and sell their crops directly to European and American chocolate manufacturers. The cocoa holdups succeeded in mobilizing much of the population against the foreign companies and demonstrated the power of mass organization and mass protest. Mass movements for national independence were not far behind.

Achieving Independence with New Leaders

The repercussions of the Second World War in black Africa greatly accelerated the changes begun in the 1930s. Many African soldiers who served in India had been powerfully impressed by Indian nationalism. As African mines and plantations strained to meet wartime demands, towns mushroomed into cities where ramshackle housing, inflation, and shortages of consumer goods created discontent and hardship.

Western imperialism also changed. Both the British and the French acknowledged the need for rapid social and economic improvement in their colonies; for the first time both began sending money and aid on a large scale. The principle of self-government was written into the United Nations charter and was supported by Great Britain's postwar Labour government. Thus the key question for Great Britain's various African colonies was their rate of progress toward self-government. The British and the French were in no rush. But a new breed of African leader was emerging. Impatient and insistent, these spokesmen for modern African nationalism were remarkably successful: by 1964 almost all of western, eastern, and central Africa had achieved statehood, generally without much bloodshed (Map 33.2).

These new postwar African leaders formed an elite by virtue of their advanced European or American education, and they were profoundly influenced by Western thought. But compared with the interwar generation of educated Africans, they were more radical and

□ NATIONALISM IN BLACK AFRICA

1919	Du Bois organizes first Pan-African congress
1920s	Cultural nationalism grows among Africa's educated elites
1929	Great Depression brings economic hardship and discontent
1930–1931	Gold Coast farmers organize first cocoa holdups
1939–1945	World War II accelerates political and economic change
1951	Nkrumah and Convention People's Party win national elections in Ghana (former Gold Coast)
1957	Nkrumah leads Ghana to independence
1958	De Gaulle offers commonwealth status to France's African territories; only Guinea chooses independence
1960	Nigeria becomes an independent state
1966	Ghana's Nkrumah deposed in military coup
1967	Ibos secede from Nigeria to form state of Biafra
1980	Blacks rule Zimbabwe (former Southern Rhodesia) after long civil war with white settlers
1984	South Africa's whites issue cosmetic reforms but maintain racial segregation and discrimination
1989–1990	South African government begins process of reform; black leader Nelson Mandela freed from prison
1994	Nelson Mandela elected president of South Africa

humbler in social origin. Among them were former schoolteachers, union leaders, government clerks, and unemployed students, as well as lawyers and prizewinning poets.

Postwar African leaders accepted prevailing colonial boundaries to avoid border disputes and achieve freedom as soon as possible. Sensing a loss of power, traditional rulers sometimes became the new leaders' worst political enemies. Skillfully, the new leaders channeled postwar hope and discontent into support for mass political organizations. These organizations staged gigantic protests and became political parties.

- **Pan-Africanists** People, such as W. E. B. Du Bois and Marcus Garvey, who promoted solidarity among all blacks and the eventual self-governing union of all African peoples.
- **cocoa holdups** Mass protests in the 1930s by Gold Coast producers of cocoa who refused to sell their beans to British firms and instead sold them directly to European and American chocolate manufacturers.

Viewpoints

Ghanaian and South African Leaders on Black Nationalism

• *Kwame Nkrumah led the British Gold Coast colony to independence in 1957, making it the first sub-Saharan colony to free itself from colonialism. Elected the first president of Ghana, Nkrumah is considered the father of independent Africa. His independence day speech on March 6, 1957, galvanized African nationalists across Africa, and within ten years nearly the entire continent had been liberated. One exception was South Africa, where the white apartheid regime held onto power until 1994, when Nelson Mandela became president. In May 1996 Deputy President Thabo Mbeki delivered his "I am an African" speech to celebrate the adoption of a new South African constitution that ended all discrimination.*

Kwame Nkrumah, Ghanaian Independence Day Speech

66 At long last the battle has ended. And thus Ghana, your beloved country, is free forever.... I ... thank the chiefs and people of this country, the youth, the farmers, the women who have so nobly fought and won this battle. I want to thank the various ex-servicemen who have also struggled with me in this mighty task of freeing our country from foreign rule and imperialism....

From today, we must change our attitude—our mind. We must realize that from now on we are no more a colony but a free and independent people. But ... that also entails hard work. I am depending upon the millions of people to help me to reshape the destiny of this county.

We are prepared to build an African nation that will be respected by every other nation in the world.... I can see that you are here in your millions, so that we can prove to the world that when an African is given the chance he can show the world that he is somebody.... We shall show the world that the African is ready to fight his own battle and that the African man is capable of managing his own affairs....

We have done the battle and we again rededicate ourselves not only in the struggle to emancipate all the countries in Africa; our independence is meaningless unless it is linked up with the total liberation of the African continent.

Ghana is free forever! 99

Thabo Mbeki, "I Am an African"

66 On an occasion such as this, we should, perhaps, start from the beginning. So, let me begin. I am an African....

I have seen what happens when one person has superiority of force over another, when the stronger appropriate to themselves the prerogative even to annul the injunction that God created all men and women in His image. I know what it signifies when race and colour are used to determine who is human and who subhuman. I have seen the destruction of all sense of self-esteem, the consequent striving to be what one is not, simply to acquire some of the benefits which those who had imposed themselves as masters had ensured that they enjoy. I have experience of the situation in which race and colour is used to enrich some and impoverish the rest....

All this I know and know to be true because I am an African!

Because of that, I am also able to state this fundamental truth: that I am born of a people who are heroes and heroines. I am born of a people who would not tolerate oppression.

Whatever the setbacks of the moment, nothing can stop us now! Whatever the difficulties, Africa shall be at peace! However improbable it may sound to the sceptics, Africa will prosper!

Whoever we may be, whatever our immediate interest, however much baggage we carry from our past, however much we have been caught by the fashion of cynicism and loss of faith in the capacity of the people, let us say today: Nothing can stop us now! 99

Sources: Felix M. Kiruthu, *Voices of Freedom: Great African Independence Speeches* (Colorado Springs: International Academic Publishers, 2001), pp. 27–29; Thabo Mbeki, "Statement of Deputy Resident TM Mbeki ... on the Occasion of the Adoption ... of 'The Republic of South Africa Constitutional Bill 1996.'" Reprinted by permission of the South African Government Information website.

QUESTIONS FOR ANALYSIS

1. What does Nkrumah believe Ghanaians must do now that they have independence?
2. What is it that gives Mbeki the confidence to say that now Africa will prosper and be at peace?
3. What does it mean to be African according to these documents?

The Opening of Parliament in Ghana As part of an ancient ritual, two medicine men pour out sacred oil and call on the gods to bless the work of the Second Parliament and President Kwame Nkrumah, standing on the right. The combination of time-honored customs and modern political institutions was characteristic of African states after they secured independence. (Wide World Photos/AP Images)

Eventually they came to power by winning the general elections that the colonial governments belatedly called to choose their successors.

Ghana Shows the Way

Perhaps the most charismatic of this generation of African leaders was Kwame Nkrumah (1909–1972). Nkrumah spent ten years studying in the United States, where he was deeply influenced by European Socialists and Marcus Garvey. He returned to the Gold Coast after the Second World War and entered politics. Under his leadership the Gold Coast — which he rechristened "Ghana" — became the first independent African state to emerge from colonialism. (See "Viewpoints: Ghanaian and South African Leaders on Black Nationalism.")

Nkrumah came to power by building a radical mass party that appealed particularly to modern elements — former servicemen, market women, union members, urban toughs, and cocoa farmers. He and his party injected the joy and enthusiasm of religious revivals into their rallies and propaganda: "Self-Government Now" was their credo, secular salvation the promise.

Rejecting halfway measures — "We prefer self-government with danger to servitude in tranquility" — Nkrumah and his Convention People's Party staged strikes and riots. Arrested, the "Deliverer of Ghana" campaigned from jail and saw his party win a smashing victory in the 1951 national elections. Called from prison to head the transitional government, Nkrumah and his nationalist party defeated both westernized moderates and more traditional political rivals in free elections. By 1957 Nkrumah had achieved worldwide fame and influence as Ghana became independent.

After Ghana's breakthrough, independence for other African colonies followed rapidly. The main problem in some colonies, such as Algeria, was the permanent white settlers, not the colonial officials. Wherever white settlers were numerous, as in Kenya, they sought to preserve their privileged position. But only in Southern Rhodesia and South Africa were whites numerous enough to prevail for long. Southern Rhodesian whites declared independence illegally in 1965 and held out until 1980, when black nationalists won a long liberation struggle and renamed the country Zimbabwe. Majority rule in South Africa took even longer.

French-Speaking Regions

Decolonization took a somewhat different course in French-speaking Africa. The events in the French North African colony of Algeria in the 1950s and early 1960s help clarify France's attitude to its sub-Saharan black African colonies.

France tried hard to hold onto Indochina and Algeria after 1945. Predominantly Arabic speaking and Muslim, Algerian nationalists were emboldened by Nasser's great triumph in Egypt in 1952 and by France's

▢ Mapping the Past

MAP 33.2 Decolonization in Africa, 1947 to the Present Most African territories achieved statehood by the mid-1960s, as European empires passed away, unlamented.

ANALYZING THE MAP How many African states achieved independence after 1945? How many experienced some sort of postcolonial conflict?

CONNECTIONS How did the imperialist legacy serve to complicate the transition to stable, independent nations in Africa and Latin America?

defeat in Indochina in 1954 (see page 988). But Algeria's large, and mostly Catholic, European population — known as the **pieds-noirs** ("black feet") because its members wore black shoes instead of sandals — was determined to keep Algeria part of France. In November 1954 Algeria's anticolonial movement, the **National Liberation Front** (FLN), began a long, bitter, and bloody war for independence. Besides being the most violent of the anticolonial wars in Africa, the war also nearly tore France apart as French anticolonialists fought with French pro-imperialists. Finally, in 1962, the FLN won, and Algeria became an independent state. An estimated 900,000 of the 1,025,000 Eu-

ropeans and indigenous Jews fled Algeria in the first few months of 1962.

While the terrible war raged on in Algeria, France upped its aid to its sub-Saharan African colonies, but independence remained a dirty word until Charles de Gaulle came to power in 1958. Seeking to head off radical nationalists and receiving the crucial support of moderate black leaders, de Gaulle chose a divide-and-rule strategy. He divided the French West Africa and French Equatorial Africa federations into thirteen separate governments, thus creating a "French commonwealth." Plebiscites were called in each territory to ratify the new arrangement. An affirmative vote meant continued ties with France; a negative vote signified immediate independence and a complete break with France.

De Gaulle's gamble was shrewd. The educated black elite — as personified by the influential poet-politician Léopold Sédar Senghor, who now led Senegal's government — loved France and dreaded a sudden divorce. They also wanted French aid to continue. France, in keeping with its ideology of assimilation, had given the vote to its educated colonial elite after the Second World War, and about forty Africans held French parliamentary seats after 1946. For both cultural and practical reasons, therefore, French Africa's leaders tended to be moderate and in no rush for independence.

In Guinea, however, a young nationalist named Sekou Touré (1922–1984) led his people to overwhelming rejection of the new constitution in 1958. Inspired by Ghana's Nkrumah, Touré laid it out to de Gaulle face-to-face: "We have to tell you bluntly, Mr. President, what the demands of the people are. . . . We have one prime and essential need: our dignity. But there is no dignity without freedom. . . . We prefer freedom in poverty to opulence in slavery."[2]

The Belgians, long-time practitioners of paternalism coupled with harsh, selfish rule in their enormous Congo colony (see page 758), had always discouraged the development of an educated elite. When they suddenly decided to grant independence in 1959 after wild riots, the fabric of government broke down. Independence was soon followed by violent ethnic conflict, civil war, and foreign intervention. The Belgian Congo was the great exception to sub-Saharan black Africa's generally peaceful and successful transition to independence between 1957 and 1964.

> "We have one prime and essential need: our dignity. But there is no dignity without freedom. . . . We prefer freedom in poverty to opulence in slavery."
>
> **SEKOU TOURÉ**

Sub-Saharan Africa Since 1960

☐ What are some of the common features of independent Africa since 1960?

The facility with which most of black Africa achieved independence stimulated buoyant optimism in the early 1960s. But within a generation democratic government and civil liberties gave way to one-party rule or military dictatorship and widespread corruption.

The rise of authoritarian government in Africa after independence must be viewed in historical perspective. Representative institutions on the eve of

independence were an imperial afterthought, and the new African countries faced tremendous challenges. Above all, ethnic divisions threatened civil conflicts that could tear the fragile states apart. Yet this did not happen. Strong leaders used nationalism, first harnessed to throw off foreign rule, to build one-party regimes and promote unity. Unfortunately, nation building by idealistic authoritarians often deteriorated into brutal dictatorships, frequent military coups, and civil strife. Then, in the early 1990s, a powerful reaction to this decline, inspired by the eastern European revolutions, resulted in a surge of democratic protest that achieved major political gains and rekindled in part the optimism of the independence era.

Striving for National Unity

Africa's imperial legacy is more negative than positive. Although some countries left generally better legacies than others — Britain's was better than Belgium's or Portugal's, for example — overall the "civilizing mission" did more harm than good. On something of a positive note, the forty or so states (see Map 33.2) inherited varying degrees of functioning bureaucracies, some elected political leaders, and some modern infrastructure — transportation, communication systems, schools, hospitals, and the like. And every country inherited the cornerstone of imperial power — a tough, well-equipped army to maintain order. But other features of the imperialist legacy served to torment independent Africa.

The disruption of traditional life had caused real suffering and resulted in unobtainable postindependence expectations. The prevailing export economies were weak, lopsided, and concentrated in foreign hands. Technical, managerial, and medical skills were in acutely short supply. Above all, the legacy of political boundaries imposed by foreigners without regard to ethnic and cultural groupings weighed heavily on post-independence Africa. Nearly every new state encompassed a variety of peoples who might easily develop conflicting national aspirations.

Great Britain and France had granted their African colonies democratic governments as they prepared to depart. Yet belated Western-style democracy served the new multiethnic states poorly. After freedom from

---

• **pieds-noirs** The predominantly Catholic French population in the French colony of Algeria, called "black feet" because they wore black shoes instead of sandals.

• **National Liberation Front** The victorious anticolonial movement in Algeria.

imperialism no longer provided a unifying common objective, political parties often coalesced along regional and ethnic lines. Many African leaders concluded that democracy threatened to destroy the existing states and to prevent social and economic progress. Thus these leaders maintained the authoritarian tradition they had inherited from the imperialists, and free elections often gave way to dictators and one-party rule.

After Ghana won its independence, for instance, Nkrumah jailed without trial his main opponents — chiefs, lawyers, and intellectuals — and outlawed opposition parties. Nkrumah worked to build a "revolutionary" one-party state and a socialist economy. By the mid-1960s his grandiose economic projects had almost bankrupted Ghana, and in 1966 the army suddenly seized power while he was visiting China.

The French-speaking countries also shifted toward one-party government to promote state unity and develop distinctive characteristics that could serve as the basis for statewide nationalism. Mali followed Guinea into Marxist radicalism. Senegal and the Ivory Coast stressed moderation and close economic and cultural ties with France.

Like Nkrumah, many of the initial leaders at the helm of one-party states were eventually overthrown by military leaders. The rise of would-be Napoleons was lamented by many Western liberals and African intellectuals, who often failed to note that military rule was also widespread in Latin America, Asia, and the Near East in the 1970s and 1980s.

As elsewhere, military rule in Africa was authoritarian and undemocratic. In Uganda, for instance, the brutal Idi Amin (1925?–2003) seized power in 1971, packed the army with his ethnic supporters, and terrorized the population for a decade. Yet military regimes generally managed to hold their countries together, and many, like their Latin American counterparts, were committed to social and economic modernization. Drawing on an educated and motivated elite, they sometimes accomplished much. As economic and social conditions stagnated and often declined in African countries from the mid-1970s to the early 1990s, however, army leaders and dictators became more and more greedy and dishonest. By the late 1980s military rulers and one-party authoritarian regimes were coming under increasing pressure to hand over power to more democratic forces.

Nigeria, Africa's Giant

Nigeria's history illustrates just how difficult genuine nation building could be after independence was achieved. "Nigeria" was a name coined by the British to designate their nineteenth-century conquests in the Niger River basin, which encompassed many ancient kingdoms and hundreds of ethnic groups. Also for ad- ministrative convenience, the British consolidated the northern Muslim territories and the southern Christian or animist areas. Despite this diverse population, by 1945 Nigeria had spawned a powerful independence movement, and independence was achieved in 1960 (see Map 33.2).

The key constitutional question was the relationship between the central government and the various regions. Ultimately Nigeria adopted a federal system, whereby the national government at Lagos shared power with three regional or state governments in the north, west, and east. Each region had a dominant ethnic group and a corresponding political party. The parties were expected to cooperate in the national parliament, and the rights of minorities were protected by law.

After independence Nigerians' bright hopes gradually dimmed because of growing ethnic rivalries. In 1967 these intense rivalries erupted into a civil war. The crisis began in 1964 when some young military officers, many of whom were Ibos from the southeast, seized the government and executed its leaders.

At first the young officers were popular, but the Muslim northerners had long distrusted the hard-working, clannish, non-Muslim Ibos. When the Ibo-led military council proclaimed a centralized dictatorship, frenzied mobs in northern cities massacred thousands of Ibos. When a group of northern officers then seized the national government in a countercoup, the traumatized Ibos revolted and proclaimed the independent state of Biafra in 1967.

The Biafran war lasted three years. The Ibos fought with heroic determination, believing that political independence was their only refuge from genocide. Heavily outnumbered, they were gradually surrounded. Perhaps millions starved to death as Biafra became a symbol of monumental human tragedy.

Having preserved the state in the 1960s, Nigeria's military rulers focused on building a nation in the 1970s. Although the federal government held the real power, the country was divided into nineteen small, manageable units to handle local and cultural matters. The defeated Ibos were pardoned, and Iboland was rebuilt with federal oil revenues.

Except for a couple of brief periods of civilian rule, combinations of Hausa-Fulani Muslim army officers ruled until 1998, when the brutal military dictator General Sani Abacha suddenly died, giving Nigeria renewed hope for unity and democracy. A new constitution was adopted in 1999 and that same year Nigerians voted in free elections and re-established civilian rule. The April 2003 elections marked the first civilian transfer of power in Nigeria's history, ending thirty-three years of military rule, and elections in 2007 marked the first civilian-to-civilian transfer. Democracy is still not firmly entrenched in the country, however, and cor-

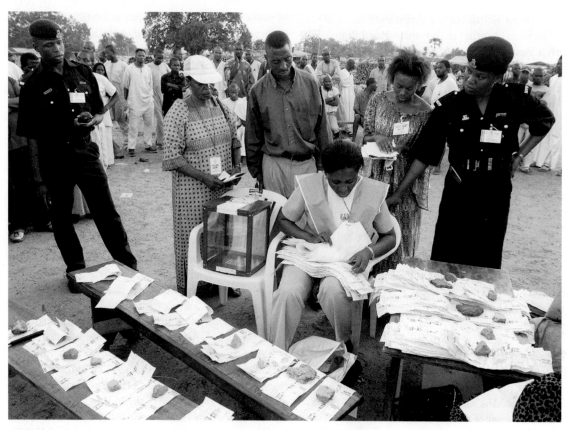

Nigerian Presidential and Parliamentary Elections, April 2003 In April 2003 Nigeria held its first presidential and parliamentary elections since the end of military rule in 1999. Over 60 million voters turned out across the country to choose among candidates from thirty political parties. Here federal police watch as election officials begin counting the ballots after sorting them by party. (Reuters/Corbis)

ruption and mismanagement remain widespread and systemic.

Nigeria is the world's eleventh largest oil producer and a member of OPEC. Oil provides about 20 percent of Nigeria's GDP, 95 percent of its foreign exchange earnings, and about 65 percent of its budgetary revenues. From the first oil boom in the 1970s, Nigerian politicians have squandered the massive oil revenues. Also, like Venezuela, Nigeria's leaders ran up huge debts in the 1970s when oil prices were high, only to be unable to repay these loans when oil prices dropped precipitously during the 1980s oil glut. Although there should be plentiful income from oil revenues to fund social programs, Nigeria's education and health care systems have continued to decline since the liberal spending in these areas in the 1970s.

Nigeria needs to diversify its economy if it is to overcome massive poverty and become economically stable. Nigeria's leaders must also calm the religious strife that continues to divide the country. Since 2000 riots between Muslims and non-Muslims have left thousands dead in the predominately Muslim northern Nigerian states. Much of the violence can be attributed to the introduction of shari'a (Islamic law) as the

law of the state of Zamfara in 1999. Since then, eleven other northern Nigerian states have also adopted shari'a. The implementation of shari'a is one of the major causes of anger among the non-Muslim populations in these states.

The Struggle in Southern Africa

Decolonization stalled after the great rush toward political independence in the early 1960s. Southern Africa remained under white minority rule, largely because of the numerical strength and determination of its white settlers.

In Portuguese Angola and Mozambique, white settlers using forced native labor established large coffee farms, and the white population increased from 70,000 to 380,000 between 1940 and the mid-1960s. As economic exploitation grew, so too did resentment. Nationalist liberation movements arose to wage unrelenting guerrilla warfare. After a coup overturned the long-established dictatorship in Portugal, African liberation forces seized control in Angola and Mozambique in 1975. Shortly thereafter a coalition of nationalist groups also won in Zimbabwe after a long struggle.

The battle in South Africa threatened to be still worse. The racial conflict in the white-ruled Republic of South Africa could be traced back in part to the outcome of the South African War (see page 761). After the British finally conquered the inland Afrikaner republics, they agreed to grant all of South Africa self-government as soon as possible. South Africa became basically a self-governing British dominion, like Canada and Australia. English and moderate Afrikaners ruled jointly and could also decide which nonwhites, if any, should vote.

In 1913 the new South African legislature passed the **Native Land Act**, which limited black ownership of land to native reserves encompassing a mere one-seventh of the country. Poor, overpopulated, and too small to feed themselves, the rural native reserves served as a pool of cheap, temporary black labor for white farms, gold mines, and urban factories. Legally, the black worker was only a temporary migrant who could be returned to the native reserve at will by the employer or the government. The native reserves system, combining racial segregation and indirect forced labor, formed the foundation of white supremacy in South Africa.

Some extreme Afrikaner nationalists refused to accept defeat and any British political presence. They elaborated an even more potently racist Afrikaner nationalist platform of white supremacy and racial segregation that between 1910 and 1948 gradually won them political power from their English-speaking settler rivals. After their decisive 1948 electoral victory, Afrikaner nationalists spoke increasingly for a large majority of South African whites.

Once in control, successive Afrikaner governments wove the somewhat haphazard early racist measures into an authoritarian fabric of racial discrimination and inequality. This system was officially known as **apartheid**, meaning "apartness" or "separation." The population was divided into four legally unequal racial groups: whites, blacks, Asians, and racially mixed "coloureds." Although Afrikaner propagandists claimed that apartheid served the interests of all racial groups

South African Native Land Act of 1913

by preserving separate cultures and racial purity, most observers saw it as a way of maintaining the lavish privileges of the white minority, which accounted for only one-sixth of the total population.

After 1940 South Africa became the most highly industrialized country in Africa. Rapid urbanization followed, changing the face of the country, but good jobs in the cities were reserved for whites. Whites lived in luxurious modern central cities. Blacks, as temporary migrants, were restricted to outlying black townships plagued by poverty, crime, and white policemen.

South Africa's harsh white supremacy elicited many black nationalist protests from the 1920s onward. By the 1950s blacks—and their coloured, white, and Asian allies—were staging large-scale peaceful protests. A turning point came in 1960, when police at Sharpeville fired into a crowd of demonstrators and killed sixty-nine blacks. The main black nationalist organization—the **African National Congress (ANC)**—was then outlawed but sent some of its leaders abroad to establish new headquarters. Other members, led by a young black lawyer named Nelson Mandela (b. 1918), stayed in South Africa to set up an underground army to oppose the government. Captured after seventeen months, Mandela was tried for treason and sentenced to life imprisonment. (See "Listening to the Past: Nelson Mandela, The Struggle for Freedom in South Africa," page 1028.)

By the late 1970s the white government had apparently destroyed the moderate black opposition in South Africa. Operating out of the sympathetic black states of Zimbabwe and Mozambique to the north, the militant ANC turned increasingly to armed struggle. South Africa struck back hard and forced its neighbors to curtail the ANC's guerrilla activities. Fortified by these successes, South Africa's white leaders launched a program of cosmetic "reforms" in 1984. For the first time, the 3 million coloureds and the 1 million South Africans of Asian descent were granted limited parliamentary representation. But no provision was made for any representation of the country's 22 million blacks, and laws controlling black movement and settlement were maintained.

The government's self-serving reforms provoked black indignation and triggered a massive reaction. In the segregated townships young black militants took to the streets, attacking in particular black civil servants and policemen as agents of white oppression. Heavily armed white security forces clashed repeatedly with black protesters, who turned funerals for fallen com-

- **Native Land Act** A 1913 South African law that limited black ownership of land to native reserves encompassing only one-seventh of the country.
- **apartheid** The system of racial segregation and discrimination that was supported by the Afrikaner government in South Africa.
- **African National Congress (ANC)** The main black nationalist organization in South Africa, led by Nelson Mandela.

Greenpoint Stadium, Cape Town, South Africa This modern stadium, complete with a retractable roof, was built especially for the 2010 soccer World Cup and seats 68,000 people. The 2010 matches marked the first time the World Cup was held in Africa. South Africa's successful handling of this global event became a matter of great pride for the country and the continent. To the left of the stadium is Cape Town, with the famous Table Mountain in the distance. (AfriPics.com/Alamy)

rades into mass demonstrations. Between 1985 and 1989 five thousand died and fifty thousand were jailed without charges because of the political unrest.

By 1989 the white government and the black opposition had reached an impasse. Black protesters had been bloodied but not defeated, and their freedom movement had gathered worldwide support. The U.S. Congress had applied strong sanctions against South Africa in October 1986, and the European Common Market had followed. The white government still held power, but harsh repression of black resistance had failed.

The political stalemate ended in September 1989 with the election of a new state president, Frederik W. de Klerk (b. 1936), an Afrikaner lawyer and politician. A late-blooming reformer, de Klerk cautiously opened a dialogue with ANC leaders. Negotiating with Nelson Mandela, whose reputation had soared during his long years in prison, de Klerk lifted the state of emergency, legalized the ANC, and freed Mandela in February 1990. Mandela then courageously suspended the ANC's armed struggle and met with de Klerk for serious talks on South Africa's political future. They reached an agreement calling for universal suffrage, which meant black majority rule. They also guaranteed the civil and economic rights of minorities, including job security for white government workers.

Elected South Africa's first black president by an overwhelming majority in May 1994, Mandela told his jubilant supporters of his "deep pride and joy — pride in the ordinary, humble people of this country. . . . And joy that we can loudly proclaim from the roof tops — free at last!"[3] Heading the new "government of national unity," which included de Klerk as vice president, Mandela and the South African people set about building a democratic, multiracial nation. The new constitution guaranteed all political parties some legislative seats until 1998.

In an imaginative attempt to heal the wounds of apartheid, the new black majority government established the Truth and Reconciliation Commission. This commission let black victims speak out and share their suffering, and it also offered white perpetrators amnesty from prosecution in return for fully confessing their crimes. Mandela's ministers repudiated their earlier socialist beliefs and accepted global capitalism as

Listening to the Past

Nelson Mandela, The Struggle for Freedom in South Africa

Many African territories won political freedom in the mid-1960s, but in South Africa the struggle was long and extremely difficult. Only in 1990 did the white government release Nelson Mandela from prison and begin negotiations with the famous black leader and the African National Congress (ANC). In 1994 Mandela and the ANC finally came to power and established a new system based on majority rule and racial equality.

Born in 1918 into the royal family of the Transkei, Nelson Mandela received an education befitting the son of a chief. But he ran away to escape an arranged marriage, experienced the harsh realities of black life in Johannesburg, studied law, and became an attorney. A born leader with a natural air of authority, Mandela was drawn to politics and the ANC. In the 1950s the white government responded to the growing popularity of Mandela and the ANC with tear gas and repression. Betrayed by an informer, Mandela was convicted of sabotage and conspiracy to overthrow the government in 1964 and sentenced to life imprisonment. Mandela defended all of the accused in the 1964 trial. The following selection is taken from his opening statement.

"At the outset, I want to say that the suggestion made by the State in its opening that the struggle in South Africa is under the influence of foreigners or communists is wholly incorrect. I have done whatever I did, both as an individual and as a leader of my people, because of my experience in South Africa and my own proudly felt African background, and not because of what any outsider might have said.

In my youth in the Transkei I listened to the elders of my tribe telling stories of the old days. Amongst the tales they related to me were those of wars fought by our ancestors in defence of the fatherland. . . . I hoped then that life might offer me the opportunity to serve my people and make my own humble contribution to their freedom struggle. . . .

It is true that there has often been close cooperation between the ANC and the Communist Party. But cooperation is merely proof of a common goal—in this case the removal of White supremacy—and is not proof of a complete community of interests. . . . What is more, for many decades communists were the only political group in South Africa who were prepared to treat Africans as human beings and their equals; who were prepared to eat with us, talk with us, live with us, and work with us. . . . Because of this, there are many Africans who today tend to equate freedom with communism. . . .

I turn now to my own position. I have denied that I am a communist. . . . [But] I am attracted by the idea of a classless society, an attraction which springs in part from Marxist reading and, in part, from my admiration of the structure and organization of early African societies in this country. The land, then the main means of production, belonged to the tribe. There were no rich or poor and there was no exploitation. . . .

[Unlike communists] I am an admirer of the parliamentary system of the West. . . . [Thus] I have been influenced in my thinking by both West and East. . . . [I believe] I should be absolutely impartial and objective. I should tie myself to no particular system of society other than of socialism. I must leave myself free to borrow the best from the West and from the East. . . .

Our fight is against real, and not imaginary, hardships or, to use the language of the State Prosecutor, "so-called hardships." . . . Basically, we fight against two features which are the hallmarks of African life in South Africa and which are entrenched by legislation which we seek to have repealed. These features are poverty and lack of human dignity, and we do not need communists or so-called "agitators" to teach us about these things.

South Africa is the richest country in Africa, and could be one of the richest countries in the world. But it is a land of the only way to develop the economy and reduce widespread black poverty.

The magnitude of the problems facing Mandela and his successors in availability of health care, housing, electricity, water, and the other amenities necessary for a decent standard of living in the twenty-first century were truly daunting, but significant progress was made. Much still needs to be done, all under the heavy burden of the worst AIDS crisis in the world (see page 1064). The highly controversial ANC leader Jacob Zuma (b. 1942) became president following elections in 2009. Zuma has had significant legal problems, having been charged with rape, racketeering, corruption, and fraud. His personal life, his contentious remarks on matters such as homosexuality, HIV/AIDS, and religion, and continued irregularities relating to his personal finances have all made him a lightning rod of debate in South Africa. He has sometimes described extremes and remarkable contrasts. The Whites enjoy what may well be the highest standard of living in the world, while Africans live in poverty and misery. . . . Poverty goes hand in hand with malnutrition and disease. . . .

The lack of human dignity experienced by Africans is the direct result of the policy of White supremacy. White supremacy implies Black inferiority. Legislation designed to preserve White supremacy entrenches this notion. . . . Because of this sort of attitude, Whites tend to regard Africans as a separate breed. They do not look upon them as people with families of their own; they do not realize that they have emotions. . . .

Africans want to be paid a living wage. Africans want to perform work which they are capable of doing, and not work which the Government declares them to be capable of. . . . Africans want a just share in the whole of South Africa; they want security and a stake in society.

Above all, we want equal political rights, because without them our disabilities will be permanent. I know this sounds revolutionary to the Whites in this country, because the majority of voters will be Africans. This makes the White man fear democracy.

But this fear cannot be allowed to stand in the way of the only solution which will guarantee racial harmony and freedom for all. It is not true that the enfranchisement of all will result in racial domination. Political division, based on color, is entirely artificial and, when it disappears, so will the domination of one color group by another. The ANC has spent half a century fighting against racialism. When it triumphs it will not change that policy.

This then is what the ANC is fighting. Their struggle is a truly national one. It is a struggle of the African people, inspired by their own suffering and their own experience. It is a struggle for the right to live.

During my lifetime I have dedicated myself to this struggle of the African people. I have fought against White domination, and I have fought against Black domination. I have cherished the ideal of a democratic and free society in which all persons live together in harmony and with equal opportunities. It is an ideal which I hope to live for and to achieve. But if need be, it is an ideal for which I am prepared to die. 99

Source: Slightly adapted from Nelson Mandela, *No Easy Walk to Freedom: Articles, Speeches and Trial Addresses* (London: Heinemann, 1973), pp. 163, 179–185, 187–189. Reprinted by permission of the Nelson Mandela Foundation.

Nelson Mandela at the time of his imprisonment in 1964. (Mohamed Lounes/Gamma)

QUESTIONS FOR ANALYSIS

1. How does Nelson Mandela respond to the charge that he and the ANC are controlled by Communists?

2. What factors influenced Mandela's thinking? In what ways has he been influenced by "both East and West" and by his African background?

3. According to Mandela, what is wrong with South Africa? What needs to be done?

4. What are Mandela's goals for South Africa? Are his goals realistic, idealistic, or both?

himself as a Socialist — he had been a member of the South African Communist Party at one time — and it remains to be seen how he will deal with South Africa's many problems. Still, South Africa today has a better education system, a more viable infrastructure, and a more diversified economy than any other African country. Many people across southern Africa, and even farther north, are looking to South Africa to be the economic engine that drives the continent.

Political Reform in Africa Since 1990

Democracy's triumph in South Africa was part of a broad trend toward elected civilian government that swept through sub-Saharan Africa after 1990. Political protesters rose up and forced one-party authoritarian regimes to grant liberalizing reforms and call national conferences, which often led to competitive elections

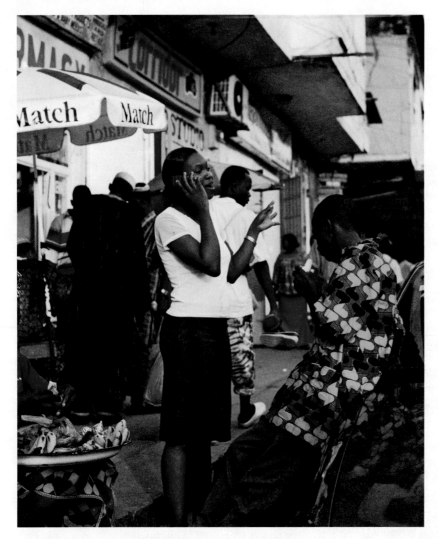

The Communications Revolution in Africa A young woman with a cell phone pressed to her ear in a street in Monrovia, Liberia, illustrates the communications revolution that has transformed economic and social life across Africa. (Tim Hetherington/Panos Pictures)

and new constitutions. These changes occurred in almost all African countries.

Many factors contributed to this historic watershed. The anticommunist revolutions of 1989 in eastern Europe showed Africans that even the most well-entrenched one-party regimes could be opposed, punished for prolonged misrule, and replaced with electoral competition and even democracy. The decline of military rule in Latin America and the emerging global trend toward political and economic liberalism worked in the same direction.

The end of the Cold War also transformed Africa's relations with Russia and the United States. Both superpowers had viewed Africa as an important Cold War battleground, and both had given large-scale military and financial aid to their allies as well as to "uncommitted" African leaders who often played one side against the other. Communism's collapse in Europe

brought an abrupt end to Communist aid to Russia's African clients, leaving them weakened and much more willing to compromise with opposition movements.

American involvement in Africa also declined. During the Cold War U.S. leaders had generally supported pro-Western African dictators, no matter how corrupt or repressive. This interventionist policy gave way to a less intense (and much less expensive) interest in free elections and civil rights in the 1990s. A striking example of this evolution was the end of steadfast U.S. support for the "anticommunist" General Mobutu Sese Seko (1930–1997) after he seized power in 1965 in Zaire (the former Belgian Congo, renamed the Democratic Republic of the Congo in 1997). Mobutu looted and impoverished his country for decades before the United States cut off aid in the early 1990s, thereby helping an opposition group topple the dying tyrant in 1997.

If events outside Africa established conditions favoring political reform, Africans themselves were the principal actors in the shift toward democracy. They demanded reform because long years of mismanagement and repression had delegitimized one-party rule. Above all, the strength of the democratic opposition rested on a growing class of educated urban Africans, for postindependence governments had enthusiastically expanded opportunities in education, especially higher education. In the West African state of Cameroon, for example, the number of students graduating from the French-speaking national university jumped from a minuscule 213 in 1961 to 10,000 in 1982 and 41,000 in 1992.[4] The growing middle class of educated professionals — generally pragmatic, moderate, and open to new ideas — chafed at the ostentatious privilege of tiny closed elites and pressed for political reforms that would democratize social and economic opportunities. Thus after 1990 sub-Saharan Africa participated fully in the global trend toward greater democracy and human rights.

The world's media have generally focused on the African governments and economies that failed in the years since 1990. Eleven years into the twenty-first century, however, many African countries continued to make significant progress in the consolidation of democracy and human rights. Even some of the countries that experienced horrible civil wars and nearly complete disintegration in the 1990s and early 2000s — such as Sierra Leone, Liberia, Angola, the Central African Republic, and Guinea-Bissau — began to pull back from the abyss. The Ivory Coast experienced years of civil war after its first-ever military coup in 1999. Rebels continue to control the country's northern half, but they and the government met and signed the Ouagadougou Agreement in March 2007, committing themselves to disarmament, reunification, and elections sometime in the future. In the meantime, Laurent Gbagbo held the presidency from October 2000 to April 2011. Gbagbo lost in elections held in November 2010 but refused to turn over the presidency to the winner, Alassane Ouattara. A tragic second civil war then broke out, which also saw military intervention by troops of the African Union, France, and the United Nations. Gbagbo was finally arrested on April 11, 2011, and Ouattara assumed the presidency.

Clearly, democracy is still a long struggle away in many African countries. Recent populist revolutions have brought down some of North Africa's one-party authoritarian rulers, but Eritrea, Ethiopia, Equatorial Guinea, Zimbabwe, and Swaziland have increasingly brutal dictatorships. Sudan's authoritarian Islamic rulers ended their long civil war with the Christians and animists in the south, only to have pro-government Arab militias attack Muslim ethnic Africans in the western Darfur region. The genocidal attacks have caused tens of thousands of deaths and an estimated 2 million refugees.

In January 2011, 98 percent of the electorate in southern Sudan voted to break away from Sudan and form a new country. If the results are upheld, the new country of South Sudan will come into being on July 9, 2011. Unlike the generally poor countries across Africa's Sahel region, South Sudan has a major revenue source: it possesses around 80 percent of Sudan's oil wells. Nearly the entire petroleum infrastructure, however, is in the north. According to the terms of the peace agreement, Sudan and South Sudan will share oil revenues equally. There remain important questions, therefore, about the transparency of the process. Many in the south worry that after the crude oil heads north to the refineries, revenues from the sale of the refined petroleum products will not be reported properly.

Congo-Kinshasa, Rwanda, and Burundi remain perilously close to the abyss of the horrendous violence that they experienced in the 1990s. The Second Congo War in Congo-Kinshasa that began in 1998 has involved nine African nations and twenty-five armed groups, and it has affected more than half of the country's 71 million people. While peace accords supposedly brought an end to the war in 2003, there has been no end to the violence in the eastern part of the country, where the war continues. By 2007 an estimated 5.4 million had died, and hundreds of thousands more have died in the four years since, making it the world's deadliest conflict

since World War II. In this war rape and sexual violence have become weapons. Although it is impossible to know precisely, observers place the number of women and young girls who have been raped by soldiers from both sides of the conflict in the tens of thousands. While the war is complex and the motivations of the many countries involved, including Rwanda, Uganda, and Burundi, are varied, possession of the Congo's abundant natural resources — including timber, diamonds, and other minerals of all kinds in great quantities — is sought by all the combatants. While the Congo is nearly the poorest country in the world, along with Burundi and Somalia, it is arguably the richest country in the world in terms of raw minerals and other natural resources, with the total mineral value estimated at $24 trillion.

Second Congo War, 1998 to the Present

Belligerents

Since the Somali civil war in 1991, no central government has existed to rule over this country that bends around the Horn of Africa. In effect, there is no Somalia, which has been labeled a "failed state." Somalia has some of the worst poverty and highest rates of violence in the world. Somali pirates operating off the Horn of Africa have been seriously disrupting international shipping since 2007.

Riots following the bitterly contested and questionable re-election of Mwai Kibaki (b. 1931) as president of Kenya on December 27, 2007, resulted in over 250 deaths in the first week after the election. Often considered one of Africa's most stable nations, Kenya unexpectedly erupted into chaos, with interethnic violence forcing hundreds of thousands to flee their homes. Former UN Secretary General Kofi Annan and a group of "eminent African personalities" came to Kenya to mediate an end to the election violence. They successfully promoted a power-sharing agreement known as the National Accord and Reconciliation Act 2008. Kenya remains heavily dependent on agriculture and tourism, and its tourism industry was hurt by the election violence of 2007 and the global economic downturn in 2008–2009. The economy picked up again in 2010; with significant increases in the tourism, telecommunications, transport, and agricultural export industries, Kenya's GDP grew at over 4 percent in 2010.

Many of the most stable democratic countries are in southern Africa. Botswana, South Africa, Zambia, and Namibia have all made the transition from

> **"**Europe is literally the creation of the Third World. The wealth which smothers her is that which was stolen from the underdeveloped peoples.**"**
>
> **FRANTZ FANON**

colonialism to democracy. With a few stops and starts, Malawi, Nigeria, Niger, and Madagascar are also making good progress. Much of the political progress is closely linked to economic progress. As Zimbabwe's authoritarian regime under Robert Mugabe (b. 1924) has created a corrupt, immoral human rights nightmare, it has also suffered total economic collapse. More politically stable countries such as Ghana have seen their economies grow and foreign investments increase. Countries in western and central Africa may soon undergo revolutionary political and economic change as a result of the oil and natural gas boom in those regions. Chad, Mauritania, Angola, Nigeria, Gabon, São Tomé and Príncipe, Congo Brazzaville, and Equatorial Guinea could all benefit from complete economic turnarounds, and others will follow.

Interpreting the Experiences of the Emerging World

□ How do contemporary writers seek to understand and represent the common experiences of peoples in the emerging world?

Having come of age during and after the struggle for political emancipation, numerous intellectuals embraced the vision of Third World solidarity, and some argued that genuine independence and freedom from outside control required a total break with the former colonial powers and a total rejection of Western values. This was the message of Frantz Fanon (1925–1961) in his powerful study of colonial peoples, *The Wretched of the Earth* (1961).

According to Fanon, a French-trained black psychiatrist from the Caribbean island of Martinique, decolonization is always a violent and totally consuming process whereby one "species" of men, the colonizers, is completely replaced by an absolutely different species — the colonized, the wretched of the earth. During decolonization the colonized masses mock colonial values, "insult them, and vomit them up" in a psychic purge.

Fanon believed that throughout Africa and Asia the former imperialists and their local collabora-

tors — the "white men with black faces" — remained the enemy:

> During the colonial period the people are called upon to fight against oppression; after national liberation, they are called upon to fight against poverty, illiteracy, and underdevelopment. The struggle, they say, goes on.
>
> . . . We are not blinded by the moral reparation of national independence; nor are we fed by it. The wealth of the imperial countries is our wealth too. . . . Europe is literally the creation of the Third World. The wealth which smothers her is that which was stolen from the underdeveloped peoples.[5]

Fanon's passionate, angry work became a sacred text for radicals attacking imperialism and struggling for liberation.

As countries gained independence and self-rule, some writers looked beyond wholesale rejection of the industrialized powers. They too were anti-imperialist, but often also activists and cultural nationalists who applied their talents to celebrating the rich histories and cultures of their peoples. Many did not hesitate to criticize their own leaders or fight oppression and corruption.

The Nigerian writer Chinua Achebe (b. 1930) rendered these themes with acute insight and vivid specificity in his short, moving novels. Achebe sought to restore his people's self-confidence by reinterpreting the past. For Achebe the "writer in a new nation" had first to embrace the "fundamental theme" that Africans had their own culture before the Europeans came and that it was the duty of writers to help Africans reclaim their past.

In *Things Fall Apart* (1958) Achebe achieved his goal by vividly bringing to life the men and women of an Ibo village at the beginning of the twentieth century, with all their virtues and frailties. Woven into the story are the proverbs and wisdom of a sophisticated people and the beauty of a vanishing world:

> [The white man] says that our customs are bad; and our own brothers who have taken up his religion also say that our customs are bad. How do you think we can fight when our own brothers have turned against us? The white man is very clever. He came quietly and peaceably with his religion. We were amused at his foolishness and allowed him to stay. Now he has won our brothers, and our clan can no longer act like one. He has put a knife on the things that held us together and we have fallen apart.[6]

In later novels Achebe portrays the postindependence disillusionment of many writers and intellectuals, which reflected trends in many developing nations in the 1960s and 1970s: the rulers seemed increasingly corrupted by Western luxury and estranged from the rural masses.

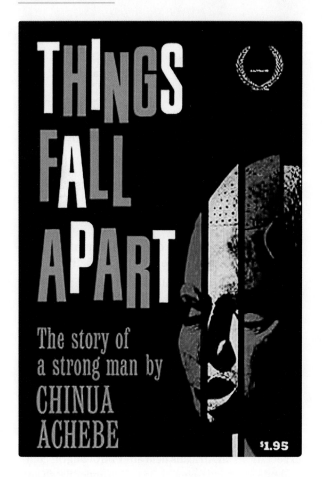

From the 1970s onward Achebe was active in the struggle for democratic government in Nigeria. In his novel *Anthills of the Savannah* (1989) he calls upon Africa to take responsibility and realize that widespread corruption is frustrating hopes of progress and genuine independence. Yet in recent essays and speeches he also returns to his earlier theme of the West's enduring low opinion of Africa — ever the "dark continent," the savage, non-Western "other world."

The Nobel Prize–winning novelist V. S. Naipaul, born in Trinidad in 1932 of Indian parents, also castigated governments in the developing countries for corruption, ineptitude, and self-deception. Another of Naipaul's recurring themes is the poignant loneliness and homelessness of people uprooted by colonialism and Western expansion.

Things Fall Apart Published in 1958, Chinua Achebe's most famous novel concerns the changing world of an Ibo village in late-nineteenth-century Africa. Achebe's powerful novels focus on complex and believable individuals caught up in the unfolding drama of colonialism, independence, and nation building in Africa. (First paperback edition cover: Chinua Achebe, *Things Fall Apart* [London: William Heinemann, 1958])

CONNECTIONS

In the last half of the twentieth century many Latin America countries broke free from their neocolonial ties with the United States and Europe. This freedom gave them the economic independence they desired to go along with the political independence they had gained in the early 1800s. Nationalist leaders in sub-Saharan Africa meanwhile were busy gathering the masses behind them to push for political independence from the colonial powers that had occupied their lands during the scramble for Africa in the late 1800s. Leaders on both continents had to decide whether to take sides in the superpower conflict of the Cold War. And when the Cold War ended, their citizens demanded more civil and human rights, democracy, and an end to corruption and rule from above.

We will see in the last chapter that the countries of Africa and Latin America played important roles in the newly formed United Nations, setting agendas in matters that were of the most concern to them: poverty, illiteracy, fair trade, globalization. The populations of these countries and those of Asia make up two-thirds of the world's citizens. In Chapter 34 we will discuss the global changes, developments, and problems that directly affect these people every day: disease, the environment, education, telecommunications, urban growth, and the agricultural revolution.

◻ CHAPTER REVIEW

◻ **What kind of government was most prevalent in Latin America during the twentieth century, and how did this change after 1980? (p. 1008)**

Politically throughout most of the twentieth century, Latin American countries were ruled by conservative, authoritarian leaders, some of them harsh and cruel dictators supported by the West. Economic nationalism was successfully practiced in countries such as Mexico and Brazil, but after the Cuban Revolution, conservatives established military rule across most of Latin America as a way to block the spread of communism. Marxist socialist reforms were implemented in Nicaragua, Chile, and Venezuela, but most successfully and thoroughly in Cuba under Fidel Castro. By the end of the 1970s only Costa Rica, Venezuela, Colombia, and Mexico had some form of democratic rule. In the 1980s much of Latin America turned toward free elections, civil liberties, and freer markets, abandoning the long-standing commitment to economic nationalism.

◻ **What factors influenced decolonization in sub-Saharan Africa after World War II? (p. 1018)**

Sub-Saharan Africa decolonized rapidly after World War II, fueled by the experience of Africans during the war and by a black nationalist movement influenced by W. E. B. Du Bois. Reacting against imperialism, Pan-Africanists such as Marcus Garvey promoted the expulsion of Europeans from Africa and the eventual establishment of a unified Africa. The Great Depression and the Gold Coast cocoa holdups of the 1930s accelerated independence, and in black Africa a generation of nationalist leaders successfully guided colonial territories to self-rule by the middle of the 1960s. The father of independent Africa was Kwame Nkrumah, a Ghanaian who, like many African nationalists, had spent many years studying in the West. He returned to Ghana after World War II and led a successful independence movement against British rule. Decolonization took a different path in the countries of French-speaking Africa. While France fought a vicious war against Algerian nationalists in North Africa, it sought more peaceful separation from its black African colonies. Most of the former French colonies elected to remain French commonwealths. Decolonization in the Belgian Congo, alone among the colonies of French-speaking sub-Saharan black Africa, was violent and chaotic.

KEY TERMS

economic nationalism (p. 1008)
Cuban Revolution (p. 1011)
Pan-Africanists (p. 1018)
cocoa holdups (p. 1019)
pieds-noirs (p. 1022)
National Liberation Front (p. 1022)
Native Land Act (p. 1026)
apartheid (p. 1026)
African National Congress (ANC) (p. 1026)

◻ **What are some of the common features of independent Africa since 1960? (p. 1023)**

By the mid-1960s nearly all African countries had won independence. The two largest colonial powers, Britain and France, had tried, although belatedly, to set up democratic governments in their former colonies. The new leaders of these countries, however, soon turned their backs on democracy and resorted to authoritarian one-party rule. Opposition parties were outlawed, and political opponents were jailed, sent into exile, or killed. Many of these early dictators were overthrown by military juntas, as happened, for example, in Ghana and Nigeria. Despite the high expectations all Africans held after throwing off colonial rule, most have continued to live under harsh and corrupt authoritarian governments.

◻ **How do contemporary writers seek to understand and represent the common experiences of peoples in the emerging world? (p. 1032)**

Many artists in the emerging world have described the common experiences of peoples living under colonial rule and in newly independent nations. Frantz Fanon in *The Wretched of the Earth* urged Third World solidarity and a rejection of Western values. One of the most famous artists is Chinua Achebe, a Nigerian writer whose novels seek to reinterpret the past by emphasizing the African cultures that existed before the Europeans arrived and tried to force their own values on the peoples they colonized. V. S. Naipaul, like Achebe, explores the disillusionment felt by many postcolonial people with the corruption and authoritarian rule of postindependence governments. Naipaul's novels also deal with the loneliness and homelessness of people uprooted by colonialism.

SUGGESTED READING

Beck, Roger B. *The History of South Africa.* 2000. Introduction to South African history with emphasis on the twentieth century.

Collins, Robert O., and James M. Burns. *A History of Sub-Saharan Africa.* 2007. Clearly written introduction to the continent's history.

Davidson, Basil. *The Black Man's Burden: Africa and the Curse of the Nation State.* 1993. A thought-provoking reconsideration by a noted historian.

Du Bois, W. E. B. *The World and Africa.* 1947. A classic text by the distinguished black American thinker.

Kenyatta, Jomo. *Facing Mount Kenya.* 1953. Powerful commentary and autobiography by one of Africa's foremost revolutionary and political leaders.

Lowenthal, Abraham F., and Gregory F. Treverton, eds. *Latin America in a New World.* 1994. Analyzes the move toward regional cooperation and market economies.

Meade, Teresa A. *A History of Modern Latin America: 1800 to the Present.* 2009. A comprehensive history and analysis of the continent and its peoples.

Meredith, Martin. *The Fate of Africa: A History of Fifty Years of Independence.* 2006. A very accessible study of modern independent Africa that spans the entire continent.

Reid, Richard J. *A History of Modern Africa: 1800 to the Present.* 2008. A concise, clearly written history of modern Africa from independence to colonialism to independence once more.

Skidmore, Thomas, Peter Smith, and James Green. *Modern Latin America,* 9th ed. 2009. The classic study of the region.

NOTES

1. Quoted in Jonathan C. Brown, *A Brief History of Argentina,* 2d ed. (New York: Facts On File, 2010), p. 243.
2. Quoted in R. Hallett, *Africa Since 1875: A Modern History* (Ann Arbor: University of Michigan Press, 1974), pp. 378–379.
3. *Chicago Tribune,* May 3, 1994, section 1, p. 5.
4. D. Birmingham and P. Martin, eds., *History of Central Africa: The Contemporary Years Since 1960* (London: Routledge, 1998), p. 59.
5. F. Fanon, *The Wretched of the Earth* (New York: Grove Press, 1968), pp. 43, 93–94, 97, 102.
6. C. Achebe, *Things Fall Apart* (London: Heinemann, 2000), pp. 124–125.

For practice quizzes and other study tools, visit the **Online Study Guide** at bedfordstmartins.com/mckayworld.

For primary sources from this period, see *Sources of World Societies*, **Second Edition**.

For Web sites, images, and documents related to topics in this chapter, visit **Make History** at bedfordstmartins.com/mckayworld.

• **Indian UN Peacekeeper** An officer with the first all-female unit of United Nations peacekeepers stands before her troops in Liberia's capital, Monrovia, in January 2007. More than a hundred peacekeepers were stationed in Liberia following a brutal fourteen-year civil war, and the female unit has become a model for the stationing of other female UN peacekeepers at troubled spots around the globe. (Issouf Sanogo/AFP/Getty Images)

34

Communism's collapse in Europe in 1991 opened a new era in world history — one that arrived with promises of peace, democracy, and economic prosperity. Millions of people still living under repressive, authoritarian, corrupt regimes were inspired to start pressing their governments for political and human rights. (See "Individuals in Society: The Dalai Lama," page 1040.) The post-1991 optimism soon faded as new tensions, conflicts, and divisions arose. Two decades later, however, the people are again taking to the streets to demand change. Africa and the Middle East have witnessed the toppling of two dictators. Perhaps more will fall, and the promises of 1991 will finally be realized.

A New Era in World History

We live in a global age. Economic cycles, international treaties and agreements, multinational organizations, and global threats connect the world's citizens in complex networks. Every day around the world billions of individuals are confronted with similarly complex global issues that impact each of them in an immediate and personal way. As we bring our history of the world's societies to a close, let us look at our interconnected planet once again, this time focusing on ordinary people and the global changes and challenges they face.

Because people living in developing nations make up at least two-thirds of the earth's population, many of the people discussed here live in the so-called Third World, where the changes and challenges of the new millennium are perhaps greatest. We should not forget, though, that there really is no Third World. There is only a set of conditions — such as poverty, disease, hunger, and unemployment — that are at their worst in the poorest or developing countries but that exist in all countries. •

Global Unity or Continued Division?
□ What is the multipolar nature of world politics today, and how do competing nation-states address common problems?

Global Interdependence
□ What are some of the benefits and drawbacks of increasing global interdependence?

The Growth of Cities
□ What factors spurred the growth of cities in Africa, Asia, and Latin America, and what were some of the main consequences of urbanization in the late twentieth century?

Science and Technology: Changes and Challenges
□ What key technological and scientific developments have had the greatest impact on life at the beginning of the new millennium?

Social Reform and Progress
□ What social problems facing women and children are the focus of reformers in the new millennium?

The United Nations in Action These soldiers are part of a French battalion serving in a United Nations peacekeeping operation in Cambodia (Kampuchea), a country wracked by war and civil conflict since 1970. United Nations forces usually provide humanitarian aid as they try to preserve fragile cease-fires after warring armies agree to stop fighting. (J. F. Roussier/Sipa Press)

Global Unity or Continued Division?

□ What is the multipolar nature of world politics today, and how do competing nation-states address common problems?

The end of the Cold War superpower confrontation brought dramatic changes to the global political situation. Yet nation-states, the traditional building blocks of global politics, continued to exist. An astonishing aspect of recent scientific and technological achievements is the lack of any corresponding change in the way the human race governs — or fails to govern — itself. Sovereign nation-states continue to reign supreme, reinforced by enormous military power. The embryonic growth of an effective global political organization that could protect nations from themselves appears permanently arrested, although efforts to control weapons of mass destruction, global warming, and other universal threats have sometimes led to global agreements.

The United Nations

As we have seen, the rise of the nation-state and the global triumph of nationalism have been grand themes of modern world history. The independent territorial nation-state — sometimes containing separatist ethnic groups striving for nationhood in their own right — remains the fundamental political organization in the early twenty-first century. Yet as the horrors of the conflicts of the twentieth century suggested, there was a need for a form of global authority transcending sovereign states as a way to maintain peace worldwide.

With a main purpose of maintaining international peace and security, the World War II generation founded the **United Nations** in San Francisco in 1945. The UN charter prohibits any member nation from using armed force except for self-defense. The charter also gives the UN **Security Council** the authority to examine any international conflict, impose economic and political penalties on an aggressor, and use force as necessary to restore peace and security. In theory, the Security Council has the power to police the world. In practice, however, this power is severely restricted. The Security Council's five permanent members—China, France, Great Britain, Russia (formerly the Soviet Union), and the United States—have to agree on any peacekeeping action.

Every "peace-loving" state is eligible to join the United Nations and to participate in its **General Assembly**. Founded with 50 members, the General Assembly comprises 192 members in 2011. Each member state, whatever its size, has one voice and one vote on all General Assembly resolutions, but General Assembly resolutions become legally binding on states only if all five permanent members of the Security Council agree to them.

The founders of the United Nations gave voice to an emerging vision of global interdependence. According to its charter, the United Nations is "to achieve international cooperation in solving international problems of an economic, social, cultural, or humanitarian character, and in promoting and encouraging respect for human rights and for fundamental freedom for all without distinction as to race, sex, language, or religion."

During the Cold War, the original hopes for the creation of an effective world body were stymied by Security Council members, most often the Soviet Union, using their veto power to block actions they felt would harm their national interests. With the Security Council often deadlocked, the General Assembly claimed ever-greater authority. As decolonization picked up speed and the number of member states grew, a nonaligned, anticolonial African-Asian bloc emerged. Reinforced by sympathetic Latin American countries, by the mid-1960s the bloc succeeded in organizing within the General Assembly a Third World majority that concentrated on economic and social issues.

With a large numerical majority, the developing nations succeeded in broadening the organization's mission. By the 1970s an alphabet soup of United Nations committees, specialized agencies, and affiliated international organizations were studying and promoting health, labor, agriculture, industrial development, and world trade, not to mention disarmament, control of narcotics, and preservation of endangered species.

1945 United Nations founded

1945–present Explosive growth of cities; rapid urbanization; increasing gap in wealth between rich and poor nations

1950s Beginning of green revolution

1970 Treaty on the Non-Proliferation of Nuclear Weapons

1980s–present HIV/AIDS global epidemic

1989 United Nations Convention on the Rights of the Child

1994 Internet becomes available to general public

1997 Chemical Weapons Convention bans the production of chemical weapons; Kyoto Protocol on global warming

2000 United Nations Millennium Project initiated

2000–2010 Warmest decade in recorded history

2001 Al-Qaeda attacks on World Trade Center and U.S. Pentagon

2003 North Korea withdraws from 1970 nonproliferation treaty; U.S.-led coalition invades Iraq; Human Genome Project completes sequencing of human genome

2004 Bombing of train station in Madrid

2005 Bombing of London subway and bus systems

2007 Assassination of Pakistani politician Benazir Bhutto

2011 U.S. begins troop drawdown in Afghanistan; bin Laden killed

- **United Nations** Founded in 1945, its main purpose is to maintain international peace and security; its expanded mission is to work with the international community to solve economic, social, cultural, and humanitarian problems.
- **Security Council** The UN body that has the authority to examine international conflicts, impose economic and political penalties on an aggressor, and even use force, if necessary, to restore international peace and security.
- **General Assembly** The second main body of the United Nations; each "peace-loving" state is eligible to join and participate in it.

The Dalai Lama

SHORTLY BEFORE HE DIED IN 1933, THUPTEN Gyatso (1876–1933), the "Great Thirteenth" Dalai Lama of Tibet, had a vision of the future. He predicted that if the Tibetans did not protect their territory, their spiritual leaders would be exterminated, their property and authority would be taken away, and their people would become slaves. For fifty-seven years he had ruled over a country treated like a pawn in the "Great Game" played by Russia, Britain, and China for territory and power. He feared the Chinese the most.

After his death, a mission of high officials went in search of his successor. Tibetans believe that each succeeding Dalai Lama is the reincarnation of the previous one. In 1937 the mission came to a peasant village in northeastern Tibet to question a two-year-old boy, Tenzin Gyatso. When he passed all the tests, they took him and his family to Lhasa, the Tibetan capital. There, in 1940, he was enthroned as His Holiness the Four-teenth Dalai Lama.

In Lhasa the boy spent much of his time studying, eventually earning a doctorate in Buddhist philosophy at age twenty-five. His youth ended abruptly in October 1950, when the thirteenth Dalai Lama's vision came true: eighty thousand Chinese soldiers invaded Tibet. In November the fifteen-year-old Dalai Lama assumed full political power. In 1954 he traveled to Beijing for peace talks with Mao Zedong. Although he was impressed by Mao's promise to modernize Tibet and intrigued by socialism, he was stunned by Mao's last words to him: "But of course, religion is poison."*

This remark was deeply troubling because the Tibetans are an intensely religious people. For centuries they lived in near isolation, practiced Buddhism, and looked to the Dalai Lama as both their political and their spiritual leader. After returning to Tibet, the Dalai Lama tried to negotiate a peaceful settle-ment with the Chinese, to no avail. In March 1959 the Chinese army crushed a massive demonstration in Lhasa, and the Dalai Lama had to flee for his life. The Indian prime minister, Jawaharlal Nehru, gave him political asylum, and he established a Tibetan government in exile at Dharamsala, India. More than 120,000 Tibetan refugees live there today.

Since the Chinese occupation began, all but twelve of more than six thousand monasteries in Tibet have been destroyed, and thousands of sacred treasures have been stolen or sold. An estimated three thousand political or religious prisoners are in labor camps in Tibet, and the Chinese have been directly responsible for the deaths of 1.2 million Tibetans. Over 7 million Chinese settlers have poured into Tibet. Tibetan women are routinely forced to undergo sterilization or have abortions.

To counter this destruction, the Dalai Lama has campaigned for Tibetan self-determination and basic human rights. He has established programs abroad to save the Tibetan culture and language and to shelter the refugees. There are Tibetan educa-tional systems for refugees, a Tibetan Institute of Performing Arts, agricultural settlements for refugees, and over two hundred new monasteries to preserve Tibetan Buddhism and to train new monks. In his quest for justice, the Dalai Lama travels around the world seeking support from world leaders, institu-tions, and common citizens. Although he describes himself as a simple Buddhist monk, few individuals in human history have spoken for the downtrodden and oppressed and for universal justice and human dignity with such moral authority.

In December 1989 the Dalai Lama received the Nobel Peace Prize. In accepting, he said that he did so on behalf of all oppressed peoples—those who struggle for freedom and work for world peace—as well as for the people of Tibet. The prize, he said, "reaffirms our conviction that with truth, courage and determination as our weapons, Tibet will be liberated. . . . Our struggle must remain nonviolent and free of hatred."†

Source: *Freedom in Exile: The Autobiography of the Dalai Lama* (London: Little, Brown, 1990).

QUESTIONS FOR ANALYSIS

1. In what ways do Tibet's history and the Dalai Lama's life reflect many of the major issues and events of the twentieth century?
2. The world's response to China's occupation reflects what political and economic factors?

*Tenzin Gyatso, the Dalai Lama, *My Land and My People* (New York: McGraw-Hill, 1962), p. 117.

†Nobelprize.org: The Official Web Site of the Nobel Prize. The Nobel Peace Prize 1989: The 14th Dalai Lama, Acceptance Speech. http://nobelprize.org/nobel_prizes/peace/laureates/1989/lama-acceptance.html.

● **The Dalai Lama in Germany promoting freedom for Tibet.** (Roberto Pfeil/AP Images)

Without directly challenging national sovereignty, Third World members of the General Assembly pressure for international cooperation in dealing with global issues, and the world's major powers sometimes go along. In 2000 the United Nations issued the "Millennium Declaration," a plan of action identifying eight goals, such as eliminating hunger, for the United Nations and member nations to reach by 2015. (See "Listening to the Past: The United Nations Millennium Project Report," page 1042.)

Preemptive War in Iraq

As the Cold War ended, the United Nations participated in the largest joint military action taken since the Korean conflict in the early 1950s: the 1990 Persian Gulf War (see page 1002). Success in Iraq led some to believe that the United Nations could fulfill its original purpose and guarantee peace throughout the world. Failure to stop savage civil wars in Somalia in 1992 and Bosnia in the mid-1990s, however, caused the United Nations to scale back its peacekeeping ambitions.

In 2002 another crisis over Iraq brought the United Nations to the center of the world's political stage. U.S. president George W. Bush accused Iraq of rebuilding its weapons of mass destruction and claimed that the United States had the right to act preemptively to prevent a hostile attack. Iraq, impoverished by a decade of tough United Nations sanctions, gave no indication of plans to attack any of its neighbors or the United States. America's declaration of its right to stage a unilateral preemptive strike to prevent attack thus set a dangerous precedent, while raising questions about when and how the United Nations charter's stipulating the use of armed force would apply.

As 2002 ended UN inspectors found no weapons of mass destruction. France, Russia, China, Germany, and a majority of the smaller states argued for continued weapons inspections, and France threatened to veto any resolution authorizing an invasion of Iraq. Rather than risk this veto, the United States and Britain claimed that earlier Security Council resolutions provided ample authorization and on March 20, 2003, invaded Iraq.

Iraqi forces were quickly defeated, and President Bush announced an end to the war on May 1, 2003. Although the war did bring an end to Saddam Hussein's brutal rule, Iraq remained one of the most dangerous places on earth. So-called insurgents representing all three main factions in Iraq — Sunni Muslims, Shi'ite Muslims, and Kurds — carried out daily attacks on Iraqi military and police, government officials, religious leaders, and civilians. Estimates of Iraqi deaths since the war began through 2009 range from one hundred thousand to over 1 million.

Meanwhile, the United States, Britain, and their coalition allies maintained their forces in Iraq. In the spring of 2004 stories and photographs surfaced in the world press of American soldiers abusing and

Iraqis Celebrate U.S. Withdrawal On February 27, 2009, U.S. president Barack Obama announced that only 35,000 to 50,000 American troops, out of a total of 170,000, would remain in Iraq by August 19, 2010. In this June 30, 2009, photo from the southern city of Basra, Iraqi police and soldiers celebrate the withdrawal of U.S. troops from Iraq. Iraqi forces such as these took control of Iraqi towns and cities after the Americans' departure. (AFP/Getty Images)

Listening to the Past

The United Nations Millennium Project Report

In September 2000 the United Nations issued a Millennium Declaration — a bold statement of values and an agenda of actions to be undertaken by the United Nations and its member nations to reach eight major goals relating to global poverty and hunger, disease, education, the environment, maternal health, child mortality, gender equality, and global partnerships by 2015. In the following speech delivered the previous April, Secretary-General Kofi Annan set out the broad framework for this plan of action, which became the United Nations Millennium Project. In January 2005 the United Nations issued a five-year report that summarized the results to date and offered strategies for meeting the goals by 2015.

❝If one word encapsulates the changes we are living through, it is "globalisation." We live in a world that is interconnected as never before. . . . This has its dangers, of course. Crime, narcotics, terrorism, disease, weapons — all these move back and forth faster, and in greater numbers, than in the past. . . .

But the *benefits* of globalisation are obvious too: faster growth, higher living standards, and new opportunities — not only for individuals but also for better understanding between nations, and for common action.

One problem is that, at present, these opportunities are far from equally distributed. . . . A second problem is that, even where the global market does reach, it is not yet underpinned, as national markets are, by rules based on shared social objectives. . . .

So, . . . the overarching challenge of our times is to make globalisation mean more than bigger markets. To make a success of this great upheaval we must learn how to govern better, and — above all — how to govern better together.

We need to make our States stronger and more effective at the national level. And we need to get them working together on global issues — all pulling their weight and all having their say.

What are these global issues? I have grouped them under three headings, each of which I relate to a fundamental human freedom — freedom from want, freedom from fear, and the freedom of future generations to sustain their lives on this planet.

First, *freedom from want*. How can we call human beings free and equal in dignity when over a billion of them are struggling to survive on less than one dollar a day, without safe drinking water, and when half of all humanity lacks adequate sanitation? Some of us are worrying about whether the stock market will crash, or struggling to master our latest computer, while more than half our fellow men and women have much more basic worries, such as where their children's next meal is coming from. . . .

Many of these problems are worst in sub-Saharan Africa, where extreme poverty affects a higher proportion of the population than anywhere else, and is compounded by a higher incidence of conflict, HIV/AIDS, and other ills. I am asking the world community to make special provision for Africa's needs, and give full support to Africans in their struggle to overcome these problems. . . .

Within the next fifteen years, I believe we can halve the population of people living in extreme poverty; ensure that all children — girls and boys alike, particularly the girls — receive a full primary education; and halt the spread of HIV/AIDS. In twenty years, we can also transform the lives of one hundred million slum dwellers around the world. And I believe we should be able to offer all young people between 15 and 24 the chance of decent work. . . .

The second main heading in the Report is *freedom from fear*. Wars between States are mercifully less frequent than they used to be. But in the last decade *internal* wars have claimed more than five million lives, and driven many times that number of people from their homes. Moreover, we still live under the shadow of weapons of mass destruction.

Both these threats, I believe, require us to think of security less in terms of merely defending territory, and more in terms of protecting *people*. That means we must tackle the threat of deadly conflict at every stage in the process. . . .

[T]he best way to prevent conflict is to promote political arrangements in which all groups are fairly represented, combined with human rights, minority rights, and broad-based economic development. Also, illicit transfers of weapons, money

torturing prisoners at Abu Ghraib and other detention centers in Iraq, at the Guantánamo Bay naval base in Cuba, and at prisons in Afghanistan. Questions were raised about the willingness of the United States to abide by Geneva Convention standards for the human-itarian treatment of prisoners of war and by the United Nations convention against torture.

An earthquake in world affairs, the Iraq War split the West and was partially responsible for Republican losses in the 2008 U.S. elections. Democratic presidential candidate Barack Obama campaigned on a pledge to bring American troops home. After becoming president he kept his pledge to end the American presence in Iraq by the end of 2011. In January 2011

• **middle powers** Countries not considered part of either the First World or the developing world that became increasingly assertive regional leaders after the Cold War.

or natural resources must be forced into the limelight, so we can control them better.

We must protect vulnerable people by finding better ways to enforce humanitarian and human rights law, and to ensure that gross violations do not go unpunished. National sovereignty offers vital protection to small and weak States, but it should not be a shield for crimes against humanity. In extreme cases the clash of these two principles confronts us with a real dilemma, and the Security Council may have a moral duty to act on behalf of the international community. . . .

Finally, we must pursue our disarmament agenda more vigorously. Since 1995 it has lost momentum in an alarming way. That means controlling the traffic in small arms much more tightly, but also returning to the vexed issue of nuclear weapons. . . .

The third fundamental freedom my Report addresses is one that is not clearly identified in the Charter, because in 1945 our founders could scarcely imagine that it would ever be threatened. I mean the freedom of future generations to sustain their lives on this planet. . . .

If I could sum it up in one sentence, I should say we are plundering our children's heritage to pay for our present unsustainable practices.

This must stop. We must reduce emissions of carbon and other "greenhouse gases," to put a stop to global warming. Implementing the Kyoto Protocol is a vital first step. . . .

We must face the implications of a steadily shrinking surface of cultivable land, at a time when every year brings many millions of new mouths to feed. Biotechnology may offer the best hope, but only if we can resolve the controversies and allay the fears surrounding it. . . .

We must preserve our forests, fisheries, and the diversity of living species, all of which are close to collapsing under the pressure of human consumption and destruction. In short, we need a new ethic of stewardship. We need a much better informed public, and we need to take environmental costs and benefits fully into account in our economic policy decisions. We need regulations and incentives to discourage pollution and overconsumption of nonrenewable resources, and to encourage environment-friendly practices. And we need more accurate scientific data. . . .

But, you may be asking by now, what about the United Nations? . . .

[My] Report contains a further section on renewing the United Nations. . . . But let us not forget *why* the United Nations matters. It matters only to the extent that it can make a useful contribution to solving the problems and accomplishing the tasks I have just outlined.

• **A child is immunized against disease in a remote village in Thailand, advancing one of the United Nation's Millennium Project's goals.** (Peter Charlesworth/OnAsia Images)

Those are the problems and the tasks which affect the everyday lives of our peoples. It is on how we handle *them* that the utility of the United Nations will be judged. If we lose sight of that point, the United Nations will have little or no role to play in the twenty-first century.

Let us never forget . . . that our Organisation was founded in the name of "We, the Peoples." . . . We are at the service of the world's peoples, and we must listen to them. They are telling us that our past achievements are not enough. They are telling us we must do more, and do it better. 99

Source: Millennium Report, presented to the United Nations by Secretary-General Kofi Annan, April 3, 2000. Reproduced by permission of the United Nations Development Program.

QUESTIONS FOR ANALYSIS

1. According to Kofi Annan, what are the benefits of globalization, and what is the primary problem with it?
2. What are the three global issues and the related three fundamental freedoms that Annan hopes the Millennium Project will address?

50,000 of the one-time force of over 170,000 troops remained in Iraq.

Complexity and Violence in a Multipolar World

The sudden end of the Cold War shattered the interlocking restraints of the superpowers and their allies, removing a basic principle of global organization and order. The Cold War contributed to the ideology of Third World solidarity (see Chapter 33). Beginning in the 1980s, however, wide differences in economic performance in countries and regions undermined the whole idea of solidarity, and developing countries increasingly went their own ways.

A striking development was the growing multipolar nature of world politics. Increasingly assertive **middle powers** jockeyed for regional leadership and sometimes came into conflict. Brazil, with more than 140 million people and vast territory and resources, emerged as the dominant nation-state in South America. Mexico emerged as the leader of the Spanish-speaking Americas. France and West Germany re-emerged as strong regional powers in western Europe. Nigeria and South Africa were the leading powers in sub-Saharan Africa. Egypt and Israel were also regional powerhouses. Iran and Iraq competed and fought for dominance in the Persian Gulf. China, India, and Japan were all leading regional powers, and several other Asian countries—notably South Korea, Indonesia, Vietnam, and Pakistan—were determined to join them. The rise of these middle powers reflected the fact that most countries were small and weak, and

New York, September 11, 2001 Pedestrians race for safety as the World Trade Center towers collapse after being hit by jet airliners. Al-Qaeda terrorists with box cutters hijacked four aircraft and used three of them as suicide missiles to perpetrate their unthinkable crime. Heroic passengers on the fourth plane realized what was happening and forced their hijackers to crash the plane in a field. (Amy Sanetta/AP Images)

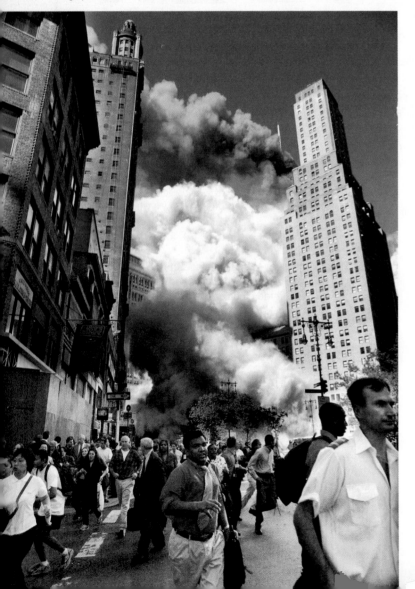

very few had the resources necessary to wield real power on even a regional scale.

Conflict and violence often bedeviled the emerging multipolar political system. In the 1990s civil wars in Bosnia, Kosovo, Rwanda, and Afghanistan killed over a million people and sent many hundreds of thousands of refugees running for their lives. Since 2000 new and continuing wars have caused millions more deaths and new refugees, particularly in Sierra Leone, Liberia, the Democratic Republic of the Congo, Uganda, Afghanistan, Burundi, Somalia, Iraq, Sudan, and Angola.

Rivalries between ethnic groups are often at the heart of the civil wars that produce so many deaths and refugees. Ethnic competition can lead to separatism—radical demands for ethnic autonomy or political independence. Only about twenty states, representing about 10 percent of the world's population, are truly homogeneous. The goal of a separate state for each self-defined people—the classic nationalist goal—could lead to endless battles and to tragedy on a global scale. The peaceful reconciliation of existing states with widespread separatist aspirations is thus a mighty challenge in the twenty-first century. The challenge of separatism seems especially great in light of the fact that civil war and terrorism often have gone hand in hand.

The Terrorist Threat

Beginning in the early 1900s and peaking in the 1960s, many nationalist movements used **terrorism** to win nationhood and political independence. This was the case in Serbia, Ireland, Israel, Cyprus, Yemen, and Algeria, among others.[1] In the post–World War II era, nationalist movements in Africa and Asia were often branded as terrorist by the imperial powers. These movements included, for example, the African National Congress in South Africa and Ho Chi Minh's Viet Minh independence movement in Vietnam. Minority ethnic groups, such as the Kurds in Turkey and the Palestinians, also attacked the powers they believed were preventing them from having their own nations. Some of the worst violence occurred in Northern Ireland, where religious differences caused Protestant and Catholic extremists to savagely attack each other's communities. Terrorist groups carried out deadly bombings, assassinations, airplane hijackings, kidnappings, and in some cases all-out war. This wave of terrorism receded in the 1980s as colonies gained independence and local and international police and security agencies became more effective in preventing attacks before they happened.

Generally successful in keeping ethnic nationalism under control in the West in the 1990s, many Europeans and most Americans believed that terrorism was primarily a problem for developing countries. In fact, terrorism had become part of a complex global pattern of violence and political conflict. As the new century opened, the global dimension of terrorism was revealed most dramatically in the United States.

On the morning of September 11, 2001, two hijacked passenger planes that departed from Boston crashed into and destroyed the World Trade Center in New York City. Shortly thereafter a third plane crashed into the Pentagon, and a fourth, believed to be headed for the White House or the U.S. Capitol, crashed into a field in rural Pennsylvania. These terrorist attacks took the lives of almost three thousand people from many countries. The United States launched a military campaign to destroy the perpetrators of the crime, Saudi-born Osama bin Laden's al-Qaeda network of terrorists and Afghanistan's reactionary Muslim government, the Taliban. Building a broad international coalition that included NATO member troops, Russia, and Pakistan, the United States joined with the faltering Northern Alliance in Afghanistan, which had been fighting the Taliban for years. In mid-November 2001 the Taliban government collapsed, and jubilant crowds in the capital of Kabul welcomed Northern Alliance soldiers as liberators. (See "Viewpoints: George W. Bush, Osama bin Laden, and the 9/11 Attacks," page 1046.)

The Taliban did not go away, however, and while bin Laden was eventually killed in May 2011, the war for control of Afghanistan continues. The Afghan government under President Hamid Karzai (b. 1957) rules tenuously from Kabul, and Taliban forces remain in the southern part of the country. The Karzai government, meanwhile, has become markedly less friendly to the United States and its allies, and critics accuse it of widespread corruption. Elections in 2009 and 2010 were marred by Taliban attacks on polling stations and claims of serious voting fraud. Karzai has become increasingly isolated, having alienated the international community, the opposition, and many of his own backers.

In December 2010 Obama significantly increased the U.S. military presence in Afghanistan, committing an additional thirty thousand forces to the sixty-eight thousand already there. The extra forces are intended to speed up the training of the Afghan Security Force so that they can take responsibility for the war. At the same time, Obama announced a troop drawdown from Afghanistan that began in 2011.

In trying to make sense of the actions of Osama bin Laden, his al-Qaeda followers, and others in this new wave of terrorism, many commentators were quick to stress the role of extreme Islamic fundamentalism as a motivating factor. But some scholars noted that recent heinous crimes had been committed by terrorists inspired by several religious faiths and sects and were by no means limited to Islamic extremists.[2] These scholars also noted that different terrorist movements needed to be examined in the context of underlying political conflicts and civil wars for meaningful understanding.

When this perspective is brought to the study of Osama bin Laden and al-Qaeda, two stages of their activities stand out. First, in the long, bitter fighting against the Soviet Union and the local Communists in Afghanistan, bin Laden and like-minded "holy warriors" developed terrorist skills and a narrow-minded, fanatical Islamic puritanism. They also developed a hatred of most existing Arab governments, which they viewed as corrupt, un-Islamic, and unresponsive to the needs of ordinary Muslims. The objects of their hostility included the absolute monarchy of oil-rich Saudi Arabia (bin Laden's country of origin), pro-Western but undemocratic Egypt, and the secular, one-party dictatorship of Saddam Hussein.

Second, when these Islamic extremists returned home and began to organize, they met the fate of many earlier Islamic extremists and were jailed or forced into exile, often in tolerant Europe. There they blamed the United States for being the supporter and corrupter of existing Arab governments, and they organized murderous plots against the United States — a proxy for the Arab rulers they could not reach. Bin Laden's network also blamed the United States for steadfastly supporting Israel and denying the claims of the Palestinians, although attempts to exploit the Israeli-Palestinian tragedy generally came later and operated mainly as an al-Qaeda recruiting tool.

Although U.S.-led forces decimated al-Qaeda camps in Afghanistan and overthrew the Taliban government, many analysts have since argued that the war on terrorism may have become more difficult as a result. Islamic extremists with only loose ties to al-Qaeda set off multiple bombs in a Madrid train station on March 11, 2004, killing 191 and wounding over 1,800. In London on July 7, 2005, 56 people were killed and more than 700 were injured by bombs detonated on three subway trains and a double-decker bus. At least three of the bombers were British citizens of Pakistani descent with unclear links to al-Qaeda. A suicide bomber who may have had links to al-Qaeda has also been blamed for the 2007 assassination of Pakistani presidential candidate Benazir Bhutto (see page 992). Thus, the war on terrorism is no longer against just the single global network of al-Qaeda. Many loosely connected cells and movements have emerged around the world, and these groups share many of the same goals but are not answerable to al-Qaeda's leadership.

Weapons of Mass Destruction

President George W. Bush justified the U.S.-led attack on Iraq in 2003 by saying that the world needed to

---

• **terrorism** The use of force or violence by a person or organized group with the intention of intimidating societies or governments, often for political purposes.

Viewpoints

George W. Bush, Osama bin Laden, and the 9/11 Attacks

- *Following the September 11, 2001, al-Qaeda attacks on the World Trade Center towers and the U.S. Pentagon, President George W. Bush addressed the U.S. Congress, telling the senators and representatives that America would respond to the attacks with a war on terror. Al-Qaeda leader Osama bin Laden initially denied any knowledge of or involvement with the attacks. Finally, in a taped statement on October 29, 2004, he accepted responsibility and described why he decided to attack the towers.*

George W. Bush, Address Before a Joint Session of Congress, September 20, 2001

❝Tonight we are a country awakened to danger and called to defend freedom. Our grief has turned to anger and anger to resolution. Whether we bring our enemies to justice or bring justice to our enemies, justice will be done. . . .

And on behalf of the American people, I thank the world for its outpouring of support. America will never . . . forget the citizens of 80 other nations who died with our own: dozens of Pakistanis; more than 130 Israelis; more than 250 citizens of India; men and women from El Salvador, Iran, Mexico, and Japan; and hundreds of British citizens. . . .

On September 11th, enemies of freedom committed an act of war against our country. Americans have known wars, . . . Americans have known the casualties of war, but not at the center of a great city on a peaceful morning. Americans have known surprise attacks, but never before on thousands of civilians. All of this was brought upon us in a single day, and night fell on a different world, a world where freedom itself is under attack. . . .

Great harm has been done to us. We have suffered great loss. And in our grief and anger, we have found our mission and our moment. Freedom and fear are at war. The advance of human freedom, the great achievement of our time and the great hope of every time, now depends on us. Our Nation—this generation—will lift a dark threat of violence from our people and our future. We will rally the world to this cause by our efforts, by our courage. We will not tire; we will not falter; and we will not fail.❞

Osama bin Laden, Statement Accepting Responsibility for the 9/11 Attacks, October 29, 2004

❝People of America this talk of mine is for you and concerns the ideal way to prevent another Manhattan, and deals with the war and its causes and results. Before I begin, I say to you that security is an indispensable pillar of human life and that free men do not forfeit their security, contrary to Bush's claim that we hate freedom. . . .

I say to you Allah knows that it had never occurred to us to strike the towers, but after . . . we witnessed the oppression and tyranny of the American/Israeli coalition against our people in Palestine and Lebanon, it came to my mind.

The events that affected my soul in a direct way started in 1982 when America permitted the Israelis to invade Lebanon and the American Sixth Fleet helped them in that. The bombardment began and many were killed and injured and others were terrorized and displaced. I couldn't forget those moving scenes, blood and severed limbs, women and children sprawled everywhere. Houses destroyed along with their occupants and high-rises demolished over their residents, rockets raining down on our homes without mercy. . . . And as I looked at those demolished towers in Lebanon, it entered my mind that we should punish the oppressor in kind and that we should destroy towers in America in order that they taste some of what we tasted and so that they be deterred from killing our women and children. And that day, it was confirmed to me that oppression and the intentional killing of innocent women and children is a deliberate American policy. Destruction is freedom and democracy, while resistance is terrorism and intolerance. . . . So with these images . . . as their background, the events of September 11th came as a reply to those great wrongs.

Should a man be blamed for defending his sanctuary? Is defending oneself and punishing the aggressor in kind objectionable terrorism? If it is such, then it is unavoidable for us.❞

Sources: George W. Bush, "Address Before a Joint Session of the Congress on the United States Response to the Terrorist Attacks of September 11," in *Public Papers of the Presidents of the United States: George W. Bush*, Book II, July 1 to December 31, 2001 (Washington, D.C.: Government Printing Office: 2003), pp. 1140–1144; uncredited government translation of the Osama bin Laden videotape, released October 24, 2004.

QUESTIONS FOR ANALYSIS

1. According to Bush, how did these attacks differ from attacks in America's past?

2. How does bin Laden justify the attacks as being "unavoidable for us"?

3. In what ways are Bush's and bin Laden's explanations of what freedom is similar or different?

destroy Saddam Hussein's weapons of mass destruction. As it turned out, Iraq had no weapons of mass destruction. Still, the fear that terrorists or rogue governments might acquire such weapons reflects global concern about the danger of nuclear, chemical, and biological attacks. (See "Global Trade: Arms," page 1048.)

After the bombing of Hiroshima and Nagasaki in 1945 (see page 937), the United States proposed the international control of all atomic weapons. The Soviets refused and exploded their first atomic bomb in 1949. The United States responded by exploding its first hydrogen bomb in 1952, and within ten months the Soviet Union did the same. Further scientific tests aroused worldwide fear that radioactive fallout would enter the food chain and cause leukemia, bone cancer, and genetic damage. Concerned scientists called for a ban on atomic bomb testing.

In 1963 the United States, Great Britain, and the Soviet Union signed an agreement, eventually signed by more than 150 countries, banning nuclear tests in the atmosphere. A second step toward control was the 1970 Treaty on the Non-Proliferation of Nuclear Weapons, designed to halt their spread to non-nuclear states and to reduce stockpiles of existing bombs held by the nuclear powers. It seemed that the nuclear arms race might yet be reversed.

This outcome did not come to pass. De Gaulle's France and Mao's China disregarded the test ban and by 1968 had developed their own nuclear weapons, although they later signed the nonproliferation treaty. India also developed weapons and in 1974 exploded an atomic device. Meanwhile, the nuclear arms race between the Soviet Union and the United States surged ahead after 1968, while the two sides also tried to set limits on their nuclear arsenals. The Strategic Arms Limitation Talks (SALT) in the 1970s limited the rate at which the two superpowers produced nuclear warheads, and in 1991 the United States and Russia negotiated the first Strategic Arms Reduction Treaty (START I), which eventually removed about 80 percent of existing strategic nuclear weapons. The New START treaty, signed by U.S. president Obama and Russian president Medvedev in 2010, requires the two countries to further reduce the number of their nuclear warheads by one-third.

India developed its atomic capability partly out of fear of China, which had manhandled India in a savage border war in 1962. India's nuclear blast in 1974 in turn frightened Pakistan, which regarded India as a bitter enemy, and by the mid-1980s Pakistan had the ability to produce nuclear weapons. In 1998 both India and Pakistan set off tests of their nuclear devices within weeks of each other, confirming their status as the world's sixth and seventh nuclear powers, after the United States, Russia, the United Kingdom, France,

and China. Both India and Pakistan have continued to increase their nuclear arsenals.

In the 1950s Israel began a nuclear weapons development program, and it is generally believed to have had an arsenal of nuclear weapons since the 1980s. Israel has never confirmed or denied this. Israel's apparent nuclear superiority was threatening to the Arabs. When Iraq attempted, with help from France, to develop nuclear capability in the 1980s, Israel responded suddenly, attacking and destroying the Iraqi nuclear reactor in June 1981.

The risks associated with the proliferation of nuclear weapons helped mobilize the international community and contributed to positive developments through the 1980s and 1990s. Argentina (1983), Romania (1989), Brazil (1998), South Africa (1990s), and Libya (2003) have all abandoned their nuclear weapons programs. Several of the former Soviet republics possessing nuclear arsenals, including Belarus and Kazakhstan, returned their nuclear weapons to Russia. Nuclear watch-guard agencies monitored exports of nuclear material, technology, and missiles that could carry atomic bombs. These measures encouraged confidence in global cooperation and in the nonproliferation treaty, which was extended indefinitely in 1995. The treaty had been signed by 189 countries as of 2010, including America, France, Russia, China, and the United Kingdom. Pakistan, India, North Korea, and Israel have not signed it.

Still, nuclear proliferation continues to threaten world peace. Iraq's attempt to build a bomb before the Gulf War highlighted the need for better ways to detect cheating. In 2003 the United States accused Iran of seeking to build nuclear missiles, and ongoing diplomatic efforts, economic sanctions, and other punitive measures by France, Germany, Britain, China, the United States, and Russia have failed to get Iran to place limitations on its nuclear program. There is also the threat that enriched nuclear materials will fall into the hands of terrorist organizations. In 2001 three Pakistani nuclear scientists were arrested following allegations that they had met with Taliban and al-Qaeda representatives. Just as ominously, the father of Pakistan's nuclear weapons program, Abdul Qadeer Khan, was charged in 2004 with passing on nuclear weapons expertise and technology to Iran, Libya, and North Korea.

In 2003 long-standing tensions between North Korea and the United States, which had never signed a peace treaty ending the 1950–1953 Korean War, reached crisis proportions over the question of nuclear arms on the Korean peninsula. As each side accused the other of failing to live up to a 1994 agreement, North Korea announced its intention to withdraw from the 1970 nonproliferation treaty, and in October 2006 North

Global Trade

Arms, with unprecedented destructive powers, command billions of dollars annually on the open global marketplace. On April 16, 1953, U.S. president Dwight Eisenhower spoke about the tremendous sums the Soviet Union and the United States were spending on Cold War weapons:

> Every gun that is made, every warship launched, every rocket fired signifies, in the final sense, a theft from those who hunger and are not fed, those who are cold and are not clothed. The world in arms is not spending money alone. It is spending the sweat of its laborers, the genius of its scientists, the hopes of its children. . . . This is not a way of life at all, in any true sense.

In the approximately sixty years since Eisenhower's speech, the spending has never stopped, not even after the Cold War's end. In 2009 global military spending exceeded $1.53 trillion; the United States accounted for nearly half of that total. Globally in 2009 the value of all conventional arms transfer agreements to developing nations was more than $45.1 billion, and deliveries totaled $17 billion. Although those numbers have been dropping since the early 1990s, global arms manufacturing and trade remains big business.

Three different categories of arms are available on the world market. The category that generally receives the most attention is nuclear, biological, and chemical weapons. After the Soviet Union collapsed, there was widespread fear that former Soviet scientists would sell nuclear technology, toxic chemicals, or harmful biological agents from old, poorly guarded Soviet labs and stockpiles to the highest bidders. Recognizing the horrific danger such weapons represent, the world's nations have passed numerous treaties and agreements limiting their production, use, and stockpiling. The most important of these are the Treaty on the Non-Proliferation of Nuclear Weapons (1970), the Biological and Toxin Weapons Convention (1972), and the Chemical Weapons Convention (1993).

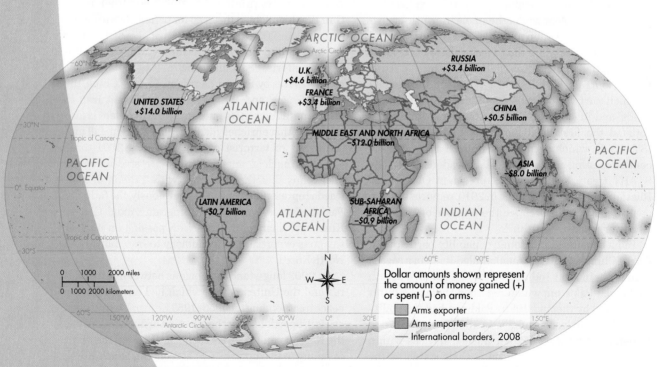

MAP 34.1 The Arms Trade

Source: Map and data from www.controlarms.org/the_issues/movers_shakers.htm, reproduced with the permission of Oxfam GB, Oxfam House, John Smith Drive, Cowley, Oxford OX4 2JY, UK, www.oxfam .org.uk. Oxfam GB does not necessarily endorse any text or activities that accompany the materials, nor has it approved the adapted text.

A second category of arms is so-called heavy conventional weapons, such as tanks, heavy artillery, jet planes, missiles, and warships. In general, worldwide demand for these weapons declined significantly after the Cold War ended. Only a few companies located in the largest industrialized nations have the scientists, the funding, and the capacity to produce them. Because the major Soviet- and Western-bloc nations had large weapon surpluses in 1991, most of the new weapons produced in this category have been made for export. In 1995 the United States for the first time produced more combat aircraft for export sales than for U.S. military use. New demand comes mainly from developing nations that are not technologically or financially capable of producing such weapons, such as Pakistan, which received fourteen F-16s in summer 2010 and has announced plans to purchase more. New or potential NATO member states have been another significant market for the United States, Great Britain, France, and Germany. In 2003, for example, the United States sold forty-eight F-16 fighter aircraft worth $3.5 billion to Poland, while Germany received $1 billion from Greece for 170 battle tanks. Many of the former Soviet-bloc countries of eastern Europe have illegally served as points of origin or transfer points for sales to embargoed nations such as North Korea and to terrorist groups such as al-Qaeda.

Amnesty International and Oxfam put up mock gravestones in central London in 2003 to represent the more than half million people killed on average each year by conventional light weapons. (Jim Watson/AFP/Getty Images)

The third category is small arms and light conventional weapons (SALWs). These are almost any remotely portable weapons including automatic rifles, machine guns, pistols, antitank weapons, small howitzers and mortars, Stinger missiles and other shoulder-fired weapons, grenades, plastic explosives, land mines, machetes, small bombs, and ammunition. SALWs make up the majority of weapons exchanged in the global arms trade. They also do the most harm. Every year, they are responsible for over a half million deaths.

SALWs are popular because they have relatively long lives and are low-maintenance, cheap, easily available, highly portable, and easily concealable. Many can be used by child soldiers. Globally, there are around 650 million guns, about 60 percent of them owned by private citizens. Fifteen billion to twenty billion or more rounds of ammunition are produced annually. Despite widespread concern about terrorists obtaining nuclear or chemical weapons, terrorists on the whole favor such small conventional weapons as truck and car bombs and automatic rifles and pistols. One of the most deadly SALWs is the land mine. Over 110 million of them still lie buried in Afghanistan, Angola, Iran, and other former war zones, and they continue to kill or injure fifteen thousand to twenty thousand people a year.

Over ninety countries manufacture and sell SALWs, but the five permanent members of the UN Security Council—France, Britain, the United States, China, and Russia—dominate. The United States and Britain account for nearly two-thirds of all conventional arms deliveries, and these two nations plus France sometimes earn more income from arms sales to developing countries than they provide in aid. The total legal international trade in SALWs is estimated at about $8 billion a year; the illegal total is about $1 billion. Of course, every legal weapon can easily become an illegal one.

In 2000 UN Secretary-General Kofi Annan observed that "the death toll from small arms dwarfs that of all other weapons systems—and in most years greatly exceeds the toll of the atomic bombs that devastated Hiroshima and Nagasaki. In terms of the carnage they cause, small arms, indeed, could well be described as 'weapons of mass destruction.'"*

*Kofi A. Annan, "Freedom from Fear," in *"We the Peoples": The Role of the United Nations in the 21st Century*, ch. 4, p. 52.

> 66In the future, warfare — highly destructive warfare —
> may be waged without the necessity for armies and
> governments, by people with little to lose.99
>
> **BRIAN JENKINS, RAND CORPORATION SCHOLAR**

Korea tested its first nuclear device. In February 2007 North Korea agreed to shut down its major nuclear facility at Yŏngbyŏn in exchange for thousands of tons of heavy fuel oil from the West and the release of $25 million in frozen North Korean funds. In April 2009, however, North Korea ended all diplomatic talks and expelled all nuclear inspectors, and in May 2009 it successfully conducted a nuclear test. Though the success of its technology remains questionable, in 2010 some observers estimated that North Korea could possess a mid-range missile capable of reaching Japan with a nuclear warhead within five years. The case of North Korea illustrates the danger of atomic war in a multipolar world of intense regional rivalries.

Chemical and biological weapons of mass destruction created similar anxieties. Since the Geneva Protocol (1925) after World War I, the use of chemical weapons has been outlawed by international agreement, but the manufacture of these terrible weapons was none-

theless permitted. In 1997 most of the world's nations signed the Chemical Weapons Convention banning the production of chemical weapons and requiring the destruction of those in existence. Inspectors received the right to make surprise searches "anytime, anywhere." As of 2010 only five countries — Angola, Egypt, North Korea, Somalia, and Syria — had not signed the agreement.

The threat of biological or nuclear weapons falling into the hands of terrorists remains a real danger. As early as 1978 Brian Jenkins, a RAND Corporation scholar, observed that

> we are approaching an age in which national governments may no longer monopolize the instruments of major destruction. The instruments of warfare once possessed only by armies will be available to gangs. . . . In the future, warfare — highly destructive warfare — may be waged without the necessity for armies and governments, by people with little to lose.[3]

Jenkins's prescient vision appears more possible than ever before. Nations think in terms of preserving themselves while destroying their enemies. But terrorists willing to become martyrs with pounds of explosives strapped to their bodies have no need for a missile to deliver a nuclear device. They will deliver it personally.

South Korean Protests Against North Korea North Korea's development of nuclear weapons has sparked angry demonstrations in the major cities of its Asian neighbors. Here a South Korean protester burns a North Korean flag and a mock atomic bomb during a rally in Seoul. (Reuters/Corbis)

Global Interdependence

☐ What are some of the benefits and drawbacks of increasing global interdependence?

Despite political competition, war, and civil conflict in the twentieth century, the nations of the world became increasingly interdependent both economically and technologically. The United States, for example, required foreign oil, China needed foreign markets, and Russia needed foreign grain. All countries and peoples had need of each other. Dependence promoted peaceful cooperation and limited the scope of violence. Yet the existing framework of global interdependence also came under intense attack. The poor countries of the developing world — frequently referred to now as the South — charged that the North (the industrialized countries) continued to receive far more than their rightful share from existing economic relationships, which had been forged unjustly to the South's disadvantage in the era of European political domination. Critics saw strong evidence of neocolonialism in the growing importance of the North's huge global business corporations — the so-called multinationals — in world economic development. Thus global interdependence was widely acknowledged in principle and hotly debated in practice.

Multinational Corporations

A striking feature of global interdependence beginning in the early 1950s was the rapid emergence of **multinational corporations**, business firms that operate in a number of different countries and tend to adopt a global rather than a national perspective. Multinational corporations themselves were not new, but by 1971 they accounted for fully one-fifth of the noncommunist world's annual income, and they continue to grow even more important in the twenty-first century.

The rise of the multinationals was partly due to the general revival of capitalism after the Second World War, relatively free international economic relations, and the worldwide drive for rapid industrialization. Multinationals could invest huge sums of money in research and development and could hold monopolies on their creations. They employed advanced advertising and marketing skills to promote their products around the world. And they treated the world as one big market, coordinating complex activities across many political boundaries and escaping political controls and national policies.

The impact of multinational corporations, especially on Third World countries, has been mixed. The multinationals helped spread the products and values of consumer society to the developing world's elites.

After buying up local companies, multinational corporations often hired local business leaders to manage their operations abroad. Critics considered this part of the process of neocolonialism, whereby local elites abandoned the national interest and made themselves willing tools of continued foreign domination.

Some poor countries found ways to assert their sovereign rights over the foreign multinationals. Many foreign mining companies, such as the extremely profitable U.S. oil companies in the Middle East, were nationalized by the host countries. More important, governments in the developing countries learned how to play Americans, Europeans, and Japanese off against each other and to make foreign manufacturing companies conform to some of their plans and desires. Increasingly, multinationals had to share ownership with local investors, hire more local managers, provide technology on better terms, and accept a variety of controls. Finally, having been denied the right to build manufacturing plants and industry as colonies, some newly independent countries also began to industrialize.

Industrialization and Modernization

Throughout the 1950s and 1960s African, Asian, and Latin American leaders, pressed by their European, American, and Soviet advisers, believed that a vigorous industrialization strategy was the only answer to poverty and population growth. To Third World elites, the economic history of the West, Japan, and the Soviet Union seemed to validate this faith in industrialization. The wealthy countries had also been agricultural and "underdeveloped" until, one by one, the Industrial Revolution had lifted them out of poverty. Modernization theories, popular in the 1960s, assumed that all countries were following the path already taken by the industrialized nations and that the elites' task was to speed the trip. Marxism, with its industrial and urban bias, preached a similar gospel. These ideas reinforced the desire of the newly independent countries to industrialize.

Nationalist leaders believed a successful industrialization strategy required state action and enterprise along socialist lines. In particular, many were impressed by Stalin's forced industrialization for its having won the Soviet Union international power and prominence. In Asia and Africa capitalists and private enterprise were often equated with the old rulers and colonial servitude. The reasoning was practical as well as ideological: socialism meant an expansion of steady government jobs for political and ethnic allies, and

---

• **multinational corporations** Business firms that operate in a number of different countries and tend to adopt a global rather than a national perspective.

The Ubiquitous Multinational Corporations Under one of the most recognized advertising symbols in the world, the Marlboro Man, Buddhist monks line up to wait for daily donations in Phnom Penh, Cambodia. (Ou Neakiry/AP Images)

modern industry meant ports, roads, schools, and hospitals as well as factories. Only the state could afford such expensive investments.

The degree of state involvement varied considerably. A few governments, such as Communist China, tried to control all aspects of economic life. A few one-party states in Africa — notably Zambia, Ghana, and Tanzania — mixed Marxist-Leninist ideology and peasant communes in an attempt to construct a special "African socialism." At the other extreme the British colony of Hong Kong downgraded government control of the economy and emphasized private enterprise and the export of manufactured goods. Most governments assigned the state an important, even leading, role, but they also recognized private property and tolerated native (and foreign) businesspeople. The **mixed economy** — part socialist, part capitalist — became the general rule in Africa and Asia.

Political leaders concentrated state investment in big, highly visible projects that proclaimed the country's independence and stimulated national pride. Enormous dams for irrigation and hydroelectric power were favored undertakings. Nasser's stupendous Aswan Dam harnessed the Nile, demonstrating that modern Egyptians could surpass even the pyramids of their ancient ancestors. These big projects testified to the prevailing faith in expensive advanced technology and modernization along European lines. Yet many of the projects were also bad investments in business terms, draining

the nation's coffers, and they were soon abandoned when expensive parts broke or energy sources failed. Long after they had rusted or fallen into disuse, the enormous national debts incurred to pay for them remained.

Still, in many ways the Third World's first great industrialization drive was a success. Industry grew faster than ever before, though from an admittedly low base in Africa and most of Asia. Nevertheless, by the late 1960s disillusionment with relatively rapid industrialization was spreading. Asian, African, and Latin American countries did not as a whole match the "miraculous" advances of western Europe and Japan, and the great economic gap between rich and poor nations continued to widen.

Most leaders in the developing countries believed that rapid industrial development would help the rural masses. Yet careful studies showed that the main beneficiaries of industrialization were businesspeople, bureaucrats, skilled workers, and urban professionals. Peasants and agricultural laborers gained little or nothing. Moreover, the poorest countries — such as India and Indonesia in Asia, and Ethiopia and Sudan in Africa — were growing most slowly in per capita terms. Industrialization appeared least effective where poverty was most intense.

Between 1950 and 1970 industrialization provided jobs for only about one-fifth of the 200 million young men and women who entered the labor force in the developing countries in that period. Most people in these countries had to remain on the farm or work in traditional handicrafts and service occupations. All-out modern industrialization had failed as a panacea.

Agriculture and the Green Revolution

By the late 1960s widespread dissatisfaction with policies of all-out industrialization prompted a greater emphasis on rural development. Governments had neglected agriculture because feeding the masses was deceptively easy in the 1950s and early 1960s. Before 1939 the countries of Asia, Africa, and Latin America had collectively produced more grain than they consumed. After 1945, as their populations soared, they began importing ever-increasing but readily available quantities from countries like the United States. Although crops might fail in poor countries, starvation seemed a thing of the past. In 1965, when India was urged to build up its food reserves, one top Indian official expressed a widespread attitude: "Why should we bother? Our reserves are the wheat fields of Kansas."[4] In the short run, the Indian official was right. When famine gripped the land in 1966 and again in 1967, the United States gave India one-fifth of the U.S. wheat crop. The famine was ultimately contained, and instead of millions of deaths, there were only a few thousand.

> **"Why should we bother? Our reserves are the wheat fields of Kansas."**
>
> **INDIAN OFFICIAL**

That close brush with mass starvation sent a shiver down the world's spine. Complacency dissolved in Asia and Africa, and **neo-Malthusian** prophecies that population would grow faster than the food supply multiplied in wealthy nations. Paul Ehrlich, an American scientist, envisioned a grisly future in his 1968 bestseller *The Population Bomb*:

> The battle to feed all of humanity is over. In the 1970s the world will undergo famines — hundreds of millions of people are going to starve to death in spite of any crash programs embarked upon now. At this stage nothing can prevent a substantial increase in the world death rate.[5]

Countering such nightmarish visions was the hope offered by technological improvements. Plant scientists set out to develop new genetically engineered seeds to suit the growing conditions. The first breakthrough came in Mexico in the 1950s when an American-led team developed new strains of high-yielding dwarf wheat. These varieties enabled farmers to double their yields, though they demanded greater amounts of fertilizer and water for irrigation. Mexican wheat production soared. Thus began the transformation of agriculture in some poor countries — the so-called **green revolution**.

In the 1960s an American-backed team of scientists in the Philippines developed a new hybrid "miracle rice" that required more fertilizer and water but yielded more and grew much faster than ordinary rice. It permitted the revolutionary advent of year-round farming on irrigated land, making possible two to four crops a year. Asian scientists, financed by their governments, developed similar hybrids to meet local conditions.

Some Asian countries experienced rapid and dramatic increases in grain production. Farmers in India upped production more than 60 percent in fifteen years. By 1980 thousands of new grain bins dotted the Indian countryside, symbols of the agricultural revolution and the country's newfound ability to feed all its people. China followed with its own highly successful version of the green revolution.

The green revolution offered new hope to the developing nations, but it was no cure-all. Initially most of its benefits flowed to large landowners and to substantial peasant farmers who could afford the necessary investments in irrigation and fertilizer. Subsequent experience in China and other Asian countries showed, however, that even peasant families with tiny farms could gain substantially. Indeed, the green revolution's greatest successes occurred in Asian countries with broad-based peasant ownership of land. The technological revolution, however, shared relatively few of its benefits with the poorest villagers, who almost never owned the land. This helps explain why the green revolution failed to spread from Mexico throughout Latin America, where 3 to 4 percent of the rural population owned 60 to 80 percent of the land.

As the practice of genetically engineered foods grew in the late twentieth and early twenty-first centuries, global opposition to the practice also grew. Many people feared that such foods would have still-unknown effects on the human body. Several European and other countries placed bans on imports of genetically modified corn and soybeans from the United States, where the practice was most common.

The loss of biodiversity was also of growing concern. When one or two genetically engineered seeds replaced all of the naturally occurring local seeds in an area, food security was threatened. With a shrinking diversity of plants and animals, farmers will find it more

- **mixed economy** An economy that is part socialist and part capitalist.
- **neo-Malthusian** Social science belief, based on the late-eighteenth-century works of Thomas Malthus, that population tends to grow faster than the food supply.
- **green revolution** The increase in food production stemming from the introduction of high-yielding wheat, hybrid seeds, and other advancements.

□ Picturing the Past

Greenpeace in Thailand The global environmental organization Greenpeace has led protests around the world against the use of genetically modified (GM) foods. Greenpeace organized this demonstration in Thailand after a government official said that he might lift a ban on such foods. The colorful genetically modified vegetables being taped off are meant to illustrate the harmful effects of GM processes on foods and the humans who ingest them. (Shailendra Yashwant/Greenpeace)

ANALYZING THE IMAGE What do the costumes suggest about the protesters' views about the effects of genetically modified foods?

CONNECTIONS What are some of the advantages and disadvantages of the scientific engineering of food crops?

difficult to find alternatives if the dominant hybrid seed in use becomes susceptible to a particular disease or pest or there is a significant climate change. Corporate ownership of seeds through patents is another worrisome outcome of this shrinking diversity: farmers will be dependent on a few giant multinational agribusinesses for their seeds. Finally, as mass-produced, genetically modified foods have become cheaper, they are eaten by the poor, while the rich are able to afford organically grown, chemically free, but more expensive foods.

The Economics and Politics of Globalization

After the 1960s there was dissatisfaction in Asia, Africa, and Latin America not only with the fruits of the industrialization drive but also with the world's economic system, which critics called unjust and in need

of radical change. Mahbub ul Haq, a Pakistani World Bank official, articulated this position in 1976:

> The vastly unequal relationship between the rich and the poor nations is fast becoming the central issue of our time. The poor nations are beginning to question the basic premises of an international order which leads to ever-widening disparities between the rich and the poor countries and to a persistent denial of equality of opportunity to many poor nations. They are, in fact, arguing that in international order — just as much as within national orders — all distribution of benefits, credit, services, and decision-making becomes warped in favor of a privileged minority and that this situation cannot be changed except through fundamental institutional reforms.[6]

The subsequent demand of the developing nations for a new international economic order had many causes, both distant and immediate. Critics of imperialism such as J. A. Hobson (see page 767) and Third World writers on decolonization such as Frantz Fanon (see page 1032) had long charged that the colonial powers grew rich exploiting Asia, Africa, and Latin America. Beginning in the 1950s a number of writers, many of them Latin American Marxists, breathed new life into these ideas with their theory of dependency.

The poverty and so-called underdevelopment of the South, they argued, were the deliberate and permanent results of exploitation by the capitalist industrialized nations in the modern era. Poor countries produced cheap raw materials for wealthy, industrialized countries and were conditioned to buy their expensive manufactured goods. Thus the prevailing economic interdependence was the unequal, unjust interdependence of dominant and subordinate, of master and peon.

The OPEC oil coup of 1973–1974 (see page 949) ignited hopes in the developing countries of actually achieving a new system of economic interdependence. But generally the industrialized countries proved to be very tough bargainers when it came to basic changes. For example, in the late 1970s the developing nations proposed a Law of the Sea based on the principle that the world's oceans are "a common heritage of mankind" and should be exploited only for the benefit of all nations. In practice this would mean that the United Nations would regulate and tax use of the sea. Some wealthy countries and their business firms were reluctant to accept such an infringement on what they judged to be their economic sovereignty and scope of action.

The great gap between the richest and poorest nations resulted from a combination of factors, ranging from colonial systems that limited economic development to the wealth-creating effects of continuous technological improvement in the developed countries since the Industrial Revolution. In the face of bitter poverty, unbalanced economies, and local elites that were generally more concerned about maintaining their own expensive living standards while catering to Western interests, people of the developing countries had reason for frustration and anger.

But close examination of our planet reveals a much more complex configuration than simply two sharply defined economic camps, a North and a South. By the early 1990s there were several distinct classes of nations in terms of wealth and income (Map 34.2). The former Communist countries of eastern Europe formed something of a middle-income group, as did the major oil-exporting states, which still lagged behind the wealthier countries of western Europe and North America. Latin America was much better off than sub-Saharan Africa but contained a wide range of national per capita incomes. Some of the largest and fastest-growing economies, as well as the highest standards of living, were found in South and East Asia. When one added global differences in culture, religion, politics, and historical development, the supposed clear-cut split between the rich North and the poor South broke down further. Moreover, the solidarity of the South had always been fragile, resting largely on the ideas of some Third World intellectuals and their supporters.

Thus a continuation of the global collective bargaining that first emerged in the 1970s seemed more likely than an international class war. The recurring international debt crisis illustrates the process of global bargaining. The economic dislocations of the 1970s and early 1980s worsened the problems of many developing countries, especially those that had to import oil.

Indifference of Rich Nations to Poor This cartoon expresses the opinion of many in the developing world that their suffering is being ignored by the better-off residents of the developed world. The focus of their anger in 2005 was the huge debts of billions of dollars owed the rich nations. These debts were so large that many countries were paying more to the wealthiest nations than they were receiving in aid. European Union and G8 members pledged during the year to reduce the debts, but it remains to be seen what will come of the pledges. (The G8 consists of the original G6 members plus Canada and Russia.) (Cam Cardow/The Ottawa Citizen)

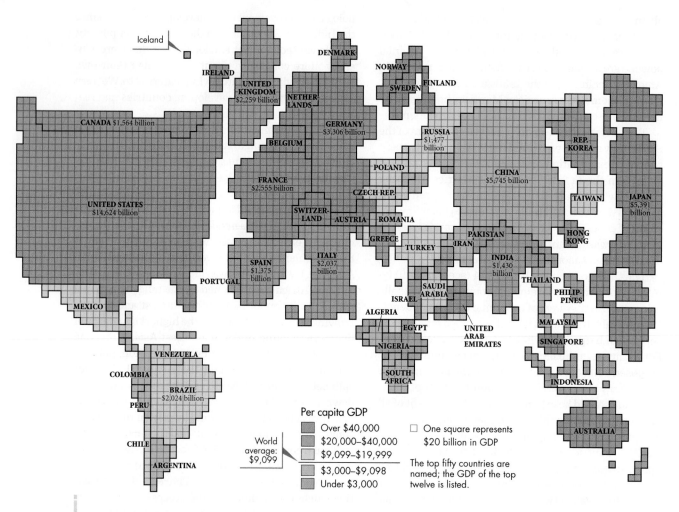

Per capita GDP

▉	Over $40,000
▓	$20,000–$40,000
░	$9,099–$19,999
▒	$3,000–$9,098
▓	Under $3,000

World average: $9,099

☐ One square represents $20 billion in GDP

The top fifty countries are named; the GDP of the top twelve is listed.

▢ Mapping the Past

MAP 34.2 The Global Distribution of Wealth, ca. 2010 This size-comparison map, arranged according to global wealth distribution, vividly illustrates the gap in wealth between the Northern and Southern Hemispheres. The two small island nations of Japan and the United Kingdom have more wealth than all the nations of the Southern Hemisphere combined, although wealth creation in India and Brazil has advanced significantly. As market capitalism expands in China, Vietnam, and other Asian countries and in Latin America and Africa, the relative size-ratios on the map will continue to change and evolve. Tiny Iceland, whose GDP is less than $20 billion, nevertheless has one of the highest per capita GDPs in the world.

ANALYZING THE MAP Which three countries are the wealthiest? Where are the poorest countries concentrated?

CONNECTIONS How were the two small nations of Japan and the United Kingdom able to acquire such enormous wealth?

Growing unemployment, unbalanced budgets, and large trade deficits forced many poor countries to borrow rapidly from the wealthy industrialized nations. By the early 1980s much of the debt was short-term and could not be repaid as it came due, so it continued to build. By 2005 the world's poorest countries were spending more on debt repayments—$100 million a day—than on health care. In 2000 the United Nations Millennium Project Report made debt relief a major goal.

Efforts to bring living standards in developing countries to levels approaching those in rich industrialized countries put tremendous pressure on global resources. American scientist and writer Jared Diamond, in his study of how societies succeed or fail, says it is therefore incumbent to ask how much of the traditional industrialized countries' consumer values and living standards we can afford to retain. Diamond is encouraged, however, by the decline in human fertility rates, and

• **TABLE 34.1** Urban Population as a Percentage of Total Population in the World and in Eight Major Areas, 1925–2025					
AREA	**1925**	**1950**	**1975**	**2000**	**2025 (EST.)**
World Total	21%	28%	39%	50%	63%
North America	54	64	77	86	93
Europe	48	55	67	79	88
Soviet Union	18	39	61	76	87
East Asia	10	15	30	46	63
Latin America	25	41	60	74	85
Africa	8	13	24	37	54

Note: Little more than one-fifth of the world's population was urban in 1925. In 2000 the total urban proportion in the world was about 50 percent. According to United Nations experts, the proportion should reach two-thirds by about 2025. The most rapid urban growth will occur in Africa and Asia, where the move to cities is still in its early stages.

also because today humans have the advantage of a global communications network and a knowledge of human history that were not available to earlier generations.[7] Throughout its history, the human race has exhibited considerable skill in finding new resources and inventing new technologies. Perhaps we can learn from the achievements and mistakes made in the human past and share our finite global resources more equitably and wisely in the future.

The Growth of Cities

☐ What factors spurred the growth of cities in Africa, Asia, and Latin America, and what were some of the main consequences of urbanization in the late twentieth century?

Perhaps no single phenomenon in the last hundred years has had a greater impact on individuals, families, and communities than the mass movement of peoples from rural areas to cities. The reasons for this migration are numerous, and the consequences for life on earth are profound. Cities represent modernity, progress, and civilization. Countries newly free from colonial rule built shiny airports, international hotels, and massive government buildings, often next to tar paper slums, as evidence of political independence and ongoing industrial development. Cities were also testimonials to increasing population, limited opportunities in the countryside, and neocolonial influence.

Rapid Urbanization

Cities in Africa, Asia, and Latin America expanded at an astonishing pace after 1945. Many doubled or even tripled in size in a single decade (Table 34.1). Moreover, rapid urban growth continued in the 1980s

and 1990s, so that by 2000 more than 60 percent of the planet's city dwellers lived in the cities of Africa, Asia, and Latin America. Rapid urbanization in the developing countries represents a tremendous historical change. As recently as 1920, three out of every four of the world's urban inhabitants were concentrated in Europe and North America. In 1950 there were only eight **megacities** (5 million or more inhabitants), and just two were in developing countries. Estimates are that by 2015 there will be fifty-nine megacities, and forty-eight of them will be outside North America and Europe.

What caused this urban explosion? First, the general growth of population in the developing nations was critical. Urban residents gained substantially from a medical revolution that provided improved health care but only gradually began to reduce the size of their families. Second, the pressure of numbers in the countryside encouraged millions to set out for the nearest city. More than half of all urban growth has been due to rural migration. Another factor was the desire to find jobs. Manufacturing jobs in the developing nations were concentrated in cities. In 1980 half of all the industrial jobs in Mexico were located in Mexico City, and the same kind of extreme concentration of industry occurred in many poor countries. Yet industrialization accounted for only part of the urban explosion.

Newcomers streamed to the cities even when there were no industrial jobs available, seeking any type of employment. Sociologists call this **urbanization without industrialization**. Many were pushed: large landowners found it more profitable to produce export crops, and their increasingly mechanized operations

---

• **megacities** Cities with populations of 5 million people or more.

• **urbanization without industrialization** A sociological phenomenon in which newcomers stream to cities seeking work even when no industrial jobs are available.

provided few jobs for agricultural laborers. The push factor was particularly strong in Latin America, with its neocolonial pattern of large landowners and foreign companies exporting food and raw materials. More generally, much migration was seasonal or temporary. Many young people left home for the city to work in construction or serve as maids, expecting higher wages and steadier work and planning to return shortly with a modest nest egg. Many young people were attracted as well by the cosmopolitan lifestyle the city offered.

Many of these developments were mirrored in the industrialized countries as well. But because industrialization had advanced in Europe and North America in the nineteenth and early twentieth centuries, people there had been drawn to urban areas at a much earlier date. By 1920 more Americans were already living in cities than in rural areas.

Overcrowding and Shantytowns

The late twentieth century saw a repeat of the problems associated with urbanization that had arisen in the cities of Europe and North America in the twentieth century (see Chapter 24), but on a larger scale. Rapid population growth threatened to overwhelm urban social services. New neighborhoods often lacked running water, paved streets, electricity, and police and fire protection. As in the early days of European industrialization, sanitation was minimal in poor sections of town. Outdoor toilets were shared by many, and raw sewage often flowed down streets and into streams.

Makeshift squatter settlements were another striking manifestation of the urban housing problem. These shantytowns, also known more positively as self-help housing, sprang up when a group of urban poor "invaded" unoccupied land and quickly threw up tents or huts. Often beaten off by the police, they invaded again and again until the authorities gave up and a new squatter beachhead had been secured.

Shantytowns grew much faster than more prosperous urban areas. In the Brazilian city of Rio de Janeiro, for example, the population of the shantytowns grew four times faster than the rest of the city's population in the 1950s and 1960s. In most developing countries, these self-help settlements came to house up to two-fifths of the urban population. Such settlements had oc-

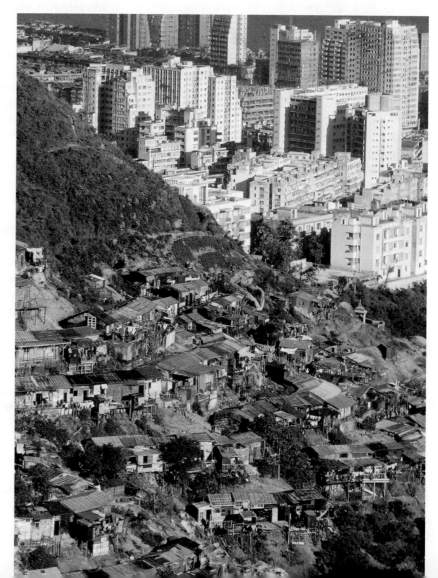

Rich and Poor in Hong Kong Global inequalities in wealth are evident in this photo of Hong Kong that shows refugee squatter housing in the foreground and modern, affluent apartment blocks behind. As a result of rapid urbanization and peasants' having to leave their land, this stark contrast between desperately poor and comfortably wealthy is found throughout the developing world. (Brian Brake/Photo Researchers, Inc.)

casionally grown in American mining towns and in Europe, but never to the extent they did in Latin America, Asia, and Africa.

Rich and Poor

At the beginning of the twenty-first century differences in wealth between rich and poor countries, and often between rich and poor individuals within those countries, were truly staggering. At the bottom end of the global income spectrum, there were sixty-one countries in which the average person made less than $750 a year; half of the world's population — 3 billion people — lived on less than $2 a day. At the other end, the U.S. state of California had the eighth largest economy in the world in 2008, and the wealth of the world's three richest people was greater than the GDP of the poorest forty-eight nations combined.

Such disparities were not new. After World War II the gap in real income — income adjusted for differences in prices — between the industrialized world and the former colonies and dependencies of Africa, Asia, and Latin America was enormous. In 1950, for example, real income in developed countries was five to six times higher than in the Third World.[8]

The gap between rich and poor was most pronounced in the towns and cities. The rich in Asia and Africa often moved into the luxurious sections previously reserved for colonial administrators and foreign businesspeople. Particularly in Latin America, upper-class and upper-middle-class people built fine mansions in exclusive suburbs, where they lived behind high walls with many servants and were protected from intruders by armed guards and fierce dogs.

Children of the elite often attended expensive private schools, where classes were taught in English or French, languages that are indispensable for many top-paying jobs, especially with international agencies and giant multinational corporations. Thus elites in the developing countries often had more in common with the power brokers of the industrialized nations than with their own people, and they seemed willing tools of neocolonial penetration and globalization.

Too often the partnership of the wealthy elite of a developing country with multinational companies and First World nations resulted in the developing country's experiencing **economic growth without economic development**. Enormous profits were being made from cash crop production or from industrial manufacturing, but few of these profits were used to benefit and raise the standard of living of the common people. Multinational companies took the majority of the profits out of the country. The remainder often went directly into the private bank accounts of the wealthy elite, who also ruled the country, in return for their maintaining

stability, keeping wages low and unions out, and allowing the companies to exploit the land and people as they wished.

In general, the majority of the exploding population of urban poor earned precarious livings in a modern yet traditional **bazaar economy** of petty traders and unskilled labor. Here regular salaried jobs were rare and highly prized, and a complex world of tiny, unregulated businesses and service occupations predominated. Peddlers and pushcart operators hawked their wares, and sweatshops and home-based workers manufactured cheap goods for popular consumption. This old-yet-new bazaar economy continued to grow prodigiously as migrants streamed to the cities, as modern industry provided too few jobs, and as the wide gap between rich and poor persisted.

Urban Migration and the Family

After 1945 large-scale urban migration had a profound impact on traditional family patterns in the developing countries, just as it had on families in industrialized countries earlier. Particularly in Africa and Asia, the great majority of migrants to the city were young men; women tended to stay in the villages. The result was a sexual imbalance in both places. There were several reasons for this pattern. Much of the movement to cities remained temporary or seasonal. Moreover, the cities were expensive, and prospects there were uncertain. Only after a man secured a genuine foothold did he marry or send for his wife and children.

For rural women the consequences of male out-migration were mixed. Asian and African women had long been treated as subordinates, if not inferiors, by their fathers and husbands. Rather suddenly, they found themselves heads of households, faced with managing the farm, feeding the children, and running their own lives. In the East African country of Kenya, for instance, one-third of all rural households were headed by women in the late 1970s. African and Asian village women had to become unprecedentedly self-reliant and independent. As a result, the beginning of more equal rights and opportunities for women became readily visible in Africa and Asia.

- **economic growth without economic development** Outcome when large profits are made from cash crop production or from industrial manufacturing and few of the profits are put back into the construction of infrastructure or other efforts to raise the standard of living of the common people.
- **bazaar economy** An economy with few salaried jobs and an abundance of tiny, unregulated businesses such as peddlers and pushcart operators.

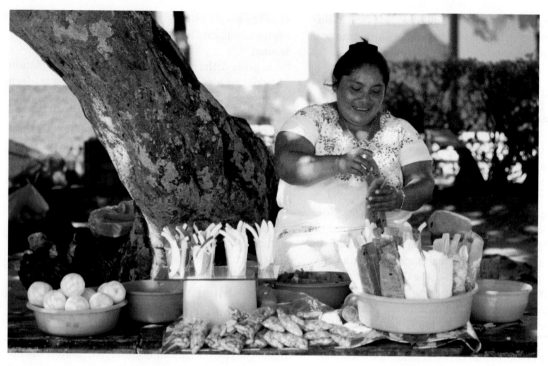

The Underground Economy This Mexican woman sells fruit and other items along the roadside. In Latin America up to 60 percent of the workforce is part of the underground, or informal, economy. Throughout the developing world, millions of people eke out a daily living by selling their labor or crops. The government loses money because it receives no taxes from them. They nearly always earn less than a worker in the formal economy, and they are constantly harassed by corrupt police and government officials, blackmailers, and extortionists. (Eric Nathan/Alamy)

In Latin America the pattern of migration was different. Whole families migrated, very often to squatter settlements, much more commonly than in Asia and Africa. These families frequently belonged to the class of landless laborers, which was generally larger in Latin America than in Africa and Asia. Migration was also more likely to be permanent. Another difference was that single women were as likely as single men to move to the cities, in part because women were in high demand as domestic servants. Some women also left to escape the narrow, male-dominated villages. Even so, in Latin America urban migration seemed to have less impact on traditional family patterns and on women's attitudes than it did in Asia and Africa.

Urbanization and Agriculture

The development of multinational agribusiness and the successes of the green revolution caused millions of small farmers and peasants to leave their land and migrate to cities. This phenomenon affected farmers in developed and developing countries alike. The decline of the family farm in the United States is as representative as any of the consequences of modern agricultural production on small farmers.

A family farm is on land owned by the family; the majority of labor is done by family members; and the business is managed by the family in an open market system. In the United States, the number of family farms decreased from 7 million in the 1930s to about 2 million in 2002. Since 1981, 750,000 farms and over a million jobs have been lost. Nevertheless, total acreage under cultivation has increased, from under 200 acres on average per family farm in 1940 to over 500 acres in 2000.

The shift from small family farms to large operations owned by private farmers owning thousands of acres — factory farms producing massive quantities of livestock products — or corporate agribusinesses has dramatically altered the American labor force. Since the 1930s the percentage of farmers in the workforce has shrunk from 21 percent to 2 percent. Half of all family farms now depend on off-farm income. The result has been the death of many small towns in America and the loss of many farm-related businesses and jobs.

Why has this happened? One simple reason is that the younger generation wants to move to the city. But there are other reasons as well. As farm-related costs — land, equipment, fuel, seeds, fertilizer, irrigation — rise, it becomes more difficult for small farmers to compete

Five Generations of the Yang Family This group portrait suggests the enduring Chinese commitment to close family ties. It also puts a human face on social transformation, for the great-great-grandmother has bound feet and the baby she holds will be an only child. In the 1980s the Chinese government prohibited couples from having more than one child, a major factor in China's falling birthrate. (Dermot Tatlow/Panos Pictures)

with the large operations. Agribusinesses have the advantages of economy of scale and can afford larger machines to farm larger acreages, can control all phases of the process — from producing the hybrid seeds to marketing the final product — and can take advantage of international markets.

Peasants in developing countries leave the land for many of the same reasons. The major difference in developing countries, though, is that these peasant farmers, usually illiterate, are often producing subsistence crops and are forced off the land by government troops or thugs hired by large landowners or companies to make way for large cash-crop production. The loss of land can also result from peasant families' possessing no documents proving ownership of the fields they have worked for generations. In industrialized countries like the United States, farmers who leave their land have educational and employment options. In developing countries, few options are available for illiterate peasants with no skills other than rudimentary farming.

Science and Technology: Changes and Challenges

☐ What key technological and scientific developments have had the greatest impact on life at the beginning of the new millennium?

The twentieth century was a time of rapid urbanization, but it was equally an era of amazing advances in science and technology. These advances were not always positive. The great excitement over the telephone, the automobile, electricity, and the airplane was quickly tempered in 1914 by the killing machines invented and used in the Great War. Totalitarian regimes exploited new developments in mass communication for mass propaganda. No sooner had the atom been harnessed than the United States released atomic bombs over Hiroshima and Nagasaki. Yet since World War II, scientists have made tremendous progress in medicine and communication technologies, though disease and environmental issues continue to present challenges.

The Medical Revolution

The medical revolution began in the late 1800s with the development of the germ theory of disease (see page 732) and continued rapidly after World War II. Scientists discovered vaccines for many of the most deadly diseases. Jonas Salk's development of the polio vaccine in 1952 was followed by the first oral polio vaccine (1962) and vaccines for measles (1964), mumps (1967), rubella (1970), chickenpox (1974), and hepatitis B (1981). Globally, these vaccines have saved millions of lives, especially those of children. According to the United Nations World Health Organization, medical advances reduced deaths from smallpox, cholera, and plague by more than 95 percent worldwide between 1951 and 1966.

Following independence, Asian and African countries increased the small numbers of hospitals, doctors, and nurses they had inherited from the colonial past. In addition, local people were successfully trained as paramedics to staff rural outpatient clinics that offered medical treatment, health education, and prenatal and postnatal care. Many paramedics were women, for many health problems involved childbirth and infancy, and many cultures considered it improper for a man to examine a woman's body.

The medical revolution significantly lowered death rates and lengthened life expectancies. Children became increasingly likely to survive their early years, although infant and juvenile mortality remained far higher in poor countries than in rich ones. By 1980 the average inhabitant of the developing countries could expect to live about fifty-four years; life expectancy at birth varied from forty to sixty-four years depending on the country. In industrialized countries life expectancy at birth averaged seventy-one years.

Since the 1980s medical science has continued to make remarkable advances. In 1979 the World Health Organization announced the worldwide eradication of smallpox. By this time, transplants of such organs as hearts, lungs, and kidneys had become routine, and in 1982 an American man became the first recipient of an artificial heart. Also important were advances in our understanding of DNA begun in the 1940s. In 2003 scientists working on the Human Genome Project announced that they had successfully identified, mapped, and sequenced the entire genome, or hereditary information, of human beings. This knowledge gives health care providers immense new powers for preventing, treating, and curing diseases and makes the completion of the project one of the most important scientific developments in history.

Despite these advances, there remains a wide gap in health care availability and affordability for the rich and the poor. Thousands of people die every day in the developing world from diseases and illnesses that are curable and easily treated. Between 1980 and 2000 the number of children under the age of five dying annually of diarrhea dropped by 60 percent through the global distribution of a cheap sugar-salt solution mixed in water. Still, over 1.5 million children worldwide continue to die each year from diarrhea. Deaths worldwide from HIV/AIDS are reaching epic proportions, while malaria and tuberculosis continue to be major killers of young and old alike. In 2010 tuberculosis remains the leading killer of women worldwide.

Population Change: Balancing the Numbers

A less favorable consequence of the medical revolution has been the acceleration of population growth. As in nineteenth-century Europe, a rapid decline in death rates was not immediately accompanied by a similar decline in birthrates. Women in developing countries continued to bear five to seven children each, as their mothers and grandmothers had done. The combined populations of Asia, Africa, and Latin America, which had grown relatively modestly from 1925 to 1950, increased from 1.7 billion to 3 billion between 1950 and 1975 and continues to grow at a similar rate.

Concerned about famine and starvation, some governments began pushing family planning and birth control to slow population growth. For a number of reasons these measures were not always successful. Islamic and Catholic religious teachings were hostile to birth control. Moreover, widespread cultural attitudes dictated that a "real man" keep his wife pregnant. There were also economic reasons for preferring large families. Farmers needed the help of children at planting and harvest times, and sons and daughters were a sort of social security system for their elders. By the 1970s and 1980s, however, population growth in the industrialized countries had begun to fall significantly. By the 1990s some European leaders were bemoaning birthrates in their countries that were below the 2.1 level needed to maintain a stable population.

The world's poor women also began to bear fewer children. Small countries such as Barbados, Chile, Costa Rica, Taiwan, and Tunisia led the way. Between 1970 and 1975 China followed, registering the fastest five-year birthrate decline in recorded history. Then other big countries, especially in Latin America and East Asia, experienced large declines in fertility. In 1970 the average Brazilian woman had close to 6 children; by 2005 she had 1.9. In 1970 the average woman in Bangladesh had more than 7 children; in 2005 she had 3.1.

There were several reasons for this decline in fertility among women in the developing world. Fewer babies were dying of disease or malnutrition, so couples needed fewer births to guarantee the survival of the number of children they wanted. Also, better living conditions, urbanization, and more education encouraged women to have fewer children. No wonder the most rapidly industrializing countries, such as Taiwan and South Korea, led the way in declining birthrates.

In the early 1960s the introduction of the birth control pill marked a revolution not only in birth control techniques but also in women taking control of their own fertility. Family planning was now truly possible. In the early twenty-first century more than half of the world's couples practiced birth control, up from one in eight just forty years earlier. However, male chauvinism, religious teachings, and conservative government leaders combined in many predominately Roman Catholic countries and in most Muslim countries to control the availability and distribution of birth control methods and abortion. Birth control and abortion were most accepted in North America, Protestant Europe, the Soviet Union, and East Asia, which explains why these regions had the lowest birthrates and population growth.

Although significant differences still exist between regions, projections of world population growth have declined sharply. By 2005 global birthrates had fallen to the lowest level in recorded history. The average woman in the developing world had 2.9 children, down from an average of nearly 6 babies in the 1970s. Fertility in most of the developing world could fall below the replacement level (2.1 children per woman) before 2100. The most recent estimates are that the world's population will "only" grow by 50 percent between 2000 and 2050, when it will reach about 9 billion. Over the next century it is then expected to level off at about 10 billion.

Global Epidemics

One of humanity's gravest fears in the early years of the new millennium comes from the threat posed by epidemic diseases. Outbreaks in Africa of the deadly Ebola and Marburg viruses; a worldwide outbreak of severe acute respiratory syndrome, or SARS, which began in 2002; ongoing avian, or bird, flu in Asia; and "mad-cow disease," which has wreaked havoc with meat production in several countries, have all raised the frightening specter of a global recurrence of a modern Black Death. Tuberculosis (TB) has also made a comeback and kills one person every fifteen seconds, thus claiming millions of lives every year, even though it is a curable disease. Malaria kills a million people a year worldwide, 90 percent of them in Africa.

Fighting the AIDS Epidemic in Asia A dramatic billboard warns people in Malaysia about the deadly dangers of AIDS. The billboard offers sound advice, focusing on the three primary ways by which the AIDS virus is spread. Can you "read" the three-part message? (Robert Francis/The Hutchison Library/Eye Ubiquitous)

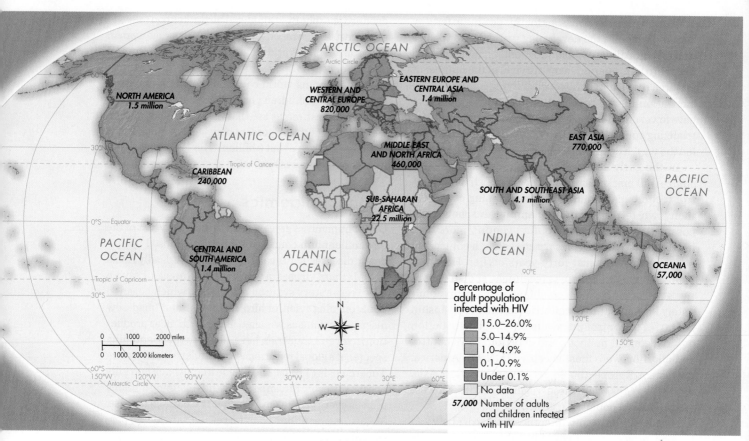

MAP 34.3 People Living with HIV/AIDS Worldwide, ca. 2010 As this map illustrates, Africa has been hit the hardest by the HIV/AIDS epidemic. It currently has fifteen to twenty times more identified cases than any other region of the world. AIDS researchers expect that in the coming decade, however, Russia and South and East Asia will overtake and then far surpass Africa in the number of infected people. (Source: Data from World Health Organization, www.whosea.org)

Few diseases in world history have been more frightening, or caused more disruption of human society, than HIV/AIDS. In 2007 the Population Division of the United Nations calculated that 36 million persons globally were infected with HIV, the virus that causes AIDS. AIDS was the world's fourth-leading cause of death.

About 90 percent of all persons who die from AIDS and 86 percent of those currently infected with HIV live in sub-Saharan Africa (Map 34.3). In Africa HIV/AIDS is most commonly spread through heterosexual sex. Widespread disease and poverty are also significant factors in that Africans already suffering from other illnesses such as malaria or tuberculosis have less resistance to HIV and less access to health care for treatment.

Another critical factor contributing to the spread of AIDS in Africa is the continued political instability of many countries — particularly those in the corridor running from Uganda to South Africa. This corridor was the scene of brutal civil and liberation wars that resulted in massive numbers of refugees, a breakdown in basic health care services, and the destruction of family and

cultural networks. The populations of countries along this corridor — Uganda, Rwanda, Burundi, Zaire/Congo, Angola, Zimbabwe, Mozambique, and South Africa — have been decimated by HIV/AIDS. South Africa currently has the largest number of HIV/AIDS cases in the world. In 2010 around 10 percent of the South African population, about 5.6 million people, were living with HIV/AIDS. Of these, over 330,000 were children under fifteen years of age. An estimated 310,000 South Africans died of AIDS in 2009. Medical health experts expect that Russia, India, China, Japan, and other countries in Asia might soon overtake South Africa in reported HIV/AIDS cases.

Although HIV/AIDS has had a devastating impact on Africa, globally the epidemic is still at a relatively early stage. Changes in behavior will be critical to slowing the spread of AIDS in the developing world. Since 2001 relatively inexpensive AIDS drugs that are widely available in the West have been dispensed freely to many of those infected in Africa and Asia, but the availability of these drugs has generally failed to keep up with the increase in cases.

Environmentalism

Like disease, the environment knows no boundaries. Some voices have always expressed concern for the environment. In the eighteenth century, for example, governments became increasingly concerned about their forests as the great demand for lumber to build ships nearly destroyed the forests of Britain, Europe, the eastern United States, and later India. The United States created the first national park in the nineteenth century. The modern environmental movement began with concerns about chemical waste, rapid consumption of energy and food supplies, global deforestation, environmental degradation caused in part by sprawling megacities, and threats to wildlife. By the 1970s citizens had begun joining together in organizations such as Greenpeace and Friends of the Earth to try to preserve, restore, or enhance the natural environment.

The environmental movement is actually several different movements, each with its own agenda. American biologist and writer Rachel Carson was an early proponent of the environmental health movement. In *Silent Spring* (1962) she warned of the dangers of pesticides and pollution:

> Along with the possibility of the extinction of mankind by nuclear war, the central problem of our age has therefore become the contamination of man's total environment with such substances of incredible potential for harm — substances that accumulate in the tissues of plants and animals and even penetrate the germ cells to shatter or alter the very material of heredity upon which the shape of the future depends.[9]

Carson and others were concerned about the effects of chemicals, radiation, pollution, waste, and urban development on the environment and on human health.

The conservation movement, represented in the United States by the Sierra Club and the Audubon Society, seeks to protect the biodiversity of the planet and emphasizes the spiritual and aesthetic qualities of nature. The ecology movement consists of different groups with somewhat similar agendas, ranging from politically active Green Parties to Greenpeace. These organizations are concerned about global warming, toxic chemicals, the use of nuclear energy and nuclear weapons, genetically modified food, recycling, saving endangered species, sustainable agriculture, protecting ancient forests, and environmental justice.

Environmentalists today are especially concerned about **global warming**, the increase of global temperatures over time. The ten years to 2010 formed the warmest decade in recorded history, followed by the 1990s. The majority of the world's scientists believe that the increase began with the Industrial Revolution

> "Along with the possibility of the extinction of mankind by nuclear war, the central problem of our age has therefore become the contamination of man's total environment with such substances of incredible potential for harm."
>
> **RACHEL CARSON**

in the 1700s. The subsequent human-generated hydrocarbons produced through the burning of fossil fuels — coal, oil, natural gas — have caused a greenhouse effect.

Possible effects of global warming over the next century include a catastrophic rise in sea levels that would put many coastal cities and islands under water; ecosystem changes that may threaten various species of plants and animals; extreme and abnormal weather patterns; destruction of the earth's ozone layer, which shields the planet from harmful solar radiation; and a decline in agricultural production. Although the exact causes and consequences of global warming are being debated, the world community is so concerned that in 1997 an amendment, the Kyoto Protocol, was added to the United Nations Framework Convention on Climate Change. Countries that ratify the protocol agree to try to reduce their emissions of carbon dioxide and five other greenhouse gases. As of July 2010, 191 countries had ratified it. The most notable exception was the United States.

Mass Communication

The invention of moving pictures, the telephone, and other revolutionary new technologies between 1875 and 1900 prepared the way for a twentieth century of mass communications and the "information age." The global availability and affordability of radios and television sets in the 1950s introduced a second communications revolution. The transistor radio penetrated the most isolated hamlets of the developing world. Governments embraced radio broadcasting as a means of power, propaganda, and education. Though initially less common, television use expanded into nearly every country, even if there was just one television in a village. Governments recognized the power of the visual image to promote their ideology or leader, and a state television network became a source of national pride. By the beginning of the twenty-first century television was bringing the whole planet into the bars and

• **global warming** The belief of the majority of the world's scientists that hydrocarbons produced through the burning of fossil fuels have caused a greenhouse effect that has increased global temperatures over time.

Evidence of Global Warming The graphics indicate the change in the seasonal melt extent, in red, of the Greenland ice sheet from 1992 (left) to 2002 (right)—a significant increase in only ten years. Of greatest immediate concern to scientists is that melting polar icecaps and Greenland glaciers are releasing cold freshwater into the northern Atlantic Ocean, which could shut down the Gulf Stream that brings warm ocean currents up from the equator to warm Europe and northeastern North America. This could produce an ice age in the northern Atlantic that would drastically affect global weather patterns. (both photos: Clifford Grabhorn/AP Images)

meetinghouses of the world's villages and was having a profound, even revolutionary, impact everywhere. Alluring television images of high living standards and the excitement of urban life stirred powerful desires in young people, who copied Western materialism, migrated to the cities, and created a global youth culture.

The third, and perhaps greatest, communications revolution occurred with the first Apple personal computers in 1976, followed by the introduction of cell phones in 1985. Mass communications have exploded

since then. Cell phones allowed individuals and nations in the developing world to bypass telephone lines, installation, and other obstacles associated with landline telephone use. Africa now has over 85 million cell phone users; equivalent landline phone use would be impossible. Cell phones have become among the most widely owned consumer products worldwide.

The Internet, or World Wide Web, has had the greatest impact on human communication. First made available to the general public in 1994, the Internet and e-mail allow for instantaneous communication to anyone, anywhere with an Internet connection. The possibilities for global access to information and knowledge are seemingly infinite. Authoritarian governments

• **feminization of poverty** The issue that those living in extreme poverty are disproportionately women.

have realized the threat that the Internet and Facebook, Twitter, and other social networking services pose to their power and control. The governments of China and North Korea, for example, have spent millions of dollars trying to restrict information traveling in and out of their countries over the Internet. For the first time in history, this type of censorship may prove impossible.

Social Reform and Progress

☐ What social problems facing women and children are the focus of reformers in the new millennium?

Just as an end to slavery became the rallying cry for social reformers in the nineteenth century, modern social reformers have sought to end global inequality, racism, and sexism and to improve human and civil rights for all. We have already described many of these developments, such as the victory of the democratic movement in eastern Europe (see pages 955–961) and the end of the racist apartheid system in South Africa (see page 1027). Much remains to be achieved, however, and nowhere is more worldwide attention being focused than on the advancement of human and civil rights for women and children.

Women: The Right to Equality

The final report for the 1995 United Nations Fourth World Conference on Women called on the world community to take action in twelve areas of critical concern to women: poverty, access to education and training, access to health care, violence against women, women and war, economic inequality with men, political inequality with men, creation of institutions for women's advancement, lack of respect for women's rights, stereotyping of women, gender inequalities and the environment, and violation of girl children's rights.[10] These are concerns that all women share, although degrees of inequality vary greatly from one country to another.

The **feminization of poverty**, the disproportionate number of women living in extreme poverty, is one of the greatest concerns facing women today. Even in the most developed countries, two out of every three

Gathering Firewood These African women in Burkina Faso bring home head-loads of wood, requiring a journey of one hour each way. In developing countries women (rarely men) make two or more such trips a week to provide fuel for cooking and heating, illustrating what has been called the "other energy crisis." As nearby forests are depleted, they must travel farther and farther to find available wood, while the denuded land becomes open to soil erosion. Women and children spend another two to three hours every day or two hauling water. (Mark Edwards/Photolibrary)

poor adults are women. In the United States, for example, half of all poor families are supported by single mothers whose average income is 23 percent lower than the poverty line. There are many causes for this phenomenon. Having principal responsibility for child care, women have less time and opportunity for work, and because they have less access to health care they are often unable to work. As male labor migration increases worldwide, the number of households headed by women increases, and thus the number of families living in poverty. Job restrictions and discrimination, plus limited education, result in women having few job options except in the "informal economy" as maids, street vendors, or prostitutes.

Despite increased access to birth control, even within developed countries, birthrates remain high among poor women, especially among poor adolescents, who make up an inordinate number of the estimated 585,000 women who die every year during pregnancy and childbirth. The poorest women usually suffer most from government policies, usually legislated by men, that restrict their access to reproductive health care.

Women have made some modest gains in the workplace, making up 38 percent of the nonfarm-sector global workforce in the early 2000s, as compared to 35 percent in 1990. But segregated labor markets remain the rule, with higher-paying jobs reserved for men. In the farm sector, women globally produce more than half of all the food that is grown and up to 80 percent of subsistence crops grown in Africa. Because this is informal labor and often unpaid, these women laborers are denied access to loans, and many of them cannot own the land they farm.

Some observers believe that violence against women is on the rise. Long part of war, rape and sexual violence were used as weapons of war during the wars in the former Yugoslavia and in Rwanda in the early 1990s. Rape and sexual violence have been subsequently labeled crimes against humanity and are considered forms of torture and genocide. Still, they have continued to be used as weapons in conflicts in Sierra Leone, Kosovo, Afghanistan, the Democratic Republic of the Congo, and elsewhere. Domestic violence appears to be on the increase in many countries, including Russia, Pakistan, Peru, and South Africa. Forced prostitution and international female slave traffic is carried on by traffickers from such countries as Ukraine, Moldova, Nigeria, Burma, and Thailand. Perhaps five thousand women a year are killed in "honor killings," when men kill their female relatives for bringing dishonor on the family's reputation, frequently because of some perceived misuse of their sexuality.

Still, some progress has been made toward equality for women. New laws have been enacted, and worldwide more girls than ever before are receiving an education. More women are now allowed to vote and to hold office, and half of all the female heads of state elected since 1900 were elected after 1990. Women also are moving across and up in the workplace, holding a wider variety of jobs and more senior positions.

Children: The Right to Childhood

In 1989 the United Nations General Assembly adopted the Convention on the Rights of the Child, which spelled out a number of rights that are due every child. These

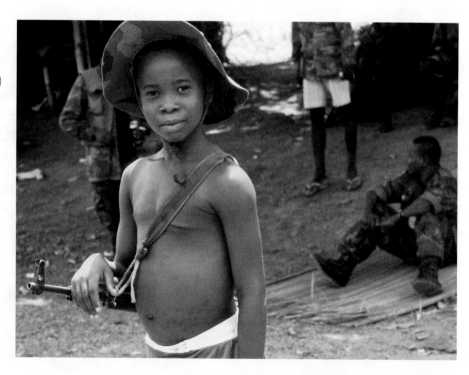

Child Soldier in Sierra Leone
This eleven-year-old boy with a rifle slung over his shoulder is a member of the Sierra Leone army and stands guard at a checkpoint during his country's civil war. Tens of thousands of boys and girls under eighteen have been used by the militaries in more than sixty countries since 2000, either as armed combatants or informally in tasks such as spying, scouting, carrying messages, and cooking. (Brennan Linsley/AP Images)

include civil and human rights and economic, social, and cultural rights. The convention has been ratified by more countries than any other human rights treaty in world history — 194 countries as of 2009. The United States and Somalia remain the only two countries in the United Nations that have not ratified it.

It is not difficult to see why such a document was necessary. Globally, a billion children live in poverty — one in every two children in the world. In the United States 16 percent of children, more than 11 million girls and boys, live in poor families with parents who earn at or below the poverty line. Worldwide, 640 million children do not have adequate shelter, 400 million do not have safe water, and 270 million receive no health care. From 10 million to 11 million children die each year before age five.

Besides poverty, the convention addresses a number of other concerns. These include children's making up half of the world's refugees, child labor and exploitation, sexual violence and sex trafficking, police abuse of street children, HIV/AIDS orphans, lack of access to education, and lack of access to adequate health care. Increasingly in the last decade, children have been recruited or kidnapped to become child soldiers, as many as 300,000 worldwide, 120,000 in Africa alone. Child sexual abuse and child soldiers have become such widespread problems that the United Nations wrote two additional protocols — one on the involvement of children in armed conflicts and the other on the sale of children, child pornography, and child prostitution — that were attached to the original convention and adopted in 2000.

As the twenty-first century began, nearly a billion people were unable to read a book or sign their names. Of the 100 million children without access to primary education, 60 percent or more were girls. Most of the global literacy problems are found in the developing world. Increasing economic globalization have put pressure on all governments to improve literacy rates and to improve educational opportunities for young people. Since the 1990s more and more countries have recognized the importance of providing a minimum level of basic education and have made it compulsory. Globally, four in five children now participate in lower secondary education (U.S. ninth and tenth grades), but discrepancies remain wide. Many countries have 90 to 100 percent participation in at least lower secondary education, but in Africa the rate is closer to 45 percent and is only 29 percent for upper secondary (U.S. eleventh and twelfth grades). Only when countries are stable and have prosperous economies will all children receive the education they deserve.

CONNECTIONS

After forty years of superpower confrontation, the Cold War's end brought renewed hope for global peace and prosperity. If we have learned anything since 1991, however, it is that neither peace nor prosperity come easily for the human race. New rifts and old animosities have set us at odds in ways that are just as dangerous and lethal as the Cold War differences they replaced. At the same time, as the twenty-first century enters its second decade, populist revolts in several countries across North Africa, the Middle East, and elsewhere have demonstrated that women and men are still ready to fight and die for freedom from authoritarian rule and for better lives.

A common feature of these recent revolts has been the use of the Internet, cell phones, and social networking sites. While these have proved innovative tools for political change, the most revolutionary advances in education in the developing world will also come through access to the Internet. Despite the initial costs — significant for many countries — the benefits of having even one computer connected to the Internet in each school are incalculable. Instantaneously, children get access to all the world's libraries, art galleries, museums, educational sites, and knowledge bases. Internet access does not make the playing field between rich and poor students exactly level, but it comes closer to doing so than any other development in history.

The study of world history will put these and future events in perspective. Future developments on this small planet will surely build on the many-layered foundations hammered out in the past. Moreover, the study of world history, of mighty struggles and fearsome challenges, of shining achievements and tragic failures, imparts a strong sense of life's essence: the process of change over time. Again and again we have seen how peoples and societies evolve, influenced by ideas, human passions, and material conditions. Armed with the ability to think historically, students of history are prepared to comprehend this inexorable process of change in their own lifetimes, as the world races forward toward an uncertain destiny.

□ CHAPTER REVIEW

□ **What is the multipolar nature of world politics today, and how do competing nation-states address common problems? (p. 1038)**

Nation-states remained the primary building blocks of political organization as the world entered the twenty-first century. But increasing interdependency and globalization led to a new multipolar nature of world politics, with a group of countries known as middle powers rising to assume regional leadership. The increasingly complex nature of world politics forced nations and peoples to come together, negotiate, and make joint global decisions more frequently than at any time in human history. The United Nations was created to maintain international peace and security, but despite some success in peacekeeping and humanitarian work, its charter has proven difficult to enforce, as the 2003 preemptive war against Iraq attests. Nuclear nonproliferation treaties and a chemical weapons ban were positive steps toward world peace, but the new wave of terrorism in the new millennium continues to challenge world security.

□ **What are some of the benefits and drawbacks of increasing global interdependence? (p. 1051)**

Increased globalization has led to a greater degree of interdependence, as global markets and resource needs tie the countries of the world ever more closely together. Multinational corporations rapidly emerged in the early 1950s, operating across political boundaries to create a single global marketplace. Criticized for being part of a neocolonial process, multinationals bring products to developing countries but keep profits in the hand of elites at the expense of national interests. A push to industrialize developing nations in the 1950s and 1960s was successful, but Third World countries found that they could not compete with the West, and the gap between rich and poor nations widened. The green revolution dramatically increased crop yields, though profits were generally limited to larger landowners and large agribusinesses. Calls for a new international order have been complicated by the complexity of world economic systems, which consist of many distinct types of wealth and income, not just a "North" and a "South."

□ **What factors spurred the growth of cities in Africa, Asia, and Latin America, and what were some of the main consequences of urbanization in the late twentieth century? (p. 1057)**

The phenomenal growth of cities over the past fifty years has had a tremendous impact on individuals,

KEY TERMS

United Nations (p. 1039)
Security Council (p. 1039)
General Assembly (p. 1039)
middle powers (p. 1043)
terrorism (p. 1044)
multinational corporations (p. 1051)
mixed economy (p. 1052)
neo-Malthusian (p. 1053)
green revolution (p. 1053)
megacities (p. 1057)
urbanization without industrialization (p. 1057)
economic growth without economic development (p. 1059)
bazaar economy (p. 1059)
global warming (p. 1065)
feminization of poverty (p. 1067)

families, and communities. Megacities, in particular, have evolved at an astonishing pace. The reasons for this urban explosion include a tremendous spurt in population growth and people's desire to find jobs, particularly manufacturing jobs that were concentrated in the cities. People also left the countryside because they were pushed off their land or, if they were young, for the excitement of the city.

The consequences of this rapid urbanization are similar to those associated with early-twentieth-century urbanization in Europe and North America, but on a larger scale. Overcrowding and shantytowns have been some of the most visible problems. Urban social services have been overwhelmed, and cities have been unable to provide the necessary police and fire protection and adequate sanitation, running water, and electricity.

□ **What key technological and scientific developments have had the greatest impact on life at the beginning of the new millennium? (p. 1061)**

Science and technology have significantly changed global society in the twentieth century. A medical revolution has discovered vaccines to treat some of history's most deadly diseases; artificial hearts and organ transplants have become routine. The successful mapping of human DNA offers unimaginable possibilities for the prevention, treatment, and cure of diseases. As we learn more about the environment, global warming has drawn more attention from government leaders and private citizens. Mass communication is another area where advances have been revolutionary. Many people around the world have access to the Internet and carry cell phones and other devices that make information exchange almost instantaneous.

◻ What social problems facing women and children are the focus of reformers in the new millennium? (p. 1067)

At the end of the twentieth century and the beginning of the twenty-first, social reformers have turned their attention to the advancement of human and civil rights for women and children. The feminization of poverty remains one of the greatest concerns, affecting women in both developed and developing countries. Contributing factors include child care demands, job discrimination, and high birthrates. Violence against women remains rampant, and rape and sexual violence have been used as weapons of war in many recent conflicts. Still, women have made important progress toward equality, and they are increasingly moving into more positions of power. Children suffer alongside their poor mothers, and the 1989 UN Convention on the Rights of the Child seeks to address childhood poverty, child labor exploitation, sexual violence, and lack of access to health care, among other issues facing children today. Globalization has pressured governments to provide public education, though access remains uneven.

SUGGESTED READING

Bales, Kevin. *Disposable People: New Slavery in the Global Economy*. 2004. Analysis of the economic exploitation of the world's poor.

Caircross, Frances. *The Death of Distance: How the Communications Revolution Is Changing Our Lives*. 2001. Discusses the global consequences of cell phones, communication satellites, and the Internet.

Chandler, Alfred D., and Bruce Mazlish. *Leviathans: Multinational Corporations and the New Global History*. 2005. A stimulating global perspective on multinational corporations and how they affect everyone's life.

Das, Gurcharan. *India Unbound: The Social and Economic Revolution from Independence to the Global Information Age*. 2002. India's leap into the age of modern technology and computers and the consequences for its population and the world.

Drexler, Maeline. *Secret Agents: The Menace of Emerging Infections*. 2003. Provides an overview of the global threat from infectious diseases, old and new.

Fishman, Ted C. *China, Inc.: How the Rise of the Next Superpower Challenges America and the World*. 2006. Explains the profound consequences of China's becoming the next economic superpower.

Gareis, Sven Bernhard, and Johannes Varwick. *The United Nations: An Introduction*. 2005. An up-to-date introduction to the United Nations.

Gore, Al. *An Inconvenient Truth: The Planetary Emergency of Global Warming and What We Can Do About It*. 2006. Reasoned discussion of the greatest threat to the planet in the twenty-first century, for which Gore won the Nobel Peace Prize.

Johnson-Odim, Cheryl, and Margaret Strobel, eds. *Expanding the Boundaries of Women's History: Essays on Women in the Third World*. 1992. Groundbreaking essays on women's history outside of Europe and North America.

Jones, Geoffrey. *Multinationals and Global Capitalism: From the Nineteenth to the Twenty-First Century*. 2005. A historical overview of the development of multinational corporations and a global capitalist economy.

Kasarda, John, and Allan Parnell, eds. *Third World Cities: Problems, Policies and Prospects*. 1993. Discusses the prodigious growth of Third World cities in the second half of the twentieth century.

Klare, Michael T. *Resource Wars: The New Landscape of Global Conflict*. 2002. Analyzes the conflict over vital resources and the impact on national military and economic policies.

Moaddel, Mansoor. *Islamic Modernism, Nationalism, and Fundamentalism*. 2005. A scholarly historical introduction to society and politics in the Middle East.

O'Neill, Bard. E. *Insurgency and Terrorism: From Revolution to Apocalypse*, 2d rev. ed. 2005. An excellent introduction to the nature of modern war.

O'Neill, John Terence, and Nicholas Rees. *United Nations Peacekeeping in the Post–Cold War Era*. 2005. Discusses the problems associated with United Nations peacekeeping efforts.

NOTES

1. D. Rappaport, "The Fourth Wave: September 11 in the History of Terrorism," *Current History*, December 2001, pp. 419–424.

2. Ibid.

3. Quoted in J. Fallows, "Success Without Victory," *The Atlantic Monthly* 295 (January/February 2005): 80.

4. Quoted in L. R. Brown, *Seeds of Change: The Green Revolution and Development in the 1970s* (New York: Praeger, 1970), p. 16.

5. P. Ehrlich, *The Population Bomb* (New York: Ballantine, 1968), p. 11.

6. M. ul Haq, *The Poverty Curtain: Choices for the Third World* (New York: Columbia University Press, 1976), p. 152.

7. J. Diamond, *Collapse: How Societies Choose to Fail or Survive* (New York: Viking, 2004), pp. 524–525.

8. P. Bairoch, *Economics and World History: Myths and Paradoxes* (Chicago: University of Chicago Press, 1993), p. 95.

9. R. Carson, *Silent Spring* (1962; repr., New York: Houghton Mifflin, 1994), pp. 1–3, 7–8.

10. United Nations, "Critical Areas of Concern," *Report of the Fourth World Conference on Women* (New York: United Nations Department for Policy Coordination and Sustainable Development, 1995), ch. 1, annex II, ch. 3, pp. 41–44; available at http://www.un.org/esa/gopher-data/conf/fwcw/off/a — 20.en. See also Population Reference Bureau, *Women of Our World 2005* (Washington, D.C.: Population Reference Bureau, 2005) for the latest data and ten-year follow-up to the Beijing meeting.

For practice quizzes and other study tools, visit the **Online Study Guide** at bedfordstmartins.com/mckayworld.

For primary sources from this period, see *Sources of World Societies*, **Second Edition**.

For Web sites, images, and documents related to topics in this chapter, visit **Make History** at bedfordstmartins.com/mckayworld.

	Africa	The Americas
10,000 B.C.E.	*Homo sapiens* evolve, ca. 250,000 years ago Farming begins in Nile River Valley, ca. 9000 Domestication of cattle; plow agriculture, ca. 7000 Unification of Egypt, 3100–2660	Possible migration into Americas begins, ca. 20,000–30,000 Farming begins, ca. 8000 Maize domesticated in Mexico, ca. 3000
2500 B.C.E.	Egypt's Old Kingdom, 2660–2180 Egypt's Middle Kingdom, 2080–1640 Hyksos migrate into Egypt, 1640–1570	First cities in Peru; earliest mound building in North America, ca. 2500 Textiles become important part of Peruvian culture, ca. 2500 Farmers in southwestern North America grow maize, ca. 2000
1500 B.C.E.	Egypt's New Kingdom, ca. 1550–1070 Ironworking spreads throughout Africa, ca. 1500 B.C.E.–300 C.E. Akhenaten institutes monotheistic worship of Aton, ca. 1360	Olmec civilization in Mexico, ca. 1500–300 Earliest cities in the Andes built by Chavin people, ca. 1200
1000 B.C.E.	Political fragmentation of Egypt; rise of small kingdoms, ca. 1100–653 Bantu migrations across central and southern Africa, ca. 1000 B.C.E.–1500 C.E. Persians conquer Egypt, 525	Olmec center at San Lorenzo destroyed; power passes to La Venta, ca. 900
500 B.C.E.	Ptolemy conquers Egypt, 323	
250 B.C.E.	Scipio Africanus defeats Hannibal at Zama, 202 Meroë becomes iron-smelting center, ca. 100	Hopewell culture flourishes in North America, ca. 200 B.C.E.–600 C.E.

Asia and Oceania	Europe	Middle East
Farming begins in Yellow River Valley, ca. 9000 Domestication of cattle; plow agriculture begins, ca. 7000	Farming spreads to Greece, ca. 6500 Smelting of copper in Balkans, ca. 5500 Farming spreads to Britain, ca. 4000	Farming begins; domestication of goats and sheep in the Fertile Crescent, ca. 9000 Invention of pottery wheel in Mesopotamia, ca. 5000 First writing in Sumeria; city-states emerge, ca. 3500
Harappan civilization, ca. 2800–1800	Minoan culture emerges, ca. 2000 Arrival of Greeks in peninsular Greece; founding of Mycenaean kingdom, ca. 1650	Smelting of iron begins in Mesopotamia, ca. 2500 Akkadian empire, ca. 2331–2200 Hammurabi's law code, ca. 1790
Shang Dynasty; first writing in China, ca. 1500–1050 Vedic Age: Aryans dominate in North India; caste system develops; the *Rigveda*, ca. 1500–500	Mycenaeans conquer Minoan Crete, ca. 1450 Greek Dark Age; evolution of the polis, ca. 1100–800	Hittites expand empire in Mesopotamia, ca. 1600 Moses leads Hebrews out of Egypt, ca. 1300–1200 United Hebrew kingdom, ca. 1020–930
Early Zhou Dynasty, ca. 1050–400 *Upanishads*, foundation of Hinduism, 750–500 Life of Confucius, 551–479 Persians conquer parts of India, 513 Founding of Buddhism and Jainism, ca. 500	Fall of Minoan and Mycenaean cultures, ca. 1000 Rise of Sparta and Athens, 800–500 Roman Republic founded, 509	Assyrian Empire, ca. 800–612 Spread of Zoroastrianism, ca. 600–500 Babylonian captivity of Hebrews, 587–538 Cyrus the Great founds Persian Empire, 550
Warring States period; golden age of Chinese philosophy, 403–221 Brahmanic religion develops into Hinduism, ca. 400 B.C.E.–200 C.E. Zhuangzi and development of Daoism, 369–268 Alexander the Great invades India, 326 Seleucus establishes Seleucid Empire, 323 Mauryan Empire, ca. 322–185 Reign of Ashoka; Buddhism spreads in central Asia, 269–232	Flowering of Greek art and philosophy, 500–400 Persian wars, 499–479 Peloponnesian War, 431–404 Roman expansion, 390–146 Conquests of Alexander the Great, 336–323 Punic Wars; destruction of Carthage, 264–146	Persian Empire falls to Alexander the Great, 330 Alexander the Great dies in Babylon, 323
Qin Dynasty unifies China; construction of Great Wall, 221–206 Han Dynasty, 206 B.C.E.–220 C.E. Han government controls Silk Road across central Asia, 114 Chinese armies conquer Nam Viet, 111 *Bhagavad Gita*, ca. 100 B.C.E.–100 C.E.	Late Roman republic, 133–27 Julius Caesar killed, 44 Octavian seizes power, rules imperial Rome as Augustus, 27 B.C.E.–14 C.E.	

	Africa	The Americas
1 C.E.	Expansion of Bantu-speaking peoples into eastern and southern Africa, ca. 100	Moche civilization flourishes in Peru, ca. 100–800
200 C.E.	Aksum (Ethiopia) controls Red Sea trade, ca. 250	
300	Christianity comes to Ethiopia from Egypt, 328 Aksum accepts Christianity, ca. 350	Hohokam use irrigation to enhance farming in southwestern North America, ca. 300 Classical era in Mesoamerican and North America; Maya and other groups develop large advanced states, 300–900 Peak of Teotihuacán civilization in Mexico, ca. 450
500	Political and commercial ascendancy of Aksum, ca. 500–700 Christian missionaries convert Nubian rulers, ca. 600 Muslim conquest of Egypt; Islam introduced to Africa, 642 Height of African Mediterranean slave trade, ca. 650–1500	Peak of Maya civilization, ca. 600–900
700	Expansion of Islam into Ethiopia weakens state, 700–800 Berbers control trans-Saharan trade, ca. 700–900 Islam spreads across Sahara, 800–900 Kingdom of Ghana, ca. 900–1300	Teotihuacán destroyed, 750 Period of crop failure, disease, and war in Mesoamerica; collapse of Maya civilization, 800–1000 Toltec hegemony, ca. 980–1000
1000	Islam penetrates sub-Saharan Africa, ca. 1000–1100 Great Zimbabwe built, flourishes, ca. 1100–1400	Inca civilization in South America, ca. 1000–1500 Peak of Cahokia culture in North America, ca. 1150 Toltec state collapses, 1174
1200	Kingdom of Mali, ca. 1200–1450 Mongols conquer Baghdad; fall of Abbasid Dynasty, 1258	Cahokia's decline begins after earthquake, ca. 1200

Asia and Oceania	Europe	Middle East
Shakas and Kushans invade eastern Parthia and India, ca. 1–100	Roman Empire at greatest extent, 117	Life of Jesus, ca. 3 B.C.E.–29 C.E.
Maritime trade between Chinese and Roman ports begins, ca. 100		
Roman attacks on Parthian empire, ca. 100–200		
Chinese invent paper, 105		
Buddhism gains popularity in China, Japan, and Korea, ca. 200–600	Life of Diocletian: reforms Roman Empire; divides into western and eastern halves, 284–305	Sassanid dynasty in Persia, 226–651
Age of Division in China, 220–589		
Fall of the Parthian empire; rise of the Sassanid, ca. 226		
Three Kingdoms Period in Korea, 313–668	Life of Constantine: legalizes Christianity; founds Constantinople, 306–337	
China divides into northern and southern regimes, 316	Christianity official state religion of Roman Empire, 380	
Gupta Empire unites northern India, ca. 320–480	Germanic raids on western Europe, 400s	
Huns invade India, ca. 450	Clovis rules Gauls, ca. 481–511	
Sui Dynasty restores order in China, 581–618	Reign of Justinian; *Code* and *Digest*, 527–565	Life of Muhammad, 570–632
Prince Shōtoku introduces Chinese-style government in Japan, 604	*Rule* of Saint Benedict, 529	Publication of the Qur'an, 651
Tang Dynasty in China; cultural flowering, 618–907		Umayyad Dynasty; expansion of Islam, 661–750
Korea unified, 668		
Creation of Japan's first capital at Nara, 710	Muslims defeat Visigothic kingdom in Spain, 711	Abbasid caliphate; Islamic capital moved to Baghdad, 750–1258
Islam reaches India, 713	Christian reconquest of Spain from Muslims, 722–1492	Height of Muslim learning and creativity, ca. 800–1300
Heian era in Japan, 794–1185	Carolingians defeat Muslims at Poitiers, 732	
Khmer Empire of Cambodia founded, 802	Viking, Magyar invasions, ca. 800–950	
Koryŏ Dynasty in Korea, 935–1392	Treaty of Verdun divides Carolingian Empire, 843	
North Vietnam gains independence from China, 939		
Song Dynasty in China; invention of movable type, 960–1279		
Construction of Angkor Wat, ca. 1100–1150	Latin, Greek churches split, 1054	Seljuk Turks take Baghdad, 1055
Muslim conquests lead to decline of Buddhism in India, ca. 1100–1200	Norman Conquest of England, 1066	
China divided into Song and Jin empires, 1127	Crusades, 1095–1270	
Kamakura Shogunate in Japan, 1185–1333	Growth of trade and towns, ca. 1100–1400	
Easter Island's most prosperous period, ca. 1200–1300	Magna Carta, 1215	Mongols conquer Baghdad, 1238
Turkish sultanate at Dehli, 1206–1526	Life of Thomas Aquinas; *Summa Theologica*, 1225–1274	Ottoman Empire, 1299–1922
Peak of Khmer Empire, 1219	Mongol raids into eastern Europe; Mongols gain control of Kieven Russia, 1237–1241	
Mongol's Yuan Dynasty in China, 1234–1368		
Mongols invade Japan, 1274, 1281		
Marco Polo travels in China, ca. 1275–1292		
Mongol conquest of Song China, 1276		

	Africa	The Americas
1300	Height of Swahili city-states in East Africa, ca. 1300–1500 Mansa Musa rules Mali, ca. 1312–1337 Ibn Battuta's travels, 1325–1354	Construction of Aztec city Tenochtitlán begins, ca. 1325
1400	Songhai Empire, ca. 1464–1591 Arrival of Portuguese in Benin, 1485 Da Gama reaches East Africa; Swahili coast enters period of economic decline, 1498	Height of Inca Empire, 1438–1532 Reign of Montezuma I; height of Aztec culture, 1440–1467 Inca city of Machu Picchu built, 1450 Columbus reaches Americas, 1492
1500	Portugal dominates East Africa, ca. 1500–1600 Era of transatlantic slave trade, ca. 1500–1900 Muslim occupation of Christian Ethiopia, 1531–1543 Height of Kanem-Bornu, 1571–1603	Portuguese reach Brazil, 1500 Atlantic slave trade begins, 1518 Cortés arrives in Mexico, 1519 Aztec Empire falls, 1521 Pizarro conquers Inca Empire, 1533 First English colony in North America founded at Roanoke, 1585
1600	Dutch West India Company founded; starts to bring slave coast of West Africa under its control, 1621 Jesuit missionaries expelled from Ethiopia, 1633 Dutch East India Company settles Cape Town, 1652 Importation of slaves into Cape Colony begins, 1658	British settle Jamestown, 1607 Champlain founds first permanent French settlement at Quebec, 1608 Caribbean islands colonized by French, English, Dutch, 1612–1697 English seize New Amsterdam from Dutch, 1664
1700	Major famine in West Africa, 1738–1756	Silver production quadruples in Mexico and Peru, ca. 1700–1800 Colonial dependence on Spanish goods, ca. 1700–1800
1750	Peak of transatlantic slave trade, 1780–1820 Olaudah Equiano publishes autobiography, 1789 British seize Cape Town, 1795 Napoleon's army invades Egypt, 1798	Seven Years' War, 1756–1763 Quebec Act, 1774 American Revolution, 1775–1783 Comunero revolution in New Granada, 1781 Haitian Revolution, 1791–1804

Asia and Oceania	Europe	Middle East
Ashikaga Shogunate, 1336–1573 Mongols defeated in China, 1368 Ming Dynasty in China, 1368–1644 Timur conquers the Delhi sultanate, 1398	Hundred Years' War, ca. 1337–1453 Black Death arrives in Europe, 1347 Great Schism, 1378–1417	
Maritime trade and piracy connects East Asia and Southeast Asia with Europe, ca. 1400–1800 Zheng He's maritime expeditions to India, Middle East, Africa, 1405–1433 Reign of Sultan Mehmed II, 1451–1481	Development of movable type in Germany, ca. 1450 Italian Renaissance, ca. 1450–1521 Age of Discovery, ca. 1450–1650 Ottomans capture Constantinople; end of Byzantine Empire, 1453 Unification of Spain; Jews expelled, 1492	Ottoman Empire conquers Byzantine Empire under rule of Sultan Mehmet II, 1451–1481
Increased availability of books in China, 1500–1600 Barbur defeats Delhi sultanate; founds Mughal Empire, 1526 Japan unified under Toyotomi Hideyoshi, 1537–1598 First Christian missionaries land in Japan, 1549 Akbar expands Mughal Empire, 1556–1605 Spain founds port city of Manila in the Philippines, 1571	Michelangelo paints Sistine Chapel, 1508–1512 Luther's Ninety-five Theses, 1517 English Reformation begins, 1527 Scientific revolution, ca. 1540–1690 Council of Trent, 1545–1563 Peace of Augsburg ends religious wars in Germany, 1555 Netherlands declares independence from Spain, 1581	Safavid Empire in Persia, 1501–1722 Peak of Ottoman power; cultural flowering under Suleiman, 1520–1566 Battle of Lepanto, 1571 Height of Safavid Empire under Shah Abbas, 1587–1629
Tokogawa Shogunate in Japan, 1603–1867 Japan closes its borders, 1639 Manchus establish Qing Dynasty in China, 1644–1911 Dutch expel Portuguese in East Indies; gain control of spice trade, ca. 1660 French arrive in India, ca. 1670	Thirty Years' War, 1619–1648 Growth of absolutism in Austria and Prussia, 1620–1740 English civil war, 1642–1649 Habsburgs expel Ottomans from Hungary, 1683–1718 Revocation of Edict of Nantes, 1685 Glorious Revolution in England, 1688–1689 The Enlightenment, ca. 1690–1789	Shah Abbas captures much of Armenia from the Ottomans, 1603
Height of Edo urban culture in Japan, ca. 1700 Christian missionary work forbidden in China, 1715 Persian invaders loot Delhi, 1739 French and British fight for control of India, 1740–1763	Growth of book publishing, ca. 1700–1789 War of the Spanish Succession, 1701–1713 Peace of Utrecht, 1713	Afghans seize Isfahan from Persians, 1722
Treaty of Paris gives French colonies in India to Britain, 1763 Cook claims land in Australia for Britain, 1770 East India Act, 1784 First British convict-settlers arrive in Australia, 1788	Watt produces first steam engine, 1769 Industrial Revolution in Great Britain, ca. 1780–1850 French Revolution, 1789–1799 Romantic movement in literature and the arts, ca. 1790s–1890s National Convention declares France a republic, 1792	Ottoman ruler Selim III introduces reforms, 1761–1808

	Africa	The Americas
1800	Muhammad Ali modernizes Egypt, 1805–1848 Slavery abolished in British Empire, 1807	Latin American wars of independence, 1806–1825 Brazil wins independence, 1822 Political instability in most Latin American countries, 1825–1870 U.S.-Mexican War, 1846–1848
1850	Suez Canal opens, 1869 Western and central Sudan unite under Islam, 1880 European "scramble for Africa"; decline of slave trade, 1880–1900 Battle of Omdurman, 1898 South African War, 1899–1902	U.S. Civil War, 1861–1865 Dominion of Canada formed, 1867 Latin American neocolonialism, ca. 1870–1929 Diaz controls Mexico, 1876–1911 Immigration from Europe and Asia to the Americas, 1880–1914 Spanish-American War, 1898
1900	Union of South Africa formed, 1910 Native Land Act in South Africa, 1913 Du Bois organizes first Pan-African congress, 1919	Mexican Revolution, 1910 Panama Canal opens, 1914 Mexico adopts constitution, 1917
1920	Cultural nationalism in Africa, 1920s Gold Coast farmers organize cocoa holdups, 1930–1931	U.S. consumer revolution, 1920s Stock market crash in U.S.; Great Depression begins, 1929 Revolutions in six South American countries, 1930 Flowering of Mexican culture, 1930s New Deal begins in United States, 1933
1940	Decolonization in Africa, 1946–1964 Apartheid system in South Africa, 1948–1991	"Mexican miracle," 1940s–1970s Surprise attack by Japan on Pearl Harbor, 1941 United Nations established, 1945
1950	Egypt declared a republic; Nasser named premier, 1954 French-British Suez invasion, 1956 Morocco, Tunisia, Sudan, and Ghana gain independence, 1956–1957 France offers commonwealth status to its territories; only Guinea chooses independence, 1958 Belgian Congo gains independence; violence follows, 1959	Cuban revolution, 1953–1959 Military rule ends in Venezuela, 1958 Castro takes power in Cuba, 1959

Asia and Oceania	Europe	Middle East
British found Singapore, 1819 Java War, 1825–1830 Opium War, 1839–1842 Treaty of Nanjing; Manchus surrender Hong Kong to British, 1842	Napoleonic Europe, 1804–1814 Congress of Vienna, 1814–1815 European economic penetration of non-Western countries, ca. 1816–1880 Greece wins independence, 1830 Revolutions in France, Austria, and Prussia, 1848	Ottoman Empire launches Tanzimat reforms, 1839
Taiping Rebellion, 1851–1864 Perry opens Japan to trade; Japan begins to industrialize, 1853 Great Mutiny/Revolt in India, 1857 Meiji Restoration in Japan, 1867 Indian National Congress, 1885 French acquire Indochina, 1893 Sino-Japanese War, 1894–1895 U.S. gains Philippines, 1898	Unification of Italy, 1859–1870 Freeing of Russian serfs, 1861 Unification of Germany, 1866–1871 Massive industrialization surge in Russia, 1890–1900	Crimean War, 1853–1856 Ottoman state declares partial bankruptcy; European creditors take over, 1875
Boxer Rebellion in China, 1900 Commonwealth of Australia, 1901 Russo-Japanese War, 1904–1905 Muslim League formed, 1906 Korea becomes province of Japan, 1910 Chinese revolution; fall of Qing Dynasty, 1911 Chinese republic, 1912–1949 Amritsar Massacre in India, 1919	Revolution in Russia, 1905 World War I, 1914–1918 Bolshevik Revolution and civil war in Russia, 1917–1922 Treaty of Versailles, 1919	Young Turks seize power in Ottoman Empire, 1908 Turkish massacre of Armenians, 1915–1917 Sykes-Picot Agreement divides Ottoman Empire, 1916 Balfour Declaration establishes Jewish homeland in Palestine, 1917
Gandhi launches nonviolent campaign against British rule in India, 1920 Jiang Jieshi unites China, 1928 Japan invades China, 1931 Mao Zedong's Long March, 1934 Sino-Japanese War, 1937–1945 Japan conquers Southeast Asia, 1939–1942	Mussolini seizes power in Italy, 1922 Stalin takes power in U.S.S.R., 1927 Great Depression, 1929–1933 Hitler gains power in Germany, 1933 Civil war in Spain, 1936–1939 World War II, 1939–1945	Large numbers of European Jews immigrate to Palestine, 1920s–1930s Turkish republic recognized; Kemal begins to modernize and secularize, 1923 Reza Shah leads Iran, 1925–1941 Iraq gains independence, 1932
Japan announces "Asia for Asians"; signs alliance with Germany and Italy, 1940 United States drops atomic bombs on Hiroshima and Nagasaki, 1945 Chinese civil war; Communists win, 1945–1949 Philippines gain independence, 1946 Independence and separation of India and Pakistan, 1947	Marshall Plan, 1947 NATO formed, 1949 Soviet Union and Communist China sign 30-year alliance, 1949	Arabs and Jews at war in Palestine; Israel created, 1948
Japan begins long period of rapid economic growth, 1950 Korean War, 1950–1953 Vietnamese nationalists defeat French; Vietnam divided, 1954 Mao announces Great Leap Forward in China, 1958	Death of Stalin, 1953 Warsaw Pact, 1955 Revolution in Hungary, 1956 Common Market formed, 1957	Turkey joins NATO, 1953 Suez crisis, 1956

	Africa	The Americas
1960	Mali and Nigeria gain independence, 1960 Biafra declares independence from Nigeria, 1967	U.S. Alliance for Progress promotes development and reform in Latin America, 1961 Cuban missile crisis, 1962 U.S. Civil Rights Act; United States starts Vietnam War, 1964 Military dictatorship in Brazil, 1964–1985 Military takeovers lead to brutal dictatorships in Argentina, 1966, 1976
1970	Growth of Islamic fundamentalism, 1970s to present	U.S. Watergate scandal, 1972 Nixon visits China; reconciliation between U.S. and China, 1972 Military coup in Chile, 1973 Revolution in Nicaragua, 1979
1980	Blacks win long civil war with white settlers in Zimbabwe, 1980 AIDS epidemic, 1980s to present South African government opens talks with African National Congress, 1989	Democratic wave gains momentum throughout Latin America, 1980s Nationalization of Mexico's banking system, 1982 Argentina restores civilian rule, 1983 Brazilians elect first civilian government in twenty years, 1985
1990	Nelson Mandela freed in South Africa, 1990 Rwandan genocide, 1994 Second Congo War, 1998 to present	Canada, Mexico, and United States form free-trade area (NAFTA), 1994 Haiti establishes democratic government, 1994 Socialist "Bolivarian revolution" in Venezuela, 1999
2000	Civil war and genocide in Darfur, 2003 to present Mugabe increases violence against opponents after losing Zimbabwean election, 2008 Populist uprisings and protests break out in Tunisia, Egypt, and elsewhere in North Africa, 2010–2011	Terrorist attack on United States, 2001 Economic, social, and political crisis in Argentina, 2002 Formation of the Union of South American Nations, 2008 Raúl Castro succeeds his ailing brother Fidel as president of Cuba, 2008 Catastrophic earthquake in Haiti, 2010 U.S. begins troop drawdown in Afghanistan, 2011

Asia and Oceania	Europe	Middle East
Sino-Soviet split becomes apparent, 1960	Building of Berlin Wall, 1961	OPEC founded, 1960
Vietnam War, 1964–1975	Student revolution in France, 1968	Arab-Israeli Six-Day War, 1967
Great Proletarian Cultural Revolution launched in China, 1965	Soviet invasion of Czechoslovakia, 1968	
Bangladesh breaks away from Pakistan, 1971	Helsinki Accord on human rights, 1975	Revival of Islamic fundamentalism, 1970s to present
Communist victory in Vietnam War, 1975	Soviet invasion of Afghanistan, 1979	Arab-Israeli Yom Kippur War, 1973
China pursues modernization, 1976 to present		OPEC oil embargo, 1973
		Civil war in Lebanon, 1975–1990
		Islamic revolution in Iran, 1979
		Camp David Accords, 1979
Japanese foreign investment surge, 1980–1992	Soviet reform under Gorbachev, 1985–1991	Iran-Iraq War, 1980–1988
Sikh nationalism in India, 1984 to present	Communism falls in eastern Europe, 1989–1990	Palestinians start the intifada, 1987
China crushes democracy movement, 1989		
Collapse of Japanese stock market, 1990–1992	Conservative economic policies, 1990s	Persian Gulf War, 1990–1991
Economic growth and political repression in China, 1990 to present	End of Soviet Union, 1991	Israel and Palestinians sign peace agreement, 1993
Congress Party in India embraces Western capitalist reforms, 1991	Civil war in Yugoslavia, 1991–2001	Assassination of Israeli prime minster Yitzak Rabin, 1995
Kyoto Protocol on global warming, 1997	Maastricht Treaty creates single currency, 1992	
Hong Kong returns to Chinese rule, 1997	Creation of European Union, 1993	
China joins World Trade Organization, 2001	Resurgence of Russian economy under Putin, 2000–2008	Israel begins construction of West Bank barrier, 2003
India and Pakistan come close to all-out war, 2001	Euro note enters circulation, 2002	Wars in Iraq and Afghanistan, 2003 to present
North Korea withdraws from 1970 Nuclear Non-Proliferation Treaty, 2003	Madrid train bombing, 2004	Hamas establishes Palestinian Authority government, 2007
Tsunami in Southeast Asia, 2004	London subway and bus bombing, 2005	Populist uprisings and protests across the Middle East, 2010–2011
Terrorist attack in Mumbai, India, 2008		
Massive earthquake in Japan, 2011		
Al-Qaeda leader Osama bin Laden killed in Pakistan, 2011		

☐ ABOUT THE AUTHORS

JOHN P. McKAY (Ph.D., University of California, Berkeley) is professor emeritus at the University of Illinois. He has written or edited numerous works, including the Herbert Baxter Adams Prize–winning book *Pioneers for Profit: Foreign Entrepreneurship and Russian Industrialization, 1885–1913.*

BENNETT D. HILL (Ph.D., Princeton University), late of Georgetown University, published *Church and State in the Middle Ages* and numerous articles and reviews, and was one of the contributing editors to *The Encyclopedia of World History.* He was also a Benedictine monk of St. Anselm's Abbey in Washington, D.C.

JOHN BUCKLER (Ph.D., Harvard University), late of the University of Illinois, authored *Theban Hegemony, 371–362 B.C., Philip II and the Sacred War,* and *Aegean Greece in the Fourth Century B.C.* With Hans Beck, he most recently published *Central Greece and the Politics of Power in the Fourth Century.*

PATRICIA BUCKLEY EBREY (Ph.D., Columbia University), professor of history at the University of Washington in Seattle, specializes in China. She has published many journal articles and *The Cambridge Illustrated History of China* as well as numerous monographs. In 2010 she won the Shimada Prize for outstanding work of East Asian Art History for *Accumulating Culture: The Collections of Emperor Huizong.*

ROGER B. BECK (Ph.D., Indiana University) is Distinguished Professor of African and twentieth-century world history at Eastern Illinois University. His publications include *The History of South Africa,* a translation of P. J. van der Merwe's *The Migrant Farmer in the History of the Cape Colony, 1657–1842,* and more than a hundred articles, book chapters, and reviews. He is a former treasurer and Executive Council member of the World History Association.

CLARE HARU CROWSTON (Ph.D., Cornell University) teaches at the University of Illinois, where she is currently associate professor of history. She is the author of *Fabricating Women: The Seamstresses of Old Regime France, 1675–1791,* which won the Berkshire and Hagley Prizes. She edited two special issues of the *Journal of Women's History,* has published numerous journal articles and reviews, and is a past president of the Society for French Historical Studies.

MERRY E. WIESNER-HANKS (Ph.D., University of Wisconsin–Madison) taught first at Augustana College in Illinois, and since 1985 at the University of Wisconsin–Milwaukee, where she is currently UWM Distinguished Professor in the department of history. She is the coeditor of the *Sixteenth Century Journal* and the author or editor of more than twenty books, most recently *The Marvelous Hairy Girls: The Gonzales Sisters and Their Worlds* and *Gender in History.* She is the former Chief Reader for Advanced Placement World History.

ABOUT THE COVER ART

Earliest Known British Portrait of a Freed Slave, 1733 British artist William Hoare's striking portrait of Ayula Suleiman Diallo (1701–1773) is the earliest known British oil painting of a freed slave and the first rendering of a named African as an individual and an equal. Born into an aristocratic Senegalese Muslim family (a Qur'an hangs about his neck), Diallo was enslaved around 1730, taken to America and then to England, where he gained his freedom. He published his memoirs, one of the earliest slave narratives, in 1734.

◻ HOW TO ANALYZE PRIMARY SOURCES

In their search for an improved understanding of the past, historians look for new evidence — written documents or visual artifacts. When they encounter a written or visual primary source, historians ask certain key questions. You should ask these questions, too. Sometimes historians can't be certain about the answer, but they always ask the question.

ANALYZING A WRITTEN DOCUMENT

- Who wrote the document? Is it a specific person or someone whose identity you can merely infer from the context of the document (for example, a parent writing to a child, a traveler writing home)?
- When and where was the document written?
- Why was the document written? Is there a clear purpose or are multiple interpretations possible?
- Who was, or who might have been, its intended audience?
- What can the document tell us about the individual who produced it and the society from which he or she came?

ANALYZING A VISUAL SOURCE

- When and where was the image or artifact made?
- Who made the image or artifact and how was it made?
- Who paid for or commissioned it? How can you tell?
- For what audience might it have been intended? Where might it have originally been displayed or used?
- What message or messages is it trying to convey?
- How could it be interpreted differently depending on who viewed or used it?
- What can this image tell us about the individual who produced it and the society from which he or she came?